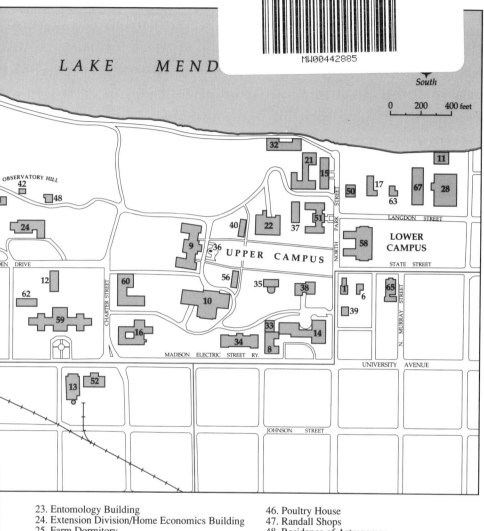

LAKE MEND

South

0   200   400 feet

MW00442885

23. Entomology Building
24. Extension Division/Home Economics Building
25. Farm Dormitory
26. Forest Products Laboratory
27. Genetics Building
28. Gymnasium and Armory
29. Hog Barn
30. Horse Barn
31. Horticultural Building
32. Hydraulic Laboratory and Pump House
33. Kitchen, University Commons
34. Lathrop Hall
35. Law Building
36. Lincoln Statue
37. Mining Engineering Laboratory
38. Music Hall
39. Music Hall Annex
40. North Hall
41. Observatory, Solar
42. Observatory, Student
43. Observatory, Washburn
44. Old Soils Building
45. Potting House

46. Poultry House
47. Randall Shops
48. Residence of Astronomer
49. Residence of Dean of Agriculture
50. Residence of President
51. Science Hall
52. Service Building
53. Sheep Barn
54. Sheep Pavilion
55. Soils Building
56. South Hall
57. Stadium
58. State Historical Society/University Library
59. State of Wisconsin General Hospital
60. Sterling Hall
61. Stock Pavilion
62. Student Infirmary
63. Student Union
64. Timber Mechanics Laboratory
65. University Club
66. Wisconsin High School
67. Y. M. C. A. Building

Merry Christmas 1996
to
Ken
from
Elaine

THE UNIVERSITY OF WISCONSIN

A History, 1925-1945

Volume III

1996 Christmas Greetings
from
Elaine

The University of WISCONSIN

1925   *A HISTORY*   1945

Politics, Depression, and War

E. David Cronon

&

John W. Jenkins

Volume III

THE UNIVERSITY OF WISCONSIN PRESS

The University of Wisconsin Press
114 North Murray Street
Madison, Wisconsin 53715

3 Henrietta Street
London WC2E 8LU, England

Library of Congress Cataloging-in-Publication Data
(Revised for vol. 3)
The University of Wisconsin : a history.
Includes bibliographical references and index.
ISBN 0-299-14430-5
Contents: v. 1-2. 1848-1925 / Merle Curti & Vernon Carstensen —
v. 3. Politics, depression, and war, 1925-1945 / E. David Cronon & John W. Jenkins.
1. University of Wisconsin—History.
I. Curti, Merle Eugene, 1897-
LD6128.C8   378.775'83   48-47638

For Jean and Marilynn

Contents

Illustrations   ix
Preface   xi
Acknowledgments   xiv
Abbreviations   xvi

Introduction   3
1.   Finding a President   13
2.   The Impresario   81
3.   Camelot by the Lake   143
4.   Unravelled Renaissance   212
5.   A Public Hanging on Bascom Hill   293
6.   The Manager   337
7.   The University at War   407
8.   "A *Faculty* University"   464
9.   A Community of Scholars   510
10. *In Loco Parentis*   551
11. A Community of Students   623
12. The Educational Enterprise   683
13. The Boundaries of the Campus   757
14. Two Difficult Decades   829

Appendices   849
Bibliographical Note   874
Photographic References   878
Index   879

Illustrations

President Birge, 1919; Board of Regents, 1924-25   321
La Follette brothers campaigning; Governor Blaine   322
President Frank, 1927; President Frank and Dean
    Sellery, 1929   323
President Frank's "trial," 1937; President Dykstra   324
Dean Russell; Dean Turneaure, 1932   325
Dean Christensen; College of Agriculture Cookout   326
Dean Sellery, 1932; Professor Ingraham   327
Dr. Middleton; Dean Snell and Chester Allen   328
Deans Goodnight and Nardin; Dean Greeley   329
Professors Leonard, Leopold, Kiekhofer, and Mathews   330
Professors Fish, Daniels, and Fred   331
Professor Steenbock; Artist-in-Residence Curry   332
University Club, 1916; University Club after 1925   333
CCC Camp Madison at Arboretum; WHA Haresfoot
    broadcast   334
President Dykstra at 1941 war convocation; Navy
    swearing-in ceremony   335
Navy Radio School, 1943; Army ROTC ski unit   336
Upper Campus, 1940; Registration line, 1928   607
Student Senate, 1926; New *Daily Cardinal* Press, 1927   608
Tripp-Adams Residence Halls complex; Elizabeth Waters
    Residence Hall   609

Illustrations

Start of Memorial Union construction, 1925; Laying first stone,
    1926; President Frank at corner stone ceremony, 1927   610
Rathskeller scene; Union Theater opening playbill, 1939   611
Experimental College Students and staff, 1927; Experimental
    College Players in *Lysistrata*, 1928   612
Haresfoot Musical, 1924; University Religious
    Conference Posters   613
Student outing, 1925; University Pier, ca. 1930   614
Sinclair Lewis with coeds, 1940; Senior Swingout, 1927;
    Pipe of Peace ceremony, 1927   615
Freshman Cap Night, 1923; Homecoming bonfire/scrap
    drive, 1942   616
Bag Rush; Bag Rush parade on State Street, 1927   617
Snowball fight on the Hill; St. Pat's Parade, 1928;
    Depression employment   618
Students Steinman, Fleming, Watrous, Owen, Murphy,
    Le Grand, and Davis   619
Coed ski class; Hoofers' toboggan slide, 1934   620
Muir Knoll ski jump; Field House boxing match   621
Work Day, 1940; Work Day, 1943   622

Preface

As a major part of its centennial celebration in 1948-49 the University of Wisconsin commissioned the first scholarly history of this remarkable institution. Written by UW history Professors Merle Curti and Vernon Carstensen, aided by a number of graduate research assistants, the large two-volume work was immediately recognized as a model for institutional histories of this sort.[1] Professors Curti and Carstensen eschewed rah-rah boosterism in favor of lively yet dispassionate, sometimes critical, but always insightful treatment of the people, issues, and forces that shaped the development of the University in its formative years. Their study showed how an enterprise that began in 1849 essentially as a small academy with an initial class of seventeen indifferently prepared male students was able by the early twentieth century to transform itself into a coeducational and graduate institution, a university in fact as well as name that was recognized around the world as one of the country's major institutions of higher learning.

For a number of reasons Curti and Carstensen chose to end their *History* in 1925. While logical in many respects, this decision meant that most of the modern history of the University has remained unexplored and untold. The present volume seeks to begin filling that void by recounting the University's development from 1925 through the end of the Second World War in 1945. A succeeding volume will treat the period from 1945 until the Wisconsin legislature merged the state's two

---

[1]Merle Curti and Vernon Carstensen, *The University of Wisconsin: A History, 1848-1925* (Madison: University of Wisconsin Press, 1949), 2 vols.

systems of higher education in the early 1970s. A post-merger volume is a more distant objective. Our study thus continues the University's story forward on approximately the same scale as the two-volume Curti-Carstensen work, although of course the University steadily became a much more complex institution in the subsequent years. While it is daunting to try to follow in our illustrious predecessors' footsteps, we have found their example, experience, and guidance invaluable. We owe much to their pioneering labors.

When Professors Curti and Carstensen began their research in the mid- 1940s there were no University archives as such. Institutional records were scattered haphazardly across the campus, squirrelled away in the basements and attics of countless buildings; others were long since destroyed or lost. Our predecessors' difficulty in recreating the University's past led in time to the decision to establish a central repository for important UW records, now known as the University Archives located in the basement of the Memorial Library and including an oral history program and smaller archives elsewhere on campus. Curti and Carstensen were often frustrated by the absence or shortage of records and documentation. Ours has been the opposite problem: how to review, digest, interpret, and retrieve the data from a vast sea of records accumulated by scores of UW instructional and service units in the more recent past.

Most college and university histories are written from the top-down perspective of the institution's leaders—the presidents, deans, members of the governing board, alumni, and in the case of public universities the governors, legislators, newspaper editors, and other representatives of the citizenry. This approach is understandable because the institutional records invariably reflect the views and actions of these influential groups. The archives rarely reveal much about the day-to-day operating life of the institution at its grass roots, the curricular and extracurricular activities of the faculty and the students—the two groups most central to its existence.

This volume seeks to combine both the top-down and the grass roots perspectives. A number of chapters deal primarily with the experience of Presidents Glenn Frank and Clarence A. Dykstra as they led the University in the years 1925-45. Their views and programs, their successes and difficulties, provide a unifying top-down focus. Since most colleges and universities function perfectly well, at least for a time, without a president or other top administrators, there are as well a number of chapters concerned primarily with the faculty, the students, and some of the important curricular and extracurricular developments of these years. By this means we hope to give a more interesting and comprehensive view of the institution. We have also sought regularly to remind the reader that a public university is very much involved in and affected by its larger environment. It cannot escape the buffeting of the political and economic currents swirling around its ivory tower.

These perspectives are reflected in the illustrations selected for the volume. There are two sections of photographs, located after Chapters 5 and 10, the first dealing with general University developments and the second emphasizing student life during the years 1925-45. In addition, scattered throughout the volume are numerous drawings, caricatures, and cartoons, most of them by students and taken from contemporary student publications. These help to show the talent and spirit of Wisconsin students in these years.

We have come to feel very much at home in the University of the years 1925-45, a much less massive and complex place than the institution we know today. Perhaps for that reason the University was, for faculty and students alike, a genuine academic *community*, one in which both groups took pride and which they defended vigorously against outside attacks. We hope our readers will come to feel the same mixture of nostalgia and respect we have developed.

E. D. C.
J. W. J.

Acknowledgments

Any scholarly work incurs a large debt of gratitude to numerous persons who helped along the way. Ours is certainly no exception. We owe a great deal to the assistance of many people—more, in fact, than it is possible to acknowledge here.

The University History Project began as a reunion initiative of the Class of 1925, two of whose members, Dorothy King Knaplund and the late John L. Bergstresser, were particularly interested and helpful. Chancellor Irving Shain was both personally and financially supportive in the project's early years, an example continued by his successors, Chancellors Donna E. Shalala and David Ward. Another alumnus, William M. Richtman, also provided unsolicited financial support.

Over the years a number of researchers have worked directly for the project: Barry Teicher, who helped initiate the research until he became the University Oral Historian and in that capacity has continued his involvement; L. Joseph Lins, who compiled a comprehensive array of University enrollment and other statistics for us; Jean Cronon, who contributed her services over two years in reading through two decades of the *Daily Cardinal* and the *Capital Times* and entering significant items into the project's computer data base; and Karen H. Cotlar, Douglas Dales, Amy M. Hielsberg, and Steven Ourada.

This book is based substantially on manuscript materials located in the University of Wisconsin Archives, whose staff, especially Director J. Frank Cook and Bernard Schermetzler, have been supportive and helpful beyond the call of their profession. We also owe much to Anne E. Biebel's expert knowledge of the UWA photographic collection. In

Acknowledgments

addition, we have made heavy use of the archives and other collections of the State Historical Society of Wisconsin and wish especially to acknowledge the generous assistance of archivists Peter Gottlieb and Harry Miller. Odessa Ofstad facilitated our research in the Glenn Frank Papers at Northwest Missouri State University, and Philip C. Bantin helped us navigate the voluminous Clarence A. Dykstra Papers at the University of California at Los Angeles. William M. Roberts, the director of archives at the University of California at Berkeley, clarified several aspects of the recruitment of President Dykstra to UCLA in 1945. Shirley E. Johnson of the UW-Extension Library helped locate materials about Extension developments in the years 1925-45. The efficient staff of the Manuscript Division of the Library of Congress speeded our research in the La Follette Family Collection.

Dean John R. Palmer of the School of Education provided office space and equipment in the early years, while the College of Letters and Science brought the project into the computer age. We owe much to the support of the L&S business staff over the years: David A. Dean, Helen Schluter, Anne C. Gunther, Karine Brager, and Michelle R. Massen. The college's Learning Support Services staff—especially Bruno Browning, Carole Turner, Colleen Brabender, and David Hytry—have invariably been prompt in keeping our computer equipment functioning and helping solve our complex software problems.

While any errors of fact or interpretation are of course ours alone, we have benefitted greatly from the knowledge and insights of a sizable number of people who read portions of the manuscript: Ira L. Baldwin, R. Freeman Butts, Vernon Carstensen, Merle Curti, Leon D. Epstein, Lowell Frautschi, Arthur O. Hove, Ralph W. Johnson, E. Robert Mulvihill, Robert B.L. Murphy, Clay Schoenfeld, Donald K. Smith, Barry Teicher, Wilson B. Thiede, John B. Washbush, Grace W. White, and H. Edwin Young.

Lastly, we want to acknowledge the assistance of literally scores of devoted alumni and retired UW staff members who generously responded to our requests for information with taped oral and written reminiscences. Their individual contributions are cited more specifically in the notes and bibliographical note, but the cumulative image of University life provided by their recollections has been of great help as we sought to recreate the years 1925-45. We hope they will find our portrayal an accurate summation of the institution they remember.

Abbreviations

The following abbreviations and short titles are used throughout:

BOR	University of Wisconsin Board of Regents
BOV	University of Wisconsin Board of Visitors
L&S	College of Letters and Science, University of Wisconsin
Press Bulletin	*University of Wisconsin Press Bulletin*
SHSW	State Historical Society of Wisconsin
UA	University Archives, University of Wisconsin-Madison
UHP	University History Project, a special project of the University of Wisconsin-Madison
UW	University of Wisconsin
WAM	*Wisconsin Alumni Magazine* or *Wisconsin Alumnus*

THE UNIVERSITY OF WISCONSIN

A History, 1925-1945

Volume III

Introduction

Our story begins in 1924 with the University of Wisconsin Board of Regents searching for a successor for President Edward A. Birge. The next year would mark the fiftieth anniversary of his distinguished service to the institution and the seventy-four-year-old president hoped to relinquish his office then. Like Birge, the University also was ripe for change. The long-time dean of the College of Letters and Science had run a cautious, caretaker administration since being drafted to take over the leadership of the campus following the unexpected death of the great President Charles R. Van Hise just after the armistice in 1918. President Birge encouraged and fully expected the regents to recruit a younger, more energetic leader to grapple with the myriad problems and opportunities of the post-war years. Enrollment was increasing dramatically, for example, from five thousand in 1916, to seven thousand in 1920, and to over seventy-five hundred by 1924. Simultaneously, advances in many fields of knowledge produced growing pressures on the University to find the money for adding new faculty, laboratories, classrooms, and library resources. Birge failed to press for improved staff salaries or badly needed facilities, other than special funding for a University hospital to round out the M.D. degree program. The legislature, badly split politically, responded with a series of static budgets. Still, the president quietly held his course. This was not the first period of significant transition he had witnessed at the University; nor would it be the last.

Edward Birge, then twenty-four, had arrived in Madison in 1875, a year after the regents had recruited Professor John Bascom from Williams College to administer the University as president. Birge was one of Bascom's first Madison faculty appointments. He had studied under Bascom at Williams and in fact was to live in the president's home until his marriage. Bascom boasted impressive scholarly credentials, with expertise in religion, philosophy, the social studies, and, to a more limited degree, the sciences. He believed in activism for social amelioration and viewed a liberal education as an important means to that end. This perspective, combined with his striking intellectual substance, made Bascom irresistible to a Board of Regents then seeking to bolster the original but largely unmet utilitarian mission of the University. Campus academic facilities, all located on the eastern slope of University Hill, then consisted of only three buildings—North, South, and Main (now Bascom) halls. They provided classroom and dormitory space for fewer than four hundred students, many of whom were enrolled in the sub-college preparatory department, taking individual courses with no degree in mind, or preparing for careers as elementary school teachers. A few well-trained faculty scholars were on hand, recruited by earlier presidents, but Bascom found the University faculty to be on the whole undistinguished, its constructive energies largely dissipated through heavy, unfocused teaching loads. To remedy this problem the new president set out to bring in capable new instructors and to allow them to concentrate on their particular areas of expertise. The youthful Birge typified this effort to change the University from an institution not much more than an academy into a respectable and socially beneficial liberal arts college.

Of course, President Bascom did not begin his labors with unlimited options; the University's as yet largely undistinguished history imposed a certain character on the process. Chartered by the first state legislature in 1848, the University had begun instruction as a preparatory school the following year in a rented downtown building. John Sterling was the professor in charge. His students—all men—hailed largely from Dane County and Madison, the seat of state government and by constitutional mandate the home of the University. The legislature also provided for a Board of Regents to oversee the University's development into an institution of higher learning that at the same time would be of practical value to the fledgling state. In 1850 the regents recruited John H. Lathrop from the University of Missouri to head UW as its first chancellor. Although enrollment increased from 27 in 1849 to 228 a decade later, the preparatory department consistently attracted the bulk of students, and Chancellor Lathrop stubbornly insisted that a classical curriculum must underlie any practical studies. Within a few years of Lathrop's appointment the legislature had become impatient with his dignified yet disappointing progress and openly attacked him until the regents finally obtained his resignation in 1859. A major point of contention during this period involved the funding of the University. Congress had provided grants of public land for new western states to use as the basis for educational endowments. The legislature had managed Wisconsin's grant poorly, however, and Lathrop and the regents found themselves constantly before the legislature seeking to augment their inadequate resources. Luckily, the regents early succeeded in obtaining state funds to purchase University Hill and construct the first three campus buildings. Otherwise, operating funds for staffing and supplies were meager.

The University remained more an academy than a college throughout the Civil War era. The regents momentarily electrified the state in 1859 with their appointment of Connecticut's Henry Barnard to succeed Lathrop. Along with Horace Mann, Barnard was one of the nation's most famous common school advocates. True to form in Wisconsin, he directed his energies to organizing teachers' institutes throughout the state and, to the regents' chagrin, virtually ignored the deteriorating situation on the campus in Madison. In 1860, faced with a directive from the regents to get more involved in University affairs, Barnard resigned and returned to New England. With the secession of the southern states in 1860-61 and the disintegration of the union, the board held off on appointing a new University head and instead placed John Sterling, the institution's original professor, temporarily in charge. Like Lathrop, Sterling administered the University much as the principal of a school, meting out advice and discipline to students and direction to the small, heavily burdened faculty. Daily attendance at chapel was mandatory for students and faculty alike. The regents kept close watch over all facets of campus life. The most significant development of this period resulted from the substantial exodus of the student body to take up arms in the early years of the Civil War. In 1863, faced with the threat of having to close the University for lack of enrollment, the regents began admitting women for study in the teacher-training department. Though they were not at first welcomed by the their male colleagues, the next year they comprised 119 of the 229-member student body.

In 1866 the legislature rechartered the University. The immediate purpose was to take advantage of the Morrill Land Grant Act of 1862, which made additional federal resources available to a designated college or university in each state for instruction in agriculture, mechanics, and military tactics. A new College of Arts would accommodate these and associated practical fields while a College of Letters would offer the traditional collegiate liberal arts curriculum. Additionally, the law forbade partisan instruction in religion and politics, created the position of president as head of the institution, and opened all University departments to women. Dane County contributed a large tract of land just to the west of University Hill, bordered on the north by Lake Mendota, for use as a University farm. The Board of Regents again looked to New England for a leader, this time to Williams College Professor Paul A. Chadbourne. A respected and widely published scientist, Chadbourne also had a solid grounding in Christian theology, which he argued was fully consistent with modern experiment-based knowledge. Viewing coeducation as out of step with democratic sentiment and the learning environment, Chadbourne resisted the regents' importunities until 1867 when they persuaded the legislature to restrict the enrollment of women students to a new Female College, housed initially in South Hall with its own preceptress. President Chadbourne quickly established productive relations with the regents and legislature, which in turn began regularly to provide small but meaningful annual appropriations in support of the institution. Most significantly, Chadbourne recruited several especially capable scholars to join John Sterling on the faculty.

In 1871 Chadbourne resigned his post at Wisconsin to accept the presidency of Williams College. As his successor the regents recruited yet another New Englander, Methodist minister John Twombly. Twombly's reputation as an effective fund-raiser may have accounted for his appointment at Wisconsin. Indeed, in 1872 the legislature agreed annually to raise $10,000 in taxes for the University's benefit. Otherwise the president was completely out of step with Wisconsin sentiment. His uncompromising fundamentalist perspective set him at odds with the faculty recruited by Chadbourne and reflected his failure to grasp the secular and scientific currents then reshaping higher education. Twombly alienated the students with his overbearing paternalistic style even as he advocated a comprehensive scheme of coeducation. It may have been this latter effort, pursued in the face of a less enthusiastic Board of Regents, that led to his forced resignation in early 1874. In Twombly's predecessor the regents had glimpsed the University's future. They now turned again to Williams College to find their next leader—Professor of Literature John Bascom, who never would have left Williams had not Chadbourne three years earlier obtained the position he so greatly coveted for himself.

Bascom turned out to be one of the great, formative UW presidents. He favored the traditional liberal arts curriculum of the recently established College of Letters at Wisconsin, showing considerably less interest in the more applied College of Arts, however. He worked hard to strengthen and focus the energies of his faculty. By the mid-1880s the University's courses in the humanities and sciences were unsurpassed in the state. The president himself taught the capstone moral philosophy course to upperclassmen, stressing their obligation to use their education to benefit the commonwealth as well as themselves. The quality of students also improved markedly, due partially to the general spread of public high schools and to new arrangements providing for admission without examination to graduates of UW-approved schools. Bascom was able to abolish the University preparatory department, an important measure in freeing the faculty for work more appropriate to their training. As a social liberal the president strongly favored coeducation, and as a better manager than Twombly he quickly and quietly arranged for equal access for women to all academic programs. Early in his administration the president helped to convince the legislature to provide a badly needed science building located at Park and Langdon streets at the bottom of the Hill. Bascom's faith in the maturity of students was reflected after Science Hall burned to the ground (due largely to an unfortunate incompatibility between fire hydrants and hoses!). The president had to transfer the displaced faculty and provide laboratory and classroom space in North Hall previously used as a men's dormitory, obliging the residents to seek unsupervised private accommodations in town. For undergraduate men, at least, the day of close *in loco parentis* supervision had ended at the University.

Considered by some of his associates as cold and austere, President Bascom could be a decisive and aggressive leader. His tight control over the College of Letters program was illustrative, as was his close supervision of faculty conduct, which extended to granting permission for even brief absences from campus. Less concerned with the College of Arts, the president essentially ignored the University's engineering and military work while quietly allowing Regent Hiram Smith and Professor William Arnon Henry to begin shaping one of the nation's premier agricultural research programs. More interested in social justice than farm production, President Bascom associated himself with movements supporting increased state government activism, the right of labor to organize and strike, women's suffrage, and prohibition. Simultaneously, he struggled with the regents over the boundaries between his and their authority, sometimes even appealing to the governor to appoint board members more to his liking. This tactic naturally created strong enemies on the board, particularly Regents Napoleon Van Slyk and Madison Republican politician Elisha "Boss" Keyes. Regent Keyes also functioned as the de facto University business officer and in that capacity often clashed with the president over expenditures. Bascom's increasingly vocal social reform activities, especially his public advocacy of prohibition, and his near-complete unwillingness to work with Keyes finally led the regents to encourage his resignation. He submitted it in 1887, declaring bitterly, "I leave the University of Wisconsin simply because I have had no sufficient liberty in doing my work."[1]

For their next president the regents appointed a Beloit College graduate and widely respected geologist, Thomas C. Chamberlin. Here was a leader fully in tune with the developments reshaping American higher education. Building upon the firm collegiate foundation completed by Bascom, Chamberlin quickly moved the institution into true university status by encouraging original faculty research and advanced study at the master's and doctor's degree levels for promising graduates. Chamberlin also was dissatisfied with what had become the increasingly anachronistic University structure as defined by the 1866 charter. He offered his own reorganization plan, which quickly gained approval by the regents and the legislature. The University reorganization of 1889 featured four distinct instructional units: the new Colleges of Letters and Science, of Agriculture, and of Mechanics and Engineering, as well as the continuing School of Law. Chamberlin's administrative triumphs were offset, however, by his unpopularity and failed relations with the students. Even less inclined to paternalism than John Bascom, Chamberlin simply expected his young charges to behave as adults or pay the consequences. This view turned out to be untenable. In 1891 the president prevailed upon Edward Birge, by now a respected teacher, faculty leader, and presidential confidant, to handle student affairs as the first dean of the College of Letters and Science where most of the undergraduates were enrolled. At the same time Chamberlin controlled all academic and staffing matters for the entire University until he left Wisconsin the next year to head the geology department at the new University of Chicago.

Chamberlin's successor was Charles Kendall Adams, who came to

---

[1] Merle Curti and Vernon Carstensen, *The University of Wisconsin: A History, 1848-1925* (Madison: University of Wisconsin Press, 1949), vol. 1, p. 271.

Wisconsin from the presidency of Cornell University—New York's land-grant institution—to which he had been recruited after distinguishing himself as an historian at the University of Michigan. Like Chamberlin, the new president established good relations with the regents and the legislature while also becoming popular with the students, in part because he was a strong supporter of intercollegiate athletics. More significantly, Adams continued to strengthen the academic side of the University by adding high-quality faculty scholars, continuing to refine the administrative structure, and playing a key role in working with the State Historical Society to obtain legislative funding for a new building on the lower campus to house the libraries of the two institutions. Although the president retained control over all personnel and most curricular decisions, he encouraged limited faculty participation in University governance by appointing several committees to address questions of educational policy and procedure. In 1894, following an investigation into charges of radicalism against Professor Richard T. Ely, the Board of Regents vindicated the prominent economist and issued a resolution, which declared in part:

> In all lines of academic investigation it is of the utmost importance that the investigator should be absolutely free to follow the indications of truth wherever they may lead. Whatever may be the limitations which trammel inquiry elsewhere we believe that the great state University of Wisconsin should ever encourage that continual and fearless sifting and winnowing by which alone the truth can be found.[2]

President Adams was very likely the author of what has become the classic assertion of the University's commitment to academic freedom.

When an exhausted Adams took leave in 1900 to recover his health the regents designated Letters and Science Dean Birge as acting president. During the previous decade the dean had functioned as Adams' principal assistant, often answering questions when the president was unavailable and occasionally making decisions when he was away. Birge had emerged as a faculty leader early in his career when he pledged with several science colleagues to share research equipment and findings and always support the University's interests above those of individuals or departments. He had demonstrated his commitment to the University's evolving public service mission by heading the new Sum-

---

[2]Report of the investigating committee, September 18, 1894, quoted in Curti and Carstensen, *University of Wisconsin*, vol. 1, p. 525.

mer Session program intended to improve Wisconsin's elementary and secondary schools. Late in 1901 President Adams, plagued by continuing poor health, felt compelled to resign. For a year-and-a-half the badly divided Board of Regents sought an outsider for the post before deciding for the first time to appoint a UW candidate. The two leading faculty contenders were Birge, already acting president, and geologist Charles R. Van Hise, a UW graduate and classmate of the current governor, progressive Republican Robert M. La Follette. La Follette let it be known that his choice was Van Hise and used the delay to muster support for his candidacy. His intervention offended some of the more conservative regents led by William F. Vilas, who had always resisted partisan interference with the University. Although the official ballot electing Van Hise president in 1903 suggested a substantial margin of regent support, in realty the board was badly split, reflecting to a considerable extent the growing division within the dominant Republican Party between the progressives and the conservatives, or stalwarts.

President Van Hise delayed his inaugural celebration until the University Jubilee of 1904, which honored the fiftieth anniversary of the first UW baccalaureate commencement. The joyful affair—whose motto was "service to the commonwealth"—included academic delegates from across North America and Europe. Dignitaries from the faculty, the state, and beyond, spoke to enthusiastic audiences, who recognized that they were in effect celebrating the University's coming of age. The high point of the five-day jubilee was Van Hise's brilliant inaugural address. After reviewing the University's rather brief history, he offered his vision of the "combination university" he intended to foster during his administration. Here would be an unprecedentedly comprehensive institution of higher education, with teaching, research, and public service as its fundamental and interrelated missions. He outlined a vital community of scholars gathering strength from a reinvigorated and modernized dormitory system and a student commons and union as the campus centers of student life. The president's address marked its author and his institution as forces to be reckoned with in American higher education.

Thanks in part to Van Hise's association with the La Follette progressives, the next few years were remarkably successful ones for the University, although complete implementation of the ideal remained elusive. The three basic missions all experienced dramatic improvement as Van Hise delegated authority to his deans, fortified increasingly important academic units such as the new Graduate School, and supported initiatives to establish general and agricultural extension agencies as dedicated instruments of University public service outreach. More subtly and of longer-run import, the president oversaw the development of a campus master plan designed to encourage scholars from the various disciplines regularly to associate with one another and to collaborate in their work when appropriate. He greatly strengthened the developing tradition of faculty participation in University governance by dramatically expanding the number of faculty committees and the responsibilities of the faculty. He was instrumental in founding the University Club, which quickly became the center of faculty social life. The close collaboration between the president and Governor La Follette led to the use of University experts—Van Hise and Birge among them—to assist in the work of state agencies and commissions, a part of what came to be known as the Wisconsin Idea of broad University service to the people of the state. To enhance the quality of student life Van Hise fostered the creation of a student government and appointed the first dean of men to oversee extracurricular student affairs. Although they remained continuing goals, he failed in his efforts to obtain state funding for men's dormitories and a student union. By the time of the First World War it seemed clear, as he had forecast in his inaugural address, that private money might have to be raised for these projects.

The driving force of the Van Hise administration was largely spent by late 1914, when stalwart Republican Emanuel L. Philipp was elected governor after a campaign in which he criticized the progressives and their use of the University for what he considered partisan purposes. Although exaggerated, the charges were to some extent valid, particularly with respect to the well-publicized University Extension Division, which operated outside the normal channels of University governance. Van Hise cultivated the new governor, however, and soon began to persuade him of UW's essentially non-partisan character and its great value to the state.

American entry into the European war in 1917 quickly transformed campus life. President Van Hise and the vast majority of the faculty strongly supported the war effort, though Van Hise's old friend, patron, and now U.S. Senator Robert M. La Follette was a major critic. In January of 1918 Van Hise, all of the deans, and most of the UW faculty signed a "round robin" resolution criticizing La Follette for his anti-war stand, which the statement implied bordered on treason. The estrangement between the two classmates remained bitter and complete when

Van Hise died unexpectedly in November, a few days after the armistice ending the war. Once again the regents called on Dean Birge to take charge of the University in this time of difficult transition.

The unsettled post-war conditions and the seemingly temporary character of the Birge presidency delayed the next major phase of the University's development. This awaited the administration of President Glenn Frank, beginning in 1925 and continuing through that of Clarence A. Dykstra ending in 1945. These years would finally bring the full flowering of Van Hise's combination university. Few would notice, however, as the hopeful outlook of the booming 1920s gave way in the face of a catastrophic economic depression and another world war.

1.

Finding a President

"The University of Wisconsin has been slipping," bluntly warned Theodore Kronshage, the recently elected president of the University's Board of Regents, in an outspoken press release early in 1925. "It is still slipping, and I want the people of the state to know it." Kronshage complained that the University was trying to teach its eight thousand students in buildings designed for half that number, that its library was built for a student body of only two thousand, that the legislature had provided no new classrooms since 1913, and that the University needed 124 full-time teachers just to bring it back to the staffing level of 1911. As a result the teaching load of many faculty members had doubled. "Some of them, who have served the state faithfully for years," he declared, "are finding conditions unbearable and are transferring to more grateful institutions." As Kronshage saw it, the University's predicament was serious, even precarious. "What," he asked rhetorically, "is the matter with Wisconsin?"[1]

What, indeed, had gone wrong since the early years of the twentieth century, when leaders at both ends of Madison's State Street had pioneered the Wisconsin Idea, asking its University to provide an expanded array of services to the people and government of the state? What had eroded the resulting broad base of popular support that had led a succession of governors and legislatures generally to give a sympa-

---

[1] Theodore Kronshage, Jr., "The University of Wisconsin," press release, February 27, 1925, Glenn Frank Papers, Northeast Missouri State University, Kirksville, and BOR Papers, 1/1/3, box 38, UA. This was the first of a series of seven press releases issued by Kronshage over the next several weeks on University budget needs.

13

thetic hearing to University budget requests? The immediate cause of Regent Kronshage's press campaign was an ominous plan to cut the University's funding drastically in the 1925 legislative session. But Kronshage and his fellow regents also realized the budget crisis would jeopardize their search for a nationally prominent successor to President Edward A. Birge, who was to retire later in the year.

Treading Water with President Birge, 1918-1925

There was no disagreement that the University was in difficult circumstances after World War I. President Charles R. Van Hise, for a decade-and-a-half the University's highly respected leader, had died unexpectedly while recovering from routine surgery just after the armistice. Both Van Hise's appointment as president and his brilliant leadership had owed much to his close association with Robert M. La Follette, Sr., the state's dominant political leader and former three-term governor, now Wisconsin's senior U.S. senator. Van Hise and La Follette had been good friends since their days as classmates at the University in the late 1870s. Van Hise and a sizable part of the faculty generally shared La Follette's progressive views and welcomed his paternalistic interest in his alma mater. During these years a town-gown Saturday Lunch Club consisting of progressive Republican legislators and officials and like-minded UW faculty members including Van Hise lunched regularly at the University Club to discuss public policy issues.[2] There were also numerous town-gown dining clubs, some of which included prominent state officials, where easy informality and warm camaraderie bridged the length of State Street.[3] The war brought a rupture in the close association of the University with the La Follette progressives, however. President Van Hise disagreed with La Follette's opposition to the war and took a leading part in marshalling faculty criticism of the senator's views and activities. Early in 1918 he and all the deans and 93 per cent of the faculty signed a "round robin" resolution denouncing La Follette's "utterances and actions, which have given aid and comfort to Germany and her allies in the present war." The condemnation deeply wounded the senator and angered his followers in the legislature and throughout the state. To them the resolution was proof that Van

---

[2]Roger W. Axford, "William Henry Lighty, Adult Education Pioneer" (Ph.D. diss., University of Chicago, 1961), pp. 7-8, 275-9.

[3]See pp. 518-27.

Hise and the University had fallen under the sway of La Follette's political enemies, the conservative or "stalwart" Republicans currently ruling the state.[4]

To succeed Van Hise the Board of Regents turned instinctively to Dean Edward A. Birge of the College of Letters and Science, naming him acting president on December 4, 1918. Two weeks later the regents voted to make Birge president, but at his insistence with the understanding the board would begin searching for "a man to whom the office may be committed with the full expectation that he may hold it for a long term."[5] During the next year the regents failed to conduct a search, and in December of 1919 they asked Birge to withdraw his condition and accept an indefinite term as president.[6] A faculty member since 1875, at the age of sixty-seven Dean Birge was an obvious choice to take over the

presidency on short notice. He was by far the most experienced campus administrator, having headed the University's largest college since 1891. He had served previously as acting president several times, had been Van Hise's chief rival for the presidency in 1903, and had recently administered the University during Van Hise's frequent wartime absences. A distinguished zoologist and the scientific father of American limnology or lake studies, Birge was known for his broad interests,

---

[4]"Round Robin" resolution, January 16, 1918, BOR Papers, 1/1/3, box 31; Merle Curti and Vernon Carstensen, *The University of Wisconsin: A History, 1848-1925* (Madison: University of Wisconsin Press, 1949), vol. 2, p. 115; George C. Sellery, *E. A. Birge: A Memoir* (Madison: University of Wisconsin Press, 1956), p. 49; Belle Case La Follette and Fola La Follette, *Robert M. La Follette* (New York: Macmillan, 1953), vol. 2, pp. 842-52; Paul W. Glad, *The History of Wisconsin*, vol. 5, *War, a New Era, and Depression, 1914-1940* (Madison: State Historical Society of Wisconsin, 1990), pp. 42-3.

[5]Birge to the Regents, December 17, 1918, BOR Papers, 1/1/3, box 32; Curti and Carstensen, *University of Wisconsin*, vol. 2, p. 123.

[6]December 3, 1919, BOR Papers, 1/1/3, box 33; Curti and Carstensen, *University of Wisconsin*, vol. 2, p. 123.

spartan tastes, and unquestioned integrity. His appointment as president represented continuity, tradition, and stability. More conservative and less innovative than Van Hise, however, Birge viewed his administration as limited in both scope and duration. Along with the other deans, Birge had endorsed the wartime round robin resolution, though evidently with some reservations. Privately he believed there might well come a time when it would be politically advantageous for the University to point out that not all of the faculty had joined in the criticism of Senator La Follette nor had the non-signers suffered any reprisals as a result.[7]

Since President Birge expected his administration to be relatively brief, he undertook no major changes nor new initiatives, even in the face of rapidly changing post-war circumstances. Indeed, with his conservative temperament Birge and his associates badly misjudged the University's needs following the war. They planned for enrollment in the fall of 1919 to return to the pre-war level of about five thousand students. Instead nearly seven thousand appeared and another five hundred enrolled during the year, or an increase of nearly 50 percent over the pre-war peak. Birge and the Board of Regents also expected the cost of living to decline after the war, yet prices rose steadily in the serious post-war inflation, generating mounting faculty unhappiness over the rapid erosion of the purchasing power of their static salaries. The University Committee in a series of reports called the situation a "crisis" and appealed for action by the Board of Regents and the legislature.[8] A man of simple wants, Birge was at first unmoved by the faculty complaints and only reluctantly recommended that the regents raise salaries out of current funds pending the appropriation of additional funds by the legislature.[9]

---

[7][Edward A. Birge,] "Edward A. Birge," chapter 10 of a series on the history of the University of Wisconsin, consisting of a letter from Birge to John Berge, secretary of the Wisconsin Alumni Association, September 21, 1942, *WAM*, 44 (November, 1942), 9-18; Curti and Carstensen, *University of Wisconsin*, vol. 2, p. 115, n. 88.

[8]See, for example, UW Faculty Document 128, "Preliminary Report of the University Committee on Salaries of the University Faculty," May 5, 1919, UA; UW Faculty Document 128A, "Supplementary Report of the University Committee on Salaries of the Faculty," May 12, 1919; UW Faculty Document 128B, "Report of the University Committee on the Salaries of the Faculty," May 10, 1919; UW Faculty Document 138, University Committee, "Annual Report for 1918-19," November 3, 1919; UW Faculty Document 158, University Committee, "Special Report on the Matter of Salaries," June 21, 1920; UW Faculty Document 166, University Committee, "Annual Report for 1919-20," October 23, 1920.

[9]For Birge's explanation of his cautious stance on the issue of raising faculty salaries after

Fortunately, Governor Emanuel L. Philipp was sympathetic to the University's plight. A stalwart Republican who had first been elected in 1914 in a campaign criticizing among other progressive reforms the La Follette-Van Hise agenda for the University, Philipp by now had swung around to a more supportive view of the state's major institution of higher education. To deal with the University's very real budget crisis, the governor agreed to call a special session of the legislature in May, 1920, presenting a broad recommendation for increased funding for UW operations and salaries as well as construction of a University hospital, without which the Medical School could not reach full development. Although the progressives and socialists in the legislature were suspicious of the governor and inclined to punish the University for its recent criticism of Senator La Follette and what they believed was its increasing conservatism, the special University appropriation bill, including separate authorization and funding for construction of the hospital, eventually passed as recommended by Governor Philipp. The increase in the University operating budget was accompanied, however, by a sharp debate over tax policy. The governor had endorsed the request by President Birge and the regents to obtain the additional funding by raising the University's share of the state mill rate tax on property. The progressives and socialists in the legislature instead amended the measure so the increased University funding would come from a surtax on individual and corporate incomes. Governor Philipp promptly vetoed the appropriation on the ground that it established a new tax policy under which the state's income tax would be used for specific rather than general purposes. Throughout Birge seemed to side with Philipp and the stalwarts against the progressives.[10]

In spite of this largely barren outcome, the 1920 special legislative session proved to be the most favorable to the University of any during the next five years. Even though enrollments continued to increase—to nearly eight thousand students by 1925—funding for University operations thereafter remained largely frozen and the legislature flatly declined to appropriate construction funds for any new classrooms or dormitories. The noisy debate over state tax policy continued, with the University's budget requests held hostage to ideology.

Following the election of John J. Blaine as governor in 1920, political power in Wisconsin increasingly passed from the stalwart to the

---

the war, see [Birge,] "Birge," pp. 13-6.
[10]Curti and Carstensen, *University of Wisconsin*, vol. 2, pp. 204-12.

progressive wing of the state Republican Party. A forty-seven-year-old native of the small town of Boscobel and a long-time La Follette disciple, Blaine had earlier served in the state senate and most recently as attorney general. Wisconsin citizens overwhelmingly reelected Governor Blaine and Senator La Follette in 1922, with the latter's triumph viewed by his followers as a popular judgment against the senator's wartime critics. The progressives also gained control of both houses of the legislature, where some vowed to use their political power to punish the University and purge it of its alleged conservative leadership. The following year, for example, both houses of the legislature adopted a resolution denouncing the wartime round robin resolution for its "libelous aspersions on the record and character of Robert M. La Follette, Wisconsin's most distinguished citizen." The circulation of the anti-La Follette petition in 1918 was condemned as "unworthy of men employed in Wisconsin's greatest educational institution." Only after the senator intervened did his supporters drop their demand that the offensive resolution be delivered up and burned.[11] Throughout, President Birge seemed largely indifferent to the need for better public relations, either for himself or the institution he headed, and he did little to consolidate political and public support for the University.[12] Birge found relations with Governor Blaine particularly trying. An ambitious politician of strong partisan views and excitable temperament, the governor was convinced the University was under the dominance of the stalwarts and was, as he told the legislature in 1923, "lacking a broad democratic viewpoint."[13] To be sure, when Blaine took office the Board of Regents was solidly conservative with a stalwart majority appointed by Governor

---

[11]Joint Resolution 19, *Laws of Wisconsin*, 1923, p. 1038; Curti and Carstensen, *University of Wisconsin*, vol. 2, p. 218. Senator La Follette's letter requesting that his supporters drop the demand to destroy the round robin resolution was in fact drafted by his twenty-five-year-old son, Philip, who was serving as his Madison lieutenant while his older son, Bob, Jr., ran his Washington office. Philip F. La Follette, *Adventure in Politics: The Memoirs of Philip La Follette*, Donald Young, ed. (New York: Holt, Rinehart and Winston, 1970), pp. 84-5. Since the Madison *Capital Times* had republished the names of the signers of the round robin, it was widely known that President Birge was prominent among them.

[12]Curti and Carstensen, *University of Wisconsin*, vol. 2, pp. 212-23. Birge had a personal acquaintance of sorts with Senator La Follette. Both the senator and his future wife Belle had enrolled in Birge's first biology laboratory course after he joined the UW faculty in 1875. Birge remembered La Follette as an indifferent student who "had no use for science work," but was impressed with Belle's interest and enthusiasm in discovering "a new and totally unexpected world—a world of new life and, still better, of new ideas." Sellery, *Birge*, p. 15.

[13]*Wisconsin Senate Journal*, 1923, pp. 41-2; Curti and Carstensen, *University of Wisconsin*, vol. 2, p. 217.

Philipp during the previous six years, but the governor's belief was not entirely fair to President Birge. A nominal Democrat, Birge did not often engage in partisan politics. He voted for Democrat Cox against Republican Harding in the national presidential election of 1920, for example, but subsequently provided a warm endorsement for Senator La Follette, his one-time student, in the latter's third-party presidential bid in 1924.[14] A more accurate view of the UW president was that on the whole he avoided politics and politicians and tried as much as possible to keep the University free of partisan alignments.

Governor Blaine and his often unruly progressive Republican supporters in the legislature, sometimes augmented by the more radical Socialist and Non-Partisan League factions, had to contend with a serious economic depression in Wisconsin agriculture during the early 1920s. State revenues were down, and Blaine and the legislature were reluctant to increase taxes, especially property taxes that would bear heavily on farmers who provided much of the progressives' support at the polls. Instead, they favored expanding the state's income tax, which would hit the wealthy individual and corporate supporters of the stalwarts. As vacancies developed, the governor gave a high priority to replacing stalwarts on the Board of Regents, beginning in 1921 with the appointment of another Boscobel native and long-time La Follette progressive, Milwaukee attorney Theodore Kronshage, Jr. A UW graduate (A.B., 1891, and L.L.B., 1892), Kronshage had a long-standing interest in education. He had previously served for ten years on the board of normal school regents and two years on the state board of education. The legislature aided in the reform of the University Board of Regents in 1923 by enlarging the board and requiring that in addition to two women its members must include two farmers and two engaged in the manual trades. By 1924 Governor Blaine had achieved a progressive majority of the regents, marked in that year by the unanimous election of his friend Kronshage to preside over the board. The author of a highly laudatory study of Wisconsin progressivism at this time predicted that the effect of the "more liberal board" would "undoubtedly as time passes be reflected in a liberalization of the faculty and of university policies."[15] Governor Blaine was careful to consult Senator

---

[14]Curti and Carstensen, *University of Wisconsin*, vol. 2, pp. 132-3, 138.

[15]Chester C. Platt, *What La Follette's State Is Doing: Some Battles Waged for More Freedom* (Batavia, N.Y.: Batavia Times Press, 1924), p. 12. Intended to support Senator La Follette's 1924 presidential aspirations, this book, by the state manager of the Wisconsin Nonpartisan League, reflected the La Follette progressives' faith in education as a tool of social

La Follette (but not President Birge) about his regent appointments and nearly always followed the senator's suggestions.[16]

Blaine remained convinced that large savings could be achieved for the state by greater University efficiencies, primarily through heavier faculty teaching loads and reduced support for research. He counted on his regent appointees to reform the institution, closely monitoring their attendance and actions at board meetings and occasionally giving them advice and meeting with them privately.[17] When even his own regents showed little enthusiasm for draconian budget cuts, the governor used the Emergency Board, a creation of the progressives to oversee state spending between legislative sessions, to withhold appropriated funds from the University and other state agencies. He boasted in 1924 that he had thereby cut $530,000 from the University's appropriation for the year.[18] Later that year Blaine raised the figure, proudly claiming in a campaign speech that he had "reduced the tax for support of the university $1,115,000,...the first reduction in state taxes in ten years."[19] The message evidently pleased the voters, for the governor was easily reelected to a third term with more votes than in either of his two previous races.

Conceding that he might have an "obsession" on the subject, early in 1925 the governor informed Senator La Follette that he intended to "get right into the entrails of the University," rooting out its "peculiar self-complacency" and "entire indifference toward public service," while at the same time reducing its budget "by hundreds of thousands of dollars." He emphasized: "It's going to be the job of the next President to make the change and the reorganization along fundamental lines."[20] To buttress his belief that the staff of the University was more interested in lucrative outside activities than in public service, the governor went so far as to ask the state assessor of incomes for information about the non-University income of leading members of the UW faculty and

---

reform.

[16]John J. Blaine to Robert M. La Follette, Sr., March 3, 1925, John J. Blaine Papers, box 46, SHSW.

[17]See, for example, Blaine to Theodore Kronshage, Jr., February 19, May 10, 1924, Blaine Papers, boxes 33 and 35; Kronshage to Blaine, March 3, 1924, ibid., box 33; Blaine to Zona Gale, February 19, 1924, ibid.; Blaine to La Follette, February 29, 1924, March 3, 1925, ibid., box 46.

[18]Press release, June 25, 1924, ibid., box 37.

[19]Campaign flyer [ca. August, 1924], ibid., box 40.

[20]Blaine to La Follette, March 3, 1925, ibid., box 46.

administration as reported on their state income tax returns. Coincidentally, most of those listed had signed the wartime round robin resolution. Whether the governor was developing some sort of purge list is not clear, but he told La Follette he intended to present information on "fifty to a hundred of the professors" to the Board of Regents, "which I think will result in a complete reorganization and a President will have to be selected who will meet that situation."[21] Blaine's letter was sufficiently ominous that Belle La Follette wrote her son Philip in Madison that "it reads as though he had softening of the brain," adding it had "caused Daddy some loss of sleep."[22] Although it does not appear the governor's activities were known at the other end of State Street, University supporters had good reason to question the depth and nature of Blaine's commitment to the institution's well-being.

The Flirtation with Roscoe Pound

As early as 1923 the La Follette family, Governor Blaine, a few regents, and even some members of the faculty were beginning to plan for Birge's likely retirement and replacement as University president. The speculation was muted and private, for the president was highly respected and gave no hint of any thought of departing his Bascom Hall office. Actually, Birge had expected to leave his post when he turned

---

[21]Ibid.; H.R. Briggs to Blaine, February 28, March 13, 1925, ibid. Following up an earlier request for information about the outside incomes of a number of top UW faculty members, Blaine expressed special interest in the tax returns of President Birge, Medical School Dean Charles Bardeen, Dean of Men Scott Goodnight, Dean of Women Louise Nardin, and Professor W.O. Hotchkiss, the state geologist, with whom he was currently feuding over the latter's support for highway development in opposition to the governor's economy drive. Blaine to Briggs, March 9, 1925, ibid.

[22]Belle C. La Follette to Philip F. La Follette, two letters, March 9, 1925, P.F. La Follette Papers, box 133, SHSW. Like her husband, Belle La Follette was a liberal arts baccalaureate graduate of the Class of 1879 and subsequently of the Law School. Also like her husband, she took an abiding interest in the University. She used her influence as the governor's wife in 1903, for example, to help secure a $10,000 appropriation to start a home economics program in the College of Letters and Science, later moved to the College of Agriculture. A quiet but determined feminist, she also campaigned for the appointment of women faculty and lobbied against University nepotism policies that discriminated against well-qualified faculty wives. See Lucy Freeman and George Zabriskie, *Belle: The Biography of Belle Case La Follette* (New York: Beaufort Books, 1986); Dee Ann Montgomery, "An Intellectual Biography of Belle Case La Follette" (Ph.D. diss., Indiana University, 1975); Maria Bode, comp., "Belle Case La Follette: A Source List" (unpublished pamphlet, 1981), SHSW; Mina Crocker, "Thirty Years of Home Economics," *WAM*, 36 (January, 1935), 107, 126.

seventy in 1922 and was surprised when the regents made no move to find a successor. He kept his own counsel, however, believing like a good soldier his superiors would let him know when his tour was up.[23] It was no secret, however, that Birge would be seventy-two at the start of the coming academic year, well past the University's traditional retirement age. The changing political complexion of the state and the Board of Regents, moreover, made it increasingly likely the progressives would determine the choice of Birge's successor, a consideration that had probably kept them from pressing the issue earlier. As prominent UW graduates, Senator La Follette and his wife Belle had always taken a proprietary interest in their alma mater, sharing the progressives' faith in education as a powerful agent for social change. While in recent years the senator had largely refrained from direct involvement in University affairs, he and his wife were clearly interested in the direction of the institution. They intended to have a hand in the selection of its next president. Governor Blaine, too, was determined to see that a new president measured up to his conception of the University's needs and mission.

Senator La Follette in particular had given considerable thought to the requisite qualities needed to lead a great university. With its dominant position at the apex of Wisconsin's educational system, La Follette regarded the University as one of the most important institutions of the state. In the right hands it could assure a steady supply of well-educated young men and women—the future leaders of the state and nation—imbued with a commitment to public service and the common good. The key ingredient, the senator told a friend, was "high moral courage":

> The greatest work of a university is to *build character*. It takes the raw youth of the state in the formation period, when the mental and moral fiber is most pliable. It should give the youth back to the state—a citizen, well grounded in scholarship; but *above and before all else*—a citizen in whom the upbuilding and *development of character* has been the *first consideration* of those who have controlled his university life. I believe that a university president should have the broadest scholarship, possess executive ability and tact,—but *more than all else*, that he should be a *great moral and spiritual power*, strong enough to make that *the dominant influence in the university over which he presides.*[24]

---

[23][Birge,] "Birge," pp. 10-1, 16-7.

[24]La Follette to A.B. Butler, July 14, 1923, quoted in La Follette and La Follette, *La Follette*, vol. 2, pp. 1153-4. Emphasis in original.

La Follette's model seemed based on his memory of former UW President John Bascom, his revered philosophy teacher, spiritual guide, and father-figure during his student days in Madison.

By early 1923 the La Follettes had settled on the family's choice for Birge's successor. He was Robert Morss Lovett, an English professor and former dean of junior colleges at the University of Chicago, whose progressive views as a member of the editorial board of the *New Republic* were well-known. From Madison, which he visited often as the family's political agent, the senator's older son and secretary, Robert M. La Follette, Jr., reported to his parents that he had "not been asleep on the University matter." His younger brother Phil had interviewed "in the strictest confidence" three UW faculty members—Roe, Kiekhofer, and Otto—before visiting Lovett in Chicago to report favorable faculty sentiment. For his part, Bob had conferred at length with Regent Kronshage as to whether the La Follette faction yet had a working majority on the Board of Regents that could assure Lovett's appointment. Kronshage listed eight progressive regents to six stalwarts, with two independents, but the progressives were not necessarily under La Follette control, and he warned that "our problem is to sell L to them." Kronshage was reluctant to move prematurely, pointing out that the stalwarts had not forced the selection of a new UW president when they controlled the board. Bob urged the appointment of another La Follette supporter, Democrat Daniel Grady of Portage, as a replacement for an outgoing stalwart member, Walter J. Kohler, and the early election of Kronshage as board president. "The Board is still too close for comfort," he reminded his parents, "and besides we need a vigorous man with experience to help hold Ted [Kronshage] up to scratch."[25]

Governor Blaine, a progressive with ambitions and a political machine of his own, quickly got wind of these La Follette maneuvers and moved to exert his authority. Writing Senator La Follette that he had picked up "a rumbling regarding a successor to President Birge," he blandly observed that his appointee, Regent Kronshage, had suggested the senator "ought to get busy on helping us find a suitable president" in view of talk about Agriculture Dean Harry Russell and physics Professor Max Mason as likely inside candidates. Blaine fig-

---

[25]Robert M. La Follette, Jr., to his parents, January 16, 1923, La Follette Family Papers, box A30, Library of Congress. Though a Democrat, Grady had admired and supported the senior La Follette for many years. Governor Blaine appointed him to the board the following year.

ured the regents were evenly split along progressive-stalwart lines and thought at least two regents "might balk at any attempt to put over an election without thorough consideration and publicity." The governor said he had reviewed and confirmed his authority to remove regents at his pleasure, and had advised Kronshage "that the Governor would not stand for the election of a president until after he had the opportunity to study the candidates and indicate his objection, if in fact not his endorsement." Without directly challenging Wisconsin's senior statesman, the governor appeared to be suggesting there should be no attempt at a La Follette coup over the UW presidency.[26]

In April Governor Blaine again wrote Senator La Follette about the University presidency. He reported that Regent Zona Gale, the Pulitzer Prize-winning Portage author and La Follette progressive whom Blaine had appointed to the board at the senator's suggestion the previous year, had passed on several suggestions from Oswald Garrison Villard, the editor of the liberal *Nation* magazine in New York. Villard proposed President William A. Neilson of Smith College ("the most successful college president in the country today....a perfect jewel; a liberal—though not out-spokenly so"), Carl Van Doren, an English professor at Columbia University and the literary editor of the *Century Magazine* ("a charming personality; is a real liberal; a complete believer in free speech and everything *The Nation* stands for, yet gives no offense"), Columbia Professors Carlton Hayes and Harold L. MacBain ("both good liberals and excellent executives"), and Illinois Professor

---

[26]John J. Blaine to R.M. La Follette, Sr., February 5, 1923, La Follette Family Papers, box B95. Three weeks later Blaine reported to the senator that he had conferred further with Attorney General Herman Ekern, a La Follette intimate, with Kronshage, and with Professor Joseph S. Evans of the Medical School about the UW presidency. Based on these talks, Blaine now believed "the attempt will be made to put over Max Mason....The gossip is that he is Birge's choice, and it was the plan of Van Hise before his death." His conferees had suggested other possibilities—the historian Frederick Jackson Turner, formerly of Wisconsin and now at Harvard, and Dean Ellwood P. Cubberley, of the Stanford College of Education—but the governor was concerned that he knew nothing about their political philosophy. In any event, Blaine said he had told Kronshage "it would be very inadvisable to elect during the session of the legislature, at least for the next two months, and I rather feel that whoever is to be elected should meet with the approval of the administration, else his tenure of office might be no more than a year, and no man would want to come here unless he had some assurance that his presence was acceptable to the administration." It was clear Blaine intended to be involved in the presidential selection and he intimated that he expected no trouble from a pliant Board of Regents. "I don't like to exercise the arbitrary power of removal of a regent," he told La Follette, "as I would fear the reaction, unless the circumstances would justify it." Blaine to R.M. La Follette, Sr., February 28, 1923, ibid.

Stuart P. Sherman ("a brilliant person; an unusual writer,...but I must confess the general effect of his writing is very conservative not to say reactionary"). Concerning Neilson, Gale had pointed out "that his being president of an old conservative institution might look good to the other people."[27]

Shortly before departing on a European vacation in the summer of 1923, Senator La Follette arranged to meet with Lovett in New York to discuss the UW presidency. Afterward La Follette noted in his diary, "All present *were most favorably impressed with Lovett.*"[28] Belle La Follette assured their daughter Mary that Lovett was "simple, direct, ready, fine sense of humor, a very pleasing smile...a scholar but nothing academic."[29] Young Bob continued to worry that things might go awry and urged his father to confer with Governor Blaine and others in Madison about the presidential succession before sailing. "The matter cannot wait until our return from Europe," he told his parents, "and it should be settled certainly before we go. It is of too great importance to be permitted to be handled without some of us looking after it."[30] During the next few months members of the La Follette family continued their pursuit of a Lovett presidency, aware that other contenders were being mentioned. In December Phil La Follette made his brother a startling proposal: to recruit Lovett, Dean Roscoe Pound of the Harvard Law School, and former Amherst President Alexander Meiklejohn—"all three one as President, another as Dean of L.&.S., and the other as Dean of Men or possibly one of the other Depts."[31] Anxiety mounted as the family continued to push for early action on Lovett. Early in the new year Belle La Follette wrote her son Bob: "Let us know about the U.W. Presidency as soon as you have anything on it. It interests me more than the U.S. Presidency and I am not sure it is not more important."[32] This was surely a striking comment from one whose

---

[27]Blaine to R.M. La Follette, Sr., April 4, 1923, La Follette Family Papers, box B95. Gale was referring to the stalwart regents.

[28]Diary entry, July 31, 1923, quoted in La Follette and La Follette, *La Follette*, vol. 2, p. 1074. Emphasis in original.

[29]Belle La Follette to Mary La Follette Sucher, August 1, 1923, La Follette Family Papers, box A29. We are indebted to Professor Bernard A. Weisberger for calling this letter to our attention.

[30]R.M. La Follette, Jr., to his parents, July 11, 1923, ibid., box A30. See also R.M. La Follette, Jr., to his parents, July 7, 10, and 14, 1923, ibid., about his efforts to persuade Governor Blaine to fill two vacancies on the Board of Regents with La Follette progressives.

[31]P.F. La Follette to R.M. La Follette, Jr., December 6, 1923, ibid.

[32]B.C. La Follette to R.M. La Follette, Jr., January 15, 1924, ibid.

husband would shortly launch an unsuccessful third-party bid for the U.S. presidency.

In late January Bob, Jr., told his parents of a plan for Governor Blaine to interview Lovett with Regent Callahan, the state superintendent of public instruction, who was considered a central figure because of his influence with educators across the state. Another key regent was Elizabeth Waters, a Fond du Lac school teacher and prominent University graduate, because of her influence with UW alumni. "If it works out well and C is strong for our man," Bob noted, "we will put C to work on Miss Waters with whom he is said to have great influence." Bob stressed he was trying to avoid any political friction with the governor and had assured Blaine the La Follettes were supporting him for re-election. "I felt the University matter was so important," he explained, "that I could not risk any trouble with him until it is out of the way."[33] Regent Kronshage also encouraged Governor Blaine to interview Lovett, especially with respect to his position on the wet-dry issue, "because I believe it might have some bearing on the situation."[34]

Although Phil La Follette assured his mother "the University matter seems to be progressing in fine shape,"[35] Governor Blaine's meeting with Lovett did not go well. After interviewing both Lovett and Van Doren, Blaine confided his reactions to Zona Gale. Of the two men, Blaine said he preferred Van Doren because in a three-hour interview Lovett had seemed reluctant to comment on the governor's blunt-spoken iconoclastic views on the problems of higher education:

> I charged the churches and universities with being materialistic and dominated by materialistic notions and thought, and left the way open, but got no response. I criticized severely the present system of education, that is a system that was attempting to develop super-specialists in large numbers, while the product as a whole developed scarcely any leadership except in the training of young men and women in methods that assisted the powerful interests of this country in cheating and exploiting. I got no response or discussion on that.

Van Doren, on the other hand, was more forthcoming. "I got a great deal of his reaction on all these propositions," Blaine noted, "and they

---

[33]R.M. La Follette, Jr., to "Dear Ones," January 27, 1924, ibid., box A31.

[34]Kronshage to Blaine, January 29, 1924, Blaine Papers, box 32.

[35]P.F. La Follette to B.C. La Follette, February 18, 1924, La Follette Family Papers, box A31.

were favorable."[36] Young Bob, however, reported to his parents his understanding that Lovett had made a good impression on both Blaine and Callahan, but noted the latter's strong interest in the candidacy of Dean Pound. He also expressed concern over Lovett's unwillingness to give definite assurance he would accept the presidency.[37]

Mindful of the La Follette family's deep interest in the UW presidency, Governor Blaine asked Miss Gale to visit the senator in Washington "to discuss the University matters," suggesting she share his letter evaluating Lovett and Van Doren. He also wrote Senator La Follette that he doubted any presidential appointment would be made soon and complained that some of his regents, including Gale herself, were not attending board meetings regularly. Off-handedly, the governor enclosed a copy of a three-page letter he had written to Alfred T. Rogers, the senator's Madison law partner, pointing out Rogers' ownership of a sizable block of *Capital Times* stock and accusing him and thus indirectly the La Follettes of tacitly supporting the Madison paper's recent editorial attacks on the Blaine administration.[38] An experienced bare-knuckle fighter himself, Senator La Follette immediately recognized the significance of the letter to Rogers. "Altogether it looks like this is to be held as a club over whole situation," he wired Bob, Jr., in Madison. "Hence doubt if any action can be taken now unless you who are on the ground can see some certain way of putting it through."[39] Meanwhile young Bob reported gloomily that Regent Callahan's informants at the University of Chicago had told him there were a hundred men at the university with more executive ability and two hundred with higher academic standing than Lovett.[40]

Given the unpredictable nature of the situation, young Bob and the

---

[36]Blaine to Gale, February 19, 1924, Blaine Papers, box 33.

[37]Except for Regent Waters, about whom he remained doubtful, Bob told his parents he was confident "the other progressive members of the Board will I am sure take programe [*sic*; i.e., follow instructions] on this matter." R.M. La Follette, Jr., to "Dear Ones," February 22 and 27, 1924, La Follette Family Papers, box A31.

[38]Blaine to R.M. La Follette, Sr., February 29, 1924, Blaine Papers, box 33, and La Follette Family Papers, box B97; Blaine to Alfred T. Rogers, February 29, 1924, ibid.

[39]R.M. La Follette, Sr., to R.M. La Follette, Jr., draft telegram, March 1, 1924, La Follette Family Papers, box A31. It is unclear whether the senator sent this telegram on March 1. In a similar draft dated March 3, after the sentence "Hence doubt if any action can be taken now" he crossed out these revealing words: "certainly unless L. ready to decide also willing to stand in a fight and the necessary eight absolutely reliable. If you are sure all these points would favor putting it through otherwise take no action and await developments." Ibid.

[40]R.M. La Follette, Jr., to "Dear Ones," March 1, 1924, ibid.

other La Follette lieutenants in Madison concluded the best strategy was the senator's fall-back option—the creation of a regent presidential selection committee chaired by Kronshage with authority to select its members, the latter proviso "in order to be sure of the committee," Bob told his parents. "My idea is that if L. says he will take it we should crowd him through the committee and the board." If Lovett declined, he added, "among all the others I am strongest for Pound."[41] The Madison La Follette advisers did not believe the governor's letter to Rogers was "sufficient evidence upon which to base a row," especially since Blaine had agreed to the Kronshage selection committee.[42] True to this plan, on March 5 the Board of Regents secretly authorized the appointment of a presidential selection committee chaired by Regent Kronshage and gave him the authority to select its other four members. Young Bob speculated that Kronshage would appoint Regents Grady, Gale, Callahan, and Butler, "which I think is the committee that you and Herman [Ekern] discussed."[43] He also expressed dismay at Kronshage's inclination to undertake a thorough national search in spite of Bob's protest that "much of this has been done." Ekern and the two La Follette brothers all believed the senator should "ask Ted to come down to Washington and talk the matter over with him and if necessary lay down the law to him." The matter was too important "for us to neglect any phase of it."[44]

Upon her return from Washington Gale reported to Blaine that Senator La Follette was "anxious to get the best man from the standpoint of outlook, attitude toward life—the man who can *communicate* visions." Her New York literary contacts had spoken highly of Van Doren as "thoroughly fine, wise, modern, dependable, sane." Although Gale had met Lovett only once, she had "an impression of great quiet powers," and said she would be "inclined to take a chance, a risk even, on the administrative ability of whomever we select." Of the two, Gale told the governor she favored Lovett, perhaps because "I found the La Follettes very strongly for him." "But why not have them both," she enthused, "one for President and one to succeed Dr. Young?" a reference to Karl Young, the long-time chairman of the English Department,

---

[41]R.M. La Follette, Jr., to "Dear Ones," March 3, 1924, ibid.

[42]R.M. La Follette, Jr., to "Dear Ones," March 4, 1924, ibid.

[43]R.M. La Follette, Jr., to "Dear Ones," March 6, 1925, ibid. Attorney General Herman L. Ekern was a lifelong La Follette supporter and family intimate.

[44]R.M. La Follette, Jr., to "Dear Ones," March 14, 1924, ibid.

who had left the University the previous year.[45]

Lovett, whose liberal politics and activism later led President Franklin D. Roosevelt to appoint him governor of the Virgin Islands, later recalled in his memoirs considerable confusion over his candidacy for the Wisconsin presidency. After his meetings with Senator La Follette and Governor Blaine, Lovett asked Professor John R. Commons, a prominent UW economist, for advice. Commons replied that while Lovett had the support of many modern language faculty members, they lacked influence; the more powerful social science departments favored Dean Roscoe Pound of the Harvard Law School. Commons also advised his friend that he anticipated a conservative reaction before long that would restore the stalwarts' control of the Board of Regents, which might then throw out a progressive like Lovett. "A Christian like you wouldn't last a week," Commons reportedly predicted. According to Lovett, at one point in the spring of 1924 Phil La Follette had "burst upon" him to report that the Board of Regents intended to appoint him to the presidency the next day. The La Follettes were evidently unaware, however, of a recent secret understanding between President Birge and the regents that he could serve the University for an even fifty years. If the Lovett backers knew about this agreement, they had miscounted; Birge was as yet a year short of his promised half-century mark.[46]

What to a later observer is intriguing about this early maneuvering is not only the extent to which it involved the top political leadership of the state but that it was mostly informal and outside the usual University governance channels. The Board of Regents did not get around to designating a presidential selection committee until March of 1924, well after the interviews with Lovett and Van Doren by top Wisconsin

---

[45]Gale to Blaine [ca. April 8, 1924], Blaine Papers, box 34. Emphasis in original.

[46]Robert Morss Lovett, *All Our Years* (New York: Viking Press, 1948), pp. 196-7; Milton Mayer, "Portrait of a Dangerous Man," *Harper's*, 193 (July, 1946), 63. In an often revealing memoir on his presidency written for the alumni association a decade-and-a-half later, Birge recalled:

> Why was my retirement put off to so late a date as 1925, especially in view of the understanding with which I came into the presidency? I did not expect to retire in 1921, as there was still much confusion in the matter of salaries; but I did expect to retire in 1922. But nothing was said to me by the regents, and following my long-time custom, I asked no questions. As time passed I determined not to stay beyond 1925, my fiftieth anniversary, and as we approached close to that date I did not wish to retire before it came.

[Birge,] "Birge," p. 17.

politicians and long after the La Follettes had decided to push Lovett's appointment. Even then the existence of the selection committee was kept secret and its chairman given the unusual authority to name the other members. The board apparently never discussed or drew up a list of qualifications and expectations to guide the search. Indeed, it is not at all clear that President Birge or most of the regents were even aware of the preliminary discussions to identify a successor to Birge during 1923 and early 1924 before the appointment of the committee. News of the presidential selection committee did not leak out until more than two months after its appointment. "I am surprised that we have been able to keep this matter confidential so long," young Bob commented to his parents.[47]   At Governor Blaine's urging the committee held its first meeting on May 21, 1924, shortly after the *Wisconsin State Journal* broke the news of the committee's existence. For once sensitive to appearances, the governor asked Kronshage to call the first meeting of the committee before its only stalwart member, Harry Butler, left the board the following month, in order to get Butler's views as to procedure and, not least, to "avoid any suggestion of unfair play or precipitate action." It would, Blaine confided, "be a great protection to me if the committee would meet as suggested."[48]

As young Bob had predicted, the initial membership of the presidential selection committee was as Senator La Follette had wanted: progressives Theodore Kronshage, Zona Gale, Daniel Grady, stalwart Harry Butler (briefly), and ex officio regent John Callahan, the state superintendent of public instruction. Especially after Kronshage was elected president of the full board in June, he quickly became its dominant member. Although the committee kept no permanent records, Callahan as its secretary did establish more orderly procedures than had been followed up to that point. He developed files on various candidates suggested by alumni and others and solicited evaluations of their qualifications and experience. Although the UW faculty had created its University Committee as a small general faculty executive body in 1916, the search committee did not seek its advice and evidently took note of faculty sentiment only haphazardly and informally, if at all.

Over the next few months the selection committee considered some

---

[47]R.M. La Follette, Jr., to R.M. La Follette, Sr., May 20, 1924, La Follette Family Papers, box A31.

[48]Blaine to Kronshage, May 10, 1924, Blaine Papers, box 35. A prominent and respected Madison corporate attorney, Butler was a conservative Democrat who had been appointed to the board by stalwart Governor Emanuel L. Philipp in 1920.

fifty candidates, among them William Washburn Child, the former editor of *Collier's Weekly* and recent ambassador to Italy, President Frank L. McVey of the University of Kentucky (about whom Kronshage reported he had heard "many good things"), A. Ross Hill, a former president of the University of Missouri, President Henry Suzzallo of the University of Washington, Glenn Frank, the rising young editor of the liberal *Century Magazine* in New York, physicist Robert A. Milliken, President Walter A. Jessup of the University of Iowa, President Frank Aydelotte of Swarthmore College, Dean Gordon Laing of the University of Chicago, Herbert J. Davenport of Cornell University, and Walter W. Stewart, formerly a professor of economics at Amherst College and currently the director of research and statistics at the Federal Reserve Board. Eventually the list was narrowed to Harvard Law Dean Roscoe Pound, Professor Otis W. Caldwell, the director of several experimental education programs at Columbia University Teachers College, Professor Robert Morss Lovett of the University of Chicago, President William Allen Neilson of Smith College, and Frank P. Graves, the New York state commissioner of education.[49] The committee sought evaluations of these candidates by mail and through interviews with a number of leading educators. Often it was advised that the individual under consideration was unlikely to be available. Most of those contacted believed Dean Pound would never leave Harvard, for example, and Boston philanthropist Edward A. Filene, for whom Glenn Frank had worked before joining the *Century Magazine*, doubted Frank could be induced to give up his prestigious and well-paid editorship in New York.[50]

The selection committee evidently gave little or no consideration to the possibility of appointing another insider, though Clough Gates, a progressive newspaperman from Superior and a future regent, did suggest a former UW faculty member, economist Balthasar H. Meyer. In 1905 as a notable illustration of what later would be known as the Wisconsin Idea, Governor La Follette had tapped Meyer to serve on the Wisconsin Railroad Commission, from which President William Howard

---

[49]See Kronshage to Callahan, May 27, 1924, Theodore Kronshage Papers, box 4, SHSW; Callahan to Lynn H. Hough, June 19, 1924; Callahan to Edward A. Filene, June 24, 1924, Michael B. Olbrich Papers, box 2, SHSW; Gustav A. Lake to Blaine, July 11, 1924, and memorandum [ca. December, 1924], Blaine Papers, boxes 38 and 45; *Wisconsin State Journal*, January 22, 1925.

[50]Memorandum [ca. December, 1924], Blaine Papers, box 45; Edward A. Filene to Callahan, October 8, 1924, Olbrich Papers, box 2.

Taft had subsequently appointed him in 1911 to his present seat on the Interstate Commerce Commission.[51] The Madison *Capital Times*, the only consistent La Follette daily paper in the state, raised the intriguing possibility of Alexander Meiklejohn, who had recently been fired as president of Amherst College for his controversial educational reforms and tangled finances, but the suggestion was evidently ignored by the committee. It nevertheless sparked a quick protest to Governor Blaine from a UW alumnus now on the faculty of the University of Montana.[52] Once the selection committee's existence was public knowledge, Governor Blaine felt obliged to deny any involvement in the selection process, which, his secretary asserted with more force than candor, was "entirely in the hands of the Board of Regents."[53]

This was not quite the case. Learning the selection committee was nearing a decision, in late December Governor Blaine asked Regents Kronshage and Gale to meet with him prior to the next board meeting, with, as Kronshage promised, "a view of going over the entire presidential situation."[54] Although the board took no action at its meeting in late December, after reading press speculation that the selection committee intended to give its recommendation at the January meeting, one of the other regents, progressive John C. Schmidtmann of Manitowoc, hastily sought Senator La Follette's views and advice, which he said "would carry much weight" with the La Follette regents.[55] The senator declined to recommend any particular candidate, but cautioned that the regents should not be stampeded into electing a president the same day they received the committee's recommendation. The selection was "of the utmost importance, not only for Wisconsin, but for the entire country," La Follette declared. In a revealing passage he went on to express at some length his deep dissatisfaction with the current state of the University, and, no doubt, his lingering hurt from the faculty's nearly unanimous wartime rebuke:

---

[51]Clough Gates to Kronshage, November 29, 1924, Kronshage Papers, box 5.

[52]John W. Nash to Blaine, July 9, 1924, Blaine Papers, box 38. Nash cautioned Blaine about "ugly rumours afloat concerning certain financial matters while he [Meiklejohn] was at Amherst." Young Bob La Follette agreed that Meiklejohn lacked executive ability "and that is much needed." R.M. La Follette, Jr., to his parents, March 3, 1924, La Follette Family Papers, box A31. For more on Meiklejohn, see Chapter 3.

[53]Frank W. Kuehl to W.R. Russell, August 12, 1924, Blaine Papers, box 40.

[54]Blaine to Gale and Kronshage, December 26, 1924, ibid., box 44; Kronshage to Blaine, December 27, 1924, Kronshage Papers, box 5.

[55]John C. Schmidtmann to R.M. La Follette, Sr., January 6, 1925, La Follette Family Papers, box B102.

Under the deadly influences which came with the war, and the evils attending the Philipp administrations, she became a veritable hot-bed for the hatching out and spreading of ideas hostile to the old democratic spirit which had prevailed at the University from the days of President John Bascom down. Every member of her faculty known as a liberal or progressive in his beliefs has been quietly discriminated against or openly persecuted.

Some of us have spent a lifetime in making the government of Wisconsin stand before all the world for liberty and equality, and today the men who control the University openly teach hostility to everything the State of Wisconsin represents before all the world....

Our University is a *state University*. It belongs to the people of Wisconsin. The state was not made for the university. The university was established to serve the state....Now is the time of greatest crisis for the University, and through the influence of the University for the state. The man chosen as President will, whether he be right or wrong, be President for the next ten years. In that time the University will have become deeply rooted in reaction or she will be established as the great exponent of all that is progressive in higher education.[56]

Concerned about rumors that Dean Roscoe Pound of the Harvard Law School had the inside track, in early January young Bob La Follette urged his brother Phil in Madison not to give up on Lovett. "We must stop action at the January meeting!" he emphasized. "You must help with our true friends on the board to put it off until February at least. They must see that to act in January is to play into the hands of the reactionaries!"[57] In response, Phil twice met with Governor Blaine, the second time with Attorney General Ekern, to stress the family's concerns and to request that the Board of Regents not take hasty action. Blaine blandly assured them that Kronshage had advised him no appointment would be made at the January regents meeting.[58]

On January 20, the day before the board's next scheduled meeting, Regent President Kronshage met again with Governor Blaine and presumably gave him an informal advance summary of the selection committee's report.[59] There is no record of the discussion at the board's meeting on January 21, but after hearing the recommendation of the selection committee the regents quickly voted to offer the University presidency to Dean Pound. The board authorized a small committee to

---

[56]R.M. La Follette, Sr., to Schmidtmann, January 13, 1925, quoted in La Follette and La Follette, *La Follette*, vol. 2, pp. 1154-5. Emphasis in original.

[57]R.M. La Follette, Jr., to P.F. La Follette, January 7, 1925, P.F. La Follette Papers, box 133.

[58]Philip F. La Follette to "Dear Ones," January 21, 1925, ibid.

[59]M.E. McCaffrey to [Kronshage], January 19, 1925, Kronshage Papers, box 5.

visit Pound in Cambridge to work out the details of the appointment. Only one regent—progressive John E. Cashman—voted against the decision; Schmidtmann protested the choice but acquiesced; and two progressive regents were absent, one of whom—Gale—had told Kronshage she was undecided. The matter was settled in less than a half-hour.[60]

Although the regents had agreed to keep their action secret until they had Dean Pound's acceptance, word of the selection quickly leaked out through the legislature to virtually universal acclaim. Significantly and perhaps ominously, the La Follette family privately expressed reservations and even betrayal. Belle La Follette described the senator as "deeply disappointed and indignant that the University matter was not postponed as he had been led to believe."[61] Phil and young Bob flatly declared they had been double-crossed by the governor. "The man must be mad to have played such a game as this over a matter about which he knew there could be no compromise," Bob, Jr., complained bitterly:

> It seems as if we were in for a series of lickings. I hope that I am a good enough sport to take them as they come, but I am damned if I will take them lying down, and when the man who helped to give us this one puts his head above the parapet I shall take extreme pleasure in endeavoring to make its conformity, his head, I mean, resemble nothing so much as a dish pan....It is my idea not to blow off any steam concerning what happened in Madison but to bide our time and keep our powder dry....There can be no harm however in keeping our rifles clean and filing off the head of the hammer and putting in a weak trigger spring.[62]

More philosophical than her sons and conscious that the La Follettes did not have firm control of the Board of Regents, Belle resignedly told her children she and their father believed "Pound is the best we can get so we hope he may accept."[63] There was always the possibility that he might decline, however, in which case the senator intended to press for a delay that might help Lovett's chances.[64]

---

[60]Philip F. La Follette to his parents, January 21, 1925, P.F. La Follette Papers, box 133; *Wisconsin State Journal*, January 22 and 23, 1925; *Capital Times*, January 22, 1925; Fred L. Holmes, news service release, January 22, 1925, UHP.

[61]B.C. La Follette to "Dear ones all," January 25, 1925, P.F. La Follette Papers, box 133.

[62]R.M. La Follette, Jr., to his parents, January 22, 1925, ibid.

[63]B.C. La Follette to "Loved Ones," January 30, 1925, La Follette Family Papers, box A31.

[64]R.M. La Follette, Sr., to R.M. La Follette, Jr., telegram, January 30, 1925, P.F. La

Other reactions to Dean Pound's selection were considerably more enthusiastic. The generally stalwart *Wisconsin State Journal* applauded the regents for their "long and patient endeavors to put a man at the head of this great institution who will maintain its traditions of education and service to the state, going hand in hand."[65] One of the other candidates, New York Education Commissioner Frank Graves, wired Kronshage that the board's "excellent choice" would be "heartily commended by the academic world."[66] President Birge, who had not participated in the board's deliberations, quickly telegraphed Pound of his "great satisfaction and pleasure in your election as president of the university." He promised to "render all the aid that I can in the transfer of the administration into your hands" and assured Pound he was not only the unanimous choice of the regents but would "also find a faculty united in welcoming you and in helping your administration."[67] Echoing the president's enthusiasm, Professor E.A. Ross, who earlier had served with Pound for five years on the faculty of the University of Nebraska, told a *State Journal* reporter that Pound was "as big a man as now occupies the presidential chair in any American university." Direct, sincere, and highly principled, yet possessed of a keen sense of humor, Pound could not be dominated by anyone. "He will feel under no obligation to head a class or factional administration," Ross declared.[68] The general view was that the regents had made an excellent choice.

Born and reared in Lincoln, Nebraska, the son of a judge and member of a family of remarkable achievers, Roscoe Pound had studied botany at the University of Nebraska before obtaining his legal education at the Harvard Law School. After admission to the Nebraska bar in 1890, he practiced law in Lincoln while completing a Ph.D. in botany. He joined the faculty of the University of Nebraska Law School in 1899, became its dean in 1903, and subsequently taught at the Northwestern and University of Chicago law schools before moving to the Harvard Law School in 1910, where he was appointed dean in 1916. Currently fifty-four, Pound was in the prime of his professional life. A leading expert on the common law, he was known for his progressive

Follette Papers, box 133.
[65]*Wisconsin State Journal*, January 22, 1925.
[66]F.P. Graves to Kronshage, telegram, January 22, 1925, Kronshage Papers, box 5.
[67]Birge to Roscoe Pound, January 23, 1925, ibid.
[68]*Wisconsin State Journal*, January 23, 1925.

views and his advocacy of sociological jurisprudence—relating judicial decisions to their social and economic context. Pound's education and interests were unusually broad. His prodigious memory, which impressed fellow lawyers and judges with his vast knowledge of case law, had enabled him to master a number of languages. He was also a botanist of note, for whom a rare lichen—*roscopoundia*—is named, and while in Nebraska he directed the botanical surveys of the state and in 1898 published a book on the *Phytogeography of Nebraska*. An outspoken civil libertarian, in 1920 he publicly denounced the anti-radical Palmer raids and subsequently expressed doubt about the fairness of the Sacco-Vanzetti trial. Given his midwestern roots and progressive outlook, it was confidently assumed in Wisconsin, as one commentator declared enthusiastically, "there is no question but what Dean Pound will accept the offer."[69]

Whatever contact the selection committee may have had with Dean Pound before the board's decision to offer him the presidency, it was quickly apparent the regents had received no assurance he would accept the post. After spending two hours with his old friend, UW economics Professor John R. Commons reported that Pound was undecided and would decline unless he received assurances as to the extent of Mrs. Pound's social responsibilities and the provision of administrative and research assistance so he could continue his scholarly work.[70] Regents Kronshage and Callahan travelled to Cambridge and were initially encouraged by the dean's apparent interest in returning to a midwestern coeducational state university. So too was Regent Zona Gale, who also visited Pound to try to sell him on the bright prospects for a reform administration at the University of Wisconsin.

At Harvard, however, various pressures were being mobilized to keep Pound from leaving. Seven hundred Harvard students stood vigil outside his home in the January cold and snow to let the dean know how much they wanted him to remain. A group of prominent members of

---

[69]*Capital Times*, January 23, 1925; *Wisconsin State Journal*, January 22 and 23, 1924; Holmes, news service release, January 22, 1925; "Roscoe Pound," *Who's Who in America, 1942-43* (Chicago: A.N. Marquis, 1942), p. 1777; N.E.H. Hull, "Roscoe Pound," *Constitution*, 2 (Fall, 1990), 68-70. Pound was a good friend of progressive U.S. Supreme Court Justice Louis D. Brandeis, who had helped to persuade him to accept the Harvard appointment in 1910. As an attorney Brandeis had drawn on Pound's ideas in marshalling extensive sociological data in his brief for the landmark *Muller v Oregon* case in 1908, which persuaded the Supreme Court to consider such evidence in upholding an Oregon law limiting the hours of women workers.

[70][Unknown] to Kronshage, telegram, January 24, 1925, Kronshage Papers, box 5.

the New York bar, including a former U.S. cabinet member, described Pound as "the acknowledged leader of legal education throughout those parts of the world where the common law prevails" and declared that his departure would be an irreparable loss to the entire legal profession. His Harvard colleagues appealed to his honor not to abandon the current campaign which he had initiated to raise endowment funds for the Law School.[71]

On January 27 Pound wrote Kronshage that in spite of the "great attraction" of the Wisconsin presidency, he had decided to decline. "I give up the idea of going to Wisconsin with the greatest reluctance," he said, "but I am afraid I have so committed myself here that I must not think of leaving." He enclosed a personal and more candid letter to Callahan in which he spelled out his reasons more fully. For one thing, he had been persuaded that he could not honorably abandon his leadership role in the Law School's unfinished endowment campaign. More important, "confidential advice has come to me from Wisconsin," Pound explained, "that I should be regarded as the choice of a party, and should have to expect political difficulties in the near future." He had asked Regent Gale about this in their meeting the previous day, and "was much disturbed at her answer." She had confirmed that he was the choice of the progressive regents but had pointed out that the present progressive majority on the board would hold for at least the next six years. Pound was not reassured:

> I could not consent to go to an institution of learning as the choice of a party, or where I would be regarded as such. I had assumed a situation entirely divorced from politics, and the information I now have as to the intimate relation of the university and its conduct to politics comes as a distinct shock.[72]

Strongly partisan herself, Gale had very likely misunderstood Pound's concern and tried instead to sell him on the great opportunities for educational reform in Wisconsin as a result of his selection by a progressive-dominated Board of Regents working with a progressive governor and legislature. That he might be concerned about political meddling in internal University affairs seems to have escaped her entirely.

---

[71]Roscoe Pound to Callahan, January 27, 1925, ibid.; *Wisconsin State Journal*, March 15, 1925.

[72]Pound to Kronshage, January 27, 1925; Pound to Callahan, January 27, 1925, Kronshage Papers, box 5.

Pound made his refusal official in a telegram to Callahan on February 1 and released the information to the press the next day.[73]   In Florida, where she and the senator were vacationing, Belle La Follette received the news with mixed feelings, noting sadly, "The University situation makes the heart ache. What to do?"[74] Attorney General Ekern reported to Senator La Follette that Governor Blaine was holding up action to fill three vacancies on the Board of Regents lest the new appointments appear to give a political coloration to the presidential search.   Besides, Blaine had confided that he "had a dark horse candidate for president who had a greater scholastic standing and more degrees than Lovett and was quite as progressive and who if his selection could be put over promptly and without previous airing would be accepted by the faculty." Ekern reminded the governor that La Follette "had this matter more at heart than anything else."[75]   Not wanting to play second fiddle, Robert Morss Lovett, whom the La Follettes had so hoped to see in Bascom Hall, abruptly withdrew his name from further consideration.   Even if the composition of the Board of Regents were changed so as to assure his selection, Lovett told Ekern, this would only "emphasize the political element in my candidacy, which is, I trust, the chief ground of objection to me on the part of the faculty."[76]   The search for a new president was back on square one.

Manning the Ramparts

As the regents pondered their next move, the question of the presidential succession was complicated by a new development. For the 1925-27 biennium the Board of Regents had requested a modest increase of somewhat less than $200,000 a year for operations and an ambitious proposal of approximately $3,000,000 for new buildings ($500,000 a year for the next six years). The state Board of Public Affairs, a watchdog body created by the progressives in 1911 to promote efficiency and

---

[73]Callahan to Kronshage, telegram, February 2, 1925, ibid.; *Wisconsin State Journal*, February 2, March 15, 1925.

[74]B.C. La Follette to "Loved Ones," February 11, 1925, La Follette Family Papers, box A31.

[75]Ekern to R.M. La Follette, Sr., February 7, 1925, ibid., box B102, and Herman L. Ekern Papers, box 67, SHSW.

[76]Lovett to Ekern, February 10, 1925, La Follette Family Papers, box B102; Ekern to R.M. La Follette, Sr., February 19, 1925, ibid., and Ekern Papers, box 67; La Follette and La Follette, *La Follette*, vol. 2, p. 1155; Lovett, *All Our Years*, p. 197.

charged with reviewing agency requests for the legislature, recommended instead a reduction of about $200,000 a year in the University's operating budget and only a token amount for construction. The budget cutters seemed to be taking their cue from Governor Blaine, who in his opening message to the legislature had again complained that too much was being spent on education.[77] President Birge was shocked at this unexpected development. "If the recommendations of the Board are carried out," he wrote Regent Kronshage, "the only thing for us to do that I can see is to discontinue the hospital and medical school or else to dismiss a corresponding number of members of the faculty in other departments."[78] Birge was referring to the new Wisconsin General Hospital, which had opened the previous fall as the clinical base for the expansion of the Medical School to a full four-year curriculum beginning in September, 1925. Both of these developments, Birge and the regents had assumed, would require more staffing, hence their request for increased operating funds.

To meet this new threat Birge and Kronshage quickly decided to mount an unprecedented counterattack. For the time being the presidential search was put on hold, for the regents were well aware they would have a hard time attracting a top-quality candidate to the presidency while the University's operating budget was at substantial risk. One Blaine-La Follette regent advised that there should be no "sugar-coating facts"; the effort should continue "until the people and the legislature are in a state of turmoil over the situation."[79] The opening salvo in the University's lobbying campaign came on February 18 at the traditional legislative banquet at which UW faculty members entertained individual legislators. Welcoming the group, President Birge observed that he spoke as a citizen rather than as president because he expected to retire from the office in June. He reminded the legislators they had always recognized the need for some regular increase in the University's operating budget, "if a strong faculty, chiefly composed of young men, is to be maintained." He also pointed out that the recent opening of the new University Hospital had brought substantial new operating costs. If the legislature were to adopt the reduced budget recommended by the Board of Public Affairs, he warned, "there is only one way to meet the situation—to close schools or departments of the University for which the

---

[77]Sellery, *Birge*, pp. 75-6.
[78]Birge to Kronshage, January 26, 1925, Kronshage Papers, box 5.
[79]Schmidtmann to Kronshage, February 7, 1925, ibid.

state is too poor to provide." Small wonder the regents had not yet found a president for the University, Birge declared. "What man of ability will leave his present position," he asked his audience, "and come to Wisconsin in order...to take an active administrative part in degrading an institution to which the legislature refuses adequate and ordinary support." After recalling past legislative generosity, the president tactfully expressed confidence that again this year the legislature would "maintain the strength of the University and the good fame of Wisconsin."[80]

Birge persuaded Regent President Kronshage to take the lead in the University's public relations campaign. "You are a politician," he is reported to have told Kronshage; "you know how politicians' minds work." Kronshage was indeed a skillful politician, and he had come to have high regard for the University he served. Over the next several months he took a great deal of time from his Milwaukee law practice to lobby individual legislators and speak to audiences around the state. More visible was the series of seven hard-hitting news releases sent out under Kronshage's name to the press of the state under the general eye-catching headline of "The Predicament of the University," with individual articles on such topics as "Where the University Dollar Comes From," "How the University Dollar is Spent," "Building Needs Pile Up Since 1913," "Wisconsin Spends Billions on Luxuries," "8000 Students in Buildings Built for 4000," and "Wisconsin's Neighbors Spend Millions on Buildings." The series was largely ghost-written by journalism Professor Grant Hyde of the University Press Bureau and sharpened by both Kronshage and Fred L. Holmes, an experienced Madison progressive newspaperman who sometimes wrote for *La Follette's Magazine*.[81] Today's UW staff members, who experience the same frustration, will smile sympathetically at Kronshage's lament over the legislature's practice of appropriating all funds to the University, even tuition and external grants not generated by Wisconsin taxes nor provided by the state. This, he indignantly complained, had the effect of artificially inflating the University's budget requests and misleading the public as to the institution's real cost to state taxpayers.[82] The first of the Kronshage

---

[80]Sellery, *Birge*, p. 76.

[81]Ibid., p. 77; Kronshage, press releases, February 25-March 7, 1925, BOR Papers, 1/1/3, box 38, and Frank Papers, Kirksville.

[82]Kronshage, press release, "Where the University Dollar Comes From," March 2, 1925, BOR Papers, 1/1/3, box 38, and Frank Papers, Kirksville.

press releases caused a considerable stir in the state capitol. Attorney General Ekern reported to Senator La Follette that Kronshage's attack on "the parsimoniousness of the administration" had the politicians asking "just what it means."[83]

What it meant was soon clear: an unrivaled University public relations campaign. Birge and Kronshage enlisted the help of George I. Haight, '99, a Chicago attorney and the current president of the Wisconsin Alumni Association. Utterly devoted to his alma mater, the blunt-spoken and hard-driving Haight used his position and the associa-

[handwritten note]

> If the financial measures now before the Legislature are enacted into law, they will not only prevent the development of the University, but they will also cripple it beyond recognition.
>
> No such recommendations have ever been made to any Wisconsin legislature during the past sixty years, nor, so far as I know, to any legislature in the group of states to which Wisconsin belongs.
>
> E. A. Birge.

tion's publications to mobilize the alumni with a dazzling display of inflammatory rhetoric. The March, 1925, issue of the *Wisconsin Alumni Magazine* was largely devoted to alerting its readers to the political threat. In the frontispiece Regent President Kronshage, '91, presented

---

[83]Herman L. Ekern to R.M. La Follette, Sr., February 7, 1925, La Follette Family Papers, box B102.

a detailed review of the budget emergency, "the like of which has not confronted the University since the far-off days of the Civil War." Also reproduced were President Birge's remarks at the recent legislative dinner. Haight appealed for contributions for an Alumni Loyalty Fund, warning: "The University is in danger....The cause is plain; the need is great." The sense of urgency was highlighted by the cover of the magazine, which carried a handwritten appeal by President Birge under the ominous heading, "A Crisis Confronts This University."[84] The resulting funds enabled the association to blanket the alumni with a pamphlet summarizing their alma mater's plight under the compelling title, *The Crisis Confronting the University of Wisconsin, a Plain Story of Fact, Addressed to the Legislature and the People of Wisconsin.*[85] During the spring of 1925 both Kronshage and Haight addressed numerous alumni meetings around the state and country appealing for support of the University.

Fully as important as these public activities was the unpublicized effort to assure favorable treatment by the press and political leadership of the state. Kronshage suggested, for example, that Haight "build a fire" under John L. Sturtevant, the publisher of the *Wausau Daily Record-Herald* for his editorial "filled with misstatements and falsehoods, and abusing President Birge and the Regents for undertaking what he calls 'propaganda'." "Unless something is done to set him right," Kronshage warned, "we will get nothing but unfair treatment from him."[86] Kronshage himself wrote to Walter S. Goodland, the publisher of the *Racine Times-Call* and a future state senator and governor, arguing that the University's needs were generally misunderstood because it had been asked by the state to undertake many functions, such as the work of the county agents and the University Hospital, not directly related to its traditional educational mission.[87] The regent president also worked on key legislators. He informed Regent Gale that Senator Staudenmeyer, a member of the important joint finance committee, was "very luke warm towards University appropriations," so she should have a "serious talk" with him. Kronshage suggested that Haight recruit U.S. Circuit Judge Evan Evans, a former Baraboo attor-

---

[84]*WAM*, 26 (March, 1925). Haight contributed several thousand dollars of his own funds to underwrite the publicity campaign. WAA Board Minutes, May 9, 1926, WAA Papers, 21/2/1, box 3, UA.

[85]Sellery, *Birge*, p. 77.

[86]Kronshage to Haight, February 25, 1925, Kronshage Papers, box 5.

[87]Kronshage to W. S. Goodland, February 21, 1925, ibid.

ney and president of the alumni association, to work further on Staude-meyer. "Should you see him yourself," he advised, "don't forget to tell him you are a product of the soil, because Staudemeyer is very loyal to anything which has an agricultural flavor."[88] Haight and President Birge both lobbied Michael Olbrich, Governor Blaine's executive counsel and chief advisor, warning of the grave damage to the University if the proposed budget cuts were implemented. Haight pointed out that Roscoe Pound's rejection of the University presidency was an outside judgment on the serious nature of the University's problems.[89]

Soon other voices were raised on behalf of the University. The editor-publisher of the *Grant County Herald* reported to Kronshage that the Lancaster Kiwanis Club had adopted resolutions "backing the University Regents in their request for funds and instructing the secretary to write our representatives, senator and Gov. Blaine apprising them of our views and action."[90] On the other side of the state the legislative educational committee of the Milwaukee Association of Commerce resolved that it was "for the best interest of the City of Milwaukee and the state of Wisconsin that the University shall again attain its former high rank as an educational institution." Hence it was "imperative that the legislature provide proper financial support not only for this, but for coming years."[91] A prominent resident of Menomonie assured Kronshage that the campaign had "sold the University to the people of this neck of the woods," while the secretary of the Wisconsin Teachers Association congratulated the regent president "for the splendid fight you have been making to save the University."[92]

Governor Blaine was harder to convince. Throughout the spring of 1925, as public support for the University mounted, he remained adamantly opposed to any tax increase and continued to believe substantial savings could be wrung from the University's budget. As noted earlier, the governor was at this time collecting tax data on the outside income of prominent University faculty and administrators, possibly with an intent to use the information against his UW critics. To counter the Kronshage press releases about University space needs, he sought

---

[88]Kronshage to Gale, March 31, 1925; Kronshage to Haight, March 31, 1925, ibid.

[89]Haight to Michael Olbrich, February 24, 1925; Birge to Olbrich, February 25, 1925, Olbrich Papers, box 2.

[90]A.L. Sherman to Kronshage, March 4, 1925, Kronshage Papers, box 5.

[91]William L. Pieplow to Kronshage, April 23, 1925, ibid.

[92]A.C. Anderson to Kronshage, March 14, 1925; Edgar G. Doudna to Kronshage, March 16, 1925, ibid.

information about the University's long-range building plans looking for evidence of grandiose expectations. When he read a newspaper report that the Iowa legislature had cut $400,000 a year from the budget of the University of Iowa, Blaine promptly wrote an Iowa legislator for details, explaining, "The University here is making quite unusual demands and many extravagant statements"; hence his need for "such information as will assist me here."[93] To a UW critic who had complained about "the blah which university authorities are in the habit of blowing around," the governor offered reassurance:

> As I see the situation now in the legislature, there isn't any danger of anyone running away with excessive appropriations for the University. It doesn't appear that the University needs more buildings or more instructors and teachers and professors. There is something else they need. It is over-organized, over-manned, super-headed, with fictitious standards, and a lot of other things that bring about unnecessary expense.
>
> That is a problem that I am trying to work out, but you know how hard it is for the Governor to do so, as the whole thing is buried under a heap of professionalism that is hard to penetrate.[94]

Meanwhile, the governor had the opportunity to strengthen his control over the University's Board of Regents with three new appointments in the spring of 1925: Dr. Adolph Gunderson of La Crosse, Victor P. Richardson of Janesville, and Michael B. Olbrich of Madison. The student newspaper, the *Daily Cardinal*, noted that all three were prominent progressives and were expected to "take an important part" in the selection of the next president.[95] Of the three, the most closely identified with the governor was Olbrich, a forty-three-year-old Madison attorney and former state deputy attorney general who had served as Blaine's executive counsel since 1921. In appointing Olbrich, Blaine by-passed Senator La Follette's candidate, his Madison law partner, Alfred T. Rogers, whose loyalty Blaine considered suspect. He thought Rogers would be too soft on the University because he believed the

---

[93]Briggs to Blaine, February 28, March 13, 1925; Blaine to Briggs, March 9, 1925; Frank Hanson to Blaine, March 5 and 7, 1925; Blaine to Hanson, March 7, 1925; Blaine to J.D. Phillips, March 9, 1925; Phillips to Blaine, March 14, 1925; Blaine to G.W. Patterson, April 11, 1925, Blaine Papers, boxes 46 and 47. Blaine's Iowa informant was of little help, reporting that he was not involved in the appropriations committee deliberations but doubted the university's budget cut was "as much as the news item report." Patterson to Blaine, April 16, 1925, ibid., box 47.

[94]Hanson to Blaine, March 10, 1925; Blaine to Hanson, March 13, 1925, ibid., box 46.

[95]*Daily Cardinal*, March 4, 1925.

governor's hard line plans "would be destructive rather than constructive."[96] Still, Olbrich's progressive credentials were unchallengeable. Twice, in 1912 and 1916, he had been selected to nominate Senator La Follette for president in the Republican national conventions. Locally he had played a major role in the development of the Madison parks system. Olbrich quickly became one of the key members of the Board of Regents and would remain so until his untimely death in 1929.

As political support for the University grew, it was evident to some Wisconsin progressives that Governor Blaine's anti-University and anti-education stance was hurting him and the Wisconsin progressive movement politically. Since it was an open secret that Blaine hoped to run against U.S. Senator Irvine L. Lenroot in 1926, he could ill afford to alienate an important bloc of Wisconsin voters. After a trip in which Kronshage conferred with school teachers and normal school staff around the state, he reported to Olbrich that these normally progressive supporters were "in an open state of revolt claiming that Governor Blaine has been the most reactionary governor in educational matters that the state has ever had." Kronshage said Herman Ekern, the state attorney general and another long-time La Follette progressive, believed the situation was serious enough so the three of them ought to meet with the governor "and endeavor to point out to him where we think he is leading the progressive party."[97] Olbrich responded in early May that he had already discussed the problem with Blaine in a preliminary way and the governor had "suggested taking it up again next week."[98]

The concerns of Blaine's own regents and other progressive leaders soon had a moderating effect on the governor, though it is not known whether, as was rumored at the time, Kronshage threatened to campaign against Blaine if he did not support his regents' budget requests. The governor plainly did not want to enter the 1926 senatorial primary labeled as anti-education, with the influential educational establishment of the state united against him. By late spring, when the legislature got down to serious work on the 1925-27 state budget, the earlier recommendation of the Board of Public Affairs to cut the University budget was forgotten. Governor Blaine even accompanied Kronshage to the meeting of the legislature's Joint Committee on Finance to urge support

---

[96]Blaine to R.M. La Follette, Sr., March 3, 1925, Blaine Papers, box 46.
[97]Kronshage to Olbrich, March 31, 1925, Kronshage Papers, box 5.
[98]Olbrich to Kronshage, May 4, 1925, ibid.

for the University's requests.[99]   Overwhelmed by the University's intensive lobbying campaign, the legislature provided not only increased operating funds but also appropriated $1 million for new buildings and authorized the construction of a field house.   In contrast with past sessions, this time there was no bitter wrangling over tax policy, with the legislators retaining the special ⅜ mill property tax for the University.[100]   It was, President Birge later remarked, the largest single appropriation for buildings in the University's history to that time.

All in all, the Kronshage-Birge-Haight public relations campaign in the spring of 1925 must be considered one of the most ambitious and successful such efforts in the history of the University.   Not only was a serious budget threat under a hostile governor beaten back, but the University received the most favorable budgetary treatment by the legislature in more than a decade.   Its alumni and friends around the state were mobilized as rarely before or since.   If this support could be consolidated under the next president, the University might be able to resume the influential and respected role in the life of the state it had held during the Van Hise-La Follette era in the early years of the twentieth century.

"The Schoolmaster Is King"

Even before legislative action on the budget was completed, the regents returned to the task of selecting a new president, confident now that the outcome of the budget deliberations would not undermine the search.   Regent Olbrich, the newest member of the board and the governor's top adviser, was added to the presidential selection committee, replacing its lone stalwart member, Madison attorney Harry Butler, whose appointment to the board had expired.   This time the La Follette family refrained from endorsing any candidate, though Ekern advised the senator to take a close look at the qualifications of the former president of Amherst College, Alexander Meiklejohn, whose reform administration had attracted a good deal of national attention.[101]   Although the

---

[99]Sellery, *Birge*, pp. 77-8.

[100]Act 334, *Laws of Wisconsin*, 1925, pp. 431-9; Act 32, ibid., pp. 91-2; Curti and Carstensen, *University of Wisconsin*, vol. 2, p. 222; Sellery, *Birge*, p. 78.

[101]Ekern to R.M. La Follette, Sr., April 6 1925, La Follette Family Papers, box B102; Ekern to La Follette, April 10, 1925, Ekern Papers, box 67.   Ekern reported that Ralph Sucher, La Follette's son-in-law and Phil La Follette's fraternity brother, was pushing Meiklejohn and believed the reports of Meiklejohn's financial mismanagement at Amherst had been

La Follettes' previous choice, Robert Lovett, was unhappily out of the running following the regents' unrequited courtship of Roscoe Pound, others under consideration by the committee earlier were still available. One name above all others kept coming up in correspondence and discussion during the spring of 1925: that of Glenn Frank, the dynamic young editor of the *Century Magazine* in New York, whose liberal views and compelling rhetoric were attracting an increasing following among progressives nationally.

There was little in Glenn Frank's background to suggest he might one day head a major university. Born in the small central Missouri town of Queen City in 1887, in Frank's thirty-seven years he had come far from his rural roots. As a boy young Glenn showed an interest in public speaking and religion, joining the Methodist Church at the age of ten and becoming a youthful evangelist at twelve. While in his teens he sharpened his forensic skills as a Methodist circuit riding preacher, ministering to three congregations at one time and touring Iowa one summer with the famed evangelist Billy Sunday. Although Frank read widely, his formal schooling was limited, and in the fall of 1909 he had to use all of his eloquence to persuade a dean to overrule the admissions committee in gaining entrance to Northwestern University, which at this time retained its original Methodist ties. At Northwestern Frank's intellectual capacity was quickly apparent as was his zest for campus extracurricular life. He joined the staff of the yearbook and the campus literary publication, the *Northwestern Magazine*, serving as the latter's editor in his senior year. He acted in dramatic productions and participated in the debating society, winning two major oratorical contests. To improve his public speaking he arranged for private lessons at the Northwestern School of Oratory, though his teachers soon declared he knew more about oratory than they. Obliged to live on a modest budget, he defrayed some of his college expenses by speaking extensively in the Evanston area, usually before religious groups, and in summers on tour as a Chautauqua lecturer. Glenn Frank was clearly a big man on campus—more mature, ambitious, and energetic than most of his fellow undergraduates. He was also popular. At graduation his classmates voted him the senior who had done the most for the school as well as the best-looking man in his class.[102]

"misrepresented." These two letters from Ekern to the senator suggest that the La Follettes still harbored a hope of influencing the UW presidential selection. See also pp. 144-9.

[102]Lawrence H. Larsen, *The President Wore Spats: A Biography of Glenn Frank* (Madison:

Although Frank was a conscientious but not an outstanding student—like Senator La Follette his extracurricular interests no doubt often interfered with his studies—he impressed his professors with his maturity and lively curiosity. Walter Dill Scott recalled him as "the most brilliant mind that I had come in contact with among the undergraduates." Concluding that Frank had all the necessary qualities—self-assurance, good organizational and speaking skills—and a background in the Methodist ministry, during his senior year President Abram Harris offered Frank the new position of alumni secretary at a salary of $1,200 a year and ample time for Chautauqua lecturing. For the next three years Frank threw himself into the task of building up Northwestern's contacts with its alumni, in the process revolutionizing the traditional approach to alumni relations. Spending most of his time on the road, he bustled about the country organizing alumni clubs, raising endowment funds, addressing high school audiences from Denver to New York, recruiting students, and editing a lively alumni magazine. The fees from his growing participation in the national lecture circuit, an activity which both he and President Harris saw as complementing his university responsibilities, soon enabled him to build a comfortable home for his parents in Missouri.[103]

Frank's travels and contacts around the country as Northwestern's alumni secretary served to enlarge his horizons, just as his student days had altered his provincial Missouri outlook. In the fall of 1915, Lincoln Steffens recommended him for the position of private secretary to Edward A. Filene, the well-known Boston merchant-philanthropist. Frank initially turned down the opportunity, telling his fiancée he was disinclined "to become a sort of intellectual man Friday to any millionaire."[104] Further negotiations satisfactorily clarified the nature of his responsibilities, and Frank accepted the position as Filene's chief assistant. Among other things, he welcomed the opportunity to live in Boston, which he regarded as the seat of American culture, and the generous salary of $7,500 a year enabled him to marry his childhood sweetheart, Mary Smith, the daughter of a prosperous hardware mer-

State Historical Society of Wisconsin, 1965), pp. 7-22; James Ward Rector, *Analysis of a Biography* (Madison: State Historical Society of Wisconsin, 1968), pp. 2-15; *Dictionary of Wisconsin Biography* (Madison: State Historical Society of Wisconsin, 1960), pp. 133-4; *Milwaukee Journal*, May 28, 1925; *Wisconsin State Journal*, May 31, 1925.

[103]Larsen, *President Wore Spats*, pp. 21-5.

[104]Frank to Mary Smith, November 11, 1915, quoted in Rector, *Analysis of a Biography*, p. 25.

chant in Glenwood, Missouri.[105]

The Franks were happy in Boston, where their only child, Glenn, Jr., was born in December of 1918. Mary Frank was a graduate of Smith College and had many friends in New England. Frank shared Filene's progressive views and identified with his internationalist activities in the League to Enforce Peace, which advocated a world organization similar to the later League of Nations. He relished his contacts with influential men like former President William Howard Taft, the titular head of the League to Enforce Peace, who he confided to Mary had "taken a very gratifying liking" to him.[106] He continued to lecture to appreciative audiences on issues of the day. In 1918 Frank published his first book, *The Stakes of the War*, in collaboration with a somewhat eccentric wealthy Harvard Ph.D., Lothrop Stoddard. It was a kind of handbook for the coming Paris peace conference in which the two authors argued that Americans must become better informed about foreign affairs—"a belated recognition of the fact that we are part and parcel of a world of interlaced interests in which no nation can play a lone hand."[107] Frank's second book, *The Politics of Industry*, appeared in 1919, and drew on his and Filene's ideas on how to develop productive labor-management relations under enlightened capitalism in the post-war era.[108]

Although he enjoyed the association with Filene and the two men remained good friends, by the end of the war Frank was ready for new challenges. Both of his books had been published by the Century Company, and parts of *The Politics of Industry* had first appeared in the *Century Magazine*, whose owner, W. Morgan Shuster, was impressed by Frank's energy, ideas, and facility with words. Late in 1918 Shuster offered him the post of associate editor of the *Century Magazine*, which in addition to loosely defined general editorial responsibilities gave him a national podium from which to express his views on current affairs each month. It also meant a move to New York City and its more exhilarating intellectual and artistic atmosphere. Frank threw himself into his new job with characteristic zeal, arguing that the magazine

---

[105]Rector, *Analysis of a Biography*, pp. 14-21; Larsen, *President Wore Spats*, pp. 26-36.

[106]Frank to Mary Frank, March 21, 1918, quoted in Larsen, *President Wore Spats*, p. 32.

[107]Lothrop Stoddard and Glenn Frank, *The Stakes of the War: A Summary of the Various Problems, Claims, and Interests of the Nations at the Peace Table* (New York: Century Company, 1918), p. vii, quoted in Larsen, *President Wore Spats*, p. 32.

[108]Glenn Frank, *The Politics of Industry: A Footnote to the Social Unrest* (New York: Century Company, 1919).

needed to abandon its traditional eclectic literary format if it were to attract new readers. By 1921 these ideas had so won over Shuster that he promoted Frank to editor-in-chief at a handsome annual salary of $13,000. Frank quickly set about revamping the *Century*, redesigning its cover, tightening its format, adding contemporary drawings, and generally targeting its contents to a literate mass audience. He used his Chautauqua and other contacts to attract articles, short stories, and poetry by prominent literary and political figures, including Wisconsin's most famous writer, Zona Gale.[109]

In his monthly essay, which he titled "An American Looks at His World," Frank touched broadly on the problems of the day, generally urging industrial harmony through enlightened capitalism, calling on the clergy for a spiritual renaissance, urging a common sense definition of Americanism, criticizing the religious hypocrisy of the resurgent Ku Klux Klan, and deploring provincial politicians and narrow nationalism. So highly regarded was Frank as a social commentator that when the University of Delaware established a university press in 1922 he was invited to give a series of inaugural lectures, which were subsequently published by the new press as its first book, along with a number of his reworked *Century* columns.[110] While not particularly original nor profound, Frank read widely and had a knack for translating complex concepts into easily understood terms, which he presented to his readers and audiences in such polished prose as to seem more memorable and significant than was usually the case. Always he revealed a deep veneration for science and scholarship. Because the scientific mind rejected meaningless labels and ideologies in its search for the truth, he remarked in one column, it was "the only sort of mind worth having."[111] A fervent internationalist, Frank in the December, 1923, issue of the *Century* denounced those who (like Wisconsin's senior senator) were opposed to the League of Nations, calling them parochial, demagogic, and possessed of "the lowest form of political intelligence."[112] An

---

[109]Larsen, *President Wore Spats*, pp. 38-45; Rector, *Analysis of a Biography*, pp. 19-23.

[110]Glenn Frank, *An American Looks at His World: Variations on a Point of View* (Newark, Delaware: University of Delaware Press, 1923); John A. Munroe, *The University of Delaware: A History* (Newark, Delaware: University of Delaware Press, 1986), pp. 253-4.

[111]Frank, "Three Pillars of Society: A Free University, a Pacific Church, a Realistic State," *Century Magazine*, 108 (August, 1924), 567.

[112]Frank, "The Wages of Complexity: On Civilization and the Biology of Death," *Century Magazine*, 107 (December, 1923), 319-20, quoted in Steven D. Zink, "Glenn Frank of the University of Wisconsin: A Reinterpretation," *Wisconsin Magazine of History*, 62 (Winter,

acknowledged Republican of clear progressive leanings, Frank nevertheless gave scant encouragement to Senator La Follette's independent presidential bid in 1924, commenting editorially, "I have never been able to muster great enthusiasm for the 'third party' movements that have arisen since I became a voter."[113] Some of Frank's views thus suggested he might bring some political liabilities to Wisconsin.

Glenn Frank was not unknown in Madison when the regents began seriously considering him for the presidency in the spring of 1925. In addition to his *Century* editorials and three books, just a year earlier he had accepted an invitation to deliver the Phi Beta Kappa initiation address at the University. So considerable was Frank's reputation as an inspiring speaker that the ceremony was moved to the armory in order to accommodate the largest possible audience. Even so, many were turned away, and in its enthusiasm the crowd spilled over into the seats reserved for the Phi Beta Kappa initiates, causing considerable turmoil at the start of the ceremony. UW sociology professor E.A. Ross compared Frank favorably with another recent campus visitor, Bertrand Russell, and a member of the philosophy faculty described him as "probably the foremost orator in America." Frank's subject, "The Probable Outlook for Western Civilization," was characteristically broad and infused with uncomplicated idealism yet delivered with such ornate flourishes as to captivate his audience. "Social, spiritual and intellectual competition must take the place of material competition," Frank told the attentive Madison crowd. "We must have economic internationalism instead of political nationalism....Politics should be rationalized, based on scientific knowledge of social problems and statistical study of the results." At the dinner for the Phi Beta Kappa initiates preceding his public address Frank offered his definition of a proper college-educated man. "He should be a liberal—and a liberal is a person who is a slave to no orthodoxy, who thinks clearly and objectively and who acts courageously in the face of the facts of the case."[114] If he revealed little about his qualifications for a major university presidency during his 1924 Madison visit, Frank at least had said nothing to tarnish his appeal to Wisconsin progressives.

1978-79), 98.

[113]Frank, "Decadence of American Politics: Some Campaign Observations," *Century Magazine*, 108 (September, 1924), 715, also quoted in Zink, "Glenn Frank," p. 98. See also *Milwaukee Journal*, May 21, 1925; *Wisconsin State Journal*, May 21, 1925.

[114]*Daily Cardinal*, April 29 and 30, May 1, 2, and 3, 1924.

Whether he might be interested in the UW presidency was another matter. Those consulted by the selection committee in its earlier round of deliberations doubted Frank could be lured away from New York, where he held a prestigious and high-salaried editorship and moved in glamorous literary and artistic circles. His former Boston employer, Edward A. Filene, thought not, but declared, "if I am wrong and you can get him, I think you would have the best man in the country for your purpose."[115] After Roscoe Pound declined the presidency, Filene advised the selection committee to take another look at Frank, assuring committee secretary Callahan that Frank was "a man who possesses a combination of high scholarship and practical business ability that would be difficult to surpass." Filene still doubted Frank would accept, but "knowing him as I do, I am sure that he would appreciate the importance and opportunities of the position and would give the matter his most earnest consideration."[116] He sent Frank copies of his correspondence with the selection committee so his friend would be aware of the Wisconsin interest.

Early in April, 1925, Regent Zona Gale, whose fiction Frank had published in the *Century Magazine* and who served with him as a member of the editorial board of the Literary Guild, took it upon herself to find out whether he might in fact be interested in the presidency. While noncommittal, the response was reassuring, enough so that Gale was ecstatic at the prospect of her good friends Glenn and Mary Frank coming to Madison. "I hold my breath at the whole idea," she responded immediately:

> Dr. Birge's resignation is to take effect at the end of this school year—and if the Legislature does not cripple us, the new president will really have the chance of the world, as universities go. It is true that the University has fallen behind in its building program, for ten years; and that it is far more conservative than it was ten years ago. But with our eight thousand students, and our campus, and our past, what a future you could give us.[117]

Frank's follow-up was even more tantalizing. "Through all this, I

---

[115]Filene to Callahan, October 8, 1924, Olbrich Papers, box 2.

[116]Filene to Callahan, March 6, 1925, ibid. Filene also sent copies of this letter to Regents Gale and Kronshage, perhaps in an effort to launch a Frank bandwagon.

[117]Gale to Glenn Frank, April 14, 1925, Frank Papers, Kirksville, and Zona Gale Papers, box 3, SHSW. A somewhat garbled version of this letter is quoted in August Derleth, *Still Small Voice: The Biography of Zona Gale* (New York: D. Appleton-Century Company, 1940), p. 168.

have suspected that when the tumult and the shouting dies we shall discover that the schoolmaster is king," he told Gale. Of course, he found the "teaching ministry of journalism" satisfying, and in fact just that week had received two attractive journalistic proposals that would give him a daily and weekly audience of several million readers while trebling his income.

> All of us who, in any way and through any medium, contrive to awaken and discipline the minds and spirits of our generation are schoolmasters. There is a vast incoordinated university of America that has no campus and whose faculty is made up of poets, novelists, publicists, business men, engineers, statesmen, and the like, who, consciously or subconsciously, see in their jobs the opportunity and the obligation to educate, organize, and infuse with more spacious meaning the life of their time. In this larger university you have for some time been a full professor, and for the last seven years at least I have been trying hard to qualify as an instructor.

Frank's disarming flattery must surely have appealed to Gale. Even more captivating was his confession that the Wisconsin prospect "awakened to new life an old dream" of a satisfying academic life. "Tonight's mood, at any rate," he confided, "tells me that if a great university opportunity should present itself in the near future, with adequate funds and freedom to move forward on a creative program, I should undoubtedly turn my back on this alluring next step in journalism."[118] "I am thrilled beyond words," replied the normally loquacious Gale.[119]

At the next meeting of the presidential selection committee on May 9, Gale abandoned her earlier view that the regents should make one more effort to recruit Roscoe Pound, who was reported to have second thoughts about his decision to turn down the Wisconsin presidency. Instead she concentrated on the Glenn Frank candidacy, sharing with the committee her exploratory correspondence and another recent endorsement from Filene. The committee had received other positive evaluations of Frank, including a letter from one of his former Northwestern teachers, Walter Dill Scott, now president of the university, who stressed Frank's ability "to win the confidence of the alumni and the citizens of the state."[120] Former Northwestern President Harris echoed Scott's evaluation, noting that Frank was "a progressive, but not given to denunciation," who would "win friends among business men, and

---

[118] Frank to Gale, April 17, 1925, Frank Papers, Kirksville.
[119] Gale to Frank, April 22, 1925, ibid.
[120] Scott to Callahan, May 5, 1925, Olbrich Papers, box 2.

political men."[121]   Prior to the meeting Gale had asked Frank for a list
of his recent outside speaking engagements on political and educational
subjects and references to "some of the specifically educational utterances, either in the Century or elsewhere, which I might have missed,
together with any of the comment on you and your work."[122]   Frank had
promptly responded with "some editorials that you will know best how
to use," adding:

> It is the needs and opportunities of the situation that have captured my
> interest. If it were simply a case of an easy berth in a thoroughly satisfied
> and smoothly running institution that presented no challenge, I would not for
> a moment consider turning my back on the very exciting and profitable
> contracts that are now awaiting my decision.
>   But I feel that there is a chance to make the University of Wisconsin
> once more the pioneer that shall give leadership to the whole field of state
> supported education. I feel that we have only scratched the surface of what
> a great university can mean to the life of a state. And I feel that once the
> plans and policy of a university are right it is possible to stir a whole state to
> sustained enthusiasm and support.[123]

If they wanted him, it was clear Glenn Frank hoped the regents would
understand hd was available, but might be expensive.

And want him they did! The members of the selection committee—Kronshage, Callahan, Olbrich, and Gale (Grady was ill)—quickly
decided that Frank was their man, with Callahan and Olbrich especially
sharing Gale's enthusiasm and Kronshage pointing out the importance of
Filene's strong endorsement. The committee arranged to meet again the
following week just prior to a special meeting of the full Board of
Regents, in order, as Gale reported to Frank, "to confer with a committee from the faculty—at least not obligatory at all, but desirable, and
there is a committee of the students which wishes to be heard." Gale
hesitated to violate the confidentiality of the committee's discussion, but
wished her friend could have been present, "for all of it was so uniquely
in your praise." While nothing was yet certain, of course, "nothing
could be more thrilling, I think."[124]

The special meeting of the Board of Regents on May 13, 1925,
with President Birge absent, turned out to be nothing short of a Glenn

---

[121]A.W. Harris to Kronshage, May 11, 1925, ibid.

[122]Gale to Frank, May 2, 1925, Frank Papers, Kirksville.

[123]Frank to Gale [ca. May 5, 1925], ibid.

[124]Gale to Frank, May 10, 1925; Gale to Filene, May 10, 1925, ibid.

Frank love feast. On behalf of the selection committee, Kronshage reported its unanimous recommendation of Frank for the presidency, and the regents gave no consideration to other candidates. Although the board kept no minutes of this meeting, Zona Gale's entertaining and revealing account to Frank the next day gives something of the flavor of the deliberations, which seem to have been more like a revival meeting, though lasting only an hour:

> Mr. Olbrich ventured the suggestion that if you came, in two years time you would be one of the best and most popularly known figures in the state. He said: "And remember, this man is not merely university presidential timber. He is Presidential timber. There is no end to the distance he can go. He has his literary and platform beginning, his ripeness of thought—he is like the figure of the young James Russell Lowell." Mr. Kronshage was reading aloud, again, at the board meeting, your "free university" section, and Mr. Olbrich held in his hand the Science of Education one, and when Mr. Kronshage stopped, he began, and when he stopped Mr. Kronshage had found something else, and Mr. Olbrich said: "I disclaim any intention of holding responsive readings with Mr. Kronshage, but listen to this!" And later: "I didn't mean to read any more, but hear THIS." And so on. Mr. Callahan, state superintendent, who had been acting as secretary to the committee on the president, then read your statement about the League of Nations—which was asked for—and that set the last doubt at rest. He read it across a file at least a foot high, of folders filled with letters about different candidates whom he had collected material to cover, for a year or more. Your folder was one of the first ones which he had prepared, and sent out letters for, but everyone said, Mr. Filene, everybody, even I, that you couldn't be had. Then at last somebody said that the thing to do would be to empower the committee to get in touch with you, with power to act, and that was the motion which was passed. There was no direct vote on you at all—it was just taken for granted. I call that viva voce, without the trouble even to viva the voce.[125]

Mindful of their embarrassment in the earlier abortive negotiations with Roscoe Pound, the regents agreed to say absolutely nothing to the newspapers until the matter of Frank's appointment "was settled beyond any doubt."[126] News of the board's selection leaked immediately, however, and was trumpeted in the afternoon editions that day. The next morning the *Daily Cardinal* carried a front-page headline: "Selection of Frank as New President Denied by Regents," quoting Regent President Kronshage as solemnly declaring that "the stories published in the papers are not true." The special meeting, board Secretary McCaf-

---

[125]Gale to Frank, May 14, 1925, ibid.
[126]Ibid.

frey explained, was solely to discuss the University's appropriation request under consideration by the legislature.[127] The denials fooled no one, and favorable reactions to the selection immediately began to arrive from around the country. An Oshkosh attorney told Regent Olbrich he had read nearly everything Frank had written and liked "his ideas, his ideals and his youth....he will bring something fresh and new and inspiring to the job."[128] A North Dakota banker and alumnus thought the appointment "excellent." Frank's editorials "disclosed a man of wide interests and comprehensive knowledge in many fields," which suggested he was "a Liberal, both in politics and religion; a combination which very seldom is found."[129] Eugenics publicist Albert E. Wiggam wrote Zona Gale from New York that he was "touched and thrilled" at the thought of Glenn Frank heading the University of Wisconsin. The citizens of Wisconsin, he predicted, would soon find that Frank's personality was as big as the state. "If you don't watch," he warned, "it is going to become in time, I am sure, as big as the nation, and you might ultimately lose him for the biggest possible service to which the nation can call him."[130]

Following the board meeting on May 13 Kronshage telephoned the news to Frank and dispatched two members of the selection committee, Regents Callahan and Olbrich, to New York to work out the details of the offer. This time there was no hesitancy on the part of the candidate, though Frank drove a hard bargain. The agreement signed between Frank and Callahan and Olbrich committed the board to pay Frank a salary of $18,000 a year (in contrast to the $10,000 paid President Birge), a rent-free furnished home in the newly acquired spacious presidential mansion at 130 North Prospect Street (which had come to the University earlier in the year from the estate of Madison attorney John M. Olin, coincidentally a classmate of Birge's at Williams College), a suitable entertainment allowance (which in September the board set at $200 a month and added to Frank's salary, bringing it to $20,400), a car and driver, and actual moving expenses from New York. The agreement also noted that Frank had committed himself to some lecture engagements for the fall of 1925: "he cannot honorably

---

[127]*Daily Cardinal*, May 14, 1925.

[128]Edward J. Dempsey to Olbrich, May 14, 1925, Olbrich Papers, box 2.

[129]Samuel Torgerson to Ben F. Faast, May 15, 1925, ibid.

[130][Albert E. Wiggam] to Gale, May 9, 1925, Frank Papers, Kirksville, also printed in *Wisconsin State Journal*, May 31, 1925.

cancel these, and so will fulfill them." Frank had also recently signed a contract to write a daily editorial for the McClure Newspaper Syndicate. Callahan and Olbrich were not entirely happy about this, and stipulated: "Mr. Frank agrees that such a schedule of writing should not be undertaken concurrently with the Presidency of the University, but he must extract himself as best he can from this contract, extract himself at once if possible, and if it prove impossible to cancel the contract at once to conclude the arrangement within the shortest possible time."[131] McClure's declined to dissolve its contract with Frank and began distributing his columns in late September, 1925. The arrangement was financially attractive for Frank, guaranteeing him a minimum of $800 a month, rising to $1,000 a month after six months, and reaching $1,500 a month or more if, as was the case, the series proved successful.[132]

On May 20 Glenn Frank issued a lengthy press statement in New York which began: "I have today accepted the presidency of the University of Wisconsin, so graciously tendered to me by the board of regents." Seeking to reassure both the faculty and the progressives of the state of his forward-looking views as well as his respect for the past, he wisely indicated he had much to learn and would forego further comment until he was better informed:

> It has been no easy matter to break the ties that bind me to the congenial and challenging field of journalism, but the University of Wisconsin presents a great tradition of sound scholarship, inspired teaching, productive research, and practical service, of freedom to investigate, and courage to follow the truth wherever it may lead. Merely to safeguard and sustain such a tradition is a high challenge.
>
> And if it should be the good fortune of any president to enhance and enrich that tradition by a progressive adaptation of it to the growing needs of an enlightened commonwealth, he should be a very happy man, indeed.
>
> Obviously I can not at this time undertake to discuss either the problems or policies for two reasons:

---

[131] "Memorandum of Agreement between the Undersigned Committee of the Board of Regents of the University of Wisconsin and Glenn Frank," n.d., BOR Papers, 1/1/4, box 96, and Business Administration Papers, 24/1/1, box 19, UA.

[132] Howard Wheeler to Frank, June 18, 1925; F. Edith O'Dell to Frank, August 25, 1925, Frank Papers, Kirksville. Years later Mary Frank added an explanatory handwritten note to the letter announcing McClure's decision not to agree to the cancellation of the contract: "Note by Mrs. Frank. Glenn wanted to cancel his contract because he was afraid that the University might be criticized if he made such a large syndicate salary, despite the fact that writing the articles took so little time and helped advertise the University & writing the articles helped lessen burden of writing speeches. He used editorials." Mary Frank note on Wheeler to Frank, June 18, 1925, ibid.

First, because the day has gone by when the policies of a free university should be determined by the secret processes of the mind of a president. The policies of a free university must ultimately come out of a sincere and sustained collaboration between the president, the members of the board of regents, the members of the faculties, the men and women who are submitting themselves to the discipline and inspiration of the university, and in a very real sense the whole people of the state and those who represent them.

A really great state university must both express and serve the deepest needs of the last man and woman and child in the state. Such universities are not created by an executive order from the office of the president; they come out of a vast cooperative enterprise in which the whole state shares.

Second, because I have not yet made a careful study of these specific problems now confronting the university.

The University of Wisconsin is dedicated to the proposition that sound policy must grow out of honest and unhampered investigation of facts. I should like to feel that my election is an expression of confidence that I shall be loyal to that proposition.

Until I have come to know the facts, therefore, my duty is a silence.[133]

Others were less constrained. President Lotus D. Coffman of the University of Minnesota expressed his surprise that the Wisconsin regents had done the "impossible" by persuading Glenn Frank to give up his editorial post, and told Regent Callahan: "You have a brilliant young man for your new leader."[134] Frank's former teacher, President Walter Dill Scott of Northwestern University, predicted that despite his lack of academic experience Frank would soon return Wisconsin to "its position of leadership among the state universities of America."[135] The Massachusetts commissioner of education congratulated the Board of Regents for its "real service to the cause of education by bringing over into the field of university administration one of the ablest intellectual leaders of our contemporary American life."[136] A New York friend assured Professor John R. Commons that if there were any doubting Thomases in Madison, "you just tell them for me that they will have to eat crow after Frank really gets into harness."[137] Press reactions to the appointment in Wisconsin and around the country were nearly all posi-

---

[133]*Daily Cardinal*, May 21, 1925.

[134]Lotus D. Coffman to Callahan, May 24, 1925, Olbrich Papers, box 2.

[135]Quoted in *Daily Cardinal*, May 27, 1925.

[136]Payson Smith to Callahan, May 22, 1925, Olbrich Papers, box 2.

[137]E.G. Draper to John R. Commons, May 21, 1925, Birge Presidential Papers, 4/12/1, box 51, UA. In a second letter Draper declared that Frank "is one of the few men that I know who is fearless without being dogmatic and really nas [*sic*] a very sensitive and idealistic spirit as well as a practical ability for accomplishment." Draper to Commons, June 4, 1925, ibid.

tive. The *Kansas City Post* predicted Frank would turn the University of Wisconsin into "the foremost educational experiment station in America," no doubt "by surrounding himself with a large number of liberal educators."[138] A United Press dispatch described Frank at thirty-seven as the youngest president in the Big Ten and probably the youngest university president in the country. "'Well, I'll be 38 when—or, rather, if, all goes well, at the time I am president,'" he was quoted, "as if anxious to emphasize the oldest age he could claim."[139]

Closer to home the reactions were also mostly enthusiastic. Mrs. Blaine told Zona Gale the governor was "quite boyishly happy" over the appointment and was confident he and Frank were "going to be of one mind."[140] The superintendent of the Wauwatosa public schools confessed to Regent Kronshage that the appointment of Frank had appeared "incongruous at first," but on further reflection it seemed "so fitting as to be almost obvious."[141] Professor E.A. Ross, to whom Madison reporters regularly turned for comment on just about any University subject, hailed Frank's common sense liberalism and especially his public speaking talents, which he saw as "a big asset at this time when the university needs to be interpreted to the people of the state, who have become a little unmindful of the faithful work going on here."[142] A Milwaukee businessman promised "wholehearted support" from the alumni. While acknowledging President Birge's "splendid work," he conceded that "the University for a number of years has been lacking in just the type of enthusiastic, human leadership which Mr. Frank is evidently so well qualified to give."[143]

For his part, President Birge called the appointment "a fortunate omen for the future of the University," emphasizing that Frank's "youth with its vigor and adaptability" and his "modern ideas and ideals of education and social advancement" would assure "we shall not only keep all of the gains of the past but also shall discover hitherto unrealized possibilities of service and progress."[144] Significantly, Birge did not assure Frank, as he had Dean Pound, that he would find the faculty united in support of his appointment. Amidst the general rejoicing over

---

[138]Quoted in *Daily Cardinal*, May 27, 1925.
[139]*Wisconsin State Journal*, May 21, 1925.
[140]Gale to Mary Frank, May 26, 1925, Frank Papers, Kirksville.
[141]William Darling to Kronshage, May 29, 1925, Kronshage Papers, box 5.
[142]*Wisconsin State Journal*, May 21, 1925.
[143]Morris F. Fox to Olbrich, June 30, 1925, Olbrich Papers, box 2.
[144]Birge, press release, May 21, 1925, Birge Presidential Papers, 4/12/1, box 51.

the appointment there were in fact some misgivings in the campus community. Far from welcoming the news that the regents had chosen an ordained minister as president, the Roman Catholic pastor of St. Paul's University Chapel thought Frank's liberalism made him suspect as a religious vagrant, not a sound theologian.[145]

Some faculty members also questioned Frank's youth and inexperience, noting that he possessed only an earned baccalaureate degree and that his sole experience in higher education administration was his youthful three years as alumni secretary immediately following his graduation from Northwestern. Indeed, Professor Max Otto of the philosophy department, a La Follette family intimate, expressed utter disbelief when Phil La Follette told him in advance of the regents' likely selection:

Max Otto's New Seal

You really didn't mean that anybody is seriously interested in that hot air artist for the job, did you? If it's really true, it shows what a joke the whole business is. They're fooling with the job! We're trying to conduct an institution of higher learning, aren't we? Then how can anyone select a man for the post of president who is persuaded that what we need to save us—university, nation, world—is a cross between a mountebank and a bully? That's been his consistently announced program. The *lord* save us if he should be elected. There wouldn't be anywhere else to turn. And alas some of us can't qualify there. With ignorance or stupidity elevated to power in politics and a tongue given the first place in our highest educational institution we'd have to live for the rest of our days some of us on Wisconsin's glorious memories.

An accomplished artist, Otto closed his handwritten note with a sketch of a new University Numen Lumen seal showing a kneeling UW faculty member with arms upraised in prayerful supplication![146] About this time

---

[145]*Wisconsin State Journal*, May 31, 1925.

[146]Max Otto to P.F. La Follette [May 12, 1925], P.F. La Follette Papers, box 133. Although Otto was aware of and shared the La Follette family's opposition to Frank, most UW

a faculty joke began circulating that the regents had gone east to buy a pound but instead had got a franc, without realizing there was a difference in the rate of exchange!

Chief among the faculty skeptics was the strong-willed dean of the College of Letters and Science, George Clarke Sellery, a close confidant of outgoing President Birge. Sellery, who would in time become one of the new president's most significant critics, offered only measured praise of the appointment:

> As editor of the Century he has been essentially a student of education in its broadest reaches. The disadvantage of lack of intimate familiarity with the intricate problems of a university is amply offset by the breadth of outside view which his talents and activities have given him. The chief thing for the public to keep in mind is that the new president must be given adequate time to produce results.[147]

Just how much time Dean Sellery would give President Frank was unclear.

Significantly, another sometime Madison resident had no comment at all on the appointment. In Washington, where the elder La Follette was entering upon what would prove to be his final illness, there was only silence on the regents' choice. Belle merely observed to her children: "The U.W. matter was a strange performance. But we are not saying anything."[148] From Madison Phil La Follette told his parents he did not share the general enthusiasm for Frank, fearing he was "Wilsonesque—too much of a phrase maker."[149] Years later, after Frank had been fired by a Board of Regents dominated by Governor Philip La Follette, the deposed president recalled that while lunching at the Player's Club in New York before moving to Madison he had run into the senator's son-in-law, the playwright George Middleton, who warned ominously: "Don't get your neck into that, it's against the wishes of the family."[150] Whether or not the incident occurred, either at all or as

---

faculty members assumed that because Frank held progressive views his selection had been dictated by Senator La Follette's followers on the Board of Regents. Ira L. Baldwin to E. David Cronon, April 2, 1993, UHP.

[147]*Wisconsin State Journal*, May 21, 1925.

[148]B.C. La Follette to "Dear Ones," May 16, 1925, P.F. La Follette Papers, box 133.

[149]Philip La Follette to his parents, May 31, 1925, La Follette Family Papers, box A32. We are indebted to Professor Bernard A. Weisberger for calling this letter to our attention.

[150]*Capital Times*, January 8, 1937; *Wisconsin State Journal*, January 8, 1937; *Milwaukee Journal*, January 8, 1937. In a revealing handwritten draft of a passage not included in his

Frank remembered it—and Middleton promptly denied the encounter—it does suggest how much importance Frank attached to the La Follette family's influence in Wisconsin and to the absence of the La Follette imprimatur on his presidency.[151]

On May 21, the day the news of Glenn Frank's acceptance of the presidency hit the Madison newspapers, and perhaps not entirely coincidentally, the Wisconsin legislature passed the generous University appropriation bill for the 1925-27 biennium. On May 24 the new president arrived in Madison for two days of meetings with regents, the governor, and University and community leaders, touring the campus, and viewing his future residence. As he descended from his railroad car, Frank was greeted by an unseasonable May snowstorm, which the members of the presidential selection committee hastily assured him was neither typical nor symbolic. Frank took it all in stride and before departing pronounced himself captivated by "the beauty and allurement of Madison."[152] Following his return to New York, almost as an afterthought, on May 29 a special meeting of the Board of Regents formally appointed Glenn Frank president of the University. It was agreed he would take up his new responsibilities in September, with President Birge remaining in office through the summer. A month later the board formally accepted Birge's resignation, effective September 1, 1925, and with unprecedented generosity recognized his half-century of distin-

---

published memoirs, Phil La Follette commented:

> My father had met Dr. Frank in 1924 and was impressed with his superficiality, glibness, and lack of strength under a very shallow veneer of "quickie New Yorkese polish." Because of his and Mother's veneration for the University he was deeply interested in who would become President of the University. It never crossed his mind that there was the slightest impropriety for him—a distinguished graduate and the State's leading citizen—to be concerned with this important appointment.
>
> For reasons which I cannot explain to this day except for "show-offness"—to prove "he wore no man's collar"—Governor John J. Blaine connived at the appointment of Frank totally without regard to my father's opinion. The first the [that] he—or any of us—knew of Frank's selection was when we read about it in the newspapers.

P.F. La Follette, draft memoirs, n.d., P.F. La Follette Papers, box 123.

[151]Zink, "Glenn Frank," p. 98. Ironically, one of the regents who helped lead the fight to fire Frank in 1937 had, prior to his board service, applauded Frank's appointment in 1925, telling Regent Kronshage: "In getting Glen[n] Frank for the Presidency, I believe you have picked a President that will be hard to beat. I miss my guess if he does not stand out within a few years as one of the strongest University presidents in the country." Clough Gates to Kronshage, May 23, 1925, Kronshage Papers, box 5.

[152]*Wisconsin State Journal*, May 25, 1925.

guished University service by appointing him president emeritus "at his present salary" of $10,000 a year.[153]

"Glenn Frank: Free President"

Throughout the long search for a new president the Board of Regents never adopted a formal job description nor developed any guiding principles for its selection committee. Unlike the elder La Follette and his wife Belle, who gave a great deal of thought to the leadership needs of the University, except for Zona Gale's exuberant musings individual regents seem not to have articulated their views as to the qualities and talents they hoped to see in President Birge's successor. Because of their faith in the ameliorative role of education and the central importance of the University in inculcating progressive ideas, the top progressive politicians of the state—Senator La Follette and Governor Blaine—sought to influence the presidential selection process to a degree that might shock later observers. It seems clear that the regent majority shared this concern to find a leader who believed the University should be a major agent of social change. The regents also recognized their institution's need for a fresh and energetic outsider—in geography and profession—who could persuasively present campus needs to the people and political leaders of Wisconsin. In the process they hoped to revitalize the University's pioneering commitment to the Wisconsin Idea of ever-expanding expert service to the state. In short, they wanted someone broadly liberal in social, economic, and political outlook so as to be able to relate comfortably to the currently dominant progressive political leadership of the state. Glenn Frank seemed to fit these unstated requirements admirably.

Michael Olbrich, though a new regent already one of the most influential members of the board, summed up the regents' hopes and expectations in an address to the state over the University's fledgling radio station WHA in mid-June. Describing the president-elect as "a Scotch Methodist marvel from Missouri with a Manhattan finish,"

---

[153]June 22, 1925, BOR Papers, 1/1/3, box 38; McCaffrey to Frank, July 2, 1925, Frank Papers, Kirksville; Sellery, *Birge*, p. 81. Birge was also eligible for a Carnegie pension of $4,000, bringing his retirement salary to $14,000 a year until the depression salary waivers and cutbacks of 1932-33, when his "normal" salary was reduced to $6,000 and subsequently cut further through waivers until it was established at $5,400 after 1936-37. His Carnegie retirement allowance of $4,000 remained unchanged throughout the depression.

Olbrich recalled that like the late revered Senator La Follette, as an undergraduate Glenn Frank also had won major oratorical contests and served as editor of the college magazine. The regents had not sought a great scientist or scholar as president, Olbrich explained, nor did they want a narrow specialist. "To have written a book or two superbly well was scholarship of quite as high an order as much reading about the writing of books"; "to have spoken from a thousand platforms, molding a thousand audiences to the speaker's mind by a master's touch was specialization of quite as significant a type as fine writing about the theory of speech"; "to have first hand contact with the people of each and every state and station might be research quite as relevant to the practical conduct of the affairs of a great university as the advancement of the hesitant hypothesis based on deciphering many cuneiform characters that psycho-analysis was an ancient Persian pastime, or that Assyrian gentlemen indulged the practice of plying their toothpicks in public places." The regents believed that "breadth of outlook was not inconsistent with depth of understanding" and that "a pleasing platform personality and a voice of gracious cadence might well go hand in hand with brain power of the highest order." Thus when it became known Glenn Frank was available, "doubt ceased and debate ended."

> For he has gone far, is bound to travel further, and Wisconsin will travel with him. He comes to lead, not to follow. Neither to take program from vested interest, nor to run the errands of party, nor echo the will or whim of faction, nor execute the orders nor serve the ends of any cult or creed shall be his function here. He was not imported as the property or protege of an association of owners. But he was invited to be president in his own right, sole proprietor of his job, authorized without condition or reservation to hang out the sign, Glenn Frank, free president of the free University of Wisconsin....
>
> Wisconsin's golden age is here. With her great young president, with financial provision for the future assured by the legislature and the Governor, who can doubt that our beloved University is on the threshold of her greatest expansion, the greatest renaissance in all her history.[154]

Olbrich and his regent colleagues, it was clear, expected much of their new leader.

For his *Century* readers during the summer Frank devoted his final three columns to a sweeping review of "The Outlook for Western

---

[154]M.B. Olbrich, "Glenn Frank, Free President," WHA radio address, June 15, 1925, reprinted in *WAM*, 26 (July, 1925), 335, 342-3.

Civilization." While denying he was advancing "any body of nicely articulated social doctrines" and claiming to have "consistently fought against the plague of premature conclusions," the essays clearly reflected some hard thought about Frank's new career.[155] Indeed, his last column, published in the September, 1925, issue as Frank was arriving in Madison and subtitled "Engineers of a New Renaissance," seemed to be written with the opportunities of his new position very much in mind. In it the president-elect called for a marriage of scholarship and statesmanship so as to "thrust the results of research into the stream of common thought and make them the basis for social action." What was needed, he declared, was "an evangelism of scholarship" to bring "the socially usable ideas that have been produced by the natural and social sciences" into the public mind. This might require laymen with facile pens to summarize and publicize the latest findings, but there were also "unusual scholars who combine the burrowing qualities of the mole with the singing qualities of the lark." To energize and orchestrate all this activity would require a new sort of practical visionary, "a great spiritual leader who will be able to capture the attention of the whole Western world and fire its imagination with the social and spiritual possibilities that are locked up in the new ideas." Such a leader "would be a sort of impresario" who could "play ringmaster to the specialists." A "combination of Francis Bacon and Billy Sunday," this impresario would need to be "an omnivorous reader" who was "at home with the great generalizations that have emerged and are emerging from the sciences, philosophies, and practical experiences of mankind." At the same time, he would also have to possess "just enough of the alloy of mountebankery in him to enable him to touch the imagination of the masses and to invest the whole adventure of the modern mind with that absorbing passion for humanity which has characterized all great epochs of civil and religious progress." Such a leader, Frank predicted, could bring about a second renaissance.[156]

This was, surely, a noble vision for a new university president. Frank nominated no candidate for this daunting super-leader role, perhaps because he hoped his more discerning readers would need no prompting. He did suggest that the task would require "a man whose

---

[155]Frank, "The Outlook for Western Civilization: I—the Literature of Despair," *Century Magazine*, 110 (July, 1925), 371.

[156]Frank, "The Outlook for Western Civilization: III—Engineers of a New Renaissance," *ibid.* (September, 1925), 626-36.

official position gives to his voice a sounding board with world-wide resonance and gives to his pronouncements an obvious and automatic prestige"—and here he modestly turned aside any speculation for the moment—someone such as "a British Premier or an American President."[157] But who could forget that Woodrow Wilson had recently moved to the White House after serving as president of Princeton University, that Glenn Frank had once toured and preached with Billy Sunday, and that this series of articles once again demonstrated its author's impressive facility at interpretive scholarship and evangelical expression? However fanciful Frank's vision or unlikely that he would be called from Madison to lead a national renaissance, the next few years at Wisconsin promised to be very, very interesting.[158]

New Tools for the New Spirit

With Glenn Frank's reflections on the bright future of western civilization as a backdrop, several important developments were occurring in Wisconsin that presaged a new forward-looking era for the University. On June 30, 1925, the officers of the new Wisconsin University Building Corporation filed for and received a charter from the state. The WUBC constituted a fundamental breakthrough for the

---

[157]Ibid., p. 634.

[158]Frank was not the only one to call for new academic leadership. Albert Edward Wiggam, in *The New Decalogue of Science* (Indianapolis: Bobbs-Merrill Company, 1922), not only recognized the same need but had no doubt about Frank's special leadership qualities. In his preface Wiggam thanked Frank for reading the manuscript and predicted that Frank's career "will be one of the world-events of the coming generation" since his "genius, scholarship, poise and insight represents the new type of statesman, of whom I have endeavored to write." Later, on pages 132 and 133, Wiggam continued his extravagant praise: "We already have enough science right at hand to bring the world into an earthly paradise. It remains for all men...to apply it. I know of no man who has seen all its intellectual implications, its difficulties and possibilities so clearly as Mr. Glenn Frank, the publicist, a man who is rising among the younger men of his generation as the new type of scientific statesman, who must shortly replace the older type if the world is to reap in social organization, in industrial development and political achievement the happy possibilities for the common man which the scientist has laid at our feet. With such power over nature what could we not do for the common man if only our leadership itself could enter completely into that spiritual surrender to truth and that exacting intellectual method by which this power was by the scientist discovered. Speaking with a truly continental eloquence, Mr. Frank has called this next great intellectual step, 'The Spiritual Renaissance of the Western World.'...In a book, shortly to be published,...Mr. Frank has outlined the bases, motives and objectives of this rapidly gathering movement toward a new spiritual spring-time in the hopes and hearts of men. It is already bending like a new bow of promise across the sky of human hope."

University in finally acquiring a means to construct the men's dormitories that President Van Hise had called for in his 1904 inaugural address. The corporation provided a solution to two vexing and up to now insoluble problems: the unwillingness of the legislature to provide funds for any but the most pressing instructional needs, and the prohibition of the Wisconsin constitution forbidding state agencies to incur any debt, even for facilities like dormitories that had assured operating revenues to cover amortized construction and operating costs. To break this logjam, under Kronshage's astute leadership the Board of Regents came up with the WUBC, an imaginative quasi-public but legally private corporate entity whose officers—the University business manager, comptroller, and regent secretary—were under the direct control of the board yet legally distinct and therefore able to borrow the necessary construction funds and perform other customary corporate activities. It was elegantly simple: the regents could now lease to their captive corporation the tract of land designated for dormitories in the 1908 campus architectural plan; the WUBC in turn could borrow funds from the state annuity board against the prospective operating revenue stream, construct and furnish the dormitories, and then lease them back to the University for a rental sufficient to cover the payments on principal and interest. Tripp and Adams halls and the adjacent Van Hise Refectory were soon under construction, opening in the fall of 1926.[159] Four decades after the Science Hall fire in 1884 had obliged the University to reclaim North Hall for academic purposes rather than for continued use as a men's dormitory, male students once again would live on campus.

Next came the regents' famous—some said infamous—Grady resolution "that no gifts, donations, or subsidies shall in the future be accepted by or on behalf of the University of Wisconsin from any incorporated Educational endowments or organizations of like charac-

---

[159]See "The University of Wisconsin Financing and Construction of Men's Dormitories," December, 1926, Business Administration Papers, 24/1/1, box 31; "The Wisconsin University Building Corporation," presented to the Board of Regents on October 14, 1939, BOR Papers, 1/1/3, box 54; and Barry Teicher and John W. Jenkins, *A History of Housing at the University of Wisconsin* (Madison: UW History Project, 1987), pp. 24-5. Although the regents established WUBC for the purposes described in the text, it is interesting to note that their first use of the corporation, decided at their June 25 meeting, was to have it purchase and lease back to them the new furniture for Olin House, President Frank's new home. President Van Hise's inaugural address calling for University dormitories appears in *The Jubilee of the University of Wisconsin: In Celebration of the Fiftieth Anniversary of Its First Commencement Held at Madison June the Fifth to June the Ninth Nineteen Hundred and Four* (Madison: Jubilee Committee, 1905), pp. 98-128.

ter." Offered by Regent Daniel Grady, a Portage Democrat and long-time La Follette supporter, the measure implemented a recent editorial in *La Follette's Magazine* warning of the need to protect colleges and universities from the selfish dictates of corporate wealth.[160] The Grady resolution had the immediate effect of spurning about $800,000 in pending grants from the Rockefeller-funded General Education Board for the construction of medical school research facilities and support of the work of prominent UW economist John R. Commons. For the future it asserted a progressive intention, as the debate described it, to steer clear of the perverting influence of "tainted" money. If UW research was really needed to solve a particular problem, Grady, Gale, and other supporters argued, the state of Wisconsin could be counted on to sponsor and fund it. The Grady prohibition, which will be discussed further in the next chapter, generated spirited controversy among members of the progressive-dominated Board of Regents and ultimately spilled over to involve UW faculty, administrators, students, and alumni, as well as the politicians and press of the state. While the debate produced no consensus, ideological or otherwise, with progressives lining up on both sides of the issue, in a sense the resolution reflected the optimistic mood of the day. Grady and his backers were seeking to lay the foundation for an unfettered administration under the University's youthful new president, whose idealistic leadership they believed would provide a model for all of American higher education.[161]

On August 22, with Glenn Frank not yet in Madison, the regents took another momentous action, coincidentally related to the import of the Grady prohibition. They approved a second unique and legally distinct agency whose dual purpose was to acquire and market patents resulting from the scientific discoveries of UW scholars and to dispense the proceeds in support of further research. Two years earlier President Birge had rebuffed agricultural chemistry Professor Harry Steenbock's offer of the patent rights for his potentially valuable nutrition-related research on vitamin D. By mid-1924 Steenbock saw evidence of a greater breakthrough, an inexpensive irradiation process to enhance the vitamin D content of various foods. The Steenbock discovery promised an end to the currently widespread nutritional disease of rickets in humans and animals. This time Steenbock's consultations with Agricul-

---

[160]Editorial, *La Follette's Magazine*, 17 (January, 1925), 2-3.

[161]BOR Minutes, August 5, 1925, UA. See also Martin Kenneth Gordon, "Wisconsin and the Foundations, 1925-1931" (M.A. thesis, University of Wisconsin, 1965).

ture Dean Russell, Graduate Dean Slichter, and several astute UW alumni produced agreement that patenting was necessary to assure proper application of the new process, especially in view of Steenbock's concern that its use to enhance oleomargarine might undermine Wisconsin's important dairy industry. Any University mechanism to hold and market the Steenbock patent, however, needed the approval of the Board of Regents. After quiet lobbying this was soon forthcoming. In fact Regent Grady, who clearly had no qualms about this sort of private educational foundation, himself offered the successful motion: "that the plan of organizing the proposed non-stock, non-profit corporation to be known as Wisconsin Alumni Research Foundation, together with its articles as presented be approved."[162] The scheme called for the foundation to be operated by UW alumni as a private and legally independent corporate entity, yet with the intent of using any profits resulting from the Steenbock or other patents to support University research.

WARF, as the new agency soon came to be known, is arguably the single most important reason why the University of Wisconsin emerged as one of the nation's great research universities in the second half of the twentieth century. In 1925, however, no one had any idea just how significant the new venture would turn out to be. The key issue, confronted by the regents with uncharacteristic boldness, was the highly controversial decision to patent and thereby restrict access to a faculty discovery developed in a publicly-funded university laboratory. Even more audacious was the idea that the University should profit from this life-saving breakthrough, and do so through a revolutionary captive research-funding agency the likes of which had never before been contemplated by an academic institution. Intrigued yet evidently skittish at the prospect, the full board had referred the controversial Steenbock scheme to its Executive Committee on April 22 with power to act. Only late in the summer, with Glenn Frank's exhilarating proclamations as background and the new president about to take office, did Executive Committee members Grady, Callahan, Olbrich, and Kronshage vote official approval for launching the Wisconsin Alumni Research Foundation.[163] It would prove to be one of the most pivotal acts in the Univer-

---

[162]BOR Minutes, April 22, 1925.

[163]Ibid. The executive committee voted approval of the general plan for WARF on May 8 (see Executive Committee papers for that date in BOR Papers, 1/2/2, box 20, UA) and approved the proposed articles of organization, as well as the general plan, on August 22, ibid. A good account of Steenbock's work appears in Howard A. Schneider, "Harry Steenbock (1886-1967)—A Biographical Sketch," chapter 5 in David L. Nelson and Brook Chase

sity's history.

The Summer Interregnum

Throughout the late spring and summer the *Daily Cardinal* and the Madison press kept close tabs on Glenn Frank, who the *Cardinal* predicted would "soon be ranked as one of the leading presidents of the day." As Frank's three "Civilization" articles appeared in the *Century* and he reiterated their main themes in public addresses, the *Cardinal* speculated on the likely implications for Wisconsin, though with a trace of skepticism about the president-elect's call for the blending of scholarly expertise and statecraft. "Perhaps," the paper commented, "he can explain more fully how he would choose his experts and how he would put his theories into practice." Still, the *Cardinal* looked forward to exciting days ahead under Glenn Frank's leadership. "Under his program," the editor enthused, "Wisconsin's future as a guiding and beneficent force in the life of the community and nation seems bright indeed."[164] This certainly was the new president's intent. When the publisher of the *Wisconsin State Journal* wrote pledging his paper's support, Frank assured him that the University and the state of Wisconsin would shortly become "the social, political, and economic laboratory to which the whole nation will look for intelligent, progressive, and responsible leadership."

> I do not mean that I think the University should be a propagandist agency for any particular point of view, except the scientific point of view, by which I mean simply the point of view from which men ask, first, what are the facts of the case, second, what is the horse-sense conclusion to be drawn from the facts, and, third, how can we put this horse-sense conclusion into effect. That, after all, is the progressivism and the liberalism that we want, isn't it?
>
> My feeling is that a state University should be kept wholly out of politics, in the party sense, but plunged as deeply into politics, in the Platonic sense. That is to say, a state University should, out of its studies and researches, constantly be throwing up the raw materials of fact upon which

---

Soltvedt, eds., *One Hundred Years of Agricultural Chemistry and Biochemistry at Wisconsin* (Madison: Science Tech Publishers, 1989), pp. 45-64. The best discussion of the founding of WARF published to date appears in Mark H. Ingraham, *Charles Sumner Slichter: The Golden Vector* (Madison: University of Wisconsin Press, 1972), pp. 176-93.

[164]See *Daily Cardinal*, May 27, June 27, July 2, 4, and 30, 1925.

sound political judgment can be formed.[165]

In spite of Frank's announced intention not to comment on or involve himself in University matters until taking up his new post on September 1, he found it impossible to remain entirely aloof. President Birge occasionally discussed University business with him, as when the International Education Board requested that Agriculture Dean Harry Russell be granted a leave during 1925-26 to conduct a study of educational needs in Asia.[166] Surprisingly, the regents seem not to have consulted the new president much about their unusually important actions during the summer. Frank's friend and patron, Zona Gale, a supporter of the Grady resolution, did send him a rambling account of the board's debate on that controversial issue, including President Birge's acid comment that "if he were an incoming president, and such action was taken, he should resign!" Others also alerted Frank to the need to think about how he would deal with this politically tricky matter when he moved into Bascom Hall.[167]

Amidst the high expectations there was in fact plenty of unsolicited advice, so much, in fact, that the president-elect might be pardoned for deciding to withhold judgment on most of it. Regent Olbrich passed on a warning from Justice Marvin B. Rosenberry of the Wisconsin Supreme Court of a plan by some stalwart Republicans to try to get Frank to commit himself on various issues before his arrival in Madison. Olbrich and Rosenberry thought Frank ought "to be on your guard."[168] Frank gratefully accepted President Birge's caution about the hazard of accepting an invitation to provide a statement about religious educa-

---

[165]Frank to A.M. Brayton, June 5, 1925, Frank Papers, Kirksville.

[166]Frank eventually gave his approval, but only after meeting with Russell in New York. See Birge to Frank, June 9, 1925, ibid., and Birge Presidential Papers, 4/12/1, box 51; Frank to Olbrich, June 12, 1925; Frank to Olbrich, telegram, June 24, 1925; Olbrich to Frank, telegram, June 24, 1925, Frank Papers, Kirksville; Edward H. Beardsley, *Harry L. Russell and Agricultural Science in Wisconsin* (Madison: University of Wisconsin Press, 1969), p. 160.

[167]Zona Gale to Frank, August 6, 1925; Charles R. Bardeen to H.J. Thorkelson, August 7, 1925; Bardeen to Frank, August 8, 1925; John Callahan to Frank, August 8, 1925; M.B. Olbrich to Frank, August 11, 1925; Edwin E. Witte to Frank, September 29, 1925, Frank Papers, Kirksville. Frank almost certainly had been forewarned in June of the regent action by Medical School Dean Bardeen, the University official who had applied for the disputed grant. See Bardeen to Glenn Frank, June 24, 1925, and [Bardeen] to Theodore Kronshage, June 26, 1925, ibid.

[168]Olbrich to Frank, June 4, 1925, ibid. Olbrich pointed out that Rosenberry was himself a stalwart, but wished Frank well and wanted him to get off to a good start.

tion.[169] He likewise withheld a commitment on Dean of Men Scott H. Goodnight's proposal, which the dean conceded "does not, it is true, demand immediate attention," to remove student discipline from his responsibilities.[170] Psychology Professor Joseph Jastrow cautioned Frank that he would be bombarded with conflicting advice when he reached Madison, but then proceeded to offer some of his own: "For myself," Jastrow declared, "I have long ago reached the conclusion that the methods of managing Universities were essentially wrong." He therefore urged Frank to study his essay, "Administrative Peril in Education," in a 1913 book on *University Control*: "Whatever you do in preparation for the new office, read that book," Jastrow advised. "Make all the allowance you wish and dissent as forcibly as you care to; but after all it is the only document that comes near to telling the true story. It isn't Upton-Sinclairish in the least; yet he finds some support in it."[171]

Law Professor Howard L. Smith, an old-fashioned generalist who eventually left the University a substantial bequest to promote humanistic learning, sounded the most ominous note, bluntly warning that the University needed a thorough house-cleaning and spiritual rebirth. The materialist leadership of the late President Van Hise, with its stress on applied research and training, had bred "an atmosphere that is absolutely poisonous, the sordid atmosphere of the market place." President

---

[169]Frank to Birge, July 9, 1925, Frank Presidential Papers, 4/13/1, box 2. See also Frank to Birge, June 11, 1925, ibid.

[170]S.H. Goodnight to Frank, May 27, 1925, ibid. The attachment was a letter from Goodnight to E.A. Birge, dated March 20, 1925, which argued the dean's case in detail. Frank also received communications from other UW staff members hoping to influence their new leader. These included a telegram on August 22 from John R. Commons pointing out a staffing opportunity with the resignation of the prominent agricultural economist H.C. Taylor from the U.S. Department of Agriculture as well as a letter from engineering faculty members E.W. Wines and L.E. Blair recommending their colleague Ben G. Elliott to replace University Extension Division Dean Reber, whose resignation had been widely rumored. Frank followed up the Commons lead, urging Taylor "to give me a chance to talk to you before you commit yourself elsewhere." Frank to Taylor, August 24, 1924, ibid.

[171]Joseph Jastrow to Frank, June 21, 1925, ibid. See J. McKeen Cattell, ed., *Science and Education*, vol. 3, *University Control* (New York: The Science Press, 1913). The volume included Cattell's proposed plan to reorganize institutions of higher education on a more democratic basis, as well as responses to the plan by named and unnamed critics. Several unsigned letters from UW faculty were included. The reference to Upton Sinclair pertains to his *The Goose-Step: A Study of American Education* (Pasadena, California: The Author, 1922), a severe indictment of American higher education in general and including criticism of President Birge and the University of Wisconsin.

Birge, though a professed champion of the liberal arts, had done little to counter the Van Hise emphasis on mundane pursuits. What the University sorely needed was "a president who will lift our eyes from the ground, and give us ideals that are not wholly sordid," Smith declared. "In short, Mr. Frank, the University of Wisconsin just now needs for its President, a prophet. Gird on your robes and come to us."[172]

The Coming

Garbed instead in a conservative blue suit, dotted blue shirt, black tie, gray felt hat, and highly shined black shoes, Glenn Frank stepped from the train in downtown Madison on September 1, 1925, ready to assume the University presidency. Only his tan spats, "for which he is famous," a reporter pointed out, were missing on this especially warm summertime Circus Day afternoon.[173] With the new president was his wife Mary, his six-year-old son Glenn, Jr., and the family dog, a mutt named Jonesy. The official greeting party included President Birge, who offered a welcoming hand to his successor in office, Regent and Mrs. Daniel Grady, University Business Manager J.D. Phillips, and Regent Zona Gale,

[172]Howard L. Smith to Frank, July 14, 1925, Frank Papers, Kirksville. Smith weakened his defense of the liberal arts by a scathing attack on Van Hise, who, he declared, was "a crude, uncultured man, an expert on Cambrian rocks, whose excursions into economic geology had taught him that there was at least one kind of education that had a readily convertible money value....He was almost incapable of weighing values, except in terms of dollars and cents."

[173]*Milwaukee Journal*, September 2, 1925. The *Capital Times* also reported on September 1: "his inevitable spats were absent. 'They're too hot'," Frank responded to a question about their omission.

who hugged and kissed her friend Mary. Rather than squander his famed eloquence on this small group of friends and reporters, Frank distributed copies of a press release and followed Birge to a waiting sedan that carried the newcomers to the nearby Loraine Hotel and its Governor's Suite. This would accommodate the family for much of September while workers finished remodeling Olin House, the recently acquired presidential residence overlooking the campus from University Heights. Before the day was out Frank took possession of the president's office in Bascom Hall, atop "the Hill" with its fabled view of the state capitol a mile east up State Street, met with the few UW officials on hand during this traditionally slack vacation period, and checked more than once on progress at the Olin mansion.[174]

President Frank's press release seemingly appealed to everyone. Perhaps recalling Regent Olbrich's summertime warning about the stalwarts' scheme to test his judgment, Frank opened with a humble refusal to speculate about specific future developments, instead asserting that "the determination of the policies of the University is, as I see it, a cooperative enterprise in which the whole state must share." This populist approach (which incidentally was much more inclusive than the "democratic" plan recommended by Professor Jastrow), certainly carried no "guaranty of wise and effective action," Frank pointed out, and would require "a high quality of sportsmanship on the part of all concerned." It might at times result in slower progress than a benevolent despotism acting with greater promptness and precision. "But this is part of the price we pay for democracy," Frank cautioned. "And when the books are balanced we are likely to find that the mistakes of democracy are, in the long run, less costly than the mistakes of despotism."

> I am here now and eager to get to work. I shall not attempt to disguise my sense of elation at the prospect of having a share in the development of education in Wisconsin. I would not know where to look for a challenge more inspiring than the one that today brings me to Wisconsin. The strategic significance to the life of the state and to the life of the nation of the work of this great University can hardly be over-estimated.

Although the new president's agenda for the University remained vague, Frank made no secret of his intention to be an activist leader in support of several first principles:

---

[174] *Capital Times*, September 1, 1925; *Wisconsin State Journal*, September 1, 1925.

the ideals of sound scholarship and inspired teaching, of productive research and practical service, of freedom to investigate and courage to follow the truth wherever it may lead. Here certainly is sure guidance for the future. We cannot dispense with any of these ideals and still have a great University.[175]

Madison quickly welcomed President Frank and his family to the community. The local press painted a warm portrait of affectionate domesticity. In what would turn out to be a considerable misreading of Mary Frank, the *Capital Times* reported that she was "a typically American woman of the home," who had "immediately reflected the woman's point of view in being somewhat overwhelmed" by the size of Olin House and "the problems presented from a housekeeping point of view in such a large building." Even the Franks' favorite hobbies did not escape notice: Glenn, Sr., relished golf; Mary cherished Glenn, Jr.; and Glennie enjoyed the cartoons he somehow had discovered in the *Capital Times.* Here indeed was a "happy family" whose members "truly love each other."[176] A few days later the *Wisconsin State Journal*'s society reporter described Mary Frank as "youthful and vivacious with a magnetic personality." She and her husband already had dined with Governor and Mrs. Blaine at the executive residence. But mostly "Mrs. Frank has given much of her time since being here to the opening of the residence and her interest in it assures a social administration as a gracious hostess." The advent of the Franks promised "a return of many brilliant social functions of the university, such as have not been held in recent years."[177] Subsequent articles reinforced this expectation by noting the numerous dinners, luncheons, and teas that Mrs. Frank was attending as the guest of honor.[178]

Both Madison newspapers soon editorialized about the new president. Reflecting its progressive leanings, the *Capital Times* predicted that "Dr. Frank will be the guiding spirit in a program that will not be made FOR Wisconsin in advance but will come OUT of Wisconsin." Ever preaching economy, editor William T. Evjue applauded Frank's assumption "that the big job of the educator is to make people THINK

---

[175]For the text of the statement see *Capital Times,* September 1, 1925, and *Wisconsin State Journal,* September 1, 1925.

[176]*Capital Times,* September 2, 1925.

[177]*Wisconsin State Journal,* September 9, 1925.

[178]Ibid., September 13, 18, and 20, 1925; *Capital Times,* September 18, 1925; *Milwaukee Journal,* September 20, 1925.

with their own equipment and on their own initiative unfettered and unshackled by the ghosts and dogmas and prejudices of the past." The University needed to return to basic principles, and not simply chase after "big appropriations and wonderful buildings." Once on the right path, this foremost champion of the Grady resolution promised, "Dr. Frank will find that the people of this commonwealth will be generous, as they always have been, in furnishing the university with every aid adequate to maintain the further progress of this great institution."[179]

The senior Madison newspaper, the stalwart *Wisconsin State Journal*, offered a somewhat less partisan set of expectations for the new leader. "A few Wisconsin people, we fear, may be disappointed," the paper observed, reflecting the new president's assurances to its publisher: those who hoped that under Frank's administration the University could be used to promote "the theories of one or another political faction." President Frank would disappoint them.

> The essential thing in his career has been pursuit of truth. He has not sought truths that could be used in one way, and ignored truths that could be used in another. Rather he has sought the truth and permitted the truth to be responsible for its own consequences.

Frank's style as editor of the *Century Magazine* had been to analyze the data and draw conclusions without regard to ideological preconceptions, sound training for his new position:

> We predict that President Frank will bring to the University of Wisconsin this painstaking scholarship and this inflexible surrender of everything to the truth. University service can hope for no more than this from any man. To think straight, to see straight, to act straight—that makes the ideal citizen....And the finished product for which the state maintains the university is the good citizen.[180]

President Frank quickly took to the hustings to begin establishing

---

[179] *Capital Times*, September 4, 1925. The final quote concerning Wisconsin's generosity to the University also referred to the emerging debate over the Grady resolution, whose supporters, including the *Capital Times*, argued that foundation aid was unnecessary because the state always had and always would supply the requisite funds. The paper ignored the fact that President Birge, Regent Kronshage, and others had only recently completed a hard-hitting and ultimately successful campaign to convince the legislature and governor to approve a minimally adequate budget for the institution after a decade of fiscal neglect. For more on the lingering controversy over the Grady resolution see Chapter 2.

[180] *Wisconsin State Journal*, September 13, 1925.

his persona throughout Wisconsin. The day after his arrival he addressed the Rotary Club of Madison, conveniently meeting at the Loraine Hotel, on the prospects of western civilization and American patriotism. Appealing strongly to his audience of businessmen and civic leaders in the age of Babbitt, he asserted: "The highest social service that any man can render is to mind his own business."[181] At another point in his hour-long address, Frank offered one of his typical catchy, simplistic, but obscure aphorisms: "If a man stresses production of wealth only, he is a slave. If he stresses distribution only, he is a plutocrat, and if he stresses consumption of wealth only, he is a parasite. We can build a durable civilization only by the amalgamation of all three."[182] The next week he spoke in Milwaukee before the convention of the National Association of Professional Men's

Clubs, which opened the doors of the Pabst Theater so the general public might hear the new president as well. Frank addressed himself to the prospects for civilization in light of the recent carnage in Europe, concluding: "God and time alone can tell whether this aversion to war, born in the bitterness of experience, will stay the coming of another world war until the race breeds a few world statesmen big enough to lure us into the common sense policy of some common administration of the common interests of the world."[183] As if to emphasize his continuing interest in national and international affairs, Frank also helped sponsor and took part in a conference on Chinese-American

---

[181]Quoted in *Capital Times*, September 3, 1925.
[182]Quoted in *Milwaukee Journal*, September 4, 1925.
[183]Quoted in *Wisconsin State Journal*, September 12, 1925.

relations in Baltimore.[184]   On September 22 the new president addressed an audience at the Interstate Fair in La Crosse.   The *Milwaukee Journal* correspondent marveled at how "he held their attention by the very intensity of his manner, telling them of the kind of men and women the university hopes to produce."

> They are friendly folk hereabouts, and when the president had gone they asked each other how they liked his speech. They liked it. It is evident, very evident, that Glenn Frank gets on with people. For the consensus of opinion seemed to be, as one man put it—"The main thing is we've got a president who can come out and say 'hello' to the people."[185]

As if to demonstrate his determination to get right down to business, Frank refrained from a formal inauguration.   Instead he shrewdly used the campus-wide Varsity Welcome ceremony on September 25 as a kind of working presidential inaugural.   The Varsity Welcome—first held in 1913 in the University armory—had over the years since developed into an important tradition at the University.   Professor Julius E. Olson, himself a member of the Class of 1884 and the long-time chairman of the Faculty Committee on Public Functions, had conceived of the program as a means of cultivating loyalty and devotion to the University—to Varsity.   With the large influx of students following the World War, the welcome moved outdoors and began to take fuller advantage of the opportunities for institutional pageantry.   Each class gathered at its assigned position—seniors, graduate, and law students at the Lincoln Terrace in front of Bascom Hall, juniors and sophomores lining the north and south sides of the Hill, and the freshmen grouped near the clock tower on Music Hall at the bottom of the Hill.   When all were in place, the senior class paraded down the Hill and then back up, escorting the newest class to an honored position at the top, where the freshmen sang, cheered, and gave "skyrockets" to prove their worthiness to join the UW family.   All then listened to welcoming addresses by state and campus dignitaries.   President Frank's use of the ceremony to present himself to students, staff, and townspeople was a showman's recognition of the public relations value of the event in highlighting the University's most prominent freshman.

---

[184]*Capital Times*, September 17, 1925. Frank's co-sponsors included former U.S. Supreme Court Chief Justice John Clark, President S. Parkes Coleman of the Federal Council of Churches, Mrs. John D. Rockefeller, Jr., and President William Green of the American Federation of Labor.

[185]*Milwaukee Journal*, September 23, 1925.

As a result, the 1925 exercises drew a record crowd and, in keeping with Frank's publicist intent, for the first time became a multi-media event, as it was extensively covered in the local press and recorded on film to be shown subsequently at the Strand Theater in downtown Madison.[186]

The new president's address emphasized the University's scholarly traditions and quality while offering clarifying insights into some of the inspiring themes he had proclaimed earlier in the summer in his "Civilization" series. "From slightly different angles," he told the freshmen, "you and I are together setting out on a great adventure this morning."

> Together we are going to find out whether it is possible for young men and young women to make themselves really at home in the modern world, able to work in harmony with the creative forces of their time instead of at cross-

---

[186]See *Daily Cardinal*, September 25, 1925; *Capital Times*, September 25, 1925. For background on the Welcome, see "The Varsity Welcome," editorial, *WAM*, 15 (October, 1913), 27-8; "The Varsity Welcome," editorial, ibid., 16 (October, 1914), 1-2; Charles I. Corp, "The Varsity Welcome," ibid., 17 (November, 1915), 14-5; "The Varsity Welcome," ibid., 18 (November, 1916), 4-6; "Hear the President," ibid., 27 (November, 1925), 5. Printed programs for several of the Welcomes may be found in General University Materials, 0/9/1, UA. The films have been lost or destroyed, and the identities of the people who produced them is unknown. Some sense of the solemn pageantry that had developed around the Varsity Welcome by the 1920s can be seen from the following summary of the speech by Letters and Science Dean George Sellery at the 1929 ceremony. Sellery had spoken extemporaneously, but at the request of Professor Max Otto later summarized his remarks in a handwritten letter, which, Sellery said, were "somewhat along this line, although, I think, less stiltedly."

 Mankind has always used ceremonials to mark important epochs in the life of the individual. From the most savage tribes to the most civilized peoples the story is the same....[*sic*] To celebrate fittingly, to give utterance to sentiments too deep or too poignant to be expressed in words, ritual is called upon. Birth, marriage, death, the attainment of manhood, admission to the army, the Church, the throne—these at all times and in all places, have demanded the aid of ceremony, pageantry, ritual, sacrament.

 The same universal sentiment has decreed that the place chosen for the celebration of the rites shall be noble. Whether the vaulted aisle of the forest glade, the high-place of the elders, the parish church, the cathedral of the bishop, or the palace of the king, dignity has marked it as a fitting spot for the celebration of the high event.

 We of this University have our ceremonies and our sacred places, and this is one of them. Here, in the presence, we trust, of the spirit of Lincoln, within the shadows of the Hall named for John Bascom, in this high-place under the bright Wisconsin sky, with pageantry, music, and speech, it is our custom to welcome the freshmen into the fellowship of the University of Wisconsin."
George C. Sellery to Max Otto, October 1, 1929, Max Otto Papers, box 2, SHSW.

purposes to them.

Happily, the faculty stood ready and willing to aid the process:

> The University of Wisconsin is not interested in teachers who are mere
> merchants of dead yesterdays; it covets and captures men who are guides into
> unborn tomorrows, men who have objects as well as subjects, men who
> refuse to put conformity to old customs above curiosity about new ideas, men
> who are not content to be peddlers of petty accuracies when they are called to
> be priests and prophets of abundant living.

The cultivation of a lifelong social concern and commitment to civic
improvement was, Frank declared, the fundamental objective of
University life.

> In the class rooms of this University you will hear many doctrines discussed,
> but in the deepest sense of the word it is not the business of this University to
> fill your minds with doctrines. As I have said many times and in many
> places, it is not the business of a University to teach its students what to think
> but to teach them how to think, and then to trust them to decide what to think
> as year by year they face the changing facts of a changing world....The
> University of Wisconsin does not exist merely to train you to be clever
> competitors in the world as it is; it exists to help you to become creative
> cooperators in the making of the world as it ought to be.[187]

Only a few days short of his thirty-eighth birthday, Glenn Frank
had met his first class. He was ready to bring the promised renaissance
to Wisconsin.

---

[187]*Capital Times*, September 25, 1925; *Daily Cardinal*, September 26, 1925.

2.

The Impresario

Regent President Theodore Kronshage's series of hard-hitting articles on the financial plight of the University produced a classic public relations triumph early in 1925. The Kronshage publicity effort, coupled with skillful lobbying, persuaded a reluctant governor and legislature to provide an unusually generous appropriation for the 1925-27 biennium just as the regents were announcing Frank's selection. Although caretaker President Birge had encouraged and assisted in the campaign, he previously had given little serious attention to the University's declining image.[1] The lesson was not lost on Kronshage and his fellow regents, however, and they expected Birge's successor aggressively to foster public and legislative support for the University. Glenn Frank seemed the ideal choice for this role, and he responded to his

---

[1]Curti and Carstensen remarked on the decided contrast between Presidents Van Hise and Birge with respect to public relations. Van Hise sought publicity and made skillful and effective use of the print media. Birge, on the other hand, was reticent and secretive, seemingly "indifferent" and "suspicious" of University public relations activities and the press and occasionally drawing an editorial rebuke. Editor William T. Evjue of the *Capital Times* regularly complained about University secrecy under Birge, as in a March 23, 1921, editorial: "We believe that the whole method of publicity pursued at the university is wrong. Nothing can ever be gained for the university by seeking to cover up and distort the real facts. The university will gain in the long run by being absolutely frank and open with both the newspapers and the people of the state. This is a people's university and the people are entitled to the fullest knowledge concerning what happens at the university. If the university authorities expect to receive fair treatment from the newspapers the university authorities must be equally fair in giving the newspapers the real facts." Quoted in Merle Curti and Vernon Carstensen, *The University of Wisconsin: A History, 1848-1925* (Madison: University of Wisconsin Press, 1949), vol. 2, p. 133.

charge by cultivating the image of an impresario of academic and social affairs. Whether through his acceptance statement in May, his summertime "Civilization" series in the *Century* magazine, or the press release issued when he took up his duties as president on September 1, the message remained the same: Frank intended to enlist the University's many constituencies in a well-publicized collaborative quest for an academic "renaissance."

Selling the University

President Frank stressed this theme of collaborative renewal in his initial address to a packed University faculty meeting at the start of the fall semester. As the *Daily Cardinal* reported, Frank's vision was all-embracing: "The rule of this university will be a democracy composed of the voices of every single person involved in its welfare." Secretary of the Faculty Charles A. Smith summarized Frank's message in his official report of the president's remarks:

> Selling the University to the people must be a collaboration in which every man and woman who has one spark of interest in the University must share. [Frank] suggested that we do for the present what Diderot and the Encyclopedists did for the eighteenth century in gathering up the findings of pure and social sciences and putting it into a language that the people can understand.[2]

This challenge, combined with affirmations of the "ideals of sound scholarship and inspired teaching, of productive research and practical service, of freedom to investigate and the courage to follow the facts wherever they may lead," impressed at least some initial faculty skeptics.[3] As a member of the history department grudgingly conceded to his young fiancée, "he made, on the whole, a rather favorable impression."[4]

---

[2]UW Faculty Document 275, "President's Address," October 5, 1925, UA; *Daily Cardinal*, October 6, 1925.

[3]In his address to the first University faculty meeting the following academic year, Frank referred indirectly to the reception of his October, 1925, speech: "I cannot begin a consideration of any of the issues that may underlie the work of the University during the year now begun without stopping to express my deeply felt gratitude for the considerate graciousness you accorded to me during my first difficult year of orientation to this University scene. I was sensitively aware of the fact that I had not come to the University of Wisconsin as a result of your active choice, and that I had come without the credentials of long academic service." October 4, 1926, Glenn Frank Papers, Northeast Missouri State University, Kirksville.

[4]Paul Knaplund to [Dorothy King], Monday night [October 6, 1925], Paul Knaplund

Frank worked with the University Press Bureau as he shaped the public relations side of his administration. President Van Hise had established the bureau in 1904 with a similar purpose in mind, and over the years it had flourished as it issued its weekly collection of releases in the *University of Wisconsin Press Bulletin*. Caretaker President Birge had allowed the bureau to languish, however, and by 1924 Editor Grant M. Hyde reported to his uninterested boss that "few university professors or officers have a very clear conception of news, and many of them are averse to using newspaper publicity." Consequently, concluded Hyde, "success has been harder and harder to attain."[5] In the last few years only Andrew W. "Andy" Hopkins had made full use of the *Press Bulletin*, sometimes filling more than half its columns with stories about the many triumphs of his so-called Wisconsin College of Agriculture.[6] Frank appreciated Hopkins' accomplishments and by 1927 was trying to broaden the effective scope of the bureau by making it "the neck of the bottle through which shall flow out to the newspapers and through them to the people of the state, the benefit of *all* knowledge that is bottled up here in our laboratories and libraries and the cortices of our staff."[7] Or as Ralph Nafziger, journalism professor and *Press Bulletin* editor, observed in 1930: "Ideal press bureau activity concerns itself with a full and continuous explanation of the many good things which are being attempted and accomplished, and which contribute to the profit and happiness of hundreds of thousands of citizens."[8]

The *Daily Cardinal* and the Wisconsin Alumni Association also helped to spread the good news.[9] In addition to its main constitu-

---

Papers, 82/5, UA.

[5]Grant M. Hyde, "The Press Bureau," September, 1924, Frank Presidential Papers, 4/13/1, box 8, UA.

[6]"75th Department History" (unpublished manuscript, n.d.), Departmental Files, Agricultural Journalism, UA; Andrew W. Hopkins, "'Andy' Hopkins, One of the Founding Fathers, Talks about the Editor's Job," in American Association of Agricultural College Editors, *ACE* (September-October, 1963), 4-5, ibid.

[7]Quoted in Morse Salisbury, "Handling Scientific News for the Press" [ca. September, 1927], Frank Presidential Papers, 4/13/1, box 66. Emphasis added.

[8]Ralph O. Nafziger, "Shall It Be News or Scandal? How the Public Gets News of the University as Told by the Man Who Tells Them All About It," *WAM*, 31 (January, 1930), 179; "New Press Bureau," ibid. (June, 1930), 367.

[9]The *Daily Cardinal* was founded in 1892 as the successor to several earlier student-owned papers, most importantly the *University Press*. Curti and Carstensen, *University of Wisconsin*, vol. 1, p. 686. See the *Daily Cardinal*, September 21, 1927, for a short summary of its history. On November 10, 1928, the directors of the General Alumni Association changed their organization's name to the Wisconsin Alumni Association. To avoid confusion the latter

ency—University students—the *Cardinal* reached faculty members, city residents, parents, and the commercial press. As Frank sought to promote the University, the *Cardinal* played a useful role by publishing press bureau news releases and by producing its own complimentary reports. Inspired by the president, in October of 1926 the staff issued a new *Weekly Cardinal*, which appeared throughout the following academic year and sporadically thereafter in the form of a special Sunday edition. "It shall be our purpose," pledged the editors, "to present to parents of students and friends of the university throughout the state and nation accurate information and news concerning student life at Wisconsin, new developments in education, and the coming of great professors, political struggles concerning the university, and its students, our advances and accomplishments."[10] The alumni association also published supportive articles in its *Wisconsin Alumni Magazine.* Frank spoke frequently to gatherings of University alumni and cultivated association leaders, particularly WAA President and Chicago attorney George I. Haight, who had cooperated energetically with Regent Kronshage in the publicity campaign of early 1925. Haight soon was arranging meetings for Frank with "men who are really doing things" and keeping his "ears wide open...to hear of Wisconsin and the new President....In the main, the feeling and thought is everything that it should be. There are some places here and there where we must do some work."[11]

WHA's New Patron

President Frank quickly developed an appreciation of the public

name is used throughout the text of this volume. Minutes of the Meeting of the Wisconsin Alumni Association, Book I, November 10, 1928, WAA Papers, 21/2/1, UA.

[10]*Weekly Cardinal*, October 30, 1926; *Press Bulletin*, November 3, 1926.

[11]George I. Haight to Glenn Frank, December 7, 1925, Frank Presidential Papers, 4/13/1, box 7.

relations potential of fledgling campus radio station WHA, to which he thereafter lent unprecedented administrative support. He also, of course, used it for his own purposes, as on March 1, 1926, when he broadcast a talk about the University to numerous special "radio parties" arranged at public schools and municipal facilities across the state by WHA program director William Lighty. Exhorted Frank:

> I challenge every man and woman throughout Wisconsin to a common team-play that shall make this university not only a place where great teachers shall awaken the latent powers of eager youth and where creative scholars shall by patient research push out beyond the frontiers of the new unknown, but a dynamic center from which there shall go out those forces of information and inspiration that shall make for the economic betterment, the intellectual stimulation, and the spiritual enrichment of the last man, woman, and child in Wisconsin.[12]

The program, effectively advertised in advance through the *Press Bulletin*, attracted WHA's largest audience to date as well as enthusiastic listener responses.[13] Frank's message also was heard on campus, and later in the month two leading members of the faculty radio committee asserted their intention "to secure complete and representative support and cooperation from all parts of the university, in order that the broadcasts may as effectively as possible reflect the life, the work, the spirit and the aspirations of the university."[14]

Regardless of the medium involved, it soon became clear that President Frank would be the centerpiece of any campaign to sell the University to the public. As he addressed parents at fathers' and mothers' weekends or alumni at homecoming celebrations, the president successfully touched on difficult and thorny issues by redefining them according to his own intriguing, if not scholarly, perspective. Soon after arriving in Madison, for example, he dramatically described himself as a "realist" who intended to pursue the truth wherever it

---

[12]*Daily Cardinal*, March 3, 1926.

[13]*Capital Times*, March 6, 1926. Wrote the principal of the Mauston High School: "President Frank made a real hit with the hundred students present and we trust we will be able to hear him again in the near future." A woman from Columbus thanked Frank "for the complimentary remarks he made about the state of Wisconsin and the young people at the university with whom he is coming in contact." A listener from Manitowoc said Frank's was "the most interesting talk I've heard since the inauguration of President Coolidge." *Daily Cardinal*, March 6, 1926.

[14]E.M. Terry and W.H. Lighty, "Memorandum" [ca. March 8, 1926], Frank Presidential Papers, 4/13/1, box 12.

might lead: "If the facts warrant, I am willing to be as reactionary as the czar of Russia on Monday or as radical as Leon Trotzky on Thursday."[15] Recalling the Wisconsin Idea of University service to the state, Frank reminded the 1927 Wisconsin Press Association banquet that "both the press and the university are servants of the public and depend upon the public for confidence and support."[16] He impressed a group of businessmen by explaining his notion of a "new Wisconsin Idea" that would link the state and University through the faculty's research.[17] The prospect seemed exciting and reflected well upon the speaker, who apparently did not know or had forgotten that faculty research was the University's earliest major public service function. Failure to acknowledge the University's past achievements sometimes alienated the president's academic colleagues on campus, but the public was captivated by his compelling oratory and his inspiring vision of a renascent institution.

Frank soon evolved into a celebrity of higher education and beyond, one perhaps like Woodrow Wilson destined for the U.S. presidency. In June, 1927, H.L. Mencken proclaimed this possibility in his *American Mercury* column. "There is surely no lack of men among us who would make intelligent, conscientious and even brilliant Presidents," Mencken noted. "I heave a brick at random, and after hitting Glenn Frank, Litt.D., president of the University of Wisconsin, it bounces from him to kiss" five other possibilities. "Here are six highly intelligent and industrious men," Mencken declared, "each of them adept at some difficult art, science or craft, and all of them beyond the slightest whisper of corruption."[18] While Mencken's endorsement hardly translated into convention delegates, it both reflected and nurtured Frank's growing national reputation. Thereafter references to Frank's suitability for high political office regularly appeared in his private correspondence and the press.[19] Meanwhile, the student editors

---

[15]*Capital Times*, October 20, 1925.

[16]*Daily Cardinal*, February 12, 1927.

[17]*Press Bulletin*, May 9, 1928.

[18][H.L. Mencken], editorial, *American Mercury*, 11 (June, 1927), 159. Mencken also mentioned Daniel Willard (Baltimore and Ohio Railroad), James Branch Cabell (Virginia), Captain William G. Stayton (U.S.N. retired and of the Association Against the Prohibition Amendment), U.S. Supreme Court Justice Louis D. Brandeis, and J. McKeen Cattell (editor of *Science*). For reports of the Mencken statement see *Capital Times*, May 25, 1927, and *Daily Cardinal*, May 26, 1927.

[19]On April 9, 1928, for example, A.M. Brayton, editor and publisher of the *Wisconsin State Journal*, wrote to Frank about the recent primary election, urging that the time was right for the University president to "make a beginning," the first step being "to make the race for

of the *Badger* (issued in the spring of 1926) dedicated their annual to
the new president:

> Because he so nearly fulfills his own prophecy of the Leader of a New
> Renaissance who shall combine a Bacon's devotion to science with a Roose-
> velt's power of popular appeal,—matching the "Evangelism of Superstition"
> with an "Evangelism of Scholarship,"—it is to Glenn Frank,—the Man,— on
> the dawn of his arrival at the University of Wisconsin, that we confidently
> dedicate this forty-first volume of The 1927 Badger.

Clearly, the University of Wisconsin and Glenn Frank, its young president, were on the rise.

The Experimental College

Frank went out of his way during his first semester at Wisconsin to
criticize the current state of undergraduate education, presumably at UW
and elsewhere, and to call for curricular reform. At least as reported in
the press, his comments offered few specifics and embodied catchy
phrases over more substantive analysis. The *Daily Cardinal*, for one,
found Frank's generalized indictment appealing, praising his lament that
"the curriculum of today is a hodge-podge of unrelated specialisms."
"The ring and tone of Dr. Frank's speeches is encouraging and impressive," the editor exulted more enthusiastically than grammatically.
"The prospects for constructive service are bright."[20]   Professional
journalists also noted Frank's criticism, but tended to transmit only his
most colorful and striking observations.   Thus the Associated Press
report of Frank's address to the Missouri state teachers' convention in
November, 1925, observed that he "condemned the American tendency
to 'Fordise the brain and opinions of the nation'."[21]   Precisely what
Frank meant was left unstated, but it was clear he believed something

---

governor this year." On November 5, 1929, Edward L. Conwell, previously an instructor in
the English department, wrote to encourage "the possibility of making the race for the Presidency of the United States at some future time...." Both letters in the Frank Papers, Kirksville. Meanwhile, according to the *Daily Cardinal* of November 22, 1928, Frank had recently
visited President Calvin Coolidge at the White House. On January 4, 1929, the *Daily Cardinal*
reported that a commercial newspaper in Chicago had recently advocated a Frank Presidency,
and on January 10, in a follow-up editorial, the *Cardinal* asserted that Frank was fit for the
post, even if he did speak proper English and sometimes wear spats.

[20]*Daily Cardinal*, October 13, 1925.

[21]*Capital Times*, November 13, 1925.

was seriously wrong with American education.

A few UW students paid close attention to their new leader and liked what they heard. In December, 1925, they began a new publication, *The Issue*, subtitled "A Forum of Student Opinion."[22] Frank's inspiration and influence were obvious. Founding editor John Schindler's front-page forward included an ambitious promise "to help the Wisconsin student to a clearer consciousness of the present day tendencies in education, politics, economics, literature, science, industry, psychology, religion, philosophy." Inside, an editorial entitled "President Frank" proclaimed:

> Again there is to be the creative spirit [at Wisconsin], building something where there was nothing, catching the imagination of a populace, inspiring men to give to a cause higher than the interests of self....The university has also a man with the sort of spirit and faith that has been known to stimulate and move institutions greater than a university.

Schindler's enthusiasm echoed the president's promise to the University community that "the days of its greatest creative development are ahead."[23]

Educational reform was very much a national issue by the time Glenn Frank started his administration. The ferment in education was part of the larger progressive movement that sought to improve American life and institutions after the turn of the century. One of its most influential intellectual leaders was the philosopher John Dewey, whose work and writings both reflected and shaped the general movement and its concern to use the schools and colleges to help create a more democratic, just, and caring society. Dewey was among those who organized the Progressive Education Association in 1919. Much of the attention of the progressive educators was directed at the primary and secondary

---

[22]A letter to the editor of the *Capital Times*, published November 28, 1925, announced and explained *The Issue*: "There is a movement of revolt against present day standardized methods of education in evidence throughout America....The undercurrent of revolt at the University...has swelled into open criticism....The Issue,...motivated by a 'feeling of disgust for the students who pursue and live on a mental diet of teas, petting and dancing' will appear on the campus within a few days....It is a favorable sign. It indicates an intellectual awakening at the University of Wisconsin among the students."

[23]The UW Archives has three numbers of *The Issue* on file, and the collection is presumed complete. The third and final number, for November, 1926, further indicates Frank's support of this committed if not enduring venture: "...we are indebted to President Frank for his kind permission [to reprint the speech, 'The Revolt Against Education'], and for his enthusiastic cooperation in this, as well as in all other matters pertaining to the Issue."

schools, but the movement also had a considerable influence on higher education, especially in rethinking the traditional liberal arts undergraduate curriculum. There was growing dissatisfaction with the lack of focus in the free elective system popularized by Harvard in the late nineteenth century, which Harvard President A. Lawrence Lowell sought to correct after 1910 through the tutorial system earlier pioneered by Woodrow Wilson while president of Princeton. Other notable experiments included the development of keystone humanities and civilization courses at Columbia after the World War, the creation of honors programs at Swarthmore, Alexander Meiklejohn's experiments with unified curricula at Amherst, and the founding of a number of new progressive experimental colleges, such as Bennington, Sarah Lawrence, Bard, and Black Mountain. Altogether there were more than a hundred major efforts by American colleges and universities to reform their undergraduate general education programs in the inter-war period. President Frank's initiative at Wisconsin was thus very much a part of the larger movement.[24]

Just how Frank intended to revitalize undergraduate education became apparent late in 1925 with rumors of the appointment of the well-known educational reformer Alexander Meiklejohn. First to break the news in Madison, was the semi-official voice of La Follette progressivism, the *Capital Times*, which featured a special dispatch from Chicago on its front page. "The announcement of his proposed appointment," enthused the report, "has literally startled the educational world."

> With Dr. Frank and Dr. Meiklejohn, two of the nation's most liberal educators, putting into practice their advanced views on teaching, it is freely predicted here that the University of Wisconsin will become one of the leading laboratories of the nation in educational procedure and that the eyes of pedagogues throughout the land will be fixed on that school.

The account offered a summary of the "needed changes" Frank hoped

---

[24]See Lawrence A. Cremin, *American Education: The Metropolitan Experience, 1876-1980* (New York: Harper & Row, 1988), especially pp. 153-272; Cremin, *The Transformation of the School: Progressivism in American Education, 1876-1957* (New York: Knopf, 1961); Patricia Albjerg Graham, *Progressive Education: From Arcady to Academe: A History of the Progressive Education Association, 1919-1955* (New York: Teachers College Press, 1967); Frederick Rudolph, *Curriculum: A History of the American Undergraduate Course of Study Since 1636* (San Francisco: Jossey-Bass, 1977); R. Freeman Butts, *The College Charts Its Course: Historical Conceptions and Current Proposals* (New York: McGraw-Hill, 1939).

to accomplish:

> The present course in liberal arts is obsolete. Educators everywhere realize that fact. As subjects are taught nowadays, the student gets a scattered supply of information on a dozen or more subjects. Education must be an intelligible whole in order to fit the student for life.[25]

Frank evidently intended to look outside the University of Wisconsin for help in its renaissance.

Speculation continued throughout the first few weeks of the new year. The *Daily Cardinal* at first confessed its inability to confirm the appointment of Meiklejohn, who, it emphasized, "is ranked with the most brilliant men of the educational and philosophical world."[26] In mid-month, the *Cardinal* quoted Meiklejohn on the timidity of American scholars: "They have not a lively enough sense of that for which they are responsible, or, if you like, of their own importance." "Wisconsin," the *Cardinal* editors declared, "needs men who say things like that." While "an excellent start" had been made with the recruitment of President Frank, more was required:

> One man cannot handle an institution that is constantly growing larger and increasing in complexity daily. The selection of personnel for the purpose of developing larger policy is the essence of administration. Let us hope that Dr. Meiklejohn will soon be a part of the personnel at Wisconsin.[27]

On January 23 speculation ended as the *Cardinal* proclaimed in a banner headline, "DR. MEIKLEJOHN ACCEPTS FACULTY POST." Without spelling out Meiklejohn's responsibilities, an elated Glenn Frank declared: "I think Wisconsin is to be congratulated on Mr. Meiklejohn's appointment. From him we expect productive scholarship and provocative teaching."

Frank and Meiklejohn had conferred—conspired is probably not too strong a term—regularly and privately during the past year about founding an experimental program under the direction of the former Amherst College president. In January, 1925, while still editor of the *Century Magazine,* Frank had published Meiklejohn's "A New College: Notes on a Next Step in Higher Education."[28] A year later, with Meiklejohn

---

[25]*Capital Times*, December 31, 1925.

[26]*Daily Cardinal*, January 7, 1926.

[27]Ibid., January 16, 1926.

[28]Alexander Meiklejohn, "A New College: Notes on a Next Step in Higher Education,"

now a member of the UW faculty, the two were ready to move ahead with the idea on which they had long since agreed. As always President Frank used the local press to maximum effect. The *Daily Cardinal* proudly announced on February 27, 1926, that Frank would shortly present a major address on the "Junior College" before students of the Harvard Graduate School of Education emphasizing "The Revolt Against Education." The subject, the paper noted, was an issue of growing national concern.[29] "Although this will be President Frank's first discussion of the matter," observed the *Cardinal*, "he has given plenty of thought to the problem." At a meeting of the general University faculty on March 1, Frank announced the appointment of an All-University Commission to study and report on the problems of "articulation" in undergraduate education at Wisconsin and elsewhere. Frank underscored the importance of the commission by stating that he himself would chair the group, with Meiklejohn and key deans and faculty leaders comprising its membership. The president also distributed copies of a "confidential" memorandum that essentially contained the text of what he would later present to his Harvard audience.[30]

The memorandum crystallized the previously inchoate thrust of Frank's public statements on educational reform. On the one hand, he characterized Meiklejohn's plan presented in the *Century* article as "a definite suggestion of teaching by situation rather than by subject in the college," and asked rhetorically, "Could it be made to work throughout our college and university world?" The task of the All-University Commission, it was becoming increasingly clear, was to answer this question in the affirmative by recommending that the University sponsor a showcase program to be organized and run by Meiklejohn himself. Meiklejohn's convenient presence gave Wisconsin a unique opportunity to test his reform ideas. If it did not, the only option was for undergraduate liberal arts education to continue suffering from "the disease of departmentalism."[31] Who could object to experimentation intended to

---

Century Magazine, 109 (January, 1925), 312-20.

[29]*Daily Cardinal*, February 27, 1926. The *Cardinal* pointed to the current issue of *The Nation* discussing current thinking about badly needed changes in programming at the freshman-sophomore level, including highly critical comments from the presidents of Johns Hopkins and Harvard universities. Now, the editors noted, President Frank would have his say.

[30]UW Faculty Minutes, March 1, 1926, UA.

[31]Glenn Frank, "An Experiment in Education," part 1, *WAM*, 28 (December, 1926), 50. Also see Glenn Frank, "The Revolt Against Education," an address delivered at Harvard

bring improvement? "I covet for the University," Frank declared, "the honor of being the institution in which the last twenty-five years of educational disillusionment and educational inventiveness shall come to fruition."[32]

The memorandum also defined Frank's generalist view of the relation between "civilization" and the supposedly low state of higher education. The fault, Frank believed, lay in the elective system of undergraduate education, developed at Harvard in the late nineteenth century and now in effect at Wisconsin and most American colleges and universities. In Frank's confident view, the elective system represented "essentially a strategic retreat of educators from an increasingly unmanageable mass of modern knowledge." It could not be reformed; it must be replaced: "We cannot meet the contemporary educational challenge by negotiating another strategic retreat. We must contrive to effect a successful advance toward a more adequate correlation of modern knowledge and a more adequate comprehension of modern life."[33] At Harvard, Frank intended his message as a challenge to discuss and debate, presented as it would be within the fortress of the long-time enemy. At Wisconsin, Frank's manifesto could only be read as a lay outsider's wholesale rejection of the University's established liberal arts curriculum, the views of most of its faculty, and especially the academic leadership of the College of Letters and Science, the unit responsible for educating the great majority of UW undergraduates.[34]

Members of the University community reacted variously to this and similar messages from the president. Many rejected Frank's simple either-or imagery. A *Daily Cardinal* editorial placed Frank on one end of the continuum between general and specialized education. "We can hardly reconcile ourselves to either extreme," the paper observed. "Both, we believe, are essential to a university....A happy medium would be more acceptable."[35] Faculty reaction may be judged by the pervasive skepticism expressed during the L&S faculty debates over the All-University Commission's recommendation to establish an Experimental College within the larger college. Ultimately its purpose would be "to formulate and to test under experimental conditions, suggestions

University, March 20, 1926, Frank Papers, Kirksville.

[32]Glenn Frank, "An Experiment in Education," part 2, *WAM* (January, 1927), 90-1.

[33]Frank, "Experiment in Education," part 1, p. 53.

[34]Frank referred to himself "as a layman in the field of education...I am only a journalist on parole." Ibid., p. 89.

[35]*Daily Cardinal*, March 27, 1926.

for the improvement of methods of teaching, the content of study, and the determining conditions of undergraduate liberal education."[36] The four faculty meetings during April, 1926, were spirited and well-attended, with those present reacting with a bemused skepticism to the new president's rather nebulous scheme. Simultaneously, the faculty sought to guard against the possibility that Frank and Meiklejohn might try to graft the practices of their Experimental College onto its dubious host college without explicit faculty approval. One professor skipped the final faculty meeting with the comment, "I simply have no time to waste on all that nonsense."[37] Recognizing the new president's naïveté, L&S Dean Sellery, a commission member, gave luke-warm backing to the plan and then sat back to await its implementation (and eventual collapse).

"A real step in the realization of the spirit of education in the 'new Wisconsin' became a reality last night," the *Cardinal* proclaimed in late May, 1926, "when the faculty...approved the general plan of Dr. Alexander Meiklejohn for an experimental college at the university." The *Cardinal* rightly credited Glenn Frank for initiating the reform:

> Several months ago the president startled Eastern educators by his talk at Harvard in which he discussed the junior college. The action of the Letters and Science faculty last night is another step in carrying out the idea of developing Wisconsin as one of the leaders in progressive educational institutions.[38]

Once launched, President Frank's involvement with the Experimental College consisted primarily of public speeches and writings in support of the project as an inspiring Wisconsin example of curricular reform. While the president provided occasional and limited behind-the-scenes administrative assistance, he gave essentially no substantive direction, leaving the experiment in the hands of Professor Meiklejohn. As will be discussed more fully in the next chapter, Meiklejohn spent the 1926-27 academic year planning and recruiting faculty members for the venture, most of whom he had previously known as students and colleagues during his tenure at Brown University and Amherst College. From first to last it was essentially a Meiklejohn experiment that opened with 119 male freshmen in the fall of 1927 and, after a tumultuous five

---

[36]L&S Faculty Minutes, April 30, 1926, UA.
[37]Knaplund to [King], Sunday night [May 16, 1926], Knaplund Papers.
[38]*Daily Cardinal*, May 27, 1926.

years, folded in 1932. By that time the bright image of Glenn Frank's Experimental College as a reflection of his renascent University had been overshadowed by the great depression.

Undergraduate Education and the Progressive Schoolmen

The sad annual phenomenon of mass underclass failures plagued leading American public universities throughout the early twentieth century. Born of the inherent conflict between providing open access for qualified secondary school graduates while at the same time maintaining rigorous academic standards, the resulting attrition rates among freshman and sophomore regularly alarmed observers. Wisconsin's experience reflected the national pattern, and it seemed that nearly everyone had an explanation or answer to the problem.[39] Professor William H. "Wild Bill" Kiekhofer, whose popular introductory economics class attracted hundreds of students, complained in 1926, for example, that students themselves were at fault because of their failure to work hard enough.[40] Others deplored "careless statements that a large proportion of students come here only for a good time with no idea of work or study."[41] Concern over the high attrition typically arose after first-semester grades resulted in a considerably diminished student body for the second semester. In February, 1926, the *Wisconsin State Journal* claimed an unnamed University official had stated that because first semester enrollments had exceeded housing accommodations by eight hundred therefore that number of students had been dropped. "Every year at this time," retorted a University spokesman after the *State Journal* recanted its bogus report, "we have the same flood of rumors about wholesale flunking. They are always wildly exaggerated and with no more foundation than the present ones." The fact remained, however, as a *Daily Cardinal* editorial pointed out, that eight hundred students that year had indeed "failed to make the grade and that the university cannot afford to harbor them any longer."[42]

Glenn Frank initially kept out of this debate over student retention.

---

[39] For national and UW statistics on the dropping of underclassmen, see L&S Papers, 7/2/3, box 3, and 7/1/7, box 1, UA.

[40] *Daily Cardinal*, January 21, 1926.

[41] Letter to the editor, *Capital Times*, December 30, 1927.

[42] Junior Dean of Letters and Science Harry Glicksman was the misquoted official. See page 1 and the editorial page of the *Daily Cardinal*, February 11, 1926, for discussion of this incident.

For one thing, there was nothing approaching a campus consensus as to what if anything was wrong or needed correcting. No single faculty or administrative agency existed to assume general responsibility for student academic progress. One clear voice did stand out, however, that of the University Board of Visitors. Charged with monitoring University affairs and reporting to the regents, this body of distinguished alumni traditionally concerned itself primarily with the problems of undergraduate education. Because of the background of several of its influential members, during the twenties the visitors tended to view these from a professional schoolman's perspective, which by this time reflected the same progressive educational values held by Glenn Frank.[43] Favoring scientific reform through educational psychology and management improvements to produce maximum educational efficiency, the progressive education movement sought to adapt the school to the needs of the student while simultaneously streamlining and rationalizing the entire schooling process from kindergarten through the university.[44] Recent Boards of Visitors had operated very much in terms of this orientation, and their recommendations consequently struck a responsive chord in the new University president.[45]

The visitors' annual reports for 1924 and 1925 defined their ideas and objectives for the remainder of the decade. They exhibited a clear and rather compelling logic. The visitors based their 1924 report on a year-long inquiry into the "purpose and functioning" of teacher education in Wisconsin and throughout the nation. The board had gathered voluminous testimony from members of the Wisconsin City Superintendents' Association who argued that improved teacher training at the

---

[43]See Frank's draft of the Harvard address in UW Faculty Minutes, March 1, 1926. For a short history of the Board of Visitors, see Edrene S. Montgomery, "That All May Act Harmoniously in the University's Interests: The Board of Visitors of the University of Wisconsin" (unpublished manuscript [1985]), Departmental Files, Board of Visitors, UA.

[44]For discussions of the "efficiency" aspect of the progressive education movement during the 1920s, see Raymond E. Callahan, *Education and the Cult of Efficiency* (Chicago: University of Chicago Press, 1962); Edward A. Krug, *The Shaping of the American High School, 1920-1941* (Madison: University of Wisconsin Press, 1972); Herbert M. Kliebard, *Forging the American Curriculum: Essays in Curriculum History and Theory* (New York: Routledge, 1992). See also fn. 24.

[45]Loyal Durand joined the Board of Visitors in 1920 and served as president from 1924 through the end of the decade. Milwaukee's leading insurance man, Durand held baccalaureate and law degrees from the University, and, among his many civic activities, served on the Milwaukee Board of Education. J.G. Gregory, *History of Milwaukee* (Chicago/Milwaukee: S.J. Clarke Publishing Company, 1931), vol. 4, pp. 693-4; Board of Regents resolution, BOR Minutes, October 12-13, 1927.

University would require institutional reorganization. Reflecting a mounting concern of professional schoolmen, the visitors complained that the UW School of Education languished because it was little more than a minor department within the College of Letters and Science. Giving it independent status, on the other hand, would demonstrate the substantial equality and status of education training vis-à-vis other professions—engineering, agriculture, medicine, and law—all of which were served by free-standing schools or colleges within the University. In support the report cited the recent experience of the Universities of Michigan, Minnesota, and Illinois. It also claimed general backing within the University for the visitors' and the superintendents' preferred educational "policies," although UW officials to date had argued that the existing institutional structure could accommodate any needed reforms. The visitors concluded their 1924 report by affirming the University's good intentions but formally recommending that the regents grant independent status to the School of Education.[46] Under President Birge, the first dean of the parent College of Letters and Science, the University did nothing.

The visitors' report for 1925 addressed the student failure issue, defined as a problem of poor articulation between the high schools and the University. The analysis covered "Matriculation, the Advisory System and the Instructional System, with special reference to the incoming freshman students." With regard to matriculation, the visitors declared: "We believe that if closer coordination could be established, secondary school principals might provide the University in advance with some very valuable information concerning the student's ability and habits." Based on interviews with UW staff and students, the visitors also concluded that underclassmen were left too much on their own in establishing themselves on campus. Even L&S Dean Sellery, under whose auspices most undergraduate advising took place, conceded that

---

[46]"Report of the Board of Visitors" [March, 1924], Frank Presidential Papers, 4/13/1, box 7. The visitors' argument for an independent school of education reads as follows: "If, however, the personnel of the present School of Education who have the confidence of the profession of the state and whose leadership as individuals is recognized, can be a greater force in bringing educational leadership to our University, if the University can render a greater service to the youth of the state, if the communities of the state can be assured better teachers and hence greater returns upon their large investments in education by a change in the organization and administration of the Department of Education, as it would appear might be the case from the experience of neighboring state universities, we would earnestly urge early and careful consideration of the changes by the President, the Dean of the College of Letters and Science, the Director of the School of Education, and the Board of Regents."

"the Advisory System is not working very well." Apparently the better and more experienced advisors regularly gravitated toward the less demanding and more sophisticated juniors and seniors. The report also pointed to "some very interesting experiments that are being tried in various colleges to acclimate freshmen students to relieve the handicap with which they must start their work." For example, freshmen at the University of Chicago were "required to report a week in advance of the opening of school for the purpose of becoming acquainted with the methods of instruction employed at the University and of learning of other duties and responsibilities in connection with their work." Finally, the visitors reiterated complaints about the poor quality of undergraduate instruction as expressed most recently in their annual report of 1922, which argued that "the freshmen need better teachers."[47] Again the University administration failed to act, with caretaker President Birge no doubt believing this was an issue for his successor.

Frank waited until the end of the 1926-27 academic year, when he quietly and without public explanation began to address the concerns expressed in the 1925 visitors' report. He recommended that the regents approve two staff appointments and create a special agency within the campus central administration to deal with articulation matters.[48] The regents concurred, appointing Frank O. Holt as University registrar and director of a new Bureau of Educational Records and Guidance.[49] Currently the superintendent of schools in Janesville, Holt had served as president of the Wisconsin Education Association in 1925-

---

[47]"Report of the Board of Visitors," June 19, 1925, BOV Papers, 2/1/1, box 1, UA, and Birge Presidential Papers, 4/12/1, box 55, UA.

[48]BOR Minutes, May 18, 1927.

[49]William D. Hiestand had died on April 23, 1925, after serving since 1887 as the University's first and only registrar. The position remained vacant until Holt's appointment. Personnel Cards, UA; *Capital Times*, April 23, 1925.

26 and recently had declined an offer to head the state teachers college at La Crosse.[50] He enjoyed the high regard of UW alumni and professional educators alike.[51] The second appointment was that of Professor V.A.C. Henmon, a psychologist and also a prominent figure in Wisconsin's professional education circles. He had resigned as the first director of the UW School of Education the previous June to accept a professorship at Yale University.[52] While Henmon was considering the Yale offer President Frank had received numerous pleas from Wisconsin school principals, superintendents, and normal school officials to find some way to retain his services at Wisconsin. The only negative comments noted Henmon's long-time opposition to an independent School of Education.[53] Frank's blandishments and Henmon's brief exposure to the Ivy League convinced the latter that he preferred Wisconsin over Yale. He returned the following year as a professor of psychology, with a promise the discipline would be separated from philosophy under Hen-

---

[50]Mary Holt Segall and Fred Holt, "Biography of Frank O. Holt" (unpublished manuscript, n.d.), Biographical Files, UA.

[51]After learning of the Holt appointment, one alumnus wrote to Frank, "He will bring to his new work an understanding of its problems that probably few men in similar positions have had an opportunity to acquire." Frank responded, "It is gratifying to know that his appointment has brought satisfaction to the alumni." J.T. Seafor to Frank, June 1, 1927; Frank to Seafor, June 6, 1927, Frank Presidential Papers, 4/13/1, box 34.

[52]Henmon had first joined the University as an associate professor of education in 1910. The regents promoted him to full professor in 1913. After service in World War I, he returned to campus with the expanded title of Professor of Education and Director of the School of Education. Personnel Cards.

[53]Frank Presidential Papers, 4/13/1, box 7. In a document prepared for the Board of Visitors in 1923, Director Henmon described a number of advantages of the school's association with the College of Letters and Science, and observed:

> In view of these facts the maintenance of an intimate contact with the College of Letters and Science seems very desirable. It keeps the problem of teacher training alive in the college instead of setting it apart in a separate institution. In a state university it is just as much the responsibility of the departments of English, history, Latin, mathematics, etc., to see to it that the state is provided with trained teachers as it is that of the department of education....So long as the college faculty meets fairly its obligations and responsibilities in the training of teachers we have, with our present organization at Wisconsin, everything that a [separate] college organization could provide.

The visitors' report, submitted to the Board of Regents the following March, quoted extensively from Henmon's statement and noted his strong opposition to an independent school, in sharp contrast to the views of a number of school superintendents and teachers around the state. V.A.C. Henmon, "The School of Education at the University of Wisconsin," September 25, 1923; "Report of the Board of Visitors," March, 1924, Birge Presidential Papers, 4/12/1, box 42, and Frank Presidential Papers, 4/13/1, box 7.

mon's charge and with the assignment to join forces with Holt as the scientific director of the new bureau.[54]

These changes resulted from a series of influences and events. First, of course, was the 1925 visitors' report, which spoke Frank's language and represented the views of a constituency he respected and sought to please. Also influential was a letter from Bart McCormick expressing concern over Professor Henmon's threatened departure to Yale. A member of the Board of Visitors, McCormick reminded Frank of the visitors' concerns over the problems faced by UW freshmen and hinted at a partial solution: "It is evident that with a sufficient amount of help, the Registrar"—whose office was currently vacant—"may be an important factor in any re-adjustment that may take place, since he is the first officer of the University with whom students come in contact."[55] Here was an insight to ponder, particularly in light of a letter the president had received from Frank Holt the previous week. Holt had written to introduce himself and express interest in the University Extension Division deanship soon to be vacated by Louis E. Reber. Frank, who may have had another candidate in mind, responded that a quick decision about Extension was unlikely because he intended to wait "to find the man who will best insure and promote such development, regardless of all considerations save the one consideration of the utmost educational efficiency."[56] But Frank was interested in Holt. The two kept in touch, becoming better acquainted and sharing ideas. Frank simultaneously maintained contact with Henmon, who added his thoughts to the mix. During the spring of 1927 a mutually agreeable plan took shape and the president proposed that he and Holt "talk turkey," while he simultaneously negotiated Henmon's return to Madison.[57] Regent approval followed quickly.

A week later Frank issued an informative statement about Holt's and Henmon's new agency:

---

[54]Frank offered several important inducements: first, he raised Henmon's salary from $6,000 (in 1925-26) to $7,500; second, he changed Henmon's title from Professor of Education to the more prestigious Professor of Psychology; third, he arranged to split the Department of Philosophy and Psychology into two distinct units, placing Henmon in charge of the latter; and fourth, to accommodate Henmon's research interests, he organized the Bureau of Educational Records and Guidance.

[55]B.E. McCormick to Frank, April 2, 1926, Frank Presidential Papers, 4/13/1, box 7.

[56]F. O. Holt to Frank, March 25, 1926; Frank to Holt, April 5, 1926, ibid.

[57]Holt to Frank, April 8, 1926, ibid.; Holt to Frank, November 12, 1926; Frank to Holt, November 19, 1926; Holt to Frank, February 17, March 1 and 8, 1927, ibid., box 25.

> The bureau of educational records and guidance will go beyond the mere keeping of grades to the assembling of a wide range of information respecting the life and work of the students as the background and basis for the development of an effective service of counsel and guidance to the students—an end that is not always achieved by the prevailing system of advisers....
>
> The bureau likewise will be the assembly point for a richly detailed fund of information regarding the nature and results of the educational processes to which the students are subjected. This will provide facilities that will make it possible for the university to keep up a continuous study of the results of its enterprises and to take its own educational pulse.[58]

Taken together, the reorganized registrar's office and the new Bureau of Educational Records and Guidance represented the major thrust of Glenn Frank's effort to address the problem of better articulation between the University and the high schools of the state. Although ostensibly separate in nature, the two units would function from the start as a single agency, the first effort to combine comprehensive student services and quantitatively-based institutional research. The bureau was another manifestation of Frank's interest in scientific academic experimentation of the sort he expected from the Experimental College.

The Holt-Henmon combine produced impressive results during the next few years. Beginning with the fall semester of 1927, for example, the bureau initiated a program of freshman aptitude testing by which college success might be predicted.[59] Later in 1927 Holt and Henmon helped organize what became known as the Committee on Cooperation, with membership including all of Wisconsin's institutions of higher education as well as representation from the various school professional associations. Holt chaired the group, which instituted in 1929 a statewide aptitude testing program to be administered to all high school seniors.[60] The test sought to identify potentially successful college students, and UW officials then made use of this information in encour-

---

[58]Quoted in *Press Bulletin*, May 25, 1927.

[59]*Capital Times*, October 18 and 27, December 27, 1927; *Daily Cardinal*, October 20, 1927, October 1, 1929.

[60]*Daily Cardinal*, December 15, 1927, April 7, November 26, 1929; "State Contacts through High Schools" [ca. May, 1928], Frank Presidential Papers, 4/13/1, box 44; Holt to Miss [Julia] Wilkinson, May 12, 1928, ibid.; Holt to Henmon, January 2, 1929, L&S Papers, 7/28/4, box 21; Holt to Frank, January 22, 1929; Holt to Frank, June 25, 1929, including "Cooperative Testing Program, 1929: Report," June 25, 1929, Frank Presidential Papers, 4/13/1, box 60.

aging their enrollment at the University.[61] During 1928 the bureau organized for the first time campus counseling sessions during the summer for matriculating freshmen and their parents.[62] Also in 1928 the bureau added Professor of Education Alanson H. Edgerton to its staff as director of vocational guidance. He sought to smooth the transition from college studies to gainful employment.[63] Throughout President Frank characteristically offered his blessing, support, and public applause, while allowing Holt and Henmon to develop the bureau as they saw fit. In 1931 the bureau moved beyond aptitude testing with the Wisconsin Achievement Testing Program. Working closely with high school principals, superintendents, and teachers from around the state, UW faculty over the next few years helped to develop a battery of achievement tests for placing entering students in appropriate University courses.[64] All of these collaborative efforts helped to strengthen the University's ties and influence with the high schools of the state.

The Freshman Days orientation program, first offered in 1928, further demonstrated the Frank administration's commitment to addressing the articulation problem.[65] The University faculty created this program in December, 1927, in response to a formal recommendation from the Bureau of Educational Records and Guidance. The University of Maine had established the first such endeavor in 1923, and a 1926 University of Iowa study identified similar programs in twenty-seven

---

[61]See, for example, Frank to My Dear High School Graduate, form letter, June 25, 1929, Frank Presidential Papers, 4/13/1, box 60. The University sent copies to the 1,427 Wisconsin high school seniors scoring in the top 25 percent of the scholastic aptitude test. The statewide testing program opened in 1929, administering the Ohio State University Psychological Test to 16,619 seniors in 434 public and 14 private Wisconsin high schools. For the next three years the program used the aptitude test developed by the American Council on Education. With the inauguration of statewide testing of high school sophomores as well as seniors, Wisconsin began using the Henmon-Nelson Test of Mental Ability developed specifically for this expanded purpose. Gustav J. Froehlich, *The Prediction of Academic Success at the University of Wisconsin, 1909-1941*, Bulletin of the University of Wisconsin, General Series No. 2358, Serial No. 2574, October, 1941, pp. 11-2.

[62]"Rough Draft of Facts Concerning First, 'Freshman Period' and Second, The Service to be Rendered By the Bureau of Guidance During the Summer Months of 1928," n.d., Frank Presidential Papers, 4/13/1, box 59; *Capital Times*, July 3, 1929; *Daily Cardinal*, July 16, 1929; "From Mr. Holt," a report describing the 1930 summertime program that served over nine hundred families [ca. October, 1930], Frank Presidential Papers, 4/13/1, box 97.

[63]A.H. Edgerton to Frank, December 24, 1927; "Services in Vocational Guidance and Counseling," Frank Presidential Papers, 4/13/1, box 57.

[64]Froehlich, "Prediction of Academic Success," pp. 31-6.

[65]The program later became variously known also as Freshman Period and Freshman Week.

major institutions, with all but one of them functioning successfully. Wisconsin's four-day orientation tried to accomplish a number of specific objectives aiming to assist the new student in a successful transition from high school to college. During this period entering freshmen could find housing, register for classes, and pay fees. Their faculty advisors had available to them high school records, frequently presented on standardized forms developed in association with the Committee on Cooperation, to be used in helping the new students plan their courses of study more intelligently. Health service and bureau personnel administered physical examinations and aptitude tests. Talks on how to study and use the library complemented social and cultural activities. The substantial faculty participation demonstrated a concern for the entering freshmen and a desire to help them gain a feeling for "what it's all about" at Wisconsin.[66] President Frank explained this and the other bureau programs in a letter to twelve hundred high school principals, concluding:

> The university cannot give strength to the essentially no-account weakling and wastrel; but it is obligated to leave no stone unturned to awaken and discipline latent strength that might remain latent in the absence of intimate counsel and informed guidance. And the program at which I have here hinted is a token of the university's determination to live up to this obligation.[67]

Freshman Week instantly took root as the University's foremost orientation tool.

In spite of the progress made, the Board of Visitors' reports of the latter 1920s took on an increasingly quarrelsome tone, even as they acknowledged the Frank administration's achievements in the Experimental College, the registrar's office, the Bureau of Educational Guidance and Records, and Freshman Week. Broader improvements in undergraduate advising and instruction, responsibilities falling primarily on the College of Letters and Science, had not materialized, at least to the satisfaction of the visitors. The problem, after all, was nebulous and ill-defined and therefore difficult to address institutionally. At bottom it involved the behavior of individual faculty members, a group of semi-autonomous professionals with numerous educational and scholarly perspectives and obligations. To be sure, as the visitors favored, it

---

[66]UW Faculty Minutes, December 5, 1927; UW Faculty Document 318, "Freshman Days," December 5, 1927; BOR Minutes, December 7, 1927.

[67]*Press Bulletin*, May 30, 1928.

would be *possible* to reward advisors and teachers of lower classmen as generously as the University's leading scholars. But the likely academic dislocations were so great as literally to challenge the fundamental nature of the institution. This would be dangerously disruptive. Almost no one on campus, certainly not Glenn Frank nor his administrative and faculty colleagues, ever seriously considered attempting the requisite structural changes that might have pleased the visitors. Only with respect to an independent school of education, hinging again on a clear presidential policy decision, did the Board of Visitors and its professional schoolmen supporters essentially get their way.

It was probably during the winter of 1927-28 that President Frank finally decided to do something substantial about the School of Education. In November he sent Acting Director Willis L. Uhl, who had succeeded Henmon in 1926, a description of the autonomous College of Education at the University of Iowa, and on the file copy added a handwritten reminder to himself: "This problem should be settled before end of this semester."[68] The following month he weighed a number of strategies to win over the opposition.[69] By April Frank had decided Uhl was unsuited to the task of reforming the school. With uncharacteristic dispatch, the president told Uhl of his respect for

him as a scholar but also his concern about Uhl's leadership abilities, which Frank thought might be inadequate during the coming "long pull of distasteful work in whipping the internal situation into a coherent and cooperative enterprise."[70] Frank's strong hint had its intended effect: in early summer Uhl resigned to accept the education deanship at the

---

[68]"Organization of the [Iowa] College of Education," with Frank's handwritten reminder, November 16, 1927, Frank Presidential Papers, 4/13/1, box 57.

[69]Two unsigned memoranda, December 16, 1927, and n.d., ibid.

[70]Frank to Willis L. Uhl, April 26, 1928, ibid., box 53.

University of Washington, and Frank quickly promoted Associate Professor Charles J. Anderson, with whom he had for some months been consulting about the plan for an autonomous school, to the rank of professor and director.[71]

Director Anderson lost no time drawing up plans for reform of the school. In November he sent a memorandum to Frank discussing the complex nature of teacher training and the dire need in the profession for a new rank of "master teacher," comparable in accomplishment and distinction with possessors of advanced scholarly degrees, which he argued the University should assume responsibility for preparing.[72] Two weeks later Visitors McCormick, Kircher, and Durand submitted a special report to the regents. It pleaded "that immediate steps be taken by the President and the Board of Regents to make such changes as will permit of the organization and development of an independent College of Education."[73] The following March the visitors reported Anderson's appearance before a joint meeting of their board and representatives of several Wisconsin school organizations to discuss "his plan of reorganization which had already been presented to the President of the University and the Board of Regents."[74] The visitors, of course, endorsed Anderson's call for independence.

Submitted to the president on January 1, 1929, the plan had two parts. The first outlined, in Frank's words, "specific actions and interpretations" necessary for establishing an independent school of education. The second included "a more elaborate discussion of the whole School of Education problem."[75] Two features of the document stand out. One presented Anderson's five-part argument for an independent school:

1. Education is now recognized as a profession.

---

[71]Uhl to Frank, June 18, 1928, ibid., box 55; Personnel Cards.

[72]C.J. Anderson, memorandum, November 8, 1928, Frank Presidential Papers, 4/13/1, box 55.

[73]B.E. McCormick, H.W. Kircher, and Loyal Durand to the Board of Regents, November 24, 1928, BOV Papers, 2/1/1, box 1.

[74]"Board of Visitors Annual Report," March 6, 1929, ibid.

[75]The two documents are typed and undated, but clipped together in Frank's files preceded with a sheet, in the president's hand, headed "Memoranda re the School of Education." The date may be established by reference to another, more formally and carefully prepared, but also undated, document that had been produced sometime prior to July, 1929, and which referred to the "program presented to you [Frank] on January 1, 1929." Frank Presidential Papers, 4/13/1, box 70.

2. Teachers trained wholly in liberal arts colleges are academic rather than professional in view point.
3. Public education sorely needs professional leadership.
4. Other professions have found it necessary to establish independent colleges in order to create a craft spirit.
5. Education needs the same opportunity.

Director Anderson concluded with the other key section:

> The legislature has created nine state teachers colleges thus expressing its confidence in the importance to the state of teacher training by giving them college status. These state teachers colleges have established four year courses for high school and elementary teachers. Graduates of these courses, after a few years of experience in teaching, will come to the University to continue their training. The establishment of an independent School of Education will make possible a closer integration of the whole teacher training system of the state.[76]

Here was a vision and opportunity that appealed to the visitors, the schoolmen, and Glenn Frank.

Two related problems challenged the president, however. First, how to satisfy the general faculty that an independent school would not concentrate on producing practice-oriented educational professionals at the expense of scholarship-based subject matter education? That is, would the education graduates of the future simply know *how* to teach, and not *what* to teach? Second, how to convince the schoolmen that academic interests would no longer retard the development of professional education and teacher training at Wisconsin? The January 1 memorandum contained Anderson's answer, which was to include within the school faculty "one member from each academic department offering courses which are included in a teaching major." Frank, realizing that such an approach would be unacceptable to the standards-conscious letters and science faculty, apparently suggested to Anderson that the several functions envisioned for an independent school might instead be consolidated under one budget line and remain as a single unit within the parent L&S college. On March 6 Anderson replied to this idea in writing:

> Dear Chief:
> I have thought over our discussion of yesterday. Budgetary autonomy

---

[76] A letter dated March 11, 1929, from Burton E. Nelson, president of the Stout Institute, Menomonie, Wisconsin, to Frank indicates the appeal of this passage. Ibid, box 64.

alone will do little for teacher training. Our hands will still be guided by the academicians when dealing with such vital problems as staff appointments and promotions, the teacher training program, advisory responsibility for teacher training candidates, the selection of candidates for teacher training, the academic prerequisites to teacher training, etc.[77]

Anderson's objections were reasonable, but they failed to respond adequately to Frank's political problem with respect to Dean Sellery and the L&S faculty.

Perhaps in normal times Anderson's reply would have convinced the president that independence should immediately be pursued. But two days later, on March 8, 1929, conditions changed radically as Dean Sellery attacked Frank's cherished Experimental College in a major freshman convocation speech. The president responded with public silence while behind the scenes he planned Sellery's ouster. Suddenly independence for the School of Education became relatively inconsequential when an L&S dean of Frank's choosing might be willing to satisfy the visitors and others who favored ridding the college of all of its professional training units—Commerce and Journalism, among others, as well as Education. The president pondered his options during the next few weeks and let it be known that he would have something to propose at the regents meeting in June. With his tendency to avoid hard administrative decisions, however, Frank surprised both Sellery and some regents by failing to recommend the dean's dismissal.[78] The School of Education issue thus reverted to its previous unresolved status. Finally, toward the end of the year Frank called a meeting with Anderson and Sellery and announced, according to Sellery's recollection, that he intended to "cut the School of Education loose."[79] After some conversation about how to implement this decision, the three agreed that Sellery and Anderson should develop a proposal to take before the L&S faculty. Although the dean's account does not claim it, Frank may have learned that Sellery had devised a way to handle the seemingly intractable political problems that had up to this time frustrated the establishment of an independent School of Education.

Sellery's solution was positively brilliant. Transcending the dependent-independent dilemma, the dean's plan proposed instead a

---

[77]C.J.A. to Dear Chief [March 5 or 6, 1929], ibid., box 70.

[78]George C. Sellery, *Some Ferments at Wisconsin, 1901-1947: Memories and Reflections* (Madison: University of Wisconsin Press, 1960), p. 38.

[79]Quoted in ibid., p. 45.

"coordinate" School of Education. Institutionally occupying the same distinct status as Engineering, Law, Medicine, and other separate professional units, the school would automatically include within its faculty *all* letters and science faculty who taught upper level academic courses applicable to education majors! On January 31, 1930, Frank, Anderson, and Sellery circulated the proposal, now in the form of Letters and Science Document 44, to the college faculty for consideration on February 17. Sellery formally presented the measure, and he and Anderson described and defended its nine sections. The vote for adoption was unanimous, as was that of the general University faculty on April 7. The regents gave their approval on April 23, and the new School of Education went into operation in the fall of 1930, with Anderson as its first dean. The Board of Visitors, speaking for themselves and the schoolmen, immediately applauded the "coordinate" structure:

> It gives us very great pleasure to commend the recent action of the faculty of the College of Letters and Science in recommending the establishment of a separate School of Education....We believe that the step taken by the faculty...constitutes an advance which the people of the state of Wisconsin will approve most heartily.[80]

The School of Education quickly achieved a position of respect and productivity that endures to the present day. It has retained as well the unusually close relationship with the faculty of its parent College of Letters and Science, a fruitful association unique to Wisconsin in American higher education.

Adult Education

On President Frank's recommendation, on April 28, 1926, the Board of Regents named Chester D. Snell to head the University Extension Division. Snell had previously directed the extension program of the University of North Carolina, where he had developed an innovative arts outreach program. Initially appointed acting dean at his predecessor's annual $7,500 salary, the youthful but hard-driving Snell soon received the permanent dean's designation. By 1928 he was making the impressive salary of $9,000—$1,500 more than such veteran campus

---

[80]"Board of Visitors Annual Report for 1930," March 7, 1930, BOV Papers, 2/1/1, box 1.

administrators as L&S Dean George Sellery and Graduate School Dean Charles Slichter, and only $1,000 less than Frank's other recent recruit, Professor Alexander Meiklejohn. In fact, President Frank sought in 1928 to bring the Extension dean's salary up to the level of the Experimental College director, but the regents, probably sensitive to the hard feelings such generous compensation would produce, compromised on the lower figure. Snell's predecessor, Dean Louis Reber, had given yeoman service to the University, particularly during the Van Hise years. Under the Birge administration of the early 1920s, however, Reber had for the most part followed a complacent outreach policy. Abandoning its aggressive pre-war "Wisconsin Idea" style, the division now quietly functioned primarily as a correspondence school of limited scope. Fully aware of the regents' public relations expectations of his fledgling administration, Glenn Frank wanted Chester Snell to revitalize University Extension and make it more of a conduit for University-wide service to the people of the state.[81]

Frank intended to reshape the Extension Division according to the related themes of public service and adult education, expanding on the outstanding model developed over the years by the outreach activities of the University's College of Agriculture. The key to Agriculture's exceptional and comprehensive utility to the state had been its well-structured organization that placed University professors, researchers, and agricultural extension specialists in department-based proximity to one another. This encouraged close and effective working relationships that had hastened the development of modern commercial agriculture throughout Wisconsin.[82] Meanwhile, Dean Reber's extension unit, a separate agency from the cooperative extension work of the College of Agriculture, tended to cloister its staff away from the academic departments. While it succeeded in offering well-presented and focused adult education programs, at the same time it failed to encourage rigorous scholarly attention by the regular University faculty to important problems faced by the people of the state. "Roughly speaking," Glenn Frank promised in the 1927 *Wisconsin Blue Book*, "it may be said that the new period of Extension development upon which we are now entering will be marked by an effort to make Extension less

[81]For a fuller discussion of Extension developments in the period see pp. 784-815.

[82]See, for example, W.H. Glover, *Farm and College: The College of Agriculture of the University of Wisconsin, A History* (Madison: University of Wisconsin Press, 1952), pp. 250-68 and passim; Edward H. Beardsley, *Harry L. Russell and Agricultural Science in Wisconsin* (Madison: University of Wisconsin Press, 1969), pp. 83-101.

and less a separate arm of the University and more and more a channel through which the whole University will function in the life of the State."[83]

Progress on the public service side quickly became evident, although some of the improvement may have been more apparent than real. One well-publicized effort was a joint program between the Extension Division and the College of Engineering to transmit the findings of campus applied research to Wisconsin industry. Unlike the College of Agriculture, which enjoyed solid and substantial federal funding to support its work, Engineering at Wisconsin was and remained a relative pauper, its research needs largely ignored by state and federal legislators. Yet President Frank insisted that as much as possible be done, and the *Press Bulletin* soon began issuing glowing stories of progress.[84] One report, entitled "Badger Science: Engineers Work at Industrial Problems," described recent faculty work:

> Investigations into chromium plating, attempts to case-harden steel by means of gas, the development of methods of treating waste products from pea canneries and creameries to make them inoffensive, and the designing of a double-speed induction motor for use in certain industrial operations are among the current research activities of the College of Engineering at the state university.[85]

Engineering also followed in Agriculture's footsteps by setting up industrial fellowships to support the college's research in areas of mutual interest. In mid-1928, for instance, the *Press Bulletin* announced that the regents had accepted $15,000 from a group of Wisconsin foundries to support three years of metallurgical study.[86] The provision of adequate laboratory facilities was basic to the research mission,

---

[83]Glenn Frank, "The University of Wisconsin—A Look Backward and Forward," *Wisconsin Blue Book, 1927* (Madison: State of Wisconsin, 1927), p. 368; Glenn Frank, "Future Policies and Programs in University Extension," manuscript of speech presented at the University Extension Division faculty meeting, May, 1927, Frank Papers, Kirksville.

[84]As President Frank optimistically put it: "Far-reaching plans are maturing for the placing of the College of Engineering upon a basis that will enable it to serve the rapidly developing industrial life of Wisconsin as the College of Agriculture has served the developing agricultural life of Wisconsin....These plans involve...the provision for adequate laboratories for the College of Engineering and the focussing of the research facilities of the College upon the pressing problems of Wisconsin's industrial production." Frank, "A Look Backward and Forward," p. 366.

[85]*Press Bulletin*, December 7, 1927. See also ibid., April 11, 1928.

[86]Ibid., June 6, 1928.

however, and Frank worked energetically to remedy this long-standing deficiency, which was partly overcome in 1931 with the opening of the new Mechanical Engineering Building.

Dean Snell committed the Extension Division to Frank's objective of developing improved channels between the University and the public. Again the College of Agriculture model proved instructive, with its long-standing programs of Farmers' Institutes, the Farm Short Course, and Farm and Home Week, each in its way bringing the expert and the practitioner together for periods ranging from a single day to fifteen weeks for instruction and exchange of views and ideas.[87] Glenn Frank seemed always to be proposing "institutes" of various sorts that Extension might co-sponsor with the appropriate University department or other agency. Perhaps his most ambitious suggestion, offered in mid-1927, was for the campus to host an annual Wisconsin Institute on the Affairs of the Commonwealth. The idea was to gather leaders from key sectors of the economy and, in conjunction with faculty experts, identify and plan how to eliminate basic problems of the state.[88] While the commonwealth institute never took shape as Frank envisioned it, Extension did cooperate with the College of Engineering, as well as with the Journalism, Commerce, Education, and Library schools, among others, to sponsor useful professional conferences.[89] Extensive short courses in such disparate fields as community recreation leadership and electrification also helped forge constructive links between community and academe.[90]

But it was the adult education orientation that came to characterize University Extension under Frank and Snell most fully. In this they were very much reflecting the broader progressive education movement. Through adult education the progressives hoped to instill progressive social and cultural values among America's working classes; their approach was thus mass liberal education with a social activist twist. Advocates openly proclaimed this ameliorative objective. William H. Lighty, the long-time UW director of extension teaching and 1926

---

[87]The Farmers' Institute (off campus) and the Farm Short Course (on campus) began operating during the mid-1880s; Farm and Home Week first opened on campus in 1904 as a ten-day farmers' course.

[88]*Capital Times*, July 18, 1927; *Daily Cardinal*, July 19 and 21, 1927; *Press Bulletin*, July 27, August 10, 1927.

[89]See, for example, *Daily Cardinal*, April 21, October 30, 1929, November 20, 1930; *Capital Times*, July 22, 1930.

[90]*WAM*, 29 (June, 1928), 318; *Capital Times*, September 24, 1930.

president-elect of the National University Extension Association (NUEA), made no bones about his commitment to social reform. "In the area of adult education," he told one audience, "lies the greatest efficiency of education to make contemporary changes in our institutions."[91] Lighty organized the April, 1927, NUEA convention. It featured addresses by himself, Glenn Frank, and Edward A. Filene, Frank's one-time patron. Each lauded the adult education movement as a key component of extension.[92]

Joseph K. Hart soon emerged as another important figure in the Wisconsin effort. Appointed acting professor of the philosophy of education in 1927, Hart was a much-published national advocate of adult education. His arrogance soon alienated many of his UW faculty colleagues, but he nevertheless functioned as Extension's equivalent of Alexander Meiklejohn, whose views he shared and lauded.[93] Hart saw opportunities for progressive education everywhere. In his first semester at Wisconsin Hart urged a meeting of state librarians to make the most of their educational role. "Your whole work is of the nature of adult education, for you are helping to make children adults of some sort," he reminded his audience. "You must spend your energies, at least in part, in helping to provide your community with all the materials it needs for the furtherance of life and civilization in every direction."[94]

Dean Snell sought to instill the adult education movement's influence throughout the Extension Division. The February, 1928, issue of the *Wisconsin Alumni Magazine* described several major departures. First were "new study courses and lectures on topics of adult interest,"

[91] *Press Bulletin*, July 21, 1926. Lighty, whom President Van Hise had hired in 1906, a year before appointing Reber, had organized and run the division's correspondence instruction program and otherwise functioned as the dean's second in command.

[92] *Capital Times*, April 20, 1927; *Press Bulletin*, April 27, 1927.

[93] Hart left the University in 1930 after C.J. Anderson recommended that Frank not reappoint the difficult colleague. Although the *Capital Times* had defended Hart in 1929 when Anderson first tried to be rid of him, editor Evjue later admitted that Hart had transformed himself from a "gadfly" to a "hornet" and probably deserved to be let go. *Capital Times*, February 11 and 13, 1930.

[94] *Press Bulletin*, October 12, 1927. In 1928 T.J. Mosley offered this definition of adult education: "As nearly as a layman can analyze it, it means that every intellectual or social specialty of the academic cloister shall be available on demand in the market place, so that education may become a life process in the community, not merely an affliction of adolescence. In other words, Adult Education is University Extension hitting on all six and being used as a vehicle for social service rather than institutional propaganda." T.J. Mosley, "University Extension Widens Its Scope," *WAM*, 29 (February, 1928), 159.

such as those presented by Professor Hart in Monroe on "educational forces of the American community." Another development was the appointment of Chester Allen to head Extension's "field force." Allen's task was to improve staff training and mobility and enhance Extension's ability to "assist working girls." There were also several altogether new Extension units, such as the Bureau of Economics and Sociology and the Bureau of Business Information. Snell expected each to consult with and assist community chest agencies, retailers, manufacturers, and other local social and commercial enterprises throughout the state. The Bureau of Dramatic Activities under Ethel T. Rockwell quickly made itself a major presence in the cultural life of the state, helping during its first year to produce over 250 plays and pageants. Finally, and unique in the nation, the new Medical Library Service and associated lectures by medical school faculty members strove to combat the traditional isolation felt by physicians in rural Wisconsin.[95] Meanwhile, William Lighty's correspondence study office overhauled its methods and materials and consequently enjoyed swelling enrollments.[96] As Lighty summarized the overall division perspective in 1930, "Wisconsin expects every citizen to go forward in rebuilding educationally, which in adult life must be done largely...without suspending the daily obligations of one's craft or profession."[97]

The heart of Wisconsin's adult education effort was to be located at the new Extension Center building in Milwaukee that opened in September of 1928. The *Daily Cardinal* heralded what it described as a "Wisconsin adult education experiment" to serve Milwaukee area residents, offering certificates "in liberal education" to students who successfully completed ten of its semester-length, non-credit courses. Among those on the planning and oversight committee were Glenn Frank, Chester Snell, Alexander Meiklejohn, V.A.C. Henmon, and J.K. Hart. Not surprisingly, a decided Experimental College tone characterized the endeavor:[98]

---

[95]Mosley, "University Extension Widens Its Scope," p. 159.

[96]*Press Bulletin*, January 9, 1929.

[97]*Capital Times*, September 24, 1930.

[98]In his address before the extension faculty in May, 1927, President Frank declared:

> The people of the State are restless and expect something different—they know not what—but the fact remains that they are not entirely pleased with the present results of higher education. Experimentation in liberal arts education is needed and will be carried on in Wisconsin through the Experimental Junior College. I see an opportunity for the Extension faculty to carry on experimental teaching work through

The principal aims of this educational plan will give an opportunity to acquire an education which will broaden a person's general outlook in the field of modern ideas and world movement, and develop a spirit of self-criticism and individual thinking. In applying this type of study the university is following an idea which has been successful in other states and in several European countries.

Courses will be given in philosophy, social science, history, language, art, bio-physical sciences, business, engineering, and home economics.[99]

Unlike the Experimental College, however, the Milwaukee program was destined to live well beyond its formative experimental stage.

The Spirit of Academic Adventure

During the early Frank years curricular and instructional experimentation was common throughout the University. The president initiated little of this directly, but in a more general sense his enthusiasm for accomplishing beneficial change and his willingness to support interesting and even controversial ideas nurtured a hospitable environment for innovation. President Frank's faculty detractors may not have seen things in this light, but they could hardly deny that nearly everyone, at least for a few years, seemed to be trying to do something different or better. The students, too, caught the mood of the times. Most strikingly, during 1929 and 1930 they engaged in an extensive dialogue among themselves and with the faculty that led to the formal approval of major curricular revisions within the College of Letters and Science.

The large and diverse College of Letters and Science hosted the bulk of innovation. In February, 1926, a committee chaired by Professor Kiekhofer recommended that the faculty "encourage the development of greater initiative and self-reliance in their studies among our superior students."[100] As approved by the faculty on March 15, the

correspondence-study and particularly to attempt a new contribution in education in Milwaukee as soon as the new building is completed. It seems to me that you have a fine opportunity to build up adult education almost removed from the "bugaboo" of college credits and degrees. Something of the spirit and technique of the Denmark folk schools developed in a business and industrial area like the Lake Shore would be a marvelous contribution to American education.

Frank, "Future Policies and Programs in University Extension."

[99]*Daily Cardinal*, April 20, 1928; *Press Bulletin*, April 25, 1928.

[100]L&S Faculty Minutes, February 16, 1926.

Student Initiative Plan allowed selected students to substitute individually guided study for traditional classroom work and to earn graduation credit through examinations on it.[101] In 1929, following the Experimental College model, the faculty approved a request from the Chi Phi fraternity to employ a live-in instructor to teach a year-long three-credit course at the house.[102] Toward the end of the 1925-26 academic year, with prodding from the business community, the L&S and University faculties approved the reorganization of the old Course in Commerce into a new School of Commerce with programs leading to B.A. and M.A. degrees, thereby giving the new school separate departmental status from economics.[103] Subsequently, the college and the University faculties accepted a revised undergraduate curriculum for commerce that made its requirements simpler and more flexible.[104] Journalism, too, acting with alumni and doubtless with strong behind-the-scenes support from journalist Glenn Frank, undertook similar institutional and curricular improvements.[105] Finally, during the 1927 summer session Professor of Music Edgar B. Gordon opened his School of Creative Arts for Wisconsin elementary school children. Begun as a teaching methods demonstration project, it soon evolved into a regular program emphasizing continuing experimentation. Gordon's work attracted a good deal of national attention and respect.[106]

Other UW schools and colleges also reflected the educational ferment. In 1926 the College of Agriculture expanded its undergraduate curriculum for students in the four-year Long Course to include two

---

[101]Ibid., March 15, 1926; *Capital Times*, March 16, 1926; *Daily Cardinal*, September 29, October 15, 1926.

[102]L&S Faculty Minutes, May 20, 1929; *Daily Cardinal*, May 24, September 25 and 28, 1930.

[103]L&S Faculty Minutes, June 14, 1926; UW Faculty Minutes, June 18, 1926; UW Faculty Document 284, "Organization of the School of Commerce with One Graduate Year," June 18, 1926.

[104]L&S Faculty Minutes, March 18, 1929; L&S Faculty Document 41, "Proposed Modification of the Curriculum of the School of Commerce," March 18, 1929, UA; UW Faculty Minutes, April 1, 1929; UW Faculty Document 339, "Modifications of the Curriculum of the School of Commerce," April 3, 1929.

[105]*Press Bulletin*, September 2, 1925; L&S Faculty Minutes, March 21 and 28, 1927, March 18, 1929; L&S Faculty Document 35II, "Requirements for the Degree of Master of Arts in Journalism in the School of Journalism," March, 1927; L&S Faculty Document 42, "Modification of the Requirements of the Curriculum of the School of Journalism," March, 1929; *Capital Times*, April 5, 1927; *Daily Cardinal*, April 14, September 21, 1927.

[106]*Daily Cardinal*, July 16, October 7, 1927, July 20, 1929. Faculty members from speech, art, and education cooperated.

distinct options. The original curriculum continued to emphasize strict scientific preparation; the new more flexible one offered training in related "economic, journalistic, educational, or mechanical phases of agriculture."[107] The Law School concentrated on raising standards, deciding in October, 1926, to require completion of three years of the L&S curriculum before admission to legal studies, which themselves remained in a constant state of flux.[108] The College of Engineering experimented with improved instructional methods during the summer of 1927, and in 1930 the faculty debated the merits of replacing the L&S freshman English course with one specially designed for engineering majors.[109] In the Medical School, the inauguration of a full four-year M.D. degree program in 1925 naturally produced great interest in curriculum and instruction. For example, in 1926 Dean Charles R. Bardeen—a Meiklejohn supporter who asserted that "the leading medical schools are all essentially experimental colleges"—created the Wisconsin Preceptor Plan, which actively involved some of the state's practicing physicians in the training process while providing advanced students with invaluable clinical experience.[110] Even the large College of Letters and Science, where there was considerable faculty skepticism about the Experimental College, conducted a major review of its curriculum in 1929-30 under the leadership of history Professor Carl Russell Fish. The Fish Committee reforms aimed to provide a richer, more flexible, and more rigorous learning environment for undergraduate students.[111] The early Frank years thus involved a good deal of educational change across the campus.

---

[107]*Press Bulletin*, June 2, 1926; Agriculture Faculty Document 279, "Revision of the Curriculum of the College of Agriculture," May 3, 1926, UA. In 1931 the College of Agriculture dropped the old Curriculum A option, which few students any longer elected, and modified Curriculum B to make it standard for all students in the Long Course. UW Faculty Document 376, "Curriculum Changes in the Four-Year Course in Agriculture," January 12, 1931.

[108]UW Faculty Minutes, October 4, 1926; *Capital Times*, January 1, 1928.

[109]On instruction see *Capital Times*, April 26, 1927; *Daily Cardinal*, April 27, 1927. On Freshman English see *Daily Cardinal*, April 27 and 29, May 7, 8, and 16, June 5, October 2, 1930.

[110]*Press Bulletin*, August 24, 1927; Paul F. Clark, *The University of Wisconsin Medical School: A Chronicle, 1848-1948* (Madison: Published for the Wisconsin Medical Alumni Association by the University of Wisconsin Press, 1967), pp. 32-5; Bardeen to Frank, February 13, 1930, Frank Presidential Papers, 4/13/1, box 70.

[111]See pp. 750-2.

Student Life and Educational Progress

Glenn Frank believed that the extracurricular side of student life was a crucial part of a vital educational experience, and as a former Methodist preacher he considered religion as central. Since 1917 the campus-area YWCA and YMCA had organized annual religious conferences. Although held on campus, they were strictly unofficial in nature.[112] In October of 1925, the two Ys hosted one of these events—now called the All-University Religious Convocation—which featured a telling address by the new president:

> I am glad that, at the beginning of my administration as president of the University of Wisconsin, you have given me this opportunity to express my belief in the central significance of religion in the lives of modern men and women.
>
> This is a state university. On its campus men and women of all creeds and of no creed meet and mingle. Catholics and Protestants, Buddhists and Baptists, Mohammedans and Methodists may alike entrust themselves to its care and to its discipline. Supported by all, it is the servant of all. This university cannot be partisan of any particular creed, but unless it cultivates in its sons and its daughters a sensitiveness to the spiritual issues of existence it becomes a danger instead of a defense to the state.
>
> In these all-university services meet not the divergent demands of conflicting creeds but the common cry of human needs and human aspirations.
>
> Every year I find myself falling more and more under the spell of the radiant realism of Jesus. I find in Him a refreshing freedom from the artificialities and superficialities into which we so easily fall when our minds consciously approach the elusive matters of the spirit.[113]

Glenn Frank thus early sought to identify his administration with non-sectarian religious values.

The president thereafter took personal charge of the religious convocations, effectively transforming them into official University activities.[114] The first event under these new auspices occurred in

---

[112]*WAM*, 26 (April, 1925), 213.

[113]Frank called his talk "The Radiant Realism of Religion." *Press Bulletin*, October 21, 1925.

[114]*Press Bulletin*, March 3, 1926; *Daily Cardinal*, February 10, 1926; *Capital Times*, February 22, 1926. The *Wisconsin Alumni Magazine* nicely characterized the new arrangement: "The tenth All-University Religious Convocation arranged by the Young Women's and Young Men's Christian Associations, was a major campus event of February. President Glenn Frank assumed personal charge of the conference, presided at the meetings and

February, 1926, at the Armory/Gymnasium and featured addresses by Frank, Alexander Meiklejohn, and liberal theologian Reinhold Niebuhr, the minister of the Bethel Evangelical Church of Detroit. Soon monthly programs dotted the calendar, and the theological purview successively broadened from non-sectarian Protestant to non-sectarian Christian to non-sectarian Judeo-Christian with a decided tinge of skepticism. Thus Professor Max C. Otto, the widely known philosopher and agnostic, set the tone of the February, 1928, convocation by using his keynote address to raise basic questions about the nature of religion rather than to offer theological interpretations and spiritual advice.[115]

This was too much for Father Harry C. Hengell, the Roman Catholic priest at St. Paul's University Chapel adjacent to the campus. He angrily proclaimed to his congregation the following Sunday that for Catholics to cooperate further with the UW religious convocations was to commit treason against the Church of Rome.[116] Father Hengell may have had a point. President Frank himself had recently urged students to rethink their religious values while at the University:

> Unless you are but lifeless masses of blood and bone and the university a mere mechanism bereft of spirit, you will leave this university changed men and women....all that you brought with you will, at one time or another, suffer a sort of judgment day assessment....
>
> In this reassessment of the issues of life, which authentic education implies, religion cannot be exempt....You cannot lock your spirit in quarantine for four years while you educate your mind. Your religion will feel the same impact of inquiry and valuation that your politics and your economics will feel.[117]

As Glenn Frank conceived them, the All-University Religious Convocations reflected just how far the University should extend its educational reach into the students' personal lives and value systems.[118]

At the same time the president believed in treating UW students as thoughtful adults. "I would be delighted at any time," he declared in October of 1930, "to give a student self governing body as much power

---

delivered one of the principal addresses." *WAM*, 27 (April, 1926), 152.

[115]*Daily Cardinal*, February 28, 1928.

[116]Ibid.

[117]Ibid., February 26, 1928.

[118]The *Badger*, 1930, p. 538, commented acidly in its satirical section: "'Watch out for this guy Frank,' says Father Hengell. 'He wants you to think for yourself instead of letting me think for you.'"

as it will absorb, provided that it will be a real governing group, firmly face each problem brought before it, and not shrink from doing its duties in a crisis."[119]   The president's comment reflected the fact that the Student Court and the Student Senate had disbanded themselves in 1926 and 1927, respectively, due primarily to the indifference of the student body to general self-government.[120]   Frank and the faculty, awaiting initiatives from the students, had allowed events to drift.   As a result Dean of Men Scott Goodnight found himself essentially responsible for dealing with most extracurricular student misconduct.   This he did with

A Student View of the Rocking Chair Incident

considerable zeal, including the well-publicized apprehension and expulsion of a trysting student couple in a Sterling Court apartment toward the end of December, 1929.   The next month the romantic poet and English Professor William Ellery Leonard learned of this "rocking chair" incident, so named because Goodnight had sat in a rocking chair while waiting for the miscreants to emerge.   Leonard considered Goodnight's conduct a violation of student privacy rights and wrote the president demanding that he bar the dean from such interference in the future.   Frank ignored the letter, whereupon the indignant Leonard sent a copy to the local press for publication.   The resulting public uproar reflected badly on the president, who some were beginning to believe

---

[119]*Daily Cardinal*, October 21, 1930. See also the editorial on the demise of student self-government, *WAM*, 32 (November, 1930), 62.

[120]Coeds, through the venerable Women's Self-Government Association, continued to work with the dean of women in the conduct of their extracurricular activities.

spent too much time away from Madison and his University duties. Frank's call for the resumption of student self-government thus represented a politically clever response to the supporters of both Leonard and Goodnight. Its immediate effect was nil, though it did reflect the president's genuine belief in responsible student self-governance. As in other matters, however, Frank awaited the action of those concerned to put the concept into effect.

While in this instance his challenge was ignored, throughout his presidency Frank consistently allowed students considerable freedom in their extracurricular lives, even when he sometimes found their behavior ill-considered or even reprehensible. In 1929, for example, members of several gentile sororities and fraternities established the Apex Club to sponsor off-campus dances barred to Jewish participants. Although Frank was an outspoken opponent of anti-Semitism and racism he refused to interfere, arguing that while the University would not tolerate discrimination within its boundaries, it also must not dictate the personal associations of its students. The following year when women residents of Barnard Hall objected to a new dining room dress code, the president declined to intervene on the ground that the issue was one of self-governance; the women must decide for themselves. The 1928 "Dora Russell affair" seemed to call Frank's consistency into question after the president cancelled a campus address by a prominent advocate of companionate marriage and free love. As it turned out, Frank acted in accordance with a request of the student organizers of the event, who had changed their minds about the suitability of Mrs. Russell for a campus appearance. The local Unitarian Church then agreed to sponsor her rather innocuous talk. Frank's liberal image suffered permanent damage, however, as many observers never fully comprehended his motives or action.

The opening of the impressive Tripp and Adams men's residence halls on Lake Mendota in the fall of 1926 heightened President Frank's interest in the educational possibilities inherent in an expanded system of campus living accommodations for much of the student body. The new facilities offered well-designed opportunities for cooperative social and cultural experiences. With the handsome Tripp-Adams complex very much in mind, the president declared optimistically in the spring of 1926, "I do not believe that the parents of Wisconsin students will or should be satisfied until all freshmen have an opportunity for community living in dormitories."[121] The assignment of half of Adams Hall for use by the Experimental College beginning in 1927 further emphasized the educational potential of residence hall life. Moreover, the brilliant success of the Wisconsin University Building Corporation—the regents' mechanism for circumventing the constitutional prohibition of University indebtedness—seemed to suggest a way to fund more ambitious constructional initiatives. Thus on March 3, 1928, the *Daily Cardinal* reported Frank's intention to establish "a program for housing all the university students in dormitories, with the exception of the organized groups."

Meanwhile, President Frank's closest friend and supporter among the regents, Michael Olbrich, quietly studied Harvard's graduate student housing program and prepared a report to the board that fleshed out Frank's vision. Spurred on by Olbrich, in March, 1929, the regents approved the appointment of a special joint regent-faculty committee "to continue the study of the fraternity, sorority and student housing situation." Regent and committee chairman John Schmidtmann expressed the committee's outlook when he asserted that "the student leaving the campus is just as much the product of his way of living here as he is in his class work."[122] The Schmidtmann committee submitted its report to the full board in November, paradoxically just after the stock market crash. The report contained an extremely ambitious two-phase plan for the residential development of the western campus, stretching along Lake Mendota from Observatory Hill to Picnic Point, all to be funded through the WUBC. New facilities ultimately were to include men's and women's dormitories, fraternity and sorority houses, recreational areas, "and perhaps even faculty homes." The area, concluded the committee, "properly platted, landscaped, and planted with trees and shrubs, can be developed into a 'university city' that will be picturesquely unique in the United States."[123] The "University City" plan graphically affirmed Glenn Frank's vision. Unfortunately, the great depression soon made its achievement impossible.

The Memorial Union, long in planning and construction, opened its doors in the fall of 1928. The handsome facility promised to enhance

---

[121]*Press Bulletin*, July 14, 1926.

[122]John C. Schmidtmann, "Is Housing Its Students a Proper Obligation of the University?" November 11, 1929, BOR Papers, 1/1/4, box 97, UA.

[123]Untitled report submitted to the Board of Regents, November 22, 1929, Lawrence Halle Papers, Division of Residence Halls, UW-Madison.

student self-determination while at the same time providing a "living room" for the campus community. Construction of the lakefront edifice had begun in mid-1926, even before all of the necessary funds and pledges for its cost were in hand. The next two years witnessed a succession of emergency fund-raising projects and labor troubles that constantly seemed to put the realization of President Van Hise's dream in jeopardy.[124] Recent graduates John Dollard and Porter Butts worked full-time to coordinate fund-raising for the project. As the building neared completion, President Frank named physiological chemist and champion of the student community Harold Bradley as chairman of a forty-member all-University committee to plan for the governance of the Memorial Union. The most important issue confronted by the Bradley committee was the extent to which students should control the programming and management of a building they had largely initiated and generously helped to fund. Both Bradley and Frank favored giving the responsibility to the student body.

On May 16, 1928, Professor Bradley presided over a ceremony transferring control of union affairs to a new student-dominated Union Council, which for most of the next decade would be the most important student government agency on campus. Bradley first described the history of student unions, noting that Wisconsin's would join twenty-eight others among the major universities. He then passed the "Union gavel" to Union President Lauriston Sharp of the Class of 1929 with these words:

> At this time...we see the dissolution of the university committee as the responsible group for the conduct of Union affairs and the assumption of that responsibility by the Union council. It is a momentous change. Up to now the Union has been nursed and cared for, nurtured, clothed, taken care of in one way or another by a parent or a foster-parent. Now it steps out on its own. It has attained its majority, its own individuality.
>
> In token of the abdication of the university committee as a guiding force, in token of the assumption of its own majority and competency to run

---

[124]Van Hise had declared in his 1904 inaugural address: "The union should be a commodious and beautiful building, comfortably, even artistically, furnished. When the students are done with their work in the evening, the attractive union is at hand, where refreshments may be had, and a pleasant hour may be spent at games, with the magazines, in a novel, or in social chat. The coarse attractions of the town have little power in comparison." *The Jubilee of the University of Wisconsin: In Celebration of the Fiftieth Anniversary of Its First Commencement Held at Madison June the Fifth to June the Ninth Nineteen Hundred and Four* (Madison: Jubilee Committee, 1905), p. 113. For a more extended discussion of the development of the Memorial Union, see pp. 589-606.

itself, I turn over this gavel to the first president of the Union council and to the council as a group.

With power always goes responsibility. It is up to this council—especially the student members—to make this first year a record of effective organization, of great accomplishment, of fine quality, of fine taste—a record that other councils will strive to live up to.[125]

As the *Daily Cardinal* recognized, a "new era in the social and cultural life of the university community" had begun.[126] It was also a new era in student government.

The Memorial Union building celebrated its official dedication the following October. Chicago alumnus George Haight, who had helped mightily to raise the construction funds, officiated at the ceremony, and President Frank offered a dedicatory prayer:

Give us to see it as a memorial to Youth....Give us to realize that the minds and spirits of men and women will be made and molded in the hours of light and laughter they spend here no less than in the more sober processes of laboratory and seminar.

Later, at the dedication dinner, Frank elaborated on the potential of the Memorial Union to enhance campus life, because it would

afford facilities for social contact and co-operation, hitherto available only to students who created their own sororities and fraternities...give temple and tools and tasks to the spirit of self government...supplement the more formal associations of the class rooms with a common meeting ground for teachers and students.[127]

While Frank had not initiated nor participated in planning the union project, he had made its completion a high campus priority. He rightly saw the Memorial Union as a key extracurricular vehicle for student growth and cultural enrichment.

---

[125]*Daily Cardinal*, May 17, 1928.

[126]Ibid., May 17, 1928.

[127]"Dedicate Memorial Union Building," *WAM*, 30 (November, 1928), 43. The self-government function was an important one, as the *Daily Cardinal* editorial for May 17, 1928, observed: "The opportunity is inestimable in that it places almost wholly in the hands of a student body the management of a $1,250,000 project, the Memorial Union Building. It has been charged, and the charge has not been so ably refuted, that student self government at the University of Wisconsin has been on the decline with the abandonment of the Student Court and the Student Senate. Now is presented the chance for student leaders in the new council to put beyond doubt the fact that student government is a live and vital force at the University of Wisconsin."

The first few years of the Frank administration thus witnessed educational ferment and accomplishment unequalled since the early Van Hise years a quarter-century before. The president occasionally took the lead in advocating and implementing certain developments, but ultimately he remained true to his promise to function in the impresario role. Even with respect to his most dramatic and prominent initiative, the Experimental College, he made certain to seek the advice of leading faculty members and the formal approval of the faculty as a whole before launching the venture. And while the college benefited from Frank's moral support and applause, once the project was under way he refrained from intruding in its operation even after Director Meiklejohn disappointed him by failing to test various curricular reforms or validate his experimental curriculum scientifically. As other initiatives emerged from within and outside the campus, Frank recognized their potential, nurtured them as required, but kept hands off their operation. This was certainly the case with two of his pet projects, the Bureau of Educational Guidance and Records and the Freshman Days orientation program, both of which he left to others to develop. Where Frank inherited established programs, he appreciated their value to his collaborative vision, encouraged their leaders, and saw that important assets—for example, the Tripp and Adams men's residence halls and the Memorial Union—brought maximum benefit to the University.

Regent Grady's Protective Resolution

The early Frank years witnessed a competition in Wisconsin between opposing notions of academic freedom and scholarly integrity. Prominent in one camp were the followers and family of Robert M. La Follette, Sr., who had created and led the Wisconsin progressive movement from before the turn of the century until his death in 1925. La Follette progressives tended to view issues in black and white moral terms, with a stern and single-minded logic pervading their thinking on policy matters. They saw themselves as the champions of the poor and oppressed against "the interests"—the powerful monopolistic corporations and wealthy capitalists who enriched themselves at the expense of ordinary people and who, if permitted, would ruin the nation's character and intellectual leadership through the subversion of its colleges and universities. With their strong faith in the ameliorative value of education, the issue of who controlled the University was of prime importance.

Faculty members might share progressive objectives, but most of them were certain their work would have professional integrity and social value only to the extent they were able to conduct their teaching and research objectively without regard to partisan influences and ideology. To be sure, each professor might not endorse the research and conclusions (or, for that matter, the political views) of any particular colleague, but most believed that honesty, adherence to the technical canons of scholarship, and rigorous colleague review and criticism were the best guarantees that academic scholarship would remain free to pursue the truth wherever it might lead. To oversimplify only slightly, many of the La Follette progressives thought they already knew how the world worked and what was needed to right its wrongs. Many of the scholars, even those of progressive inclinations, on the other hand, saw their research as considerably more open-ended and tentative, particularly with respect to social, political, and economic conclusions. The potential thus always existed for conflict. It was in this context that the controversy over the so-called Grady resolution of the Board of Regents took place during the opening months of the Frank administration.

Senator La Follette himself prepared the way early in 1925 when he warned ominously in *La Follette's Magazine*:

> The time is at hand when the American people must meet this issue of Monopoly control over higher education. More particularly, the University of Wisconsin...must take the lead in restoring that fearless "winnowing and sifting of truth" which is paralyzed by the subsidies, direct and indirect, of the Monopoly System.[128]

La Follette's admonition might soon have been forgotten, except for three nearly simultaneous events occurring a few months later. In May came the announcement of Glenn Frank's appointment to the UW presidency, with the knowledge at least among some progressives that he was not La Follette's choice. Then on June 18 came news of the senator's death and a heightened desire among his followers to honor their leader's memory. A week later the Board of Regents decided by a narrow six to five margin, with lame-duck President Birge breaking

---

[128]*La Follette's Magazine*, 17 (February, 1925), 19-20. See also ibid. (January, 1925), 2-3; Martin Kenneth Gordon, "Wisconsin and the Foundations, 1925-1931" (M.A. thesis, University of Wisconsin, 1965), p. 9.

the tie, to accept a $12,500 grant from the Rockefeller-funded General Education Board to support Dr. Arthur S. Loevenhart's research on syphilis.[129] Soon an angry Milwaukee socialist proposed that the State Federation of Labor censure the regents for their action, declaring: "It is a mistake for the University which is maintained by the people, to accept money from the Rockefeller Foundation or from similar sources....Let wealth gain a foothold and wealth will expect something in return."[130] Echoing La Follette's warning, the *Capital Times* demanded that the regents return the grant: "The soul of the University of Wisconsin is not for sale to interests that are in the business of buying colleges and universities."[131]

As discussion continued among the public, the press, and the board, Regent Daniel H. Grady, a Democrat and long-time La Follette progressive who had voted against the grant to Loevenhart, drafted a resolution for consideration at the board's meeting on August 5. The ensuing debate lasted five hours, for it was common knowledge among the members that through the persuasive efforts of Medical Dean Bardeen the General Education Board was ready to provide $600,000 for a badly needed medical research building. As finally adopted by the regents over the objections of retiring President Birge and on a divided vote of nine to six, the resolution stated: "Resolved, that no gifts, donations, or subsidies shall in the future be accepted by or on behalf of the university of Wisconsin from any incorporated educational endowments or organizations of like character."[132] The contest had been rancorous and split the progressive members of the board. President Birge had vainly argued that the policy would unfairly constrain Glenn Frank when he arrived on campus the following month, but Regent John Cashman replied that the regents and not the president were responsible for making University policy. Regent Olbrich noted that the University had a long tradition of accepting "gifts from almost similar sources," such as the Rockefeller agency that was sponsoring Agriculture Dean Russell's imminent trip to the Far East. Regent Kronshage referred to the heavy financial drain of the University on the state coffers and asserted that private sources of support were needed,

---

[129]BOR Minutes, June 25, 1925.
[130]Letter to the editor, *Capital Times*, July 25, 1925; Gordon, "Wisconsin and the Foundations," p. 22.
[131]*Capital Times*, July 24, 1925.
[132]BOR Minutes, August 5, 1925.

especially for research. In response Regent Casperson denied that the legislature would fail to meet University needs, while Frank's friend Regent Gale emphasized that in Wisconsin the people, as individuals or through their government, should be the only ones to support their state university.[133]

The Wisconsin Alumni Association quickly mounted an attack against the Grady resolution by naming a study commission, chaired by George Haight, with whom Regent Kronshage had worked on the recent public relations campaign. Its hearings became the key platform for University faculty members and administrators (not including the recently arrived President Frank), who testified nearly unanimously that legislative funding of research had been and in all probability would remain inadequate, that private foundation support for research should be encouraged to make up the deficiency, that proper safeguards were in place to protect the public interest, and finally that scholars were by nature seekers after truth and were fully capable of withstanding any contaminating influences. Only the *Capital Times'* editor, William Evjue, appeared in support of the resolution, as individual regents declined to testify. Evjue's argument emphasized the La Follette progressives' view that a public university, to be true to its basic purpose, must derive its support exclusively from the public, whether through the state government or the open-handed generosity of individual citizens. In late December the association issued a report highly critical of the Grady resolution—along with a minority opinion—but to no effect.

The following May the regents, now fully aware of the potentially damaging implications of the resolution, accepted a $30,000 grant from the Engineering Foundation for furnace slag research. This decision effectively limited the applicability of the Grady resolution to those agencies created by Andrew Carnegie and John D. Rockefeller, in progressive eyes the twin symbols of evil monopoly capitalism. As implemented over time, the gift policy thus inconsistently maintained University access to most of its traditional private sources of support while simultaneously affirming the La Follette view of the nature and integrity of the University and faculty scholarship. Meanwhile, Evjue's

---

[133]Zona Gale to Frank, August 6, 1925, Frank Papers, Kirksville. See also Regent John C. Schmidtmann, "Passing the Tin Cup for Gifts: University Regent Opposes Subsidizing University of Wisconsin by Corporation Endowments: People Will Support a Service Institution," *La Follette's Magazine*, 17 (November, 1925), 175, 178.

Capital Times continued to publish articles and editorials during the next few years seeking to prove the danger of entanglements between higher education and commercial interests. The emasculated Grady resolution remained in effect until 1930 when a more conservative Board of Regents rescinded it.

Recognizing the irreconcilable and highly volatile nature of this dispute, which had been joined before his arrival in Wisconsin, Glenn Frank initially avoided taking a clear stand. Instead he issued high sounding general statements of principle. "We must see to it that this university is ever kept a genuine home of learning," he announced as he stepped from the train on September 1. "We must see to it that this university ever provides encouragement and equipment for research, made possible by a state-wide realization that generous support" is necessary.[134] In his first address to the University faculty on October 5, while the WAA hearings on the Grady resolution were in progress, the president called for governance of the institution by "minds both flexible and informed," adding that "policies must come out of collaboration and not from any one group of this institution." Without mentioning the Grady restriction directly, he warned:

> It is impossible to build or to maintain a great university in the fullest sense of that word unless research is assured two things—support and freedom....We must assure to the research of this institution as nearly complete freedom as is humanly possible in an organized society; and, as I see it, freedom of research in this institution implies freedom from the influence and dictates of organized wealth, and freedom from the influence and dictates of organized politics....I would not be interested in remaining even one single hour after it had become clear that it was not possible in the matter of research to secure for [UW] both support—adequate and continuous—and freedom both from the dictates of organized politics on the one hand, and from organized wealth on the other.[135]

Following this talk, the *Daily Cardinal* proclaimed Frank an opponent of the Grady resolution, while the *Capital Times* applauded his neutrality.[136]

President Frank avoided public comment on the new gift policy until November 9, when the University hosted the annual meeting of the National Academy of Sciences. Noting "speculation" among the

---

[134]*Press Bulletin*, September 9, 1925.
[135]UW Faculty Document 275.
[136]Editorials, *Daily Cardinal* and *Capital Times*, October 8, 1925.

country's leading scholars regarding "certain local academic legislation on the future of sciences and research at this university," Frank asked that they wait "for all the facts" and avoid drawing "hasty conclusions." "Speaking for the plans and purposes of the administration and for the scientific staff, I can assure you that the University of Wisconsin will neither cut itself off from the vast co-operative efforts of American and European scholarship nor retrench on its own research program."[137] Addressing the likely effect of the Grady resolution rather than the policy itself, President Frank remained safely outside the raging debate while putting the best face on an exceedingly difficult situation he had no power to alter. In office only a few weeks, with no expectation at the moment of accomplishing any change, the new leader would have been foolish to join one camp or the other.

While Glenn Frank declined to challenge the regents over the Grady resolution, he nevertheless gradually proved himself a strong defender of academic freedom and civil liberties for the faculty and students. Whenever possible, he took only the minimal action needed to accomplish his objective, but he did not shrink from a more forceful and forthright stand when necessary. He followed this strategy during a 1926 dispute over the World Court and the League of Nations, which the La Follettes and their mostly isolationist Wisconsin progressive followers viewed with deep suspicion. In March of that year John Cashman—a La Follette progressive, state legislator, and re-gent—charged that Professors Pitman Potter, William G. Rice, and Carl Russell Fish were subjecting their students to "propaganda" in support of these world government agencies. He demanded their dismissal.[138] A journalistic firestorm ensued, while a silent President Frank success-fully countered Cashman's demand simply by ignoring it.

The following December Governor Blaine, who had recently been elected to the U.S. Senate, called on the regents to fire Associate Professor Fred H. MacGregor, a political scientist and the director of the Extension Division's municipal reform bureau. In his role as secretary of the Wisconsin League of Municipalities, MacGregor had published a pamphlet entitled *A Taxation Catechism*, which Blaine claimed was biased and full of "lies." Ever alert for a good scrap, the *Capital Times* carried a number of articles, editorials, and letters to the

[137] *Capital Times*, November 9, 1925.
[138] Ibid., March 12, 1926; *Daily Cardinal*, March 14, 1926.

editor, some of them critical of the governor.[139] President Frank appreciated the seriousness of Blaine's attack and responded with a ringing endorsement of academic freedom, which deserves to be quoted at length:

> As long as I am president of the University of Wisconsin, complete and unqualified academic freedom will not only be accorded to the members of its faculties but will be vigorously defended regardless of the pressure, the power, or the prestige that may accompany any challenge of this inalienable right of scholarship. The University of Wisconsin cannot permit political interests, economic interests, or religious interests to censor the opinions of its teachers without sacrificing its self-respect and destroying its value to the state that supports it.
>
> The university has the right and the duty to require from the members of its faculty scientific accuracy and intellectual honesty in their handling of facts. In their expressions of opinion, the university has no right to require from the members of its faculties conformity to any prevailing theories or policies of the state in particular or of society in general—whether the theories in question be political, economic, social, or religious.
>
> Any member of a faculty of the University of Wisconsin is and must remain as free to agree with or dissent from any political or economic policy of the state of Wisconsin as he is free to agree with or dissent from a religious rite in Liberia.
>
> And as long as I am president of the University of Wisconsin, this complete freedom of thought and expression will be accorded with utter impartiality alike to teachers who entertain conservative opinions and to teachers who entertain radical opinions. The fact that I may think, that an official of the state may think, or that a citizen of the state may think a teacher's opinions wrong-headed or even dangerous will not alter this policy. For the whole of human history presents unanswerable proof that only through the open and unhampered clash of contrary opinions can truth be found.
>
> To put the matter bluntly: A teacher's opinions, however widely they may differ from prevailing policies and beliefs at the moment, cannot, with my consent, be made a subject of university discipline....
>
> The administration of the University can consider the case of Mr. MacGregor only in the light of the charges that Mr. Blaine has made against him of incompetence as a scholar.[140]

The statement was blunt and unequivocal. The fact that the president waited to issue it until after Blaine had vacated the governor's office need not detract from its force. The timing was after all a matter of tactics not principle, and merely illustrated Frank's skill in minimizing

---

[139]*Capital Times*, December 24, 28, and 31, 1926, January 4, 5, 6, and 7, 1927.
[140]*Press Bulletin*, January 19, 1927.

damaging confrontations.

President Frank was particularly eloquent during this period, too, in dealing with a noisy controversy over the Reserve Officer Training Corps program. The issue of University participation in the program was hotly debated throughout the inter-war period, with student activists regularly challenging the ROTC presence on campus. Throughout the fall of 1927, for example, the *Daily Cardinal* sparked a heated campus debate over whether enrollment in ROTC should be voluntary or compulsory or indeed whether the University should sponsor such a militaristic program at all. The *Cardinal* thought not, and seemingly opened its columns to anyone who had something to say on the subject. The controversy attracted the attention of the Chicago *Tribune*, which published highly critical articles about the debate in Madison, claiming the University was indoctrinating its students with unpatriotic pacifist beliefs.[141] At the urging of several deans, following the second attack President Frank defended Wisconsin's commitment to free speech and inquiry at a special all-University convocation in the Stock Pavilion.[142] He told the students:

> You are the beneficiaries of a university that is willing, if need be, to pay the price of open opposition to any person or to any organization, public or private, political, religious, or economic, that might seek to dictate or delimit its search for truth....When a purblind press tries to dragoon you into its own particular brand of swashbuckling by calling you radical or questioning your patriotism, there is little to be gained by insisting upon the redness of your blood or recounting the valor of Wisconsin's sons on battlefields.[143]

The controversy died within a week of his comments, after a *Daily Cardinal* referendum to abolish ROTC lost by a huge 80 to 20 percent margin. Even the *Tribune* had to concede grudgingly that the UW student body seemed "almost" sound.[144]

President Frank's occasional ringing manifestoes did not, of

---

[141]Chicago *Tribune*, November 9 and 22, 1927.

[142]Frank also had issued an earlier statement in defense of the *Daily Cardinal* and the University. *Capital Times*, November 11, 1927.

[143]*Daily Cardinal*, November 23, 1927; *Press Bulletin*, November 30, 1927. On November 25, 1927, the *Capital Times* discussed a resulting Chicago *Tribune* editorial: "Of 'college professor' discussions such as those which Dr. Frank delivered Tuesday the editorial says, 'When he reaches the limit of his applied common sense he tailspins off into voids to which he hopes that the unmistakable nobility of what he thinks will make up for the utter inexplicability of what he says'."

[144]*Daily Cardinal*, November 26 and 30, 1927.

course, cause all problems of partisan politics and threats to academic freedom to vanish. Far from it. While few critics directly challenged his basic assumptions, events often demanded important interpretations. In early 1927, for example, state Senator Sauthoff carried on in the Blaine tradition by ruthlessly attacking Engineering Dean Frederick E. Turneaure for his allegedly anti-progressive behavior as an ex officio member of the state Highway Commission. Agriculture Dean Harry Russell was also a perennial target and worthy opponent of the progressives, who charged that he ran his college according to the conservative agricultural policies of the U.S. Department of Agriculture. Russell regularly faced angry demands that he resign his post, which he finally did in 1930, though perhaps for other reasons. In these cases the criticism involved disputes over policy rather than faculty academic freedom or civil rights, and President Frank chose not to get involved.

In 1928 Frank broadened his view of faculty rights to include the basic citizen right to engage in political activity, issuing a statement approving the partisan activities of Professors Malcolm Sharp and Joseph Russo. The next year Alexander Meiklejohn, a progressive with pronounced socialist leanings, joined with Zona Gale, John Dewey, and others to establish the League for Independent Political Action. In 1930 economics Professor Harold Groves won election to the state assembly with strong progressive and labor backing, and Philip F. La Follette, a part-time lecturer in the Law School, took the governorship. While the president expected UW faculty members to be scrupulously objective in their teaching and scholarship, Frank's view of the Wisconsin Idea included the faculty's right as citizens to engage in partisan political activity and to hold elective office if its demands did not interfere with their University responsibilities.

In January of 1929 Walter J. Kohler was inaugurated as governor, the first stalwart Republican to win that office since the war. Although progressive Republicans viewed him with hostility, Governor Kohler had already earned a solid reputation as a friend of the University through his service as an alumnus and a member of the Board of Regents between 1918 and 1924. He and Glenn Frank established instant rapport, with the president participating prominently in Kohler's inaugural festivities and subsequently socializing regularly with him in the Town and Gown dining club and on the golf course of the exclusive Maple Bluff Country Club.

Kohler's electoral triumph had bitter repercussions, however. His progressive foes, led by youthful Phil La Follette, the younger son of the late senator, and Madison attorney Harold Wilkie, filed a law suit alleging illegal campaign spending in an ultimately unsuccessful effort to have the election overturned. Frank's friendship and association with the governor generated mounting concern among some progressives. William T. Evjue, the acerbic editor of progressive *Capital Times*, concluded toward the end of Kohler's term that the UW president "has been gradually revising his earlier enthusiasms and policies and going over to the side of the old, reactionary group that has dominated the university before he assumed his duties as president."[145]   When Kohler subsequently announced the appointment of three stalwart regents, two of them replacing progressives Daniel Grady and John Cashman, the *Capital Times* mournfully headlined the news: "The Governor Gains Control."[146]   "With the watchful eyes of Messrs. Butler, Mead, and Clausen exercizing supervisory control," Evjue warned a few days later, "there is little likelihood that anything but smug economic views will pierce the class and lecture rooms." No longer would the political science and economics faculty "dare to discuss the implications of the centralization of wealth, monopoly control, the chain bank and chain store, public utility exploitation and other present day evils," he lamented. "The governor has invited reaction and wealth to sit on the knee of old Abe at the top of the Hill."[147]

The fears of Wisconsin progressives were to some extent realized when the new stalwart majority on the Board of Regents voted to rescind the 1925 Grady resolution barring foundation gifts.[148] Lieutenant Governor Henry Huber, a long-time La Follette progressive, angrily declared that the "God of the dollars" was back in control, and Bill Evjue predicted that the University would soon again be passing its "tin cup to monopoly."[149]   Within a week, in fact, Graduate School Dean Charles S. Slichter quietly mounted a campaign to start recouping the losses accrued over the past half-decade.[150]   More eager even than Dean Slichter to regain foundation support, President Frank had already

---

[145]*Capital Times*, February 9, 1930.
[146]Ibid., February 14, 1930.
[147]Ibid., February 16, 1930.
[148]BOR Minutes, March 5, 1930; *Daily Cardinal* and *Capital Times*, March 5, 1930.
[149]*Capital Times*, March 6, 1930.
[150]Charles S. Slichter to Frank, January 25, 1929, Frank Presidential Papers, 4/13/1, box 67; Mark H. Ingraham, *Charles Sumner Slichter: The Golden Vector* (Madison: University of Wisconsin Press, 1972), p. 175. Slichter had consistently favored industrial support of research.

persuaded the regents to approve the creation of an All-University Research Council—consisting of social science, natural science, and associated sub-councils of faculty scholars—to consider all proffered gifts "in terms of the scientific needs of the university and the social needs of the public, and to make appropriate recommendation to the regents respecting the acceptance or rejection of such gift and the manner of administering it."[151] Frank had anticipated the demise of the Grady resolution and evidently believed the new faculty research council could reassure skeptics that the public interest would be protected.

The president also expected the All-University Research Council to help attract renewed foundation support as part of a broad organizational restructuring he had in mind. This became evident in March, 1930, when he distributed for consideration by the faculty an eighteen-page position paper entitled "A Functional Organization of Faculty Forces." Frank proposed to change the names of the University's various faculty "divisions" and "conferences" to "institutes," and further to expand their narrow focus from graduate degree programming to include matters of research and instruction at both the graduate and upper division undergraduate levels. Each of the new institutes would include one of the new research council's sub-councils. Faculty members would retain their departmental and school or college affiliations to satisfy the institution's academic program needs, while simultaneously participating in institute activities so they might more easily function collectively as "coherent guild[s] of scholars."

The University should have, in other words, "an administrative organization chart and an intellectual organization chart." Pointing to the Institute of Human Relations at Yale, the Institute for the Study of Law at Johns Hopkins, the Food Research Institute at Stanford, and the Institute for Research in Social Sciences at North Carolina, the president noted two key advantages of this sort of focussed but interdisciplinary organizational structure. First, the collaborative programs of these institutes had proved appealing to outside funding agencies. Second, "the integration of their personnel is attractive to working scholars." In noting the important advantages of interdisciplinary collaboration, Frank emphasized that his proposal actually called for only a modest "shift in

---

[151]BOR Minutes, January 15, 1930; *Daily Cardinal*, January 16, 1930; *Press Bulletin*, January 22, 1930. Frank and Graduate School Dean Slichter had been discussing this possibility since at least mid-1926. See Slichter to Frank, June 21 and 28, 1926, Frank Presidential Papers, 4/13/1, boxes 15 and 34.

emphasis" at Wisconsin. The introduction of the "institute" plan, he explained, would hardly be more than "a purely practical consideration."[152] After considerable debate the faculty approved the naming of a committee of deans, divisional leaders, and other faculty members to consider the proposal further.[153] Whether the faculty thought the idea too "revolutionary," as Dean Sellery later characterized it, or for other reasons, the deepening economic depression distracted Frank and the University community from serious consideration of the scheme.[154] It would remain for Frank's successor, using a more indirect strategy, to persuade the University faculty to adopt a similar interdisciplinary structure. In any case, the proposed institutes, in conjunction with the research council, constituted Frank's long-delayed response to the Grady resolution. In doing so he effectively affirmed that foundation support might safely sustain the University and its scholarly enterprise *and* benefit society in the process. The president had taken a stand, but in his own time and on his own terms.

University Administration

Frank's administrative responsibilities were demanding. Among the most important and trying were the preparation and defense of the University's biennial budget requests, a complicated process involving multiple levels of approval. Frank's initial effort, for the 1927-29 biennium, spanned nearly eight months and was impressive. He first described the University's needs in a general way in December, 1926, at a meeting of the State Board of Affairs.[155] The president used this forum to begin preparing the public and the legislature for a substantial budget increase, necessitated, in his view, by a growing student body, the demands of the recently expanded medical school program, an enlarged public service effort (including extension and research components), and a badly needed building construction program. The Board of Regents approved Frank's budget request the following month. The next step in the budgetary process occurred in May, 1927, as the legislature's Joint Committee on Finance opened hearings on the

---

[152]UW Faculty Document 360, "A Functional Organization of Faculty Forces," April 7, 1930.

[153]UW Faculty Minutes, April 7, 1930.

[154]Sellery, *Some Ferments at Wisconsin*, p. 51.

[155]*Press Bulletin*, December 15, 1926.

University's request. The *Wisconsin Alumni Magazine* later characterized President Frank's testimony as graceful, calm, and convincing.
"His exposition of the field and function of the University, the sources
of receipts, items of expenditure of the budget, and the building needs
of the University, demonstrated a keen power of analysis and a marvelous understanding of all phases of University activity." The president
used "a vocabulary shorn of all technicality and ambiguity."[156] Leaving
nothing to chance, Frank brought with him a number of colleagues.
The University business manager and comptroller were prepared to
answer technical questions, and members of a special committee—including Regents Wild and Olbrich as well as Carl Johnson, Philip
La Follette, and former Regent Theodore Kronshage—stood ready to
explain other parts of the proposed budget.

The University request languished through much of the summer as
a tumultuous legislative session and a recalcitrant Governor Zimmerman
delayed final action.[157] During July there were many charges and
recriminations but little apparent progress. In the first week of August
the governor publicly accused the legislature of voting a number of
excessively large appropriations in the omnibus state budget bill in an
effort to force his vetoes and political embarrassment. The University
request thus remained in jeopardy. But on August 9, after denying a
number of other appropriations, Zimmerman finally approved the
generous $11 million UW allocation, though reserving the right to delay
certain capital improvements until sufficient funds accumulated in the
state treasury. Frank's hard work had resulted in an impressive 13
percent increase in funding amounting to approximately $1.3 million.[158]
This meant, the delighted president explained, "that 'marching orders'
held in abeyance for the last ten years can now be issued. The State has
done its part in a magnanimous and statesmanlike manner. It now

---

[156]*WAM*, 28 (June, 1927), 281.

[157]Zimmerman, a self-proclaimed progressive, had been elected governor with the support
of the stalwart Republicans against a La Follette-endorsed progressive candidate. As governor,
Zimmerman emphasized moderation and careful fiscal responsibility, which led him into
conflict especially with the progressive-dominated assembly. Neither faction's preferred
candidate, Zimmerman was dropped by the stalwarts in favor of Walter Kohler, who won the
Republican gubernatorial nomination and the election in 1928. See Paul W. Glad, *The History
of Wisconsin*, vol. 5, *War, a New Era, and Depression, 1914-1940* (Madison: State Historical
Society of Wisconsin, 1990), pp. 314-5, 320-1; Robert C. Nesbit, *Wisconsin: A History*,
second edition revised and updated by William F. Thompson (Madison: University of Wisconsin Press, 1973, 1989), pp. 468-9.

[158]*Capital Times*, August 9, 1927.

remains for the University to prove itself worthy of this new note of confidence." The University had succeeded beyond all expectation. Exulted the *Alumni Magazine*:

> The approval of the university budget by the state legislature is regarded throughout the state as a great victory for President Frank, whose straight forward presentation impressed the legislature. The appropriation covered all of the requests of the regents and the president, including an amount for "elbow room," as it was expressed by President Frank in his presentation.[159]

In January of 1929 the *Milwaukee Journal* ran a front-page feature article on "Dr. Glenn Frank, the best lobbyist...the university ever had." According to reporter Fred Sheasby, the president frequently spent his evenings "mingling with the political boys in the hotel lobbies" of Madison's capitol square. Sometimes he motored down with Mrs. Frank, and other times he walked "through the snow and wind, his ears tingling from the weather." Avoiding back-room logrolling, "he moves about shaking hands and chatting as one might meet up with neighbors in most any evening." Frank easily recalled everyone's name, "and greets people with as much warmth as if he were running for something and was in the midst of a campaign. He greets them with derby in hand and a gracious bow, a sparkling gentleman interested in those about him and equally interesting to everybody." Soon he would appear before the legislature's joint finance committee with the 1929-31 biennial budget request. Once again he would avoid talk of figures as much as possible:

> He will give more of a story picture of what the university needs—sketchy, bright and entertaining, for no one in this neck of the woods has a more fascinating play on words. Here comes the value of the acquaintances he makes. Here comes the value of informal handshaking in hotel lobbies.

Even legislators intent on cutting spending at every opportunity were apt to respond generously. "Great is the power of personality, and great the power of words," declared Sheasby, predicting Frank would easily get all the support the University needed. "That is his job. Moreover, the legislature will feel honored in giving it to him."[160]

So it was again on September 4, 1929, when Governor Kohler signed into law a budget that essentially granted the entire University

---

[159]*WAM*, 29 (October, 1927), 9.
[160]*Milwaukee Journal*, January 30, 1929; *Capital Times*, January 31, 1929.

request. Contrary to Fred Sheasby's rosy prediction, however, the journey to this destination had been beset by the hazards and detours usually associated with politics in Wisconsin. Progressives in the senate and assembly, loudly backed by the *Capital Times*, had strenuously resisted Frank's request for improved faculty salaries, demanding a detailed report from the president on faculty outside income. Frank consistently refused to produce this information, which he did not possess and declined to collect. Senator John C. Schumann countered by bringing to light the embarrassingly high income of Dean Harry Russell, whose University salary had amounted to only a modest fraction of his total earnings the previous year. The salary question remained a side issue, however, as the legislature was disposed to approve the University request. Much of the debate centered on the best method of financing it. Not surprisingly, the progressive-dominated assembly resurrected the income surtax idea of the early 1920s, while the more conservative senate refused to consider it.

Ultimately, after much angry debate and protest among legislators, students, faculty, and UW administrators, the legislature agreed to raise tuition significantly for out-of-state students from $124 to $200. This measure, combined with judicious culling of a list of proposed construction projects and the cancellation of an earlier appropriation for a new University library (partly because the regents had been unable to decide whether to put up an addition or construct an entirely new facility), enabled the legislature to approve a budget acceptable to all except some of the students. Throughout the process President Frank remained centrally involved, calling emergency meetings of the regents, cancelling a planned European vacation, spending countless hours downtown lobbying with legislators, and conferring with Governor Kohler. In the end his efforts paid off.

The president's success was neither accidental nor due to his action alone. In keeping with his earliest statements about his administrative style, whenever possible he sought assistance from others. His recruitment of progressive leaders Theodore Kronshage and Philip La Follette to support the 1927 biennial budget request helped produce success that year. He turned to La Follette again in 1929, when the University's budget request seemed in jeopardy. La Follette, who had mixed feelings about the president, reported to his vacationing wife: "Glenn Frank was in yesterday. His University Budget is all up in the air, and it rather looks as if it may get caught in a jam between the two houses in a fight over the method of raising money for it. If it fails, the

University will be in a tight place."[161]   Frank regularly sought the advice and counsel of Regent Michael B. Olbrich, a progressive activist with wide contacts in Madison legal and business circles and in the legislature.   With Olbrich's help he managed to maintain cordial relations with both the La Follette and Blaine factions of the state's progressive movement and with the stalwart Kohler administration.   The appointment of Frank Holt to the Frank administration was a master stroke in public relations.   The new registrar had extensive contacts with professional schoolmen throughout the state, and he provided guidance to President Frank in his lobbying and in his leadership of an influential support group, the Association of Wisconsin Presidents and Deans. Another key associate for Frank was engineering Professor J.D. Phillips, the University's business manager since 1921.   He was consistently a source of sage counsel and advice, and his quiet professionalism and competence won the respect of regents, legislators, and faculty alike.   No one in the University possessed such detailed knowledge of the institution as Phillips, and Frank regularly deferred to his wise judgment on fiscal and budget policy matters.[162]

Frank's record with respect to educational administration was mixed.   No academic himself, he tended to defer to his faculty colleagues whenever possible.   This certainly was the case with Alexander Meiklejohn's Experimental College, as were the president's deferential dealings with the deans of Agriculture, Engineering, Law, Medicine, and the Graduate School, all of whom were in office when Frank arrived on campus.   In appointing Chester Snell to head the Extension Division, the president recruited a man who seemed to share his enthusiasm for a broadened University outreach effort.   But as with

---

[161]Philip F. La Follette to Isen La Follette, August 7, 1929, P.F. La Follette Papers, box 134, SHSW.

[162]James David Phillips (1868-1949) served as an assistant professor and then professor of engineering at UW from 1902 through July, 1921, when he became acting business manager. The regents appointed him business manager, effective July 1, 1923. He retained the position until retiring in 1938.   He was a founder and first treasurer of the Memorial Union Building Committee beginning in 1919, and was a founder of the Wisconsin University Building Corporation. The faculty memorial resolution on the death of Phillips characterizes his service through the trying years of the 1920s and 30s: "Throughout those diverse troubles, J.D. Phillips' excellent judgment and his business acumen helped immeasurabl[y] to guide the affairs of the University along sound lines of administrative policy.   He believed that the function of the business office is to serve the educational departments of the University, and he put that philosophy into actual practice in all his administrative decisions.   His effective leadership promoted a spirit of cooperation among Regents, faculty, and administrative staff."   UW Faculty Document 927, December 5, 1949.

the other deans, Frank refrained from interfering with Snell's activities. Harry Russell's troubles with the progressive politicians in the late twenties were well publicized, and he eventually tendered his resignation in 1930. Whether Frank encouraged Russell's departure is unknown, although he quietly explored possible successors as early as 1928. There is no record, however, of any presidential displeasure with Dean Russell. In 1928 Frank privately and in a general sort of way urged young Philip La Follette to succeed Law Dean Harry Richards, who had given no public indication he intended to leave his post. After Richards' unexpected death the next year, Frank more formally offered the deanship to La Follette, who declined in favor of a political career. By the end of the decade the University administration included only one new dean recruited by President Frank, but vacancies in Agriculture and Law offered him further opportunities to reshape the University administration.

President Frank's most significant and enduring administrative personnel problem involved George Clarke Sellery, Birge's hand-picked successor as letters and science dean. Neither man tried very hard to accommodate the other. The scholarly yet crusty Sellery, who as Birge's protégé may have been disappointed when passed over for the presidency, early viewed Frank as a shallow publicist who was out of his depth in a major university. Sellery's memoirs may be read as a comprehensive and sometimes bitter refutation of the Frank administration by one who saw no need to smooth the young president's path.[163] One especially revealing passage describes how the recently arrived president entertained Sellery for dinner and then proudly showed him a dossier containing reports on prominent University, civic, and political leaders. Sellery's own unflattering portrait offended the dean, as did the thought that Frank would hire a detective to gather such information. Sellery kept his feelings to himself, however, and missed a crucial opportunity to clarify his almost certainly mistaken assumption about the document's origin. In all probability Frank knew nothing about the origin of the report, which a well-meaning east coast alumnus had apparently sent to him as an unsolicited guide to the University and Wisconsin political scene. Still, the episode helped to sour Dean Sellery permanently on the youthful president. For his part, Frank persisted in publicly attacking the dean's college at least indirectly in his unabashed and uncritical advocacy of Meiklejohn's and his own views about liberal

---

[163]See Sellery, *Some Ferments At Wisconsin*, pp. 51-5 and passim.

education. Behind the scenes, moreover, on numerous occasions the president uncharacteristically intervened in the internal administration of the college to a degree unknown in the other units of the University. Frank's well-publicized but aborted plan to fire Sellery in 1929 was only one of many unwise slights committed by the president against his influential senior dean.

Trouble Ahead

On October 9, 1929, Frank's patron and major supporter on the Board of Regents, Michael B. Olbrich, hanged himself. Despondent over financial problems and in poor health, Olbrich's self-destructive act was a sign that trouble also lay ahead for President Frank and the University. "He was my friend," mourned the president in a moving eulogy.

> And I am still too deeply moved by his passing to weigh in words the richness and depth of his life as I felt its impact upon mine. It was but a little more than four years ago that he walked into my life bearing...an invitation to me to throw in my life with the life of this Commonwealth that he lived in and loved. That May morning marked the beginning of a relationship that was, from the start, more than an official relationship. I say again, he was my friend.

Over the years, Frank recalled, the two men had spent many hours together before the winter fire, with Olbrich's "informed and incisive mind play[ing] upon the problems that vex our time in church and state and school." In the president's view, Olbrich was "an authentic liberal," whose convictions rested upon "three profound convictions":

> He believed that life and society should be directed by the conclusions of intelligence. He believed that, without freedom of thought and expression, intelligence would never become the controlling force in our social order. And he believed that life and the social order should be kept experimental, free from the blight of finality and dogmatism. Of such liberals and of such liberalism is the kingdom of a creative civilization![164]

Because Frank shared his friend's convictions, with Olbrich's passing went some of the vitality of their vision for the University.

---

[164]Glenn Frank, "Michael Balthasar Olbrich, 1881-1929," *WAM*, 31 (November, 1929), 56. See also *Capital Times*, October 10, 1929; *Daily Cardinal*, October 11, 1929.

Less than a fortnight later the utter collapse of the stock market made clear that the Frank administration was about to enter a new and less friendly environment. "One brokerage house crashed with the fall," reported the shaken *Daily Cardinal* on October 30. "All Wall street was thrown in a state of panic by the crushing force of the millions lost. Police guards were thrown around the exchange." Economics Professor William Kiekhofer called the fall an "inevitable stabilization" but predicted that stocks soon would assume their "normal values." Less convinced was Governor Kohler who warned a few weeks later that because of declining state revenues he might have to delay funding for construction of the recently approved Mechanical Engineering Building.[165] By December, conditions had deteriorated to the point where the *Cardinal* charged Kohler with callously raising tuition, refusing faculty salary raises, and holding up several building projects. "Has the business administration become political?" asked the editors. "Is a big general fund on election day more important than a healthy support of the state university?"[166] President Frank recognized the genuinely precarious economic situation, however, and publicly supported Kohler's actions.[167] Shortly before Christmas the Union Board sponsored the first of many campus-based charity programs to assist a growing number of hard-pressed students.[168] The great depression was under way.

Declining social and economic conditions increasingly absorbed Frank's attention. He worked effectively with Governor Kohler to arrange the release of state building funds. At the same time he offered his own interpretation of the economic collapse. He told a meeting of contractors that unwise mergers had caused the business slump.[169] In March he tried to explain the growing unemployment problem in an article for the *Cardinal*, and a week later outlined problems of the "machine civilization" before a graduate student dinner.[170] In May he predicted a major urban-rural schism and denied the utility of simplistic moral reform efforts.[171] The next month he discussed "business statesmanship" before a convention of commercial secretaries and told

---

[165]*Daily Cardinal*, November 23, 1929.
[166]Ibid., December 6, 1929.
[167]*Capital Times*, December 7, 1929.
[168]*Daily Cardinal*, December 14, 1929.
[169]*Capital Times* and *Daily Cardinal*, February 14, 1930.
[170]*Daily Cardinal*, March 16 and 25, 1930.
[171]Ibid., May 10, 1930; *Press Bulletin*, May 21, 1930.

farmers that to survive they must organize financial cooperatives.[172] After a summer that included charges and denials of communist influences on campus, Frank encouraged his Freshman Welcome listeners to liberate themselves from the tyranny of the "crowd mind."[173] If any doubt remained as to the growing dominance of the depression on campus affairs, the president's annual address to the faculty in October, 1930, settled the matter. His topic was "the economic situation and its relation to the University."[174] This would remain the major underlying theme for the remainder of Glenn Frank's years at Wisconsin.

[172]*Capital Times*, June 17 and 20, 1930.
[173]*Daily Cardinal*, September 25, 1930.
[174]UW Faculty Minutes, October 6, 1930.

3.

Camelot by the Lake

By far the most important and controversial of Glenn Frank's educational ventures was the Experimental College, which operated for five years between 1927 and 1932. It remains today the most commonly cited example of Wisconsin's contributions to curricular change and educational innovation. As such the experiment deserves extended treatment as the centerpiece of the Frank renaissance. Its launching reflected the heady atmosphere and bright promise of the early Frank years; its demise foreshadowed the end of the Frank era at Wisconsin.

Even before he arrived in Madison in the fall of 1925 to take up his presidential office, Frank had decided to undertake a bold reform of undergraduate education. Through his initiative once again the University of Wisconsin would demonstrate its national leadership. While editor of the *Century Magazine*, he had revealed his interest in educational reform, calling for curricular change and publishing articles by progressive educators critical of current instructional methods. The challenge for professors, he declared, was to teach their students not just *what* to think, but *how* to think: "the main business of the university is to rid men's brains of the ancestral ghosts that haunt them."[1] Decrying the intellectual "hodge podge" and lack of focus in most undergraduate education, Frank joined the chorus of those critics who lamented the excessive freedom of the elective system introduced by Harvard University in the late nineteenth century. American colleges and universities, he told a reporter shortly after arriving in Madison, were "intellectual department stores" and "charnel houses where cre-

---

[1] Glenn Frank, "Three Pillars of Society: A Free University, a Pacific Church, a Realistic State," *Century Magazine*, 108 (August, 1924), 570.

ative education dies."[2] The new president clearly intended the hallmark of his administration to be curricular and pedagogical reform, with Frank himself recognized as an inspirational leader of the progressive education movement nationally.

"A Sense of the Human Process as a Whole"

Of the various critics of American higher education, Frank was most influenced by the controversial reform president of Amherst College, Alexander Meiklejohn. Born in Rochdale, England, the son of a Scottish textile worker, Meiklejohn and his family had emigrated to Rhode Island in 1880 when he was eight. After receiving A.B. and A.M. degrees from Brown University and a Ph.D. degree from Cornell University in 1897, Meiklejohn returned to his alma mater to teach philosophy. At Brown he quickly became one of the most popular members of the faculty. Although he was an inspiring speaker, no matter how large Meiklejohn's classes he rarely lectured, preferring to generate dialogue and discussion through his unrivaled talent for socratic teaching. Small in frame and stature but a champion of physical fitness and competitive sports, Meiklejohn impressed students with his near-professional athletic skill, especially in cricket, soccer, ice hockey, bowling, tennis, and squash. In 1901 his popularity in class and out led to a part-time appointment as dean of students, followed quickly by promotion to full professor. Increasingly his reputation as a master teacher and his ideas about educational reform gained attention throughout New England and even the nation. Looking for a leader who could revitalize their faltering institution, in 1912 the trustees of Amherst College elected Alexander Meiklejohn as president. He was just forty years old, eager for the challenge of reforming a rather stuffy and complacent small liberal arts college.

Amherst had been founded in 1821 as a stronghold of puritan orthodoxy in western Massachusetts. For most of the nineteenth century the college saw itself as the conservative defender of the faith in opposition to Harvard's growing secularism and unitarian apostasy. Amherst was known for the substantial proportion of its graduates who entered the clergy, often for service in foreign missions. By the early twentieth century, however, some Amherst faculty and students were questioning

---

[2]*Daily Cardinal*, October 13, 1925; *Capital Times*, October 26, 1925.

the traditional emphasis on classical learning and piety, and the college seemed ready for a new educational vision.[3] This Meiklejohn quickly set about to provide. In his inaugural address the new president called for a radical reform of the curriculum to make Amherst a citadel of more relevant learning, a course of study "fully and unreservedly intellectual" but one "unified and dominated by a single interest, a single purpose,—that of so understanding human life as to be ready and equipped for the practice of it."[4]

For Amherst the Meiklejohn vision meant adding offerings in the social sciences and contemporary social problems—he created a new freshman course on "Social and Economic Institutions"—and revitalizing the teaching of the humanities through a more integrated and interdisciplinary curriculum. To speed these changes the new president brought in younger faculty members who shared his commitment to integrated learning and socratic dialogue. By 1922-23 half of the Amherst faculty had been appointed by Meiklejohn, and their classes were attracting three-quarters of the students. Inevitably a rift developed between the new Meiklejohn men and the older faculty, most of whom felt a proprietary interest in traditional Amherst ways. Although as at Brown Meiklejohn was immensely popular with the students, he was unfortunately more a visionary prophet than a tidy or tactful administrator. His ideas and innovations gradually polarized the Amherst faculty and aroused the alumni, some of whom feared Meiklejohn's vaguely socialistic ideas about contemporary issues. While supportive of his educational reforms, the trustees eventually lost confidence in the president over his misrepresentation of faculty views and his mismanagement of his personal finances, including his frequent overdrawing of his salary—by a full year at one point! Reluctantly, in June of 1923 the board asked for Meiklejohn's resignation, an action bitterly opposed by the great mass of the student body and many of the younger faculty. In protest, thirteen Amherst seniors refused their degrees at the 1923 Commencement ceremony and eight members of the faculty—loyal Meiklejohn men—resigned. The affair attracted national attention, mostly unfavorable to the Amherst trustees, who chose to keep silent about the varied reasons for their dissatisfaction with their controversial

---

[3]See Thomas Le Duc, *Piety and Intellect at Amherst College, 1865-1912* (New York: Columbia University Press, 1946).

[4]Alexander Meiklejohn, "Inaugural Address," October 16, 1912, in Norman Foerster, Frederick A. Manchester, and Karl Young, *Essays for College Men: Education, Science, and Art* (New York: Henry Holt, 1913), pp. 28-59.

president.[5] After visiting Amherst and interviewing trustees, faculty, and students, Walter Lippmann summed up the college's dilemma admirably:

> Amherst has lost a fine educator and a great spiritual leader of youth because he was an unsuccessful leader of men. He did magnificently with students. He failed lamentably with the grown ups. He could inspire but he could not manage. He was lots of Woodrow Wilson and none of Lloyd George.[6]

Glenn Frank was one of those who saw Meiklejohn as a martyred prophet. More than a year before Meiklejohn's troubles became a national cause célèbre, Frank had considered publishing an article by the embattled Amherst leader, perhaps the piece calling for unity of the undergraduate curriculum that appeared later that year in the *New Republic*.[7] Within weeks of Meiklejohn's dismissal, Frank hastily negotiated a contract for a book of the Amherst president's addresses on education, published later in the year under the title *Freedom and the College*.[8] He also accepted an article by Meiklejohn for the *Century Magazine*. Pointedly asking "To Whom Are We Responsible?" and with his own recent experience at Amherst clearly in mind, in it Meiklejohn argued that the faculty and presidents of colleges and universities should not be viewed as responsible to the students, parents,

---

[5]See Lucien Price, *Prophets Unawares: The Romance of an Idea* (New York: Century, 1924); *New York Times*, June 17, 20, and 23, 1923; Boston *Herald*, June 24, 1923; *New York Herald*, June 24, 1923; Robert Morss Lovett, "Meiklejohn of Amherst," *New Republic*, 35 (July 4, 1923), 146-8; John Merriman Gaus, "The Issues at Amherst," *Nation*, 117 (July 4, 1923), 12; "The Meiklejohn Case," *Public Affairs* (August, 1923), 16; Walter R. Agard to Frank L. Babbott, June 17, 1923, Alexander Meiklejohn Papers, box 1, SHSW; John Gaus to Walter Lippmann, June 29, 1923, ibid., box 53; Thomas Le Duc, "Alexander Meiklejohn," *Dictionary of American Biography*, Supplement 7 for 1961-65, John A. Garrity, ed. (New York: Scribner's, 1981), pp. 523-4.

[6]Walter Lippmann, "The Fall of President Meiklejohn," New York *World*, June 24, 1923.

[7]Paul Kennaday to Alexander Meiklejohn, March 31, 1922, Meiklejohn Papers, box 8; Meiklejohn, "The Unity of the Curriculum," *New Republic*, 32 (October 25, 1922), 2-3.

[8]See Glenn Frank to Meiklejohn, June 18, July 3, 11, and 14, 1923; Joseph Anthony to Meiklejohn, June 20, 1923; Lyman B. Sturgis to Meiklejohn, July 13, 1923; Meiklejohn to Frank, July 2, 5, 9, 13, and 25, 1923; Meiklejohn to Sturgis, July 16, 1923, Meiklejohn Papers, box 8; Alexander Meiklejohn, *Freedom and the College* (New York: Century, 1923).

public, donors, alumni, or even to their institution's trustees except in a narrow legal sense; rather they should be held answerable only to the ideals of the academy—the search for truth. Frank was impressed with Meiklejohn's idealistic but iconoclastic views, telling him his argument went "directly to the heart of an important matter."[9] Fully accepting the Meiklejohn view of his dismissal as an academic freedom issue, Frank arranged for the Century Company to publish a very pro-Meiklejohn book on the Amherst schism the following year.[10]

During the fall of 1924 the former Amherst president announced that he was trying to raise funds—which he estimated at $3 million—to launch a new experimental liberal arts college under his leadership. He approached financier Bernard Baruch with no success, and got no more than encouragement from Abraham Flexner, the secretary of the Carnegie Foundation for the Advancement of Teaching.[11] More promising was the support of Herbert Croly, the editor of the *New Republic*, who had followed Meiklejohn's career closely and supportively. Croly offered to use his influence with the ailing Mrs. Willard Straight, whose fortune bankrolled the liberal magazine. Mrs. Straight was willing to provide a small planning grant, but she and her financial advisors insisted on a concrete plan for establishing the new college before considering major funding.[12] Glenn Frank was recruited into the Croly-Meiklejohn group, which also included the prominent journalist Mark Sullivan and Professor Alvin Johnson of the New School for Social Research.

To attract national support for the proposed Meiklejohn venture, in January, 1925, Frank published another Meiklejohn article in the *Century Magazine*. In it the former Amherst president called for a bold

---

[9]Frank to Meiklejohn, June 2, 1923, Meiklejohn Papers, box 8; Meiklejohn, "To Whom Are We Responsible: A Memorandum on the Freedom of Teachers," *Century Magazine*, 106 (September, 1923), 643-50.

[10]Price, *Prophets Unawares*.

[11]Meiklejohn to Bernard M. Baruch, draft, n.d.; Abraham Flexner to Meiklejohn, November 14, 1924, Meiklejohn Papers, box 8.

[12]Herbert Croly to Meiklejohn [ca. November, 1924]; Anna Bogue to Meiklejohn, December 2, 1924, ibid.

next step in higher education, the creation of a new experimental liberal arts college devoted to the socratic teaching of an integrated general education curriculum. The new college should be small, Meiklejohn said, with not more than twenty-five or thirty faculty members and perhaps three hundred students. Students would be expected to learn for themselves; "we should like to substitute for lecturing a scheme of tutorial instruction." He suggested that the first two years be devoted to the broad study of two different civilizations: in the freshman year an examination of the society of ancient Athens in the golden age of Aristotle and Pericles, and for contrast in the sophomore year the investigation of a more recent civilization such as that of modern Britain or the United States. "Out of these two views of western civilization, first at its beginnings and then at its next to the latest point," Meiklejohn explained, "the student would get a sense of the human process as a whole." Furthermore, since the faculty could not be expected to be scholarly experts on every aspect of these two civilizations, students and faculty would be learning together, creating a closely knit academic community in the process. Meiklejohn admitted he had not fully worked out his thoughts about the course of study in the third and fourth years, indicating merely that it should continue the emphasis on general education while allowing for some concentration in "special studies" or "subjects." The chief defect of modern undergraduate education, he argued, was its almost accidental content resulting from the excessive freedom of the elective system. The new college would assure "that young men and women think about the right things and think about them well." [13]

Meiklejohn's vision of a new experimental college drew a good deal of favorable editorial comment across the country, reflecting the current public interest in curricular reform and especially in the general education content of the first two years of undergraduate study. It also attracted some applications for employment and offers of available real estate. Believing that philanthropists would need something more concrete than the general sketch in the *Century* article, however, the Croly group kept pressing Meiklejohn, first privately and then publicly in a *New Republic* editorial, to spell out his ideas more fully—to provide something specific, which, one of the group told him bluntly, should "be in the nature of a college catalogue with running commentary on the

---

[13]Meiklejohn, "A New College: Notes on a Next Step in Higher Education," *Century Magazine*, 109 (January, 1925), 312-20.

various items."[14]   Never much interested in administrative detail, Meiklejohn proved unwilling or unable to draft a concrete plan of how he hoped to recruit and pay his faculty, attract and house his students, and implement the specifics of his new curriculum.[15]   Although he continued to dream of the new college, by the spring of 1925 Croly, Frank, and his other backers had given up hope of raising an endowment for the venture.

"I Think I Have Found a Way"

At this juncture Glenn Frank accepted the presidency of the University of Wisconsin. Almost immediately he began to think about how his new situation might advance the Meiklejohn vision of a fresh approach to undergraduate education. Even before moving to Madison, during the summer of 1925 Frank visited Meiklejohn in New England and explored with him the possibility of the latter's accepting a special professorship at Wisconsin, in order, he said, to create "a new sort of college, where students would form a community, and would really learn 'to understand,' by means of liberal education." Both men agreed that the scheme would require time to work out arrangements with the Wisconsin regents and faculty.[16]   Over the next several months while President Frank was settling into his new University routine, he kept up a steady stream of letters, telegrams, and had at least two meetings with Meiklejohn away from Madison to continue their secret negotiations.

Appointing a professor, Frank quickly discovered, was not a simple presidential prerogative. In early November he wired his friend not to come for a scheduled campus visit: "Absence of certain regents for coming week and an unusual budget situation make it impossible for me to get financial decision and conclude other administrative

---

[14]See, for example, Frank to Meiklejohn, December 17, 1924; Croly to Meiklejohn, December 24, 1924; Charles P. Howland to Meiklejohn, January 2, 1924 [1925]; Alvin Johnson to Meiklejohn, January 7, 1925, Meiklejohn Papers, box 8; "Dr. Meiklejohn Proposes," *New Republic*, 41 (January 28, 1925), 246-8.

[15]Meiklejohn did not respond to the *New Republic*'s call for a detailed plan for more than a year, long after Croly and Frank had abandoned their efforts to raise funds for the scheme and after Frank had recruited him for a similar venture at Wisconsin. Even then, his plan was nearly as general as that presented in his 1925 *Century* article. Meiklejohn, "A New College," *New Republic*, 46 (April 14, 1926), 215-8.

[16]Frank to Meiklejohn, telegram, August 27, 1925, Meiklejohn Papers, box 32; Meiklejohn to Frank, August 30, 1925, Frank Presidential Papers, 4/13/1, box 10, UA; *Capital Times*, May 10, 1927.

arrangements that must be determined in advance of our action. It would be useless for you to come for a day now for final action can not be taken this week."[17] The problem was partly financial, for Frank had discovered there was no provision in the University budget for a high salaried special professorship of the sort he had discussed with Meiklejohn. "To date have not found way to handly [*sic*] more than full professorship beginning second semester," he wired Meiklejohn on November 13. "Could you afford to take professorship second semester pending my other arrangements."[18]

The question seems somewhat odd, for Meiklejohn since leaving Amherst had held no regular position and in fact had been reduced to earning an uncertain and even precarious living by lecturing and writing. Frank's problem was nevertheless more complex than it might appear. In their discussions in the summer of 1925 Frank had promised Meiklejohn a special high-salaried professorship befitting both his status as a former college president as well as his intended role as the director of a new undergraduate educational experiment. Unfamiliar with Wisconsin salaries, Frank had evidently mentioned the figure of $10,000, half his own presidential salary and allowances but far above the regular UW faculty scale. Once in Madison Frank discovered he had neither the funds nor faculty and regent approval for the position, the salary, or the program. Meiklejohn's response indicated the former Amherst president understood Frank's dilemma. "My guess is," he speculated shrewdly, "that the matter has gotten into a position in which faculty action is needed, and that faculty action is slow if not reluctant." Meiklejohn indicated he might be willing to accept a lower professorial salary for a time but expressed unwillingness to hold a regular faculty appointment teaching philosophy "while the wider arrangement is still pending." It was clear that Meiklejohn's chief interest was not teaching philosophy but curricular reform.[19] "Every day my enthusiasm grows," Frank responded, "but I have a very difficult financial situation and also want to proceed so that the work will have all possible backing."[20]

To assure "all possible backing," Frank decided to make use of a suggestion in the annual report of the faculty's University Committee

---

[17]Frank to Meiklejohn, telegram, November 3, 1925, Meiklejohn Papers, box 32, and Frank Presidential Papers, 4/13/1, box 10.

[18]Frank to Meiklejohn, telegram, November 13, 1925, and Meiklejohn Papers, box 32.

[19]Meiklejohn to Frank, November 14, 1925, ibid.

[20]Frank to Meiklejohn, telegram, November 27, 1925, ibid., and Frank Presidential Papers, 4/13/1, box 10.

for 1924-25. Noting the recent recommendation of the University's Board of Visitors calling for improved undergraduate instruction, the prestigious executive committee of the general faculty expressed concern about "the large courses of the first two years, in which it is claimed that the students do not get as good teaching as is reasonably possible to give." It therefore recommended that the new administration appoint an "All-University Commission" to study the "problems of articulation of the University in its several parts, but in particular to study problems of improvement of instruction and more helpful contacts between students and faculty." The general faculty routinely approved this pious recommendation for a study commission at its meeting on November 2, 1925, not yet aware of Frank's plan for a new educational unit.[21]

Frank discussed how to implement the commission scheme with Meiklejohn when the latter visited him in Madison briefly over the weekend of November 28-29, 1925. The commission would be, the president saw, a convenient vehicle for winning faculty approval of Meiklejohn's reform scheme. It would thus be vital for Meiklejohn to participate in its work. To Frank's undoubted surprise and dismay, his friend now raised new concerns. Meiklejohn was willing to begin his appointment with the coming spring semester, but he did not want to teach philosophy. Instead he proposed that he be assigned to work full-time for the commission in drawing up a plan for curricular reform involving tutorial instruction. "In that case," he suggested, "I would want to go to Oxford and Cambridge and study during term time just

---

[21]UW Faculty Document 273, University Committee, "Annual Report for 1924-25," November 2, 1925, UA. The Report of the Board of Visitors was sent to individual regents and presumably to President-elect Frank on July 2, 1925. Among other suggestions for improving teaching, the Board of Visitors called attention to an experiment at the University of Minnesota to teach a limited number of freshmen in small classes "that dove-tail together the fundamentals of the various natural sciences and social sciences with sufficient historical background to make them intelligible, and to give a basis for their interpretation." M.E. McCaffrey to Regents, July 2, 1925, enclosing Board of Visitors, "Annual Report for 1924-25," June 20, 1925, BOR Papers, 1/1/3, box 39, UA, and BOV Papers, 2/1/1, box 1, UA. L&S Dean George C. Sellery later speculated that President Frank himself was responsible for the idea of an "All-University Commission," since the title seemed decidedly not UW language. Years later while writing his memoirs about the period, Sellery asked Professor Paul F. Clark, the acting chairman of the University Committee in 1925, where the idea of the commission had originated. Clark could not recall, but remembered that he had had a number of conferences with President Frank while writing the report. Clark agreed that the term All-University Commission "wasn't our verbiage." Sellery, *Some Ferments at Wisconsin, 1901-1947: Memories and Reflections* (Madison: University of Wisconsin Press, 1960), pp. 10-1.

how they do it all—in detail."[22]

Meanwhile, other players were getting into the game. Probably at Frank's prompting, on December 2 Professor E.B. McGilvary, the canny chairman of the Department of Philosophy, wrote inquiring if Meiklejohn would accept an offer of a professorship of philosophy at a salary of $6,000, teaching two lecture courses and a seminar. "The Dean generally expects a professor to give about ten hours a week to class-room work," he noted, "but I have no doubt that suitable adjustments could be made in this matter if you would come."[23] (The proposed $6,000 salary would put Meiklejohn on a par with McGilvary himself, and well ahead of the other senior members of the philosophy department.) Meiklejohn was nonplussed to receive an offer whose salary and expected service were so out of keeping with his discussions with Frank. "Position becoming exceedingly difficult," he wired the president. "Can we not get whole situation in hand and come to decision."[24] Frank's return telegram was reassuring:

> Suggest you wire McGilvary you are interested but would like conference with him and me before giving definite answer. I have almost completed arrangements for creation of three distinguished professorships at special salaries. My plan is to allot one of these to you if you agree. We must then decide in conference whether to create policy commission at once or defer that until a local faculty commission has spent next semester on a preliminary study. Maybe a semester of residence and teaching prior to specific work on curriculum would solidify support and hasten results.[25]

Meiklejohn accordingly assured McGilvary that "the teaching of philosophy appeals to me with very great force now," and suggested a meeting "with all of you who are concerned in the matter" in order that "we all make sure that we are agreed about our arrangements."[26] Writing to President Frank the same day, he expressed relief over the

---

[22]Meiklejohn to Frank, Sunday [November 29, 1925], received December 2, 1925, Frank Presidential Papers, 4/13/1, box 10.

[23]E.B. McGilvary to Meiklejohn, December 2, 1925, ibid.; UW Budget, 1925-27, UA.

[24]Meiklejohn to Frank, telegram, December 6, 1925, Frank Presidential Papers, 4/13/1, box 10, and Meiklejohn Papers, box 32.

[25]Frank to Meiklejohn, telegram, December 6, 1925, Meiklejohn Papers, box 32. Frank's initial draft of this wire specified "special salaries from eight to ten thousand," a commitment he evidently decided to omit in the telegram as sent. Frank Presidential Papers, 4/13/1, box 10.

[26]Meiklejohn to McGilvary, December 8, 1925, Frank Presidential Papers, 4/13/1, box 10. Meiklejohn sent Frank a copy of his response to McGilvary.

clarification of McGilvary's unexpected initiative and appreciation for the proposed special professorship, but observed, "I gather from your telegram that the immediate appointment of a commission *with me in charge* seems to you inadvisable." Skilled in the ways of academic bargaining, even from a weak hand, Meiklejohn noted he had recently received a new proposal to establish "The College" and urged a quick resolution of the arrangements for a Wisconsin appointment, whatever his immediate responsibilities. "But the first thing is, of course, the permanent arrangement and I think it will be well for all of us, deans, heads, professors, et al if we can get it settled. I know it will be good for me."[27] Frank's response was unequivocal. "I think you are entirely safe in turning down all other proposals," he promptly wired, "with full assurance that the special professorship at special salary will be open to you beginning next semester....We can make this the most thrilling adventure in America."[28]

President Frank's more immediate adventure involved selling the high-priced Meiklejohn appointment to the regents and the University community. McGilvary made clear the philosophy department's expectation that Professor Meiklejohn would cover its general course on the history of philosophy and provide specialized courses on Locke, Berkeley, Hume, and Kant.[29] Even after a quick visit to Madison on December 17, Meiklejohn continued to insist that he should be free of any teaching responsibilities for the spring semester while he worked out the plan for curricular reform. Frank grew increasingly exasperated over his friend's new coyness and inability to appreciate the delicate political problems facing the president. Above all, the success of their curricular reform scheme would require careful "internal preparation," the president wired Meiklejohn the day after Christmas. "I want no beating of drums until company is really ready to march. Trust my judgment on this."[30] Meiklejohn continued to hold out for a leave, at one point even raising the unlikely threat that he might not come if it were not granted, but Frank remained adamant. Meiklejohn, he insisted, needed to be in Madison, actively teaching while he played a leading part in the study commission's review of undergraduate

---

[27]Meiklejohn to Frank, December 8, 1925, ibid. Emphasis in original.
[28]Frank to Meiklejohn, telegram, December 11, 1925, Meiklejohn Papers, box 32, and a copy dated December 10, 1925, in Frank Presidential Papers, 4/13/1, box 10.
[29]McGilvary to Frank, December 10, 1925, Frank Presidential Papers, 4/13/1, box 10.
[30]Frank to Meiklejohn, telegram, December 26, 1925, Meiklejohn Papers, box 32, and Frank Presidential Papers, 4/13/1, box 10.

education during the spring semester. "When we talked this summer there was no suggestion of a half-year's wait before light teaching schedule began," Frank reminded his friend. "At any moment plans for policy study may change and you should be on the ground."[31]

The issue of Meiklejohn's immediate responsibilities remained unresolved up to the time he arrived in Madison on January 20 for a visit with the Franks and a meeting with the Board of Regents. For the occasion Frank had spelled out for his friend his plans for the grand Wisconsin experiment. The letter may have been written as much to create a record as to persuade Meiklejohn, for it was the first comprehensive statement of the president's intentions and expectations. "I think I have found a way to create and sustain an 'experimental college of liberal arts' inside the University," Frank declared. "I am concerned that the University of Wisconsin shall provide for the higher education of the United States the first really experimental laboratory of higher education." Contrary to Meiklejohn's hope, the venture would not be a wholly separate college, as this would require a multi-million dollar endowment. Instead a cross-section of the regular student body—"say one hundred students, not all superior students"—would live together in one dormitory so as to give a residential character to the experiment and would be taught by "a small staff of five or six specially selected professors," who were not only experts in some field but also "men of general scholarship and broad culture." Because of the small size of the experimental group the faculty would have "complete freedom to set up a wholly new curriculum and wholly new teaching methods without any regard whatever to prevailing academic traditions." Frank suggested that a parallel group of one hundred students taking the regular curriculum be studied as a control group to evaluate the value and effectiveness of the experimental curriculum and pedagogy. This experimental college need not mean "the indefinite postponement of fairly prompt and far-reaching readjustments in the regular college procedure," the president reassured Meiklejohn. On the contrary, "I am confident that such an experimental laboratory set up inside one of our great universities will more quickly and effectively provide leadership for the whole system of higher education in America

---

[31]Meiklejohn to Frank, telegram, December 27, 1925, Frank Presidential Papers, 4/13/1, box 10; Frank to Meiklejohn, telegram, December 31, 1925, Meiklejohn Papers, box 32; Meiklejohn to Frank, January 4, 1926, Glenn Frank Papers, Northeast Missouri State University, Kirksville; Frank to Meiklejohn, telegram, January 11, 1926, Meiklejohn Papers, box 32, and Frank Presidential Papers, 4/13/1, box 10.

than would a separate experimental college."[32] These plans were not, however, shared with anyone in Madison as yet.

On January 23, 1926, President Frank proudly announced the appointment of Alexander Meiklejohn as the first Brittingham Professor of Philosophy, holding a new chair funded by the estate of the late Thomas E. Brittingham, a wealthy lumberman and former University regent. Frank described Meiklejohn as "one of the great and gifted teachers of this generation" from whom the University could "expect productive scholarship and provocative teaching." Press comment about the appointment was favorable, speculating that the former Amherst president would very likely play a leading role in curricular change at the University.[33] Referring to the still-smoldering controversy over the Board of Regents' recent Grady resolution banning gifts from private foundations, in praising the Meiklejohn appointment the *Capital Times* was careful to make a rather strained distinction between the Brittingham Trust and other private philanthropies such as the Rockefeller Foundation.[34] In view of the constraints of the regular University budget, the availability of the Brittingham funds was highly fortuitous for Frank. Brittingham had died in 1924, establishing in his will a family-controlled trust for the benefit of the University. Frank's decision to obtain Brittingham funds to create a new distinguished professorship for Meiklejohn represented the University's first use of Brittingham trust funds. It required not only the approval of the Board of Regents but also of the Brittingham family trustees, which Frank secured in a casual conversation with Mary Brittingham, Thomas Brittingham's widow.

Meiklejohn's salary, which for understandable reasons was not announced, was set at $9,000. Six months later the Regents approved Frank's recommendation that Meiklejohn receive an additional $1,000 for directing the Experimental College, thus honoring the salary figure

---

[32]Frank to Meiklejohn, January 16, 1926, Meiklejohn Papers, box 32, and Frank Papers, Kirksville.

[33]Frank press release, January 23, 1926, Frank Presidential Papers, 4/13/1, box 10; *Capital Times*, January 23, 25, 27, and 28, February 4 and 10, 1926; *Daily Cardinal*, January 23 and 24, February 13, 1926. See also extensive press clippings in the Meiklejohn Papers, box 32. The enterprising editors of the *Cardinal* had uncovered and reported rumors of the negotiations with Meiklejohn as early as January 7, praising him in an editorial on January 16 as an eloquent champion of academic freedom and curricular reform, reporting the next day that he would soon visit the University, and asserting on January 20 that he was expected to accept a faculty appointment as early as the spring semester.

[34]*Capital Times*, January 25, 27, and 28, 1926.

Frank had mentioned in his initial negotiations with his friend in the summer of 1925. With his usual understatement, L&S Dean Sellery commented drily in his memoirs that the Meiklejohn salary was "out of line with the prevailing college scale."[35] In fact, Meiklejohn would be second only to Frank as by far the highest paid faculty member in the University.[36]

To considerable fanfare on February 11 the new Brittingham professor began teaching a section of McGilvary's course on the Introduction to Philosophy to a hundred enthusiastic students. "I abominate lectures," the champion of socratic dialogue told the class. "The only way to really learn this subject is by having you talk; and if you won't discuss, we'll just have to wait until somebody does talk."[37] A recent widower with largely grown children, Meiklejohn from the first threw himself unreservedly into campus life, freely commenting on student issues to *Daily Cardinal* reporters and speaking frequently to University and Madison groups. He initially took a room at the University Club but soon told President Frank he was looking for an apartment so he would "have a place to which students can come."[38] It was clear his reputation as a charismatic teacher and student champion was well deserved.

"Situations Rather Than Subjects"

Meiklejohn and Frank were also continuing to pursue the experi-

---

[35] Sellery, *Some Ferments at Wisconsin*, p. 11.

[36] L&S Dean Sellery and Graduate School Dean Charles S. Slichter (mathematics) were each currently receiving $7,500 as top University administrators, as was Professor Michael F. Guyer, the chairman of the zoology department, the highest-salaried regular L&S faculty member. A sense of "the prevailing college scale" can be seen in the 1925-26 salaries of some of the top L&S faculty members: Carl Russell Fish (history), $6,500; Charles E. Mendenhall (physics), $6,500; Grant Showerman (classics), $6,000; John R. Commons (economics), $6,000; Edward A. Ross (sociology), $6,000; Alexander Hohlfeld (German), $6,000; and Edward B. Van Vleck (mathematics), $6,000. Most faculty members were paid far less. UW Budget, 1926-27. In recruiting a senior chemistry faculty member from the University of Michigan in 1929, Dean Sellery and President Frank agreed that $6,000 was "our normal maximum salary" and that $7,000 should be considered "the super-class." Sellery to J.H. Mathews, February 5, 1929, Frank Presidential Papers, 4/13/1, box 66.

[37] *Capital Times*, February 12, 1926.

[38] Meiklejohn to Frank, February 1, 1926, Frank Presidential Papers, 4/13/1, box 10. For Meiklejohn's rapid immersion into campus life see *Daily Cardinal*, February 17, 18, 19, 22, 26, and 27, 1926.

mental college idea, circumspectly at first and more openly after March 1 when the president announced to the faculty his appointment of the All-University Commission to study "the problems of the articulation of the University in its several parts," a direct response to the University Committee's recommendation four months earlier. The high-powered character of the commission, which the president said he would chair, indicated its importance in his eyes: Deans Sellery and Slichter, and Professors Harold C. Bradley (chairman of physiological chemistry), Commons, Guyer, Meiklejohn, and William H. Page (law). Apart from the two newcomers—Frank and Meiklejohn—all were respected faculty leaders of long-standing.[39] The president clearly wanted the commission's recommendations to be received by the University faculty with respect.

Frank elaborated on his objectives in an accompanying memorandum, which was so long that probably few faculty members bothered to read it through. Denying any desire to be a "corporate academic Mussolini who would undertake to dictate the future educational policies of the University," he repeated his objections to the free elective system and echoed Meiklejohn's complaint about what Frank called "the disease of departmentalism," which fostered narrow specialization and discouraged general education. The time had come to rethink the nature and content of the first two years of liberal arts education, he said, and perhaps to teach students "situations rather than subjects." Frank recalled that while editor of the *Century Magazine* he had published an article by Meiklejohn suggesting a "way out of the confused wilderness of unrelated specialisms." Briefly describing Meiklejohn's proposed curriculum, Frank declared: "Here at any rate is a definite suggestion of teaching by situation rather than by subject," a proposal for "a program of study in which the rigid departmental boundaries would be ignored," and one that might "be carried on concurrently with our regular teaching by subjects." The Meiklejohn plan was advanced so tentatively and so late in Frank's lengthy memorandum that few were likely to recognize it as the president's real agenda for the All-University Commission.[40]

---

[39]UW Faculty Minutes, March 1, 1926, UA. At the previous meeting, the faculty had approved Frank's request to enlarge the commission beyond the limit of five faculty members originally specified, suggesting a range of from seven to twelve members. UW Faculty Minutes, February 1, 1926. See also *Capital Times*, March 2 and 20, 1926; *Daily Cardinal*, March 19, 1926.

[40]Frank, "An Experiment in Education," part 1, *WAM*, 28 (December, 1926), 51-3, 55;

The All-University Commission met but three times during the spring of 1926 in the presidential mansion in University Heights. It considered nothing but the experimental college project, Dean Sellery later recalled, even though a special faculty committee on student discipline later recommended that the commission study the recurring problem of student dishonesty.[41] (Evidently President Frank regarded the commission only as a tool to gain faculty approval of his plan, or perhaps was confident the Meiklejohn experiment would itself point to a solution for a variety of problems.) In April Professor Meiklejohn submitted to the commission what he described as "a very hurried and tentative draft of a plan for experimentation in the teaching of a selected group of Freshmen and Sophomores from the College of Letters and Science."[42] As Dean Sellery noted without surprise in his memoirs, in its broad outlines the proposal was "true to the blueprint of the January, 1925, article in the *Century Magazine*."[43] To assure that his proposed "Experimental College of Liberal Studies" would be "a unified community," Meiklejohn again recommended contrasting a comprehensive study of Periclean Athens in the first year with that of a contemporary civilization in the second. He suggested a limited enrollment of 150-200 male freshmen students in the first year, drawn from the College of Letters and Science and living together in one of the new Tripp-Adams men's dormitories along Lake Mendota west of Observatory Hill.[44] While the method of instruction "would be fundamentally tutorial," the teaching staff would hold regular faculty appointments and would also teach a regular course each semester in a University department. Meiklejohn emphasized that every effort should be made to test the validity of the curricular experiment by assuring that the Experimental

---

ibid., part 2, *WAM*, 28 (January, 1927), 87-91.

[41]Sellery, *Some Ferments at Wisconsin*, p. 12; UW Faculty Document 317A, "Report of Special Committee on Discipline," December 5, 1927.

[42]Meiklejohn, "Report on Experimental College of Liberal Studies," April, 1926, Meiklejohn Papers, box 55, and Frank Presidential Papers, 4/13/1, box 10.

[43]Sellery, *Some Ferments at Wisconsin*, p. 12.

[44]The availability of Adams and Tripp halls was fortuitous for Frank and Meiklejohn, not only because they were the first men's dormitories since the reassignment of North Hall to academic use following the Science Hall fire in 1884. The faculty committee charged with planning their construction in 1925 had given careful attention to how this living space could enhance the residents' academic experience. Influenced by the Oxford and Cambridge colleges, each hall consisted of eight smaller "houses" with separate entrances and a den for meetings and communal discussion, and with the whole complex served by a common refectory for dining.

College students were "representative in character, ability, and preparation, of the student community as a whole." Although the students would not be subject to regular L&S degree requirements, their curriculum would seek "to achieve the ends which the requirements are intended to serve." To reassure any skeptics, Meiklejohn declared:

> It will be essential to provide a scheme of examinations or other tests by which (1) the giving of college credits may be justified, and (2) the value of the experimental teaching may be measured. At this point the experimental college must submit itself to the judgment, not only of its own teachers, but also of the wider University, and, if so desired, of judges of educational values from the outside.[45]

President Frank presented the one-page report of the All-University Study Commission—Frank had changed the name perhaps to emphasize its tentative character—to a special meeting of the letters and science faculty on April 30, 1926. Noting that few universities provided either facilities or encouragement for curricular experimentation, the president explained that the commission believed an effort should be made to improve the education provided to freshman and sophomore students. It therefore proposed creating a pedagogical laboratory for this purpose, a true scientific endeavor in the "spirit of those who set up a laboratory for the study of cancer." The commission's formal report was sketchy, simply recommending the creation of an Experimental College within the College of Letters and Science "to formulate and to test under experimental conditions, suggestions for the improvement of methods of teaching, the content of study, and the determining conditions of undergraduate liberal education." Apart from a few stipulations about the full transferability of the academic work taken in the Experimental College when its students entered the parent College of Letters and Science as juniors, the report provided no curricular details. These Professor Meiklejohn offered in the discussion that followed, once again drawing on the ideas he had developed in his *Century* article. Faculty comments were generally supportive of experimentation in principle, but several speakers requested more detailed information about what was intended and at least one questioned the need for a special college. Recognizing they would have to allay faculty concerns, Meiklejohn and Frank promised to distribute a fuller description of the proposed experiment for

---

[45]Meiklejohn, "Report on Experimental College of Liberal Studies," April, 1926.

discussion at a subsequent faculty meeting.[46]

The L&S faculty met four more times before finally approving in amended form the commission's recommendation for the creation of the Experimental College. Debate was spirited, indicating considerable faculty skepticism and uneasiness over the vagueness of Meiklejohn's scheme. After the first meeting a dubious Professor Paul Knaplund—reflecting his Norwegian fisherman background—wrote his fiancée: "I couldn't resist the temptation to say that they were apparently ready to rig up a ship, provide captain, crew and passengers but take chart and compass away and send it into a fog guided by a fog horn. Which remark brought down the house."[47] President Frank felt obliged to offer assurance at the next meeting that the purpose of the Experimental College was merely to "set up machinery for hypotheses, not to apply to [the L&S] College on the whole." The proposal was "simply one item," he said, under consideration by the All-University Study Commission.[48] (In fact, after winning faculty approval of the Experimental College Frank did not call any further meetings of the commission and it neither considered nor presented any other recommendations.)

Several faculty members, led by Professor Frederick W. Roe of the Department of English, expressed concern about maintaining the integrity of letters and science baccalaureate degrees if Experimental College students were exempted from meeting regular L&S degree requirements. Since Roe was also the so-called junior dean responsible for L&S student advising, it was unclear whether he was speaking for himself or was a surrogate for Dean Sellery. Others questioned whether the experiment would yield any scientifically valid results. Psychology Professor C.L. Hull scoffed at the large number of variables inherent in the Meiklejohn plan and pointed out that scientists tried to control their experiments so they could deal with one variable at a time. He pointed out that students enrolling in the Experimental College were likely to be self-selected, and asked pointedly, "What are you going to compare them with?" History Professor Carl Russell Fish remarked that the biggest variable was the prophet and his disciples; he wondered, "How

---

[46]L&S Faculty Minutes (draft and final), April 30, 1926, UA. See also *Capital Times*, May 1, 1926; *Daily Cardinal*, May 1, 2, and 5, 1926.

[47]Paul Knaplund to [Dorothy King], Tuesday [May 4, 1926], Paul Knaplund Papers, 8/25, UA.

[48]L&S Faculty Minutes (draft), May 17, 1926.

much can we rely on the prophet?" Evidently stung by this query, President Frank responded that the Experimental College would not be Meiklejohn's personal enterprise; his job would merely be to supervise the investigation. O'Neill of the speech department observed that while he did not object to experiments, this one struck him as "adventure but not experimentation." The second meeting adjourned without voting on several proposed motions, one to refer the report back to the commission "for further definition," another to safeguard existing L&S degrees, and a third to assure careful faculty scrutiny of the experiment and limit of its scope and duration.[49] Professor Knaplund declined to attend the meeting. "I simply have no time to waste on all that nonsense," he wrote his fiancée.[50] The next day he reported: "From what I hear there was quite a scrap at the L&S faculty meeting yesterday. I wasn't there. It's over Meiklejohn's scheme—his folly."[51]

Before the third faculty meeting, a worried President Frank and the members of the commission marshalled faculty support and added three amendments to their report intended to allay some of the faculty concerns. Two of the changes sought to protect the L&S bachelor of arts degree by stipulating that only those Experimental College students who met "the full foreign language requirement" would be eligible for the B.A. degree. The third amendment provided for ongoing L&S faculty review of the Experimental College:

> It is understood that the detailed set-up of the experiment, when completed, will be submitted to the Letters and Science Faculty for discussion and suggestion, and that periodic reports of progress of the work of the Experimental College will be presented to the Faculty.[52]

Speaking both as chairman of the meeting and as a member of the commission, Dean Sellery highlighted the changes, explaining that the commission thought it wise not to require L&S faculty "approval" in the new paragraph inasmuch as "changes would want to be made and approval for each change would be difficult." The L&S Executive Committee "would handle the questions of irregularities that may come up." All in all, the dean declared, it was "a sound proposal adequately

---

[49]Ibid.
[50]Knaplund to [King], Sunday night [May 16, 1926], Knaplund Papers.
[51]Knaplund to [King], Tuesday [May 18, 1926], ibid.
[52]L&S Faculty Document 31 (revised), "Report of the Study Commission," May 22, 1926, and Frank Presidential Papers, 4/13/1, box 113.

protected." Dean Slichter, another member of the commission, emphasized that "we shall never get the approval of the majority of the faculty for any particular set-up," and argued for reasonable flexibility in setting up the Experimental College. For himself, Slichter believed the success of the experiment was assured. A third respected member of the commission, Professor John R. Commons, declared if he were younger he would like to serve on the college's staff, since he thought it worthwhile to synthesize the work of the first two years. In any event there would be, Commons stressed, various checks on the experiment, including the L&S Executive Committee as well as the academic departments into which the students would eventually matriculate as majors.

Not all of the critics were persuaded by this high-powered support. Dean Roe continued to argue that the commission's amendments did not adequately protect the integrity of L&S degrees because they dealt only with the foreign language and not with the mathematics and science requirements. He objected that never before had the faculty been asked to approve a course of study in advance of its development and detailed specification. Professor O'Neill continued to argue for L&S faculty "approval" of the curriculum of the Experimental College, and moved to insert that word in new paragraph in the commission's amended report. In response, Kahlenberg (chemistry) pointed out that Meiklejohn and his colleagues would and should want to change plans as they went along, and E.A. Ross (sociology) worried that monthly L&S faculty meetings would "be cluttered up by discussion of alterations in the new plan." The O'Neill motion lost decisively. Nor did Roe win support for his motion stipulating that Experimental College students must meet all requirements in order to earn a regular L&S degree.[53] Knaplund complained afterward about the two hours of time wasted at the meeting, where the "few amendments to limit the powers of the proposed new college were voted down so that thing has now a smooth sailing."[54]

Before giving approval to the commission's amended report on May 26, the L&S faculty voted down as unnecessary a motion to set a two- or a five-year limit on the experiment, but it did adopt two additional amendments offered by Professor Alexander Hohlfeld, the respected chairman of the German department. The first required periodic reports not just from the staff of the Experimental College but "by the

---

[53]L&S Faculty Minutes (draft), May 24, 1926.
[54]Knaplund to [King], Monday night [May 24, 1926], Knaplund Papers.

Executive Committee of the College of Letters and Science or some other committee of that College specially chosen to study the work of the Experimental College." The second Hohlfeld amendment stipulated that any curricular changes adopted by the Experimental College could be incorporated into the curriculum of the parent College of Letters and Science "only by vote of the Faculty of that College after it has specifically passed on the results of the experiment in question."[55] Clearly, the faculty was skeptical about the academic value of the new experimental curriculum and suspicious of the wider Frank-Meiklejohn agenda. Its approval, as Dean Sellery later remarked, could be interpreted as not only "a gesture of good will to the new president" but also "a certain friendly wariness."[56] Local press and student reaction to what reporters called the UW's new "Junior College Plan" was considerably less hesitant and more positive than that of the L&S faculty.[57]

To put the L&S faculty's "wariness" in perspective, one must know about the relatively new interdisciplinary Course in Humanities that had been created by the College of Letters and Science in 1920 as part of its most recent curriculum review. Administered by an interdisciplinary faculty committee, the humanities course was a more structured four-year bachelor of arts degree option designed to challenge students seeking a broad general education. Because of the similarities with the goals of the vaguely defined Meiklejohn plan, it is worth quoting part of the 1925-26 catalog description of the L&S humanities baccalaureate degree:

> Students may here secure substantial introductions to the four great fields of learning: language and literature; history and its correlated branches; science; philosophy and mathematics. They will come into vital contact with at least one of the great civilizations of the ancient world. They will acquire the power to acquaint themselves with at least one of the great foreign civilizations of the modern world. They will have training in English composition and spend at least a year with the masters of English literature. They will be given the opportunity in courses in history, economics and political science to gain knowledge regarding the institutions of the past and present, and to study methods of analyzing social facts. An introduction to one of the sciences will open to them the world of natural phenomena, and bring to them some experience in scientific method. Courses in mathematics and philosophy will serve to induce in them habits of close reasoning.[58]

---

[55]L&S Faculty Minutes, May 26, 1926.
[56]Sellery, *Some Ferments at Wisconsin*, pp. 13-4.
[57]*Daily Cardinal*, May 25, 26, and 29, 1926; *Capital Times*, May 27, 1926.
[58]*University of Wisconsin Catalog, 1925-26*, Bulletin of the University of Wisconsin, Serial

In none of the discussions about the experimental college scheme in 1925-26 did Glenn Frank or Alexander Meiklejohn give any indication they were aware of this existing L&S degree option, which was attracting some of the ablest students in the college.[59] It probably did not matter; their vision was both different and free of any existing faculty watchdog committee.

Following the guarded and unenthusiastic endorsement by the letters and science faculty, the proposal to create the Experimental College easily gained approval from the general faculty and the Board of Regents.[60] Glenn Frank had won his first major victory in Madison, one that was shrewdly conceived, conducted, and executed. It nevertheless was achieved at some cost in raising faculty suspicions about the president's larger objectives. Dean Sellery had smoothed the way, but his misgivings had also been heightened by the proposal's vagueness and expansive rhetoric. Much would depend on how the Experimental College developed under the direction of Frank's import, Alexander Meiklejohn.

"We Are Going to Set You Free"

During 1926-27 Meiklejohn set about preparing for the opening of the Experimental College the following year, devoting most of his time to recruiting a faculty and planning the curriculum. At Meiklejohn's request, on November 15 President Frank and Dean Sellery formally appointed him chairman of the new enterprise "with primary responsibility for assembling the teaching group and, with the members of the group, developing the detailed basis upon which the experimentation is to proceed." The Board of Regents confirmed the appointment the following month.[61] Meiklejohn and Frank also began promoting the

---

No. 1354, General Series No. 1130, August, 1926, p. 85.

[59]It is of interest that the Course in Humanities option both antedated and long survived the Experimental College. In fact, by the end of the period of this volume the secretary of its supervising faculty committee was one of the key Experimental College faculty, Professor Walter R. Agard. *General Announcement of Courses, 1944-46 (Catalog)*, Bulletin of the University of Wisconsin, Serial No. 2771, General Series No. 2555, June, 1945, p. 69.

[60]UW Faculty Document 282, "The Experimental College," June 17, 1926; UW Faculty Minutes, June 7, 1926; BOR Minutes, June 19, 1926, UA.

[61]Sellery and Frank to Meiklejohn, November 15, 1926, Meiklejohn Papers, box 32, and L&S Papers, 7/1/13, box 9, UA; BOR Minutes, December 8, 1926; Sellery, *Some Ferments at Wisconsin*, pp. 14-5. Frank prepared the appointment letter for Sellery's and his signature,

new college in articles and public addresses around the state and nation. The president predicted that the Experimental College might "lead us out of [the educational] wilderness," by ending the current tendency toward "suicidal specialization" and "suicidal smattering."[62] In an article in the 1927 official *Wisconsin Blue Book* Frank highlighted the Experimental College as a key part of his program for the University, which he expansively asserted had been approved "by a virtually unanimous vote [of] the faculty of the College of Letters and Science."[63] In December he published his long memorandum to the faculty at the time of the appointment of the All-University Study Commission, laying out the academic and intellectual foundation for the experiment in a two-part article in the *Wisconsin Alumni Magazine.*[64] Meiklejohn was somewhat more cautious in his predictions but issued a press statement promising "a genuinely radical attempt to study all available procedures and to find a way of making the first two years of college a vital contribution to the teaching of American students." He denied rumors that he planned to staff the Experimental College from outside, promising that most of its teachers would be regular letters and science faculty.[65]

This was not really the case. Even before the Experimental College proposal was presented to the letters and science faculty for initial discussion, let alone approval, Meiklejohn was trying to recruit a former Amherst colleague—political scientist John M. Gaus—for the venture, explaining that "Frank wants me to get the Amherst group so far as possible."[66] Key to Meiklejohn's plans for the new undertaking was the recruitment of Gaus and Walter R. Agard, who both had resigned from the Amherst faculty in protest against the trustees' treatment of Meiklejohn in 1923. Meiklejohn and Frank had little trouble getting the politi-

---

and in an accompanying letter to the dean explained: "There would probably be no need for my signature at all were it not, in a sense, a university venture as well as a Letters and Science venture in view of the university-wide implications of possible results." Frank apparently wanted Sellery to have no doubt about the president's deep interest in the experiment. Frank to Sellery, November 13, 1926, L&S Papers, 7/1/13, box 9.

[62]*Capital Times*, July 13, 26, and 28, 1927.

[63]Frank, "The University of Wisconsin—A Look Backward and Forward," *Wisconsin Blue Book, 1927* (Madison: State of Wisconsin, 1927), pp. 365-6.

[64]Frank, "An Experiment in Education," pp. 51-3, 55, 87-91.

[65]Meiklejohn, press statement, February, 1927, Frank Papers, Kirksville; *Daily Cardinal*, February 15, 1927. See also *Capital Times*, May 10, 1927, January 1 and 17, 1928.

[66]Meiklejohn to John Gaus, April 24, 1926, Meiklejohn Papers, box 14. Meiklejohn repeated this assertion in a follow-up letter: "But Frank wants me to get as many as I can of the Amherst men. That means 5 or 6." Meiklejohn to Gaus, April 28, 1926, ibid.

cal science department to agree to the appointment of Gaus as a full professor at a salary of $5,000, but the classics department balked at first at offering Agard a full professorship at the same substantial salary.[67] Similarly, Law Dean Harry S. Richards informed the president he had with considerable reluctance and against his better judgment agreed to Meiklejohn's request for a high salaried ($4,250) assistant professorship for Malcolm Sharp, because he did "not wish by my attitude or actions to embarrass either Mr. Meiklejohn or yourself in carrying through the project." He said he doubted the joint appointment would work well, however, and stipulated that its cost should not be at the expense of other Law School needs and that it carried no implication of permanent tenure.[68]

It was a tribute to Meiklejohn's magnetic personality that of the initial Experimental College staff of eleven—three full professors including Meiklejohn, three associate professors, two assistant professors, one instructor, and two graduate assistants—most had a prior Meiklejohn association, either as faculty members or as students at Brown and Amherst during the Meiklejohn years.[69] As might be expected, there

---

[67]See Meiklejohn to Gaus, April 24 and 28, May 7 and 17, 1926, January 27, February 24, March 7 and 26, 1927; Gaus to Meiklejohn, "Tuesday" [April 27, 1926], May 3, 1926, ibid. Upon their initial appointments Gaus and Agard, with salaries of $5,000, became the second-highest paid members of their respective departments, although neither could be considered senior in age, experience, or scholarship.

[68]Frank to H.S. Richards, March 23, 1927; Richards to Frank, April 8, 1927, Frank Presidential Papers, 4/13/1, box 33.

[69]Besides Meiklejohn, the initial Experimental College teaching staff consisted of John M. Gaus, professor of political science (former Amherst student and faculty member); Walter R. Agard, professor of Greek (former Amherst student and faculty member); Percy M. Dawson, associate professor of physiology; Laurance J. Saunders, associate professor of history (former Amherst faculty member); Samuel G. A. Rogers, associate professor of French (a student in Meiklejohn's last year at Brown); Malcolm P. Sharp, assistant professor of law (former Amherst student and the son of Meiklejohn's UW philosophy department colleague, Frank C. Sharp); Paul Raushenbush, assistant professor of economics (former Amherst student); William B. Phillips, instructor in English; Carl M. Bögholt, assistant in philosophy (former Amherst graduate student); and John W. Powell, assistant in philosophy. Of the group, six had known Meiklejohn at Amherst and one at Brown; four of these—Agard, Gaus, Saunders, and Sharp—were brought to Wisconsin by Meiklejohn to play leading roles in the Experimental College; Dawson, Rogers, and Raushenbush already held UW faculty appointments; and Bögholt had independently enrolled for graduate work in philosophy at Wisconsin at the time of Meiklejohn's appointment. Of the dormitory fellows assigned to the four Experimental College houses in Adams Hall in the first year, one—Delos S. Otis, a graduate student in history who subsequently was promoted to the Experimental College teaching staff—was also a graduate of Amherst College in the Meiklejohn era. Meiklejohn's sensitivity to appearances was not well-honed. During the last two months of 1927-28, he appointed his father-in-law

was some resentment on the part of the regular UW faculty at this influx of Meiklejohn men, a number of whom were appointed at a higher rank and salary than their departments might have recommended had they been in charge of the search. The relationships between the Experimental College and the regular academic departments were, as Meiklejohn admitted to Gaus, "intricate and tricky," and Meiklejohn and Frank did not always handle them smoothly or collegially.[70] Perhaps the chief problem, which as outsiders neither Frank nor Meiklejohn recognized and certainly did little to address in their exuberant statements about the high purpose of the experiment, was that the newcomers—whose competence was not questioned—were perceived as being brought to Madison to show the regular L&S faculty how to teach.

With the exception of Meiklejohn, who held membership in the philosophy department but was the full-time Experimental College chairman, as a general rule the "Ex-College" faculty members were expected to teach a regular course and devote a third of their time each semester to their home academic departments on the Hill. In an early decision the Experimental College faculty decided to refer to themselves as "advisers" in order to lessen the gap between teacher and student in the new unified academic community. Graduate assistants received the same title, since faculty rank was to have no special meaning in this democratic endeavor. In practice, of course, the more senior advisers played a larger role in curricular decisions. Although the form was democratic in what

The Experiment as Seen by Hill Students

and former Brown University philosophy colleague, Walter G. Everett, to the staff of the Experimental College to take over Meiklejohn's day-to-day student advising so he could concentrate on administrative work. By 1930-31 the Meiklejohn men among the Ex-College teaching staff had grown to include one of the chairman's sons, Donald Meiklejohn, who as a first-year graduate student could hardly be considered a seasoned instructor.

[70]Meiklejohn to Gaus, March 26, 1927, Meiklejohn Papers, box 14; Sellery, *Some Ferments at Wisconsin*, p. 16.

became a seemingly endless round of planning meetings, throughout the five-year history of the venture Meiklejohn provided the most influential vision and voice, always true to the general blueprint of his 1925 *Century Magazine* article. So skillful and charismatic was the chairman in conducting the free-wheeling planning sessions, however, that the group nearly always adjourned believing it had developed its consensus through the discussion, when in fact it rarely decided anything much differently than Meiklejohn intended.[71]

The Experimental College opened with much fanfare in September of 1927, its 119 male freshmen occupying four of the eight "houses" or sections of Adams Hall, one of the two new men's lake shore dormitories opened the previous year. There was considerable public interest and expectation regarding the venture. "If we were a high school student graduating this year," declared the editor of the *Ashland Daily Press* in the far north of the state, "we should make a tremendous struggle to be one of those enrolled in the new experimental college at the University this fall."[72]   The *Daily Cardinal* called the opening "a courageous take-off" and described the endeavor as a "crusade."[73]   "We are going to set you free," Meiklejohn told the first class at its initial welcoming meeting, and that remained a key objective of the college.[74] This was, in fact, to be a guiding principle of the experiment—freedom for the students to develop their intellectual powers and social sensibilities to the fullest with only guidance and not coercion from their advisers.

The initial enrollment was probably something of a disappointment to Frank and Meiklejohn. Frank at least had hoped for an enrollment of 125 drawn from a sufficiently large pool of applicants to get a true cross-section of the wider student body in order to make comparisons with a control group of regular L&S students. Instead, nearly all Experimental College applicants from the regular freshman class were admitted by Chairman Meiklejohn in the order of their application.[75]   As Professor Hull had predicted in the faculty debate, from the beginning

---

[71]Carl Bögholt, oral history interview, 1973, UA.

[72]Editorial, *Ashland Press*, quoted in *Capital Times*, June 7, 1927.

[73]Editorial, *Daily Cardinal*, September 20, 1927. See also ibid., September 19, 21, 22, and 24, 1927; *Capital Times*, September 21, 1927.

[74]*The First Year of the Experimental College: An Informative Resumé* (Madison: University of Wisconsin Experimental College, 1928), p. 10.

[75]"Preliminary Report of the Faculty of the Experimental College to the Faculty of the College of Letters and Science," October 17, 1927, L&S Papers, 7/1/1-2, box 2.

the Ex-College students were mostly self-selected rather than carefully chosen as participants in a controlled experiment, a condition that grew ever more pronounced in subsequent years. There was nothing wrong with this, of course, but it suggested the experiment would be hard to evaluate.

In many respects the first year was both characteristic and the high point of the Experimental College's five-year history. From the first day there was a contagious esprit among the students and staff as they set about creating their largely self-contained and closely knit academic community on the shores of Lake Mendota. Chairman Meiklejohn and the faculty advisers were readily available and spent much of their time meeting with students individually or in small groups in their offices in Adams Hall. The method of instruction was primarily tutorial; lectures, even by guest experts, were discouraged in favor of searching discussion and dialogue. All-college meetings were held several times a week in the nearby Soils Building, sometimes to discuss the work and views of a visiting specialist, at other times to consider college business. To Meiklejohn's dismay, early in the fall after a series of meetings the students rejected his suggestion that they adopt some form of self-government for the college. Some students argued for anarchism or communism and others questioned whether they ought to appear even more separate from the larger University community. Eventually, they voted 49-46 against even a loose town meeting form of government, yet then rejected by 40-30 a motion to abandon the effort to form a student government for the college![76] In later years the students established an Experimental College student council with limited powers and responsibilities. Most of the Ex-College students welcomed the sense of exclusiveness and elitism, proudly accepting the nickname of "guinea pigs" assigned them by the other students. The following spring, to emphasize the college's distinctiveness within the University, they designed an official Ex-College blazer (dark blue with pearl grey edging and the Athenian owl embroidered on the front pocket), which was promptly purchased by over half the students and several of the faculty advisers and dormitory fellows. Such un-Wisconsin affectation probably struck Meiklejohn and his predominantly Ivy League staff as a useful morale-booster, but it was bound to raise eyebrows elsewhere on the

---

[76]*Daily Cardinal*, October 12, 13, 18, and 19, November 10 and 11, 1927; *Capital Times*, October 12, 1927; *WAM*, 29 (December, 1927), 89; *First Year of the Experimental College*, p. 38.

campus.[77]

Although there were refinements in the readings and assignments over the years, throughout the experiment the curriculum followed the general outline prescribed in Meiklejohn's 1925 *Century* article. During the freshman year the students investigated all aspects of Athenian civilization in the fifth and fourth centuries, B.C., using Plato's *Republic* as the basic text and reading widely about Athenian literature, art, law and government, philosophy, religion, economics, science, and the history and geography of ancient Greece. In the sophomore year they turned the same searching scrutiny to the development of American civilization in the nineteenth and twentieth centuries, with *The Education of Henry Adams* as the basic text supplemented by a variety of other readings.[78] John Gaus had argued unsuccessfully for beginning the first year with a more general introduction covering the rise and fall of various ancient civilizations and providing some understanding of the origins of the Greeks, but joked to Meiklejohn that he recognized "you mystics will want to convey the impression that they sprang full armed and spouting Kant from the then equivalent of an Earl Carroll bathtub."[79]

Gaus was, however, more successful in determining the format and specifics of the sophomore year, in which Meiklejohn had less interest. The most important Gaus contribution was the major research project each student was assigned to begin over the summer after the freshman year: a wide-ranging study of the development of some American region or community—usually the student's home town—to be completed as a sophomore thesis by the beginning of the following spring semester under the direction of one of the advisers. The regional study was an imaginative attempt to sharpen the students' research skills and have them apply their general knowledge of the unfolding of the Athenian and American civilizations to the development of a particular American

---

[77]*Daily Cardinal*, April 1 and 29, May 2, 6, 8, and 10, 1928; *WAM*, 29 (May, 1928), 283; *First Year of the Experimental College*, p. 44.

[78]John Gaus was responsible for selecting the Adams autobiography as the basic text for the second year and remained enamored of its pedagogic value throughout his teaching career at Wisconsin and Harvard after World War II, though others thought its sophisticated skepticism and cynicism made it more appropriate for upperclassmen and graduate students. Following its publication in the year of Adams' death, the book achieved widespread popularity as assigned reading on college and university campuses across the country for the next several decades. *The Education of Henry Adams: An Autobiography* (Boston and New York: Houghton Mifflin, 1918).

[79]Gaus to Meiklejohn, August 15, 1927, Meiklejohn Papers, box 14.

community. For most students the regional study proved to be one of the most challenging and valuable parts of their Experimental College experience.[80] Many years later Meiklejohn told Gaus he thought it "came nearer to expressing the basic intention of the College than did any other feature of our planning."[81] These regional studies are still on file with the Experimental College records and remain an interesting, valuable, but largely unknown and unused source.

Chairman Meiklejohn and the other Experimental College advisers did not believe in regular class examinations any more than in classroom lectures, both of which they thought tended to emphasize specific facts over broader understanding. Each student was required to keep a notebook throughout the year as a record of his reading and thinking and to turn in written papers regularly. Aside from a rare multiple choice or short answer quiz on some topic under investigation, which was intended for teaching rather than grading purposes, the Ex-College students escaped the terrors of six- and twelve-week and semester final exams, much to the envy of their counterparts on the Hill. Instead, they were assigned in groups of about a dozen students to one of the advisers for regular tutorial conferences about their reading and course work. Each adviser was also expected to have weekly group discussion sessions for his advisees and occasional specialized sessions for other students on topics in the adviser's area of special expertise. The assignment of advisers was changed every six weeks to enable the faculty to know all of the students. The advisers kept a notebook on their tutorial conferences and wrote up a detailed report on each advisee's progress at the end of the six-week advisory period. These reports were passed on to succeeding advisers and provided the basis for Chairman Meiklejohn's annual letter to each student's parents about their son's intellectual, academic, and social progress. At the end of the sophomore year students who had completed the Experimental College course received a letter grade for sixty academic credits based on three accomplishments: the regional study, a second major term paper completed at the end of the sophomore year on some aspect of *The Education of Henry Adams*, and an individual oral examination conducted by two of the advisers. While in keeping with Meiklejohn's

---

[80]One member of the Board of Regents whose son was in the first Experimental College class was so proud of his offspring's sophomore regional study of Manitowoc, that he arranged to have it published in serial form in the *Manitowoc Daily Herald*. John C. Schmidtmann to Carl Russell Fish, December 16, 1929, Carl Russell Fish Papers, box 8, SHSW.

[81]Meiklejohn to Jane and John Gaus, April 5, 1962, Meiklejohn Papers, box 14.

educational philosophy, little was absolutely required of the students, the emphasis was on constant reading and discussion, structured and unstructured. Most but by no means all of the Ex-College guinea pigs welcomed and flourished under this free regimen.

In addition to their work in the college, students were permitted to take a regular course on the Hill each semester. Many did so, especially those who wanted to meet the foreign language requirement of the L&S bachelor of arts degree, those who needed preparatory work in mathematics and science for their future majors, or those who simply chose to broaden their education beyond the Experimental College curriculum. To meet the concern of the foreign language departments, Frank and Sellery blocked an initial plan of the Experimental College advisers to offer elementary foreign language instruction, limiting the college to some specialized advanced language work and Professor Agard's voluntary and remarkably successful college class in elementary ancient Greek. From the first the advisers recognized that their curriculum was weak in science and that its brief treatment of the scientific achievements of the ancient Greeks gave the students little understanding of the development and importance of modern science. They sought to remedy this defect with the addition of physicist Robert J. Havighurst in 1928-29, who began offering a unit on modern physical science in the sophomore year (eventually expanded to six weeks, including an opportunity for four weeks of laboratory experience). As in other Experimental College classes, attendance was not required and only averaged around 65 percent for the laboratory during the three years it was offered, 1929-30 through 1931-32. Coverage of science remained weak throughout the five-year experiment, with a cursory treatment of biology provided only in the final two years of the college.[82]

---

[82]After Meiklejohn's first report to the L&S faculty, chemistry Professor Louis Kahlenberg sent him a detailed curricular plan for the teaching of science in the Experimental College and offered further assistance, but there is no indication Meiklejohn took advantage of the offer. [Kahlenberg] to Meiklejohn, January 21, 1928, P.F. La Follette Papers, box 134, SHSW; Robert J. Havighurst, "Report on the Physics Period," November 12, 1931, Meiklejohn Papers, box 55. In this report Havighurst elaborated on the continuing debate among the Experimental College advisers over the nature of the learning process:

> The usual type of university course places all too much emphasis upon the getting and memorization of facts, we say. Indeed, one reason that we are fairly sure of our fidelity to human nature in separating the getting of facts from their interpretation is that we see what passes for getting facts so thoroughly separated in the classroom from interpreting facts that one goes on completely without the other.

To broaden the intellectual horizons of the students, Meiklejohn brought in occasional guest experts to discuss their work and interests as they related to the Ex-College curriculum. Often these were UW faculty members with specialized expertise, as when A.K. Lobeck described the climate and geography of ancient Greece, when UW scientists Charles Slichter, Chauncey Leake, and Joel Stebbins outlined the Greek contributions to the fields of mathematics, science, medicine, and astronomy, or when E.B. McGilvary and Max Otto elaborated on various philosophic ideas originally explored by the Greeks. Often Meiklejohn used his considerable contacts and persuasive powers to attract distinguished outside guest speakers to the college, occasionally able to get some extra funds from President Frank for this purpose. Professor A. Eustace Haydon of the Department of Comparative Religion of the University of Chicago was a regular visitor, commenting on the religious ideas and practices of the Greeks. Dr. Aleš Hrdlička of the Smithsonian Institution reviewed the reasons for the decline of Greek civilization. In the spring of 1929 the Columbia University philosopher Irwin Edman and the well-known social commentator Lewis Mumford each gave five talks to the students over several days and afterward publicly praised the educational approach of the Experimental College. The following year Frank provided $500 to bring the Chicago painter Morris Topchevsky to be an artist-in-residence in the college for two months and another $500 for Dr. Frankwood Williams, a New York psychiatrist and UW alumnus, to spend two weeks in residence advising on how to improve the social/emotional life and group dynamics of the college.[83] Speakers who came expecting to give a

---

The tendency of the Experimental College has been toward emphasis upon interpretation of facts or upon the methods of interpretation of facts. Our students do not get many facts about Athens, but they are supposed, in the freshman year, to learn to interpret such facts when they do get them. We do say that in our second-year work it is somewhat more important that we get facts as well as learn to interpret them. Someone will ask, "How can you learn to interpret facts without first or at the same time getting or learning them?" I confess that I do not know the answer, yet I think we have been trying to do just that, and perhaps we have had some success. I think Mr. Meiklejohn would answer, "By studying logic."
On his copy of the report Meiklejohn made a marginal rejoinder: "Science is not always logical. Assumptions are often made the only justification for which is that they give results." See also *Daily Cardinal*, January 20, 1928, February 12, March 3, June Commencement issue, October 20, 1929; *Capital Times*, May 6, 1928, June 19, 1929.
[83]Dorothy Crowley to Warner Taylor, May 2, 1929, L&S Papers, 7/16/20, box 10; Meiklejohn to Frank, November 12, December 11, 1930; Julia Wilkinson to Miss F.G.

formal lecture were often surprised and even nonplussed at the unabashed freedom with which the Ex-College guinea pigs interrupted them with questions and comments.[84]

Freed from most of the fixed time commitments facing students in regular University courses, the guinea pigs were expected to devote at least their mornings to their reading assignments, writing, course discussion, and other college work. This still gave them a great deal of free time for their own pursuits, which they immediately began to fill with a rich variety of extracurricular activities in the college and in the wider campus community. The range of interests among members of first class was typical. A few of the students took over an available basement room in Adams Hall for a carpentry workshop, scrounging for furniture and tools. Their project dovetailed neatly with the effort of another group of students to form a drama group and produce a Greek play, Aristophanes' *The Clouds*. The workshop group agreed to construct the sets for the play if they could share in the proceeds so as to acquire more tools. The production budget of *The Clouds* was a modest $20, borrowed from several of the advisers, but its performance in the Stock Pavilion in mid-December, 1927, was acclaimed a great creative success and produced enough revenue to cover costs, meet some of the workshops equipment needs, and fund a more ambitious production in the spring semester of Euripides' *Electra*, which the *Capital Times* pronounced "solemn, weird," but "excellently staged, acted."[85]

The Experimental College Players then began offering a regular schedule of mostly classical Greek plays, with one, Sophocles' *Antigone*, performed in February, 1930, in a modern translation by Maurice Neufeld, a sophomore Ex-College student in Professor Agards informal class in ancient Greek. The Neufeld translation was deemed so fresh and imaginative that it was published with an introduction by

Sanford, March 7, 1929; G.C.S. [Sellery] to Miss Wilkinson, March 11, 1929, Frank Presidential Papers, 4/13/1, boxes 66 and 100; *First Year of the Experimental College*, pp. 27-8; *Daily Cardinal*, March 30 and 31, April 27, 1929. See also Morris Topchevsky, "Report Submitted to the Advisers of the Experimental College," February 12, 1931, Meiklejohn Papers, box 55. In one instance Dean Sellery told Julia Wilkinson, President Frank's executive secretary, that Meiklejohn's "proposed compensation for Mr. Edman seems excessive." G.C.S. to Miss Wilkinson, March 11, 1929, Frank Presidential Papers, 4/13/1, box 66.

[84]David G. Parsons, oral history interview, 1987, UA.

[85]*Capital Times*, October 12, December 10, 1927, March 24, 1928; *Daily Cardinal*, December 1 and 15, 1927, February 25, March 15, 23, and 24, 1928; *First Year of the Experimental College*, pp. 29-30, 33-4.

Meiklejohn and remained in use for a number of years.[86] When the players produced *The Bacchanals of Euripides* in 1931, an enterprising student, Richard Weil, sent George Bernard Shaw a form asking him to "heartily endorse the undertaking." Weil was really seeking an autograph, but Shaw wrote back in some puzzlement: "I do not understand why they should make such a fuss about it; why shouldnt they produce the Bacchae?"[87] In addition to reinterpreting classical drama, the players on occasion produced an original play. In the spring of 1932 members of the last Ex-College class performed "A.D. 29," their own contemporary social commentary on the life of Christ.[88]

Another extracurricular group organized by some Ex-College students in the first year was the Forum, to which guest experts were invited to discuss their views on topics of interest to the group. The students recognized that in a sense they were competing with the college's own program of guest speakers, which, they conceded, was "something of a forum itself." Other similar discussion groups were more specialized. The law group met weekly during the second semester to discuss legal institutions and problems under the leadership of faculty adviser and law Professor Malcolm Sharp. The philosophy club met weekly at the Meiklejohn home for some of Helen Meiklejohns "dialectical cookies" while its members wrestled with the chairman over such metaphysical imponderables as the dualism of mind and matter, freedom and determinism, appearance and reality, the nature of truth, and the insights of the great philosophers from Socrates, Plato, and Aristotle to Kant and Hegel.[89] Such heady fare helped to establish the image of the Experimental College, at least among its members, as a place of round-the-clock verbal sparring and serious talk.

The flexible academic schedule of the college also gave its students time to participate in wider University student activities, and many did. Although there was an initial feeling that Experimental College students

---

[86]*Daily Cardinal*, January 10 and 15, February 13, 19, 27, and 28, 1930. After his two years in the Experimental College, Neufeld took his B.A., M.A., and Ph.D. degrees at Wisconsin in labor history and economics and went on to a distinguished career as a professor of industrial relations at Cornell University.

[87]Ibid., March 13, 1931; Sam Steinman, "No-Credit Courses," *WAM*, 32 (April, 1931), 294.

[88]*Daily Cardinal*, March 27, April 14, 1932.

[89]*First Year of the Experimental College*, pp. 30-2. The production of this well-written, edited, and illustrated 48-page booklet was another extracurricular project of a group of Ex-College students in the initial class.

should not join social fraternities because of the requirement that they live in Adams Hall for two years, a considerable number did join and participate in one or another of the Greek letter organizations. Others were active on the *Daily Cardinal* and other student publications, worked for the Union Board, and participated in campus forensic and musical organizations. Six of the twenty members of the Freshman Glee Club in 1927-28, for example, were from the Experimental College. The first sophomore student ever elected to serve as editor of the *Wisconsin Literary Magazine*, Frederick Gutheim, was from the Experimental College. Ex-College students were also to be found on University athletic teams, with a substantial number winning numeral sweaters as freshmen. One member of the first class, Carroll Blair, who later achieved considerable notoriety for his radical views and political activities, earned two sweaters as a freshman in cross-country and track, and another, Sam Behr, earned three—in football, basketball, and track. Behr also was elected captain of the freshman basketball team and was awarded the W Club cup as the best all-around athlete in spring football practice.[90] Considering their small number, the Ex-College guinea pigs were disproportionately active and successful in campus extracurricular activities. Their visibility and willingness to assume leadership roles undoubtedly helped somewhat to dispel the view among Hill students that the college was isolated and aloof from the larger campus community.

"Simply So Unbelievably Vulgar"

Students on the Hill did, however, tend to believe that the Experimental College students were more radical in their political views than the campus as a whole, perhaps in part because Meiklejohn and several of the Experimental College advisers were known to be active in the socialist League for Industrial Democracy. The *Cardinal* expressed surprise when a straw ballot revealed in the fall of 1928 that a plurality of Ex-College students favored Republican presidential candidate Herbert Hoover over Democrat Alfred E. Smith, Socialist Norman Thomas, and Communist William Z. Foster, and commented that maybe

---

[90]Ibid., pp. 39-42. Behr subsequently graduated from the UW Medical School with an excellent academic record and practiced medicine in Rockford, Illinois. Paul F. Clark, oral history interview, 1972, UA.

the guinea pigs were a cross-section of the campus after all.[91] Perhaps to preserve their reputation, in another poll several weeks later the guinea pigs perversely endorsed comedian Will Rogers for the White House![92]

A Couple of Hill Students in the Ex College Era

In fact, the great majority of the Experimental College students were probably not much different in their political views than the student body as a whole.[93] The radical image of the college came from a relatively small minority of students attracted to it because of its well-publicized freedom and unconventional curriculum and from an occasional well-publicized incident, which because of the high visibility of the experiment attracted more attention and unfavorable comment than would ordinarily have been the case. Such coverage fed the anti-University rhetoric of critics like John Chapple, the politically ambitious editor of the *Ashland Daily Press*, who charged that the Experimental College was "a cleverly disguised scheme to instill revolutionary ideas into student minds without arousing the suspicion of the citizens of the state."[94] Conservatives expressed alarm (and had their negative view of Meiklejohn's venture confirmed) when an Ex-College "radical" allegedly hung a red flag from his dormitory window to celebrate May Day in 1931. Even the progressive *Capital Times* reported disapprovingly that "the red flag of communism waved at Adams Hall."[95]

---

[91]*Daily Cardinal*, October 1 and 3, 1928.

[92]Ibid., October 27, 1928.

[93]In his final report, Meiklejohn conceded that although most of the Experimental College students were conservative, "the minority of 'radicals' was undoubtedly larger than is usual in such groups....For a time the College had a very active group of communists in its midst." "Report of the Advisers of the Experimental College," January, 1932, p. 115, Meiklejohn Papers, box 55.

[94]*Daily Cardinal*, November 17, 1931.

[95]*Capital Times*, May 2, 1931. Feeding the growing belief that the Experimental College

While the meaning and significance of this event was questionable—it was probably a practical joke[96]—there were several genuinely radical Experimental College students who attracted considerable notoriety during their years at the University. Carroll Blair, a member of the first college class from Redgranite, Wisconsin, seems to have been politicized by his studies at the University and especially by the collapse of the American economy in the great depression. He became active in the Communist Party and while still a student worked as a labor organizer at the International Harvester plant in Milwaukee. In August of 1930 he was sentenced to a year's imprisonment in the Milwaukee house of correction for attacking a policeman during an unemployment demonstration. Law Professor Malcolm Sharp, one of the Experimental College advisers, immediately sought Blair's release, for which Sharp was roundly criticized by the *Milwaukee Journal.* "The experimental college is not to be charged with making this young man a communist," the paper conceded.

> But it certainly did fail in its opportunity to make a human being....And Prof. Meiklejohn, surveying the work he is doing, may well reflect that all the freedom he granted to the student in this case, and all the examination of the philosophy of society which he brought to bear on him, was a flat failure as a builder of intellect.[97]

While Blair was serving his sentence he ran unsuccessfully for governor

---

attracted a disproportionate number of Jewish students, some of whom were also radicals, the *Capital Times* identified the dormitory room as "occupied by Justin A. Silverstein, Experimental College student."

[96]There is some question about the meaning of this event. In later years an Experimental College alumnus remembered the affair as harmless horseplay rather than a political statement: some of Silverstein's friends had taken advantage of his absence to hang his red winter underwear from his window; his friends hadn't realized there was any political significance to their practical joke until they read the newspapers the next day. Parsons, oral history interview. Support for Parsons' recollection of the affair may be found in the *Daily Cardinal,* May 4, 1932, and February 12 and 16, 1935, when one of the perpetrators, W.W. Blaesser, confessed that he and his friends had not known the "the potentialities of red underwear" until the press construed their prank as "dastardly rebellion."

[97]Quoted in *Capital Times,* August 21, 1930. See also ibid., August 20 and 22, September 2, 1930. When he was arrested, Blair initially gave the name of Fred Bassett, which his home town friends speculated might have been because he knew the former treasurer of Berlin, Wisconsin, of that name, who had recently been imprisoned for misappropriating city funds. Ibid., August 23, 1930. Blair continued to use the name of Bassett interchangeably for a time. After repeated unsuccessful campaigns for political office on the Communist ticket in Wisconsin, for many years he operated a left-wing book store in downtown Milwaukee.

on the Communist ticket in 1930 and later for mayor of Milwaukee in 1932.[98] In spite of Meiklejohn's expressed hope that little notice would be taken of the effort, the press highlighted his and Sharp's unsuccessful appeal before Governor Kohler the following December to grant Blair a pardon.[99] Blair was freed a few months later by the new governor, progressive Republican Philip F. La Follette.[100]

One of Blair's classmates in the first Experimental College class attracted even more notoriety for his radical political activities. David Gordon, recruited to Wisconsin from New York on one of the new Zona Gale creative writing scholarships, may have been a Communist before arriving in Madison but certainly was a radical activist in his first year at the University. In the spring of 1928 he was imprisoned in New York for publishing an allegedly obscene poem, "America," in the Communist *Daily Worker* in which he denounced capitalism with graphic imagery.[101] At first University officials doubted Gordon would be jailed, since he had published the poem as a precocious seventeen-year-old well before enrolling in the University. The real objective of the New York authorities may have been the *Daily Worker*, which was fined $500 for printing the poem, but after a brief trial Gordon received an indeterminate sentence as a juvenile.[102] Gordon supporters, including the American Civil Liberties Union and leftist writers John Dos Passos and Max Eastman, promptly rallied to his support, with Heywood Broun describing the draconian sentence in his newspaper column as "a piece of judicial folly."[103] In Madison, students held a mass rally in

---

[98]*Daily Cardinal*, October 3, 1930, February 27, 1932. In his 1932 mayorality race Blair/Bassett condemned the University as "a pretty bad place to get an education," since it was peopled by bewhiskered professors who were "dull capitalists" and students who were "equally dull, uninteresting and passive." Ibid., March 3, 1932.

[99]*Milwaukee Journal*, December 4, 1930; *Capital Times*, December 4, 1930; unidentified newspaper clippings, Meiklejohn Papers, box 56.

[100]*Capital Times*, April 14, 1931. The *Marinette Eagle-Star* praised the move because it would prevent this "good clean American boy" from becoming a Communist martyr. "It is a pity that Blair should have fallen into the company of Communists at the University of Wisconsin experimental college—many of them from New York's ghetto." Ibid.

[101]The poem would hardly be considered obscene by today's standards. It read in part: "America is a land of censored opportunity./ Lick spit; eat dirt,/ There's your opportunity;...You're everything aren't you, America?/ Of course./ You're even a neat whore house/ Standing on the sidewalk of the world./ Two dollars a woman:/ Nice bed/ Warm room./ But most important:/ A fleshy woman/ To make you feel you're giving away your life's water/ For a healthy bastard./ Why not?" *Daily Worker*, March 12, 1927.

[102]*Capital Times*, April 3, 11, and 12, 1928.

[103]Ibid., April 15 and 24, 1928.

Gordon's behalf, with three hundred supporters signing a petition urging his release.[104] Professor Michael V. O'Shea, the head of the Zona Gale scholars selection committee, called for Gordon's parole so he could return to Madison where additional University education "would go much farther to reconstruct his attitude toward his fellows and his country."[105] William Ellery Leonard, the poet laureate of the English department, described a new Gordon poem, "The Song of Life," written from his cell in Tombs Prison, as the product of "a thoughtful, brooding young spirit with a sense of beauty and a gift of speech." "He certainly belongs with the University of Wisconsin," Professor Leonard declared, "and not at a New York reformatory."[106] After reading his offending poem, however, not all members of the campus community enlisted in the Gordon camp. Some two hundred dormitory and fraternity students signed an anti-Gordon petition denouncing his obscenity and sent it to the New York Parole Commission to counter the pro-Gordon appeal.[107] In May, after languishing for more than a month in jail, Gordon was placed on three years' probation and allowed to return to the University, where the Board of Regents approved the continuation of his Zona Gale scholarship for the fall semester.[108]

Professor O'Shea's expectations notwithstanding, this was not the end of Gordon's radical activities. A year later he disrupted a campus meeting by denouncing as a "capitalist plot" the engagement of Anne Morrow, daughter of a J.P. Morgan banking partner, to Charles A. Lindbergh, a one-time UW student who had recently received a University honorary degree following his epochal flight across the Atlantic. The disapproving *Daily Cardinal* chided Gordon to keep his views to himself, "so the University will not be disgraced."[109] In the

---

[104]Ibid., April 20, 1928; *Daily Cardinal*, April 20, 1928.

[105]*Capital Times*, April 29, 1928; *Daily Cardinal*, April 29, 1928. The *Janesville Gazette*, somberly viewing recent student activities at the University, doubted that O'Shea's prescription for curing "radical enemies of the government" would do much good. Instead of jail, the paper declared, "what should have been done to David was to give him a spanking with a paddle sans clothing and have his mouth washed out with soap three times a day for a year." Quoted in *Capital Times*, May 2, 1928.

[106]*Capital Times*, May 7, 1928.

[107]*Daily Cardinal*, April 19 and 22, 1928.

[108]*Capital Times*, May 10, 11, and 12, 1928; *Daily Cardinal*, May 9, 11, 12, and 17, June 28, 1928. The following month a federal obscenity charge against Gordon was dropped by the U.S. attorney. *Capital Times*, April 12, June 6, 1928.

[109]*Daily Cardinal*, February 20, 1929; *Capital Times*, February 21, 1929. See also *Daily Cardinal*, February 22 and 24, 1929; *Capital Times*, February 22 and 23, 1929.

spring of 1930 he was arrested after leading a march of unemployed workers in downtown Madison under the auspices of the local council of the Communist National Trade Union Unity League. Gordon complained that the UW athletes who disrupted the parade were "bourgeois hoodlums" and denounced the police and University for their "fascist terror."[110] After leaving Madison Gordon moved to Cleveland where in 1932 he organized "The Workers School," whose purpose was to train workers for the class struggle under Lenin's motto: "Without revolutionary theory there can be no revolutionary practice."[111] His description to Meiklejohn of his teaching methodology revealed how much he had absorbed the socratic dialogue of his Experimental College experience:

> The method of teaching is the "question-discussion"form. In this manner the instructor draws from the student himself the logical explanation of a problem. A system of question-asking, when supported by sufficient and proper reading material, gives the student the method of dialectic thinking, of proceeding to solve problems causally, in relation to each other, etc.[112]

By 1937 Gordon, still an enthusiastic radical, had joined the Loyalist army in Spain, from which he wrote requesting that Meiklejohn give his regards to "Ex. Col. alumni and faculty" and send him books on the Greek philosophers and the history of philosophy.[113] Clearly, this young man's life had been touched significantly by his association with Alexander Meiklejohn and the Experimental College.[114]

In at least one instance Meiklejohn and the Experimental College were criticized as too conservative. In a letter to the editor of the *New Republic*, the feminist leader Edith Abbott complained in the summer of 1928 about a recent article by Robert Morss Lovett praising the male-

---

[110]*Capital Times*, March 6, 7, and 12, 1930; *Daily Cardinal*, March 2, 12, 13, and 18, 1930.

[111]David Gordon to Meiklejohn, February 4, 1933, Meiklejohn Papers, box 15.

[112]Gordon to Meiklejohn, March 21, 1933, ibid.

[113]Gordon to Meiklejohn, August 12, 1937, ibid.

[114]Gordon survived the Spanish Civil War and eventually became a science writer living in New Jersey. In 1962 he wrote an affectionate greeting to Meiklejohn on the occasion of the latter's ninetieth birthday, recalling how Meiklejohn had always referred to him as "Mr. Heraclitus" after the Greek philosopher who taught that permanence is an illusion and the only reality is transition and change. "And I cannot forget that you invited 'Mr. Heraclitus' to discuss and answer questions about Heraclitus-brought-up-to-date before the assembled student body and faculty and that you permitted this to go on for six hours." Gordon to Meiklejohn, April 27, 1962, ibid., box 32.

only Experimental College. "Is the University of Wisconsin coeducational or is it not?" she asked pointedly. She wondered why the regents should "suddenly abandon the fine tradition of the pioneers—equal opportunities for all students, women and men alike."[115] Meiklejohn candidly conceded that his Experimental College was not ready for coeducation.[116] In fairness, though Meiklejohn's previous experience was with male-only institutions, he was certainly not opposed to equal education for women. He simply considered the residential aspect of the college so important a part of its educational life that it took precedence over the admission of women. In the 1920s no American college or university—especially a state-supported one—could have considered allowing undergraduate women to live side-by-side in the same dormitory with men. A hint of the University's difficulty in preserving a Victorian double standard in the age of the flapper came in the fall of 1928, when the Experimental College Players staged a production of Aristophanes' ribald comedy, *Lysistrata*, a play about how the Athenian women persuaded their men to end war-making by declaring a boycott of love-making.[117] In an editorial headlined "What Are They Learning?" the Cincinnati *Enquirer* subsequently charged that a young UW coed from Indiana had been scandalized by her experiences in Madison—in particular by the free-thinking comments and reading assignments of an unnamed UW English instructor and by her attendance at an unnamed play. According to the newspaper, she had told her mother "there was some kind of a 'Research Club' functioning at the university that did not recite, but simply discussed all questions in class." This club had put on a Greek play that was "simply so unbelievably vulgar that she could not relate the story; in fact, it made even old-timers blush."[118] The editorial was forwarded to President Frank from Fond du Lac Regent Elizabeth Waters, who had received it from her state senator, William A. Titus, himself a member of the University's Board of Visitors. He in turn had been sent it by his son-in-law, a Cincinnati physician and UW alumnus, who suggested that Titus bring it "to the attention of some of 'the powers that be' in Madison, who are always shouting for 'Freedom and Liberalism'."[119]

[115]Edith Abbott, to the editor, "Meiklejohn at Wisconsin," *New Republic*, 55 (August 15, 1928), 334; *Capital Times*, August 14, 1928.
[116]*Daily Cardinal*, February 17, 1928.
[117]Ibid., October 11, 1928, November 3 and 28, 1928.
[118]Cincinnati *Enquirer*, July 10, 1929.
[119]John H. Skavlem to W.A. Titus, July 11, 1929; Titus to Elizabeth Waters, July 13,

President Frank took the complaint seriously and had his executive secretary try to identify the student and the circumstances. Both Professor Henry B. Lathrop, the chairman of the English department, and Dean of Women Louise Nardin were inclined to discount the vague reference to the English instructor, but they concluded that the *Enquirer's* complaint must refer to the recent Experimental College production of *Lysistrata*. Both strongly condemned the decision to perform the play. "In my opinion the *Lysistrata* is a scandalous play," Lathrop declared flatly, "and I think it was a mistake to permit it to be presented."[120] Dean Nardin was equally blunt. "The presentation of that play seems to me a deplorable mistake," she reported to the President, "which we can not defend when such criticism as this is made. I know from the hostesses in our dormitories that some girls who attended the play were amazed and shocked at its coarseness."[121] To some on the Hill, it seemed, freedom for and within Frank's and Meiklejohn's Experimental College ought to have some limits.

"I Wish You Would Say We Instead of They"

Another Bascom Hill observer who looked askance at the free-wheeling activities of the Experimental College was George Clarke Sellery, the crusty dean of the College of Letters and Science. The Experimental College had been created as an L&S administrative unit, but Sellery quickly discovered that his supervisory responsibility for Meiklejohn's venture was more nominal than real. On most matters, including budgets and staff appointments, Meiklejohn by-passed the dean and dealt directly with his patron, President Frank. To preserve the formalities, sometimes Julia Wilkinson, the presidents executive secretary, referred Meiklejohn's requests down to Sellery, asking that the dean recommend them to the president. Usually Sellery did so without comment, but once he responded tartly: "I have no basis for judging these recommendations. I have not heard of the proposals before....Will you please put in *as if coming from me* such recommendations as Dr. Frank has agreed to?"[122] Sellery understandably resented

1929; Waters to Frank, July 19, 1929, Frank Presidential Papers, 4/13/1, box 56.

[120]H.B. Lathrop to Julia M. Wilkinson, July 25, 1929, ibid.

[121]F. Louise Nardin to Wilkinson, July 26, 1929, ibid.

[122]Wilkinson to Sellery, November 24, 1928; Wilkinson to Sanford, March 7, 1929; G.C.S. [Sellery] to Wilkinson, March 11, 1929; Sellery note on Wilkinson to Miss F.G.

Frank's habit of assuming the dean's budget should cover many of Meiklejohn's special requests, usually passing this message through Miss Wilkinson.[123] On one occasion Dean Sellery had to remind the University business manager that the College of Letters and Science "desperately" needed its $500 reimbursement under Frank's arrangement that Sellery would provide half of the funds required for some additional furniture for the Experimental College.[124] The president also intervened occasionally to secure favorable treatment for Ex-College students who did not meet L&S regulations. "I am sure you will be willing to concur in this suggestion," he pointedly told the dean in 1929 in recommending that six poorly-prepared freshmen be admitted to the Experimental College, "even if our opinions differ on it."[125]

All this no doubt rankled in South Hall where Dean Sellery guarded the interests of the College of Letters and Science. Sellery was by nature a team player and at first believed the new president deserved support for a curricular experiment so dear to his heart. But the dean had also been an active member of the L&S instructional faculty since 1901, continuing to teach his popular history courses after becoming dean. He was recognized as one of the University's dedicated teachers. Sellery was first and last a faculty man, proud of the quality, professionalism, and devotion of his L&S colleagues. He increasingly came to resent Frank's and Meiklejohn's exuberant praise of their new approach to learning, which they asserted would cure all of the ills of American higher education. The problems the Experimental College

Sanford, ibid., box 66. Empahsis in original.

[123]See, for example, Wilkinson to Sellery, November 24, 1928, ibid.; Frank, office memorandum [ca. late March, 1928], ibid., box 40.

[124]Sellery to J. D. Phillips, May 17, 1928, ibid., box 51.

[125][Frank] to Sellery, June 19, 1929, ibid, box 66. See also Sellery to Frank, September 20, 1928; Sellery to Frank, July 10, 1929; Frank to Sellery, May 20, 1929, ibid.; Frank to Sellery, September 24, 1929; Frank to Sellery, February 20, 1930; Sellery to Frank, September 25, 1929, ibid., box 85; Sellery to Frank, October 1, 1930; Wilkinson to Sellery, April 2, 1931, ibid., box 103.

was addressing, they declared repeatedly, were general and endemic, the result of the narrow specialization and indifference to teaching of most faculty members in American colleges and universities. Dean Sellery was especially offended by Frank's sweeping assertion of the need to clear out faculty "dead wood." The president never thought to exempt his own institution from this indictment, yet as a newcomer he had no real knowledge of the Wisconsin faculty, the quality of its teaching, or even of its academic programs. On one occasion early in his administration Frank asked Dean Sellery how he was doing. Sellery replied pointedly: "You are doing very well, but when you are lecturing on universities I wish you would say we instead of they. That will remind you that the old days of free swinging at the universities are over for you." The advice had little effect.[126]

By the spring of 1929 Sellery felt compelled to speak out in defense of his faculty even if it cost him the deanship. He chose as the occasion an address to the freshman class at its spring convocation in the great hall of the Memorial Union. Sellery told President Frank afterward that the *Cardinal's* rather full coverage of his extemporaneous remarks was accurate, though in later years he conceded that some of his words now struck him as perhaps "a trifle provocative." He began his talk by deploring the current tendency of Americans to depreciate themselves, and reminded the freshmen they were attending one of the greatest universities in the world. All education was self-education with direction, he noted, and that was exactly what took place all the time in the College of Letters and Science. The rumor had somehow gotten abroad that the faculty of the College of Letters and Science was engaged in the task of pouring standardized information into student minds. "We have not done so," Sellery flatly declared. Indeed, "one of the forces protecting the world from standardization is the freedom—the clash of ideas—in the universities." As for the Experimental College, it was attempting a number of worthwhile things, but Sellery questioned the experiment on four grounds: its lack of required classes, its effort to study civilizations in the large, its insistence on a self-contained residential dormitory life, and its cursory treatment of science. Above all, Sellery questioned whether the experiment was not too sharp a break from the fixed requirements of high school, as he doubted whether freshmen and sophomores were ready for such complete freedom. Much to the enjoyment and quiet satisfaction of a large part of

---

[126]Sellery, *Some Ferments at Wisconsin*, p. 15.

the faculty, the Sellery convocation speech hit the campus like a bomb-shell. "SELLERY DECLARES EX COLLEGE IDEAS WRONG," headlined the *Capital Times*; "EXPERIMENTAL COLLEGE TECHNIQUE ASSAILED BY DEAN G.C. SELLERY," echoed the *Daily Cardinal*.[127]

Asked by the editor of the *Wisconsin Alumni Magazine* to elaborate on his extraordinary public criticism, Dean Sellery responded that he simply wanted to defend the L&S faculty and "to give their recent critics the salutary even if novel experience of a little taste of their own medicine." The L&S faculty was fully committed to improving its methods and procedures; it had proved that in authorizing the Experimental College.

> It hoped and still hopes to derive help from the experiments there undertaken. But that is no reason, as I see the situation, for telling university and teacher audiences here and there over the country that Liberal Arts faculties—and that is understood to mean our faculty in the first instance—are mossbacks or worse. There will be occasion enough for that if and when better methods and processes are demonstrated and proved and the faculty shows itself unwilling to employ them. That time has not yet arrived.[128]

Sellery submitted a draft of his *Alumni Magazine* statement to President Frank for review before publication, emphasizing that his intent was not to attack the Experimental College, only to defend the College of Letters and Science.[129] Despite having solicited a response from the dean, the editor of the *Alumni Magazine*—probably with encouragement from President Frank—decided not to mention Sellery's criticism or print his explanation. Instead, the *Magazine* published an editorial acknowledging the existence of "controversy, and bitter controversy, concerning the college," but expressing hope that "alumni will withhold judgment as to

---

[127]*Capital Times* and *Daily Cardinal*, March 9, 1929; Sellery, *Some Ferments at Wisconsin*, pp. 36-7. See also *Daily Cardinal*, March 8, 10, and 12, 1929. Sellery made minor typographical corrections in the *Cardinal* account for President Frank on May 2, 1929. Frank Presidential Papers, 4/13/1, box 66. After Sellery published an account of this incident in his memoirs in 1960, Professor Paul Clark, whose 1925 University Committee report had called for the All-University Study Commission that Frank used as his vehicle for launching the Experimental College, wrote Sellery: "I wish you could have made a little more of your masterly rebuttal (pp. 37-39) but of course you couldn't without being guilty of too much self-praise. It was not only in L&S that the courage and quality of your remarks were appreciated. We all were uplifted." Paul F. Clark to Sellery, January 10, 1960, L&S Papers, 7/16/18, box 1.

[128]G.C.S., "Draft for consideration with President Frank," May, 1929, Frank Presidential Papers, 4/13/1, box 66; Sellery, *Some Ferments at Wisconsin*, p. 37.

[129]G.C.S., "Draft for Consideration with President Frank," May, 1929.

the worth of the experiment."[130]

Sellery's blunt-spoken views might have been popular with the faculty, but they hardly endeared him to President Frank or to the students and staff of the Experimental College.[131] Early in his administration Frank had thought well enough of Sellery to ask him to serve as acting president in his absence, as had President Birge before him.[132] At the same time he had expressed private reservations about Sellery and several of the other deans to Regent President Kronshage.[133] By 1929 relations between Frank and Sellery had cooled and the president had begun to worry about Sellery's commitment to the president's reforms.[134] In December of 1928 Sellery appointed a faculty committee chaired by Professor Paul Knaplund of the history department to review the Experimental College in accordance with the L&S faculty's stipulation in authorizing the experiment. Although Knaplund had criticized the venture in the L&S faculty debate over the establishment of the college two years earlier, the Knaplund Committee had a reasonable balance, with at least two of the five members sympathetic to the Meiklejohn reforms.[135] The following month the president sent a handwritten

---

[130]"Judgment of the Experimental College," *WAM*, 30 (April, 1929), 222.

[131]*Daily Cardinal*, March 10, 12, and 27, 1929.

[132]See Frank to Sellery, July 4, 1926, Frank Presidential Papers, 4/13/1, box 15, in which the president jocularly asked Sellery "to keep the seal, lay the corner-stones, and look out for the few technical necessities that may require official blessing during my absence." See also Birge to Sellery, July 18, August 5, 1922, Birge Presidential Papers, 4/12/1, box 36, UA. President Clarence A. Dykstra continued the practice of asking Dean Sellery to be responsible for University affairs in his absence, commenting one time: "I leave knowing that there will be smooth sailing in my absence." Dykstra to Sellery, November 7, 1938, Dykstra Presidential Papers, 4/15/1, box 37, UA. See also Dykstra to Sellery, July 25, 1940, ibid., box 55.

[133]See Kronshage to John C. Schmidtmann, May 6, 1927, Theodore Kronshage Papers, box 6, SHSW, cited in Edward H. Beardsley, *Harry L. Russell and Agricultural Science in Wisconsin* (Madison: University of Wisconsin Press, 1969), p. 213, n. 61.

[134]That the president's regard for Dean Sellery had begun to cool may be inferred from the fact that Sellery's name was conspicuously omitted on a guest list for a luncheon Frank asked his secretary to arrange at the Madison Club for visiting President Harry W. Chase of the University of North Carolina in March, 1928. All of the other deans were to be invited, along with Governor Zimmerman, President Emeritus Birge, several regents, a number of leading faculty members (including Meiklejohn), and the editors of the two Madison newspapers. Frank to Miss Wilkinson, memorandum, March 22, 1928, Frank Presidential Papers, 4/13/1, box 40.

[135]The need for such a review had been discussed at the meeting of the L&S faculty on November 19, 1928, and in response Sellery had appointed a special faculty committee on December 17 "to report on the progress of the work of the Experimental College." The committee consisted of Paul Knaplund (history) as chairman, and Bayard Q. Morgan (German), Max C. Otto (philosophy), Warner Taylor (English), and Henry R. Trumbower (economics).

note to his secretary suggesting that he did not trust the L&S reviewers:

> Remind me that I must draft a statement on why reform of "liberal education process" should not, in a University, be determined by the College of Liberal Arts alone, but by the whole University, showing the interlocking of the future of professional education with the pre-professional liberal training. (See Assn of Am. Med. Colleges Proceedings 1925 Cabot's Address) It is important that I draft this statement as soon as possible, and set up a committee, representing all the University, to consider the Experimental College. Otherwise the L&S committee ~~will~~ may fail to see the problem whole.[136]

As in other situations, Frank failed to follow through on this resolve, but Dean Sellery's well-publicized criticism at the freshman convocation a month later was a challenge the president felt he could not ignore.

Over the next several months Frank gave serious thought to removing Sellery as dean. He dispatched a faculty emissary to sound out the L&S department chairmen on the faculty's reaction if Sellery were replaced. He recruited Warren Weaver, the chairman of the UW mathematics department, as Sellery's replacement. Upon the president's assurance the deanship would soon be vacant, Weaver agreed to accept the appointment, but told Frank he would not help to depose Sellery. The president said not a word of this to Sellery, but his coolness toward the dean indicated his deep displeasure. Sellery soon heard ominous reports of Frank's undercover maneuvering, and at least one friend urged him to resign the deanship before he was fired. At the commencement exercises in June, Sellery was seated next to Regent Schmidtmann, whose son was an Ex-College student. In parting, Schmidtmann remarked that it would seem strange to attend the exercises without Sellery in the future. Much to the dean's surprise, however, at the meeting of the regents the next day Frank presented no recommendation about Sellery, the board took no action on his appointment, and he continued as dean as if nothing had happened. Subsequently, Frank told intimates he should have gotten rid of Sellery when he first arrived in Madison, but explained that after the dean's

---

Otto's presence on the committee indicated its balance, for he was known to be a friend of Meiklejohn and sympathetic to his ideas for curricular reform. Indeed, one of Otto's friends told him his membership "insures a sympathetic report on the college." Otto responded that "my job was what you suspected it to be." L&S Faculty Minutes, November 19, 1928; Sellery to C.A. Smith, December 17, 1928, L&S Papers, 7/1/1-2, box 2; Boyd H. Bode to Max C. Otto, May 3, 1929; Otto to Bode, May 10, 1929, Max C. Otto Papers, box 2, SHSW; *WAM*, 30 (February 1929), 161.

[136]Frank to Miss Wilkinson, January 22, 1929, Frank Presidential Papers, 4/13/1, box 72.

public criticism it was impossible to fire him. Many years later Max Otto offered another explanation. He had gone to Frank to point out that there was a good deal of faculty dissatisfaction with the president; consequently, he thought it would be a serious blunder to give the malcontents a leader by ditching the widely-respected dean.[137]

Whatever the reasons for Frank's failure to act, in the fall of 1929 the *Capital Times*, ever alert for campus gossip, published an account of Frank's abortive plan to fire Sellery, attributing the president's failure to act to "considerable" faculty opposition.[138] Both Frank and Sellery issued "amused denials," with Frank hailing Sellery as "one of the university's most distinguished scholars and one of its greatest teachers," and claiming that the two enjoyed "the most intimately cordial friendship."[139]

That Sellery was not alone in his resentment of Frank's and Meiklejohn's aspersions on the faculty was to be seen in a complaint by Professor Grant Showerman of the classics department to the Knaplund Committee as it began studying the Experimental College in the spring of 1929. Showerman, a distinguished Latin scholar, asked the committee to include in its investigation "the method and the substance of Alexander Meiklejohn's publicity work in support of the Experimental College," which Showerman described as vilification and condemnation of existing faculty teaching. "I am one of many earnest men on this campus," Showerman pointed out, "who resent the outrageous abuse to which their institution is subjected, but who, because of courtesy and because of deference to administrative wishes, have not so far made the protest I am here expressing."[140] The members of the

---

[137]See *Capital Times*, October 15, 1929; Clark to Sellery, January 10, 1960, L&S Papers, 7/16/18, box 1; Sellery, *Some Ferments at Wisconsin*, pp. 38-9; Mark H. Ingraham, "The University of Wisconsin, 1925-1950," in Allan G. Bogue and Robert Taylor, eds., *The University of Wisconsin: One Hundred and Twenty-Five Years* (Madison: University of Wisconsin Press, 1975), p. 63; Lawrence H. Larsen, *The President Wore Spats: A Biography of Glenn Frank* (Madison: State Historical Society of Wisconsin, 1965), p. 102. After his firing in 1937 Frank claimed he had been told by Regent Kronshage at the time of his appointment as president that one of his first acts should be to fire Sellery. *New York Times*, January 11, 1937.

[138]*Capital Times*, October 15, 1929.

[139]Ibid., *Wisconsin State Journal*, *Daily Cardinal*, and *Milwaukee News*, all October 16, 1929. Sellery observed drily in his memoirs: "I noticed that he made no reference to me as dean, but I doubt that many appreciated the discrimination." Sellery, *Some Ferments at Wisconsin*, p. 39.

[140]Grant Showerman to the Committee of the College of Letters and Science on the Experimental College, February 16, 1929, L&S Papers, 7/7/12, box 1. When he could get no

committee prudently decided Showerman's suggestion was outside their province,[141] but they did spend several months interviewing Meiklejohn and the staff and some of the students of the Experimental College, reviewing reading lists and other curricular materials, and studying enrollment and student performance data.[142]

The Knaplund Committee's report in May, 1929, deliberately refrained from passing judgment on the Experimental College, arguing that the venture had "not yet found itself in either content of study or method of procedure" and was still too new and transitional for a valid appraisal. The report included two paragraphs written not by Knaplund but by Max Otto, a close friend and philosophy colleague of Meiklejohn and the committee member most sympathetic to the experiment. Otto saw to it that the report praised the experiment for trying to address "a major problem in contemporary education"—how to help students achieve "a unified comprehension of the highly specialized types of knowledge," how to "stimulate intellectual curiosity and to further the power to think objectively and creatively," how to "develop the sense of social responsibility," how to develop a new system of evaluation and grading, and how to "secure a more personal working relationship

---

satisfaction from the Knaplund Committee, Showerman made his grievance public in a stinging attack on Frank, Meiklejohn, and the Experimental College published in *School and Society* in 1931. The sarcastic and highly personal nature of Showerman's criticism no doubt offended some readers—Max Otto told Showerman he deeply deplored "its illiberality of spirit and its tone of assumed intellectual superiority"—but the enthusiastic applause Showerman received from readers in Madison and around the country showed how much others also resented Frank's and Meiklejohn's sweeping attacks on current educational practices. Arthur Stanley Pease, who had succeeded Meiklejohn as president of Amherst College, told Showerman: "I have been wondering when someone would say these things, for much has appeared on the other side of the question. What you have written will be read with much interest, and, outside of Madison, in few places more than here." Interestingly, quite a number of Showerman's correspondents assumed Frank would soon fire him for daring to speak out. Showerman, "A Most Lamentable Comedy," *School and Society*, 33 (April 11, 1931), 481-8; Otto to Showerman, April 16, 1931; Pease to Showerman, April 28, 1931, L&S Papers, 7/7/12, box 1. Another outspoken UW faculty critic was philosopher Eliseo Vivas, who publicized his criticism of the educational philosophy of the Experimental College (absence of discipline, over-emphasis on the individual, and lack of specialized advisors) in a debate with Meiklejohn in the *Nation* magazine in the spring of 1931. *Daily Cardinal*, March 22, November 29, 1931.

[141]Minutes of the Committee on the Experimental College, March 5, 1929, L&S Papers, 7/16/20, box 10.

[142]See, for example, Knaplund to F.O. Holt, January 8, 1929; Holt to Knaplund, January 18, 1929; Dorothy Crowley to Warner Taylor, May 2, 1929; Minutes of the Committee on the Experimental College, January 8 and 18, March 5, 1929, ibid.

between teacher and student." The fact that the committee refrained from passing judgment on the experiment at this point did not mean, Otto's paragraphs declared, "that we assume a neutral attitude as regards this basic problem, or that we suggest such an attitude as the proper one for university teachers to take." On the contrary, it was the very importance of this entire matter, "which seems to us to demand long and profound study on the part of the faculty, that induces us to withhold judgment until that study has produced a larger body of fact and a clearer vision." The committee called for "a closer relationship than at present exists" between the Experimental College and the larger University and recommended that the college be reviewed again the following year.[143]

In discussing his committee's report at the L&S faculty meeting on May 20, 1929, Knaplund emphasized its tentative character and called attention to the data presented by the committee showing higher average scores by Experimental College students on English placement and psychological tests than by L&S students in general. He noted that hopes for the college to enroll a cross section of the student body had not been realized; its students were instead mostly self-selected. Meiklejohn conceded his disappointment in this regard as well as concern about declining enrollment, especially of students from Wisconsin. After some questions and considerable discussion, largely led by Meiklejohn, the faculty voted to receive the Knaplund report as presented.[144] Subsequently, the faculty voted twice to delay the further review recommended by the Knaplund Committee, until 1931-32.[145] The L&S faculty also agreed to allow the Experimental College to

---

[143]Undated draft of the two quoted paragraphs with the handwritten notation by Otto, "Not written by P.K. but by M.C.O.," Otto Papers, box 2; L&S Faculty Document 43, Knaplund Committee Report, May 10, 1929. Many years later the widow of Professor Knaplund offered an explanation for the committee's carefully neutral, even partly supportive, report. Her husband, she said, was convinced the Experimental College was a failure, having been influenced in part by his history department colleague, Carl Russell Fish, who had withdrawn from the Experimental College instructional staff after only one semester. Fish, one of University's great teachers, was upset at the lack of discipline and structure in the college. Mrs. Knaplund said her husband believed that with its enrollment declining the Experimental College would soon fall of its own weight, and its supporters should not be given an opportunity to claim that its demise was caused by the hostility of the L&S faculty. He did not want to give any impression that Meiklejohn had been martyred at Wisconsin as had happened at Amherst. Dorothy K. Knaplund, oral history interview, 1991, UHP.

[144]L&S Faculty Minutes (draft), May 20, 1929; *Daily Cardinal*, May 21, 1929; *Capital Times*, May 21, 1929; *Press Bulletin*, May 29, 1929.

[145]L&S Faculty Minutes, February 17, December 15, 1930.

award departmental honors to its best sophomores, though it declined to grant L&S sophomore honors to such students.[146]

"Uncouth Behavior in the Dining Rooms"

Declining enrollment and to some extent its special character were indeed a serious disappointment and problem for the backers of the experiment. While Meiklejohn had always envisioned a small experimental group, he and President Frank had planned for an entering class of 125 students each year, with a steady-state enrollment of 250 when the college reached full operation. The Experimental College never attained this level, however, and enrollment figures for its five-year life showed instead a steady and embarrassing decline in student interest, as indicated in Table 1.

Table 1
Experimental College Enrollment, 1927-1932

Year	Freshmen	Sophomores	Total
1927-28	119	—	119
1928-29	92	103	195
1929-30	79	76	155
1930-31	74	64	138
1931-32	—	66	66

Worse yet from the standpoint of a hoped-for cross section of the regular student body, to say nothing of public relations in the state, Wisconsin students never showed much interest in the Experimental College, whose enrollment came predominantly from outside the state. In fact, the proportion of resident and non-resident students in the Experimental College was just about the opposite of that of the University as a whole, where Wisconsin residents regularly comprised about 70 percent of the total enrollment during these years. Table 2 shows the disproportionately heavy out-of-state enrollment in the Experimental College throughout its life.

---

[146]Ibid., October 21, 1929.

Table 2
Experimental College
Percentage of Resident and Non-Resident Enrollment, 1927-31

Year	% Resident	% Non-Resident
1927-28	38	62
1928-29	37	63
1929-30	14	86
1930-31	31	69

While the University's data about the religious affiliation of students are incomplete and imprecise, the Bureau of Guidance and Records estimated in a 1932 report that the percentage of Jewish students in the Experimental College ranged from approximately 20 percent in the first class to 40 percent in the 1930-31 class, as compared to a level of about 10 percent in the student body as a whole.[147] Meiklejohn lamented in his final report that because the Experimental College had attracted a few radicals and a larger number of Jews, it had appeared "as something 'queer' and 'hostile' and 'alien' in the larger

---

[147]"Report of the Bureau of Guidance and Records on the Experimental College," February, 1932, pp. 1-3, L&S Papers, 7/1/1-2, box 2; Annual Reports of the Experimental College, October 17, 1927, June, 1930, February, 1931, L&S Papers, 7/1/1-2, box 2, and Frank Presidential Papers, 4/13/1, boxes 74 and 100. The bureau's report estimated the proportion of Jews in the general student body as 10-15 percent. This may be somewhat high. The two religious censuses conducted by the University in 1928 and 1929 reported a Jewish enrollment of about 9 percent. Meiklejohn's annual reports were understandably vague about the Experimental College enrollment after the first report and he omitted any enrollment data at all in the 220-page final report submitted to the letters and science faculty in January, 1932, and published by Harper & Brothers later in the year. "Report of the Advisers of the Experimental College," January, 1932; Alexander Meiklejohn, *The Experimental College* (New York: Harper & Brothers, 1932), reprinted by the Arno Press in 1971, and again in an abridged version edited by John Walker Powell, one of the Experimental College advisers, by the Seven Locks Press in 1981. In this final report Meiklejohn commented: "The percentage of Jews was, quite naturally, unusually large, and it has tended to increase." Again: "For several reasons the percentage of Jewish students was unusually large." "Report of the Advisors of the Experimental College," pp. 116, 150. Interestingly, in view of the great publicity about the Experimental College in the Madison newspapers during its life, the college attracted very few students from Madison. The first and largest class included only one Madison student—Gordon Meiklejohn, the son of the chairman, for whom Meiklejohn waged a successful campaign for a special exception to gain resident status and tuition. Harold C. Bradley to M.E. McCaffrey, June 1, 1926; Bradley to Alexander Meiklejohn, June 2, 1926, Frank Presidential Papers, 4/13/1, box 2; *First Year of the Experimental College*, p. 24.

student community."[148]	The college may have fulfilled Frank's dream of creating "the first really experimental laboratory of higher education," but the president's expectation that it would consist of "students representing a cross section of our regular student body" was certainly not realized.[149]

Frank, Meiklejohn, and the Experimental College advisers worried especially about the lack of interest by students from Wisconsin. To attract more Wisconsin residents, the college pursued a number of strategies. From the beginning Meiklejohn saw to it that the *Wisconsin Alumni Magazine* carried regular reports of college activities, including an account of the first two years of the experiment in June, 1929. That same month the University sent Alumni Recorder John Bergstresser and Ex-College student Campbell Dickson on an extensive trip around the state to promote the college among high school students and educators. After visiting Fond du Lac, Oshkosh, Neenah, Menasha, Appleton, Green Bay, Manitowoc, Sheboygan, Baraboo, Fort Atkinson, Eau Claire, Chippewa Falls, Merrill, Wausau, Stevens Point, and Wisconsin Rapids, Bergstresser reported decidedly mixed results. "Not a single student was found who had definitely decided to enter the college," he told President Frank, although twenty showed "real interest" and were sent promotional literature and "hundreds of graduating seniors who had probably never heard of it before were told rather fully about the college."

The strikingly perceptive questions asked by principals and teachers were revealing. They were worried about the reported antagonism of the regular UW faculty and wondered how the graduates of the Experimental College would adapt to the regular UW curriculum as juniors. They asked how Ex-College students would be able to meet their degree requirements, especially in the professional programs, and questioned the adequacy of the study of science in the college. They thought the Experimental College might be better adapted to exceptional

---

[148]"Report of the Advisers of the Experimental College," p. 150.

[149]Frank to Meiklejohn, January 16, 1926, Meiklejohn Papers, box 32, and Frank Papers, Kirksville. For example, the Experimental College attracted some of the very brightest students who took the 1929 scholastic aptitude test administered by the University to Wisconsin high school seniors planning to attend college the next year, second only to the humanities course and nearly twice the median intelligence percentile of those enrolling in agriculture. V.A.C. Henmon and F.O. Holt, *A Report on the Administration of Scholastic Aptitude Tests to 34,000 Wisconsin High School Seniors in Wisconsin in 1929 and 1930*, Bulletin of the University of Wisconsin, Serial No. 1786, General Series No. 1570, 1931, p. 51.

students, and asked whether in fact it had not "attracted exceptional students? and otherwise unusual ones?" Finally, they believed most freshmen were too immature to handle so much freedom.[150] Bergstresser followed up his trip with a letter to all alumni living in Wisconsin enclosing a four-page bulletin about the college which he pointed out "might be interesting to you and to any high school graduates you know who are planning to attend the University." He urged the alumni to correct "a widely prevalent, but erroneous, impression that for enrollment in the Experimental College a student must have special training and superior scholastic aptitudes."[151]

There were a number of reasons for the reluctance of Wisconsin parents to send their sons to the Experimental College. One, certainly, were the negative reports, soon passed around Madison and the state, of the excessive freedom and disrespect for rules and authority the college allowed impressionable eighteen-year-olds. Meiklejohn believed passionately in individual freedom and assumed it went hand-in-hand with collective responsibility. He had been disappointed when the first Ex-College class rejected any form of self-government, but thought it would be only a matter of time before the students recognized the need for some form of individual and collective self-restraint. This lesson, he was convinced, was an important part of their education. The problem was that the Experimental College did not exist in isolation. Its students occupied only part of Adams Hall, which was adjacent to the other men's dormitory, Tripp Hall. All of the Adams-Tripp students ate in a common dining hall and were generally under the responsibility of the UW dormitories and commons staff and the faculty Committee on Dormitories. Regular students soon came to resent the excessive noise and violation of dormitory quiet hours by the Ex-College students, their exuberant practical jokes and unrestrained high jinks, including well-publicized biscuit fights in the dining room, and their general disregard of dormitory regulations. Meiklejohn had secured from President Frank full authority over the Experimental College, including exemption for its students from normal UW disciplinary procedures. He considered their youthful enthusiasm harmless, reflective of the development of a desirable esprit de corps among the members of the college.

Others thought the young savages needed taming. Chief among

---

[150]John L. Bergstresser to Frank, June 24, 1929, Frank Presidential Papers, 4/13/1, box 55.

[151][Bergstresser] to John Smith, draft, July 18, 1929, ibid., box 74.

these was Professor Harold C. Bradley, the chairman of the Dormitories Committee, who with another long-time committee member, Graduate Dean Charles S. Slichter, had waged the lengthy fight to build the first two men's dormitories along the shore of Lake Mendota. That effort had taken more than a decade, eventually succeeding when the regents agreed to borrow $300,000 from the bequest of J. Stephens Tripp for part of the construction costs and to borrow the rest through their new captive agency, the Wisconsin University Building Corporation, established for this purpose. Both Slichter and Bradley were impressed by the Oxford-Cambridge residential colleges and their system of dons. Believing the new men's facilities should be more than simply a place to eat and sleep, they designed not simple dormitories but two large quadrangles—Tripp and Adams halls—each consisting of eight smaller houses having a common room or den and staffed with a resident house "fellow." Nearby was a two-story refectory or commons serving meals to students from the entire complex. The intent was to provide not only room and board but a vital experience in living and learning together, which would be an important supportive adjunct to the students' academic work at the University.[152]

Both Bradley and Slichter were members of the All-University Study Commission on the Experimental College and they supported President Frank's decision to assign half of Adams Hall to Alexander Meiklejohn for the college when it opened in the fall of 1927. The Dormitories Committee further agreed that Meiklejohn could use all of Adams Hall for the Experimental College when it was scheduled to be at full strength in 1928-29. As a courtesy the committee allowed Meiklejohn to appoint his own house fellows—paid from general dormitory funds—without following the customary screening and training procedures used for the regular house fellows. What Professor Bradley and his colleagues had not anticipated was how Meiklejohn's commitment to complete freedom and separatism for his guinea pigs would affect the operation of the entire Adams-Tripp complex.

Bradley's committee chose to ignore the first rumblings of trouble during 1927-28, until at mid-year one of Meiklejohn's house fellows, who was also an Experimental College adviser, left town for two weeks without notifying the dormitories staff of his absence. At this Bradley

---

[152]Mark H. Ingraham, *Charles Sumner Slichter: The Golden Vector* (Madison: University of Wisconsin Press, 1972), pp. 114-9; Barry Teicher and John W. Jenkins, *A History of Housing at the University of Wisconsin* (Madison: UW History Project, 1987), pp. 21-33.

called a meeting of the committee with Meiklejohn and the Adams-Tripp house fellows to try to reach a common understanding about life in the halls and the responsibilities of the house fellows. The notes kept by Bradley of the discussion made clear there were irreconcilable differences. Meiklejohn and his Experimental College fellows declared that they expected and welcomed a certain amount of non-conformity in their students:

> They wanted their men to think things out for themselves and arrive at their own conclusions without too much insistence on conformity. It was felt by others, however, that a certain minimum in good manners could be expected, and was indeed part of the training which the Dormitories were expected to give their students. It was not believed that table manners and dress which conforms to a reasonable standard would interfere with intellectual freedom of thought.[153]

The meeting left unresolved the question of how the Experimental College house fellows would be appointed in the future, with Bradley and Donald L. Halverson, the director of dormitories and commons, insistent that all house fellows should be appointed and trained in the same way, and with Meiklejohn equally adamant that he must select and be responsible for his own fellows.[154]

Bradley considered the differences serious enough to write a long letter of complaint to Frank requesting a conference with the president for his committee to review the disruptive behavior of the Experimental College students. He first sent a draft to his friend Slichter for comment. Slichter responded that he had "no suggestions to make, because I think there is no way of approaching this subject except with the utmost frankness and with all the facts before the president....I quite agree that the success of the Experimental College cannot be bound up in any substantial way with lax manners or a weak recognition of the comfort of others."[155]   In his letter to Frank, Bradley reviewed at considerable length the problems caused by the presence of the free-spirited Ex-College students in the Adams-Tripp housing complex.

---

[153]"Notes on Dormitories Committee Meeting with the Dormitory Fellows," February 19, 1928, Graduate School Papers, 6/1/2, box 14, UA, also Business Administration Papers, 24/1/1, box 41, UA.

[154]D.L Halverson to J.D. Phillips, February 21, 1928, Business Administration Papers, 24/1/1, box 36.

[155]Bradley note to Slichter on Frank letter draft, March 5, 1928; Slichter to Bradley, March 7, 1928, Graduate School Papers, 6/1/2, box 14.

They were a disruptive element in the new men's dormitories, which were trying with some success to establish a system of self-government and a communal social life. Meiklejohn and his house fellows were failing to exercise appropriate supervision over their charges to the detriment of living conditions for other residents. Bradley summarized the unsatisfactory result of the recent meeting of his Dormitories Committee with Meiklejohn and his house fellows:

> (1) The Experimental College desires as complete segregation and isolation as possible from the rest of the Dormitory students in order to build up a social life about a community of intellectual interests. Dr. Meiklejohn considers anything which accentuates the dissociation of the Experimental group to be advantageous. He even thinks the calling of the men "guinea pigs" has been beneficial in emphasizing this separation and so in developing group consciousness.
> (2) Uncouth behavior in the dining rooms is considered evidence of intellectual non-conformity, and so apparently is of no moment, and perhaps by implication a good sign. This would apparently explain why the Experimental Fellows do not attempt to restrain food-throwing, excessive noise, etc., in the dining rooms.
> (3) The same attitude will explain the disregard of the quiet hour observance, which has proved disturbing to the non-Experimental houses in Adams and even to Tripp.

Bradley reminded the president that the extent of property damage in the Experimental College houses was five times higher than in the rest of the Tripp-Adams complex.[156]

As was often the case, President Frank preferred not to get involved, though after a meeting with Meiklejohn he jotted down a cryptic note and query:

> 1. State principle re discipline in Adams Hall when Ex. College takes it over....
> 2. Is it right to have Halverson responsible for discipline in Dormitories? This is job for educator or dean of men.[157]

In his final report on the experiment Meiklejohn made brief reference to this conflict, pointing out that the behavior problems had eventually

---

[156]Bradley to Frank, draft, March 5, 1928, ibid., box 4, also reproduced (in slightly garbled form and dated March 8, 1928, which indicates that Frank gave a copy to Meiklejohn) in Appendix XI, "Report of the Advisers of the Experimental College," p. 219.

[157]Frank, office memorandum [ca. late March, 1928], Frank Presidential Papers, 4/13/1, box 40.

diminished, "but only as the College, in the two later years, gave ground, submitting to the necessities of the situation."[158]

After the college's proportion of Wisconsin students fell to only 14 percent in 1929-30, more aggressive recruiting measures seemed clearly to be required. A committee of Experimental College advisers, including John Bergstresser, the alumni recorder, recommended a multi-pronged strategy "to make the people throughout the state aware of what the College means and willing to support it." Their first suggestion was that President Frank send a letter to all high school principals and school superintendents in the state "explaining our failure to get Wisconsin boys, the importance of the experiment, his confidence in it as an established part of the University, and his request for co-operation in making it significant for the state as a Wisconsin cross-section." The president should also speak out for the college and perhaps send a letter to all alumni in the state. Among many other suggestions were having Professor and Mrs. Meiklejohn speak to every AAUW chapter and to other Wisconsin women's groups, scheduling statewide extension lectures on the college by the advisers, having

---

[158]"Report of the Advisors of the Experimental College," p. 151. Behavior problems and the appointment of house fellows were not the only issues on which Meiklejohn and the Dormitories Committee and staff continued to disagree during the life of the Experimental College. After the first class completed the two-year program of the Experimental College, Meiklejohn insisted that its members, regardless of non-resident status, should have preference in room assignments in the Adams-Tripp complex, including preference for vacant rooms in Adams Hall. The Dormitories Committee and staff believed the regent-mandated priority rules should govern room assignments, thus giving preference to Wisconsin residents and to previous residents. Since Meiklejohn had always insisted that the Experimental College students were to be kept separate from and treated differently than the other residents, the Dormitories Committee believed that residence in the Experimental College did not give its students priority as previous dorm residents. The issue was discussed with the regents, who declined to change the policy or make an exception. Nevertheless, Meiklejohn told the Dormitories Committee in May, 1929, that "Dr. Frank had authorized the assignment of this year[']s Experimental College Sophomores who will return as Juniors in Adams Hall without following order of application or legal residence." Evidently Meiklejohn was determined to try to fill up Adams Hall for the Experimental College by one means or another! D.L.H. [Halverson] to "Pete" [A.W. Peterson], May 24, 1929, and enclosure; Halverson to Meiklejohn, May 24, 1929, Business Administration Papers, 24/1/1, box 45. See also Halverson to J.D. Phillips, February 19, 1929, ibid.; Halverson to Peterson, June 17, 1929; [Phillips] to Halverson, July 1, 1929, ibid., box 56. During the Ex-College's final year, with many of its students suffering from the depression, Meiklejohn sought and received permission from the Board of Regents to use the students' dormitory room deposits as a loan fund, "with the understanding that Professor Meiklejohn will be personally responsible for damages to property, normally protected by the individual student deposits, for the remainder of the year, when such deposits will not be available." BOR Minutes, January 1, 1932.

University officials and other "friendly" counselors "help to guide boys here" during the fall registration, and improving faculty and student opinion on the Hill "so as to avoid propaganda against the College."[159] President Frank cannot be faulted for lack of support; his public acclaim of the experiment was constant and unflagging. In June of 1930, for example, he announced that if his eleven-year-old son Glenn, Jr., were old enough he would enroll him in the Experimental College.[160]

"A Fresh Turn on the Road of Experimentation"

Throughout most of its history the Experimental College was plagued with rumors of imminent demise, which understandably helped to undermine its enrollment. Belatedly, Meiklejohn and the advisers realized that the name of their venture—so important for winning initial approval from a skeptical L&S faculty and for connoting change to the wider academic world—also conveyed a sense of transition and impermanence that confused the public on which the college depended for students and support. Sometimes even the experiment's top booster, President Frank, said it was but a passing phase in the development of a new undergraduate curriculum. In responding to questions from a legislative committee in December, 1929, about the value and cost of the college, for example, Frank conceded that it had produced no savings but also explained it had not been created as a permanent unit. It was created merely to test certain ideas about teaching and to explore a possible revision of the freshman-sophomore liberal arts curriculum. Frank speculated that perhaps the time had come to consider adapting some of the lessons of the experiment to the University as a whole. "ALL U.W. TO BE 'TEST COLLEGE,'" headlined a Madison newspaper's account of his testimony: "PLAN EXPERIMENTAL METHODS ON HILL; MAY USE 60 PER CENT OLD METHODS, 40 PER CENT MEIKLEJOHN SYSTEM."[161] The president was obliged to issue a hasty press release denying any intention either "to discontinue the Experimental College" or that "the College of Letters and Science was to be transformed into

---

[159]"Experimental College Enrollment Program," report of a committee consisting of Sharp, Bergstresser, Havighurst, and Agard [1930], Frank Presidential Papers, 4/13/1, box 74.

[160]*Daily Cardinal*, June 3, 1930. In fact, shortly after Glenn, Jr.'s birth Frank had signed him up at Groton, the exclusive New England preparatory school, to begin his studies in 1932. In the fall of 1936, when Glenn, Jr., reached college age, the Franks sent their son to Harvard.

[161]*Capital Times*, December 6 and 8, 1930.

a replica of the Experimental College." Even Frank's disavowal left some ambiguity, however, when in the final sentence he emphasized that he wanted "to remove any suggestion that I announced anything new about the Experimental College—any new decision regarding its *immediate* future."[162]

By early 1930 Meiklejohn had begun to consider ending the experiment. He consulted his friend Phil La Follette, who, as the latter told his wife, tried "to be helpful without giving advice on subjects I know not of."

> As I see it it comes down to a question of what Alec can do with the problem in view of his inherent character. It is useless to try and force or expect one of a given temper[a]ment to do things, which though *essential*, are not possible for him. Alec has the psychological twist where he personally identifies the College with himself; consequently he cannot fight for it because he senses or feels that he is fighting, to put it crudely, for his meal ticket.[163]

There was no doubt that Meiklejohn regarded the Experimental College as his personal contribution to curricular reform, just as it was impossible to disassociate the college from the ideas and personality of its founder. There could also be no denying the problem of declining enrollment. When only 128 freshmen and sophomores registered for 1930-31, less than half of the College's planned capacity, Meiklejohn's forebodings were understandable.[164]

Shortly after Christmas of 1930 Meiklejohn and a group of the advisers appealed to Dean Sellery for a public expression of support. After an evening of discussion Sellery agreed to speak out for the college, but on condition the advisers hold final examinations for each

---

[162]Glenn Frank press release for Monday, December 9, 1929, Frank Presidential Papers, 4/13/1, box 74. Emphasis added. See also *Capital Times*, December 12, 1929.

[163]Philip F. La Follette to Isen La Follette, February 2, 1930, P.F. La Follette Papers, box 134. Emphasis in original.

[164]When the editor of the *Nation* suggested an article on the demise of the Experimental College as a reflection of the decline of Wisconsin progressivism, Max Otto denied that either was true. "The college is to go on at least for the coming year," he stressed. "Whether it will continue after that depends upon a number of circumstances, among which is the size of the attendance by students from the state." Otto to H.R. Mussey, May 3, 1930, Otto Papers, box 2. In a follow-up letter Otto remarked: "If the college is discontinued after the coming year, which seems to be the impression of people who ought to know about its future, I think it will not be correct to attribute this fact to the triumph of illiberal forces." Otto to Mussey, May 22, 1930, ibid.

year of the course. This they flatly refused to do.[165] Conscious of the deepening depression and its likely effect on the University's budget and on the Experimental College's heavy out-of-state enrollment, and especially in light of Dean Sellery's withholding of public support for the venture, Meiklejohn persuaded the reluctant advisers the time had come to terminate their noble experiment. He would rather declare victory with banners held high than either surrender to hostile foes or simply wither away.

Accordingly, in February, 1931, Chairman Meiklejohn on behalf of the Experimental College advisers recommended to the parent letters and science faculty that no freshmen be admitted to the college the next fall and that 1931-32 be its final year of operation. He further urged that the advisers be directed to report on the experiment and posed a number of questions to be considered in such a report, suggesting also that a faculty committee be designated to evaluate the advisers' report and the lessons of the experiment.[166] The L&S faculty accepted these recommendations with little discussion on February 16.[167] The same day President Frank issued a press release denying that he or anyone outside the college had pressured Meiklejohn and the advisers to reach their decision. He hailed "this striking example of a university project that does not care to crystallize itself into a vested interest after its administrators feel that it has achieved measurable completion." It was, the president declared reassuringly, "but a fresh turn on the road of experimentation."[168] There were few regrets around the state. The *Milwaukee Journal* applauded the University's willingness to experiment, but agreed that the time had come to end this one.[169] The *Janesville Gazette* was more bluntly critical. Complaining of Meiklejohn's "maze of sesquipedalian verbiage," the newspaper asserted that his report to the faculty was really a confession of failure because the Experimental College had contained "every element of the hobo in

---

[165]Sellery, *Some Ferments at Wisconsin*, p. 28.

[166]L&S Faculty Document 48, "Report of the Experimental College," February, 1931.

[167]L&S Faculty Minutes, February 16, 1931. *Capital Times*, February 16 and 17, 1931; *Daily Cardinal*, February 17 and 18, 1931. At the February 16 faculty meeting Meiklejohn apologized for premature publicity about the recommendation to end the Experimental College, no doubt alluding to a report carried by the *Capital Times* that day. That he may have been the source of the leak is suggested, however, by the fact that the same issue had also carried a long article written by Meiklejohn under the heading: "Dr. Meiklejohn Tells Why He Would End Ex-College." *Capital Times*, February 16, 1931.

[168][Glenn Frank,] press release, February 16, 1931, Frank Papers, Kirksville.

[169]Editorial, *Milwaukee Journal*, quoted in *Capital Times*, February 19, 1931.

education. "[170]

Following the decision to end the college, Meiklejohn promptly set to work on the promised final report. He intended it to be a large work—not only a comprehensive review of the experiment, but also a vigorous defense of the educational and pedagogical philosophy underlying the college along with a set of recommendations and advice for future experimentation and curricular change. It would, of course, be addressed to the letters and science faculty, but its real audience was meant to be much wider—the academic community and educated public across the country. Even as he worked on the report, therefore, Meiklejohn entered into negotiations with Harper and Brothers to publish his report on the Experimental College as a book immediately after its submission to the faculty in Madison.[171]

Dean Sellery selected the membership of the new faculty committee on the Experimental College with unusual care, first presenting Meiklejohn with a list of a dozen candidates from which Sellery proposed to appoint the five-member committee, and asking if he regarded any as unsuitable. Meiklejohn offered no objections, so the dean proceeded to appoint a committee consisting of respected senior faculty members under the leadership of journalism Professor Willard Bleyer.[172]

As with the Ex-College itself, the 220-page final report on the experiment was mostly Meiklejohn's doing, with the chairman writing its twenty-one chapters and selecting its eleven appendices. As expected, the report was for the most part a glowing endorsement of the experiment and its educational vision of tutorial instruction centered around the broad interdisciplinary study of two distinct civilizations widely separated in time. Though he solicited comments and criticism from the other Ex-College advisers, Meiklejohn got mostly encourage-

[170]Editorial, *Janesville Gazette*, quoted in *Capital Times*, February 21, 1931.

[171]Meiklejohn told President Frank: "I would suggest that I be authorized to negotiate with a publisher to bring out the book in my own name but with the arrangement that the University be supplied with the number of copies it desires in 'bulletin' form. Either those copies would be supplied at minimum cost or, it might be, free. If there were money in the project, I'd gladly have them supplied free, but however it may be done, I do want to provide for the proper advertising and circulation of the book." Meiklejohn to Frank, October 7, 1931, Meiklejohn Papers, box 32.

[172]Sellery, *Some Ferments at Wisconsin*, p. 29. The committee consisted of Professors Homer Adkins (chemistry), V.A.C. Henmon (psychology and Bureau of Guidance and Records), Harry Jerome (economics), Kimball Young (sociology), and Willard G. Bleyer (journalism) as chairman.

ment and approval from them and few suggestions for changes. One of the most thoughtful and penetrating of the in-house reviews was from John Bergstresser, who had developed an interest in the college first as alumni recorder promoting the enrollment of Wisconsin residents and subsequently in evaluating the experiment in his later position as assistant director of the University Bureau of Guidance and Records. To rein in the high spirits of the Experimental College students, moreover, Bradley and the Dormitories Committee had prevailed upon Bergstresser to serve as the head fellow in Adams Hall during the college's last two years, where he also acted as Meiklejohn's assistant and managed the college office in the summer. His views, then, were those of a friendly insider yet one who was not fully involved in nor committed to all of the educational aspects of the experiment.

While Bergstresser made clear his respect for the college and his great admiration for its leader—he thought Meiklejohn's report contained "the words and wisdom of a modern Socrates" about "one of the greatest of educational adventures"—he nevertheless offered some telling observations. "It is easier for sophomores to understand *The Education of Henry Adams*," he noted, comparing the challenging second-year text with Meiklejohn's narrative, "than it will be for many university faculty members to understand this report. My prediction is that not 50% of them will read it; and that not half of those who read it will 'get' it." Bergstresser admitted some ambivalence about Meiklejohn's reluctance to impose any discipline on the Experimental College students. "I can't get rid of a lurking and will-o-the-wisp conviction," he confessed, that "it is possible to use a minimum amount of discipline without thwarting or stunting the growth of qualities of responsibility, initiative, and self-direction."

> I am afraid that of all the things proposed by the Report that this matter of discipline will receive the most opposition—if not verbal, then at least emotional. Other suggestions of great value may be dropped or ignored, I fear, because of the reactions against the discipline discussion, a reaction which for most people will be based upon a few specific instances and observations without any broad, philosophical thinking on the subject.

Similarly, while Bergstresser conceded he "might be 'all wet' on this," he disagreed with Meiklejohn's opposition to examinations, which, well aware of Meiklejohn's passion for competitive sports, he shrewdly compared to the spur and challenges of athletic competition.

Bergstresser said he thought the "community of learning" had become most real while the Ex-College students were working on their required regional studies or the *Henry Adams* paper, "partly because of the challenges, the competitive elements, and the fellowship in effort resulting from these 'examinations'."

> Personally, I like examinations because they are an effective spur to thorough work, integration of ideas and subject matter, and the *thinking thru* process. The report on the Experimental College is *your* examination. Won't you admit the necessity of writing it forced you (or stimulated you) to think through, integrate your ideas, put forth your best effort, etc?[173]

Another thoughtful but probably unwelcome critique was provided by Eugene S. Duffield, the 1929-30 executive editor of the *Daily Cardinal* and subsequently a graduate student in history who served half-time on the college teaching staff for 1930-31. Based on his year's experience as an Ex-College adviser, Duffield offered some telling suggestions for the final report. He questioned the college's emphasis on generalities largely unsupported by factual knowledge. "One of the last things on which I should think of examining an Experimental College freshman," he declared, "would be an exact historical knowledge of fifth century Athens." Duffield expanded his argument using Meiklejohn's own discipline of philosophy:

> If you are a Realist maintaining that essences exist prior to particulars, you may agree with the method. But there are still in the world stubborn, pedestrian Nominalists who insist that only particulars generate essences. They will undoubtedly say that the Experimental College puts too much stress on interpreting and too little on knowing, that empiricism is too lightly abandoned for *a priori* generalizations.

Conceding the value of the tutorial method in teaching highly motivated, superior students, Duffield nevertheless questioned whether the loosely structured Experimental College had much effect on those who were "lethargic or indolent or baffled or pathetically helpless." He quoted excerpts from the advisers' reports for a number of such students he had known over a two-year period, arguing that for at least some of the members of the college these comments demonstrated little or no educational progress.

---

[173][John Bergstresser,] "Notes on the Experimental College Report," n.d., Meiklejohn Papers, box 55. Emphasis in original.

I can not say definitely how many the College reaches and how many it fails to reach. All that I can do is to point out that I have been able to cite seven illustrations from a group of acquaintances numbering 50 at the outside. If the College has recognized that some failures are inevitable, it has stopped there and failed to develop a technique for measuring them or ridding itself of them.

Anti-social student behavior was also a problem the college failed to recognize and address, Duffield thought, resulting from its unwillingness to apply its education to its communal living. "Studying Plato, the students follow Nietzsche," he commented, "not because they know anything about him, but because they have desires which they aim to satisfy, society to the contrary notwithstanding." Contrary to Meiklejohn's expectation, in reality the education offered by the Experimental College "may be fostering rampant individualism rather than social pliability."

> Just how it works in this direction is illustrated by the following account of a discussion which took place in the last sophomore meeting.
> Mr. Meiklejohn: If you are asking me the general question: "Are there circumstances in which the individual should refuse to conform to or be coerced by the world?" my answer is, yes.
> Eberiel: How is one to know when to conform and when to rebel?
> Mr. Meiklejohn (shaking his head): I have no formula for that.
> Where does this discussion leave a Fellow trying to handle 30 immature, wilful youngsters? They are too likely to understand Mr. Meiklejohn's answer as meaning there is no formula except that given by their own viscera. His democracy will be understood in a way which will reinforce this impression. The students will procede [*sic*] to do what they jolly well please as far as they are allowed.[174]

The Bergstresser and Duffield comments, it should be emphasized, were intended to be friendly and supportive, offered by Ex-College staff members to aid Meiklejohn in drafting his report.

The Meiklejohn final report on the Experimental College was distributed to the letters and science faculty in February, 1932, and published as a book the following May.[175] It contained few surprises,

---

[174]E.S. Duffield, memorandum [1931], ibid., box 56.

[175]"Report of the Advisers of the Experimental College"; Meiklejohn, *Experimental College*. The *New Republic*, an early Meiklejohn backer, promptly published a sympathetic

consisting of a lengthy review of the experiment—its origins, philosophy, curriculum, teaching methods, and lessons learned—plus a number of suggestions for reorganizing the College of Letters and Science and for continued curricular experimentation. The report's tone was mostly dispassionate, though at points it seemed a trifle defensive or even combative. Meiklejohn offered a strong defense of the educational philosophy underlying the experiment: tutorial instruction, a broad interdisciplinary curriculum, self-contained residential living and learning, and an emphasis on student freedom. He admitted to few mistakes in either the operation of the college or its relations with the larger University of which it was a part. He clearly considered himself more sinned against than sinning in his dealings with most of those on the Hill. While Madison readers might have developed a different perspective based on a fuller knowledge of the situation, the overall effect of the report was to leave outsiders with the impression that once again a gentle, far-seeing prophet had been stoned by the educational pharisees. It was Amherst all over again.

Having fulfilled its charge by reviewing Meiklejohn's final report with care and discussing it and the companion statistical report of the University Bureau of Guidance and Records with the Experimental College advisers, the Bleyer Committee presented its recommendations to the letters and science faculty on April 18, 1932. Its report was debated that day and again a week later. The committee noted, as had the Bureau of Guidance and Records,[176] that an objective appraisal of the Experimental College was impossible, given "the large number of uncontrolled, and for that matter uncontrollable, variables in such a complex, large-scale experiment." It paid tribute to "the especially chosen group of unusually able Advisers" and praised them for "a thoughtful and courageous attempt to solve some of the important problems in higher education." Still, the committee did not accept the advisers' recommendation in their final report to set up four new experimental units within the College of Letters and Science. This, it

---

but not totally uncritical review of Meiklejohn's Experimental College report by John Dewey, one of the founders of the Progressive Education Association and a long-standing champion of educational reform. Dewey, "The Meiklejohn Experiment," *New Republic*, 72 (August 17, 1932), 23-4. Meiklejohn continued to promote the Experimental College idea after publishing his report. Early in 1933, for example, he sought unsuccessfully to interest the Carnegie Foundation for the Advancement of Teaching in evaluating the experiment. W.S. Learned to Meiklejohn, April 1, 1933, Meiklejohn Papers, box 8.

[176] "Report of the Bureau of Guidance and Records on the Experimental College."

pointed out, would require the enrollment of a greater fraction of the incoming freshman class and enlisting the service of a larger group of faculty than past experience indicated would voluntarily choose to participate in such an experiment. The resulting uncertainty about student-faculty participation "would demoralize the plans of the University for 1933-34. "

Instead, the Bleyer Committee recommended the creation of a single unit—coeducational and non-residential, and with its students taking half of their academic work in special integrated courses and the other half in regular Hill courses—"if the faculty believes that another project should be undertaken on the basis of the experience of the Experimental College. " The committee also recommended that the dean appoint a committee to consider how to improve the curriculum, teaching methods, and conditions of life of the freshman and sophomore years in light of the recent experimentation at other colleges and universities around the country.[177] Meiklejohn protested that these recommendations amounted to a virtual repudiation of his experiment and recommendations, and offered an amendment to reduce the number of freshmen in the experimental unit from two hundred to a hundred, to require integration of the course of study as a whole and not just its experimental component, and to limit the regular Hill courses to not more than five credits a semester.[178]

Preferring not to debate either the general question or the details of a new experimental unit, a week later the L&S faculty voted instead to refer the entire matter to the proposed new committee recommended in the final section of the Bleyer report. President Frank then entered the discussion for the first time, reading a long list of suggestions and questions he wanted considered by the new committee. Evidently concerned the president was trying to slant the committee's agenda toward the approach of the Experimental College, Dean Sellery suggested that this new matter be held over for the May meeting, but Professor Kahlenberg moved instead "that the committee not be limited to any set of questions, but that the material read by President Frank be accepted for substance of doctrine only. " The Kahlenberg motion

---

[177]L&S Faculty Document 56, "Report of the Committee on the Experimental College Report," April, 1932; L&S Faculty Minutes, April 18, 1932.

[178]"Amendment to the Bleyer Report Proposed by the Advisers of the Experimental College," April 25, 1932, L&S Papers, 7/1/1-2, box 2; *Daily Cardinal,* April 19 and 20, 1932; *Capital Times,* April 19, 1932.

carried with no debate.[179] In the fall of 1932, with the depression now requiring substantial University retrenchment, including faculty salary reductions, the L&S faculty voted unanimously to postpone the appointment of the new committee "until the present economic crisis is over." Much to the continuing dismay of the *Daily Cardinal*, it was never appointed.[180] The faculty mood and the times were hardly propitious for another sweeping curricular experiment.

◇   ◇   ◇

How, more than three-score years later, shall we appraise Glenn Frank's and Alexander Meiklejohn's short-lived Experimental College? First, we must agree that for many of the participants something magic occurred along the shores of Lake Mendota between 1927 and 1932, an exciting educational adventure that deeply affected students and advisers alike and changed their lives forevermore. For them, it must have seemed they were recreating Camelot. That said, one must nevertheless fault Frank and Meiklejohn, not for undertaking their bold experiment, but for doing so in a way that undermined its chances for any lasting success. In this regard Frank was not well served by his friend Meiklejohn.

Frank had expected a genuine experiment—or preferably several experiments—that would be tested and validated against a control group of regular letters and science students. (The students enrolled in the L&S humanities baccalaureate degree option might have served as such a control group.) More a prophet and self-promoter than a true experimenter, Meiklejohn wanted the college to be a self-sustaining intellectual community as isolated as possible from the larger University. He was quite willing to give his guinea pigs battery after battery of intelligence tests, which showed that in their range of knowledge the Experimental College sophomores ranked well above the norms of graduating college seniors from around the country. The high scores demonstrated that the college was able to attract a group of exceptionally bright and articulate students, but they revealed little about the role of its curriculum and pedagogy in producing the results. To

---

[179]L&S Faculty Minutes, April 18 and 25, 1932; *Daily Cardinal* and *Capital Times*, April 26, 1932; Sellery, *Some Ferments at Wisconsin*, pp. 30-2.

[180]L&S Faculty Minutes, November 21, 1932; Sellery, *Some Ferments at Wisconsin*, p. 32; *Daily Cardinal*, November 2, 3, 22, and 23, 1932, January 6, 15, and 21, 1933, June 3, 1934, November 12, 1936, May 19, 1937.

Meiklejohn, however, the flattering scores and even more the devotion of his students proved the validity of his experiment.

The University of Wisconsin was hardly unique in experimenting with a new approach to general education in the 1920s, for there were more than a hundred such ventures launched by American colleges and universities between the two world wars. Meiklejohn's insistence on a residential college, however, made Wisconsin the first major university—ahead of Harvard's undergraduate houses or Yale's similar residential colleges of the next decade—to attempt to integrate living and learning in its dormitories. In practice, this exacted a high price from the faculty advisers, who were expected to spend most of their time with the students in Adams Hall. The decision that each adviser should teach all parts of the curriculum, so faculty and students alike would be learning together, no doubt produced some well-informed generalists in both groups, but it was enormously time consuming for conscientious faculty members who also had to run individual and group tutorials, offer personal counseling on any and all subjects, and give specialized lectures in the Experimental College and in their regular courses on the Hill. In the end the advisers recommended that in the future such teaching assignments be rotated frequently to avoid faculty burnout.

The heavy emphasis of the advisers on their work in the Experimental College, moreover, weakened their ties to their academic departments and contributed to the isolation of the college within the larger University. This created a special problem for the non-tenured advisers who needed to be concerned about earning tenure through scholarship and service in their home departments. Since Meiklejohn desired this isolation, he did not recognize it as a problem until too late. Neither he nor President Frank gave sufficient thought to the question of how to fit the Experimental College into the University in a way that might bring lasting influence and success from its experience. After the president skillfully manipulated the faculty governance structure so as to gain grudging approval from the letters and science faculty for the experiment, neither he nor Meiklejohn did anything to build interest or a base of support for the Experimental College among the University faculty generally. Quite the contrary. Their decision to bring in a number of outsiders—Meiklejohn men—to staff the college, to impose them on the academic departments sometimes at a higher rank and salary than the departments thought appropriate, and thereafter to imply that their purpose was to show the rest of the faculty how to teach, reflected an insensitivity that virtually guaranteed hostility to the project.

Their determination to keep the Experimental College a special presidential initiative was also a blunder. While helpful to Meiklejohn in running the college and useful in promoting Glenn Frank as an educational reformer, it meant the enterprise never took root either administratively or academically within its nominal parent, the College of Letters and Science.

But the demise of the Experimental College cannot be blamed only on the lack of interest and even hostility of the letters and science faculty or its champion, Dean Sellery, though both were a factor. If they failed to support and promote the college, it was because they had some genuine concerns about what they considered its excessive freedom and lack of focus and academic accountability, features Meiklejohn regarded as essential parts of his educational philosophy. That these apprehensions were shared by an increasing number of Wisconsin parents and high school teachers and principals was reflected in the college's ever-declining enrollment, especially from Wisconsin. No doubt the advent of the great depression after 1929, with its negative effect on the college's heavy proportion of out-of-state students, helped to bring on its closing. This is not sufficient reason, however, to explain why the college failed to attract more student and parental interest throughout its five-year life. One must always return to the free-spirited experience it offered, which plainly did not appeal to everyone. Yet we must also not forget that for some students it was a mind-stretching, ennobling experience, unlike any other.[181]

Whatever the many reasons for the death of the college or however one chooses to evaluate the experiment, the closing signalled beyond doubt that Glenn Frank's promised academic renaissance was in trouble.

---

[181]See Appendix 3.

4.

Unravelled Renaissance

As we have seen, for the most part Glenn Frank enjoyed an extended honeymoon during his first five years in Madison. Through his syndicated newspaper column and his frequent speeches around the country, he quickly became an eloquent and highly visible national spokesman for the University and for higher education generally. Although his rhetorical trademark was more often generalized and catchy phrases than substantive specifics, his reputation was that of a champion of educational reform and academic freedom. Even when his major project, the Experimental College, did not work out as well in practice as he anticipated, the venture generated an enormous amount of favorable publicity across the country for Frank and the University. Nor did he neglect Wisconsin. No previous president worked more diligently in building University support through speeches to alumni, parents, and other audiences around the state and in successfully lobbying the legislature for more funds. As a veteran legislator commented with some disbelief, "When Dr. Frank tells his story the boys want to throw money at him in $100,000 lots."[1]

---

[1]*Milwaukee Journal*, January 30, 1929. Another contemporary indication of Frank's success as a lobbyist came from UW Registrar Frank O. Holt, who told the president in March of 1929 of meeting with some Madison residents:

> The discussion centered about yourself and a very prominent insurance man in the city suggested that he had heard you present your budget to the Joint Finance Committee and he said this: "I don't see how the legislature can help but give Mr. Frank everything he asked for because everything was so clearly stated, so splendidly organized and so fairly put that even a man who could neither read nor write and who could neither add nor subtract ought to be able to understand how perfectly justified the President is in asking what he did ask for in the budget." Another gentleman in the crowd added this: "Not only that but Governor Kohler

212

Like most presidents Frank found it difficult to develop close friendships with individual faculty members, but he was considered genial and easily approachable. When he lunched at the University Club, he made it a point to sit at the large round table with a group of faculty, joining comfortably in the general banter, stories, and small talk. It was hard not to like Glenn Frank as a person. Even when he differed with a dean or a professor, he never seemed to hold a grudge. Although Mary Frank impressed many as a social snob,[2] both of the Franks worked hard at town-gown relations. The president golfed regularly at the Maple Bluff country club, was an active member of the prestigious Town and Gown dining club, and was readily available to speak to local service and church groups on just about any subject. The Franks entertained frequently in the presidential mansion, Olin House, often hosting some famous guest whose presence in Madison attested to the president's wide contacts and national stature. Mary Frank's dinner parties were usually glittering social occasions—frequently black- or white-tie formal affairs the like of which Madison had rarely seen.[3]

---

is entirely with him."
Holt to Glenn Frank, March 6, 1929, Frank Presidential Papers, 4/13/1, box 60, UA.

[2]Shortly after the Franks arrived in Madison, Mary Frank called on the wife of William G. Rice, a very junior member of the law faculty. "We could not imagine why Mrs. Frank had come to call so elegantly on an unknown assistant professor's wife," Professor Rice recalled many years later. "After consulting with others we came to the conclusion, never verified however, that she searched the New York Social Register and had found our address—my father being a New York State officer—and that of a few other faculty folk so listed, and counted these people of so exceptional social standing as to deserve her special consideration." William Gorham Rice, oral history interview, 1974, UA. Dorothy Knaplund, the wife of a more senior member of the history faculty, recalls that the Knaplunds were not invited to parties at Olin House until after she and Mary Frank attended the same high society wedding in Chicago where Mrs. Frank discovered that Mrs. Knaplund came from a socially prominent Oak Park family. Dorothy King Knaplund, oral history interview, 1991, UHP.

[3]Madison guests were not used to some of Mary Frank's social innovations, such as having a servant formally announce the arrival of guests. In his memoirs Philip F. La Follette describes one such white-tie dinner given by the Franks in La Follette's honor after his inauguration as governor in 1931. For the occasion Mrs. Frank had rented fancy footmen's uniforms for the student help—black trousers, blue dress coats, and red vests. One of the dinner courses was imported Russian caviar served from a large mound on a huge hollowed-out ice cake lighted from within. Just as the student "footman" was serving Senator John J. Blaine, the tray accidentally tilted enough "to pour what seemed like a small Niagara of ice water down John's neck, drenching him fore and aft." Apart from this embarrassing fiasco, La Follette made clear his disapproval of such lavish entertaining during the general hardship of the great depression. Philip F. La Follette, *Adventure in Politics: The Memoirs of Philip La Follette*, Donald Young, ed. (New York: Holt, Rinehart and Winston, 1970), pp. 236-7. For similar versions of this incident, see La Follette, draft memoirs, n.d., P.F. La Follette Papers,

This is not to suggest that the president was without critics, though complaints were infrequent and muted in the early years of his administration. Very nearly from the beginning some of the faculty scorned him as an outsider, were amused at his intellectual pretensions, resented his high salary and lavish life style, and were skeptical of his ideas about educational reform. In part this reflected the deeply ingrained element of snobbery in academe. Frank had earned no advanced degrees, had no research "field," and, though he published two books on national and world affairs in two years while serving as president, was not a scholar.[4] Consequently, he received little credit for his undeniable skill as a generalist drawing on his wide reading, keen memory, facile pen, and above all his golden tongue. His efforts to simplify and popularize knowledge merely made him seem shallow to the faculty. Among campus administrators, Letters and Science Dean George Sellery was an early Frank skeptic, though he mostly kept his doubts to himself. Not long after Frank's arrival in Madison a joke began circulating among the faculty that this was the second time in history a virgin had brought forth a savior—a reference to Regent Zona Gale's reported key role in the president's selection. Frank's tendency to obscure issues with lofty but balanced phrases led to the cynical observation that he fitted his own definition of a mugwump: a man with his mug on one side of the fence and his wump on the other. Other faculty scoffers dismissed him as "the great glibberal."

Frank preferred to preside rather than to administer, to generate ideas for others to implement if they chose, and above all to promote the University around the state and nation. He selected strong deans and other top administrators and then let them handle their responsibilities without much presidential interference or second-guessing. He disliked dealing with knotty personnel problems and usually tried to ignore or defer acting on them unless they reached a noisy stage that could no longer be overlooked. Even then he sometimes pulled back, as when in 1929 he abandoned his plan to remove Dean Sellery for publicly criticizing the president's pet project, the Experimental College.[5] Frank's smooth, cheerleading style of presidential leadership worked

---

box 124, SHSW.

[4]Glenn Frank, *Thunder and Dawn: The Outlook for Western Civilization with Special Reference to the United States* (New York: Macmillan, 1932); Frank, *America's Hour of Decision: Crisis Points in National Policy* (New York: Whittlesey House, McGraw-Hill, 1934).

[5]See pp. 183-9.

well enough at first, but gradually its deficiencies became more evident. The coming of the great depression in late 1929 brought troubled times to the University as well as to Wisconsin and the nation. The depression caused not only economic hardship but also increasing turbulence in the political life of the state, both of which had serious ramifications for the University. The depression began during the administration of stalwart Republican Governor Walter J. Kohler, Sr., who had been elected in the Hoover landslide of 1928, thus ending eight years of progressive rule. Because President Frank worked effectively with Kohler, who also was a member of the Town and Gown dining club, progressives were suspicious of Frank's professed devotion to liberalism. When Philip F. La Follette, the younger son of the late senator, defeated Kohler in the bitterly fought gubernatorial election of 1930, Wisconsin progressives were again in a position to take a hard look at Glenn Frank's leadership of the University. The La Follettes had always taken a proprietary interest in their alma mater and the family had not welcomed the selection of Frank as president in 1925. An attorney, Phil La Follette served as a part-time lecturer in the UW Law School from 1927 until his election as governor three years later. He had many faculty friends and was confident he knew the University well. Whatever his private doubts about the president, however, up to this time his relations with Frank were good enough for the president twice to offer him the deanship of the Law School in 1928 and 1929.[6]

The End of the Frank Honeymoon

A law enacted in the waning months of the Kohler administration required a governor to hold budget hearings with the heads of state agencies before submitting his budget recommendations to the legislature. Governor-elect La Follette decided to hold such hearings in

---

[6]Philip F. La Follette to Louis D. Brandeis, March 14, 1928; Brandeis to La Follette, March 17, 1928; La Follette to "Bob, Ralph, Mary, and Fola" [La Follette family], May 7, 1929; Belle C. La Follette to Mary Frank, October 3, 1930, P.F. La Follette Papers, box 134; P.F. La Follette, draft memoirs, n.d., ibid., box 124; La Follette, *Adventure in Politics*, p. 118. Frank's persistence over more than a year in trying to recruit Phil La Follette for the law deanship no doubt reflected the president's concern for good relations with the La Follette family rather than his sober judgment of the legal stature of this youthful and relatively inexperienced part-time lecturer. One can attribute the same motivation to Mary Frank's warm letter of congratulation to Belle La Follette after her son Phil's election as governor. See B.C. La Follette to Mary Frank, October 3, 1930, P.F. La Follette Papers, box 134.

December, 1930, even before his inauguration. The worsening economic conditions dictated a tight state budget, and La Follette accordingly subjected agency heads to withering scrutiny, seeking to ferret out waste, inefficiency, and overstaffing. Because of the size of its budget, he gave special attention to the University, first asking Milwaukee attorney Theodore Kronshage, a former regent and prominent progressive, to analyze the UW budget request, which on Frank's recommendation had been approved by the Board of Regents in October.[7]

When President Frank suggested an informal meeting on his budget request the evening before the University's scheduled hearing, the governor-elect invited him out to the La Follette family farm in Maple Bluff for a private session with Kronshage and himself. Many years later La Follette recalled in his memoirs how Kronshage had proceeded to grill Frank on his request, demonstrating both a broad knowledge of the University and a detailed mastery of its budget:

> Kronshage had the university budget on his lap, and strips of paper seemed to stick out from nearly every page. Over the years I have heard some, and read many, cross-examinations; however, none surpassed Kronshage's cross-examination of Glenn Frank that night. It was devastating, calm, cold, and relentless. Kronshage went through the university's budget item by item. It produced a shock. He exposed Mr. Frank—not in public, but before the three of us in that room. When it was finished, he had revealed the man, his mind, his character, his spirit—everything there—naked. It was most unpleasant, almost sickening. All this without one word that was not most proper and precisely relevant to the job of the president of the university.
>
> For more than three hours Kronshage asked questions like this: "You told the regents that Professor _____ was deadwood, that you could not fire him because he had tenure. But you promised to tie him to a salary post. Why do I now read here in your budget, page ___, line ___, that you have increased his pay by two thousand dollars a year?"
>
> Questions like this by the hour, all seeking an explanation of what the president had done with an extra million dollars a year of the people's money. When it was over, a stark fact stood out: the president, out of weakness, had put a jack under the entire university payroll and boosted it willy-nilly one million dollars a year.[8]

---

[7]BOR Minutes, October 11, 1930, UA.

[8]La Follette, *Adventure in Politics*, p. 234. For similar versions of this account, see also La Follette, draft memoirs, n.d., P.F. La Follette Papers, boxes 123 and 124. It must be remembered that La Follette wrote his memoirs in the 1950s and early 1960s in part to justify his role in the firing of Frank in 1936-37. There is no contemporary corroboration of this meeting in either the La Follette or the Kronshage Papers (also at SHSW), although press accounts reported Kronshage's presence and active participation in the public budget hearing

It must have been, to say the least, an unexpected and humiliating experience for President Frank. His previous lobbying success at the capitol had hardly prepared him for such an inquisition, especially at the hands of a former regent who had helped engineer his appointment five years before and a governor-elect whom he had recently sought to honor with the Law School deanship.[9]

At the public hearing the next day, attended by members of the legislature's Joint Committee on Finance, La Follette and Kronshage subjected Frank to a relentless six-hour cross-examination on the University's budget request for the 1931-33 biennium. The regents and Frank were asking for an operating budget of $9.1 million for the two years, or nearly $1 million more than the current level, plus a special capital fund of more than $3.5 million for new buildings to be constructed over the next several years. Of the latter needs, the major request was $1.5 million for a new library, which had been the University's top building priority for a number of years (and which would remain so for the next two decades).

La Follette raised questions about the value of higher education in an age of evident social irresponsibility and sought to learn whether the University had reassessed its programs and mission in light of changing times and needs. Why, he demanded, was the University admitting and retaining students whom Frank had described as "cake-eaters" lacking any serious interest in learning? After consulting his aides, Frank conceded that perhaps as much as 15 percent of the student body fell into this category. At what point, La Follette asked, would the University's ever-increasing size—now 9,400 students—adversely affect the quality of instruction and learning? If the cake-eaters were eliminated, would not the University have adequate funding without seeking any increase? "Well, we wouldn't be pinched," Frank admitted. Why, demanded former Regent President Kronshage, was the budget of the College of Agriculture up 20 percent while enrollment was down by 20 percent, especially after the Board of Regents, with three agricultural representatives, five years earlier had questioned the value of some of the college's activities and had voted to freeze its budget pending a

---

the next day. See *Capital Times*, December 5 and 6, 1930; *Wisconsin State Journal*, December 11 and 12, 1930.

[9]That Frank counted on La Follette's interest in the University is suggested by his asking for La Follette's help when the University's budget request was stalled in the legislature in 1929. See P.F. La Follette to Isabel "Isen" La Follette, August 7, 1929, P.F. La Follette Papers, box 134.

review and determination of its mission? Frank could only emphasize somewhat defensively the useful extension services of the college and the research strength of its scientists, warning that without the ability to pay competitive salaries the most eminent faculty members might leave.

This opened the way to sharp questioning by both La Follette and Kronshage about the apparently haphazard way salary increases were granted under Frank. Without citing examples, Kronshage complained that large increases had gone to men Frank had described to the regents as deadwood, "whom it was decided five years ago were unfit to be on the faculty." La Follette in turn asserted that in contrast some of the ablest UW faculty members, "who are of immeasurable value to the institution," had received disproportionately smaller increases in Frank's budget. What seemed to rankle La Follette and Kronshage most was the president's handling of the $1 million increase in the University's operating budget granted in 1927 and which had been carried forward thereafter, ostensibly to enable him to revitalize the faculty with new appointments. Apart from normal attrition, few of these could be identified except for the handful in Alexander Meiklejohn's Experimental College.

It was, the *Capital Times* headlined, an unprecedented "grilling," in which the governor-elect charged the UW president with weak administration, lacking any long-range plan, and failing "to cope with big problems."[10] From Washington, where he now occupied his father's senate seat, elder brother Bob La Follette expressed quiet satisfaction, telling Phil's wife her husband had "handled the cross examination of Frank with great skill."[11] The *Wisconsin Alumni Magazine* predicted that requests for increased funding would "be met with stern opposition by the Progressive faction," though it professed considerable surprise that the governor-elect—an alumnus and former UW law lecturer—"could be so nearsighted as to not realize the needs of the school."[12]

The Frank honeymoon was over.

---

[10]*Capital Times*, December 6 and 7, 1930; *Wisconsin State Journal*, December 11 and 12, 1930.

[11]Robert M. La Follette, Jr., to Isen La Follette, December 9, 1930, P.F. La Follette Papers, box 134. See also R.M. La Follette, Jr., to P.F. La Follette, December 18, 1930, ibid., box 2.

[12]"La Follette Questions the Budget," *WAM*, 32 (January, 1931), 158. By the following month the magazine was predicting "a sweeping inquiry into the university and all of its activities" by the progressives. Ibid. (February, 1931), 198-9.

Mounting Budget Woes

Far from any increase in its appropriation, over the next few months the University had to fight hard to minimize the reduction of its budget. In late January, 1931, Governor La Follette recommended a decidedly austere budget for the state's operations over the next two years. For the University he proposed a budget reduction of $513,365 or about 6 percent less than its state funding in the 1929-31 biennium. La Follette warned against any "temptation to dodge realities" or "an uncritical retrenchment by some crude form of long-division cutting of everybody and everything" or an attempt "to pass on the decrease by increasing fees." Rather, he demanded a fundamental cost-benefit appraisal of the work of the University.[13] The *Capital Times*, the only consistent La Follette supporter among Wisconsin daily newspapers, applauded the governor for his willingness to cut the state's education budget, which showed his "courage to meet a problem whose consideration as he says is 'long overdue'."[14] Other papers, however, criticized the harsh treatment of the University. Both major Milwaukee papers, the *Sentinel* and the *Journal*, thought La Follette had gone too far, with the *Journal* doubting "that this is the reasoned recommendation of the governor or that it will be his reasoned conclusion when he has gone more thoroughly into the subject."[15] The stalwart Republican editor of the Wausau *Record-Herald* echoed President Frank's plea not to cut the budget of the College of Agriculture, citing its value to the hard-pressed farmers of the state.[16]

As another indication of his distrust of the president, before determining his budget recommendations Governor La Follette asked to meet with three other senior UW administrators, Deans Charles Bardeen, George Sellery, and Charles Slichter. Afterward, Graduate Dean Slichter told Frank he should seize the opportunity to adjust his budget request rather than leave its reshaping entirely in the hands of the

---

[13]*Capital Times*, January 29, 1931; P.F. La Follette, "A Challenge to Educational Leadership," *WAM*, 32 (February, 1930), 186, 211.

[14]*Capital Times*, January 30, 1931. Earlier, in an editorial entitled "Time to Scrutinize Education Humbuggery," *Capital Times* editor William T. Evjue had called for a legislative investigation of the University: "The waste of public funds starts at the university and goes down into the public school system." Ibid., January 7, 1931. For pro and con reactions from its readers, see ibid., January 9, 13, 14, and 17, 1931.

[15]Ibid., February 4 and 8, 1931.

[16]Ibid., February 12, 1931.

governor and legislature.[17] There is no evidence that Frank took the advice, other than to announce he would accept budget cuts under protest provided the reason for them was the depression and not the administration of the University.[18]

Appearing together before the legislature's Joint Committee on Finance on February 25, Frank and La Follette got into several sharp exchanges about the effects of the governor's proposed cuts on the University. Vainly did the president plead that the regents' budget request was reasonable and represented the lowest level of funding needed to maintain the institution's quality. Under pressure he conceded the University might be able to absorb a $50,000 cut but asserted the governor's much more drastic reduction, including a further decrease in the second year of the biennium, would do serious harm. He particularly deplored the proposed cutback in agricultural extension work, which La Follette argued could be absorbed by administrative cutbacks and enrollment shifts. No doubt reflecting his earlier meeting with Dean Slichter, the governor had recommended an increase in the small state fund for faculty research, explaining that it was prudently administered (under Slichter's direction) and represented a wise investment in the future. Frank objected that this was not really new funding but merely a shift between categories that only increased the reduction of the University's general operating budget. Pleading with the legislators not to cut faculty salaries, Frank noted that over the past five years he had tried with only partial success to bring the faculty salary scale back up to the purchasing power represented at the turn of the century. To the charge that he had failed to clean out faculty deadwood, Frank declared he had changed his mind about some members of the faculty after getting to know them better. Besides, the purpose of tenure was to protect academic freedom, which was essential to a free university. Throughout, committee members and especially the governor questioned Frank sharply, endeavoring to show that he was unfamiliar with the details of the University's budget and programs.[19]

In coping with this suddenly more hostile atmosphere at the state

---

[17]Charles S. Slichter to Frank, January 23, 1931, Frank Presidential Papers, 4/13/1, box 103.

[18]*Capital Times*, February 7, 1931.

[19]"Exchanges between President Frank of the University and Governor Philip La Follette before the Joint Committee on Finance on Wednesday, Feb. 25, 1931," Glenn Frank Papers, Northeast Missouri State University, Kirksville; Frank, "The University Answers the State's Challenge," *WAM*, 32 (February, 1931), 187-9, 218-20.

capitol, the best President Frank and the University's friends could do was to try to minimize the damage. Governor La Follette's influence over the legislature made this a difficult task. The University's friends, led by first-term progressive assemblyman Harold Groves, a UW assistant professor of economics, managed to defeat a bill cutting all state salaries above $4,000 by 10 percent, which would apply mostly to UW faculty members.[20] In other respects, however, they succeeded only in restoring $80,000 to the University's operating budget. The governor more than nullified this modest gain by using for the first time his item veto powers authorized by Wisconsin voters in the 1930 general election. La Follette vetoed five UW special budget items totaling $115,000, explaining that he was reluctantly approving the legislature's general $80,000 increase over his UW budget request only because to veto it would require vetoing the main University appropriation, thereby leaving intact the much higher University funding level of the previous biennium.[21] To make sure the University community understood that retrenchment was now the order of the day, he appointed President Frank to a new governor's commission to study how to reduce state expenses further.[22]

---

[20]*Daily Cardinal*, March 11, 19, and 21, 1931.

[21]University Budget, 1931-32, UA; *Daily Cardinal*, April 22, 1931; "Governor Vetoes Appropriations," *WAM*, 32 (June, 1931), 356. Although most budget categories were pruned somewhat, the legislature approved the governor's sizable increase in the University's small faculty research budget (from $73,000 to $105,000). One of La Follette's item vetoes was of the entire $30,000 appropriation for the separate state Geological and Natural History Survey. He argued that this research activity, begun in 1873, had always been conducted by UW staff and thus should be a part of the University's budget, though neither he nor the legislature funded it there, unless the governor intended the increase in the UW research fund to cover whatever support the University cared to give the survey. It may be that this veto was aimed at President Emeritus Edward A. Birge, who had directed the survey from its inception until he became president in 1919 and was still actively engaged in its studies of Wisconsin lakes. Birge had been one of the prominent signers of the "round-robin" resolution criticizing the wartime views of the governor's father in 1918. It was probably no accident that after the adoption of the biennial budget Harold Wilkie, a long-time La Follette progressive and Governor La Follette's first appointment to the Board of Regents, tried to persuade the regents to review Birge's $10,000 retirement salary but failed on a narrow 8-6 vote. BOR Minutes, executive session, June 30, 1931.

[22]*Daily Cardinal*, April 21, 1931. One of Frank's assignments was to chair a subcommittee considering whether the state should attempt to spread employment by adopting a nepotism rule forbidding both married partners from holding a state job. For many years the University had followed such a nepotism policy with respect to faculty appointments. It is of interest that Belle La Follette, a lifelong feminist, was strongly opposed to such nepotism rules, which she thought usually worked against women, and once urged her son Phil when he was on the law

The fight over the University's budget in the spring of 1931 was but the forerunner of a seemingly never-ending series of funding trials for Frank and the University as the economic crisis deepened. The need to relieve depression-born frustration and find scapegoats made the University fair game for critics on a variety of fronts. Probably the president regretted more than once his failure to pursue an invitation at this time from his old friend and patron, Boston philanthropist Edward A. Filene, to leave Wisconsin and direct a wide-ranging study on the causes and cure of the depression.[23] Following the 1931 budget fight *Time* magazine reported that because of his uneasy relations with Governor La Follette Frank had asked a friend, Chicago attorney Silas H. Strawn, to help him find a more attractive position. Both men quickly denied the story, with the president declaring flatly: "There is absolutely nothing to it. I am under indefinite contract here."[24] That the rumor received national circulation, however, highlighted Frank's suddenly changed circumstances in Wisconsin politics.

As it became ever more apparent that state tax revenues would not be sufficient to fund even the smaller appropriations approved for the 1931-33 biennium, Governor La Follette directed the University and other state agencies to reduce their spending further. The Emergency Board, consisting of the governor and the co-chairmen of the legislature's joint finance committee, became the vehicle for releasing appropriated funds and in the process extracting new savings. In the fall of 1931 the governor called a special session of the legislature to deal with budget and depression problems, indicating the need for a drastic reduction of state expenses, including salaries. To avoid a general state property tax, the legislature authorized the Emergency Board to cut the original appropriations for state agencies by up to 20 percent.

Quite apart from this threat, Frank and the UW business manager, J.D. Phillips, were forced to struggle with an unanticipated $100,000

---

faculty to try to do something about the University's policy. Ibid., November 29, 1931; Belle C. La Follette to Philip F. and Isen La Follette, April 4, 1927, P.F. La Follette Papers, box 134.

[23]Edward A. Filene to Frank, February 28, 1931, Frank Papers, Kirksville. Filene's inquiry was exploratory, based on Frank's syndicated column, which an associate had described as showing "the best thinking that is being done today." He reported that a large unidentified foundation was interested in the project to the extent of providing $10-$20 million. "May I suggest," he cautioned, "that if you intend to break your custom of not answering letters and answer this one, you do so rather promptly?"

[24]"The Smoke at Madison," *Time*, 17 (May 11, 1931), 30; *Daily Cardinal*, May 9, 1931; *Capital Times*, May 13, 1931.

deficit caused by an enrollment decline of more than six hundred students for the fall semester. During the fall football attendance also dropped off, precipitating a crisis in the athletic department's budget. Some economy was achieved by reassigning the responsibilities of the bursar's office to Phillips' business office, in the process forcing the resignation of Bursar G.L. Gilbert and his assistant.[25] Other savings were achieved by cutting out University inspection of accredited state high schools, dropping instruction in Hebrew and Semitic languages, which had never drawn much enrollment, reducing supplies and clerical support, and slashing the athletic budget by 26 percent—all without reducing salaries.[26] One of Governor La Follette's new appointees to the Board of Regents, Madison attorney Harold M. Wilkie, urged the regents to go further by sharply curtailing free tickets for athletic events and by charging UW faculty members for campus parking. Wilkie no doubt endeared himself to the faculty by arguing that they could well afford to pay for their campus parking because faculty salaries had not been cut.[27]

In fact, as the governor and legislature wrestled with the problem of declining state tax receipts, consideration of cutting not merely salaries but the faculty itself mounted. In December of 1931 Senator Ben Gettleman of Milwaukee introduced a resolution demanding a detailed report from President Frank on what was being done to eliminate the faculty deadwood noted by former Regent Kronshage in his testimony before the joint finance committee. Eventually Gettleman withdrew his bill, but it was an ominous straw in the wind. He had more success in persuading the senate to launch an investigation of high athletic salaries at the University.[28] When enrollment declined further for the second semester of 1931-32, UW Business Manager Phillips warned the regents the University was "skating on thin ice" financially, and the board instructed the deans to cut back on spending.[29]

At the other end of State Street, there was continuing talk of the

---

[25]*Daily Cardinal*, September 23, 26, 27, 29, and 30, 1931; *Capital Times*, September 29, 1931.

[26]*Daily Cardinal*, October 6, November 19, December 1, 2, and 3, 1931; *Capital Times*, December 2, 1931; "Solving the University's Financial Crisis," *WAM*, 33 (December, 1931), 74, 97.

[27]BOR Minutes, December 2, 1931; *Daily Cardinal*, December 2, 1931; *Capital Times*, December 2, 1931; "Solving the University's Financial Crisis," p. 74.

[28]*Capital Times*, December 2, 1931; *Daily Cardinal*, December 2, 3, 10, and 17, 1931.

[29]*Capital Times*, January 20, 1932; *Daily Cardinal*, January 21, 1932.

need to cut out faculty deadwood and slash UW salaries. Chairing the Emergency Board, Governor La Follette in late February began a series of meetings with state agencies seeking further retrenchment.[30] At the hearing on the University, President Frank revealed plans to cut more than $400,000 from the UW budget largely by reorganizing the curriculum for the first two years to eliminate some elementary discussion and laboratory sections. Responding to the charges he had done nothing about deadwood, Frank pointed out that since he had assumed the presidency in 1925 a total of 299 staff members had left University employment and 407 new appointments had been made, rather meaningless figures without any comparison with normal attrition and staff turnover. Frank's economy plan would have the greatest impact on the University's largest undergraduate unit, the College of Letters and Science, which was estimated to lose about 25 percent of its instructional staff at the junior level. The president nevertheless denied a complaint by the *Capital Times* that his savings would be accomplished "by trimming off young sprouts on the university faculty tree, instead of clearing the deadwood."[31]

Governor La Follette believed more substantial savings were required and could be achieved by reducing faculty salaries. He asked the regents to look particularly at staff members with the highest salaries, including the president.[32] In his memoirs the governor recalled that at this time he summoned the Board of Regents to a private meeting in his capitol office and bluntly expressed his dissatisfaction with Frank's administration of the University, warning that he and the legislature had a duty to see that the regents fulfilled their responsibilities.[33] The regents' response was to give UW Business Manager Phillips much greater control of the University budget. Among other things, Phillips was authorized to merge certain appropriations into lump sums for more efficient use, directed to establish a more centralized accounting system, required to provide monthly estimates of revolving fund income and quarterly revisions of departmental budgets, and given personnel management authority over the wage rates and working hours of non-in-

---

[30]*Daily Cardinal*, February 13, 16, and 24, 1932.

[31]Ibid., March 1, 2, 3, and 5, 1932; *Capital Times*, February 29, March 2, 1932.

[32]*Capital Times*, March 3, 4, and 6, 1932.

[33]La Follette, *Adventure in Politics*, pp. 235-6. La Follette noted that not all of the board welcomed his intervention: "My remarks were ill-received by some regents. Indeed, an older man—highly respected and a Progressive—complained privately that he objected to being scolded by a youngster."

structional staff.[34]

President Frank's intention to drop most elementary quiz sections stirred an immediate uproar on campus. Several hundred instructors and assistants, mostly from the College of Letters and Science, held a mass meeting to protest the move and petitioned the president to find economies less detrimental to undergraduate education and the junior staff. At a meeting on March 7 the general faculty adopted a resolution asking the president to appoint a consultative committee with representation from all faculty ranks to advise on ways of meeting the crisis, pointing out that "serious budget reductions inevitably affect educational policy."[35] The president did so the following month.[36] Meanwhile, there was growing state support for cutting faculty salaries as a depression economy move. This course was strongly urged by the La Follette progressive organ, the Madison *Capital Times*, which ran a series of articles complaining about high faculty pay, noting that 271 UW staff members received annual salaries above $5,000. The paper reserved its sharpest criticism for President Frank's $20,400 salary and assorted fringe benefits, as well as the $10,000 retirement pay granted former President Birge in 1925.[37] The editors of both the *Daily Cardinal* and the *Wisconsin Alumni Magazine* urged caution, warning that harsh salary treatment might lead to the loss of the University's best faculty mem-

---

[34]J.D. Phillips, "Report by the Business Manager on Purchasing and Personnel Problems," March 8, 1932, BOR Papers, 1/1/3, box 44, UA; BOR Minutes, March 9, 1932; "University Faced with Drastic Budget Slash," *WAM*, 33 (April, 1932), 228.

[35]UW Faculty Minutes, March 7, 1932, UA; *Daily Cardinal*, March 5, 6, 8, and 9, 1932; *Capital Times*, March 5, 6, 7, 8, and 9, 1932; "University Faced with Drastic Budget Slash," pp. 205-6, 228. The motion offered originally by Professor John Gaus of the Experimental College and Department of Political Science was modified in the debate. President Frank objected to a section that deplored the proposed cut of the junior faculty, pointing out that his plan would not affect the salaries or jobs of any faculty members, only graduate assistants. L&S Dean George Sellery persuaded the faculty to delete another provision limiting the scope of the committee to salary reductions, arguing that it ought to have more leeway.

[36]At the April 4, 1932, meeting of the general faculty President Frank announced the membership of this Consultative Committee on Retrenchment Policies: Professors E.B. Fred, Ralph Linton, J.B. Kommers; Associate Professors Phillip G. Fox, R.J. Roark, B.A. Beach; Assistant Professors C.W. Thomas, Grayson L. Kirk, V.W. Meloche; Instructors C.T. Caddock, Phyllis Bartlett, L.J. Haworth; Assistants W.E. Chalmers, Daniel Gerig, and Phillip Fehlandt. When the committee made its report at the faculty meeting on June 6, Professor Max C. Otto and Instructor Ragnar Rollefson were listed as members, evidently replacing Linton and Haworth. UW Faculty Minutes, April 4, June 6, 1932; *Capital Times*, April 5, 1932; *Daily Cardinal*, April 14, 1932.

[37]*Capital Times*, March 3, 4, 6, 7, 8, 9, 11, 13, and 20, April 7, 13, 21, and 22, May 14 and 21, June 22 and 23, 1932.

bers. The anti-La Follette Milwaukee *Sentinel* also denounced what it called the governor's "great leveling movement projected into the field of higher education," which would "establish mediocrity as the goal of the University of Wisconsin."[38]

Salary Waivers

Responding to declining state revenues, in May of 1932 Governor La Follette and the Emergency Board slashed the budgets of all state agencies. The cut from the University's already reduced appropriation for the 1931-33 biennium amounted to more than $700,000. At a meeting at the state capitol on May 16, the governor and the heads of the various state agencies, including President Frank of the University, agreed that part of the reduction must come from salaries. In a statement issued that evening they declared that every state employee would be required to "waive" a minimum of one week's salary, "with the remainder of the reductions [to] be absorbed by heavier waivers on the salaries ablest to carry the reduction."[39] Thus was born Wisconsin's salary waiver system, named no doubt with the pious hope that the cuts would be temporary and the old salaries restored when better times returned. Its progressive philosophy befitted the state that had been the first to enact a progressive income tax.

By now events were clearly outrunning the work of the faculty's Consultative Committee on Retrenchment Policies, appointed only a month earlier in response to the junior staff's concern over the possible loss of their jobs. The committee's report to the faculty in early June was hardly a clarion response to the latest developments, making no mention at all of the impending salary cuts or how they should be applied. Instead, it concerned itself chiefly with the problem of finding jobs or other support for the instructors and graduate assistants who would be affected by the University's decision not to fill about 160 junior staff positions in 1932-33. The committee recognized that such appointments turned over regularly and estimated that only about 10 individuals who would normally be continued were currently without any employment or support for the coming year. It urged that they "be

---

[38] *Daily Cardinal*, March 8, 1932; *Milwaukee Sentinel*, quoted in ibid., March 9, 1932, and in *Capital Times*, March 7, 1932; C.L. Jamison, "Should Faculty Salaries Be Deflated?" *WAM*, 33 (March, 1932), 176-7.

[39] *Daily Cardinal*, May 17, 1932; *Capital Times*, May 17, 1932.

now given such assurance of appointment as lies within the power of the Administration." Noting that 133 UW graduate students were expected to receive a Ph.D. degree later in the month, the report also stressed that "it would be unfortunate should any of our Ph.D.s be forced into professional inactivity either by unemployment or by taking positions whose work is unrelated to their special capacities developed by long and severe training." To avert such tragedies the report recommended that the Graduate School develop a list of unemployed Wisconsin Ph.D.s and that "a co-operative effort be made to place these persons" either at the University or elsewhere.[40] The 210 faculty members present accepted this rather innocuous report but also spent some time in inconclusive discussion of how any salary reductions should be handled. A quite unrealistic resolution was offered but not adopted calling for the exemption of assistants and instructors from either salary cuts or abnormal terminations. Instead, any required salary savings should be achieved by the "voluntary relinquishment of part of their salaries by the members of the staff above the rank of instructor."[41] While the sentiment was no doubt popular with the junior staff, acceptance of such selfless idealism by their senior colleagues could hardly be expected even in an institution that had long emphasized a service ideal in its faculty.

The task of how to administer the salary cuts was left to President Frank and the Board of Regents, which at the end of an extraordinary six-day meeting approved a graduated salary reduction plan on June 21, 1932. The regents were sharply divided over the issue of how steeply graduated the waiver scale should be, with Regent Har-

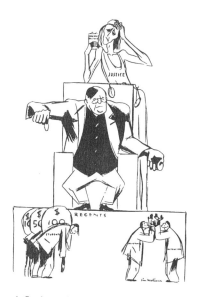

A Student View of the Depression Cuts

---

[40]UW Faculty Minutes, April 4, June 6, 1932; UW Faculty Document 413, "Report of Consultative Committee on Retrenchment Policies," June 6, 1932, UA; *Daily Cardinal*, May 6, 10, 17, 19, 25, and 28, June 4 and 5, 1932; *Capital Times*, May 17 and 21, 1932.

[41]Undated draft resolution, Alexander Meiklejohn Papers, box 54, SHSW.

old Wilkie, who was emerging as the leader of the La Follette faction on the board, arguing for larger cuts for the higher-salaried faculty and staff. As adopted, the reductions ranged from 3 to 13 percent, depending on salary level, with the result that President Frank and about a hundred of the deans and senior faculty members would generate a third of the savings.[42] William T. Evjue, the combative editor of the *Capital Times*, praised Wilkie for "fighting the battles of the lower salaried members of the university staff" against "many high salaried members of the faculty who were for the straight 10% cut." This drew a sharp retort from philosophy Professor Max C. Otto, a prominent progressive and long-standing friend of the La Follette family and the governor. Asserting that there was a general desire among the faculty for a salary reduction plan that was fair to all, Otto characterized Evjue's straight 10

[42]BOR Minutes, June 18, 1932; *Daily Cardinal*, June 18 and 28, 1932; *Capital Times*, June 17, 18, 22, and 23, 1932. The UW salary waiver plan, which the regents estimated would generate savings of approximately $300,000 in 1932-33, was scaled as follows:

$7,000 - up	13%	$3,001 - $3,500	8%
$6,001 - $7,000	12½%	$2,501 - $3,000	7%
$5,001 - $6,000	12%	$2,001 - $2,500	6%
$4,501 - $5,000	11%	$1,501 - $2,000	4%
$4,001 - $4,500	10%	$ 1 - $1,500	3%
$3,501 - $4,000	9%		

"Slash Salaries to Save Budget," *WAM*, 33 (July, 1932), 313. The regents authorized a few exceptions to the waiver plan. Married persons on salaries of $1,500 or less were exempted, as were a few named individuals. The most prominent of the latter was Law School Dean Lloyd K. Garrison, a prominent New York attorney who had been appointed only the previous March and had not yet arrived on campus. Although his $10,000 annual salary was highly visible, it was understandable why the board decided to leave it intact. By setting the top 13 percent bracket at $7,000 and above, the waiver plan was a good deal less progressive than it appeared. Only a few professors had salaries above $7,000, of whom Alexander Meiklejohn, Frank's recruit to establish the Experimental College, was unique at $10,000 for an academic year appointment. Biochemist Harry Steenbock, whose work on vitamin D had led to the creation of the Wisconsin Alumni Research Foundation in 1925, had the next highest faculty salary in 1931-32, $7,750. Except for Medical School Dean Bardeen ($9,000), the deans Frank had inherited (Sellery of L&S, Turneaure of the College of Engineering, Slichter of the Graduate School, and Acting Law School Dean Rundell) were still being paid at the prevailing $7,500 dean's rate in effect when Frank arrived in 1925. Frank's own dean appointees were paid considerably better: College of Agriculture Dean Christensen received $11,000, University Extension Division Dean Snell, $9,000, and, as noted, Law Dean Garrison, $10,000. It was immediately evident that Frank's own substantial $20,400 salary would be subject to the same 13 percent waiver reduction as a top faculty member like Steenbock, who received only a little more than a third as much. UW Budgets, 1931-32 and 1932-33. Later in the summer the regents decided to drop the waiver exemption for married persons earning less than $1,500 if both spouses were employed, whether by the University or some other employer. *Capital Times*, August 3, 1932.

percent advocates, at least among the faculty, as "purely mythical":

> I do not know exactly what took place at the meeting of the Board of Regents, but I am persuaded that the difference of opinion over salary cuts which developed there was not of the nature suggested by you....I am sorry that in a matter of such importance you were willing to trust to rumor. Why didn't you send someone out to get the facts? If you had, you would, I think, have found the members of the university faculty have shown themselves quite ready to cooperate with the administrative officers to make the salary cut as just all around as possible.[43]

At the marathon June meeting the Board of Regents also approved a creative use of the as yet rather limited research funds being generated by the fledgling Wisconsin Alumni Research Foundation. The regents endorsed a plan by the Graduate School for one-year WARF post-doctoral research fellowships for newly minted Wisconsin Ph.D.s unable to find professional employment. Recognizing the urgency of the crisis, the WARF directors took the unusual step of providing a $10,000 grant for such fellowships, the first use of foundation funds for other than faculty research. The regents also approved a plan for senior faculty research leaves, to be funded by personal savings or WARF or other foundation grants, in order to generate additional University salary savings.[44] These special WARF grants were expanded considerably during the worst years of the depression. Between 1933 and 1935, for example, WARF cut back on the development of its endowment and gave the University $317,000 to support research in the natural sciences; in contrast, the foundation had previously provided no more than $45,000 in any two-year period. During the depression years the University used most of its WARF grants for research leaves for a total of sixty-one faculty members in the natural sciences, thereby freeing

---

[43]Max C. Otto to W.T. Evjue, July 11, 1932, Max C. Otto Papers, box 2, SHSW.

[44]See Charles S. Slichter to Frank, June 17, 1932, Frank Presidential Papers, 4/13/1, box 121; BOR Minutes, June 18, 1932; *Daily Cardinal*, June 28, 1932; "Research Foundation Helps Solve University's Financial Problems," *WAM*, 33 (July, 1932), 316. During 1932-33 a total of twenty-three new UW Ph.D.'s, four of them women, received modest stipends ranging between $300 and $500 from this $10,000 WARF grant. In a notable departure from the existing policy, eligibility for this research support was broadened to include the social sciences and humanities disciplines as well as the natural sciences, with grants given to support projects in sociology, history, and comparative literature. Ibid., 34 (January, 1933), 112. The basic policy of the WARF trustees to restrict the foundation's support to the natural sciences remained in place, however, even though WARF Executive Director Harry L. Russell unsuccessfully urged the trustees in 1932 to broaden their scope to include the "social and historical sciences."

regular University salary funds to maintain staffing levels and faculty strength in many areas across the institution.[45]

After two stormy years of dealing with Phil La Follette, President Frank very likely hoped the results of the 1932 election might bring improved relations between the University and the state capitol. La Follette's bid for a second term failed when he lost decisively in the primary election for the Republican gubernatorial nomination to his old stalwart foe, industrialist and former governor Walter Kohler. In an unusual upset in normally Republican Wisconsin, Kohler in turn lost the regular election to the Democratic mayor of Madison, Albert G. Schmedeman, who swept into office on the long presidential coattails of Franklin D. Roosevelt. During the campaign Schmedeman had defended the University from Republican attacks and there was reason to hope he might be more sympathetic to campus needs than his predecessor.[46]

While Frank's personal relations with Governor Schmedeman were warmer than with La Follette, the severity of the economic crisis gripping the state and nation meant continued hard times for the University. In presenting his biennial budget request to the governor-elect in December, 1932, Frank therefore stressed its bare-bones character, noting it was 22 percent below what the legislature had approved for 1929-31 and 14 percent under the appropriation for 1931-33. (He neglected to point out that both appropriations had subsequently been cut substantially as the depression deepened.) Frank conceded that student enrollment had declined, but emphasized that the reduction in teaching staff and overall University expenditures was proportionally even greater. The enrollment decline was a more serious problem than might be assumed, he said, since most of the drop was among non-resident students, each of whom paid $200 more a year in tuition and fees than Wisconsin residents. With almost exactly the same number of students as in 1925, Frank observed, the University was asking for less than the state had

---

[45]Edward H. Beardsley, *Harry L. Russell and Agricultural Science in Wisconsin* (Madison: University of Wisconsin Press, 1969), pp. 165-8.

[46]See *Daily Cardinal*, May 25, 1932. Schmedeman was a lifelong Madison resident who owned a clothing store and dabbled in Democratic politics, which required considerable optimism in a traditionally Republican state. After service on the Madison city council, he campaigned for Woodrow Wilson in 1912 and was rewarded with the post of minister to Norway. Returning to Madison in 1921, he was recognized as the leading Democrat of the area and ran unsuccessfully for governor against Walter Kohler in 1928. No Wisconsin Democrat had been elected governor since George Peck in 1890, so even Schmedeman must have been surprised at his decisive victory in 1932.

provided that year and much less than it had appropriated in subsequent years. The president closed by noting that his proposed budget continued the recently imposed salary waivers ranging from 3 to 13 percent but did not make any further salary adjustments. He said he assumed "that problem will arise in later budget discussions when the whole picture of the state's financial problem has been assembled." Frank elaborated on these arguments during the University's budget hearing before the Joint Committee on Finance in February, where his own high salary came under discussion. He told the legislators the drastic cuts of the recent past and the lost income from a 10 percent enrollment decline during the current year had "pretty thoroughly exhausted possible means of retrenchment other than by further salary and wage reductions." Three years of the worst depression in American history had made Glenn Frank a political realist.[47]

Since there was some evidence the University had imposed larger salary cuts than other state agencies, President Frank may have hoped this argument would insure more favorable consideration of his budget request. If so, the strategy backfired. Facing an estimated state deficit of $24 million, Governor Schmedeman could be no more generous than his predecessor. He accordingly recommended a 15 percent reduction in the University's request. Furthermore, the finance committee and the legislature cut the governor's recommendation by more than $300,000, approving an appropriation for the 1933-35 biennium that was more than 19 percent below the University's request and 29 percent under the amount originally appropriated by the legislature for the 1931-33 biennium.[48] It was clear that a much more drastic reduction of salaries would be required for the University to operate within this greatly shrunken appropriation.

Even as the University's biennial budget was under consideration, the faculty made clear it expected to be consulted about how to handle any further cuts. At its meeting in November, 1932, the general faculty directed its executive body, the University Committee, to undertake as

---

[47]Frank, "Text of University Budget Presentation to Governor-elect Schmedeman," December 13, 1932, Frank Papers, Kirksville; *Daily Cardinal*, September 21, 1932; J.D. Phillips, "The Depression and the University," *WAM*, 34 (January, 1933), 99-100; J.D. Phillips, "Budget Facts: University Administration Slashes Budget Requests to Minimum in Effort to Cooperate with State Program," *WAM*, 34 (March, 1933), 161-2, 187; *Capital Times*, February 10, 1933.

[48]"State Recommends Drastic Budget Cut," *WAM*, 34 (April, 1933), 194-5. In addition, the legislature cut the projected University receipts from fees by 12 percent.

its chief project for the year a detailed study of the "essentiality and relative costs" of various University activities "in order that the members of the faculty may gain a better understanding of the whole budgetary situation and thus be enabled to assist the administrative officers more intelligently than is now possible, in meeting emergencies and effecting economies."[49] Present-day faculty members may not see this for the unusual and even revolutionary directive that it was. A logical extension of the charge to the previous year's Consultative Committee on Retrenchment Policies, this action laid the foundation for a significant expansion of the faculty's role in institutional governance. Never before had the faculty presumed to involve itself in budgetary matters, which had previously been the exclusive province of the administration and the regents. President Frank offered no opposition to this initiative and indeed probably welcomed it.

The University Committee took its charge seriously, meeting forty-five times and conferring with a variety of campus administrators before producing a lengthy report in May of 1933. Because of the report's sensitive nature, the committee directed that it not be made public and that it be distributed only to the legal (or professorial) faculty. After detailing the source and expenditure of various University funds, the report offered a number of recommendations. Any system of salary waivers should be on a progressive sliding scale similar to that used for the state's income tax. Because more than a third of the salary costs of the University were incurred for persons earning less than $1,000 and about two-thirds for persons receiving less than $2,000, the committee concluded "it is clear that a considerable portion of the waivers must be derived from the first and second thousand dollars of a person's salary." The committee noted the cost of living was conservatively estimated to have declined by about 15 percent since the start of the depression. It therefore recommended that the waiver reduction applied to the lowest salary bracket should only be "commensurate with the decrease in the cost of living." The waiver policy should also take into account reduced employment. The committee separately provided President Frank with scales of waivers netting various amounts illustrating its principle of progressive reductions applied to salaries up to $8,000. The committee pointedly observed that it chose not to deal with salaries above this level (chiefly that of the president) because it was inappropriate for the

---

[49]UW Faculty Minutes, November 7, 1932; *Daily Cardinal*, October 21 and 22, November 9, 1932; "Faculty Asks Voice in Budget Retrenchment," *WAM*, 34 (December, 1932), 80.

faculty to make recommendations concerning the salaries of top administrators.

The University Committee report stressed the importance of maintaining faculty tenure and honoring all fixed-term contracts—a position
seven years in advance of the famous tenure statement of the American
Association of University Professors in 1940. It also urged that any
waiver schedule should provide enough financial leeway to permit some
promotions and associated salary increases for outstanding faculty
members in order to fend off outside offers and keep up morale in these
difficult times. As for savings through greater faculty efficiency, the
committee steered clear of a detailed analysis of teaching loads across
the campus, contenting itself with the observation that current practices
were "as heavy as is consistent with continued effectiveness of instruction." Similarly, the report recommended against any substantial shift
away from the lecture-quiz section format of instruction, except in
science courses where a distinction could reasonably be made between
lecture-demonstration courses for students needing only a generalized
knowledge of the subject and more advanced courses with associated
laboratory work for students requiring more professional experience.
The University Committee confessed that it had been unable to give
adequate attention to the question of the possible waste of resources
resulting from duplicate, overly specialized, and under-enrolled courses,
and it recommended that this matter be studied by committees from each
of the seven faculty divisions during the coming year.[50]

The report was a thoughtful and thoroughly statesmanlike piece of
work, the most important of any document issued by the University
Committee since its creation in 1916. Its recommendations were approved with little discussion on a voice vote by the general faculty on
June 5, 1933.[51] Many years later Mark Ingraham, one of the first-year
members of this 1932-33 University Committee, declared that there was
no action by the faculty during his long University service of which he
was more proud than its endorsement of the basic principle that retrenchment should be achieved not by across-the-board cuts or the firing
of worthy colleagues but rather by graduated salary reductions affecting
all UW staff members. Ira Baldwin, another respected faculty member

---

[50]UW Faculty Document 432, Special Report of the University Committee, "Appraisal of
University Activities to Help Meet Emergencies and Effect Economies," May 9, 1933. The
University faculty at this time was divided into seven broad divisions, used mostly in connection with graduate study.
[51]UW Faculty Minutes, June 5, 1933.

who like Ingraham was beginning to show the leadership qualities that would bring him to high administrative responsibilities during the next few years, later cited this report as an important step in the evolution of responsible faculty governance at the University of Wisconsin. Both men believed it was unique in the country at this time.[52]

Before adopting a new waiver schedule on August 2, 1933, the Board of Regents was subjected to an organized campaign by the graduate assistants and instructors to preserve their jobs and salaries, presumably at the expense of the professorial faculty. This threat so disturbed Letters and Science Dean George Sellery that he fired off a blunt handwritten memo to President Frank early on the morning of the regents meeting. Sellery warned against any action that might "increase the 'tenure'" of the junior staff, whose teaching positions were temporary and merely related to undergraduate enrollment and program need:

> Instructors & assts. come to Wisconsin to study under our professors. They wouldn't come otherwise. Are we now to soak those professors in order to keep up the pay of the assistants? How preposterous!...
>
> From time to time we add to the professorial group those instructors who promise best results. They are now professors. It is proposed to soak these selected former instructors for the benefit of the undifferentiated mass. How absurd!...
>
> Finally: if the proposal to exempt from the waiver those instructors and assistants whose ~~work~~ time has been reduced seems likely to prevail, I should suggest that this bonus should be restricted to those who have got their Ph.D.s, *i.e.*, *to those who are no longer graduate students*.
>
> Lastly: The analogy of the stenographers is no good. These are at their livelihood job: they are properly comparable with people in a factory. The junior staff members are training for a livelihood, they're grad. students who get some teaching to do when the University needs them.[53]

Whether Frank presented Sellery's arguments to the regents is unknown, but the board substantially followed them and the faculty

---

[52]Ingraham was a mathematician who began his UW teaching in 1919 as an instructor and served as L&S dean from 1942 to 1961. Baldwin was a bacteriologist who joined the faculty as an assistant professor in 1927, was appointed assistant dean of the College of Agriculture in 1932, and served successively as graduate dean, dean of agriculture, and University vice president. Mark H. Ingraham, oral history interview, 1972, UA; Ira L. Baldwin, oral history interview, 1974, UA. For Ingraham's account of this episode see Mark H. Ingraham, "The University of Wisconsin, 1925-1950," in *The University of Wisconsin: One Hundred and Twenty-Five Years*, Allan G. Bogue and Robert Taylor, eds. (Madison: University of Wisconsin Press, 1975), pp. 71-3.

[53]George C. Sellery to Frank, August 2, 1933, Frank Presidential Papers, 4/13/1, box 137.

recommendations in devising the next round of salary reductions. The new waiver schedule, to be applied on the normal (pre-waiver) 1931-32 salary rates, was more progressive than the previous plan. It remained in effect substantially unchanged for the next three years and in modified form for nearly a decade:

First	$ 500	of each salary	12%
Next	500	or fraction	16%
Next	2,000	or fraction	17%
Next	2,000	or fraction	19%
Next	2,000	or fraction	21%
Next	2,000	or fraction	23%
Next	1,000	or fraction	25%

Frank's salary, the only one above $10,000, was cut a flat 20 percent, the maximum total reduction for any full-time appointment.[54] Afterward Sellery became a strong campus voice in support of the regents' progressive waiver scale, which he argued was both wiser and more humane than the flat 15 percent cut imposed by the federal government on its employees.[55]

Not all of the regents agreed with the new waiver plan, however. Harold Wilkie in particular thought it favored the higher-salaried administrators and senior faculty and thereafter tried regularly to persuade the board to provide exemptions or reduce the salary cuts for the junior staff and to increase the size of the waivers for the higher brackets.[56] Wilkie was especially critical of President Frank for not taking the lead and voluntarily sacrificing more of his substantial salary, a complaint echoed by the progressive *Capital Times*, which repeatedly publicized

[54]BOR Minutes, August 2, 1933; J.D. Phillips, "The University Budget for 1933-34," *WAM*, 35 (October, 1933), 4-5; *Capital Times*, August 6, 1933. The board voted to empower a committee consisting of President Frank, regents President Fred Clausen, Business Manager Phillips, and the regents executive committee to adjust the budget and waiver scale "to prevent injustice." From 1932-33 through 1936-37 the University budget listed the nominal salary less the waivered amount as a way of keeping track of the original intended salary level. In 1937-38 the budget began listing only the "net" salary, recognizing that it was unlikely the state would ever restore the old salaries. By this time there had been some promotion and other salary increases so that some faculty members were above their old pre-waivered salaries.

[55]G.C. Sellery, "The University and the Assistants," *WAM*, 35 (October, 1933), 6-7. For a critical response to Sellery's views by an unhappy assistant, see *Capital Times*, October 12, 1933.

[56]See, for example, Wilkie's unsuccessful effort (over Frank's objections) to persuade his fellow regents to modify the waiver plan in *Capital Times*, October 11, 1933; "Salary Waivers Not Changed by Regents," *WAM*, 35 (November, 1933), 46.

the president's high salary and extensive outside income from writing and speaking. This view was shared by much of the faculty, including the members of the University Committee, who were surprised when Frank did not extend their progressive scale in determining the size of the waiver on his salary, which was more than double the highest faculty rate. Probably nothing during Frank's nearly twelve years as president was so damaging to his reputation and support within the University and across the state as his perceived unwillingness to cut his salary and moderate his lavish life style during the depression.

A Tempest over the Brittingham Trust

In the spring of 1931, still smarting over the Board of Regents' decision a few months earlier to overturn its Grady resolution rejecting outside foundation support, editor William T. Evjue of the *Capital Times* launched a vicious campaign against the so-called Brittingham Trust. Evjue had picked up a report that the Brittingham trustees, headed by Thomas E. Brittingham, Jr., had refused to continue paying the salary of Professor Alexander Meiklejohn, whom President Frank had recruited in 1926 to develop the Experimental College.[57]

The Brittingham Trust was something of an anomaly. Officially named the University of Wisconsin Trust, it resulted from a substantial bequest tacitly accepted by the regents in 1924, the year before Glenn Frank's appointment, from the estate of a wealthy Madison lumberman and philanthropist, Thomas E. Brittingham, Sr. A former regent, Brittingham provided handsomely for the University by leaving the residual portion of his estate, totaling approximately $250,000 after the addition of funds from his wife's estate, to be administered by a family-controlled trust, the income of which was to be used only for University purposes. His widow Mary and the couple's three children served as the initial trustees; in 1929, upon his mother's death, the eldest son, Tom, Jr., assumed the lead responsibility on behalf of his brother and sister. Shortly after he arrived in Madison President Frank had persuaded Mary Brittingham to allocate trust funds for the special $9,000-a-year Brittingham professorship in philosophy created for Meiklejohn in 1926. The arrangement, it appears, was an oral agreement and did not include a clear understanding of how long the Brittingham commit-

---

[57]See Chapter 3.

ment was to run.

In May of 1930 Tom Brittingham informed President Frank that the Brittingham trustees wished to withdraw their support of the Brittingham professorship in philosophy after the 1930-31 academic year in order to devote the funds to other University needs. Frank objected, claiming that Mrs. Brittingham had agreed to a permanent endowed professorship, but Tom Brittingham declared that the Brittingham children were certain their mother would never have made such a long-term commitment without consulting the other family trustees. While professing appreciation of Meiklejohn's work, he

pointed out that Meiklejohn's project had always been described by Frank and the University as experimental and argued that five years of Brittingham support for it was enough. The time had come to use the trust's funds for other short-term research projects. Brittingham did not suggest any alternative uses, leaving that decision to the University.[58]

Nine months later, casting about for ways to keep Professor Karl Paul Link, a rising young biochemist, from pursuing a job offer in California, Agriculture Dean Russell and Graduate Dean Slichter decided to create a special five-year research professorship for Link. Slichter, who chaired the University Research Committee, accordingly made a detailed proposal to the Brittingham trustees. He stipulated the yearly schedule of Link's salary over the five-year period and promised the University would allow him to use his regular UW salary for support of one or more research assistants. In return, Link would have to agree "that the program is to be continued for the complete period of five years and not interrupted by resignation or otherwise."[59] Plainly, the UW administrators hoped to use Brittingham funds to tie down Link for at least the next half-decade.

---

[58]Thomas E. Brittingham to Frank, May 8, December 12, 1930, March 27, April 13 and 15, 1931, UHP.

[59]Charles S. Slichter to Thomas Brittingham, Jr., December 10, 1930, ibid., also quoted in "The Brittingham Gift Affair," *WAM*, 33 (October, 1931), 5, 34.

This creative use of the Brittingham funds for a promising biological scientist appealed strongly to Tom Brittingham and the other trustees, who may also have had some doubts about the soundness of Meiklejohn's well-publicized educational and political views. By return mail Brittingham reported that the trustees approved the request in all particulars. This time, to leave no ambiguity, he noted the trustees' understanding of their commitment, repeating almost word-for-word the terms specified for the professorship by Dean Slichter:

> All three trustees of the Brittingham funds of which my brother, my sister, and myself are the trustees, have decided and hereby authorize you to extend this invitation to Mr. Karl Paul Link, at present Associate Professor of Bio-Chemistry in the University, for a research professorship in Bio-Chemistry to begin September 1, 1931 and extend for five years ending June, 1936. This provision is to carry a salary of $5,000 for each of the first two years, $5,250 for the third year, and $5,500 for the fourth and fifth years of the tenure of this professorship, these salaries being for the ten-month period during the year, and they do not cover work during the summer school.
>
> We make this offer with the understanding that Mr. Link will agree that he will complete the full five years of the professorship and it is not to be interrupted by resignations or desires to go elsewhere. We also want it agreed between the University and the trustees that they will continue their present contributions now made to Mr. Link's salary amounting to $2,900 a year, this money to be designated to Mr. Link's department for an assistant or assistants, as he may desire. It is also to be understood that Mr. Link carry out such a program of teaching advanced students as might be agreed upon between the President of the University and Mr. Link.
>
> It is our hope that with the position and salary question definitely settled for five years, and the fact that this salary is coming from one place only, that this will be a challenge and inspiration to Mr. Link to further carry on his research work and thus justify our action in having selected him for this professorship.[60]

The same day Brittingham wrote President Frank requesting an appointment to make sure Frank understood and approved the terms of the grant.[61] Evidently he did, for on March 27, 1931, on the president's

[60]Brittingham to Slichter, December 12, 1930, UHP, also quoted in "The Brittingham Gift Affair," p. 34.

[61]Brittingham to Frank, December 12, 1930, UHP. Link's research needs under the Brittingham grant were spelled out more fully by College of Agriculture Dean Harry Russell after sharing a train ride to Chicago with Tom Brittingham on February 14, 1931. See Russell to Brittingham, February 14, 1931; Brittingham to Russell, February 17, 1931; Russell to Frank, February 28, 1931, ibid. Brittingham told Russell he was counting on him "to see that our money receives the maximum in purchases made, and that it is not in any way allowed to slip

recommendation the Executive Committee of the Board of Regents approved both the Brittingham grant and the appointment of Link to the special research professorship.[62]

It seemed a routine action until two weeks later when the *Capital Times* ran a front page story headlined: "MEIKLEJOHN NO LONGER PAID BY BRITTINGHAM/ U. REGENTS ADVISED MONEY NOW TO BE USED FOR RESEARCH." Editor Evjue accompanied the news story with an inflammatory editorial in which he inquired:

> Would it be too much to ask of Dr. Frank to come from behind the veil of secrecy with which everything pertaining to the University is shrouded, and explain the astonishing statement that Tom Brittingham is taking time off from his stock market activities to pick faculty members who can be trusted to be safe and sane?[63]

Evjue kept up the pressure. The following week, on the eve of the regular meeting of the Board of Regents, he demanded that Frank release any correspondence specifying the Brittingham objections to Meiklejohn and asked: "Is the University to bend the knee to Mr. Brittingham?" He questioned how this action squared with the regents' assertion that "no money would be accepted by the University 'with strings attached'?"[64]

The regents took up the Brittingham gift during a long two-hour debate over the issue at the board meeting on April 15. Besides the *Capital Times'* charges, they had before them a joint resolution recently adopted by both houses of the legislature, once again under progressive control, resurrecting the abandoned Grady resolution on outside grants. It urged the regents to make clear the University would accept external funding only "when no condition shall be imposed which in any manner restricts the freedom of research or which places the University under obligations to any individual, corporation, or organizations."[65]

---

into the so called 'general pot'."

[62]BOR Executive Committee Minutes, March 27, 1931, UA, also quoted in "The Brittingham Gift Affair," p. 34. It should be noted that in addition to the Link grant, the Brittingham trustees were also contributing $2,500 a year in support of President Emeritus Birge's limnology research and $1,000 a year for zoology Professor Michael Guyer's genetic research. See Brittingham to Frank, March 27, 1931, UHP.

[63]*Capital Times*, April 8, 1931.

[64]Ibid., April 13, 1931. Actually, so far as can be determined, Brittingham had discussed the trustees' decision to discontinue paying Meiklejohn's salary with Frank in a conversation rather than by letter.

[65]Joint Resolution 34A, 1931, p. 2, BOR Papers, 1/1/3, box 43.

The day before the regents meeting Frank had received a long letter from Tom Brittingham which the president chose not to share with the board. Reacting to the *Capital Times'* criticism, Brittingham stressed that he and his fellow trustees had no desire to put strings on their grants to the University. They simply preferred to support on a temporary basis projects "the funds for which would be difficult to obtain from the ordinary budget of the University." They hoped by this means to assure that their gifts would "accomplish something definite rather than going into the common pot of ordinary University expenditures." He pointed out that the trustees had paid Meiklejohn's salary for five years without ever asking for or receiving a report on his work or even an invitation to visit the Experimental College. So much for any strings. He then added a veiled threat:

> On the other hand, the will provided that the income from this trust should be turned over from time to time and hence there is no obligation on the part of the trustees to do anything at the moment. If the regents do not care to accept the Link matter, I am sure our trustees would not object to having the money accumulate until such years in the future when this plan would be acceptable. Naturally, however, each trustee would be disappointed in seeing the present opportunities passed by for some indefinite ones of the future.[66]

During the board's discussion of the matter President Frank read a long statement detailing the history of the Brittingham Trust, which, he emphasized, antedated his administration. Rather than applauding the generosity of the Brittingham family and its commendable refusal to dictate how the trust's funds should be spent, Frank seemed to want to distance himself from the controversy. He reminded the regents he had several times in the past told them he was uncomfortable with the control of the Brittingham funds by outside trustees and would advise the board to decline any bequests with such restrictions in the future. He then recommended that the regents inform the Brittingham trustees that in the future the University would "be glad to receive regularly the total annual income" from the trust to be expended under its direction. It would not, however, "care to enter into continuous negotiations with outside judgments on every project to be supported."[67]

Under the prodding of Governor La Follette's outspoken recent

---

[66]Brittingham to Frank, April 13, 1931, UHP, also quoted in "The Brittingham Gift Affair," pp. 34-5.

[67]Frank, statement to the Board of Regents, April 15, 1931, quoted in "The Brittingham Affair," pp. 4-5; *Capital Times*, April 15, 1931; *Daily Cardinal*, April 16, 1931.

appointee, Harold Wilkie, the regents went much further than Frank intended. While the board said it welcomed the support of Brittingham funds for permanent research professorships or short-term research projects, it also stipulated that "conditions limiting the discretion of the Board of Regents cannot be accepted consistently with the duty which rests upon the Board." It therefore directed its Executive Committee to review its earlier action concerning the special research professorship for Karl Paul Link "in the light of any response of the Trustees of the Brittingham estate to this resolution."[68] "Regents Bar Brittingham Gift String," the *Capital Times* trumpeted that afternoon, gloating over Frank's defeat by Wilkie.[69]

President Frank now had the unhappy responsibility of informing the Brittingham trustees of the regents' rebuff. He did so in a long letter to Tom Brittingham on April 17, trying to put the best face possible on the rejection and regretting "that this matter could not have been settled without this ripple in the current."[70] Brittingham did not reply until July, evidently feeling he had made the trustees' position clear in his recent letter. He did, however, write Frank requesting that in releasing the correspondence about the matter he include Dean Slichter's letter of December 10 "showing that the Link matter was presented to us by your University authorities and not to you by our trustees."[71] When no response was forthcoming from the Brittingham trustees by the time of the regents meeting in June, the Executive Committee recommended that the board "decline to receive the money tendered by said trustees on the terms and conditions set forth in connection therewith and return to said trustees the money so far paid on account of the Link professorship in bio-chemistry." It was so voted, with the knowledge that the University would now have to find other funds to support the promised Link professorship as well as Meiklejohn's top faculty salary.[72]

Also at the June meeting the regents accepted a $17,500 grant from W.T. Rawleigh, a Freeport, Illinois, patent medicine manufacturer, for a study of tariff policy. Whereas the Brittinghams had agreed to fund a

---

[68]BOR Minutes, April 15, 1931; "The Brittingham Gift Affair," p. 35.

[69]*Capital Times*, April 15, 1931.

[70]Frank to Brittingham, April 17, 1931, UHP, also quoted in "The Brittingham Gift Affair," p. 35.

[71]Brittingham to Frank, May 20, 1931, UHP.

[72]BOR Minutes, June 30, 1931; "Brittingham Gift Affair," p. 35; *Capital Times*, June 20, 1931.

University-proposed project in its entirety without suggesting or modifying its nature or terms, Rawleigh had stipulated that economics Professor John R. Commons was to direct the tariff study in which his firm had an economic interest. The difference, apparently, was that Rawleigh was a long-time financial and political supporter of the La Follette family and Commons was a politically correct progressive. The irony was not lost on James S. Watrous, a perceptive graduating senior. He produced a clever cartoon for the *Wisconsin Alumni Magazine* the following month showing the regents tripping over a crystal-clear, cellophane-wrapped Brittingham gift while reaching for the Rawleigh gift (an opaque corked bottle) as Commons and Rawleigh readied themselves to pull on its attached rope.[73] The uncomfortable inconsistency was also recognized by President Frank, who tried without success to distinguish between the two grants in an effort to mollify Tom Brittingham and persuade the trustees to continue their support of University research.[74]

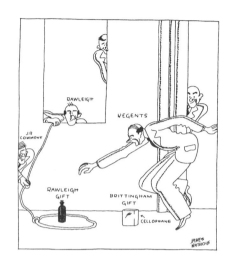

Not content with this victory, the *Capital Times* continued throughout the summer to demand that President Frank release the correspondence with Tom Brittingham.[75] The paper's tone was so shrill and insistent that another editor speculated that Evjue was after "Frank's scalp."[76] When Frank and the regents finally released the correspondence in early August, the *Times* asserted that because it dealt mostly with the Link professorship Frank must be withholding important Brit-

---

[73]*WAM*, 32 (July, 1931), 386. Relations between Commons and the La Follettes were close and long-standing. Even before Phil La Follette was inaugurated as governor in early 1931, he had Commons at work drafting various pieces of reform legislation which the progressives hoped to enact. See John R. Commons to La Follette, December 4, 1930, P.F. La Follette Papers, box 134.

[74]Frank to Brittingham, August 5, 1931, UHP.

[75]See *Capital Times*, June 18, 26, and 27, August 5, 6, 7, and 9, September 23, 1931.

[76]Ibid., August 13, 1931.

tingham letters concerning Meiklejohn. "It is this eternal tendency toward slick evasiveness and sly circumvention," the paper declared, "that is forever keeping Mr. Frank in hot water."[77]

To complete the public record, an exasperated Tom Brittingham gave the rival *Wisconsin State Journal* a copy of a letter he had written Frank on July 15, summarizing the reaction of the Brittingham trustees to the regents' rejection of the Link gift. The University's request for support of the Link professorship, he said, had "seemed a worthy one to the trustees, one which might serve humanity and could not serve any private interest, and so it must seem to any sensible man." It now appeared that Frank and the regents believed the Brittingham bequest should have been rejected by the board in 1924 and were unwilling to accept any more Brittingham grants unless the trustees would "disregard the discretionary powers and duties imposed on them by the will." He therefore requested that the trustees "be definitely informed upon this point in order that they may determine their future action with respect to the disposition of the income."[78] "Nailed," chortled editor Evjue at this confirmation that Frank had withheld some of the Brittingham correspondence. The letter, Evjue declared, "proves both directly and inferentially that Mr. Brittingham and his associate trustees did not want Brittingham money to be used for Mr. Meiklejohn, that they would prefer to have the money used by Mr. Link in the safer field of biochemistry."[79] In the fall of 1931 the *Wisconsin Alumni Magazine* offered its judgment on the stand-off:

> To an impartial observer the entire affair seems to be most regretable. There can be little question that the administrators of the University of Wisconsin Trust have the welfare of the University constantly in mind when making any bequests and their donations should not be rejected for what seem to be trivial points. An outsider can take the actions of the Regents to mean but one thing,—politics.[80]

It is hard for a later chronicler to disagree.[81]

---

[77]Ibid., August 6, 1931.

[78]Brittingham to Frank, July 15, 1931, UHP; *Capital Times*, August 7, 1931; "The Brittingham Gift Affair," p. 36.

[79]*Capital Times*, August 7, 1931.

[80]"The Brittingham Gift Affair," p. 36.

[81]Grants from the Brittingham trustees to the University did not resume until 1936, when the trustees agreed to a five-year grant of funds for the salary of John Steuart Curry to be the University's first artist-in-residence, in the College of Agriculture. In 1939 the trustees made

Deans Goodnight and Nardin and In Loco Parentis

Budget woes were only a part of President Frank's well-publicized difficulties in the early thirties. Several persistent personnel problems he had managed to gloss over up to this time reached a stage of open controversy that neither he nor the regents could ignore. One of these involved the roles of the deans of men and women, Scott H. Goodnight and F. Louise Nardin. During the roaring twenties both, and particularly Dean Nardin, were perceived by many of the students and some of the faculty to be blue-nosed guardians of outdated victorian morality. This was not quite fair, for their offices were expected to enforce the University's traditionally rather mild *in loco parentis* role in guiding the lives of the young people entrusted to its care. They operated under the policy guidance of the faculty Committee on Student Life and Interests (SLIC), which had expanded the University's role in student life considerably since its creation in 1914.[82] President Frank, moreover, gave no sign that he wanted to modify their responsibilities. Nardin was a kindhearted and gentle person but a strict disciplinarian particularly where the morals of her coeds were threatened. Goodnight had long recognized the difficulty of mixing the two major roles of their offices—student counseling and discipline. Even before Frank's arrival on

Deans Goodnight and Nardin at the Prom

a similar grant for Danish pianist Gunnar Johansen to be an artist-in-residence in the School of Music. Later that year the Brittingham trustees also made a grant to enable Curry to paint murals for the entrance and seminar room of the Biochemistry Building. In accepting the Brittingham grant for Curry's salary in 1936, the board's Executive Committee observed that the regents were "deeply gratified that any regrettable misunderstanding respecting the policy of administering these funds has been definitely cleared up." BOR Executive Committee Minutes, October 3, 1936; BOR Minutes, June 17, November 18, 1939.

[82]See pp. 564-9.

campus in 1925 he had urged the new president, as he had President Birge, to separate these functions.[83] Although on the whole the newspapers of the state supported Goodnight over his irascible critic, William Ellery Leonard, neither dean's campus image was enhanced by their roles in the famous rocking chair incident in December of 1929. By characteristically failing to move aggressively to head off Leonard's criticism, Frank allowed an incident to grow into an issue before finally taking official notice. More significantly, his belated and overly harsh response further diminished his image among the faculty and beyond.[84]

The furor over the rocking chair affair was sufficiently embarrassing to the University that afterward President Frank, at the urging of SLIC, promised the regents to overhaul student discipline policy.[85] During the fall of 1930 the Madison press reported numerous rumors—"as the ants on an ant hill," commented the *Wisconsin State Journal*—of sweeping changes Frank intended to make in the responsibilities of the two deans. There were even hints that the reorganization might involve the departure of Dean Nardin, who had been under increasing fire for two years.[86] The speculation reached the point that she felt obliged to write the president asking "the favor of receiving definite details of your plan that cover the various types of work for which our office has been responsible."[87] Frank ignored her request and instead announced his proposed reorganization to the regents on November 22 and at a faculty meeting on December 1, asking for its review by a special Joint Committee on Social Control consisting of the University Committee and the faculty Committee on Student Discipline. The faculty gave its approval to the joint committee, chaired by geology Professor William H. Twenhofel, but over two successive faculty meetings the discussion revealed suspicion on the part of some that Frank and the regents had already decided the matter.[88]

The Twenhofel Committee presented its report in the spring, proposing only modest changes in the current student affairs structure.

---

[83]See p. 72.

[84]See p. 119.

[85]BOR Minutes, October 11, 1930.

[86]*Wisconsin State Journal*, August 24, 1930.

[87]F. Louise Nardin to Frank, November 25, 1930, Frank Presidential Papers, 4/13/1, box 101.

[88]English Professor Helen White seemed particularly suspicious of the president's motives, probably reflecting sympathy for Dean Nardin. BOR Minutes, November 22, 1930; UW Faculty Minutes, December 1, 1930, January 12, 1931.

In an unusual display of independence the faculty rejected the committee's recommendations for not going far enough. Instead, by a narrow margin of 83-77 it adopted a motion by sociology Professor Kimball Young calling for the removal of the deans of men and women from any role in student discipline. Twenhofel thereupon moved that a new committee should restudy the matter and resigned from his committee, which abruptly disbanded. The split in the faculty over the Twenhofel report divided the administration as well, with L&S Dean Sellery supporting the Twenhofel Committee (and by implication Deans Goodnight and Nardin) and Dean Charles R. Bardeen of the Medical School joining Kimball Young's rebels in opposition.[89] Hard upon the faculty's rebuff of the Twenhofel Committee, a student committee issued a report strongly criticizing what it saw as the rigidity and coldly unsympathetic attitude of the two deans in handling student rules infractions, which it said created "an attitude of defiance and resentment" among students. To head off further embarrassing publicity, President Frank quickly asked Professor Young to chair a new special Committee on the Organization of the University's System of Student Counsel and Discipline.[90]

The Young Committee's report, presented first to the faculty and then to the regents in June, 1931, delicately skirted the controversial issue of the personalities and practices of the two deans. It did, how-

---

[89]*Wisconsin State Journal*, May 7, 1931. The faculty was so evenly divided over whether to reject the Twenhofel report that the vote on the Young motion was taken three times—first verbally, then on a standing vote, and finally at Dean Sellery's request on a written ballot. When English Chairman R.E.N. Dodge, a Twenhofel supporter, asked that these ballots be signed, President Frank demurred with the comment: "This is a ballot and not an inquisition."

[90]UW Faculty Minutes, December 1, 1930, January 12, April 6 and 29, May 6, 1931; *Capital Times*, January 21, March 8 and 10, May 7, 8, 10, 12, and 15, 1931; *Milwaukee News*, May 9, 1931; *Milwaukee Sentinel*, May 9 and 10, 1931; *Fond du Lac Reporter*, May 11, 1931; *Milwaukee Journal*, May 11, 1931; *Daily Cardinal*, March 10, May 7, 8, 9, 10, 12, and 13, 1931; "Faculty Votes to Curtail Disciplinary Powers of Deans," *WAM*, 32 (June, 1931), 344-5, 362. Because press reports suggested that Frank had promised the regents he would reorganize the offices of the deans of men and women to remove their disciplinary powers, the faculty was initially suspicious that the president had acted without faculty authorization in a matter related to the faculty's traditional academic responsibilities. Twice English Professor Helen C. White offered motions seeking assurances that Frank had not preempted faculty authority in the matter. UW Faculty Minutes, December 1, 1930, January 12, 1931. In an effort to assure acceptance of its report, Frank recruited some heavy hitters for the new committee. Serving with Young were E.B. Fred, M.F. Guyer, C.K. Leith, M.C. Otto, Blanche Trilling, and Warren Weaver. Frank consulted Dean Bardeen about the membership of the committee. Bardeen suggested several of its members, including Young and Trilling, who were, he said said, "both OK from my point of view." C.R. Bardeen to Frank, May 8, 1931, Frank Presidential Papers, 4/13/1, box 104.

ever, explain that its recommendations were "tied by complications involving personnel," which in "the present complex situation" made it "impossible to separate personnel from certain questions of policy and organization." The first and most important of the committee's three recommendations called for a sharp reduction in the involvement of the deans of men and women in student discipline cases. Once the deans had reviewed a case and determined that punitive discipline might be called for, they were to refer the matter to the faculty Committee on Student Conduct and thereafter have nothing to do with it. The committee also recommended that the deans reduce their involvement in supervising the details of student life and activities, which it pointed out "are often a source of friction, and which in our judgment now prevent them from utilizing to the best advantage their opportunities for leadership and counsel." In short, the committee endorsed the arguments Dean Goodnight had unsuccessfully made to Presidents Birge and Frank in 1924-25, and which Frank had finally come to accept.[91] Since the Young Committee's recommendations generally followed the policy and structure that the president had proposed six months earlier to the regents and the faculty, the board had little reason not to accept them.

Although President Frank initially denied press speculation that Dean Nardin would be ousted under the new student affairs structure,[92] in accepting the Young Committee's recommendations the Board of Regents decided not to continue the dean in her position. When word of this decision leaked out, Frank and Regent Arthur Sholts explained that Nardin had been given several choices: resignation, a resumption of her initial faculty appointment in the Department of English, or a year's leave of absence followed by teaching.[93] The dean accepted none of these options, instead publicly demanding to learn why after thirteen years her work had suddenly been determined to be unsatisfactory. She warned sarcastically that her successor would need to know "what

[91]UW Faculty Document 385, "Report of the Special Committee on the Organization of the University's System of Student Counsel and Discipline," June 1, 1931; BOR Minutes, June 20, 1931, Exhibit A.

[92]*Capital Times*, June 3, 1931.

[93]See Frank's handwritten explanation of the decision to offer Dean Nardin new responsibilities. "Shifts in administrative duties and officers are going on all the while within a large organization like the University," he pointed out. "Obviously the decision regarding such shifts rests with the Administration and the Regents, and it cannot be assumed that every administrative officer in the institution has the right to veto such decisions respecting his or her duties." Frank, draft, n.d., Frank Presidential Papers, 4/13/1, box 101.

principles Dr. Frank wanted the office conducted upon—if he himself knows."[94] Declaring that the president's answers were unresponsive, she commented acidly: "You can't nail a custard pie to the wall."[95]

Dean Nardin's Alleged Bubbler Crusade

The Nardin firing drew a good deal of press comment in Wisconsin and nationally, with speculation that she had alienated Frank and some of the regents by her victorian views, especially her alleged advice to women students in the spring of 1929 not to wear red dresses or flocked stockings or drink at bubblers in public places in order to "avoid arousing men." Although there is no proof of the allegation, *Time* magazine hinted that Nardin's ouster came at the hands of two women with more modern feminist views, Regent Meta Berger and former Regent Zona Gale.[96] Others blamed President Frank for not backing his administrative colleagues. The Rev. F.J. Bloodgood, rector of the campus-area St. Andrews Episcopal Church, issued a blunt statement during the controversy complaining of Frank's "shabby and undignified treatment" of Deans Nardin and Goodnight.

> President Frank has considerable gifts of eloquence and political adroitness. but education and administration appear to interest him little....Without

---

[94]*Daily Cardinal*, July 11, 1931. When the Nardin-Frank correspondence was released, the *Milwaukee Journal* thought Nardin had the better of the argument and criticized Frank for not providing more policy guidance for his deans of men and women in the area of student discipline. *Capital Times*, July 15, 1931; *Daily Cardinal*, July 16, 1931.

[95]*Daily Cardinal*, July 14, 1931.

[96]Ibid., July 9 and 18, 1931. At least one UW coed, Bettina Wright, defended Nardin and denied that the dean had ever warned women students to shun drinking fountains or do other things that might "arouse" male students. *Capital Times*, August 14, 1931. See also *Daily Cardinal*, May 8, 9, and 10, June 1, 1929; *Capital Times*, May 9 and 15, 1929.

conferring with his deans about their work, he has permitted attacks on them in the press under the guise of improving student discipline. Student discipline is not improved when students witness disloyalty in their president to his colleagues. No wonder the faculty is in an unhappy state.[97]

Throughout the Nardin affair Glenn Frank came across as an indecisive heavy, whose abrupt but belated replacement of a woman dean on short notice seemed needlessly harsh, and whose dithering had obliged the faculty and the regents to try to straighten out problems with the structure and mission of the two student affairs offices.[98] Although there is no evidence suggesting long-standing hostility between the president and his dean of women, neither were their relations close and cordial despite the fact that Nardin came from the same small-town Missouri background as did Glenn and Mary Frank. When Dean Nardin was appointed in 1919 two of her University of Missouri referees, while praising her teaching and administrative abilities, noted that

---

[97]*Milwaukee Journal*, May 15, 1931.

[98]This was one of the few instances where President Frank behaved uncharitably toward one of his critics. Nardin had some support in the faculty and administration among those who thought she had been treated shabbily. Both L&S Dean George Sellery and German Professor Alexander Hohlfeld, the chairman of the faculty representatives on the joint Regent-Faculty Conference Committee, sought unsuccessfully to get Nardin a semester's leave of absence with pay. Since she had "banked" her salary for serving in the summer sessions of 1925 and 1928, under University policy she was entitled to convert it into a semester of paid leave. She told Hohlfeld she felt entitled to this "as a matter of justice," but declined to make a formal request for a leave. Hohlfeld and others urged Frank to show "as much liberality in the final settlement as possible," and expressed the hope that the president and the regents would "disregard the rather undignified press publicity in which Miss Nardin has given way to a clearly wrought-up state of feeling, and arrange for a semester's leave of absence." After Frank declined to act, Nardin's administrative colleague, Dean Goodnight, confirmed her suspicions about the president's hostility:

> You are quite right that the President didn't want you to have the leave-of-abasence [*sic*] remuneration. If he had wanted it you would have received it, and we are all of the opinion that it would have been the only handsome and dignified thing to do. I much regret that it was not done, and if I could have my way about it, I assure you that you would receive it.

Goodnight contemptuously referred to Frank as "De King Fish," after the popular radio comedy character in the *Amos and Andy Show*. When the leave of absence scheme fell through, as director of the summer session Goodnight arranged for the payment to Nardin of the $1,200, without interest, of her banked past summer session salary. See Scott H. Goodnight to Nardin, September 15, 1931; Nardin to Goodnight, September 8, 1931; Goodnight to M.E. McCaffrey, J.D. Phillips, and C.W. Vaughn, September 11, 1931, Student Affairs Papers, 19/2/1-4, envelope 1, UA; A.R. Hohlfeld to Frank, July 29, 1931, Frank Presidential Papers, 4/13/1, box 97.

she lacked social polish.[99] It may well be that this was a fatal flaw in the eyes of the socially ambitious Franks, who had spent their adult lives trying to shake the dust of Missouri from their feet. In any event, with President Frank's selection of Louise Troxell as Dean Nardin's successor, concern over the Nardin affair quickly receded. Prematurely widowed, Mrs. Troxell had done graduate work at the University and was currently working as a statistician in the economics department. She was well-known and liked in the larger Madison community. Her appointment was a signal there would be a more modern and less disciplinary outlook in the dean of women's office.[100]

The Snell Episode

Another long-festering personnel problem involved the University Extension Division. The extension scandal centered around Dean Chester D. Snell, whom Frank had recruited in 1926. Snell's slight southern drawl belied his hard-driving, aggressive style of leadership. "There is a side to me which perhaps you have not seen," he told his predecessor, Louis Reber, before coming to Madison, "—when running in high gear I am quite an autocrat and a driver—you know it takes that to build an efficient organization in a short space of time."[101] In Wisconsin Snell soon came to be viewed as a young man in a hurry, an often tactless empire builder who grumbled openly about the incompetence of long-time staffers, rebuilt the extension faculty to fit his view of the changing nature of outreach education, and within a few years replaced six of fourteen major administrators in his division. He also alienated most of the other deans by trying to tighten his control over all extension activities.

The depression gave Snell the opportunity to respond to new state

---

[99]See President A. Ross Hill to Charles R. Van Hise, July 20, 1918; Dean J.C. Jones to Van Hise, July 18, 1918, Charles R. Van Hise Presidential Papers, 4/10/1, box 65, UA.

[100]BOR Minutes, August 5, 1931; *Capital Times*, August 5 and 12, 1931; *Daily Cardinal*, July 16 and 18, August 6, September 23, 1931; *WAM*, 33 (October, 1931), 15. Dean Troxell's first husband died in 1930. She remarried Dr. Hugh Greeley in 1934 and thereafter used the name Louise Troxell Greeley until about 1943, when she reverted to the name Troxell. See *Who's Who in America, 1942-43* (Chicago: A.N. Marquis, 1942), p. 941, and ibid., *1944-45* (1944), p. 2151.

[101]Chester D. Snell to Louis E. Reber, March 2, 1925, quoted in Frederick M. Rosentreter, *The Boundaries of the Campus: A History of the University of Extension Division, 1885-1945* (Madison: University of Wisconsin Press, 1957), p. 139.

needs by increasing the number of organized correspondence courses and freshman-sophomore level classes serving the unemployed and others who could not afford the expense of resident study in Madison. He contracted for after-hours space in numerous high schools across the state whose school boards were delighted to gain some extra income and prestige from association with the University. Snell saw the economic crisis as an opportunity to build a system of UW junior colleges under Extension's aegis. During the 1933-35 biennium more than seven thousand students were enrolled in extension classes in fifty-four Wisconsin cities outside of Milwaukee. Although these developments were popular in the local communities, they made President Frank uneasy. Neither he nor the Madison faculty nor influential Madison political and business leaders favored the development of University of Wisconsin "campuses" outside of Madison. Nor did the president think kindly of Dean Snell's aggressive lobbying with regents and legislators to secure more funds for his division.

A key Extension unit was the large program in Milwaukee, which for more than two decades had embodied the University's presence in the state's largest city. In Extension's early years President Van Hise had resolutely rejected suggestions that the Milwaukee program might eventually become a full-fledged branch of the University, fearing this would dilute support for the main campus in Madison. The need to provide educational services to Milwaukee-area veterans after World War I, however, led to an expansion of the Milwaukee extension activities. Over the objections of Marquette University officials, by 1923 the Milwaukee Extension Center was offering a full-time regular freshman-sophomore program in addition to the usual array of non-credit and correspondence courses. By the late twenties Milwaukee Extension had its own downtown building which some of its staff saw as the beginning of a four-year campus. Under former Dean Reber the Milwaukee Center had gradually come to enjoy semi-autonomy. Dean Snell secured funds both to complete the Milwaukee Extension Building and to expand its staff and activities, but he also began to exercise more direction and control from Madison.

As his division shared in the University-wide budget reductions of the early thirties, Snell of necessity cut back on staff and expenditures. Pointing to the unpredictable nature of extension program revenue, he tried without President Frank's permission to limit assistant professor appointments to one year rather than the traditional three. He also strongly discouraged faculty research in favor of teaching. Not surprisingly, these actions were highly unpopular with Milwaukee faculty members, who considered themselves the junior equivalent of their Madison colleagues. The latter in turn were uneasy over the dean's meddling in academic affairs and his limiting the length of faculty appointments. Many of the Milwaukee faculty belonged to Local 253 of the American Federation of Teachers and were active in progressive politics. In the spring of 1934 Dean Snell declined to reappoint Assistant Professor Donald C. Boughton, who had been on research leave, explaining that as an active researcher Boughton would find the Milwaukee Center's emphasis on lower division teaching uncongenial. Boughton responded on June 4 with an open letter warning that the dean's disrespect for faculty research, leaves, and tenure signalled a shattering of staff morale. Four days later the Milwaukee County Federation of Teachers petitioned President Frank to investigate the Snell administration, calling the dean "undemocratic, arbitrary, and discriminatory." Senior Milwaukee faculty, also members of the union, deplored the public airing of a personnel matter and declared that the AFT view was not representative of faculty feeling, but the conflict was now in the open.

Frank did nothing over the summer, but in October, citing the complaints about Snell's behavior, he asked the Board of Regents to investigate the dean's handling of his division—an action Snell later claimed was deliberately timed to occur when some of his supporters on the board were absent. A regent committee held hearings in Madison and Milwaukee, compiling a thousand pages of testimony full of recrimination and pent-up hostility. Even if one discounted most of the complaints as petty and mean-spirited, Dean Snell had clearly lost the confidence of some of his subordinates and with it his capacity for effective leadership. In March, 1935, the Board of Regents decided to ask for his resignation. Like Dean Nardin, Snell refused to resign, claiming he had never acted without consulting President Frank and charging that the attack against him stemmed from his refusal to condone "subversive activities, improper conduct and immorality on the part of a small group" of the Milwaukee staff.[102] Given the opportunity to substantiate these charges, the embattled dean offered his correspondence with Frank and an affidavit claiming that certain of his Milwaukee critics had engaged in immoral behavior aboard a yacht in Lake Michigan. Unpersuaded, the regents voted to dismiss him.

---

[102]Quoted in Rosentreter, *Boundaries of the Campus,* p. 143.

The Snell charges and counter-charges were tailor-made for the yellow press, which feasted on the scandal. Typical were the lurid headlines of the Chicago *Times* on April 25: "WISCONSIN U YACHT LOVE!/ UNIVERSITY 'FREE LOVE' QUIZ ROCKS CAMPUS/ STENO'S TRYST ON YACHT TO BE BARED/ YACHT PARTY STORY TOLD IN RECORDS/ DEAN SNELL OUSTED FOLLOWING HIS SENSATIONAL CHARGES." The embarrassing publicity was fueled for several months longer while a legislative committee chaired by Senator E.F. Brunette, which was already investigating the University for its alleged toleration of communism, looked into the Snell matter as well.[103] The board's firing of the extension dean stood, however. It is hard to assess how much damage Frank and the University sustained in shaken public confidence over the Snell affair, although a later observer is inclined to agree with those regents who believed the president ought to have acted sooner and more decisively. Frank's prompt choice of Frank O. Holt, the popular and widely respected University registrar, as Snell's successor helped to rebuild confidence.[104]

Rebuilding Badger Athletics (Twice)

Recurring problems with intercollegiate athletics during the early thirties provided additional evidence for those who sought it that President Frank's loose, easy-going administrative style was not well-suited to handling tough personnel and budget problems before they reached a clamorous crisis stage. Part of the difficulty stemmed from the lackluster performance of Badger athletic teams in these years, especially in football. The decline of Wisconsin football anguished alumni fans and

---

[103]The basis for the regents' dismissal of Snell and President Frank's response to his charges are outlined at length in BOR Minutes, April 24, 1935. The board indignantly rejected the loose criticism in the report of the Brunette committee. Ibid., November 8, 1935. The testimony of Frank and Regents Callahan and Wilkie about the Snell ouster before the Brunette committee was covered extensively by the Wisconsin press. See especially *Milwaukee Journal*, June 14, 1935; *Milwaukee Sentinel*, June 14, 1935; *Oshkosh Northwestern*, June 14, 1935; *Chicago Tribune*, June 14, 1935. The sensationalist Chicago *Times* headlined its story about Frank's testimony: "DENIES FREE LOVE/ FRANK LABELS SNELL JUST A 'DICTATOR'." Chicago *Times*, June 14, 1935. See also pp. 810-12.

[104]For the Snell affair see BOR Minutes, March 13, April 24, November 8, 1935; Glenn Frank, "The Snell Episode," Frank Papers, Kirksville; Rosentreter, *Boundaries of the Campus*, pp. 138-44; Clay Schoenfeld, *The Outreach University: A Case History in the Public Relationships of Higher Education* (Madison: University of Wisconsin-Madison Office of Inter-College Programs, 1977), pp. 105-23.

led to charges by Wisconsin sports writers that the University's high academic standards discriminated against student athletes and made it impossible to field competitive teams. The *Daily Cardinal* and student groups, on the other hand, complained about excessive professionalism in intercollegiate sports and agitated against the lower eligibility requirement set for athletes in contrast to students participating in other extracurricular activities. For athletes the University applied the somewhat lower Big Ten standard rather than its general campus requirement of a C average. In the spring of 1927 the men's Union Board published a critical pamphlet written by Jefferson D. Burrus entitled *The Present Intercollegiate Athletic System.* Burrus, a star end on the football team and crew captain—and incidentally a Phi Beta Kappa and future Rhodes Scholar—complained that professional demands had taken the fun out of sports and kept him from enjoying other aspects of campus life. For a time the Burrus complaint set off a campus debate about the place of intercollegiate athletics and even drew national attention.[105] Falling attendance in the depression intensified the athletic program's problems and threatened its ability to pay off the loan from the state teachers retirement fund that had made possible the construction of the Field House in 1930. Nor did the high salaries paid UW coaches escape critical public notice in these lean years. Since oversight of intercollegiate athletics was a faculty responsibility, in the absence of constructive faculty action the situation cried out for close presidential scrutiny and strong leadership.

If Frank was inclined to temporize, others were not. During the winter of 1931-32 a legislative committee began investigating the UW athletic program, seeking evidence of mismanagement in the handling of its financial and competitive problems. Through the three alumni representatives on the Athletic Council and its monthly magazine, the alumni association stepped up its campaign for a revival of Wisconsin sports prowess.[106] In January, 1932, the general faculty received the

---

[105]Lowell Frautschi, interview with the authors, February 26, 1993, UHP; *Daily Cardinal*, February 9 (editorial), March 25, April 26, 27, and 30, 1927.

[106]Yielding to pressure from the Wisconsin Alumni Association, the Athletic Council and the Board of Regents had agreed in 1929 to add two more alumni representatives to the council (making a total of three). This had required the appointment of a sixth faculty representative in order to maintain the principle of faculty control of intercollegiate athletics as required by the rules of the Big Ten conference. Reflecting both its origin and this principle of faculty control, the so-called Big Ten or Western Conference was officially known as the Intercollegiate Conference of Faculty Representatives.

long-awaited report of a special faculty committee elected two years earlier in response to mounting faculty uneasiness over the growing professional and commercial character of intercollegiate sports. The committee, chaired by law Professor Ray Brown and including as well George Little, Harold Bradley, Warren Weaver, and Frank Sharp, was directed to study intercollegiate athletics at Wisconsin and elsewhere, especially "the problem of the relation of intercollegiate athletics to the educational activities and policies of the University and the proper balance to be maintained between the same."[107]

The Brown Committee's report was a wise and thoughtful policy statement, which remains as perceptive and timely as when it was written more than a half century ago. It made a number of recommendations, most of which the general faculty accepted on March 21. The committee endorsed the value of intercollegiate competition and denied that athletics had come to overshadow the educational interests of the University or that student athletes as a group performed much differently than other students in their academic work. At the same time, the report expressed concern over the extent to which commercial considerations had come to dominate intercollegiate athletics in order to fund an extensive array of major and minor competitive sports, pay coaches high salaries, and construct and maintain physical facilities like the UW Stadium and Field House. It highlighted the funding problem by pointing out that in 1930-31 the state of Wisconsin provided only $61,000, or 19 percent, of the $323,600 budget for the University's physical education program, including instruction for the required freshman-sophomore physical education classes and advanced courses for P.E. majors, an extensive intramural sports program, and intercollegiate competition in a number of major and minor sports. As a result the entire program was heavily dependent on gate receipts from football and to a lesser extent from basketball.

The report warned of the growing professionalism of college

---

[107]UW Faculty Document 399, "Report of the Special Committee on the Relation of Intercollegiate Athletics to the Educational Activities and Policies of the University," January 18, 1932; George C. Sellery, *Some Ferments at Wisconsin, 1901-1947: Memories and Reflections* (Madison: University of Wisconsin Press, 1960), pp. 73-4. Little and the other members of the Brown Committee were sensitive to the possible conflict of interest inherent in his leading role in intercollegiate athletics as the director of physical education at the University. Little provided information and participated fully in the work of the committee up to the point when it began deliberating on its findings and recommendations, when he voluntarily withdrew and was not asked to sign the report.

football and basketball, whereby "the individual initiative of the player is repressed by over-coaching and an excessive specialization of function." It attributed this to "the pressure of the alumni and of the general public which demands a winner or a change of coaches" to the point where "the temptation to violate conference prohibitions is almost irresistible."

> The solution lies in a straightforward recognition and acknowledgement of the evils existing; in the growth of an enlightened public opinion; in a determination on the part of the faculties and governing bodies of the Intercollegiate Conference universities to maintain a program of sport motivated, not by the desire for championships nor for the making of money, but by the welfare of the student body; and, finally, in the appointment and support of directors and coaches who sympathetically subscribe to these views.

To reduce the win-at-any-cost pressure on coaches the committee recommended they receive the same level of job security "as that of any other member of the Faculty of similar rank" and that the University "move as rapidly as possible towards the adoption of a scale of salaries for coaching positions similar to those of other members of the Faculty having equal rank." Finally, the Brown Committee recommended the restructuring of the Athletic Council, which would continue as it had since 1915 to be a subcommittee of the faculty Committee on Student Life and Interests. The size of the council should be pruned to a more manageable seven members: the University business manager, the faculty chairman of SLIC, an alumnus chosen by the president from a list nominated by the alumni association, the president of the Student Athletic Board, and three members of the legal faculty not connected with athletics or physical education.[108]

That the Brown Committee may have gotten wind of other reorganization plans can be inferred from a motion offered by one of its members, mathematics Professor Warren Weaver, at the December, 1931, faculty meeting. As amended during debate, the resolution pointedly reminded the Athletic Council that it "owes its existence to and derives its powers from the Faculty under the authority of the Regents," and directed it first to "present to the Faculty, prior to final recommendation to the Regents, such reorganization plans as the Council may draw up."[109]

---

[108]UW Faculty Document 399; Sellery, *Some Ferments at Wisconsin*, pp. 77-8.
[109]Sellery, *Some Ferments at Wisconsin*, p. 74.

As if in response, at the following meeting of the general faculty, English Professor J.F.A. "Sunny" Pyre, the long-time chairman of the Athletic Council and a Badger football star of the late 1890s who was sometimes referred to as the faculty "sports czar," presented the council's plan for a major reorganization of intercollegiate athletics:

> The Athletic Council recommends that, beginning with the fiscal year 1932-33, Intercollegiate Athletics be administered as a separate department, distinct from the department of Physical Education as a whole. The Council further recommends that there be a Director of Intercollegiate Athletics who shall be responsible to the University Faculty, through the Athletic Council of the Faculty. The above recommendations of the Council are intended to provide a basis for a program of consolidation and retrenchment in intercollegiate athletics which is, in part, dictated by the existing financial situation and which will involve some changes of staff and staff duties as well as the transfer of certain sports activities from an intercollegiate to an intramural status. The detailed program contemplated cannot be reported in full at this time for the reason that certain arrangements as to personnel must await confirmation by the Board of Regents.

After considerable discussion the faculty approved these changes, with the proviso that a special committee would consider the status of sports not included in intercollegiate competition.[110]

Two days later, on January 20, the Board of Regents accepted the resignations of Glenn Thistlethwaite as head football coach and George Little as director of physical education. Both resignations had been requested by the Athletic Council as a means of restoring the University's credibility in football and the financial stability of the UW athletic program. "Thisty" Thistlethwaite's resignation was not unexpected, inasmuch as alumni opposition to the sorry performance of his teams had been building for more than a year and even some of his players had expressed dissatisfaction with his coaching. Little's forced resignation, on the other hand, was more surprising and controversial, generating considerable sympathy for him around the state. The Wisconsin Assembly even passed a resolution declaring that the popular athletic director's resignation was "regretted by the great majority of the members of this house and all true friends of the University," with one of the legislative investigators suggesting pointedly that he was "being made the goat" for lax oversight by the faculty's Athletic Council.[111]

[110]UW Faculty Minutes, January 18, 1932; Sellery, *Some Ferments at Wisconsin*, p. 74.
[111]Resolution 18A, adopted January 20, 1932, BOR Papers, 1/1/3, box 44; "Uteritz

Because both men held tenured full professorships, their rights as faculty members had entered into the faculty debate over the resolution offered by Warren Weaver in December. For a time this concern also led the six faculty members of the council to the rather fanciful consideration of Thistlethwaite for the new position of director of intercollegiate athletics and of Little as football coach. These ideas were dropped when the alumni representatives insisted on a clean break with the past. The regents offered Little the chance to remain as director of intramural sports, one of his great interests.[112] Rather than stay on in the reorganized independent athletic structure he had opposed, however, he instead accepted a newly created position of director of physical education at Rutgers University.[113]

The January, 1932, regents meeting revealed the extent of the board's unhappiness over the current state of Wisconsin athletics. Regent Grady presented a resolution calling for the abolition of the Athletic Council and its replacement with a new seven-member Athletic Board, consisting of the chairman of the regents Committee on Physical Education, the president of the Student Athletic Board, a representative of the Wisconsin Alumni Association, and four faculty members. An ardent Badger sports booster, Grady's obvious intent was to preempt the Brown Committee's reorganization plan and in the process assure direct regent involvement in athletics. While acknowledging that the regents could do whatever they liked, President Frank strenuously objected to the Grady motion, arguing that the Athletic Council was and had always been "a creature of the faculty." Consequently any change involving it ought to involve consultation with the faculty or at least an opportunity

Recommended for Athletic Director," *WAM*, 33 (January, 1932), 131.

[112]See p. 651.

[113]See George Little to Frank, December 14, 1931, February 13 and 27, 1932, Frank Presidential Papers, 4/13/1, box 117; Little to Fred Clausen, February 27, 1932, BOR Papers, 1/1/3, box 44; *Capital Times*, December 14, 17, 26, and 28, 1931, January 20, 1932; *Daily Cardinal*, December 3, 4, 5, 8, and 15, 1931, January 7, 20, 21, and 22, March 1, 1932; "Uteritz Recommended for Athletic Director," pp. 110, 130-2.

for the faculty to confirm the new arrangements. "A dangerous precedent will be set, not only here, but in all the Big Ten universities,"
Frank warned, "if you do not permit the faculty to consider the matter."
The president's view prevailed and the board decided to defer action on
the Grady resolution until the next meeting to permit Frank to consult
the faculty.[114]

Hardly coincidentally, on the very same day the Wisconsin legislature passed a joint resolution noting the state's "great disappointment"
that the performance of the University's athletic teams did not match its
academic stature. Mincing no words, the resolution blamed the faculty
members of the University's Athletic Council, most of whom it pointed
out had served for up to two decades on that body and who had "failed
to recognize the necessity for progress along athletic lines." The resolution called on the regents to reorganize the council "so that the department of physical education will be able to keep pace with the modern
trend in intercollegiate athletic competition."[115]

With the faculty, the regents, the alumni, and even the legislature
all actively pursuing a redirection of UW athletic affairs, there was
considerable potential for a clash between these various contenders. At
the very least the situation posed a major test of the diplomatic skills of
President Frank. There is no record, however, to indicate that he
conferred with the Brown Committee or with other representatives of
the faculty about the tabled Grady resolution, as the regents had agreed
he should.[116] It may be that Frank's forceful objection to precipitous

---

[114]BOR Minutes, January 20, 1932; "Regents Propose Athletic Council Reorganization,"
WAM, 33 (February, 1932), 144, 164-5.

[115]"Regents Propose Athletic Council Reorganization," pp. 164-5. The report of the
legislative committee investigating the athletic program was similarly critical of the faculty role
on the Athletic Council, a position echoed even more pointedly by one of its members in a
supplementary report. Ibid.

[116]In his memoirs Dean Sellery expressed surprise that Frank did not bring the Grady
resolution before the University faculty. "He may have consulted individual faculty members,"
Sellery conceded, "but I never heard of any such consultations. Why? I do not know. The
reader may guess as well as I." Sellery, *Some Ferments at Wisconsin*, p. 75. With his
extensive faculty connections, it seems unlikely that Sellery would not have known if the
president had consulted the Brown Committee or the University Committee about the Grady
resolution. The numerous competing investigations of the hapless UW athletic program were
too much for the editor of the *Daily Cardinal*, who commented sarcastically: "Action by one
agency would have been desirable. The athletic council began. The voice of the press was
added. The alumni came in. The team came in. The legislature came in. The faculty came
in. The regents came in. The meddlers came in. Quick! Won't someone please shut the door
before a Congressional committee enters. It is already a case of 'too many cooks'." Samuel

action at the January regents meeting was simply intended to remind the regents that Big Ten rules required faculty control of intercollegiate athletics and to postpone regent action pending faculty consideration of the Brown Committee report.

At the March 9 board meeting Regent Grady introduced a revised version of his resolution to replace the Athletic Council with a new Athletic Board. The new scheme reflected alumni objections to Grady's earlier division of seats on the board, which now would consist of four faculty members, two representatives of the alumni association (rather than one as called for originally), and the president of the Student Athletic Board. Instead of direct representation, the regent chairman of the board's Committee on Physical Education and the University business manager would be "advisory members without vote." The Grady resolution stipulated "that in its actions said Athletic Board shall conform in all respects to the rules and regulations of the Intercollegiate Conference governing membership therein." The regents took no formal notice of the Brown Committee report, most of which was approved by the faculty in late March. Instead, they approved the Grady reorganization on April 27 and pressed President Frank to appoint and report the membership of the Athletic Board at once. Frank's appointees, approved by the regents on the spot, consisted of Professors Andrew T. Weaver (chairman), Scott Goodnight (dean of men and chairman of the Student Life and Interests Committee), Asher Hobson, and G.L. Larson, and continuing alumni members Walter Alexander and J.P. Riordan. The advisory members without vote were Regent Harold Wilkie and Business Manager J.D. Phillips.[117]

A major reason for the regents' dissatisfaction with the old Athletic Council was its reluctance to nominate Clarence W. Spears as the new football coach. Spears, formerly at the University of Minnesota and currently the head football coach at the University of Oregon, was the favored candidate of influential alumni and key regents, who wanted a

---

Steinman, "Little Acorns," *Daily Cardinal*, January 17, 1932.

[117]BOR Minutes, March 9, April 27, 1932; Sellery, *Some Ferments at Wisconsin*, pp. 75-7. Andrew Weaver's brother, a professor of English literature at the University of Michigan, had mixed feelings about his brother's acceptance of this new responsibility. He cautioned that such service was not viewed favorably by most faculty members or by the academic profession as a whole, pointing out that Sonny Pyre's colleagues in the UW English department were not using a textbook on English romantic poetry Weaver had edited with Pyre because the latter's "connection with athletics gave him such a black eye at Wisconsin." Ray Bennett Weaver to Andrew T. Weaver, November 16, 1932, Central Administration Papers, 40/1/1/2-1, box 5, UA.

coach of national reputation. The council proposed other candidates, but eventually caved in when the regents held out for Spears. He turned out to be a tough bargainer, spurning the $8,500 salary offered by the regents on March 9. The refusal shocked his backers but led to further negotiations and a special meeting of the regents three weeks later to approve a sweetened offer, which Spears accepted, of a ten-month salary of $10,000 and moving expenses from Eugene, Oregon.[118] For a board about to be faced with the necessity to develop a system of staff salary waivers, the timing of this salary—the highest yet paid a Wisconsin coach and higher than that of any faculty member save Alexander Meiklejohn—could hardly have been worse.

Coach Spears arrived in Madison in April of 1932, in time to direct the spring practice. He was received like a conquering gladiator. Fully twelve hundred cheering fans welcomed him at a banquet in the Armory, the largest such gathering ever staged on the campus up to that time. Professor Arlie Mucks, Sr., a former UW football player and Olympic track star, who was credited with finally persuading Spears to accept the Wisconsin offer, served as toastmaster, with, as the *Wisconsin Alumni Magazine* reported, "his booming voice almost shaking the rafters of the old gym." Regents Ben Faast, Fred Clausen, and Harold Wilkie each stressed the commitment of Board of Regents to a revival of Badger athletic fortunes. It remained for Glenn Frank, however, to try to put the celebration into perspective. A poor university could have a good football team if it were willing to pay the price, Frank cautioned Spears and the crowd:

> But a great university would not have a bought-and-paid-for team as a present. A university is not an athletic club. It is a place where men's minds and bodies and spirits are disciplined for the difficult business of living and making a living. It is no credit to a university to build a great team if, in the building, it does no more than to attract to the university the support of a sport-mad crowd that is not interested in the total purposes of the institution.

Frank reminded his audience that the ancient Greeks had honored their great athletes without either "crass commercialism" or the loss of "their enthusiasm for the high enterprises of philosophy, politics, art, religion, and the beginnings of the intellectual adventure we have come to know

---

[118]BOR Minutes, March 9 and 28, 1932; *Daily Cardinal*, March 4, 12, 15, 24, 25, 26, 28, 30, and 31, 1932; *Capital Times*, March 9, 23, and 30, 1932; Sellery, *Some Ferments at Wisconsin*, p. 75.

as modern science." Turning to Coach Spears, he pledged: "I give you then as the goal towards which the Wisconsin spirit should strive to direct Wisconsin athletics, the athletics of the ancient Greeks." Observers noted that Spears seemed embarrassed by his warm welcome, but it may be that he was simply perplexed over how to react to such a lofty charge.[119]

Whether the Board of Regents' new Athletic Board met the Big Ten requirement for faculty control of intercollegiate athletics was questionable. The issue was formally and bluntly raised by the University Committee in its report to the general faculty in the fall of 1932:

> The status of the new Athletic Board in the University organization can hardly be said to be clear. Whether it has the status of a Faculty Committee as did the Athletic Council, the functions of which were transferred to it, is at least doubtful. The method of its creation, the means provided for the appointment of its members, and the introduction into its membership of a member of the Board of Regents suggests that it has no such status. It does seem clear, however, that the intent and effect of the action of the Board is to reduce, substantially, Faculty authority over and responsibility for intercollegiate athletics. The committee believes that intercollegiate athletic competition affects the educational interests of the University to such an extent that, ultimately, the best interests of the University are not served by withdrawing from the Faculty authority over and responsibility for such competition to the extent implied by the recent action of the Board of Regents. It submits its expression of belief in this respect for approval by the Faculty.[120]

In the depths of the depression the general faculty was not ready for a showdown with the regents, however. Professor Andrew Weaver, the widely respected chairman of the speech department and head of the recently appointed Athletic Board, argued eloquently that the new structure should be given time to function before the faculty passed judgment on its effectiveness. While no record of Weaver's remarks exists, he must have warned that a faculty challenge to regent authority was unwise and premature, and might in fact trigger a conference investigation that would surely undermine the new football coaching staff before it had a chance to prove itself. At Weaver's urging the faculty decided to table the explosive section of the University Commit-

---

[119]"1200 Attend Spears Welcome," *WAM*, 33 (May, 1932), 250-1, 268; *Daily Cardinal*, May 1, 1932.

[120]UW Faculty Document 423, University Committee, "Annual Report for 1931-32," October 29, 1932.

tee's report dealing with athletics.[121] Afterward, Weaver's brother Ray, an English professor at the University of Michigan, congratulated him on "the triumph of statesmanship in the faculty" and commented: "As you well said—What a time for the faculty to start a rumpus! By golly, they'd better sit quiet and feed while they can."[122]

"Doc" Spears worked a veritable miracle in his first season as the Wisconsin football coach, fully justifying the hopes of his champions. With indifferent talent, the 1932 Badgers nevertheless finished third in the Big Ten, missing an undefeated season by a single point in their 7-6 loss to favored Purdue. It was the best Wisconsin season since 1920. Wisconsin fans agreed with the Chicago *Daily News* sports writer who termed it "the outstanding coaching achievement of the year." Spears' players concurred, with the team captain calling him "as good a coach as can be found in the country."[123]

Unfortunately, Spears' 1933 team was less impressive, finishing dead last in the Big Ten. There was also a darker side to the continuing enthusiasm for the new coach. Spears was impulsive and headstrong and had an explosive temper.[124] While he was popular among alumni fans, he did not work well with colleagues in the newly independent athletic department, especially his equally strong-willed colleague Walter E. Meanwell, who had coached UW basketball since 1911. Gradually, the Athletic Board, President Frank, and the regents came to see that their decision to appoint University Business Manager J.D. Phillips as acting athletic director was not enough. Phillips had too many other responsibilities to be able to pay close attention to athletic

---

[121]UW Faculty Minutes, November 7, 1932; Sellery; *Some Ferments at Wisconsin*, pp. 78-9.

[122]R.B. Weaver to A.T. Weaver, November 13 and 16, 1932, Central Administration Papers, 40/1/1/2-1, box 5. Before the faculty meeting Ray Weaver had told his brother: "I don't see any point to Spears having to lick the Wusconsin [*sic*] faculty before he even starts on foreign animals. If you could get him a little alumni support and make the faculty lay off him you could pay for your field house—and then what? You would have your field house paid for. I can't see any sense in playing foot ball the way she is played now unless you get the old school right back of the team and start for the rose bowl." Ibid., October 30, 1932.

[123]Gregory S. Kabat, "Hats Off to 'Doc' Spears," *WAM*, 34 (December, 1932), 75-6, 95; Ronald McIntyre, "Fighting Team Finishes Third," ibid., 78-9, 95.

[124]In 1933 the *Milwaukee Sentinel* charged that Spears had assaulted its photographer during the Illinois game, knocking him to the ground and breaking his camera. A subsequent investigation by the UW Athletic Board concluded that Spears had acted under considerable provocation and cleared him of wrongdoing in what the board's chairman, Andrew Weaver, called an "unfortunate occurrence." *Milwaukee Sentinel*, October 15, 1933; "Newspaper's Charges against Coach Spears Proved Absolutely False," *WAM*, 35 (October, 1933), 15.

matters or to deal with the growing friction between the Spears and Meanwell. By the spring of 1934 the Athletic Board concluded that the post of athletic director needed to be filled on a full-time basis. At its request the regents created a temporary athletic *troika*, designating Spears, Meanwell, and track Coach Tom Jones as an executive council to direct the athletic department until a full-time director could be appointed.[125]

This clumsy arrangement ended in July, when in a complicated series of moves the board appointed Coach Meanwell as the UW athletic director, naming his assistant, Harold E. "Bud" Foster, '29, to succeed him as basketball coach. The action came, however, only after the regents rejected the first choice of a divided Athletic Board, George Downer, the athletic department's publicity director. The alumni members had held out and lobbied for making Coach Spears the director. With substantial support for Spears among the regents as well, the Board of Regents asked the Athletic Board to reconsider its recommendation of Downer. It did so, but reported that its second choice for director was Meanwell, whth the alumni members continuing to back Spears. So closely divided were the regents in the Spears-Meanwell contest that President Frank was obliged to break an 8-8 tie vote in favor of Meanwell. Frank explained that although he considered both men well-qualified he believed the only proper choice for the regents was "to approve or reject the majority recommendation of the Athletic Board charged with the administrative oversight of athletics."[126]

The Meanwell era was brief and anything but placid. The tension between the Director Meanwell and Coach Spears did not lessen with the change in their relationship. While Spears retained the support of some alumni and regents, others began to question his hard-driving, win-at-any-cost attitude and his treatment of his players. Critics complained that he encouraged unsportsmanlike conduct and unnecessarily rough play. There were allegations that he used his medical background

---

[125]Athletic Board to Board of Regents, March 14, 1934, BOR Papers, 1/1/3, box 46; BOR Minutes, March 14, 1934; *Daily Cardinal*, March 15 and 16, 1934.

[126]BOR Minutes, June 16, July 13, 1934; [Andrew T. Weaver, "Majority Report of the Athletic Board"] to Frank, June 6, 1934; Walter Alexander and Myron T. Harshaw ["Minority Report to the Board of Regents," June 16, 1934]; Weaver to Frank, July 12, 1934; John Messmer to Daniel H. Grady, July 7, 1934; C.W. Jahn to Board of Regents, July 7, 1934, BOR Papers, 1/1/3, box 47; *Daily Cardinal*, May 11, June 17, 26, 27, and 30, July 4, 7, and 14, 1934; *Wisconsin State Journal*, July 17, 1934; "Meanwell Named Athletic Director," *WAM*, 35 (July, 1934), 299.

to secure the premature release of sick or injured players from the student infirmary so they could play in a big game. There were also charges that he had his trainer give the team brandy at half time to stimulate his players to greater efforts. Some hinted that the coach himself had a drinking problem.[127]

Although the team had been billed as having the best line in the conference, Coach Spears' Badgers had a dismal 1935 season, winning but a single game and losing to South Dakota, Marquette, Notre Dame, Michigan, Chicago, Northwestern, and Minnesota. After the disheartening season, John Golemgeske, the captain-elect of the 1936 football team, circulated a petition among his teammates requesting a new coach. Then, evidently under pressure he abandoned the move, with hints that the petition had been initiated at Meanwell's urging.[128] The Milwaukee W Club demanded an investigation of the turmoil in the athletic department as did other alumni, with at least one group blaming the athletic director for not giving enough support to Coach Spears.[129]

First the Athletic Board and then the Board of Regents investigated the disarray in the athletic department, taking extensive testimony from Meanwell, Spears, and others during January and February of 1936. All the while the sports writers of the state and nation feasted on the controversy, with some blaming the faculty-dominated Athletic Board for the mess. An unhappy alumnus in New York warned President Frank that the eastern reaction to the UW controversy was "uniformly bad," enclosing a critical clipping from the *New York Sun* which he pointed out did "not do the university any good."[130] Whether supporting Meanwell or Spears, most of those contacting Frank urged a quick resolution of the controversy and an end to the negative publicity. At a meeting with the Athletic Board in mid-January, the regents indicated their backing of Spears in the controversy, while the Athletic Board supported Meanwell. The regents' response was firm—either keep

---

[127]See, for example, J.R. Richards to Frank, November 22, 1935; Dana Hogan to Harry Sheer, November 25, 1935; Maxson F. Juddll to Frank, December 7, 1935, Frank Presidential Papers, 4/13/1, box 184; R.B. Weaver to A.T. Weaver [February, 1936], Central Administration Papers, 40/1/1/2-1, box 5; Lawrence H. Larsen, *The President Wore Spats: A Biography of Glenn Frank* (Madison: State Historical Society of Wisconsin, 1965), p. 114.

[128]*Daily Cardinal*, December 6, 7, and 8, 1935.

[129]Plymouth Alumni to Frank, telegram, December 6, 1935; Elmer McBride to Frank, December 9, 1935; C.H. Gaffin to Frank, December 10, 1935; A.C. Kingsford to George C. Sellery, December 10, 1935, Frank Presidential Papers, 4/13/1, box 184.

[130]R.D. Jenkins to Frank, February 8, 1936, ibid.

Spears or both men must go.

The apparent interest of the Board of Regents in preempting the oversight responsibility of the Athletic Board prompted the general faculty to remind the regents of its key role in intercollegiate athletics. For the faculty meeting on February 3, 1936, the University Committee resurrected its predecessor's report on the subject, which the faculty had tabled in 1932 rather than risk a confrontation with the regents. The committee was now ready for a showdown:

> The present University Committee views the subsequent course of events and the existing situation as regards the administration of the control of intercollegiate athletics with such grave concern that it hereby recommends that a special meeting of the legal faculty be called for Monday, February 10, to deal with a statement of principle and policy relative to the administration and control of intercollegiate athletics.[131]

The special faculty meeting a week later drew the largest attendance in years. Professor Edward Bennett, the University Committee chairman and long-time chairman of the Department of Electrical Engineering, opened the meeting by reading a "Proposed Confidential Statement to the Board of Regents Relative to the Control and Administration of Intercollegiate Athletics." While conciliatory in tone, the statement made clear (1) that the faculty understood its control to mean that the Athletic Board had the status of a faculty committee reporting directly to the faculty, (2) that the faculty was empowered to prescribe the manner in which the Athletic Board was constituted and its members selected, (3) that the Athletic Board had responsibility for initiating actions on budget and personnel in the Department of Intercollegiate Athletics, and (4) that its recommendations on matters of budget and personnel, if approved by the president, were subject only to veto or approval by the Board of Regents. The final point was the strongest reminder to the regents: "The power to initiate an action after being exercised by the Athletic Board does not lapse in the event the recommended action fails to receive the approval of the Board of Regents, but reverts to the Athletic Board for further consideration and recommendation." The faculty members present endorsed the statement by a unanimous vote.[132]

---

[131]UW Faculty Document 496, "Recommendations of the University Committee," February 3, 1936; Sellery, *Some Ferments at Wisconsin*, p. 79.

[132]UW Faculty Document 496A, "Proposed Confidential Statement to the Board of Regents Relative to the Control and Administration of Intercollegiate Athletics," February 10, 1936;

The showdown—which one Madison sports writer called the Battle of "Fighting Hill"—came at the regents meeting on February 14-15, when the Athletic Board scathingly criticized Coach Spears for his conduct over the past four years and recommended that he be fired, at the same time praising Meanwell and urging that he be retained as athletic director. The next day the exasperated regents formally rejected the Athletic Board's recommendations. Then, in direct opposition to the recent faculty declaration, the board voted not to continue the appointments of either Spears or Meanwell, along with the brandy-dispensing football trainer, William Fallon. Fallon's dismissal was a surprise and largely an afterthought by Regent Grady, who argued for a clean sweep. Declaring the regents' action made a mockery of faculty control, that afternoon the faculty members of the Athletic Board resigned, joined by the president of the student "W" Club, Howard T. Heun.[133] From Ann Arbor, Andrew Weaver's brother congratulated him on his "right and gallant stand" and speculated that "the real fight at Wis. is to get Glennie."[134]

To look into the dispute, which had received a good deal of attention from the press nationally, the Big Ten Intercollegiate Conference dispatched two faculty investigators to Madison, Professors George A. Works of the University of Chicago and Bland A. Stradley of Ohio State. As it happened they arrived the very day of the regents meeting. After receiving their report the conference voted to require the University to demonstrate faculty control over its athletic programs by July 1 or face suspension or even expulsion.[135]

The conference ultimatum focussed the regents' attention as never before on the issue of faculty control. Clearly a high order of statesmanship was required to find a graceful way out of the box in which the regents now found themselves. On March 2 President Frank informed the faculty that the usually dormant Regent-Faculty Conference Committee would be convened to consider the situation. The committee met in

---

UW Faculty Minutes, February 10, 1936; Sellery, *Some Ferments at Wisconsin*, pp. 79-80.

[133]BOR Minutes, February 14-15, 1936; "Athletic Row Settled: Meanwell, Spears, Fallon Go: Faculty Board Members Resign," *WAM*, 37 (March, 1936), 172-4, 192; *Daily Cardinal*, February 13, 14, 15, 17, and 18, 1936; *Badger*, 1936, pp. 213-24; Sellery, *Some Ferments at Wisconsin*, p. 80.

[134]R.B. Weaver to A.T. Weaver, February 5, 9, 15, 17, 18, 20, 22, and 29, 1936, undated but postmarked February 17, 1936, Tuesday [February, 1936], Central Administration Papers, 40/1/1/2-1, box 5.

[135]*Daily Cardinal*, March 1, 3, and 4, 1936; Sellery, *Some Ferments at Wisconsin*, p. 80.

Frank's office on March 10, with board President Harold Wilkie heading the regent members and Dean George C. Sellery speaking for the faculty group. Wilkie made it clear the regents were willing to accept the principles embodied in the February 10 faculty declaration on faculty control of athletics. Sellery, in turn, indicated the faculty representatives were not demanding a return to the old Athletic Council and were agreeable to a continuation of the seven-member Athletic Board. They asked only that its four faculty members be appointed by the president in conjunction with the University Committee and that the two alumni members be selected by the president from a panel of six nominees. Their unstated objective was to reduce the possibility of regent or alumni pressure on the president for the appointment of particular members. Whether or not the regent representatives understood the motivation, they agreed to the faculty request.

The report of the conference committee, dated March 10, followed closely and quoted extensively from the University Committee's declaration of faculty authority adopted by the faculty a month earlier. It was approved unanimously by the full Board of Regents the next day and by the general faculty at a special meeting on March 13.[136] After the reconstituted Athletic Board, now chaired by neuro-psychiatrist William F. Lorenz of the Medical School, was in place, the faculty adopted another resolution, drafted by Dean Sellery, declaring "that the Faculty of the University of Wisconsin considers itself in control of the athletic affairs of this institution." The Big Ten conference accordingly lifted its threat of suspension on May 22. Wisconsin was once again a member in good standing.[137] A month earlier the regents had approved the new Athletic Board's recommendation for the appointment of Harry Stuhldreher, an All-American quarterback and one of Knute Rockne's famous Four Horsemen backfield at Notre Dame in the early 1920s, as head football coach and athletic director.[138] Another effort to rebuild

---

[136]BOR Minutes, March 11, 1936; UW Faculty Minutes, March 13, 1936; UW Faculty Document 496B, "Report of the Regent-Faculty Conference Committee on Athletics," March 13, 1936; "Our Big Ten Situation: Faculty and Regents Act to Avert Expulsion from Western Conference," *WAM*, 37 (April, 1936), 206-7; *Daily Cardinal*, March 10, 11, 12, 14, and 15, 1936.

[137]UW Faculty Minutes, May 4, 1936; *Daily Cardinal*, May 4, 7, and 23, 1936; Sellery, *Some Ferments at Wisconsin*, p. 83.

[138]BOR Minutes, April 22, 1936; *Daily Cardinal*, April 28, 29, and 30, 1936; "Meet the New Director: Harry A. Stuhldreher, Notre Dame Hero, Names Director and Coach, Sundt Assistant," *WAM*, 37 (May, 1936), 242.

Wisconsin athletics was about to begin.

A clear winner in the messy Spears-Meanwell controversy was the University faculty, which strengthened its role in campus governance and forced the Board of Regents to recognize its primary responsibility for control of Badger athletics. Another winner was Frank's sometime critic, Dean George Sellery, who had the leading part in negotiating the face-saving retreat for the regents and who in the process demonstrated his solid base of faculty support. On the other hand, Glenn Frank received little credit from either the faculty or the more impatient regents in the confrontation, even though he had steadfastly stood for responsible faculty control of athletics. In the eyes of Frank's critics, this was another instance when the president had allowed problems to fester to the point where the regents felt compelled to intervene and who then played only a marginal role in resolving the controversy.

Dean Garrison Goes to Washington

In addition to his selection of Louise Troxell as dean of women in 1931 and the promotion of Registrar Frank Holt to be dean of extension in 1935, President Frank made several other major appointments of University deans in the early thirties that were by common agreement first-rate. Frank made his selections deliberately and carefully in keeping with his management philosophy of delegating most of the day-to-day administration of the University to capable subordinates. Even George Sellery, no fan of the president, conceded that "there is no doubt that Mr. Frank deserves high marks for his selection of deans."[139]

The first of these was the appointment of Nebraska-born Chris L. Christensen, the executive secretary of the Federal Farm Board, to succeed Harry Russell as dean of agriculture in 1931 after Russell resigned to become the director of the Wisconsin Alumni Research Foundation.[140] Christensen had studied cooperative marketing in Denmark and had organized the American Institute of Cooperation in 1924 to promote agricultural cooperatives in the United States. Like Frank he admired the Danish folk high schools. With the president's enthusiastic encouragement he proceeded to adapt the wide-ranging Danish folk school curriculum to his college's Farm Short Course and other out-

---

[139]Sellery, *Some Ferments at Wisconsin*, p. 93-4.
[140]BOR Minutes, June 21, 1930, January 21, 1931; "Meet the New Dean," *WAM*, 32 (February, 1931), 193.

reach activities with the aim of enriching all aspects of rural life. The most daring manifestation of this expanded outlook was Christensen's recruitment of the prominent American regional painter, John Steuart Curry, to be the University's first artist-in-residence in 1936, very likely the first such appointment in an agricultural college anywhere.[141] Curry's assignment was to portray farming and rural life in his paintings and to travel about the state encouraging rural artists and an appreciation of folk art. Under his leadership and training, a distinctive Wisconsin school of regional painters emerged in the late thirties and forties depicting rural life. Of all his deans, Frank got along best with Chris Christensen. They golfed and socialized together, shared the same intellectual interests and the same liberal Republican politics, and in time came to the same increasingly critical view of Franklin D. Roosevelt's New Deal.

Frank selected two other key administrators from within the University. With the retirement of Dean Charles S. Slichter in 1934, Frank recommended that the regents name bacteriology Professor Edwin B. Fred to head the Graduate School, thereby beginning what was to be a long tradition of picking the graduate dean from the scientific faculty of the College of Agriculture. Fred was a strong faculty man with high scholarly standards. He rose early and worked late and expected no less of his associates. His research on nitrogen fixation had contributed greatly to the development of the rotational pattern of corn and alfalfa forage cropping by Wisconsin dairy farmers to minimize the loss of soil fertility. Soft-spoken, with still a hint of his native Virginia accent, Fred loved to tell how his Confederate grandfather had furnished General Lee with the general's famous horse "Traveller." Under Dean Fred's leadership during the depression the Graduate School made judicious use of the special WARF grants to keep newly minted UW Ph.D.s active in research while they sought scarce jobs and to expand greatly the number of WARF faculty research leaves as a way of maintaining faculty numbers and strength across the institution.

Following the death of Medical Dean Charles R. Bardeen the following year, President Frank named Professor William S. Middleton to head the school. Dr. Middleton was a specialist in clinical medicine

---

[141]BOR Minutes, July 25, 1936; BOR Executive Committee Minutes, October 3, 1936; *Daily Cardinal*, September 23, December 5, 1936, January 16, 1937. Curry's $4,000 annual salary was funded by a five-year grant from the Brittingham Trust, the first use of Brittingham funds since the unfortunate dispute between the Board of Regents and the Brittingham trustees in 1931.

who had begun working in the student infirmary in 1912, the infant Medical School's first clinic. A leading member of the Department of General Medicine, Middleton was a gifted diagnostician and exacting teacher who inspired fear as well as respect from his medical and nursing students. He was to provide the Medical School with the same driving leadership and skillful political generalship of his predecessor.

A major coup was Frank's recruitment of the liberal New York attorney Lloyd K. Garrison as dean of the Law School in February, 1932, after a search extending nearly three years following the death of Dean Harry S. Richards in the spring of 1929. Garrison was well-known as a legal reformer and expert on labor and bankruptcy law. He and his wife brought a distinguished lineage to Madison. In announcing the appointment President Frank reminded reporters that Garrison was the great-grandson of the abolitionist Civil War editor, William Lloyd Garrison, while Mary Frank, always impressed by social status, drafted a flowery press release on behalf of the University League proudly noting that Mrs. Garrison, the former Ellen Jay, was a direct descendant of the first chief justice of the United States and on her mother's side was related to the socially prominent Shaw family of Boston.[142]

Quickly supportive of the Wisconsin Idea of University public service, Garrison not only encouraged his faculty and students to use their expertise on behalf of the public but did so himself. An ardent New Dealer, he yearned to be involved in the exciting national reform activities taking place in Washington under President Franklin D. Roosevelt. He therefore jumped at the invitation in June, 1934, to be the first chairman of the National Labor Relations Board, created to administer disputes arising under the pro-collective bargaining Section

---

[142]Lloyd K. Garrison to Frank, January 15, February 3 (telegram), February 4 and 19, 1932; Frank to Garrison, February 16, 1932; Frank, press release, February 17, 1932; [Mary Frank] University League press release, n.d., Frank Presidential Papers, 4/13/1, box 114; BOR Minutes, March 9, 1932; *Daily Cardinal*, December 1, 1931, February 6, 9, 10, and 18, 1932; *Capital Times*, January 28, February 17, 1932; "Appoint Law Dean: Lloyd Garrison Named to Post Left Vacant by Death of Dean Harry S. Richards in 1929," *WAM*, 33 (March, 1932), 175. Mary Frank's flowery University League press release noted that "although born of and in society," Mrs. Garrison had "not given it much of her time and talents," being interested in modern education and teaching at the Dalton School in New York. In addition to her distinguished New York Livingston and Jay lineage, on her mother's side she was descended from the Boston Shaw family, "for generations leaders in the annals of Boston society." Her grandmother was the sister of Colonel Robert Gould Shaw, who "organized a regiment of colored troops during the Civil War" and whose statue "by St. Gaudens is opposite the State House in Boston."

7A of the National Industrial Recovery Act. Such short-term service was not uncommon among UW faculty members at this time; law Professor William Gorham Rice, for example, had just spent the spring semester as legal adviser to the labor board.[143] Garrison's service was supposed to be only for the summer while he organized the work of the board, since he had no intention of abandoning his deanship. He had not secured President Frank's approval for this summer "leave," and when the appointment was announced effective July 9, 1934, Frank was dismayed to learn that its duration was specified as three months, which meant Garrison would not be free to return until well after the start of the fall term. He also was skeptical that President Roosevelt and Secretary of Labor Perkins would be willing to let Garrison return as scheduled:

> My fear is that as we near the opening of the school year political pressure from Washington will come to extend your summer leave and thus place the University in the undesirable position of seeming reluctant to cooperate with the federal authorities.

He asked for the dean's formal assurance to the Board of Regents this would not happen.[144] Once in Washington Garrison made certain his superiors understood the temporary nature of his service. "I had a talk with the Secretary of Labor yesterday," he assured Frank two days after

---

[143] Garrison to Frank, February 19, 1934, Frank Presidential Papers, 4/13/1, box 147.

[144] Garrison to Frank, telegram, June 30, 1934; Frank to Garrison, July 3, 1934, ibid. Because Dean Garrison's administration of the Law School was so new, Frank advised against the NLRB appointment and thought he had received Garrison's assurance that he would not accept it without further discussion. Instead, Garrison wired Frank the news of his acceptance, which was followed immediately by a White House press release about the appointment. He then wrote asking Frank to "forgive me for my sins of omission and commission. I am, as you know, faithfully & loyally yours & ~~would~~ feel dreadfully about having embarrassed you as I know now that I did." Garrison to Frank, July 4, 1934, Frank Papers, Kirksville.

taking up his post. "The understanding is quite clear that I am to return to Wisconsin in time for the opening of the Law School this fall, and that no pressure will be brought to bear upon the University to extend my service here longer."[145]

As Frank had anticipated, in late August President Roosevelt made a direct personal request that Frank grant Garrison a leave of absence for a full year so he could continue his NLRB work. Frank responded that the University had been generous and had "cut red tape right and left" in arranging for some of its faculty to accept a sudden call for New Deal service. As a key administrator, however, Garrison's situation was different. His law deanship was just getting under way and 1934-35 would be a legislative budget year. "It becomes a serious matter to have the executive headship of one of the important units of the University vacant under such circumstances," Frank pointed out. Garrison would have to choose where he could give the most useful service: if he stayed in Washington it would "be necessary for him to relinquish the deanship."[146] To Garrison Frank commented: "Whatever my shortcomings in other fields, you must admit I am good as a prophet."[147]

Roosevelt and Secretary of Labor Frances Perkins did not give up easily. F.D.R. pleaded with Garrison to stay on, if not for a year at least for a few more months. Garrison wavered, not ready to give up either his deanship or the NLRB chairmanship. He suggested to Frank that he return to Madison for a week or two to open the fall term and then go back to Washington, returning again in October for a week to work on his budget request before winding up his affairs in Washington,

---

[145]Garrison to Frank, July 11, 1934, Frank Papers, Kirksville.

[146]Frank to Franklin D. Roosevelt, August 30, 1934, Frank Presidential Papers, 4/13/1, box 164, and Frank Papers, Kirksville.

[147]Frank to Garrison, August 30, 1934, Frank Presidential Papers, 4/13/1, box 164, and Frank Papers, Kirksville. Frank made clear that he would deeply regret a decision by Garrison to leave the deanship:

> You know how highly I prize your presence in the University. I do not want, however, to put any undue pressure upon you to decide other than your best judgment of relative values and relative opportunity for constructive work dictates. I have so written the President in the letter, a copy of which I enclose. When you were appointed, I told you I would not try to hold you at the post for longer than enough years to round out a decent job. I shall not even inject my personal judgment as to what I would now do were I in your place. I shall leave the matter entirely in your hands. I know you will do what you think is the right thing. If you feel that you must resign, I should know it right away, for I should, in that regrettable event, proceed promptly to fill the post.

"either by the middle of November or at absolutely the latest by the end of November."

> I know that you would rather have me back and that it would probably be better for the school if I were at my desk every day. But I am torn by a terrifying sense of my duty here and equally by a sense of what I owe to Wisconsin. If some little give and take could be worked out I would be thankful for it....
>
> The President in his talk with me intimated that if I would stay on at this job I could look forward to an increasingly important part in the Government. I think he meant it, although perhaps like so many Government servants I am getting a quite exaggerated idea of my own importance. However that may be, I would have been tempted to yield if I had felt that I had done justice to the University in my short stay in Madison. I do not think that I have, and I feel that I owe it to the University to consider no other way of life until I have at least earned my salt in Madison, by which time I shall probably never want to leave under any circumstances.[148]

In this instance the sometimes indecisive Frank was adamant. "You should make a clean-cut decision one way or another," he told Garrison by telephone and letter.[149] The Roosevelt administration next tried heavier pressure, inspiring press reports blaming Frank for not allowing Garrison to continue at his important national post. In their widely syndicated "Washington Merry-Go-Round" column, Drew Pearson and Robert S. Allen claimed, erroneously, that F.D.R. had repeatedly telephoned a stubborn Glenn Frank pleading vainly for Garrison's continued service. The White House also recruited a number of prominent Americans, some of them Frank intimates, to lobby the UW president. One was Frank's old friend and patron, Edward A. Filene, who both telephoned and sent a long telegram urging that Garrison's leave be extended as part of the Univer-

---

[148]Garrison to Frank, September 5, 1934, Frank Presidential Papers, 4/13/1, box 164.

[149]Frank to Garrison, September 8, 1934, ibid., and Frank Papers, Kirksville. Frank was sympathetic but firm:

> I appreciate the dilemma the situation puts to you. I knew perfectly well that this would be the situation in which you would find yourself. That is why I could not understand why either you would consider or the Secretary of Labor approve the assumption of a major responsibility in so crucial a post for a few summer weeks. I quite understand the President's eagerness that you should remain at your post in Washington. It may well be that you should. My only point is that it is not feasible for you to carry both jobs in view of the special circumstances here. Legislative year presents problems that are more than merely knowing how much shall be asked for the Law School and coming in at the last minute before a hearing.

sity's contribution to the national emergency. "Bury personal considerations and give it good sportedly as your contribution no matter at how
great sacrifice of personal inclinations or local university situation,"
Filene pleaded. "If you dont [*sic*] play ball now in situation critical as
this no matter what the reasons," he warned, "you shut yourself off
from too much that you may need or find important to you and your
work later."[150] Another recruit to the Garrison cause was Daniel
Grady, the most prominent Democrat on the Board of Regents, who
unsuccessfully sought to persuade the board to overrule Frank. Frank
particularly resented being portrayed as the heavy by the press. "All of
the press stories have referred to the fact that you 'have' to return to the
University unless I decide otherwise," he grumbled to Garrison. "This,
I submit is not fair."[151]

Frank remained firm and in the end Garrison decided to come back
to his law post but asked permission to make a public statement explaining his departure from the National Labor Relations Board. By now
Frank was both wary and exasperated:

> I shall not undertake to say what statement you should issue. No one else
> who has served the government and returned to the University has felt it
> necessary to issue a statement. If you feel you must issue a statement, I shall
> feel, and I think the Regents will feel that you have done something less than
> you should unless you make perfectly clear that you took the appointment for
> the vacation period without any University authority for a leave, that after
> you had taken the post, both you and the Secretary of Labor assured the
> University that you would be back at the University at the opening of the
> university year, that the University has not insisted upon your returning, and
> that you assume all responsibility for the decision to return. This, it must be
> clear to you, is only fair. To suggest that you are returning only because I
> have insisted that you must either return or resign is simply passing the buck
> to me and putting the University in a hole after I made the whole matter sun-
> clear to you before you took the post and after you assumed this responsibility
> without the further consultation which you agreed should take place before

---

[150]Edward A. Filene to Frank, telegram, September 11, 1934, ibid. See also Charlton
Ogburn to Frank, September 7, 1934; Florence C. Thorne to Frank, telegram, September 13,
1934; Thomas L. Woodward to Frank, October 3, 1934, Frank Presidential Papers, 4/13/1,
box 164; Frances Perkins to Frank, telegram, October 15, 1934; Frank to Perkins, telegram,
October 15, 1934, Frank Papers, Kirksville.

[151]Frank to Garrison, September 11, 1934, Frank Papers, Kirksville. An example is the
opening paragraph of an unidentified editorial clipped by President Frank: "Glenn Frank,
president of the University of Wisconsin, will not release Lloyd K. Garrison from academic
duties on the Madison campus to continue as chairman of the National Labor Relations Board.
So the Government is losing a valuable public servant at a critical time."

you answered Washington.[152]

The whole affair left all of the players unhappy. Frank and nearly all of the regents understandably resented the negative publicity suggesting the University was unwilling to cooperate in the national recovery effort. They blamed Dean Garrison and Washington officials for creating a no-win situation for the University. Secretary of Labor Perkins and probably President Roosevelt were indignant and suspicious of Frank's motives in refusing to grant Garrison a leave.[153] They could not help but relate Frank's stand to his increasingly vocal criticism of the New Deal, which Frank believed was eroding individual liberties and creating a dangerous centralized bureaucracy. Their suspicions may in fact have been warranted. After all, Frank had allowed the Law School to operate under the competent leadership of Acting Dean Oliver Rundell for nearly three years before Garrison's appointment. Rundell took over again while Garrison was in Washington in the summer of 1934 and eventually succeeded him as first the acting and then the regular dean when Garrison left the University permanently in 1942. Coincidentally, Frank's anti-New Deal book, *America's Hour of Decision*, was published at the height of the uproar over the Garrison affair and was reviewed in the *Daily Cardinal* the day before the dean's return to the campus in late October.[154] On the other hand, Frank had

---

[152]Frank to Garrison, October 9, 1934, ibid. Frank was reacting to a proposed press release in which Garrison explained that while Frank had offered to release him from his promise to return to Madison for the fall term, "my remaining here would require my resignation as dean and the appointment of someone else to take my place...." Garrison to Frank, telegram, October 3, 1934, ibid.

[153]See Frances Perkins to Frank, telegram, October 15, 1934; Frank to Perkins, telegram, October 15, 1934, ibid.

[154]Frank, *America's Hour of Decision*; *Daily Cardinal*, October 21 and 23, 1934. While Frank denied a partisan bias in his book, his snappy chapter titles suggested a liberal Republican point of view: "The Temper of the Crowd," "Democracy Flouted," "Freedom Invaded," "Plenty Renounced," "Science Betrayed," "Education Hamstrung," "Religion Exiled," "Nationalism Amuck," and "The Alternative to Revolution." The following passage is representative of Frank's concern about the direction the New Deal was taking the United States:

I am not at all enamored of the prospect of having my own and the nation's life ordered about by bureaucrats. I do not believe that the complex economic life of the United States can ever be run effectively from Washington....I am profoundly skeptical of many of the mutually contradictory mechanisms of the New Deal. There is, it seems to me, a rather heavy strain of Alice in Wonderland economics in much of its program. In particular, I think the New Deal, despite its protestations to the contrary, is playing fast and loose with the values of private initiative,

searched for several years to find a dean who could revitalize the Law School along more socially relevant lines, and his reluctance to see Garrison's reforms put on hold was certainly understandable. Phil La Follette, about to return to the governorship, had also sensitized him to the importance of careful preparation of the University's biennial budget requests, of which the Law School's needs were a significant part.

It is not known if President Roosevelt mentioned his unhappiness with Frank to the La Follette brothers, although it would not be surprising if he had. Their contacts with F.D.R. were close and frequent enough for this. The La Follettes had organized their Wisconsin supporters into the new Progressive Party in the summer of 1934 and were occupied with the fall campaign at this time. Roosevelt counted on Young Bob's support of New Deal legislation in Congress. Indeed, as a mark of his favor he invited the senator to ride on the Democratic campaign train during Roosevelt's visit to Green Bay shortly before the September primary election. It was clear he was not backing any Democratic challenge to the senator. Both La Follette brothers won their races that fall under the Progressive Party banner, with Bob remaining in Washington and Phil returning to the governorship after a two-year absence. Phil was friendly with Garrison, shared his political views, and relied on him for advice on labor and other issues. It thus would not be surprising if the La Follettes disapproved of Frank's refusal to grant Garrison a leave to enable him to continue his national labor board service. If so, they undoubtedly chalked up the episode as yet another mark against the president and his administration of the University.

Rebuilding Enrollment and the Campus Image

Another serious problem for Frank and the University during the early thirties was enrollment, which totalled more than 9,400 in 1929 but fell off sharply during the early years of the depression to less than 7,400 in 1933. The decline in non-resident enrollment was proportionally greater, exacerbating the budget problems since non-resident students paid significantly higher tuition than Wisconsin residents. Since

---

permitting the sins of some of its practitioners to obscure the productive virtue of the principle itself. But I am quite as convinced as any New Dealer that some factor of integration had and has to come into the picture if private initiative is to be saved for itself and for its service to the nation. (pp. 83, 84)

the legislature expected the University to generate part of its budget from student fees, the enrollment decline was a serious problem that President Frank and other campus administrators sought to counter in a variety of ways. One objective was to make it easier for students to find the means to enroll and remain in school. The University raised funds for student loans by dipping into various of its endowments and by organizing charity events from balls to football games. It cut the cost of room and board in UW dormitories, used vacant UW buildings for student housing and eating cooperatives, and promoted its low-cost tent colony on Lake Mendota for married summer session students. It sponsored a new UW credit union to provide small loans to needy staff members, especially the graduate assistants. The semi-official University League ran a used clothing exchange for the benefit of impecunious graduate assistants and junior faculty. Most important, the University created an employment office to help students find jobs on and off campus, an effort that was aided mightily when New Deal federal work relief funds became available after 1933 through the Civil Works Administration and later the National Youth Administration. The Wisconsin Alumni Research Foundation greatly expanded its support of research by faculty and graduate students during the worst of the depression. Its regular program of UW research support grew from about $15,000 a year in 1930 to more than $200,000 annually a decade later; in the dark years 1933-36 it provided additional emergency grants totalling more than $193,000.

In his concern for enrollment President Frank passed up few opportunities to sell the University to audiences of Wisconsin parents and teachers, stepping up the public relations work he had considered an important part of his responsibilities from the beginning. Speaking frequently to alumni and school groups around the state, he extolled the University and the educational opportunities it offered to the young people of the state. Frank also encouraged faculty members and student leaders to participate in these promotional activities, for he recognized that the University would have to increase its efforts to prove its value to the people of Wisconsin in these difficult times.

Sometimes it was mostly a matter of damage control, as when in February, 1932, the University made available an old house near the campus for use as a low-cost student housing cooperative. The students who moved in decided to advertise their "red" politics by putting up a sign naming it Haywood House after Big Bill Haywood, the ex-cowboy and miner who had helped organize the radical Industrial Workers of

the World early in the century and had been imprisoned for his allegedly seditious views after the World War. To some critics around the
state, the episode was convincing proof of the University's radicalism,
but Frank chose to ignore the provocation and not give martyrdom to
the youthful zealots. Instead the regents decided to raze the house after
the semester had ended.[155]

Others charged that the University promoted or tolerated atheism
and immorality among its students and faculty. Chief among these
critics was Father H.C. Hengell, the ever-vigilant Roman Catholic
pastor of St. Paul's Chapel serving the campus area. Hengell had been
openly suspicious of Frank's commitment to proper Christian values
from the beginning. He dismissed Frank's active sponsorship and
participation in the annual All-University Religious Convocation beginning in 1926, which Hengell saw as promoting modernist and liberal
religious ideas. At the opening of the 1931-32 school year he complained publicly that the University was fostering "agnostic sectarian-
ism" and was a liability rather than an asset to the community.[156] Later
in the year he objected that the Catholic Church was being ridiculed in
some of the courses of the University, prompting injured denials from
a number of faculty members.[157]

Throughout 1931-32 Hengell and other clerics criticized Professor
Max Otto of the philosophy department, whose popular course "Man
and Nature" they viewed as a threat to organized religion. In this
elective course Otto examined the evidence for and against evolution
and divine creation, the classical arguments for the existence of a personal God, and the philosophical systems of a number of religious
thinkers over the centuries. Otto was widely viewed as an atheist,
though as a Unitarian perhaps skepticism was a more accurate description of his personal religious beliefs. No one on campus, however, had
higher ethical standards or did a better job of integrating ethical values
into his teaching. Typical of the attacks on Otto was the warning in a
sermon by Rev. E.T. Eltzman of the Parkside Presbyterian Church that
young people should be protected from the professor's dangerous atheism. He urged parents to send their children to a denominational college for two years before exposing them to such insidious ideas at the

---

[155]See *Capital Times*, May 12, August 3, 1932; "Frank Discusses Criticisms of the University," *WAM*, 33 (July, 1932), 330.

[156]*Daily Cardinal*, September 23, 1931.

[157]Ibid., February 11, 12, 14, and 16, 1932.

University.[158]   Hengell's and Eltzman's charges prompted at least one
out-state newspaper to demand that Otto be fired and another to agree
that parents should not send their children to learn "such bizarre doctrines" in Madison.[159]   Even the normally supportive publisher of the
Wisconsin State Journal, Aaron M. Brayton, hinted that Otto was a
liability to the University, and President Irving Maurer of Beloit College
agreed flatly that atheists should be barred from college teaching.[160]
The public criticism of Professor Otto continued to the point where
three Madison clergymen felt obliged to issue a statement defending
"his right to express himself," even though they thought him "mistaken
in his religious position." "As a matter of justice," they declared, "we
make public our confidence in his moral integrity."[161]

The complaints about the irreligion of the campus were overshadowed in the spring of 1932 when the *Daily Cardinal* published an
anonymous letter entitled "Virginity—a Woman's View" and signed
simply "Junior Woman." Readers of a later generation would hardly be
shocked by the letter, but in 1932 it created a sensation on campus and
around the state. Junior Woman objected to warnings that those who
engaged in premarital sex would suffer a loss of self-esteem, and confessed that "we who are not virgins can smile at the notion that we have
lost our self-respect." While not advocating promiscuity, the author
proudly aligned herself with the "students who view sex, not as a sinful-
but-inevitable thing to succumb to in spite of loss of self-respect, but as
a natural and normal and wholesome method of rounding out their lives,
particularly their love lives." Laws governing intimate personal relations "are not divine and inviolable," Junior Woman concluded. "If
they outgrow their relevance why should we continue to consider them
our guides?"[162]

Readers on and off campus seem to have taken the Junior Woman
letter at face value, with no one publicly questioning whether it might
have been written by a male *Cardinal* staffer or correspondent as a joke

---

[158]Ibid., January 19, 1932.

[159]DePere *Journal Democrat* and Wausau *Record-Herald*, quoted in *Capital Times*, January
26, February 27, 1932. The *Daily Cardinal* argued that Otto deserved to be singled out not
for his ideas but because he was one of the University's most thought-provoking teachers. "To
us any denouncements of such a man are absurd," the paper declared editorially on January 22,
1932.

[160]*Daily Cardinal*, May 17, September 29, November 8, 1932.

[161]Ibid., May 19, 1932.

[162]Ibid., April 15, 1932.

to lighten a slow news day. First to weigh in was the ever-vigilant Father Hengell, who in his Sunday sermon attacked Junior Woman's advocacy of free love as a tenet of the atheist.[163] The local Unitarian minister, Rev. William O. Holloway, responded the next Sunday with a sermon defending Junior Woman's "fearless, intelligent frankness" in discussing changing moral attitudes, which Holloway predicted would eventually bring "greater sex freedom for the unmarried woman." Such libertarian prospects were too much for Rev. Heitmeyer of Madison's First Baptist Church, who denounced both Junior Woman and his Unitarian colleague. "Sex freedom as a biological necessity," he proclaimed, "exactly describes the moral status of the cattle pen."[164] An indignant 1920 alumnus denounced the *Cardinal* for becoming the voice of "unrepresentative libertarian extremists" and weighed in with a criticism of President Frank for not minding the University store:

> Badger citizens may thrill with admiration when he goes barnstorming around the national platform circuit demanding "courageous leadership" of all and sundry in miscellaneous situations. Yet sometimes it might be wondered from reading The Daily Cardinal whether he doesn't find rather large challenges to positive and constructive moral leadership right on his own campus. Or did the Rocking Chair episode signalize the dawn (or shall we say the Thunder and Dawn) of a new era of campus moral laissez faire?[165]

Vainly did Samuel Steinman, the chastened executive editor of the *Cardinal*, try to keep the matter in perspective:

> The student pastors need have no fear that their flocks are being led astray. The parents need not worry about their children's virginity. The faculty need not contemplate the situation with drawn expressions. The students need not demonstrate. No emergency measures are necessary. One co-ed wrote a letter to The Daily Cardinal—that is all.[166]

At the end of April the *Wisconsin State Journal* gave featured coverage to a letter from a wrathful mother calling upon her counter-

---

[163] *Capital Times*, April 18, 1932; *Daily Cardinal*, April 19, 1932.

[164] *Daily Cardinal*, April 26 and 28, 1932.

[165] Ibid., April 26, 1932. For other letters and two editorials pro and con on the furor over the Junior Woman letter, see ibid., April 20, 23, 24, and 26, May 3, 1932.

[166] Samuel Steinman, "Little Acorns: Wolf!" ibid., April 20, 1932. Steinman's editorship is probably most remembered for this episode and its fallout. That is unfortunate, for he was one of the ablest, hardest-working, and most thoughtful *Cardinal* editors of the inter-war period.

parts to clean up the University, which she described as "a huge broth-el," during the forthcoming Mother's Weekend. "Bring your brooms and mop pails," she advised, complaining that President Frank was ignoring the situation. "There is a great need of spring house cleaning here." The *Milwaukee Sentinel* agreed, demanding a public investigation of campus morals.[167]

A Student View of Chapple's Charges

Others were more concerned about campus radicalism. Chief among them was the politically ambitious young editor of the Ashland *Daily Press*, John B. Chapple. Although he had visited the Soviet Union in the late 1920s and come back favorably impressed by the achievements of the Bolshevik revolution, within a few years Chapple was an outspoken member of the stalwart wing of the Republican Party. In the fall of 1931 he began speaking out on various issues, hoping to build support for his candidacy for statewide office against the La Follette progressives in 1932. One of his main targets was the University, which Chapple charged was "a hot-bed of radicalism," guilty of "insidious teaching of atheism, loose moral standards, and communist doctrines."[168] Challenged by the *Daily Cardinal* to present his charges on campus, Chapple came to Madison in early November, 1931, to help organize a student League for Defense of American Principles, led by a conservative first-semester freshman and Chapple informant, John M. Schofield. Schofield had already drawn the ire of campus liberals by his anti-communist warnings in the *Cardinal*.[169]

Chapple returned in mid-November and addressed an unruly crowd of four hundred skeptical and often jeering students in Bascom Hall.

---

[167]*Wisconsin State Journal*, April 28, 1932; *Milwaukee Sentinel*, May 3, 1932; *Daily Cardinal*, May 3 and 4, 1932.

[168]*Daily Cardinal*, October 15 and 20, 1931.

[169]Ibid., October 31, November 3, 4, 11, and 15, 1931.

He named sixteen members of the faculty, including President Frank and Max Otto, as dangerous radicals who were leading their youthful charges astray. In particular he dismissed Frank's pet project, the Experimental College, as "a cleverly devised scheme to instill revolutionary ideas into student minds without arousing the suspicions of the people of the state."[170] Chapple's criticism was so extreme and his evidence so flimsy that most of the accused faculty members either dismissed the charges as absurd or declined comment. The *Cardinal*'s Samuel Steinman agreed that Chapple's wild accusations were "silly and fatuous," but he denounced "the animal-like behavior of a good portion of Mr. Chapple's large audience," which he compared to "a Mississippi lynching bee or a Ku Klux Klan night-meeting." Such conduct, he said, was "far beneath what we have come to regard as the standard of university culture."[171]

Chapple stepped up his wild charges in the months that followed. It was clear he considered the University a useful weapon for attacking the La Follette progressives' rule of the state.[172] To illustrate the grip of atheism in Wisconsin under the La Follettes, he pointed out that when Belle La Follette died in the summer of 1931, her son, the governor, had asked the atheist Max Otto to give the eulogy at the funeral services held on the campus of the University. (He neglected to point out that Professor Otto was an old and close friend of the La Follette family, that the memorial service had been in the State Historical Society Building, or that the Rev. H.H. Lumpkin, the rector of First Episcopal Church in Madison, had conducted a religious graveside service for the interment in Forest Hill Cemetery.) "All this was not aimed at the University or Professor Otto," Phil La Follette commented bitterly many years later. "It was to strike through them at us."[173]

Beginning in February Chapple's wild charges were taken up by a new anti-La Follette weekly, *Uncensored News*, published in Madison for the 1932 political campaign with the shadowy backing of unnamed

---

[170]Ibid., November 16 and 17, 1931.

[171]Ibid., November 18, 1931.

[172]See, for example, John B. Chapple, *La Follette Socialism: How It Affects Your Job, Your Savings, Your Insurance Policy, Your Rights and Your Future* (Ashland, Wisconsin: J.B. Chapple & Company, 1931); Chapple, *Is Gag Rule to be Tolerated in Wisconsin?* (Ashland: Ashland Daily Press, 1931); Chapple, *Unmasking Invisible Forces of Destruction in America* (Ashland: J.B. Chapple, 1932).

[173]P.F. La Follette, draft memoirs, n.d., P.F. La Follette Papers, box 123. See also the less forthright and detailed comments in La Follette, *Adventure in Politics*, pp. 156, 177-8.

stalwart Republicans. The Chapple and other criticism of alleged campus immorality, atheism, and radicalism galvanized some University students to strike back in defense of their alma mater. They formed a Student League for Intellectual Freedom, vowing "to fight the insidious propaganda" that was threatening their "sacred right to learn and to be taught."[174] Although campus skeptics doubted the movement would last, within a short time twelve hundred students signed a league petition expressing faith in the University. The league organized squads of UW students to trail candidate Chapple around the state, challenging his allegations and countering his anti-University propaganda.[175] They also publicized evidence that Chapple's anti-University campaign was bankrolled by Republican stalwarts seeking to undermine Governor La Follette's bid for reelection. And in a notable exposé they got John Schofield to apologize for having circulated Chapple charges against Glenn Frank that he later discovered were false. Small wonder that at an anti-Chapple rally on the lower campus some students proposed forming another organization, the Student League for the Sudden Immersion of John B. Chapple in the Waters of Lake Mendota.[176]

Whether or not President Frank was involved in the organization of the student defense of the University, he simultaneously and eloquently took the offensive himself to try to stem the flood of criticism from alarmed mothers, distressed divines, and opportunistic politicians. Dismissing classes on May 13, he summoned the students to an all-campus convocation in the UW Field House.[177] He and Frank Holt also acted to institutionalize the student truth squads for future use in University public relations. Frank arranged to have his long address entitled "Freedom, Education, and Morals in the Modern University" broadcast to a wider state audience over the University radio station, WHA, and released its text to the press and republished it in the *Wisconsin Alumni Magazine*. Speaking bluntly but with the touches of humor and graceful alliteration that were his trademark, the president excoriated the "little handful of ambitious men" whose attacks were promoting "this carnival of demagogic claptrap." He denied that he or any member of the

---

[174]*Daily Cardinal*, May 10, 1932. Although this was primarily a student effort, it had the support of some faculty members and the pastors of several campus-area churches and religious foundations. *Capital Times*, May 14, 1932.

[175]See, for example, *Daily Cardinal*, May 13, 14, 17, 18, 19, 21, 22, and 24, July 28, August 12, October 14, 1932.

[176]Ibid., May 20, 27, and 29, June 1, 2, and 3, 1932.

[177]Ibid., May 6 and 7, 1932; *Capital Times*, May 6, 7, 8, and 9, 1932.

faculty was a communist but affirmed his conviction that "just as a germ dies in sunlight...so radical ideas are less dangerous when expressed than when repressed." Those who never differ from the majority never need worry about their right of free speech, he pointed out. "But men whose Americanism is real, and not mere campaign rhetoric, do not flinch from the duty of defending the rights even of men whose opinions they despise."

As for charges that the University encouraged atheism, Frank pointed out that while he had left the pulpit, he "had no sense of having left the ministry." He and the University promoted the annual All-University Religious Convocation and welcomed the work of the nine campus-area church organizations ministering to students. Studying atheism or, for that matter, the history of the medieval church in UW courses should not be interpreted as supporting either irreligion or Roman Catholicism. The University belongs to no political group or religious sect and must be free to study any political, social, economic, religious, or moral issue. "To do less," Frank warned, "is to commit suicide as a University."

> There are stray forces in Wisconsin that are frankly afraid of a fearless University. There are some Stalwarts who would like to see every liberal mind eliminated from the faculty and administration of the University of Wisconsin and every expression of student or faculty opinion inconsistent with their conservative views ruthlessly suppressed. There are some Progressives who would like to see every conservative mind eliminated from the faculty and the University turned into a propagandist agency for their particular views of politics and economics....
>
> But this much I can say with certainty: As long as I am president of the University of Wisconsin no limited group in this state will turn the University into its tool without knowing that it has been through a fight. The University is not worth the investment of one dollar of taxpayers' money unless it maintains its freedom from the external control of cliques. And as long as I am president I shall fight for this freedom to deal objectively with the life of the mind and the life of the state regardless of personal cost to myself or political support for the University itself.

But, Frank emphasized, with freedom comes responsibility. The final section of the president's remarks dealt with the allegations of student immorality. He denied that the recent changes in the regulatory and disciplinary functions of the offices of the deans of men and women implied any relaxation of University rules or control over the lives of its students. The concern about campus immorality he blamed on "two outbursts of bad taste and indefensible indiscretion in the letter columns of the student newspaper." The president declared he was reluctant to lay down "a list of taboo topics" or otherwise censor student publications, for he knew how censorship could "lay a clammy hand upon the mind of the student body or a nation." Yet recent experience must convince any student editor that "the printing of the views of an occasional student on sex relations" was not only a violation of good taste "but gives added war materials to blatherskates and demagogues who are seeking to attack the University for other reasons." He had confidence that student journalists could draw the line between good and bad taste. But "if this confidence proves to be misplaced," Frank cautioned, "I can draw this line and draw it without infringement of that authentic freedom of speech in which I believe profoundly."[178]

While at least one student pointed out the president's inconsistency in defending both free speech and censorship,[179] most reactions to Frank's convocation speech were highly positive. Even the often critical *Capital Times* urged that it "be made accessible to the mothers and fathers of Wisconsin."[180] Frank followed up his advice to the students by quietly persuading the editorial staff of the *Daily Cardinal* to announce that the paper would no longer print anonymous letters from its readers. He also used the occasions of the Mothers' Weekend later in May and the annual reunion of the alumni the following month to make a similar ringing defense of academic freedom at the University, in particular singling out for praise Max Otto's constructive spiritual influence.[181] At the alumni meeting the president scotched a well-organized effort by some conservative alumni to demand that the Board of Regents either suppress the *Cardinal* or take "immediate steps as are necessary to keep the editorial and news policies of The Daily Cardinal within the bounds of good taste, common decency, and loyalty to our university." The anti-*Cardinal* resolution failed after Frank emphasized to the alumni that "there shall never be established, with my consent, a sweeping censorship that will convert either the University or the student newspaper into a docile house organ for any single group—pro-

---

[178]See *Daily Cardinal*, May 14 and 18, 1932; *Capital Times*, May 14, 1932; *Wisconsin State Journal*, May 14 and 15, 1932; Frank, "Freedom, Education and Morals in the Modern University," *WAM*, 33 (June, 1932), 276-81.

[179]*Daily Cardinal*, May 15, 1932.

[180]*Capital Times*, May 14, 1932. See also ibid., May 17, 1932.

[181]See *Daily Cardinal*, May 18, 1932; "Frank Discusses Criticisms of University," pp. 306-7, 330-1.

gressive, stalwart, socialist, or any other."[182]

Although President Frank managed, somewhat tardily if none the less forthrightly, to head off this move to censor the *Daily Cardinal*, the issue continued to plague his efforts to cultivate a positive image of the University throughout the state. In actuality, during the 1930s the various editors of the *Cardinal* tended to be mildly progressive rather than radical in their outlook on social and economic questions. Their stand on some issues, however, seemed to confirm the view of the University's conservative critics that the campus was imparting antisocial values and ideas to the youth of the state. The paper's biting criticism of the excessive commercialism of intercollegiate athletics, for example, its pointing out the irony of the regents' willingness to offer significantly higher salaries to coaches than to professors, and its perennial attacks on the campus Reserve Officer Training Corps (ROTC) program offended many Badger boosters and veterans' groups around the state.

As a land grant institution, the University had an obligation to offer military science in its curriculum, but the opponents of ROTC argued that the requirement could be met in other ways. Indirectly, the ROTC program was supported by the University's physical education requirement, because male students could substitute the first two years of ROTC for compulsory freshman-sophomore physical education. Once required of all Wisconsin men students, by the 1930s military training through the four-year ROTC program was optional, but the gym alternative gave its enrollment a significant boost, at least in the first two years. In March of 1932, acting on the advice of a special committee chaired by the University's chief psychologist, Professor V.A.C. Henmon, the faculty voted to replace the compulsory physical education requirement with an expanded program of intramural and recreational sports. As might be expected, the action was highly popular with students. The Board of Regents was less sympathetic, however, and referred the proposal back to the faculty the following month on the ground the new policy would affect men and women students differently.[183] Clearly, it might also affect ROTC enrollment, a consideration the regents probably had in mind.

---

[182]*Daily Cardinal*, June 28, 1932.
[183]UW Faculty Minutes, February 15, March 7, 1932; UW Faculty Documents 401, 401A, and 401B, "Report on Physical Education and Intramural Sports," February 15, March 7, 1932; BOR Minutes, April 27, 1932.

The general faculty considered the regents' rebuff at its June 6 meeting but decided to postpone the physical education issue until fall, when it voted to adopt a uniform one-year requirement for men and women.[184] To minimize the impact of this change on ROTC enrollment, on the advice of its military affairs committee the general faculty recommended on February 6, 1933, that the various schools and colleges of the University grant two academic credits for each semester of ROTC taken in the sophomore year as well as one credit per semester for sophomore band.[185] When L&S Dean George Sellery brought this recommendation to the faculty of the University's largest college, however, his rebellious colleagues voted narrowly to "non-concur."[186] Not content to leave the matter dangling, Sellery appointed a committee to study the question of ROTC credit further. He then persuaded the L&S faculty to reconsider its earlier action and to adopt the committee's report, which recommended granting four academic credits for completing freshman-sophomore ROTC and eight credits for advanced ROTC in the junior and senior years.[187] The credit policy of Letters and Science then became the standard for the campus after its approval by the regents.[188]

Students were generally disappointed the compromise retained compulsory freshman gym. Critics of ROTC, especially the *Daily Cardinal*, continued to express their unhappiness over the decision to preserve its status by giving explicit academic credit for completing the program. In the spring of 1933 the Board of Regents received two serious complaints about the student paper. Reflecting the continuing alumni unhappiness of the previous year, the directors of the Wisconsin Alumni Association, evidently with support from the University's Board of Visitors, urged the regents to create an official newspaper under the School of Journalism "to promote the best interests of the University of Wisconsin and its student body and to secure for the University proper publicity."[189] The ROTC cadet colonel presented a petition on behalf of 464 ROTC students complaining about the anti-ROTC bias of the *Cardinal*, which had "for the past several years endeavored to disintegrate the

---

[184]BOR Minutes, June 6, November 7, 1932.

[185]Ibid., February 6, 1933.

[186]L&S Faculty Minutes, February 20, 1933.

[187]Ibid., April 17, 1933; L&S Faculty Document 57, "Report of the Special Committee on R.O.T.C. Credit," April 17, 1933.

[188]BOR Minutes, June 17, 1933.

[189]Ibid., March 8, 1933.

Corps of Cadets through a campaign of malicious misrepresentation and vilification, together with unwarranted personal attacks on the instructional staff by a few radical individuals." The petitioners requested the regents "to take action to rectify this condition."[190]

Act they did, with a heavy hand. On April 27 the Board of Regents stripped the *Cardinal* of its status as the official campus newspaper. The board directed a special committee, consisting of *Cardinal* editor Frederick Noer and the paper's Board of Control, along with President Frank, Dean Sellery, and the regents' Executive Committee, "to consider the possible form of organization and control that will best safeguard both the principle of responsibility and the principle of freedom in the management of the paper."[191] Two months later the regents went further. After hearing a report about the stalemated negotiations concerning the *Cardinal*, the regents rejected a plan to reorganize the *Cardinal* Board of Control. Instead they directed their Executive Committee "to prepare plans for the creation of an official University newspaper designed to support the general University welfare and with opportunity for free expression of student opinion."[192]

Although few were willing to defend the beleaguered *Cardinal* in all respects, many considered the regents' decision excessive. The *Capital Times* chastised the board for "gagging student opinion." The action, editor Evjue declared, "not only threatens free speech and opinion at the university but will entail the expenditure of university funds for an unwarranted and all too apparent purpose."[193] At the first opportunity Regent Harold Wilkie, who usually reflected the views of Governor La Follette, newly back in office, offered a motion to restore the status of the *Daily Cardinal* as the University's official newspaper. His resolution also enlarged the paper's elected Board of Control by two members, one appointed by the regents and the other by the president of the University. With neither discussion nor explanation the board beat a hasty retreat and adopted Wilkie's resolution. This time, in contrast to his strong public denunciation of censorship the previous year, there was also no indication of forceful leadership by President Frank.[194]

---

[190]F.H. Clausen to M.E. McCaffrey, April 7, 1933, with enclosure, BOR Papers, 1/1/3, box 45.

[191]BOR Minutes, April 27, 1933; *Capital Times*, April 27, 1933.

[192]BOR Minutes, June 17, 1933; *Capital Times*, June 18, 1933.

[193]Editorial, *Capital Times*, July 30, 1933.

[194]The Wilkie motion also directed the reconstituted Board of Control to "reconsider the appointments to the staff of the Daily Cardinal for the ensuing year." BOR Minutes, August

President Frank had another opportunity to take a well-publicized stand on free speech in the spring of 1935. On the evening of May 15 a group of Langdon Street fraternity men and athletes disrupted a meeting of the Student League for Industrial Democracy in the Law School auditorium. The local group was an offshoot of the League for Industrial Democracy, a national socialist organization headed by Professor Robert Morss Lovett of the University of Chicago, once Governor La Follette's candidate for the UW presidency. The LID board included such prominent liberals as John Dewey and sometime UW Professor Alexander Meiklejohn. After heckling the speaker, Monroe M. Sweetland, a staff organizer for the LID, the intruders broke up the meeting and dragged Sweetland and others down to Lake Mendota. The student mob also attacked a meeting of the more radical National Student League being held in the YMCA building next to the Memorial Union. The *Daily Cardinal*'s headlines the following morning graphically told what happened next: "LAW SCHOOL SCENE OF CAMPUS SPREE/ 'STRONG MEN' TOSS FOUR NSL, LID INTO MENDOTA/ CROWD OF 50 GROWS TO 1,000 AS MEETINGS ARE 'ADJOURNED'."[195]

The press of the state and nation denounced the attackers, as did a number of University faculty members. Max Otto told his class of three hundred students the next morning, "If that was Americanism last night and I had been there I would have preferred to have been thrown into the lake." He also declared that any "W" Club members participating in the assault should be stripped of their letters and should "bow in shame" as they yielded up their "W"s.[196] A newly organized Committee for Constitutional Rights, headed by Dean Garrison of the Law School, scheduled a protest meeting, but President Frank preempted their gathering by calling instead an all-University convocation for the same hour on Friday evening, May 17. Frank's convocation was billed as a rally in defense of free speech and not an explicit protest against the recent disruption at the Law School. When the president asked Dean Sellery to be one of several speakers at the convocation, Sellery at first demurred, saying he felt very strongly about the Mendota dunking and would feel obliged to criticize its perpetrators. Frank nevertheless urged the dean to address the meeting.

The convocation attracted an audience of more than twelve hundred

---

2, 1933; *Capital Times*, August 3, 1933.

[195]*Daily Cardinal*, May 16, 1935.

[196]*Milwaukee Journal*, May 16, 1935; Sellery, *Some Ferments at Wisconsin*, p. 64.

which overflowed the large auditorium in Agricultural Hall. Most of the eleven speakers followed the lead of President Frank, who defended academic freedom and free speech with the generalized philosophical and constitutional arguments he had used many times in the past. Not so George Sellery. His impromptu but impassioned speech denounced the actions of the student mob, which Sellery called "the most disgraceful thing ever perpetrated at the university." He heaped scorn on the athletes wearing "W"s during the fray, pointing out that some of their victims were women. "Such chivalry!" Sellery declared sarcastically. "If the organization of the wearers of the 'W' allow individuals of that organization to display the letter in such proceedings as these, it will not be long before the emblem will no longer be a badge of honor."[197] What the *Cardinal* headlined as "Sellery's Fiery Blast" was applauded wildly by the student audience, which gave him a tumultuous sky rocket when he left the rostrum.[198] Afterward a few students disagreed. Maurice Zolotow thought Sellery was guilty of arousing mob passions, "just like the reds do—instead of quietly disciplining the 'W' attackers." A more conservative upperclassman chided Sellery for underestimating the communist menace. "I am not a 'W' man," he said, "but I wish I were. Greeting to the chaps who had nerve enough to do what the officials did not."[199]

President Frank was more interested in calming campus tensions and reducing negative publicity than in making an example of the leaders of the mob. Nor did he want to take on the influential national "W" Club. Accordingly, the Dane County district attorney gave 6 of the students arrested during the affair a verbal spanking, and Frank chose to interpret a petition signed by 147 other participants explaining their actions as a public apology sufficient to warrant dropping any further University disciplinary action in the matter.[200] Years later Herbert Jacobs, a reporter who was working for the *Milwaukee Journal* in 1935, told George Sellery that after joining the *Capital Times* the following year he had learned some interesting background information about the Mendota dunking. It seems that a youthful *Times* reporter, eager for a story on a slow news day, had visited fraternity row on Langdon Street the night of the SLID meeting. He warned the frater-

---

[197]*Wisconsin State Journal*, May 18, 1935; Sellery, *Some Ferments at Wisconsin*, pp. 66-7.
[198]*Daily Cardinal*, May 18, 1935.
[199]Ibid., May 23, June 2, 1935.
[200]Ibid, May 19, 24, and 26, 1935.

nity men, especially the athletes, of the need to break up this meeting of dangerous radicals, even suggesting it would be a good idea to throw them into the lake. The next day he boasted to his colleagues at the paper how he had generated the big story and was chagrined when they did not share his enthusiasm for manipulating the news this way.[201] Ever alert for a good news story with a moral, *Times* editor Evjue made much of the Mendota dunking as a cowardly assault on free speech without ever letting on that one of his employees might have been responsible for the student riot.

The depression years provided a sharp contrast with the contagious atmosphere of optimism and renewal that had followed Glenn Frank's appointment in 1925. No longer was he seen as the boy wonder president who was bringing about the rebirth and revitalization of the University of Wisconsin. Instead, by the mid-thirties he was increasingly on the defensive, facing a hostile governor and legislature, critical regents, cynical faculty members, and a skeptical public. His promised renaissance was long forgotten, his very relevance seemed increasingly in question.

---

[201]Herbert Jacobs to Sellery, February 5, 1960, L&S Papers, 7/16/18, box 1, UA. Interestingly, Sellery chose not to mention this revelation in his account of the dunking incident in his published memoirs.

5.

A Public Hanging on Bascom Hill

The recurring criticism of Glenn Frank and his administration of the University during the early 1930s had a cumulatively corrosive effect on his support on and off campus. Gradually, he was no longer seen by the public, the politicians, and the press of Wisconsin and the nation as the invincible young reformer who was revitalizing a complacent and stuffy institution. Never popular with the bulk of the faculty, increasingly his ideas and rhetoric seemed predictable and less relevant to current needs, his loose administrative style inadequate to deal with ever more frequent crises. The president's response to the recurring depression budget cuts, and especially his failure to volunteer for a larger salary waiver or otherwise to reduce his grand manner of living, hurt his image on campus, just as the endless negative publicity about the University damaged his reputation around the state.

In time the criticism went national. Early in 1934 the *American Mercury* magazine, in whose pages H.L. Mencken had a few years earlier identified Glenn Frank as an attractive candidate for the White House, published an appraisal of the Wisconsin president. It was by all odds the most savagely disparaging review of Frank and his University service yet to appear. Sub-titled "Journalist on Parole," the piece was written by Ernest Meyer, a *Capital Times* columnist. Offering a number of examples indicating that Frank had abandoned his one-time progressive impulses, Meyer found little to praise in the man he described as an "aging boy wonder." His caustic portrait was highly personal:

He still retains a shining school-boy face and the enduring adolescence of a confirmed optimist. He has warm, lively eyes. He is, in looks, gestures,

293

diction, and elocution, disarmingly smooth. He smokes a democratic pipe. He laughs easily, but is quite humorless. He makes you feel instantly at ease with him, relaxed, even if you came with a grudge and complaint. He laves your hurts with the balm of his voice, mellow and musical, and weaves around you the spell of his dialectic. He knows words. Good, wholesome words, trigger words that release mystical springs in you and make you itch with undefinable enterprise. But when you leave him, it takes less than an hour's walk in the crisp air to recall that your complaint was unanswered, your demands unfilled, and that once again your weapons have remained ingloriously stuck in the syrup of his eloquence....It took the campus two years to doubt him, and six to regard him with amused contempt. And today, eight years after his arrival, he has probably not a single sincere admirer left among the host who hailed his coming with hosannas.[1]

It is hard to believe that Meyer's boss Bill Evjue and other La Follette progressives—perhaps even the governor himself—were unaware of Meyer's plan for this slashing attack on the University president before a national audience.

Frank himself learned of the critical Meyer article before it appeared. "I do not know the angle from which the Mercury article proceeds to 'debunk' me," he wrote his friend Zona Gale, but he nevertheless suggested ways to counter the attack.

> I suspect it proceeds from the following points of view its author and his editorial chief on the Times have persistently held, viz:
> (1) That I am a bogus liberal and have always followed the lead of the reactionaries in the University.
> (2) That I never "take a stand" on controversial issues.
> (3) That I talk but do not act, and that, in consequence, nothing in the way of liberal reform has come to the University under my administration.
> (4) That these contentions are borne out in the following instances:
> (a) The cancellation of the sex lecture by Dora Russell.
> (b) The discontinuance of the Experimental College.
> (c) The 1933-34 budget which ranged in salary cuts from 12 percent on the lowest to 20 percent on the highest salaries.

Frank professed to be mystified how anyone could doubt his liberalism. He cited instances of his defense of academic freedom, his refusal to censor the *Daily Cardinal*, and his recruitment of such prominent liberals as Alexander Meiklejohn, Chris Christensen, and Lloyd Garrison to reform the University. He pointed out he had persuaded the

---

[1]Ernest Meyer, "Glenn Frank: Journalist on Parole," *American Mercury*, 31 (February, 1934), 149.

Board of Regents to restore the UW degrees withheld or revoked as a result of wartime intolerance, including the baccalaureate degree withheld from Ernest Meyer himself for being a conscientious objector to the war. He noted that unlike many other institutions the University had not fired large numbers of junior faculty in the depression, preferring the more humane approach of reducing and staggering employment and cutting the salaries of all staff members on a graduated basis. Certainly there were critics among the students and faculty, he conceded, but the real test of his liberalism was whether they felt free to complain. "The day we do not have discontented persons here," he commented, "I shall feel that liberalism has died here." Frank enclosed a number of documents for Gale's use in preparing a rebuttal. "And these few notes I send at the price of great personal embarrassment," he apologized, "but it seems justified in the light of the utter unfairness of the continuous attack of a little group."[2]

Gale drew heavily on Frank's material in answering Meyer's attack in the March issue of the *American Mercury*, first allowing the president to suggest revisions. As had Frank's, Gale's laudatory account of his presidency overstated the case and claimed credit for a number of developments with which Frank had actually had little to do. In closing she quoted the famous English philosopher H.G. Wells as saying on his last visit to America: "I am going to Wisconsin to see my friend Glenn Frank, because Wisconsin is a place where education still exists."[3]

On campus, even some of Frank's critics and skeptics were offended by the personal nature of Meyer's attack on the president, and for a time Frank gained greater sympathy and support among the faculty. The chairman of the faculty's influential University Committee, Mark Ingraham, told Frank the committee regretted Meyer's "undignified and unsportsmanlike attack" and predicted that "to a marked degree the faculty of Wisconsin will resent attacks of the nature to which you have been subjected, and will desire that political considerations be kept

---

[2]Glenn Frank to Zona Gale, January 4, 1934, Glenn Frank Papers, Northeast Missouri State University, Kirksville.

[3]Zona Gale, "Glenn Frank," draft manuscript [ca. January, 1934], Frank Papers, Kirksville; Gale, "Some Achievements of Glenn Frank," *American Mercury*, 31 (March, 1934), 381-3. Meyer offered a point-by-point rebuttal when Gale's article appeared. *Daily Cardinal,* March 2, 1934. Never a fan of President Frank, George Sellery felt obliged in his memoirs to point out what he regarded as exaggerations in Gale's litany of Frank's achievements before offering his own brief and more critical assessment. George C. Sellery, *Some Ferments at Wisconsin, 1901-1947: Memories and Reflections* (Madison: University of Wisconsin Press, 1960), pp. 92-4.

out of discussion of University affairs."[4] Chemistry Professor Farrington Daniels agreed that "this unwarranted attack from outside will serve
to strengthen your position with the faculty and students."[5] Graduate
Dean Charles S. Slichter, observing that his imminent retirement placed
him "beyond fear and favor," declared he and his wife were "deeply
pained at the senseless attack." He assured Frank that "in the matter
of personal esteem & affection—no president of this institution has ever
stood higher."[6] Law Dean Garrison reported he had heard a lot of
faculty talk about the Meyer article. "Without exception," he told
Frank, "they regard it as unfair and poor sportsmanship—even those
who are wont to be critical of you. You now have their sympathy—in
many cases where you did not have it before."[7] Julius Olson drew on
his long experience at the University to console Frank with the reminder
that President John Bascom had endured even greater humiliation. "The
obloquy hurled at you recently did not emanate from an authoritative
source," he pointed out. "It overshot the bounds of sane and reasonable
criticism, and the reaction has already set in, as you surely know."[8]
Harold Bradley agreed:

> I want you to know how deeply I resent the attacks that have been
> launched in your direction, and how glad I should be to do anything which in
> your judgement would be of help in the cause. It seems inconceivable that
> any reasonably motivated individual could allow himself to do so much
> damage to a great institution, in order to work out what evidently is a private
> grudge. It seems equally inconceivable that in any kind of public personal
> attack the methods and the code should be so cowardly and low.
>   I am inclined to think the personal animus and the yellow character of
> the attack has become so clear that many loyalties that were only warm
> before, have been fanned into white heat.[9]

The *Daily Cardinal* printed a long excerpt from the Meyer article
ten days after its appearance, but, surprisingly, chose not to comment
on it editorially.[10] The paper did, however, run a front-page story the

---

[4]Mark H. Ingraham to Frank, February 6, 1934, Frank Papers, Kirksville.
[5]Farrington Daniels to Frank, January 25, 1934, ibid.
[6]Charles S. Slichter to Frank, January 26, 1934, ibid.
[7]Garrison to Frank, January 30, 1934, ibid.
[8]Julius E. Olson to Frank, January 28, 1934, ibid.
[9]Bradley to Frank, January 31, 1934, ibid. For similar expressions of support from faculty
members and Madison residents, see also A.R. Hohlfeld to Frank, February 9, 1934; Alfred
W. Swan to Frank, February 28, 1934; Ethel Rockwell to Frank, March 29, 1934, ibid.
[10]*Daily Cardinal*, February 6, 1934.

next day quoting the famous Wisconsin architect Frank Lloyd Wright's defense of Frank. It also made an exception to its rule against anonymous letters by printing a long communication from an unidentified instructor complaining that "incalculable damage has been done to a worthy person and an intelli-gently and progressively administered institution."[11]

The Crumbling of the Ramparts

The Meyer attack may have backfired by generating sympathy for Frank on campus, but it suggested that some Wisconsin progressives were willing to go to considerable lengths to undermine the UW president. Frank's future would depend heavily on the attitude of Philip La Follette, who at the time of the Meyer attack was preparing to pull his followers out of the Republican Party into a new Progressive Party. The move was a bold gamble to realign Wisconsin politics more forthrightly along ideological lines, and, incidentally, was in opposition to Glenn Frank's increasingly open involvement with anti-New Deal Democrats and with the national Republican Party. Reelected as governor on the new party's ticket in 1934 after an absence of two years, La Follette won a third term by an even larger margin in 1936. The La Follette magic, it seemed clear, was still operative with Wisconsin voters. For President Frank, who had experienced Governor La Follette's hostility as early as 1930, these La Follette triumphs signalled that the governor would be able to appoint a majority of the fifteen-member Board of Regents during his third term.

During the University's budget hearings at the start of his second term, Governor La Follette had made up his mind that Frank was not up to the job of leading the University. The task, he decided, "was to get

---

[11]Ibid., February 7 and 13, 1934. A Wisconsin Rapids attorney, whose son was a student at the University, wrote Frank of his "disgust" over the Meyer attack:

> Richard was home from University last week and was terribly angry about the article. He says this is the attitude of all of the students who have read it. He says that he has not discovered that you are unpopular among the students, but quite the contrary, and that this article has strengthened your position rather than weakened it. I was not surprised at all when I learned that this man, Meyer, is a graduate of the Capitol Times cesspool. This institution has been engaged for years as a business in the assassination of character. It seems to have found this line of effort profitable in a business way.

Theo. W. Brazeau to Frank, February 3, 1934, Frank Papers, Kirksville.

the regents to 'regenting'." To this end he summoned some of the leading regents and, as he recalled many years later, "urged upon them the importance of their recognizing their responsibilities to the State and University by either remedying the errors in Dr. Frank's administration or making a change in that administration." He warned that if they did nothing the University's budget requests would get little support from the governor and the Progressive-dominated legislature.[12]

Early in 1936 Regent Harold Wilkie, La Follette's first appointee to the board and by now its president, went to see the governor. Wilkie had clashed frequently with Frank at board meetings in recent years and told La Follette he had concluded the president must be replaced. He said he had discussed this view only with Regents John Callahan, the state superintendent of public instruction and an ex officio member of the board, and Daniel Grady, a liberal Democrat and La Follette appointee. Both men had been regents when Frank was appointed in 1925, and both, Wilkie reported, agreed that Frank had outlived his usefulness to the University. The governor arranged to meet with the three regents to consider how to proceed. He later claimed he found Callahan and Grady even more emphatic than Wilkie on Frank's failings as a university leader. Callahan particularly objected to the president's lucrative outside lecturing and writing activities which he believed kept Frank from devoting full time to his UW responsibilities and which he had promised the regents in 1925 would be curtailed.

La Follette suggested that the three regents meet with Frank and tell him how they felt. Callahan instead argued that it might be better if he, as a professional educator, talked with Frank alone. He promised to do so at an education meeting both men were to attend in St. Louis shortly. Just what happened in this meeting is unclear, except that Callahan reported on his return he thought he had bungled things by admitting to Frank he was speaking for only three of the regents.[13] Frank immediately got on the telephone to mobilize support from other regents, charging that a small cabal was plotting to purge him. One of those he contacted was George W. Mead, a wealthy Wisconsin Rapids paper manufacturer and Zimmerman appointee who had served on the board since 1928. Mead promised to work on Raymond Richards, one of the five new regents La Follette had recently appointed. Richards

[12]P.F. La Follette, draft memoirs, n.d., P.F. La Follette Papers, box 124, SHSW.

[13]Ibid.; Philip F. La Follette, *Adventure in Politics: The Memoirs of Philip La Follette,* Donald Young, ed. (New York: Holt, Rinehart and Winston, 1970), pp. 237-8.

was an electrician and local politician from Wisconsin Rapids and thus was susceptible to Mead's influence. Mead declined the president's invitation to stay with the Franks during the next board meeting, pointing out he needed to be at the hotel with the other regents. "I can do more there than I can in a meeting," he told the president, "and if things should actually become lively I would want to be in close touch with the fellows and the discussion before we get there assembled in a body."[14]

There was an inconclusive showdown of sorts at a closed meeting of the board on March 10, 1936. Frank opened with a prepared statement defending his administration, which mystified at least one new regent, Kenneth S. Hones of Colfax, who had not been contacted by either the Frank critics or supporters before the meeting. Board President Harold Wilkie responded with some critical observations about Frank's leadership, citing in particular his mishandling of the Snell case the previous year and suggesting that for the good of the University Frank ought to resign. Two regents, Republican George Mead and Democrat Jessie Combs of Oshkosh, objected to Wilkie's remarks and declared his comments unwarranted and out of order. No one followed up on Wilkie's proposal, so the matter died for the time being. One of the other new regents, Clough Gates of Superior, who had praised Frank's appointment in 1925, said afterward he inferred from the discussion "there was an undercurrent of anti-Frank sentiment on the board." News of the confrontation was leaked by the anti-Frank forces immediately, and the *Daily Cardinal* headlined a front page story the next day: "FRANK LEAVES JUNE 1 — REPORT/ RUMOR REGENTS BACKING MOVE."[15] The more detailed account in the *Wisconsin State Journal* noted Wilkie's admission that Governor La Follette was behind the ouster move. There was persistent speculation that La Follette might himself be interested in the UW presidency, a rumor the governor's office promptly denied.[16]

---

[14]George W. Mead to Frank, March 4, 1936, Frank Papers, Kirksville. Mary Frank later wrote a note on Mead's letter identifying him as "Regent—one of most excellent ones."

[15]*Daily Cardinal* and *Capital Times*, March 11, 1936. See also Morris H. Rubin, "Battle Lines Hold: Sellery Acting Prexy," *Wisconsin State Journal*, January 8, 1937.

[16]*Wisconsin State Journal*, March 11, 1936. When the report of La Follette's interest in the UW presidency persisted, he felt obliged to write Regent Wilkie denouncing it as "pure fabrication" and asserting: "If there were a vacancy in the university presidency, I would under no circumstances be a candidate for it nor accept it if it were tendered to me." Ibid., March 17, 1936; *Daily Cardinal*, March 18, 1936.

Like the Meyer attack a year earlier, the challenge by the anti-Frank bloc on the Board of Regents created mostly sympathy for the UW president. At the annual campus gridiron banquet hosted by Sigma Delta Chi, the professional journalism fraternity, two days later, Frank was given a rousing ovation by the largely faculty audience, which the *Cardinal* described as "probably as dramatic and arresting a tribute as has ever been received on the campus." The editor shrewdly cautioned, however, that the applause should not be taken "lock, stock, and barrel as an expression of real faculty sentiment." It was, rather, "a sympathetic tribute to one who does not deserve to be railroaded out of office on a political rail."[17] Another student view was expressed by *The Challenge*, the outspoken organ of the Young Communist League at the University. Frank's support among the regents was evaporating, the paper asserted, because of his "clumsiness" in handling the recent athletic problems and his "notoriously unfair" salary cuts in the depression. While the president's unflagging defense of free speech was commendable, progressive regents rightly "suspected the sincerity and intellectual integrity of a liberal who has capitulated to the reactionaries in politics just as he has to those in education."[18] Most observers predicted Glenn Frank was in for a stormy spring.

If the president ever considered following Wilkie's advice to resign, he gave no hint. On the contrary, his confident demeanor and tough public statements seemed to suggest he had every intention of fighting for his post. "The day a state university sells its soul to a particular party or creed or race it would as well close its doors," he warned a nation-wide audience of UW alumni over an NBC radio hookup in April, "for it will die as a seat of learning and linger only as an agency of propaganda for the half-truths of partisanship."[19] When it became clear Frank would not leave quietly, Governor La Follette, Wilkie, and other close Progressive advisers concluded it would be, in La Follette's words, "stupid politics" to proceed with the ouster plan before the November general election. "You cannot argue the fitness of a university president before a million voters," the governor commented drily.[20]

This did not mean La Follette and Wilkie let up in the campaign to

---

[17]Editorial, *Daily Cardinal*, March 14, 1936.
[18]Quoted in *Capital Times*, April 14, 1936.
[19]Ibid., April 14, 1936.
[20]La Follette, *Adventure in Politics*, p. 238.

undermine the University president. Not in the least. At the June meeting Wilkie shamelessly used his position as board president to try to get the regents to reject Frank's proposed budget for 1936-37, which called for partially restoring the "waived" staff salaries by means of additional funding largely provided by higher tuition. At one point during the session Wilkie took a regent committee to a pre-arranged meeting of the state Emergency Board, where Governor La Follette militantly opposed the fee increase and persuaded the board to approve a $35,000 grant to help balance the University budget. Sensing a close decision, Wilkie delayed the regent vote to allow a La Follette appointee, Regent Raymond Richards of Wisconsin Rapids, to reach Madison. Richards had earlier indicated his intention to vote against Frank's budget. Whether Richards was lobbied by Regent Mead, his fellow townsman, is unknown, but to Wilkie's quite evident consternation when Richards arrived he steadfastly declined to vote on the ground he had not studied the budget nor heard the discussion about its provisions. His refusal to vote left the regents tied 7-7. Contrary to past board practice, Wilkie refused to allow President Frank to break the tie by casting what would be the deciding vote. Vainly did some of the regents protest this arbitrary ruling, with Regents Grady and Backus, both prominent lawyers, heatedly citing statutory authority for the president to vote in case of ties. Vainly did Regent Mead appeal the ruling of the chair, losing on the same 7-7 vote, with Wilkie again ruling that Frank could not vote to break a tie even on a procedural issue. To no avail did Regent Callahan offer a motion to separate Frank's salary from the main budget proposal, thus removing the basis for Wilkie's ruling against allowing the president to vote. Again the vote was 7-7, with Wilkie once more ruling that Frank could not vote on this motion either. "You're setting aside the statutes of this state," a frustrated President Frank told a grinning Wilkie.[21]

At a special meeting of the Board of Regents the following month to continue the stalemated consideration of the budget, Frank read an opinion from Democratic Attorney General James E. Finnegan holding that the UW president had been illegally deprived of his right to have his vote counted in favor of the budget at the last meeting. The budget, Finnegan ruled, had thus been adopted. "Mr. Finnegan is entitled to his opinion on the matter and I am entitled to mine," Wilkie responded, declining to change his ruling. This time there was a majority of 8-6 to

---

[21]*Wisconsin State Journal*, June 16 and 17, 1936.

support a motion by Clough Gates to have Frank's budget redrafted by the regents' Executive Committee, with the provisos that there should be no increase in student fees and that Frank's salary for the coming year should be cut to $15,000.[22] In August, after snubbing the president's input, the board adopted a revised budget. For good measure the regents argued at length whether to approve the president's and Dean Christensen's recommendation of Warren W. Clark to be associate director of agricultural extension.[23] All in all it was as brutal and humiliating a series of rebuffs of a University president since John Bascom's continuing difficulties with a hostile Board of Regents in the 1880s had persuaded him the only honorable course left was to resign before he was fired.

President Frank made clear, however, he had no intention of quietly departing. He drew cheers when he told an audience of alumni and graduating seniors in late June that Wisconsin citizens "cannot afford to let the state government run away with the university."[24] The following month to an audience of nearly two thousand summer session students, many of them teachers, Frank warned of the need to protect the independence of the schools and universities of the country. "Fight for freedom," he admonished, "for when it dies, we are doomed to be puppets—and who knows who will pull the strings?"[25] He repeated his warning in a featured address at the annual school administrators' conference in Madison in September, remarks sufficiently provocative that the *Capital Times* headlined them: "FRANK JABS GOV. LA FOL-LETTE IN ADDRESS BEFORE TEACHER BODY/ WARNS AGAINST GOVERN-MENT DOMINATION OF U.W."[26]

Frank had a major ally in the new president of the Wisconsin Alumni Association, Harry A. Bullis, '17, the vice president of General Mills, Inc., in Minneapolis. At a meeting of the presidents of UW alumni clubs in the fall of 1936 Bullis defended President Frank against "a board of regents playing dangerous politics with the school." His critical comments led one of those present, newly appointed Progressive Judge Alvin C. Reis, to complain that Bullis was trying to politicize the alumni. "I think I recognize a Republican convention when I see one,"

---

[22]*Capital Times*, July 23, 1936. The 8-6 margin was achieved at this meeting when Regent Richards voted with the anti-Frank bloc and pro-Frank Regent Backus was absent.

[23]BOR Minutes, August 17, 1936, UA; *Milwaukee Journal*, August 17, 1936.

[24]*Wisconsin State Journal*, June 21, 1936.

[25]*Capital Times*, July 23, 1936.

[26]Ibid., September 25, 1936; *Daily Cardinal*, September 26, 1936.

he commented. While Bullis agreed that the alumni association should stay out of partisan politics, he responded heatedly: "No president of a great university like this should be subject to the ill-mannered treatment handed Glenn Frank."[27] In reporting the meeting Evjue's *Capital Times* dismissed the alumni association in a front-page editorial as "a politically dominated organization" composed of "stiff-necked, hard-shelled conservatives."[28] Bullis was indeed a GOP activist who applauded Frank's growing involvement in Republican national politics and believed he had a promising political future. The day after President Roosevelt's landslide victory in the national elections of 1936, which also swept Phil La Follette back into the Wisconsin governorship for a third term, Bullis wrote Frank thanking him for sending some observations about the regents' budget for Bullis' use in the *Wisconsin Alumni Magazine.* He urged Frank to begin thinking about the next presidential campaign:

> Many of us think the Conservative or Republican Party should begin now to plan for 1940. As I told you in Madison, we are hoping that the Republican Party will begin to publicize you for the nomination four years hence. I suppose Phil would want to be your opponent. You had better grab the political rights now for the University song "On Wisconsin."[29]

A Partisan Lynching

Phil La Follette had also been thinking about Glenn Frank's future, which would not, he hoped, include the latter's continued residence in Wisconsin in either an academic or a political office. The La Follettes had never tolerated other contenders for the leadership of Wisconsin progressives, and Glenn Frank's growing interest in politics was a threat not to be ignored. Like his father, Governor La Follette was proud of his skill as a stump speaker; he did not welcome comparisons with Frank's polished oratory or the thought of having to campaign against it. With the election behind him, La Follette signalled his supporters on the Board of Regents the time had come to depose the UW president. Of the fifteen regents in December, 1936, ten had been appointed by

---

[27]*Daily Cardinal*, October 3, 1936.

[28]*Capital Times*, October 7, 1936.

[29]Harry A. Bullis to Frank, November 4, 1936, Frank Papers, Kirksville. For Bullis' call to arms for the alumni, see his "A Challenge to All Alumni—Politics Must Not Control the University," *WAM*, 38 (October, 1936), 3-4.

progressive governors, including five named by La Follette within the past year. The board maneuvering over the spring and summer had revealed that Frank had seven sympathizers among the regents, however. To La Follette's chagrin, these included John Callahan and Daniel Grady, who had joined Harold Wilkie in complaining to the governor about Frank's leadership earlier in the year, but who had since been offended by Wilkie's ruthless treatment of Frank in recent board meetings.

As things turned out, the firing of Glenn Frank as president of the University of Wisconsin was messy and protracted. At the insistence of the condemned man the lynching was carried out in public before a fascinated national audience. If the main purpose was the removal of Frank from Wisconsin as a potential political threat to the La Follette brothers, the effort was a miserable failure. Indeed, the firing of Glenn Frank blighted Phil La Follette's political prospects as had no other event of his public career, and but for the untimely automobile accident that cost Frank his life in 1940, it might very well have ended the senatorial career of his brother Bob.

The day before the regular regents meeting in December, 1936, Wilkie and Clough Gates, now firmly in the anti-Frank bloc of regents, met with Governor La Follette to discuss strategy. They agreed Wilkie and Gates should inform Frank of their intention to introduce a resolution terminating the president's appointment at the end of the academic year. Wilkie telephoned the governor later that evening to report that Frank had pleaded with them not to introduce their resolution at this meeting but instead to give him a month, or two at the most, to find another position and then resign gracefully. Wilkie was pleased the matter had been resolved satisfactorily. La Follette was skeptical and asked if they had Frank's promise to resign in writing. Wilkie said no; he trusted Frank's word. "Well, Harold," La Follette told him, "that is an awful mistake. You and I will pay through the nose for that. I wouldn't trust that fellow if he swore to it on a stack of Bibles. But I guess the fat's in the fire."[30]

The fat was indeed in the fire. Even while they spoke Glenn Frank was in touch with Zona Gale in New York and other friends around the country warning of the plot by the La Follette Progressives to remove him from office. Soon the transparently political nature of the attack

---

[30]P.F. La Follette, draft memoirs, n.d., P.F. La Follette Papers, boxes 124 and 125; La Follette, *Adventure in Politics*, pp. 239-40; *Daily Cardinal*, December 10, 1936.

against Frank was evident to all on campus. The Christmas issue of the student humor magazine, the *Octopus*, carried a full-page cartoon showing President Frank, his trade-mark spats gleaming, standing coyly under a sprig of mistletoe hoping the two La Follette brothers flanking him would take the hint.[31]

At the December 9 board meeting the regents met in a closed committee-of-the-whole discussion all morning and much of the afternoon before opening the meeting and transacting some routine business. Their most important action was a decision to have Wilkie, rather than Frank, present the University's budget request at the governor's budget hearing the following week. Wilkie made it clear that if President Frank attended the hearing he would speak as an individual rather than as the representative of the University or the board, which had rejected his budget in favor of its own. The unprecedented rebuff was highlighted by the *Daily Cardinal* in a front page

Octopus' View of the Controversy

editorial asking La Follette, Wilkie, and Gates to explain "why President Frank is being quietly shorn of his power, or why he is the victim of insults in the form of the wage cut and the open antagonism of Progressive regents." The paper wondered about the motives of Frank's opponents. "It is a sad reflection upon the Progressive party," the normally progressive *Cardinal* declared, "that it is choking a university administrator from office without making specific charges against him and allowing him to make a defense."[32]

Speaking off-the-record after the meeting, one of the regents (probably Wilkie) did in fact offer several charges against Frank: he was a "bad" administrator; he had failed to get rid of faculty deadwood and paid incompetent faculty members higher salaries than younger, more effective staff; he had lost the confidence of the regents; and in ten years had "failed to do anything for the university." The political nature of the confrontation was revealed in the comment that the over-

[31]*Octopus*, 18 (December, 1936), 15.
[32]"Open Glenn Frank's Case!" *Daily Cardinal*, December 10, 1936.

whelming vote for Governor La Follette and other Progressives in the recent elections could be taken "as nothing other than a mandate on the part of the voters of Wisconsin to oust Frank." Gordon Sinykin, one of Governor La Follette's secretaries, told reporters Frank had earlier agreed to resign so he could be replaced by July 1, but now had left the matter entirely up to the Board of Regents.[33]

When the regents met again a week later, ostensibly to review Wilkie's budget presentation, the board president used the occasion to spell out the charges against President Frank more formally and fully. They were, generally, that he was a weak and ineffective administrator who had failed to deal decisively with campus problems such as the Snell affair and the recent troubles in the athletic department, that he spent too much time on lucrative speaking and writing engagements and not enough on University business, and that he had abused his University expense account for lavish living. The board agreed to hold a later public hearing on the charges in order to allow Frank time to prepare his defense and adjourned subject to its president's call. By now even the *Capital Times*, the state's major Progressive organ and frequent Frank critic, was complaining that the anti-Frank campaign was being carried on in an atmosphere of "cheap political intrigue."[34] The national press, which with the encouragement of Zona Gale and other Frank friends had begun to cover the case, was skeptical of Wilkie's formal charges, emphasizing that Frank's supporters believed "the real reason for the drive against him is that he is persona non grata to Governor La Follette."[35]

---

[33]*Daily Cardinal*, December 11, 1936. The editors of the *Cardinal* found these explanations insufficient. In a signed editorial entitled "Has Glenn Frank Fulfilled His Duties as University President?" Lester H. Ahlswede, the paper's editorial chairman, reviewed Frank's ten years at the University and found a number of things to criticize. On the other hand, Ahlswede believed the tactics of the anti-Frank regents were disgraceful. "The means which have been employed to oust the president smell to lower depths than any faults of Glenn Frank," he declared. "We reiterate that the regents and the progressive party should bring the matter out into the open. Then, when sufficient grounds for his removal are found, put him out! Sneaking around the bush might eventually accomplish the end, but it is by far the worst method." Ibid. Stung by the *Cardinal*'s criticism, Wilkie wrote the paper denying that any regent had provided a list of reasons for opposing President Frank, but promised: "You may rest assured that the regents do not intend to have any proceeding or action unfair either by reason of notoriety or by reason of any lack of opportunity for open discussion." Wilkie, letter to the editor, December 11, 1936, quoted in ibid., December 13, 1936.

[34]*Capital Times*, December 14, 1936.

[35]*New York Herald Tribune*, December 17, 1936. On Zona Gale's activities in promoting interest in the Frank case in the New York press, see Gale to Glenn and Mary Frank [Decem-

Indeed, the regents' decision to hold a formal hearing over Frank's dismissal brought a storm of criticism from around the state and nation. Too late Phil La Follette discovered why Glenn Frank listed "publicist" as his primary occupation in his entry in *Who's Who in America*. Frank, Bullis, Zona Gale, Madison Mayor James R. Law, and Madison alumni Emerson Ela, Fred Holmes, and Robert B.L. Murphy, among others, mobilized UW alumni and used the president's academic and media contacts to generate widespread sympathy for his plight. The regents and the governor were swamped with angry telegrams and letters and critical editorial comment denouncing the action as a sordid political move, more characteristic of Huey Long's Louisiana than of Old Bob La Follette's Wisconsin. Few believed that the Wilkie bill of particulars on its face warranted the president's firing. For a time the board's secretary, M.E. McCaffrey, was overwhelmed with the task of making and distributing copies of the protesting communications that flooded in upon the board and individual regents. One such letter came from Thomas E. Brittingham, Jr., who reminded the regents how they had "leaned over backwards in our case not to accept gifts with strings attached," and then asked sarcastically how they could now "allow any chance of politics to enter this picture where the strings are so apt to become good-sized ropes?"[36] To cope with the deluge of critical mail at the state capitol Governor La Follette's office had to assign extra clerical help and develop a form response explaining that the regents, not the governor, were responsible for the administration of the University.

Desperate to counter the negative publicity, Governor La Follette seized on a suggestion by President Lotus D. Coffman of the University of Minnesota, who had declared in a protest telegram that no one in education, not even a university president, should be dismissed without a hearing by his peers.[37] On December 21 La Follette dispatched UW chemistry Professor Norris Hall, a personal friend and classmate of President James B. Conant of Harvard University, bearing a letter from the governor requesting that Conant chair a committee consisting of political science Professor Charles E. Merriam of the University of Chicago, and Justice John Wickhem of the Wisconsin Supreme Court, a former UW law professor, to review Frank's performance as president

---

ber, 1936], Frank Papers, Kirksville.

[36]M.E. McCaffrey to each regent, with enclosures, December 19, 1936, Frank Papers, Kirksville.

[37]L.D. Coffman to [unknown], telegram, n.d., ibid.

and advise whether he should be reappointed. In a personally typed letter to Hall, the governor emphasized the need for haste:

> It is vital that if there is to be such an inquirey [*sic*] it should be had at once. For the good of the University dragging this whole business on will do inestimable harm. It should begin not later than early next week....
>
> For the foregoing reason it should be clear that if Conant declines, it is difficult, if not impossible to seek further. His position, his scholarship and his personal integrity makes [*sic*] it possible to turn to him with dignity. We cannot be expected to go from University to University to get someone to take his place—thus entailing inexcusable delay, and the risk of having to accept someone who lacks the very qualities that Conant possesses, but who might nevertheless possess the *outward* paraphanalia of a university administrator.[38]

The governor failed to mention that a number of leading university presidents, including Angell of Yale, Hutchins of Chicago, Coffman of Minnesota, Chase of New York University, Lindley of Kansas, and Graham of North Carolina, as well as Willard Givens, the executive secretary of the National Education Association, and Professor Andrew J. Carlson of the University of Chicago, the president of the American Association of University Professors, had already communicated their concern over the impending dismissal of Frank.[39]

Conant responded promptly declining the delicate assignment. He pleaded the press of university business but said his main reason was that he thought "this is not a question an outside group could answer by an inquiry of two days or, indeed, two months." After the Frank matter was settled Conant promised he would be willing to participate in a review of "the relationship of the board of regents to the State and the whole problem of the independence of the university from any suspicion of political control."[40] Following this rebuff and what La Follette considered Conant's "astonishing" proposal, the governor decided to abandon this damage-control effort and to press ahead with the regents' dismissal hearing as soon as possible.[41]

---

[38]P.F. La Follette to Norris [Hall], December 21, 1936, P.F. La Follette Papers, box 65.

[39]Undated duplicated copies of communications prepared for the Board of Regents [December, 1937], Frank Papers, Kirksville.

[40]James B. Conant to P.F. La Follette, December 24, 1936, P.F. La Follette Papers, box 65; *New York Times*, January 9, 1937.

[41]In a draft prepared for but not included in his published memoirs La Follette recorded with evident satisfaction an encounter he had with Conant some years later when La Follette gave a lecture at the Harvard Business School. Harvard had recently been much criticized for

First, however, La Follette made sure the anti-Frank majority on the Board of Regents would hold. The governor's office engaged in a flurry of last-minute activity when it picked up a rumor that pro-Frank Regent Daniel Grady planned to challenge the legality of the appointment of one of La Follette's recently named regents, Edward J. Brown of Milwaukee, because a certified copy of Brown's appointment had not been filed with the secretary of state as required by law. The governor hastily corrected the omission just as the hearing was about to begin.[42]

The Frank trial took place over two days on January 6-7, 1937, in the regular regents meeting place in the anteroom of the University president's office in Bascom Hall. In order to accommodate the press and the large number of spectators who wanted to attend, initially the regents planned to hold the session in a larger room and had reserved Tripp Commons in the Memorial Union for that purpose. With encouragement from the governor's office, this was vetoed at the last minute by Wilkie on the ground the board wanted to avoid a spectacle. Pleading illness over the Christmas holidays, Frank asked for more time to prepare his defense, but the two anti-Frank members of the regents' Executive Committee—Wilkie and Gates—refused any further delay, evidently agreeing with La Follette that the president was stalling until after the new legislature convened later in the month in the hope it might take an interest in the proceedings.[43] Desperately, Frank used his limited time to develop a factual defense of his administration. He asked Dean Anderson of the School of Education, for example, to review the faculty teaching reports for evidence of recent improvement

---

not renewing the appointments of two economics instructors because of their radical views. During the luncheon Conant had hosted for him, La Follette told him he had with difficulty restrained his impulse "to wire him that I did not feel qualified to pass on those instructors' alleged radicalism but would, if requested, look over the qualifications of Harvard's administration." Conant, La Follette reported, "took it in good part and gave me a delightful lunch." P.F. La Follette Papers, box 124. Conant made no mention of either La Follette's invitation or his luncheon humor in his memoirs, *My Several Lives: Memoirs of a Social Inventor* (New York: Harper & Row, 1970).

[42]*Capital Times*, January 6, 1937; *Wisconsin State Journal*, January 7, 1937.

[43]*Capital Times*, December 21 and 23, 1936; Milwaukee *Sentinel*, December 23, 1936; Oshkosh *Northwestern*, December 23, 1936. The decision not to move the Frank trial to Tripp Commons as initially planned caught editor Evjue of the *Capital Times* by surprise and embarrassment. His regular column on January 6 applauded Wilkie for moving the proceedings to larger quarters. "Certainly the plan being used today," he declared prematurely, "is preferable to the usual plan of holding regents' meetings behind closed doors for the discussion of university policies and certainly, too, Progressive regents should always be the first to ask for the fullest publicity."

in the University's quality. Anderson responded that "any conclusions based upon an analysis of these reports could be shot full of holes." He suggested that Frank "use the declining percent of students dropped from the university as evidence that both teaching and counselling have improved."[44]

The two-day hearing was nothing if not a spectacle. Space in the jammed and sweltering room was saved for the press, a few dignitaries like former Governor Francis McGovern and Carl Beck, the author of "On Wisconsin," and a number of alumni association representatives, including Harry Bullis, Zona Gale Breese, George Haight, Myron Harshaw, and Fred Holmes. They had difficulty getting to their seats through the crush of hundreds of students massed in the hallways outside, who jammed into the open windows of the small hearing room and frequently disrupted the proceedings with applause and sky rocket cheers.

Wilkie and Gates presented the charges against Frank, detailing his allegedly ineffective and absentee leadership and seeking to prove his extravagant living at University expense by itemizing his total income and the cost of the furnishings, maintenance, and automobile use by the Franks since they moved into the unfurnished presidential residence in 1925. Grady led the defense of the president, augmented by former Regent Zona Gale Breese and a number of other alumni witnesses. Well-known as the golden-tongued orator of the board, Grady frequently discomfited Wilkie by his barbed comments suggesting the move to dismiss Frank was dictated and directed by the governor, a charge the board president hotly denied. The cut-and-dried nature of the proceedings was suggested when the board reluctantly decided it would be necessary to extend the hearing into a second day. "We've been stalling long enough," anti-Frank Regent Brown objected. "We should get down to business and get it over with." To this Grady, a strong supporter of Coach Spears in the recent athletic squabbles, snapped, "I don't see why we don't take at least one-quarter of the time in firing a president as you took in firing an athletic coach."[45]

---

[44]"Andy" [C.J. Anderson] to Frank, December 30, 1936, Sellery Presidential Papers, 4/14/1, box 1, UA. This was a slippery basis on which to argue improved institutional quality under Frank's leadership, since there was some reason to question whether University grading standards might be influenced by the need to maintain student enrollment during the depression or whether depression-era students might be more serious about their academic work and grades than their pre-depression counterparts.

[45]*Wisconsin State Journal*, January 7, 1937.

During the second day the board got into a heated argument over how much time to allow testimony from pro-Frank alumni and students. When Wilkie cut off one of the alumni speakers, attorney Harry Adams of Beloit, Adams angrily shook his fist at Wilkie, declaring, "star chambering benefits neither you nor the University." Caryl Morse, in 1936 the first woman ever elected as president of a senior class, said she spoke for the students—"the life blood of the university"—in praising the president's interest in and accessibility to students. Another student, Donald Truax, told the board how in only twelve hours he and a small group of friends had collected twelve hundred student signatures asking that Frank be retained. Immediately after Truax finished, however, James Doyle, president of the 1937 Senior Class, jumped to his feet protesting that it was "utterly presumptuous" for Truax or anyone else to pretend to represent the student body, a presumption Doyle had not hitherto held in his career as a remarkably successful student politician.[46]

Finally, for two-and-a-half hours in the afternoon of January 7 President Frank grimly read parts of an eleven thousand-word statement rebutting his critics and summarizing the achievements of the University under his leadership. He clearly had no hope of influencing the vote, only to leave a record. He chose his final words carefully and aimed them at Regents Wilkie and Gates and Governor La Follette:

> The only thing to which I have entered any protest is the attempt to pass judgment on a university administration in terms of hastily trumped-up charges and details, which even if true, would not be the real answer to the nature of the administration of a university.
>
> I have also protested that you cannot conduct a great state university from outside the board of regents.
>
> It is an unwholesome, unhealthy, anti-American, anti-educational procedure for one or two men on any board to take absolute control over this board and sit in caucus with political leadership for one or two hours preceding practically every important meeting of this board.

Board Secretary Maurice E. McCaffrey then called the roll. By the long-anticipated margin of 8-7, the regents voted to terminate Frank's appointment at the end of June and placed him on a paid leave of absence until that time. They then asked L&S Dean George C. Sellery to assume Frank's responsibilities effective immediately. Reportedly at his request Sellery, who continued his dean's responsibilities, received no

---

[46]See pp. 634-40.

additional salary for taking over as the de facto acting president.[47]

The appointment of Sellery, Frank's most prominent campus critic, was no accident, although the dean told reporters he knew nothing of the regents' intention and thought at first the news of it was a joke.[48] This was perhaps technically accurate but was by no means the whole truth. On December 13 Sellery had declined the suggestion by Regent Mead, a Frank supporter, that he organize his fellow deans to threaten their mass resignation if the regents removed Frank. Sellery told Mead the work of the University must go on and the deans should not get involved in the regents' fight with Frank. Four days later during the evening of December 17, Governor La Follette tracked Sellery down at a dinner party and sent a car to bring the dean, who did not own a car or drive, to the executive residence. La Follette wanted to know if Sellery would serve as acting president if Frank were dismissed. The answer was yes. "Obviously," Sellery later commented drily in his memoirs, "the anti-Frank regents wanted no last-minute complications."[49] Neither, evidently, did Governor La Follette. Contemporaries noted the irony of the governor's reliance on a man whose prominent role in circulating the faculty's "round robin" attack on his father in 1918 had long rankled the La Follette family.[50]

For several weeks in late December and January, the University of Wisconsin received more national news coverage than ever before in its history. The reaction to the regents' trial and dismissal of President Frank was overwhelmingly negative. Throughout Governor La Follette tried to distance himself publicly from the affair, steadfastly denying any direct involvement in the regents' decision. The day after Frank's ouster the governor issued a lengthy public statement defending his actions:

> Throughout this matter I have constantly remembered that it is not the Governor's function to decide what he would do if he were a regent. His duty is confined solely to being satisfied that the regents are acting with good cause and not from improper purposes or from bad motives.

---

[47]The Frank trial received extensive coverage in the national and local press, so much that Governor La Follette's wife Isabel filled two scrapbooks with clippings about the case. The accounts by Morris H. Rubin in the *Wisconsin State Journal*, by Havens Wilber in the *Capital Times*, and by F. Raymond Daniell in the *New York Times* were particularly detailed and comprehensive.

[48]*Wisconsin State Journal*, January 8, 1937.

[49]Sellery, *Some Ferments at Wisconsin*, p. 92.

[50]See, for example, *New York Times*, January 11, 1937.

I am fully aware of the charges of sordid motives and political bias that have been spread broadcast over this State and nation. I am satisfied these charges are unjustified and wholly without foundation. They have been an unjust, if not a malicious, attack upon individuals. But more important than anything else, they have done unwarranted injury to the great University of Wisconsin....

Upon the basis of the whole record, I was and am convinced that the Governor was in no way justified in discouraging or interfering with regents of the university, who at long last decided that a change in administration responsibility was imperative for the welfare of that great institution.[51]

Most commentators, however, blamed La Follette and his Progressive henchmen for what they interpreted as a naked attempt to assert partisan political control over the University. In his memoirs written two decades later, La Follette admitted more family interest and involvement in President Frank's firing, crediting his brother Bob with having "urged me most strongly to back the move to drop Frank at whatever cost to us personally."[52] As the anti-La Follette criticism mounted, the governor's older sister Fola expressed dismay that someone had "bungled matters in ways quite beyond your control with the result that you, Phil, simply have to sit and take it on the chin until time can sift things out....to be pounded like this for something that really isn't *your* fight is a tough break."[53]

Immediately after Frank's dismissal Governor La Follette went to Washington and with his brother, the senator, conferred with President Roosevelt at the White House, ostensibly about relief problems in Wisconsin. The governor's papers contain no correspondence about the purpose of this hastily arranged trip, although at the time the press speculated it was to request F.D.R.'s assistance in persuading Wisconsin Democrats not to join with Republicans in making the Frank case a cause célèbre when the legislature convened. The Progressives lacked a clear majority in either house of the Wisconsin legislature, holding

---

[51]Ibid., January 9, 1937.

[52]P.F. La Follette, *Adventure in Politics*, p. 243.

[53]Fola La Follette to Philip F. and Isen La Follette, P.F. La Follette Papers, box 135. Emphasis in original. The four La Follette siblings were close and corresponded regularly during their adult years. Apart from this and another letter from Fola the next day again commiserating with her brother, there is a surprising absence of family correspondence, and in particular none from brother Bob, in Governor La Follette's personal papers during the several month period surrounding the Frank firing, a time when one would have expected increased contact. The two letters from Fola, of course, supported the governor's public stance of non-involvement in the Frank affair.

only sixteen of thirty-three seats in the senate and forty-six of the hundred seats in the assembly. Whatever the purpose of the trip, enough Democrats subsequently joined with Progressives to allow the governor's party to organize both houses of the 1937 legislature. Some of the Democratic legislators "frankly admitted they had been 'advised' from Washington." Perhaps President Roosevelt likewise did not wish to see Frank's political ambitions advanced by any more Wisconsin martyrdom.[54]

The reaction of the University community to Frank's dismissal was mixed. The next day a thousand students skipped classes and marched down State Street to the capitol demanding to see the governor to protest the firing of their president. La Follette eventually agreed to meet with them in the assembly chambers and distributed to the largely hostile and jeering crowd his press release proclaiming his non-involvement but support of the regents.[55] In a front-page editorial, Wallace T. Drew, the executive editor of the *Cardinal* declined to judge the merits of Frank's presidency or of the regents' hearing, which he called "only a sop to the public." He did, however, praise Frank's firm defense of freedom of the press. "In no case," he emphasized, "even when we criticized his policies severely, has he exercised any form of censorship over us." The next president, Drew thought, would need to possess "Dr. Frank's qualities as a publicist and an administrator, plus, evidently, a quality which Dr. Frank did not have—the ability to reconcile his views with those of the ruling party in the state."[56]

In contrast, the faculty was utterly silent throughout the affair, taking its cue from the deans and the University Committee that this was a matter to be settled between the regents and the president. A few wrote Frank expressing private support and regret; a couple of others congratulated the governor on the result or offered suggestions for avoiding such governance problems in the future. The governor later claimed that Dean Sellery and former Graduate School Dean Slichter had urged him not to weaken in the face of the pro-Frank publicity.[57]

---

[54]See, for example, *New York Times*, January 10, 1937; Raymond Lonergan, "Lonergan's Comment," *Labor*, January 19, 1937.

[55]*New York Times*, January 9, 1937.

[56]Wallace T. Drew, "His Goose Was Cooked," *Daily Cardinal*, January 8, 1937.

[57]See Harold Bradley to Frank [December, 1936]; Ellen Garrison to Mary Frank, Friday [December, 1936], Frank Papers, Kirksville; Julian Harris to P.F. La Follette, January 8, 1937; William G. Rice, Jr., to P.F. La Follette, January 13, 1937, P.F. La Follette Papers, series 5, scrapbook 20 and box 68. See also P.F. La Follette, draft memoirs, n.d., P.F. La

It must have been a bitter disappointment to President Frank that not a single faculty member or University administrator defended him publicly. Not one! The bulk of the faculty had long ago written Frank off as a shallow poseur and were inclined to agree with the editors of the *Nation* that the regents had a right to file for divorce. As in some divorces it was regrettable that the ensuing recriminations were so unpleasant and highly public, but the prevailing campus view was that the proceedings were nevertheless necessary to end a marriage that was no longer the effective union both parties had originally hoped for.[58]

After the Fall

And what of Glenn Frank after the messy "divorce"? He had plainly sought and welcomed martyrdom, but for what purpose? The press was full of speculation the La Follette brothers and other leaders of the Wisconsin Progressive Party fervently hoped Frank would leave the state and pursue any political ambitions elsewhere.[59] For a time the ex-UW president was silent about his plans, enjoying his enemies' discomfiture. In the summer of 1937 he bought a $100,000 home on an eight-acre estate in the exclusive Madison suburb of Maple Bluff and announced he would continue to make his home in Wisconsin.[60] Symbolically, Frank's new home was within a stone's throw of the La Follette family farm. When Joe Coleman, who had bought a fifteen-acre home site from the La Follettes adjoining the Frank property, heard the news, he muttered in dismay: "Now for the rest of my life I'll have to be Belgium!"[61]

At the same time Frank announced he was assuming a controlling interest in and the editorship of the magazine, *Rural Progress*, a monthly publication mailed free to two million midwestern farmers. This would give him a vehicle for promoting his views about American society. "It is obvious that Wisconsin is to be the scene of a bitter duel

---

Follette Papers, boxes 124 and 125; P.F. La Follette, *Adventure in Politics*, p. 242; UW Faculty Minutes, January 11, 1937.

[58]"We Cannot Mourn Glenn Frank's Passing," *Nation*, 144 (January 16, 1937), 59.

[59]See, for example, *Wisconsin State Journal*, January 12, March 16, June 25, 1937; *Capital Times*, July 16, 1937; *La Crosse Tribune and Leader Press*, July 25, 1937.

[60]Frank paid only $40,000, although Madison insurance executive Harry French had spent more than $100,000 in building the large English gothic residence seven years earlier. *Wisconsin State Journal*, July 16 and 17, 1937; *Chicago Tribune*, July 18, 1937.

[61]*Eau Claire Telegram*, July 29, 1937.

between Frank and the La Follettes," Bill Evjue commented in his *regula Capital Times* column. "The ousting of Frank from the presidency of the University of Wisconsin and the manner in which he was ejected has left a sting and Frank will undoubtedly want to settle old scores."[62]

Absorbed in his new publishing venture, Frank stayed on the

"*Hmmm . . .*"

sidelines during the 1938 Wisconsin off-year elections, no doubt gloating as Phil La Follette was trounced for a fourth term as governor by a conservative Republican Milwaukee businessman, Julius P. Heil. Frank's magazine was dependent on advertising revenue and it did not catch hold as he and his backers had hoped. *Rural Progress* appeared at increasingly infrequent intervals during 1938 before suspending publication in the summer of 1939. Meanwhile, Frank accepted former President Herbert Hoover's invitation to head a special policy-making group known as the Republican Program Committee charged

Frank's New Role

with developing a statement of party principles to guide the Republican platform committee in 1940. Frank delayed issuing his committee's report, entitled *A Program for a Dynamic America*, until March, 1940, perhaps hoping it would ignite interest in him as a dark horse candidate for the party's presidential nomination. The report called for a watered down New Deal, one without stifling bureaucratic controls, but like its author the document was too liberal for party conservatives and too bland for many others. As a result the document had little effect on the 1940 Republican platform or the convention. On the night of the presidential balloting Frank had to listen to the cheers for another—successful—dark horse candidate, Wendell Willkie, who ironically was a distant relative of Frank's old Board of Regents adversary, Harold Wilkie.[63]

Following the Republican convention Frank returned to Wisconsin.

---

[62]*Capital Times*, July 16, 1937.

[63]Lawrence H. Larsen, *The President Wore Spats: A Biography of Glenn Frank* (Madison: State Historical Society of Wisconsin, 1965), pp. 161-8.

With only five days before the filing deadline he announced his candidacy for the U.S. senate seat occupied by Young Bob La Follette. Perhaps Frank had concluded that like Woodrow Wilson he would need to demonstrate more active political experience and success at the polls if he were to be considered a serious contender for the White House. Miraculously, in less than a week he and a group of hard-working volunteers accomplished the near-impossible feat of collecting the necessary fifteen thousand signatures comprising at least one percent of the electorate in each of Wisconsin's seventy-one counties. Next he launched a whirlwind speaking campaign, criss-crossing the state seeking to persuade Wisconsin voters to end La Follette rule once and for all. On Sunday afternoon, September 15, 1940, two days before the Republican primary election and an hour late for a speaking engagement in Green Bay, Glenn Frank's speeding campaign car failed to round a turn on Highway 57. Killed instantly were the candidate and his twenty-two-year-old driver, Glenn Frank, Jr., only a year out of Harvard; a sound technician in the back seat was thrown clear and survived his serious injuries.[64]

Thus ended, suddenly and tragically, Glenn Frank's comparatively brief but controversial association with Wisconsin. His prospects for winning the Republican senatorial nomination had been regarded as good. Whether he could have gone on to defeat Senator La Follette, the Progressive nominee, in the general election will never be known. The odds for that were much longer, given the still magical pull of the La Follette name. Nor was the senator so closely identified in the public mind with the highly unpopular action of his brother in dismissing Frank from the UW presidency. Still, Frank was well- and for the most part favorably-known throughout Wisconsin. He probably had at least as good a chance of an upset victory as did the unknown Appleton judge, Joseph R. McCarthy, who defeated La Follette six years later. Had Frank succeeded, what a different course subsequent Wisconsin and national politics might have taken!

How should we, after more than half a century, assess Glenn Frank's UW presidency? First of all, the charges and evidence introduced against him at the regents' "trial" hardly deserved a reprimand let

---

[64]Ibid., pp. 3-6, 168-9.

alone the president's dismissal. There was no attempt to conduct an objective review of Frank's stewardship nor to advise him to correct any deficiencies. Most of the complaints were so vague and petty they might have been made against just about any college or university president at any time. Once La Follette and Wilkie were satisfied they had the votes to oust Frank, their objective seemed more to persuade the public of the president's administrative inefficiency and expensive life style than to influence the Board of Regents, a majority of whose members had already agreed to make the change. One of the members of the anti-Frank majority, Mrs. Clara T. Runge of Baraboo, highlighted the political/ideological nature of the proceedings when she admitted the charges against Frank boiled down to the fact that he had "not been a very good progressive."[65]

It seems clear that Frank's dismissal as president was a political decision made by Governor Philip La Follette and his older brother, Senator Robert M. La Follette, Jr., and carried out by a loyal La Follette agent, Harold Wilkie. Their motives were never spelled out fully, but surely they included first and foremost the desire to remove Frank as a likely future political rival in the state. The La Follettes, senior and junior, had a long history of breaking with anyone they could not dominate or who posed a threat to their leadership of the Wisconsin progressive movement. Frank's liberal political views, his great gift of spellbinding oratory, and his growing involvement in the moderate wing of the Republican Party made him a serious potential threat to the political ambitions of the La Follette brothers and their new Progressive Party. The tragedy was not so much in the substitution of one president for another, for Frank and his successor Clarence Dykstra cannot be ranked with Bascom and Van Hise among the great leaders of the University. Rather the tragedy was the intrusion of raw politics into the management of the University to a degree not seen since President Bascom's battles with Boss Keyes in the 1880s. Old Bob and Belle La Follette, who had always revered their alma mater even while they sought to influence it, deserved better from their sons, whose concern

---

[65]*Wisconsin State Journal*, January 7, 1937. After Zona Gale Breese quoted this conversation at the Frank trial without attributing it to Mrs. Runge, the latter finally admitted that she had made the statement but denied she intended it to be taken in a political context. "I discussed the same question with President Frank," she said. "I don't know just how to put it. I guess I said I was a very sincere progressive, but I didn't intend it to mean anything to do with politics. It's a matter of economics. I've always wanted to protect those who are weaker than others. That's what I meant by the word progressive."

with the University was based more on self-serving politics than any educational vision.

Except for the uniqueness of his highly publicized dismissal, Glenn Frank has been largely forgotten by the University he led for more than eleven years—longer, it should be noted, than any other UW presidents save the revered Bascom and Van Hise. There are no buildings named for him. His official portrait, commissioned by friends after his tragic death, has been relegated to the University Archives rather than placed in the company of other prominent UW leaders whose likenesses grace the walls of the chancellor's office in Bascom Hall. It is as if the University community has accepted unquestioningly the verdict of the La Follette family on Frank's service.

This is another tragedy, for without glossing over Frank's short-comings or making him into something he was not, we need to judge his service fairly and remember his contributions. Such a review involves taking into account that he was hired in 1925 by a progressive-led (but not La Follette-dominated) Board of Regents that was seeking a leader with good public relations skills, one who could improve the image of the University in Wisconsin and nationally and do a better job of getting legislative support for the institution. The regents wanted a prominent outsider of liberal views, someone who was a man of affairs but not necessarily a scholar. Frank, admittedly primarily a publicist, was eminently qualified to carry out this definition of his presidential assignment. In fact, few could have accomplished it better than he did until he had to deal with a hostile Governor La Follette in the 1930s.

Frank's critics were correct in charging that he was not a strong hands-on administrator. He preferred to recruit able deans and other top campus administrators and then delegate responsibility to them for the day-to-day management of their units. Frank's interest in curricular reform stimulated campus-wide thinking about better ways to accomplish the University's educational mission. An idea rather than a detail man, he liked to suggest new approaches and trust others to explore and carry out those worthy of implementation. Whether this was a presidential defect depends on one's view of leadership. That the service of most of his administrative appointees continued to be highly regarded after he left office suggests his judgment was better than his critics allowed. Similarly, Frank did not accept the view of his outside critics that one of his assignments was to get rid of faculty "deadwood." As an outsider himself, he may initially have shared the assumption that the University might be better off without some of the faculty members who did not warm to his reform ideas. He quickly recognized the importance of the tenure system in protecting free inquiry, however, and thereafter resolutely resisted demands to fire controversial professors like Fred MacGregor and Max Otto whose views attracted criticism. His outspoken defense of academic freedom in the classroom and the student press was as much as any member of the University community had a right to expect and more resolute than many of his counterparts on other campuses. One can fault him for not being more persuasive or following up his 1930 proposal for a more functional interdisciplinary organization of the faculty. Nevertheless, in concept it was remarkably similar to the divisional structure adopted by the faculty under Clarence Dykstra's prodding in 1942 and still in effect.

Lastly, we should recognize that Glenn Frank was an early champion of the undergraduate student in a university environment that was coming increasingly to emphasize graduate and advanced professional education and faculty research. His Experimental College was flawed mostly in Alexander Meiklejohn's failure of implementation: Meiklejohn's unwillingness to use it for true experimentation and his self-destructive aloofness in dealing with the regular L&S faculty and its curricular assumptions and requirements. Still, the college's innovative interdisciplinary spirit lives on in the later Integrated Liberal Studies Program, launched after the Second World War. Perhaps *because* Frank was an outsider, a generalist, and not an academic—the very things the UW faculty most held against him—he recognized the need to refocus the undergraduate curriculum to prepare students better to deal with an increasingly complex world. The real tragedy of Glenn Frank's Wisconsin experience is that those same attributes meant his reform ideas played better around the country than they did on Bascom Hill, thereby minimizing his legacy to the University.

President Edward Asahel Birge in 1919

The Board of Regents in 1924-25
Theodore Kronshage second from left; Zona Gale third from right

The La Follette brothers campaigning
Phil and Bob, Jr.

Governor John J. Blaine at Varsity Welcome in 1921

President Glenn Frank in 1927

President Frank and Dean Sellery at Varsity Welcome in 1929
Note their evident coolness

323

The Regents' "Trial" of President Frank in 1937
Note the students jammed into the room

President Clarence Addison Dykstra

324

Agriculture Dean Harry Lumen Russell

Engineering Dean Frederick Eugene Turneaure in 1932

Agriculture Dean Chris Lauriths Christensen

Dean Christensen hosting a cookout in 1941
With Biochemistry Professor Edwin B. Hart and former Dean Russell

Letters and Science Dean George Clarke Sellery in 1932

Mathematics Professor Mark H. Ingraham
Appointed Letters and Science Dean in 1942

327

Dr. William Shainline Middleton
Director of Student Health and Dean of the Medical School after 1935

Extension Dean Chester D. Snell (right)
with Chester Allen, Director of Extension Field Staff

Dean of Men Scott H. Goodnight
Dean of Women F. Louise Nardin

Dean of Women Louise Troxell Greeley

William Ellery Leonard

Aldo Leopold

William H. Kiekhofer

J. Howard Mathews

Carl Russell Fish at Varsity Welcome in 1925

Farrington Daniels

Edwin B. Fred

331

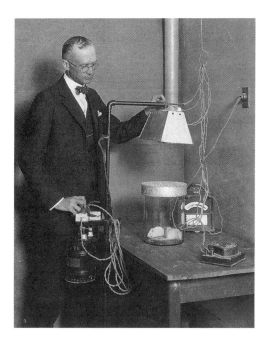

Harry Steenbock

John Steuart Curry and student assistants

The University Club in 1916

The completed University Club after 1925

CCC Camp Madison in the Arboretum

An early WHA Haresfoot broadcast

President Dykstra addressing the war convocation
December 12, 1941

A mass Navy swearing-in ceremony in Great Hall

335

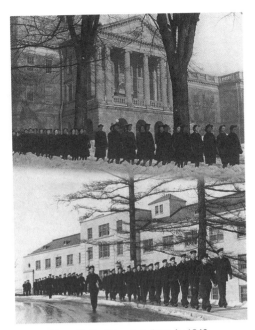

Navy Radio School students in 1943

Army ROTC ski unit on Lake Mendota

6.

The Manager

Governor La Follette's recent electoral triumph notwithstanding, the highly publicized firing of Glenn Frank, almost universally condemned by columnists and editorial writers in Wisconsin and around the country, was a dangerous threat to the governor's further political ambitions. La Follette shrewdly believed the best damage control for the University and his administration was prompt action by the Board of Regents to name a distinguished presidential successor. Meanwhile, he was assured that University affairs were in the capable hands of Letters and Science Dean George Clarke Sellery, whom the regents had asked to fill in for deposed President Frank until a successor could be found. Sellery, it will be recalled, had been recruited by the governor for this role in mid-December of 1936, three weeks before Frank's trial and dismissal.[1]

"Sursum Corda!"

Dean Sellery made it clear to colleagues and reporters he was only "pinch hitting for a semester at most."[2] One of his first acts was to call a special meeting of the University faculty on the afternoon of January 11 to begin the healing process even as the regents set about selecting a new leader. A sizable gathering of two hundred faculty members assembled on short notice to hear Sellery's brief remarks, which lasted

---

[1]Technically, the Board of Regents neglected to give Sellery the formal title of Acting President, merely designating him to carry on the responsibilities of the presidency temporarily while continuing his deanship.

[2]*Wisconsin State Journal*, January 8, 1937.

337

less than fifteen minutes. There were no questions or comments from the floor. Noting that he would not "pass judgment" on the "recent upheaval," Sellery expressed "profound admiration and gratitude" for the way the faculty had kept out of the fight. In this way "the heart and soul of the university" had remained unscathed in what actually was nothing more than an administrative "snarl." It was sometimes forgotten, the dean reminded his audience, that administrators exist "for the sole purpose of enabling the teaching and research staffs to do their jobs. The administrators are in the strictest sense helpers."[3]

Adding that he had accepted this "tough assignment" for the good of the University, Sellery concluded his address with a four-part "profession of faith." First, speaking always as a "faculty man," he reiterated his belief in "the superior wisdom of faculty conclusions in the matters entrusted to the faculty by the laws of the university." He pledged that while acting as president he would try faithfully to represent the "decisions and desires" of his colleagues before the regents. Second, he stressed his commitment to "faculty tenure," mostly as a tool in recruiting "young men of promise and capacity." Third, he dedicated himself to "straightening out certain salary inequities as fast as our means permit." Finally, President Frank's severest faculty critic offered a parting affirmation:

> I believe in the greatness and worth of the University of Wisconsin and of the State of Wisconsin, which created and nurtures it. We are still a great university and we shall continue to advance in greatness and worth with the state. We are both, state and university, sound in heart and head. Do not, I beg of you, sell the University or the State of Wisconsin short! Sursum corda! (Lift up your hearts!)

While these latter professions spoke to nagging faculty concerns, Sellery's first point was a distinct departure. Combined with his introductory remarks, George Sellery as president had proclaimed that henceforth the faculty should occupy the "superior" position in its relations with the administrative "helpers."[4]

---

[3]UW Faculty Minutes, January 11, 1937, UA. For the press release issued by the UW News Bureau, see Sellery Presidential Papers, 4/14/1, box 19, UA, and *Wisconsin State Journal*, January 12, 1937.

[4]Mark H. Ingraham, Sellery's successor as L&S dean in 1942, recognized the implications of Sellery's address: "This was clearly an implied criticism of Glenn Frank and a sermon for his yet unselected successor." Mark H. Ingraham, "The University of Wisconsin, 1925-1950," in Allan G. Bogue and Robert Taylor, eds., *The University of Wisconsin: One Hundred and*

The impetus for greater faculty participation in University governance gained strength as the presidential search proceeded. The regents' resolution dismissing Frank on January 7 included four sections: relieving the president of his duties and responsibilities, designating Sellery temporarily to carry on, defining the presidential search-and-screen process, and requiring that the full board consider any recommendations for the next president. The third point read:

> That the executive committee is instructed to consider and consult with candidates for the office of president of the university but that before making any recommendations to the full board as to a new president, *the committee shall consult the university committee of the faculty.*[5]

This consultative provision established a precedent that in expanded form remains in effect to the present. Ironically, the previous day the faculty members of the Regent-Faculty Conference Committee, whose ranks included Dean Sellery, had issued a statement proclaiming the faculty's collective neutrality with respect to Frank's status.[6] Now the regents—evidently as a quid pro quo as well as a sensible effort to keep peace on campus—were for the first time formally involving the faculty at the beginning (if not the termination) of a presidential appointment.[7]

Only five days after Frank's dismissal the *Wisconsin State Journal* featured on its front page a photograph of Clarence A. Dykstra, the city

---

Twenty-Five Years (Madison: University of Wisconsin Press, 1975), p. 61.

[5]BOR Minutes, January 6-7, 1937, UA. Emphasis added. The full text of the resolution appeared in the *Wisconsin State Journal*, January 8, 1937.

[6]The text read: "Because of the wide circulation in the press of the statement that the silence of the members of the university faculty in the present situation indicates their endorsement of the charges made respecting the administration of the university by Pres. Frank, we, the faculty members of the regent-faculty conference committee, deem it proper to advise you that it is our belief that this statement does not fairly represent the opinion or attitude of the members of the faculty, but that their silence represents rather a considered judgment on their part that the welfare of the university, their highest concern, can best be served under existing conditions, by refraining from public expression of personal convictions." Signers included: Oliver S. Rundell, I.L. Baldwin, R.F. Dvorak, V.C. Finch, E.B. Fred, E.M. Gilbert, E.G. Hastings, W.B. Hesseltine, Asher Hobson, C.L. Jones, A.T. Lenz, E.L. Sevringhaus, M.O. Withey, and George C. Sellery. *Wisconsin State Journal*, January 6, 1937.

[7]One member of the University Committee for 1936-37, historian John D. Hicks, stated in his memoirs: "Our committee was assured by the regents—quite unofficially, of course—that if we would not come to Frank's defense we would be given a voice in the choice of his successor. Actually, we couldn't do anything for Frank—he was beyond help, and we were too divided on that subject anyway." John D. Hicks, *My Life with History: An Autobiography* (Lincoln: University of Nebraska Press, 1968), p. 208.

manager of Cincinnati, accompanying a United Press dispatch reporting he had been contacted about the UW presidency. Revealingly, neither Dykstra nor Regent President Wilkie denied the report, merely declining comment.[8] Claiming authoritative knowledge, the same day the Madison *Capital Times*, which usually had better Progressive sources than the *State Journal*, included the Cincinnati city manager's name among a list of fourteen presidential contenders.[9] The *State Journal* subsequently reported on February 1 that Dykstra remained the leader after the regents Executive Committee had interviewed him and two other men in Chicago. Although Dykstra had by now emerged as the favorite, stated the source, a final decision was some time off.[10] Three days later the paper printed a list of twenty-eight candidates, Dykstra among them, and news that Regents Wilkie, Callahan, and Gates would soon travel east for interviews in New York, Pennsylvania, and Massachusetts.[11] Whether the case or not, it appeared the presidential search had begun to wander.

In company with George Sellery, the University Committee also moved decisively to involve the faculty in the selection process. "CHOOSE PERMANENT PRESIDENT SOON, UNIVERSITY FACULTY ASKS

---

[8]*Wisconsin State Journal*, January 12, 1937.

[9]The presidential contenders were: David E. Lilienthal, Walter Jessup, Robert M. Hutchins, E.B. Fred, John M. Gaus, Lloyd K. Garrison, George C. Sellery, James Landis, Felix Frankfurter, C.A. Dykstra, E.A. Gilmore, George Counts, John Wynant, and Winfred Leutner. Lilienthal was "most prominently mentioned," according to the paper, but Regent President Wilkie declared that no consideration would be given to Frank's successor until after the board meeting of January 20. *Capital Times*, January 12, 1937.

[10]The other two candidates were George A. Works, executive assistant to University of Chicago President Robert Hutchins, and Ernest Oscar Melby, dean of the School of Education at Northwestern University. The article added that the two had been eliminated from further consideration for their own and other reasons.

[11]Interviews with five men had been arranged in advance: Kirtley F. Mather (Harvard), Payson S. Wild, Jr. (Harvard), Warren Weaver (formerly of UW and currently with the Rockefeller Foundation), Ralph Hetzel (Pennsylvania State University), and Ned H. Dearborn (New York University). The other names on the list, about some of whom the regents knew almost nothing, included: C.J. Anderson (UW), Harold Benjamin (University of Minnesota), C.L. Christensen (UW), E.G. Doudna (Wisconsin state normal schools), Dykstra, E.A. Fitzpatrick (Marquette University), E.B. Fred (UW), L.K. Garrison (UW), John Gaus (UW), A.D.S. Gillette (Minnesota public schools), Lynn H. Harris (Bridgewater, Massachusetts), J.D. Hicks (UW), E.O. Melby (Northwestern University), Raymond C. Osborn (Ohio State University), William J. Robbins (University of Missouri), George Selke (St. Cloud College, Minnesota), J.R. Shannon (Indiana State College), J.J. Tagert (University of Florida), J.P. Vaughan (Chisholm, Minnesota), George A. Works (University of Chicago), James B. Taylor, Jr., and J.V. Breitwate (University of North Dakota).

REGENTS," the *State Journal* headlined on February 10. The accompanying article reported a memo recently transmitted to the regents Executive Committee by the University Committee. Forcefully worded, the document urged quick action to forestall institutional drift and defined the faculty's expectations for a leader. "He should be an individual influenced by no loyalties to any political, economic, or social group or doctrine except the doctrine of unbiased inquiry and education based thereon," the committee declared. Nor should any autocrats apply:

> It is the right of the president of the university to attempt to influence the faculty in the direction of his views, but he should not govern by regent mandate or by mere virtue of his presidential office....[He] should give allegiance to the democratic policy of rule.
>
> Any matter of educational policy, or any matter which will directly influence educational policy, should be adopted only after the administration has considered the matter with the faculty.

The ideal candidate should be someone, preferably a scholar, who shared the democratic values of the University of Wisconsin.[12] It appeared that Clarence Dykstra, who was known nationally as the "dictator of Cincinnati" for his forceful leadership during the 1936 Ohio River flood emergency, might not qualify in faculty eyes.

What happened next is unclear. A report in late February told of an offer to Ralph Hetzel, a UW alumnus and the current president of Pennsylvania State University. He apparently declined, however, reportedly because of uncertainty about the tenure he might expect at Wisconsin.[13] On March 2 the *State Journal* quoted a somewhat ambiguous telegram it had received from Hetzel: "Have not presumed to make any statements relative Wisconsin presidency since talk with committee of regents." By now "campus speculation" had begun to center on E.B. Fred, the highly regarded agricultural bacteriologist and dean of the UW Graduate School, "who is said to be the choice of a very large group of the faculty." Fred met all of the criteria set down by the University

---

[12] As traditionally had been the case, the presidential search committee failed to preserve the record of its proceedings, and University Committee papers for this period were not saved. Thus a full text of the University Committee memo probably does not exist, and the *Wisconsin State Journal* article quoting from it is as authoritative a source as there is.

[13] Hetzel had recently served as president of the National Association of State Universities as well as on the executive committee of the Association of Land Grant Colleges and Universities. See *Who's Who in America, 1942-1943* (Chicago: A.N. Marquis, 1942), p. 1062; *Wisconsin State Journal*, February 26, 1937.

Committee, and he boasted an impressive record of faculty citizenship reaching back to 1913. But he also had worked closely with President Frank and owed his appointment as dean to Frank in 1934. His loyalty to Frank might not endear him to some of the regents, particularly in the face of Governor La Follette's enthusiasm for Dykstra. In several meetings with the regents committee, the members of the University Committee stressed the need for a president with strong scholarly qualifications, someone like Dean Fred or physicist John T. Tate, the respected liberal arts dean at the University of Minnesota.[14] The committee's initial coolness toward Dykstra diminished, however, after some members made inquiries in Cincinnati and learned the city manager had "no particular educational theories."[15] In late February the *Capital Times* reported that Dykstra had been or was about to be named president. Asked about the report, Regent Callahan, the lonely pro-Frank member of the Executive Committee, observed with some uncertainty: "I don't know anything about it. Dykstra wasn't offered the job unless the other two members of the committee acted in my absence."[16]

On March 11 the Executive Committee made its oft-heralded decision. That afternoon the *Wisconsin State Journal* published a special extra edition with a banner headline: "Dykstra To Be Offered U. Of W. Post." Although the candidate's willingness to accept a substantial cut in pay—from $25,000 in Cincinnati to the $15,000 limit set by the regents[17]—remained in doubt, the University Committee's concurrence had cleared the way for an offer. As described by the press, Dykstra seemed well qualified to head the University. Though like Glenn Frank he lacked a Ph.D. degree, he had taught at Ohio State University, the University of Kansas, and the University of California at Los Angeles prior to accepting the nation's premier city manager post in Cincinnati. He had continued an active connection with the University

---

[14]*Wisconsin State Journal*, March 3, 1937. For an overview of Tate's career at Minnesota see James Gray, *The University of Minnesota, 1851-1951* (Minneapolis: University of Minnesota Press, 1951), pp. 416-9.

[15]*Milwaukee Journal*, March 14, 1937, and in Clarence A. Dykstra Papers, box 76, UCLA Archives; *Capital Times*, March 9, 1937.

[16]*Capital Times*, February 26, 1937. See also *Wisconsin State Journal*, March 10, 11, and 12, 1937.

[17]President Frank's $20,400 salary had always seemed exorbitant to many Wisconsin citizens on and off campus. Even after the salary was cut by 20 percent in the depression salary waivers, Frank's critics like Governor La Follette and Regent Wilkie thought it still too high. In searching for a successor the La Follette-dominated board accordingly set a lower salary limit of $15,000.

of Cincinnati after moving to Ohio, moreover. His membership in the appropriate scholarly organizations—the American Political Science Association, the American Academy of Political and Social Sciences, and the American Association of University Professors—further confirmed his academic bona fides. Numerous glowing letters of reference had resolved any remaining concerns. One reassuring testimonial, written privately to a UW faculty member, was published in a Madison newspaper:

> He has a fine presence and carries himself well at any social or academic event. He has a good sense of humor and of relative values, both of which have not suffered a bit by the difficulties which he has had to meet. While he is especially fitted academically in sociology and its related fields, he is very widely informed. He could be counted upon to be sympathetic in every phase of university work really worth while. I should say he is a conservative liberal or liberal conservative, whichever you choose, but he has never let his politics enter into his job.[18]

The full Board of Regents ratified the choice a week later on March 18, appointing Clarence Addison Dykstra president at a salary of $15,000. Dykstra was reportedly willing to accept the $10,000 salary reduction for the opportunity to head a major university and, not least, because of political uncertainty about his future in the Cincinnati post. As the Executive Committee noted in its recommendation, the faculty's prerogatives had been respected, indeed expanded:

> We have gone into the matter thoroughly; have investigated and considered many men who appeared to have strong qualifications; have interviewed a considerable number and have conducted a considerable correspondence. *We also, on several occasions, conferred with the University Committee of the Faculty. They made their own investigation and gave us the benefit of their views and the information they had.* We are unanimously of the opinion that Clarence A. Dykstra of Cincinnati, Ohio, is the best qualified of all persons of whom we have any information for the position. We are further of the opinion that he would be an ideal choice. His educational and administrative experience, in our judgment, preeminently fit him for the position. His record is one of great competency and highly successful achievement in every piece of work he has undertaken. His record of public service amply justifies our confidence that he can and will cooperate fully with the ideals and spirit

---

[18]The *Wisconsin State Journal* for March 12, 1937, published the entire letter from which this excerpt is taken. Its author was Herman Schneider, dean of engineering and commerce at the University of Cincinnati, and it was addressed to Schneider's UW friend, F.E. Turneaure, dean of the College of Engineering.

of Wisconsin. *We are fully satisfied that as president he would fully and cordially cooperate with the faculty, regents, staff, alumni, students and all the people of Wisconsin in promoting the best interests of the University and the state.*[19]

The choice was not unanimous, however. Three of the pro-Frank regents—Grady, Gundersen, and Christopherson—abstained, with Grady objecting that despite an earlier understanding, the full board had not been kept advised of the candidates under consideration or of the selection of Dykstra except through the press. "I want to make it very plain that I have never heard the discussion of anyone else, nor have I heard any discussion of the recommendations and qualifications of Mr. Dykstra except through the press," Grady explained with considerable emotion, "and I feel that I am not in a position to vote either in approval or disapproval of this recommendation." Gundersen, a fraternity brother and appointee of Governor La Follette, asked sarcastically whether the appointment had the approval of the governor, to which Wilkie retorted: "It certainly does not have his disapproval." Grady and Gundersen also objected to the plan to put Dykstra on salary before June 30 while Dean Sellery was serving as acting president.[20]   The members of the University Committee subsequently confirmed their part in the selection process, both in comments to reporters and in a report to the faculty.[21]

---

[19]"Report of the Executive Committee to the Board of Regents," March 18, 1937, BOR Papers, 1/1/3, box 50, UA; BOR Minutes, March 18, 1937. Emphasis added. With the messy Frank "divorce" no doubt in mind, the executive committee reminded the board that "this appointment would, of course, be for the year 1937 to 1938 (July 1 to June 30) as is customary in such cases."

[20]BOR Minutes, March 18, 1937. The minutes initially did not include the objections, which were added through an amendment on June 7, 1937, at Regent Grady's insistence. See also *Capital Times*, March 11, 18, and 19, 1937; *Cincinnati Enquirer*, March 12, 1937; *Daily Cardinal*, March 12, 13, 14, 16, and 19, 1937; *New York Times*, March 18, 1937.

[21]Professor Edwin G. Hastings, the University Committee chairman, told reporters he and his colleagues appreciated "the consideration paid them by the Board of Regents executive committee." *Capital Times*, March 10, 1937. Hastings and his five colleagues (Brown, Daniels, Hicks, Roark, and Trumbower) were even more effusive in their annual report to the faculty the next fall:

> The Regents directed its Executive Committee to confer with the University Committee regarding the men who were being considered for the presidency of the university. A number of meetings were held with the Executive Committee of the Regents, and correspondence was had with personal acquaintances of the members of the committee in institutions with which persons being considered for the presidency were connected. The committee received every consideration from

"No Crystallized Ideas or Attitudes"

In contrast to his predecessor, whose arrival in Madison was preceded by months of publicity over his intention to orchestrate an educational renaissance, Clarence Dykstra's approach seemed different. "As yet," the president-elect told a well-wisher, "I have no crystallized ideas or attitudes on the general subject of education. I do have a point of view, and it is this point of view which I must explore further in order to come to conclusions which will give me a direction in which to steer."[22]

Faculty reaction to Dykstra's appointment was mixed. The enthusiasm of one of the "best known and most popular professors," as quoted anonymously by the *Milwaukee Journal*, was at best restrained: "I am rather disappointed in the choice, but I see no good in revealing such." The general view, however, was to withhold judgment and give the new leader a chance. A future colleague in the political science department assured Dykstra of fair-minded support: "John Hicks is now completely 'converted'! You will find him a loyal co-worker. In fact, most of the 'academic' opposition is disintegrating now that it is learning how 'academic' you've really been!" George Sellery sent his felicitations, observing that Dykstra was "certain of a genuine welcome and of cordial and solid support." The *Daily Cardinal* urged the student body to lend its backing, at least initially: "We cannot judge his ability before we know what he will do. Give him a year's chance; then speak the piece. Until

the Executive Committee of the Regents. It has reason to believe that its services were helpful to the Regents and appreciated by them.
UW Faculty Document 537, "Report of the University Committee for the Year, 1936-37," November 1, 1937, UA.
     [22]Dykstra to Morris A. Black, March 31, 1937, Dykstra Papers, box 22, UCLA. The letter does not elaborate on Dykstra's "point of view."

then—cooperate."[23]

President Dykstra quickly began to cultivate the University community. On March 24 the *Daily Cardinal* announced that all faculty members and instructors would soon receive formal invitations to attend a reception for the new leader on Tuesday, March 30, in the Memorial Union's Tripp Commons. To emphasize the unified nature of the welcome, the receiving line would include President-elect and Mrs. Dykstra, Governor and Mrs. La Follette, the regents and their spouses, Acting President and Mrs. Sellery, and President Emeritus Birge and his daughter Anna.[24] The event came off splendidly, with Dykstra steadily shaking hands and exchanging greetings for two-and-a-half hours. In the process he met about two-thirds of the entire UW faculty. As for the press, he knew exactly what to say: "What are my plans? I haven't any on earth except to go to work as soon as I can."[25] Dykstra then returned to Ohio to wind up his affairs there.

"Just So You'll Feel at Home, Mr. Dykstra"

On May 1 President Dykstra and his family were back in Madison to stay, residing temporarily in rooms at the Memorial Union while the Franks prepared to move out of the presidential mansion. The Dykstras' son Franz, the newspapers reported, would enroll at the Wisconsin High School on campus for his senior year. Unlike Glenn Frank, Jr., who had gone to the exclusive Groton prep school before enrolling at Harvard, Franz expected to attend the UW. "I have not yet had time to become as

[23]*Milwaukee Journal*, March 14, 1937; Walter R. Sharp to Dykstra, March 16, 1937, ibid. John D. Hicks, a member of the University Committee, reported in his memoirs that he had favored E.B. Fred for the presidency, but that his opposition to Dykstra had been soft. Hicks, *My Life with History*, p. 208. See also G.C. Sellery to Dykstra, March 20, 1937, Sellery Presidential Papers, 4/14/1, box 15; *Daily Cardinal*, March 25, 1937.

[24]A widower, Birge lived with his daughter Anna, who customarily served as his social hostess.

[25]*Daily Cardinal*, March 31, 1937.

acquainted with Wisconsin's problems as I must be to express very definite opinions," the elder Dykstra modestly told reporters, "but I shall shortly apply myself to an intensive study of them....My chief job is to manage the administration of the university, but I firmly intend to keep my feet on the ground, so to speak, by keeping in contact with all educational trends and problems." Tacitly referring to Glenn Frank's tendency to reorganize the University, particularly Dean Sellery's domain, Dykstra reassuringly added: "The general consensus is that the Letters and Science colleges should retain their integrity...." As for undergraduate education at Wisconsin, the new leader was comfortingly vague: "I am definitely in favor of a solid, substantial education. Education is a serious business and every student should realize this when he starts his college career."[26]

President Dykstra was more assertive in his first formal address to the faculty on October 4, 1937, but his words were just as encouraging. "I need your counsel in orienting myself for the task that lies ahead," he told the gathering.

> It is relatively easy to get acquainted with the history of the University and I have been doing so. It is a magnificent story and its meaning for the university world needs no comment or emphasis from me....But I do not find it quite so simple to analyze and know the university of today or to project its future.

In the body of his talk Dykstra described the cynical yet potentially idealistic generation of depression-era college students whose single remaining faith in institutional life probably resided in the university. Very few would become cloistered scholars. Rather, "ninety nine out of one hundred of our students will become part and parcel of the working world that is to be—the great controlling force in our society." The implications for the University's mission were clear: "the prime obligation of sending out into an unacademic world an increasing number of young people equipped to meet the issues of life in a growingly complex society with high standards of intellectual workmanship." The need was urgent, the challenge great. "And so I ask you," concluded the new president humbly, "to think with me about the problem of where we are in education and where and how we are going. I do not have the answers. Perhaps together we can find them....We are a

---

[26]Ibid., May 1, 1937.

community of scholars."[27]

Lillian Dykstra was also a welcome contrast to her predecessor. Unlike Mary Frank, whose social pretensions had alienated many, Mrs. Dykstra seemed effortlessly to draw the University together. Neighbors recalled that Mrs. Frank had instructed UW grounds keepers to shoot noisy birds out of her trees so she could sleep undisturbed,[28] but after meeting Lillian Dykstra no one could imagine her giving such a brutal order. As the *Daily Cardinal* reported, the new mistress of Olin House soon become known on and off campus as the "gracious first lady of the university." Even more down-to-earth and friendly than her business-like husband, Lillian Dykstra astonished people by apparently remembering the name of every person to whom she was introduced. The Dykstras entertained regularly, but much less formally than the Franks. Monthly "at homes" or "open houses" for the students quickly provided a warmer tone to campus student life. There were also many Dykstra-hosted informal gatherings for the faculty and other University staff members at Olin House, the University Club, and the Memorial Union. Students and staff alike soon came to appreciate the warm simplicity of both Dykstras and their genuine interest in the University, both for what it *was* as well as for what it might *become.*[29]

"The Tradition of Democratic Participation"

"It is the desire of the president not only to maintain the tradition of democratic participation in university affairs by members of the faculty but also to extend and make more general such participation," President Dykstra declared in a memo distributed at the opening of the University faculty meeting on April 4, 1938. More specifically, the president wanted to remind faculty members of an unusual privilege not available to their colleagues at most other universities:

---

[27]UW Faculty Document 534A, "President Dykstra's Address to the Faculty," October 4, 1937. Emphasis in original.

[28]Gertrude Wilson, oral history interview, 1990, UA. On the general problem of rumors about Mary Frank, see Lawrence H. Larsen, *The President Wore Spats: A Biography of Glenn Frank* (Madison: State Historical Society of Wisconsin, 1965), p. 126.

[29]*Daily Cardinal*, October 4, 1938. See also, for example, ibid., June 4, 1939; Erna Brambora Rollefson, oral history interview, February, 1984, UHP; Ira L. Baldwin, oral history interview, 1983, UHP; Gunther W. Heller, oral history interview, 1984, UA; Fannie T. Taylor, oral history interview, 1982, UA.

It is the sincere hope of the president that all will participate to the fullest extent in making nominations [for chairman] within the departments. This procedure will be one of the ways in which a new president may know something of the trends of opinion throughout the colleges.

Dykstra then quoted a University regulation adopted by the regents in 1920:

> The Departmental Committee [consisting of assistant, associate, and full professors] of any department may by ballot express its preference for its chairman, and the entire ballot shall be transmitted by the chairman to the dean of the school or college concerned. The university faculty may prescribe rules governing the nomination of departmental chairmen. The dean of the college or school to which a department belongs, after consultation with the president and after receiving the ballot as herein provided or after affording opportunity for such ballot, shall appoint a chairman from the members of professorial rank....The term of appointment shall be for one year, but there shall be no limit upon the number of consecutive appointments.[30]

No new rule was in effect; the president had merely reminded the faculty of one of its rights, which had mostly been overlooked or ignored for the past two decades.

Dykstra's reminder was of more than symbolic importance, however, and owed much to that staunch defender of the faculty, Dean Sellery. The first rule calling for departmental consultation in the appointment of chairmen, but not including a balloting provision, had come into being in 1910. Adopted by the faculty in June of that year and later included among the University regulations approved by the regents, the provision was one of several contained in the "Final Report of [the] Committee on Improvement of Organization."[31] This report reflected the commitment of then President Charles R. Van Hise to

---

[30]Dykstra, "Memorandum for Announcement on the April 4, 1938, Faculty Calendar," attached as enclosure to "Calendar, Regular University Faculty Meeting, Monday, April 4, 1938," General Presidential Papers, 4/2/2/1, box 4, UA.

[31]"Final Report of Committee on Improvement of Organization, adopted June 6, 1910," UW Faculty Papers, 5/2/2/2, box 3, UA. The BOR Minutes for June 21, 1910, declared: "The dean of the school or college to which a department belongs shall, after consultation with the President of the University and with the departmental committees, appoint a chairman...." Evidently unaware of these earlier actions, in their history of the University, Curti and Carstensen erroneously reported that the regents first adopted the rule in 1920. Merle Curti and Vernon Carstensen, *The University of Wisconsin: A History, 1848-1925* (Madison: University of Wisconsin Press, 1949), vol. 2, p. 351. The 1920 board action, which grew out of a dispute over the chairmanship of the chemistry department, was in reality a restatement of the earlier policy. See BOR Minutes, March 5, 1920; General Presidential Papers, 4/0/3, box 2.

increase faculty participation in University governance and to develop a vital community of scholars at Wisconsin.[32] How often the departments were actually consulted or balloted for their chairmen is unknown, for the latter tended to hold their appointments for many years and even decades in this period. Certainly by the time of Glenn Frank's arrival in 1925 the general practice was for the president and appropriate dean to appoint departmental chairmen without any reference to formally expressed faculty opinion. In 1930, probably despairing of Glenn Frank's frequent meddling in L&S affairs, Dean Sellery sent the president a strong admonitory letter referring to the faculty-regent action of 1910.[33] Frank ignored the message. With a more receptive leader now in office, Sellery thought it time bring up the consultative policy once more:

> May I recall your idea of having all departments unobtrusively asked to make nominations for chairmen this Spring?...Your remarks might well include a hint that you, newly here, would like to know, through these nominations, the slant of opinion in the departments.[34]

Dykstra agreed, thereby helping further to enhance his reputation as a dedicated faculty man.

From the start Dykstra consulted widely with his new colleagues about conditions on campus and possible future directions for University development. An effective manager, he respected the chain of command. One of his earliest assignments to the deans and directors was for each to prepare a status report on his or her unit. The president repeated the request in 1940 and 1942. The result was a continuing institutional self-evaluation that quietly drew numerous faculty members into the process. Equally important, the president read the reports and used them as the basis for writing his own overview papers on the institution. Returning to a long tradition abandoned by President Birge, Dykstra's several biennial reports reflected well on the UW and its scholarly staff. Although intended to inform the regents and the public

---

[32]Among President Van Hise's notable initiatives in this connection were his energetic efforts to establish the University Club in 1906, his oversight of the preparation of the ambitious Campus Plan of 1908, and his support for creating the faculty University Committee in 1916.

[33]Mark H. Ingraham, "The University of Wisconsin," p. 54; [Sellery] to Dr. Frank, n.d., marked received June 11, 1930, Frank Presidential Papers, 4/13/1, box 85, UA.

[34]G.C.S. [Sellery] to Dykstra, March 25, 1938, Dykstra Presidential Papers, 4/15/1, box 17, UA.

regarding the University, the self-evaluations and presidential reports must also have reassured faculty members as to their importance in Dykstra's eyes while at the same time encouraging them to think and act constructively about the institution.[35]

True to his word, President Dykstra took the initiative in educational affairs only after careful consideration. His first major effort began quietly on December 9, 1938, in a meeting with the University Committee. In the course of more general discussion, Dykstra suggested that the committee conduct a formal study "of teaching aims and methods, with special reference to the long-time objectives of university instruction." No decision was reached that day, but the committee took the matter under advisement. The next month Chairman Raymond J. Roark sent the president an "informal memorandum" giving the committee's "tentative opinion." Its advice was both procedural and substantive. Agreeing that the project was entirely desirable, the committee thought "the only question concerns the means by which such study can best be accomplished." Owing to the diversity and dissimilarities of the several schools and colleges, no all-University agency could effectively do the job. Each unit should therefore evaluate its own program, in close collaboration with the appropriate dean, and formal "college committees" should be established to carry on this important function in the future.[36] Dykstra wisely followed this strategy, quietly encouraging curricular reform in several of the undergraduate colleges, especially Letters and Science and Engineering.[37]

Amidst the several curricular reviews in the schools and colleges, especially that of the so-called Daniels Committee of the College of Letters and Science,[38] the University faculty voted on January 8, 1940, to establish a broader and more ambitious study group, the Committee

---

[35]Dykstra to All Deans, Directors of Schools, Directors of Co-ordinate Services, the Comptroller, and Superintendent of Buildings and Grounds, April 2, 1938, General Presidential Papers, 4/0/2, box 7; Dykstra to All Deans and Directors, June 10, 1942, ibid., box 11. See also "Reports of the President of the University of Wisconsin to the Board of Regents and Citizens of the State" [titles vary slightly], December, 1938, December, 1940, January, 1943, May, 1943, and 1944, ibid., box 12.

[36]Raymond J. Roark, for the committee, to Dykstra, January 23, 1939, General Presidential Papers, 4/0/3, box 2. The "teaching aims and methods" quotation is from this letter and thus are Roark's words, not the president's. Other University Committee members at this time were: Charles Bunn, George W. Keitt, Hans Reese, Henry R. Trumbower, and W.F. Twaddell.

[37]See pp. 728-31, 752-5.

[38]See pp. 752-5.

on the Quality of Instruction and Scholarship. There were several recent developments behind its formation. One was that the University was currently under siege by a hostile state government led by stalwart Republican Governor Julius P. Heil. Heil's election in 1938 was partly the result of a backlash against Phil La Follette for having engineered the firing of Glenn Frank.[39] Following Heil's election the Republican legislature and governor purged the Board of Regents of its progressive membership through a forced reorganization and Heil invoked stringent budget-cutting measures, all the while hurling personal recriminations at President Dykstra, whom he doubtlessly saw as the creature of the discredited Progressive governor. Memory of the grave budget crisis of 1932-34, with its precedent-setting involvement of the University Committee in the resulting budget deliberations, stirred faculty leaders to action. In December of 1939 the University Committee proposed that the faculty elect a Special Committee on Financial Stringency to review the situation. The faculty put off conclusive action until its next meeting.[40]

About this same time President Dykstra conferred with and received a draft report from the L&S curriculum review committee. Although its chairman, chemistry Professor Farrington Daniels assured the president that "we have tried to meet in a practical way nearly all the points which you have raised," the scope of the committee's recommendations was more narrow than the president had hoped.[41] He therefore welcomed the recommendation for another special committee, this one able to deal with University-wide issues. In the faculty debate over its establishment Dean Sellery and University Committee Chairman George W. Keitt emphasized the need to study the University's precarious finances. Dykstra, on the other hand, advocated a standing institutional research committee "to study educational problems" more broadly, perhaps in part so he would be better able to respond to critical

---

[39]Paul W. Glad, *The History of Wisconsin*, vol. 5, *War, a New Era, and Depression, 1914-1940* (Madison: State Historical Society of Wisconsin, 1990), p. 558.

[40]UW Faculty Minutes, December 4, 1939; UW Faculty Document 587, "Request for Special Committee on Financial Stringency," December 4, 1939.

[41]Farrington Daniels to Dykstra, December 18, 1939, General Presidential Papers, 4/0/3, box 2. Attached to this transmittal letter was a draft copy of the "Report of the Committee on Curriculum and Educational Procedure (as of December 9, 1939)." See also "Memorandum to Appraisal Committee," n.d., in which President Dykstra expanded his views on educational reform at the University, suggested the formation of a standing committee on institutional research, and offered his evaluation of the December 9 draft of the Daniels Committee report. Ibid.

questions from the Heil administration or possibly to work on University-wide curricular issues. The resulting compromise was approval of a motion requesting the president to appoint a special committee with a loosely defined mission to consult with the University Committee and ultimately to report to the University faculty as a whole.[42]

With this broad faculty approval the University Committee took the initiative and worked closely with the president in setting up the new panel. The central feature was a "Memorandum on the Action and Concept of the University Committee In Recommending the Creation of the Committee on Quality of Instruction and Scholarship." This four-page brief contained two pages of narrative and a four-item appendix outlining the legal basis for the investigation, including quotations from legislation affirming faculty prerogatives in the shaping of educational policy. The University Committee also explained the reason for its December proposal recommending the study: "The reduction in funds appropriated to the University for the current biennium necessitated rapid adjustments within the University, some of which necessarily involve questions of educational policy." The investigation should be wide-ranging—"flexible enough in its organization to permit any reorientation of lines of emphasis or methods of procedure that may seem needful to the new Committee as its work progresses." Since the new committee would "necessarily have both fact-finding and policy-making functions," its personnel should be "broadly representative both as to departments and rank" and inclusive of the "major sub-divisions or fields of concentration in the University," though each member would "be a representative of the entire University." On March 4, "in conjunction with the University Committee," President Dykstra announced the appointment of the twenty-member body, including a five-person executive group, with both bodies chaired by mathematics Professor Mark H. Ingraham.[43]

---

[42]UW Faculty Minutes, January 8, 1940. The successful motion, presented by Professor Hicks, read as follows: "That a Special Committee of the Faculty, to be appointed by the President acting in conjunction with the University Committee, undertake the study recommended by the University Committee, said Special Committee to consist of as many members as the President and the University Committee shall jointly determine. It shall be the duty of this Special Committee to submit for the consideration of the Faculty and the Administration both its findings of fact and its recommendations for the future."

[43]Ibid., March 4, 1940. The continuity between the Daniels and Ingraham committees is illustrated by the fact that on March 4 the University faculty both accepted the L&S-approved report of the former and received word of the appointment of the latter. Also see Dykstra to Dear Sirs (and Madame), March 4, 1940, letter of appointment naming the general committee

As much as anything, the appointment of Mark Ingraham to chair this important committee demonstrated Dykstra's willingness genuinely to share policy-making responsibility with the faculty. Born in Brooklyn, New York, in 1896, Ingraham had earned his Ph.D. in mathematics from the University of Chicago in 1924 after taking his M.A. in the same subject at Wisconsin in 1922. Between 1919 and 1922 he had held various UW instructorships and fellowships, and was assistant professor of mathematics from 1924 to 1926, before accepting a similar position at Brown University. After only a year he was brought back to Wisconsin in the fall of 1927 as a full professor. By 1940 he had developed into one of the two or three most highly respected and experienced faculty citizens with a good deal of University-wide experience.[44] Among other responsibilities, he had served on the University Committee during the severe budget crisis of the early 1930s, on the Graduate School Research Committee from 1935 to 1937, and more recently during 1938-39 had been the president of the American Association of University Professors, the prestigious national faculty organization.[45] In 1939 his proposal resulted in a University Committee study on UW faculty tenure that stood essentially as the last word on the subject locally until the early 1970s.[46] Now Mark Ingraham would oversee the most wide-ranging and substantive institutional self-study yet conducted at the University of Wisconsin.

The Ingraham Committee began work at the University Club in the spring of 1940, consulting first with the University Committee and soon thereafter with President Dykstra.[47] Both, recalled the chairman, "made statements to this Committee which broadened rather than narrowed the

---

and its executive committee (indicated by *): *Mark Ingraham (chairman), J.H. Beuscher, Carl M. Bögholt, George S. Bryan, Norman Cameron, *S.M. Corey, Gilbert H. Doane, William Ebenstein, C.A. Elvehjem, *E.B. Fred, *Einar Haugen, *William B. Hesseltine, F.O. Holt, Merritt Y. Hughes, W.H. Kiekhofer, William B. Sarles, C.H. Sorum, W.E. Sullivan, M.O. Withey, and Frances Zuill. General Presidential Papers, 4/0/3, box 3.

[44] Deans E.B. Fred and George C. Sellery were the other two leading faculty citizens.

[45] Besides serving on the University Committee since 1933, Ingraham had been a member of the Regent-Faculty Conference Committee, the Nominating Committee, a Special Committee on Length of Summer Session, a Special Committee on Group Insurance, and a Special Committee on Sabbatical Leaves. Furthermore, with the exception of 1935-35, when he was on research leave, Ingraham had been the chairman of the mathematics department since 1932.

[46] UW Faculty Minutes, May 1, 1939; UW Faculty Document 584A, "Revised Report on Faculty Personnel Policies," May 6, 1940.

[47] Mark H. Ingraham to Members of the University Committee, March 15, 1940, General Presidential Papers, 4/0/3, box 3.

possible field of its activity."[48] Before long a rigorous program of data gathering and analysis was under way which lasted for months. A year later, on April 7, 1941, the UW faculty received and accepted the committee's general report and a special report on the evaluation of instruction. In November of 1942 the committee submitted an updated general report. The faculty accepted this third and final committee document with little discussion, its attention by now focussed on the Second World War and the rapid changes it was bringing to the campus.[49]

The Ingraham Committee took into account the desires of both the University Committee and the president, although the faculty perspective predominated. Part I of the General Report, for example, spoke mostly to the budgetary themes raised by University Committee Chairman Keitt and Dean Sellery during the faculty debate in January of 1940. This thirty-seven-page document was intended to be informational, consisting of a series of statistical analyses of "changes in income and expenditure and their relationship to enrollment over the past decade, and...how these changes were reflected in altered educational methods." It offered no recommendations for action, suggesting instead that it serve primarily "as a basis for Faculty discussion." Similarly, rather than presenting specific conclusions and recommendations the shorter report on Evaluation of Instruction merely summarized "the present status of objective procedures for comparing the effectiveness of various methods of instruction" and then proposed possible topics of investigation suitable for "one or more interested departments." The committee saw its role more as a stimulus than a shaper of change, noting in the introduction to Part II of the General Report that it expected as much from the "indirect result" of the meetings with various departmental staffs and "the process of self-analysis stimulated thereby as it does from the direct outcome of its report." Ultimately, Ingraham and his colleagues declined to recommend any new faculty legislation, asserting that existing policies were fully adequate to support appropriate faculty and administrative action. Furthermore, "as far as new curriculum changes should be made...the machinery of the faculty

---

[48]UW Faculty Document 615, "Committee on the Quality of Instruction and Scholarship, General Report, Part I," April, 1941, p. 1.

[49]UW Faculty Minutes, April 7, 1941, and November 2, 1942; UW Faculty Document 615; UW Faculty Document 615A, "Report of Sub-Committee on Evaluation of Instruction," April 7, 1941; UW Faculty Document 615B, "General Report of the Committee on the Quality of Instruction and Scholarship, Part II," November 2, 1942.

divisions seems more appropriate than further general faculty action."[50] The report was thus more a victory for responsible faculty governance than for presidential leadership, though this result may not have offended Dykstra.

The four faculty divisions referred to by the Ingraham Committee had recently been organized on an experimental basis in the spring of 1942 and represented a major triumph of the collaborative relationship between President Dykstra and the faculty. The previous fall Dykstra had suggested to the University Committee that it look into "the problem of divisional organizations that might supplement the present college and departmental structure." The challenge was analogous to the institute proposal offered unsuccessfully to the faculty by former President Frank in 1930.[51] This irony was not lost on the *Capital Times*, which in reporting the faculty's adoption of the new divisional structure pointed out that it "was proposed 12 years ago by the late Dr. Glenn Frank."[52] The new scheme, relying on arguments reminiscent of Frank's, established four broad faculty divisions (replacing the seven former graduate divisions): biological sciences, humanities, physical sciences, and social studies. Individual departments and faculty members would be assigned membership in a division according to their teaching and research interests, with overlapping membership possible in interdisciplinary fields like history, philosophy, and mathematics. In grouping faculty with similar interests, the intent was to encourage the exchange of information and ideas across departmental and college lines and thereby promote interdisciplinary collaboration. Each division was expected to administer itself through an elected executive committde according to procedures largely of its own design. The divisions would function primarily as advisory bodies on educational policy and faculty personnel matters, supplementing the academic departments and the several schools and colleges.[53] As the new structure evolved, the four

---

[50]UW Faculty Document 615, p. 2; UW Faculty Document 615A, pp. 1, 2; UW Faculty Document 615B, pp. 2, 21.

[51]See pp. 133-4.

[52]*Capital Times*, March 19, 1942.

[53]UW Faculty Document 643, "Report of the University Committee (Corrected)," March, 1942, p. 1. The desire to create a faculty structure that would encourage and support cross-departmental contacts and interdisciplinary collaboration was a major objective underlying the new divisional structure and explains the unusual provision for membership by individuals and departments in more than one division—a feature abandoned in the late 1960s out of a concern for orderliness and fear of deviating from the "one man-one vote" principle. Largely forgotten by the faculty today, this original objective for more cross-departmental interaction is still

divisional executive committees assumed primary responsibility for advising deans on problems of course duplication and quality and on the qualifications of faculty candidates for tenure. After the initial three-year experimental period, the faculty voted in 1945 to make the divisions permanent.[54] Clarence Dykstra had triumphed where Glenn Frank had failed.

Undoubtedly both President Dykstra's restrained but skillful leadership and his genuine interest in faculty government account for the faculty's approval of the new divisional structure. In 1930 Dean Sellery had effectively opposed President Frank's institutes proposal as a presidential assault on the existing department/college governance structure. In 1942 the dean raised no objection as Mark Ingraham, whom the faculty had re-elected to the University Committee in 1939, presented and successfully defended a remarkably similar plan. Perhaps Sellery and other faculty members had now come to recognize the need for a new faculty structure to deal with the growing complexity and specialization characteristic of the modern research university, a problem to which Glenn Frank had frequently pointed. The crucial difference, however, was Dykstra's willingness to give the faculty control over the planning process, a factor absent in Frank's top-down initiative. Even so, some faculty skepticism remained and was reflected in the debate over the proposal and the addition of a requirement that it be considered experimental until evaluated by the University Committee and reviewed again by the full faculty in 1944-45. President Dykstra may have proposed the divisions, but it was clear they essentially belonged to the faculty.

Another development in 1942 confirmed Dykstra's solid commitment to the "superior" faculty role proclaimed by George Sellery after the firing of Glenn Frank. Ironically, the problem was to select a successor to Sellery himself, who that year had reached the mandatory retirement age of seventy, a limit he had persuaded the regents to adopt while serving as acting president in 1937. A careful administrator, Dykstra developed a list of eleven criteria he thought any successful candidate should possess, and he worked closely with a special regent search committee charged with making the final recommendation to the

---

reflected in the annual spring banquet of the Physical Sciences Division, in which the faculty of this division dine together, receive a report from their elected divisional executive committee, and listen to an after-dinner speaker on some topic of general interest.

[54]UW Faculty Minutes, May 7, 1945.

board. Six letters and science faculty members emerged as leading contenders and the president carefully canvassed the college through its department chairmen. There was a clear consensus: the L&S faculty wanted Mark H. Ingraham to succeed George Sellery as dean.[55] And so a classic faculty man was succeeded by another, one who if possible commanded an even higher degree of respect and allegiance from his fellows. Ingraham shared Sellery's faith in Dykstra's commitment to faculty rule. Many years later Ingraham recalled that Dykstra had "kept raising questions—important ones," but he "clearly believed in faculty control of educational policy and, although he would like to influence, he did not wish to subvert it."[56]

The Legacy of La Follette's "Augean Stables"

The storm over Governor La Follette's decision to fire Glenn Frank left deep political scars in Wisconsin—within the Board of Regents, the legislature, and ultimately the electorate. President Dykstra had been appointed by the La Follette majority among the regents and was in reality the governor's candidate. Inevitably he was tied in the public mind to the La Follette administration. At first this seemed to work to the new president's advantage, as reflected in the quick and easy passage of the governor's biennial budget for 1937-39. Probably to ease the new president's path, for a change La Follette was in a generous mood, recommending that the University receive $770,000 of the $900,000 budget increase it had requested through a series of cordial communications involving the governor, Sellery, Dykstra, and others. Long-time capitol observers must have been reminded of the similarly generous budget accompanying the appointment of Glenn Frank in

---

[55]President Dykstra's list contained these items: "1. One who by hard committee work and devotion to U. has the most intimate knowledge of work of the College. 2. One who has shown flair for admin. even tho recog. scholar & teacher. 3. Capacity for growth. 4. Demonstrated co-operative talents. 5. Well known among universities generally. 6. Has worked with Wisconsin Teachers Assoc. & has their confidence. 7. Has confidence of the faculty of Univ. 8. Has confidence of other deans. 9. Has real grasp of emerging educational problems. 10. Sure footed & man of good judgement. 11. Believes in high standards and also practical education." Dykstra Presidential Papers, 4/15/1, box 80. Dykstra's file on the search and screen process includes resumes of Walter Agard, Farrington Daniels, John Gaus, Mark Ingraham, Robert Reynolds, and W.F. Twaddell, all then serving on the L&S faculty. The file also contains letters from eighteen department chairmen and a list indicating that each chairman had been consulted and his preference. Ibid.

[56]Ingraham, "University of Wisconsin," p. 64.

1925. Thanks to the timely assistance of President Roosevelt, the La Follette Progressives had been able to organize the legislature, which as a result spent little time debating the governor's budget proposals. In mid-April, for example, the assembly debated only ten hours before approving the La Follette budget by a vote of 74 to 19.[57] The senate followed suit in early May, after which Senator Merwyn Rolands, the co-chairman of the Joint Committee on Finance, observed with a mixture of awe and surprise, "We've given the university the best treatment they've ever had in their lives."[58] This was something of an exaggeration, but it reflected the suddenly favorable legislative mood.

Still, resentment over Governor La Follette's heavy-handed tactics in the legislature, at the University, and elsewhere was building. Ultimately it would lead to his defeat and the end of his political career in Wisconsin. The distrust of La Follette was suggested by several legislative proposals concerning the University's Board of Regents. The first of these, introduced in late February by Progressive Senator John E. Cashman and Republican Senator Conrad Shearer, would require senate confirmation of the governor's appointments to the board. Cashman had served as a regent from 1923 to 1930 as an appointee of Governor Blaine but recently had broken with La Follette by defending Frank. He admitted the bill was a direct response to "an incident which took place early this year."[59] Expected La Follette-inspired fireworks failed to materialize at the hearings on the Cashman-Shearer bill, but the *Daily Cardinal* correctly predicted the measure's demise at the hands of the Progressive-controlled assembly, "since it is a back-handed censure of the governor's tactics during the Glenn Frank ouster."[60]

The governor's forces also beat back other bills that reflected growing legislative concern over La Follette's meddling in University affairs. In March Senator James Callan, a Milwaukee Democrat, proposed that the Board of Regents be reconstituted to include fifteen

---

[57]*Daily Cardinal*, April 15, 1937.

[58]Ibid., May 6, 1937.

[59]1937 Senate Bill 136, *Legislative Journal Index*. As reported in the *Daily Cardinal*, March 13, 1937, Cashman explained that the Cashman-Shearer bill was intended to "remove the appointment of members of the board of regents from political maneuvering." Cashman had been a staunch supporter of Robert M. La Follette, Sr., and following the senator's death in 1925 had worked tirelessly, though unsuccessfully, for state funding for a new University library to be named in honor of his political hero. Like Regent Grady, however, Cashman's loyalty to the father did not always extend to his younger son.

[60]*Daily Cardinal*, April 8, 1937.

members, five to be named by the governor, five by UW alumni, and five by the general public.[61] On April 15 Senator Joseph Clancy, a Racine Democrat, supported Callan's measure, calling Frank's ouster "one of the disgraces in the history of the state."[62] Two weeks later the moderate Republican *Wisconsin State Journal* came out in support of the Callan bill, predicting that "political control of the university will remain as long as the chief executive of the state can appoint whom he minds to the board of regents." The *Journal* favored this measure over the Cashman-Shearer plan as well as one recently offered by Assembly-man Francis T. Murphy, a Milwaukee Democrat, that provided for a twelve-member non-partisan Board of Regents elected from the state at large. "In our judgement," the paper declared, the Callan bill "would bring about the best balanced and most representative board of regents possible, and by its divided sources of emanation, would present the best balanced and most stable organization which we could arrive at by democratic political methods."[63]

Senator Edward J. Roethe, a Fennimore Republican, and Assem-blyman James D. Millar, a Menomonie Progressive, co-sponsored the most extreme measure. The Roethe bill proposed to abolish the University Board of Regents along with seven other major and four minor educational governing bodies in favor of a single state board of education. Following the Cashman-Shearer model, the nine members of the new centralized agency would be named by the governor and confirmed by the senate. In late April, the *Daily Cardinal* published pro and con articles, with John Garton of the Young Communist League observing in opposition: "It seems obvious that Senator Roethe's bill is not so

---

[61]1937 Senate Bill 221, *Legislative Journal Index*; *Daily Cardinal*, March 23, 1937. The *Cardinal* also favored regent appointments by three agencies: the governor, the alumni, and the faculty. See editorials in *Daily Cardinal*, January 9, April 28, 1937.

[62]Senator Clancy summarized his fears for the University in crude language: "The quickest way to wreck this institution is to throw it into politics....Huey Long tried it in Louisiana, and I think your governor is trying it here....I wonder if your present president [Dykstra] isn't going to sail into rough waters. I smell a nigger in the woodpile and so do the alumni." *Daily Cardinal*, April 15, 1937.

[63]Like the Cashman-Shearer bill, the Callan bill was, as the *Daily Cardinal* noted on March 23, "another repercussion" of the Frank firing, intended "to take the selection of the board of regents out of politics." See also "Balance the Regents," editorial, *Wisconsin State Journal*, April 29, 1937. In offering his bill on April 12, Assemblyman Murphy promised that "selection of a board through a nonpartisan election is bound to provide only high type, civic-minded men as candidates and ultimate members." *Daily Cardinal*, May 20, 1937; 1937 Assembly Bill 800, *Legislative Journal Index*. The Milwaukee *Sentinel* also advocated the non-partisan election of regents in an editorial reprinted in *WAM*, 38 (April, 1937), 276.

much the product of his love for the masses as it is the byproduct of his enmity for the Progressive governor."[64]

Although the *Wisconsin State Journal* reported that Governor La Follette had instructed his followers to quash the Roethe bill, its supporters kept it alive and under consideration in both houses through July 2, the last day of the legislative session.[65] While the bill never came close to passage, the governor's heavy-handed lobbying with respect to it and other measures inflamed many legislators. Thus when Harold M. Wilkie—a close La Follette advisor and the governor's chief agent on the Board of Regents—testified at a senate hearing against a controversial insurance bill, he was the target of unusually bitter insults and recrimination. At one point Senator Maurice Coakley, a Beloit Republican, sarcastically recalled Wilkie's role in the Frank ouster: "Harold had the job of cleaning the governor's Augean stables, when there was dirty work to be done." Senator Michael Kresky, a Green Bay Progressive, complained that Wilkie was "the high priest" of the Progressive Party and charged he was "enjoying the finest, the fattest retainers ever handed out, while the progressives are in the saddle."[66] It was clear that President Dykstra would have to take into account the lingering political bitterness and division over his predecessor's ouster and his own appointment by Glenn Frank's enemies.

Not surprisingly, Dykstra worked cordially and productively with the La Follette-dominated Board of Regents throughout the remainder of the governor's term. In mid-July Dykstra and Regent President Wilkie jointly presented for board approval the 1937-38 University operating budget. The governor's generous budget recommendation, recently approved by the legislature, for the first time made it possible to reduce the salary waivers in effect since 1932, as well as to provide pay raises to 687 UW employees.[67] Regent Grady had not forgotten the Frank

---

[64]1937 Senate Bill 284, *Legislative Journal Index*; *Daily Cardinal*, April 29, 1937. Leo W. Roethe, the senator's son and a representative of the campus Young Republican Club, supported the measure.

[65]*Wisconsin State Journal*, June 10, 1937; *Capital Times*, June 3, 1937; *Daily Cardinal*, June 4, 1937. By July 2, defeat finally seemed certain, so Senator Roethe filibustered in the successful effort to have his measure die through inaction rather than rejection. *Capital Times*, July 2, 1937.

[66]*Wisconsin State Journal*, May 28, 1937.

[67]BOR Minutes, July 10, 1937. All waivers on the first $3,000 of salary were removed, thus eliminating the burden for 2,300 of the University's 2,700 employees. A modified scale remained in effect for the remaining 400, involving a 15 percent cut on the next $1,000 in salary over $3,000, 20 percent cut on the next $1,000 in salary over $4,000, and 25 percent

affair, however, and regularly reminded his colleagues of their ugly deed until his term expired in early 1938.[68] At the October meeting of the board, for example, Grady strongly objected to Dykstra's proposed salary increase for Dean Sellery because of the latter's cooperation with the La Follette forces in deposing Glenn Frank. Dykstra responded with logic and data, convincing all of the board except the recalcitrant critic.[69] Apart from Grady, Dykstra and the regents carried on with cool efficiency, negotiating with the state Emergency Board over occasional fiscal problems, streamlining the University administrative structure, reinvigorating the depression-ravaged campus building program with federal funds, and generally coping with rising student enrollments.[70]

Meanwhile, Phil La Follette's political support was eroding, though the governor's hubris kept him from sensing his danger. Calling a special legislative session in October, 1937, the governor resorted to even harsher tactics than in the regular session to push through a series of laws informally known as Wisconsin's "Little New Deal." La Follette viewed these measures as the culmination of his administration and a model for reform at the national level. This was probably true enough, but instead of universal praise there were cries of outrage over his heavy-handed tactics. Every daily newspaper in the state denounced the governor's actions. Even the usually supportive *Capital Times* agreed:

> The rights of the minority were swept aside. The last few days were characterized by tactics of the Huey Long variety, and the legislation was railroaded through in shotgun style. Bills were put through the legislative hopper under gag rule that never had an adequate hearing. Members voted on bills they had never read.
>
> It was a week in which we had legislative decrees through pressure exerted from the governor's office. It was a week in which democratic processes were abandoned and an executive dictatorship was in the saddle....there was too much that smacked of Hitler and Mussolini.[71]

---

cut on any salary over $5,000. *Daily Cardinal*, July 13, 1937.

[68]*Daily Cardinal*, January 19, February 3, 1938.

[69]BOR Minutes, October 29, 1937; *Daily Cardinal*, October 30, 1937.

[70]*Press Bulletin*, May 11, 1938; *Daily Cardinal*, June 4, 1938.

[71]Quoted in William T. Evjue, *A Fighting Editor* (Madison: Wells Printing Company, 1968), p. 562. No date; ellipsis in original. For a discussion of the special legislative session of 1937 see John E. Miller, *Governor Philip F. La Follette, the Wisconsin Progressives, and the New Deal* (Columbia: University of Missouri Press, 1982), pp. 101-26.

The portents were not good.

The following year Governor La Follette compounded his problems in Wisconsin by launching a new national party, the National Progressives of America, announcing its formation at a rally on April 28 at the University Stock Pavilion. The full house included many rank-and-file Wisconsin progressives. Ominously, only one of the state's Progressive congressmen and only one prominent progressive from elsewhere attended the rally. Editor Evjue of the *Capital Times* was pointedly absent, as was the governor's brother, U.S. Senator Robert M. La Follette, Jr., whose support for the venture was plainly more formal than enthusiastic. The governor's hundred-minute address was rambling and frequently ambiguous if not incoherent. Toward the end, pointing to the huge blue banner with its white cross-in-circle symbol hanging behind him, La Follette proclaimed: "What we believe in and what we propose is so clear, and so fundamental it can be told without words. It is expressed by a symbol."[72] His meaning was far from clear, however. Critics and troubled supporters alike thought they detected an alarming shift toward fascism, symbolized by what they called the "circumcised swastika" on the new party's banner. Following the official unveiling, La Follette set out to organize party chapters across the country. Nearly everywhere he found reluctant progressives and other liberals, who were much more interested in working with rather than against Roosevelt's New Deal administration. Although discussed widely for a time, the National Progressives of America effectively died aborning.

The La Follettes, father and sons, had always personified and dominated the political movement they led. Relying heavily as had his father on informal support, Phil La Follette lacked a professional grassroots organization to turn out the vote once his image was tarnished. His efforts to organize a national third party in the spring and summer of 1938, moreover, sharply reduced the time and involvement he could devote to campaigning in Wisconsin. He had expected to retire from the governorship at the conclusion of his third term, but reluctantly decided to run again when he discovered that no prominent Wisconsin

---

[72]Quoted in Miller, *Governor Philip F. La Follette*, p. 135; see also ibid., pp. 127-62 for a detailed account of the National Progressives of America. Surprisingly, La Follette thought the Stock Pavilion speech one of his best. He also resented criticism of the "circumcised swastika" symbol, which he and his wife Isabel had devised to indicate the party's commitment to abundance through reform at the ballot box. Philip F. La Follette, *Adventure in Politics: The Memoirs of Philip La Follette*, Donald Young, ed. (New York: Holt, Rinehart and Winston, 1970), pp. 246-56.

Progressive was willing to chance the race in 1938. La Follette's enemies derived much of their considerable energy from the governor's arrogant behavior during the 1937 legislative sessions. A coalition of conservative Republicans and Democrats accordingly dedicated themselves to throwing La Follette and his Progressives out of the state house. They succeeded spectacularly on November 8, when Wisconsin voters elected Milwaukee stalwart Republican Julius P. Heil governor by a 5-3 margin and shifted the political complexion of the legislature well to the right. Although in the past the La Follettes had been able to count on a good share of the Democratic vote, tens of thousands of Wisconsin Democrats crossed party lines to insure Heil's victory.[73] President Dykstra, who in the eyes of many was a creature of the La Follette Progressives, now faced a very different and likely more hostile political environment.

"Come Down To Earth, Mr. Heil"

Julius Heil was hardly a typical Wisconsin politician. Blunt-spoken, quick-tempered, full of bluster, this self-made industrialist had been born in 1876 in Düsmond-on-the-Mosel, Germany, from which his family emigrated to New Berlin, Wisconsin, when he was five. Heil concluded his formal education at the age of twelve to go to work in the local general store. Two years later he became a drill-press operator at the International Harvester works in nearby Milwaukee. Energetic and physically strong, as a young man Heil spent much of the 1890s traveling throughout South America installing welded steel track for street railway systems. Back in Milwaukee in 1901 he founded the Heil Rail Joint Welding Company, which eventually developed into a major manufacturer of dumptruck bodies, road machinery, heating units, and associated heavy equipment. Originally a Democrat, Heil had given his only public service prior to the 1938 election as state director of President Roosevelt's business-oriented National Recovery Administration, which he initially viewed as a "patriotic and stirring program for recovery."[74] During his short NRA tenure Heil managed to raise the ire of at

---

[73]William F. Thompson, *The History of Wisconsin*, vol. 6, *Continuity and Change, 1940-1965* (Madison: State Historical Society of Wisconsin, 1988), pp. 401-13; La Follette, *Adventure in Politics*, pp. 254-6.

[74]Julius P. Heil to General Hugh S. Johnson, telegram, August 2, 1933, Julius P. Heil Papers, box 1, SHSW. For short biographies of Heil see *Dictionary of Wisconsin Biography*

least one official at the Wisconsin Department of Agriculture and Markets for "urging the various lines of trade to organize outside of the N.R.A. code."[75] Heil was his own man.

Like many conservatives, by 1938 Heil was thoroughly disenchanted with both Roosevelt's New Deal and Phil La Follette's progressive programs. In January he told a northern Wisconsin audience he was willing to run against La Follette on the Republican ticket for governor. If elected he promised to "conduct government much as he conducted his own business" and promised "to eliminate unnecessary public jobs," reported the Superior *Evening Telegram.*[76] As the September primary approached, candidate Heil proclaimed a simple platform:

> Wisconsin is a big corporation and needs a man of wide experience. I honestly feel that I have the qualifications and can cut out expenses by this experience. Taxes are piling up so terrifically that we are unable to cope with the situation. Unless the good citizens of our State take a personal interest in the matter we know not when the end will come....Honest labor, farmers and industry have no fight excepting as the politician makes one, for the three are all interested in the same thing—good business. When business is good we all get our part of it.[77]

With the Republican nomination in hand and with Democrats pledged to cooperate, Heil campaigned according to tactics summarized perfectly by one supporter: "Recognize the fact, as the people do, that this should be a campaign primarily to beat La Follette and to replace him with efficient administration, and that you are the man logically to

---

(Madison: State Historical Society of Wisconsin, 1960), p. 166, and *Who's Who in America, 1942-43*, p. 1043.

[75]J.D. Beck to Heil, September 28, October 17, 1933, Heil Papers, box 1. The quotation is from the first letter.

[76]Superior *Evening Telegram*, February 1, 1938.

[77][Heil] to Tom Wileman, August 12, 1938, Heil Papers, box 1. This was a standard statement Heil used in correspondence with his supporters.

render an efficient business administration."[78]

Heil's stunning personal victory in the November 8 general election also carried over into the legislature. The Republicans doubled their previous eight senate seats, leaving them one vote short of an absolute majority, while the GOP captured full control of the assembly.[79] The new administration had a mandate, but exactly for what remained unclear. A Democratic supporter summarized the hopes of Heil's supporters: "It seems the people have faith in you and that you will give them a business administration instead of playing politics as the little 'Fuehrer' of the East Wing in the Capitol has been doing and trust you will clean house properly when you get started."[80] No doubt recognizing the liability of his association with the La Follettes, President Dykstra sent formal congratulations to the governor-elect but remained publicly silent on the election. Heil, who had refrained from making the University an issue in the campaign, replied: "I am very elated over the fine vote of confidence the citizens of Wisconsin gave me, and I want you to know that under my leadership it will be my aim to see that Wisconsin will again take its rightful place among the States." Although the governor-elect concluded by offering his "kindest regards," Dykstra may well have questioned the value of this sentiment in that Heil's signature was stamped rather than signed.[81]

A month after the election the *Daily Cardinal* published a letter from Victor F. Weiss, a Sheboygan junior in the College of Letters and Science. Weiss's progressive leanings were obvious. Headed "Tales of Julius," the piece took the economy-minded governor-elect to task for making a start at accomplishing his major campaign pledge—to reduce state government spending. "Already he has driven 'hard bargains' with the banking commission, the public service commission, and the state board of health," observed Weiss. "Republican papers are hailing him as a politician who keeps his promises." On the other hand, con-

---

[78]Gilbert L. Klein to Heil, September 21, 1938, ibid., box 2. On November 1, on the eve of the election, the Heil campaign sent a form letter to supporters that referred to Phil La Follette as "Emperor" and pleaded: "If you are a believer in a Christian society, such as this Constitution is giving us, won't you please do everything possible to rid this State of such obnoxious men as are heading the Progressive Party at this time?...I am writing this letter because I know you are sincere and want to protect your business and good family for the future." Ibid., box 3.

[79]Thompson, *Continuity and Change*, pp. 401-2.

[80]Jos. M. Theisen, Assemblyman from Sheboygan, to Heil, November 12, 1938, Heil Papers, box 4.

[81]Heil to Dykstra, December 3, 1938, Dykstra Presidential Papers, 4/15/1, box 30.

tinued Weiss, "Julius" had recently promised at the November 30 UW football banquet to recruit championship-caliber high school gridders for the team, regardless of cost, while simultaneously casting "dubious eyes on Wisconsin's safety measures for the prevention of silicosis in industries." While the election was over and Wisconsin citizens should "bury the hatchet and pitch in," Weiss was nevertheless already "fed up" with these and other Heil "adventures."

> But Mr. Heil should also cooperate instead of acting as a brainless idiot....After all, there is a limit to which the intelligence of the electorate may be insulted....Come down to earth, Mr. Heil. The party is over. The people of Wisconsin have placed a great trust in you and it is up to you to try to live up to their expectations.[82]

Informed of Weiss's letter during a budget hearing at the capitol two days later, Heil abruptly halted the proceedings to offer his impromptu reaction. "I wish one of the smart young men from the campus who called me an idiot would come up here and tell me how to do it," exclaimed the offended governor-elect.

> I wish they would help an old fool, these kids who live here on the taxpayers' dollars....If these young people who come to the university, which is supported by the taxpayers' money, would stay there and learn their lessons and not come up here and try to be smart and sarcastic, things would be better.

A seasoned politician might have stopped at this point or ignored the provocation altogether. But Heil, a self-made and free-swinging businessman, was a political neophyte, and he was angry:

> I'm going to have that young man brought before me and if he doesn't belong to the state of Wisconsin I'm going to kick him out of the school....It only makes my blood boil and I resent it, and when it comes to dishing out funds for the university to keep this type on the campus, I won't be so free....I hope this gets back to the university.[83]

It did, immediately.

By press time the next day Clarence Dykstra had already begun trying to manage the potentially dangerous situation. Weiss's letter could not have appeared at a more inopportune time, coming as it did

---

[82]*Daily Cardinal*, December 13, 1938. See also Victor F. Weiss, oral history interview, 1991, UA.

[83]Quoted in *Milwaukee Journal*, December 16, 1938.

only a day after Dykstra had submitted the University's budget request for the 1939-41 biennium to the governor-elect.[84] Informed of Heil's comments, Dykstra immediately spoke with the *Cardinal*'s editor about the "carelessness of the department which receives these letters and asked him whether it would not be wise to keep irresponsible statements, such as this letter, from seeing the light of day." The next day Dykstra issued a press release lamenting "that freedom of speech and freedom of the press result sometimes in an individual expression of pique or animus which gets a publicity all out of proportion to the importance of the individual who utters it." Besides, noted the president, the *Cardinal* had earlier printed a more positive editorial on the governor-elect. "I hope Mr. Heil will see this editorial. It is a representative sentiment. The letter which appeared was the work of an individual and was neither intelligent nor in good taste." At the same time Dykstra wrote directly to Heil. After reiterating his points about freedom of the press and the positive *Cardinal* editorial, the president spoke to his primary concern—the budget: "The case of the University rests on the needs of almost 12,000 students and the requirements of the people of the State as set by the Legislature. We are doing our best to live up to these responsibilities." Dykstra concluded by stressing his cautionary advice to the *Cardinal* and declaring that he looked "forward to further cooperation with you in the near future."[85]

The Weiss incident overshadowed any more positive aspects of the evolving University-Heil relationship. While the governor-elect had attended and spoken enthusiastically at the annual gridiron banquet only three weeks after the election, the context was athletics and Heil's exuberant remarks were meaningless hyperbole.[86] Prior to the publica

---

[84]Dykstra, for the Regents of the University of Wisconsin, to Heil, December 12, 1938, BOR Papers, 1/1/3, box 52; *Daily Cardinal*, December 13, 1939.

[85]A copy of the press release and Dykstra's letter of December 16 to Heil are in Dykstra Presidential Papers, 4/15/1, box 30. This file also contains many press clippings reporting the Weiss incident. The account of Dykstra's admonitory conversation with the *Cardinal* editor appears in Dykstra's letter to Heil.

[86]On December 2, 1938, following the November 30 banquet, Howard I. Potter, president of the Wisconsin Alumni Association, assured Heil: "As mentioned, the University is a great business enterprise (the greatest in the State by far) as well as a great educational institution (and recognized as such throughout the world),—with sympathetic and simple human understanding needed most at this stage of its existence, on the business side." On December 1, 1938, John Berge, executive secretary of the Wisconsin Alumni Association, wrote Heil, construing the Governor-elect's remarks as positively as possible: "Many members from both groups talked to me last night after your speech and told me that they were genuinely grateful

tion of the Weiss letter, Heil probably had known or thought very little about the University apart from its athletic teams. He was not an alumnus; indeed, he had not even attended high school. In his eyes the University was just another of many state agencies whose appetite for public funds needed to be curtailed. Now, suddenly and unexpectedly, the insulting words of a brash young student had brought the University to his attention. The state press gave wide coverage to Heil's emotional reply to Weiss, which in turn triggered many critical editorials and letters. The governor-elect did receive some public and private support, but most commentators sided with the University, questioning Heil's judgment and intentions. For the first time since venturing into politics Heil found himself on the defensive. Soon his attitude toward the University and especially its leadership began to take on a strikingly negative cast.

"The New Broom Has Begun to Sweep"

Governor Heil omitted any direct reference to the University in his inaugural address on January 2, 1939, but the signs were nevertheless ominous. For one, the governor-elect designated Glenn Frank to serve as master of ceremonies. The deposed University president opened the proceedings with his usual graceful but ornate style: "The free people of a free commonwealth, through a free ballot, have chosen the men who are to lead for two years to come." In his own remarks Governor Heil may have had in mind the recent controversy over the Weiss letter: "Some of the individuals have already kicked me over, but I am still the farmer boy blacksmith who intends to cut the costs of Wisconsin state government. At the same time I intend that we shall give efficient and full service to the people." His critics would not deter him from his goal:

> Rigid economy must and will be practiced. Waste and extravagance are at an end. Idleness and indifference in public office must stop. A just and honest administration of state government is imperative. A business government, rather than a political state government, is at hand.

"I am a Christian man," the governor concluded. "I believe in God. I

---

to you for the fine support you pledged the University of Wisconsin." Heil Papers, box 4. Heil's credentials as a sportsman were confirmed by his personal sponsorship of the American bowling team in the 1936 Olympics.

believe in prayer....I pray now to the Almighty God that divine help might be given us all in re-awakening the immortal spirit of 'On Wisconsin'!"[87]

Governor Heil and his staff spent most of January preparing the 1939-41 biennial budget. It proved to be a trying time for both the Heil administration and the University. On January 6, for example, President Dykstra provided some materials and answers to questions raised by the Heil's staff. The only information lacking, he noted, involved "the teaching hours of members of the faculty and the breakdown in time spent for the State at State expense." Dykstra argued that this required an individual-by-individual analysis, but he offered to make himself available to discuss the matter. "We want Mr. Heil and yourself," he told a Heil assistant, "to have every bit of information which you think necessary for an understanding of the University problems." As for the regents' budget request: "The University is asking for nothing for itself either as an institution or as a group of State employees. It is asking only for the funds which seem to be necessary to conduct the public service given to us as a responsibility by the State."[88]

A week later Dykstra met with the governor about the budget. While Heil was cordial enough, Dykstra sensed that the meeting did not go well. Afterwards the concerned president wrote thanking Heil for their conference, adding: "The last word which you dropped while I was in your office this morning troubled me as I made my way out of the Capitol." Contrary to what the governor seemed to believe, Dykstra emphasized that the proposed University operating budget would amount to less than the actual state support for the UW during 1929-31; the only request for increased assistance involved legislatively mandated public service programs.[89] Communications continued at various levels until January 27, when Acting Budget Director Giesel telephoned UW Comptroller Peterson to advise the University to desist in its lobbying. According to a secretary's summary note concerning the conversation, Peterson concluded that things were "'getting frayed along the edges and pretty irritable.' He thinks any effort we might make would be waste effort and do more harm than good—with the governor."[90]

---

[87]A report of the inaugural festivities and the full text of Governor Heil's address appear in the *Wisconsin State Journal*, January 3, 1939.

[88]Dykstra to J.F. Horn, January 6, 1939, Dykstra Presidential Papers, 4/15/1, box 30.

[89]Dykstra to Heil, January 13, 1939, ibid.

[90]Summary note, January 27, 1939, ibid.

By this time the governor had evidently decided how to deal with the University's budget request. The previous evening he had addressed a highly enthusiastic Association of Commerce banquet in Sheboygan. Heil pleased his audience, which included radio listeners, by announcing: "I've started out at the capitol. The new broom has begun to sweep." One area scheduled for sweeping was highway construction. Another was public education:

> We've got to level off the school, university and normal school expenditures. They're too high. I am just as much a sympathizer with education as anyone, but I believe we have gotten to a spot in education where we have to level off....
> I want boys and girls to be educated, to be doctors, chemists, engineers and scientists. But I don't want the universities to make one of every one. Our good professors admit that they have many students down there that haven't any right to be there. Also I believe it is not proper to conduct a solicitation to find students in the 48 states of the Union, just as I told the president of the university.[91]

Four evenings later the governor hinted further of his intentions, this time before the Chamber of Commerce in Kenosha. The University suffered some harsh words. The professors, declared Heil, should be put to work "at least an hour a day, and not like some we've got who work only an hour a week." He was willing to pay for an honest day's work. "I want the finest professors we can get," he said, "and I want the best salaries for our professors, but I want to know that they work for their pay." Concerning President Dykstra's reported ambition to make UW the largest university in the country, Heil noted that it already was sixth while the state ranked only fourteenth in population. "It would be fine to have the largest university," Heil observed skeptically, "if we had the money." Referring to his recent meetings with UW officials over the University's budget request, Heil reported:

> I asked Dr. Dykstra how much does it cost to educate a fellow?...They told me how much money they wanted and how many students they had. They figured out it cost $143 per student.
> Now I don't need a pencil to find out they don't know what they're talking about. They knew I didn't go to school so they thought "we can fool that boy."

Queried by the *Wisconsin State Journal* about his reaction to this

[91]Sheboygan *Press*, January 27, 1939.

charge, President Dykstra wisely had "nothing to say."[92]

Dykstra did respond privately to the governor. He had seen news reports on the Kenosha address, and he realized that inaccuracy in press accounts is common. "I am distressed, however," he told Heil, "with just one item, namely, that you are quoted as having said that the president of the University tried to fool you on figures." Dykstra's denial was categorical: "I want you to know in all sincerity that I never have attempted in any public reporting anywhere or at any time to fool any individual or the public at large." He regretted "that because of the extreme pressure upon your time you and I have not had time to sit down and go over the figures which are in your office." Everything there was accurate. The president expressed confidence that Heil's budget analyst "who has gone over figures with us somewhat, will assure you that we have all of our cards on the table and that we intend to keep them face up." Concluding on a positive note, Dykstra told of repeated efforts by reporters to solicit his reactions to Heil's Sheboygan and Kenosha attacks:

> I have told them just one thing,... "I believe that the Governor and the Legislature will treat the University fairly". I still believe this and am more than anxious to keep in close touch with you and your staff in matters affecting educational policy and educational expenditure in this State. My record elsewhere testifies to economical administration....I am at your service at any time and for any purpose that conceivably might be useful to you.[93]

The appeal came too late.

The next day, February 1, 1939, Governor Heil submitted his proposed 1939-41 biennial budget and addressed a joint session of the legislature. He reported that taken together the state agencies had requested support totaling approximately $96 million. This, he declared, was unacceptable and he had therefore slashed the budget back to $66.75 million, or nearly two-thirds of the requested level. The state, he pointed out, had been operating consistently "in the red for nine straight years" by means of sleight-of-hand accounting maneuvers. Indeed, "it is only by the grace of God and the supreme court that the state general fund is not now completely bankrupt." The sensible way to resolve this scandalous situation, concluded the businessman-governor, was for the state to decrease expenditures and increase revenues.

---

[92]*Wisconsin State Journal* and Milwaukee *Evening Post*, January 31, 1939.

[93]Dykstra to Heil, January 31, 1939, Dykstra Presidential Papers, 4/15/1, box 30.

This he proposed to do forthwith. The bulk of Heil's savings were at the expense of the state penal and correctional institutions, the public teachers colleges, and the University of Wisconsin. For the University, the governor recommended cutting legislative support by slightly more than $1 million below the appropriation for the previous biennium. Viewed another way, the governor had pared the UW request by nearly $7 million.[94] Hard times had returned, and with a vengeance!

During the next month the University administration quietly prepared to fight for its needs. The *Daily Cardinal* published a number of articles and editorials on Heil's budget proposal. The emphasis was critical but the tone largely reasoned and restrained.[95] The governor, for his part, delivered an upbeat UW Founders' Day address over a national NBC radio broadcast. His message emphasized the standard litany of University contributions to the public good: triumphs in vitamin research, advances in dairy science, accomplishments of the School of Commerce and the Bureau of Business Information, and more. Only in one brief passage did Heil allude to his budget treatment of the University:

> The State has been, and always will be, fair in its support of its University. It asks that its contributions be well spent. It asks, as it should ask, for fair returns in service and in teaching for the outlays which it makes. On this philosophy, the University can, and will, continue its success,—a success of which we are all so proud.

Sharing the Founders' Day podium with Heil, President Dykstra made only a single reference to the budget debate by characterizing the University request as merely seeking minimal "sustenance."[96] Dykstra pursued this conciliatory strategy further by hosting a "fete in honor of Heil" at Olin House.[97]

On March 1 Dykstra testified before the legislature's Joint Committee on Finance, arguing in support of a larger but hastily trimmed UW budget proposal. Continuing his conciliatory approach, the president suggested the unpleasant possibility of raising student fees as a means of reducing the University's reliance on state taxpayers. He refused,

[94]The full text of Heil's address appeared in the *Wisconsin State Journal*, February 1, 1939.

[95]*Daily Cardinal*, February 2, 7, 8, and 17, 1939.

[96]Heil, "Founders' Day Address," delivered over NBC Red Network, commemorating 90th birthday of UW, February 6, 1939, Dykstra Presidential Papers, 4/15/1, box 30; *Daily Cardinal*, February 7, 1939.

[97]*Daily Cardinal*, February 26, 1939.

however, to accept criticism of so-called frill language programs in Gaelic and Polish, both of which the legislature itself had recently mandated. This stand brought an eruption of partisan anger in the senate. One Democrat charged that Dykstra's observation was an "intentional slap at the Irish and Polish citizens of the state." Two Progressives retorted that the Heil administration was cynically out to get Dykstra so Glenn Frank could resume the UW presidency.[98] Meanwhile, a diverse and apparently unorchestrated lobbying campaign developed in support of the University involving individual students, parents, the campus Teachers' Union, and the women residents of Barnard Hall.[99] Governor Heil took note of this effort in a Milwaukee speech in mid-March, resurrecting his allegation of the University's intention to become the nation's largest. He added: "I feel this way about Brother Dykstra. It'd be nice if he tended to the affairs of the university instead of trying to spread propaganda throughout the state and try[ing] to coerce me."[100] Once again the president refused public comment. Heil's foot-in-mouth propensity for outrageous comments showed up again in a speech to the Manitowoc Chamber of Commerce, when he declared flatly: "One-third of the 13,000 at Madison ought not to be in school."[101]

The governor did not limit his attention just to the next biennium, moreover. On March 31 he and his two legislative colleagues on the state Emergency Board summarily imposed a 10 percent cut in the University's state funding for the last quarter of the current fiscal year, ignoring the fact that by this time most of the University's costs were fixed for the year. A shocked President Dykstra conferred with the faculty and regents and within the week halted most purchases and imposed a general hiring freeze.[102] On April 4 Dykstra sent a strongly worded protest to the Emergency Board outlining the problems involved in abruptly reducing expenses at an institution whose costs largely involved staff salaries based on contractual obligations. He asserted among other things that the University was being asked to provide a third of the state's savings when it received only a tenth of its funding from state taxes. "May I respectfully request," he concluded in a rather

---

[98]Ibid., March 4, 1939.
[99]Ibid., March 12, 15, and 18, 1939.
[100]Ibid., March 18, 1939.
[101]Ibid., March 29, 1939.
[102]UW Faculty Minutes, April 3, 1939; *Daily Cardinal*, April 5, 1939.

less conciliatory tone, "that since the Legislature is our original responsible financial authority that this problem be put up to it with the suggestion that the cut be applied to all State operations equitably."[103] Ten
days later the frustrated president wrote again to the Emergency Board,
denying Governor Heil's public statement that "even President Dykstra
did not object" to the recent cut. He was, he explained to Heil, confronted with an unpleasant dilemma:

> If I flood the State with protests and stories about the University budget, I
> become a non-cooperator. If I work quietly with you and the Joint Finance
> Committee, word goes out that the University is not in a difficult financial
> position. My attempt to be helpful, therefore, rather than antagonistic reacts
> against the University either way....I am still anxious to work with you for
> the best interests of the State, and I shall continue to try to cooperate if you
> will allow me to.[104]

The governor remained unmoved and on April 25 the Board of Regents
took formal notice of the $86,644 reduction in the current state appro-
priation for the University.[105]

In mid-April the joint finance committee sent its recommended
budget for the next biennium to the assembly for debate. Even though
the committee had raised the University's appropriation by $385,000
over the governor's recommendation, the figure still represented a
reduction of $661,000 from the previous biennium. At the board's
April meeting President Dykstra explained to the regents the "disastrous" implications of this budget, which promised to emasculate both
on-campus instruction and extension programs. Following the governor's lead, joint finance also had rejected the entire UW building appropriation request of slightly over $4 million. The president observed
soberly: "Here in Wisconsin education, rather than other services, is
taking the cut. This is not a wholesome situation." Understandably,
the regents began consideration of alternative revenue sources, of which
the most likely was raising student fees.[106]

This possibility quickly generated strong student opposition, expressing itself in numerous *Daily Cardinal* articles and editorials, a

---

[103]Dykstra to Emergency Board, April 4, 1939, Dykstra Presidential Papers, 4/15/1, box
30.

[104]Dykstra to Heil, April 14, 1939, ibid.

[105]BOR Minutes, April 25, 1939.

[106][Dykstra] to Board of Regents, April 25, 1939, BOR Papers, 1/1/3, box 53; BOR
Minutes, April 25, 1939.

campaign to encourage parental lobbying of the legislature, and, finally, a noisy protest march to the capitol. Attempts by the Progressive minority in the legislature to restore the University's funding to the 1937-39 level backfired in the face of the governor's successful counter-campaign to cut the joint finance recommendation by 5 percent. On May 18 the legislature dealt the University a staggering blow as Heil's "Republican economy bloc" approved a biennial budget that essentially followed the governor's initial request. The result effectively reduced the University's state funding level to that of 1922, a time the institution was teaching half as many students.

Not only did President Dykstra face an extremely challenging fiscal problem, he also had to contend with a rising level of animosity on all sides. Angry students were ruthless in their attacks on the governor. They chided him for his recent off-hand suggestion that the University could save considerable money by canceling all freshman instruction, which he erroneously thought the state normal colleges could easily provide. The May issue of the campus humor magazine *Octopus* included an especially biting "Heil Page," which the *Capital Times* delightedly reprinted for the benefit of off-campus readers. Of Heil's tight-fisted fiscal policy, his characterization of Dykstra as a "politician" and a "stranger," and yet his seemingly inconsistent willingness to send the UW band on a national tour, the *Daily Cardinal* wrote apprehensively: "We are concerned about the attitude of a Wisconsin governor toward the educational resources of this state. A great school can be hurt in two years so seriously that it will take many years to bring it back." For his part Dykstra downplayed such concern, assuring a gathering of parents that "no adversity kills a firmly rooted university."[107] A *Cardinal* reader, no doubt speaking for many on campus, predicted that "Governor Heil's wrecking campaign will fall on him like a load of bricks in 1940." Unfazed by his youthful critics and buoyed by the support he perceived from the general citizenry, the governor threatened to cripple UW construction plans by abolishing the Wisconsin University Building Corporation, which he thought violated the constitutional prohibition against state agencies incurring debt.[108]

---

[107] *Daily Cardinal*, May 21, 1939.

[108] Ibid., May 26, 1939. W.B. Rundell, the cashier of the Farmers State Bank of Hillsboro, assured Governor Heil: "You are absolutely correct about the university and the whole school teacher racket. Let Dykstra squawk all he wants. It is time these school teachers are finding out they are just 'hired hands' like the rest of us. Our directors and stockholders and farmers customers all comment favorably on your policies." May 23, 1939, Heil Papers, box 5.

In this context a beleaguered University administration set about constructing a workable operating budget for the 1939-40 fiscal year. President Dykstra stated the problem in detail before the regents on June 16. The most difficult challenge was to avoid salary cuts in the face of a $323,000 reduction, in the operations category, which supported the instructional program. This was an especially touchy subject for the senior faculty, whose depression salary waivers remained largely unrestored. As Dykstra saw it, two steps were necessary merely to maintain support at its current insufficient level even as enrollment continued to rise. First, the regents must take the unpleasant and controversial step of increasing student fees by $5 per semester. Second, the University must convince the Emergency Board to hand over a $100,000 appropriation (derived from unexpended 1938-39 balances and later raised to $130,000) which the legislature had earmarked for operational and extension uses. The board generally supported this strategy, although Regents Hones and Miller ultimately voted against the budget to protest the need to raise student fees.[109] On June 20 Dykstra wrote the Emergency Board seeking its concurrence.[110] At the same time the president and Comptroller Peterson worked out the final details of the budget, which the regents formally approved on July 11. A subdued President Dykstra told the board, "It is hoped that what has been done to meet our financial situation will be well received by the people of Wisconsin and their official representatives."[111]

This is not to suggest the University was alone in its budget travails; nearly every state agency shared in the misery to some degree and mobilized its defenses as best it could. The legislative deliberations

---

[109]Regent Hones explained his negative vote in the following statement, concurred in by Regent Miller:

I believe the student fee increase is (1) unfair to prospective students whose parents represent the low income workers of the state who sadly need higher educational opportunities to prevent a serious social problem in the future in the state and nation; (2) a violation of the principle of a free educational system; (3) setting a precedent for loading costs of education on students from year to year, reverting our school system back to the old tuition system (this can easily go as far as the rural schools); (4) uncalled for because the Legislature is still in session and I as a member of the Regents do not admit that this deficiency budget is our problem.

BOR Minutes, July 11, 1939.
[110]Dykstra to Emergency Board, June 20, 1939, Heil Papers, box 30.
[111]BOR Minutes, July 11, 1939; Dykstra to the Regents, July 11, 1939, BOR Papers, 1/1/3, box 54.

over the biennial budget and associated appropriation bills were noisy and rancorous, though usually resolved largely to the satisfaction of the parsimonious governor. In the process, however, the Republican-Democratic coalition that had defeated Phil La Follette showed early signs of its ultimate dissolution. Also, old-line Republican leaders were beginning to realize their maverick governor was not a party team player who could be counted on to advance the GOP standard. The governor was plainly his own man—one who too often spoke his mind, frequently even before he made it up. His off-hand proposal to eliminate the freshman class at the University or his undignified name-calling of President Dykstra were embarrassing illustrations of this tendency. They indicated, though, less a deep-seated animosity toward the University than a single-minded, say-anything commitment to the basic goal of reducing state spending.

A Non-Partisan Board of Regents

While anti-La Follette sentiment remained strong, there was still one partisan score involving the University to be settled. On July 18, 1939, the Republican-Democratic coalition in the senate approved a bill introduced by Senator Roethe to revise Chapter 36.02 of the statutes in order to reconstitute the University Board of Regents.[112] Roethe, it will be recalled, had been one of several legislators to advocate a change in the composition of the board in the aftermath of Glenn Frank's dismissal. Now, two years later, he had resurrected a modified and less extreme version of his plan, which called for a board of nine members serving staggered nine-year terms, each appointed by the governor and confirmed by the senate.[113] Senator Nelson (Progressive, Maple) opposed the bill, charging that it would lead directly to the firing of Glenn Frank's successor. "The fate of Pres. Dykstra is not involved in my bill," responded Roethe. "I can see the harassing and haranguing given Dykstra by the governor," countered Nelson. "What other conclusion can you draw? It is just as plain as day."[114] The coalition held firm in

---

[112]All fourteen Progressives voted in opposition. *Capital Times*, July 18, 1939.

[113]Roethe had introduced this revised bill on January 27, 1939, at which time it had been referred to the Senate Committee on Education and Public Welfare. It languished there until July 6, when the senate finally took it up for consideration. Like the 1937 bill, this measure concerned itself only with the University, rather than with the entire state educational establishment. 1939 Senate Bill 41, *Legislative Journal Index*.

[114]*Capital Times*, July 21, 1939. In reporting on the anticipated assembly action on the

the assembly, which on July 27 in the face of bitter Progressive opposition approved the Roethe bill, adding only an amendment providing for the continuing ex officio membership of the State Superintendent of Public Instruction. Declared Assemblyman Andrew J. Biemiller, a Milwaukee Progressive: "This is a political bill. It attempts at one fell swoop to take this university over and put it in charge of people to be appointed by Gov. Heil." Ultimately, he feared, "the purpose of this bill is to give Glenn Frank a job."[115] Roethe characterized such charges as "too ridiculous to warrant more than passing mention." The *Wisconsin State Journal*, which had supported a change in the selection of regents in the aftermath of the Frank firing, agreed: "The governor is aware of the demand throughout the state that the university be divorced from politics. We believe he can be trusted to make appointments of regents that will ensure the separation."[116] The senate approved the amended Roethe bill on August 1, and Governor Heil signed it into law a week later.[117]

The governor had thirty days to name the new board, which he did on August 30th. On September 9 the senate confirmed eight of the nine nominees. The approvals were by wide margins, affirming to some extent the *State Journal*'s sanguine prediction. Only Milwaukee Judge August C. Backus, a sitting regent originally appointed by Republican Governor Walter Kohler, failed of approval. The senators declined to explain their close rejection of this respected veteran regent who had voted against the motion to fire President Frank.[118] This left only Regent Arthur J. Glover to serve as a bridge to the old board. Governor La Follette had named this influential dairyman and editor, a moder-

---

bill, the *Capital Times* of July 26, 1939, offered this editorial warning: "Enactment of the bill will give Gov. Heil power to appoint an entirely new board and obtain the discharge of Pres. Clarence A. Dykstra. Heil has stated that he believes there should be a change at the university."

[115]Ibid., July 27, 1939. Biemiller also predicted: "You say we will have outstanding men appointed to the board. You'll have appointment of Milwaukee Athletic Club type of men with outstanding fronts and that's as far as 'outstanding' will go."

[116]*Wisconsin State Journal*, August 1, 1939. According to this report, Glenn Frank had endorsed the plan as "an honest attempt to create a procedure that will permanently safeguard the state's greatest public institution, its university, from personal or political manhandling by any governor of any party."

[117]Chapter 310, *Wisconsin Statutes*, 1939.

[118]The *Capital Times* for September 6, 1939, reported that Backus was unpopular among the senators and that he might recently have lost support for testifying against a bill to tax certain University property.

ate Republican, to the board in 1937.[119] Mrs. Barbara M. Vergeront, a social service-oriented Republican from rural Veroqua also had an agricultural background. There were four attorneys on the new board: Republican Michael J. Cleary, a onetime state assemblyman and insurance commissioner and currently president of the Northwestern Mutual Life Insurance Company in Milwaukee; A. Matthias Werner, a Sheboygan attorney and businessman and New Deal Democrat; Republican Arthur T. Holmes, the secretary and patent counsel for the Trane Company in La Crosse; and Herman L. Ekern, a long-time La Follette progressive and former state official, now practicing law in Madison and Chicago. Two industrialists rounded out the original list: Walter J. Hodgkins, president of the Lake Superior District Power Company and Michigan Gas and Electric Company; and Frank J. Sensenbrenner, the president of Kimberly-Clark Company of Neenah and almost certainly the most conservative new regent. On September 14 Governor Heil named Judge Backus' replacement, attorney Leonard J. Kleczka, a Milwaukee Democrat, whom Governor La Follette had appointed to a brief term as a regent during 1934-35.[120] Although the new board had a more conservative cast than its predecessor, for those who had feared a board consisting exclusively of hard-shell Republican stalwarts, the caliber and mix of Heil's nominees was a pleasant surprise.

The reconstituted Board of Regents convened for the first time on Wednesday, September 20, 1939, the first day of the new semester. Senator Roethe and Governor Heil were on hand to offer greetings and best wishes. The governor announced that he had selected no one "to repay political debts or to accept dictation from the state capitol." He emphasized: "I am not a dictator and I don't want to be a dictator. All I am interested in is efficiency and that we might have in this efficient set-up a great University that we might make great men and women for tomorrow." Heil advised the board to "be courageous and to mete out justice as you would have justice meted out to you." As for President Dykstra (who had kept his own counsel throughout the reorganization process), he "has done a dynamic job." Dykstra in fact was "an out-

---

[119]Glover had replaced Dr. Gunnar Gundersen of La Crosse, a UW classmate, fraternity brother, and one-time good friend of Governor La Follette, whom La Follette declined to reappoint for a second term because of Gundersen's outspoken defense of President Frank and criticism of his firing. At the same time La Follette had reappointed anti-Frank Regents Harold Wilkie and Robert Baker.

[120]A series of biographical sketches of the new regents may be found in BOR Papers, 1/1/3, box 54, and in *Capital Times*, September 20, 1939.

standing citizen and I like him," proclaimed the now-conciliatory governor. "I don't blame him for fighting for money for the University. That is his job to get the money to run the University of Wisconsin in unhampered fashion."[121]   The board quickly organized itself, naming hold-over Regent Glover as its presiding officer. Adjournment came two hours later, following a productive session that included decisions to seek $150,000 in set-aside funds from the Emergency Board and to inform the assembly of problems associated with an administration-backed bill proposing mandatory military training for all male freshman and sophomore students. Neither of these actions promised to delight the governor, but they were a signal the new board and President Dykstra could work cordially and productively on behalf of the University.[122]

Although many Progressives at first feared the reorganization would transform the University into a docile puppet of the conservative Republican governor and lead to Dykstra's ouster, these concerns evaporated as the president and regents collaborated in defense of UW interests against another Emergency Board assault in the fall of 1939. Dykstra may have had a premonition of further trouble when he prepared his annual presidential address to the faculty on October 2. His tone was pessimistic, his theme the generally dismal outlook at home and abroad. In Europe war was spreading and might engulf much of the continent; at home enrollments and appropriations were down, curricular and facilities problems were mounting, and the legislature had not even fully funded the miserly UW budget. Four days later the Emergency Board highlighted Dykstra's foreboding by warning UW Comptroller Peterson to expect a further 25 percent reduction in state budget allotments for the second half of the fiscal year beginning in January. Official notification of the cut came in mid-November, along with news from Regent Glover that Heil had suggested the regents survey the University, presumably to determine its fiscal "efficiency." Glover demurred, opting instead to continue the new board's emerging practice of being primarily the advocate of University interests and needs rather than playing the watchdog role it had often assumed for the La Follette administration under former Regent Wilkie's leadership. In December the regents quietly negotiated an agreement with the Emer-

---

[121] *Capital Times*, September 21, 1939; *Press Bulletin*, September 27, 1939; *Daily Cardinal*, September 21, 1939.
[122] BOR Minutes, September 20, 1939.

gency Board that accepted the threatened 25 percent cut but also provided $130,000 of the previously withheld set-aside appropriation. The end result was a modest net gain for the University. Under the circumstances it was a considerable triumph.[123]

This episode was indicative of the precarious financial condition of the state treasury throughout 1939-40.[124] Under these exigencies President Dykstra managed University affairs rather well. The new board lent strategic backing, as when in January of 1940 the regents approved Dykstra's resolution clarifying University gift policy as a means of attracting increased funding for research and other activities. Formerly this issue was guaranteed to ignite verbal fireworks, but with Daniel Grady and other La Follette progressives no longer on the board the policy of seeking private support no longer seemed so controversial.[125] The regents also quietly cultivated the governor and his colleagues on the Emergency Board, thereby heading off any further mid-year allotment cuts and providing for a minimally adequate 1940-41 operating budget.[126] Appreciating the power of public opinion, President Dykstra also quietly encouraged students, faculty, and alumni to do what they could.[127] When State Senator W.A. Freehoff (Republican, Waukesha) interpreted these efforts as an "insidious propaganda campaign" against the governor, the president responded innocently, "I haven't heard of such a thing." A *Daily Cardinal* columnist, Gordon Dupee, was more forthright: "Why shouldn't students and faculty members criticize

---

[123]UW Faculty Minutes, October 2, 1939; BOR Minutes, November 18, 1939; Heil, Otto Mueller, and P.B. McIntyre to A.W. Peterson, October 6, 1939; E.C. Giessel to Dykstra, November 18, 1939; Glover, for the Regents, to State Emergency Board, December 6, 1939; Dykstra to State Emergency Board, December 15, 1939; [Dykstra] to State Emergency Board, December 18, 1939, Dykstra Presidential Papers, 4/15/1, box 48. Reports of the set-aside fund varied over time. Beginning at $100,000, the figure rose to $150,000. Ultimately $130,000 ($100,000 for operations and $30,000 for extension programming) were released to the University.

[124]One estimate predicted a statewide revenue deficit of $800,000 by January 30, 1940. See Herman Seide to Heil, December 29, 1939, Heil Papers, box 5.

[125]BOR Minutes, January 19-20, 1940. This policy statement on the acceptance of gifts reaffirmed the 1930 regent action overturning the Grady resolution of 1925, which had spurned support from incorporated educational foundations, especially those funded with "tainted" money by Rockefeller and Carnegie.

[126]Dykstra to Heil, February 29, 1940; "Governor Heil's Speech Before the Rotary Club, Milwaukee, Tuesday, March 12, 1940"; Dykstra to Heil, April 4, 1940, Dykstra Presidential Papers, 4/15/1, box 48. See also BOR Minutes, May 11, 1940; Dykstra to the Board of Regents, May 11, 1940, BOR Papers, 1/1/3, box 55.

[127]Ray Roark to Tom [McLean Jasper], March 1, 1940, Heil Papers, box 5.

Heil's administration if they feel it is not to the best interests of the university?"[128]

The realistic answer was that this governor was temperamental, unpredictable, and dangerous when aroused. In the interest of amicable relations, Clarence Dykstra was not above disingenuous and even groveling behavior in his dealings with Heil. In October, 1939, for example, the president tried to explain away a report that he had associated the governor with Hitler and Mussolini. Speaking to a radio audience about the funding needs of the University, he had observed, "The first step taken in the dictator states has been to cut down university opportunities." The comment was general, but the press immediately interpreted it in the Wisconsin context. "It never once occurred to me that any newspaper would attempt to twist such a statement into an attack on Governor Heil," the president told a Heil assistant afterward. "When I wrote [this passage], Governor Heil never came into my mind at all."[129] With the University's annual budget pending, the following June Dykstra sent the governor two photos from the recent Law Library dedication ceremony, "so that you can see...what a good looking Governor Wisconsin has and how he looks behind a pulpit."[130] Dykstra also sent Heil a printed copy of the governor's commencement address later that month, emphasizing: "The attention you received indicated how completely [the graduates] appreciated what you had to say to them."[131] In response to what was really only a form letter from the Emergency Board thanking Comptroller A.W. Peterson (and other state budget officers) for their cooperation during the 1939-40 fiscal year, Dykstra responded effusively: "I am glad to say...that we have attempted in every possible way to co-operate with the State of Wisconsin...in making our funds do the utmost work for the State. I should like to say further that we shall continue to do this for we want to be helpful in every possible way." He addressed the letter, "Attention: Governor Julius P. Heil."[132]

Sometimes the president stood his ground against the governor.

---

[128]*Daily Cardinal*, March 7 and 9, 1940.

[129]Dykstra, "Station WIBA Broadcast," October 19, 1939; Dykstra to Colonel W.C. Maas, October 12, 1939, Dykstra Presidential Papers, 4/15/1, box 48.

[130]Dykstra to Heil, May 7, 1940, ibid.

[131]Dykstra to Heil, June 19, 1940, ibid.

[132]Heil, Mueller, and McIntyre to Peterson, June 21, 1940, Business Administration Papers, 24/1/1, box 152, UA; Dykstra to Emergency Board, June 24, 1940, Dykstra Presidential Papers, 4/15/1, box 48.

Dykstra resisted Heil most consistently over proposed legislation requiring military training for all male University students. Governor Heil favored it, but Dykstra, whose credentials as an advocate of national preparedness fortunately were unassailable, opposed the idea as unnecessary and impractical. Heil's concern for national security led him to require that all state employees wear photo identification cards while on the job. Dykstra simply declined to enforce this politically unpopular edict until the governor abandoned it.[133] The president was also quick to defend the faculty against criticism from members of the Heil administration. He sent a strongly worded protest to Colonel W.C. Maas, the governor's executive assistant and chief spokesman, after Maas had made extravagant claims that the faculty was under-worked and overpaid:

> Under the circumstances, it seems to me that when you make a statement that you are after the professor who gets $8,000 a year [the top faculty salary at the time was $6,900] and teaches one hour and in that way has time for lecturing and writing books for his own glory and income, you do the faculty of the University irreparable harm and I can find no possible basis for your statement. It is a generalization which does not have even one instance upon which to stand.[134]

Dykstra was more diplomatic in dealing with Governor Heil directly, but he nevertheless sometimes stood firm. When, for example, Heil charged financial malfeasance on the part of University officials in the purchase of lamps for the new Elizabeth Waters women's dormitory, Dykstra quickly defended the University and explained in detail what had actually happened. He concluded, "Minor misunderstandings doubtless arise from time to time, but I am sure they will not be of your or my making."[135]

"No Sectarian or Partisan Tests"

By the late thirties events abroad were obliging the United States to pay increasing attention to world affairs. Italy's attack on Ethiopia, the Spanish Civil War, the creation of the Rome-Berlin Axis, Japanese

---

[133]August Frey, Division of Departmental Research, to All Department Heads, December 8, 1939; Dykstra to Frey, December 14, 1939, Dykstra Presidential Papers, 4/15/1, box 48.

[134]Dykstra to Maas, December 14, 1939, ibid.

[135]Heil to Dykstra, June 6, 1940; Dykstra to Heil, June 7, 1940, ibid.

expansion in Asia, and Germany's incursions into central and eastern Europe concerned many Americans. Public sentiment across the country as well as at the University consistently favored American neutrality in the face of the collapsing world order, however. During the fall of 1939 concern changed to alarm with the startling Nazi-Soviet non-aggression and trade pacts, the lightning conquest and partition of Poland by Hitler and Stalin, the resulting declaration of war against Germany by Great Britain, France, and their allies, and the Soviet invasion of Finland in the winter of 1940. In the United States the Roosevelt administration and Congress edged away from strict neutrality by approving the cash-and-carry sale of munitions to friendly belligerents.

To bolster domestic defenses the House Committee on Un-American Activities—popularly known as the Dies Committee after its chairman, U.S. Representative Martin Dies—mounted a well-publicized domestic search for fascists and especially communists.[135] In November, 1939, Dies Committee investigator Major Hampden Wilson testified about a survey he claimed to have made of fifty colleges and universities, the University of Wisconsin among them. He alleged that a national organization, the American Student Union, was the primary agency for spreading communism on American campuses. Typically, declared Wilson, the ASU opposed ROTC programs and arranged speaking engagements at colleges for "Red" speakers.[136] The *Daily Cardinal* investigated and refuted some of Wilson's claims. President Dykstra and those deans who could be reached either denied any contact with the investigator or could not recall ever hearing of him.[137] As for the ASU, it maintained no chapter in Madison, though the University League for Liberal Action was both an ASU affiliate and an accredited student organization. League President Donald Thayer affirmed ULLA opposition to compulsory military training, but he refused to condemn ROTC, whose program was voluntary at Wisconsin.[138]

---

[135]The Dies Committee was active from 1938 to 1944.

[136]*Daily Cardinal*, November 28, 1939.

[137]A survey of the correspondence files of President Dykstra, L&S Dean Sellery, and Dean of Men Goodnight has revealed no indication of Wilson's presence in Madison nor any contacts with these key UW officials.

[138]*Daily Cardinal*, November 29, 1939. It should be noted that some student liberals at the time suspected ULLA President Thayer of being a secret communist activist who was following the Communist Party's current popular front policy of trying to unite all liberal groups under an anti-war, anti-fascist, pro-U.S.S.R. banner. A native of Cedar Rapids, Iowa, Thayer was

The ULLA was well-known locally for advocating progressive politics, civil rights for Negroes and other minorities, and the peace movement, along with increased state funding of the University. In the spring of 1939 the league had renounced its status as a chapter of the increasingly controversial American Student Union while nevertheless remaining an affiliate. During the Christmas break of 1939 the league hosted the fifth annual national ASU convention, indicating to some observers a closer continuing association with the ASU than appeared on the surface and perhaps a ULLA affinity for communism. Delegates from across the country attended the gathering, with a preponderant representation from New York and the east coast. Robert Lampman, a sophomore from Plover and later a distinguished UW economist, was a Wisconsin delegate and wrote his parents a revealing description of the gathering:

> A few impressions of the convention—it is predominantly an eastern group—mostly New York. Harvard sends one of the outstanding delegations. New York alone can swing anything. I feel (although I have no basis) that the convention has a great majority of people sympathetic to the Young Communist League. The executive secretary, Joe Lash, is leading what seems to be a militant *minority* in opposition to the pro-Soviet group.[140]

One of the invited speakers was Earl Browder, the leader of the American Communist Party, whose well-reported address to an audience of eleven hundred in the new Memorial Union Theater, promised that his party "always will keep us out of war."[141] The *Wisconsin State Journal* reported that John E. Waters of the conservative Constitutional Educational League had asked the U.S. Justice Department to investigate the meeting because the ASU was "on record as planning to sabotage our national defense," including an attempt to "bury the Dies

---

older than the typical UW student and had served in the American Abraham Lincoln Brigade on the loyalist side during the Spanish Civil War. Thayer's behavior in the subsequent fight over ASU affiliation seemed to some of his opponents to involve classic communist tactics. Although Thayer took a prominent role in peace rallies and other ULLA activities in these years, he remains something of a shadowy figure. There are no photographs of him in the annual *Badger*, for example, even in the senior class section of 1942, his graduation year. Leon D. Epstein and Robert J. Lampman, conversations with the authors, December, 1991.

[140]Robert J. Lampman to "Dear Folks," December 29, 1939, Robert J. Lampman Papers, UHP. Emphasis in original.

[141]*Wisconsin State Journal*, December 28, 1939; American Student Union, *Student America Organizes for Peace: Proceedings of the Fifth Annual Convention, Madison, Wisconsin, December 27-30, 1939* (Madison: ASU, 1939).

committee six feet under the ground."[142] For many delegates and observers, the key litmus test for the convention was the debate over the recent Soviet attack on tiny neighboring Finland.[143] The test came up pink as the leadership easily beat back an attempt to brand the U.S.S.R as an aggressor. This, the *Daily Cardinal* declared bitingly, "proved, we believe, more decisively than any Dies committee just what shade of carmine tinctures its ranks."[144] ULLA member and *Cardinal* columnist Leon Epstein agreed: "The ASU now stands, not as a liberal front for peace and democracy, but as a Communist front for the apology of Russia's foreign policy."[145]

The controversial ASU convention assured wide campus interest in a ULLA meeting called for Friday evening, January 12, to elect officers and to consider disaffiliation from the ASU. It promised to be a showdown between the leftist supporters of the Soviet Union and those members of more moderate liberal views.

A Common Student View of Campus Radicals

---

[142]*Wisconsin State Journal*, December 28, 1939.

[143]UW delegate Lampman described the issues and strategy of the debate to his parents before the matter was settled:

> This afternoon the real fight begins—the set-up is this. Side number 1 says—we must denounce Russian aggression because we will be called Communist if we do not. Side number 2 says we must not condemn Russia because by doing that we will be playing directly into the hands of pro-war factions in this country that want us to fight an anti-Soviet war. Now this issue is complicated by the fact that side number 1 (in part) has threatened to walk-out of the convention if we do not condemn Russia—as we have other aggressors in the past (*Germany, Italy, Japan*). Also it is complicated by the difficulty of making the public understand why we take either stand—also by the unfriendliness of the press. The Wisconsin delegation is going to take the lead in a compromise proposal this afternoon. This will be for the sake of unity within the ASU.

Lampman to his parents, December 29, 1939, Lampman Papers. Emphasis in original.

[144]*Daily Cardinal*, January 3, 1940.

[145]Ibid., January 9, 1940.

ULLA member Lampman, who had sought a compromise in the heated debate at the ASU meeting, was now increasingly disillusioned. "I'm pretty disgusted with the ULLA," he wrote his parents the day before the meeting, "and all the talking and arguing and name-calling and howling going on both inside and out."[146] The day of the meeting the *Cardinal* published results of a national student opinion poll that included UW respondents. The featured conclusion was that the great bulk of American college students supported the Dies Committee and thus presumably its suspicion of the ASU. A *Cardinal* editorial set the stage for the evening's confrontation: "If the ULLA quashes the rapidly growing internal desire to 'wash our hands of the ASU,' the campus may proudly point to a haggling band of chronic malcontents and soapbox intellectuals. We hesitate to predict what their 1940-41 dogma will be. Orders from Moscow are so vaciliatory [*sic*] these days."

At the ULLA meeting Leon Epstein, a Beaver Dam senior, offered the formal motion and led the fight to disaffiliate from the ASU. The ensuing four-hour debate, like that at the ASU gathering, was bitter, legalistic, and convoluted. In the end the decision—by a vote of 103 to 74—was to retain the ASU affiliation.[147] Lampman described the meeting as "a very disgusting show of parliamentary mess and argumentative morass."[148] The next day an obviously unhappy President Dykstra declared the league's action was "not representative of student opinion." Dean of Men Goodnight agreed with this assessment, and L&S Dean Sellery commented tersely, "I am disappointed."[149] Leon Epstein's reaction was less reserved. "The University League for Liberal Action now appears primarily as a chapter of the American Student Union," he declared. "The Communists and their sympathizers are entitled to it as their organization, and I hope their liberal 'friends' will let them have it."[150] He thereupon resigned from the organization, followed by Lampman and a good part of the membership.

Shortly afterward Dean Goodnight, the UW official most directly responsible for supervising student affairs, spoke over a local radio

---

[146]Lampman to his parents, January 11, 1940, Lampman Papers.

[147]*Daily Cardinal*, January 13, 1940.

[148]Lampman to his parents, as an addendum to his January 11 letter previously cited, January 13, 1939. He observed with considerable frustration: "In any sort of political organization the hardest thing in the world seems to [be to] get any 2 people talking about the same issue at the same time."

[149]*Daily Cardinal*, January 14, 1940.

[150]Ibid., January 16, 1940.

station. Intending to reassure the public of the moderate character of most UW students, the dean told his listeners that of the eleven thousand young men and women enrolled at Madison, only a tiny fraction—perhaps thirty or forty—were communists. Their numbers were so few, in fact, they "could be put in one end of a box-car for convenient shipment back to New York"![151] Perhaps inadvertently, Dean Goodnight had given public voice to a question that was troubling many: How far should the constitutional guarantee of free speech be extended to communists and others who advocated eliminating that freedom? The dean seemed implicitly to favor some restrictions, with his box car allusion probably intended to reassure Wisconsin parents that their children were not included among the few leftist troublemakers. Surprisingly, no one seemed to read any anti-Semitic or nativist implications into his comment.

The *Cardinal* considered Goodnight's comment worthy of a rare front-page editorial the next day but confessed to some puzzlement about the policy issue involved. "If the dean's statement is sustained," the editors pointed out, "a vital principle of democracy is thrown to the theoretical wolves, and our way of living is undermined. Yet if Communists are protected, our way of living is again undermined. What to do?" *Cardinal* interviews with faculty members revealed on the whole a sturdy devotion to the Bill of Rights. Classics Professor Walter Agard's answer was clear: "I believe in civil liberties and stand by the Bill of Rights." Dean Sellery agreed and would limit this policy only to the extent that legal action became necessary to counter "overt action to overthrow the government." Political scientist Grayson Kirk, soon to leave for Columbia University where he would in time become its president, thought democratic principles should apply: "There should be no abrogation of civil liberties except as the majority of the people feel a need for such action." No fan of Dean Goodnight, the opinionated English Professor William Ellery Leonard took a pragmatic view. The more the communists talk, he observed, the "more ridiculous they become." That being so, how could "any sane man" argue that they should be deported?[152] It remained for *Cardinal* editorial chairman and columnist Edwin Newman, later a nationally prominent television journalist, to put the affair into perspective. Newman had been a UW delegate to the ASU convention, and like Epstein and Lampman he

---

[151]Ibid., January 18, 1940.
[152]Ibid., January 18, 1940.

subsequently resigned from the ULLA when it declined to end its ASU affiliation. Newman nevertheless felt constrained to point out that the recent ASU gathering had broken no laws. If some of its stands ran counter to the views of most Wisconsin residents, "that is no crime: it is, in fact, the essence of democracy to allow disagreement.... We must remember that if, to protect democracy, we deliberately abrogate the civil liberties of any individual or group, we no longer have the democracy we set out to protect."[152]

Whatever his feelings at the time, Clarence Dykstra kept his own counsel until February. "Intolerance is like an epidemic," he then declared in a statement prepared for the national American Legion, an organization hardly noted for its defense of the civil liberties of radicals. "It seems clear to me that the American Legion can do no finer thing for our country than to stand through thick and thin for tolerance and civic liberties."[153] He also gave his support to the new Campus Liberal Association, formed by those who had bolted from the ULLA after its refusal to disaffiliate with the ASU. Dykstra stressed the practical benefits of academic freedom at the University of Wisconsin: "Passage of time has demonstrated that what was called pinkness in Wisconsin was in fact leadership in thinking plus courage to blaze the trail."[154] Without ever publicly rebuking Dean Goodnight, Dykstra made clear his commitment to unfettered civil liberties. After Dies Committee investigator John C. Metcalfe charged at a foundryman's convention in Milwaukee that communists had made great inroads into educational institutions, Dykstra disagreed when he later spoke at the same meeting. "I am convinced that we can get rid of isms and quirks when we get at the causes," replied the president. "Not only is the university the very place where it is most necessary to hear all opinions, but also the place where the reasons for hearing them ought to be advanced."[155]

---

[152]Ibid., January 19, 1940.

[153]Dykstra, "The Dangers of Intolerance," statement prepared for the National Headquarters of the American Legion, Dykstra Presidential Papers, 4/15/1, box 139.

[154]Dykstra, "The University's Challenge to a Liberal Club" [February 28, 1940], ibid., box 155. On the founding and purposes of the Campus Liberal Association, see *Daily Cardinal*, February 24, 25, 27, 28, and 29, 1940; Milwaukee *Sentinel*, February 20, 1940; *Milwaukee Journal*, February 28 and 29, 1940; *Capital Times*, February 26, 1940; *Wisconsin State Journal*, February 29, 1940.

[155]Quoted in Leon Epstein's column, *Daily Cardinal*, February 20, 1940. See also the Milwaukee *Sentinel*, February 17, 1940, for the Metcalfe charge and the following response by President Dykstra: "There are many under the impression that universities are in the business of producing discontent....if we maintain the freedom we prize, then we must exercise the

Dykstra's support of civil liberties needs to be seen in the context of his oft-repeated advocacy of American-style democracy, a theme of his talks around Wisconsin and throughout the country from the start of his presidency. The European war led him to expand his efforts to promote American democratic values, in the process placing the University at the head of a burgeoning national citizenship training movement. In Wisconsin this took the form of a two-month program of talks, classes, and discussion groups directed at preparing young people for the exercise of their rights and responsibilities as voters when they reached full citizenship at the age of twenty-one. The program functioned simultaneously on campus and in nineteen counties, all under the auspices of the University Extension Division. President Dykstra, Wisconsin Supreme Court Justice Rosenberry, and University Extension Dean Holt launched the program before an audience of seven hundred on March 19, 1940. Coincidentally, the student planning committee had chosen the Memorial Union Theater, site of the recent controversial ASU convention, to stage the kick-off event, which WHA Radio broadcast throughout much of the state.[157] The first training program culminated on Citizenship Day, Sunday, May 19, at a colorful voter induction ceremony at the Stadium presided over by Dykstra and witnessed by thousands of Dane County residents and Parents Weekend visitors.[158]

The previous evening the president had spoken to a well-attended banquet of parents and students at the Memorial Union. His words were forceful and timely. "Only this hemisphere is at peace," he pointed out. "Everywhere else throughout the world there is strife, contention, the ugliness of war and the black-out of those qualities and ideals which we here hold dear." Quoting from Hitler's *Mein Kampf*, Dykstra rejected its doctrines for a free people:

> We want to develop men who will get up from their knees, who will stand on their feet, their own feet, who will see with their own eyes, who will think with their own minds, who will speak what they believe, without

---

rights of expression. Only the giving of more light gives us greater desires to understand, and understanding make[s] it possible for us to sit down together and arrive at solutions." The *Milwaukee Evening Post*, *Capital Times*, *Wisconsin State Journal*, and *Sheboygan Press*, all carried reports of Dykstra's comments on February 17, 1940.

[157]The effort resulted from the initiative of University Extension Division Professor Roy J. Colbert, who had run a successful model program in Manitowoc the year before. *Daily Cardinal*, March 19 and 20, 1940.

[158]A total of 591 new voters were scheduled to participate in the induction ceremony, with Justice George B. Nelson administering the oath of citizenship. Ibid., May 19, 1940.

fear or fawning, men competent to act without being driven, men whose souls
are their own. It is because of such a belief that we at the University must
guard freedom as well as truth....In guarding freedom on a university campus
we guard the freedom of all everywhere....

The doctrine of force and of violence has no use for a free educational
system. It closes the door to freedom of teaching and freedom of utterance.
It goes further. It closes the ears of those who might listen to another voice
or another teaching....here on this campus let us adhere to the belief that
freedom makes the free man and the free man helps to guarantee freedom....

Let us, in Wisconsin, have faith in the guiding principle of this University
in the sifting and winnowing process which goes on here in our search
for light and truth. The University is both lighthouse and experiment station.
Let us keep it that way. Unless we preserve the freedom of the University
there will be no freedom outside of its walls. Democracy cannot be preserved by totalitarian processes, even when they pretend to be the very
bulwarks of freedom. Freedom is either sacred and to be maintained at all
hazards, or it is in process of being lost.[159]

Here was the president's response to those, like Dean Goodnight and
Governor Heil, who proposed to cut corners in their defense of liberty.
Dykstra pointed to the Citizenship Day celebration as a more
accurate indicator of student commitment to democratic values: "Tomorrow you will see a ceremony which signalizes the entrance of our
students into the voting obligation. Let those who think of this campus
as a subversive spot consider and ponder these things before repeating
such charges. Let us cultivate the tolerance to which we give lip service."[160] Unfortunately, Governor Heil was unable to attend this event
as he had earlier planned. Had he listened to Dykstra's comments
perhaps he might have been less worried about the threat of student
radicalism.[161]

During the next two weeks German forces overran Belgium,
invaded France, and forced the evacuation of thousands of British and
allied soldiers from Dunkirk in a daring rescue across the English
Channel. Throughout the United States college students responded to
news of the deteriorating international situation with energetic protests
against the growing likelihood of U.S. involvement in the conflict.
Springtime peace rallies had occurred annually at Madison and elsewhere since the mid-thirties. In previous years the tone had strongly

---

[159]Dykstra, "Parents Week-End," notes marked "incomplete," May 18, 1940, Dykstra
Presidential Papers, 4/15/1, box 155.

[160]Quoted in *Milwaukee Journal*, May 19, 1940.

[161]*Chicago Tribune*, Milwaukee *Sentinel*, and *Wisconsin State Journal*, May 19, 1940.

favored neutrality over preparedness, although a free exchange of ideas and viewpoints had flourished to a remarkable degree. In 1940, however, the tone was increasingly strident, with the rallying cry, "Stay Out of Europe!" On May 21 the campus Peace Federation asked the UW Student Board, the recently established student government, to help sponsor an emergency campus rally "to give the student body a chance to protest actively any drift of sentiment toward again involving America in a European war."[162] Numerous other student organizations gave their support for such a meeting. "I see no reason why young people cannot get together to discuss the whole problem of peace and war," commented President Dykstra. "Such a facing of the problem is certainly a good thing, if it is faced and thought out realistically and if their interest is in the future of America rather than in the success of an European ideology."[163]

According to the highly supportive *Daily Cardinal*, the May 23 protest attracted eight hundred participants and supposedly was "the biggest anti-war rally" in University history. Student, labor, and church speakers "were unanimous

The Referee

A Typical UW Anti-War Cartoon

in expressing a determination to 'keep out of foreign wars'," and "almost equally unanimous" in opposing "'huge and hasty increases in military expenditures'." Many of the speakers argued that American resources should be devoted exclusively to solving American problems. Thus Edward Nestigen, secretary of the campus YMCA and a ULLA activist, promised: "We must fight for democracy at home, and not on a European battlefield." Similarly, the former president of the Youth Committee Against War invoked fears of a conscripted army, declaring, "while we have the freedom to talk against war, we must fight it."

---

[162]*Daily Cardinal*, May 21, 1940.
[163]Ibid., May 23, 1940.

ULLA President Donald Thayer offered the ULLA/ASU slant on why neutrality was the right policy for America: "Labor and students have long been crushed in France, and now even England has become a totalitarian state."[164] The two Madison newspapers reported the rally as if it were two different events. The *Wisconsin State Journal* emphasized the failure of inclement weather to dampen the size or ardor of the crowd. On the other hand, editor William Evjue of the *Capital Times*, whose view of European events had changed after the Germans earlier overran his beloved Norway, claimed only five hundred attended a bogus event that had originated "in university Communist circles." In response Clarence Schoenfeld, the executive editor of the *Daily Cardinal*, lamented that "for no reason at all another editor had to drag the old red herring across his edit page again."[165] On reflection the *Cardinal* did concede that the affair might have provided too much of "a sounding board for those opposed to any and all preparedness."[166]

By mid-June Paris had fallen to the German blitzkrieg and Italy had entered the war against the Allies. President Roosevelt responded by stepping up American preparedness. On June 16, as the Soviet Union began its occupation of the Baltic states, he signed a naval expansion bill providing for the construction of a two-ocean U.S. Navy. He also appointed a National Defense Research Committee, whose job it was to enlist America's colleges and universities in the effort. The next day as the new French premier, Marshall Henri Pétain, announced French surrender talks with Hitler's generals, the University held its 1940 commencement ceremony. Governor Heil gave a short address to the graduates, including this advice:

> I would like to give this thought. Keep your feet on the ground! No matter how the present erratic conditions of the world may disturb you and the rest of us, let us stay sane. Let us not be swayed by fantastic, spectacular leadership untried and generally unsound. Do not sell your birthright as Americans. Preserve this democracy at all cost. Keep America sane. Live your lives with the full realization that we, the people of America, are the government of America. Orderly means are available, through the Constitution of the United States, to make adjustments in our government as the needs of the times require. The American Way is the best way.[167]

[164]Ibid., May 24, 1940.
[165]Ibid., May 25, 1940.
[166]Ibid., May 26, 1940.
[167]Heil, "University of Wisconsin Commencement," June 17, 1940, Dykstra Presidential Papers, 4/15/1, box 45.

The governor's warning conveyed the gravity of the moment without suggesting what sort of "adjustments in our government" he thought might be required.

The following day a worried resident of Minneapolis wrote Governor Heil expressing concern about radical influences at the University of Wisconsin. He may have been motivated by news reports that the House Un-American Activities Committee was stepping up its anti-communist activities.[168] Chairman Dies now planned to open regional offices throughout the country to investigate "fifth column" activities and hold secret hearings to gather testimony for the use of law enforcement agencies. Horn informed the governor that earlier in 1940 President Dykstra had joined twelve other college presidents in signing a statement criticizing the Dies Committee. "The Universities of Wisconsin and Minnesota," concluded the Minnesota writer, "are hotbeds of liberalism and should be cleaned up and you might start on your President who runs around the country talking about democracy." Horn sent Dykstra a copy of this message along with a cover letter. "You must feel embarrassed and say, 'Is my face red?' after the present turn of events," he told Dykstra. "You are one of the liberals who tried to destroy the Dies Committee....Many of us are tired of this thing called 'Academic Freedom'."[169]

Dykstra received a copy of this complaint on June 20 and immediately sent a note to the governor defending himself. The UW president explained that Horn's concern "dates from a statement made originally by a committee of Americans to the committee in Congress which was considering a further appropriation for the Dies Committee." Dykstra had declined to participate, however, because the group might say things he did not believe. Rather, he had prepared his own short public statement, a copy of which he now enclosed. "I think the sentiment which I suggested here is almost precisely the sentiment of your own Commencement speech at the University," claimed the president, "namely, that we have laws, a Department of Justice and courts that are open to everybody. Neither you nor I likes witch hunts and at the time...the [Dies] committee was actually on a witch hunt." As things turned out, moreover, congressional debate over continued appropriations did in fact produce beneficial changes in the committee's practices.

---

[168] *Saint Paul Pioneer Press*, June 18, 1940.

[169] Charles L. Horn to Heil, and Horn to Dykstra, both dated June 18, 1940, Dykstra Presidential Papers, 4/15/1, box 48.

"I am quite sure that you and I see our international problem in something of the same light. At least I was persuaded of that after the little talk we had Monday noon [of Commencement day] under the tree at our house."[170] Although written in a confident tone, President Dykstra's hasty response suggested that he was not entirely sure the unpredictable governor shared his commitment to civil liberties.

Meanwhile, Dykstra's nearby colleague President Alexander G. Ruthven of the University of Michigan was setting a rather different example. In his commencement address on June 15 Ruthven warned: "Michigan welcomes only students who are convinced that democracy is the ideal form of government for a civilized people. She will not be confused by sophistries built around meaningful but ill-defined phrases such as 'freedom of the press' or 'freedom of speech,' but will deal firmly, without fear or favor, with subversive or so-called fifth-column activities."[171] Ruthven meant business. Two weeks later he notified nine students they were unwelcome to return to the campus in the fall. Their transgressions apparently included attendance as delegates at the 1939 national ASU convention in Madison and participation in peace protests in Ann Arbor during the spring of 1940. Ruthven was acting according to policy he had promulgated since 1935:

> Attendance at the University of Michigan is a privilege and not a right. In order to safeguard its ideals of scholarship, character, and personality the University reserves the right, and the student concedes to the University the right, to require withdrawal of any student at any time for any reason deemed sufficient to it.[172]

Michigan's policy was in direct opposition to the student freedoms defended so forcefully by UW Presidents Dykstra and Frank.

Shortly after Ruthven's action, Governor Heil wrote to Regent President Glover describing an impromptu meeting with several reporters. They wanted to talk about "the activities of communists, nazis and

---

[170]Dykstra to Heil, June 20, 1940; Franz Boaz to Dykstra, December 27, 1939; Dykstra to Boaz, January 8, 1940; Dykstra, statement to American Committee for Democracy and Intellectual Freedom, January 8, 1940, ibid., boxes 43 and 48.

[171]Quoted in *Time*, 36 (July 8, 1940), 38.

[172]Quoted in Howard H. Peckham, *The Making of the University of Michigan, 1817-1967* (Ann Arbor: University of Michigan Press, 1967), 191-2. Peckham describes Ruthven as a no-nonsense president: "He had no tolerance for students who came not for what the University had to offer, but for such other purposes as exhibitionism, drinking, and playing, or devotion to off-campus controversies."

fascists," a subject certain to arouse the interest of the Wisconsin chief executive. In the course of the discussion the journalists had informed Heil of President Ruthven's notice to certain students with "socialistic tendencies" that he would not readmit them to the University of Michigan in the fall.

> And so the newspaper boys wanted to know whether we were doing anything to guard against those young men and women making application at the University of Wisconsin. I told them that we had not up to this time, but that I was going to ask the president of the Board of Regents and the Board to consider whether it would be advisable to interest themselves in trying to eliminate obnoxious minds from entering our University and by chance infest the pure minds who love their America and their constitution and their flag.

The governor further thought "it would be nice to ascertain just how many we have on the faculty of our University who are teaching the gospel of communism and its affiliates." With German and Soviet forces seemingly triumphant in Europe, Heil was convinced "that at this crucial moment we ought to know the enemies in our midst, and so I hope and pray that you and your good Board will find a solution to the problem confronting our state and nation."[173]

To underscore the request, under separate cover the governor sent a copy of the same day's *Wisconsin State Journal*, whose main front-page headline read: "HEIL ASKS REGENTS TO BAR U.W. REDS/ FACULTY, TOO, WILL FEEL HIS PURGE." The article, and a similar one appearing in the *Capital Times* that day, reported Heil's meeting with the press. Both stated the governor was intent on ridding not only the University but the entire state of all communists, nazis, fascists, and anyone else whose patriotism was questionable (excepting only foreign students). "By American I mean a united people who love the constitution, the stars and stripes, the country and its institutions," the *State Journal* quoted the governor, "and people who don't believe in America are not fit subjects to associate "[174] The *Capital Times* described the governor as wanting the regents to exclude all "Reds" and anyone else "not 100 per cent American." Adding a note of immediacy, the *State Journal* also carried a letter to the editor signed "Irate Citizen" discuss-

---

[173]Heil to Glover, July 2, 1940, Dykstra Presidential Papers, 4/15/1, box 48.

[174]The *Capital Times*, July 2, 1940, offered a more coherent quotation from the governor: "By American we have got to have a united people who love the constitution, the Stars and Stripes and democracy. People who don't believe in that are not good subjects to associate with in a democracy called America." See also *Wisconsin State Journal*, July 2, 1940.

ing a forthcoming meeting of the UW chapter of the Young Communist League: "All the wild-eyed cranks on the campus will be there," complained the anonymous writer. "Why don't they go back to Brooklyn during the summer months, at least, and give the good citizens of Madison's West side a respite from the ravings of the numerous un-American trouble makers who infest the campus?" The *Capital Times* reported that Heil planned to send an observer. It was clear the governor expected the regents to deal with such problems. It was also evident that his concern had shifted from economic depression to national security.

Governor Heil was not educated in the formal sense, nor was he familiar with the culture and tradition of academic freedom at Wisconsin. A self-made man who had shouldered his way to industrial and financial success in Milwaukee, he considered himself eminently practical. As governor he now had to worry about the effects on his state and country of a world rushing headlong into total war. Extraordinary measures in defense of America's and Wisconsin's interests were fully warranted. Hence his interest in President Ruthven's action and his belief that the University of Wisconsin might reasonably be expected to follow suit. Regent Arthur Holmes promptly wrote President Dykstra in full support of the governor. "I think that any student or teacher who advocates the overthrow of the present government of the United States by force, and the substitution therefor of another form of government," he declared, "should be immediately expelled or discharged." No meeting of the board was necessary to consider this drastic policy, asserted attorney Holmes:

> I think a statement by the head of the University, setting forth a strong position on Americanism, is all that is required. I am sure that the students of the University of Wisconsin and the faculty will, themselves, purge the University of any foreign influences.[175]

The regents did convene privately on July 13 to consider Governor Heil's suggestion. Regents Hodgkins and Sensenbrenner were absent. The rest of the board unanimously approved a response to Heil that cordially but firmly declined either to bar students with "'obnoxious minds'" or to survey the faculty for those teaching "'the gospel of Communism and its affiliates.'" The regents believed in the overwhelming loyalty of the people of the state, the faculty, and students to

---

[175]Arthur T. Holmes to Dykstra, July 6, 1940, Dykstra Presidential Papers, 4/15/1, box 48.

"the principle that a democracy is the ideal form of government for a civilized people." They pointed "to the important program of citizenship training which originated at the University of Wisconsin and is now spreading rapidly to all states throughout the nation....It is a high compliment to our faculty that such a program was initiated by our University."[176]

Noting that those students who were "impressed with other forms of government" might well benefit from exposure to UW's "program of American education," the regents' response got to the heart of the matter:

> The question of political and religious tests for admission to the University is covered by Section 36.06 of the Statutes which reads as follows: "no sectarian or partisan tests shall ever be allowed or exercised in the university, or in the admission of students thereto or for any purpose whatever". The Regents are bound by this Statute.[177]

That was that. While ideas could not be policed at UW, the board assured the governor that "disloyal acts" could, and when discovered, would be reported "to the proper legal authority for action." The regents appealed to "all Wisconsin citizens" to maintain their "faith in our American institutions," and concluded by reaffirming the famous board resolution of 1894, "that here at Wisconsin we 'should ever encourage that continual sifting and winnowing by which alone the truth can be found'."

At a press conference on July 16, Governor Heil grudgingly acquiesced in the regents' decision without accepting their larger argument that essentially all was well at the University:

> Those laws were made before we ever had anybody dissatisfied with our democratic way of living....We're in a streamlined age now, and it's not impossible the legislature may see fit to broaden the powers of the regents in the future. Of course, the members couldn't do anything about my request,

---

[176]BOR Minutes, July 13, 1940.

[177]In an apparent effort to sharpen their stand, the regents abridged and in the process misquoted Section 36.06, which actually read: "The board of regents shall...determine the moral and educational qualifications of applicants for admission to the various courses of instruction; but no instruction, either sectarian in religion or partisan in politics, shall ever be allowed in any department of the university; and no sectarian or partisan tests shall ever be allowed or exercised in the appointments of regents or in the election of professors, teachers or other officers of the university, or in the admission of students thereto or for any purpose whatever."

but it served its purpose in getting the matter before the people and waking them up to the dangers facing them.

Heil offered one last suggestion (but no formal recommendation) as to how the University could legally encourage patriotism while keeping the pressure on the enemy:

> I'm not so sure it wouldn't be a good idea to have all students take an oath of allegiance to support democratic ideas and government. Certainly, no one would refuse to take such an oath if he was a good American citizen. That wouldn't be against the statutes, and I'm sure everyone would be glad to affirm his faith in America and its customs.[178]

President Dykstra had managed the potentially serious confrontation with characteristic style and effect. For it was he who has quietly orchestrated the regents' response to the governor, including the brilliant and probably unprecedented invocation of Section 36.06's prohibition against any partisan or sectarian test. Even Regent Holmes, who had initially argued for a purge, eventually succumbed to Dykstra's calm logic. Though a comparative newcomer to the state, Dykstra appreciated the importance of the underlying commitment to academic freedom as it had evolved at the University of Wisconsin. He never missed an opportunity at critical moments like this one to remind his audiences, including the regents, of their invaluable heritage.

Toward "Total Preparedness"

Happily for the University, the summer of 1940 marked a turning point in relations with Governor Heil. As the United States moved ever closer to direct participation in the war, the governor came to appreciate the value of the University in Wisconsin's and the national defense effort. During the week preceding the regents' rejection of the governor's red purge, Dykstra and six other university presidents petitioned the U.S. Senate in qualified support of the pending Burke-Wadsworth Selective Service Training Bill.[179] On July 11 Dykstra addressed a UW

---

[178] *Capital Times*, July 17, 1940. The earliest variation of Section 36.06 containing references to religious *and* political beliefs occurred in Title VII, Chapter 21, Section 7, *Wisconsin Statutes*, 1866. Title VII, Chapter 18, Section 17 *Wisconsin Statutes*, 1849, protected only religious thought.

[179] Senate Bill 4164/House Bill 10132, June 21, 1940, Dykstra Presidential Papers, 4/15/1, box 154. The petition is reported in *Capital Times*, July 12, 1940.

Summer Session convocation on "The Problem of the Burke Bill," which he criticized as too narrow by virtue of its over-emphasis on the "military" aspects of preparedness.[180] Dykstra argued that the effort should be comprehensive, involving essentially the entire citizenry in all aspects of national life. His message was too subtle, however, and the president soon complained that the press had misunderstood his support for universal national service. "Evidently the reporters assumed I meant *military* service," he protested, "and my mail has been full of the thought."[181] Dykstra reserved his most powerful comments for the University's freshman convocation on September 21. He described the spread of war throughout the world and listed American responses, including the enactment of the draft the previous month, through which "every young man of twenty-one is liable to call under certain conditions and with certain exemptions." True to the democratic spirit, opinion varied about exactly what to do, but "the vast majority in America are for what is called 'all aid short of war.'" Although risk and uncertainty abounded, one thing was certain: "This is a day of total war and total preparedness," Dykstra soberly told his youthful listeners. "Live this year through upon the premise that it is the most important year of *your* life, not only, but also the most important year in the life of the nation. It may well be the solemn truth."[182]

President Roosevelt appreciated Dykstra's support for the draft and was well aware of his administrative skills. On September 29 a *Daily Cardinal* headline announced, "Dykstra Rumored as Draft Leader." Speculation mounted while Dykstra visited the White House and then agreed to serve as the first director of the selective service program.[183]

---

[180]Dykstra, "The Problem of the Burke Bill," Dykstra Presidential Papers, 4/15/1, box 154.

[181]Introductory comments in Dykstra, "Implications for Education from European Scene," address before the UW Summer Session Education Conference, July 17, 1940, ibid. Emphasis in original. The *Capital Times*, July 12, 1940, headlined Dykstra's remarks: "Forced Army Training, Is Dykstra Plea."

[182]Dykstra, "Freshman Convocation," September 21, 1940, Dykstra Presidential Papers, 4/15/1, 154. Emphasis in original.

[183]*Daily Cardinal*, September 29, October 9, 10, and 11, 1940; *New York Times*, October 10, 1940; *Milwaukee Journal*, October 12 and 14, 1940; *Capital Times*, October 12, 1940; *Wisconsin State Journal*, October 9 and 12, 1940. Harvard President James B. Conant also was an academic advocate of the draft. In his autobiography Conant reported that President Roosevelt had considered him for the directorship but rejected the idea on the ground that Conant was busy in other preparedness-related activities. James B. Conant, *My Several Lives: Memoirs of a Social Inventor* (New York: Harper & Row, 1970), p. 238.

Dykstra did not seek this assignment and in fact commented somewhat morosely, "The die is cast and there seems to be nothing for me to do but to respond to this national call."[184] On October 12 the regents gave informal approval.[185] The appointment was praised around the country and in Wisconsin, although the radical University League for Liberal Action predictably urged the UW president to reject the offer which ULLA leaders characterized as a ruse to subvert midwestern liberal opposition to the draft.[186] At the regents meeting on October 26 the board officially granted permission for Dykstra to accept the federal post. They also designated a three-member committee consisting of Comptroller A.W. Peterson, L&S Dean George Sellery, and Graduate School Dean E.B. Fred to perform the president's administrative duties under his guidance in his absence.[187] Dykstra assured the board he would return to the campus regularly. Here was an opportunity to exemplify his "total preparedness" theme, and the *Cardinal* agreed that the arrangement could work. "If Mr. Dykstra sits in Bascom hall reasonably often, if his regency functions as a cooperative unit, if every student and faculty member continues to do his part, the University of Wisconsin can face the challenges of this school year undaunted."[188]

President Dykstra's tenure in Washington continued through the 1940-41 academic year. He served as head of selective service until March when at President Roosevelt's behest he resigned to accept the chairmanship of the new eleven-member National Defense Mediation Board. Three months later he returned full-time to Wisconsin while remaining "on call" with the government.[189] While logging many hours on trains, throughout this nine-month period Dykstra juggled his federal and University responsibilities effectively. He attended the monthly meetings of the Board of Regents, presided over most of the general University faculty meetings, and remained actively involved with the

---

[184]Dykstra to Charles B. Rogers, telegram, October 14, 1940, Dykstra Papers, box 32, UCLA.

[185]Regents Glover, Holmes, Sensenbrenner, Vergeront, Cleary, Kleczka, Werner, and Callahan attended the hastily called October 12, 1940, meeting and agreed unanimously that Dykstra must answer the call and that the University would grant him a leave of absence. *Daily Cardinal*, October 13, 1940.

[186]See correspondence and clippings in Dykstra Papers, boxes 32 and 78, UCLA; *Daily Cardinal*, October 13, 1940.

[187]BOR Minutes, October 26, 1940; *Daily Cardinal*, October 27, 1940.

[188]*Daily Cardinal*, October 30, 1940.

[189]*Capital Times*, June 17, 1941. Dykstra's appointment with the federal government lapsed on June 30, 1941.

administration of the University. In contrast to President Frank, who was criticized by some of the faculty and regents for his extensive speaking engagements away from the campus, there was little or no grumbling about Dykstra's Washington service. In normal times these dual responsibilities would have seemed extraordinary if not unacceptable.[190] But as the country moved inexorably onto a wartime footing, other UW staff members and students also found themselves thrust into government service. A spirit of make-do cooperation and inner strength was steadily eclipsing the depression doldrums.

Not since 1925, if indeed ever, had the regents involved themselves so actively and comprehensively in fashioning the 1941-43 biennial budget. They worked closely with Comptroller Peterson and others in shaping the request and defending it before the legislature and the public at large. As one student commentator noted approvingly in December of 1940:

> Those who feared that the industrialists Heil placed on the board of regents would turn out to be a reactionary hatchet-squad need worry no longer. That men who are busy handling the affairs of some of the largest industries in the world should take the time to master the intricacies of university administration and finance in order to pull this school out of its nose-dive is a tribute to their character and patriotism.[191]

Governor Heil's bid for reelection was successful in November, 1940. At a tumultuous budget hearing the following month he promised unequivocally to support the University's request.[192] When he unveiled his omnibus biennial budget for the state on January 9, 1941, it totalled more than $74 million, the largest in Wisconsin history. He proposed that the University receive its requested $7.8 million for operations.

---

[190]As part of the regents' official action on October 26, 1940, approving Dykstra's federal service, the board stipulated that the president would continue to receive his regular UW salary and that Dykstra in turn would hand over to the University his federal salary, minus expenses. Secretary of State Fred Zimmerman blocked payment of Dykstra's UW salary, however, arguing that the state constitution prohibited any state officer from simultaneously holding a federal position. Consequently, from November, 1940, through March, 1941, Dykstra received no UW salary. Meanwhile, the dispute worked its way through the courts until the Wisconsin Supreme Court upheld the regents' action on December 2, 1941. The justices ruled that the constitutional prohibition did not apply to Dykstra because he was an employee and not an officer of the state. For a summary of this drawn-out controversy, see A.W. Peterson to the Board of Regents, December 5, 1941, BOR Papers, 1/1/3, box 57.

[191]Jerry Sullivan, "It's My Nickel," *Daily Cardinal*, December 10, 1940.

[192]*Daily Cardinal*, December 7, 1940.

The legislature generally concurred, and on April 29 the governor signed this generous budget into law. President Dykstra used a radio address to celebrate the triumph:

> Wisconsin citizens and public officials have rallied to the support of the University with great enthusiasm this year....Governor Heil has stood 100 per cent with our institution. We have had real teamwork from Alumni, Faculty, Student Body, Governor, Legislature, and Citizens which some might say is unusual. For this situation the president of the University is grateful. This is, and must be, a day when each is for all and all for each. We must stand together for the things we believe in. We are doing it in Wisconsin and at the University.[193]

With quiet but effective coaching from Dykstra and his supportive regents, Governor Heil had come a long way in only two years in appreciating the value of the University to the state and nation.

The growing state commitment to preparedness during the first half of 1941 did not, of course, eliminate all differences of opinion, painful compromises, and even bitter disagreements. When the University proposed a new capital building fund of nearly $2 million, Governor Heil first blessed it, then eliminated it from his budget proposal, and finally became one of its staunchest supporters. The legislature remained unconvinced, however, and failed to vote the funds. As American involvement in the war seemed increasingly likely, the legislators probably saw University needs as less pressing than others more directly associated with national defense. Another disagreement involved Governor Heil's perennial call for mandatory military training at the University. He raised this issue again in his budget message to the legislature, warning that "nothing should be allowed to interfere with the re-arming of America....The safety of the people is the highest law."[194] Subsequently the governor campaigned for the requirement, while students protested and Dykstra and other University authorities argued that compulsory ROTC was unnecessary and unworkable. In late April the legislature passed and Heil approved the ROTC bill, but only after it had been radically amended to give the regents broad authority to grant exemptions.[195]

In May Heil rekindled the campus loyalty debate. Previously he had advocated legislation to bar Communists from the Wisconsin ballot.

---

[193] *Press Bulletin*, May 21, 1941.
[194] For the full text of Governor Heil's message see *Capital Times*, January 9, 1941.
[195] *Daily Cardinal*, April 29, 1941.

Law Dean Garrison and others on the faculty had opposed this measure while also expressing other opinions the governor interpreted as anti-American. Heil took particular offense at a WHA radio program, "Wake Up America," which considered the international situation from various perspectives. He objected to the views of certain speakers so strongly that he asked the regents to investigate faculty involved. When the board declined to act, the governor remained suspicious of the ideological purity of the campus.[196]

In spite of the Heil's concerns there was no question but that the University community was gradually preparing for war and reshaping itself accordingly. The Extension Division early took the lead on the educational side by offering pilot training and citizenship programming. By late 1940 the College of Engineering had set up a special program to prepare recent high school graduates for work in defense industries.[197] Meanwhile, University scholars focussed their intellects and expertise on the nation's defense needs. In July of 1940 President Dykstra appointed a Special Committee for Research on National Defense charged with the task of identifying the campus research projects and facilities involved in work related to the defense effort. Dykstra submitted the resulting 309-page report to the regents in September.[198] During the next year various status reports described developments in the production of atomic energy, hemp, and high test aviation fuel. In November, 1940, Secretary of War Frank Knox notified the Medical School that he had designated it to sponsor and organize an Army reserve unit, the 44th General Hospital. The following May the Wisconsin Institute for National Defense brought community leaders from across the state to the campus to discuss their various preparedness efforts. New York Mayor Fiorello La Guardia called the institute a "model for the nation."[199] By October, the campus-based U.S. Forest Products Laboratory had over a hundred of its employees at work on defense projects.

---

[196]William J. Morgan to Heil, May 14, 1941, Heil Papers, box 7; BOR Minutes, May 27, 1941; *Capital Times*, May 19 and 24, June 5, 1941; *Daily Cardinal*, May 28, 1941; *Wisconsin State Journal*, June 5, 1941; Thompson, *Continuity and Change*, p. 488; James F. Scotton, "Loyalty and the Wisconsin Legislature" (M.A. thesis, University of Wisconsin, 1966), pp. 113-6 and appendix.

[197]*Press Bulletin*, December 4, 1940, July 2, 1941; *Daily Cardinal*, June 28, 1941; *Capital Times*, June 29, 1941.

[198]*Press Bulletin*, July 17, October 9, 1940; *Daily Cardinal*, September 29, 1940; BOR Minutes, September 28, 1940.

[199]*Press Bulletin*, May 7, 1941; *Daily Cardinal*, May 13, 15, 16, and 17, 1941, September 24, 1941; *Capital Times*, September 23, 1941.

Following the passage of the Selective Service Act in the summer of 1940, the military draft and government defense work began taking University students and staff as early as the fall semester of that year, a trend that accelerated steadily thereafter. The regents responded by returning fees, approving modified graduation requirements, and promising reentry or reemployment upon completion of service. By late October, 1941, President Dykstra reported to the regents that 160 UW staff members were on leave for government defense work. Thus when on December 7 Japanese bombs fell on Pearl Harbor, the University in many respects was already at war.

7.

The University at War

The Japanese bombing of the American naval base at Pearl Harbor, Hawaii, on Sunday, December 7, 1941, quickly and dramatically transformed nearly all aspects of University and national life. "Winter and war, both long overdue, dropped out of the clouds hand in hand Sunday night with a suddenness that struck the town dumb," somberly observed David Gelfan in the *Daily Cardinal*.

> The Memorial Union...became a counting house of death as the lounge radio stopped its flow of afternoon music to pour out the tidings of war. Half-dozing students were jerked out of their seats by the incredible news, and casual passersby were drawn into the room by the solemn expressions of those clustered around the radio.... From the Union the word of the war spread to the lodging houses and dorms, many of which had already heard the news from their own radios. From Chadbourne hall to the Kronshage houses the campus took one convulsive gasp, and dived for the nearest radio.[1]

Even among campus pacifists, hope had vanished that somehow direct American participation in the bloodshed could be avoided. For everyone the insistent question was, what happens next?

President Dykstra's partial answer was to call an all-University convocation for Friday, December 12, at the Field House to try to quell the distracting rumors and speculation about the future. A capacity crowd of students, faculty, and townspeople attended the gathering, broadcast throughout the state over WHA radio. After the singing of Christmas carols, "Varsity," and "America," followed by numerous "skyrocket" cheers, Dykstra took the podium. "This is a momentous

---

[1] *Daily Cardinal*, December 9, 1941.

week in American history," he declared, stating the obvious in solemn tones. He explained that although he had consulted with selective service officials in Washington, he unfortunately could report no concrete plans nor predict exactly what might happen next to UW men. For the present, he advised, they should follow their consciences in deciding what to do, but Dykstra stressed the virtue of "staying on the job until our country sees fit to call us." He announced that a cadre of special faculty counselors would soon be ready to provide advice and information about draft deferment policy and service options as they became clear. For their part, University women had an important role to play in "the great field of civilian defense and community activity," involving such campus programs as the recently organized Women's Elective Service. As for campus life generally, "sobriety, courage and industry" were the new watchwords, although sensible recreation, too, was important, "if we are to remain calm and sane in times of crises." "This is a time for consecration in the high purposes to which America was dedicated," Dykstra concluded somberly. "This is a time for faith, for belief in our leadership, for the cherishing and the brightening up of our ideals and our hopes. We have closed ranks. From this day on we march together, calmly, deliberately and with united purpose."[2]

Mobilizing for War

President Dykstra and his University colleagues moved quickly to place the campus on a wartime footing. The challenge was daunting and unprecedented. The only comparable recent experience was the relatively brief mobilization of 1917-18 during the First World War. Then the demands on the University and American higher education generally involved some unpleasant dislocation but only minimal structural adjustment. By 1941 the technology of war had become more sophisticated and the threat to the western hemisphere seemed considerably more serious. As the first director of selective service in 1940 and a prominent spokesman for national preparedness, Dykstra had participated in discussions within the federal government concerning the

---

[2]Clarence A. Dykstra, "All University Convocation," December 12, 1941, Dykstra Presidential Papers, 4/15/1, box 153, UA. Filed with this speech text are notes from two members of the audience, Susan Davis and Mr. Kivlin. Davis declared: "The address was magnificent. It came over the air with extraordinary clearness. It is one of the most outstanding and valuable services rendered this State and the Nation." Kivlin termed the speech "Excellent."

organization of manpower to meet wartime military, industrial, and agricultural needs. He and other administrators in Washington and on the campuses, however, had given less attention to the question of specifically how the colleges and universities might best contribute in any general mobilization or their role in continuing to educate the nation's future leaders in a protracted conflict. Prior to Pearl Harbor, the University had organized draft registration exercises and identified UW faculty members and research projects with military utility, but otherwise the campus was largely unprepared for the massive dislocations to come.

Tacitly acknowledging the fundamental principle of faculty participation in University governance, Dykstra appointed a special Committee on Emergency Educational Policy. The committee, initially involving thirteen faculty members and the six academic deans, received the charge to make "provision in the largest possible way for the preparation of students to serve our country in the near future." Chemistry Professor J.H. Mathews chaired the committee, which first met on December 18 and concluded most of its business by February 2, 1942. Curriculum and the calendar issues were the main considerations. By early January the committee had developed a list of thirteen new war-related courses and numerous modified ones to be offered during the spring semester. A supplementary time table was issued, and on Sunday, January 11, the committee sponsored a student meeting at Memorial Union to explain the changes. More than a thousand students attended the event, which included general lectures in the Union Theater and more intimate question-and-answer sessions in Great Hall. The committee also developed revised 1942 spring semester and summer schedules that moved commencement up three weeks to June 1 and extended the summer term to twelve weeks. With regard to future calendars, the committee, in cooperation with President Dykstra, surveyed other Big Ten institutions as to their plans and considered switching UW to a tri-semester or perhaps a quarter plan. The committee finally decided to continue the modified semester plan, with a lengthened summer session capable of accommodating fifteen-week (full semester) courses. With these changes diligent UW students—like many of their counterparts across the nation—could reasonably expect to complete a full undergraduate program in two years and nine months.[3]

---

[3]For the full text of President Dykstra's charge to the committee and a detailed record of its operations, see "Committee on Emergency Educational Policy, Committee on Student Defense Problems, Emergency Courses," notebook, General Presidential Papers, 4/0/1, box 39,

Meanwhile, the University Personnel Council joined the mobilization effort by organizing the faculty counseling service referred to by President Dykstra in his convocation address. Dean of Men Scott Goodnight had established the council in 1938 to coordinate the many separate student service programs that had developed since Frank Holt and V.A.C. Henmon had pioneered with the Bureau of Guidance and Records in 1927. By 1941 Assistant Dean of Men Willard Blaesser, who had been instrumental in shaping the group, was officially administering the UPC, and he now took the lead in accomplishing its new mission. Within a week of Pearl Harbor the UPC office had distributed an informational document to the faculty counselors outlining their duties. The document also included information on military, government, and educational service opportunities available to UW men. In mid-January Blaesser issued a comprehensive twenty-seven-page revision, for the first time describing a bewildering array of Army and Navy enlisted reserve programs, which would allow students to continue their studies under military auspices until needed for active service. Throughout the spring semester Blaesser distributed various updates to the document, which persisted as the counselors' bible until July, 1942, when another fully revised edition took its place. Particularly during this first semester of war the special counseling program—acknowledged by officials in Washington as "one of the best"[4]—was of the utmost importance to at least two thousand UW men students who found themselves struggling to make informed decisions in the context of a rapidly-changing nation at war.[5]

Two days after Pearl Harbor the UPC steering committee, including Chairman Frank Holt and Assistant Dean Blaesser, met with student representatives from the Wisconsin Student Association, the Wisconsin Union, the Women's Self-Government Association, the *Daily Cardinal*, the House Presidents' Council, and the senior class. As the *Cardinal* reported, they discussed "what students should do in relation to the

---

UA. The University faculty approved UW Faculty Document 640, "Revision of the University Calendar for the Emergency Caused by War," on February 2, 1942. Document 640 formally established the policy of speeding up the educational process, but specific calendars for succeeding academic years remained to be arranged. Professor Mathews and his fellow committee members helped to make these arrangements.

[4]*Daily Cardinal*, February 21, 1942.

[5]Willard Blaesser to Special Faculty Counselors, January 17, 1942, General Presidential Papers, 4/0/1, box 42. For an overview of the counseling program and a discussion of Blaesser's central part in it, see *Press Bulletin*, August 12, 1942.

national emergency." An informal joint war council resulted that among other things helped President Dykstra prepare for the all-University convocation on December 12. Several days later, recognizing the ad hoc council's ability to influence the key student organizations, Dykstra officially rechristened it the Committee on Student Defense Problems—although it became popularly known as the University War Council as well as the Faculty-Student Committee on Student Defense Problems. As events transpired the full joint committee spawned many ideas while the student contingent actually supervised the implementation of programs by the various campus organizations. In mid-February President Dykstra designated this group of student leaders the Student War Council.[6]

Student enthusiasm was high for war-related activities, particularly early in the conflict. Ten days after the Pearl Harbor attack, for example, the *Daily Cardinal* announced the formation of a program called University Elective Service, suggested by the defense problems committee and operating under the auspices of the Student Board, the official student  government. Some months earlier the Women's Self-Government Association had sponsored a Women's Elective Service project to function as the principal women's volunteer service organization. WES had assisted Red Cross and British War Relief efforts, sent candy and letters ("Wiskits") to men in the American armed forces, and organized non-credit courses in home nursing and first aid. UES now would replace WES, adding to the services offered and

---

[6]*Daily Cardinal*, December 10 and 11, 1941. Original members of the Student War Council were President Carl Runge (Student Board), President Robert Lampman (Wisconsin Union), President Betty Biart (WSGA), Editor Robert Lewis (*Cardinal*), Chairman Benoni Reynolds (House Presidents' Council), and President Burleigh Jacobs (Senior Class). Membership eventually expanded to eight. S.H. Goodnight, Blaesser, and Blanche B. Stemm, Office of the Dean of Men, "Biennial Report, 1940-41 and 1941-42," November 10, 1942, General Presidential Papers, 4/0/2, box 11. On the subsequent development of the Student War Council see *Daily Cardinal*, February 17, 1942, and *Badger*, 1942, p. 115.

including men among the volunteers. The initial task was to recruit replacements for about 60 defense research project student helpers whose depression-era National Youth Administration funding had in mid-December been suddenly and drastically curtailed by the federal government. History Professor Robert Reynolds—himself soon to depart for military intelligence work in Washington—assured student volunteers their assistance would involve "the sort of abstract experimental work that means victory in the long run."[7] UES, which remained dominated by University women, soon was sponsoring classes in typing, first aid, and nutrition and canteen work. Other campus organizations, such as the Wisconsin Union or the University YMCA, sponsored similar activities, and duplication and overlap became a problem. The Student War Council, as the designated agency responsible for coordinating student war activities, soon had its hands full.

The extent and tempo of military activity on campus increased markedly in the months following Pearl Harbor. The war brought new challenges to the Department of Military Science and its Reserve Officer Training Corps (ROTC) program. Although the draft, new enlisted reserve programs, and spontaneous enlistments promised eventually to diminish ROTC participation, enrollment remained at record levels throughout 1942.[8] Meanwhile, well-publicized marching drill and maneuvers, the establishment of special ski and commando training units, and the first wartime graduation exercise kept

"He Says He's a History Major"

---

[7]*Daily Cardinal*, December 19, 1941.

[8]Reports varied widely as to enrollments. The *Press Bulletin* of March 11, 1942, put the figure at 1,881, while an official report late in the war claimed an enrollment of 2,481, which excluded over 100 advanced cadets. "Activities of Department of Military Science, 1942-1945," UW Faculty Papers, 5/100, box 1, UA. The ROTC roster for November, 1942, included 2,592 cadets. Herbert H. Lewis to Dykstra, November 19, 1942, General Presidential Papers, 4/0/2, box 11. According to the *Press Bulletin*, October 7, 1942, ROTC enrollment at the time was 2,574. These statistical disparities were typical of nearly all military-related activities on campus throughout the war.

the corps in full campus view.[9] Expanding its instructional role, the military department helped twelve academic departments adapt selected courses to wartime needs. Department staff lectured on such topics as military public relations, aerial photography, army administration and supply, military law, and chemical warfare. During the 1942 summer session the department continued its instructional assistance effort and regular ROTC training activities while also offering a non-credit evening course in Morse code, cryptography, and other aspects of signal communications for local townspeople and students. The department also offered military instruction for naval reservists enrolled in the Extension Division's Civilian Pilot Training program, for members of the Dane County Civilian Air Patrol, and for 60 advanced ROTC cadets who expected soon to receive their commissions. Finally, working through the office of Wisconsin Adjutant General Ralph M. Immell, the department provided instruction and advice to units of state guardsmen and troopers.[10]

The University's Civilian Pilot Training program attracted a good deal of interest as it adapted to wartime needs. Established in late 1939 by the University Extension Division, the program initially prepared civilian flyers, ground crew workers, and instructors for commercial and military employment. Training facilities included two Madison-area airfields and classroom space in the Mechanical Engineering Building. In March, 1942, as the program graduated its third class of 25 men into active duty with the Naval Air Service, the number of UW-trained flyers now exceeded that of any other school in the country. The Navy representative at the graduation ceremony in the state capitol congratulated the "Flying Badgers" and applauded the University and the state for their "patriotic, all-out effort."[11] In July the program was transferred from University to Navy control, and with certain exceptions enrollment was limited to 70 naval reserve students preparing for combat pilot duty. In the process the Navy contracted with the University to provide 30 of these men, who were training on a full-time basis, with sleeping accommodations at the campus YMCA and dining service next door in Memorial Union's Tripp Commons.[12]

---

[9]The student Hoofers Club provided the leadership and instructors for the ROTC ski patrol and other interested campus groups. *Badger*, 1943, p. 62.

[10]For an overview of Department of Military Science activities at this time see Lewis to Dykstra, November 19, 1942.

[11]*Press Bulletin*, March 11, 1942; *Daily Cardinal*, May 15, 1942.

[12]This and other discussions of the Navy at the University during the war rely heavily on

In March, 1942, the War Department designated the University as headquarters for a new United States Army Institute correspondence study program. The University Extension Division, which had pioneered with correspondence study since the turn of the century and was perhaps the most experienced such agency in the country, would oversee the undertaking. Although initially the new institute permitted only limited registration by Navy and Coast Guard personnel, it was evident that providing correspondence study for American soldiers was a potentially massive undertaking. The Wisconsin legislature, moreover, had recently mandated that Extension provide free courses for state citizens on active military duty. Already 592 Wisconsin servicemen had enrolled. Thirty soon-to-be-assigned military personnel would help extension staff members run the institute and increasingly take over everything but the grading of papers, which would remain the responsibility of resident extension faculty members. The first USAI catalog listed sixty-four available UW Extension Division courses as well as many others sponsored by seventy-six affiliated universities and colleges. As of June, 1942, the roster included about a thousand students in uniform, but authorities expected the total to grow to between twenty and seventy thousand soldiers eventually. The most popular subjects were arithmetic, bookkeeping and accounting, algebra, shorthand, English grammar, railroad rate study, radio and telephony, trigonometry, typewriting, and cost accounting.[13]

The pilot training program and the Army institute increasingly contributed active military personnel to the UW campus population. But the most striking influx of men in uniform began on April 1, 1942, with the opening of the Navy Radio School, the first such university-based training unit in the country. By July a full complement of over twelve hundred sailors was on campus, not counting the Navy support staff. The University provided room and board as

John B. Washbush, "The Campus and the Navy in World War II: Naval Training at the University of Wisconsin, 1939-1946" (unpublished manuscript, 1968), UHP, and Departmental Files, ROTC, UA.

[13]Four officers and 26 enlisted men had been assigned to the program as of June, 1942, with an anticipated full complement of 120. *Wisconsin State Journal*, June 14, 1942.

well as instructional and recreational accommodations. The Navy furnished personal supplies, specified the curriculum, and generally supervised the young men, many of whom had never before lived away from home. The radio program was essentially self-contained, involving short-term technical training and little college-level instruction. The sailors initially bunked in makeshift lodging at Camp Randall Stadium and in World War I-vintage barracks, which since 1918 had seen service as chicken coops and then as quarters for College of Agriculture Farm Short Course students. When the semester concluded in June the radio men replaced the departing civilian residents of the two oldest and largest men's lakeshore dormitories, Tripp and Adams halls. The sailors studied and played hard. By summer their antics were occasionally producing angry complaints from parents of local high school girls, who were attracted by the glamour of this large body of energetic young men in uniform.[14] The solution was to designate the Tripp-Adams complex, the adjacent playing fields, and the Stadium as an official military reservation. The unfamiliar concept of "off limits," enforced by signs and Navy shore patrols, had taken over part of the campus.

At the close of the first wartime semester, President Dykstra offered a solemn commencement charge to the Class of 1942. Many of the graduates already were in uniform, while others—including Dykstra's son Franz, a letters and science graduate—soon would be:

I have faith in this generation; it is already living up to the promises we have made for it; it has courage, intelligence and understanding; it faces realistically but with high idealism the challenge ahead; it is putting aside all of its personal plans and hopes to undertake grimly a terrible assignment.[15]

The president's words followed five months of dedicated effort by Uni-

---

[14]On May 5, 1942, the *Daily Cardinal* editorialized that it was the parents' responsibility to control their children. J.L. Miller, instructional director of the Navy Radio School, however, notified Dykstra on May 19, 1942, that "considerably more Navy supervision and control" was needed. Quoted in Washbush, "The Campus and the Navy," p. 15.

[15]"Charge to the Class," June 1, 1942, Dykstra Presidential Papers, 4/15/1, box 152.

versity staff and students to mobilize the campus. Even at this early stage of the conflict, the effort had become complex, time-consuming, and often confusing. The Student War Council faced new challenges daily. Similarly, the University administration encountered a seemingly endless round of vexing problems that nearly always demanded immediate solutions. The establishment of the Navy Radio School that spring was typical. It had involved complex negotiations with Navy authorities and quick action by the Board of Regents, President Dykstra, individual faculty members, the comptroller, the superintendent of buildings and grounds, the director of dormitories and commons, and the director of Memorial Union, all of whom had a part to play before the school was a reality. As the Army and Navy expanded their training activities at the University with bewildering speed in the months ahead, the campus would be tested as never before.

Continued national mobilization resulted in frequent and insistent demands from the military for special technical training. Often Washington planners made their requests for University assistance by telephone and expected an instant response. Recognizing that the emergency did not allow for normal deliberation by the full Board of Regents at its regular monthly meetings, on June 27, 1942, the regents adopted a new policy authorizing the Executive Committee and President Dykstra to enter into military-related agreements without first consulting the full board. While the war contracts involved many parts of the University, the College of Engineering was called on frequently, sometimes merely to provide classrooms and laboratories if not actual instruction, but always diverting engineering faculty members into administrative and supervisory roles. Such was the case with three successive classes of 30 Naval officers studying diesel engine operation and for a training program for 156 Army Air Corps mechanics from Chanute Field in Illinois. On a different front the U.S. Surgeon General contracted with the Medical School for a series of special twelve-week anesthesiology courses. The most unusual request from Washington came to Donald Halverson's Department of Dormitories and Commons, which in October, 1942, opened the first-of-its-kind university-based school for Navy cooks and bakers.[16]

---

[16]BOR Minutes, May 30, June 27, September 26, 1942, UA. The cooks and bakers school opened with nine sailor students. Donald Halverson was director of instruction and Helen Giessel was the chief teacher. The course lasted sixteen weeks, involving nine hours of kitchen work and one hour in class daily. Washbush, "The Campus and the Navy," p. 6.

Military women invaded the campus on October 9, 1942, as the first contingent of Women Accepted for Voluntary Service (WAVES) arrived to begin training in the Navy Radio School. The Navy wanted female radio operators to replace sailors at shore stations, thereby freeing the men for combat duty at sea. While the WAVES would receive the same instruction as the sailors, their classes—contrary to long tradition at Wisconsin—were separate. The mood in Madison was festive that Friday as small groups of women, finally totalling 480, disembarked from trains and made their way to quarters on the lower campus in Barnard and Chadbourne halls. (Prior to the WAVES' arrival the dean of women's office had relocated all civilian coeds into private off-campus housing.)[17] The next day the women cheered Badger stars Pat Harder and Elroy Hirsch and their teammates in their 17-9 football victory over Missouri. The University band serenaded the female volunteers at halftime. Classes soon started, but the WAVES remained in civilian clothes until the 19th when seventy-five Marshall Field Company employees turned Memorial Union's Great Hall into a "factory assembly line" for outfitting 58 future radio operators every ninety minutes.[18] Later during an orientation ceremony at Memorial Union, Extension Dean Frank Holt assured the female "bluejackets" of their sincere welcome to campus. "There should be no difference here in the attitude towards the WAVES, from that toward the regular coeds. This University has always seen its responsibility, not only in terms of those enrolled on the campus, but in reaching other groups beyond those enrolled."[19]

Relations between the University and the armed services were not always smooth. Evidence of friction occurred as early as May, 1942, when an Army officer accused President Dykstra of encouraging an "obvious and harmful lack of enthusiasm" among students over an Air Corps recruiting program on campus.[20] Dykstra had hardly put out this brush fire when he received notification that the Navy had decided for technical reasons to disaccredit the University's Navy enlisted reserve

---

[17]As word of the WAVES assignment arrived during the summer, Assistant Dean of Women Zoe Bayliss and a student helper relocated the coeds who had planned to live at Barnard and Chadbourne. Halverson to Dykstra, "Report on Student Housing Situation," September 25, 1942, BOR Papers, 1/1/3, box 58, UA.

[18]*Capital Times*, September 20, 1942.

[19]*Press Bulletin*, October 21, 1942.

[20]*Wisconsin State Journal*, May 1, 1942; *Capital Times*, May 2, 3, and 4, 1942; editorial, *Daily Cardinal*, May 6, 1942.

program. The president managed to have this decision reversed in June, but only after considerable effort. In addition, University officials gradually realized that the military technical training programs, which were heavily vocational in nature, were monopolizing campus living facilities while allowing the academic resources of the institution to languish. This was certainly true of the largest program, the Navy Radio School, for which Dykstra came to think the University served primarily as its "hotel."

Such problems were not limited to Wisconsin, of course. On November 12, 1942, President Robert Hutchins of the University of Chicago addressed a complaint to the Navy bluntly criticizing the low quality of officers in charge of trainees on his campus and at Minnesota, Indiana, and Wisconsin.[21] A week later Dykstra jotted a cryptic note: "Complete frustration Naval Radio School." Perhaps due to Hutchins' letter, on November 27 the Navy assigned a new leader at Wisconsin. Commander Leslie K. Pollard would remain in Madison for the duration and he eventually earned widespread respect. But at the beginning his decisions troubled Dykstra. In direct opposition to the president's wishes, he significantly diminished civilian involvement with the radio school. Next, giving disconcertingly short notice, he announced on December 5 that the Navy diesel training program would close in February.[22] How could UW authorities plan for the rational use of their facilities and staff under such chaotic circumstances?

An experienced administrator, President Dykstra worried about what he diplomatically termed the emerging "confusion" in federal manpower policy and began advocating college-level work for military personnel.[23] Like his colleagues throughout higher education, Dykstra believed that somehow the nation's colleges and universities must find a way to use their classrooms for academic students rather than short-term technical trainees. After all, the nation would require a pool of well-educated leaders after the war, even as the armed services needed a greatly expanded officer corps now. With the decline of the regular

---

[21]Washbush, "The Campus and the Navy," p. 20. President Dykstra believed the University ought to make a more valuable contribution than merely housing a radio school: "Is it not of greater value to the Navy to use the University of Wisconsin for higher educational training where the regular faculty could be employed, rather than to have dormitory space occupied by radio students necessitating a different faculty particularly in view of the fact that such radio training could be supplied efficiently at smaller colleges." Quoted in ibid., p. 26.

[22]Quoted in ibid., pp. 21, 22-3; *Daily Cardinal*, November 28, 1942.

[23]*Capital Times*, September 23, 1924; *Daily Cardinal*, September 25, 1942.

student body, moreover, many liberal arts faculty members had little work to do. Dykstra therefore argued for a "single coherent policy" to be established by a national manpower council.[24] Meanwhile, the problem of shrinking enrollment worsened in the fall of 1942 when the draft began taking 18- and 19-year-old men. Since women previously had constituted only about a third of the undergraduates at Wisconsin, the likelihood of making up much of the decreased male enrollment seemed depressingly slight. Wisconsin's enrollment problems were reflected across the country, and the tempo of the dialogue among the college presidents increased, as did their discussions with federal manpower authorities and military officials. By early November there was public speculation that selected servicemen might be assigned to university campuses for baccalaureate studies eventually leading to commissioning as officers. On November 13 President Dykstra quietly informed Navy officials of his intention to pursue the new, more academic officer-training programs he thought would develop in the near future.

There was further discussion of this long-range manpower issue the following month. The *Daily Cardinal* reported Dykstra's discussion of a proposal to enroll a quarter-million servicemen for "specialized" academic instruction at selected colleges and universities. The University undoubtedly would participate, he stated, and UW faculty would do the teaching.[25] Contradictory rumors abounded, however, and Dykstra scheduled a convocation of all military reservists on campus to clarify the situation. Twelve hundred students attended the Memorial Union event and welcomed the president's prediction that a "uniform-and-pay" course of studies would replace many of the enlisted reserve programs. Dykstra also provided his audience with the latest information about their expected "call to the colors" dates, ranging from January 1 for ROTC seniors, to end of the fall semester for Army enlisted reservists, to "a date to be announced" for the Navy reservists, to June 1 for medical and engineering students. Although details of the expected new academic programs at Wisconsin and other campuses remained undefined, Dykstra expected them to involve both Army and Navy personnel. Once the reservists had completed basic training, he explained, many would be ordered to UW or some other campus for continued study. The next day

---

[24]*Daily Cardinal*, October 10, 1942.

[25]Ibid., December 3, 1942. The recommendation was issued by the Educational Policies Commission of the National Education Association.

Dykstra distributed a memorandum to the faculty describing what he knew about the planned specialized training initiative and the part the faculty would be expected to play in it.[26] A mutually beneficial military personnel policy was coming into focus.

In early January, 1943, University officials, like their colleagues across the country, urged all Army reserve students to enroll for the spring semester after learning that call-up dates were again being delayed. As an incentive for cooperation, Dykstra pledged the University would refund the fees of anyone ordered to service during the term. Meanwhile, Dykstra had been appointed to a distinguished committee charged with advising the War Manpower Commission on the selection of institutions to host the much-discussed specialized programs and their operation.[27] On January 11 the University faculty voted approval of a plan suggested by L&S Dean Mark Ingraham (who had succeeded Dean George Sellery on July 1, 1942) to create an "unclassified" category for "soldier-students" and to make available academic credit for work completed.[28] The next month President Dykstra announced that the prototype Army Specialized Training Program—soon universally known as ASTP—would include curricula in area studies, psychology, medicine, and engineering. Simultaneously, federal officials announced a revised manpower plan intended to raise twenty-eight new Army divisions every four weeks. By the end of February, 23 UW student Army reservists had received orders to report for active duty by March 13. Similar orders followed throughout the spring.

The logjam began to break in March. Early in the month President Dykstra addressed the faculty, reporting that a Navy counterpart to the Army's ASTP would begin operation in a few months and be called V-12. Meanwhile, an Army Air Corps meteorology training program—one of the earliest specialized academic programs anywhere—would open at the University in few days with an initial contingent of 350 students.

---

[26]Ibid., December 18, 1942; Dykstra, memorandum to faculty, December 18, 1942, General Presidential Papers, 4/0/1, box 44.

[27]War Manpower Chief Paul V. McNutt, acting on the advice of the Army and Navy secretaries, appointed the committee, to be chaired by Owen D. Young of the General Electric Company. Other members included: Presidents Edmund E. Day (Cornell), O.C. Carmichael (Vanderbilt), James B. Conant (Harvard), Dykstra (Wisconsin), F.D. Patterson (Tuskegee), Robert G. Sproul (California), E.V. Stanford (Villanova), and William P. Tolley (Syracuse); Associate Justice Wiley Rutledge (U.S. Court of Appeals) also served.

[28]UW Faculty Minutes, January 11, 1943, UA; *Daily Cardinal* and *Capital Times*, January 12, 1943; *Press Bulletin*, January 27, 1943. The regents soon approved these arrangements. BOR Minutes, January 23, 1943.

"These weather boys are the first regular collegiate men to be here in uniform," explained the president. The program would function under College of Letters and Science auspices with geography Professor Glenn T. Trewartha as course director.[29] The first class, including 5 former UW students, arrived in groups of a few dozen after March 8, taking over three of the Kronshage men's dormitories on the lake shore to the west of the Tripp-Adams complex. As the meteorology trainees were arriving in Madison, the American Council on Education issued a pamphlet generally describing ASTP. The Army program would involve both basic and specialized academic studies, with terms lasting twelve weeks, the number of terms required for completion varying according to the particular field of study. Selection for ASTP would require a high score on the Army's standardized aptitude test, approval by a military personnel board, and assignment to a field of study whose quota remained unfilled. The Navy issued similar information about its V-12 program in April, although at Wisconsin only the upper level courses would ever become available.[30]

In September, 1942, Donald Halverson, the director of residence halls and chairman of the University Housing Committee, had reported to President Dykstra that so far the University had managed to arrange accommodations for all of its regular students as well as the military trainees. This was impressive news, considering that the campus was then housing and feeding 40 percent more students than in "normal" times. Conditions became more difficult in March of 1943 when the influx of meteorology students could only be met by fitting each room in the Swenson, Jones, and Chamberlin houses of the Kronshage complex with a double bunk bed and cot. Within a month additional meteorologists moved into Conover House, requiring that its original residents squeeze into the Showerman, Mack, Gilman, and Turner houses, the last enclave of male civilian students living on campus. This

---

[29]In November the regents approved an Army Air Force request that the University set up a "course for meteorologists." BOR Minutes, November 21, 1942. The program was scheduled to open February 1, 1943, at five universities, including UW. It would accept high school graduates and college students, with instruction lasting fifteen to twenty months. The host institutions would provide room, board, and uniforms, and the students would receive pay. See the *Daily Cardinal*, November 24, 1942, for an overview of the program. See also UW Faculty Minutes, March 1, 1943; *Capital Times*, March 3, 1943; Dykstra, notes for address to the faculty, March 1, 1943, Dykstra Presidential Papers, 4/15/1, box 152.

[30]*Daily Cardinal*, April 13, 1943; Washbush, "The Campus and the Navy," pp. 39-41. According to Washbush the Army and Navy had an agreement that no institution could run general programs for both ASTP and V-12.

apparently was the limit, however, and with the anticipated opening of the ASTP and V-12 programs extraordinary measures were now required. Thus on March 27 the regents authorized Halverson to negotiate agreements "with off-campus organizations or enterprises such as clubs, fraternities, etc. for the purpose of operating such units as auxiliary housing units for government trainees sent to the University for instruction." The regents also ordered that "the director of residence halls is to have final supervisory authority over all housing and food service for trainees at the University." By summer Director Halverson's division was housing and feeding almost all of the 3,200 service men and women then assigned to campus.[31]

Throughout the 1942-43 academic year the University attempted to maintain a semblance of its regular instructional program for the rapidly diminishing civilian student population. The problem was exacerbated by unprecedented demand for courses in engineering, the physical sciences, medicine, and nursing. Yet these were exactly the fields whose faculty members were being drawn away in large numbers for research, administrative, and military service. Law and Agriculture, for their part, maintained a relatively comfortable balance, with enrollments decreasing in concert with increasing departures and non-instructional demands on their faculty members. Liberal arts enrollments, on the other hand, languished except in certain war-related foreign language courses. As the conflict dragged on, many male students either dropped out of school to await the draft or shifted along with the women into relatively more technical or applied studies. This left growing numbers of L&S professors essentially out of work and with few immediate prospects for using their expertise in support of the common struggle. The University, in other words, simultaneously faced severe staffing shortages and surpluses across its severely dislocated curricula. At the national level, this imbalance led to mounting pressure for including a basic or general studies component in the new ASTP and V-12 programs. In Madison, while Professor William F. Steve shoe-horned a trebled enrollment into his hugely popular Physics 1 course, President Dykstra and the deans surveyed their underused faculty members (and spouses) in search of people to teach high-demand subjects like basic mathematics. Retooling and flexibility were becoming watchwords of the day.[32]

[31]Halverson to Dykstra, September 25, 1942, BOR Papers, 1/1/3, box 58; *Daily Cardinal*, October 10, 1942; BOR Minutes, March 27, 1943; *Press Bulletin*, June 16, 1943.

[32]On the problem of faculty employment, see Dykstra, speech notes for "Faculty Meeting,"

Curricular and related academic policy concerns also consumed faculty energy. By the fall of 1942 staff members were offering forty-five specially designed wartime courses for credit. Whenever possible the regular curriculum in such fields as mathematics favored application over theory. The faculty significantly increased the physical education requirement for both men and women in an effort to accommodate the students' diverse needs, ranging from rigorous basic military training to general personal fitness. The new Contemporary Trends course, a product of the 1940 Daniels Curriculum Committee,[33] afforded an unusual opportunity in these hectic times for students to reflect on the war and anticipated problems of the post-war world. The Schools of Medicine, Nursing, Commerce, and Journalism began offering shortened practice-oriented, non-degree programs for students soon to enter service. Tinkering with admission, course, and degree requirements, as well as planning and staffing for a full-blown three-semester annual calendar, required almost constant activity of the various schools and colleges and the University faculty as a whole. They reflected the faculty's multi-faceted attempt to balance effective responses to wartime demands with the longer-term obligation to maintain the basic integrity of the instructional program at Wisconsin.

The effort to maintain a reasonable semblance of the regular academic program was not always appreciated. Already during the spring of 1942 UW officials were contending with unusually high levels of frivolous behavior on the part of men students who expected to depart soon for military service.[34] Crusty L&S Dean George Sellery, soon to retire, had no sympathy for such behavior. In late May the *Capital Times* quoted Sellery as offering this advice to the slackers: "You came to the university to get an education," he declared. "If you remain at the university you're going to get one whether you like it or not. If you

---

December 7, 1942, Dykstra Presidential Papers, 4/15/1, box 152; *Badger*, 1943, p. 349. The *Daily Cardinal*, October 16, 1942, reported that Professor Evans had recently recruited two astronomers (Huffer and Stebbins), two hydraulic engineers (Woodburn and Borchardt), one agricultural bacteriologist (Wilson), and several wives (Huffer, Johnson, Evans, and Sokolnikoff) to help with mathematics department teaching. On December 16, 1943, the *Daily Cardinal* reported that faculty shortages in mathematics and physics were critical.

[33]See pp. 752-5.

[34]In April, 1942, Dean of Men Goodnight prohibited open house parties, "in which conduct seems to have been most reprehensible. We are at war, and now we have an even greater obligation to maintain high standards in our campus community." *Daily Cardinal*, April 11, 1942. Two days later a *Cardinal* editorial criticized this policy. See also *Capital Times*, April 12, 1942.

don't like it you don't belong at the university so make room for another student who's got some gumption."[35] The uncertain call-up dates for enlisted reservists further increased the temptation for a last civilian fling. By November of 1942 the problem, which plagued campuses throughout the country, led to a stern warning by L&S Assistant Dean Chester H. Ruedisili:

> It is time to begin to distinguish between men at the university who are here to train themselves to serve their country in a leadership capacity, and those who are here merely to mark time. There are students now in school who are doing a poor job through negligence and indifference. These same students...should be doing a good job somewhere else.[36]

The situation continued to deteriorate until February, 1943, when the UW military authorities called an emergency meeting of enlisted reservists to condemn what the *Cardinal* characterized as the nefarious and demoralizing cutting of classes. To underline this message, reservist Donald Meves, who recently had been dropped from the University for failing to attend class, urged the 160-man audience to attend to their studies.[37] Such warnings were mostly futile and the problem persisted throughout the term until the call-up of essentially all eligible male students substituted military discipline for the distractions of civilian life.

While some University students may not have taken their studies as seriously as the faculty wished, the great bulk of campus extracurricular behavior was thoughtful, constructive, and forward-looking. As in the first days of the war, the tone of life at UW continued to reflect demanding wartime conditions that were quite different from the recent depression. The Pan Hellenic and Inter-Fraternity Councils, for example, curtailed their social programs to demonstrate support for those in military service and to conserve resources. In the fall of 1942 the Greek-letter fraternities and other student groups donated hard-won

---

[35]*Capital Times*, May 20, 1942. On February 17, 1942, the *Daily Cardinal* ran a guest editorial written by Dean Sellery, entitled "Buckle Down to Your Jobs, Students: This is WAR!" He argued: "You are your chief war work. Are you doing better, steadily improving, focussing your energy on this war work? Don't tell me; tell yourself and act accordingly."

[36]*Daily Cardinal*, November 12, 1942. Declared Junior Dean Harry Glicksman, the deputy L&S administrator: "It would be unfair to the war effort, to our institution, and to the students to impair standards of scholarship at this critical time. The nation will need officers: we must help to train them. The country will continue to require standards of efficiency and integrity: our faculty and administrators should therefore encourage excellence as never before."

[37]Ibid., February 20, 1943.

trophies accumulated for decades that helped produce a huge hundred-ton scrap pile at the foot of Bascom Hill. The impressive mound replaced the traditional homecoming bonfire that year and eventually became part of the nation's war machine. Recurring war bond and stamp drives soaked up any surplus cash. One blood drive in November, 1942, exceeded its quota of 600 quarts by 214. In an unprecedented display of solidarity, the *Daily Cardinal* joined with four hundred other college newspapers in December of 1942 in taking a "Voice for Victory" pledge fully to support the United States war effort. A few months later UW student Josie Cohen announced that the campus Social Post wartime volunteer organization was launching an experimental dating bureau to match coeds with servicemen. Commented one pleasantly surprised veteran of a previous dating program: "Astounding. I didn't realize there were girls left at this university who just drank cokes."[38]

The Memorial Union, the focal point of extra-curricular student life since opening in 1928, issued special guest cards to military personnel. At first the cards were limited to participants in college-level academic training programs, although they were eventually offered to any campus-based service man or woman. The Union sponsored "At Ease" programs on Sunday afternoons and "servicecraft nights." Service dances were common, and USO hostesses offered instruction in folk dancing. In January, 1943, Navy Radio School WAVES and sailors joined forces to stage a musical show, "Look Alive." The Union Forum series for 1942-43 emphasized "public discussion in wartime."[39] In February of 1943 the Wisconsin Union Directorate established a military relations committee to establish and maintain liaison with the recreation directors of the military branches on campus. For its first project the committee organized a much-appreciated orientation program for all newly arrived service people. The service use of the Memorial Union was sufficiently great that by the end of 1943 officials announced that because of the Union's responsibility for feeding upwards of a thousand military personnel each day, the facility could host no more civilian banquets for the duration.

Soon after the attack on Pearl Harbor, UW students and faculty began discussing and planning for the post-war world. The Student War Council sponsored a series of lectures on the topic in February, 1942.

---

[38]Ibid., March 6, 1943.
[39]*Badger*, 1943, p. 214. On the Memorial Union as a USO, see *Daily Cardinal*, May 21, 1942.

Many of the organized houses followed suit with their own discussion programs. Strong support expressed itself for some kind of unifying world organization that would transcend the weaknesses of the League of Nations. After economics Professor Selig Perlman outlined his views at a unity forum in late 1942, one of the students present declared in a letter to the *Cardinal*: "We need more intelligent discussion of this sort on our campus, and the professors, experts in their field, are the ones which should take the lead." The interest was great, the discussions intense. At one point, in fact, the *Daily Cardinal* editorialized that the many student forums needed better coordination to avoid wasteful duplication. During the spring of 1943 the *Cardinal* launched a semester-long series of articles by UW faculty members on "America and the War." The series aimed to provide information and stimulate discussion of "the problems affecting the student body after the war." Topics included: "social aspects" of the war and post-war world, U.S. foreign policy, the "philosophical climate of the post-war world," "international status of labor," "war debts and reparation," and "post-war selective service." The faculty authorities recruited for this ambitious venture included Merle Curti (history), Gaines Post (history), Chester V. Easum (history), Selig Perlman (economics), William L. Sachse (history), Arthur C. Garnett (philosophy), and Philo M. Buck (comparative literature), as well as President Dykstra. The impressive series ran on Tuesdays and Fridays throughout the semester.[40]

As the enrollment of civilian male students and their role in extracurricular activities declined, University coeds took up the slack. The *Daily Cardinal* launched an "intensive program to train women for staff positions," and the Women's Self-Government Association (WSGA) reoriented its activities "in keeping with the increased importance of women on the campus." The all-female home economics Euthenics Club provided USO hostesses, raised money for British War Relief, and mounted a "Share the Meat for Victory" campaign.[41] In October, 1942, the Student War Council sponsored an unprecedented all-University convocation for women in anticipation of the registration of all UW coeds with the new Women's Emergency National Training Service (WENTS). Three hundred women signed up to take a six-week non-credit emergency first aid course sponsored by the UW School of Nursing. Graduates would be prepared to respond in the event of a

---

[40]*Daily Cardinal*, November 11, December 1, 1942, February 23, 1943.
[41]*Badger*, 1943, pp. 248, 280, 291.

much-feared flu epidemic and generally to assist professional physicians and nurses. In November University women participated in the national Women at War fund-raising week. "Never before," observed the *Cardinal* of the many vacant jobs in society, "has the woman student been presented with such opportunities and such demands for specialization."[42] By January, 1943, increasing shortages in the domestic work force led to national discussion of extending the draft to include women. In anticipation of such a call (which never came), Beulah Larkin, an assistant dean of women, encouraged UW coeds whenever possible to redirect their studies into high-demand technical areas such as mathematics, physics, chemistry, geography, statistics, and accounting. Yet while many women energetically answered the call, like their male reservist counterparts at the time, more than a few failed to sustain the commitment. As one *Daily Cardinal* editorial asked plaintively, "Where are the WENTS?"[43]

For many years UW student leaders had actively opposed prejudice and discrimination. Now, with wartime propaganda emphasizing the superiority of American democratic ideals over the racist ideology of the Axis powers, the local civil rights movement gained fresh momentum.[44] On the day of the Pearl Harbor attack, as outrage against the Japanese attack mounted, some students organized the Wisconsin Liberal Council to back the U.S. war effort while also opposing any illegal retaliation against Japanese people living in America. UW students subsequently condemned mistreatment of American citizens of Japanese descent and expressed support for admission to the University of some whom the federal government was relocating from the west coast. Students also stepped up the pressure against race-based rental discrimination practiced in Madison by many Greek-letter chapters and private rooming houses.[45]

---

[42]*Daily Cardinal*, December 5, 1942.

[43]Editorial, *Daily Cardinal*, February 16, 1943. On the lack of interest among coeds for WSGA work see *Daily Cardinal*, April 21, 1943. On coed war efforts see *Daily Cardinal*, March 26, 1943, and *Press Bulletin*, April 21, 1943.

[44]*Daily Cardinal* columnist Bob Lewis wrote on March 21, 1942: "White civilization must turn its weight behind world democracy—political, economic, and social. It must free its slaves or they will enslave him." The next day a *Cardinal* editorial supported a Council Against Intolerance proposal to the U.S. War Department that a racially mixed Army division be formed and advocated "racial equality and democracy" throughout the United States.

[45]Discrimination in housing had a long history in Madison. With few black students enrolled, student concern prior to 1940 focussed mostly on instances of anti-Semitism. Disapproval of housing discrimination against blacks increased significantly during the spring term of 1942. Editorial, *Daily Cardinal*, May 8, 1942. With the beginning of the 1942-43

When a southern sailor on campus for training publicly insulted a black UW student at Memorial Union in October of 1942, the ensuing campus protest led to stern warnings by Navy authorities against any repetition.[46] When student activists learned of a UW Medical School policy of declining to admit Negroes into the clinical sequence of the M.D. degree program because of the difficulty of placing them in hospital residencies, there was a similar noisy student condemnation.[47] In 1943 the Wisconsin Players canceled their production of "According to Law" because some of the black actors found it offensive.[48] A month later the Wisconsin Union film committee similarly canceled the showing of "Lucky Ghost" because of its alleged racial insensitivity. Well-attended forums, artistic performances, and cultural activities provided an affirmative image of and vision for the future of American Negroes. Perhaps the most successful undertaking of this sort was the nineteenth annual UW Negro History Week, celebrated on campus during February, 1943.[49] As L&S Junior Dean Harry Glicksman summarized the growing campus consensus in March, "The pending war has crystallized the thoughts and resolves of many people who have long been shocked by the incursion

---

academic year the campaign against local racial injustices, involving both students and faculty, gained momentum. *Capital Times*, September 23, 24, and 25, 1942; *Daily Cardinal*, September 23, 24, 25, 26, and 29, October 1, 1942. President Dykstra declared in early October: "We cannot control the housing policy of private homes in Madison. We can only regret that discrimination exists, and use such good offices and persuasion as we have to ask for liberality. We have done this in the past and have attempted to open houses to students in every class, group, race and religion." *Daily Cardinal*, October 2, 1942.

[46]Editorial, *Daily Cardinal*, October 14, 1942. The editors stated in part: "To that one sailor we wish to point out that he is a guest here at the university, and that here at Wisconsin we strive to treat men of all races alike." Two days later the *Cardinal* quoted Commander Green's statement on the matter: "The navy men are guests in Madison, and will conduct themselves as such, regardless of any personal ideas they may have. The entire personnel has been informed that they must observe the customs of the city and of the university while they are here. There must be no friction." Two days later the paper published a letter declaring: "If this war does nothing else it must end race prejudice here and abroad....no matter what color a man's skin may be, he is a man—and every other man's equal." A similar incident, this time involving a beating on Langdon Street, occurred in April, 1943. Commander Pollard dealt with it swiftly and effectively. Ibid., April 24, 1943.

[47]*Capital Times*, January 13 and 15, 1943; *Daily Cardinal*, January 16, February 12, 1943.

[48]*Daily Cardinal*, November 7, 1942. The play had previously received an award from the American Civil Liberties Union for its portrayal of southern racial problems.

[49]*Daily Cardinal*, February 3 and 12, 1943; editorial, *Capital Times*, February 7, 1943. One letter to the editor exhorted: "In your history week you will place in full view evidences of not only your right to have equal treatment but proof of your capabilities as well. Perhaps you will be able to advance farther in your aim for democratic treatment as a result. In any case, we hope with you that you will be able to do so." *Daily Cardinal*, February 6, 1943.

of hateful bigotry into areas like ours, where tolerant breadth rightfully belongs."[50]

Many University faculty members were involved in war-related research and extension activities. Special federal contracts for research and off-campus training fueled much of the effort. As of November, 1942, more than a hundred UW scientists were at work on national defense problems, many in University laboratories.[51] Although most of the projects were secret at the time, enough information was available to generate good public relations for the University. The U.S. Geological Survey effectively functioned as the outreach arm of the UW geology department. The Extension Division helped Wisconsin businesses and municipalities subdue their most pressing wartime building problems. College of Agriculture agronomists issued their new rust- and smut-resistant Vicland oats variety at this time, enabling farmers to maintain high dairy feed levels and thereby to avoid wintertime milk shortages. Professor Gustav Bohstedt, a leading meat and animal scientist, issued recommendations for emergency hog rations, which resulted in highly efficient feeding in a national context of severe protein shortages. Chemical engineering faculty members developed non-corroding brass cartridge cases for Navy use. Medical School scholars studied diseases and wounds common in theaters of war. UW social scientists applied their expertise to war problems, too, as when the famed anthropologist Margaret Mead visited campus to consult with Professor H. Scudder Mekeel of the anthropology department about her project on "Food Habits in Relation to the War."

In October, 1942, President Dykstra announced the creation of the University of Wisconsin Emergency Inventions Development Council. Physics Professor Hugo B. Wahlin chaired the group, which also included members from the Departments of Mining and Metallurgy, Bacteriology, Medicine, and Biochemistry. The committee solicited ideas from anyone on campus and throughout the state. "These ideas will be collected and transmitted to those persons or organizations where we feel they will do most good in the war effort," explained Wahlin.

---

[50]The student board's adoption of a strong statement on housing was the occasion for Glicksman's remarks. *Daily Cardinal*, March 24, 1943.

[51]*Press Bulletin*, November 18, 1942. Observed the *Daily Cardinal* on December 5, 1942: "What these [research] problems are, and who is working on what, is a matter of military secret and cannot be told here." Even the Board of Regents remained largely uninformed. In February, 1943, for example, the regents received only a list, but not descriptions, of secret and confidential government contracts in effect at the University. BOR Minutes, February 17, 1943.

"The committee will welcome any ideas on anything from a better anti-tank shell to a substitute for tin foil wrapping for cheese."[52] In January, 1943, Wahlin reported that the committee had received more than a hundred ideas from across Wisconsin. They ranged from suggestions for military strategy to plans for modernized airplane and submarine detectors. Probably operating more as a public relations and morale-building tool than as an effective device for identifying and channeling technically important ideas, the council encouraged all segments of the Wisconsin population to identify with the University and its wartime effort.

The University Extension Division and WHA radio engaged fully in the conflict. In the spring of 1943, for example, the Madison-based Army Institute broadened its mission to provide correspondence study to personnel of the Navy, Marines, and Coast Guard, in addition to the original Army clientele. In the process its title was changed to the United States Armed Forces Institute (USAFI). By mid-1943 enrollment exceeded thirty thousand. In May, 1942, the University and the federal government entered into a contract for Extension to run an Engineering, Science, and Management Defense Training program throughout the state. Within six months the program had worked with more than a thousand Wisconsin businesses, involving two hundred classes and enrolling six thousand individuals.[53] Extension also offered many less technical but nevertheless worthwhile defense courses and with federal encouragement set up a war information center for civilian defense. A more glamorous extension activity, the Civilian Pilot Training Program, was by the fall of 1942 monopolized on campus by military personnel, but it soon expanded to serve civilian and military trainees in a total of seven Wisconsin cities. The program also eventually provided glider pilot training for the Marines. WHA radio broadcast a steady round of lectures, interviews, and forums that informed and challenged its listeners on matters of war and peace and generally encouraged serious dialogue about the post-war world. By 1943 the University was fully mobilized.

---

[52]Committee members included: Wahlin, Edwin R. Shorey (mining and metallurgy), Perry Wilson (bacteriology), Frederic E. Mohs (medicine), and Marvin J. Johnson (biochemistry). *Press Bulletin*, October 21, 1942.

[53]"War Training Program for Wisconsin War Industries and Other Essential Industries and Businesses: ESMDT and ESMWT Programs, 1941-1945," July 31, 1945, UW Faculty Papers, 5/100, box 1.

Boom and Bust

The military occupation of the University reached its peak in the summer of 1943. In late May a group of 150 pre-meteorology "C" students joined the 363 "B" weathermen previously in residence since April. The new men would study mathematics, physics, geography, and English on "the Hill" in their year-long course and their arrival assured the continued military occupation of the Kronshage dormitory complex. At the same time a group of 35 women Marines arrived from Hunter College in New York, where they had recently completed their preliminary training. They joined the Navy's WAVES and a few Coast Guard SPARS in the female section, now numbering about 500, of the Navy Radio School and took up residence at Barnard and Chadbourne halls on the lower campus. These uniformed students, combined with the 1,200 male radio school sailors residing at the stadium and Tripp and Adams dormitories, and the 110 Navy and Marine student pilots housed in three Lake Street fraternity houses, comprised the expanded original detachments of service trainees on campus. This was impressive enough, but in early June the first contingents of the long-awaited Army Specialized Training Program began arriving in Madison, moving into thirteen fraternity houses along Langdon Street and the dormitory wing of University Club on State Street.[54]

By the first day of classes on June 14, 428 ASTP men were in residence. Of these, 316 were enrolled in the basic phase of the engineering program, which involved three 12-week semesters of English, history, mathematics, physics, and engineering drawing. Another 112 soldiers, all of whom were fluent in at least two foreign languages, began work in the area and languages program, envisioned as leading to wartime assignments behind enemy lines and leadership of the post-war occupation of enemy territory.[55] (Contrary to President Dykstra's earlier expectation, the University received no ASTP trainees for a program in personnel psychology.) Late arrivals during the term pushed the final ASTP enrollment to nearly 650. Colonel Herbert H.

---

[54]*Summer Cardinal*, June 4, 1943; *Press Bulletin*, June 2, 1943. As of mid-June, 112 area studies men resided at the Delta Tau Delta and Beta Theta Pi houses; 316 basic engineering men lived at the University Club and the Phi Kappa Sigma, Psi Upsilon, and Phi Epsilon Phi houses. *Summer Cardinal*, June 15, 1943.

[55]Area and languages was one of the advanced programs—along with personnel psychology, medicine, and engineering—open to men with liberal arts backgrounds or who would qualify after two terms of basic ASTP work. *Summer Cardinal*, June 29, 1943.

Lewis, the commanding officer, warned the ASTP trainees that their studies would not be easy: "The hours will be long and the subjects intensive."[56] Within a month unanticipated deficiencies in mathematics among the basic engineering students led to the establishment of a remedial program. The ASTP *Specializer* section of the *Cardinal* advised its readers—whatever one's educational background—to follow a simple motto: learn "the mostest in the quickest time."[57] Enrollment for the second ASTP term, beginning in September, jumped to 902.

In addition to the khaki-clad ASTP trainees, 500 V-12 apprentice seamen landed in Madison on July 1, 1943. Fresh from civilian life, these officers-in-training preceded their uniforms to campus. Nearly all of the new arrivals began their course work the next week in the College of Engineering. Their academic calendar involved three sixteen-week terms, and, as with ASTP, University faculty members taught the classes, with the students receiving full academic credit for their work. The V-12s filled the remaining vacancies in the Kronshage dormitories adjacent to the Navy Radio School reservation to the east. They were free to participate in intercollegiate athletics and involve themselves in any campus organization or activity that did not interfere with their studies, which included the rudiments of Navy drill. They remained on active duty, however, subject to Navy supervision and discipline.

The UW Medical School also participated in the ASTP and V-12 programs at several levels. In mid-June the first involvement began when most of the University's male medical students left the campus for Army or Navy reception centers—138 to the Army and 79 to the Navy—where they received uniforms, equipment, and the "bare rudiments of military training."[58] Two weeks later they returned to Madison and resumed their studies, only now in uniform. Due to the severe housing shortage as well as their special status, the ASTP and V-

---

[56]*Daily Cardinal*, June 15, 1943. The fluid situation made keeping track of programs and enrollment information very difficult. The two issues of the *Press Bulletin* for June, 1943, for example, reported that 350 pre-medical ASTP students were studying on campus. The fact was, however, that although the Army had informed the regents of its intention to establish such a program, it had been canceled before opening due to the unavailability of students. On June 26, 1943, UW Comptroller A.W. Peterson addressed a memorandum to the regents on military programs at the University. Peterson listed 499 basic and 144 area studies enrollments, figures which he said were approximate. BOR Minutes, June 26, 1943.

[57]*Specializer*, June 22, 1943.

[58]Many conflicting enrollment figures were announced. The figures used here are from an official regents document regarding the extending of training contracts. BOR Minutes, October 16, 1943.

12 medical students enjoyed the privilege of arranging for their own accommodations and paying for them with government stipends. In addition to handling the heavy load of regular ASTP and V-12 medical students, the Medical School also operated as one of eighteen institutions in the country providing advanced instruction in internal medicine, surgery, and dentistry to Army and Navy medical personnel.

The Army presence on campus grew further during the second half of 1943. On July 9 the *Summer Cardinal* announced the creation of a new Army Specialized Training Reserve Program (ASTRP). It would provide scholarships in the ASTP basic engineering sequence for qualified high school graduates under eighteen years of age. Participants would begin the program before taking basic military training, and they would wear civilian clothes. In August President Dykstra announced that the University would open its ASTRP course on September 13. The youthful recruits would reside in several of the Kronshage houses in quarters to be vacated by a group of meteorologists soon to graduate. The young men would wear uniforms only while attending military department activities with the few remaining ROTC cadets on campus.[59] Each ASTRP student would leave the program at the end of the term following his eighteenth birthday (when he would reach the minimum age for active military service), complete thirteen to seventeen weeks of basic training, and if qualified be returned to UW or sent to some other ASTP institution for continued study. The ASTRPs began arriving on campus during the last week of August. As the term opened in September, 292 of them took their places in class.

Several additional Army training programs were initiated in the fall of 1943. On October 1 the University opened a program to train 16 Women's Army Corps (WAC) members in physical therapy. The first of three envisioned two-month Army Civil Affairs Training School classes, approved by the regents for between 90 and 125 officers and actually enrolling 92, began their studies on October 25. On December 12 a new pre-professional ASTP program to fit students for medical and dental studies opened with 51 men enrolled. On December 27 ASTP Company "I" began operation with a complement of 200 recently arrived

---

[59]With ASTP and V-12 soon to open, the campus ROTC program changed drastically. The transition was complete in June, 1943, with ROTC now emphasizing the basic preparation of men for military service on a "branch immaterial" basis. As of December, 1943, ROTC enrollment involved 96 special students, all of whom resided with the ASTP students. Their numbers fell to zero in March, 1944. "Activities of Department of Military Science, 1942-1945," pp. 3, 28-9.

men for advanced area and languages study. It was difficult to keep track of the service enrollments because of the variety of programs and the constant movement of trainees to and from the campus. Still, their importance to the University was clear in view of the precipitous decline in regular student enrollments during the war.

University and military officials cooperated in smoothing the way for the various specialized academic programs, which not only made use of campus housing, dining, and classroom facilities but also relied on regular University instructional staff. It will be recalled that President Dykstra had doubted the appropriateness of the large Navy Radio School at an institution like the University of Wisconsin. Increasingly he believed this and other technical training programs ought to be located at less comprehensive educational institutions, reserving UW resources for providing more advanced academic work. With the ASTP and V-12 programs in place and the likelihood of their continued growth, Dykstra tried to curtail the radio school. On August 24 the Navy responded by notifying the University it would phase out the female section of the school (the WAVES, women Marines, and Coast Guard SPARS), closing it in December. The Navy also promised to withdraw two hundred sailors, leaving about a thousand male radio men on campus.[60] Barnard and Chadbourne halls would now be available to house male ASTP, ROTC, and civil affairs students. A few days later the Army notified University Comptroller Peterson that it would not replace the several hundred meteorology students who were completing their studies late that summer.[61]

While the effort continued to make all military trainees feel welcome at the University, official policy now favored a more focused attempt to integrate the ASTP, V-12, and meteorology students into the full scope of University life. While they were subject to military discipline and control, their academic work was similar to that of many of the civilian students they encountered on campus. In August, 1943, the Wisconsin Student Association extended honorary membership to the students in these programs.[62] The next month the faculty and regents

---

[60]A total of 1,179 WAVES, Spars, and women marines attended the radio school, 929 graduating and 410 receiving ratings. Washbush, "The Campus and the Navy," pp. 26-7; *Daily Cardinal*, September 25, 1943; *Badger Navy News*, December 17, 1943.

[61]BOR Minutes, August 30, 1943. According to the "Report of the Comptroller at Informal Conference," presented at the Board of Regents meeting, December 3-4, 1943, 120 meteorology "C" students remained on campus in December, 1943. BOR Papers, 1/1/3, box 60.

[62]On August 17, 1943, the Student Board of WSA voted honorary membership to ASTP and

affirmed earlier Athletic Board actions that allowed the specialized academic trainees to participate in intercollegiate athletics—now defined as "essentially activities of the armed services."[63] Every two weeks the Wisconsin Union Service Committee met with social committee members of each campus training unit to discuss program possibilities at Memorial Union. The Wisconsin Union committee also set up an information center for service men and women near the main entrance to the Union building. The staff of the 1944 *Badger* dedicated a quarter of the yearbook to military students and made a special effort to raise subscriptions among them. Home economics major Betty Vallier led a late-fall effort to establish a "co-ed canteen" at Memorial Union. "I felt it might be the solution to the problem of entertaining the servicemen on campus," Vallier explained to the *Daily Cardinal*.[64] Early in 1944 two ASTP trainees joined the Junior Prom planning committee to try to assure full ASTP involvement in that major spring social event.

Perhaps not surprisingly, during the fall of 1943 civilian students began to express some tension and resentment over the seemingly overwhelming military occupation of the campus. On October 2 the *Cardinal*, now largely under female direction, praised the outpouring of student support for the servicemen but also reminded its readers of the basic "student" (i.e., "civilian") character of the Memorial Union. The paper warned:

> ...low mumblings of complaint are beginning to sound forth from the student body because it feels that the military groups are being given precedence in the Union. Before these mumblings turn into open rebellion you ought to provide facilities and activities at which students will not feel out of place.[65]

V-12 students. The board excluded all other military personnel on campus on the grounds they were not, in the *Cardinal*'s words, "college men." The meteorologists protested that they too earned college credit for their work and in fact included among their numbers more highly educated students than did ASTP or V-12. At a special meeting on August 23, the Student Board reconsidered its decision and agreed to include the meteorologists. *Daily Cardinal*, August 20 and 24, 1943.

[63]BOR Minutes, September 18, 1943.

[64]*Daily Cardinal*, November 19, 1943. "I am very much interested in doing everything I can for the servicemen," explained Vallier, "and I think that everyone should and does feel that way. That is why I am so enthusiastic about the plans for the co-ed canteen and why I feel it will be a great success."

[65]Ibid., October 2, 1943. The friendly attitude toward the military on campus was never unanimous. At the opening of the fall semester, 1942, for example, John Wickhem, worrying that service men would overrun the Memorial Union, urged that a system of passes for "special guests" be established as a way of maintaining emphasis on students at the facility. Ibid.,

The negative feelings also found expression on campus sidewalks when resentful civilian students sometimes refused to step aside for marching columns of ASTP and V-12 trainees heading to or from class.[66] The friction was severe enough that Bill Brown, the acting UW military-civilian coordinator, was forced to concentrate most of his attention on resolving disputes between the two groups. Civilian resentment continued, however, when the Student War Council met to reformulate the military relations board and included six military and only three civilian students. Participants on both sides exchanged angry words. One particularly bitter soldier-student urged his colleagues-in-arms to seek their social enjoyment anywhere but the Memorial Union.

Several factors contributed to this increasingly unfriendly attitude toward military students on campus. For one, by the fall of 1943 the civilian student body numbered only about 4,500—half as large as it had been only a year earlier and about 40 percent of its pre-Pearl Harbor size.[67] At the same time the number of ASTP, V-12, and Army meteorology students had mushroomed to more than 3,000, rivaling the regular student population. Unlike the Navy radio trainees, these men were in most cases former college students taking college-level academic courses for which they would receive post-war academic credit. They tended to think of themselves as regular—if uniformed—members of the campus community. Many of them also had a relatively more conservative outlook compared with some of the more radical UW civilian students. This became apparent in November of 1943 when the service-dominated Military Relations Board considered launching an unprecedented public relations program to counter, as the *Cardinal* summarized it, the "undue amount of bad publicity concerning actions of radical individuals on the campus."[68] Finally, as the fortunes of war began to turn in the Allies' favor, some civilian students began to take a more casual view of the UW war effort. This was evident in the *Daily Cardinal*'s call for a return to the traditional campus social life:

September 25, 1942.

[66]This behavior led the Student War Council to approve a plan whereby marching formations would be limited to the extreme right side of any walkway and that all formations would be broken up within seventy-five feet of a classroom entrance. Ibid., October 7 and 8, 1943.

[67]Total civilian enrollment on September 28, 1942, was 9,088; a year later the number had fallen to 4,567. "Comparison of Registration Through September 28, 1943 and the Corresponding Day of Last Year," October 16, 1943, BOR Papers, 1/1/3, box 59; L. Joseph Lins, "Fact Book for History of Madison Campus," notebook, 1983, UHP.

[68]*Daily Cardinal*, November 18, 1943.

More formal social events are important to both the civilian and military students as individuals. They are important to Wisconsin, in order to preserve a part of the color that was Wisconsin's, a color that will be easier to restore after the war if proms and dances are continued on a slightly reduced scale at this time.[69]

War need not be unbearably grim; warriors (and their dates) required an occasional diversion!

President Dykstra's vision of a more suitable and stable military presence at the University was soon dashed. At the Teheran Conference in mid-December, 1943, the Allied leaders agreed to open a major front against Germany in western Europe as soon as possible. The Army's top priority now shifted to organizing the nation's ground troops for the coming major offensive. ASTP and associated Army programs with long-term training objectives suddenly were superfluous. Soon the *Daily Cardinal* was reporting that academic training programs would shortly be scaled back throughout the country. Within a month of enrolling the second group of UW officer-students, the Army abruptly terminated the Civil Affairs Training School on January 20, 1944, transferring essentially all of the personnel to European staging areas. On February 19 the War Department—pleading the "increased tempo of offensive operations with the mounting casualties demanding immediate replacement"—ordered huge reductions in ASTP enrollments nationwide to take effect no later than April 1. Wisconsin officials first expected to lose half of the Army men, leaving about 660 on campus for the spring term. The actual cutback was much more severe, however, leaving only the pre-medical, medical, and ASTRP programs viable. "The War Department needs certain units activated at once," explained Lt. Col. Franklin W. Clark, the UW Army commandant. "The manpower situation is so critical that the only source from which these units can be filled is the ASTP. This being true, the only justifiable action is the one being taken."[70] The majority of the ASTP men soon left Madison, with the remaining Army students in the specialized academic and technical training programs continuing their studies until they too departed at intervals.

The military pullout from the University involved primarily the Army. In early March, 1944, the UW Navy V-12 engineering program completed its second term and started its third with an influx of 160 new

---

[69]Editorial, ibid., October 13, 1943.
[70]*Specializer*, February 24, 1944.

students. According to Commander Pollard, because of the pressing need for Navy officers no curtailment of the program was contemplated. In the spring of 1944 the Navy celebrated its second anniversary as a major campus tenant. Commander Pollard and President Dykstra issued statements praising the work of the several training units, most of which continued in operation. By this time more than fifty-eight hundred men and a thousand women had passed through the radio school, the V-12 program, the cooks and bakers school, the diesel engine school, flight training, and the engineering and medical education programs. On July 1, 1944, a new contingent of 150 V-12 sailors entered UW classrooms. About a fifth of these men were veterans of the war in the Pacific who had been selected for training as engineers. They were quartered in the four eastern houses of the Kronshage complex. Navy radiomen occupied the remainder of the Kronshage units, recently vacated by the last remaining Army meteorologists.[71]

The Army's hasty deactivation of ASTP created problems and eventually opportunities in Madison and elsewhere across the country. By the spring of 1944 many college and university officials were complaining about the dislocation and financial losses entailed in the unexpected ending of the program. For the UW faculty members assigned to instruct the ASTP servicemen, the 1944 spring term was nothing if not chaotic. Similarly, the thirteen fraternity houses serving as ASTP billets found themselves suddenly bereft of their lodgers and of the income needed for mortgage payments. In mid-April, 1944, the regents considered turning the former ASTP quarters in the University Club over to the University Extension Division, but they finally decided instead to return the dormitory wing to the club for rental to civilian students if any could be found. A glimmer of good news appeared later that month when Commander Pollard announced that the UW Navy Radio School would expand into the largest agency of its kind in the nation. Unlike the pre-ASTP/V-12 days, however, University officials now welcomed the chance to produce "hotel" income with their increasingly underused physical plant. Radio school enrollment eventually soared to over seventeen hundred, while UW-Navy relations flourished and Commander Pollard announced to a friendly Madison Rotary Club audience that he favored the establishment of a permanent Navy ROTC unit on campus. The NROTC campaign would continue well into 1945 before its eventual success, but the revitalization of the

[71]*Badger Navy News*, March 3, July 14, 1944.

radio school following the collapse of ASTP was a crucial early step. The scaling back of military training programs at the University continued throughout the balance of 1944 and into 1945. During the latter part of 1944 the Navy withdrew from Extension's pilot training program, the Army closed its pre-professional ASTP course, and the War Department reduced the number of advanced medical trainees on campus from 38 to 20. The fifth Army term closed with a total of 129 AStRPs enrolled. In January of 1945, 119 ASTP men continued with their medical studies, 49 of them scheduled to graduate in June. As the allied armies closed on Berlin during the spring, discussion increasingly focused on the tidal wave of veterans that was expected soon to inundate the country's colleges and universities. In April the Bureau of Naval Personnel announced that the UW radio school would close in September, although the V-12 and medical training programs would continue. By this time fifteen thousand sailors and WAVES had been trained at the University, at least nine thousand of them graduating from the various programs. By war's end the University had acquired a significant body of blue-jacketed alumni. "Yes, we are moving toward a peace-time campus," the *Daily Cardinal* reminded its readers, "but in doing so we do not want to lose the sight of the navy blue."[72] Meanwhile, University officials began arranging with the government for the resumption of the peacetime Army ROTC program and the establishment of a new Navy reserve unit in the fall. On September 15, 1945, University President E.B. Fred, who had succeeded President Dykstra early that year, reported to the regents that UW's Navy medical program would close in February, 1946, and that the V-12 engineers would become part of the Navy ROTC program opening on November 1.

Even as University administrators were adjusting to the curtailed military presence on campus, they had begun planning for the rehabilitation and education of returning war veterans. In September of 1943 the regents authorized a contract with the U.S. Veterans Administration to offer rehabilitative instruction for men designated by the VA under the Public Law 16 (1943), "Rehabilitation and Vocational Education of Disabled Veterans." The initial course would run from September 15, 1943, to June 30, 1944. In February, 1944, the regents authorized arrangements to admit shell-shocked veterans to the Wisconsin General Hospital. Two months later the board approved a contract with the Veterans Administration to provide services under PL 16 in Milwaukee

---

[72]*Daily Cardinal*, April 25, 1945.

through the Extension Division and during the summer of 1944 in Madison for vocational rehabilitation training of disabled veterans. In June the VA contracted with the University to provide correspondence study courses to disabled veterans through June of 1945. "The returning students will be a mature, hardy, seasoned group of folks," observed President Dykstra during a welcome session at the 1944 summer session. "So we here on this campus are glad you share this opportunity with us. We need your help, counsel, and guidance." At a University-hosted Institute on Vocational Rehabilitation in the summer of 1944 UW staff members debated the virtues of psychological therapy for veterans. By September, 1944, with the veterans clearly headed home in the foreseeable future, the regents authorized Comptroller Peterson to sign new contracts with the VA in accordance with PL 16 and Public Law 346, the so-called GI Bill of Rights.[73]

Good news from the war fronts combined with a dwindling military presence on campus encouraged the reassertion of peacetime values in student life. A prime example was the 1944 Junior Prom. The affair monopolized the entire Memorial Union, boasted three orchestras, and recalled the elegance of traditional campus social life. On the negative side, many civilian students were clearly becoming inured to wartime appeals for campus solidarity. In April of 1944 the Student Board and nine student groups planned a large "Toward a Better World Rally." Although the organizers recruited a prominent University of Chicago professor to speak in the Memorial Union Theater and arranged for President Dykstra to introduce him, only eighty-two persons of the eight or nine hundred expected turned out. The sparse rally was indicative of a general campus malaise the *Cardinal* lamented toward the end of the semester: "Students on the whole have been entirely too apathetic toward any sort of campus action... leaving it up to a small minority to work in war activities, to run their student government, and to attend convocations and lectures on current events and problems."[74]

The judgment seems somewhat off the mark. The regular civilian students had no difficulty keeping occupied with their studies under the accelerated wartime curriculum. They continued to participate enthusiastically in the annual campus work days and otherwise consistently demonstrated a concern for University and societal problems. In

---

[73]BOR Minutes, February 12, April 15, June 15, September 18 and 30, 1944. President Dykstra's remarks were reported in the *Summer Cardinal*, July 11, 1944.

[74]*Daily Cardinal*, May 12, 1944.

October, 1944, for example, a storm of student protest erupted over the University Club's refusal to accommodate Arthur E. Burke, a Negro graduate student planning to complete his doctoral studies in English. Student and faculty pressure forced a vote by the club membership on the matter that effectively and for the first time placed the faculty on record against racial discrimination at the University.[75]

Gradually the University community began to turn its attention to post-war life. An early structural accommodation came in December, 1943, when the faculty formally established a standing Committee on Student Personnel. This more broadly based and academically substantive group replaced Dean Goodnight's Personnel Council, which had been so helpful in smoothing student adjustments to wartime dislocation in the dark days following Pearl Harbor. In early 1944 the *Daily Cardinal* announced that Wisconsin would cooperate with the U.S. Committee on Educational Reconstruction as it placed foreign students at American universities to prepare themselves to help rebuild their devastated nations. Discrimination at UW on the basis of sex, race, or creed would not be tolerated. Alert to emerging opportunities for enrolling more students, at least three of the University's modern language departments urged faculty advisers to remind students of the value of language skills in preparing for international public service and corporate careers. In February, 1944, the regents approved a thoroughly revised and updated College of Agriculture undergraduate curriculum. The board also directed its Regent-Faculty Conference Committee to evaluate and report on the extent to which current instructional practices met appropriate scholastic standards. A month later the University faculty voted to lower entrance requirements for promising veterans and agreed to admit students to the Medical School after two, instead of three, years of college work. Similar adjustments followed as the campus prepared for peace and a new era in American life.

Wartime Governance and Administration

As we have seen, the University's involvement in the war was energetic, all-pervasive, and by any standard highly effective. While essentially every University staff member participated to some extent in the effort, it was President Dykstra who provided important leadership on campus, in the state, and nationally. Dykstra's prominent role in the

---

[75]See pp. 542-50.

national manpower debate contributed significantly to the founding and shaping of the academically-oriented ASTP and V-12 programs. Throughout the conflict he worked productively with the American Council on Education, the National Association of State Universities, and the Association of Land Grant Colleges and Universities to develop appropriate post-war educational policies. Sometimes he participated as the University's designated representative, often he served on special committees, and usually he held high leadership positions. In all of these roles his counsel was regularly sought and he frequently was called to Washington to consult with education and government leaders. He was also in regular demand—both at home and in Great Britain—to speak on the role of the nation's colleges and universities in the war effort and in shaping the post-war world.[76] Throughout much of 1943-44 Dykstra headed the Wisconsin State Defense Council, which oversaw all phases of civil defense in the state except the direct protection of life and property.

These external demands on President Dykstra naturally limited to some extent his ability to perform his normal presidential duties. Perhaps least affected were his regular meetings with his various University constituencies. In an age when most long-distance travel was still by train, Dykstra managed somehow to satisfy his off-campus obligations while at the same time arranging to preside over most University faculty meetings and to confer regularly with the Board of Regents, a feat that must have presented a scheduling nightmare for his office staff. He also participated regularly in Founders' Day and other alumni activities, and he and Mrs. Dykstra maintained their traditional practice of hosting receptions and "at-homes" for legislators, faculty members, and students. The president also contributed occasional articles to the *Wisconsin Alumnus* magazine. Though frequently away from Madison, President Dykstra did not become the object of open grumbling as had his predecessor, Glenn Frank.

Inevitably some administrative adjustments had to be made. The

---

[76]In late 1942 the British government had invited Dykstra for a visit. Governor-elect Loomis' untimely death in December had forced the president initially to delay the trip and other problems kept him in the U.S. until spring, when the U.S. Office of War Information assumed responsibility for designating American representatives to foreign countries. Dykstra then cancelled the trip because he wished only to make the visit as a guest of the British. In any event, the British invitation to Dykstra is a good indication of his stature abroad as well as at home. See Mrs. Herbert S. Roswell to Dykstra, October 8, 1943, and Dykstra to Roswell, October 9, 1943, Dykstra Presidential Papers, 4/15/1, box 131.

most important was the gradual transfer of fiscal authority from Dykstra to Comptroller A.W. Peterson, who previously had worked closely and effectively with both the president and the regents. Demands from the War Department and other federal agencies followed no predictable schedule, and therefore the president simply was not always available for the instant reaction often called for. It therefore fell to Comptroller Peterson to work out the University's response, sometimes with the full Board of Regents and more often with its Executive Committee. Thus without anyone consciously planning the change, by the war's end Peterson had solidified his standing with the regents and greatly enlarged the administrative and budgeting functions of his office. Similarly, notwithstanding Dykstra's effective work with the alumni, the president also required help dealing with outside civilian constituencies. The president and regents discussed this problem throughout 1943 and finally agreed to establish the position of University Vice President for External Relations. The post was in fact tailor-made for Frank O. Holt, whom President Frank had originally appointed as registrar and who later had replaced Dean Chester D. Snell at the helm of the troubled University Extension Division. Holt's appointment in the fall of 1943 as head of the new Public Service Department gave Dykstra a popular and widely respected associate who could, according to the regents' plan, "represent the President in Alumni Association matters, and in contacts with educational organizations, schools and colleges of the state."[77]

The wartime period also witnessed heavy turnover in the University's academic administration, some of it directly related to the conflict. This was the case with the Medical, Law, and Graduate schools, whose deans spent much of the war on leave away from campus. Medical Dean William S. Middleton served primarily in England as a colonel with the U.S. Medical Corps, while Law Dean Lloyd K. Garrison was general counsel and then executive director of the War Labor Board. Graduate Dean E.B. Fred headed the nation's biological warfare research program. Happily for the University, the deans' associates—Walter Meek, Oliver Rundell, and Harold Stoke—were able to fill in effectively for their chiefs. More crucial for the ongoing work of the University were the deanships of the College of Letters and Science and the College of Agriculture. L&S Dean George C. Sellery, who had occupied his office since 1919, left University service in 1942 after reaching the

---

[77]"Report of the Regent Expansion Program Committee" [October 16, 1943], BOR Papers, 1/1/3, box 59.

mandatory retirement age of seventy.[78]   President Dykstra and the regents easily agreed on mathematics Professor Mark H. Ingraham as Sellery's successor after consulting extensively with the L&S faculty. Ingraham's credentials as chairman of the mathematics department, as past president of the American Association of University Professors, and as two-time University Committee member and chairman provided ample assurance that he would maintain the college's traditional commitment to high academic standards and faculty participation in University governance.   Agriculture Dean Chris Christensen resigned his post in 1943 after accepting the vice presidency for post-war development of the Celotex Corporation in Chicago.   The times seemed to call for a reorientation of the college that would continue Christensen's depression-era emphasis on the social and economic aspects of rural life while paying renewed attention to Dean Harry Russell's earlier emphasis on the scientific and technological underpinnings of agricultural production.[79]   The regents unanimously approved the appointment of recently returned bacteriologist and Graduate Dean E.B. Fred for the job at Agriculture.   Fred's credentials as a University citizen and scholar, while configured somewhat differently than Ingraham's, were every bit as substantial.   His ascendancy to the College of Agriculture deanship assured the continued development of the college's already robust physical and biological science research and extension programs.

One sad break in the University's long-time administrative structure deserves note.   On August 9, 1943, Julia Wilkinson, the highly respected executive secretary to every UW president since the early days of the Van Hise administration, suffered a fatal heart attack while eating her lunch in the president's office.   Modest and self-effacing, deeply loyal to and protective of each of her presidential chiefs, Wilkinson over the years had also quietly championed the cause of students in difficulty of one sort or another.   The tribute adopted by the Board of Regents was more than pro forma; its sentiments were widely shared across the campus:

> The death of Miss Julia M. Wilkinson of our President's Office staff has left a void in our University community which will be difficult, if not

---

[78] As Chapter 6 explains, Sellery served as the de facto acting president following the firing of Glenn Frank in early 1937. Ironically, his major initiative had been to designate seventy as the University's mandatory retirement age.

[79] See Chapter 13 for an extended discussion of the policies and perspectives of College of Agriculture Deans Russell and Christensen.

impossible, to fill....

...In her position in the President's office, she inevitably participated in the entire program, and often aided and abetted the University's progress in ways little known to most of us.

To this University's cause, as exemplified in its freely translated motto, "The Light of the World", she gave unstintingly of her good judgment and wisdom; of her great personal courage and tact and sense of humor; and of her rare gift of tolerance and sense of justice.

She will live long in the memories of all of us as an exemplification of this University itself—sincere and honest devotion to high ideals; conscientious and realistic application to daily duties; seeking always to serve and serve well the needs of our great state.[80]

The following October the regents agreed to frame a special memorial prepared by Mary Frank, the widow of Glenn Frank, entitled "Five Gifts of Julia Wilkinson," and to hang it permanently on the wall of the secretary of the president.[81]

As he had from the beginning of his presidency in 1937, Dykstra continued to cultivate and expand faculty participation in University governance. The appointments of Deans Ingraham and Fred affirmed his commitment to the process. He saw to it that essentially every important matter of educational policy came before one or another official faculty body. The creation of the four Faculty Divisions in the spring of 1942 provided for greatly increased and regularized influence and responsibility for safeguarding the quality of the faculty itself as well as for watching over the curriculum. The new Committee on Student Personnel helped focus faculty attention on questions of academic student services. The rapidly changing needs of the war led Dykstra and the regents to consult frequently with the faculty on an unusually wide range of issues. Sometimes this occurred on an ad hoc basis through the Special Committee on Educational Problems appointed in the spring of 1944 and charged with planning for the massive influx of military veterans expected at war's end. At other times standing faculty bodies,

---

[80]BOR Minutes, September 18, 1943. Wilkinson was a bulwark of the president's office. She comprehended the institution as perhaps few ever had and enjoyed the respect and admiration of many for her wise insights and advice. Argyle Stoute, president of the UW Negro Culture Foundation, observed: "And I will always remember her words of counsel when during a very trying situation she said, 'Don't you allow yourself to do the same thing that others are accused of doing to you. Justice in the end will triumph over all injustices.' No further word was said because both of us knew and understood." *Daily Cardinal*, August 13, 1943.

[81]BOR Minutes, October 16, 1943.

such as the Committee on Student Life and Interests, met the new circumstances with energy and imagination. Under the guidance of Dean of Men Scott Goodnight, SLIC spent long hours debating plans for the post-war integration of all Greek-letter houses into the campus residence hall house fellow system and associated reforms. Although few concrete changes resulted at this time, the broadly inclusive effort produced considerable dialogue and generally heightened the faculty's consciousness of the challenges to come.

Another adjustment to wartime conditions was the unprecedented expansion of regent participation in University administration. The regents' resolve to lend increased assistance came early in the conflict and was evident at the conclusion of what came to be known as the Whitehead's God affair. The dispute began quietly enough on the day before the Pearl Harbor attack, when the board decided to delay action on a proposed contract between the University of Wisconsin Press and philosophy Assistant Professor Stephen L. Ely for publication of his book-length manuscript entitled "The Religious Availability of Whitehead's God." The regents normally did not involve themselves with such details, merely receiving a report on the press's activities. Indeed, President Dykstra had brought the contract to the board only because it contained an unusual yet minor financial provision, of which he thought the board might wish to take official note. But with the contract on the table Regent Kleczka became intrigued with the study's title and requested a postponement to investigate. The following month Kleczka informed his colleagues he had found the manuscript unobjectionable, although the title was misleading. Regent Ekern now asked for a clarification of the board's responsibilities vis-à-vis the UW Press. Dykstra urged immediate approval and raised the specter of regent censorship. Ekern sharply denied any such intention, commenting offhandedly, however, that the University probably had better things to do at this time than to cultivate ancient controversies as Ely's study seemed to do. The regents then unanimously granted Ekern's request. The matter next came before the board at its February meeting and again a postponement resulted, this time on the motion of Regent Hodgkins that a subcommittee prepare a formal statement on the entire issue, which by this time had generated considerable public controversy. Finally, on March 14 the board received and approved the special subcommittee report, which, among other things, provided for the publication of Professor Ely's book.

For some who feared wartime intolerance and censorship, the

regents' behavior seemed ominous. Philosophy Professor and Chairman Max Otto, who had been among the lonely minority refusing to sign the faculty's "round robin" censure of Senator Robert M. La Follette, Sr., in the First World War, was one. After the first tabling of the Ely contract by the board on December 6, Otto wrote President Dykstra warning that, "if correctly reported," the regent action might have an "important political bearing on University research." With the decision laid over again the next month Otto reiterated his mounting concern in a statement he released to the *Daily Cardinal*. He argued that the regents should exercise control only over the finances of the University press. To interfere with publication because of content was to usurp the proper authority of the faculty publications committee, which already had duly approved Ely's manuscript. Otto said he was shocked at Regent Ekern's purported view that the University must avoid controversy. "In a world which has become one huge controversy, what is more important to talk about than the controversial issues in which we are involved?" The Rev. Alfred W. Swan of Madison's First Congregational Church publicly concurred the next day, as quickly did emeritus Professor W.H. Lighty and the editors of the *Daily Cardinal*. As Swan put it, "While the signing of contracts may be a necessary part of book publishing, that a board charged with managerial responsibility should pass on the competence and character of material to be published, seems to me a highly questionable invasion of academic responsibility."[82] Following the regents' apparent capitulation in March, a *Daily Cardinal* editorial jubilantly proclaimed victory: "for probably the first time in the past decade, students on this campus have seen that their liberties and rights as students cannot be threatened...without an advance guard of strong and able men rising to defend those rights and liberties."[83]

The regents viewed the Ely case very differently. Ironically, the initial delay in approving the contract had occurred because of Regent Kleczka's concern to *protect*, not attack, the University's academic integrity. As George Sellery later agreed in his analysis of the controversy, the term "availability" in the manuscript title was ambiguous and Kleczka might reasonably have wondered if it conveyed a sectarian message. And as the regent subcommittee reported to an approving

---

[82]*Daily Cardinal*, January 24, 1942.

[83]Otto's letter to Dykstra is dated December 10, 1941, and is quoted in George C. Sellery, *Some Ferments at Wisconsin, 1901-1947: Memories and Reflections* (Madison: University of Wisconsin Press, 1960), p. 104. See also *Daily Cardinal*, January 19 and 24, March 17, 1942.

board on March 14, Section 36.06 of the state statutes—the same provision invoked earlier by the regents against Governor Heil's attempted Red purge—proscribed exactly such "instruction" by the University. The subcommittee made several additional points. First, by law the regents "represent and speak for the people of the state" and possess the "duty, power and full responsibility for the operation and control of the University." Duties might occasionally be delegated, but the board could not "foreclose itself from acting in delegated matters." Otto and his supporters, in other words, were misinformed as to the limited extent of regent authority. Second, the regents categorically denied that their behavior involved censorship or threatened academic freedom, or that their deliberations provided any basis for Dykstra's concern and Otto's charge. Finally, they wanted everyone to understand that "matters which, in the future, will come before the Board of Regents for their consideration will be given such consideration as the Regents believe should be given."[84] This latter assertion was more than merely an aggrieved response to overly suspicious critics. Already the University's transition to a wartime footing had proceeded far enough to demonstrate the extraordinary administrative and policy effort that would be required by the board.

Not since 1925 had members of the Board of Regents worked so diligently and effectively to obtain an adequate operating budget as they did in 1942-43. With enrollments falling and programs in limbo, with UW faculty members and deans taking leave on short notice, and above all with President Dykstra needed in too many places at once, the University was in turmoil. The situation became even more uncertain in December of 1942 when Progressive Orland S. Loomis died unexpectedly of multiple heart attacks after unseating Governor Julius Heil in the November election. Confusion reigned for a time until the Wisconsin Supreme Court ruled that Republican Lieutenant Governor Walter S. Goodland should be inaugurated in early January as acting governor. Little known to most and objectionable to few, Goodland maintained a grip on the state administration that was tenuous at first, particularly in light of his octogenarian age. Indeed, he had been considering retirement until the Republican state convention infuriated him the previous

---

[84]Sellery, *Some Ferments at Wisconsin*, pp. 105-6; "Report of the Special Committee Appointed to Consider Publications of the University of Wisconsin Press," adopted by the Board of Regents on March 14, 1942, BOR Papers, 1/1/3, box 57. "The Regent Report...is a document of high importance to the University. It is written with restraint that does honor to the Board's responsibilities." Sellery, *Some Ferments at Wisconsin*, p. 111.

summer by failing to endorse his re-election. Undaunted by the controversy over his unexpected elevation, Goodland followed Loomis' schedule of hearings on the various state agencies' budget requests in December. Meanwhile, Regent Michael J. Cleary, the chairman of the board's finance committee, had orchestrated the University request while keeping his colleagues fully informed and involved to the extent they might be helpful. The request included a $2.7 million increase over the previous biennium, $2 million of which was earmarked for a post-war building program. Goodland's reaction was equivocal; he promised that the state would not allow the University to "disintegrate," but he refused to support the building proposals because they contradicted Republican campaign promises for strict economy. Later, thanks to sustained regent importunities, Goodland agreed to recommend the establishment of a special state building fund to provide for the University's pressing physical plant needs.[85]

While encouraging a spirit of unity sorely lacking in recent sessions, the war nevertheless seriously complicated the legislative agenda. On the one hand, legislators could agree that state agencies such as the University deserved help in their support of the war effort. The value of the expanded UW summer semester was obvious, for example, and its additional cost had to be met. At the same time, competition for state funding was fierce and well organized, partially due to former Governor Heil's much-resented draconian treatment of state agencies and local governmental units. Exacerbating this political problem was the uncertain state economy, which had suddenly become highly inflationary and, if possible, even more difficult to predict than during the depression. As in the early 1920s, Governor Goodland and the legislature spent so much time and energy battling over tax policy that they paid inadequate attention to legitimate state funding needs. Regent Cleary and his colleagues maintained the pressure as University advocates, however, appearing at joint finance committee hearings and lobbying individual legislators. The result was a reasonably generous University biennial operating budget that slightly exceeded Acting Governor Goodland's request and avoided any serious program or staff reductions.

---

[85]For a discussion of the Loomis-Goodland transition see William F. Thompson, *The History of Wisconsin*, vol. 6, *Continuity and Change, 1940-1965* (Madison: State Historical Society of Wisconsin, 1988), pp. 424-6.

During the 1943 session the legislature also authorized the regents to establish an independent School of Commerce at the University. Created in 1900 as a sub-unit of the Department of Political Economy (later the Department of Economics), the school (known as the Course in Commerce from 1904 to 1926) had always been a part of the College of Letters and Science. Although oriented toward practice, the school's first three directors—Professors William A. Scott (1900-1927), William Kiekhofer (acting, 1927-1931), and Chester Lloyd Jones (1931-1935)—had nevertheless valued their close association with the more scholarly economics faculty. This changed in 1935 when President Frank selected accounting Professor Fayette H. Elwell to succeed Jones, who returned to full-time teaching. Elwell envisioned an expanded School of Commerce that would serve Wisconsin business as the College of Agriculture had for so many years effectively assisted the rural homes and farms of the state. Elwell's other model was the School of Education, which had been severed from the college in 1930. He first convinced a skeptical L&S Dean Sellery to grant the school departmental status, with its own distinctive programs of study and cross-listed courses going into effect at the start of the 1935-36 academic year. Elwell then proceeded to lobby Wisconsin trade associations and business groups to support his campaign for full independence. An eight-year struggle ensued between members of the economics department, other L&S faculty, Dean Sellery, President Dykstra, and the regents on one side, and the resourceful and indefatigable Elwell and his staff on the other. Outflanked within the University, Elwell continued to cultivate business, civic, alumni, and political support off campus, which finally produced the enabling legislation of 1943.[86]

---

[86]This discussion of the School of Commerce relies heavily on [Fayette H. Elwell], "School of Commerce History: Early Chapters" (unpublished manuscript, n.d.), UHP, and Departmental Files, School of Business, UA; Elwell, oral history interview, 1972, UA.

Elwell's secession efforts benefitted from the director's clever strategy and from fortuitous wartime social and economic conditions. Throughout the late 1930s the campaign proceeded quietly. At this time Elwell cultivated his Rotary colleagues and other business-oriented outsiders, whose support did not appear threatening to the director's scholarly opponents on campus. Then in 1941 Elwell formally proposed to the L&S faculty that economics and commerce break away from the college and form a separate "coordinate" unit loosely tied to the College of Letters and Science like the School of Education. The issue was now joined. As Elwell expected, his L&S colleagues focussed on the threat of losing economics, effectively forgetting about commerce. Meanwhile, American entry into the war brought new vitality to Wisconsin business and industry, whose contributions to the war effort were crucial. Business standing in public opinion and influence over public policy expanded accordingly. Respectful legislative hearings on Elwell's proposed enabling bill during mid-June, 1943, demonstrated this fact for all to see, and regent hearings on the proposed separation the following October reaffirmed it.

Reading the handwriting on the wall, the regents referred the mechanics of separation to the Regent-Faculty Conference Committee, which in turn recommended that a special faculty committee be convened to study the matter. The seven-member special committee included L&S Dean Ingraham and two members selected by him, Director Elwell and two additional members of his choice, and School of Education Dean C.J. Anderson appointed by Dykstra. On January 8, 1944, the special committee reported, unanimously affirming Elwell's public service mission statement for the school while voting four to three in favor of separate coordinate status. The regents approved these recommendations and directed President Dykstra to consult with the faculty about how to implement the reorganization.[87] With faculty concurrence Dykstra reconvened the special committee, which developed a variation of the School of Education scheme of organization. This innovative plan, it will be recalled, had been conceived by George Sellery and C.J. Anderson in 1930 to provide for a broad-based education faculty with continuing formal ties to the College of Letters and Science. The committee's plan for the new School of Commerce significantly left

---

[87]"Report of the Committee on the Program and Status of the School of Commerce," January 7, 1944, BOR Papers, 1/1/3, box 60. The board approved the report a week later. BOR Minutes, January 15, 1944.

economics with L&S. The University faculty approved it on April 3. Twelve days later, after President Dykstra lobbied quietly but unsuccessfully against the decision, the regents named Fay Elwell as the first dean of the School of Commerce effective July 1. As the *Capital Times* observed, "Prof. Elwell now steps into the job that he has carved out for himself in years of off-campus campaigning and maneuvering."[88] Time would show that he was considerably less interested in maintaining a close coordinate association with his school's parents—the Department of Economics and the College of Letters and Science—than were Education Dean Anderson and his successors.

Although the legislature approved a reasonably generous 1943-45 operating budget, it again failed to provide for new and improved campus buildings. The problem was not so much opposition as timing. With the war in full swing, building for civilian needs, however important, had to wait. Governor Goodland and most legislators agreed that University facilities had become woefully neglected since the last significant infusion of state funds, for the Mechanical Engineering Building in 1929. Moreover, few questioned the University's predictions of a massive influx of returning veterans after the war. While the regent Constructional Development Committee lobbied hard throughout the 1943 session and beyond, it probably was unreasonable to expect any legislature to approve Acting Governor Goodland's proposal to set up a special post-war building fund when it was impossible to know when appropriations would be spent and what they could buy. Undaunted, the regents sought planning advice from an ad hoc committee including President Dykstra, the state architect, the state engineer, and the University comptroller and superintendent of building and grounds. In August the legislature created an interim building study committee under Senator William A. Freehoff that maintained close liaison with University officials during the remaining months of the year. During the fall of 1943 the faculty and regents received and discussed the devastating Metcalf-Blegen report on University library facilities. To nobody's surprise, this commissioned analysis by prominent librarians from Harvard University and the University of Minnesota established beyond any reasonable doubt the need for a new library, which had been among the University's top building priorities for two decades.[89] In 1944

---

[88]*Capital Times*, April 16, 1944. The first public report of the disagreement between Dykstra and the regents appeared in the *Capital Times*, January 25, 1945.

[89]See pp. 685-700 for a full discussion of the Metcalf-Blegen report and the enduring library

the Freehoff Committee recommended immediate post-war funding for University construction in the range of $5 million and in August an internal committee of UW deans and administrators drew up a building needs list totalling nearly $18.4 million. As in the past, however, the legislature remained unwilling to appropriate even a single dime for post-war construction.

This was the situation on October 28, 1944, when President Dykstra announced his resignation, effective in January, to accept the position of provost—chief administrative officer reporting to the president in Berkeley—of the Los Angeles and La Jolla campuses of the University of California.[90] Dykstra had taught at UCLA earlier in his career, had many friends and contacts at the university and throughout southern California, and had maintained a vacation home at Laguna Beach. Although UCLA was smaller and did not yet approach the academic stature of Wisconsin, its post-war prospects were bright. California President Robert G. Sproul's recruitment of Dykstra, beginning the previous February, had been secret, relentless, and accommodating. Dykstra hesitated at first because the position would involve some reduction in salary, stature, and responsibility. Still, the appeal of a fresh and relatively open-ended challenge in friendly and familiar circumstances must have been appealing as the sixty-year-old UW president contemplated his future.[91] The immediate prospects at

---

problems at the University.

[90]BOR Minutes, October 28, 1944; *Capital Times*, October 28, 1944. Early reports of Dykstra's possible resignation appeared in the *Capital Times*, October 25 and 26, 1944, and *Daily Cardinal*, October 26 and 27, 1944.

[91]Materials in the Dykstra Papers at UCLA, the Dykstra Presidential Papers in the UW Archives, and President Sproul's Papers in the Bancroft Library at Berkeley provide a sketchy but revealing account of the California courtship of President Dykstra. Until nearly the end Sproul and Dykstra managed to keep their negotiations secret through obscurely worded telegrams, handwritten personal letters, and off-campus meetings in Chicago and elsewhere. Dykstra visited Sproul in Berkeley in late August of 1944, necessitating, as he confessed to Sproul, that he "fake" the reason for traveling to the west coast. Dykstra initially rejected the California opportunity. His $15,000 salary at Wisconsin was the same as Sproul's, and the UCLA provost position was budgeted at $10,000. Dykstra worried, moreover, about constraints on his freedom of action in campus administration and in dealing directly with regents and legislators in a position that was under the California president. Sproul persuaded the California regents to raise the provost salary to $12,000 for Dykstra and to guarantee him an annual $3,000 retirement salary, plus assurance that the California rule requiring top administrators to retire at sixty-five would be extended by three to five years in Dykstra's case. Sproul also promised Dykstra he would have full administrative authority over the UCLA campus. Dykstra to Robert G. Sproul, n.d., President Sproul Papers, University of California Archives, Berkeley. The authors are indebted to California University Archivist William M. Roberts for

Wisconsin, though positive, probably did not seem as good as in California's expanding system of higher education. And it must not have been coincidental that Dykstra reached his decision as the legislature was again declining to fund what he believed was an absolutely crucial building program. The University of Wisconsin, moreover, was a relatively mature institution with fewer opportunities to make a presidential mark than at UCLA. Finally, Dykstra had been on the job in Wisconsin during seven lean years spanning the turmoil of depression and war; he may simply have favored a more focussed administrative challenge devoted to shaping a young institution in his final years before retirement.[92]

Dykstra's departure was uniformly cordial. His final presidential message, issued just prior to his resignation, emphasized the need for more generous legislative support of the University, his one area of major disappointment. At a time when his resignation was only rumored, the *Daily Cardinal* published a series of highly complimentary letters on his administration of the University. After Dykstra formally submitted his resignation on October 28, regent President Hodgkins, speaking for the board, warmly praised the president's leadership. The

---

providing copies of the Sproul-Dykstra correspondence in this collection.

[92]President Dykstra was not immune to criticism, some of which has been reported in Chapter 6, concerning his dealings with the legislature and Governor Heil. Some faculty members and perhaps some regents thought he spent too much time away from the campus and neglected his University responsibilities while completing various federal assignments. The campus mythology holds that the conservative regents were displeased with Dykstra and encouraged his departure and may even have forced it. The board and the president sometimes disagreed, as in the Whitehead's God controversy of 1941-42, the School of Commerce drive for independence, and the appointment of Elwell to be commerce dean in 1944. This latter defeat—the most significant during his tenure as president—may definitely have played a part in Dykstra's decision. Disagreement does not necessarily produce disenchantment, however. Similarly, throughout the war the regents expanded the discretionary powers of Comptroller A.W. Peterson and involved themselves heavily in certain aspects of University administration, including the budgeting process. This, too, does not prove regent dissatisfaction with the president, only a reasonable accommodation to the times. The authors have found no contemporary evidence of regent unhappiness with President Dykstra's performance. His son Franz confirms that he never heard either of his parents complain about their interactions with the Board of Regents, only about occasional budgetary difficulties with the governor and legislature. Franz Dykstra, telephone interview with E. David Cronon, February 21, 1992, UHP. In any event, in reporting Dykstra's departure from Wisconsin *Time* magazine commented that Wisconsin farmers sometimes thought Dykstra was "too much of a city fellow," the legislature as "too much of a professor," and the faculty as "too much of a Rotarian type." Thus Dykstra's resignation "will take him where folks consider him one of their own." *Time*, 46 (November 6, 1944), 48-9.

frequently critical *Capital Times* awarded the Dykstra administration high marks and could suggest no major difficulties that might have produced a forced resignation. For his part, the always genial UW president had nothing but friendly comments about the University and the state, emphasizing repeatedly that the UCLA position was the only one in the country that could have attracted him away from Madison. In its January, 1945, issue the *Wisconsin Alumnus* ran a laudatory review of Dykstra's tenure. Students had always found President and Mrs. Dykstra friendly and approachable, appreciating their custom of monthly "at homes" for the student body. The *Daily Cardinal* expressed a typical student reaction to the UW president when it declared in an editorial shortly after his departure: "We hope that he will not forget us of the University of Wisconsin, who owe much to his work, his interest, and to his friendship."[93]

Preparing for Peace

The Board of Regents now faced the problem of finding a new president to guide the University through the coming demobilization and rapid restructuring as the campus faced the inevitable challenges of the post-war era. The selection process involved two notable features. The board now accepted as standard practice the formal participation of the faculty in the search and screen process, with the University Committee as in 1937 acting as the official representative of faculty opinion.[94] There was also now a general reluctance on the part of regents and faculty alike to seek another outsider as president. "We believe,"

---

[93]*Daily Cardinal*, October 27 and 31, 1944, January 9 and 24, 1945; *Capital Times*, October 28 and 29, 1944, January 7 and 9, 1945; BOR Minutes, October 28, 1944; Philip H. Falk, "President Clarence A. Dykstra," *WAM*, 46 (January 15, 1945), 10.

[94]In late November the regents officially requested involvement of the faculty and deans in the selection process: "Voted, That the Deans and Faculty be invited to appoint or elect a committee from their membership with which the Regent Committee may consult and advise in connection with the selection of a University President." BOR Minutes, November 25, 1944. See also *Capital Times*, November 26, 1944. The University faculty officially received the regent resolution in early December and, as in 1937, designated the University Committee as its agent. UW Faculty Minutes, December 4, 1944; *Daily Cardinal*, December 5 and 6, 1944. The two committees—representing the deans and the University Committee—essentially acted as one, and Dean Ingraham requested that Agriculture Dean E.B. Fred no longer attend meetings because he was clearly a leading candidate. Mark H. Ingraham, "The University of Wisconsin, 1925-1950," in Allan G. Bogue and Robert Taylor, eds., *The University of Wisconsin: One Hundred and Twenty-Five Years* (Madison: University of Wisconsin Press, 1975), p. 59.

explained Regent Matt Werner, chairman of the board's Personnel Committee, "that we should explore what possibilities there are on the university campus...and should give such candidates first consideration."[95] This disposition to look inside may have reflected a desire to return to the familiar Van Hise-Birge vision of the University before Glenn Frank and Clarence Dykstra brought their outsider perspectives. Or it may also have revealed a belief that an insider would be more likely to concentrate on University administration and spend less time on national affairs than the two most recent presidents.

The search took several months to complete. According to rumors at the time, the only serious outside contenders were UW alumni with close campus connections: Harvard economist Sumner H. Slichter, the son of Graduate Dean Emeritus Charles S. Slichter; Warren Weaver, possessor of three UW degrees and a former UW professor of mathematics now working for the Rockefeller Foundation; and Pennsylvania State University President Ralph D. Hetzel, who held UW baccalaureate and law degrees and who had received serious consideration for the presidency in 1937. Although press reports in December speculated that Slichter had been offered and turned down the job, apparently all that transpired was that both Slichter and Weaver were approached and declined to be considered. Each also told the regents that Agriculture Dean E.B. Fred was their obvious choice. By early January, 1945, the board seemed inclined to name an acting president as their deliberations continued. President Dykstra departed for Los Angeles on the 22nd and two days later the *Capital Times* reported that Fred had now emerged as the presidential front runner. The next day the board unanimously affirmed this prediction, naming the fifty-eight-year-old Fred as president effective February 15. "His inter-

---

[95]On October 29, 1944, the *Capital Times* reported that the board already had named a selection committee and that one external and five internal candidates were being considered. On November 21, 1944, the *Daily Cardinal* reprinted a *Milwaukee Journal* editorial that advised: "Search for a scholar to command the intangible field of ideas; then give him a practical man to transmute these ideas into the living, moving, tangible plant that is the university. Such a team is usually a success." According to the *Daily Cardinal* on December 19, search committee chairman Matt Werner had stated the "first consideration...will be given, everything else equal, to a man with a Wisconsin background in residence and education. 'We believe that we should explore what possibilities there are on the university campus....and should give such candidates first consideration.'" These candidates, according the *Cardinal*, included Chris Christensen, E.B. Fred, Frank Holt, Ingraham, William Kiekhofer, and C.J. Anderson. *WAM*, 46 (January 15, 1945), 4, speculated that the leading candidates were Ingraham, Fred, Anderson, Holt, Kiekhofer, Sumner Slichter, and Warren Weaver.

est in the University and its program was not limited to his particular field," observed the regents. "His knowledge of the whole University, its personnel, its facilities and equipment as well as its obligations and objectives is as broad as, if not broader than, that of any living person."[96]

The choice of Fred pleased virtually everyone.[97] While a few social scientists and humanists wondered if his administration would favor the hard sciences, over the years Fred had developed a respectful following throughout the faculty for his distinguished scholarship, sound judgment, and devotion to the University as a whole. Student opinion as expressed through the *Daily Cardinal* was enthusiastic. Even the *Capital Times* had no criticism of the choice. "The thing that strikes us about the Fred administration," the paper observed, "is that the major emphasis has been placed upon scholarship in the choice of a head

for this state's great institution of higher education."[98] On the day of his election Fred tried to eat lunch at the University Club with his wife, but instead he spent his time there working through an impromptu reception line of his many well-wishing colleagues. The legislature, where Fred was popular with rural representatives who appreciated the value to farmers of his research on nitrogen fixation, quickly issued a congratulatory joint resolution. General Mills executive Harry Bullis, Class of '17,

---

[96]BOR Minutes, January 25, 1945, quoted in *Daily Cardinal*, January 25, 1945.

[97]Regent Werner and some other regents may have supported Fred from the start. President Emeritus Edwin Young was a prominent faculty member on the joint faculty-deans search committee in 1958 seeking President Fred's successor. Young remembers a cryptic comment by Regent Werner at the initial meeting with the regents to discuss search procedures. "This time," said Werner to his fellow board members, "I think we should play square with the faculty." Edwin Young, conversation with E. David Cronon, October 29, 1992.

[98]Editorial, *Capital Times*, January 26, 1945.

who had helped mobilize support for the beleaguered Glenn Frank in 1936-37, spoke for many of the alumni when he stated:

> Dr. Edwin B. Fred will make a great president for the University of Wisconsin. He is a man of the highest character and integrity, a distinguished educator and scholar, with an international reputation in his own specialty. He is a sincere advocate of academic freedom, an able administrator, and an inspiring leader.[99]

Not since Van Hise had the University boasted a leader with such a broad and enthusiastic base of support within the institution.

As the regents searched for a new president, they also were developing and lobbying for their requested 1945-47 biennial operating budget and stepping up the pressure for legislative action on a post-war construction program. In November, 1944, with the election of Walter Goodland in his own right to the governorship, prospects for favorable treatment of the University seemed better than in many years, particularly with the end of war in sight. Regent Michael J. Cleary, chairman of the finance committee, had primary responsibility for managing the operating budget request, which received friendly consideration by Goodland in December. The influential *Milwaukee Journal* helped by running a series of articles that same month deploring the legislature's perennial failure to provide an adequate physical plant for the University. The first installment concluded by endorsing the regents' anticipated request of over $12 million for new buildings, including $1.7 million for a new library.[100] Meanwhile, Regent John D. Jones' politically sophisticated Constructional Development Committee appointed a broad-based "Advisory Committee" of University staff, state officials, and one regent "to assist in the preparation of a definite plan for the future development of the campus." The two bodies began working together on a common strategy in early January.[101] On January

---

[99]"Edwin B. Fred the 12th UW President," *WAM*, 46 (February 15, 1945), 3.

[100]*Milwaukee Journal*, December 17, 1944.

[101]"Report of the Constructional Development Committee to the Board of Regents," January 9, 1945, BOR Papers, 1/1/3, box 61. Membership included the University president, the academic deans, the chairman of the Athletic Board, the director of residence halls, the superintendent of buildings and grounds, the state chief engineer, the state architect, the secretary of the state planning board, the secretary of the regents, and the comptroller of the University. The regent minutes refer to the advisory committee as the University Planning Commission. This informal designation should not be confused with the Campus Planning Commission, which the board later formally established as a continuing advisory body.

10 Governor Goodland presented his budget request to the legislature. Regarding the University, he proclaimed:

> The University cannot properly serve the needs of the state unless we provide it with the men and facilities to do so. For the last two decades the University has remained almost at a standstill with respect to growth and facilities. This session of the legislature, if it does its simple duty, must meet this problem squarely and adequately.[102]

Goodland's warm support of the University recalled the productive La Follette-Van Hise and Kohler-Frank partnerships earlier in the century. With the governor's favorable budget proposal before the legislature, the regents and UW officials stepped up the pressure. On the day the board named E.B. Fred president, one regent committee attended hearings at the capitol and another met with the University advisory committee on building needs. Simultaneously, the *Wisconsin State Journal* and the *Daily Cardinal* joined the *Milwaukee Journal* in publishing articles on the problems and inadequacies of the campus physical plant. The regents remained active as hearings on the operating budget proceeded. On February 15 the board gave the advisory committee standing status and renamed it the Campus Planning Commission. Regents Jones, William J. Campbell, and Frank J. Sensenbrenner were named to the new commission.[103] A few days later Regent Cleary attracted widespread attention by declaring that over the preceding fifteen years the University's physical plant had been allowed to degenerate to a disgraceful condition. Recently appointed President Fred promptly joined the campaign. In March Regent Walter J. Hodgkins published an article entitled "Is Our University Slipping?" in the *Wisconsin Alumnus*. The *Daily Cardinal* urged its readers to bombard the legislature with requests for support of the building budget.[104] The well-coordinated lobbying effort was reminiscent of Regent Kronshage's public relations campaign of 1925, and the results were nearly as impressive. In late June, following the end of war in Europe, the legislature appropriated almost $9 million each for University operations and construction during the next biennium.

---

[102]*Daily Cardinal*, January 11 and 17, 1945; *Capital Times*, January 11, 1945. See also "Gov. Goodland Approves UW Building Program," *WAM*, 46 (February 15, 1945), 4.

[103]BOR Minutes, February 15, 1945. For reports on the standing commission see *Capital Times*, February 15, 1945; *Daily Cardinal*, February 16, 1945.

[104]*WAM*, 46 (March 15, 1945), 3-6.

In June of 1944 Congress enacted a generous post-war educational program for returning veterans as part of the Servicemen's Readjustment Act, a measure that quickly came to be known as the GI Bill. UW Registrar Curtis Merriman predicted that between 125 and 150 men would enroll under the new federal program as early as the fall semester of 1944. "The deluge will not come until after the war," cautioned Merriman, but his estimate turned out to be conservative when at least 170 veterans were on hand at the start of the fall term.[105] Reflecting the national discussion about how best to handle the returning veterans, during 1944 UW administrators, faculty, and civilian students debated what might be the most appropriate educational and counseling programs for the ex-servicemen. On the day President Fred took office the *Daily Cardinal* reported the formation of a new Veterans' Council to meet with and advise returning soldiers.[106] This innovative UW effort, though experimental and as yet largely untested, soon received widespread attention. In late April the regents accepted a comprehensive report of the Committee on Student Personnel on student-veteran issues and adopted revised admission rules that assured generous access for veterans who could demonstrate any sort of Wisconsin background as well as for non-resident veterans. President Fred watched closely as the University readied itself for the anticipated deluge of GI Bill students later in 1945.

Other signs of the new era at the University were evident in the wake of President Dykstra's resignation. In February, 1945, Dean of Men Scott Goodnight, since 1915 the first and only occupant of his office, announced his retirement effective July 1. Goodnight's departure foreshadowed major policy changes, inasmuch as he had been the architect of much of the expanded *in loco parentis* role of the University in student life over the past three decades. Not as publicized but nevertheless of great importance, the regents consolidated and streamlined the University's fiscal affairs under the enhanced control of Comptroller A.W. Peterson, whose new title became Director of Business and Finance. The regents had grown accustomed to working directly with Peterson during President Dykstra's wartime absences and evidently thought the post-war expansion of the University would require

---

[105]The *Daily Cardinal* of October 18, 1944, reported 170 veterans, while the *Capital Times* for September 24, 1944, reported 200.

[106]*Daily Cardinal*, February 15, 1945. On the attitudes and problems of returning veterans, see *Daily Cardinal*, March 30, April 3 and 4, 1945.

a more centralized fiscal structure.[107] President Fred would spend the next several years trying to reestablish his control over University financial matters. Also in March of 1945 President Fred orchestrated the creation of the University of Wisconsin Foundation. This new agency joined the earlier pioneering Wisconsin Alumni Research Foundation (1925) as a private, single-purpose UW support group. Its mission was to organize sustained fund-raising efforts to provide vital financial support for University programs.[108]

During the spring of 1945 President Fred began to outline his vision of the post-war University. Although not a spellbinder like Glenn Frank nor as comfortable before an audience as Clarence Dykstra, the new president conveyed a sense of integrity and devotion to traditional University ideals that commanded the respect of his listeners, whatever their backgrounds. Even before officially taking office, he gave a brief summary of his views in his first presidential address to the faculty. To his former colleagues he repeatedly asserted his dedication to the "Wisconsin Idea," referring to the long tradition of University service to the state. He also emphasized his faculty background and his appreciation of the central role of his fellow scholars in all phases of University life, a commitment reminiscent of Dean Sellery's pledge at the time he became acting president in 1937. In early April, coincident with the unexpected death of President Franklin D. Roosevelt, Fred explicitly staked out a leading place for the University in post-war higher education. News of Germany's surrender on May 8 signalled the imminent end of the long conflict. Almost spontaneously the University community gathered in a packed convocation presided over by the president in the Field House, a meeting rivaling the post-Pearl Harbor convocation in emotional intensity but now embodying a contagious spirit of jubilation and triumph. The end of the semester provided another opportunity for both celebration and sober reflection. President Fred responded with major addresses to the alumni and the Class of 1945 on "The Purpose of the University." The time had arrived, he told both groups, to get to work on the challenges of the post-war era.

◇   ◇   ◇

[107]BOR Minutes, March 21, 1945; "Suggested Report of the Committee on Organization," March 20, 1945, BOR Papers, 1/1/3, box 62. See also *Capital Times*, March 21, 1945; *Daily Cardinal*, March 22, 1945.

[108]For a characteristically suspicious view of the new foundation by the *Capital Times* see, editorial, March 25, 1945.

The Second World War brought an unprecedented upheaval to the University. More than 12,500 UW students and alumni donned military uniforms for service in all parts of the globe, and over 500 of them sacrificed their lives in the conflict. At least 150 University faculty members worked in their campus laboratories and elsewhere on important problems of national defense and others entered military service in a variety of roles. The two UW nuclear accelerators, popularly known as atom smashers, and several UW scientists, for example, were drafted for service at Los Alamos, New Mexico, on the top secret Manhattan Project to develop the atomic bombs that ended the war with Japan. Much of the clinical staff of the Medical School departed the campus en masse to serve in the South Pacific as the Army's 44th General Hospital. Similarly, a substantial part of the law faculty spent the war years helping to staff various federal agencies. Both units of University Extension—general and agricultural—responded well to the national emergency, extending the University's influence throughout the armed services and across the state.

On campus the regular instructional program also changed to meet the challenge. Whenever possible the curriculum stressed practical learning with new courses developed to address special wartime needs. Law, Engineering, Nursing, and Medicine made major curricular adjustments to emphasize war-related training. The College of Agriculture stopped worrying about crop surpluses and returned to its more congenial pre-depression focus on the efficient mass production of food. Responsible for instructing the bulk of civilian undergraduate students, the College of Letters and Science faculty also taught the uniformed students enrolled in the meteorology, ASTP, and V-12 programs. Though less closely related to the University's traditional academic mission, the several technical training programs—particularly the large Navy Radio School—filled University classrooms, dormitories, and walkways. Together the various service programs gave a distinctly military appearance to the campus, coloring extracurricular life no less than the classroom. According to one estimate the Memorial Union averaged over 3,200 visits by service personnel daily throughout the war. The most dramatic illustration of the wartime era was the designation of a significant part of the campus—the men's lakeshore dorms and the Stadium—as a military encampment, with signs posting the area off limits to unauthorized personnel.   In short, the years 1941-45 encompassed probably the most distinctive and sweeping changes the University had experienced during its entire first century.

The war years were nothing if not chaotic.   Never before had the institution had to adapt so quickly to so many changing circumstances. Regular enrollment plunged by more than half between 1941 and 1943. At the same time the various military and naval training programs expanded and contracted, beginning and ending so rapidly that it became an administrative nightmare to keep track of them and meet their instructional and housing needs.   For the regular civilian students the war demanded countless adjustments.   The truncated calendar fueled an academic speed-up and a temporary end of any leisurely pursuit of knowledge for its own sake.   In the absence of most University men, for the first time women students predominated and enjoyed an unparalleled opportunity to run the *Daily Cardinal*, the *Badger*, and other student organizations and activities.   The need for on-campus housing for the service programs preempted most of the residence halls on campus. Indeed, for much of the war only two women's dormitories—Elizabeth Waters Hall and the student Nurses Dormitory—were available for civilian students.   By 1945 the University had taken over fifteen vacant fraternity houses, using nine of them for civilian women students, two for WAVES enrolled in the radio school, three for Army trainees, and one as an officers' club.   As much as anything these changes on Langdon Street symbolized the war's profound break with peacetime campus life. Notwithstanding the predicted influx of GIs, newly installed President Fred and his associates must have looked forward with some relief in the summer of 1945 to a return to more normal University pursuits.

8.

"A Faculty *University*"

"Ours is a *faculty* university," College of Letters and Science Dean George Sellery liked to remind his colleagues and campus newcomers.[1] By this he meant that at Wisconsin the faculty was much more than the intellectual heart of the University; it also had a substantial role in institutional governance. Faculty authority began to develop early in the twentieth century and matured steadily thereafter. A major reason for this was that Presidents Van Hise and Birge had come from the faculty and respected their colleagues' collective wisdom and devotion. Van Hise, the first to earn a Wisconsin Ph.D. degree in 1892, was also the first native of Wisconsin and the first UW alumnus to head the University. At the outset of his administration he set a democratic tone by telling the faculty he supposed he would have to be addressed as "President" when presiding at faculty meetings; otherwise he preferred to be called simply Mr. Van Hise. In administering the University he consulted and usually deferred to the judgment of his colleagues. Van Hise stressed that UW departments did not have "heads" appointed for indefinite terms, but instead were led by "chairmen" whose role was more to represent than direct their departmental colleagues.[2] Birge had

[1] John D. Hicks, *My Life with History: An Autobiography* (Lincoln: University of Nebraska Press, 1968), p. 201.

[2] Van Hise incorporated this extraordinarily democratic view of departmental administration into the compilation of University regulations issued by the Board of Regents under his leadership in 1907. Chapter II, section 8, entitled "Duties of the Professors," declared:

> The professors and associate professors of any department shall constitute a committee which shall have direct charge of all the interests of the department. The chairman of the committee for any department shall be designated by the Dean of the College in consultation with the President. The special duties of such chairman shall be those ordinarily exercised by the chairman of a committee.

464

the same philosophy.[3] By 1925 Wisconsin was known throughout the country as a university with an unusually well-developed system of faculty governance where the faculty played a major part in setting academic policy.[4]

Glenn Frank's background in journalism made him a superb publicist for the University but had by no means prepared him for the ways of an academic community, especially one where the faculty was accustomed to viewing its president as a colleague no more exalted than first among equals. The faculty regarded Frank as a glib but shallow dilettante and received most of his proposals with suspicion and even dis-

---

University of Wisconsin By-Laws and Laws of the Regents (Madison: University of Wisconsin, 1907), p. 104.

The 1914 revision of the *Laws*, also under Van Hise, expanded the democratic character of departmental administration by establishing departmental committees, consisting of all faculty members of professorial rank, including assistant professors, which were responsible for "the immediate governance of each department," including the "power to determine all questions of educational and administrative policy pertaining thereto." Although the senior members were not yet designated a departmental executive committee, their authority was also enlarged:

> Departmental recommendations regarding the annual budget and matters ordinarily associated therewith, such as appointments, dismissals, promotions, and salaries, shall be made by the full and associate professors, and shall be transmitted through the chairman to the appropriate dean.

Ibid. (1914), pp. 132-3.

[3]In another extraordinarily democratic move, under President Birge the Board of Regents expanded the authority of the departmental committees to include consultation in the appointment of departmental chairmen:

> The Departmental Committee of any department may by ballot express its preference for its chairman, and the entire ballot shall be transmitted, by the chairman thereof, to the dean of the school or college concerned. The University Faculty may prescribe rules governing the nomination of departmental chairmen. The dean of the college or school to which a department belongs, after consultation with the president and after receiving the ballot as herein provided or after affording the opportunity for such ballot, shall appoint a chairman from the members of professorial rank. The term of appointment shall be one year, but there shall be no limit upon the number of consecutive terms.

UW Faculty Document 149, University Committee, "Resolution on Nomination of Department Chairmen," March 1, 1920, UA; BOR Minutes, March 5, 1920, UA.

This action was an outgrowth of a bitterly contested palace revolt against the autocratic leadership of the long-time chairman of the Department of Chemistry, Louis Kahlenberg. Ironically, Kahlenberg's more diplomatic successor, J. Howard Mathews, went on to serve as chairman for the next thirty-three years, in the process building one of the country's great chemistry departments. See Aaron J. Ihde, *Chemistry as Viewed from Bascom's Hill: A History of the Chemistry Department at the University of Wisconsin in Madison* (Madison: Department of Chemistry, 1990), pp. 401-13.

[4]Mark H. Ingraham, oral history interview, 1972, UA.

dain, in part because they usually were promulgated from the president's office atop "the Hill" rather than developed through collegial discussion and consensus. Apart from the short-lived Experimental College, which the faculty accepted grudgingly as a goodwill gesture to its new leader, many of Frank's other ideas—like his 1930 call for a "functional organization of faculty forces"—were ignored and died stillborn. Ironically, the president's hands-off administrative style tended to strengthen the faculty's role in institutional governance and would have been applauded in a more scholarly leader like Van Hise or Birge. Frank's forbearance did little to endear him to his associates. Rather, it was seen as weakness or, worse, aloofness. By the time Frank ran into political difficulties with the La Follette progressives in the 1930s, he had come to understand better how to work with the faculty governance structure and to accept its limits on his presidential prerogatives. By then, however, he had irretrievably lost most of whatever faculty support he might have won earlier through a more down-to-earth collegial approach.

Like Frank, Clarence Dykstra lacked a Ph.D. and his academic experience and credentials were only marginally stronger than those of his predecessor. No scholar, he was a practitioner in the field of public administration, probably the least academically respected sub-field of political science. Dykstra's most recent work as a city manager might have conditioned him to authoritarian management; indeed, during the great flood of early 1937 he was approvingly dubbed the Cincinnati Dictator. In Madison, however, his leadership style was more to reign rather than rule. In the process he, too, strengthened faculty governance.

The circumstances of Dykstra's appointment probably led him to recognize early on that he needed faculty allies. Selected in early 1937 by Governor Philip La Follette and appointed by his compliant Board of Regents, Dykstra soon found both gone. Stalwart Republican Julius Heil, who succeeded La Follette as governor the next year, may not have had preconceived views about the University other than as a voracious consumer of state tax dollars whose appetite must be curbed, but he was suspicious of anything and anybody tied to the La Follettes. Consequently, at first Dykstra had a decidedly rocky relationship with Heil, and perhaps at least partly for this reason the new president went out of his way to cultivate faculty support. He and his wife Lillian displayed a refreshing simplicity that quickly won the faculty favor denied the more aloof and snobbish Glenn and Mary Frank. As president, Dykstra occasionally led, more often followed, but never tried to impose his will on the faculty. Unlike his predecessor's ambitious agenda, Dykstra's goals were rather more modest, or at least indirect, and he made sure they did not upset the faculty.[5]

The Expansion of Faculty Authority

Throughout the Frank and Dykstra administrations the faculty's role in University governance expanded significantly. On occasion this resulted from a direct faculty challenge to the president or the regents. The most dramatic example of a confrontational approach was the abrupt resignation of the faculty members of the Athletic Board in 1936 to protest regent meddling in intercollegiate athletics during the Spears-Meanwell controversy. To end the embarrassing impasse (and avoid possible expulsion from the Big Ten Conference), the regents backed down and explicitly recognized faculty control over intercollegiate athletics.[6]

Faculty authority also developed because the president and regents recognized the advantages of sharing their power with a responsible faculty. Thus President Frank agreed to faculty consultation on how to deal with depression budget cuts, and both he and the regents readily accepted the University Committee's carefully crafted plan for a graduated system of salary reductions or waivers during the emergency. The scheme called for the higher salaried staff members to bear steeper pay cuts, but it also, significantly, guarded the principle of tenure for the two senior faculty ranks and the contractual obligation to honor the term of other appointments.[7]

If the University managed to avoid outright dismissals during the darkest years of the depression, it did reduce the number of instructional

---

[5]Mark Ingraham liked to recount an experience that to him illustrated the unusually democratic atmosphere at Wisconsin, rare among American universities in the 1930s. He was lunching with a group of academics at a national professional meeting when someone asked one of those present how he liked his university's new president. The reaction was enthusiastic because, it was reported, the president lunched at the faculty club once in awhile and talked to those present "just like he's one of us." Ingraham commented that Wisconsin was a little different. It too had a new president, Clarence Dykstra, and when he came to the club the faculty talked to him "just like he's one of us." Ingraham didn't think much about his comment at the time, and was surprised that it quickly made the rounds of the country as an example of Wisconsin's unique collegial spirit. Ibid.

[6]See pp. 253-69.

[7]Ibid., pp. 226-36.

positions and failed to reappoint some expectant members of the junior faculty. For the most part, such terminations were limited to graduate assistants and instructors whose positions traditionally rotated among advanced graduate students to prepare them for teaching appointments elsewhere. It was to assist such depression victims that the Graduate School created the special program of postdoctoral research grants funded by the Wisconsin Alumni Research Foundation beginning in 1932.

There were, nevertheless, a few instances where instructors of long-standing were not reappointed. These painful cases caused considerable uneasiness in the faculty and helped to generate support for a small but lively faculty union, Local 223 of the American Federation of Teachers, which developed during the thirties. One such controversial termination occurred when a reorganization of the School of Music in 1939 resulted in the non-reappointment of Florence Bergendahl, an instructor since 1925. The tenure committees of both the faculty union and the more substantial local chapter of the American Association of University Professors investigated the case, calling the attention of the University Committee and President Dykstra to the fact that the associate and full professors of the music school had not been consulted as required by regent policy. Professor Walter Agard of the faculty union undoubtedly spoke for many when he complained that "something in the administrative setup is radically wrong when a staff member is flatly dismissed after 14 years of service."[8] At the next meeting of the general faculty Mark Ingraham, currently the national AAUP president, offered a motion directing the University Committee to develop a policy statement on faculty tenure.[9]

In December of 1939 the University Committee submitted its initial tenure report to the faculty, which referred it back for further work and clarification.[10] The revised document, produced the following May, stressed that the report was merely an effort to clarify and codify traditional University practice. The University Committee conceded there

[8] *Daily Cardinal*, March 21 and 22, 1939; UW Faculty Document 583, "Annual Report of the University Committee for 1938-39," November 6, 1939. Agard expressed frustration to his friend and former colleague Alexander Meiklejohn that "Miss B— refuses to allow her personal case to be fought," and added: "Sellery slipped in this business, I am sure, and will regret it." Agard to Meiklejohn, March 25, 1939, Alexander Meiklejohn Papers, box 1, SHSW.

[9] UW Faculty Minutes, May 1, 1939, UA.

[10] Ibid., December 4, 1939.

were no immediate problems concerning tenure and academic freedom at the University. Nor was there any threat to the indefinite appointment of senior faculty—"that degree of security that is now, by established practice and tradition, accorded associate professors and professors." While there were no legally binding guarantees of such tenure protection, the report noted, they seemed unnecessary at Wisconsin. (Perhaps more likely the committee thought it politic not to seek them from a new and more conservative Board of Regents.)[11]

Most UW tenure problems, the report pointed out, involved instructors and assistant professors holding annual appointments for long periods. Accordingly, the committee recommended that as of July 1, 1941, instructors should be appointed annually for no more than eight years before being terminated, promoted to assistant professor with tenure, or tenured in rank, with a decision and notification by the end of the fifth year. Assistant professors should have a probationary period not to exceed six years, or eight in combination with service as an instructor, and might receive tenure with or without promotion beyond that rank. In setting limits to the probationary time of the junior staff, the report stressed the importance of care in appointment, reappointment, training, and promotion, and the need for early evaluations and necessary terminations. It also prescribed procedures for termination of tenured faculty for adequate cause, stipulated that tenure could not be won simply by length of service, and, no doubt with an eye on skeptics outside of academe, emphasized that tenure should not protect inefficient faculty members. These might be terminated after other remedies and written notification had been tried to no avail.

Quoting the regents' famous 1894 "sifting and winnowing" statement, the University Committee concluded its report with a ringing

---

[11]The concept of tenure—indefinite appointments for the two senior faculty ranks—had been recognized by the regents as early as the Van Hise administration. Chapter II, section 13, of the *By-Laws and Laws of the Regents* published in 1907 provided:

> All deans, directors, professors, and associate professors shall hold their positions at the pleasure of the Board, assistant professors for the term of three years, if so appointed, instructors, assistants, and fellows for the term of one year, but all subject to termination at the pleasure of the Board.

Although other parts of the *By-Laws and Laws* underwent substantial revision over the next three decades, the language of this section remained unchanged. Still, the meaning of tenure remained vague and inchoate for some years. In the dispute over Dean Snell's refusal to make three-year appointments at the Milwaukee Extension Center, for example, the term tenure was used with respect to the junior staff's expectation of three-year contracts. See pp. 251-3, 810-12.

affirmation of tenure as a bulwark of academic freedom. Its purpose was to "give staff members a degree of security of employment that will protect them from unjust discharge, and so to warrant men of superior ability in undertaking the training, toil, and financial limitations commonly attendant upon a life of public service as a university professor." Small wonder the ninety-four faculty members in attendance at the meeting approved the tenure statement unanimously.[12] Although the Board of Regents took no formal notice at the time of the faculty's tenure statement, the provisions regarding the length of probationary service by non-tenured faculty were with minor modifications incorporated into the next edition of University regulations and were henceforth regarded as established University policy.[13]

By 1945 much of the modern faculty governance structure and personnel policies were in place, respected by the administration and the regents. Since its establishment in 1916 the University Committee had increased its oversight and stature considerably, gaining by common consent the right to examine any aspect of the University's operation in which the faculty had an interest. Its reports were respected because they were factual and collegial—that is, they were neither confrontational nor adversarial in nature or tone. The committee sometimes led in raising issues of national concern. Characteristically, it began the study of faculty tenure policy even before the issue was addressed at the national level in the 1940 tenure statement of the American Association of University Professors, whose influential guidelines were thereafter increasingly adopted by colleges and universities across the country. Although the regents ignored the faculty entirely in the appointment of Glenn Frank in 1925, in the selection of Frank's successor in 1937 the University Committee won the right for the faculty to be consulted on the appointment of the president and soon by Extension on the choice of deans as well. At the department level, at Dean Sellery's suggestion Dykstra began enforcing the existing but largely ignored 1920 regent rule calling for annual faculty consultation on the appointment of departmental chairmen. In the reorganization of the faculty into the four interdisciplinary divisions created in 1942, President Dykstra and the

---

[12] UW Faculty Minutes, May 6, 1940; UW Faculty Document 584A, "Revised Report on Faculty Personnel Policies," May 6, 1940; *Daily Cardinal*, May 7, 1940.

[13] *Rules of the University of Wisconsin* [ca. 1940], BOR Papers, 1/00/2, box 1, UA. Dean Sellery cited the new regulations in notifying a music school staff member in 1941 of the terminal nature of her appointment. Sellery to Helene Stratman-Thomas, May 14, 1941, Dykstra Presidential Papers, 4/15/1, box 72, UA.

regents agreed that the four elected divisional executive committees should advise deans on the quality of course proposals and tenure recommendations. Also on the recommendation of Sellery while he was serving as acting president in 1937, the Board of Regents established the policy of mandatory retirement for faculty members when they reached the age of seventy, a policy designed to assure a regular turnover and renewal of faculty ranks. Thus by the end of our period the University was even more explicitly a faculty-run institution than it had been twenty years earlier. In this regard it was much ahead of other major institutions across the country.

Faculty involvement took time, of course, especially on the part of the senior faculty; there were innumerable committees, meetings, reports, and deliberations. In these years the general faculty customarily met monthly during the academic year and sometimes held special meetings in addition. So, too, did the faculty of some of the schools and colleges, though in 1926 the letters and science faculty authorized its dean to dispense with a meeting in any month lacking substantial business.[14] When President Frank created the independent School of Education out of the College of Letters and Science in 1930, the school continued the L&S practice of monthly faculty meetings. Faculty meetings were less frequent in the other professional schools, whose deans exercised more authority and where democratic collegial government was less developed. At the college level, faculty meetings dealt almost exclusively with academic and curricular issues. This was often the case at the campus level as well, although the general faculty meetings also addressed broader questions of University policy and structure, along with such minutia as the academic calendar, grading standards, women's hours, and, regularly, student discipline and intercollegiate athletics.

Business came to the faculty through a well-developed system of standing committees, whose recommendations were ordinarily but not always accepted without scrutiny and occasional modification. Some important issues were brought for faculty consideration after study by special ad hoc committees appointed for that purpose. Examples are the All-University Study Commission's proposal for the Experimental College in 1926 or the curricular reforms recommended by the Fish Committee in 1930 and the Daniels Committee in 1940.[15] Like these,

---

[14]L&S Faculty Minutes, January 18, 1926, UA.
[15]See pp. 150-2, 156-64, 750-5.

many issues came first to a college faculty meeting for consideration before being recommended to the general faculty. Some faculty committees, such as the Committee on Student Life and Interests, which had a number of subcommittees, the Athletic Board, and the Research Committee, required major commitments of time from their members.

The Research Committee illustrated the increasingly substantial faculty role in institutional policy and governance at Wisconsin in this period. When the regents began budgeting a small amount for the support of research in 1916, the University faculty responded the following year by creating a research committee to advise on the use of flexible University research funds.[16] From the outset the faculty considered the committee a prestige assignment, its composition invariably consisting of senior faculty members of considerable scholarly distinction. When mathematics Professor Charles S. Slichter became graduate dean in 1920, he expanded the role of the Research Committee. Although at first the members generally followed the persuasive Slichter's suggestions in approving research grants, gradually as the amount of state and especially WARF research funding increased, the committee's work and the role of its members in making the allocation decisions expanded. In 1936 the faculty voted to recognize formally the close relationship between the committee and the graduate dean by making it a standing Graduate School committee charged with administering "the special research fund and...the WARF fund and other monies assigned to the Graduate School."[17] By this time the members of the Research Committee were deciding how to spend sizable and growing sums each year to support the research projects of individual faculty members. At other universities such decisions were typically made by a single individual—the president or a dean, as was the case with the federal funds for agricultural research dispensed by Dean Harry Russell in his role as director of the UW Agricultural Experiment Station. But for two out of the three major sources of University research funding in these years—state Fund Number 9 and the WARF funds—the allocation decisions were made by a committee of faculty peers rather than by an administrator. At no other American university at this time did a faculty committee have such substantial spending authority. And al-

---

[16]This action was also in response to a call by the National Research Council of the National Academy of Sciences asking major universities to establish research committees to facilitate cooperation with the NRC on national defense problems. UW Faculty Document 30, University Committee, "Resolution for UW Faculty," March 5, 1917.

[17]Note attached to UW Faculty Document 30 and dated November 2, 1936.

though the committee occasionally invested in dead-end projects, it is unlikely that any other university could match the quality over time of the collective decisions made by the members of the UW Research Committee.[18]

Wisconsin faculty members took their governance responsibilities seriously, though depending on the business to be considered attendance at general faculty meetings fluctuated widely. There were only eleven participants at one meeting in 1936 when President Frank was away and the agenda contained little business, for example, but five hundred, or nearly the entire faculty, turned out in the fall of 1925 for Frank's first faculty meeting and again in 1931 when the discussion centered on depression budget cuts and changes in the state teachers retirement system.[19] Attendance at the monthly general faculty meetings averaged above a hundred, or more than 20 percent of the faculty, throughout this period. At faculty meetings of the College of Letters and Science, home of about half of the faculty, attendance was of course lower. Still, Dean Sellery could count on well over a hundred L&S colleagues turning out to discuss important issues and a hard core of twenty to thirty senior faculty regularly coming to deal with an agenda containing

---

[18]The legislature first appropriated $23,000 for general research as a continuing line item, Number 9, in the 1919 University budget, thereby giving rise to the name "Number 9" used for many years thereafter to identify the University's state-funded research budget. By 1931-32 the Number 9 fund had increased to $75,000. Although the Wisconsin Alumni Research Foundation was incorporated in late 1925, the Steenbock patent was not approved until 1928. The first WARF grant was $1,200 in 1928-29 to support Professors E.B. Fred's and W.H. Peterson's studies of bacteria. WARF support increased to $9,700 the following year and expanded steadily thereafter, more than replacing the series of reductions in state funding of Number 9 during the depression. By 1933-34, for example, Number 9 had been cut to $36,000, but a total of $146,663 in WARF funds was supporting eighty-five research projects. By 1945 WARF support had grown to $230,000 annually. In keeping with Harry Steenbock's original vision, throughout our period WARF funds were used primarily to support research in the natural sciences. To provide a better balance, the Number 9 funds, originally intended for support of physical and biological research, were used for work in the humanities and social sciences. For a good discussion of the early innovative use of these flexible research funds, see Mark H. Ingraham, *Charles Sumner Slichter: The Golden Vector* (Madison: University of Wisconsin Press, 1972), pp. 139-93. For a detailed history of WARF support see E.B. Fred, *The Role of the Wisconsin Alumni Research Foundation in the Support of Research at the University of Wisconsin* (Madison: Wisconsin Alumni Research Foundation, 1973); Fred, "The Year of Decision, 1925: The Early Days of WARF" (unpublished manuscript, April 14, 1961), General Presidential Papers, 4/16/4, box 17, UA; Clay Schoenfeld, "The W.A.R.F. Story: The Wisconsin Alumni Research Foundation, Sixty Years of Research and Realization—1925-1985" (unpublished manuscript, 1986), UHP.

[19]UW Faculty Minutes, June 19, 1936, October 5, 1925, April 29, 1931.

only routine matters. At Wisconsin, the faculty liked to say, faculty government was by and for the *concerned*, and there were many in that category.

Increasing Faculty Authority over Staffing

During the inter-war years faculty ranks were relatively stable and the turnover of the senior faculty was low, probably fewer than a dozen changes University-wide in some years. As student enrollment slowly grew during the twenties and latter thirties, there was a modest increase in size of the faculty, enabling some departments to add new fields of study. Like enrollment, faculty numbers declined during the early years of the depression, especially at the junior level, but to its credit the University weathered the depression without the major staff layoffs that occurred at some institutions. It also managed, through WARF research grants and judicious if reduced staffing, to keep a number of especially able younger scholars in Madison. Even in the worst of the depression years, the administration and regents accepted the University Committee's advice that it was important for faculty morale to retain enough budgetary flexibility to allow some promotions and modest merit-based salary increases.

The overwhelming impression of the UW faculty in these years is that of a comparatively small, stable, friendly, homogeneous, and overwhelmingly male academic family, whose leaders—deans and department chairmen—held their offices for long periods, often for decades. Relationships among faculty and campus administrators were easy and informal, with most faculty members preferring to be on a first-name basis and eschewing the title Dr. in favor of Mr. or Professor in more formal settings. The Second World War brought considerably more staff and administrative turnover and temporary curricular changes, but still within the general context of pre-war student and faculty values and customs. In 1945 the University of Wisconsin was recognizably the same institution in size, scope, and character that it had been twenty years earlier. Its great expansion and change were yet to come.

Throughout the nineteenth century UW presidents were centrally involved in the recruitment and appointment of faculty members, which the regents considered a purely administrative and regent function. This changed under President Van Hise, whose democratic instincts led him to delegate a good deal of his presidential authority to the academic deans and the faculty. Under Van Hise the academic deans took over much of the responsibility for staffing their schools and colleges, leaving the president freer to concentrate on broad institutional policy and relations with the regents and the state.

Gradually, as departments grew in size the senior faculty or at least the department chairman also played a role in selecting candidates for appointment. Department involvement in staffing decisions—faculty appointments, promotions, and tenuring—developed first in the College of Letters and Science, encouraged by Deans Birge and Sellery. Both men believed strongly in faculty governance and rarely acted on a personnel matter without the recommendation of the affected department, though both also considered the department's role advisory and believed the dean's and president's judgments must prevail. In the professional schools departmental participation in faculty recruitment developed more slowly and unevenly. Strong-willed Harry Russell made the personnel decisions in the College of Agriculture during his twenty-four years as dean until 1930. Similarly, Dean Frederick E. Turneaure handled staffing matters in the College of Engineering for more than three decades from 1903 until his retirement in 1937. And while Professor Paul Clark remembered Dean Charles Bardeen as open and easily approachable, Clark also recalled that Bardeen saw no need to consult his colleagues about faculty recruitment or many other matters during his nearly three-decades-long direction of the Medical School from 1907 until his death from cancer in 1935. Clark once asked Bardeen why he did not discuss some issue with the faculty, only to be reminded that since the final decision rested with the dean he saw no reason to waste the faculty's time![20]

By 1925 it was still assumed that the president had the authority to recommend faculty appointments directly to the regents, but at least in Letters and Science the faculty had also come to expect prior discussion with the dean and department concerned. Thus President Frank and Dean Sellery consulted the chairmen of the affected departments about the appointment of Alexander Meiklejohn and other faculty recruited for the Experimental College in the late 1920s. Throughout the inter-war years it was generally accepted that the administration had the authority

[20]Paul F. Clark, oral history interview, 1972, UA; Clark, *The University of Wisconsin Medical School: A Chronicle, 1848-1948* (Madison: University of Wisconsin Press, 1967), p. 45.

to overrule the wishes of a departmental faculty. As faculty involvement in University governance grew during the 1920s and 1930s, however, the Board of Regents gradually came to assume prior departmental endorsement of faculty appointments brought to the regents for approval.[21]

The increasingly important role of departmental faculty in personnel decisions was highlighted by Dean Sellery's and President Dykstra's ill-fated effort to appoint Milton Friedman as an associate professor of economics in 1941. The episode is instructive both as an example of the complexities of academic politics and as an illustration of growing faculty authority.[22] Friedman, later to win a Nobel Prize for his work in economic theory at the University of Chicago, was appointed as a part-time visiting lecturer in the Department of Economics in 1940-41 to teach two courses a semester while also assisting Professor Harold Groves on a research project concerning Wisconsin income tax policy. Only twenty-six, Friedman was already recognized as a scholar of considerable promise. He did not yet have a Ph.D. degree, but he had published a number of articles and book chapters and had completed the preliminary doctoral exams at both Chicago and Columbia Universities. He confidently expected that his already completed doctoral dissertation would be accepted by Columbia in 1940. (Actually, because of a controversy over some of his interpretations this did not happen until 1946 following its revision and publication as a book.)

At Wisconsin Friedman proved to be a stimulating teacher. He quickly developed an enthusiastic following among the economics junior staff and graduate students, including Groves' research assistant, Walter Heller, a future chairman of the National Council of Economic Advisors under Presidents John F. Kennedy and Lyndon B. Johnson. Of the senior economics faculty, from the first Harold Groves acted as Friedman's major patron. Groves soon began to explore the possibility of getting his protégé a regular faculty appointment in the department. At

---

[21]While not giving primacy to departmental recommendations, the 1920 regents rule nevertheless called for consultation by deans with the senior departmental faculty on all personnel actions. By 1977, this departmental role had so expanded in practice and was so deeply ingrained that neither the administration nor the regents objected to a faculty revision of the *Faculty Policies and Procedures* requiring that all faculty appointments must be *initiated* by a department, a significant expansion of departmental authority.

[22]The authors are greatly indebted to Professor Emeritus Robert J. Lampman, the chief author and editor of *Economists at Wisconsin, 1892-1992* (Madison: Department of Economics, 1993), for information about the Friedman affair.

Groves' request, sometime during the winter Friedman prepared an analysis of the department's courses in economic theory and statistics. He reported that the instruction was too elementary for students to do sophisticated statistical work and offered a blunt and damning conclusion:

> A student cannot secure training at UW sufficient to qualify him to teach advanced statistics or to do independent work in the field of statistical methods. Even if he takes all the work offered, he will be but indifferently qualified to do research involving the application of modern statistics.[23]

Groves' scheme was for Friedman to handle the work of the late Professor Harry Jerome, who had taught statistics for the department from 1915 until his death in 1938. Since that time his statistics courses had been taken over by two faculty members in the School of Commerce, Professors Erwin Gaumnitz and Philip G. Fox. Like the economics department, the commerce school was a distinct departmental unit of the College of Letters and Science. It had loose ties to economics through several joint faculty appointments, though not including Gaumnitz and Fox. Groves no doubt hoped both to keep Friedman at Wisconsin and in the process to recapture the economics department's control over its statistics courses, which served students in economics, commerce, and agricultural economics.

If this was the strategy, it backfired. Friedman's outspoken memo criticizing the Gaumnitz-Fox handling of statistics instruction understandably offended the commerce faculty and some senior members of the economics department. Both groups resented the upstart youngster's blunt condemnation. Thus when the economics executive committee met on March 22 to consider whether to offer Friedman an assistant professorship, the motion was supported by only four of the nine members present and after considerable discussion was withdrawn by its author, Professor Don Lescohier, without a formal vote.[24]

Groves was not willing to drop the matter, however, and managed to persuade L&S Dean Sellery that Friedman would help to restore the economics department's lustre, which had been fading since the retirement of its famous institutional economist, John R. Commons, in

---

[23] *Capital Times*, May 14, 1941.

[24] Walter A. Morton, unofficial notes of economics budget committee meeting, March 22, 1941, UHP; Edwin E. Witte to George C. Sellery, April 1 and 15, 1941, Dykstra Presidential Papers, 4/15/1, box 74; Morton, oral history interview, 1978, UA.

1933.[25] Sellery readily agreed that it was not healthy for the commerce faculty to determine economics appointments even indirectly. A strong civil libertarian, he also evidently suspected that anti-Semitism might be involved in the department's decision not to recommend the appointment of Friedman.[26]

With President Dykstra's approval, Sellery accordingly offered Friedman a three-year appointment as an associate professor of econom-

---

[25]Following his appointment in 1904, Commons and his students, a number of whom subsequently joined the UW faculty, had made the economics department the leading center of institutional economics, stressing a pragmatic and interventionist rather than a theoretical approach to the problems of modern capitalism. Commons' commanding personality and views dominated departmental deliberations for several decades, and nothing of substance was decided without his approval, including his choice of Edwin E. Witte, the director of the Wisconsin Legislative Reference Bureau, as his successor. Witte soon assumed the chairmanship, but after Commons' retirement the department lacked a commanding leader of Common's stature—though it had several strong personalities—and had fallen into increasing dissension and disarray. For Commons' account of his remarkably active and productive life, see his *Myself: The Autobiography of John R. Commons* (New York: Macmillan, 1934; Madison: University of Wisconsin Press, 1963).

[26]It is impossible to determine whether anti-Semitism played a part in the Friedman deliberations, although Sellery apparently thought so, probably persuaded by Groves, Selig Perlman, and perhaps Elizabeth Brandeis, all of whom supported Friedman. In discussing the case with Walter Morton, one of Friedman's departmental opponents, Sellery indicated that he planned to recommend Friedman's appointment regardless of the department's wishes, explaining cryptically, "This is not the Third Reich." Morton always denied anti-Semitism was involved, arguing that the issue was simply that Friedman's interests in statistics and economic theory did not fit the department's staffing needs. The majority did not want to offend its two commerce colleagues, Gaumnitz and Fox, by implying that they were not competent to teach the statistics courses, nor to upset the department's young theorist, Assistant Professor James S. Earley, by bringing in another theorist. It is worth noting that the economics department had two Jews on its teaching staff at this time, both of whom favored the Friedman appointment: Professor Selig Perlman, a Russian immigrant and prominent labor economist who had joined the department in 1921, and Elizabeth Brandeis, the daughter of the famous reformer and U.S. Supreme Court justice, who had been a part-time lecturer since the late 1920s specializing in unemployment issues, especially unemployment compensation. Perlman's son Mark, also an economist, later cited the Friedman case as a "blatant" and "overtly anti-Semitic" example of university hiring discrimination at this time, perhaps an indication that his father also shared this view. See Mark Perlman, "Jews and Contributions to Economics: A Bicentennial Review," *Judaism*, 25 (Summer, 1976), 307. For Morton's denial, see Morton to Mark Perlman, April 28, 1981; Morton, "The Friedman Affair of the Economics Department in the Spring of 1941" (unpublished manuscript, September 18, 1979), UHP; Morton, oral history interview. See also Leonard S. Silk, *The Economists* (New York: Basic Books, 1976), pp. 58-9, which also assumes that anti-Semitism was behind the opposition to Friedman. Silk was a 1940 UW baccalaureate graduate with a major in economics. He would have had an interest in the Friedman affair but very likely had no direct knowledge since it occurred the year after he left Wisconsin.

ics without the department's endorsement. Friedman balked at the non-tenured character of the appointment, however, asking for assurance he would not again be a victim of departmental politics when the appointment ran out. Unable to make such a promise or refute his logic, Dykstra and Sellery raised the offer to a tenured associate professorship, conditional as always on approval by the Board of Regents. Upset by this decision to second-guess his department, economics Chairman Edwin E. Witte tactfully conceded "the right of the University Administration to proceed contrary to the wishes of the majority of our department," but in a strongly worded three-page letter to Dykstra and Sellery he emphasized that with the exception of two of the nine tenured economics professors (Groves and Selig Perlman), the department believed the Friedman appointment would be a serious mistake:

> Whatever may be the faults of the professors in the department of economics, I do not believe that they justify disregard of the democratic policies which the University has always pursued in making appointments....Without criticizing anyone, it is undeniable that many unfortunate incidents have occurred in connection with the promotion and consideration of Mr. Friedman for a position in our department, which have aroused extreme bitterness, both within the department and in the associated departments of agricultural economics and the School of Commerce. The situation is such that the appointment of Mr. Friedman will intensify the bitterness within the department and render impossible any effective cooperation. It may even result in the resignation of some of the most valuable members of the department and may lead to a row which may reach not only the Regents but the Governor and the Legislature.[27]

In response Sellery reminded Witte of his key concern: "I do not believe it necessary to allow other departments to determine our judgment in such matters." He amplified this point in a handwritten note added to Dykstra's copy of the dean's letter to Witte: "I have already told Friedman the job was his & he has accepted—none too gladly. To let him out I will not agree to. It wd. force me to let Gaumnitz get a strangle hold on economic statistics & Commerce dominate Economics. That wd. be dangerous."[28]

Following conferences by Dean Sellery with the senior members of the economics faculty, Witte again informed President Dykstra that the

---

[27]Witte to Dykstra and Sellery, April 15, 1941, Dykstra Presidential Papers, 4/15/1, box 72.

[28]Sellery to Witte, April 16, 1941, ibid.

great majority of his colleagues were "of the opinion that the appointment of Mr. Friedman will not be to the best interests of the department, but, on the contrary, very destructive of its morale."[29] Witte's fear (or perhaps threat) that the row might become public was soon borne out when the Madison *Capital Times* featured the story on May 14 under a large front-page headline: "FIREWORKS IN U.W. ECON DEPARTMENT AS INSTRUCTOR MAY GET $3500 PROF'S JOB/ DYKSTRA, SELLERY SAID TO FAVOR APPOINTMENT OF FORMER COLUMBIA UNIVERSITY INSTRUCTOR TO ASSOCIATE PROFESSOR OF ECONOMICS." The story quoted Friedman's critical comments about UW statistics instruction, and without identifying the source other than "one prominent professor of economics" it also included lengthy extracts from Chairman Witte's April 15 letter protesting the plan to appoint Friedman.[30]

The following day President Dykstra and Dean Sellery met with the senior economics and commerce faculty members. Contrary to advance press speculation, the Friedman appointment was not discussed. Instead the focus was on a renewed call for an independent School of Commerce under its own dean. This idea had been promoted periodically since the early thirties by Professor Fayette H. Elwell, the commerce school director, following the separation of the School of Education from the College of Letters and Science. Elwell probably concluded that the controversy over the Friedman appointment offered an opportunity to push for separation, for he and his colleagues informed Dykstra and Sellery they were considering asking the legislature to establish an independent school.[31]

---

[29] Witte to Dykstra, May 12, 1941, UHP.

[30] *Capital Times*, May 14, 1941. One should not assume that Witte, a circumspect and loyal team player, was the source of the story. He had informed Sellery and Dykstra that he was distributing copies of his letter to his colleagues, "so that they will have an opportunity to inform you if I am wrong on any point." The leaker was probably Walter Morton, the most vocal critic of the Friedman appointment and a close friend of William T. Evjue, the equally irascible editor of the *Times*. See also similar coverage of the Friedman controversy by the *Daily Cardinal*, May 15, 16, and 27, 1941, and the *Wisconsin State Journal*, May 15, 1941.

[31] *Capital Times*, May 15 and 16, 1941. Prior to this meeting Dean Sellery had written a long letter to President Dykstra summarizing his objections to separating commerce from his college. He pointed out that the commerce curriculum was "overwhelmingly made up of regular Letters and Science materials handled by Letters and Science professors."
  To have commerce "annex" economics would be a very objectionable thing, for economics is a central element in a liberal arts education; it is one of our grand old departments and the subject is best taught in a college of letters and science, because it deals not only with this application and that but with the broad field. Where would labor economics figure in a separate school of commerce? Where

When on May 27 President Dykstra recommended that the Board of Regents appoint Milton Friedman as a tenured associate professor, one of the regents asked if the proposal had the endorsement of the economics department. Embarrassed, Dykstra of course had to answer in the negative, and after some discussion about the importance of faculty support of personnel recommendations the regents decided to table the appointment. Friedman thereupon withdrew his name from further consideration and left Wisconsin to pursue his soon-to-be distinguished career elsewhere.[32] Within the University there was speculation that commerce Director Elwell, who had many business contacts around the state and on the Board of Regents, had sabotaged the appointment by priming one of the regents to ask Dykstra the fateful question about departmental support. It was, however, a perfectly reasonable question even if answering it flustered the president.[33]

There are a number of ironies in the Friedman affair beyond the loss of a future Nobel Laureate. Friedman later became the chief architect of the Chicago libertarian free market school of economics, much opposed to the interventionist doctrines of the Wisconsin institutionalists. Yet in 1941 his support came from the more liberal institutionalists in the department—Groves, Perlman, and Brandeis—and his opponents were mostly political conservatives with whom Friedman would in time be more in ideological sympathy. The proposed appointment also got entangled in the running political battle over an independent School of Commerce, which finally was achieved in 1944

---

would "pure economics" come in? It would seem that it would have to be bootlegged. If one adds up the courses that are peculiar to commerce one discovers that there are only a handful. Of these accounting is central. Sellery to Dykstra, May 14, 1941, Dykstra Presidential Papers, 4/15/1, box 72.

[32]Friedman to Dykstra, June 2, 1941; Dykstra to Friedman, June 10, 1941, Dykstra Presidential Papers, 4/15/1, box 64; Witte to James S. Earley, June 6, 1941, UHP. The minutes for the May 27 regents meeting make no reference to the controversy over the Friedman appointment.

[33]Morton, oral history interview. Although in his oral history recollections Morton speculated that Elwell was behind the regent's question, as the leading Friedman opponent in the economics department he himself was certainly capable of such prompting. Like Elwell, he had excellent business and political contacts and in addition was the most likely source of the initial leak to the *Capital Times*. On the other hand, the regents may simply have been reacting to the considerable press coverage of the controversy. In his unpublished autobiography, Harold Groves blames both Elwell and Morton for the "political pressure and intrigue" that derailed the Friedman appointment. Groves, "In and Out of the Ivory Tower" (mimeographed, 1969), p. 183, UHP.

over President Dykstra's objections after Dean Sellery's retirement removed the most formidable obstacle to the separation. Within the economics department some of the conservatives, including Friedman's chief opponent Walter Morton, tended to favor a merger with commerce and may have seen the Friedman appointment as a barrier to these plans because his work in statistical methodology impinged on the interests of commerce Professors Gaumnitz and Fox.

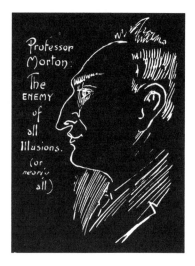

Morton as Seen by Max Otto

The chief lesson to be drawn from the Friedman affair was its revelation of how far faculty authority for selecting candidates for faculty appointments had evolved during the early twentieth century. Several times during the controversy economics Chairman Witte acknowledged that Sellery and Dykstra had both the right and the authority to overrule the department's wishes and promised he and his colleagues would respect their decision. In the end, however, the faculty managed to prevail over these two respected top administrators. In retrospect one may question the soundness of the department's motives and judgment in this case, but the Friedman affair helped to cement a department's primacy in making faculty appointments.

Maintaining Faculty Quality

Other faculty recruitment efforts during the period were more successful, no doubt because they had at least the acquiescence if not in all cases the enthusiastic support of the departmental faculty. President Frank's and Alexander Meiklejohn's determination to staff the Experimental College with committed undergraduate teachers brought a number of gifted instructors to Wisconsin in the late twenties, although at unusually high salaries that caused considerable resentment among the regular faculty of their home departments. A half century later Walter

Morton still remembered with bitterness how he and Harold Groves, both possessing Ph.D. degrees, were appointed as assistant professors in the economics department in 1927 at the standard academic year salary of $2,500. Their colleague Paul Raushenbush, who did not have a Ph.D., also began an assistant professorship in the department that same year. Because Raushenbush was also teaching in the Experimental College, however, his patron Meiklejohn persuaded President Frank to pay him a salary of $3,300, or a third more than Morton and Groves received.[34]

Raushenbush left the University in 1932 to direct the Wisconsin unemployment compensation program he had helped to create, but some of the Experimental College faculty—John Gaus in political science, Walter Agard in classics, and Carl Bögholt in philosophy—remained as popular and innovative teachers long after the demise of the college. Like Meiklejohn the Experimental College staffers were activist and progressive or even radical in their political views. Along with Raushenbush, Gaus was a close friend and political adviser of Governor Philip La Follette; though less active, Bögholt was also a staunch progressive; Agard was one of the organizers and leaders of the faculty union in the thirties and shared Meiklejohn's interest in the socialism.

It is noteworthy that even in the depth of the depression when the University was suffering from sharply reduced budgets and "waived" faculty salaries, neither the regents nor the state imposed a rigid hiring freeze. As long as the deans operated within their shrunken budgets, they were able to fill key faculty vacancies. Often they made such replacements at the less expensive assistant professor level, but, remarkably, in every depression year there were some senior appointments as well. If faculty numbers declined for a time, this was regarded as a temporary contraction resulting from smaller enrollments and budgets; the chief consideration was that the depression must not be permitted to weaken the quality of the faculty over the long run.

The experience of the Department of History illustrates the importance of this depression strategy, for history suffered several major losses that might have damaged it irretrievably under a less flexible staffing policy. Regarded as one of the top history programs in the nation since the days of Frederick Jackson Turner in the early twentieth century, by 1925 the department consisted of eight regular

---

[34]UW Budget, 1927-28, UA; Morton, oral history interview.

faculty members, one of whom, the renowned ancient historian
Alexander A. Vasiliev, had joined it
that fall, replacing Michael I.
Rostovtzeff who had accepted an
appointment at Yale.[35] The department's senior modern European
historian, Carl Stephenson, resigned
in 1929, but in effect had already
been replaced two years earlier by
another full professor of comparable
stature, Chester P. Higby. At the
same time the increased University
funding of the late twenties enabled
the department to replace one
assistant professor and add
another—Curtis P. Nettels in early
American history and Chester V.
Easum in modern German history. When another full professor, the
medievalist Eugene H. Byrne, resigned in 1931 to head the history
department at Barnard College, he was replaced by a promising assistant
professor from the University of Nebraska, Robert L. Reynolds.

Vasiliev as Seen by Max Otto

    In 1932, just as Governor La Follette was mandating the first
round of salary waivers, the department suffered two major blows.
Professor Frederic L. Paxson, one of the two senior American historians
whose history of the American frontier had won the 1924 Pulitzer Prize,
resigned to accept a $9,300 professorship at the University of California
at Berkeley. The *Beloit Daily News* was not alone in wondering how
the University could justify its recent decision to hire a $10,000 football
coach when it was unable to fend off a lesser offer to one of its great
scholar-teachers.[36] Two months later, the other senior American
historian, departmental Chairman Carl Russell Fish, died unexpectedly
from pneumonia. Fish was one of the University's most popular
lecturers on and off campus. Only a year earlier he had declined an

[35]The 1925-26 roster of the history department consisted of Dean and Professor George C. Sellery, Professor and Chairman Carl Russell Fish, Professors Frederic L. Paxson and Alexander A. Vasiliev, Associate Professors Eugene H. Byrne, Paul A. Knaplund, and Carl Stephenson, and Assistant Professor James L. Sellers.

[36]*Beloit Daily News*, quoted in *Daily Cardinal*, May 5, 1932. See also *Daily Cardinal*, May 3, 4, 5, and 6, 1932.

attractive offer from Berkeley to remain at Wisconsin.[37] His untimely death, coming on top of the loss of Paxson, was a major test of the department's ability to maintain its national stature.

Before Fish's death he and Dean Sellery had moved quickly to replace Paxson with another senior historian, John D. Hicks, currently the dean of the College of Arts and Sciences at the University of Nebraska. A fellow Missourian and classmate of Glenn Frank at Northwestern, Hicks had done his graduate work at Wisconsin, receiving the Ph.D. in 1916; as an alumnus he was receptive to an appeal from his alma mater. An engaging and witty teacher, his 1931 book, *The Populist Revolt*, would soon be regarded as the classic study of that third party political reform movement of the 1890s. Dean Sellery was on vacation in Canada when Fish died, but he moved quickly to consult Paxson and his successor Hicks about how to deal with the emergency. He also arranged to bring Professor Paul Knaplund, the department's British historian who was teaching for the summer at the University of Michigan, back to Madison over a weekend to review departmental options and subsequently appointed Knaplund to the departmental chairmanship until Hicks could take over. Knaplund would serve again in that capacity on and off for a total of seventeen years. Much of the credit for the quality of the history staffing during this period must go to Knaplund's strong leadership, high standards, and care and skill in faculty recruiting. Rather than seek a senior scholar on short notice, the department decided to replace Fish with a gifted and equally flamboyant assistant professor, William B. Hesseltine. An American Civil War specialist, Hesseltine took over Fish's legendary course on "Representative Americans" and immediately captivated its large undergraduate clientele with his wry humor and unorthodox interpretations of historical figures. He also quickly began to attract and train some of the ablest history doctoral students ever produced by the department.[38]

---

[37]Fish had been at Wisconsin since 1900 and was slated to receive a Carnegie pension rather than one from the State Teachers Retirement Fund. The size of the Carnegie pensions had been greatly reduced in recent years because of lower investment income, so he found the higher California salary especially attractive. Fish's popularity around the state was such that a considerable campaign developed to keep him at Wisconsin. He decided to turn down the California offer when his salary was increased sufficiently to make up for the reduction in his likely Carnegie pension. See *Capital Times*, January 10 and 13, 1931.

[38]See Sellery to Marion Richardson, telegram, July 11, 1932; Richardson to Sellery, telegram, July 12, 1932; Sellery, "Recommendation to Regents," August 5, 1932, Frank Presidential Papers, 4/13/1, box 121, UA. For a number of positive views of Paul Knaplund's

Under Hicks' and Knaplund's confident leadership, over the next decade-and-a-half the department maintained and in fact added to its strength, mostly through a remarkable ability to identify promising younger scholars who could be recruited as assistant professors at modest salaries. Its record was impressive: Gaines Post (medieval history) in 1934, and Charles F. Edson (ancient history, replacing the retiring Vasiliev), Fred Harvey Harrington (American foreign relations), and William L. Sachse (Tudor-Stuart English history) all in 1937. Harrington, a future president of the University, left to take a position at the University of Arkansas in 1940 but returned to Wisconsin as an associate professor in 1944. That same year another associate professor, Merrill Jensen, joined the department to succeed Curtis Nettels, who had departed for Cornell University. Jensen would make Wisconsin the major center for the study of the American Revolution. In 1942 Knaplund and the department made a key senior appointment in American history to replace John Hicks after the latter accepted a chair at Berkeley.[39] The choice was Merle E. Curti of the Columbia University Teachers College, already regarded as one of the major figures in the new field of American social and intellectual history. The department's judgment was quickly validated when Curti's pioneering intellectual history, *The Growth of American Thought*, won a Pulitzer Prize in 1944.

By 1945, at the end of our period, the history department had grown by three to a total of eleven regular faculty members.[40] Of its 1925 roster of eight, only the chairman, Paul Knaplund, remained, the rest having died, retired, or left for positions at other universities. Though somewhat younger in age, as in 1925 the department was nevertheless overwhelmingly senior, with only one non-tenured

long service to the University and the history department see *Paul Knaplund* (Madison: State Historical Society of Wisconsin for the Department of History, University of Wisconsin, 1967). John Hicks' recollection of his experience at Wisconsin as a student and faculty member may be found in his *My Life with History*.

[39]In his post-retirement memoirs Hicks noted his great reluctance to leave Wisconsin despite its low salary scale and the attractions of California. "I loved the University of Wisconsin as I have loved no other university," he confessed a quarter-of-a-century later, "and I still find it difficult to account for my decision to leave it." Hicks, *My Life with History*, p. 210.

[40]The 1944-45 roster of the department consisted of Professor and Chairman Paul A. Knaplund, Professors Merle E. Curti, Chester V. Easum, William B. Hesseltine, Chester P. Higby, Gaines Post, and Robert L. Reynolds, Associate Professors Charles F. Edson, Fred H. Harrington, and Merrill M. Jensen, and Assistant Professor William L. Sachse.

member. It would be hard to make the case that its quality had declined over the twenty-year period, for it had expanded its coverage of the field, replaced its losses with a number of first-rate scholars and devoted teachers, and had acquired at least one genuine star. Across the country it continued to be recognized as one of the best history graduate programs. On campus, history was also regarded as one of the University's premier departments with, it was often said, an independent foreign policy vis-à-vis the rest of the institution. The department's continued high stature resulted mostly from its own esprit and determination to be great, of course. Still, one cannot overlook the crucial importance of the University administration's selective replacement policy during the dark years of the depression, when it must have been tempting to cope with massive budget cuts by imposing a hiring freeze, as occurred for a time at a number of less far-sighted institutions.

Another of the University's top-ranked departments used a somewhat different strategy to maintain and enhance its strength during this period. The College of Agriculture's Department of Agricultural Chemistry, which changed its name to the Department of Biochemistry in 1938,[41] was already famous the world over for its basic research on nutrition. Its chairman throughout the inter-war period, Edwin B. Hart, pioneered in the study of vitamins and the role of copper as an essential element of human life. His colleague Harry Steenbock specialized in the study of vitamin D. As we have already seen, Steenbock's decision to patent his epochal discovery of how to irradiate food with ultraviolet light to give it vitamin D properties led to the creation of the Wisconsin Alumni Research Foundation in 1925 to market the patent and use the income for the support of UW scientific research. Another of the department's four faculty members in 1925, William H. Peterson, studied fermentation and identified the factors for the growth of bacteria; during World War II his expertise helped make possible the secret UW research project to increase the production of penicillin.

Under Hart's wise leadership, over the two decades between 1925 and 1945 the department grew from four to ten faculty members, all the while building on its strength in nutritional studies. Unlike the history department and other letters and science units which generally declined to appoint their own graduates until they had first established a solid reputation at other universities, all of the faculty members added to

---

[41]BOR Minutes, March 9, 1938.

biochemistry over the period were UW graduates. Although most of the new recruits were selected from among the department's own top students, biochemistry had close ties with the L&S Department of Chemistry and its sister Departments of Agricultural Bacteriology and Genetics and it occasionally recruited from them as well. Hart believed the Wisconsin biological science departments attracted some of the ablest graduate students in the country; consequently there was little need to look outside the University for top quality new faculty. Since there was a close association between the work of the College of Agriculture's basic scientists and the applied research of the UW Agricultural Experiment Station, moreover, it made sense to recruit as new faculty members the ablest of the advanced students who were already working on these projects while engaged in their graduate work.

In 1926, for example, the department appointed as an instructor one of its most promising graduate students, Conrad A. Elvehjem, promoting him to a regular faculty appointment as an assistant professor in 1930. Elvehjem quickly showed his star quality, exploring the vitamin B complex and the curative uses of nicotinic acid, and in the process discovering a cure for the dreaded nutritional disease pellagra. In 1944-45 he took over from Hart as departmental chairman and later became dean of the Graduate School and president of the University. Another home-grown star was Karl Paul Link, appointed as an assistant professor in 1927. As already noted, the University's effort to retain Link by creating a special research professorship for him with Brittingham Trust funds triggered an unfortunate confrontation between the Board of Regents and the Brittingham trustees in 1931.[42] The great discovery in Link's laboratory of the blood anti-coagulant dicumarol, isolated from spoiled sweet-clover hay, illustrated the often fruitful relationship between pure science and practical applications at Wisconsin. It also gave WARF its second major patent; as a blood thinner dicumarol quickly became a standard treatment for the prevention of strokes and also was the basis for WARF's highly effective and lucrative rat poison, Warfarin.

The department added another Wisconsin Ph.D., Paul H. Phillips, as an assistant professor in 1935. Phillips was interested in the problem of how to preserve bull semen, an essential part of any program to improve the state's large dairy herd. Eventually, he and one of his graduate students, Henry A. Lardy, who joined the biochemistry faculty

---

[42]See pp. 236-43.

in 1946, discovered a method for the easy collection and preservation of semen using materials readily available to farmers. This became the basis for the widespread artificial breeding and genetic improvement of cattle and other large farm animals in Wisconsin and elsewhere in the years that followed. Another important addition was Associate Professor Marvin J. Johnson in 1942. An outstanding scholar-teacher, Johnson developed procedures for producing antibiotic drugs quickly and efficiently, a major wartime concern. His students were soon to be found in key research and development positions throughout the rapidly growing antibiotic drug industry. Two years later, at the end of our period, the department appointed one of its recent Ph.D.s, Robert H. Burris, to an assistant professorship. Burris would subsequently be elected to the National Academy of Sciences for his distinguished work on nitrogen fixation.

Even more successfully than the history department, biochemistry not only maintained but significantly increased its stature over the two decades, becoming the best such department in the country and probably the world. In this endeavor it was aided by the WARF research funds its own faculty helped to create, as well as by the increased federal funding for agricultural teaching and research that became available in the depression. Three of its four members at the start of our period were still active twenty years later, and its faculty roster—all but one tenured—had grown to ten, or two-and-a-half times the department's size in 1925. If one could designate two of its 1925 faculty—Steenbock and possibly Hart—as stars, to them could be added Elvehjem, Link, Johnson, and potentially Burris at the end of our period twenty years later. Without question the department weathered the storms of depression and war exceptionally well.

We should not overlook some other notable faculty appointments across the campus in these years. A number of these enabled the University to move into new fields of learning. Dean Sellery recruited Oskar F. Hagan from Germany in 1926 to begin building a program in the history of art. Hagen was not only a distinguished art historian but an eminent musicologist as well, a world authority on the music of George Frederick Handel. During the thirties Hagen gave both training and teaching appointments to a graduate student and later instructor in the art department, James S. Watrous, who among other projects painted the Paul Bunyan murals in the Memorial Union. Watrous eventually joined the art history department as an instructor in 1941, in a sense succeeding the German-born Wolfgang F.E.G. Stechow, who was appointed an assistant professor in 1936 and promoted to associate professor the following year but who left for a distinguished career at Oberlin College in 1940. Another new program began with Philo M. Buck's appointment in 1926 and his development of what became the first department of comparative literature in the country. The appointment of the Swiss-born linguist Alfred Senn as a full professor in the Department of German in 1932 launched a program in comparative philology, the forerunner of the present linguistics department.

Sometimes special funds made possible new ventures. In 1933, for example, the College of Agriculture used a five-year WARF grant to appoint Aldo Leopold, who had joined the campus-based U.S. Forest Products Laboratory staff as assistant director in 1924, to serve as the country's first professor of game management in the Department of Agricultural Economics. Thereafter until his tragic death in 1948 Leopold proceeded to develop a pioneering program in wildlife management that eventually grew into the present Department of Wildlife Ecology. In 1935, while the Democrats briefly controlled the Wisconsin Senate, a group of Polish legislators succeeded in earmarking an appropriation for the teaching of Polish at the University. Instruction began the following year with a visiting scholar from Poland, Professor Jerzy Kurylowicz of the University of Lvov, and led in time to the creation of the present Department of Slavic Languages in 1942.[43] Not to be outdone, an Irish bloc in the 1937 legislature added an appropriation for a chair in Gaelic and Irish studies, which was filled by a talented and courtly Irish linguist, Myles Dillon, the son of the famous Irish revolutionary, John Dillon. Dillon's broad knowledge of classical and modern languages strengthened Senn's developing program in linguistics.[44] Using primarily Brittingham gift funds, the University also

---

[43]1935 Senate Bill 534, *Legislative Journal Index;* Chapter 494, *Wisconsin Statutes,* 1935; *Daily Cardinal,* February 22, March 3, 1936. Kurylowicz taught only one semester before returning to Poland. He was succeeded by two other visiting Polish faculty members, Professors Witold Doroszewski (1936-37) and Jozef A. Birkenmajer (1937-39). Birkenmajer returned to his homeland to fight and later die in World War II. In 1939 the first American-born Pole, Edmund I. Zawacki (1939-78), took over Polish instruction as a lecturer in what was still a one-man department. Ironically, although leaders of the large Wisconsin Polish population had agitated for years for the inclusion of Polish in the University curriculum, there proved to be little student demand for it, even among students of Polish extraction, after it became available, a pattern that has continued to the present. A Polish department at the Milwaukee Extension Center was established in 1934.

[44]1937 Senate Bill 199, *Legislative Journal Index;* Chapter 296, *Wisconsin Statutes,* 1937; *Daily Cardinal,* September (registration issue) and September 29, 1937. Since there were even

pioneered with several distinguished artist-in-residence appointments during these years: the regional painter John Steuart Curry in the College of Agriculture (1936), the Danish pianist Gunnar Johansen (1939), and the Belgian Pro Arte String Quartet (1940) in the School of Music. The touring Pro Arte Quartet was performing in the new Memorial Union Theater on Sunday afternoon, May 10, 1940, the day the German army suddenly attacked and began overrunning its homeland. In sympathy for the plight of the stranded quartet in a world gone mad, President Dykstra arranged to give it first a temporary and then a permanent home in the UW School of Music, thereby making Wisconsin the first American university to sponsor a world-famous string quartet for teaching and concert purposes.[45]

By the start of our period investigators in several UW departments were studying cancerous tumors, including Director William D. Stovall of the State Laboratory of Hygiene, Joyce Riker in plant pathology, and Michael F. Guyer in zoology. During the 1930s cancer research moved forward rapidly as a consequence of two major infusions of private funding. The $420,000 Jennie Bowman bequest in 1934 enabled the Medical School to develop an increasingly strong program in cancer research, reflected initially in the appointments of Frederic E. Mohs and Harold P. Rusch to the first Bowman cancer research fellowships in 1935. Both men subsequently joined the UW faculty, with Mohs developing an innovative chemosurgery treatment for skin cancers. A second major bequest, from Michael McArdle in 1935, combined with a depression Public Works Administration grant, resulted in the construction of the McArdle Laboratory in 1940 to house the Medical School's cancer research programs under the overall direction of Harold Rusch. The appointment of biochemist Van R. Potter to the McArdle staff in 1940 brought additional strength to the oncology faculty through his investigations of complex enzyme systems and metabolism in tumor tissue. As early as 1936 Wisconsin had achieved enough stature in the field to host a major cancer research conference, which attracted more than five hundred participants from around the country and the world.[46]

---

fewer students interested in Gaelic than Polish, Dillon sometimes taught other languages in the Department of Classics. His versatility added considerably to the University's developing strength in linguistics.

[45]See Martha Blum, *The Pro Arte Quartet: Fifty Years* (Madison: University of Wisconsin-Madison School of Music, 1991), pp. 2-39.

[46]BOR Minutes, January 16, 1935; Charles R. Bardeen to Frank, February 14, 1935, Frank Presidential Papers, 4/13/1, box 160; *Daily Cardinal*, March 14, 1934, January 15,

On the whole, Dean Sellery of the College of Letters and Science preferred to have the benefit of a long probationary period before recommending L&S faculty members for tenure.[47] With its need for a sizable junior faculty to teach Freshman English, for the most part the Department of English could afford to pursue this grow-your-own-stars approach, sometimes keeping its own best graduates, but mostly recruiting from outside. Its significant assistant professor appointments in these years included Miles L. Hanley and Ricardo B. Quintana (1927), Harry Hayden Clark (1928), Mark Eccles (1934), Madeleine Doran (1940), and Frederic G. Cassidy (1942). Following several retirements and deaths of senior faculty members in the mid-thirties, Dean Sellery allowed the department to recruit two full professors, Merritt Y. Hughes (1936) and Henry A. Pochmann (1937). Sellery's willingness to allow English to recruit at the senior level very likely reflected his perception that the department had slipped in quality and needed stronger leadership at the top. Hughes took over the departmental chairmanship in his second year, 1937-38. This concern about quality was certainly shared by some of the better students and a sizable proportion of the English junior staff at this time, and came to a head in their public outcry over the department's decision in 1937 not to retain an instructor, William M. Card, a faculty union activist who had

---

1935, August 5, September 19, 1936, March 10, November 2, 1940; *Press Bulletin*, March 27, August 28, 1940; *WAM*, 38 (October 1936), 18.

[47]Sellery was certainly not averse to recruiting senior faculty members when an attractive opportunity arose or program needs called for more experienced staffing. Nor did he have a blanket policy against appointing UW graduates in order to avoid inbreeding, though L&S departments were much less inbred than those in the Colleges of Agriculture and Engineering. John R. Commons, who brought a number of his former students into the Department of Economics during his long tenure from 1904 to 1933, defended the practice in economic terms, reducing it to a behavioristic labor theory of value, which, he pointed out, benefitted the University in several ways. In spite of its comparatively small size and resource base, he noted, Wisconsin had long provided more funding for education than other states. Even so, the University, with a relatively low salary scale, could not hope to "pull teachers with established reputations away from other universities."

> Consequently we have to run our own seed-bed for future professors and take them when they are young. Curiously enough, our own product will often stay with us, notwithstanding offers of several thousand dollars more elsewhere. I figured this out and often illustrated it to my students according to the legal theory of the value of service....What is a professor "worth" to the university? He is worth as much as he can get elsewhere. How much does a professor donate to the university? He donates as much as the excess salary he could get elsewhere.

Commons, *Myself*, pp. 131-3.

criticized departmental policies and evidently had offended some of his senior colleagues. One of Card's supporters was Frederick Bracher, a Berkeley Ph.D. who resigned his Wisconsin instructorship after only a year, in protest, he told President Dykstra and the regents, "against the policies of a senior staff majority of little men and pedants, who fear and hate the genuinely distinguished minority among their colleagues, and who favor those younger men who flatter their vanity while ignoring their inadequacies."[48]   On the other hand, William Ellery Leonard, who had voted for Card's retention, denied that the case involved academic freedom or union hostility.[49]   No matter, the *Cardinal* saw it as further proof of the timidity and low standing of the department.[50]

The substantial enrollment in Freshman English allowed the English department the luxury of more visiting appointments than most departments. In 1937, for example, it hired Wallace E. Stegner as a temporary instructor, unwisely letting him go two years later to pursue his distinguished literary career first at Harvard and then Stanford. The department showed more interest in another visitor, the Nobel Laureate novelist Sinclair Lewis. Driving cross-country in the fall of 1940, Lewis paused while passing through Madison to look up an old acquaintance, the equally quixotic William Ellery Leonard. The next day Leonard hastily arranged a luncheon for the famous guest with some of his colleagues, dinner with President Dykstra, and a meeting and tour of the campus with some graduate students. Entranced, Lewis impulsively offered his services as an unsalaried "professorial lecturer in English," to be in residence for three or four months of the year. He wrote a friend enthusiastically of the general agreement "that it would be dandy to have Uncle Harry come to teach the boys and girls to be novelists." He reported his delight at what he found here:

---

[48]Frederick Bracher to Dykstra, June 26, 1937, BOR Papers, 1/1/3, box 50. See also Harold M. Groves, Walter R. Agard, and N.P. Feinsinger, University Teachers' Union Special Committee on the Investigation of the Case of William Card, "Communication to the Board of Regents," n.d., for Board of Regents meeting of May 5, 1937, BOR Papers, 1/1/3, box 50; *Daily Cardinal*, February 28, March 1 and 2, 1934, April 28, May 1, 4, 5, 6, 7, 8, 9, and 11, July 24, September 23, October 12 and 29, 1936; BOR Minutes, May 5, June 19, July 10, October 30, 1937.

[49]*Daily Cardinal*, May 8 and 18, 1937.

[50]"The English Department Is Not Above Criticism," editorial, ibid., May 5, 1937. See also a spirited response to the *Cardinal* attack by eleven English department junior staff members in ibid., May 7, 1937.

Madison a sweet town—60,000; big enough to buy records, small enough to make country quiet available within a mile; the dome of the State Capitol at one end of town and the University's towers at the other end, and all this on a green peninsula between two large blue, bluff-rimmed lakes, and nice keen youngsters, along with older shepherds, in the English Department. I was tempted. (And—later bulletin—I have since done fell, hurray!)[51]

Although Lewis subsequently considered the language of the Board of Regents' approval of his appointment—"with no pay, no tenure, and no official rank"—to be offensive and threatened to leave, he was eventually mollified after a long meeting with President Dykstra and several senior members of the English department. He promptly rented the largest house he could find, at 1712 Summit Avenue in University Heights.[52]

News of the Lewis appointment occasioned great excitement on campus and in the city, with some faculty members speculating apprehensively that the novelist might be using his stay to gather material for a satirical novel attacking academic life in general and their university in particular. Although Lewis decided to limit the enrollment in his writing seminar to fifteen, after holding interviews and reviewing the writing samples submitted by the applicants he agreed to take on twenty-two ecstatic creative writing students, with the proviso that reporters would be kept away and the students would not discuss the work of the class with the press. For the most part he declined social invitations and restricted his contacts to faculty members of a similar artistic bent—the regional painter John Steuart Curry, the prize-winning novelist in the French Department, Samuel Rogers, and the Danish pianist and artist-in-residence Gunnar Johansen, whom he persuaded to give him beginning lessons on a specially rented Steinway grand piano.

In mid-October Lewis' youthful actress protégé and mistress, Marcella Powers, arrived for a two-week visit. The novelist hastily persuaded the University Theater to recast its production of *Stage Door* to give his "niece" a part during its four-night run, October 23-26. Then, impulsively and without warning, at the fifth class meeting on November 6 Lewis announced he was leaving. He had, he explained to the bewildered students, taught them all he knew. The next day he was

---

[51]Lewis to Marcella Powers [late September, 1940], quoted in Mark Schorer, *Sinclair Lewis: An American Life* (New York: McGraw-Hill, 1961), pp. 665-6.

[52]BOR Minutes, September 28, 1940; *Daily Cardinal*, September 28 and 29, October 3, 1940; Schorer, *Sinclair Lewis*, p. 666.

gone, leaving his huge rented house to be occupied rent-free for the remainder of the year by a graduate student couple who had assisted him briefly, and obliging Merritt Hughes, the perplexed English chairman, to sort out the tangled schedules of twenty-two unhappy students. No one ever found out what prompted Lewis' sudden decision to abandon his class. Perhaps he had simply concluded that teaching was more demanding and less interesting than he expected; or maybe he found his departmental colleagues less stimulating and deferential than at first meeting; or possibly he sensed that Madisonians were not ready for the flaunting of a "niece" considerably less than half his age. For the University the whirlwind courtship and divorce with Sinclair Lewis remained a puzzling mystery, the stuff of campus legends.[53]

The English department was one of the few University units where women played increasingly prominent roles on and off campus in this period. Helen C. White (1919) and Ruth C. Wallerstein (1920) had joined the department as junior faculty members by the start of the inter-war period. They subsequently gained wide respect for their teaching, scholarship, and outside professional activities, as did Madeleine Doran subsequently. In 1956 White became the first woman to be elected as national president of the American Association of University Professors. During her long career at Wisconsin she received dozens of honorary degrees and other awards for her distinguished scholarship and professional leadership. English was the first UW department to begin the now common practice of changing its chairman every three years, for a time rotating the post regularly among White, Hughes, and Quintana.[54]

Other notable faculty additions to the College of Letters and Science throughout these years included Chester Lloyd Jones, a foreign trade expert who joined the commerce school as a professor in 1928 and became its director the following year; Einar J. Haugen, an up-and-coming assistant professor who succeeded the venerable Julius E. Olson in Scandinavian language and literature in 1931; Edwin E. Witte, the

---

[53]*Daily Cardinal*, October 5 and 10, November 7, 8, and 9, 1940; Schorer, *Sinclair Lewis*, pp. 667-70.

[54]White, who earned her Ph.D. at Wisconsin in 1924, was a feminist of sorts, but she had little patience with female colleagues who protested that they were held down in a male-dominated university. She believed her own experience refuted this. If women academics spent less time complaining and more time on scholarship, she argued, they would find they could command the respect of their male colleagues. Mark H. Ingraham, oral history interview.

director of the Wisconsin Legislative Reference Bureau, who was appointed a full professor in the economics department in 1933 as John R. Commons' hand-picked successor; Robert O. Roeseler, recruited from Ohio State as a professor of German in 1934 to bolster the department following the retirement of Max Griebsch and the imminent retirement of its long-time chairman, Alexander Hohlfeld; and Raymond Dvorak, appointed in 1934 to direct the University band following the untimely death of "Major" E.W. Morphy. Antonio G. Solalinde had already begun to build a strong program in Spanish literature by 1925, subsequently developing the world-famous Spanish Seminary within the Department of Spanish and Portuguese to study medieval Spanish texts. Solalinde recruited Eduardo Neale-Silva as an instructor in 1928 to provide the department with expertise in Latin American literature. Lloyd A. Kasten followed in 1929, and his medieval interests made him a natural to take over the direction eventually of both the seminary and the department from Solalinde.

Like biochemistry, the L&S chemistry department, for decades one of the University's strongest academic units, was confident of its ability to pick able young scholars and preferred a long apprenticeship. Consequently, the department mostly recruited its new faculty at the assistant professor level in these years: Villiers W. Meloche (1928), Norris F. Hall and C. Harvey Sorum (1929), M. Leslie Holt (1936), Joseph O. Hirschfelder and John E. Willard (1942). In mathematics distinguished recruitments brought Rudolph E. Langer (1927) and Cyrus C. MacDuffie (1935) as full professors and Stephen C. Kleene as a promising young instructor in 1935. Kleene became a world-renowned mathematical logician and later served five years as letters and science dean from 1969 to 1974. Major appointments in physics included John H. Van Vleck, recruited as a professor in 1928 and lost to Harvard in 1934, Gregory Breit, who joined the department as a full professor in 1934 and was elected to the National Academy of Sciences five years later, and Julian E. Mack (1929), Ragnar Rollefson (1936), and Raymond G. Herb (1937), all appointed initially as assistant professors. Other important L&S science appointments were John H. Stauffer in botany (1934) and Roland K. Meyer (1935) and Arthur D. Hasler (1936) in zoology. Besides President Dykstra who held a faculty appointment in political science, other notable additions to that department in these years included Assistant Professors Walter R. Sharp (1926), Grayson L. Kirk (1929), and Llewellyn Pfankuchen (1934), Associate Professor John T. Salter (1930), and Professor Harold W.

Stoke (1939). A frequent campus lecturer on world affairs, Kirk left Wisconsin in 1940 to be head of the political science department and later president of Columbia University; after serving briefly as acting dean of the Graduate School, Stoke departed in 1944 to be president of the University of New Hampshire. The philosophy department also provided seasoning for a couple of future college presidents, Frederick H. Burkhardt (1937) and Harold A. Taylor (1939), both appointed initially as instructors, but who left after World War II for other posts, Burkhardt to be president first of Bennington College and then of the American Council of Learned Societies and Taylor as president of Sarah Lawrence College. Other key social science appointments included the anthropologist Ralph Linton, recruited as a full professor in 1928 but lost to Columbia in 1937; the psychologist Harry F. Harlow, who made Wisconsin a leading center for primate research after his appointment as an assistant professor in 1930; and in sociology Kimball Young (1926), Samuel A. Stouffer (a talented social statistician who was appointed as an assistant professor in 1931, promoted to professor only three years later, and lost to Chicago in 1935), Howard Becker (1937), and Hans Gerth (1940).

By 1925 Dean Harry Russell had already established the College of Agriculture as very likely the best in the country. An unusual feature of the college was the fact that its applied production programs and extension activities were buttressed by strong basic science departments—agricultural chemistry (biochemistry), bacteriology, genetics, and plant pathology. The production departments often had a direct link to relevant basic science through joint faculty appointments or the research of their own staff members. Professors Laurence F. Graber of agronomy and Clinton J. Chapman of soils were known to Wisconsin farmers as "Mr. Alfalfa" and "Mr. Fertilizer," respectively, for their work in improving forage yields for the state's important dairy industry.[55] As we have seen in biochemistry, the College of Agriculture tended mostly to recruit its faculty at the junior level, often from its own best graduate students. Exceptions to this general policy were George S. Wehrwein (rural sociology, 1927), Gustav Bohstedt (animal husbandry, 1928); Benjamin M. Duggar (plant pathology and botany, 1929); Walter Wisnicky (veterinary science, 1938); Walter W. Wilcox (agricultural economics, 1944), all appointed initially as full professors. In addition, Asher Hobson (1931) and Olaf S. Aamodt (1934) were

---

[55]*Press Bulletin*, April 10, 1929, October 8, 1930.

recruited as full professors to chair the Departments of Agricultural Economics and Agronomy, respectively. Some of the more significant junior appointments in agricultural economics in these years included: Rudolph K. Froker (1930), Walter H. Ebling and Kenneth H. Parsons (1937), and Clifford M. Hardin (1942); in agricultural bacteriology Ira L. Baldwin (1926), Elizabeth Mccoy (1930), William B. Sarles (1932), and Perry W. Wilson (1933); in agricultural genetics Malcolm R. Irwin (1933) and Lester E. Casida (1934); in agronomy Norman P. Neal (1936), Hazel L. Shands (1937), and James H. Torrie (1941).

The Law School, especially under Dean Garrison's leadership after 1932, moved to a broader social science and activist approach to the study of the law in the inter-war years.[56] This was reflected in some of its appointments: Assistant Professors Alfred L. Gausewitz and Howard L. Hall (1929), Nathan P. Feinsinger and Richard V. Campbell (1930), Jacob H. Beuscher (1935), John C. Stedman (1936), and J. Willard Hurst (1937), and the prominent St. Paul attorney, Charles W. Bunn, recruited as a full professor in 1933.[57]

C. R. Bardeen

The Medical School developed rapidly after it introduced a full four-year curriculum in 1925.[58] Charles Bardeen, the first dean until his death in 1935, was the University's first professor of anatomy. Especially during the school's first two decades when it offered only a two-year scientific curriculum without clinical training, Dean Bardeen concentrated on building solid medical science rather than clinical

---

[56]See also pp. 733-9.

[57]It says something about contemporary attitudes that Dean Garrison, the great-grandson of the prominent abolitionist editor William Lloyd Garrison, felt it worth pointing out to President Dykstra and Acting President Sellery that Hurst was not only the most promising candidate but was not Jewish—"not that it makes any difference." Garrison to Dykstra, June 30, 1937, Sellery Presidential Papers, 4/14/1, box 8, UA.

[58]See also pp. 717-23.

departments. Bardeen's successor, William S. Middleton, was a clinician who had been recruited in 1912 to help staff the new Student Health Service. He believed the chief mission of the Medical School should be to train doctors and other health professionals, and less so to conduct basic scientific research. During Middleton's deanship the needs of the clinical departments took precedence over basic science, with the major exception of the growing program in cancer research. This difference in emphasis was reflected in Medical School appointments in these years. Some of the more significant faculty recruits included German-born Ernst A. Pohle as professor of radiology in 1928 to develop this important clinical and research field, Edgar J. Witzemann (1927) and Philip P. Cohen (1941) in physiological chemistry, Arthur L. Tatum (1928) and Maurice H. Seevers (1929) in pharmacology and toxicology, Ralph M. Waters (1927) in surgical anesthesia, Harland W. Mossman (1927) and Otto A. Mortensen (1930) in anatomy, Joseph W. Gale (1927) in thoracic surgery, Theodore C. Erickson (1941) in neurosurgery, Herman W. Wirka (1935) in orthopedic surgery, John W. Harris (1928) and Madeline J. Thornton (1934) in obstetrics and gynecology, Mabel G. Masten (1930) and Annette C. Washburne (1935) in neuropsychiatry, and Ovid O. Meyer (1932), Reuben H. Stiehm (1933), Marie L. Carns (1934), Helen A. Dickie (1941), all in general medicine.

From its inception the College of Engineering had considered its primary mission to be the training of engineers and to a lesser extent the provision of consulting and testing services for the state.[59] The applied research undertaken by the college faculty in these years mostly dealt with practical problems of concern to Wisconsin industries and communities. Unlike Deans Russell and Bardeen, who believed in the importance of basic science disciplines underpinning their applied agricultural and medical programs, Dean Turneaure saw no such need in Engineering during his long administration of the college from 1903 to 1937. Like most of the engineering educators and professionals of his day he thought practical experience was more important than advanced study. He was accordingly parsimonious in handing out the college's limited research funds, especially for projects without an immediate practical application, and he discouraged Ph.D. training. While typical of engineering educators of the period, this limited view of the college's mission influenced Dean Turneaure's decisions about

---

[59]Ibid., pp. 723-32.

staffing needs. During his long administration of the College of Engineering he recruited few faculty members with Ph.D. degrees. When he retired only seven of the seventy-eight full-time members of the engineering faculty possessed a Ph.D. degree, four of them in chemical engineering, the most scholarly of the college's academic departments. The College of Engineering was also heavily inbred. Nearly half of the sixty-seven college graduates on the faculty (some faculty members did not have even a baccalaureate degree) were UW products, most of whom had been hired immediately or within two years of their graduation.[60]

An example of Turneaure's lack of imagination was his view of chemical engineering, which in the years after the Second World War became the college's most distinguished department. The dean was skeptical that chemical engineering was an important engineering field and limited it to a single full professor, Otto Kowalke, who as the long-time chairman of the department shared Turneaure's view of the importance of practical experience and applied work. O.P. Watts retired in 1937 still an associate professor. Olaf A. Hougen, who joined the chemical engineering faculty as an assistant professor in 1920, persisted in completing a Ph.D. degree in 1925, the department's first since 1912. He eventually persuaded Kowalke of the value of research and graduate training. Despairing of ever reaching a full professorship under Turneaure and Kowalke, however, Hougen resigned in 1936 to take a position at the Armour Institute of Technology in Chicago. Chemists across the campus viewed his departure with dismay, so much so that the chemistry department, Graduate Dean Fred, and L&S Dean and Acting President Sellery undertook a campaign to persuade Kowalke and Turneaure that chemical engineering could justify more than one full professor. Hougen was thereupon brought back at that rank in 1937 to resume his increasingly successful efforts to build the department to the national distinction it achieved by mid-century.[61]

---

[60]F. Ellis Johnson, "Report on the Administration of College of Engineering, 1938-1944" [ca. January 13, 1945], Fred Presidential Papers, 4/16/1, box 32, UA; *General Announcement of Courses, 1938-1939 (Catalog 1937-1938)*, Bulletin of the University of Wisconsin, Serial No. 2347, General Series No. 2131, August, 1938, pp. 276-300.

[61]See [E.B. Fred?] unsigned memo, June 22, 1936; F.E. Turneaure to Sellery, January 13, 1937, Sellery to Tuneaure, March 31, 1937; Turneaure to Hougen, March 29, 1937; O.L. Kowalke to Hougen, March 27, 1937, all in Sellery Presidential Papers, 4/14/1, box 17; Hougen, "The Situation in Chemical Engineering Relative to My Return," memorandum of conference with Sellery and Fred; Hougen to Kowalke, April 20, 1937; Hougen to Dykstra, May 26, 1937; Dykstra to Hougen, May 27, 1937, all in ibid., box 11; Ihde, *Chemistry as*

Turneaure's successor as dean, F. Ellis Johnson, was a Wisconsin alumnus, most recently the dean of engineering at the University of Missouri. Johnson had a considerably broader view than Turneaure of the needs of engineering education. He quickly decided to push the faculty into more basic and significant research and to reorganize and consolidate the departments of the college. Though it made an enemy of his old classmate, Kowalke, Dean Johnson pressed him to give up the departmental chairmanship after twenty-four years in favor of Hougen. Johnson then persuaded the WARF trustees to make a special ten-year grant to the department of $10,000 a year for flexible support of research. This enabled Hougen to go on a half-time research appointment beginning in 1941 and hand over the chairmanship responsibilities to Roland A. Ragatz, a promising younger colleague whom Hougen had encouraged to complete a Ph.D. while serving as an assistant professor in the late 1920s. In 1942 Johnson and Hougen recruited Kenneth M. Watson, a former UW faculty member and Hougen Ph.D. currently working for the Gulf Oil Company, as a teammate for Hougen on a similar half-time research appointment.[62]

This is not to suggest that under Turneaure's leadership the College of Engineering made few significant faculty appointments, only that he viewed the college's mission as primarily one of instruction and service and shaped it accordingly. Several notable engineering faculty appointments by Turneaure included Harold F. Janda, a UW graduate brought back as a full professor to head the program in highway engineering and city planning in 1928, James G. Woodburn, appointed as a professor of hydraulic engineering in 1937, and Kurt F. Wendt, kept on as an instructor in engineering mechanics after his graduation in 1927. Promoted slowly through the faculty ranks as his work on materials testing gained recognition, Wendt eventually became associate director of the Engineering Experiment Station in 1948 and engineering dean in 1953. It was under Dean Wendt's leadership that the College of Engineering, like its counterparts elsewhere in the country, began to move from the traditional emphasis on practical training to an engineering technology

Viewed from Bascom's Hill, pp. 554-6. With Hougen came four of his Armour students, one of whom, W. Robert Marshall, subsequently joined the Wisconsin faculty and eventually became director of the Engineering Experiment Station in 1946 and dean of the college in 1971.

[62]Johnson, "Biennial Report of the College of Engineering, 1940-42" [ca. December 3, 1942], General Presidential Papers, 4/0/2, box 11; Johnson, "Report on the Administration of College of Engineering, 1938-1944."

and science-based curriculum. Dean Johnson had shared this vision but unfortunately moved too aggressively to accomplish it after his appointment in 1938. Suspicious of his motives and resentful of his perceived autocratic style, the engineering faculty rejected his several suggestions for curricular reform. At least two of the longstanding departmental chairmen he replaced—Otto Kowalke of chemical engineering and Edward Bennett of electrical engineering—led a campaign against Johnson's efforts to reorganize and redirect the college. Their criticism culminated in a decision by President E.B. Fred and the Board of Regents to ask for Dean Johnson's resignation in 1945-46.[63]

If old timers on campus and in Madison believed the University's golden age ended with the death of President Van Hise in 1918,[64] there is in fact little evidence that the overall quality of the faculty declined in the inter-war period and much to suggest that the institution was strengthened in a number of areas. In 1940 the general faculty, acting on a suggestion by the University Committee, directed that a special committee be appointed to study the effect of the depression

---

[63]Johnson, "Report on the Administration of College of Engineering, 1938-1944"; Johnson to Dykstra, January 13, 1945; Edward Bennett to James W. Watson, October 8, 1943; Johnson to Fred, May 21, 1945; "Memorandum of Conferences with Dean Johnson Concerning the Deanship of the College of Engineering," June 5 and 9, 1945; Johnson to Fred and the Board of Regents, July 21, 1945; "Memorandum of Conference with Dean Johnson," November 27, 1945; Johnson to Fred and the Board of Regents, November 26, 1945; Johnson to Fred, December 17, 1945; "Memorandum of Conference with Professor M.O. Withey Concerning the Future of the Engineering College," December 27, 1945; "Memorandum of Conference with Departmental Chairmen on Deanship of College of Engineering," January 2, 1946; "Memorandum of Conference with Dean Johnson," January 8, 1946, Fred Presidential Papers, 4/16/1, box 32. Johnson retained the nominal title of dean on paid leave during the second semester of 1945-46 while he sought another position, and Withey took over the college administrative responsibilities until the regents formally confirmed his appointment as dean later in the year. See also pp. 728-32.

[64]See, for example, Gertrude Wilson, oral history interview, 1990, UA. In 1944 former Milwaukee Socialist Mayor and UW alumnus Daniel W. Hoan asserted that the University had declined to the point where it was only "a third rate college." He blamed the deterioration on Governor Heil's industrialist-dominated Board of Regents, leading the surprised and pained *Wisconsin Alumnus* magazine to protest that Hoan had his facts wrong both about the composition of the regents and the quality of the institution. John Berge, "'Third Rate College'...Dan Hoan, '05," *WAM*, 46 (November 15, 1944), 10. For another response to Hoan, see Walter J. Hodgkins, "Is Our University Slipping?" ibid. (March 15, 1945), 3-6. An assessment of the nation's top colleges and universities in 1957 by Chesly Manly, a *Chicago Tribune* reporter, also concluded that the University had "declined from its golden age in the first part of this century," which Manly attributed to a UW commitment to democracy and its consequent lack of a selective admission policy. The *Tribune* nevertheless ranked Wisconsin as ninth best among American universities. *Chicago Tribune*, April 21 and May 19, 1957.

retrenchment on the quality of the University.[65] This broadly-based blue ribbon Committee on the Quality of Instruction and Scholarship consisted of a number of prominent faculty leaders under the leadership of mathematics Professor Mark H. Ingraham, who would shortly be named dean of the College of Letters and Science upon veteran Dean George Sellery's retirement in 1942. The first part of the committee's report, issued in April of 1941, made a careful study of University funding during the past decade as related to instructional staffing, salaries, and quality. While faculty numbers had fluctuated down and then up with enrollment changes, the proportions among the various faculty ranks had remained relatively stable, with graduate assistants showing the greatest decline. Especially at the lower faculty ranks it was clear the depression had enabled the University to recruit a more experienced teaching staff. Whereas in 1931 only 15 percent of UW instructors possessed a Ph.D. degree, ten years later the figure was 39 percent. In Letters and Science, which taught the bulk of the undergraduates, 69 percent of the instructors had a Ph.D. degree in 1940. While the Ingraham committee chose not *"to appraise the nicety of adjustment secured by the University"* in meeting the depression budget cuts, its report made clear that in terms of faculty quality the institution had weathered the crisis rather better than one might have expected:

> The proportional increase of instructors having the doctor's degree, the slow rate of promotion during the last ten years, and the "buyer's market" for academic services have combined to give the University a more mature and, in the lower ranks, a more highly trained staff than it had ten years ago.[66]

The committee stressed, however, that the University had lost ground in salary competitiveness during the decade, which it warned might erode the institution's ability over time to attract and retain top quality faculty members. Although the University began to restore the old faculty salary scale in 1937, the task was complicated by the extremely tight state funding and the renewed budget cuts during the Heil administration. Much of the effort was consequently based on holding the growth of the instructional staff below the increase in student enrollment in order to free more funds for higher salaries. The

[65]UW Faculty Document 583; UW Faculty Minutes, December 4, 1939, January 8, 1940.
[66]UW Faculty Document 615, "Committee on the Quality of Instruction and Scholarship, General Report, Part I," April, 1941; *Daily Cardinal*, July 1, 1941.

increased tuition revenue from growing enrollment was thus used only in part for additional instructional staffing but also gradually to restore faculty salaries. Across the University, student credits had increased by 24 percent during the decade while the teaching staff declined by 4 percent; in Letters and Science the increase in credits was 29 percent compared to a decline of 15 percent in instructional personnel over the decade. The inevitable result was heavier teaching loads and larger class sizes. Even so, the committee reported that as of the spring of 1941 the University had not yet been able to restore the old salaries completely: "There are still about 150 members of the Faculty whose salaries now are not as high as they were in 1930, and in the case of about fifty of these the amount of reduction is over $500 per annum."[67] It would in fact be more than a decade from the imposition of waivers in 1933 until the pre-waiver salaries were fully restored across the University. In the meantime, of course, some faculty members had moved beyond their 1932 salary level through promotions or other advancement and new appointees had been hired at salaries generally lower than the pre-depression scale.[68]

Much of the credit for getting through the depression without a serious erosion of faculty quality or morale must go to the faculty itself for devising and accepting a graduated system of salary reductions that honored tenure and appointment contracts. The salary waivers achieved substantial savings—about 60 percent of the total reduction of the University budget in the depression years. This determination to share the pain of the depression cuts as fairly and humanely as possible and without the trauma of layoffs surely helped to mitigate more damaging

---

[67]UW Faculty Document 615.

[68]In 1944 the University Committee applauded the Board of Regents for accepting President Dykstra's recommendation to restore all salary waivers, but pointed out that the University was nevertheless at "a substantial salary disadvantage" compared with other leading state universities, a problem exacerbated by the significant increase in the cost of living during the past five years. The committee's report to the faculty noted:

> Only among instructors has the average salary regained and risen above the 1929-32 average. The average salary for instructors for 1944-45 is about $200 higher than the 1929-32 figure. For assistant professors the average salary this year is about $70 below the 1929-32 level, and that for associate professors is about $200 below. Full professors salaries for 1944-45 are about $300 below the pre-waiver figure.

UW Faculty Document 714, University Committee, "Report on Faculty Salaries at the University of Wisconsin," November 6, 1944; UW Faculty Document 761, University Committee, "Report on Faculty Salaries," April 1, 1946; "Faculty Salaries Too Low," *WAM*, 46 (December 15, 1944), 5.

consequences of the crisis. Equally important was the willingness of the regents to forego a hiring freeze and instead allow the president and the academic deans to pursue a flexible staffing policy that permitted some promotions and selective senior appointments where necessary to maintain faculty quality, program depth, and morale. It would be wise to recall this lesson when the University and the state confront future budget crises.

The determination to recruit and retain a strong faculty even in adversity was only one indicator of the quality of the University in the inter-war years. Another was the distinction of the faculty as viewed by the wider academic world outside of Wisconsin. Although reputational surveys are suspect, here the judgment was generally positive. Twice during the period—in 1925 and again in 1941—the University hosted meetings of the prestigious National Academy of Sciences. In 1925 five UW scientists served as local hosts by virtue of having achieved the signal honor of election to the country's most distinguished scientific body: botanist C.E. Allen, plant pathologist L.R. Jones, physicist C.E. Mendenhall, astronomer Joel Stebbins, and mathematician E.B. Van Vleck. By the time of the 1941 meeting four other UW members had been added to the academy: botanist and plant pathologist B.M. Duggar, bacteriologist E.B. Fred, physicist Gregory Breit, and geologist C.K. Leith. In its number of academicians the University ranked ninth in the country and first in the Big Ten at this time. At the 1941 gathering, moreover, nearly a third of the sixty-seven scientific papers were given by UW scientists, including an explanation by physicist Raymond G. Herb, a future academy member, of the University's new four-and-a-half million volt accelerator or atom smasher which he had recently designed and built.[69] Another quality indicator was the stature of the University's graduate programs, which regularly placed the University among the top ten American universities in national rankings throughout this period.[70]

---

[69]*Press Bulletin*, November 4 and 18, 1925, September 24, October 8 and 10, 1941; *Capital Times*, November 9, 10, and 11, 1925, October 14 and 15, 1941; *Daily Cardinal*, November 7, 10, 11, and 12, 1925, September 24, October 7, 10, 14, and 16, 1941.

[70]While one should not make too much of reputational surveys, see Raymond M. Hughes, "A Study of the Graduate Schools of America," Association of American Colleges *Bulletin*, 11 (May, 1925), 237-45 and accompanying data; American Council on Education, *Report of the Committee on Graduate Education* (Washington: 1934); "Report of the Committee on Graduate Instruction," *Educational Record*, 15 (April, 1934), 192-234. It is difficult to compare these two surveys, both directed by Hughes, since they sought to measure different things and used somewhat different methodologies. The 1925 survey ranked the quality of graduate programs

Although an incomplete sampling will have to suffice, in addition to the increasing number of Wisconsin scientists elected to the national academy in these years, other faculty members received scholarly awards and professional honors that recognized their stature and brought credit to their institution. Two UW historians won Pulitzer prizes for their distinguished scholarship: Frederic Paxson in 1925 for his *History of the American Frontier* and Merle Curti in 1944 for his path-breaking *The Growth of American Thought.* In 1933 the Pulitzer selection committee also awarded a special posthumous prize to former UW historian Frederick Jackson Turner, an alumnus who did his major scholarly work as a Wisconsin faculty member.[71] Geologist Charles K. Leith, a frequent participant in international scholarly conferences, received a number of honors in company with his election to the National Academy of Sciences: the Penrose medal of the Society of Economic Geologists in 1935 and of the Geological Society of America in 1942, as well as the presidencies of the former society in 1925 and the latter in 1933, and election as a fellow of the American Academy of Arts and Sciences. Astronomer Joel Stebbins similarly garnered a

---

in twenty different disciplines, omitting fields in agriculture and engineering. The broader 1934 survey, which included agriculture and engineering for a total of thirty-five disciplines, listed the programs in each field that ranked as "distinguished" without differentiating among them. Wisconsin could claim that its university ranked seventh in the nation in the rankings of the 1925 survey, whereas it ranked second only behind the University of California in the number of its "distinguished" programs (seventeen) in 1934. Although this was mixing quality and quantity considerations with questionable comparative validity, both surveys clearly indicated the University's high stature among major American graduate institutions. The most significant change in UW rankings in the two surveys involved the history department, which ranked sixth in 1925 and was not listed among the distinguished programs in 1934, no doubt reflecting the loss of its two senior Americanists, Paxson and Fish, in 1932. The department would regain its distinguished ranking in the next ACE survey in 1966. See also Walter C. Eells, "American Graduate Schools," *School and Society,* 39 (June 2, 1934), 708-12; Edwin R. Embree, "In Order of Their Eminence—An Appraisal of American Universities," *Atlantic Monthly,* 155 (June, 1935), 652-64; *Chicago Tribune,* April 21, May 19, 1957. President Frank understandably liked to cite the 1925 and 1934 surveys as proving how much the University had improved under his leadership, an assumption hard to demonstrate from the data and which his regent critics were quick to challenge at the time of his dismissal. See Clough Gates, *Certain Claims of President Frank Concerning the Progress of the University of Wisconsin under His Leadership* (pamphlet, January 6-7, 1937), pp. 21-31, Biographical Files, UA.

[71] *Press Bulletin,* May 6, 1925; *Capital Times,* May 5, 1933; *Daily Cardinal,* May 3, 1944. Interestingly, both Paxson and Curti were tied to Turner. Paxson's award was for his work extending Turner's study of the American frontier. Curti was Turner's last doctoral student at Harvard and would shortly be elevated to the Frederick Jackson Turner professorship, one of the University's first named chairs, in 1947.

number of honors, including the Bruce gold medal, for his discoveries.[72] King Victor Emmanuel III of Italy decorated classicist Grant M. Showerman in 1928 for his studies on ancient Rome; in 1932 the German Academy in Munich honored historian Chester V. Easum for his biography of Carl Schurz; the German government similarly honored art historian Oscar Hagen in 1935 for his work on G.F. Handel's opera scores; and King Haakon VII of Norway knighted Professor Julius Olson and otherwise honored him for his leadership in Scandinavian studies.[73] Throughout the period UW faculty members regularly won research fellowships from such competitive national sources as the Guggenheim Foundation, the Social Science Research Council, and the Huntington Library.

Engineering Professor Daniel W. Mead received many honors for his pioneering contributions to hydraulic and sanitary engineering: among them, in 1928 President Coolidge appointed Mead to the Colorado River Board to advise on the feasibility of the Boulder Canyon dam project, and the American Society of Civil Engineers awarded him its Norman medal in 1936 for his distinguished leadership and contributions to the field.[74] Biochemist Conrad A. Elvehjem was recognized increasingly for his pioneering work on the vitamin B complex, receiving among other awards the $1,000 Mead Johnson prize from the American Institute of Nutrition in 1939 and the prestigious Willard Gibbs medal from the American Chemical Society in 1942.[75] Several faculty members, among them Professors Samuel G.A. Rogers of the French department and Helen White and Wallace E. Stegner of the English department, gained recognition for their creative writing. Rogers' novel *Dusk at the Grove* won the $10,000 Atlantic prize in 1934, an astronomical sum at the time, and Stegner's novelette *Remembering Laughter* won the $2,500 Little Brown prize in 1938.[76]

[72]*Capital Times*, December 30, 1932, February 14, 1941; *Daily Cardinal*, February 17, 1935. See also Sylvia W. McGrath, *Charles Kenneth Leith: Scientific Adviser* (Madison: University of Wisconsin Press, 1971); Richard J. Lund, *Memorial to Charles Kenneth Leith, 1875-1956* (New York: Geological Society of America, 1957); S.W. Bailey, ed., *The History of Geology and Geophysics at the University of Wisconsin-Madison, 1848-1980* (Madison: Department of Geology and Geophysics, 1981), p. 74.

[73]*Capital Times*, November 16, 1925, December 22, 1928, January 23, 1929, April 15 and 16, 1932; *Daily Cardinal*, November 17, 1925, April 16, 1932, September 28, 1932, November 17, 1932, March 27, 1935.

[74]*Daily Cardinal*, November 20, 1935, January 21, 1937, April 14, 1942.

[75]Ibid., March 17, 1939, February 27, 1943.

[76]Ibid., May 8, 1934, November 22, 1935, June 30, 1938. Professor White regarded her

The Belgrade Academy of Sciences elected historian Alexander A. Vasiliev to membership in 1934 for his distinguished scholarship on the Byzantine empire; the same year the British Royal Historical Society named his colleague Paul A. Knaplund as a fellow for his work on nineteenth century British politics; art historian Oskar Hagen received similar European recognition as an honorary fellow of the University of Göttingen and election to the British Royal Society of Arts in 1937.[77]

UW faculty members played an active part in national scholarly associations throughout the period. For example, Mark Ingraham was named associate secretary of the American Mathematical Society in 1927 and secretary of its board of trustees in 1937, a fellow of the American Association for the Advancement of Science and a member of its council 1929-37, and president of the American Association of University Professors in 1938-39.[78] Political scientist Frederic A. Ogg played a leadership role in the American Council of Learned Societies and the Council on Foreign Relations, served as managing editor of the *American Political Science Review* throughout most of the period, and was elected president of the American Political Science Association in 1941. His UW colleagues President Clarence A. Dykstra and John M. Gaus served terms as APSA president in 1938 and 1945 respectively.[79] Medical School Professor and Assistant Dean Walter J. Meek was elected president of the American Physiology Society in 1929; bacteriologist Ira L. Baldwin became secretary-treasurer of the Society of American Bacteriologists in 1935 and president in 1938; mechanical engineer Morton O. Withey was elected president of the American Society of Engineering Education in 1943; French Professor Casimir D.

---

creative writing as only a sideline, which she and her departmental colleagues considered no substitute for genuine scholarship. This attitude may help to explain why the English department made no effort to keep Stegner, who taught at Wisconsin as a young instructor for only two years before moving on to develop his literary career at Harvard and Stanford, a career of such distinction that Wisconsin tried to make amends a half century later by awarding him an honorary degree. For Stegner's semi-autobiographical account of his Wisconsin years, see his novel *Crossing to Safety* (New York: Random House, 1987). Rogers continued to intersperse fiction with his scholarly writing. One of his later novels was set at a poorly disguised midwestern university with a big red Science Hall, on the third floor of which the villain, a medical student, practiced necrophilia with the cadavers in the anatomy lab. See Rogers, *Don't Look Behind You* (New York: Harper, 1944).

[77]*Daily Cardinal*, April 29, May 29, 1934; *Press Bulletin*, March 17, 1937.

[78]*Press Bulletin*, January 11, 1928; *Daily Cardinal*, February 24, 1938.

[79]*Press Bulletin*, February 15, 1928, February 2, 1938; *Daily Cardinal*, January 8, 1941, February 20, 1945.

Zdanowicz headed the National Federation of Modern Language Teachers in 1931 and American Association of the Teachers of French in 1939.[80]

In short, there is ample evidence of the professional esteem accorded Wisconsin faculty members throughout the academic world both in America and abroad during the inter-war period. UW faculty members took leadership roles in the professional organizations of their various disciplines or earned research support and scholarly recognition at the national level, thereby gaining widespread respect for their institution. While the reputation of individual departments may have risen or fallen somewhat as a consequence of personnel changes over the period, collectively the image of the University remained strong, with many members of its faculty recognized as among the intellectual leaders of the country. Meanwhile, the growing WARF endowment was positioning the campus to remain a major research center in the post-war era.

[80]*Press Bulletin*, April 9, 1930; *Daily Cardinal*, January 9, 1935, October 6, 1938, January 13, 1944, September 26, 1945. For other indications of UW faculty prominence in general, see individual entries in *Who's Who in America*.

9.

A Community of Scholars

One of the most striking features of the University of Wisconsin in the inter-war years is the degree to which the faculty functioned as a genuine and close-knit *community* of scholars. We have already seen how this sense of community manifested itself through a maturing faculty governance structure at the college and campus levels. But the formal organization of the UW academic community was only one part of the community's many dimensions. There were numerous informal opportunities for faculty discourse and socialization on and off campus that shaped decisions and developed consensus within the formal University governance structure.

It must be remembered that at this time the academic departments of the University were at once small enough to allow frequent personal contact while large enough to provide for some diversity of personalities, expertise, and viewpoints important for a stimulating and productive intellectual interchange. The Departments of Agricultural Chemistry (later Biochemistry) and Bacteriology were ranked among the country's top biological science programs during the 1930s, yet throughout that decade neither department had more than seven tenured faculty members at any time. Turnover was negligible, moreover, with only one member—a bacteriologist—leaving UW employment. The pattern was similar in other College of Agriculture units. Agricultural economics had a maximum of thirteen tenured faculty during the decade; genetics, four; and plant pathology, eight. Even in the College of Letters and Science, where the heavier student enrollment necessitated a somewhat larger faculty, departments were small compared to the post-World War II period. In no year did botany have more than seven tenured faculty; chemistry, twelve; English, twelve; history, nine; physics, five;

and sociology and anthropology, ten. The College of Engineering operated on an even smaller scale. Chemical engineering made do with only three tenured faculty; electrical engineering, six; mining and metallurgy, three; and steam and gas engineering, five. In such an intimate environment it was easy for faculty members to talk knowledgeably and share ideas with their immediate colleagues about their professional work and interests.

Of course, as departments expanded in size they could and did add specialists in new areas of their disciplines. The growing complexity and compartmentalization of knowledge also made it more difficult for scholars in one field to keep abreast of developments in another. This led to a number of efforts to share findings and insights more generally and in the process to nurture the concept of an integrated scholarly community. In the Medical School, for example, the anatomy department ran a journal club in which faculty members and invited graduate students took turns reporting on major articles in assigned scientific periodicals. The physics department of the College of Letters and Science had a weekly colloquium for the same purpose. Many of the science departments developed variants of these models.

Scholars from different departments also met to share knowledge. An organization of faculty and graduate students called Gamma Alpha drew its members from physics, botany, agricultural chemistry, bacteriology, plant pathology, soils, and electrical engineering. Meetings were usually held at a host department which organized the program to cover the research under way there. Typical introductory remarks included a review of the "state of the art" for the discipline under discussion. Another illustration of this sharing of research findings was the plant science conference organized by Professor James Johnson, a senior member of the horticulture department, in 1936 for the benefit of botanists and agriculturalists from several departments. In addition to discussing the latest research developments the group also lobbied for new greenhouse facilities for their common use. The journal clubs, colloquia, and campus conferences served not only to share knowledge but to help faculty members in different departments get to know one another and make use of each other's expertise. This organized interchange was more characteristic of faculty in the natural sciences than in the social sciences and humanities, where scholars typically tended to conduct their research individually rather than in groups or teams.[1]

---

[1]On the anatomy department see Harland Mossman, oral history interview, 1983, UA. On

The tradition of cross-departmental collaboration was deeply ingrained at Wisconsin, where joint faculty appointments were common and the walls between departments and schools and colleges were low and porous. Ira Baldwin recalled his surprise on visiting Cornell University in the 1930s in order to consult with two fellow bacteriologists who held appointments in separate units of the university, one in agriculture and the other in veterinary medicine. Much to Baldwin's astonishment, he found that although the two men were friends they did not know where each other's offices were and never saw one another on campus. Rather, they worked exclusively in their own departments, around which "fences" had developed, neither collaborating nor discussing their work although they had similar interests. Baldwin and others have made the point that at Wisconsin it would be quite unlikely for two faculty members in the same general field, whether or not personal friends, to be unaware of the other's work if not actually involved in it in some way. Collaboration at Wisconsin was common and frequently involved researchers from different yet related fields of study. Professor Gustav Bohstedt emphasized in his memoirs how he and his colleagues in animal husbandry worked with researchers throughout the College of Agriculture, an experience and attitude echoed by botanist John Stauffer and others.[2]

This pattern of a loose administrative structure, open relationships, easy joint appointments, and mutually beneficial interdepartmental and interdisciplinary collaboration, while perhaps not unique to Wisconsin, was probably more highly developed here than at any other major American research university. It is impossible to determine precisely when this Wisconsin characteristic of close interaction across disciplinary lines began to develop, but it is clearly deep-rooted. Edward A. Birge, whose active UW career spanned an even half-century following his appointment to the faculty in 1875, recalled that soon after his arrival in Madison he and several more senior colleagues in various

the physics department and Gamma Alpha, see Ragnar Rollefson, oral history interviews, 1983 and 1984, UHP. On the plant science conference see Glenn Pound, oral history interview, 1982, UHP. A notable exception in the social sciences was the "Friday Nights" hosted by economist John R. Commons for colleagues and students. Jean S. Davis to John W. Jenkins, March 21, 1984; Charles A. Pearce to John W. Jenkins [May, 1984]; Joseph E. Shafer to John W. Jenkins, March 20, 1984, UHP.

[2]Ira L. Baldwin, oral history interview, 1982, UHP; Gustav Bohstedt, *Early History of Animal Husbandry and Related Departments of the University of Wisconsin-Madison* (Madison: Gustav Bohstedt, with assistance from the UW Saddle and Sirloin Club, 1973); John R. Stauffer, oral history interview, 1983, UHP.

departments dedicated themselves, as Birge described it, "to promoting the University as a whole, even if it meant sacrificing our own departments." This involved putting the common good ahead of individual or departmental interests and sharing not only scarce laboratory equipment but ideas and expertise as well. William O. Hotchkiss, a UW graduate and the state geologist from 1909 to 1925 while on the University faculty, remembered his surprise when he mentioned his research plans to friends at a geological society meeting, only to be warned that someone might steal his ideas. "That was my first intimation," he noted in dismay, "that the scientific atmosphere I was brought up in was not universal."[3] As befitted an increasingly faculty-centered institution, by the early twentieth century the UW management philosophy was to adjust the administrative structure to meet the teaching and research needs of the faculty, not the other way around.[4]

The University's pioneering commitment to extension education also promoted collaborative research. Extension service was most highly developed in the College of Agriculture, which had the financial resources and contacts within the agricultural community to identify and solve many important applied research problems through its Agricultural Experiment Station and Cooperative Extension Service. Budgeted as an integral part of agriculture faculty members' workloads, Extension and Experiment Station responsibilities drew research and applied agriculture faculty together to work on common problems. Dean Harry Russell's insistence on including an appropriate array of basic science units as well as the usual applied and production departments in his college also helped to assure fruitful collaboration on solving the problems confronting Wisconsin farmers.[5]

[3]George C. Sellery, *E.A. Birge: A Memoir* (Madison: University of Wisconsin Press, 1956), p. 19; Mark H. Ingraham, oral history interview, 1972, UA.

[4]An example was the ambitious Cret-Laird-Peabody campus plan of 1908, which reflected President Van Hise's determination to nurture collegial relations across school/college/department lines through carefully planned campus expansion and development. Although University of Pennsylvania architect Warren P. Laird, the chairman of the three-member regents Architectural Commission, had presented the report as merely a "preliminary draft" without formal board action on its recommendations, the regents and University administration nevertheless used it as an authoritative guide for many years thereafter. "Preliminary Draft of the Report of the Architectural Commission on the General Design of the University of Wisconsin for Examination by the Members of the Board of Regents," December 16, 1908, BOR Papers, 1/1/3, box 22, UA.

[5]Edward H. Beardsley, *Harry L. Russell and Agricultural Science in Wisconsin* (Madison: University of Wisconsin Press, 1969), pp. 64-82; John W. Jenkins, *A Centennial History: A*

This structural support for collaboration was less developed or absent in other parts of the University. While the College of Engineering maintained a similar extension and experiment station organization, it lacked the federal and state funding required to operate on anything like the scale of the College of Agriculture. In the College of Letters and Science, home of the social scientists who played a key role in formulating some of the major economic and political reforms of the progressive era, little structural or financial aid existed to support collaborative research projects. The letters and science and engineering teaching loads were heavier than in the College of Agriculture, where faculty members had more time for research, better support, and their responsibilities directed them to applied problems requiring collaborative efforts. Still, the commitment to faculty cooperation was strong across the entire University and helped to build and maintain the sense of a close-knit academic community.[6]

A notable example of this interdisciplinary spirit during the 1930s was the Science Inquiry, a faculty response to President Glenn Frank's call for academic leadership in solving important societal problems. Organized as an informal ad hoc committee in 1933 by C.K. Leith (geology), Graduate School Dean E.B. Fred (bacteriology), Chester Lloyd Jones (economics and political science), and Harry Steenbock (agricultural chemistry), the group set for itself the mission of reviewing campus-based teaching and research in the natural and social sciences as related to major political, economic, and social questions, especially in Wisconsin. In their first report, the members of the Science Inquiry explained to President Frank:

> The procedure has been informal and flexible. Individuals and groups have been called on for consultation and for preparation of reports, without formal organization of subcommittees. First and last, possibly two hundred people have taken part.

The Science Inquiry continued until the early 1940s, when the University turned its attention to the more specialized life-and-death needs of

---

History of the College of Agricultural and Life Sciences at the University of Wisconsin-Madison (Madison: College of Agricultural and Life Sciences, 1991), pp. 52-60; Merle Curti and Vernon Carstensen, *The University of Wisconsin: A History, 1848-1925* (Madison: University of Wisconsin Press, 1949), vol. 2, pp. 400-10; W.H. Glover, *Farm and College: The College of Agriculture of the University of Wisconsin, A History* (Madison: University of Wisconsin Press, 1952), pp. 269-86.

[6]Benjamin G. Elliott, oral history interview, 1983, UHP.

World War II. While the effort lasted, faculty members from across the campus worked together to study and prepare bulletins and reports on such topics as *The Erosion Problem, Lakes, Wildlife Management, The Transportation Problem, Public Utility and Power Regulation,* and *The Fight against Crime and Delinquency.* The exercise embodied the long-standing tradition of the University's community of scholars in the service of state and nation.[7]

Another mark of the unusually strong faculty commitment to this evolving community of scholars was Professor Harry Steenbock's pivotal decision to patent his vitamin D irradiation process. Steenbock could easily have pocketed all of the proceeds from his potentially lucrative discovery, which eventually totalled more than $40 million. Instead, he helped to develop an innovative non-profit organization, the Wisconsin Alumni Research Foundation, to market the patent for the support of research at the University. Steenbock might also have restricted the WARF research funds to his own department, agricultural chemistry, or to the College of Agriculture. Taking a broader view, he directed that the Steenbock patent income be used to support scientific research generally at the University. In time WARF funds effectively came to support research in the social sciences and humanities as well, first by freeing up other UW research funds for this purpose in the depression-era emergency postdoctoral fellowships and more directly in support of faculty research in all parts of the University after 1962. The importance of Steenbock's generous vision can scarcely be over-stated. In the years after 1925 and especially after World War II, WARF became probably the single most important reason why the University was able to develop and maintain its position as one of the nation's and indeed the world's major research universities, in the process building one of the most productive and broadly based biological sciences research community in the country. Without Harry Steen-bock's concern to share the fruits of his research with his colleagues—his community—the history of the University of Wisconsin would have been very different.[8]

---

[7]C.K. Leith and others to Glenn Frank, May 31, 1934, Science Inquiry Bulletins, 0/15, UA. See also Leith, "The Science Inquiry: Faculty Members Establish Correlating Agency for Campus Research Program," *WAM*, 38 (December, 1936), 88-9, 118-9; Edwin B. Fred, oral history interview, 1973, UA; Sylvia W. McGrath, *Charles Kenneth Leith: Scientific Adviser* (Madison: University of Wisconsin Press, 1971), pp. 120-4.

[8]The two best published accounts of the creation of the Wisconsin Alumni Research Foundation are in Beardsley, *Harry L. Russell*, pp. 155-71, and Mark H. Ingraham, *Charles*

The Informal Community

Another distinctive feature of Madison in these years was the informal but far-reaching social network that infused the University community and underlay the institution's more formal governance structure. A host of cultural offerings, literary societies, recreational groups, and dining clubs regularly brought faculty members of diverse interests and backgrounds together for entertainment, enlightenment, and fellowship. The School of Music's several student orchestras, bands, glee clubs, and smaller ensembles, the Wisconsin Players, Professor Margaret H'Doubler's innovative dance-drama group, Orchesis, and the annual all-male student Haresfoot Club revue ("All of our girls are men, yet everyone's a lady") provided a rich and varied campus cultural life for town as well as gown. Nationally-acclaimed artists such as Pablo Casals, Sergei Rachmaninoff, Marian Anderson, and the Chicago and Minneapolis Symphony Orchestras regularly performed in the Stock Pavilion or the Armory until the completion of the Memorial Union Theater in 1939 provided a more appropriate setting. The campus boasted the oldest university foreign film society

A Haresfoot Chorus "Girl"

Sumner Slichter: The Golden Vector (Madison: University of Wisconsin Press, 1972), pp. 176-93. See also Clay Schoenfeld, "The W.A.R.F. Story: The Wisconsin Alumni Research Foundation, Sixty Years of Research and Realization—1925-1985" (unpublished manuscript, 1986), UHP; [H.L. Russell,] *A Decade of Service, 1925-1935: Report of the Director* (Madison: Wisconsin Alumni Research Foundation, 1936); Fred, "The Year of Decision, 1925: The Early Days of WARF" (unpublished manuscript, April 14, 1961), General Presidential Papers, 4/16/4, box 17, UA; E.B. Fred, *The Role of the Wisconsin Alumni Research Foundation in the Support of Research at the University of Wisconsin* (Madison: Wisconsin Alumni Research Foundation, 1973); Robert Taylor, "The Birth of the Wisconsin Alumni Research Foundation" (unpublished manuscript based on interviews with Harry Steenbock, 1956), General Presidential Papers, 4/16/4, box 17, UA; Jenkins, *Centennial History*, pp. 81-4; Glover, *Farm and College*, pp. 293-5; Curti and Carstensen, *University of Wisconsin*, vol. 2, p. 413.

and with the opening of the Union building in 1928 the first student art gallery in the country.[9]

Other tastes also received attention. There was the Get-Away Club, which met regularly during the inter-war period to hike throughout Wisconsin and hear about adventuresome international and American travel. Its 1931-32 roster included faculty members from physiological chemistry, botany, comparative literature, forestry, engineering, sociology, and chemistry, as well as the chief justice of the Wisconsin Supreme Court and the director of Wisconsin Alumni Research Foundation.[10] For other tastes there was the Faculty Bowling League, in existence at least as early as 1919 and still operating at the present time with a membership spanning the entire University. Some of these groups made a conscious effort to link the University with the wider Madison community—for example, service groups like the Madison Rotary Club with its substantial University membership, the Madison Literary Club and the Town and Gown Club, both dating from the 1870s, the University Heights Poetry Club, the University West End Club, the Friday Noon Luncheon Club, and the Ygdrasil Literary Society for those of Norwegian descent.[11]

---

[9]See Fannie T. Taylor, oral history interview, 1983, UA; Ragnar Rollefson, oral history interviews; Angeline G. Lins, oral history interview, 1984, UHP; Fannie T. Taylor, *The Wisconsin Union Theater: Fifty Golden Years* (Madison: Memorial Union Building Association, 1989).

[10]See Get-Away Club logs in College of Agriculture Papers, 9/1/22-3, boxes 1 and 2, UA.

[11]Many of these town-gown clubs, some of which date back to the nineteenth century, are still functioning. The currently active Madison Literary Club and the Town and Gown Club were founded as deliberate town-gown ventures in 1877 and 1878, respectively. Their archives are deposited in the State Historical Society of Wisconsin. President Frank belonged to both clubs and read three papers before the literary club—in 1926, 1932, and 1939—during his years in Madison. The Ygdrasil Literary Society was named and organized in December of 1896 by Rasmus B. Anderson, then an insurance company president and the first UW professor of Norwegian, as a vehicle for promoting the Scandinavian heritage and providing fellowship for Norwegian-Americans living in the Madison area. Over the years a number of prominent UW faculty members, including Julius Olson, Einar Haugen, Olaf Hougen, Paul Knaplund, Ragnar Rollefson, Harald Naess, and Conrad Elvehjem participated in its activities. The University Heights Poetry Club also began in 1896 under the leadership of several UW families living in the new University Heights subdivision west of the campus. Unlike some of its contemporaries, from the first it welcomed women members on an equal footing and soon expanded its geographical reach. The club celebrated its fiftieth anniversary in 1946 with a gala dinner at the Madison Club at which one of the founding members, Mrs. Amos A. Knowlton, recalled the early days of the club and life on University Heights. The University West End Club grew out of an initiative by Dean Frederick Turneaure of the College of Engineering in 1898 to establish an organization to promote enlightenment and fellowship for University residents and later others living in the west end of Madison, then defined as the

The community also included some organizations exclusively for women, in which the relatively few female faculty members and more numerous University wives played important roles. The College Women's Club, the Madison chapter of the American Association of University Women, thrived throughout these years. Beginning in 1923 it operated its own club house for women in the former Vilas home on Gilman Street, offering sleeping rooms and serving two meals a day in its dining room. Another active group was the University League, an organization of UW women (faculty and wives) founded in 1901. Both of these groups provided an opportunity for University women to meet, socialize, and work on common projects. Occasionally husbands were invited to social or cultural events that nourished the broader University community. An example of a more restricted women's group was the Smith Club, for graduates of Smith College in Massachusetts, which for a time owned a house on Gilman Street as a meeting place for its thirty or so members. President Frank's wife Mary, a Smith alumna, hosted at least one tea to introduce a newly arrived young Smith graduate to her Madison sisters. Other social groups for women were sponsored by some of the schools and colleges—in the Colleges of Agriculture and Engineering in particular—or various academic departments.[12]

"A Soviet of Dining Clubs"

The dining clubs are a particularly interesting and important Uni-

---

immediate campus area. The club's emphasis and membership area changed somewhat over the years, but it is still in existence, its archives held by the State Historical Society. Younger than the others, the Rotary Club of Madison was started in 1913 by a group of Madison businessmen, but soon came to include a significant University representation, both as speakers and as members. The still functioning Friday Noon Luncheon Club began in the late 1920s as a small women's group consisting of women faculty and faculty and town wives who met regularly for lunch at the Memorial Union and then retired to one of its member's home for an afternoon of bridge and dessert. Ygdrasil Literary Society, "Seventy-Fifth Anniversary" (unpublished pamphlet, 1971), UHP; Chester P. Higby, "History of the University Heights Poetry Club" (unpublished manuscript, 1956), L&S Papers, 7/36/14, box 24, UA; "History of the University West End Club" (unpublished manuscript, n.d.) and records, SHSW; John W. Jenkins, *History of the Rotary Club of Madison* (Madison: Rotary Club of Madison, 1990); Gertrude Wilson, oral history interview, 1990, UA.

[12]See *The College Club Bulletin* (January, 1930, through November, 1941), UHP; Mrs. Theodore W. Zillman, *A History of the University League, 1901-1966* (Madison: University of Wisconsin, 1966); Julia Bögholt, oral history interview, 1983; Mrs. Arno T. Lenz, oral history interview, 1983; Ira L. Baldwin, oral history interview, 1983; Erna Brambora Rollefson, oral history interview, 1984, UHP.

versity tradition, reflective and supportive of the strong sense of faculty community during the first half of the twentieth century. Such social groups were not unique to Wisconsin, of course, but probably no other American university city could equal Madison with respect to the number and longevity of the dining clubs flourishing in this period and in a number of cases still in operation. It is impossible to say how many such groups existed at any time or what percentage of the faculty belonged to them, as only a few kept records of their activities. Impressionistic evidence suggests, however, that while membership in a particular group was by invitation the clubs were ubiquitous, and such fellowship was available essentially to any faculty member with a friendly demeanor and interesting personality. It was not uncommon for an individual to belong to more than one club.

Typically, the clubs met monthly during the academic year for dinner, usually at a member's home but sometimes at the University Club, the Memorial Union, or a local restaurant. Their membership was usually tenured and almost exclusively male, although some of the clubs had an occasional ladies night to which the wives of members were invited. At least two all-women dining clubs were operating by the late 1920s with a membership consisting of women faculty and University and town wives. One couples dining club has also come to light, though there may have been more. Some of the clubs included members from the town; others were limited to University staff. In the early years some of the club dinners were rather formal affairs with the specified dress often black tie and the host serving cigars and perhaps port during the discussion following an elaborate dinner. Nearly always there was a post-dinner program of serious intellectual content involving a talk, the reading of a paper, or organized discussion about some topic of common interest. Upon being consulted about the formation of a dining club, Dean Birge gave blunt advice: "If you want your club to have a long life, you must have some serious motive, otherwise it will degenerate into a gossip club and soon die."[13] All of the UW dining clubs of any duration took Birge's advice to heart.

The oldest and most prestigious of the dining clubs, still in operation, was the Town and Gown Club, formed in 1878 by two Madison attorneys, Burr W. Jones and Charles W. Gregory, and a University speech professor, David B. Frankenburger. For well over a century the

[13]Ira L. Baldwin, "The Chronicles of the University of Wisconsin Inefficiency Club" (unpublished manuscript, 1976), UHP.

Town and Gown membership has included a long line of distinguished faculty members, University presidents, regents, governors, supreme court justices, bankers, attorneys, and businessmen. It is noteworthy that all of the seventeen members who belonged to the club during its first quarter-century were members of the equally venerable Madison Literary Club, founded a year earlier and also still in existence. Town and Gown's practice was to meet for dinner in a member's home approximately twice a month on Saturday evenings throughout the academic year for fellowship and enlightenment, the latter through an after-dinner program of structured discussion led by one of the group. Each host was responsible for writing up a page of minutes summarizing the evening's activities, which have been preserved in the club's archives in the State Historical Society of Wisconsin. By September of 1931 the club statistician was able to report that the club had thus far met 901 times over fifty-three years and had produced seven hundred pages of minutes![14] A similarly prestigious but younger dining group was the X Club, whose diverse members in the 1920s—including President Frank, a regent, and faculty leaders from a variety of departments—dined together monthly for the purpose of joining one of their number designated as "chief conversationalist" in unravelling some issue of current concern.[15]

An example of a more single-mindedly serious purpose was the Q Club, known commonly as the Fourth Tuesday Club after its monthly meeting schedule, which a group of senior science faculty members organized in 1931 to dine together regularly at the University Club in order to learn about each other's research. The founders stipulated that programs "must be entirely informal" and "quality" membership should be "limited in numbers in order to prevent reticence for free discussion." To the original members from bacteriology, agricultural chemistry, mathematics, chemistry, physiology, and pharmacology, the group quickly added colleagues from botany, genetics, geology, horticulture, zoology, and physics. Characteristically, the club paid no attention to

---

[14]For an illuminating account of the early years of the Town and Gown Club, see Ingraham, *Charles Sumner Slichter*, pp. 214-21.

[15]See, for example, H.S. Richards, memorandum, March 9, 1926, and 1926-27 Dining Club schedule, Frank Presidential Papers, 4/13/1, boxes 14 and 22, UA. Besides President Frank, the X Club membership in 1926-27 included Regent Michael Olbrich, Joel Stebbins (astronomy), Arnold Dresden (mathematics), Dean Harry Richards (law), Oliver Rundell (law), Alexander Meiklejohn (philosophy), Max Otto (philosophy), Walter Meek (physiology), and James O'Neill (speech).

school/college divisions, drawing members from Agriculture, Letters and Science, and the Medical School. The handwritten minutes of the January, 1933, meeting recorded by botanist Benjamin Duggar give something of the flavor of the club's activities:

> All present. Fourth Tuesday Club met as usual at dinner at Univ. Club. Prof. E.G. Hastings gave an illuminating discussion of the group of tubercli bacilli, with special reference to the bearing of scientific work on problems of tuberculosis eradication in dairy husbandry. He emphasized the significance of the tuberculin test and showed why all animals reacting to this test are not actually tuberculous on slaughter but react often because sensitized by some slight infections from other forms of closely related bacilli. The curious workings of the state laws were developed. Cultures were exhibited of half a dozen "forms" of "tubercli" bacilli including human, bovine, avian, and saprophytic soil forms. Discussion was general and lively, especially relating to the significance of Eradication, Pasteurization, etc.[16]

The Inefficiency Club was yet another faculty dining group with a broader membership and purpose. Organized in 1916 and taking its name defiantly in protest against the efficiency called for by the critical Allen Survey of the University the previous year,[17] for many years the club limited its membership to nine persons, with an unwritten rule that there could be only one from any department. Its charter members included the University business manager and the director of the state historical museum located on the campus, plus seven faculty representatives of fields as diverse as genetics, mathematics, physics, geology, music, engineering, and zoology. The founders were in the prime of their professional lives, ranging in age from thirty-six to forty-nine. Those from the faculty were mostly senior and tenured, although two—geologist Warren J. Mead and zoologist George Wagner—were still assistant professors. The Inefficiency Club's modus operandi was similar to that of most of the dining clubs. Following the monthly dinner at a member's home, a member or often an invited speaker would share insights and lead discussion about a topic of current interest. Members of the club valued its fellowship highly. Most remained active in it for many years, even after retirement, with the result that the club had only twenty-seven members during its first sixty years of existence. Charter member Charles N. Mills, the director of the School of Music, once declined an attractive offer to return to the

---

[16]Fourth Tuesday Club Minutes Book, UHP.
[17]See Curti and Carstensen, *University of Wisconsin*, vol. 2, pp. 267-84.

University of Illinois primarily because Illinois offered no counterpart to the stimulating fellowship he found in the Inefficiency Club. An important rule of the club, common to most of the dining clubs, stipulated that discussion at meetings was privileged so members could feel free to express their views with a frankness they might not care to have attributed to them elsewhere. Ira Baldwin, who joined the club in 1939, has emphasized how useful he found such candor in formulating policy and otherwise administering the University while serving first as a dean and later as vice president for academic affairs.[18]

A rather different sort of dining group, Ye Olde Warre Clubbe, of which Baldwin was also a member, grew out of a suggestion at a dinner party hosted by Professor Asher Hobson, the chairman of agricultural economics, at his home early in 1939. The club's roots went back to the daring faculty confrontation with the Board of Regents in the mid-thirties, when the four faculty members of the Athletic Board resigned in protest after the regents ignored their advice in the Spears-Meanwell controversy.[19] That searing experience made the four rebels—Hobson, Andrew Weaver (speech), Robert Aurner (business administration), and Gus Bohstedt (animal husbandry)—lifelong friends. Hobson, Weaver, and Aurner were the prime movers in organizing the new club, while Bohstedt decided not to participate. In addition to the battle-scarred trio, other charter members were Ira Baldwin (bacteriology), Aldo Leopold (chairman of wildlife management), Alfred W. Peterson (UW comptroller), and Milton H. Frank, (vice president of the Wisconsin Power and Light Company). As Frank's membership suggests, from the beginning the club sought compatible members from the town as well as the University, with its prime purpose, as Baldwin recalled, "that of bringing together on a regular basis a group of *congenial people* for a *private, friendly* and *intimate discussion* of the many critical issues which at that time were crowding in from all sides."

A listing of the Ye Olde Warre Clubbe membership requirements stipulated that members "must be liberally educated, self or otherwise" and "able and qualified to converse intelligently on any subject—ancient, modern, and future space." As for politics, they "must be conservative—all American in every way; no Dealers." Discussion at club meetings was thus more general than research-focussed, as was the case in some of other dining clubs, and the purpose

---

[18]Baldwin, "Chronicles of the Inefficiency Club."
[19]See pp. 258-69.

of the group was more social than professional. While University members predominated at first, in later years the club sought to achieve a rough balance of one-third University, one-third business, and one-third government members. The dress specified by Asher Hobson in a 1941 club invitation of "dinner jacket, black tie—and sox" soon gave way to less formal attire, and the club eventually began to schedule an occasional ladies night for spouses and even meetings away from Madison at the vacation homes of some of its members. During the forty years after the first exploratory dinner in 1939, Ye Olde Warre Clubbe met at least 320 times, ordinarily on the second Tuesday of the month. That its members valued their fellowship highly is attested by the fact that after his retirement charter member Frank flew from his winter home in Arizona a number of times in order to attend club meetings.[20]

Still another long-lasting dining club began in a different way in 1930 under the initiative of Robert B.L. Murphy, a 1930 L&S graduate and currently a student in the UW Law School, and Lowell E. Frautschi, a 1928 graduate who had been obliged to abandon his graduate work in history in order to help in his family's Madison furniture store. The two youthful founders invited several other graduate students to dine regularly at the Memorial Union for discussion and talks by University faculty members and others about their work. Initially, the members whimsically referred to themselves as the Royal Bengal Bicycle Riders Club, but Frautschi, who served as secretary-treasurer, thought this title too frivolous and cumbersome and started calling the group the Academy, a name that has continued to the present day. Always restricted to men, for the first few years the composition of the club changed frequently as its youthful members left Madison, but enough of the core remained to keep it going. During the club's second year, law student Jacob Beuscher joined briefly before returning in 1936 as a Law School faculty member. Similarly, Perry Wilson was recruited in 1934 as a graduate student and remained a member after graduating to a faculty appointment in the bacteriology department. Closely tied to the University through its twice-monthly meetings in the Memorial Union, the club gradually took on a definite town-gown character by the end of the 1930s with a composition balanced between

---

[20]Milton H. Frank, "History, Battles, Dinners & Picnics of Ye Olde Warre Clubbe" (unpublished manuscript, 1968); Baldwin, "I Remember: Forty Years of Ye Olde Warre Clubbe" (unpublished manuscript, 1978), UHP.

University and town members. Unlike many of the dining clubs, in 1936 the Academy began to keep records of its meetings, and the list of its several hundred speakers and their topics provides a fascinating insight into University-town problems and concerns over the decades since.[21]

On the distaff side, the still-functioning Walrus Club began in the spring of 1911 as a women's dining club, taking its name from the invitation of the loquacious Walrus in Lewis Carroll's *Through the Looking Glass*: "The time has come...to talk of many things."[22] From the first the club had a town-gown membership, though University women—faculty members and faculty wives—predominated. They were an intellectually lively and elite group, and for a time spawned a second Walrus Club in Palo Alto, California. Initial members included Alice R. Van Hise, wife of the University president, Althea H. Bardeen, wife of the dean of the Medical School, Gertrude E.L. Slaughter, a prolific author and wife of a distinguished UW classicist, Anna M. Ely, wife of the founder of the UW economics department, Dorothy R. Mendenhall, a medical doctor and nationally prominent pediatrician and the wife of a UW physicist, and Dean of Women Lois Kimball Mathews, who resigned her University appointment but not her membership in the club after her marriage to Wisconsin Supreme Court Justice Marvin B. Rosenberry in 1918. As vacancies occurred the club invited others to join, including Professor Abby L. Marlatt, who for many years chaired the home economics department (1921), Alice S. Clark, like her husband a medical bacteriologist (1924), Rachel Szgold Jastrow, an active Zionist and wife of the first UW psychologist (1924), Rosamond E. Rice, a young mother whose husband was a rising law professor (1926), Dean of Women Louise Troxell Greeley (1931), Lillian K. Dysktra, wife of the new University president (1938), and Elizabeth Brandeis Raushenbush, the daughter of U.S. Supreme Court Justice Louis D. Brandeis and a UW lecturer in economics (1940). Normally the club limited itself to a dozen members so they could be seated at one table and participate in a single common conversation. In fact, an early

---

[21]See Lowell Frautschi, "Dinner Club: Annals of the Academy," vol. 1, "1930-1980" (unpublished manuscript, September, 1980), and vol. 2, "1980-1990" (unpublished manuscript, September, 1990), UHP. The club's members believe that its unbroken patronage of the Memorial Union's dining service for more than sixty years is unrivalled and has made it the Union's most faithful customer.

[22]Lewis Carroll, *The Complete Works of Lewis Carroll* (New York: Modern Library, n.d.), p. 186.

club rule stipulated: "All conversation shall be addressed to the entire table. There shall be no duologues."[23] Other strictures forbade gossip or discussion of purely personal matters except at the October meeting, when members reported on their summer activities. The club met monthly throughout the academic year, usually for luncheon at a member's home, occasionally for dinner.

In 1913 the Walrus Club adopted the practice of having each hostess write up a detailed record of the monthly meetings. These accounts offer a revealing glimpse into the interests and concerns of a group of exceptionally well-informed and intellectually curious women. Sometimes the hostess asked one or more of the members to lead the table discussion on recent national and international events. Rarely did the conversation turn on University or Madison matters, though Dean Greeley's minutes of December 15, 1937, record that the meeting would long be remembered "as coinciding with a period of great strain because of the removal of Mr. Frank as president of the university," a topic that "took precedence over all others."[24] On another occasion Mrs. Clark led a spirited discussion of the standards to be used in evaluating faculty merit, especially the contest between teaching and research—perennially revisited issues familiar to modern readers.[25] Following the meal the club listened to a talk or paper delivered by one of the members on some subject of personal interest or expertise—art, literature, history, diplomacy, science, education, legal and constitutional issues, and the like—followed by general discussion. These were ambitious presentations, as suggested by the minutes of a meeting in 1930 recorded by one of the town members, Katherine M. Jones, the wife of Burr W. Jones, a former member of the law faculty, Wisconsin congressman, and supreme court justice:

> After luncheon Mrs. Slaughter introduced Cassiodorus of Squillace, a perfectly new gentleman to most of us. Cassiodorus, called the last of the Romans and the first of the Italian patriots, was born in Seyllactirium about 468 and died in Calabria in 560. Under Theodoric and his successors he labored for forty years as confidential minister to re-establish the civilization of the earlier better days of the Roman Empire, to save Italy from the domination of the Eastern Empire, to preserve the culture of the past for the future and toward the end of his life, when political power was no longer his, to combine with the religious ideas of the time the pursuit of knowledge, by

---

[23]Record books of the Walrus Club, vol. 1 [ca. December, 1913], p. 5, UHP.
[24]Ibid., vol. 2, p. 178.
[25]Ibid., vol. 2 (December 11, 1928), p. 39.

creating a library for the preservation of the old literature and founding a monastery where work was begun, later carried on by all the monasteries of Europe where libraries were created, manuscript copies annotated[,] adorned and "clothed in beautiful garments." We know Cassiodorus through his Letters mostly written in the name of the King. They reveal wide diversity of interests, curiosity about the natural world, undiscriminating love of literature, art, architecture, enthusiasm for bookmaking.[26]

The same could be said of the members of this club.

Another all-female town-gown dining club—also still in existence—emerged in the late 1920s, which like the Walrus Club normally met for lunch followed by an afternoon of cards once a month on Fridays throughout the academic year. There was some overlap between the two groups; Lillian Dykstra and Elizabeth Brandeis belonged to both. Conversation at meetings of the Friday Club had less structure than in the Walrus Club and often dealt with University and Wisconsin politics, thanks to the absorbing political interests of some of its early members, especially Isabel La Follette, Rhoda Otto, Jane Gaus, Dorothy Walton, and Brandeis.[27] Max and Rhoda Otto's long-standing association with the La Follette family and Jane and John Gaus's close friendship with Isabel and Philip La Follette helped to assure that the sentiment of the Friday Club was solidly behind the governor's effort to oust President Frank in 1936-37. Years later a disgruntled faculty member—Walter Morton of economics—charged that the University was to some extent run by an unofficial matriarchy during the Dykstra years, with members of the Friday Club, especially Brandeis, using their influence with Lillian Dykstra to gain the president's ear.[28]

There were probably dozens of similar but mostly male dining clubs—some with names like the Six O'Clock Club, Logos, and the Society for Promotion of Research and Conversation (SPRC); others without a name. One can only speculate on their influence on University affairs in these years, but it is hard to dispute Ira Baldwin's

---

[26]Ibid., vol. 2 (January 6, 1930), p. 61.

[27]Gertrude Wilson, oral history interview.

[28]Walter Morton, oral history interview. Gertrude Wilson, a "town" member of the Friday Club and also a friend of Morton, agrees that the club functioned as a behind-the-scenes matriarchy, especially during the campaign to get rid of Glenn Frank. Part of the hostility to President Frank was rooted in the active dislike of Mary Frank, whose social pretensions and snobbery were offensive to many campus women. Mrs. Wilson remembered the extreme partisanship of some of the Friday Club activists in the 1930s as the most distasteful aspect of the club, but exempted Lillian Dykstra from this failing. Wilson, oral history interview.

belief that it was substantial. Like Baldwin, Letters and Science Dean Mark Ingraham belonged to two faculty dining clubs, one scientifically focussed and the other more general and broadly interdisciplinary. Ingraham was one of the most widely respected faculty leaders of his generation. Upon his retirement in 1966 after a UW career spanning more than four decades, he stressed the unusually strong sense of faculty community he had enjoyed at Wisconsin and the role of the clubs in sustaining it. "To me the University has not just been a community of scholars," he told a group of well-wishers:

> For me it has been "a society of friends."...Within this life of friendship, clubs have meant a great deal: The University Club, where I take my daily defeat in billiards, and whose level of food has varied from year to year but whose standard of conversation has remained stimulating; the Madison Literary Club, where the gown welcomes its contact with the town, and which provides the pleasantest way to appear before our jurists; and two dining clubs. It is my experience, as a member of these two dining clubs and as a guest at many others, that has led me to declare that the government of this University is a soviet of dining clubs. One of the two has had five chairmen of the University Committee without, I believe, having had membership on the committees that nominated them. All of these clubs are but a little of the connective tissue within the body of friendship.[29]

The Supreme Soviet

If, to use Dean Ingraham's illuminating phrase, the informal government of the University in his experience was a soviet of dining clubs, then the University Club might be described as the supreme soviet. Organized in response to President Van Hise's call in 1906 for a faculty club to promote fellowship and unity in the campus community, the University Club opened its doors at the corner of Murray and State Streets two years later. Built in three stages, with the final section completed in 1924, the club's impressive four-story building included two large and several smaller dining/meeting rooms, a well-equipped regular and a separate pastry kitchen, a library and reading lounge, game rooms for cards, billiards, and table tennis, a

---

[29]Mark H. Ingraham, "Retirement Dinner Talk," May 24, 1966, in Ingraham, *From a Wisconsin Soap Box* (Madison: Mark H. Ingraham, 1979), pp. 193-4. Ingraham used the phrase "a soviet of dining clubs" on a number of occasions in emphasizing the clubs' role in the informal governance of the University. See Ingraham, "Sub-Groups and the Faculty," speech text, April-May, 1937, L&S Papers, 7/1/6/2/2, box 1; Ingraham, oral history interviews, 1972 and 1978, UA.

ladies parlor, and eighty-five single sleeping rooms and five two-room suites available for rent to male faculty members and graduate students, one of whom resided there for forty-five years! A number of single faculty members found the club a convenient place to live, and the club reserved a few of its sleeping rooms for campus guests. Historian Paul Knaplund, for example, lived at the club until his marriage in 1926; his older bachelor colleague, Alexander Vasiliev, lived there throughout his faculty service from 1925 to 1939 and beyond. President Van Hise promoted the club and was one of the charter members, but it began as an entirely private venture with no University subsidy, funded through the sale of shares of stock to faculty and alumni members and through short- and long-term loans including eventually a sizable mortgage from the State Annuity and Investment Board. The club house was located on one of the choice sites in the lower campus area; by the late twenties it was conservatively valued at $300,000.[30]

The significance of the University Club, as its then president Ira Baldwin remarked in 1938, was its role as "a very valuable agency in bringing and holding together the University faculty."[31] In its early years the club primarily served social and residential purposes. The club's dinner programs, musical entertainments, lectures, films, and dances were popular, sometimes selling out within hours after reservations opened. Indeed, so great was the demand that some dinner programs had to be limited to members only. Occasionally attendance was restricted for other reasons. On February 21, 1935, for example, the club sponsored a forum on UW athletics moderated by President Frank and featuring Athletic Director Walter Meanwell and Professor

---

[30] The University Club was built on the site of the substantial brick home of Professor John B. Parkinson, an alumnus and former regent who joined the faculty to teach mathematics and then political science beginning in 1867 and who served for a time as University librarian and vice president. The Parkinson home had been damaged by fire in late 1905 and thus was available at a distressed price to be rebuilt as part of the first unit of the club. In 1912 the club added a south wing, and in 1922-24 the old Parkinson house was replaced by the central lobby and east addition. Construction and ownership of the building was through the University Club House Association, which leased the premises to the University Club for a rental covering the interest and amortization of the club house mortgages. Although legally separate, both organizations were controlled by UW faculty who were University Club members. Indeed, during its first quarter century the club itself acquired a majority of the stock of the association through gift or bequest. See UW Faculty Document 429, "Report of the President's Committee of Nineteen," April 21, 1933, UA; E.G. Hastings, memorandum, October 18, 1933, UHP; Mildred Lindquist, oral history interview, 1982, UA; *Daily Cardinal*, February 21, 1907; Barbara J. Wolff, "Small Island in Time," *WAM*, 81 (January-February, 1980), 4-9.

[31] Baldwin to J.H. Moore, January 20, 1938, UHP.

Andrew Weaver, the embattled chairman of the University Athletic Board then engaged in a confrontation with the Board of Regents.[32] The monthly club bulletin noted that attendance would be limited to members and faculty guests of members, in order to have "a sort of 'family discussion'."[33] At first the club's dining room was small, because most members lived near the campus and typically walked home for lunch. Gradually, as the University staff moved westward from the campus into the developing University Heights section and beyond, more members lunched at the club and the dining service expanded to include several entrée choices at lunch and dinner seven days a week.

With members spending more time at the club, its services expanded accordingly. By 1926 its library was subscribing to fifty-five American and foreign magazines and ten newspapers. Even in the midst of the depression a decade later the club was still subscribing forty-seven American and foreign magazines and seven newspapers, including the *Illustrated London News*, *Leipziger Illustrierte Zeitung*, and *Manchester Guardian Weekly*. During the 1920s zoology Professor George Wagner annually paid $15, which he later expanded to a share of largely unmarketable club house stock, for the right to select old copies of the club's magazines and newspapers for his use at home.[34] Recognizing belatedly that these back issues represented a source of income, during the 1930s the club began holding an auction annually at which members could bid for the yearly right to take home the copies of a particular magazine after four weekly or two monthly issues had been put out for members' perusal. In 1936 the magazine auction raised more than $100 for the club's subscription fund. Before the 1937 auction the Magazine Committee informed club members of a growing problem of "lost" issues of certain periodicals, which it pointed out was "a gentle euphemism for what is, in fact, theft of personal property which belongs to the Club or one of its members and has been paid for."

> In general, this loss has occurred among the more expensive magazines; for example, we have had to buy two numbers of *Fortune*, replacing stolen copies. The French *Le Sourire*, which has been objected to by some people on the ground that it was likely to corrupt the morals of the members, seems

---

[32]See pp. 258-69.
[33]University Club Bulletin #4, February 8, 1935, UHP.
[34]See, for example, University Club Board Minutes, January 21, 1927, UHP.

to have corrupted somebody in an unexpected way, since every number of that magazine during the present year has disappeared within a week after its receipt. Whether the anonymous criminal is an unofficial scout of the Legion of Decency or just someone with whom esthetic considerations outweigh ethical ones, we don't know, but members are asked to search their consciences and their rooms for possible clues.[35]

Even among gentlemen, it seemed, honor was sometimes elastic and elusive.

From the University's standpoint, the congenial social life of the club was valuable because it promoted faculty interaction across departmental and college lines, as Van Hise had anticipated in 1906. More important, however, was the growing trend of using the club for official departmental and committee meetings in addition to the inevitable informal discussion of University matters during meals and over a game of bridge or billiards. By the 1920s a great deal of formal University business was being conducted at the club. In 1933, after a quarter century of the club's existence, a faculty committee reported:

There can be no question that the University Club has played a most important part in the life of the University. Faculty members who use it regularly deem it indispensable. A very large part of the administrative business of the University is transacted in the informal conferences and formal meetings held at the Club house. Statistics taken from the records of the Club show that during the past five years the average number of weekly meetings held at the Club was 29 with an aggregate attendance of 350. Of these meetings 80 per cent were meetings of official committees or departments of the University. Most of these meetings were luncheon gatherings attended by non-members of the Club as well as by Club members. No record is kept of the much larger number of informal conferences which observation shows is held at the Club every day.[36]

Through the 1920s the club was in a healthy financial condition, enrolling more than half the faculty and a substantial majority of the senior professors.[37] Club president Grant Hyde gave an unqualified rosy report to the members at their annual business meeting late in 1929, ironically just a month after the stock market crash. "From every

---

[35]Ibid., November 22, 1930; Miles L. Hanley, memo to club membership, January 21, 1936; University Club Calendar, March and April, 1936; Magazine Committee, memo to club membership, January 27, 1937, UHP.

[36]UW Faculty Document 429.

[37]In 1930 the club had 406 members, including 58 junior or graduate student members, at a time when the University faculty numbered less than 600. Membership data, UHP.

point of view, the financial future of the club seems promising," he declared. "The physical plant is in fine condition with no large needs in view in the near future, and the income and patronage of all departments are very gratifying."[38] Club members had in the past occasionally talked about the possibility of turning the club house over to the regents in view of its growing use for University business and, not incidentally, to be able to purchase cheaper University heat and electricity and escape Madison property taxes. While the club prospered, able to complete the club house in 1924 and reduce its mortgage indebtedness, most members were reluctant to give up the autonomy that ownership of their club house represented.[39]

With the onset of the great depression, however, the option of University ownership seemed increasingly worth exploring. Club membership and revenues declined as the depression deepened, especially after the University staff began to feel the bite of salary waivers in 1932-33. Even before waivers, during 1931-32 the club ran an operating loss of more than $3,200. At their annual meeting in October, 1932, club members had an extended but inconclusive discussion on whether to approach the regents about taking over the property.[40] Always open to town residents who were college graduates, the club instead launched an aggressive drive for new members, especially from among officials in state government, but with little effect. In desperation the board successfully negotiated with city officials for a modest reduction in the club's property tax assessment and explored the purchase of steam heat and electricity from the University. They learned that while there would be significant operating savings through the purchase of University heat and power, it would cost the club about $3,500 for a tunnel to connect with the University's utilities. Hard-pressed to pay current operating costs, the club was in no condition to undertake this capital improvement. Reluctantly, the board began borrowing short-term operating funds and assigned long-delinquent accounts of former members to a finance

---

[38]Grant M. Hyde, "President's Report," November 15, 1929, UHP.

[39]For an extended discussion of the possibility of turning the club over to the University in the mid-twenties see *Capital Times*, May 8, 17, 18, 19, 20, 21, 22, and 25, December 8, 1926.

[40]Henry R. Trumbower, treasurer, "University Club Operating and Financial Statements for 1931-32," October 22, 1932; University Club Minutes of Annual Meeting, October 22, 1932, UHP.

company for collection.[41]   By the spring of 1933, with its dormitory rooms only two-thirds rented, with the club obliged to delay payments to various creditors, and with the club house association about to default on its mortgage with the state investment board, the enterprise faced imminent bankruptcy. The directors had good reason to fear wholesale resignations of the remaining members in the face of possible assessments to meet the club's mounting debts.

At its regular meeting on February 17, 1933, the board decided to appeal to President Frank to save the club by turning its club house over to the University. Three days later the officers met with Frank and informed him that in their judgment the club could not continue beyond the current year without major University assistance. A frequent user of the club himself, Frank agreed with the importance of preserving this symbol of faculty unity and center of campus fellowship, though he also knew the Board of Regents would balk at assuming the club's debts outright.   He therefore arranged a meeting of the usually inactive Regent-Faculty Conference Committee on March 7, at which both he and the club officers presented the case for University ownership of the club house property.   The reaction of the regent members was encouraging, so the directors scheduled a meeting of the club membership to approve the transfer.[42]

The club was fortunate to have as its president at this crucial time Professor Edwin G. Hastings, the long-time chairman of the bacteriology department, an efficient and hard-headed leader who was wise in the ways of University administration and campus politics. Hastings needed all of his considerable organizational skills to shepherd the transfer proposal through the necessary approvals before May 1, when the club house property would again be entered on the city of Madison property tax rolls for the 1933 tax year.

The first hurdle was to persuade the club membership that the financial crisis was grave enough to demand University intervention if the club were to be saved, a painful decision reached at a special meeting held at the club on the evening of March 21. The members authorized the transfer of the club house and grounds to the Board of Regents, "subject to the existing indebtedness of the University Club

---

[41]University Club Board Minutes, October 28, November 18, December 9, 1932, January 19, February 17, 1933.

[42]University Club Board Minutes, February 17, March 14 and 20, 1933; Hastings, memorandum summarizing the reasons for the reorganization, October 18, 1933, UHP.

House Association" and with the understanding that the property would "continue to be used as a center for such official and recreational activities of the University Community as the regents may determine." The members also directed the officers to vote the club's majority holding of stock in the club house association, the legal owner of the property, in favor of the transfer. As anticipated, the association stockholders, most of them active club members, gave their approval on March 30, at the same time authorizing the refunding of the association's bonded indebtedness.[43]

The next hurdle was higher and more difficult. To strengthen the case with the Board of Regents, Professor Hastings sought endorsement of the action of the club's membership at a general University faculty meeting on April 3. There was little disagreement over the desirability of continuing to use the club house for some sort of faculty club and the need for more general faculty participation. The faculty also recognized the regents would need to be assured that any faculty club would be able to generate enough revenue to cover both operating expenses and the mortgage indebtedness on the property before agreeing to a landlord role. The questions of possible compulsory membership and an equitable dues structure generated considerable discussion, however. In the end the faculty recognized that such issues could not be settled in floor debate and requested President Frank to appoint a committee "of not less than fifteen members of the Faculty to confer with and assist the Regents" in the reorganization of the club, with instructions "to submit the resulting plan for ratification to a meeting of all faculty ranks involved."

Frank quickly appointed a broadly based group, the so-called Committee of Nineteen, to represent the general faculty's interest in the matter. The president selected its members with care from all parts of the University, asking economics Professor William H. Kiekhofer to chair the committee and including among its members such faculty leaders as Edwin B. Fred, Harold C. Bradley, Oliver S. Rundell, Walter R. Agard, John G. Fowlkes, and John D. Hicks. He was careful to include four women—Lelia Bascom, Helen I. Denne, Hazel

---

[43]University Club notice of special membership meeting, with attached resolutions, March 21, 1933; University Club House Association, notice of special meeting, March 23, 1933; University Club Board Minutes, March 24, 1933, UHP. There was little reason to doubt the approval of the association stockholders, inasmuch as the club owned about 68 percent of the stock, mostly acquired through gift or bequest over the years. Hastings, memo, October 18, 1933, ibid.

Manning, and Helen C. White—as well as representatives of the junior faculty, Assistant Professors Edmund D. Ayres and V.W. Meloche. Some of the committee members were active in the club—for example, Kiekhofer, Bradley (a charter member), Fowlkes, Fred, Joseph W. Gale (a resident), Rundell, and Philip G. Fox; others were not.[44]

The Committee of Nineteen presented its report at an extraordinary special meeting of the faculty in the Music Hall auditorium on the

evening of April 21, 1933. Because of the nature of the recommendations, in addition to the legal faculty members of professorial rank all instructors and assistants earning $1,500 or more were invited to take part in the discussion and vote, an action that probably contributed to the attendance of 275 at the meeting. After reviewing the history and current financial difficulties of the University Club, the committee declared its belief in the great value of the club to the University community. The savings resulting from University ownership of the property would make possible the continuation of the club, the committee argued, "provided members of the Faculty are willing to support a faculty club in much larger numbers than at present and at the greatly reduced dues which university ownership would make possible." The committee warned, however, that "the Regents cannot accept the property for the purpose of a faculty club unless assured of sufficient receipts to meet operating costs, including the amortization of the debt over a period of years." To provide such assurance the report recommended that membership dues for the reorganized faculty club be reduced in order to encourage broad voluntary membership across the campus. It suggested an annual rate of ¾ of 1 percent of a member's actual UW academic-year salary, with a minimum of $10 and a maximum of $45 per year. A more controversial second recommendation pledged that "if at any time the plan of voluntary membership fails to procure the necessary financial support, the

---

[44]UW Faculty Minutes, April 3, 1933, UA.

Regents will have the approval of the Faculty in making faculty membership obligatory." In this event the dues would drop to ½ of 1 percent of salary with a minimum of $10, a maximum of $30 per year, with a further exemption for persons paid less than $1,500 a year.[45]

The University Club had been organized at a time when there were few women staff members at the University. It very likely never occurred to its founders that the club should be anything but a male haven. Consequently, its membership, facilities, and programming had always been male-oriented. Women could be admitted only as "women associate members" (at token dues of $10 a year, the same as for non-residents), with the result that in 1933 only six women belonged to the club. Club rules requested ladies to use the Murray Street entrance leading to the ladies parlor, the club's major concession to the female sex. In general women were treated as guests in the club and had only limited use of its facilities. Such discrimination was clearly not possible in a reorganized, more broadly based club operating under University sponsorship. Kiekhofer therefore proposed that women henceforth should be admitted as regular members. Until the club house facilities could serve them more adequately, however, their dues should be limited to ½ of 1 percent of their academic-year salaries, subject to a minimum of $10 and a maximum of $45 annually. If conditions should ever require compulsory membership, he proposed that women be exempted until appropriate facilities, including residential space, were available to them.[46]

As in the April 3 faculty meeting, the issue of obligatory membership in the event the reorganized University Club were to fall upon hard times generated most of the debate and parliamentary maneuvering, as it had in the committee's deliberations.[47] By common consent the

---

[45]UW Faculty Document 429. Under the existing dues structure, all regular members paid $50 a year regardless of salary level, associate members (non-tenured faculty in their first three years of UW service) paid $40, and junior members (graduate students, mostly residents of the club dormitory) paid $20.

[46]Ibid.; UW Faculty Minutes, April 21, 1933. It should be recalled that since 1923 the Madison chapter of the American Association of University Women, in which University women staff members played a large role, had operated a club house for women on Gilman Street not far from the campus. Though considerably smaller in size, the AAUW club was essentially a female version of the largely male University Club. As the latter's financial woes deepened, its directors went so far as to explore the possibility of renting space and perhaps merging with its women's counterpart. University Club Board Minutes, October 28 and November 18, 1932.

[47]Within the committee, members had also been sharply split on the issue of voluntary

meeting changed the length of obligatory membership to "during any period" rather than "if at any time" so as to emphasize its temporary character, though it also voted down a motion limiting the duration to one year at a time. When an instructor proposed that married staff members earning less than $2,000 be exempted from compulsory membership, his motion lost on a vote of 81-151. Acknowledging the need for quick action, the meeting also rejected a delaying motion for a mail referendum. Helen White, now a recently promoted and tenured associate professor and already showing a gentle determination to achieve equality of treatment for women, moved to strike out the provision exempting faculty women from compulsory membership. Her motion lost on a vote of 35-86, with a substantial number of her male colleagues obviously preferring not to take a stand on such a complicated women's rights issue. Finally, after nearly four hours of debate, at 11:15 P.M. the faculty wearily approved the provision for obligatory membership by a substantial margin of 163-42, but only after directing the president to appoint a standing committee each year to consider exemptions from the requirement and to allow remission of dues without loss of membership.[48]

Not quite. Meeting with the Board of Regents on April 27, Professor Kiekhofer reported the faculty's endorsement of the recommendations of his Committee of Nineteen, emphasizing the faculty's pledge of obligatory membership should the reorganized University Club require this for financial viability. After stipulating in executive session that the action should not appear in the minutes of their public meeting, the regents gave conditional approval to the scheme:

> That the Regents approve the University's assuming the property and operation of the University Club as a Faculty Union, with complete faculty membership on a graduated fee basis, contingent upon the administration's working out a self-liquidation plan of organization and operation that will commend itself to the faculty and conserve the value of the club for the University and the State; That the Executive Committee of the Regents be empowered to act for the Regents in the review and adoption or rejection of such plan.[49]

---

versus compulsory membership. Meloche got no support for his motion to offer the faculty only an obligatory membership plan, whereas Agard got four other members (Ayres, Bascom, Gale, and Fred) to support his motion for a voluntary-only plan. See [Philip G. Fox?], "Votes of the Committee," vote summary, n.d., UHP.

[48]UW Faculty Minutes, April 21, 1933; *Capital Times*, April 22, 1933.

[49]BOR Executive Committee Minutes, April 27, 1933, UA. By taking the action in a

After meeting with Professor Kiekhofer and Engineering Dean Turneaure representing the club house association the following day, the regent Executive Committee authorized the University's acceptance of the club house property on April 29 so as to avoid the 1933 Madison property tax assessment due to be entered on May 1. The regents drove a hard bargain, however. Almost certainly at the prompting of Regent Harold Wilkie in whose law office the meeting was held, they stipulated that the club's second mortgage bondholders—most of them senior faculty members or faculty relatives—must agree to accept fifty cents on the dollar for the $46,000 face value of their bonds before the University could accept the property.[50] Over the next two months the bondholders tendered their bonds for payment under this requirement. At the same time the investment board agreed to increase its first mortgage to $140,000 at 4½ percent interest in order to pay off the second mortgage bondholders and provide funds for a tunnel to connect the club house with the UW utility system.[51]

Lorenz as Seen by Max Otto

The next step was to draw up plans for the reorganized club, a task closed meeting the regents were probably reflecting some sensitivity to public criticism of the inconsistency of their cutting the University budget and at the same time taking over the "mismanaged" University Club. See "A Taxpayer," letter, *Capital Times*, April 11, 1933.

[50]Hastings to J.D. Phillips, April 24, 1933; Hastings to Frank, April 29, 1933; Second Mortgage bondholders transfer form, April, 1933; UW Faculty Minutes, May 1, 1933, UHP; BOR Executive Committee Minutes, April 28, 1933; *Capital Times*, April 25, 26, 27, 28, and 30, 1933. The bondholders had little choice; with the club house association in default on its first mortgage, if the club went bankrupt the second mortgage bonds would very likely be worthless.

[51]George Wagner to M.E. McCaffrey, June 14, 1933, BOR Papers, 1/1/3, box 46, UA; Hastings to Frank, April 29, June 2, 1933; University Club House Association loan amortization schedule, April 28, 1933; Wagner to second mortgage bondholders, form letter, May 22, 1933; Alfred W. Peterson to Albert Trathem, June 17, 1933; McCaffrey to Wagner, C.R. Acley, State Annuity and Investment Board, and University Club Secretary, July 19, 1933; "Agreement between the State Annuity and Investment Board and the University Club House Association," July 29, 1941, UHP; McCaffrey to Phillips, July 10, 1933; Peterson to McCaffrey, July 12, 1933, and reply same date, Business Administration Papers, 24/1/1, box 103, UA.

President Frank entrusted to a committee chaired by Dr. William F. Lorenz, the well-known chairman of neuropsychiatry in the Medical School and a member of the house committee of the old club. At the same time interested faculty launched an intensive and successful drive for new members for the reorganized club, which the Lorenz committee decided should continue to bear the name of the University Club. The gratifying growth in membership laid to rest at least for the time being fears the provision for obligatory faculty membership might have to be invoked. To meet the fiscal concerns of the regents, the Lorenz committee established a three-member Board of Financial Control, with representatives of the regents, the University administration, and the club to monitor its financial condition.

In recognition of the broader base of the reorganized club, the Lorenz committee promptly held an election to add six new members representing all faculty ranks to the club's current board of directors. Only one of the two women nominated, Blanche Trilling, the chairman of women's physical education, was elected, so thereafter for a number of years the club used paired nominees on its ballot to assure the election of at least one woman director. In the next regular election in the fall of 1933 Helen White joined Trilling on the board and remained an influential leader for a number of years thereafter, eventually serving as the club's first woman president in 1941.[52] One of the first actions of the new board, no doubt reflecting its broader membership and constituency as well as its fiscal concerns, was to approve renting accommodations to married couples during the summer.[53] Another effort to attract women members was the introduction of weekly women's teas begin-

---

[52]University Club Board Minutes, May 8 and 17, 1933; W.F. Lorenz, memo and ballot, May 9, 1933, UHP. For the first regular election of directors after the reorganization President Hastings gave some explicit suggestions to the nominating committee:

It would seem wise to have some of the present Directors of the Club retained in order that there may be a certain degree of continuity in the management of the organization. It might be that some of the old members could be nominated for a one year period; the new members for the two and three year periods. The present organization is one which includes both the men and women of the faculty. It is believed that the nominations should be so arranged as to assure the election of at least one woman and possibly two. There would seem to be no question but that the role which the women members of the Board of Directors can play would be a very important one, especially in increasing the attractiveness of the Club to the women, and, undoubtedly, to the men.

Hastings to the Committee on Nominations, September 25, 1933, UHP.
[53]University Club Board Minutes, June 9, 1933.

ning in the fall of 1933.[54]

The following year the club's directors proposed that the regents acquire the Phi Kappa Psi fraternity house at 811 State Street immediately adjacent to the University Club property. The fraternity had collapsed under the depression and was in default on its mortgage. The club's proposal called for the University to borrow $75,000 over fifty years to acquire the property, including $10,000 for remodeling to include accommodations for women members of the University Club as well as a home for the AAUW's College Club. The scheme, which the directors noted was only "a basis for negotiations," also called for the University to pay an annual rental of at least $4,000 "for facilities used by the University in the combined University Club houses."[55] From the club's standpoint the proposal made a good deal of sense, for it would solve the problem of providing comparable facilities for women members, though whether the regents could be persuaded as landlords to pay rent to the club was at best a tenuous assumption. They were in any event skeptical of the club's ability to take on an additional financial burden and gave no serious consideration to the proposal at this time.

In the extremely depressed real estate market of the mid-thirties the Phi Psi property remained available, with its mortgage holder, the Guardian Life Insurance Company, eager to unload this rather large white elephant at a sacrifice price. In the fall of 1936 the club decided to try again to acquire the property in order to expand the club's facilities and provide living accommodations for women members and graduate students. A committee consisting of Oliver Rundell, Helen White, and Charlotte Wood was charged with developing a plan for the property's acquisition and use.[56] The confusion and administrative uncertainties following the firing of President Frank shortly thereafter held up further consideration of the scheme until the fall of 1937, when club President Ira Baldwin reopened the matter with the club directors and the new Dykstra administration. This time there was more urgency because of the reported intention of Guardian Life to remodel the building for its corporate headquarters. Hoping to forestall this development, early in January the club's board urged the regents to acquire the property and pledged its cooperation to that end. The regents were less persuaded of the need to expand the facilities of the University Club,

[54]Ibid., October 27, November 17, December 15, 1933.
[55]Ibid., April 20, May 18, 1934.
[56]Ibid., November 19, December 18, 1936.

however, than to head off a business development in prime campus expansion space. They consequently authorized the purchase of the Phi Psi property by their Wisconsin University Building Corporation for $53,000, but decided to use the building to house the Wisconsin Library School which the state government had proposed putting under the University's management. Thus ended the dream of a women's branch of the University Club, never a realistic possibility in these depression years.[57]

One reason for the regents' lack of enthusiasm for underwriting an expansion of the club was no doubt their awareness of its continuing shaky financial condition. While the problems were never so serious nor protracted as to require invoking the obligatory membership provision agreed to by the faculty in the reorganization of 1933, throughout the thirties the University Club struggled to operate in the black. In May of 1935 the club's directors decided they would have to defer the next mortgage payment to the state investment board and make only partial payments to the club's other creditors, including the University.[58] Shocked, President Frank and the University business office promptly intervened, insisting that the schedule of mortgage payments be maintained and installing a business manager, Edward A. Thomas, who was charged with the responsibility for managing the club on a more business-like basis.[59] With Thomas scrutinizing expenditures and budgeting more tightly, the club's financial health gradually improved. As funds became available one of his first steps was to undertake needed repairs to the club house and to upgrade its maintenance. A persistent problem was collecting the past-due accounts of members, especially the residents, and the board regularly wrestled with the problem of how Thomas should deal with tardy colleagues. Eventually the board authorized such drastic steps as the posting of names and amounts owed prominently in the club lobby, notifying the University administration of delinquent staff members, evictions, and turning long-overdue accounts

---

[57]Ibid., October 29, 1937, January 7 and 10, February 25, 1938; I.L. Baldwin to C.A. Dykstra, January 11, 1938, UHP; BOR Minutes, October 30, 1937, January 19, March 9, 1938.

[58]University Club Board Minutes, May 27, 1935.

[59]Ibid., June 13, 1935. At least one of the club directors, Philip G. Fox, favored an assessment on the membership over surrendering operational control to a University-designated manager, but the majority of the board did not feel there was enough time to implement an assessment. In the end the board decided to hire Thomas as club manager on a 6-2 vote, with Fox and Dr. William F. Lorenz in opposition.

over to a collection agency. A more positive inducement was the board's 1935 decision to develop a grill room in the basement and to sell beer there. The latter turned out to be more an expression of intent than a reality, however, for as late as 1941 the directors were still seeking without success to get regent permission for a license to serve beer and light wines in the club dining rooms.[60]

As for the University as a whole, the advent of the Second World War brought significant changes in the University Club's operation. After the United States entered the conflict a growing number of members departed for civilian or military war service, leaving the board to wrestle with increasingly complex budgetary, membership, staffing, and rationing problems. Club Manager Thomas, who had done so much to keep the club functioning effectively since 1935, himself left with a Navy commission in mid-1943. During his absence the board assigned the management of the club to a triumvirate of women staff members.[61] One of the first signs of the changed atmosphere was the board's decision immediately following the Pearl Harbor attack to purchase a globe for the club library. Soon thereafter the directors decided to extend club membership to any eligible members of the armed forces assigned to Wisconsin at the special rate of $2.00 a month, later dropped to $1.50.[62] Staffing was difficult during the war, leading the club to make greater use of women student help and to offer full-time employment to Japanese-Americans relocated from west coast internment camps.[63]

In the spring of 1943 the board decided to make some of its dormitory rooms available to help house the growing number of military trainees on campus. This patriotic gesture may have been interpreted more broadly than intended, for a month later the University requested the entire club dormitory for use by soldiers assigned to the University under the new Army Specialized Training Program. Club President Asher Hobson informed the members:

> The Club is now in the Army. At least its dormitories are. The Army has made no payments for these facilities. We do not know *when* the Army will

---

[60]See University Club Board Minutes, July 30, December 6, 1935, January 24, 1936, March 29, 1937, March 30, 1938, January 27, June 2, October 26, November 23, 1939, January 19, March 29, May 3, October 4, 1940, May 16, June 20, September 27, 1941, January 16, March 27, April 23, 1942; Edward A. Thomas to Lorenz, July 30, 1935, ibid.

[61]University Club Board Minutes, May 4 and 10, 1943; "Report of the Special Committee on University Club Management," May 7, 1943, UHP.

[62]University Club Board Minutes, March 27, October 16, 1942.

[63]Ibid., May 22, 1942, March 26, 1943.

pay. We do not know *what* the Army will pay. One is forced to conclude that the Club's financial situation is not altogether clear. It is hoped that we will soon know the when and the what. The suspense is rather trying but the officers and directors refuse to become pessimistic.[64]

The ASTP occupation lasted about a year, for which the federal government eventually paid the University a rental of less than half of the average annual income from the dormitory during the past three years. The club directors considered this unfair, arguing that while the club had no wish to profit from its patriotism, neither did its members feel they could afford to subsidize the Army. The regents agreed and directed the University comptroller to increase the settlement by about $5,000, "on a basis that will leave the University Club in the same financial position it was when the University took over the Club dormitory," using for this purpose "funds received from the government for other services."[65]

The Burke Affair

The University Club managed to survive the trials of the great depression and a variety of wartime dislocations, but another event in the fall of 1944 shook the club to its foundations and threatened its very existence. It began innocuously enough on July 10 with a letter from one Arthur E. Burke to the club management explaining that he was a graduate student in English language and literature who planned to return to the University in the fall to complete his Ph.D. residency requirements. He asked to rent "a single room, not too expensive."[66] Inasmuch as the Army had by this time largely vacated the club dormitory, its manager, Mildred Lindquist, routinely responded notifying Burke that the club accepted him as a resident to share a double room. Whether Miss Lindquist took any note of Burke's Howard University address is unclear, but in any event she knew the club's constitution and by-laws made no mention of any racial exclusionary policy and was

---

[64]Ibid., April 23, May 4 and 10, October 22, 1943; University Club Minutes of membership meeting, May 14, 1943; Asher Hobson, "Finances," *University Club News*, 6 (October 22, 1943), 2, UHP. Emphasis in original.

[65]BOR Minutes, May 26, 1944, UA; *University Club News*, 7 (June 1, 1944), 1. In 1942 the regents also voted to provide $1,500 for needed maintenance of the club house. BOR Minutes, March 14, May 30, 1942.

[66]Arthur E. Burke to the Management of the University Club, July 10, 1944, UHP.

aware that it had entertained Negro guests in the past. When Burke, to whom the University had given an Adams fellowship, arrived in Madison on September 21 he was assigned to Room 324, after which the desk clerk notified the house chairman, State Geologist Ernest F. Bean, that the club now had a black resident. Professor Bean called on Burke the next day and informed him the club did not accept Negro residents. He offered to help Burke get accommodations at the nearby University YMCA and take care of the transfer of his luggage. He also told him the club would not charge him for his brief occupancy, an offer Burke politely declined as both "an affront" and "a violation of my integrity to accept."[67]

That might have been the end of the matter had not Burke enrolled in Professor Merle Curti's course in recent American history. After the first class meeting Curti casually asked Burke how he was getting on and was shocked to hear about his housing misadventure. Curti assured him there were many in the club who would disapprove of any such discriminatory policy, especially during a war presumably being fought against racism. He then mobilized a number of his liberal friends in the club—among them former presidents Helen White and Paul Clark, Ray Agard, Elizabeth Brandeis, Harry Glicksman, and Elmer Sevringhaus— to press for a reversal of the House Committee's policy. When neither President Hobson nor the directors showed any disposition to act, Curti, White, and several others confronted the board at its next monthly luncheon meeting on October 17. Curti's recollection of the encounter three decades later recaptured some of its drama:

> I'll never forget Miss White. She was just wonderful. She said, "Gentlemen"—they were all men, of course—"there was a time in this University Club when women weren't admitted into it at all. But," she said, "you know, you really couldn't keep us out. We're here. And you might as well make up your mind to it. Negroes are going to be here and why don't you just accept the fact gracefully." Well, this was terrific. She said it in her sweet and charming way, and finally it was agreed that a referendum of the membership could be held and that then the management would abide by the majority vote.[68]

---

[67]Burke to Ernest F. Bean, September 24, 1944; Burke to Miss Lindquist, n.d., ibid.; Mildred Lindquist, oral history interview. It later developed that at least one other Negro student had roomed at the club in the past without incident; hence the decision to evict Burke was probably made ad hoc by House Committee Chairman Bean, perhaps in consultation with President Hobson.

[68]Merle Curti, oral history interview, 1973, UA.

Contrary to Curti's recollection, the board did not yield gracefully at this meeting, agreeing only to consider the issue at its next meeting. Three days later it voted inconclusively on a motion to ratify the informal decision of the previous month not to admit Burke to club membership. The directors approved this motion at still another special board meeting the following day, then adopted one to refer the question of Negro membership in the club to the membership at large.[69]

As the Burke affair gradually became known on campus, a number of other club members expressed their dismay to the officers and directors. Professor Lelia Bascom, one of the more active women members and a distant relative of the former University president, told Hobson that race prejudice not only destroyed "that fairness for which we say we are fighting" but was all the more disquieting "at a university known for its liberality."[70] Farrington Daniels, a chemistry professor on wartime service with the top secret atomic bomb project at the University of Chicago, echoed this sentiment, urging the directors "to prevent accentuation of the race problem." "I realize that accepting a person into a club is more complicated than renting him a room," he wrote Hobson, "but I do feel strongly that our faculty club in a liberal university must not draw a color line."[71] Assistant Professor John Paul Heironimus of the classics department wrote on behalf of the Madison meeting of the Society of Friends:

> We deplore this deviation from the principle of equal treatment of all races, and find it the more distressing because of the University Club's previous record of enlightenment in its policy of receiving guests without discrimination as to color and creed. The shifts of population caused by the war have brought racial prejudice into many regions where it was not found before. This makes it all the more important that responsible elements of the community such as are represented in the University Club should hold fast to the principles of equality and justice which have brought honorable distinction to the University and the state in the past.[72]

The University Club directors' lengthy debate over a referendum on the question of Negro membership brought the controversy into the open, leading the two Madison newspapers belatedly to publicize the story of Burke's eviction. This in turn triggered shocked protests from

[69]University Club Board Minutes, October 17, 20, and 21, 1944.
[70]Lelia Bascom to Hobson, October 11, 1944, UHP.
[71]Farrington Daniels to Hobson, October 11, 1944, ibid.
[72]J.P. Heironimus to Hobson, October 12, 1944, ibid.

the *Daily Cardinal* and a number of liberal student organizations, which demanded that the faculty show enlightened leadership for basic human rights.[73] The student reaction was predictable, because for more than a decade activist student groups, including the *Cardinal*, had consistently shown more concern about housing discrimination in the city than had the faculty or the University administration. As early as 1940 the Student Board, the official representative of the student body, had established a standing committee on student housing after the well-publicized eviction of a Negro woman graduate student from a State Street rooming house.[74] UW students had reacted indignantly to the decision by the Daughters of the American Revolution in 1939 not to allow the famous Negro contralto Marian Anderson to sing in their Independence Hall in Washington, a rebuff that drew nationwide protests. Anderson was well-known on campus, having performed the previous year in the Union Concert Series. After the United States entered the war student leaders consistently championed ideals of equality of treatment and opportunity,

Octopus' Protest

calling for an end to racial segregation in the armed forces and the acceptance of Japanese-American students relocated from west coast internment camps.[75] The *Cardinal* launched a campaign to address the housing discrimination faced by black and Jewish students when thousands of workers building the Badger Ordnance plant at Baraboo flooded the Madison housing market in 1942. The paper also condemned the de facto racial discrimination practiced by the Medical School, which discouraged Negro students from going beyond the first two years of

---

[73]*Capital Times*, October 22, 23, 24, 25, 26, and 28, 1944; *Daily Cardinal*, October 24, 25, 26, and 27, 1944; UW Chapter, United States Student Assembly, "Statement of Housing," October 18, 1944; Negro Cultural Foundation to the Directorate and members of the University Club, October 20, 1944; "Negro Student Ouster from University Club," USSA leaflet, n.d.; Ruby K. Kubola, for the residents of Groves Women's Co-operative House, to University Club, October 23, 1944; University Religious Council to University Club, October 24, 1944, UHP.

[74]*Daily Cardinal*, April 25 and 27, May 1, 1940.

[75]Ibid., April 22, May 13 and 20, November 8, 1942.

medical training in Madison because of the difficulty of finding clinical experience for them during the final two years.[76] In the spring of 1943, after a year-long study by its housing committee, the Student Board unanimously adopted a fifty-five-page report outlining and condemning racial and religious bias in student housing.[77]

Burke's shabby treatment by a quasi-official University organization the next year understandably galvanized student support. "UNIVERSITY CLUB REFUSES ROOM TO NEGRO/THREAT TO DEMOCRATIC INSTITUTIONS MUST BE CRUSHED," headlined the *Cardinal* in a lead editorial on October 24:

> ...it is not uneducated, bigoted, or misguided Southerners throwing up their ideals of white supremacy at any move to enlighten or free Negroes from discrimination who are involved. No, some of our own professors, whose words we are to accept as gospel, who are educating us to take our place in this democracy of ours—it is they who now attempt to prevent a Negro from making his home in Madison to continue his advanced education at our university.

To emphasize its disapproval of the University Club's practice, the student directorate of the Memorial Union pointedly declared a non-discrimination policy for its sleeping rooms and other facilities.[78]

Much of the student protest activity was directed at influencing the vote of University Club members in the referendum on Negro membership. So, too, were the efforts of Professor Curti and his fellow faculty dissidents, who addressed an open letter to the membership reminding them of their club's public character in a University with a long-estab-

---

[76]For the concern about housing see ibid., February 26, March 5, 13, 19, 20, and 31, April 9, 11, 14, and 22, May 8 and 12, September 17, 22, 23, 24, 25, 26, and 29, October 1, 2, 8, 14, and 16, 1944; *Capital Times*, September 23, 24, and 25, 1942. The concern about Medical School discrimination see *Capital Times*, January 13 and 15, 1943, April 9 and 16, 1944; *Daily Cardinal*, January 15 and 16, February 12 and 20, 1943.

[77]*Capital Times*, March 23, May 19, 1943; *Daily Cardinal*, March 23, 24, and 25, April 9, 13, 14, 21, 22, 23, and 30, May 4, 6, and 7, 1943. Although President Dykstra publicly praised the zeal and idealism of the students, privately he criticized the inaccuracies and loose generalizations of the report and its authors' failure to consult University administrators knowledgeable about student housing matters. As a result the University's student housing committee decided to take no action on the Student Board report, much to the unhappiness of student activists. See Sub-Committee on Student Living Conditions and Hygiene Minutes, May 17, 1943, and draft response to the student report, May 22, 1943; "Housing Report Rejected," flier, n.d., Dykstra Presidential Papers, 4/15/1, box 105, UA.

[78]*Daily Cardinal*, October 27, 1944.

lished tradition of liberalism and democratic rights.[79]   Not all of the faculty agreed with the Curti group, of course.   Professor Joel Stebbins, the University astronomer and a recent president of the club, made clear to the directors his concern that some members were trying to impose their social values on the club through the housing issue, since membership for housing purposes included eligibility for all club facilities and activities.   "A group of colored students and their guests could easily grow to reserve several tables at one of our club dinners," he warned, "with subsequent intermingling with other members and their guests during the evening." He doubted that a majority of the club members "would care to insist upon such a situation."[80]   Curti has recalled how his department chairman, the formidable Paul Knaplund, angrily accused him of trying to destroy the University Club, because no matter how the referendum came out Knaplund expected some members to resign.[81]

On October 28 the club announced that a majority of the members voting in the referendum had declared their support for the admission of Negroes.[82]   The directors decided to leave it up to the three tellers—Professors Clark, Holt, and Rundell—whether to release the breakdown of the vote. They chose not to, no doubt because the referendum revealed a significant split in the membership.   The vote was 150 in favor and 98 against, or a margin of only 60 percent in favor of integration, and with the resident and non-resident members voting in about the same proportions.   Of the fifty residents of the club house, nineteen objected to extending membership (and resident privileges) to blacks.[83] Burke promptly wrote Hobson inquiring about the status of his room

---

[79]Curti and others to the Members of the University Club, October 23, 1944, UHP. The other signatories were: Walter R. Agard, Lelia Bascom, Carl M. Bögholt, Elizabeth Brandeis, Paul F. Clark, L.E. Drake, A.C. Garnett, John M. Gaus, Harry Glicksman, Harold Groves, Norris F. Hall, Max Otto, Selig Perlman, Robert C. Pooley, Robert L. Reynolds, C.H. Ruedisili, Leonard A. Salter, Jr., E.L. Sevringhaus, Ruth Wallerstein, and Helen C. White. Although the open letter was labeled "Confidential," it was quickly reproduced and featured in the local press. *Capital Times*, October 26, 1944; *Daily Cardinal*, October 27, 1944.

[80]Joel Stebbins to the President and Directors of the University Club, October 19, 1944, UHP. See also H. Johnson to Hobson, October 25, 1944, ibid. For a similar point of view, see an anonymous letter to the editor, *Capital Times*, October 31, 1944.

[81]Curti, oral history interview, and conversation with the authors, 1991. Curti believes that Knaplund, a Norwegian immigrant and long-time club member who had lived there until his marriage in 1927, was motivated more by his concern for the preservation of the club than by racial prejudice.

[82]*Capital Times*, October 29, 1944; *Daily Cardinal*, October 31, 1944.

[83]Rundell, Holt, and Clark to the President and Board of Directors, October 31, 1944; Rundell to Hobson, November 4, 1944, UHP.

reservation and membership, and after consideration of what Hobson called this "demand," the board instructed Secretary Leslie Holt to send Burke an application form, which he promptly submitted. On November 24, as an item of business separate from other routine membership actions, the directors voted to accept Burke as a member and to offer him a room the following month. They also decided in the future to make clear to all applicants for rooms that their requests would need the approval of the board and that all resident graduate student members must have their membership in the club formally renewed by the board each September.[84] The club might be integrated, but its leaders were determined that it should not be regarded as just another campus dormitory.

The Burke affair was significant as a turning point not only in the history of the University Club but of the University as well. The officers and some of the long-time members of the club, well aware of its precarious financial condition, saw the issue primarily as a threat to the club's continued existence. They consequently failed to provide moral leadership, justifying their timidity and in some cases their racial prejudice in terms of preserving the club and its prerogatives as a private membership organization. Burke's supporters, led by Professors Curti, White, and Clark, felt so strongly about the immorality of racial discrimination at the University that after being rebuffed by the directors they were willing to force the divisive question to a vote by the club's membership, even if the result was the break-up of the organization. Curti was perhaps viewed by some as an upstart troublemaker inasmuch as he had been at the University only two years, but most of his associates in the Burke protest were long-time members of the UW faculty and of the club. In fact, two of them—Helen White and Paul Clark—had recently served as club presidents, and two others—Max Otto and Elmer Sevringhaus—were former club directors. Thus although they were newcomers to the campus Burke and Curti were catalysts for a broad reaffirmation of old Wisconsin values of equal treatment and fair play. Fred Harvey Harrington, who in the 1960s would serve as president of the University, had just rejoined the UW faculty as a young associate professor of history when the Burke episode

---

[84]Burke to Hobson, October 31, 1944; Hobson to Burke, November 3, 1944; Hobson to Board of Directors [November 3, 1944]; M.L. Holt to Burke, November 8 and 28, 1944; Board of Directors Minutes, November 7 and 24, 1944, ibid.; *Capital Times*, November 2, 1944. It is interesting to note that the normally crusading *Capital Times* made no editorial comment on the Burke affair.

occurred in the fall of 1944. His role in the protest was limited to soliciting affirmative votes in the referendum, but he later remembered the affair as helping to crystalize his determination as president to combat discrimination within and outside of the University.[85]

For many students, too, the Burke affair kindled an interest in civil rights and non-discrimination in housing that remained long after the immediate question of Burke's admission to the club had been settled. Even as University Club members were voting on the issue of Burke's membership, a group of fifteen campus student organizations met to organ-ize the Committee for Democratic Housing, which pledged itself to expose and eliminate housing discrimination in the immediate campus area. The new organization had some difficulty fending off efforts by leftist students to seize control and several of the founding groups withdrew to pursue their efforts alone.[86] But the student proponents of fair housing practices continued thereafter through rallies, speeches, and housing surveys to educate the University and Madison communities to the existence of racial and religious intolerance in their midst.[87] The Burke affair was thus an important element of the growing civil rights movement that would involve so many UW students during the next two decades.

◇   ◇   ◇

For students and faculty alike the goal and very often the reality in these years was a close-knit but open University community. A dedicated teacher-scholar, mathematics professor and L&S Dean Mark

---

[85]Fred Harrington to John W. Jenkins, November 3, 1984, UHP. As UW president, Harrington later resigned from the Madison Club when it blackballed a prominent Jewish attorney and University alumnus for membership. He also refused to attend meetings of higher education associations in the Chicago and New York University Clubs because of their ban on blacks or Jews as members and declined to attend UW alumni meetings around the country if they were held in restricted facilities.

[86]See especially *Wisconsin State Journal*, October 26, 1944; *Daily Cardinal*, October 26, November 9, 10, 14, 28, 29, and 30, 1944. The domineering tactics of the Wisconsin Liberals Association, the campus chapter of the Communist-front American Youth for Democracy, led several groups, including the only black student organization, to withdraw from the CDH in its first month. Arthur Burke himself deplored the disruptive behavior and hidden agenda of the WLA-AYD activists. "Honest facing of all issues, more than anything else," he warned, "is the crying need." Burke, letter to the editor, *Daily Cardinal*, December 5, 1944.

[87]See *Daily Cardinal*, December 6 and 8, 1944, March 30, May 1, 3, 4, 8, and 10, 1945; *The New Guard* (journal of the UW chapter of the United States Student Assembly [November, 1944]), UHP.

Ingraham spelled out at the end of his long career the close relationship between student and professor in a community of scholars that defined itself as an extension of Wisconsin democracy:

> I am glad the University of Wisconsin has many brilliant students, but I am also glad it is not composed only of brilliant students. It must be very frustrating for a superior mind to meet nothing but outstanding minds. The birthright of excellence is to excel, not to be humiliated....It is fun to spark brilliance and see it soar out of sight. It is also fun to develop breadth and depth in the minds of those who are called "solid citizens."

Above all, Ingraham valued the University's willingness for its faculty to do more than engage in teaching and research—to be dilettantes part of the time—and to structure their community in such a way as to facilitate the sharing of ideas and learning:

> Frankly, I could not and would not drive myself to let Gibbon and *Alice in Wonderland* gather dust while I spent all my evenings exploring the gizzard of a matrix, although truly a beautiful bit of anatomy. Once I symbolized a decision to remain at Wisconsin by the realization that if I left and if I wanted to know some fact concerning the relation between Dante and Giotto, I would have to travel hundreds of miles for an answer, while here the answer was right at the same luncheon table with me at the Club. The freely shared wealth of knowledge and thought at Wisconsin is taken for granted.[88]

We will examine the student component of this remarkable community next.

---

[88]Ingraham, *From a Wisconsin Soapbox*, pp. 190, 191.

10.

In Loco Parentis

Like the faculty, UW students in the inter-war years also constituted a cohesive academic community with a high degree of unity and esprit. To be sure, they had their own distinct identities and goals as individuals and as members of a multitude of often competing student organizations and living groups. But they also possessed an underlying devotion to their University that later generations of students, confronting a much larger and more impersonal institution, would probably consider quaint and naive. This loyalty expressed itself in many ways: pride in faculty and student achievements, a decided preference for campus authority over that of the Madison politicians and police, a multitude of all-campus events and activities, enthusiastic support for even mediocre Badger athletic teams, student-organized truth squads to counter criticism of the University and to promote its support around the state, and even annual student work days to beautify the campus. Another indication was the strikingly high degree of student participation in the campaign to raise funds to build the Memorial Union, itself a continuing monument to responsible student involvement in institutional governance. The University, in turn, took an increasingly parental interest in all aspects of student life, developing an array of supervisory and support services far more comprehensive and professional than those available to earlier generations of UW students.

The Student Body, 1925-45

Two external events had a profound impact on UW students during these years—the great depression of the 1930s and the Second World

551

War. Each altered the size and mix of the student body, changed traditional patterns of faculty staffing and instruction, and in the process influenced curricular and extracurricular activities. Not since the dark days of the Civil War had the University been so profoundly shaped by external forces. The flux in campus life lasted for nearly two decades until the early 1950s, when more traditional academic conditions finally returned.

University enrollments rose steadily in the 1920s. The student body grew from a little over 7,000 in 1920 (a figure itself 40 percent higher than the pre-World War I peak of 5,000 in 1916) to more than 9,400 in 1929. The number of undergraduates increased 26 percent during the years 1920-29. Total University enrollment increased even more—35 percent—as the number of graduate and advanced professional students in law and medicine more than doubled in the decade. The number and proportion of women students also grew during these years and was especially noticeable at the undergraduate level, where by the late twenties women constituted more than 40 percent of the total student body. On the other hand, the number of non-resident students—greater at Wisconsin than in most state universities—grew at about the same rate as the student body as a whole, amounting to about 28 percent of the undergraduate and 45 percent of the graduate enrollment in 1929.[1] It was no wonder University authorities in the 1920s placed such emphasis on increasing the University's operating budget and expanding its physical plant to handle this seemingly inexorable growth.

The virtual collapse of the American economy following the stock market crash in late 1929 quickly reversed this trend, especially at the undergraduate level. At this time Wisconsin residents paid no tuition (non-resident tuition was $100 a semester), but all students were charged a fee of $21.50 per semester and had to meet expenses for board, room, books, and incidentals, which were estimated to average $600 a year in 1933. Even though these latter costs declined by 10-20 percent in the early years of the depression, the expense was more than many students and their families could afford in the general hard times.[2]

---

[1] L. Joseph Lins, "Fact Book for History of Madison Campus," notebook, 1983, UHP.

[2] *General Announcement of Courses, 1933-34 (Catalog 1932-33)*, Bulletin of the University of Wisconsin, Serial No. 1880, General Series No. 1664, July, 1933, pp. 15-8. The semester fee was raised 28 percent to $27.50 in 1934 to help offset the drastic reduction in state support for the University's operating budget. Ibid., *1934-35 (Catalog 1933-34)*, Bulletin of the University of Wisconsin, Series 1972, General Series No. 1756, May, 1934, p. 15.

Consequently, undergraduate enrollment dropped by 26 percent between 1929 and 1933. The overall enrollment decline was somewhat less drastic—22 percent—because enrollments in the Graduate, Law, and Medical schools grew in the early years of the depression before declining later in the thirties. For the more advanced students, the hope of increasing one's marketability in the shrinking job market evidently had the effect of keeping students enrolled as long as they could manage the costs. Women were affected disproportionately more by the depression, as many hard-pressed families chose to educate sons over daughters. The women's share of total enrollment fell from 37 percent in 1929 to 31 percent a decade later; at the undergraduate level the proportional decline was from 40 percent to 34 percent. The group most drastically affected by the depression was that from out-of-state. These students faced both a tuition charge and often higher living expenses because Wisconsin residents had priority for the limited number of University dormitory rooms. Non-resident enrollment fell by more than half between 1929 and 1934. From 32 percent of the total enrollment in 1929 the proportion of out-of-state students declined to only 16 percent of the campus total in 1935. Not since 1905 had the proportion of non-

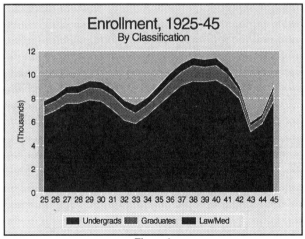

Figure 1

resident students been as low. The depression had an equally devastating effect on the smaller number of foreign students attending the University; their ranks declined by 60 percent between 1930 and 1935.

The University continued to deserve its reputation for a highly diverse student body, attracting students from all forty-eight states and more than a score of foreign countries throughout the depression, but their diminished numbers meant it was a somewhat more provincial institution during these years.[3]

World War II had an even greater effect on student demographics. After falling to a low of 7,400 in 1933-34, enrollment rose again, surpassing its 1929 high in 1936 and reaching 11,400 in 1940. During the war years it fell precipitously by more than half by 1943-44 or about the level at the time of the First World War. Although enrollment then began to rise again with the early return of a few veterans, during the last year of the war the University had 15 percent fewer students than at the start of our period in 1925. The number of graduate and advanced professional students decreased to an even greater extent than the undergraduates. The non-resident enrollment total was not much affected by the war owing to a large increase in women non-residents. In 1943-44, the number of non-resident students was slightly over 2,000 or almost identical to the total in 1939-40, but the proportion of non-residents in the student body jumped from 18 to 34 percent during these years, reflecting the sharp drop in Wisconsin male students.

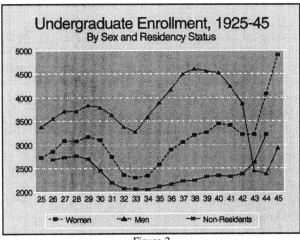

Figure 2

---

[3]Lins, "Fact Book"; Curtis Merriman, "Registrar's Report to the President of the University," November, 1942, General Presidential Papers, 4/0/2, box 11, UA.

Whether through enlistment or the draft, men abandoned their studies for wartime service in overwhelming numbers. Their ranks dropped more than threefold from about 7,700 in 1940 to less than 2,300 in 1944 and some of these were younger men awaiting their draft calls. In contrast, the number of women students increased sharply, from about 2,700 in 1940 to approximately 4,400 in 1944. For the first time in the University's history women made up more than half of the regular student body—58 percent of the total in 1943 and 66 percent in 1944.[4] If UW coeds of these years remember the University as less of a nunnery than these figures suggest, it is only because of the presence of a considerable number of campus-based military training programs during the war. Many of these uniformed students were not in regular courses or degree-programs, however, and most marched to and from their own specialized classes in a body, mingling with the regular UW students only during their limited free time. Throughout the entire period the University remained a largely undergraduate institution, with graduate students on average comprising only about 10 percent of the enrollment and students seeking advanced professional degrees in fields such as law and medicine only 5-6 percent. Figures 1 and 2 provide a graphic portrayal of the dramatic changes in enrollment patterns over the two decades.

Although the University of Wisconsin was one of the elite public institutions, its students in these years hardly came from elite backgrounds. Many of them were the first in their families to attend college and some were the children of immigrants. Even before the great depression devastated student finances, UW administrators estimated that more than a third of the student body was wholly or partially self-supporting. During the fall semester of 1927, a year of general prosperity, fifteen hundred students sought part-time jobs through the University's Student Employment Office.[5] University press releases regularly emphasized the diversity of the student body, probably at least partially to counter any suspicion the campus chiefly served the wealthy and powerful. The *Press Bulletin* reported in late 1929, for example, that "one out of each 10 students in the freshman class...comes from the farm, one out of each four comes from the home of a tradesman, and one out of seven is the child of a worker in manufacturing or mechani-

---

[4]Lins, "Fact Book."

[5]"Army of Students Seek Work," *WAM*, 29 (January, 1928), 126. See also "Students Labor at Odd Tasks," *WAM*, 30 (October, 1928), 13.

cal industries." In fact, the data showed there were "more children of carpenters, of grocers, of mechanics than of bankers, more children of unskilled laborers than of officials of manufacturing and mechanical industries, more children of farmers than of a combined total of bakers and brokers, physicians and surgeons, lawyers, and manufacturers."[6] In short, though there might be a substantial representation from the middle class, for the most part these were not the sons and daughters of the aristocracy.

Nor was the University elite in its admission requirements. Throughout this period it was essentially an open admissions institution, which operated under the democratic philosophy that all qualified and ambitious young people, no matter how humble their origins, ought to have an opportunity to test their competence and stretch their minds at the state's major center of higher learning. Accordingly, the University welcomed any graduate of an accredited secondary school who had taken at least ten specified units of college preparatory work (reduced to nine in 1943) and who was recommended by his or her high school principal. In 1942 the registrar estimated that 90 percent of the freshman class was admitted simply by certificate of high school graduation. This did not mean that once admitted a student was assured of a degree, however; far from it. The University relied on the rigor of its academic work and degree requirements, especially the difficulty of some of its introductory courses, to weed out the laggards, dullards, dilettantes, and hedonists, and to maintain reasonably high academic standards. At the end of the first semester of 1927-28, for example, the University dropped 433 students, or more than 5 percent of the student body (and nearly 11 percent of the freshmen class!). Even so, some faculty members thought the standards should be even tougher; sociology Professor E.A. Ross argued in 1926 that as many as a thousand students deserved to be dropped. The flip side of the open admissions policy was that only about 46 percent of entering freshmen in these years ever received a UW degree.[7]

With the establishment of President Frank's new Bureau of

---

[6]*Press Bulletin*, December 25, 1929. See also ibid., January 16, 1929.

[7]*Daily Cardinal*, March 15, 1928. The University normally did not release exact figures on the number of dropped students, but did so this year because of rumors that the number was unusually large. Campus officials were accordingly careful to stress that the number and percentages were normal. See *Press Bulletin*, March 21, 1928; "U.W. Drops But 443 Students," *WAM*, 29 (April, 1928), 245; Merriman, "Registrar's Report." For the Ross comment see *Capital Times*, February 9, 1926; *Daily Cardinal*, February 10, 1926.

Records and Guidance in 1927, the University stepped up its articulation efforts with Wisconsin high schools to improve the academic background and qualifications of entering students. Psychology Professor V.A.C. Henmon, the bureau's research director, helped to develop a scholastic aptitude test and promoted its use throughout the state to assist secondary school teachers and principals in assessing their graduates' likelihood of academic success in Madison. By the end of the 1930s some thirty thousand Wisconsin high school seniors were taking either Henmon's test or the similar American Council Test (ACT) each year. The test scores of entering UW freshmen improved steadily throughout the period, suggesting either the economic hard times of the period made parents less willing to risk the expense of higher education on offspring of marginal academic interest or capability, or more likely the schools were recommending fewer students of questionable ability. Whatever the reason, the rising scores correlated well with the high school performance of the matriculants. In 1933, 22 percent of the entering freshmen came from the top 10 percent of their high school classes. By 1941 the corresponding figure had risen to 27 percent, and the number in the bottom tenth had declined from 2.3 percent to 1.5 percent over the nine-year period.[8]

In spite of the considerable enrollment fluctuations of the depression and war years, the UW student body retained a highly cosmopolitan character. Even in the dark depression year of 1932 the campus was home to students from every state and the District of Columbia and from twenty-seven foreign countries. Neighboring Illinois led the states, and Canada and China the foreign countries, but beginning in the late twenties New York regularly provided the second largest out-of-state contingent, some of whose members were attracted initially by the Experimental College.[9] Indeed, it was often activist students from New York and New Jersey, many of them Jewish with liberal-to-radical political views, who contributed a good deal of the leadership of campus organizations and gave the student body an avant-garde image. In the process they often aroused the concern —frequently veiled, sometimes open—of conservative Wisconsin editors, politicians, clergymen, and parents.

Although Jewish students were represented at the University to a much greater extent than in the population of the state as a whole

---

[8]Merriman, "Registrar's Report."

[9]*Daily Cardinal*, October 9, 1931, September 21, 1932; Merriman, "Registrar's Report."

(where practicing Jews were considerably less than 1 per cent of the total in 1936), they nevertheless constituted a relatively small minority of the student body. In 1928 the University conducted for the first time a census to determine the religious affiliations of its students. Participation was voluntary, but more than two-thirds of the students responded, reporting adherence to thirty-four different religious faiths. Based on these findings the student body was overwhelmingly Christian, with Jews (9 percent) and a tiny handful of Moslems, atheists, and agnostics constituting the remainder. The two largest church groups were Roman Catholic and Lutheran (all synods), each with 16 percent, but other main-line Christian churches were also well-represented: Methodist (15 percent), Congregational (14 percent), Presbyterian (10 percent), Episcopal (7 percent), Baptist (4 percent), and Christian Science (3 percent).[10] Although the University ceased these religious surveys after the next year, there is no reason to think the religious composition of the student body changed significantly over the next decade.

University authorities did not permit sectarian proselytizing on campus and firmly resisted proposals by local clergymen for a department of religion or for courses in theology or religion as such. At the same time, the University supported the religious lives of its students in a number of ways. Many faculty and staff members took an active role in the campus-area churches attended by many students. Other faculty served on the boards of the University YMCA and YWCA, both of which placed a greater emphasis on non-sectarian religious programming at this time than in later years. As a former clergyman, after his arrival in 1925 President Frank enthusiastically embraced the annual all-University religious convocations sponsored by the two campus Y's, virtually turning them into official University functions. For a number of years Frank spoke at these convocations and helped bring major religious leaders to the campus to participate in the week-long events. He likewise gave strong support to the religious emphasis week and religion day programs begun in the early 1930s by the ecumenical University Religious Council. Organized in 1930 as the Inter-Church Council, the group consisted of representatives of the two Y's and the more liberal campus religious groups; its purpose was to

[10]*Press Bulletin*, December 26, 1928, January 15, 1930; *Daily Cardinal*, January 4, 1929, January 15, 1930; *Capital Times*, December 24, 1928; "Take Census of Faiths," *WAM*, 30 (February, 1929), 161.

facilitate all-campus religious services on special occasions like Thanksgiving and Easter and other joint programs. President Frank repeatedly urged students to understand, develop, and test their faiths, and made clear his own belief in a personal god and his commitment to humanistic religious values. Each year the University erected lighted Christmas trees on Bascom Hill and in the dormitories, while groups from the music school regularly performed a well-attended program of Christmas music. Thus while the University itself did not explicitly endorse any particular religion or creed, throughout this period its leaders and staff by their example let students know religion was a valued adjunct to campus life.

While in most respects upholding the separation of church and state as understood at the time, University leaders welcomed and cooperated with the churches established by various denominations in the immediate campus area to serve the student community. The oldest and largest of these was St. Paul's Roman Catholic Chapel, built in 1910 at 723 State Street a block east of the campus. St. Paul's claimed to be the first church of any denomination designed specifically to serve the students of a state university. Its first priest was the outspoken Father Harry C. Hengell, who until his death in 1937 ministered to generations of UW Roman Catholic students and kept a wary eye on what he regarded as the dangerous religious liberalism and skepticism of President Frank and some members of the UW faculty. Just east of St. Paul's was Calvary Lutheran Church, built in 1920 by the Missouri and Wisconsin Evangelical Lutheran Synods to serve primarily the students of these conservative Lutheran churches. Nearby was the Presbyterian Student Center at 731 State Street, established earlier but subsequently housed in a handsome stone edifice dedicated in February, 1933, in a program featuring President Frank as the main speaker. "Pres House" boasted that it was the only regularly constituted all-student-directed church in the United States.

Just west of the engineering campus on the corner of University Avenue and Breese Terrace was the imposing First Congregational Church, which traditionally had a large University component in its membership and whose minister in this period, Rev. Alfred W. Swan, was a popular and outspoken figure in the campus community. In addition to its own student programming, the church had helped to establish a Congregational Student Association in 1906, which operated a student center (known to generations of students as the "Congo") southeast of the campus at 429 North Murray Street. Other campus-area churches in a single block along University Avenue included the University Methodist Church, sponsor and host of the student Wesley Methodist Foundation, the Episcopalian St. Francis House, and Luther Memorial Church (affiliated with the synods comprising the United Lutheran Church in America). From its beginning in 1907 as the first Madison Lutheran church to offer all-English services, Luther Memorial was always closely tied to the University community. It was also more liberal and ecumenical than its campus rival, Calvary Lutheran, and thus more comfortable with its campus associations. In 1923 Luther Memorial moved from a site at Lake and University to its large new church building at 1021 University Avenue between St. Francis House and University Methodist Church.[11] Baptist students were served by the Wayland Baptist Student Center, located in these years at 429 North Park Street. In 1924 the Hillel Foundation of B'nai B'rith established a center for Jewish students at 508 State Street, directed at first by Rabbi Sol Landman and subsequently during most of the period by Rabbi Max Kadushin.

Church Attendance in 1925

By the start of our period in 1925, then, the campus was ringed by a variety of churches and religious centers intended primarily to serve the University community and representing the major faiths reflected in the student body. The importance of the campus religious centers in the extracurricular lives of UW students in these years should

---

[11]Luther Memorial fell on hard times during the depression. Unable to meet its debt service, the congregation declared bankruptcy and the property was sold by court order in 1937. The only interested buyer was the Board of American Missions of the United Lutheran Church, which transferred the property back to the congregation under a more favorable $50,000 mortgage. In 1944 the church helped to purchase a house at 228 Langdon Street as a general Lutheran Student Association center, which was eventually relocated to the Luther Memorial site on University Avenue in the 1960s.

not be underestimated. As the religious surveys of 1928 and 1929 revealed, most students at this time came from church-going homes and found it easy and natural to continue their religious involvement in a student center or church sponsored by their faith in Madison. They were not ashamed to show an interest in religion nor to discuss religious issues. A 1934 analysis of the use of leisure time, carefully structured to involve more than 10 percent of the entire student body, revealed that about half of the students surveyed attended church regularly, which, the report commented drily, was "a record equal to or better than the average community."[12] Apart from formal worship, the campus-area churches and religious centers also offered fellowship and recreation, an easy opportunity to meet and socialize with like-minded young people of both sexes, and student-organized programs of general and often secular interest. Until the University began offering a course on marriage and the family in the late 1930s, the ministers of the student churches were the best source of information and advice about this subject of enduring interest to young people.

The University gave unofficial but powerful support to the student churches by serving only two meals on Sunday—breakfast and noon dinner—in campus dormitories. Consequently, students flocked to the Sunday evening low-cost suppers offered by the campus churches. At these gatherings the emphasis was more on fellowship than religion and the meal was ordinarily followed by a serious talk and discussion. Often a popular faculty member was invited to share supper and speak afterward on some topic of interest to the student audience. One student in the late twenties remembers deciding which Sunday evening church supper to attend by choosing among the faculty members featured for the evening programs.[13] During the depression a number of the student religious centers began sponsoring inexpensive eating cooperatives. Typical was the Three Squares Club, organized by the Wesley Methodist Foundation in 1933. By 1936 the club had expanded to serve 75 members at a cost of $.43 a meal, with some of its members paying partly in produce from their family farms. Congo's eating co-op got by for less, charging $3.50 for twelve meals a week and returning surplus "dividends" monthly ranging from 8 to 22 percent. The Wayland

---

[12]Porter Butts, "Summary of the Main Findings and Conclusions from a Study of Student Residence and Student Use of Leisure Time at the University of Wisconsin," p. 8, BOR Papers, 1/1/4, box 97, UA.

[13]Henry Ahrnsbrak, oral history interview, 1976, UA.

Center co-op charged its 20 members only $2.25 a week.[14]   In 1936 Congo regularly drew 100-150 students to its Sunday night suppers, which cost only $.15.[15]   Other religious centers were equally popular. This is not to suggest that the University did not attempt to keep meal costs low in its own student dining facilitiess during the depression. Commons Director Donald Halverson did wonders in providing nutritious low cost meals in the dormitory dining rooms and the Memorial Union throughout the depression.   Indeed, the Union advertised in 1932 that students could eat three meals a day in its cafeteria for only 53 cents:

53¢ A DAY FOR THREE MEALS AT THE UNION
SAMPLE MENU

Breakfast - 8¢
Prunes
Toast and Coffee

Lunch - 20¢
(after 12:30)

Dinner - 25¢

Braised veal	Noodles	Roast Pork	Mashed Potatoes
Beet relish	String beans		Salad
	Bread and butter		Bread and butter
	Cherry Pie		Cocoanut Cookies
	Coffee or Milk		Coffee Or Milk

This is a sample menu for one day. There is a change every day in the menus.

These specials are served in the Cafeteria of the Union. Each meal is carefully planned by the Union dieticians.

In Place of Parents

During the latter part of the nineteenth century the University took its *in loco parentis* responsibilities rather casually, if indeed anyone accepted the charge.   Most of the students were men, who were assumed to be young adults capable of handling their extracurricular lives without much supervision or assistance from campus authorities. When the first Science Hall burned down in 1884, there was little objection when President Bascom, who was as concerned about developing the moral character of his youthful charges as any parent could wish, casually reassigned North Hall to academic purposes rather than for continued use as a men's dormitory, obliging its residents to

---

[14]*Milwaukee Journal*, November 1, 1936.
[15]Ibid.

find lodging off campus. This left the University with no men's dormitories and only one for women, Ladies Hall (later renamed Chadbourne Hall). Since it was easier to persuade the always parsimonious legislature to provide housing for women students than for men, President Van Hise was able to secure funds to construct a second women's dormitory—later named Barnard Hall—in 1912. Although he tried hard, Van Hise had no success in getting similar facilities for the men. Not until the Adams-Tripp complex opened in 1926—more than four decades after the loss of North Hall—did the University again provide a limited amount of campus housing for male students. Even so, a report by a special regents committee in 1930 emphasized that less than one-eighth of the student body could be accommodated in University residence halls.[16] This meant most students, men and women alike, had to seek rooms in the town, either in the Greek-letter fraternities and sororities that were proliferating east of the University, or, for the great majority of students, in the many private rooming and boarding houses that continued to multiply around the campus.

Until the Van Hise era the University paid scant attention to the private lives of its students as long as their behavior was not scandalous or excessively rowdy. No aspect of student life cried out more for University attention than the rooming houses in which most students—men and women alike—lived, where caveat emptor ruled and the landlords charged whatever the traffic would bear. In 1905 a committee of the Board of Visitors discovered sixty-three rooming houses occupied by both men and women students. A number of these houses had no parlors and female residents were obliged to entertain callers in their bedrooms, a potentially scandalous situation the committee believed demanded University attention.[17] The Women's Self-Government Association, the official representative of women students, voted in 1908 to develop a list of rooming houses whose owners agreed to rent only to women and to provide first-floor parlor privileges. The following year the Board of Regents provided funds to hire an official to inspect student rooming and boarding houses at least twice a year, a move reflecting the University's growing interest in student health following an epidemic of typhoid in the student district. The same

---

[16]Untitled report of the Special Regents Housing Committee, November 22, 1930, Business Administration Papers, 24/1/1, box 137, UA.

[17]The Board of Visitors had been urged to make this investigation by the University League, an organization of faculty wives and University women, which since its establishment in 1901 had campaigned for more University supervision of women students' housing.

concern led to the appointment of Dr. Joseph S. Evans as the first professor of clinical medicine and his development beginning in 1910 of a University-operated student health clinic, the second in the country.[18]

Up to this time the faculty had concerned itself primarily with working with student groups in an advisory way to try to assure that student social and other extracurricular activities supported and did not interfere unduly with their academic progress. Academic misconduct was dealt with severely by a faculty committee and the deans. Other disciplinary problems were handled by the faculty, deans, and the president on an ad hoc basis, but under a general policy of encouraging students to regulate their own out-of-class lives. With the appointment of the first dean of women, Annie Crosby Emery, in the 1890s, extracurricular matters involving women students were generally handled separately under the dean's leadership. In 1910 the faculty decided to restructure its committee on student social affairs into a new Committee on Student Interests, which quickly developed subcommittees for such extracurricular areas as athletics, debating, publications, hygiene, fraternities, and entertainments. This committee established some regulations for fraternity rushing and pledging, developed policies for chaperoning, and issued permits for student dances, public events, and trips out of town.

This arrangement was not entirely effective, however, and in 1914 the faculty replaced it with a more comprehensive Committee on Student Life and Interests (quickly known as SLIC). President Van Hise named Associate Professor of German Scott H. Goodnight chairman of the committee and two

----

[18]See Merle Curti and Vernon Carstensen, *The University of Wisconsin: A History, 1848-1925* (Madison: University of Wisconsin Press, 1949), vol. 2, pp. 497-9, 518-9. The original plan was to charge students a health service fee of $1 a semester to fund Dr. Evans' position. Evans objected to this arrangement as likely to complicate his relations with the student body, however, and his wishes were respected. Ibid., p. 519, n. 89.

years later also appointed him as the first dean of men. The dean of women, by now Lois Kimball Mathews, served as SLIC's assistant chairman. For a number of years SLIC consisted of seven members: the deans of men and women, plus five faculty members, each of whom chaired one of its subcommittees (Athletics, Living Conditions and Hygiene, Music and Dramatics, Journalism and Oratory, and Society, Fraternities, and Politics). The faculty chairman of the Athletic Council (reconstituted by the regents as an independent Athletic Board in 1932)[19] chaired the SLIC subcommittee dealing with athletics, which included intramural as well as intercollegiate athletic issues. The subcommittees had administrative responsibility for their respective areas and were linked together and operated under general policies developed by the parent committee. Unlike previous fragmented efforts to regulate student activities, the new committee embraced all aspects of student life outside the classroom.

In establishing the Committee on Student Life and Interests the faculty underscored its belief that suitably controlled extracurricular activities could play a constructive role in the education of students. The problem was to achieve a proper balance between academic and non-academic endeavors. By bringing all organized student extracurricular activities under SLIC's purview, the faculty hoped to emphasize the constructive side of extracurricular activities through extensive but essentially benign regulations. If the regulative aspect sometimes appeared (at least to students) more important than the constructive side of SLIC's activities, the latter concern was never absent. By 1925 SLIC with its subcommittees was one of the largest and most active faculty committees. It remained so throughout the period of this volume, operating continuously under the strong leadership of Dean of Men Goodnight (until he retired in 1945) and Deans of Women F. Louise Nardin (from 1919 to 1931)[20] and Louise Troxell (after 1931). The University at last possessed an effective mechanism through which to assert some surrogate parental authority.

Students after 1914 felt the impact of SLIC in a variety of ways. SLIC rules required all student organizations to register and list their officers annually in order to gain official University recognition and the right to use University facilities for meetings and other activities. Each

---

[19]See pp. 258-60.
[20]For an account of President Frank's controversial firing of Dean Nardin in 1931, see pp. 247-50.

such use had to be authorized in advance by the dean of men's office. SLIC limited student late-night events to Friday and Saturday and otherwise enforced the hours restrictions developed in conjunction with the Women's Self-Government Association for the women's dorms, sororities, and houses, no doubt under the assumption that controlling the after-dark hours of one sex regulated the other as well. SLIC was behind the dress code enforced in the dormitories and Greek-letter houses for evening and Sunday dinners (coats and ties for men, dresses or skirts and blouses for women). SLIC reviewed and could disallow outside speakers invited by student groups to speak on campus, a proscriptive right exercised in conjunction with the president with decreasing frequency in the period, however. Through its all-University calendar of approved events SLIC controlled the timing of student dances, plays, concerts, and other activities in order to prevent excessive concentration and duplication. The committee required chaperons (registered with the dean of men or women in advance) at all mixed student dances and parties and it maintained a list of approved chaperons.

SLIC also concerned itself with academics. It established and enforced minimum grade point and credit levels for eligibility to participate in extracurricular activities, including athletics. At first the committee ruled that freshmen were not permitted to pledge a fraternity or sorority or be in an organized student activity in their first year, but later this requirement was reduced to the first semester and then abandoned entirely during World War II. Each semester SLIC released comparative data on student grade point performance by sex, class, college, and organized living unit, the latter designed to focus attention on segments of the student body (usually some of the fraternities) needing to party less and study harder.

A recurring problem was the financial mismanagement, petty graft, and occasional bankruptcy of student classes, organizations, and publications, leaving unhappy creditors looking to the University for succor. As the committee pointed out in seeking reform, within the University even department chairmen had no access to cash funds, whereas student groups often handled large amounts of cash. To reduce temptation and help assure the solvency of student publications, major dances, and other enterprises, in the 1930s SLIC created the position of Student Financial Adviser under Ray L. Hilsenhoff in the dean of men's office to handle and audit the accounts of student groups. By 1939 Hilsenhoff, formerly an accountant in the University business office, was supervising the expenditure of about a half million dollars annually of student organizational funds.[21] Earlier, in 1932 Dean Goodnight helped to organize and headed a Fraternity Buyers Cooperative to help the depression-weakened Greek houses save money in purchasing food and supplies.[22]

Although the 1914 faculty report establishing the Committee on Student Life and Interests did not discuss student self-government, SLIC's objective over the years became more and more to encourage responsible student management of student activities, as the financial adviser and the buyers cooperative indicate. The committee, with its two agents in the persons of the deans of men and women, thus became the University's chief proxy in providing "parental" supervision and encouragement of the extracurricular life of its youthful charges. As Goodnight put it in a 1931 report, SLIC's mission was "to supervise the rapidly increasing student activities on the campus, to promote wholesome participation in them by a larger number of students, to curb them insofar as they were hurtful to academic work, and to rid them of abuses."[23] To foster this "wholesome participation," during the 1930s the committee added a student member to each of its subcommittees. As the University developed more and more student services during the twenties and thirties, the need for better coordination was increasingly evident. In 1938 President Dykstra approved the formation of the University Personnel Council under Dean Goodnight's leadership to share information and develop common policies among the various campus offices dealing with students.[24]

---

[21]*Press Bulletin*, November 8, 1939.

[22]*Daily Cardinal*, February 11, 1931, March 30, 1932; "Fraternity Buyers Cooperative Makes Successful Campus Debut," *WAM*, 33 (June, 1932), 297. The cooperative had its inception in the fall of 1931 when a student, Rolf Darbo, experimented in buying coal and laundry services for twelve fraternities. The substantial savings Darbo achieved for these fraternities persuaded Goodnight to help expand and formalize the venture, incorporating it in March, 1932. Darbo served as the co-op's first student manager, with Goodnight heading the Board of Governors along with four other UW faculty and staff members.

[23]"Outline of the Duties of the Office of the Dean of Men" [ca. March 31, 1931], Frank Presidential Papers, 4/13/1, box 96, UA.

[24]The UPC reflected Dean Goodnight's long-standing belief in the value of exchanging information and ideas among student advisers. In 1918 he had hosted the first meeting and helped to organize what became the National Association of Deans and Advisers of Men. Although Goodnight provided the stimulus for the creation of the personnel council, within a short time the leading figure in its development was Willard W. Blaesser, assistant director of the Memorial Union, who moved to Goodnight's office as assistant dean of men with responsibility for coordinating the work of the council.

Student Housing

A major part of SLIC's responsibilities concerned student housing, the special province of its Sub-Committee on Living Conditions and Hygiene chaired by Dean Goodnight. In this there was some overlap with the faculty Committee on Dormitories, which had been created to plan and supervise the operation of the two men's residence halls—Tripp and Adams—constructed in the mid-twenties. SLIC required undergraduate women students to live only in approved housing and maintained lists of approved houses for both men and women students. To protect the interests of landlords, SLIC required student tenants to sign leases by the semester and used University suasion and even sanctions to help assure they met their financial obligations. Staff members of the dean of men's and dean of women's offices annually inspected private housing occupied by UW students, including the Greek-letter houses. With the vast majority of students obliged to live off campus, this review of the many hundreds of private lodging houses was a formidable responsibility. Each year the housing inspector in Dean Goodnight's office visited and filed a report showing the location, capacity, prices, grade, and names of lodgers in about fourteen hundred private lodging houses and fraternities occupied by men students. The smaller number of women undergraduates and their preference for living in larger groups made the problem of keeping track of their housing arrangements somewhat more manageable. Even so, the dean of women's office annually inspected and maintained information on upwards of a hundred organized women's houses (sororities, private dormitories, and lodging houses) plus scores of smaller housing units and rooms approved for women students. Several large privately owned women's dormitories were constructed near the campus in the 1920s: Villa Maria (1925), Langdon Hall (1929), and Ann Emery Hall (1930). The dean of women worked closely with the operators of these halls. She also reviewed the qualifications of the adult women chaperons required to live in every house approved for women students.[25]

---

[25] See, for example, "Outline of the Duties of the Office of the Dean of Men"; "W.S.G.A. Organized Houses, 1935-36," list, and dean of women's materials, Frank Presidential Papers, 4/13/1, boxes 96 and 180. For the benefit of President Dykstra, Blanche Stemm, the inspector of men's housing, produced a lengthy report of her activities during 1937-38, which provided details of how SLIC attempted to monitor student housing. Using the fall registration cards Mrs. Stemm determined that the 7,571 men students were living in approximately 1,400 housing units. Time did not permit her to visit each one during the year, she reported, and she

Under regent authority SLIC could order students to move from unapproved housing even in mid-term, a potentially powerful weapon occasionally useful in persuading reluctant landlords to upgrade their properties. The invariable shortage of enough approved housing to accommodate all students vitiated its force, however. Given the relatively small number of University dormitory rooms, during most of the period of this volume private landlords were able to rent just about any room or apartment in the immediate campus area to student tenants, even if the property was not on the approved University housing list. Only when enrollment declined sharply in the early years of the depression were there vacancies in all categories of student housing, including the University residence halls. During this brief period of surplus housing Dean Goodnight in 1933 asked the regents for authority to require undergraduate men as well as women to live only in University-approved housing, but the board recognized the University's long-run dependence on the private landlords and failed to act.

The lack of effective University control over the housing occupied by male students led to problems and even occasional tragedies. In 1936 Donald Ranney, a twenty-two-year-old former student, died of smoke inhalation after being trapped in a fire at his apartment at the rear of a shoe repair shop at 651 University Avenue. Ranney had dropped out temporarily while working nights to accumulate funds to continue his education. He shared the small windowless ground floor apartment with his younger brother and two other student roommates who were in class at the time of the fire. Firemen were able to rescue one of the other student tenants living on the upper floors of the building, a coed who escaped into the crowd before being identified,

---

was obliged to omit 119 houses occupied by 133 students. Still, she managed to inspect every student housing unit within a mile-and-a-quarter of the campus, where the vast majority of students lived, and interviewed the house mothers of 4,183 students! She reported that a total of 1,188 students were living in 265 unapproved houses, a reflection of SLIC's policy not to require men, in contrast to women, to live in University-approved housing. Reasons for not approving houses included such things as women tenants, inadequate bath and exit facilities, crowding, poor facilities and furnishings, double beds, basement rooms, and lack of supervision. Mrs. Stemm noted some feeling by owners of approved housing that they received little assistance from the University over that given to owners of unapproved housing, who were free to rent suddenly vacated rooms to anyone—women or transients—whereas the former were unlikely to find another male student on short notice. She recommended allowing students to move from unapproved to approved housing in mid-semester as a way of making the approved listing more valuable to owners and house mothers. "Report of the Office of the Dean of Men," August 2, 1938, UHP.

probably to keep University authorities from learning she was living in unapproved quarters. Three days later a second fire routed seven students from another unapproved lodging house, a private home at 117 North Orchard Street.[26] These fires, especially the Ranney tragedy, sparked a sustained student drive for more University dormitories and stricter city enforcement of the housing codes governing private lodging houses, since the windowless Ranney apartment had only one exit and was in flagrant violation. A number of student groups, led by the two-year-old House Presidents Council representing all men's and women's organized student houses, and senior class President James E. Doyle, pressed the regents for action to protect student interests by developing better and safer housing. The students established a general student housing committee, which with support from the *Daily Cardinal* kept the issue alive for a number of months. The *Cardinal* went so far as to publish a special housing edition to be sent to legislators and parents around the state in order to drum up support for better student housing. The issue included a full page of photos of unsafe, unhealthy, and decrepit facilities, including a hard-to-believe picture of one student's quarters in a small unheated panel truck.[27]

The Ranney tragedy came just as Deans Goodnight and Greeley were seeking regent approval of a request to construct additional men's and women's dormitories on the west campus. This was within the framework of an ambitious long-term campus plan for a large array of residence halls, fraternities and sororities, student housing cooperatives, and perhaps even faculty homes, all adjacent to ample recreational space and located along the shores of Lake Mendota from Observatory Hill westward to University Bay. Under this scheme women students would be housed closest to the hill and the men further west, with the new Tripp-Adams men's dormitories eventually becoming women's halls. With exquisitely bad timing, a special housing committee of the Board of Regents had developed the plan in 1929-30, coincident with the arrival of the depression, arguing for the creation of "a 'university city' that will be picturesquely unique in the United States." The board gave the plan tentative approval late in 1930, subject to funding.[28] Falling

---

[26]*Daily Cardinal*, December 1, 2, 3, and 4, 1936. There was one other victim of the Ranney fire, a small scottie dog found suffocated on a sofa in the second floor apartment.

[27]Ibid., December 5 and 6, 1936, February 24 and 25, 1937.

[28]Untitled report of the Special Regents Housing Committee, November 22, 1930, Business Administration Papers, 24/1/1, box 137; BOR Minutes, November 22, 1930, UA; "'University City' for Students Seen in Long-Term Plan," *WAM*, 33 (October, 1931), 28; "'University City'

enrollment and the depressed state economy made the scheme fanciful in 1930, of course, but the circumstances were enough different six years later to lead the two deans to try to resurrect at least part of the earlier plan. If not a University City, they envisioned a large women's dormitory on the lake just below the Washburn Observatory and one or more men's residence halls near Tripp and Adams Halls.[29] The dormitory proposal had the backing of President Frank, but it came before the board on December 9, 1936, just as the regents were taking up the more hotly contested question of the dismissal of the president. Consequently, the board deferred consideration of the housing problem for several months, though University administrators, prodded by the student housing committee, did work with city officials in the meantime to crack down on housing code violators in the student area.

---

of the University of Wisconsin," *School and Society,* 34 (July 18, 1931), 87. The regents had periodically discussed the growing need for more student housing in the late twenties before appointing a special housing committee on April 4, 1929, to study the problem thoroughly. Its chairman, Regent John C. Schmidtmann of Manitowoc, gave the board a preliminary report later that year, which in many respects foreshadowed the proposal adopted by the board in 1930. See BOR Minutes, January 16, 1928, January 16, April 24, October 9, 1929; Schmidtmann, "Is Housing Its Students a Proper Obligation of the University?" November 11, 1929, BOR Papers, 1/1/4, box 97.

Not all of the regents thought the University City scheme, if it involved relocating most or all student housing onto the west campus over the long run, was practical. Regent George W. Mead, a paper manufacturer from Wisconsin Rapids and a member of the special committee, doubted that many of the existing sororities and fraternities, a number of which had constructed substantial houses in the twenties, would be willing to relocate from Langdon Street even to escape high property taxes. "No one of the old established groups would be likely to accept a free site on University grounds west of the hill," he cautioned, "and newly organized groups would have hard sledding alone in that location." He proposed instead building University dormitories "sufficient to lodge all Freshmen, both men and women, and obliging all Freshmen to live in these buildings throughout their first year in college....The large percentage of Freshmen failures would certainly be cut down heavily by this dormitory system." Mead, "Student Housing Plans," memorandum, December 6, 1929, BOR Papers, 1/1/4, box 97.

At this time the University owned most of the land extending westward from the Stock Pavilion and lying between the Milwaukee railroad tracks and University Bay, including the Eagle Heights area, and thus had ample space to accommodate the proposed University City. Still in private hands was the large undeveloped tract along the lake that included Second Point and Picnic Point, the latter used by generations of students for recreational purposes though it was not owned by the University. The Board of Regents discussed buying Picnic Point from time to time, but did not act until 1939. It took nearly another half-century before the University was able to acquire the adjacent Second Point tract through a generous gift from the Walter Frautschi family.

[29]Scott Goodnight and Charles Dollard, "The Student Housing Situation," October 14, 1936, BOR Papers, 1/1/3, box 49; BOR Minutes, December 6, 1936.

During much of 1937 the regents pondered what to do about student housing. The general student housing committee created in the aftermath of the Ranney tragedy twice urged the board to revive its 1930 University City plan, pointing out that over half of the male students were obliged to live in private lodging houses, many in "overcrowded and unsatisfactory conditions." The students stressed the need for a federal or state subsidy of any new dorms "if such housing is to be within the reach of those students most in need of it."[30]   UW Business Manager J.D. Phillips, however, cautioned the regents there was "practically no possibility of obtaining a State appropriation for dormitory construction at this time." The two women's residence halls—Chadbourne and Barnard—had been built with state funds, and the University owned them free and clear. On the other hand, the two men's halls—Tripp and Adams—had been constructed by the Wisconsin University Building Corporation in 1925 through long-term loans with many years yet to run. Even though the director of dormitories and commons, Donald L. Halverson, had tried to keep the Tripp-Adams rates as competitive as possible—so much so that over these halls' first ten years they had "not paid the full amortization of debt in addition to operating expenses"—rooms in Tripp and Adams still cost more than many of the private sleeping rooms available near the campus lacking the amenities offered in the dorms. Except for 1932-33 there had been no problem keeping the two women's halls filled, Phillips reported, but "until 1935 there always was more or less of a struggle to fill the men's dormitories." As long as the dormitories were expected to be self-supporting through good times and bad, Phillips estimated no more than 27 percent of the value of the UW dormitory plant could be amortized from operating revenues. On this basis he thought the University could safely borrow $475,000 for the construction of additional dormitories. He warned, however, that if enrollment were to go beyond the current level of ten thousand students "additional housing facilities appear to be imperative."[31]

The Board of Regents agreed the need for more student housing was urgent. In June it authorized Phillips to amend the University's application to the federal Public Works Administration to include,

---

[30]"Report of the General Student Housing Committee to the Regents of the University of Wisconsin," February 2, 1937, BOR Papers, 1/1/3, box 49; BOR Minutes, February 3, March 18, 1937.

[31]J.D. Phillips, "Proposals for Additional University Dormitories: An Analysis by the University Business Office," March 15, 1937, BOR Papers, 1/1/3, box 50.

among other projects, a $500,000 grant to aid in the construction of additional women's dormitories. The application was feasible because the legislature had recently approved a change in state law making it easier for the University to identify the required matching funds for such federally assisted projects.[32] During the summer the board created a special housing committee under the leadership of Regent Clough Gates and including Phillips, Halverson, Dean Greeley, and Albert Gallistel, the superintendent of buildings and grounds, to develop specific plans for a new women's dormitory. After consulting with the faculty Dormitory Committee, the student housing committee, and the SLIC Subcommittee on Living Conditions and Hygiene, the group also began planning additional men's housing. It concluded that market considerations required cheaper and more spartan accommodations for men than for women, but a new women's dorm should have "more of the recreational and cultural features than would be provided in the men's residences."[33] Planning for the additional men's dorms moved swiftly thereafter, with students urging low cost construction to accommodate more residents and keep room rates down. President Dykstra, on the other hand, argued for some form of subsidy to avoid despoiling the campus with inexpensive prefabricated or barracks-type units, which Regent Gates initially favored.[34] Fortunately, a majority of the regents agreed with the president. In March of 1938 the board approved plans for as many as eight new men's dorms, depending on availability of funding, and the following month it authorized the Wisconsin University Building Corporation to receive bids, sign contracts, and borrow funds from the state annuity board for the first three units, each capable of housing eighty men. As construction of what were at first simply called Units A, B, and C proceeded on a crash basis so as to be ready for the fall semester, the Public Works Administration notified the University it would contribute $229,909 for new

---

[32]BOR Minutes, May 5, June 19, 1937.

[33]Minutes of a joint meeting of the Regents Business Committee, the Student Housing Committee, and the Faculty Dormitory Committee, June 7, 1937; "Report of the Committee on Living Conditions and Hygiene," October 11, 1937; "Report of the Special Committee on Dormitories," October 12, 1937, BOR Papers, 1/1/3, box 50; BOR Minutes, October 14, 1937.

[34]BOR Minutes, October 12-13, 1937. Regent Gates for a time pressed for inexpensive prefabricated frame units, but eventually came around to Dykstra's view that the new dorms should be constructed of stone like the adjacent Tripp-Adams complex. For economy reasons the new units contained mostly double rooms, as opposed to the more numerous single rooms in Tripp and Adams.

men's dormitories. The PWA windfall enabled the regents to authorize construction of the remaining five units, plus the associated kitchen and dining facilities, to be ready in the fall of 1939.[35]

In June of 1939 the regents approved naming the new men's residence complex after former Regent President Theodore Kronshage. He more than anyone had helped to gain legislative approval for the innovative Wisconsin University Building Corporation, the private-public hybrid that had made possible most of the University's construction program in the 1920s and 1930s despite the state's constitutional ban on debt. The regents also named each of the eight new dorms after a prominent figure in the history of the state or the University.[36] Of simple rectangular design but substantial stone construction, the eight Kronshage houses were grouped together on the lake just west of the older men's dormitories. They offered a multi-tiered rate structure inaugurated by Director Halverson when Units A, B, and C opened in the fall of 1938. Halverson had for some time wanted to experiment with lower cost cooperative living arrangements in the dormitories similar to those in some of the private student houses. Accordingly, some of the Kronshage houses offered full daily maid service as in Tripp and Adams; others operated on a cooperative basis with few or no cleaning services and were priced accordingly.[37] To further keep down costs to students, the Board of Regents established a new policy waiving charges for heat and electricity in any University dormitory where a substantial part of the residents' payments went for debt service. The regents also agreed that part of the residence halls staff was engaged in instructional activity, broadly defined, and could therefore be put on the instructional rather than the dormitories and commons budget.[38] By the fall of 1939 when the five remaining

---

[35]BOR Minutes, June 3, June 17, August 26, October 14, 1938.

[36]Ibid., June 16 and 17, 1939.

[37]*Daily Cardinal*, October 1 and 7, 1938. In the first year of the experiment Unit A operated on a regular basis offering full daily maid and janitorial service at a cost of $96, Unit B offered weekly maid service for $75, and Unit C had no cleaning services at a cost of $70. When the five other Kronshage houses opened in 1939, Halverson allowed the residents to determine the level of services. They voted to drop the semi-cooperative middle option. In 1940-41 four of the houses—Turner, Showerman, Conover, and Chamberlin—offered full services; the other four—Jones, Swenson, Gilman, and Mack—were cooperative houses with no services for an annual savings to each resident of $30. Lee Burns to H.L. Wells, July 10, 1941, UHP.

[38]BOR Minutes, February 11, 1939. This was a logical follow-up to the board's 1935 decision to designate the Memorial Union as a separate Division of Social Education, with

Kronshage units opened, the University was able to accommodate nearly 1,200 men in modern, well-appointed, and fire-proof residence halls.[39] Meanwhile, plans for the new women's dormitory, though slower to develop and more complex in nature, had also been moving ahead. Apart from the initial decision that the women's dormitory should contain more recreational and cultural features than were needed in a men's residence, there was at first little agreement on the size and scope of a new women's hall. For one thing, the University had not constructed a women's dormitory for a quarter-century and neither Chadbourne (1871) nor Barnard (1912) Hall offered the sort of modern amenities desired in the new dorm. Consequently, more discussion and study were required than in the case of the simpler Kronshage houses. At first Dean of Women Greeley favored a single three-story building overlooking the lake below Observatory Hill, citing medical advice that young women could climb up to three flights of stairs without physical harm. Several months later she advocated three separate fireproof units, each with its own dining room. Even after construction began in April of 1938 planning remained fluid. It was not until the following August, when the Public Works Administration agreed to provide $363,088 for the project, that the final configuration was set. This federal grant, combined with $443,774 borrowed by the Wisconsin University Building Corporation, made possible a much larger complex than anyone had contemplated originally.[40]

The new Elizabeth Waters Hall, named for a distinguished UW alumna and highly respected regent who had died while in her third term in 1933, opened for public inspection on May 19, 1940, during the annual Parents' Weekend. Everyone marvelled at this triumph of modern dormitory planning, which provided the University with a student residence facility easily the equal of any in the country. Far

---

House Director Porter Butts and Steward Donald Halverson given faculty status as assistant professors of social education. Two years later the regents approved President Dykstra's recommendation that Halverson, who was older and had more responsibility as director of dormitories and commons, be promoted to the rank of professor of institutional management. Ibid., June 22, 1935, October 29, 1937.

[39]*Daily Cardinal*, September, October 1, 1939.

[40]Louise Troxell Greeley to A.W. Peterson, July 23, 1937, Business Administration Papers, 24/1/1, box 137; Greeley to Dykstra, November 18, 1937, BOR Papers, 1/1/3, box 51; BOR Minutes, May 5, June 18-19, July 10, October 12-13, December 7-8, 1937, June 17, October 14, December 13-14, 1938, January 17-18, February 11, March 7-8, 1939; H.A. Gray, Assistant Administrator of the Federal Emergency Administration of Public Works, to Board of Regents, March 7, 1939, BOR Papers, 1/1/3, box 53.

more than a single hall, the building consisted of five connected units on seven levels cascading down the side of the hill below Observatory Drive. The complex could accommodate 478 residents, more than doubling the spaces available for women students in campus dormitories. Compared with any other University residence hall, Elizabeth Waters was massive and truly palatial, amply deserving its immediate nickname of the "super-dorm" and later "The Rock." Its fifteen lounges, four dating parlors (soon dubbed "passion pits"), ten small kitchens and ten laundries for use by the residents, music room, library, built-in radios and paging system, sun roof lounge, and waiter service in a large dining room overlooking the complex's own private beach and pier on Lake Mendota, made it seem more like a luxury resort hotel than a college dormitory.[41] President Van Hise would have been startled yet gratified to see how his call for gracious on-campus living had been realized nearly four decades later.

Laura Trafell Greeley

Construction of Elizabeth Waters Hall brought to a head a long-simmering conflict between dormitories and commons Director Halverson and Dean Greeley. Operating under the University business manager, Halverson had since 1924 been responsible for the staffing and physical operation of all UW dormitories and after it opened in 1928 the Memorial Union. Greeley, on the other hand, had long believed she should appoint and supervise the directors (variously called hostesses or head residents) of Chadbourne and Barnard halls as part of her responsibility for the extracurricular lives of UW coeds. Much involved in planning the new Elizabeth Waters Hall, she viewed its opening as a chance to enlarge her empire. Halverson challenged her intention to select the head resident for Waters, pointing out: "You have the social set-up for the private dormitories, the sororities, and the girls' rooming houses; I have the same responsibility for the university dormitories." He thought it "incredible that you would appoint a person in my department any more

---

[41]*Daily Cardinal*, May 12, 25, and 28, 1940; *Summer Cardinal*, June 22, July 4, 1940. See also *Daily Cardinal*, August, 1940.

than I should select one of your staff."[42] When the dean persisted in her challenge, Halverson complained to UW Comptroller A.W. Peterson that she "just hops and skips all around the point and ends by saying 'you have enough to do in running the men's dormitories now you just let me have a hand in the women's, etc.'"[43] Halverson favored moving Ruth Campbell, the experienced head resident of Chadbourne, to take charge of Elizabeth Waters when it opened. Greeley backed another candidate, who presumably favored her view that the dean of women ought to have more control over "the social set-up" in the campus women's dormitories. Although Halverson won this skirmish, the war was far from over.[44]

Continuing the practice begun with the Tripp and Adams houses in 1926, Halverson and the Dormitory Committee routinely selected house fellows to live in each of the men's halls, including the new Kronshage units. They were proud of Wisconsin's pioneering house fellow system, which they believed had contributed to greater discipline and responsible self-government in the men's houses. The fellows were advanced graduate students who were responsible for maintaining order and developing a healthy intellectual and social life in their respective houses, in return for which they received free board and reduced room rent. The faculty Dormitory Committee, which had come into existence to plan the men's dormitories and the Memorial Union and had no oversight responsibilities for the social life of the women's residence halls, thought the house fellow system should be extended to the women's halls. Dean Greeley was supportive of the concept—though she preferred the title dormitory counselor—and indeed sought to persuade the two largest private women's dormitories on Langdon Street, Langdon and Ann Emery halls, to employ such counselors. She was adamant, however, that she, rather than Halverson, ought to select, appoint, and supervise the women house fellows in consultation with the student Women's Self-Government Association. She and WSGA leaders accordingly worked out a house fellow selection arrangement for the women's dorms in the spring of 1941, which she submitted to President Dykstra. To her great dismay, the following year Halverson informed

---

[42]Halverson to Greeley, April 13, 1939, Business Administration Papers, 24/1/1, box 145.

[43]Halverson to Peterson, April 12, 1940, ibid., box 152.

[44]Miss Campbell's appointment as the director of Elizabeth Waters still rankled Dean Greeley three years later. See Greeley to Dykstra, February 28, 1942, Dykstra Presidential Papers, 4/15/1, box 83.

her of Dykstra's approval of a plan under which Halverson's newly renamed Division of Residence Halls would have responsibility for the selection and supervision of all UW residence halls staff, including the head residents and house fellows. While he welcomed Dean Greeley's advice on women's issues, Halverson told her, in staffing the dormitories the "lines of authority are clear."[45]

Dean Greeley heatedly wrote to and subsequently sought an audience with the president to "register a vigorous protest" at this disregard of "the right of women to do their own job on the government and personnel side." Inasmuch as she was held responsible for any trouble involving women dormitory residents, Greeley emphasized, "it seems to me imperative that the choice and direction of my first line of assistance must be handled primarily through this office."[46] In response Dykstra made clear he was "disheartened" by this evidence that relations between Halverson and Greeley were "not more harmonious." He pointed out Halverson had agreed Dean Greeley or her representative could sit in on the selection of women house fellows. But the president was above all a tidy administrator. His letter reflected more than a trace of exasperation at the thought of dividing the operational responsibility for the women's dorms, as Greeley's plan contemplated.

> The mere physical task of counseling more than three thousand women is tremendous and you have told me often that your staff is hard put to get this done. To throw upon you operational responsibility I think is to overload your office. I think our conception of residence halls at the University includes more than housing and feeding students. That is the reason for having head residents in the various halls. Either these women will have to be responsible for running the halls or your office will. They are on the ground and you are not. They have decisions to make from hour to hour which certainly you cannot be bothered with. They must supervise the work of the fellows in the various units or you must. It would seem to me, therefore, that if your office sits in on the study of the various qualifications of candidates and you come to an agreement as to who shall be appointed that there should not be operational difficulty.[47]

Following a meeting with a still-persistent Dean Greeley, President

---

[45]Halverson to Greeley, February 26, 1942, ibid.

[46]Greeley to Dykstra, February 28, 1942, ibid. See also Greeley to Dykstra, March 4, 1942, ibid.

[47]Dykstra to Greeley, March 2, 1942, ibid.

Dykstra reminded her it was his "responsibility to declare a policy and to ask all concerned to cooperate in every possible way to carry it out." He announced he was resolving the immediate issue by appointing a separate women's house fellow selection committee, to be chaired by Director Halverson, consisting of the head residents of the three women's residence halls (who reported to Halverson), Dr. Annette Washburne, a UW psychiatrist in the student health center who worked closely with Dean Greeley, and Dean Greeley or one of her staff members. "We should have one common desire," Dykstra reminded his unhappy dean, "to serve the women on this campus, and to create a unity among all women students....If we cannot develop a real unity on the campus even in time of national emergency, then the world situation will become hopeless."[48] Neither Halverson nor Greeley chose to react to this non sequitur, since the president's irritation over the continuing conflict for control of the women's halls was plain. Dykstra's compromise nevertheless suggested that this Halverson-Greeley skirmish must be counted at least a partial draw in a continuing conflict.[49]

Greeley's dogged determination on this issue highlighted the overlapping areas of University operational and "parental" responsibility for various kinds of student housing. This multiplicity of administrative oversight was reflected even more in the supervision of the various student cooperative houses approved and in some cases sponsored and even owned by the University. Beginning in 1914 with the organization of the German House for women, the University helped to create a variety of cooperative living units. *Deutsches Haus*, as it was also called, was sponsored by faculty members of the German department and was the University's first foreign-language residence. The timing

[48]Dykstra to Greeley, March 4, 1942, ibid.

[49]Halverson's continuing difficulties with Dean Greeley probably triggered his letter of resignation two years later, which he assured President Dykstra was not "the result of an explosion following a high point of emotion." The letter reflected Halverson's unhappiness over continuing jurisdictional disputes:

I have had almost complete freedom to choose a staff and to build the kind of educational division I believe the State wants. I am proud of my associates and of my employees. We work with never a thought of friction or jealousy, in complete harmony. However, I feel I cannot continue. There are countless important reasons which are woven into the fabric of my decision. I am therefore handing you my resignation effective November 1, or, if you should prefer, I am willing to stay until December 1.

Halverson to Dykstra, September 29, 1944, UHP. Halverson's frustration must have been great, for this sort of gambit was not his style. Dykstra must have realized this and prevailed upon him to withdraw the resignation.

of the experiment was unfortunate, and the venture did not survive the inflamed patriotic passions of World War I. Reestablished in 1923, German House moved to larger quarters the following year. In 1918 several French faculty members launched a similar foreign-language house, *La Maison Française*, also for women students. Indeed, Halverson, then a French instructor and graduate student, had originally gotten into the dormitory business as manager of the French House. Not to be outdone, in 1925 the Spanish faculty sponsored *La Casa Cervantes*, or Spanish House, which provided quarters for sixteen Spanish-speaking women students and also offered meals for non-residents seeking to develop their language skills and knowledge of Spanish culture and cuisine.

Also in the 1925 the English department established Arden House as a meeting place for its Arden Club, an organization open to men and women students with literary interests. Arden House was also a housing cooperative that rented rooms to seven women and offered meals to a larger number of men and women boarders. About the same time journalism faculty established a similar cooperative, Coranto House, at 509 North Henry Street, as a residence and headquarters of the journalism professional women's sorority, Coranto. By the early 1930s there were several other professional sororities and fraternities representing different academic disciplines—in agriculture, commerce, engineering, home economics, law, and medicine—with houses serving both as cooperative residences and meeting places. Sponsorship by an academic department was essential in helping to organize these academic cooperative houses. Interested faculty provided continuity of leadership and support as well as financial backing. Typically, the latter involved the creation and leadership of a private corporation to own the house, usually purchased on a land contract or mortgage with a minimal down payment. The student residents were responsible for cleaning and maintenance, with their room and board payments covering the costs of operation and amortization of the loan.

Some of the earliest cooperative houses began with encouragement by the dean of women. Examples were Mortar Board House (1915), Tabard Inn (1919), and Charter House (1921), which began by renting University-owned houses in order to provide inexpensive cooperative housing for women students. Andersen House, a cooperative for twenty women students, was named after the then secretary of the campus branch of the Young Women's Christian Association who helped to organize it in 1921. Fallows House, another cooperative for women, was established in 1924. Both Tabard Inn and Andersen House were eventually owned and operated by a legal entity called the University Women's Building Corporation, whose officers were the dean and assistant dean of women and the secretary of the Board of Regents.[50] Dean Greeley was less enthusiastic about a WSGA proposal early in 1943, which she described to President Dykstra as "a social experiment," to establish an interracial women's cooperative house. Privately, Greeley worried that an interracial house would attract radicals and upset the neighbors.[51] The idea came originally from two women students—Virginia Wicks and Elizabeth Hunt—whose boy friends lived in a men's co-op house and were departing for war service, leaving the women with a good deal of their furniture. In spite of Greeley's initial misgivings, Groves House, named after its chief faculty sponsor and patron, Professor Harold Groves of the economics department, opened successfully at 150 Langdon Street for the spring semester in 1943.[52] Although there were plenty of skeptics, the "social experiment" proved both successful and durable. The 1944-45 residents were a mix of Jewish, gentile, black, and two Japanese-American women students who were warmly enthusiastic about "the compensation received from cooperative, inter-racial, and inter-religious living."[53] As the *Daily Cardinal* noted approvingly, Groves House was "a model for Wisconsin," helping Americans "of different racial and religious backgrounds break the traditions of prejudice and segregation."[54]

---

[50]For an account of the development of Tabard Inn see Berenice Zander, "The Tabard Inn—Wisconsin's First Cooperative House," *WAM*, 27 (May, 1926), 194-5.

[51]Greeley to Dykstra, January 4, 1942 [1943], Dykstra Presidential Papers, 4/15/1, box 104; Harold Groves, oral history interview, July 26, 1966, SHSW. In response Dykstra did not comment on what he called "the housing experiment," other than to caution that the building must meet city fire and housing code standards. Dykstra to Greeley, January 12, 1943, Dykstra Presidential Papers, 4/15/1, box 104.

[52]*Daily Cardinal*, January 7 and 8, 1943.

[53]*Badger*, 1945, p. 33.

[54]*Daily Cardinal*, April 30, 1943. Actually, according to Harold Groves' recollection, things did not go as smoothly as the founders hoped. As Dean Greeley had feared, the experiment attracted a number of free spirits, including in the second year about ten radical students who were part of a Communist cell on campus. There was enough friction over their activities that they resigned from the house en masse in mid-year, leaving the remainder of the group to scramble for replacements. Groves credited one of the two Japanese-American women, Ruby Kubota from Walla Walla, Washington, with helping to hold the group together. The co-op survived this disruption, however, and relocated to a succession of houses until it was able to purchase its own property on West Johnson Street after the war. Along the way it

Most of the early housing cooperatives aimed to alleviate the housing problems of women students, but the depression soon spawned a number of inexpensive men's cooperative houses as well. When the legendary Professor Stephen M. Babcock died at the age of eighty-seven in 1931, he left his Lake Street home to the College of Agriculture, which used it thereafter for a number of years as a cooperative house for thirty to forty of its men students.[55] With the bankruptcy of some of the social fraternities during the depression, the University was able to acquire several other houses in the lower campus area and turn them into men's housing cooperatives. Four of these houses (White, Squire, Sterling, and Hodag), between them accommodating more than a hundred residents, were situated near each other on Sterling Court and Murray Street and were known collectively after their opening in 1932 as the Badger Club.[56] As another part of the effort to help students live more cheaply, in February of 1932 Dean Goodnight arranged for a group of free-spirited bohemians to use an old University-owned house as a low-cost men's cooperative. The students proceeded to name their quarters Haywood House, after Big Bill Haywood, one of the founders of the radical Industrial Workers of the World, who had served a prison sentence for criminal syndicalism after World War I. Haywood House and its left-wing residents attracted a good deal of notoriety and criticism from around the state, but President Frank and the regents wisely refrained from any reaction until after the group disbanded at the end of the semester, at which time the board decided to forestall any more problems by demolishing the run-down structure.[57] During the Second World War, when all of the regular University dormitories except Elizabeth Waters and the Nursing Dormitory were occupied by military trainees, the University leased a number of vacant fraternity houses for military use and as cooperative houses for both men and women students.[58]

---

organized a cooperative restaurant, the Green Lantern, where students could eat inexpensively. Groves, oral history interview.

[55]*Daily Cardinal*, December 19, 1934.

[56]For a laudatory view of this experiment see "Cooperative Houses for Students at the University of Wisconsin," *School and Society*, 36 (September 3, 1932), 294-5.

[57]See *Capital Times*, May 12, August 3, 1932; "Frank Discusses Criticisms of the University," *WAM*, 33 (July, 1932), 330.

[58]Occupancy of the men's cooperatives was especially fluid. Just before leaving for Army service in 1943 the house fellow of one of these cooperatives, Halburn House, wrote to Halverson expressing appreciation for the cooperative experience.

After the war, I hope that you will carry on other such houses as Halburn....You

Much more significant than the University's dormitories and cooperatives in helping to house the student body in the 1920s and early 1930s were the social sororities and fraternities. The first UW chapter of a national fraternity, Phi Delta Theta, was chartered in 1857, and the first sorority, Kappa Kappa Gamma, in 1875. Despite initial opposition from some students, faculty members, and especially from President Bascom, who deplored the groups' secret and undemocratic character, there were three national Greek-letter societies on campus by the mid-seventies and their numbers had doubled by the time of Bascom's resignation in 1887. The first fraternity house appeared in 1888 and within a half dozen years there were ten such chapter houses in Madison. By the turn of the century the "Greeks" were organized in eleven fraternities and seven sororities, most with their own houses providing living space for some of their members. Their numbers continued to proliferate, with thirty-one fraternities and fifteen sororities added by 1930, twenty-one in the previous decade alone. The Greek houses tended to offer the most attractive, if most expensive, student housing.[59] During the twenties a number of the chapters moved from the original Greek "ghetto" around Park and Murray Streets, Irving

---

know better than I the fun of living in a homogeneous group, where the men are on the same side of the fence. We had that at Halburn. We knew that we were indebted to you and to the Division for many favors; we knew that our success at Halburn would mean future co-operative houses, houses enjoying the same breaks that we got. Out of it I think we became better men, living among friends in a place we were glad to call home. Halburn has meant a lot to us....For both social and educational reasons the idea of Halburn can't be beat.
Gerald O. Dahlke to Halverson, June 2, 1943, UHP.

[59]Porter Butts, who enrolled in the University with his older brother Robert in 1920, recalled spending a miserable first semester "huddled in a little first floor room in a rooming house on Dayton Street" where they had to share the bathroom with the host family.
It was rather dreary. It really was, and we shortly found that our experience consisted of moving from our rooming house to class and back for a detour for breakfast somewhere and lunch and so on, wherever we could find it, and the disappointment was quite real; and since we had both been presidents of our senior class, my brother as well as myself, and highly socially motivated and active, this sudden isolation was a new experience and frightening, I must say. Well, it didn't last long because one of the fraternities that didn't seem to be attractive to us as members, one or two members of it nevertheless told another fraternity that we were on the loose and that fraternity that needed members rather badly to fill the partly empty house, came around and did ask us to join and we did and so this established us as part of what was really the mainstream of student life.
Porter Butts, oral history interview, 1979, UA.

Place, and Sterling Court to the Langdon Street area, which came to be called the Latin Quarter. This shift was part of a great building boom during the 1920s in which a considerable number of the better-established and wealthier chapters acquired lake-front property and proceeded to construct large, even magnificent, houses, in a few cases at a cost of $100,000 or more. Several large privately owned dormitories for women were also constructed in the Langdon area at this time. The location was convenient to the campus and downtown. Land costs were so high, however, that most of the sumptuous new structures were sited on relatively small lots lacking adequate space for recreation or even to set off their impressive architecture. Like much of the Babbitt boosterism of the twenties, the frantic expansion of the Greek houses was imprudent and excessive. Even before the stock market crash, in 1928 and 1929 UW fraternities had a 20 percent vacancy rate and the sororities 10 percent. When the great depression hit, the Greek houses could accommodate approximately two thousand residents—or more than a quarter of the undergraduate student population—considerably in excess of their historic share of the student body.[60]

The truth about Fraternities

Burdened by heavy indebtedness resulting from the costly expansion as well as by the expense of operating their larger houses, many of the Greek chapters were poorly prepared to cope with the economic devastation of the next decade. As campus enrollment declined in the early years of the depression, so too did the number of members and new pledges, a trend accelerated as students and their parents sought less expensive living. Active sorority membership dropped 23 percent

---

[60]Curti and Carstensen, *University of Wisconsin*, vol. 1, pp. 392, 665; *Badger*, 1933, pp. 57-9, 64.

and new pledges 36 percent between 1930 and 1934; fraternity actives declined 27 percent and pledges 31 percent in the same period. Unable to attract enough members to stem the flood of red ink, nine fraternities and three sororities gave up and disbanded. More cautious about expansion and more conservative in their financial management than the fraternities, most of the sororities were able to keep up their mortgage payments and meet their operating costs. By 1934, when enrollment began to rise again, none of the active sororities had lost its house. This was not true of the fraternities, which had expanded more recklessly in the previous decade. Because only three fraternities had clear title to their houses in 1929, during the depression's first four years 40 percent of the fraternity houses were taken over by their mortgage holders, which, lacking a market for the properties, in most cases were willing to allow the chapter to continue to occupy the facility on a rental basis. Another indicator of the Greek distress was the fact that thirty-eight of the chapter houses (twenty-nine fraternities and nine sororities) were delinquent on their Madison property tax bills in 1934.[61] It was to help the beleaguered Greek houses economize in order to survive the depression that Dean Goodnight took the lead in organizing the Fraternity Buyers Cooperative in 1932.

Regardless of the hard times of the thirties, the Greek chapters remained a powerful force in student life throughout the inter-war years. Grouped in an area convenient to the campus, their houses were indispensable in providing living accommodations for a substantial part of the undergraduate student body. Most of the time their members furnished the leadership of major student organizations, controlled student government, and dominated the social life of the campus. This activity came at a price, of course. Whereas the average academic performance of sorority women was usually about as high and occasionally exceeded that of non-sorority women students, the grade point average of fraternity men was invariably below any other group of undergraduates. The occasional fraternity with some high academic achievers was the rare exception. In building group loyalty and esprit, the Greek chapters also encouraged snobbery, elitism, and intolerance in their members that ran counter to the essentially open and democratic spirit of the campus. The expense of Greek life also inevitably accentuated economic class differences. Even after the Greek houses were obliged to cut their dues and room-and-board rates sharply in

---

[61]*Badger*, 1934, pp. 24-6.

order to attract members in the depression, the costs of initiation, membership, and an expensive social life were still beyond the reach of many students. Quite apart from the hazing of new pledges, which try as he might Dean Goodnight was never able to stamp out completely, the Greek system was cruel to those it rejected. While it was probably possible during this period for most students who really wanted to join a fraternity or sorority to gain acceptance by one of the many competing chapters, there were nevertheless far too many cases of personal heartache and lowered self-esteem after would-be pledges were blackballed by the most popular and prestigious chapters.[62]

Student Government

Student organizations—of classes, forensic societies, athletic teams, and the like—existed from the earliest days of the University, but it was not until the late nineteenth and early twentieth centuries that efforts to create all-campus student government mechanisms developed. In 1897 Dean of Women Ann Emery established the Women's League (renamed the Women's Self-Government Association, or WSGA, the following year). The new organization was part of the faculty effort to get students to take more responsibility for governing their extracurricular lives. Dean Emery modeled the association after a similar one at her alma mater, Vassar College, but it was the first of its kind at a public university.[63] All women students were automatically members of WSGA, whose officers represented student attitudes and interests in dealing with the dean of women's office—at first chiefly in determining the quiet and closing hours for women's residences—and were expected to communicate University policies and regulations to their constituents.

At first students viewed WSGA as the creature of the administration; consequently, the men saw no reason to follow suit. At the beginning of his administration, therefore, President Van Hise asked the major men's organizations to name a representative to a men's student Conference, a group with no formal structure or mandate other than to exchange views with the president. Van Hise gradually overcame initial suspicion by soliciting the students' opinions and passing on their suggestions to the faculty. In 1910 he and the students reorganized and

---

[62]See Butts, oral history interview.

[63]Lois Kimball Mathews, *The Dean of Women* (Boston: Houghton Mifflin, 1915), pp. 127-49; *Daily Cardinal*, February 27, 1938.

formalized the Conference on an elective basis with representation by classes and colleges and made it a quasi-legislative body, a sort of male counterpart of WSGA.   In 1916 the regents formally chartered the group as the Student Senate representing undergraduate men.   Also in 1910, on Van Hise's recommendation the faculty and Board of Regents approved the creation of a men's Student Court of nine upperclassmen to handle minor cases of misconduct with the exception of those involving academic dishonesty.   (Women's infractions were handled by WSGA and the dean of women.)   The court's activity expanded with experience, and soon it was dealing with cases involving hazing, mishandling of student funds, election irregularities, failure of students to pay bills, scalping of football tickets, and the like.   The decisions and sentences of the court were advisory to the faculty.   Those convicted had the right to appeal to the faculty Committee on Student Discipline, which could overturn or modify the court's recommended penalty (but rarely did) and which retained original jurisdiction over cases involving academic misconduct.[64]

Student interest in and support for the organs of general student government tended to wax and wane over the years.   During much of the period the student body seemed more interested in elections for class offices, king of the Junior Prom, or specialized bodies like the *Daily Cardinal* Board of Control than for the Student Senate or the Student Court.   Indeed, the nine justices of the Student Court abruptly resigned their posts in May of 1926, protesting the court's general ineffectiveness and inability to get evidence or convictions.   They declared flatly: "The male student body does not want student self-government, at least in respect to its disciplinary aspects."   The court remained unstaffed and inactive thereafter until reconstituted on a somewhat different basis after a student referendum in 1941.[65]   The Student Senate followed suit in October, 1927, turning its charter back to the regents with the

---

[64]Maurice M. Vance, *Charles Richard Van Hise: Scientist Progressive* (Madison: State Historical Society of Wisconsin, 1960), pp. 98-103; Curti and Carstensen, *University of Wisconsin*, vol. 2, pp. 76-81; Van Hise, "Self Government at the University of Wisconsin," National Association of State Universities, *Transactions and Proceedings* (1912), pp. 256-63; Van Hise, "Self Government at the University," *WAM*, 14 (March, 1913), 276-9.

[65]Robert H. Paddock and others to the Secretary of the Board of Regents, May 25, 1926, BOR Papers, 1/1/3, box 39; *Capital Times*, May 26, 1926; *Daily Cardinal*, May 26, 1926, March 11 and 14, May 6, 7, 19, and 21, October 14, 21, 25, and 26, November 8, 1941. One of the issues in the effort to recreate the Student Court in 1941 was whether the student government would get to keep parking and other traffic fines levied by the court. The regents eventually agreed to this.

explanation that it had no influence or power, particularly over the five elected subsidiary student boards governing most extracurricular activities (athletics, forensics, Union, *Cardinal*, and *Badger*). Dean Goodnight, the senate's faculty adviser, opined that these twin suicides did not at all mean the end of student government on the campus. "Things will go on much as they did before," he emphasized, through the continued functioning of the more specialized student governing organizations.[66] Following widespread campus discussion of the issue a decade later, in the spring of 1938 the students voted in favor of another attempt at broadly based representative student government through an elected Student Board, which functioned more or less successfully throughout the rest of this period.[67]

Women students were more successful than the men in their efforts at self-government. The Women's Self-Government Association remained the oldest and probably most successful student government unit throughout these years. Its officers were used by the dean of women as a student advisory group with considerable authority over University regulations governing women students. WSGA was organized to embrace all UW women students, especially the under-graduates. Its governing board included the presidents of the largest women's houses; in 1926 there were 110 members, one from each house with at least three women residents. The WSGA Council included the organization's officers, the chairmen of major committees, and the women class presidents. The WSGA Keystone Council consisted of the presidents of all campus women's organizations.

---

[66]UW Faculty Minutes, January 9, 1928, UA; BOR Minutes, January 18, 1928; *Daily Cardinal*, October 20, 21, 25, and 26, 1927, January 19, 1928; *Capital Times*, January 10, 1928; "Student Senate Expires," *WAM*, 29 (December, 1927), 90.

[67]A key actor in this effort to reform student government was James E. Doyle, who based his campaign for president of the senior class in the fall of 1936 on an attack on the men's Union Board, which by this time had evolved into a de facto men's student government through its many activities and key role in the programming of the Memorial Union. Doyle, an independent, was concerned about Greek domination of campus politics. Another proponent of change at this time was Horace Wilkie, the head of the House President's Council and son of Regent President Harold Wilkie. In the week-long referendum on the so-called Johnson Plan completed on March 1, 1938, the sororities and fraternities voted heavily against the change, but were outvoted by the independents in balloting that drew more than four thousand voters, the highest number of participants in any student election to that time and nearly half of the entire undergraduate student body. For an understanding of the lengthy campaign to create (and control) the Student Board, see *Daily Cardinal*, October 8, 10, 17, and 30, November 13, 17, and 30, 1936, March 12 and 27, April 11 and 30, 1937, February 15, 17, 18, and 27, March 2 and 24, October 12, November 22, December 9, 1938.

Through these bodies WSGA thus had organizational ties to all UW women students.

Before moving to the Memorial Union in 1928, the WSGA headquarters were in Lathrop Hall, built in 1908 as the women's counterpart to the men's Gymnasium/Armory building to provide space for the women's physical education program. Lathrop had a gymnasium, swimming pool, and office and meeting space and served as a recreation and social center for women students as well. Indeed, it served the function and was often referred to as the Women's Union Building before the construction of the Memorial Union in the late twenties. WSGA provided women students with an active social life: in the 1920s there were regular Friday night dances, costume parties, teas, and instruction in such popular pursuits as bridge, mah jong, and the latest dance steps. Lathrop was also home to another active and long-lived women's group, the Women's Athletic Association (WAA), organized in 1913 under the sponsorship of the women's physical education faculty to promote an active women's sports program. WAA had its own cottage on Lake Mendota, built in 1923-24 on University land below Eagle Heights through the sale of stock to members, friends, and alumnae. The two-story cottage provided enviable overnight recreational opportunities for as many as forty students from WAA, WSGA, or other women's groups, always suitably chaperoned by women faculty members. Lathrop Hall also contained the offices of the women's physical education faculty and the dean of women.

A Home for Wisconsin Spirit

In his inaugural address in 1904 President Van Hise called for a men's union as a center of campus fellowship and social life. The idea was taken up by the Iron Cross, the influential men's honorary society represented on Van Hise's men's Conference group, which in 1907 created the Wisconsin Men's Union. The Union was headed by an elected Union Board responsible for sponsoring an active program of social events—mixers, dances, concerts, and other entertainments. For the next decade the Wisconsin Men's Union leased the ground floor of the University YMCA building (on the site of the present Memorial Union parking lot) to provide club and meeting rooms with billiard and card tables, soda fountain, cigar and newsstand, and lounging space. Eventually a new YMCA director objected to the Union's sale of cigars and its smokers, so the board moved its headquarters next door to a University-owned house providing offices for various student publications and organizations. After 1925 it relocated into the former University president's house on the corner of Langdon and Park Streets. The Union Board very quickly became a prestigious group, sponsoring more activities, handling more funds and dispensing more patronage, and in general commanding more respect than most other student leadership positions. The Union's frequent mixers and dances filled a need particularly for the independent students—the "barbs" or barbarians—who were left out of the more exclusive Greek social life. For many years its annual Union Vodvil show played to sold-out houses, first at the Armory and later at the Fuller Opera House downtown. Gradually the Wisconsin Union Concert Series gained the patronage of faculty and townspeople as well as students, and by the 1920s it was bringing nationally prominent concert artists, major symphony orchestras, touring theatrical companies, and famous lecturers to Madison. In 1927-28, for example, the last year before the opening of the Memorial Union building made possible an expanded program, the Union sponsored six concerts, including performances by the Ukrainian National Chorus and such eminent artists as Pablo Casals, Serge Rachmaninoff, and Fritz Kreisler, as well as a dance program by the Dennishawn Dancers.[68] For a time the Union organized a series of ambitious quadrennial all-University expositions to demonstrate the work of UW departments to admiring Wisconsin residents.[69]

Almost from the first, the Union Board emphasized the need for more suitable facilities for its burgeoning activities. It regularly complained there was no central meeting place for its members or for other men's organizations, no stage or theater, no auditorium large enough for all-campus convocations, expositions, or mass meetings. Consequently, the board was obliged to hold most of its dances in the women's social center, Lathrop Hall, and its concerts and dramatic productions in the Armory, the Stock Pavilion, or a downtown theater.

---

[68]*Badger*, 1928, p. 351. The hard-working president of the Wisconsin Union in 1927-28 was a Madison senior, Lowell E. Frautschi, a three-year veteran of the men's Union Board, who during his undergraduate years helped with the fund-raising campaign for the Memorial Union building project and for many years thereafter was a leader of the Memorial Union Building Association.

[69]For the origins of the Union Board, see Butts, oral history interview; Butts, "Diary of the Union" (unpublished manuscript, April 15, 1949), UHP; *Badger*, 1914, p. 310, and ibid., 1922, p. 196.

The 1915-16 report of its president, Crawford Wheeler, declared plaintively, "There is no other need so urgent as that for a Union building, which will combine in one place the facilities at present so entirely lacking."[70] The lament was echoed by other campus organizations, including the Wisconsin University Players, a student dramatic group sponsored by the speech department, and the men's Haresfoot Club, which from 1898 onward annually produced a popular "female" musical comedy or song-and-dance revue under the catchy motto, "All of our girls are men, yet everyone's a lady."

President Van Hise tried without success to secure state funding for a men's union building and died in 1918 without seeing the realization of this dream. After his death the drive for a union facility was taken up by Dean of Men Goodnight, with powerful support from Regent President Walter J. Kohler, Sr., a prominent Wisconsin industrialist. Kohler had provided a similar American Club for his employees and appreciated the value of constructive social and recreational facilities. Kohler, Goodnight, and others decided to launch a campaign to raise private funds for the building as a memorial to the UW men who had given their lives in the recent war. As president of the regents Kohler appointed a Memorial Union Building Committee and assumed the vice-chairmanship.[71] At first Goodnight was released part-time from his other duties to direct the effort. This was the first major private fund-raising campaign in the University's history, and Kohler, Goodnight, and the rest of the committee found it tougher going than anticipated. For one thing, the University lacked up-to-date records on its alumni. The Wisconsin Alumni Association had addresses only for its membership, about two thousand of the approximately ninety thousand living alumni. The need for better information about UW alumni for purposes of the campaign led eventually to the creation of the Alumni Records Bureau in 1924 and a subsequent tug-of-war over whether it should be run by the University or by the alumni association. Another

---

[70]Butts, *The College Union Idea* (Stanford, California: Association of College Unions, 1971), p. 13.

[71]The Board of Regents never discharged this committee, even after completion of the theater wing in 1939, and the committee continued to function as a Union support group, filling its own vacancies. At the urging of University Business Manager A.W. Peterson, a member of the committee, it was legally incorporated in 1951 as the Memorial Union Building Association, with the redoubtable George Haight as its first president and the other committee members serving as trustees. This board has continued as a useful and sometimes influential adjunct of the Union Council, and has independent control of the funds derived from the sale of annual and life memberships in the Wisconsin Union.

problem was the lack of any tradition of financial support for the University among its alumni and friends, apart from pride in the success of Badger athletic teams or other student endeavors. The solicitors discovered that many alumni were unwilling to contribute to the campaign, arguing as a matter of principle that it was the state's responsibility to provide University buildings.

The drive required an energetic, dedicated, and persuasive salesman to educate alumni, students, and parents to the need for private financial support. This role was soon filled by English Professor Edward H. "Ned" Gardner, ironically an Amherst and not a UW graduate, who took over Goodnight's role and spent the next several years crisscrossing the country seeking out alumni and enthusiastically garnering donations and pledges under the slogan, "Build a Home for Wisconsin Spirit." Gardner recruited John Dollard, '22, first as an assistant and then as his successor in 1923. Other prominent faculty members involved in the campaign were Max Mason and Harold Bradley. Dollard helped to set up the Alumni Records Bureau with another recent graduate, Porter F. Butts, '24, but also galvanized the Union Board, class presidents, and other student leaders and organizations to get donations, pledges, and life memberships from the current student body. The Union Board set aside part of the proceeds of its profitable concert series and Vodvil performances and other activities for the project and conducted annual building promotions among the students. In the end the students contributed more than the alumni, with one of every two students pledging $50 or more for a life membership in a building most of them knew they would never see completed in time for their use as students. It was a remarkable demonstration of the students' commitment to their community.

The appointment of President Glenn Frank in 1925 marked a turning point of sorts in the Memorial Union building campaign. By then enough money had been raised to clear the Langdon Street site as a sign of visible progress. An experienced publicist, the new president was aware of the importance of symbols in a venture of this sort. Accordingly, at 11:00 A.M. on Armistice Day in 1925, exactly seven years after the guns had fallen silent on the western front in France, a crowd of five thousand watched while ROTC howitzers boomed a round of salutes and President Frank turned the first shovel of dirt for the University's memorial to its own fallen sons. The event was purely symbolic, however, for the project still lacked enough money to start construction. Even before this ceremony, Frank's appointment had led

Max Mason, the leading inside candidate for the UW presidency and one of the faculty members on the Memorial Union Building Committee, to accept the presidency of the University of Chicago. A year later Mason recruited John Dollard, by then serving in the key role of executive secretary of the building project, to be his assistant. To meet this leadership crisis the committee recruited Porter Butts from his job as alumni recorder to finish the campaign under the slogan, "Let's Dig." The Butts appointment proved to be fortuitous.

The Board of Regents authorized bids for the first two wings of the Union in the late summer of 1926. Because of the current construction boom even the lowest bid—from the Pfeffer Construction Company of Duluth, Minnesota, for $773,000—was more than $100,000 higher than the available funds. And in addition to being from out-of-state, Pfeffer was an open shop firm. The next lowest bid, several hundred thousand dollars higher, was from a union contractor in Janesville, who promptly pledged $15,000 for the building campaign (Dollard called it a bribe) and waited for the pro-union progressive majority

Preliminary Sketch of the Great Hall

on the Board of Regents to reject the low bid and order the project scaled back to fit the available funds. The building committee resolutely rejected the thought of either sacrificing the beauty or quality of the proposed building—one member declared he wanted no part of planning a memorial barracks—or of delaying construction. Instead it launched an emergency drive for additional contributions, with Dollard calling on the seventeen thousand subscribers to increase and advance the schedule of payment on their pledges. For their part, the students organized a new round of fund-raising endeavors, including a ball attended by four hundred couples in the new Hotel Loraine ballroom. These activities raised about $23,000 in ten days.

When the Board of Regents met on October 13, 1926, with the building fund still short of the full amount needed to cover the low bid, the building committee recommended deferring several sub-contracts while the main construction proceeded as pledges were collected. The regents insisted the project must have the full $773,000 in hand, but agreed to delay action for a week while the committee reviewed the plans and the funding problem. Determined neither to lose the low Pfeffer bid nor to cut back on the quality and scope of the building, the committee came up with a desperate last-minute scheme to raise the missing $90,000. Two devoted Chicago alumni members, George Haight and Israel Shrimsky, both of whom had already made large contributions, persuaded seven other wealthy men each to borrow $10,000 from a friendly Madison banker on unsecured notes, to be used as the building committee's advance against unpaid pledges. At the critical regents meeting on October 22—only two weeks before Dollard's resignation to accept the University of Chicago position—he innocently asked if the only problem holding up acceptance of the low bid was the lack of sufficient funds. When assured the board had no other concerns, Dollard triumphantly presented a bank draft for the missing $90,000, offered with his building committee's explicit understanding the regents would award the contract to the firm whose bid was "very substantially lower than any of the others...so that there will be no further delay in proceeding to construction." Whatever uneasiness some of the members may have had about accepting the bid of an out-of-state and open shop contractor, the board voted 13-1 to authorize construction on this basis. The margin seemed overwhelming, but to the building committee the victory was in reality a near thing.[72]

---

[72]John Dollard to the Board of Regents, October 21, 1926, BOR Papers, 1/1/3, box 41; BOR Minutes, April 28, October 13 and 22, 1926; George I. Haight and Edward H. Gardner reminiscences, Memorial Union Building Committee Minutes, September 28, 1951, UHP; Butts, oral history interview; *Daily Cardinal*, September 22, 23, 24, and 26, October 1, 4, 5, 6, 7, 8, 9, 10, 12, 13, 14, 15, 16, 17, 21, and 22, 1926; *Capital Times*, October 13 and 22, 1926. Besides this $90,000 last-minute loan against pledges, the building committee had raised nearly a half million dollars in cash and the regents had earlier pledged $200,000 from the Tripp Estate. Haight, '99, served on the Memorial Union Building Committee for many years, contributing generously of his time and wealth to this and other University endeavors. In the eyes of many he was the embodiment of UW spirit and devotion. It will be recalled that a year earlier he played a key role in the successful regents' public relations campaign to avert a

Construction of the central social/recreational unit and the adjoining dining or commons wing began at once, there not being enough money to build the projected Memorial Union Theater wing at this time.[73] Meanwhile, the fund-raising campaign continued under Butts' direction, since the unexpectedly high construction costs had left no money to equip, furnish, and decorate the interior of the building. As a result there was understandable concern the structure would stand idle upon completion. Eventually, three ingenious attorneys—George Haight, Regent Theodore Kronshage, and Philip F. La Follette, the latter a former Union Board president while an undergraduate and now a part-time Law School lecturer—came up with the idea of expanding the mandate of the new Wisconsin University Building Corporation, which had been created in 1925 to borrow funds and construct the Adams-Tripp men's dormitories. The WUBC borrowed $400,000 from the state Commissioner of Public Lands on a fifteen-year mortgage at 4½ percent interest to equip and furnish the Union; the regents agreed to lease the site to the WUBC for a dollar a year until its loan was repaid through a Union rental payment of $36,000 a year; and the Wisconsin Men's Union Board and the Women's Self-Government Association agreed to petition the regents to establish an annual $10 Memorial Union membership fee to be paid by all students, enough to cover the loan payments with a margin for operating costs. A friendly opinion by the state attorney general and ruling by the Wisconsin Supreme Court established the legality of the arrangement. It was creative financing at its best, a worthy climax to the entire bootstrap campaign for the $1,250,000 Memorial Union building.[74]

There were soon some discordant notes, however. During the spring of 1927 a labor dispute erupted over the open-shop Pfeffer firm's use of four out-of-town non-union workers. Some local union workers refused to work with them and walked off the job. The Madison craft unions involved then threw up picket lines around the building site, garnering a good deal of student support in the weeks to come. After a series of incidents Pfeffer erected a bunk house on the site so his non-

---

draconian budget cut.

[73]For an interesting discussion of some of the engineering and design problems of the building by the project engineer see C.A. Willson, "The Structural Design of Our Memorial Union Building," *Wisconsin Engineer*, 31 (April, 1927), 221-3, 252.

[74]BOR Minutes, June 18, August 27, 1927, January 18, April 25, 1928; *Capital Times*, June 20, September 10, 1927; *Daily Cardinal*, April 22, May 30, 1928; Porter Butts, "The Union Building Is Up!" *WAM*, 29 (October, 1927), 7.

union workers would not be harassed in crossing the picket line. Over the next few weeks there were a number of increasingly violent skirmishes, involving stone-throwing, fisticuffs, threats to throw the non-strikers into the lake, and damage to building materials. University and city officials made futile efforts to mediate the conflict, while at the same time trying to keep from direct involvement in the dispute. A state legislative committee launched an investigation. On the night of May 20 a large mob attacked the site, roughed up the non-strikers, tossed several into the lake, demolished their bunk house, and threw ink over the exterior stone work of the building. Porter Butts was working late in his Union Annex office in the former president's home next door when the attack began. He and others telephoned four times for the city police, most of whose members were unionized, but found them unconcerned and unresponsive until the affair was over. Following the fracas the state attorney general reminded Madison Mayor Albert G. Schmedeman he could be held responsible for property damage occurring when the city police did not answer a legitimate call for protection. Thereafter Schmedeman saw that a substantial police guard was posted at the site around the clock, until Pfeffer finally got a permanent federal court injunction at the end of the summer barring any further interference with construction.[75]

Another sour note was struck when the building committee won a test suit in Milwaukee to collect an unpaid pledge by a student for the building drive. Most students paid their pledges willingly and often in advance, but in its zeal to complete the project the committee wanted to establish the legal basis of the pledged funds for possible use as collateral. The *Daily Cardinal*, an unflagging booster of the Union project, complained editorially that the law suit was too heavy-handed, but other students agreed the building pledges were binding obligations that ought to be paid.[76]

Other disagreements arose over the future governance and use of the Memorial Union. The project had been conceived originally by Van

---

[75]Under his open-shop philosophy Pfeffer evidently preferred to hire Madison workers, union and non-union alike, but insisted on using his own foremen and supervisors. After the strike developed, objections to a compromise settlement seemed to come more from several of the sub-contractors rather than from the Pfeffer firm. Throughout the long and acrimonious dispute President Frank managed to keep uninvolved and uncriticized. For coverage of the dispute see *Daily Cardinal* and *Capital Times*, April 16-August 31, 1927; Butts, oral history interview; Butts, "Diary of the Union."

[76]*Daily Cardinal*, February 16, 17, and 18, 1928.

Hise and the Union Board to secure suitable quarters for the Wisconsin Men's Union, to provide space comparable to Lathrop Hall as the campus center of women students' social and recreational activities. As construction proceeded, the Union Board understandably assumed it would have a major role in operating the building. Women students and alumnae had contributed generously to the building campaign, however, and it was clear even before the building was finished that to some undefined extent it had become a general student endeavor rather than a strictly men's union. In February of 1927 President Frank asked Professor Harold Bradley, the experienced chairman of the faculty Dormitories Committee, to head a broadly based committee, whose forty members included alumni as well as faculty, students, and administrators, to develop plans for the administration of the Union when it opened the next year.[77] The Bradley committee had little difficulty agreeing in principle that women students should have a role in the building, which would provide office space for WSGA as well as for the men's Union Board. A much more difficult issue was the extent to which students, and in particular the men's Union Board which had initiated the project, should direct the operation of the facility. A key player in these sometimes heated deliberations was Clyde K. Kluckhohn, the 1927-28 president of the Union Board, who after graduation went on to be a Rhodes Scholar and ultimately a distinguished Harvard anthropologist. Kluckhohn held out doggedly and successfully against Deans Goodnight and Nardin and University Business Manager J.D. Phillips for effective student control of this student enterprise.[78]

The Bradley Committee's report, submitted in the spring of 1928, offered a constitution for the Union reflecting the chairman's longstanding commitment to encouraging responsible student self-government.[79] The report established various membership categories, including one for alumni, and called for a governing council consisting of

---

[77]Ibid., February 19 and 22, 1927.

[78]At one point Kluckhohn's persistence overcame the University Committee's inclination to put the Union under Dean Goodnight's Student Life and Interests Committee. See Clyde Kluckhohn to Lowell Frautschi, January 25, 1928, UHP.

[79]Bradley had played a leading role in developing the innovative house fellow system used in the new men's dormitories, in which older students—typically graduate students—were employed to live in the undergraduate houses to provide leadership and peer counseling and to serve as role models in developing well-rounded social and intellectual interests. He saw the Memorial Union as a similar vehicle for promoting responsibility and healthy extracurricular activities in the student body as a whole.

eight students, two faculty and two alumni members, plus the Union steward (Donald Halverson, the director of dormitories and commons) and the house director (Porter Butts). Thus, the student members of the council would constitute a clear 8-6 majority in governing the Union. Kluckhohn jubilantly reported to his predecessor, Lowell Frautschi, that the outcome was "more favorable from the point of view of real student government than I had thought possible."[80] Following the approval of this constitution by the faculty and the regents, at a memorable ceremony on May 16, 1928, Bradley turned over control of the as yet unfinished Memorial Union building to the elected student president of the new Union Council, Lauriston Sharp, '29, the son of philosophy Professor Frank Sharp and another future Rhodes Scholar.[81] After reviewing the history of college unions generally and the Wisconsin effort in particular, Bradley gently reminded Sharp that "with power always goes responsibility." It was, as the *Cardinal* acknowledged, an unparalleled advance in student self-government at Wisconsin and nationally.[82]

Not everyone thought students capable of exercising such power responsibly, however. Deans Goodnight and Nardin continued their skepticism about the wisdom of student control of the council. In 1930 the alumni association, which tended in these years to take a dim view of student politics and student government generally, tried to persuade the Board of Regents to amend the Union constitution to give the alumni and faculty a majority on the council. In keeping with his basic view that students ought to take responsibility for their community, President Frank successfully opposed this move and was supported by the alumni members of the Union Council.[83]

The Memorial Union opened for use with a simple dedication

---

[80]Kluckhohn to Frautschi, January 25, 1928.

[81]Sharp was the first to occupy the living quarters provided in the Memorial Union for the use of the student president. A similar furnished apartment was provided for the house director, Porter Butts.

[82]UW Faculty Minutes, March 5, 1928; UW Faculty Document 322A, "Constitution of the Wisconsin Union," March 5, 1928, UA; BOR Minutes, March 7, 1928; *Daily Cardinal*, March 5, 8, 9, and 11, May 16 and 17, 1928; *Capital Times*, March 28, 1928. In approving the Union constitution the regents suggested that the "operating group" of the Bradley Committee continue for the time being as a steadying influence over the student-controlled Union Council until the latter got more experience.

[83]BOR Minutes, August 6 and 19, 1930; *Daily Cardinal*, March 30, April 5, August 4, November 15, 1930; *Capital Times*, August 6, 1930; "Student Government," *WAM*, 32 (November, 1930), 62; Butts, "Diary of the Union"; Butts, oral history interview.

ceremony on the lakeshore terrace on the evening of October 5, 1928. Lauriston Sharp presided and called on George Haight, the ever-loyal alumnus and member of the building committee who had done so much to make the project a reality, to dedicate the building to the memory of the UW men and women who had served in the nation's wars—"in confidence," Haight declared, "that it will urge upon all who come within its walls depth of character, breadth of vision, and the will to carry on." President Frank offered a dedicatory prayer asking that the Union be thought of as a memorial to past and future students—not as a memorial to war but "as a memorial to youth"—so future students "may bring to the affairs of their time a clarity of mind, a cleanness of purpose, and a courage of action that shall make it unnecessary for young men ever again to face the barbarity of war."[84] The doors were then thrown open to the several thousand people in attendance, and over the next few weeks many thousands more Madison and Wisconsin residents came to inspect and marvel at the two completed wings of the ornate Italian renaissance-style structure. Twelve thousand visitors came on one Sunday alone. They found a truly impressive memorial. The dining wing contained modern kitchens and a stately two-story dining hall—Tripp Commons—as well as several smaller dining/meeting rooms. The larger central commons unit housed on its ground floor several game rooms and the sprawling low-ceiling Rathskeller reminiscent of a German beer hall for casual lounging and snacks. The second floor contained a central lounge and smaller library, art gallery, and music rooms. A massive domed Great Hall dominated the third floor, leaving space for offices for student publications and organizations as well as the alumni association. Throughout, the project's interior decorator, Leon R. Pescheret of Chicago, had managed to give the building a rich and stately character more mindful of the buildings of the ancient European universities than of a utilitarian midwestern state institution.[85]

The Bradley Committee's constitution for the Union spelled out neither the future roles of the existing Wisconsin Men's Union and its Union Board nor the extent to which women would be able to share the

---

[84]"Dedicate Memorial Union Building," *WAM*, 30 (November, 1928), 43.

[85]For a good description of Pescheret's designs see Butts, "The University Furnishes Its 'Living Room'," *WAM*, 29 (February, 1928), 162-3. For the engineering design problems encountered in constructing the building, see Willson, "The Structural Design of Our Memorial Union Building," and "The Engineer of Yesteryear: The Structural Design of the Memorial Union Building," *WAM*, 65 (January, 1961), 28-9.

Memorial Union's facilities and activities. By establishing a new governance mechanism—the Union Council—the committee was clearly circumscribing the Union Board's claim to primacy in the operation of the building. Sensitive to this issue, the Board of Regents explicitly encouraged the Men's Union to continue as a student organization. It promptly filed articles of incorporation with the Wisconsin secretary of state as a non-profit, non-stock corporation comprising all men students at the University. The elected Union Board continued as the agency for carrying out the corporation's purpose "to promote all things socially and culturally of value to students," chiefly through continuing to schedule most of the activities and events in the Memorial Union, including the board's traditional Union Concert Series.[86] This potentially confusing parallel administrative structure continued until 1939, when the student body adopted a new governance system effectively replacing the men's Union Board, which had served as the de facto campus-wide student government since the late twenties, with a broadly based elected Student Board.[87] The Memorial Union Council and Directorate (which thereafter included women as well as men) then assumed responsibility for the concert series and other union programming. At about the same time the Union took over the administration of its food service from Halverson's Department of Dormitories and Commons. Designated by the regents as a separate Division of Social Education in 1935, with the House Director Porter Butts and Steward Donald Halverson given faculty status as assistant professors of social education,[88] by the end of the thirties the Memorial Union had evolved into a largely autonomous educational and recreational center of considerable and growing influence and force in the campus community.[89]

---

[86]"Men's Union Incorporated," *WAM*, 29 (July, 1928), 356.

[87]By this time the Union Board had become tarnished in the eyes of many students as well as the faculty and University administration. Usually the fraternities were able to maintain control of the board, sometimes amidst charges of corruption and ballot-stuffing. The last straw came when the 1938-39 president of the board, Ed Fleming, was apprehended after he and two friends stole most of the copies of the *Daily Cardinal* for January 8, 1939, and hid them under a lakeshore pier in order to block publication of an unflattering story. The trio was fined and put on probation by the faculty Discipline Committee, and Fleming resigned his board post in disgrace. In a rare angry outburst, President Dykstra declared he would not tolerate any more chicanery in student politics. *Daily Cardinal*, January 10 and 15, 1939.

[88]BOR Minutes, June 22, 1935. Maintaining the confusing parallel structure, the 1935 regent action included both "the Wisconsin Union and the Memorial Union Building" in the new Division of Social Education.

[89]See Butts, "Diary of the Union"; Butts, oral history interview.

As for the women, their right to use the Memorial Union, though partial at first, expanded steadily over time. The headquarters of the Women's Self-Government Association moved at once from Lathrop Hall to the Union building, where the WSGA president served automatically as the vice president of the Union Council. The fee of $2 a year paid by all women students to support WSGA activities was abandoned, with a portion of the women's $10 annual Union membership fee assigned to replace it. Lathrop Hall continued for a time as a women's social center, in which the Memorial Union's food service operated a tea room for women. Still, there was no denying that Lathrop Hall was no substitute for the magnificent Union building, nor that the women did not at first have full access to the latter's facilities. In particular, the ground floor barber shop, billiard room, and Rathskeller were restricted to men except on dance nights and other special occasions when the latter was open to couples. Women were permitted in the adjacent Katskeller, organized and named by the Union's Women's Affairs Committee as a tongue-in-cheek protest, but they could obtain food and beverages from the Rathskeller only through waiter service. To even the score somewhat, when the Great Hall was not used for other events it was initially reserved and set up as a women's lounge offering afternoon tea service, which later moved downstairs to the more intimate Georgian Grill. These gender distinctions were hard to maintain, of course, though as late as 1939 the students voted by a 6-4 margin (with half the women in support) to keep the Rathskeller as a male sanctuary. The Union Board did agree in 1936 to admit women to the Rathskeller on movie nights and the following year to open it to women generally during the summer. By late 1941, with the old men's Union Board no longer in existence to protest and with the University gearing up for war, the Union Council decided to allow women into the Rathskeller on an unrestricted basis. Normally outspoken Dean Sellery,

𝔇𝔢𝔰 𝔖𝔱𝔲𝔡𝔢𝔫𝔱𝔢𝔫𝔰 𝔗𝔯𝔞𝔲𝔪

A STUDENTS DREAM.

One of the Rathskeller's Germanic Murals

an old Rathskeller habitué, professed to be too upset to comment about the invasion of the fairer sex, but the traditional male haven was clearly gone forever.[90]

The early plans for the Union building provided for a third wing housing a large modern theater, intended to fill a long-standing campus need. Much to the disappointment of campus arts groups, the Union Theater wing was dropped when the project had to be scaled back to fit within the available construction funds. Instead, the University remodeled a large classroom in Bascom Hall to give it a stage, and the room was thereafter used for student dramatic productions, especially those of the Wisconsin Players sponsored by the Department of Speech. But the room's basic use for instruction limited rehearsal time, its second-floor location was inconvenient and its wooden seats noisy and uncomfortable, and the inadequate lighting and shallow depth of the stage imposed serious technical limitations. Large student productions like the Haresfoot revues had to rent the Fuller Opera House or Parkway Theater downtown, in which rehearsals could be scheduled only after the final movie showing at night. The stage of the Union's Great Hall was too small for dramatic productions, but the room was used for small concerts and lectures. The inconvenience of setting up and taking down hundreds of folding chairs in Great Hall was a major headache, however. At best the room was only marginally better as a concert hall than the Armory or the Stock Pavilion, and in any event only the latter could handle large performing groups like visiting symphony orchestras.

The availability of construction grants through the federal Public Works Administration in the mid-thirties enabled the Union Council and the Memorial Union Building Committee to reopen the question of the deferred Union Theater wing. In 1937 the Board of Regents agreed the Union could develop plans for the third unit and authorized the University to apply for a PWA grant to help with its construction. Like the earlier effort, the theater wing was another patchwork of creative financing: a $266,000 PWA grant, $135,000 from the Union's operating surplus and additional gifts from students and alumni, and $585,000 from a long-term loan secured by the compulsory student membership fee. Planning for the third unit was already extensive: Butts and the

---

[90]See *Daily Cardinal*, December 12, 1936, July 8, 1937, November 18, December 14, 1939; *Capital Times* and *Wisconsin State Journal*, November 23, 1941; *Press Bulletin*, December 3, 1941; *WAM*, 38 (July, 1937), 366; Butts to Ted Crabb, memo, "Original Provisions for the Use of the Memorial Union Building by Women," May 16, 1990, UHP.

Union staff had surveyed students, faculty, and potential user groups as to what facilities they most wanted in the structure. A large theater continued to be the top priority by a wide margin, followed more distantly by a bowling alley, work shops, and special interest club rooms. Further consultation with user groups and with music and speech faculty led to the decision to have two theaters: a spacious balconied hall seating thirteen hundred patrons for concerts, plays, ballet, and musical revues, and another smaller theater with a seating capacity of about three hundred for lectures, movies, and more intimate dramatic and musical presentations. Throughout, Butts consulted extensively with Lee Simonson, one of the founding members of the New York Theater Guild and an expert on theater design, in order to get facilities that would work well in multiple use.

Because in the end the PWA grant had to be spent quickly, Butts was able to persuade the state architect to hire Michael Hare, a New Yorker recommended by Simonson, as the design architect for the project. Hare produced a full set of detailed working plans in three months. There was considerable opposition to his exterior design, which called for a modern facade on a wing attached to the existing Italian renaissance-style building. Eventually, the highly respected Harold Bradley, who as chairman of the planning committee had worked closely with Simonson and Hare, was able to persuade the regents to approve the design with some modifications to the Langdon Street facade to make it harmonize better with the older part of the Union. (The regents evidently worried less about architectural harmony on the lake side.) These changes, unfortunately, also reduced the capacity of the small theater—the Play Circle—to only 168 seats.[91]

The Union Theater wing opened for public inspection on Sunday, Octnber 8, 1939, to an estimated fifteen thousand people, who toured the facility and listened while Hare and Simonson on the stage of the large theater demonstrated its superb acoustics. The following night America's famous theater couple, Alfred Lunt and Lynn Fontanne,

---

[91]Butts, oral history interview, 1976, transcribed by Nancy Bintz and Jim Rogers, in Fannie T. Taylor, *The Wisconsin Union Theater: Oral Histories* (Madison: Wisconsin Union, 1989), pp. 27-34. Bradley reminded the regents of the changing styles in women's hats with each new season. So, too, with buildings, he said. He didn't necessarily like the new styles when they first came out, but he kept an open mind and after getting used to the new hats (or buildings) found them attractive. For a contemporary discussion of the design problems of the theater wing see John J. Huppler, "The New Union Wing," *Wisconsin Engineer*, 43 (March, 1939), 96-7.

formally dedicated the theater with a special première performance of their new touring production of Shakespeare's *The Taming of the Shrew*. The Lunts were persuaded to take part in the theater dedication by Professor Andrew Weaver, the speech department chairman, who had roomed with Alfred Lunt at Carroll College many years before. They agreed to end a show in New York and mount this new production as their part of this major achievement in the state where they were summer residents. For Madisonians, who had hoped for a proper city theater for decades, the gala formal-dress opening was the social event of the year, drawing a sold-out house. It was preceded by a festive celebration dinner in Tripp Commons for some three hundred guests, including many of the alumni, students, and faculty who had helped to make the project a reality. Governor Heil grumbled about high cost of the $5.00 opening night tickets, which he thought ruled out student attendance, but the *Daily Cardinal*, for once more practical than the businessman governor, defended the price because it helped underwrite the fifty-cent-tickets for students at the Lunts' three later performances.[92]

Thus, an even twenty years after Dean Goodnight and Regent Kohler had launched the Union building campaign in 1919, the dream was at last a full reality: an elegant multi-purpose structure whose scenic location, comprehensive facilities, luxurious furnishings, and range of activities were equal to or better than those at any university in the country. It would be hard to overstate the importance of the Memorial Union in the life of the student body. If, as Van Hise had hoped, the Union was to be a unifying force in the student community, in practice it was far more. It enriched student life exponentially through facilities and programming few students had ever before experienced in their own homes or communities. As President Frank liked to say, the building's purpose was to provide a "living room" to convert the University from a house of knowledge into "a 'home' of learning."[93]

The Memorial Union was one of the first comprehensive student social centers in the United States, and Porter Butts deserves a great deal of credit for expanding the vision of what a union might be as a central unifying and educational force for the campus. In this he soon

---

[92]*Capital Times*, October 5, 1939; *Daily Cardinal*, October 7, 1939. See also Taylor, *Wisconsin Union Theater: Oral Histories*, pp. 35-7; Taylor, *The Wisconsin Union Theater: Fifty Golden Years* (Madison: Memorial Union Building Association, 1989), pp. 27-30.

[93]*Badger*, 1928, p. 355.

became a nationally recognized authority and innovator. Involved in planning the Union building almost from the beginning, Butts as house director subsequently played a leading role in developing the Union's ever-expanding array of activities after it opened in 1928. Restlessly energetic, creative and innovative, always open to new ideas, he was constantly trying new things to expand students' cultural experiences. An early example was his decision to launch the country's first student art gallery with its own permanent art collection and annual juried art competition—the Wisconsin Salon of Art—to identify new talent. This led in turn to the development of a program to lend students original works of art for a modest rental fee each semester. Butts was equally innovative in promoting wholesome recreational activities. In an effort to provide inexpensive entertainment and keep students on campus, in 1932 he opened a nightclub, the Club 770 (named for the Union's street address), in Tripp Commons every Saturday night, complete with a dance orchestra and floor shows. The Union provided a home and workshops for a variety of special interest groups concerned with photography, crafts, music, outdoor recreation, and other activities, and offered instruction and tournaments in subjects ranging from contract bridge and billiards to social dancing, skiing, and sailing. The Union Forum Committee regularly sponsored lectures and debates on topics of current interest and brought in speakers of national prominence.

After the third wing was added in 1939, Butts made sure the Union Theater was booked to the fullest possible extent—eventually averaging more than one use a day throughout the year—to present a variety of concerts, dance and theatrical performances by student and road show groups, lectures, illustrated travelogues, conferences, and the like. Butts stressed that Memorial Union was not simply a student facility but a *Wisconsin Union*—for UW staff and alumni members as well as for students. He also genuinely believed in the primary role of students in the Union's governance and program planning. Most of the time he worked easily and effectively with the student-dominated Union Council and student-run Union Directorate, the latter consisting of the student chairmen of the many Union program and other committees. Usually his persuasive and intense leadership commanded student respect and support, but on the rare occasions when it did not he was adroit enough to avert any damaging confrontations or lasting ruptures. The Memorial Union was often held up as a rare model of responsible student self-government, thanks in no small part to Butts' encouragement and skill in working with an ever-changing succession of student leaders.

◇   ◇   ◇

From a state approaching benign neglect, the University's *in loco parentis* role mushroomed from the turn of the century through the Second World War. Working with the faculty Committee on Student Life and Interests, the deans of men and women took on responsibility for supervising nearly every aspect of student extracurricular life. New buildings like the Memorial Union, the WAA cottage, the Field House, and a variety of outdoor sports facilities provided support for wholesome recreational activities undreamed of by earlier generations of UW students, while the Varsity Welcome, Freshman Week, and the Bureau of Guidance and Records sought to integrate new students more smoothly into the University family and aid their academic success. Increasingly, the emphasis was less on paternalistic regulation and discipline and more on fostering student responsibility and maturity. In this objective the chief architects—Frank, Dykstra, Goodnight, Troxell, Butts, Halverson, and Bradley—were implementing the Van Hise vision of a closely knit, mutually supportive academic community concerned with education in the broadest sense.

The Upper Campus at class break in 1940

Registration line in September, 1928

607

Student Senate meeting, January 8, 1926
With President Frank and Dean Goodnight

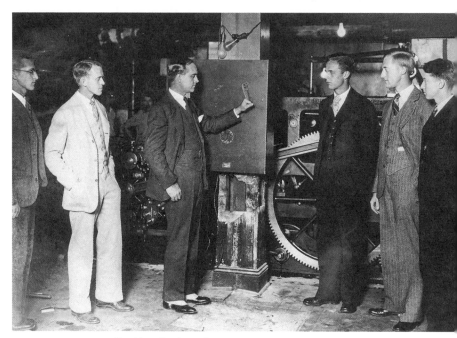

President Frank starting the new *Daily Cardinal* press
September 19, 1927

Tripp-Adams Men's Residence Halls
Constructed 1925-26

Elizabeth Waters Women's Residence Hall
Constructed 1938-40

609

Starting construction of the Memorial Union
December 9, 1925

Laying the first stone of the Memorial Union
Porter Butts, Lowell Frautschi, Harold Bradley
February 23, 1926

President Frank laying the Union corner stone
May 30, 1927

610

The Union Rathskeller as a male haven

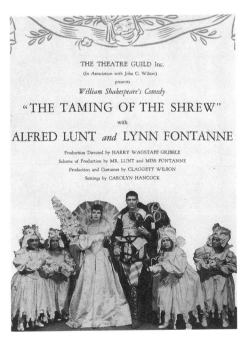

Playbill for the Union Theater opening
October 9, 1939

611

The first Experimental College class in 1927
Alexander Meiklejohn in center of second row

The Experimental College Players in *Lysistrata*
December 2, 1928

612

The 1924 Haresfoot musical, *Twinkle, Twinkle*

Posters for the annual University Religious Conference

A student outing in the fall of 1925

The University pier about 1930

Sinclair Lewis with admiring coeds in October, 1940

Senior Swingout in 1927

Pipe of Peace ceremony in 1927

615

Freshman Cap Night in 1923

Homecoming bonfire/scrap drive in 1942

An especially muddy Bag Rush

Triumphal Bag Rush parade on State Street in 1927

Engineers-lawyers snowball fight on the Hill

Engineers' St. Pat's parade float in 1928

A depression survival skill

Sam Steinman

James Fleming

Jim Watrous

Sally Owen

Bob Murphy

Roger Le Grand and Dick Davis

619

Coed ski class on Observatory Hill

The Hoofers' toboggan slide in 1934

The Muir Knoll ski jump

A sold-out boxing match in the Field House

At the 1940 Work Day
Nat Heffernan exhorting his troops

At the 1943 Work Day

622

11.

A Community of Students

Although UW students had from the earliest days of the University spent their free time in a variety of organizational and recreational pursuits, limited mostly by their imagination and resources, as the University and the student body grew in size and scope in the early twentieth century, these activities also expanded in number, kind, and quality. They had the effect of creating a distinctive and increasingly noticeable campus-based student community. By 1925 the student body was sufficiently large and diverse to support a considerable number of quite sophisticated student endeavors of increasingly professional or near-professional quality. This was reflected in the growing quality and ambitious character of student musical and dramatic productions, in the high standards of the Union's Concert and Lecture Series, in the increasing professionalism if not always success of Badger athletic teams, and even in student social life, where it was common to engage nationally prominent orchestras for major dances. Student life was increasingly big time.

Student Publications

The student community in the inter-war years was tied together by an extensive interlocking network of student publications, which enjoyed more freedom and editorial independence than was the case in many colleges and universities of the period. These included a general purpose daily newspaper, the *Daily Cardinal*, established in 1892; an annual yearbook, the *Badger*, launched in 1884 by the junior class under the name *Trochos* but called *Badger* after 1888; an irreverent monthly humor magazine, the *Wisconsin Octopus* (1919-59), and a number of special purpose periodicals, some with a University subsidy: the monthly *Wisconsin Engineer* (1896-present), sponsored by the College of Engineering for its students; the *Wisconsin Literary Magazine* (1904-29), sponsored by the Department of English and known affectionately as the "Lit" by its student editors; the *Wisconsin Country Magazine* (1906-59), produced by students in the College of Agriculture and circulated around the state; the *Commerce Magazine* (1917-29) published by students in the commerce course; the *Wisconsin Law Review* (1920-present), edited by law students; and the *Wisconsin Athletic Review*, published six times a year during the 1920s by the athletic department with student editors and writers.

After the demise of the Lit, in 1933 a group of Arden Club members started a new literary magazine called the *Rocking Horse* under the leadership of John Moe, Winifred Haynes, and Margedant Peters, three undergraduate English majors, and S. Ichiye Hayakawa, an English graduate assistant and adviser of the Arden Club. The following year the magazine's English department faculty advisers resigned in a huff over its publication of Haynes' article criticizing what she saw as the department's dull courses and outdated curriculum. Finances were always a problem and the editors also had trouble deciding whether the magazine should be a vehicle for local student writing or an outlet for the work of the best younger authors in the country. In spite of a brave start and Dean Sellery's urging President Frank to provide a temporary University subsidy, the magazine folded in the fall of 1935 along with Arden House itself, both of them victims of the depression.[1] There were a number of other short-lived student publications, mostly offering commentary on current campus and national or world issues, such as the *Wisconsin Student Independent*, which appeared for several years in the late twenties, the *Wisconsinite* (1928), the *New Student* and *Action* (both appearing briefly in the mid-1930s), the *W.S.G.A. Bulletin* and the *H.P.C. Bulletin* (both published for a time around 1940 by the organized women's and men's houses for their respective memberships), and the eccentric *"I" Gotist* (1944).

---

[1] *Daily Cardinal*, February 28, March 1 and 2, 1934, March 5, October 16, December 11, 1935; Margedant Peters and Gordon Sylander to George C. Sellery, March 17, 1935; Sellery to Glenn Frank, March 20, 1935, Frank Presidential Papers, 4/13/1, box 170, UA. Hayakawa later had a colorful career as the embattled president of San Francisco State University during the turbulent 1960s and subsequently as a U.S. senator from California.

The oldest of the long-lived and more official student publications, the annual *Badger*, had achieved impressive proportions by the 1920s. The quarto-size volumes generally ran more than six hundred pages and included embossed leatherette covers, heavy glossy paper, colored art work, and several thousand photographs of the members of the senior class, student organizations, and campus activities. Usually more than a hundred students devoted countless hours throughout the year to its production late in the spring. Originally undertaken as the major project of the junior class, after 1931 the *Badger* was published by the senior class; in making the transition, for the first and only time in its history the editor-in-chief and business manager, Jack Thompson and Gerhard Becker, served in their posts for two years in a row. Although initially the *Badger* and certain other student publications received a small subsidy from the Board of Regents, essentially they were expected to be self-supporting student enterprises, generating enough income through sales and advertising to cover their costs. Because the *Badger* charged a fee for including photos of graduating seniors and student houses and organizations in the yearbook, it cannot be viewed as a comprehensive record. More often than not the *Badger* staff was dominated by members of the Greek-letter fraternities and sororities; in consequence some of the independent students played down its importance and a few declined to pay for graduation photos. On rare occasions the *Badger* ran a deficit, leading to tighter fiscal controls by the Student Life and Interest Committee. In some years there was enough profit for the student editors to vote themselves a bonus.

Student annuals are often overlooked by historians as source material, yet they provide a unique window on student life and point to the year's events the student editors considered most memorable. Certain volumes of the *Badger* are especially valuable in this regard. For example, the editors of the 1934 *Badger* soberly recognized they were survivors of sorts—theirs was the first class whose members had experienced the University only during the worst years of the great depression. They therefore focussed their volume on how the depression's "many-sided ramifications have ruthlessly pushed their way into life at the University of Wisconsin." A thoughtful essay, "The Four Lean Years," summarized their broad investigation of the impact of the depression on the University in general and student life in particular, and provided a variety of information not readily available from other sources.[2]

Another of the long-lived general student publications was the *Wisconsin Octopus*, more familiarly known as "Octy," a humor magazine launched in 1919 in time to welcome home the veterans of the First World War. The magazine suspended publication in 1942 during World War II, but resumed again in 1946 before finally dying in 1959. It flourished particularly in the 1920s, with glossy quarto-sized issues running as many as sixty-four pages, colored covers, clever cartoons and graphics by student artists, and humorous prose and poetry. The editors mostly aimed to reach the more affluent Langdon Street Greek

student audience, though their satirical treatment of fraternity and sorority life was often sharp and biting. For a number of years the magazine annually printed a cartoon first published in 1931 labeled "The Truth about Fraternities," which portrayed Langdon Street as a Potemkin village lined with impressive but shallow facades behind which the Greek residents were living in threadbare tents.[3] At first the *Octopus* was able to charge $.25 for each of its nine monthly issues throughout the academic year, plus an occasional tenth summer issue. The depression brought a sharp drop in advertising revenue as well as a decline in circulation, however, leading the magazine to use cheaper paper and cut back to as few as sixteen pages during 1932-33, at the same time reducing its price to $.10 before raising it to $.15 in 1937. Generally the *Octopus* centered each issue around a particular campus theme: Freshman Welcome, Homecoming, Christmas, the Junior Prom and the Military Ball, and the annual Haresfoot show, with some of the cartoons and humor reflecting the topic. A regular feature of each issue in the late twenties and early thirties was a section of short book reviews by English Professor Paul Fulcher along with notes of recent classical and popular musical recordings.

Increasingly, the editors modeled their publication after the sophisticated *New Yorker* magazine, though they complained their eastern rival sometimes stole some of their work without attribution. In 1941 Octy

[2]*Badger*, 1934, pp. 8, 13-31.
[3]*Octopus*, 13 (December 9, 1931), 12.

ran two *New Yorker* cartoons reflecting what the editors pointed out was a remarkable similarity to two *Octopus* cartoons published months earlier, a resemblance the *New Yorker* airily dismissed as "purely coincidental."[4] At its best, Octy's scrutiny of campus personages and life was deft, clever, and ironic; sometimes, however, its double-entendre humor was simply sophomoric, heavy-handed, or even bawdy. In 1928, for example, the magazine's faculty censor, English Professor Finley K.M. Foster, ordered changes in a story before clearing it for publication. Later in the year the editors' publication of a risqué cartoon led for a time to a closer review of all material by the magazine's faculty majority on the Octy board of directors.[5] By 1931 the *Octopus* masthead listed Dean of Men Goodnight as president of the board of directors, and for several years it added the title "Censor" as well. In 1940 L&S Dean Sellery succeeded Goodnight as head of the board.

The Passion Play

The Naughty Cartoon

Still, both Presidents Frank and Dykstra were reluctant to impose censorship on student publications and the University's scrutiny was increasingly half-hearted and indirect. Frank, in fact, declined an invitation to write an editorial for the *Octopus* upon his arrival in 1925, explaining he thought it improper for the University administration "to appear to dictate the editorial policy of a student publication."[6]

While the *Octopus* ordinarily tried to elicit a smile or even a guffaw, occasionally it took a serious editorial stand. In the fall of 1926 the magazine came to the support of its campus rival, the *Daily Cardi-*

---

[4]Ibid., 22 (April, 1941), 14.

[5]*Capital Times*, January 11 and 15, December 7, 1928; *Daily Cardinal*, December 7, 1928. The offensive cartoon, entitled "The Passion Play," showed a couple engaged in a passionate embrace, with the young man's left hand on his willing date's knee and his right hand unobtrusively but nevertheless unmistakably cupped around one of her breasts. On the same page was another cartoon showing two bow-legged coeds dressed in riding garb with a horse with the double-entendre caption, "Just a Couple of Girls with Bad Habits." *Octopus*, 11 (December 5, 1928), 12.

[6]*Octopus*, 7 (September, 1925), 16.

nal, after officials of the Women's Christian Temperance Union had called for punishment and censorship in response to a *Cardinal* story about illegal student drinking. The *Octopus* agreed with the *Cardinal* that some UW students did drink in spite of prohibition and suggested the WCTU was about as realistic as the Red Queen in its approach to the issue.[7] Several years later the magazine printed two identical cartoons by a talented sophomore, Jimmy Watrous, showing a group of mostly inebriated students whooping it up at the prom. The first was labeled "Prom as People Think It Is" and the other "As It Really Is."[8] During the depression when Watrous served first as art editor and then editor of the magazine, his cartoons and the editorial policy of the magazine took on a more somber tone, leading the *Cardinal* to complain about the absence of humor even as it applauded Watrous' greater attention to serious issues.[9] Watrous' savage reaction to the salary waivers in 1933 was a cartoon showing a heartless regent piling increased fees on the bowed backs of students even as graduate assistants and instructors waited vainly for salary relief, while overall a dismayed figure labeled Justice tried to cure her massive headache with large bottle of bromo seltzer.[10]

As the Board of Regents prepared to fire President Frank in December of 1936, Octy published a cartoon showing Frank, white spats gleaming, coyly standing under a sprig of mistletoe desperately hoping the two La Follette brothers on either side would rise to the bait.[11] The magazine's graphic portrayal of the birth of Phil La Follette's national third party in 1938 sought to remind its readers of the uncomfortable parallel with Adolf Hitler's National Socialism.[12] Less subtle but equal-

---

[7]Ibid., 8 (October, 1926), 16-7.

[8]Ibid., 10 (January 9, 1929), 10. For a similar Watrous cartoon spoofing excesses at the prom under the watchful eyes of its chaperons, Deans Goodnight and Nardin, see ibid., 11 (January 15, 1930), 20-1.

[9]*Daily Cardinal*, September 23, 1932, September, October 21, 1933. Watrous had a longer association with the *Octopus* than any other student, working on it three years as an undergraduate and later as editor while a graduate student. By 1940, now on the faculty of the art history department, he was back as vice president of the Octy board of directors.

[10]*Octopus*, 15 (September, 1933), 11.

[11]Ibid., 18 (December, 1936), 15.

[12]Ibid., 19 (May 20, 1938), 15. A clever but sardonic spoof, "The Man Behind the Third Party," accompanied the graphic portrayal of La Follette and his National Progressives as American fascists. It was written by *Octopus* editor Leonard S. Silk, a New Jersey native who went on to earn a Ph.D. degree in economics at Duke University in 1947. After teaching at several universities he became editor of *Business Week* magazine and later a financial writer for

ly telling was the indignant *Octopus* reaction to the 1939 decision by the Daughters of the American Revolution not to allow the famous Negro contralto Marian Anderson to sing in their Independence Hall in Washington. Anderson was well-known on campus, having performed the previous year in the Union Concert Series. Ed Mayland, a regular Octy cartoonist, portrayed her as a forlorn black waif, singing even while she was booted out by a pompous DAR lady wearing a sash labeled "Equality-Liberty."[13] By the thirties, then, Octy's purpose was not simply to entertain but also to use humor to make a serious point.

Of the various student publications, the *Daily Cardinal* was by far the most important and influential, being read regularly by a high proportion of the student body, the faculty, and even some alumni and Madison residents. In 1926, for example, at a time when the University had fewer than seven thousand undergraduates, the *Cardinal* had a paid circulation of just under thirty-five hundred, including about five hundred alumni subscribers spread across the country and in several foreign countries.[14] Like the *Badger*, the *Cardinal* regularly had a staff of about a hundred students—many of them journalism majors or hopefuls—handling all of the functions of a regular daily newspaper: news reporting, editorials and opinion columns, letters to the editor, circulation, and advertising. The staff was mostly unpaid, though after a good year some of them might get a bonus, and the business staff got a small commission for selling advertising. By the early 1940s the two top staff members—the executive editor and the business manager—were each paid a salary of $25 a month.

Over the years of this volume the *Cardinal* staff experimented with a number of innovations, not all of which survived for more than a brief period: a literary section, a weekly edition for parents and alumni, a page of news about the College of Agriculture to address the "aggies'" perennial complaint that the paper generally ignored their activities, an expanded Sunday edition featuring a commercial rotogravure section of news and feature photographs, and a broadcast campus news program over the University radio station WHA and later over the Madison commercial station WIBA. In the fall of 1927 the *Cardinal* installed its own printing press in the basement of the YMCA building. The press

---

the *New York Times*, both of which no doubt helped to control his youthful interest in ironic humor.

[13]Ibid., 20 (March, 1939), 12.

[14]*Badger*, 1927, p. 382.

was moved a few years later to the paper's own building at 823 University Avenue.[15] Shortly after the outbreak of war in September of 1939, the *Cardinal* began subscribing to the wire service reports of the International News Service in order to bring its readers up-to-date coverage of world developments.[16] One of the earliest student dailies, the paper was generally a credit to the University, regularly winning awards as one of the best student newspapers in the country.

The editors of the *Cardinal* in these years prided themselves on the paper's professionalism. While on most issues the editorial policy was unabashedly progressive and reformist, the staff tried to report the news objectively and fairly, and generally succeeded in restricting opinion to the editorials, columns, and letters section of the paper. Indeed, they occasionally chided their grown-up rival, the *Capital Times*, for lapses in this regard. Some of the *Cardinal* editors and columnists were noteworthy for the time and intellectual talents they devoted to the paper.

While by no means unique, the executive editor for 1931-32, Samuel Steinman, was particularly impressive in this regard. In addition to writing most of the *Cardinal* editorials throughout the year, in nearly every issue Steinman contributed a column of personal opinion entitled "Little Acorns" in which he raised issues and commented thoughtfully on a wide variety of campus, state, national, and even world problems. He was quick to defend the University against external critics and to expand student rights, but always in a reasoned, respectful, and sometimes satirical way. Steinman's targets included criticizing the Madison police for unfairly singling out student cars for overnight parking tickets, chiding Wisconsin progressives and Governor La Follette for abandoning their historic commitment to the University and the Wisconsin Idea, rejecting John Chapple's sensational charges of UW radicalism and immorality, urging the senior class to take over production of the *Badger* in order to assure a more experienced staff and better yearbook, arguing for consistency in the University's eligibility rules for student extracurricular activities and for treating men and women in the same way with respect to dormitory hours, denouncing the decision of

---

[15]*Daily Cardinal*, September 21, 1927.

[16]Ibid., September 20, 1939. Some students objected to this as a costly frill, so the editors dropped the service after a trial period. In 1940 and 1941, however, the *Cardinal* subscribed to the United Press, a similar teletype news service. Ibid., June 22, 1940, September 30, 1941.

the national forensic honorary society Delta Sigma Rho not to admit a champion UW orator because he was black, and opposing ROTC and militarism and the excesses of intercollegiate athletics. On a number of occasions Steinman reprimanded the *Capital Times* for its inaccuracies and yellow sensationalism in covering the University, leading the *Times* on one occasion to remind its readers huffily that Steinman was "a native of New Jersey" who "thinks Wisconsin taxpayers and newspapers have no right to interest themselves in the affairs of their state university."[17]

Overseeing the production of a 12-page newspaper six days a week and a 56-page 40th anniversary edition while writing insightful editorials and columns in nearly every issue was a formidable accomplishment, so it is remarkable Steinman had time for other interests as well. He was also president of the Wisconsin Players, secretary or "keeper" of the Haresfoot Dramatic Club, vice president of the journalism honorary society Sigma Delta Chi and chairman of its annual Gridiron dinner, *Badger* satire editor, and a member of the *Cardinal* and *Badger* boards, the prestigious White Spades and Iron Cross honorary societies, and the campus elections committee. Still, he managed to graduate in four years with his class in 1932, appropriately producing a senior thesis on "The Influence upon Public Opinion of Signed Daily Newspaper Columns"![18]

The *Cardinal* was governed loosely by a Board of Control consisting of three faculty members and seven students, five of them elected by the student body at large. The name was something of a misnomer, for the paper was essentially free of University control over its editorial and news content. The paper was technically owned by a corporation of which all students were stockholders, so the Board of Control functioned approximately as a corporate board of directors. The faculty members on the board could offer advice but their role was essentially to watch over the *Cardinal*'s financial health and their participation was limited to budgetary and personnel decisions. For the most part, the

---

[17]*Daily Cardinal*, March 11, 1932. For other Steinman criticism of the *Capital Times*, see ibid., May 8, 23, and 27, December 3, 1931, February 19, 1932. For a representative sampling of Steinman's insightful observations on a variety of other issues, see ibid., May 9, 15, 19, 28, and 30, June 3, October 7, 11, 13, 20, and 22, November 5, 8, 10, 11, 17, 25, and 26, December 1, 2, 3, 5, 6, 17, and 18, 1931, January 10, 13, 17, and 22, February 16, 19, and 20, March 5, 9, 13, 15, 17, 23, 27, 30, and 31, April 2, 14, 16, 20, 21, and 29, 1932.

[18]*Badger*, 1932, p. 112.

board restricted its oversight to filling the paper's two top positions—the executive editor and business manager—and then ratifying their choices for the other staff positions.

A Critical View of the *Cardinal*

This did not mean everyone thought the paper should be free of University censorship or that it always handled its editorial freedom responsibly. Periodically, the *Cardinal* aroused the ire of some readers, especially clerics, parents, alumni, and politicians, by its outspoken editorial criticism or the iconoclastic views of some of its columnists and letter-writers. The paper's reluctance to impose censorship sometimes landed it in hot water, especially when it printed anonymous letters of questionable taste. In December, 1927, for example, the *Cardinal* published a letter from "Sis," purportedly a senior coed, explaining students often drank at the Junior Prom in order "to make an 'impossible' date temporarily bearable." She declared her intention to continue the illegal practice "even if Gov. Zimmerman is there in person to enforce the eighteenth amendment," a reference to the scheduled location of the prom in the rotunda of the state capitol. In the resulting furor state authorities threatened to withdraw their permission to use the capitol for the prom, eventually leading several male students to confess they had written the letter as a prom publicity stunt. They were forced to apologize personally to the governor, lectured by President Frank, and banned from attending the prom. The embarrassed top editors of the *Cardinal* lamely claimed the offending letter had been slipped into the paper by junior staff members, who lost their positions on the paper as a result.[19]

---

[19]*Daily Cardinal*, December 7, 9, 11, 13, and 14, 1927, January 6, 1928; *Capital Times*, December 10, 11, 12, 14, 19, 23, 25, and 28, 1927; "The 'Sis' Letter," *WAM*, 29 (January, 1928), 135. At the height of the uproar over the "Sis" letter, Dean Goodnight ordered a page torn out of the current bound issue of the *Wisconsin Literary Magazine* before it was released, because in the judgment of the *"Lit's"* faculty adviser, English Professor Finley Foster, the offending parody of Sherwood Anderson was in poor taste. *Daily Cardinal*, December 16, 1927; *Capital Times*, December 16, 1927.

An even bigger uproar developed over another anonymous letter several years later from a "Junior Woman," who scoffed at virginity and smugly defended premarital sexual activity. In this instance no one admitted authorship, and under pressure from President Frank the editors of the *Cardinal* decided in the future the paper would print only signed communications. Some of the criticism of the *Cardinal* came from alumni who, as is their wont, tended to be skeptical of the patriotism, reliability, and morality of the younger generation. Under pressure from the alumni association and the Board of Visitors, in 1933 the Board of Regents briefly terminated the *Cardinal*'s status as the official University newspaper because of general unhappiness with the paper's perennial opposition to the Reserve Officer Training Corps (ROTC) program and its biting criticism of the commercial aspects of intercollegiate athletics. The regents even toyed with the idea of establishing a rival campus newspaper. After their heavy-handed reaction drew criticism from some state newspapers, including the progressive *Capital Times* and the socialist Milwaukee *Leader*, they settled for adding two additional adult members to the *Cardinal* Board of Control (one appointed by the regents) before restoring the paper's imprimatur several months later. Unchastened, the *Cardinal* staff vowed to maintain their newspaper's traditional independence, a course made easier by the fact the paper was a financially independent private corporation that owned its own printing press.[20]

---

[20]BOR Minutes, April 27, June 17, August 2, 1933, UA; *Daily Cardinal*, March 26, April 1, 13, 19, 20, 21, and 28, May 2, June 18, July 12 and 22, September 19, 1933; *Capital Times*, April 27, May 3, June 18, August 3 and 5, 1933; "Official Status of Cardinal Revoked," *WAM*, 34 (May, 1933), 225-6, 252; "Important Actions of the Board of Regents," ibid. (July, 1933), 291. The board's decision to require two additional adult members of the *Cardinal* Board of Control apparently was never implemented. One of the complaints about the *Cardinal* at this time was that it was dominated by a self-perpetuating clique, especially by a majority of out-of-state Jewish students on its editorial board. Addressing this concern, the 1932-33 executive editor, Frederick J. Noer, a political science major from Menomonie, pointed out that only nine of fifty-four students working on the news-editorial side of the paper were Jewish, to which Regent President Fred Clausen, a Horicon industrialist, responded in a lengthy open letter to the paper:

It isn't a question of race, but of attitude. I suspect this criticism is based on the fact that the dominant majority on the editorial board hail from the east without any particular respect or sense of obligation for the traditions of our university. Their state of mind seems to be to find fault with everything that is and to assume that those who have gone before and those now charged with responsibility are to be pitied for their limitation of knowledge and outlook. There is often a disdain for our present economic order which has made the existence of our university possible. This is the indictment I have heard. It is for you and others to judge

A more serious threat of a different sort occurred in the spring of 1938 in a student dispute over the staffing and editorial policy of the *Cardinal*. In the mid-thirties a movement to break the traditional Greek dominance of student government developed, led in substantial part by a politically astute undergraduate from Oshkosh, James E. Doyle, '37. Doyle and his friends realized if the far more numerous but scattered non-Greeks, or "barbarians," could be mobilized, they could easily out-vote the fraternities and sororities and make the organs of student government more responsive to the interests of the independent students. The trick was to organize the barbs living in the dormitories and the larger private residence halls. What was sometimes called the Doyle machine succeeded in electing a majority of independents to the *Cardinal* Board of Control in 1936, with Doyle himself named to head the board. The GDIs (or God Damned Independents, as they proudly called themselves) next elected Doyle president of the senior class by a 2-1 margin in the fall of 1936, in a campus election that for once saw the utter collapse of the normally smooth-functioning Greek machine. For the Senior Prom that year, Doyle selected as his queen Ruth Bachhuber, a junior history major from Wausau and a member of the Doyle faction on the *Cardinal* Board of Control. This was the first time in a decade an independent had been chosen prom queen, an improve-ment Bachhuber proudly noted that now made it "an all-university affair."[21] In 1937-38, with the Doyle machine still in power following its leader's graduation, Bachhuber was elevated to the post of president of the *Cardinal* board.

The board's choice for the 1937-38 *Cardinal* executive editor was Morton Newman, a talented independent student from New York. Like most of the Doyle-Bachhuber GDIs, Newman was progressive in his political views. During the next few months he proceeded to give the paper a decidedly more social activist outlook, generally endorsing the program of the new University League for Liberal Action, a coalition of left-leaning student groups including the campus communists, now operating under Moscow's popular front strategy. Under Newman's editorial leadership the paper championed peace marches, housing

---

how much truth there is in it.

Fred H. Clausen to the editor, *Daily Cardinal*, April 19, 1933; "Official Status of Cardinal Revoked," pp. 226, 252. Actually, the staff of the *Cardinal* was a good deal more diverse than the student membership of its Board of Control, which was usually dominated by Greeks.

[21]*Daily Cardinal*, May 25, 1937.

reform, improved wages and hours for student workers in local restaurants, and reform of the Union Board and student government generally. Newman also worried about the declining fortunes of the Spanish loyalists and regularly warned of the rise of the fascist dictatorships in Europe. While some readers complained the paper was too one-sided politically and was devoting too much attention to foreign affairs, in reality the difference was more one of degree than a sharp break with the past. Previous editors had taken similar liberal stands, although perhaps not to the same degree or breadth of concern. Nor was the fact Newman was Jewish particularly noteworthy; Jewish students had worked on the *Cardinal* for many years, and Newman was not the first to rise to the top post as executive editor. Perhaps the most valid complaint was that under Newman the paper had become deadly serious.

As the end of Newman's term as editor neared in the spring of 1938, the Greeks mounted a spirited campaign to recapture the organs of campus government and in particular the *Cardinal* board, promising a return to a less activist, more traditional stance for the paper. In the spring elections they succeeded in electing two fraternity men to the *Cardinal* board, Wade H. Mosby, '39, and John M. Witte, '40, thereby gaining a majority of the student members. Newman's *Cardinal* blamed the defeat on the nefarious Greek practice of compulsory voting and warned the new Board of Control—"which peculiarly will be dominated by one clique—that the sentiment for a liberal Cardinal was found to be strong this year."[22]

A month later, as the old board headed by retiring member Ruth Bachhuber prepared to name the next executive editor, a disenchanted former *Cardinal* staffer and prominent fraternity and campus leader, Allen Jorgenson, cautioned her against appointing a Newman protégé to the post. Jorgenson warned that if the Bachhuber board did so the new Greek-led board would very likely oust the editor-elect in order to carry out its mandate. Bachhuber and her allies nevertheless named Richard Davis, another New York Jewish student and Newman ally, as executive editor. At the *Cardinal* annual banquet that evening, Newman and other staffers predicted the likely ouster of Davis and circulated a loyalty and unity petition among those present. To the paper's subscribers Newman warned of an anti-Semitic plot to remove Davis.[23] True to

[22]Ibid., March 29, 1938.
[23]Ibid., April 28 and 29, 1938.

Jorgenson's warning, the new board promptly dismissed Davis, leaving the new managing editor, Roger W. Le Grand, an experienced *Cardinal* staff member (and Greek), in charge. (Sadly, Davis and Le Grand had worked closely together on the paper for two years, and the 1938 *Badger* would carry a picture of them seated at the same desk.)[24]

With the ouster of Davis, a substantial part of the *Cardinal* staff went on strike and began publishing a rival newspaper under Davis' editorship, eventually called the *Staff Daily* after the Committee on Student Life and Interests ruled there could not be two papers using the *Cardinal* name. Funding the strike paper was precarious and relied on a combination of the strikers' personal funds, advertisements, and day-to-day contributions from supporters on and off campus. For nearly a month, from April 30 to May 27, the student body was split into two camps, each supporting one of the rival papers. Charges and counter-charges reverberated across the campus, with even some of the faculty drawn into the fray. Ruth Bachhuber continued to press Newman's charge that anti-Semitism was behind the ouster of Davis, an accusation vehemently denied by the new board members, who claimed their only concern was Davis' objectivity in handling campus news. Several faculty members gave vocal and financial support to the strikers, of whom L&S Dean George Sellery was the most vocal and prominent. Several times Sellery, ever alert to complaints of bigotry, contributed money to the strikers, once paying for an entire issue after a discouraged Bachhuber told him the strike paper was about to fold for lack of funds. Sellery eventually issued a public manifesto in support of the strikers. "When the effort to put The Daily Cardinal into the hands of a different group for next year is supported by an appeal to race prejudice, I am in arms," he explained in an open letter entitled "As I See It."[25] Rex Karney, the 1935-36 executive editor of the *Cardinal*, responded that Sellery had been "taken in":

> He can state no facts or argument in support of his assertion—he simply shouts the words RACE PREJUDICE—and hides behind a blatant and ill-chosen argument against fascism....Miss Bachhuber and her independents have dragged a smelly but effective red herring across the dean's desk. Her independent machine, bequeathed her by Jim Doyle, couldn't stand up under a beating.[26]

---

[24]*Badger*, 1938, p. 135.

[25]*Daily Cardinal*, May 15, 1938; *Staff Daily*, May 15, 1938.

[26]*Daily Cardinal*, May 17, 1938. Another former executive editor, Wallace Drew, who

After the *Milwaukee Journal* sent a reporter to investigate and he reported he could find no persuasive evidence of anti-Semitism behind Davis' dismissal, the paper suggested editorially that Sellery "should act his age."[27] Some faculty members also thought the controversy was rather more complex than Sellery recognized.[28] Max Otto, Sellery's old friend who had tried to avoid controversy since the efforts by Chapple and others to fire him in 1932-33,[29] declared he was "devastated" by the spirit of intolerance in Sellery's statement. "Sellery's philosophy, as voiced in this letter," Otto declared, "is the 'either-or' philosophy which has caused endless trouble in this world, the philosophy which says, 'I'm right and you're wrong, and that's that.'" Clearly upset at Sellery's giving legitimacy to the anti-Semitism issue, President Dykstra dismissed the charge by pointing out there were Jewish students on both sides of the controversy.[30]

As the strike dragged on, pressure mounted for the University administration to work out a settlement. At first President Dykstra was reluctant to get involved, believing this was a student matter that ought to be settled by the students themselves. If the *Cardinal* were to maintain its traditional independence, he thought the University should intervene only as a last resort. Dean Goodnight and the Student Life and Interests Committee were convinced the new *Cardinal* Board of Control had the authority to make a personnel change and were reluctant at first to ask for a student referendum on the decision. They were firm, however, in their view there could be only one *Daily Cardinal*. The new Board of Control rejected an early Dykstra suggestion that Davis be reinstated for a trial period until October 15, after which the

---

served in the post in 1936-37, reminded the campus that the *Cardinal* had been "attacked many times by racially-prejudiced groups in recent years on the grounds that a great majority of its staff members have been Semites." On the contrary, he pointed out, "there have always been proportional representations on the staff from all races, and we have found that all races have produced equally as good staff members. Since the opportunity to work on the Cardinal staff is extended to all students, the complaint that there are too many of one race on its staff is totally unjustified." Ibid., May 1, 1938.

[27]*Milwaukee Journal*, May 24, 1938.

[28]Referring to Sellery's earlier suggestion for a student referendum to solve the dispute, Dean Goodnight, who zealously guarded the turf of his Student Life and Interests Committee, told the *Milwaukee Journal* reporter: "Sellery is silly. Dean Sellery has the right to donate his money to any cause he wants to....But he knows well that he has no right, directly or indirectly, to authorize a referendum." *Staff Daily*, May 3, 1938.

[29]See pp. 282-4.

[30]*Daily Cardinal* and *Staff Daily*, May 17, 1938.

board would review his performance. Both sides consulted attorneys about their rights and the legality of a referendum or a recall election of the new board. Acting on legal advice, the student Elections Board rejected either a referendum or a recall election, suggesting instead a meeting of the Daily Cardinal Corporation, of which all students were de facto stockholders, to settle the dispute over the management of the paper. Six strikers promptly filed such a request. Shuddering at the thought of a potentially unruly gathering of thousands of student stockholders, Dean Goodnight instead urged both sides to accept a campus referendum on the issue of Davis' editorship. The new board naturally rejected the Goodnight plan; the strikers accepted it only if the anti-Davis student members of the Board of Control would agree to resign if the Davis forces won a majority. Goodnight and SLIC gloomily foresaw endless legal maneuvering over the *Cardinal*'s outdated articles of incorporation, litigation that probably would bankrupt the paper.

Dean Goodnight's fears were heightened when various student groups flooded the campus with competing proxy ballots for absentee voting at the meeting of the Cardinal corporation scheduled for May 26 in the Stock Pavilion. To head off a gathering over which he was expected to preside but which promised to be chaotic at best, on May 20 President Dykstra, flanked by Deans Sellery and Goodnight, pressured representatives of both sides to drop the plan for a stockholders' meeting and instead abide by the results of a new election—to be closely supervised by the UW registrar—for the five elected student members of the Board of Control. The sole issue would be whether Richard Davis should serve his term as executive editor. Elated over what both factions saw as a moral victory for the Davis forces, the strikers went to great lengths to put together a slate of new board candidates designed to attract votes across the campus. Their slate included three Greeks and for the first time in memory a student representative of the College of Agriculture. This clever strategy and vigorous campaigning proved of no avail, however, when the slate of anti-Davis incumbents won a narrow victory, 2,681-2,600, in an election that drew well over half of the undergraduates, an amazing turnout that is surely an all-time record for modern campus elections. The revalidated Board of Control promptly named Roger Le Grand as executive editor and he set about the difficult task of healing the most acrimonious dispute in the *Daily Cardinal*'s history. "FORGIVE AND FORGET—IT'S ALL OVER," headlined the paper the day after the election.[31]

The 1938 *Cardinal* strike may have been forgiven but it has yet to be forgotten, at least by the participants. To most of the strikers and their sympathizers as well as present-day *Cardinal* staffers, it remains a high point in the paper's long history, recalled as a heroic battle against the forces of bigotry and reaction, a brave if temporarily unavailing struggle to build a socially conscious paper of the left. Like most fondly held memories, this version of the strike seems considerably over-drawn. Although the strikers sought to make anti-Semitism the cause célèbre, the issue worked both ways and seems to have been more a tactic as the dispute developed than a basic cause at the outset. There were several *Cardinal* staff members—Le Grand for one—as qualified as Richard Davis for the executive editorship, and apart from political considerations Davis was not the clear-cut, obvious choice for the paper's top post. No doubt there were bigots and anti-Semites in the student body and faculty at this time, but it must be remembered that Jewish students had worked harmoniously on the *Cardinal* for many years and had risen through the ranks without evident discrimination to the paper's top managerial positions. That Richard Davis was Jewish seems to have been less an issue initially than that he was the protégé of the outgoing executive editor, Morton Newman, and could be expected to continue Newman's leftist policies. These were tending toward what later generations of *Cardinal* reporters would applaud as advocacy journalism, but this approach was more controversial in 1938. Not all of the *Cardinal* staff or the student body approved of the paper's greater partisanship and stress on social action issues under Newman's editorship. As one of the last acts by the outgoing Board of Control, the Davis appointment struck many students as a cynical effort by the old Doyle GDI machine to nullify the clear shift of political power back to the Greeks in the recent campus elections, in which the direction of the *Cardinal* had been a major issue.

A later observer is inclined to agree with President Dykstra, Dean Goodnight, the faculty members of the Committee on Student Life and Interests, and the *Milwaukee Journal* that the strike was basically an extension of student politics. As such it was more a continuation of the recent election campaign between the Greeks and the independents than a simple struggle against bigotry and reaction, though the latter view became an important issue for some students as the strike developed.

---

[31]*Daily Cardinal*, May 27, 1938.

To the extent the strike was an ideological contest between campus liberals and conservatives, the difference between the two sides was surely more one of degree than a sharp dichotomy. After the strike the staff of the *Cardinal* remained as committed to student rights and liberal causes as the paper had been historically. By the time of the Davis referendum on May 26 so many lurid charges and counter-charges had been aired that Greeks and independents were themselves divided, enough that the election defies easy analysis. In the end the student body very likely judged the Davis forces not so much on straight partisan or religious or residency grounds as on their actions and credibility during the strike.[32]

One post-strike development deserves mention. Jim Doyle, whose independent machine had dethroned the Greeks in 1936-37, thereby setting the stage for the *Cardinal* strike, studied law at Columbia University following his graduation. Upon earning his law degree in 1940 he married his Wisconsin prom queen and campus political lieutenant, Ruth Bachhuber. Drawing on their campus political experience and contacts, during the 1950s the two Doyles played leading roles in revitalizing and rebuilding the Wisconsin Democratic Party as a latter-day reincarnation of the old La Follette progressive movement, with Ruth Doyle serving for a time in the state legislature and later on the Madison School Board and with her husband becoming a partner in the old La Follette law firm. Soon regarded nationally as one of the top Wisconsin Democratic leaders, Jim Doyle was appointed to a federal district judgeship in Madison by President Lyndon Johnson in 1965. Thus while Doyle's GDI machine did not long survive his departure from the campus political scene, the experience surely was valuable training for his future career.

In all the furor over the allegations of anti-Semitism in the rejection of Richard Davis as editor, there was another more obvious form of discrimination in the *Cardinal* staff that seems to have escaped notice entirely at this time. No matter how liberal its editorial views, throughout its history the paper had been very much a bastion of male supremacy. On both the news-editorial and the business-advertising

---

[32]Although the 1938 strike is still sharp in the memories of the participants and contemporary observers, their recollections tend to be shaded by their partisan support for one side or the other. Probably the best sources for the background and development of the strike are the two papers involved, the official *Daily Cardinal* and the strikers' paper, which appeared under several names during the strike and was eventually called the *Staff Daily*. See also "Report of the Office of the Dean of Men," August, 1938, pp. 36-8, UHP.

sides, its staff consisted mostly of men. Women had never held any of the top leadership posts, being relegated to lower level reporting and feature writing, work on the women's and society pages, selling advertisements, or menial clerical tasks. This was partly—but only partly—explainable by the University's night-time hours restrictions on women undergraduates, constraints that did not apply to the men. As a morning paper, the *Cardinal* required a great deal of evening and night work by its staff, in which only the older women with more generous hours and key privileges could participate. It probably never occurred to anyone in this period—especially the women members of the Board of Control or even that great civil libertarian George Sellery—that a woman ought to be considered seriously for the paper's top leadership posts.

This situation changed radically during World War II, but not because of any greater sensitivity to women's rights. The rapid departure of men students for war service gave women increasing opportunities to move into the higher level *Cardinal* staff positions. Anticipating the depletion of its predominantly male staff, in the fall of 1942 the paper began an intensive program to recruit and train women replacements. By this time the *Cardinal* already had its first female managing editor, Dorothy Browne, and when the executive editor,

A Popular Wartime Freshman

Stan Glowacki, resigned to enter service in mid-year Browne succeeded him, the first woman to serve in the paper's top position in its fifty-one years. The next year women held all but one of the top editorial posts and all of the business staff positions, with only a lone male serving as sports editor. The female dominance was nearly as great during 1944-45, when Eileen Martinson, who had served as managing editor and then for most of a semester as executive editor the previous year, served again as executive editor.[33]   "Manning" the paper with only

---

[33]Martinson has recalled her *Cardinal* and campus experiences during the war years in an illuminating oral history interview. Coming as she did from a New York Jewish background, her comments about the social stratification and underlying anti-Semitism in most of the sororities and fraternities are of special interest. She experienced no prejudice on the *Cardinal* nor in her dealings with the University faculty and staff, however, and was agreeably surprised

inexperienced women to draw on was a difficult and nerve-wracking responsibility, and during 1943-44 the *Cardinal* had a succession of three different women executive editors and three women business managers. Because of rising costs and especially the shortage of staff, in November of 1943 the staff decided to drop the Tuesday issue and publish only four times a week. In defense of this unpopular decision, they placed the blame squarely on their male predecessors:

> If the fault lies with anyone, it is with those people who have guided the destinies of the *Cardinal* for the past four years. Successive editors and business managers, in spite of the ever-lowering clouds of war which could not help but reduce the male population on the *Cardinal*, did nothing to encourage women to work on the staff. They did not do enough to teach those women the ins and outr, the technicalities, and the arts of the business.[34]

Not surprisingly, during the war years women similarly dominated the other general student publication, the annual *Badger*, and even invaded the specialized *Wisconsin Engineer*, which in 1944-45 also had its first woman editor ever.[35]

Intercollegiate Athletics and Recreational Sports

Organized athletic competition developed haphazardly under student initiative and leadership in the first decades of the University's existence—first baseball and rowing, and later tennis, track and field sports, football, and basketball—but initially without encouragement or support from the University. At first the contests were informal and intramural, between campus organizations and classes. Gradually UW athletes took to the field against teams from Madison or nearby colleges like Beloit and Racine, but such contests were mostly limited to baseball through the 1880s. During the next decade student interest in football and in intercollegiate competition grew rapidly, encouraged by President Charles Kendall Adams, himself an avid sportsman who believed physical and intellectual development went hand-in-hand in promoting

---

when she was selected over two gentile women for the Wisconsin Alumni Association's outstanding student award in her senior year. Eileen Martinson Levine, oral history interview, 1984, UA.

[34]*Daily Cardinal*, November 17, 1943.

[35]For an indication of the extent to which women dominated student publications during the war, see the *Cardinal* mastheads and the *Badger* sections on the campus press for the years 1942-45.

character and self-reliance. The Wisconsin Student Athletic Association hired its first paid football coach, Parke H. Davis, in 1893, and two years later he was joined by Andrew O'Dea as football trainer and rowing coach. After a campaign by the *Daily Cardinal*, the association created the position of yell master (or cheer leader) to organize student support at the games; pre-game pep rallies soon followed. Also in 1893 the University acquired Camp Randall for a playing field and the following year completed the fortress-like Men's Gymnasium and Armory.[36] Dr. James C. Elsom was appointed as professor of physical culture to supervise the Gymnasium and develop a program to satisfy the new requirement of two years of physical education for all students.

---

[36]As conveyed to the University in 1893, the Camp Randall site encompassed about 40 acres covering the area between University Avenue and Monroe Street, and between Randall Street and Breese Terrace. The tract had originally been used by the Wisconsin Agricultural Society for horse races and the annual state fair. During the Civil War it was used as the primary site to train Wisconsin troops, receiving its name from the governor of the time, Alexander W. Randall. Following the war the Camp Randall site reverted to its pre-war use as the state fair grounds, until the fair was moved to Milwaukee in the 1870s, after which the grounds were used for a time for the Dane County fair. After the legislature appropriated $25,000 to purchase the site for the University in 1893, specifically for athletic purposes, the regents gradually used it for other needs, first deeding to the city of Madison a thirty-foot strip on the western edge for a street, Breese Terrace. In 1909, after beating out the University of Michigan in a competition for the new Forest Products Laboratory, the board turned over an acre of land along University Avenue to the federal government for the lab's original location. Two years later, in response to the powerful Civil War veterans lobby, the legislature set aside 6.58 acres as a Memorial Park, although it left the land under the control of the University with the express provision that the park could be used "for military drill and athletic purposes." Not long after this the University built a switch track near the Milwaukee Railroad line on the northeast corner of the property and began using the site for its large coal pile. During World War I the Army constructed a number of barracks, a barn, and other buildings near the Memorial Park to house the short-lived Student Army Training Corps. After the war some of these structures were taken over by the University's ROTC program. Wartime technical needs also led to the decision to assign much of the northern part of the tract, the area north of the proposed extension of Johnson Street, for the future expansion and development of the College of Engineering. These various decisions, which absorbed much of the northern part of the Camp Randall grounds, necessitated the relocation of the Stadium further south and realignment of the football field on a north-south axis following the collapse of part of the old wooden bleachers in 1915. This in turn subsequently restricted the location of the Field House. The various encroachments on the Camp Randall site precluded the construction of either the Field House or a gymnasium and natatorium at the corner of University Avenue and Breese Terrace as originally planned. Small wonder that Tom Jones, the athletic director and chairman of the Department of Physical Education, pleaded with President Birge and the Board of Regents in 1923 against any further use of Camp Randall for non-athletic purposes. T.E. Jones to E.A. Birge and the Board of Regents, April 23, 1923, and George E. Little to Birge, April 29, 1925, Birge Presidential Papers, 4/12/1, boxs 42 and 53, UA.

In President Adams' mind there was undoubtedly a link between physical training and athletic competition, but at first the two activities were administered separately and the latter left for the time being as a student enterprise. As intercollegiate contests drew ever larger crowds and revenues, however, University authorities and their counterparts elsewhere in the country could not ignore the abuses accompanying an increasingly professional sports program. The Wisconsin faculty established a special committee on athletics as early as 1889, but its supervision was limited initially to scheduling the use of the lower campus playing field and approving absences from class for athletic events. In 1894 the faculty created the Athletic Council to approve the scheduling of intercollegiate contests and enforce eligibility rules in an effort to curb the growing practice of recruiting graduate students and "adult special" students, often hired, for Badger teams. Nor could the University ignore the financial side of intercollegiate competition. The student athletic association occasionally ran a deficit and its chaotic bookkeeping frequently defied an audit. In 1900 President Adams informed the regents the athletic manager had handled more than $27,000 the previous year, far too large a responsibility, he warned, for a single student to bear.

During the 1890s there were several attempts to form an association of some of the midwestern universities to exercise a measure of control over intercollegiate athletic competition. While Wisconsin did not take the lead in this endeavor, the UW faculty strongly supported the movement to adopt intercollegiate regulations curbing athletic professionalism, and some faculty members were sharply critical of President Adams' lukewarm support of the joint effort. As a result Wisconsin was one of the charter members in 1896 of the Intercollegiate Conference of Faculty Representatives, joining Minnesota, Illinois, Northwestern, Purdue, Michigan, and Chicago in establishing what later became known informally as the Western or Big Ten Conference, which after the eastern conference was the second such intercollegiate athletic organization in the country. Indiana and Iowa joined the conference in 1899 and Ohio State in 1912. As its official name implied, the conference reflected faculty determination to take control of an increasingly chaotic, brutal, and even scandalous football competition. Although there were some stormy disagreements in the early years (Michigan withdrew for nearly a decade in 1908), the conference and its counterparts elsewhere in the country, including an umbrella organization that became the National Collegiate Athletic Association

(NCAA), gradually established rules governing player eligibility, residency, length of season, and the like. The game of football itself underwent significant changes: the field was shortened from 110 to 100 yards, each half was cut back from forty-five to thirty minutes, only six players plus the center were permitted on the line of scrimmage, the value of field goals was reduced from five to three points, and in 1906 the forward pass was legalized. The latter did not come into wide use until after 1910, however, when the 15-yard penalty for incomplete passes was abandoned. The violence of the game was reduced by allowing only four players in the backfield and prohibiting such dangerous plays as the flying wedge. Football provided the impetus for the creation of the new intercollegiate conferences, though after the turn of the century they gradually began to promote and regulate other conference team sports as well.[37]

President Charles Van Hise, who took office in 1903, shared the faculty concern that intercollegiate athletics, and especially football, needed to be reformed and controlled. He nevertheless thought some of the UW critics such as history Professor Frederick Jackson Turner were unrealistic in demanding that football be suspended for two years or even abolished in order to de-emphasize large spectator sports in favor of more wholesome amateur athletics. Instead, under a compromise engineered by Van Hise in 1906-7, control over intercollegiate athletics at Wisconsin was taken from the students and assigned to the faculty Athletic Council, one of whose members was the University's representative to the western intercollegiate conference. Wisconsin's first faculty representative had been L&S Dean E.A. Birge followed by mathematics Professors Charles S. Slichter and Turner. From 1912 to 1931 the chairman of the Athletic Council and conference

---

[37]For an account of the origin and early years of the game of football, written by the man who coached Wisconsin in 1893, see Parke H. Davis, *Football: The American Intercollegiate Game* (New York: Scribner's, 1911). See also John Hammond Moore, "Football's Ugly Decades, 1893-1913," *Smithsonian Journal of History*, 2 (Fall, 1967), 49-68. On the development of the Big Ten conference see Carl D. Voltmer, *A Brief History of the Intercollegiate Conference of Faculty Representatives, with Special Consideration of Athletic Problems* (New York: Western Intercollegiate Conference, 1935). See also *Daily Cardinal*, March 12, 1895, March 4, 1896; Walter Byers, *The Western Conference Rebnrds Book* (Chicago: Western Conference Service Bureau [1947]); Oliver Kuechle with Jim Mott, *On Wisconsin: Badger Football* (Huntsville: Strode Publishers, 1977).

faculty representative was English Professor James F.A. "Sunny" Pyre, a star Badger tackle in 1895 and 1896 while enrolled as a graduate student.[38] As part of the 1906-7 reforms for the first time there was an

athletic director, Dr. C.P. Hutchins, whose official title was director of physical education. To restore some balance to Wisconsin athletics, the faculty cut back the football schedule to five games, prohibited for a time the so-called big games with Chicago, Minnesota, and Michigan, and abolished spring training.[39]

Of course, as Van Hise had understood, the faculty's attempt to de-emphasize football ran counter to prevailing popular sentiment in Wisconsin and the nation at large. The faculty resolve simply could not withstand continuing pressure from students, alumni, regents, and the public for a competitive (that is, winning) football team. The ban on scheduling Minnesota lasted only a year, and in 1911 the faculty agreed to follow the rest of the conference in reestablishing a seven-game schedule, extending it to eight games in 1926. Meanwhile, the training table reappeared, along with full-time salaried coaches, the concerted recruitment of talented players, and beginning in 1924 spring practice.

All this required money, so there was mounting pressure to expand the Camp Randall Stadium, where permanent concrete risers gradually replaced the original wooden stands. By 1921 the Stadium could accommodate a crowd of 25,000 spectators, or more than three times the

---

[38] At the time Pyre was also an instructor in the English department, a situation that gave the Athletic Council some concern. In the fall of 1895 the council referred the issue of Pyre's eligibility to the faculty without recommendation, but with the sense that "it is inexpedient that a person holding an instructorship should play on a university team." After reflecting on the matter, and perhaps pondering Pyre's value to the team, the council decided that he should be permitted to play. Athletic Council Minutes, September 27, October 11, 1895, UW Faculty Papers, 5/21/1, box 1, UA.

[39] See UW Faculty Minutes, October 1, November 9, December 10, 1906, April 8, May 6, 1907; UW Faculty Papers, 5/21/1, box 1.

size of the student body; further expansion in 1923 brought the capacity to 36,000 through a combination of permanent and temporary bleachers.[40] The expansion of the Stadium was not universally popular. In 1923 the University had to fend off a bill in the legislature introduced on behalf of an unhappy Breese Terrace resident who sought to enact strict height limits on any structure within two hundred feet of that street.[41] Yet nothing could slow the growing importance of football among UW sports. Funded solely by gate receipts and concession sales, the entire Badger intercollegiate athletic program depended on the football team's ability to fill the expanding Stadium and hence its won-loss record. In 1928-29, the last year before the depression began to curtail intercollegiate athletic competition, football receipts totaled $251,069, or 88 percent of the athletic department's annual income that year.[42] Football, a sport run entirely by the students only a quarter century earlier, was by this time a major

---

[40]The original Camp Randall Stadium consisted of low wooden stands on either side of a field with an east-west axis, and located nearer University Avenue north of the present Stadium. The knoll along Breese Terrace was known as Poverty Hill, because many spectators used it to view the games free of charge. During the Minnesota game in 1915 part of the north stands collapsed, miraculously without many injuries though the game was delayed for a time. This near-tragedy persuaded the legislature to provide a small appropriation for some permanent seating, and the following year the football field was moved to its present site and laid out with a north-south axis, with the wooden stands gradually being replaced by concrete bleachers as funds became available. The process was speeded by a fire that destroyed the old wooden stands on the east side of the field in 1922, the replacement of which brought the capacity of the newer bleachers on concrete risers to 27,000, though temporary wooden stands also continued to be used for many years. During the 1920s and 1930s the University continued to expand and improve the Stadium. In 1937 all of the wooden stands on the west side of the field were replaced by concrete risers and a modern press box added. The following year a more substantial project added 7,400 seats and enclosed much of the space under the east stands to provide office, practice, and dormitory facilities. The improvements were financed entirely without state tax funds, using a combination of borrowing, athletic revenues, and federal construction funds under the New Deal PWA and WPA programs. See Walter S. Nathan, "Camp Randall Yesterday and Today," *Wisconsin Engineer*, 22 (December, 1917), 85-92; "The Proposed Stadium," *Wisconsin Athletic Review* (May 27, 1921), p. 24; "A Stadium with a History," ibid. (November 11, 1922), pp. 34-5; "Stadium Work to Be Continued," ibid. (February, 1924), p. 28; UW Faculty Document 647, "Annual Report of the Athletic Board," May 4, 1942, UA; UW Faculty Document 728, "Annual Report of the Athletic Board," May 7, 1945.

[41]Jones to Phillips, March 8, 1923, Birge Presidential Papers, 4/12/1, box 42.

[42]UW Faculty Document 446, "First Annual Report of the Athletic Board," December 4, 1933.

University business in which student interests (and claims on seating) were secondary to the needs of an increasingly costly athletic overhead structure.

Badger teams were also an important public relations tool for the University. Especially in the case of football, basketball, and later  boxing, intercollegiate competition was popular entertainment, and as an Athletic Board report conceded candidly in 1938, it was "to the interest of the University that the program shall be reported to the public in such a manner as to secure their sympathetic understanding."[43] This cultivation of public support took a number of forms. As early as the 1890s there were unorganized efforts to encourage alumni to return to their alma mater on football Saturdays. These were formalized in 1911 when the athletic department began promoting the annual alumni homecoming Saturday, complete with commemorative buttons, pre-game rally, and all the promotional hoopla familiar to later generations of students and alumni. Soon the homecoming festivities came to include a noisy torch-light parade through the student Latin Quarter, a contest for the most imaginative and elaborate theme decorations of the student houses, a Friday night rally and band concert (first in the open-air theater behind Bascom Hall and later on the steps of the Memorial Union), a mammoth bonfire on the lower campus, and the surreptitious nighttime painting of the Kiekhofer wall on Langdon near Frances Street, usually by members of the Cardinal Key honorary society.[44] After the football team itself, one of the most popular student organizations was the 140-member University marching band, which entertained at football and basketball games led by the music school director, "Major" E.W. Morphy and,

---

[43]UW Faculty Document 562, "Report of the Athletic Board," December 5, 1938.

[44]"Looking Back on Homecomings," *Wisconsin Athletic Review* (November 11, 1922), 10-1. The Kiekhofer wall surrounded an extensive property owned by the wife of Professor William H. Kiekhofer, whose lectures in his popular introductory economics course invariably drew "sky rocket" cheers from the students in attendance. The wall made a tempting target on which to paint homecoming and other slogans, and fraternity men delighted in outwitting the Madison police assigned to guard the wall at homecoming and other festive times. Occasionally the perpetrators were caught, lectured by Dean Goodnight and city authorities, and forced to repaint the wall. No matter how hard he tried, Kiekhofer was never able to persuade the students that despite the wall's name it did not belong to him.

following his death in 1934, by Professor Ray Dvorak.[45] In recognition of the importance of this increasingly vital support group, in 1928 the faculty agreed to give freshman and sophomore musicians required physical education credit for participating in the marching band.[46] Although the marching band was a strictly male organization in this period, music Assistant Professor Orien E. Dalley organized an all-women's concert band in the fall of 1933, the first such at any Big Ten university.[47]

By the twenties the football team also had a series of animal mascots to boost spectator and team spirits at the games, first a succession of ill-tempered badgers, then a more captivating black bear cub named Violet, and finally a monkey named Oscar, whose activities were sharply restricted after he bit the leading lady when cast in a dramatic production of the Wisconsin Players. These mascots generally wound up in the Vilas Park Zoo after their student owners tired of their care and mischief.[48] In 1921 the athletic department began publishing the monthly *Wisconsin Athletic Review*, which replaced the earlier *Athletic Bulletin* and was intended, according to an editorial by Track Coach Tom Jones in the inaugural issue, "to show the respect and appreciation which Wisconsin feels toward its athletic sons."[49] Two years later the department created the "W" Club to honor its letter-winning athletes and began encouraging their return to the campus at homecoming each year in order "to foster and promote the general welfare of the university and its athletics in particular."[50]

---

[45]See John B. Miller, "Wisconsin's Band among the Best," *Wisconsin Athletic Review* (December, 1929), 9, 29; *Daily Cardinal*, May 15 and 19, July 28, August 1, 1934; Mel Adams, "Hail to the Bands! 1935 Homecoming to Honor Fiftieth Anniversary of University's Bands," *WAM*, 37 (November, 1935), 43, 64.

[46]UW Faculty Document 325, "Report of the Committee on Military Affairs Re Band Option," May 7, 1928; UW Faculty Minutes, May 7, 1928.

[47]Clara E. Richter, '36, to Barry J. Teicher, February 16, 1994, UHP.

[48]John B. Miller, "Popularity of Wisconsin Football Mascots Shortlived," *Wisconsin Athletic Review* (November, 1927), 9; "More Monkey Business," ibid., (May, 1928.), 16.

[49]Tom E. Jones, "The Wisconsin Athletic Review" ibid. (March 8, 1921), 13. For background on UW athletics before 1925 see Curti and Carstensen, *University of Wisconsin*, vol. 1, pp. 693-710; ibid., vol. 2, pp. 533-48.

[50]Al Buser, "Alumni 'W' Men Organized," *Wisconsin Athletic Review* (February, 1924), 10.

By the early thirties three commercial radio stations were broadcasting Badger football games.

The growing popularity of football as a spectator sport coincided with some glorious early seasons for the Badger gridders. Especially noteworthy were the late nineties, when Wisconsin claimed two conference championships and the legendary Pat O'Dea helped lead his teammates to a string of twenty-seven victories in three years against only four losses. In the process the team racked up a total of 792 points to its opponents' 64 and held the latter scoreless in 23 games. An Australian, O'Dea excelled as a fullback and especially as a kicker, routinely getting off punts of 50 and 60 yards and once kicking over 100 yards against Yale in New Haven. His range and accuracy with both drop- and place-kick field goals were equally impressive. He made a 62-yard drop-kick goal against Northwestern in a blizzard in 1898 and a phenomenal 55-yard drop-kick goal against Minnesota the following year, the latter at a difficult angle on a dead run to his left while kicking with his right foot! After leaving Madison O'Dea dropped out of sight, and eventually the alumni association concluded he had joined an Australian regiment and been killed in the First World War. He resurfaced in California in 1934, however, and a student campaign raised funds to bring him back to Madison to preside triumphantly over the homecoming celebration that year. By this time the popular State Street student hangout of his day, Dad Morgan's, had closed, but its famous round table had been moved to the Rathskeller of the Memorial Union, where O'Dea triumphantly carved his name in it surrounded by a throng of youthful admirers.[51]

The Legendary Pat O'Dea

---

[51]See Kuechle and Mott, *On Wisconsin*, pp. 47-55; *Daily Cardinal*, September 26 and 27, October 6, 12, and 18, November 8, 15, 16, 17, 18, 20, 24, and 25, December 7, 1934; "School Days," *WAM*, 36 (October, 1934), 3; "Homecoming," ibid. (November, 1934), 42, 63; "The Great Homecoming," ibid. (December, 1934), 76. Ironically, when O'Dea first enrolled as an adult special student, the faculty Athletic Council ruled him ineligible for any

Following an undefeated season and another conference championship in 1912, Wisconsin football had only sporadic success under a series of coaches, leading to repeated calls by the press, alumni, regents, and even politicians to fix the problem. Especially distressing was the team's inability to win the big games against arch-rivals Minnesota and Michigan. Seeking more than a new president in 1925, the regents in that year also hired George Little, Fielding Yost's assistant at Michigan, to be both athletic director and football coach. Little managed to reverse the long decline in his first year (6-1-1), though his team lost to Michigan and only tied Minnesota. After a less successful second year of coaching, he decided to concentrate on his duties as athletic director, where he worked with considerable success to build up the intramural sports program. To take over his coaching duties, Little recruited Glenn Thistlethwaite, whose Northwestern team had just tied Michigan for the conference championship. "Gloomy Glenn" or "Thisty," as he was sometimes called, had mixed success over the next five years. His best seasons were 1928 (7-1-1) and 1930 (6-2-1), and overall his teams won 26 games, lost 16, and tied 3. Against conference teams, however, he won only 10, lost 14, and tied 3, with 4 of the victories against now perennially weak Chicago, which was soon to give up intercollegiate football competition.

Under heavy pressure from disgruntled alumni and concerned about declining football receipts in the depression, late in 1931 the Board of Regents accepted the resignations of both Little and Thistlethwaite. Little had recommended replacing Thistlethwaite, and despite the athletic director's popularity around the state both the Athletic Council and the regents thought he should go as well. In the hope of reversing the Badgers' faltering fortunes, the regents opted for a clean sweep, scrapping the Athletic Council as well and seeking a football coach of national stature. Their choice, virtually forced on the faculty members of the newly organized Athletic Board, was Dr. Clarence W. Spears, formerly the head coach at Minnesota, where he had beaten Wisconsin regularly, and more recently for two years at Oregon, where his teams had a sparkling 13-4-2 record and had defeated conference heavyweights UCLA and Washington. Spears' initial season at Wisconsin was his best. With what the sportswriters agreed was lackluster talent at best, his 1932 team won 6, lost 1, and tied 1, finishing third in the

---

athletic team, "not having resided at the University for one year and being deficient in scholarship." Athletic Council Minutes, March 13, 1897, UW Faculty Papers, 5/21/1, box 1.

conference behind Michigan and Purdue. For this miracle Spears was hailed nationally as coach of the year. The next three seasons were disappointing, and after a dismal 1-7 record in 1935 and a history of continued intra-departmental bickering, the regents fired Spears and replaced him with Harry Stuhldreher, the quarterback in Knute Rockne's famous Four Horsemen backfield at Notre Dame in 1924.[52]

Stuhldreher remained as football coach throughout the rest of the period covered by this volume, retiring from his coaching duties under pressure after the 1948 season to concentrate on his work as athletic director. In only three of his thirteen years as coach did he have winning seasons and only once did he produce a championship contender. His legendary 1942 team (8-1-1) ranks with the best in the University's history, however, tying Notre Dame 7-7, and losing only to lowly Iowa 6-0. It was in the Notre Dame game Wisconsin's star halfback, Elroy Hirsch, gained the nickname "Crazy Legs" for his 35-yard touchdown run that tied the contest. But for the heartbreaking Iowa loss, the Badgers would have won their first conference title since 1912. Instead, they had to settle for second behind Ohio State, a team they had beaten handily, 17-7. Nine of the eleven starting members of the 1942 Wisconsin team received All-American honors, ranging from honorable mention to first team. Every rating service named UW end Dave Schreiner, who was later killed in the Battle of Okinawa, to its All-America first team that year, and three other Badgers—Hirsch, Pat Harder, and Fred Negus—joined Schreiner on the Associated Press All-Conference first team. With more than half of his starting team intact, normally Stuhldreher could have counted on another good season the following year. This was wartime, however. By midyear eleven of his best men were in military service, including several—Hirsch and Negus among them—sent to a Marine Corps officer training program at the University of Michigan where ironically they helped the Wolverines beat Wisconsin 27-0 and give Michigan a tie with Purdue for the Big Ten championship in 1943.[53]

It should be evident that by the start of this period the earlier faculty decision to de-emphasize intercollegiate athletics was largely ignored, though the concern appeared periodically in faculty discussion

---

[52]For an account of the messy firing of Coach Spears, see pp. 263-9.

[53]For a more detailed account of the legendary 1942 football season, see Robert A. Witas, "'42 Badgers among School's All-Time Best," *Badger Plus* magazine, Milwaukee *Sentinel*, September 1, 1992.

and reports.[54] In addition to football, by 1925 the University competed in a broad array of other major and minor sports: basketball, baseball, track and field, cross country, tennis, golf, wrestling, boxing, rowing, swimming, ice hockey, gymnastics, fencing, and even the new Big Ten sport of water basketball (quickly replaced by water polo). Football was solidly entrenched as the University's preëminent spectator sport and as the primary source of financial support for the whole range of intercollegiate and intramural men's sports. The only other varsity sport to bring in any revenue was basketball, but the comparatively small seating capacity (2,200) of the Gymnasium/Armory limited this source. This deficiency was remedied after 1925 when the legislature authorized the University to build a field house using the same device, the Wisconsin University Building Corporation, created to construct the Tripp-Adams men's dormitories.

Planning and arranging the financing for the Field House took several years and its construction on a site just south of the Camp Randall Stadium was not completed until late 1930. After heavy lobbying by UW athletic boosters, in 1927 the legislature by a wide margin appropriated $300,000 for the construction of the Field House, but Governor Fred Zimmerman pocket-vetoed the measure as an unnecessary state expense. Undaunted by this setback, the Board of Regents then leased the Stadium and Field House site to the WUBC and authorized it to borrow the necessary construction funds from the state annuity board, pledging repayment from athletic receipts and other University revolving funds, including eventually some dormitory revenue. Construction was further delayed while a friendly lawsuit tested the legality of the loans from the annuity board for the Field House and for furnishing the Memorial Union, but the Wisconsin Supreme Court eventually ruled in the University's favor. Both because of funding constraints and because the basketball coach, Dr. Walter E. Meanwell, had a large role in planning the eventual facility, the result was not so much a true field house as a basketball arena, with a two-court floor and an initial seating capacity of 8,500, later expanded to nearly 13,000 with the addition of the upper balcony in 1937.[55]

---

[54]See pp. 253-69.

[55]For a discussion of the design of the Field House by the project engineer see C.A. Willson, "University Field House," *Wisconsin Engineer*, 34 (March, 1930), 197-8. The costs and financing of the Field House and Stadium improvements are summarized in UW Faculty Document 593, "Annual Report of the Athletic Board," May 6, 1940, and UW Faculty Document 618, "Annual Report of the Athletic Board," June 2, 1941. Beginning in 1934

The successful campaign for the Field House was in large part the result of Coach Meanwell's remarkable achievement in quickly building a winning basketball tradition at Wisconsin after taking over the coaching duties in 1911. A medical doctor who was more interested in coaching than medical practice, Meanwell was an astute tactician of the game whose teams developed a new type of offense involving frequent short passes and set plays designed to work the ball under the basket for sure goals. The Meanwell teams also played a rugged defensive game. Meanwell's early years remain the golden age of Wisconsin basketball. His first team won 15 games and lost none. The next year the Badgers lost but one game, and in Meanwell's third season they were again undefeated. During the coach's first two years opposing teams averaged only 16 points a game; the 1923-24 team never allowed more than 20 points throughout the season. In Meanwell's first decade at Wisconsin his teams won 133 games while losing only 36, in the process capturing seven championships. Small wonder the Gymnasium could not accommodate all the fans clamoring to share in the glory of Wisconsin basketball under a man hailed as one of the top coaches in the country.[56]

Meanwell's last years at Wisconsin were considerably less happy. Willful and headstrong, something of a martinet with his players, he was thought by some to be manipulative as well. The departure of his patron, Athletic Director George Little, in 1931 left him with no buffer in his clashes with the equally imperious new football coach, Clarence Spears. Spears, like Meanwell, was a medical doctor, and his arrival meant the basketball coach no longer enjoyed a unique and privileged status in the athletic department. Both men made up in self-confidence and ambition for their short stature, and like two jealous bantam cocks they feinted and maneuvered for dominance within the department. Their hostility and explosive tempers made for frequent clashes, especially after the Board of Regents decided to elevate Meanwell to the athletic directorship in 1934. The increasingly open bickering between Spears and Meanwell led eventually to an embarrassing, drawn out, and more or less public investigation and a decision by the regents to fire

these reports provide an excellent summary of the intercollegiate and intramural sports activities for the period.

[56]See Chris Steinmetz, "Early Badger Basketball History," *Wisconsin Athletic Review* (February, 1928), 16-7, 20-1; Walter E. Meanwell, "Basketball: Amateur vs. Professional Tactics," ibid., 22-3; George Downer, "'Doc' Meanwell," *WAM*, 32 (January, 1931), 150, 178.

both men in 1936.[57]

Before this, however, the Athletic Board adopted a new (and temporary) policy precluding the athletic director from simultaneously holding coaching responsibilities. When Meanwell resigned as coach in 1934, he chose as his successor Harold "Bud" Foster, an All-Conference and All-American center on the 1929 and 1930 Badger squads and more recently the Wisconsin assistant coach. Foster's first team tied with Illinois and Purdue for the conference championship, but in the next five years the Badgers were unable to finish higher than seventh. After a slow start in 1940-41, however, the team won fifteen straight games and both the Big Ten and NCAA championships, beating Dartmouth, Pittsburgh, and Washington State for the national title. Two members of that team, center Gene Englund and forward John Kotz, were voted All-American and "most valuable player" honors in the conference during their UW careers, and Kotz, only a sophomore in the 1941 NCAA tournament, was chosen its outstanding player. Another Foster team won the conference championship in 1947, making a total of thirteen Big Ten basketball titles won or shared to that time.

Of all the Wisconsin intercollegiate sports, the boxing teams had by far the greatest competitive success over the years, eventually building a loyal following that sometimes surpassed basketball in numbers of spectators and revenue. Beginning on an intramural basis in 1920, the sport grew in popularity over the following decade and achieved varsity status in 1933. Almost immediately Badger boxers became the undisputed masters of college boxing. The 1933 varsity team was organized by George Downey, the athletic publicity director, who recruited John J. Walsh as coach. Walsh had been a successful boxer at St. Thomas College as an undergraduate and had then enrolled in the UW Law School. Apart from a two-year wartime break, for the next twenty-five years, first as a law student and then as a practicing Madison attorney, Walsh coached Wisconsin boxing. In 1960 Charles Mohr, a UW boxer who had won a national championship the previous year, died of a brain hemorrhage after being hit in a bout. There had already been some UW faculty criticism of boxing, but a recent investigation had concluded the soft gloves and required headgear made it a safe college sport. Mohr's shocking death quickly provoked a faculty vote to terminate the sport at Wisconsin, a course soon followed throughout the country as well. In spite of the Mohr tragedy, the

---

[57]See pp. 263-9.

remarkable record of Walsh's teams is likely to remain unsurpassed in Wisconsin athletic history. In nine of sixteen seasons Wisconsin boxers were undefeated and untied. Eight times they won NCAA team championships, with thirty-eight Badger boxers gaining individual national titles and another twenty-seven becoming runner-ups. Small wonder boxing quickly became one of the University's most popular spectator sports, drawing 3,500 fans for the first match in 1933 and soon thereafter often filling the Field House to its maximum 15,000 capacity (including floor seats).

Even a cursory review of Badger athletics must include rowing or crew, probably the most truly amateur of all team sports and one unique to Wisconsin among Big Ten universities. Rowing at Wisconsin dated from the 1870s and with baseball was one of the very first competitive team sports. The Madison lakes made rowing an obvious recreational activity for UW students, though the long Wisconsin winters and lack of nearby teams slowed the development of intercollegiate competition. Interested students and alumni established the University Boat Club in 1886 and within six years raised funds to construct a boat house and purchase two eight-oared shells for class races each spring. In 1895 the club hired Andrew O'Dea as the first salaried crew coach. O'Dea was a native of Australia who had rowed for the Yarra Yarra Boat Club of Melbourne and he taught the Badger crews a technique known as the yarra yarra stroke. His younger brother Pat visited him the following year and decided to enroll in the Law School, becoming, as already noted, a Wisconsin gridiron legend. Under Andy O'Dea's tutelage Badger crews began competing nationally. They first entered the top national race, the annual Intercollegiate Regatta at Poughkeepsie, New York, in 1898, finishing third. In each of the next two years the Badgers managed to win second place at Poughkeepsie behind Pennsylvania.

In 1913 the sport suffered a major setback when the varsity crew captain was obliged to quit after developing a heart condition while working out on the practice rowing machines during the winter months. Medical advisors worried that four-mile varsity races were too strenuous for immature young men, so the faculty banned intercollegiate competition and limited the sport to intramural status. Crew supporters blamed the action on Doc Meanwell—who also held the title of athletic surgeon—suspecting he wanted a monopoly of tall students for the basketball squad. The faculty relented in 1920, and crew enjoyed a revival under the coaching of Harry "Dad" Vail until his death in 1927.

Vail's 1924 varsity crew was one of the best in Wisconsin history. Led by stroke Howie Johnson, at Poughkeepsie that year the Badgers staged a heroic finishing sprint bringing them from last place at the two-mile mark to within a half length of the victorious University of Washington shell at the finish. Some Wisconsin students made the trip to New York to cheer their classmates, and hundreds more met the team at the train station with the famous Little Red Wagon for a triumphant parade around the Square and back to the campus. Budget cutbacks during the depression kept Wisconsin crews from competing nationally between 1931 and 1937, and World War II halted intercollegiate competition once more, but the Badgers took to the water again to win their first national championship in 1946.[58]

Accompanying the rise of intercollegiate athletics was a sharp increase in the popularity of intramural and recreational sports among both men and women students, with the numbers participating far exceeding those involved in intercollegiate competition. Following George Little's appointment as athletic director in 1925, he launched an ambitious "Athletics for All" campaign designed to build up the University's intramural and recreational sports programs. The objective, Little declared in 1927, was "to enable as many men and women to participate in some form of exercise as possible." A major inducement was the faculty's decision that year to grant gym credit for participation in supervised team sports, an attractive option for freshmen and sophomores subject to the two-year physical education requirement.[59] By 1930 Wisconsin claimed to offer a wider range of intramural team sports than any other American university: in the fall, football (both regulation and touch), cross country, and bowling; in winter, basketball, indoor track, swimming, wrestling, boxing, water polo, free throwing, and hockey; and in the spring, baseball, softball, outdoor track, tennis, golf, and trap shooting. During 1929-30 a total of 6,359 men engaged in intramural competition on 604 recreational sports teams, participating on average in three different sports over the year. Altogether nearly

[58]For a history of Wisconsin varsity competition in various sports see *Badger*, 1949, pp. 177-81.

[59]See George E. Little to Glenn Frank, October 19, 1927, Frank Presidential Papers, 4/13/1, box 46; Little, "The Aims of Our Department of Physical Education," *Wisconsin Athletic Review* (October, 1927), 8, 26; "Director Little and His Program of Athletics for All," ibid. (November 12, 1927), 8, 30; Harold W. Dubinsky, "The Story of Thistlethwaite's Appointment," ibid. (November, 1927), 2-3, 27; "Athletics for All—A Reality," *WAM*, 31 (November, 1929), 58, 88; "Intramurals Score Heavily Again," ibid., 32 (October, 1930), 22.

2,600 men participated in the program, or 43 percent of the male student body. Adding to this number the approximately 1,000 students on the varsity, junior varsity, and freshman intercollegiate teams, well over half of the men students were participating in some form of organized athletics.[60]

There were, of course, a number of other popular recreational sports outside of the formal intercollegiate and intramural programs. The Memorial Union's bowling alleys got heavy use as did its billiard tables. In 1932 the Union organized a billiard contest played by telegraph between a number of university unions, with Michigan beating out the Badger team in the first year. In 1935, however, the UW billiards team won the national championship, defeating Purdue, Minnesota, Cornell, Indiana, Michigan State, Brown, Michigan, Kansas, and Rochester. The telegraphic matches led to a series of home and home matches as well, often watched by as many as five hundred spectators. Wisconsin defeated Purdue in the first such contest, set up to determine which team could claim second place nationally.[61]

Much of the outdoor recreation was naturally focussed on Lake Mendota, which offered tempting opportunities for swimming, canoeing, and sailing in the summer, and skating and ice boating in winter. For many years Carl Bernard operated a popular concession out of the University Boat House alongside the Armory, renting canoes and boats of various types to enable his primarily student clientele to enjoy the lake in summer and winter alike. Bernard's Madison-built iceboats were among the fastest in the midwest. Gradually over the years the Union's Hoofers Outdoor Club acquired a fleet of sailboats for the use of its members. Equally popular were the twin toboggan slides maintained by the Department of Physical Education running down Observatory Hill out onto the lake and illuminated for night-time use. The department also offered instruction in skiing and had some equipment to lend for recreational use. Because snow and rough ice made the lake unpredictable for skating, the University maintained hockey and recreational skating rinks on the lower campus playing field across from the Memorial Union. In 1919 Athletic Director Tom Jones helped a group of students build a wooden ski jump atop Muir Knoll,

---

[60]"With the Badger Sports," *WAM*, 32 (October, 1930), 22. See also "Athletics for All—A Reality," pp. 58, 88.

[61]"Billiards Gets a College Degree, and Wisconsin Wins the National Intercollegiate Championship," ibid., 36 (April, 1935), 202, 225.

with the landing slide extending down the hill onto the lake. Gradually the sport gained popularity, though the best UW jumpers were usually students from Norway until the jump's deteriorating condition led to its removal in 1931.

The loss of what had become a favorite campus viewpoint and nocturnal trysting spot gave the Memorial Union's newly formed Hoofers Club its first project, a campaign to replace the old homemade wooden ski jump with a professional steel structure. Students volunteered days of labor to regrade and improve the hill, the Union Board con-

"It's Unconventional, But It Sure Gets Results"

tributed $300, the Class of 1932 added $700 as a class gift, and the Hoofers collected the balance through solicitations and various money-raising activities. The *Daily Cardinal* complained that in the depth of the depression the project offered little campus benefit, and it urged the members of the junior class to be more serious next year and devote their class gift to the student loan fund.[62] The Hoofers were undeterred by this criticism, and on February 11, 1933, some four thousand spectators watched while President Frank, Governor Schmedeman, Mayor Law, and other notables dedicated the new jump—56 feet high and 108 feet long. Then fifty of the best ski jumpers in the middle west, led by Johanna Kolstad, a world champion from Norway, held a dedication tournament. Although the sport never achieved varsity status at Wisconsin, Badger jumpers regularly hosted and participated in midwestern and national tournaments. One, Lloyd Ellingson, won first place in intercollegiate jumping at Lake Placid in 1930, third in 1931, and second in 1932, when he was also a member of the U.S. Olympic Team.[63] Later in the decade two other UW students (and brothers),

---

[62]For the majority of students, the paper declared, the ski jump was "but a gaunt frame whose only purpose is to disfigure the campus." It would be far better "for a class to leave with the knowledge that though nothing concrete stands to blazon their name for posterity,...a generation of young people seeking knowledge will be given a much-needed hand in accomplishing their mission." "Leaving a Memorial in Our Wake," editorial, *Daily Cardinal*, October 13, 1932.

[63]Porter Butts, "The University Adds the Lake to Its Campus: Revival of Winter Sports

Paul and Walter Bietila, also achieved national stature in ski jumping, a sport they loved for its excitement and danger. Paul, a junior, fell during a practice jump in 1939 in a meet in St. Paul, Minnesota, while trying out for the 1940 Olympic team. He later died of complications from his injuries and is memorialized in a bronze plaque in the Hoofers lounge in the Union.[64] Incidentally, the Class of 1933 shrugged off the *Cardinal*'s condemnation of the frivolity of the ski jump project. Its class gift also went to the Hoofers: to help construct a new concrete toboggan slide on Observatory Hill, complete with water lines for icing the chute, safety gates, and an automatic toboggan release, all designed to achieve greater speed and safety than in the old dirt chutes.[65] Unhappily, the new toboggan slide was in use only four years until the construction of Elizabeth Waters women's residence hall necessitated its removal.

Professor Blanche M. Trilling, the director of women's physical education from 1912 to 1947, shared George Little's belief that recreational sports promoted physical and mental well-being, no less for women than for men. Trilling was a leader in women's physical education at the national level and organized and hosted in Madison the first meeting of the Athletic Conference of American College Women in 1917, which subsequently evolved into a national organization, the Athletic Federation of College Women. While she favored competitive recreational activity for women, Trilling had no wish to get caught up in the professionalism characteristic of men's athletics. Consequently, she strongly opposed intercollegiate competition for women. As part of the two-year physical education requirement, she and her staff taught freshman and sophomore women students the fundamentals of a number of team sports. In response to Little's "Athletics for All" campaign in 1925, Trilling expanded the existing program of intramural and class competition through the student Women's Athletic Association.

Brings Greater Zest to Snowy Weather," *WAM*, 35 (January, 1934), 100-1.

[64]*Wisconsin State Journal*, February 9, 1939; *Daily Cardinal*, February 28, 1939.

[65]Butts, "University Adds the Lake to Its Campus," p. 101. The Muir Knoll ski jump was taken down in the early 1960s and relocated to Madison's Hoyt Park so the University could construct the Lake Mendota laboratory for the limnology program. While the jump existed, however, it was a major source of income for the Hoofers. During tournaments the club constructed walls restricting the view from both Lake Mendota and Observatory Drive, so it could charge $.50 admission to as many as fifteen hundred spectators within the enclosed space. Another two thousand often watched free from further out on the Lake Mendota ice. Kent Hemele, "You Did It, Doc: The Hoofers 50th Birthday," *WAM*, 82 (March/April, 1981), 5-7.

Though separate, the WAA intramural program soon rivaled that of the men. In 1927-28, for example, only two years after the inception of the Athletics for All program, WAA sponsored intramural tournaments in basketball, bowling, hockey, horse shoes, softball, swimming, tennis, track, and volleyball. A total of 1,694 women and 52 organizations participated, encompassing about half of the total number of women enrolled in the University that year. The highlight of the year was WAA's annual winter carnival involving teams from sororities, dormitories, independent houses, and women's organizations competing in tobogganing, sledding, skiing, speed and figure skating, and ice hockey. The multi-sport winter carnival was so popular that soon WAA extended it to an annual field day each spring during Mothers' (later Parents') Weekend, involving competition and demonstrations of various warm weather sports: softball, tennis, golf, riding, gymnastics, and archery.[66] The association also sponsored a number of specialized recreational groups: the Outing Club for recreational hiking, bicycling, roller and ice skating, skiing, boating, and swimming; the Dolphin Club for synchronized swimming; Orchesis for interpretive dance; and the Riding Club for experienced and would-be equestriennes. Wisconsin women in these years thus enjoyed far more sports options than their predecessors in the early years of the University, when about the only athletic endeavor open to them was a sedate game of croquet. One fearless coed, Sally Owen, the daughter of engineering Professor Ray S. Owen, became in 1929 the first woman student to navigate the new campus ski jump successfully. Her daring feat led the *Cardinal* to proclaim approvingly if not idiomatically: "Another precedent for women has been broken."[67]

High Spirits and Good Hearts

Student extracurricular life involved much more than sports, of course, though the two were often closely intertwined. There was always an all-University dance during the homecoming weekend, for example, and impromptu parties to celebrate the victories of Badger teams. The first heavy snowfall invariably brought hundreds of students

---

[66]Henrietta Kessenich, "Blanche M. Trilling—a Leader," ibid., 39 (November, 1937), 8-10; Mathilda Fink, "A Sport for Every Girl," ibid., 29 (January, 1928), 14, 17; Margaret A. Sherwin, "Physical Education for Badger Women," ibid., 30 (December, 1928), 80-1, 98; Sherwin, "Outdoor Winter Sports for Women," ibid. (March, 1929), 187.

[67]*Daily Cardinal*, February 28, 1929. See also *Capital Times*, March 2, 1929.

out for snowball fights and for sledding and skiing on Bascom and Observatory hills. The Department of Physical Education maintained a pier for recreational swimming near the Union, as did the Division of Residence Halls adjacent to the Kronshage, Tripp-Adams, and Elizabeth Waters dormitories. Students often canoed or hiked over to Picnic Point for swimming and outings, especially after it was acquired by the University in 1941.[68] Much studied by President Emeritus Birge and his limnology assistants and students, the water of Lake Mendota was in these years much cleaner and more inviting than it would become after area farmers and Madison homeowners began to use increasing amounts of chemical fertilizers following World War II. Each year throughout the period students in the College of Agriculture staged a rodeo and livestock show—the Little International—in the Stock Pavilion, complete with demonstrations of trick riding and contests in livestock judging, bronco busting, and calf roping.

Although inter-class and inter-college rivalry was diminishing by 1925, there was still a good deal of this traditional competitive spirit throughout the inter-war period. Class and college loyalties remained strong even as some of the older campus customs disappeared. In the early decades of the University sophomores delighted in catching un-wary freshmen and holding them under the University pump located on Bascom Hill between North and South halls for an official baptism into campus life, a ritual usually preferable to total immersion in the lake. The baptism rite probably gave rise later in the nineteenth century to the lake rush, a contest between the freshman and sophomore classes on and around the pier in front of the University Boat House. The intent was to see which class could throw the most opponents into the lake. The

---

[68]Except when one owner closed it for a time, Picnic Point had been used for decades by students and townspeople for swimming and picnics in summer and skiing in winter. University authorities had long coveted the tract of land along Lake Mendota that included the slender half-mile peninsula of Picnic Point in order to round out the campus acreage around University Bay to the University's Eagle Heights farm. In 1939 the Board of Regents paid $10,000 for an option to purchase Picnic Point to be sure it remained undeveloped. Difficulties in arranging financing delayed the actual purchase until two years later when the board agreed to pay $279,000 for the 120 acres of Picnic Point proper through its private subsidiary, the Wisconsin University Building Corporation. The transaction did not, however, include the larger tract running from the base of the point along the lake past Second Point to the eastern boundary of the Eagle Heights tract. This would not come into University hands for nearly another half century, when a generous gift of $1,500,000 from the Walter Frautschi family made possible its purchase by the University of Wisconsin Foundation. See BOR Minutes, March 4, 1925, March 15, 1939, June 21, 1941, UA; UW Foundation Records, UWF office.

dangers inherent in the lake rush led to its prohibition by the University after the turn of the century and the substitution of the bag rush, a similar land battle between the two classes each fall. In the bag rush fifteen huge straw-filled gunny sacks were spaced evenly in the center of the lower campus playing field. In some years the more experienced sophomores would surreptitiously dig shallow ditches and soak the freshman side of the field with water beforehand to turn it into a sea of mud. At the starting whistle the two classes would rush onto the field to try to capture as many bags as possible and carry them back to their goal lines, all the while seeking to prevent their opponents from doing the same. The players got gloriously muddy, as did many of the thousands of spectators in attendance, and some usually wound up in the lake to clean off. Afterward the two disheveled classes—victors and vanquished alike—paraded with their trophy bags down State Street and around the Square, where on one occasion they swarmed into the Fuller Opera House and persuaded the startled manager to put on an unscheduled third performance for their entertainment.[69]

In 1901 the members of the freshman class decided to wear a distinctive cap, a dark green Eton with a cardinal pennant bearing the word Wisconsin in small white letters. The freshman rules committee and the student Conference subsequently formalized this tradition by requiring freshmen to wear the caps at all times throughout their first year except in the worst of the winter cold. The caps were topped by a button (which gave rise to the name "beanie") on which freshmen were supposed to put an index finger when addressing an upperclassman. Failure to comply, or to be properly respectful and obedient, resulted in charges before the Student Court and penalties ranging from five minutes of singing University songs at noon on Bascom Hill to being thrown into the lake. Such hazing was tolerated by the University authorities, but within controlled limits. The carrying out of lake dunking sentences, for example, was delayed until the director of the student health clinic ruled the water was warm enough.[70] Few of the

---

[69]Undated recollection of Julia Hanks Mailer; *Daily Cardinal* accounts, 1901 and 1914, quoted in Robert E. Gard, *University, Madison, U.S.A.* (Madison: Wisconsin House, Ltd., 1970), pp. 108-13. According to campus lore, as a new young instructor historian Carl Russell Fish was mistaken for a freshman while observing the lake rush and was tossed unceremoniously into the lake. Climbing out unperturbed, he remarked to the horrified spectators, "Well, my name is Fish, I should feel right at home." *Daily Cardinal*, 1949, quoted in ibid., pp. 126-7.

[70]*Daily Cardinal* accounts, 1901 and 1912, quoted in ibid., pp. 117-9.

frosh beanies have survived, because at the end of the year the freshman class held a rally on the lower campus with a giant ceremonial bonfire into which they gratefully tossed their caps, followed by a plunge into Lake Mendota to prove their immersion in the Wisconsin spirit.

The ceremonial Varsity Welcome of the freshman class by the faculty and the rest of the student body began in 1913. By 1920 it had outgrown the Armory and was moved outdoors to Bascom Hill, where it continued at the start of each fall semester as one of the most impressive campus spectacles until World War II brought its end.[71] In 1929 the faculty turned over to the three upper classes the planning and staging of Freshman Orientation Week just prior to the start of the fall semester and the Varsity Welcome. The orientation activities involved several hundred upperclass students in introducing the newest members of the University community to the campus and advising them about student life. While faculty members handled academic advising, the older students no doubt informed the frosh about which professors deserved a sky rocket acclamation.[72] Whether through these rather elaborate official welcomes or the informal and frowned-upon hazing, no UW freshman could complain of being ignored.

A rather different and colorful form of hazing occurred on "W" Day, when members of the "W" Club, armed with towels, spread out across the campus to wipe the lip stick and make-up from the faces of unwary coeds. In 1941, having been invited by Professor Kiekhofer to carry out their mission in his large Economics 1 class (where the women students were always seated together on one side of the Music Hall Auditorium), the athletes found the women ready to defend themselves with squirt guns until they ran out of ammunition. A Kiekhofer class was always entertaining and sometimes enlightening, but one suspects there was little attention paid to supply and demand curves that

---

[71]For a description of the 1925 Varsity Welcome see pp. 78-9.

[72]The sky rocket cheer was an old Wisconsin tradition, used not only at athletic rallies and contests but also to show approval of a professor, a lecture, or a class. It began with a low "Hiss," like the burning fuse on a rocket, followed by an explosive "BOOM!" as the rocket exploded, then by a hushed, drawn-out "Ahhhhh" in admiration of the beauty of the "fireworks," and finally concluding with a loud cheer, "Wisconsin!" at a rally (or the name of the professor in class). Some popular faculty members like "Wild Bill" Kiekhofer rated at least one sky rocket after nearly every lecture. Campus legend holds that physics Professor Benjamin W. "Benny" Snow, who retired in 1925, always found an excuse not to start his lecture until he had received the expected sky rocket. Many a visiting professor was understandably startled and disconcerted when he heard the low hiss at the beginning of his first sky rocket.

day. Elsewhere on campus the Union announced that its regular after-noon coffee hour would host the Spanish department faculty and provide shelter for women who wanted to violate the "W" Club ban on make-up. One coed carried a rifle to class to protect her rights; another thought the attention was fun but unsanitary; still another complained that no one had tried to scrub her face even though she had worn lots of lipstick in anticipation of the attempt. It was all good fun, of course, followed by an afternoon "W" Club sweater dance at the Armory reigned over by a suitably scrubbed queen, freshman Jean Durgin, who was chosen as "Miss No Make-Up."[73]

The class rush and green cap traditions died out during the twen-ties, but another long-standing class tradition—the annual Pipe of Peace Ceremony—was a regular feature of commencement week for nearly a half century until 1940. The ceremony symbolized the end of rivalry and strife between the men of the junior and senior classes as the latter departed from the University. Modeled after what the students believed was an ancient Winnebago Indian ceremony, the officers of the two classes buried a red-colored war hatchet deep in the campus soil and smoked the sacred calumet pipe of peace, with the junior class leaders pledging to preserve and hold sacred the honor and traditions of the University passed on by their elders. In its peak years the ceremony was held in a large brush-enclosed council ring on the lower campus where upwards of a thousand or more students, faculty, alumni, and townspeople gathered to hear speeches and songs as the senior men transmitted the lore and traditions of the campus to their successors. In later years the ceremony took place on the Union Terrace.[74]

Senior Swingout was another long-standing class ritual, this one involving all of the undergraduate women students of the University. Like the men's peace pipe cerelony, the swingout was traditionally held at the end of the school year. Beginning in 1925 it was staged during Mothers' (later Parents') Weekend in May as part of a two-day series of campus events that included the WAA field day competitions. At the start of the swingout the senior women, clad in white dresses, marched up Bascom Hill through a special arch between long lines of underclass women dressed in pastel colors. There was a long unbroken daisy chain symbolizing the unity of the women of the campus. In the early years representatives of the junior class paid a symbolic tribute to the seniors

---

[73]*Capital Times*, December 5, 1941; *Daily Cardinal*, December 5 and 6, 1941.
[74]Undated recollection of Charles E. Brown, quoted in Gard, *University*, pp. 105-8.

with an intricate march around several large beribboned May poles. The seniors used the occasion to say farewell and pass on the torch of leadership to their younger sisters, including a ceremony announcing the new members of Mortar Board, the prestigious senior women's honorary society, and other honors and awards. An even more colorful event usually held that same weekend was the Venetian Night celebration, when lighted boats and canoes paraded on Lake Mendota before the decorated and illuminated piers of the Greek houses and the Union, all against a backdrop of spectacular fireworks over the lake. Regrettably, the peace pipe, swingout, and Venetian Night traditions were abandoned during World War II and were not resumed in the more serious and impersonal atmosphere of the much larger University after the veterans returned in 1946.

Less pronounced than the inter-class rivalries but nevertheless present was a friendly competition between students of the different schools and colleges. Those in the College of Letters and Science professed to look down on the "aggies" from the College of Agriculture and the engineers or "plumbers," whose degree requirements did not include exposure to the arts and humanities or a foreign language and whose studies as a result were thought to be narrowly practical and plebeian. Rivalry between the engineering and law students was considerably more intense. Originally the two schools were located across from each other on either side of Bascom Hill until the construction of the Mechanical Engineering Building in 1930 began the gradual development of the present engineering campus at Camp Randall. Every year around St. Patrick's Day in the spring students from the two schools staged parades on Langdon and State streets honoring St. Pat as either an engineer or a lawyer, depending on one's point of view. The members of each school tried to disrupt the other's parade by squirting water and hurling insults, rotten fruit, eggs, and sometimes snowballs from ambushes along the route. Usually the Madison police tolerated the yearly fracas provided the combatants cleaned up the mess afterward.

As undergraduates, the "plumbers" took the St. Pat rivalry more seriously and staged more parades and other escapades than the somewhat older and more mature "shysters." They were also a good deal more creative in their deviltry. In 1933, for example, a group of engineers waylaid the night watchman, tied him to a tree while they took his keys to gain entry into the Law Building, and hung a "St. Pat Was an Engineer" banner from the top of the roof, carefully spreading grease and crankcase oil over the roof tiles as they climbed down to make the banner's removal more difficult. In departing they jammed all the locks and padlocked the main door with a heavy steel chain. The next morning, as indignant law faculty members and students waited to gain access to their building amidst the catcalls of the watching engineers, a brawny engineering student and football player eventually offered to break the chain. To the amazement of the watching lawyers and physical plant staff, after much straining and a mighty heave he finally succeeded. (In reality he had merely opened a solder link the engineers had concealed in the chain.) Concerned about potential for violence, the Polygon board, representing the professional engineering societies, stopped the engineers' parading in 1929, but after the shysters resumed the tradition again in 1932 the plumbers quickly followed suit. After a particularly destructive parade in 1938, the new College of Engineering dean, Ellis Johnson, decided to divert his students' attention by putting on an ambitious Engineering Exposition each spring to demonstrate to the campus and the state the latest developments in the various fields of engineering. This new challenge, along with the declining engineering presence on the hill, pretty well ended the ancient plumber-shyster rivalry. By 1940 St. Patrick's Day was celebrated only by a major campus dance at the Union.[75]

A more enduring Law School tradition—still followed—was the custom of the seniors lunching together and then parading the length of the Camp Randall football field before the start of the homecoming game to toss their canes over the north goal post. Legend held that catching the cane assured one of winning his or her first case. The practice began during the Van Hise era, with a popular senior law professor invited to lead the march. For twenty-five years, throughout the entire period of this volume, the formidable but beloved William "Herbie" Page had the honor.[76]

---

[75]The St. Patrick parades were often held in April when the weather was warmer than in March. For accounts of some of the more notable parades see *Daily Cardinal*, April 24, 1927, April 20, 21, and 22, 1928, April 28, 1929, March 17, 1932, April 3 and 4, 1935, April 4, 1936, March 15, 17, 19, and 20, May 14, 1938, March 18 and 19, 1939. For an account of the padlocking of the Law Building, see *Capital Times*, March 20, 1933; James R. Villemonte, one of the engineering student participants, conversations with E. David Cronon, 1991-92. For the end of the parades, see *Daily Cardinal*, October 24 and 25, 1929; November 5, 1939, March 17 and 19, 1940; *Press Bulletin*, January 17, 1940.

[76]Gard, *University*, pp. 68-71. Page was one of the few faculty members for whom an exception was made when the Board of Regents adopted a mandatory retirement age of seventy in 1937. Earlier, when weighing the attractions of an outside offer, he had once been assured

Not all student extracurricular activities took place on campus, of course. Until the opening of the Memorial Union with its Great Hall ballroom, major student dances such as the Junior Prom and the Military Ball often were held in the rotunda of the state capitol after the student planners obtained permission from the governor and the superintendent of the capitol. These were elaborate formal affairs, featuring a prominent name band, long gowns for the women and white-tie-and-tails or full dress uniforms for the men, and private tables on the balcony overlooking the dance floor below. Less formal or smaller dances might be held in the ballroom of a downtown hotel. Until the construction of the Union Theater in 1939, the popular Haresfoot Club review was usually staged each spring for two weeks on the road and at the Fuller Opera House or the Parkway Theater in downtown Madison. The 1931 Haresfoot production, "It's a Gay Life," was perhaps typical, though less a musical comedy and more a review than most of its thirty-two predecessors. Directed by William H. Purnell, '22, the entire production—music, lyrics, story, and choreography—was created and performed by the exclusively male student members of the club, with many of them as usual playing female roles as dancers, singers, and show girls. During two weeks in April the show toured Wisconsin and Illinois by train, performing in Oshkosh, Wausau, Menasha, Milwaukee, Green Bay, Sheboygan, Kenosha, Peoria, Chicago, Rockford, and Janesville, before returning to Madison for four shows at the Parkway Theater. The club obviously had a great time on tour, if one can believe the accounts in its daily mimeographed newspaper, *The Gay Life Gazette* ("For the troupe, the whole troupe, and no one but the troupe") produced en route.[77]

Other off-campus entertainment was to be found nearby on State Street at the magnificent Capitol and Orpheum movie theaters, in such popular gathering places as the Chocolate Shop and the Palace of Sweets or Thomas "Dad" Morgan's eatery and billiards parlor, where one could relax with one of Dad's famous chocolate malts or after the end of prohibition with a glass of beer. During the twenties those with a determination to live up to the decade's "flaming youth" image ventured into the "Bush"—the Italian section located in the Greenbush area

---

by Dean Richards that if he stayed at Wisconsin he could teach as long he wanted. When he reached seventy in 1938 the regents felt obliged to honor this promise. As a result Page taught until he was eighty-three, probably a University record. BOR Minutes, January 19, June 3, 1938.

[77]Haresfoot Club, "It's a Gay Life," scrapbook, 1931, UHP.

around Regent and Park Streets—where there were several illegal speakeasies. One favorite hangout was an Italian restaurant on Regent Street run by the Territori family, whose members were always able to supply wine and other alcoholic beverages to their customers. Even after the parents were jailed for violating the Volstead Act, their teen-age daughter continued to operate the restaurant (and speakeasy). So grateful were the Experimental College regulars for this filial devotion that in later years they always invited her to attend their Madison re-unions.[78] Popular nightspots further from the campus included Frank's in Middleton, Mother Metz's in Pheasant Branch, and later the Cuba Club on University Avenue on the western outskirts of the city. Enter-prising farmers at Nob Hill and Middleton offered hay- and sleigh-rides for student parties throughout the year.

University author-ities regularly worried about students' seeking night life at distant road houses and dance halls where even dur-ing prohibition alco-holic beverages were available and social pressure to drink was high. Following a head-on collision of two cars filled with young people on the University Avenue via-

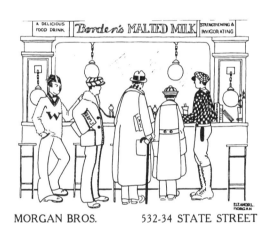

MORGAN BROS.   532-34 STATE STREET

duct west of the city in 1941, an accident that killed the sixteen-year-old daughter of Dean Ira Baldwin and injured eight others, a student com-mittee explored the possibility of a young people's night club within the city limits so high school- and college-age students would not be tempt-ed to leave town. Strangely, no one asked why the Memorial Union's

[78]David G. Parsons, oral history interview, 1987, UA. The Bush had an unsavory reputation as the center of Madison's illegal liquor traffic during prohibition. Its relatively high crime and murder rates as well as its proximity to the campus, gave Dean Goodnight considerable concern, but he was never able to devise a way to keep the more venturesome students out of the area. Periodically Madison, state, or federal authorities would launch raids against the speakeasies, most notably while Philip La Follette was serving as district attorney in 1926, but they never succeeded in drying out the area.

Club 770 did not fill such a need. Dean Goodnight, on the other hand, more realistically tied both the attraction and the problem to lax enforcement of drinking regulations in out-of-town night spots. In response to the Baldwin tragedy he proposed restricting the student use of cars and prohibiting the sale of liquor within a half mile of the campus. Student leaders were unwilling to concede that easy access to alcohol in rural areas was a problem meriting their concern, and understandably argued against any additional restrictions on student social life. The Goodnight proposals died a largely unlamented death.[79]

Wisconsin, after all, was already famous as the first university in the country to authorize the sale of beer on campus. This decision did not come easily, however, even in a heavily German state with scores of breweries large and small all racing to get back into production after the end of prohibition in March of 1933. UW students lost no time adjusting to the new era. That same month the men's literary society Athenae adopted a resolution demanding beer in the Memorial Union. The *Daily Cardinal* came out strongly in support, agreeing it was time "to render unto the Rathskeller those things that are the Rathskeller's."[80] A group of men's dormitory residents quickly raised the ante by petitioning the Board of Regents for permission to sell beer in the refectory serving Tripp and Adams halls. The regents were in no hurry to take up the issue, recognizing there were thorny questions of state and municipal regulatory policy to be settled. Sensitive to the political and public relations aspects of the question, they put off a decision until they could get an opinion from the Wisconsin attorney general. He provided little help, merely referring the problem back to the regents by advising them they had the authority to set University policy.[81]

At the board's October, 1933, meeting most of the regents were inclined to turn down the student beer petitions. Before voting on the issue, however, they broke for lunch in one of the private dining rooms at the Memorial Union. Arnold Dammen, '32, who later became assistant director of residence halls, was one of the Union waiters serving them that day. As he took the beverage orders one of the regents—whether innocently or by design is unclear—ordered a glass of beer. Nonplussed, Dammen asked Don Halverson, the Union steward, what to do. Halverson told him to run out quickly to a nearby tavern

---

[79]See *Daily Cardinal*, November 9, 12, 16, 28, and 30, December 3, 1941.
[80]Ibid., April 13, 1933.
[81]BOR Minutes, April 27, August 2, 1933.

and buy several bottles of beer. After Dammen served the beer, several other regents said they would like beer as well. *Mirabile dictu*, when the board reconvened after lunch there was only a lone vote against a motion authorizing the sale of 3.2 beer in the Union and in the Tripp-Adams refectory. Perhaps the board had undergone a miraculous conversion over lunch, or more likely the regents recognized they would be vulnerable to the charge of hypocrisy for ordering something denied the students in their own union! After the attorney general informally advised University authorities they did not need a city liquor license, on October 15 the Union began selling bottled beer in the Rathskeller. The low-ceilinged room with its heavy oak tables and colorful murals could at last function as a real German beer cellar, very likely the first such on an American college campus following the end of prohibition.[82]

The board's action was applauded by the students, of course, but it raised a number of eyebrows elsewhere in the state. The often critical *Janesville Gazette* commented sourly that President Frank was now "the world's leading tavernkeeper," while the *Stanley Republican* predicted the University would lose "the estimation of many who until now have supported its much vaunted liberalism."[83] An unidentified critic circulated photographs and a press release purporting to show UW coeds drinking beer in their dormitory rooms. This outraged the Women's Self-Government Association, which after an investigation was able to prove the photos were faked in a studio, but the exposure did not undo the damaging publicity.[84] Ironically, in criticizing the regents' action the Women's Christian Temperance Union found itself in a strange alliance with the Madison tavern owners, who also protested angrily against this unexpected competition by a public establishment that paid no taxes. The tavern association hired an attorney and threatened litigation, at the same time attempting to mobilize support from other Madison businesses—hotels, restaurants, barber shops, billiards parlors, dance halls, and the like—whose owners in the past had complained about the loss of student patronage to the Union.[85] The *Cardinal* waxed

---

[82]Ibid., October 11, 1933; *Capital Times*, October 11 and 12, 1933; *Daily Cardinal*, October 12 and 14, 1933; Lawrence Halle memoir, 1992, UHP.

[83]*Daily Cardinal*, November 11 and 15, 1933.

[84]Ibid., November 2, 3, and 4, 1933.

[85]*Capital Times*, October 15, 1933; *Daily Cardinal*, October 14 and 17, 1933. Not everyone in the University community agreed with the *Cardinal*'s criticism of the WCTU ladies as tiresome busybodies. Professor C.M. Jansky responded with a letter to the editor urging students to take seriously the WCTU's warnings about the dangers of alcohol. The

righteously indignant at the thought Madison businessmen should try to coerce students into getting their beer in "less clean and wholesome places" than the Rathskeller:

> If the tavern keepers of this city think for one moment that they can dictate where students should drink, they will find that they are sitting upon a keg of dynamite. The students refuse to be told what to do, especially by tavern keepers, and since they want beer in the Union, they will have beer in the Union, and no amount of pussyfooting, nor camouflaging on the part of the keepers of the vats will influence them to the contrary.[86]

For a time there was talk of a student boycott against the offending establishments, but tempers on both sides cooled as it became apparent the taverns could thrive in spite of beer in the Rat.

Wisconsin students, like young people generally, tended in these years to be more idealistic, more open to new ideas and supportive of change, than their elders. They embraced the liberal causes—political and economic reform, opposition to foreign entanglements, and peace at just about any price—that flourished on college campuses across the country during the twenties and thirties. The La Follette progressives dominated Wisconsin politics during most of the period, and they usually received strong support from the student body except when Phil La Follette's political interference and budget cuts were perceived as harming the University. Even then there was always an active student Progressive Club ready to defend the La Follette brothers and drum up student support for their political movement. President Roosevelt's New Deal was also popular, more so on campus than in some parts of the state. The benefits of federal PWA funds were readily apparent to students in the campus buildings constructed and remodeled during the thirties, while hundreds of appreciative students were able to remain in school during the depression only because of their CWA and NYA work-study jobs. Students had reason to believe in the political process and to have faith in a caring government during the 1930s.

Pacifism exerted a powerful appeal to many UW students in the inter-war years, in keeping with the general American disillusionment

---

issue of unfair competition by the Union had been litigated in 1930 and was the subject of a legislative investigation the following year, but the University's right to offer competing services in the Memorial Union was upheld since they were available only to Union members and their guests, not to the public as a whole. See Porter Butts, "Diary of the Union" (unpublished manuscript, April 15, 1949), UHP.

[86]*Daily Cardinal*, October 17, 1933.

over the outcome of the First World War. As the war clouds lowered again over Europe in the thirties, anti-war sentiment grew more vocal in Madison as on college campuses generally, expressed in frequent rallies and peace marches. UW students were by no means of one mind about how the United States should avoid involvement in another European conflict, however. In spite of regular campaigns by the *Daily Cardinal* and student militants against the Army Reserve Office Training program, the University's cadet corps never lacked recruits. On one occasion a *Cardinal* news editor, himself an ROTC cadet, felt obliged to dissent publicly from one of the paper's many editorials criticizing the program.[87]   No doubt some students signed up mostly for the welcome financial support during the depression, but others believed military

A Surprise Guest at an Anti-War Meeting

preparedness was an effective anti-war strategy. Even at the height of the anti-ROTC campaigns during the 1930s, the members of the cadet corps always enjoyed considerable campus prestige. They provided part of the leadership of many student organizations, including the *Cardinal*, and their annual Military Ball rivaled the Junior Prom as one of the high points of the campus social season.

Besides anti-war concerns, student liberalism was reflected in other ways, too. On questions of human rights, student thinking was usually more open and generous than that of most of their elders, if less developed and consistent by today's standards. Like most Americans of the period, students enjoyed ethnic and gender humor their present-day counterparts would find offensive in the extreme. They put on black-face minstrel shows, published Sambo and anti-Semitic cartoons, and laughed at dumb flapper jokes. Most students (and their elders) also took for granted the anti-Semitic and other discrimination practiced by most of the fraternities and sororities in picking their members. Clay

---

[87]Robert Taylor, "Woe Is Me!" letter to the editor, ibid., June 4, 1936.

Schoenfeld recalls with amusement what happened when he pledged the Sigma Nu fraternity in the late 1930s. Suspicious of his Jewish-sounding name, the chapter held up his election until one of the brothers had visited Clay's father in Lake Mills to check whether Clay really was, as he claimed, the son of the local Congregational minister![88] Selectivity was accepted as part of the Greek raison d'être, and it was after all applied with equal consistency by the Jewish fraternities and sororities and several of the Jewish-owned private dormitories on Langdon Street. On the other hand, Jewish and gentile students worked harmoniously together in campus organizations, especially the *Daily Cardinal*, and often formed close friendships. These rarely included inter-faith dating or other social interaction during this period, however. The alumni of the Greek chapters generally felt more strongly about the membership purity issue than did the actives, who occasionally chafed openly at the eligibility constraints placed on them by their national charters or alumni members. Alumni support was crucial to many of the Greek chapters, as new members were sometimes recruited with the promise that a wealthy backer would pay the pledge's room and board bill.[89]

It is dangerous, of course, to generalize broadly about student attitudes, but it seems likely that throughout the inter-war years most Wisconsin students, including the few blacks and somewhat larger number of Jews, did not believe in inter-racial and inter-faith dating or rooming, and preferred to live and socialize with students of their own general background. In 1944 a survey by the Student Board's housing committee found only a bare majority of the students polled willing to live with members of any race or creed; 49 percent said they would object. The *Cardinal* professed shock at this indication of the continuing extent of prejudice "on a supposedly liberal minded campus," but one suspects the survey may if anything have exaggerated the tolerance of the student body.[90] What is noteworthy is not the findings of a particular survey but the extent and consistency with which student leaders condemned racial and religious intolerance and discrimination when it came to their attention. And although such sensitivity increased markedly during the depression and Second World War, the concern existed earlier as well. Frequently it went beyond the more conven-

---

[88]Clay Schoenfeld to E. David Cronon, February 27, 1992, UHP.
[89]Ibid.
[90]*Daily Cardinal*, January 6, 1944.

tional attitudes of University faculty and administrators.[91]

In January of 1929, for example, the *Capital Times* ran a series of page-one stories about the formation of the Apex Club by fifteen UW fraternities. The club was avowedly anti-Semitic; its purpose, according to the leaders, was to stage private dances for its members at a downtown ballroom because of the belief Jewish students had taken over the dances at the Memorial Union. The official Apex Club membership card, signed by Chi Psi and club founder John Leigh, '28, bluntly acknowledged the document was "issued to members only in order to prevent the entrance of 'undesirables'."[92] The *Cardinal* ridiculed the group as "the apex of assininity," but also criticized the *Times* for muckraking and sensationalism.[93] While Jewish students seemed surprised but not resentful of the club, Dean Goodnight quickly made clear Apex was not a University-approved student group, and President Frank declared in a press release the University tolerated neither race nor class discrimination in its facilities and in the varied social functions under its direct control. He added a qualifier: "The University does not, however, presume officially to dictate the intimate social associates of any student or of any student group."[94] Some students were more forthright in their condemnation of Apex. Two non-Jews, Emerick Korecz and Alfred Rinelli, formed the Racket Club to publicize and embarrass the Apex gatherings. Their ridicule and the criticism of other students first drove Apex underground and then out of existence. Although the Apex Club did not survive for long, the outspoken *Wisconsin Student Independent* concluded everyone—President Frank, Dean Goodnight, the *Cardi-*

---

[91]While some faculty members quietly held racist or anti-Semitic views, a few were more outspoken in their bigotry, as when the leaders of the University Club initially evicted a black graduate student in 1944 simply because of his race. See pp. 542-9. Faculty support for the eugenics movement to improve the quality of the human species was common in the twenties and thirties, and it was easy for such views to take on a tinge of racism. Professor Emeritus Edward A. Ross, a famous UW sociologist, got into hot water with liberal students by taking a public stand against race-mixing in a campus debate in 1943. The current national chairman of the American Civil Liberties Union, Ross argued that democracy did not imply racial equality. "I'm not at all prejudiced," he declared, "but I'm still glad my three sons married white girls....I cannot feel that inter-marriage is a possible solution to the end of Negro-White discrimination until I see a statement signed by 80 per cent of America's anthropologists proving that the Negro is not an inferior race." For this he was roundly rebuked by the *Daily Cardinal*, May 4 and 5, 1943.

[92]*Capital Times*, January 11, 12, 13, 14, and 17, 1929.

[93]*Daily Cardinal*, January 12 and 13, 1929.

[94]Press release, January 11, 1929, Frank Presidential Papers, 4/13/1, box 55; *Daily Cardinal*, January 12, 1929; *Capital Times*, January 14, 1929.

nal, and Hillel director Rabbi Landman—ought to have been more aggressive in stamping out such unhealthy prejudice.[95]

Student agitation led eventually to a change in the membership requirements of the national speech honorary fraternity, Delta Sigma Rho, whose charter barred "colored persons." In 1931 the UW chapter voted to admit G. James Fleming, '31, a popular black student from the Virgin Islands, only to find that under the national rules he was ineligible for the honor. Fleming was a talented debater and orator, winner of the prestigious Frankenburger oratory prize, and a member of the Phi Beta Kappa scholastic honorary society. Student leaders were outraged at this insult, and the *Cardinal* and even the state legislature pressed the local chapter to seek a change in the national rules or withdraw. Under continuing pressure from the Wisconsin chapter, finally in the spring of 1935 a majority of the Delta Sigma Rho chapters agreed to drop the color bar. A month later the Wisconsin chapter admitted its first Negro student member, Hilton Hanna.[96]

Similarly, student and faculty pressure forced the Badger track team to withdraw from a triangular meet at the University of Missouri in the spring of 1939 because Missouri's segregation policy would prevent the participation of Ed Smith, Wisconsin's Negro hurdler. In demanding the team refuse to take part without Smith, the *Cardinal* summarized the general campus sentiment:

> If the University of Wisconsin, long proud of its liberal heritage, allows the "Southern Gentlemen of Missouri" to dictate race discrimination, it will be violating one of its sacred precepts and encouraging racial prejudice, even though it be recognized that such prejudice is a dominant factor in southern life.

After Wisconsin withdrew, Notre Dame did so as well.[97]

Although students generally supported the right of individuals or groups to select their living mates, they expected University housing facilities to be open to all students without discrimination, except for the

---

[95] *Capital Times*, January 22 and 25, 1929; *Wisconsin Student Independent*, January 24, 1929.

[96] *Capital Times*, May 21 and 28, 1931; *Daily Cardinal*, May 15, 16, 17, 19, 20, 22, 23, 28, and 29, September 24, December 10, 1931, February 10, March 13, 1932, March 27, May 9, November 22, 1934, April 19, May 19, 1935.

[97] "Track Team Should Not Take Part in Meet," editorial, *Daily Cardinal*, April 4, 1939. See also ibid., April 2, 3, 5, 8, 11, and 13, May 5, 1939; UW Faculty Minutes, April 3, May 1, 1939.

preference given to Wisconsin residents. Jewish students often sought to room in the University dormitories because they were accepted without question, though throughout this period the UW housing staff assigned roommates on the basis of perceived racial and religious compatibility. Student leaders were increasingly suspicious that University authorities condoned, or at least failed to use their leverage against, the discriminatory rental policies of many of the private landlords and house mothers ringing the campus. After receiving a number of complaints, in 1942 the *Cardinal* condemned the apparent practice of the University's housing adviser of asking certain students if they were Jewish before referring them to private housing.[98] Student concern over housing discrimination and other forms of prejudice was particularly keen during World War II, when the Madison housing market was especially tight and such practices seemed to make a mockery of the Four Freedoms and other American war aims. In this their sensibilities were more acute than those of some members of the faculty, as the Arthur Burke-University Club affair demonstrated in 1944.[99]

Student leaders were quick to condemn the University when it failed to meet their idealistic expectations, but they were also fiercely loyal and protective when it was unfairly criticized by outsiders. The *Daily Cardinal* regularly challenged editors, governors, legislators, and clergymen whom it considered hostile to the University. Perhaps the best example of this loyalty was the reaction to John Chapple, the politically ambitious Ashland editor who ran for governor in 1931-32 on a platform attacking President Frank and the University for allegedly championing radicalism and immorality. Students responded with indignation and anger, heckling Chapple at every opportunity and forcing him to retract some of his wilder charges. They also organized a Student League for Intellectual Freedom—a truth squad in today's terminology—to follow Chapple around the state and refute his criticism. So effective was this ad hoc group of student defenders that President Frank and University Registrar Frank Holt decided to continue the student speakers program with modest University backing thereafter. Each year the Student Speakers Bureau (later called the Student Public Relations Committee), with an office and some staff support in the Memorial Union, recruited as many as two hundred student volunteers to speak at high schools and at parent, alumni, and club meetings

---

[98]*Daily Cardinal*, October 2, 1942.
[99]See pp. 542-9.

around the state. The students served as very persuasive examples of the advantages of a University of Wisconsin education. When enrollments began to increase substantially in the mid-thirties, Holt credited the student lobbyists for much of the growth. In 1937 the SPRC began offering a guide service for visitors to the campus and organized a student-legislator dinner to urge larger University appropriations. The following year SPRC members contacted and interviewed the top 10 percent of high school seniors in the state to encourage them to attend the University. The committee also mounted a campaign to make legislators more aware of University achievements. When the Heil administration proposed a draconian reduction in the University's budget in 1939, SPRC chairman Leon Epstein, '40, quickly mobilized student forces against the cuts. As the *Daily Cardinal* commented approvingly during one of the earlier SPRC campaigns, "The students strengthen the University's cause."[100] They certainly did—and did it well.

The campus work days provided other evidence of student spirit and devotion to the University in this period. Although student labor made possible earlier projects like the Hoofers' ski jump and toboggan slide, the idea of students helping to beautify the campus began about 1940, when horticulture Professor Franz Aust recruited a number of College of Agriculture student volunteers to plant eight hundred black locust seedlings on Muir Knoll.[101] The following year a Student Board committee under the leadership of Robert Avery, '41, organized the first all-campus work day to widen and resurface the lake path between the men's dorms and the Union with cinders from the University heating plant. Calling themselves the campus WPA—"We Pave Anything"—the students collected steam rollers, graders, a large supply of shovels and rakes, and seventeen hundred cubic yards of cinders for the undertaking. "The project deserves the support of every student," the *Cardinal*

---

[100]*Daily Cardinal*, May 3, 1935. On the student reaction to Chapple's attacks and the formation of a speakers bureau, see ibid., May 8, 10, 14, and 22, August 12, September 23 and 29, October 27, 1932. For the later development of the student speakers bureau and other student lobbying efforts, see ibid., March 6, December 13, 1934, January 19, February 20 and 21, March 8, April 10, 12, May 1, 2, 3, 9, 12, 14, and 25, June 4, 5, 6, and 9, July 31, November 13, 14, 15, 16, 17, and 20, December 4, 18, and 20, 1935, February 28, March 24 and 26, April 16, May 14 and 27, September 29 and 30, October 13, December 5 amd 15, 1936, January 10, 14, and 21, April 27, May 13 and 23, July 31, August 4, October 14, December 4, 1937, January 6, March 22, April 8, 10, and 12, December 3 and 13, 1938, May 11 and 12, June 27, 1939, April 10, 1941, May 14, November 13, 1942, March 31, 1944, March 13, 1945.

[101]Ibid., May 9, 1940.

declared:

> All will be immediately repaid in the good time to be had working with
> hundreds of men and coeds in the open air, the free eats, and the street dance
> after the day's work. And on top of that, it is more than ordinary fun—it will
> leave a finished road behind.[102]

On Saturday, May 17, 1941, the Greeks from Langdon Street gathered
at Wisconsin Avenue and the "dormies" at the men's residence halls.
Both groups marched behind two brass bands to meet at the eastern
terminus of the lake road at the Hydraulic Lab, where President Dykstra
threw the first shovel of cinders. The students then pitched in—twelve
hundred men and women—and worked so industriously they ran out of
cinders before the day was out. Albert F. Gallistel, the superintendent
of buildings and grounds, estimated their labor had saved the University
$5,000.[103] So impressed was the Board of Regents that the members
voted a special resolution of appreciation to the student body for this
"valuable service."[104]

Although students were heavily involved in war-related activities
through their Wisconsin Elective Service program after Pearl Harbor,
the Student Board mounted another all-campus work day effort in the
spring of 1942 under the direction of an energetic junior, Francis
Bouda. This time the target was the corn field along Observatory Drive
adjacent to the College of Agriculture dean's residence. Some eight
hundred students cleared and graded this open space for use as a women's intramural athletic playing field. Once again Bouda and his
committee provided free food, beer, and entertainment to make the day
go easier, followed by an open air dance that evening on the nearby
tennis courts.[105] In 1943 and 1944 the work day projects involved
planting trees in the University Arboretum. Again the organizers
offered entertainment and free refreshments, and a contest for a "blue
jean queen" to reign over the festivities. The *Cardinal* promised her
highness would wear a smudge of dirt for make-up and a shovel for a
scepter. This feminine touch was a fitting symbol of the wartime
changes on a campus now increasingly dominated by coeds. The 1944
work day got off to a bad start when Robert Burke and Robert Claus,

---

[102]Ibid., May 11 and 13, 1940.
[103]Ibid., May 16, 17, 18, 19, and 22, 1941.
[104]BOR Minutes, May 27, 1941.
[105]*Daily Cardinal*, April 22 and 30, May 2 and 5, 1942.

the two organizers, were arrested at 7:30 A.M. while driving around the University area calling the students to work by means of a loud speaker on the roof of their car. They eventually were able to persuade Madison Police Chief McCormick it was all for a good cause and were released without charges. Even with this mishap nearly a thousand students, including some of the campus Navy V-12 cadets, turned out to plant two thousand trees, a disappointing ratio owing to the wartime shortage of gasoline and trucks to transport seedlings from the nurseries.[106] The following year the student volunteers concentrated on cleaning up Picnic Point. This time the slumber patrol to rout out lazy students was more circumspect.[107]

Despite the rivalries between Greeks and barbs, between plumbers and shysters, between aggies and Bascom Hill denizens, and regardless of the sometimes hard-fought competition for campus office, students in this period constituted a close-knit group whose members cared about each other and about the well-being of the student body. They were also proud of and devoted to the larger University of which they were a part. Like the faculty they thought of themselves as part of a vibrant academic community of national stature and import. Wisconsin students were known to play hard and party often, but there was also a serious purpose in much of their campus life. For some it involved learning the exacting craft of journalism in order to put out an award-winning daily newspaper; for others it meant sharpening forensic or athletic skills to engage competitors in campus and intercollegiate contests; for still others it included long hours of practice before staging dramatic and musical entertainments; for many it simply entailed service in the myriad groups that operated the Memorial Union or the living units or the student churches or were concerned with campus and community betterment.

Most students found their University academic work to be a mind-expanding experience that carried over into their extracurricular life. While student-faculty relations were on a more formal basis than in later years, there was also much more out-of-class contact between the two groups than later. Student bull sessions in the Rathskeller, whether over

---

[106]Ibid., April 22, May 6, 1943, March 30, April 26 and 27, May 9 and 11, 1944.
[107]Ibid., April 10, 18, and 24, 1945.

a cup of coffee or a beer, often dealt with serious topics and sometimes drew in faculty participants and expertise. Faculty members regularly invited small groups of students into their homes for conversation and tea or supper. President and Mrs. Dykstra had monthly drop-in teas for students at Olin House. Student organizations and living units routinely asked the faculty to chaperon their mixed parties or to address them on some topic of student concern. Even Dean of Men Goodnight, whose disciplinary summons struck terror into the hearts of miscreants, inspired admiration and affection among those students he worked with in campus organizations. These frequent contacts helped tie the students and staff together in ways that became difficult after the University more than doubled in size following the Second World War.

"Boy oh boy, it's Dean Goodnight!"

There are, of course, examples of UW student idealism and concern about societal problems well before Old Bob La Follette and his sons brought a heightened interest in reform to Wisconsin and the University in the early twentieth century. Yet the La Follettes captured the interest and allegiance of UW students as have few Wisconsin politicians before or since. Even as the La Follette progressives were losing their hold on the Wisconsin electorate in the late 1930s, however, student political activism was shifting further leftward. A key indicator was the growing concern about racial and religious discrimination, especially in student housing. Bigotry as such had never been a major concern of Wisconsin progressives, so in this respect the students were leading their elders. The work of the Student Board's Housing Committee after 1940, especially its major report in 1943-44, did much to expose bigotry to public view and lay the basis for post-war efforts to get the University to take a leadership role in ending discriminatory practices. Jewish students played a major part in this effort and deserve much of the credit for raising campus sensitivity to the issue.

Indeed, while it would be too much to credit the relatively small number of Jewish students with determining the student agenda, there is little doubt about their significant leavening role in this regard. The increased Jewish enrollment beginning in the 1920s, coming especially from New York and other eastern states with well-developed traditions of Jewish radical activism, clearly helped to heighten the University's reputation as a bastion of liberal thought and action. Thus any consideration of student life in the period 1925-45 must take into account the growing Jewish presence in the student body in these years. Although Jews never comprised more than about a tenth of the student population, they tended to play a more active role in student politics and on student publications, especially the *Daily Cardinal*, than their numbers would suggest. They thus very likely had a greater impact on student thought and action than any other student group. Their efforts to create a more socially aware and caring academic community are surely part of what made Wisconsin distinctive among the great public universities in these years.

12.

The Educational Enterprise

We have already noted President Glenn Frank's concern to reform undergraduate education, especially in the freshman and sophomore years and in the liberal arts generally, following his appointment in 1925. Frank's interest was mainly with the work of the University's large liberal arts college, Letters and Science, which served most of the undergraduates, and not with the smaller professional schools. With one or two exceptions he largely ignored the professional schools or at least refrained from offering suggestions about their instructional programs. Frank's pet project, the Experimental College (whose history is recounted in Chapter 3), lasted but five years, and was neither the only nor the most important educational development during the years 1925-45. President Frank's interest in curricular reform probably helped to stimulate some of the changes, as did President Clarence Dykstra's support of interdisciplinary ventures, but it must be remembered that there is nothing less static than a university curriculum, regardless of presidents or deans. The one constant is change; there are always new or updated courses incorporating the latest findings, modified requirements, and occasionally fresh degree programs. The UW faculty, in Letters and Science and in the various professional schools, launched a number of significant educational initiatives throughout the inter-war years. Many of these had a more lasting impact than the Experimental College and thus should not be overlooked in the greater attention paid to that highly publicized venture during its brief operation and since.

Some of the curricular initiatives resulted from administrative restructuring or changes in the campus physical plant. With few exceptions University facilities lagged seriously behind the enrollment growth of the period, and the regents' efforts to deal with the problem were

683

largely frustrated by the depression and the war. Still, with the limited new construction and remodeling that could be accomplished with scarce state, federal, and private funds the faculty found opportunities for some new or expanded instructional programs. The most striking example of the positive effect of improved facilities on the curriculum was the opening of Wisconsin General (or University) Hospital in 1924, which provided the clinical facilities and patients needed for the Medical School to expand to a full four-year curriculum the following year. The hospital also enabled the creation of the School of Nursing in 1924, whose students lived and studied in the new Nurses Dormitory at 1402 University Avenue beginning in 1926. These developments led in turn to the construction in 1928 of the Service Memorial Institutes building adjoining the hospital to provide more space for medical research and clinical training and of the adjacent Orthopedic Children's Hospital two years later. By 1930 there was a substantial medical-clinical complex along University Avenue west of Bascom Hill housing a full program of medical and nursing education, clinical treatment, and research.

Similarly, the completion of the Mechanical Engineering Building in 1931 began the shift of the College of Engineering to the Camp Randall area. This was followed the next year by the relocation of the college's Department of Minerals and Metals to the old Forest Products Laboratory building nearby. By the end of the decade the migration of the College of Engineering westward had progressed to the point where the School of Education could take over much of the original Engineering Building on Bascom Hill built in 1901, the first real space of its own since achieving independence in 1930. The building was thereupon renamed Education and Engineering until the last of the engineering programs on "the Hill" moved into a new Engineering Building at Camp Randall in 1951.[1] While other curricular developments of the period in most cases did not involve new facilities, nevertheless the tie between educational advancements and the changing physical resources of the campus often was clear. Conversely, in spite of the substantial enrollment growth of the inter-war years, the inability of the state to provide much in the way of additional classroom and other instructional

---

[1]For a student account of the expansion of engineering facilities over the years see Francis Hyland, Harry Hanson, and June Hartnell, "University of Wisconsin Engineering Buildings," *Wisconsin Engineer*, 49 (November, 1944), 10-2, 26. Dean C.J. Anderson of the School of Education lost no time in staking out his school's claim for the Engineering Building following the construction of the Mechanical Engineering Building in 1931. See Anderson to Glenn Frank, May 21, 1931, Frank Presidential Papers, 4/13/1, box 89, UA.

facilities during the depression and war years seriously challenged the academic enterprise. It also left the University ill-prepared to handle the massive influx of veterans after the Second World War.

An Elusive Phantom

The most conspicuous example of the negative effect of inadequate facilities on the institution's educational mission during the inter-war years was the compelling but unmet need for a larger and more comprehensive general University library. In 1900 the University Library was moved from Library Hall (now Music Hall) across Park Street to the north wing of the new State Historical Society of Wisconsin Building. This stately limestone and marble structure, whose neoclassical grandeur made it one of the handsomest buildings in the state, had been authorized by the legislature in 1895 after a lengthy campaign by UW Presidents Chamberlin and Adams and Historical Society Superintendent Reuben Gold Thwaites to solve the growing space problems of their two libraries. Adams' hope to build up the University's book collection following his appointment in 1892 was limited not only by funding but by the cramped space in Library Hall, which by the 1890s lacked both the study and stack space adequate for current University needs. The Historical Society's much larger collection had by this time also overflowed its space in the state capitol. Although there were serious problems inherent in trying to meet the needs of two quite different libraries administered by two separate agencies in the same building, it was clear to both governing boards that they could make a more compelling case for a new facility if they joined together. Moving the society's library to the campus also represented a major scholarly gain for the University, for the collection included the finest holdings of Americana and newspapers west of the Alleghenies and also boasted considerable strength in related fields of history, economics, geography, and literature.

President Adams and Superintendent Thwaites collaborated closely in planning the new facility so it would serve the needs of both institutions. Indeed, the strain of supervising the project was one of the reasons for Adams' nervous exhaustion and extended medical leave beginning in 1900. By stipulation of the society's Board of Curators, the society held title to and administered the new building, but the University provided the land, shared the cost of utilities and janitorial service, and used about 40 percent of the space. Thwaites treated the University as a co-equal tenant. When opened in 1900 the new library was by far the largest and most impressive such structure in Wisconsin and the immediate region. There were two six-level stack wings—one each for the society and the University—a spacious two-story central reading room, smaller reading and seminar rooms elsewhere throughout the building, and a museum for the society's historical artifacts. The two book collections remained legally and physically separate, each with its own card catalog and staff. Adams, who had previously helped plan new libraries while a history professor at the University of Michigan and subsequently as president of Cornell University, was justifiably proud of the Wisconsin library he had done so much to bring about, boasting to University of California President Benjamin Ide Wheeler in 1900 that he would not exchange it for the combined libraries of Princeton and Columbia.[2]

What had seemed an ideal facility at the turn of the century, however, was increasingly inadequate even after the completion of a northwest wing in 1914, owing to the continued growth in student enrollment and especially in the size of the two collections. A quarter century of experience had also highlighted the problems of trying to operate two libraries in one building, each with separate purposes, regulations, catalogs, clienteles, and staffs. There were inevitable administrative disagreements: Thwaites thought the University should share the costs of sprinkling Park Street to keep down the dust and complained that University users wasted electricity or turned on lights deliberately left darkened to conserve his tight operating budget for the building. University readers—students and faculty alike—chafed at the differing regulations governing access and use of the two collections, while society librarians had reason to worry about student theft and damage to their valuable research materials. The noise from the adjacent student playing field was another irritant. Especially during the depression, book thefts became a serious problem, leading to a decision to control and eventually to restrict undergraduate access to the stacks. By the mid-1930s the two collections had outgrown the available shelf space and some books and other materials had to be piled on the window sills,

---

[2]Charles Kendall Adams to Benjamin Ide Wheeler, March 19, 1900, cited in Merle Curti and Vernon Carstensen, *The University of Wisconsin: A History, 1848-1925* (Madison: University of Wisconsin Press, 1949), vol. 1, p. 656; Clifford L. Lord and Carl Ubbelohde, *Clio's Servant: The State Historical Society of Wisconsin, 1846-1954* (Madison: State Historical Society of Wisconsin, 1967), pp. 101-10.

floors, and even hallways throughout the building.[3]

A more serious problem was the poorly defined division of collecting responsibility between the two libraries. During the nineteenth century the first two directors of the Historical Society, Lyman C. Draper and Thwaites, had collected aggressively, seeking materials not just about Wisconsin and the Mississippi Valley but also about American history very broadly defined. They construed the latter to embrace the history of Great Britain and the New World generally and had even developed a significant collection on Shakespeare and old English drama. From the first the society's library surpassed that of the University, whose catalogs beginning in 1867 regularly boasted of the access its students had to the society's holdings. By the nineties the society reported that more than 90 percent of the users of its library in the state capitol were UW staff and students. In 1900, when the two libraries were moved into the new building, the society's collection greatly overshadowed the University's more modest holdings, even though the latter aimed to cover a broader range of subjects: approximately 230,000 society titles versus 75,000 UW titles.[4]

The partial merger in 1900 led the two institutions to try to work out a division of collecting responsibilities to avoid overlap and duplication, but Thwaites' zeal made him reluctant to cut back the society's scope. Even after the collecting agreement was further clarified in 1907 and reaffirmed in 1912, the society still claimed as its areas of interest the history of North, Central, and South America, the United Kingdom, and the British colonial possessions of the Western Hemisphere. While Thwaites was willing to cede certain subjects within this vast bibliographic empire to the University, it gradually became evident that his acquisitions appetite exceeded the society's financial resources. Much of the acquisitions growth came from gifts and bequests; indeed, the society did not receive any state support for acquisitions until 1901,

---

[3]See UW Faculty Document 427, "Report of the Library Committee on Loss of Books and Filing of Theses," January 30, 1933, UA; UW Faculty Minutes, February 6, 1933, ibid.; *Daily Cardinal*, December 15 and 18, 1932, January 10 and 11, February 6, 7, 8, 9, and 25, September 23, October 8 and 14, November 16 and 28, 1933, October 3 and 7, 1934; Lord and Ubbelohde, *Clio's Servant*, pp. 127-8; *Louis Kaplan and the University of Wisconsin Library at the University of Wisconsin-Madison* (Madison: Friends of the University of Wisconsin-Madison Libraries, 1992), p. 5.

[4]Elsie A. Fansler, "The University of Wisconsin Library: A History, 1848-1953" (manuscript, n.d.), p. 94, Departmental Files, Library, UA; sections published serially in *UW Library News*, 10 (1965-66).

when the legislature established an annual $5,000 book fund.[5]   UW Librarian Walter M. Smith liked to refer to the combined libraries as "one great state library," but its greatness was spotty and deceptive.   In the long run the association proved to be a mixed blessing for both institutions.   While clearly beneficial and convenient for University users, the presence of the society library on the campus reduced the pressure on the University to develop its own holdings.   The society's overly ambitious but ambiguous collecting scope, moreover, virtually guaranteed that some fields would be inadequately covered or would fall between the acquisitions mandates of the two institutions.

Throughout the period 1925-45 the faculty repeatedly ranked a new or expanded library building as the University's most pressing construction need.   The best opportunity for a new facility came during the Glenn Frank honeymoon period when for a brief time the legislature was unusually well-disposed toward the University.   As part of the favorable University budget adopted at the time of Frank's appointment in 1925, the legislature appropriated $550,000 for "an addition to the library and equipment."[6]   The University's intent in asking for these funds was to add a transverse wing to the society's building along Park Street to provide stack space for 300,000 volumes, a large reading room for seven hundred readers, and additional seminar rooms and library studies.   Inexplicably, University authorities had evidently neglected to inform Joseph Schafer, the society superintendent, or its Board of Curators that they were requesting this appropriation.   At least one member of the society, Chicago attorney John Thomas Lee, was outraged at this evident disregard of the society's rights to its own property, fearing a challenge to its independence and perhaps even a takeover by the University.   Lee threatened to take the issue to the membership and the governor if Schafer and the Board of Curators did not take steps to protect the society's interests.   The planned $550,000 building addition was put on hold while a seven-member society committee set about negotiating with the University.[7]

Meanwhile, the death of Senator Robert M. La Follette in June, 1925, had set Wisconsin progressives searching for an appropriate way to honor the founder of the state's progressive movement.   The idea of a memorial library at his alma mater was appealing, especially to his

[5]Lord and Ubbelohde, *Clio's Servant*, pp. 130-5.
[6]Section 20.41 (n) (1) *Wisconsin Statutes*, 1925.
[7]Lord and Ubbelohde, *Clio's Servant*, pp. 277-9.

widow Belle, who with her husband had always taken a keen interest in the University.[8] In the 1927 legislative session Senator John E. Cashman, a leading progressive and a UW regent, introduced a bill to construct a $3 million La Follette Memorial Library on the campus. The proposal was quickly endorsed by UW Librarian Smith as meeting a "pressing need."[9] Although the reaction of the anti-La Follette stalwart wing of the Republican Party ranged from unenthusiastic to downright hostile, in late June the progressive-dominated joint finance committee recommended the $3 million appropriation for the library project.[10] The La Follette memorial was considerably more controversial in the legislature as a whole, however, and the stalwart opposition more determined. Throughout the next month both houses debated and voted on the matter several times, with the proposal eventually being defeated in the senate on a bitterly fought 13-12 vote.[11] Apart from the library project, in other respects the University was treated in what President Frank hailed as "a magnanimous and statesmanlike manner," with the regents' operating budget request emerging largely intact.[12]

There still remained the question of what to do with the controversial $550,000 appropriation approved by the legislature in 1925 but which had remained unspent while the issue of a larger memorial library was under consideration. Following the defeat of the Cashman bill, the Board of Regents established a special committee consisting of Regents Olbrich, Gale, and Schmidtmann to consider how to provide more library space. They were soon joined in the study by the board's standing Constructional Development Committee and the faculty Library Committee chaired by history Professor Frederic L. Paxson.[13] The society's questions about the legality and propriety of the 1925 appropriation for a time strengthened the position of those arguing that the funds should be spent on a separate library building. Regent and Senator Cashman, a member of the Constructional Development Committee, insisted on a separate structure that presumably could become a La Follette memorial in the future, and he castigated Paxson and UW Librarian Smith for suggesting that the limited funds might better be

---

[8]See Chapter 1 for a discussion of the elder La Follettes' interest in the University.

[9]See *Capital Times*, March 19, 22, and 30, 1927; *Daily Cardinal*, March 20, 1927.

[10]*Capital Times*, June 27, 1927; *Daily Cardinal*, June 30, 1927.

[11]*Capital Times*, July 14, 20, 22, 25, and 26, 1927; *Daily Cardinal*, July 16, 19, 21, 23, 26, and 28, 1927.

[12]"Governor Approves Increased Budget," *WAM*, 29 (October, 1927), 9.

[13]BOR Minutes, August 27, December 7, 1927, UA.

used on an addition to the Historical Society Building.[14]   The Smith-Paxson view was shared by Superintendent Schafer, who by now realized this course of action was probably the only realistic hope of the society's sharing any expanded space.   He therefore opposed a separate University Library, while still pressing for legislative clarification of the issue of the society's clear title to its building.[15]   Armed with an opinion from Wisconsin Attorney General John W. Reynolds that the smaller appropriation could be used for a separate building connected by a tunnel to the main library, the regents continued to debate the issue for several months before deciding in March of 1928 to ask for the release of the $550,000 appropriation for construction of the first unit of a new and separate University Library.   They gave force to this decision by promptly purchasing a lot for part of the site of the new structure, to be located on the corner of Park and State streets across from the Historical Society Building.[16]   The board realized the available funds would allow construction of only the first unit of what would need to be a larger building in the future, but its enabling resolution emphasized that the project "is feasible and will relieve the reading room congestion at the University."[17]

The issue now depended on Governor Fred R. Zimmerman, whose approval was required to release the 1925 appropriation, but whose sympathy for a La Follette memorial project, open or disguised, was questionable.   Zimmerman, a sometime progressive and the former secretary of state, had been elected in 1926 as an independent Republican in opposition to the La Follette-endorsed candidate, Herman Ekern.

---

[14]*Daily Cardinal*, December 10, 1927.

[15]*Capital Times*, January 19, 1928; Lord and Ubbelohde, *Clio's Servant*, pp. 280-1.

[16]Franklin E. Bump and John W. Reynolds to the Regents of the University of Wisconsin, December 22, 1927, BOR Papers, 1/1/3, box 41, UA; BOR Minutes, January 18, March 7, 1928; *Capital Times*, December 23, 1927, January 1, 17, 18, and 19, March 7, 1928; *Daily Cardinal*, January 18, 19, and 21, March 1, 6, 8, 10, and 31, 1928. The board's Constructional Development Committee, including Regent Cashman, argued that the $550,000 appropriation would allow only a narrow addition across the west end of the society building that would provide only nine thousand square feet and 780 additional seats, and would be insufficient to complete an enclosed court between the two stack wings. The committee rejected this "rigid, inelastic plan" in favor of a separate structure across the street designed as "a flexible plan capable of expansion with the growing need of the University." This was a tenable position, certainly, but it was also politically suspect and probably reckless, given Cashman's advocacy of the La Follette memorial scheme, recent legislative history, and Governor Zimmerman's likely reaction. "Report of the Constructional Development Committee," January 18, 1928, BOR Papers, 1/1/3, box 41.

[17]BOR Minutes, March 7, 1928.

The La Follette family and supporters considered him an unreliable political light-weight and usurper; their continuing hostility would help to assure his defeat for reelection later in the year.[18] In spite of heavy lobbying by President Frank and the Constructional Development Committee, on April 17 the governor advised Frank that he would not release the funds for construction of a separate library building. He rejected the attorney general's reasoning, citing preliminary plans prepared by the University in 1925 in support of its request for an addition to the Historical Society and other evidence of legislative intent, including the legislature's recent rejection of a separate library. "The legislature having definitely refused to make an appropriation for a *new* library at that time," Zimmerman declared, "the governor and regents would be violating the clear direction of the legislature, if this appropriation of $550,000 were released for the purpose now proposed." He promised, however, to release the appropriation if Frank and the regents agreed to spend the funds on an addition to the Historical Society Building.[19]

Smarting from this rebuff, the regents decided not to use the 1925 appropriation for an addition but to hold out for approval of a separate library building in the next biennium.[20] This proved to be a serious political miscalculation after the progressives did poorly in the 1928 elections, losing the governorship to stalwart Republican Walter J. Kohler. Although the board identified more than $3.3 million in construction and remodeling needs in the University's 1929-31 budget request, including the top priority of $950,000 for a new library, and though President Frank lobbied hard for the library appropriation as the University's "outstanding building need," the legislature was unmoved. The joint finance committee cut back the regents' request to $1.1 million for building purposes, and after a good deal of political maneuvering the legislature slashed that amount to only $300,000 during each of the next two years for all construction, utilities, and land purchases. Worse, it returned to the state general fund the unused 1925 appropriation of $550,000 for a library addition.[21] The solons evidently wanted

---

[18]See Philip F. La Follette, *Adventure in Politics: The Memoirs of Philip La Follette*, Donald Young, ed. (New York: Holt, Rinehart and Winston, 1970), pp. 123-6.

[19]Fred R. Zimmerman to Glenn Frank, April 17, 1928, BOR Papers, 1/1/3, box 41; *Daily Cardinal*, March 24, April 12, 15, 18, and 19, 1928; *Capital Times*, April 14, 1928. Emphasis in original.

[20]*Daily Cardinal* and *Capital Times*, April 26, 1928.

[21]"Frank Asks $9,581,990 for 1929-31," *WAM*, 30 (December, 1928), 71, 104; Frank,

to make sure the La Follette memorial scheme was dead. Cashman continued to argue for a separate library building and with other members of the board disputed whether the legislature had actually repealed the 1925 appropriation, suggesting a court test, but the attorney general held that the appropriation had lapsed.[22] Thereafter the state's worsening fiscal condition in the deepening depression made state funding for large construction projects fanciful, even though the University faculty and administrators continued to push for a new library. Budget cuts rather than new buildings were the order of the day under all of the state administrations of the next decade, whether progressive (La Follette), Democratic (Schmedeman), or stalwart (Heil). After the state's economy and tax base finally began to improve, the war ruled out any non-essential construction.

The failure to deal with the problem of increasingly inadequate storage and study space in the Historical Society Building led the University to make a number of ad hoc incremental adjustments that tended to vitiate the 1895 plan for a central research library serving the entire campus. One casualty of the library storage problem was the undergraduate senior thesis. To save library stack space, in 1934 the L&S faculty decided not to require the permanent deposit of senior theses in the library. Two years later the college faculty urged departments to permit only exceptional students to write theses; only those receiving honors would be accepted by the library.[23] For the more motivated undergraduates the senior thesis had provided valuable training in research and writing. Effectively downgrading and eliminating the requirement for most students diminished the quality of their educational experience.

Another consequence was the proliferation of smaller specialized libraries. The larger professional schools (Agriculture, Medicine, Engineering, and Law) had for many years supported specialized libraries housed, funded, and administered separately from the general University Library. So had a number of the academic departments. The growing pressures on the main library fed the ever-present centrifugal

"The Gist of the University Budget," ibid. (February, 1929), 143-5; Frank, "New Library Is Outstanding Need," ibid. (April, 1929), 215-6; Harry Thoma, "How the University Fared," ibid., 31 (November, 1929), 51-2, 90; *Capital Times*, September 8, 1929; *Daily Cardinal*, October 3 and 10, 1929.

[22]*Daily Cardinal*, December 5 and 6, 1929; BOR Minutes, January 15, 1930.

[23]L&S Faculty Minutes, May 21, 1934, March 16, 1936, UA; *Daily Cardinal*, May 22, 1934.

tendencies to spawn libraries around the campus. An addition to the Engineering Building in 1909 enlarged the reading room and enabled the University Library to transfer about twelve thousand engineering books and periodicals from its collection. The engineering collection was subsequently moved to the Mechanical Engineering Building at Camp Randall after remodeling in 1939, the collection having grown to about forty thousand volumes by that time.[24] In the late 1920s an addition to Agricultural Hall expanded the space for up to fifty-five thousand volumes for the growing agriculture collection, while about the same time another addition on the west end of Bascom Hall created a reserve library and reading room for undergraduate use.[25] Depression-era federal Public Works Administration funds made possible a large library addition to the Law School in 1939, thereby unwittingly locking a totally self-contained graduate program into what in future years would be seen as prime undergraduate space. What had begun as a small departmental library in the Biology Building (later renamed Birge Hall) gradually became institutionalized as the main biology collection of the campus, operating after 1941 as a branch of the general University Library. A similar arrangement incorporated the libraries of the geology and geography departments in Science Hall as another branch, which after remodeling in 1930 held fifteen thousand volumes and a growing map collection. In 1933 the economics library opened in remodeled quarters in Sterling Hall. The library was named for Professor Emeritus John R. Commons, who with his predecessor Richard T. Ely during their long careers at the University had developed an outstanding collection on European socialism and American labor. In 1938 the School of Music established a library in honor of its late director, Charles H. Mills. Other remodeling the following year added library space for the School of Education in what had come to be called the Engineering and Education Building on the Hill. By the early thirties the *Daily Cardinal* was boasting that students were served by fourteen campus libraries.[26] What this meant in reality was a confusing patchwork of collections, some independent of the main University library in

---

[24]See "Through the Years," *Wisconsin Engineer*, 81 (October, 1976), 16-7.

[25]There was some departmental resistance to moving the reserve book collection from the main reading room in the Historical Society Building to the Bascom Hall library. For more than a decade the Department of History, always known for its independent foreign policy in University and especially library affairs, insisted on continuing its old practice of using the society reading room for its reserve books.

[26]*Daily Cardinal*, September 27, 1933, April 19, 1935.

the Historical Society Building and others operating as its branches. Coordination among them was poor or non-existent, service was uneven, and there was wasteful duplication of holdings and administrative costs across what could hardly be called a library system.

Even more disturbing to the faculty was the gradual but noticeable decline in the quality and comprehensiveness of the collections of the Historical Society and the main University Library following the partial merger in 1900. This was partly a result of a failure to revise and tighten the early agreements dividing the respective collecting responsibilities of the two organizations. More critical was the inadequate funding of both libraries. Increasingly, the society's resources proved insufficient to cover its broad collecting mandate, though without a substantial infusion of funds the University would have been unable to pick up much of the slack even if the agreements were modified. In particular *belles lettres* suffered because of the peculiar assignment of old English drama and Shakespeare to the society while the University covered American and other fields of literature. The acquisition budgets of both libraries failed to keep up with the proliferation of new titles and fields of knowledge, especially after the sweeping budget cuts of the depression years. State appropriations for the society's annual book fund, for example, declined by 43 percent from $10,700 to $6,000 during the depression. The library reductions became a source of great faculty concern. The special faculty committee appointed in the spring of 1932 to advise on the first round of depression budget cuts urged that the library be protected as much as possible by continuing to purchase the most important works and by avoiding duplication of books and periodicals.[27] The University Committee's special report the next year on how to meet the budget crisis, usually remembered chiefly for its plan of graduated salary reductions, nevertheless recommended there be no cut that would cripple the library; if anything it needed an increased allotment.[28] This appeal went largely unheard. The general University Library served primarily the research needs of the humanities and social sciences, disciplines for the most part lacking the prestige and clout of campus scientists in influencing budget priorities. Neither of the presidents of the period, Glenn Frank and Clarence Dykstra, held an ad-

---

[27] UW Faculty Document 413, "Report of the Consultative Committee on Retrenchment Policies," June 6, 1932; UW Faculty Minutes, June 6, 1932.

[28] UW Faculty Document 432, Special Report of the University Committee, "Appraisal of University Activities to Help Meet Emergencies and Effect Economies," May 9, 1933; UW Faculty Minutes, June 5, 1933.

vanced degree or was a scholar; each seemed more interested in relieving library study and storage deficiencies than in building research collections.

In 1943 Gilbert H. Doane, the University librarian who had succeeded Walter Smith in 1937, and Edward P. Alexander, the new superintendent of the Historical Society, commissioned an external review of their two libraries. Doane hoped the study would focus attention on his space and budgetary needs; Alexander was seeking professional backing to reduce his library's collecting scope to only the history of North America. The two consultants, Graduate Dean and historian Theodore G. Blegen of the University of Minnesota, and Keyes DeWitt Metcalf, the director of the Harvard University Library and president of the American Library Association, made a careful assessment of the holdings, budgets, and staffing of the two collections, including comparisons with the major university libraries in surrounding states. Their hard-hitting report presented shocking evidence of the relative decline since 1900 of Wisconsin's once-vaunted "great state library." The consultants emphasized that while the society and UW libraries made good use of available space both were "disgracefully overcrowded" to the point of endangering the collections from physical damage under poor storage conditions and theft from unsupervised areas. They pointed out that in "both books and reading room facilities" the University Library made "very inadequate provision for undergraduates compared to what is done by most of the better colleges and universities of the country." Prompt steps were needed to alleviate the space problem: a larger undergraduate library and more reserve book rooms perhaps as an addition to Bascom Hall, an addition to fill in the U-shaped court between the two stack wings of the Historical Society, a central University science library to consolidate the specialized science libraries proliferating around the campus, and in the more distant future a second Historical Society building to serve as a museum and repository for the society's holdings of manuscripts, newspapers, and state archives. "There is a marked tendency to library proliferation in the University of Wisconsin," the consultants warned, making a distinction between small working departmental libraries and the unusually large number of separate specialized science libraries on the campus. "No one understanding the financial obligations that are bound to come with research libraries would seriously advocate the building up of ten or more research libraries in the sciences on the same campus."

The consultants expressed grave concern over the failure of the

University and the society to maintain and build their collections at an acceptable rate over the past several decades. The University was spending far less on its library collections than its major competitors in the surrounding states. Including the relevant part of the Historical Society's budget, the consultants estimated that Wisconsin was expending no more than $200,000 annually on the various campus libraries. This compared with $250,000 at the University of Minnesota, $400,000 at the University of Illinois, and $450,000 at the University of Michigan, to say nothing of another $60,000 at Michigan State College. Even Iowa, a state with a smaller population and fewer resources, was spending more on the libraries of each of its two universities, Iowa and Iowa State, than was Wisconsin. In the twenty years since 1922, the UW Library's collection had increased by only 68 percent. In contrast, the four largest state university libraries in 1922 (Illinois, Michigan, Minnesota, and California at Berkeley) had grown by an average of 160 percent. The average growth of the state university libraries next smaller than Wisconsin's (Ohio State, Missouri, Iowa, Nebraska, Kansas, and Indiana) was about the same, 159 percent. If the Historical Society's library was included with the University, the growth rate over the period was even worse, dropping to 58 percent. The expenditures for books by the various state university libraries in 1941-42 highlighted Wisconsin's niggardly support of its research university.

Comparative Expenditures for Books, 1941-42[29]

Illinois	$157,000	Iowa State	$46,000
Michigan	140,000	Iowa	40,000
Berkleley	123,000	*Wisconsin*	38,000
Minnesota	102,000	Nebraska	37,000
Ohio State	90,000	Missouri	35,000
Indiana	74,000	Kansas	30,000

---

[29]The consultants noted that Missouri's expenditures in 1941-42 evidently represented a temporary drop, as the figure was $98,000 the year before and the appropriation for 1942-43 was $90,000. They also pointed out that Purdue, Indiana's engineering college, regularly spent $25,000 on books and that Kansas State Agricultural College spent $11,000, figures that should be taken into account in calculating those states' support of their research libraries.

"The library has fallen so far behind," the consultants warned, "that it will take additional appropriations for some years to restore it to a reasonable position."[30]

So damning was the Blegen-Metcalf report that University authorities did not release it immediately, leading ever-vigilant editor Evjue of the *Capital Times* to complain editorially "Why the Secrecy?" and to warn: "The welfare of the university libraries will not be advanced by suppressing facts about their defects and inadequacies. The way to progress is to get the facts out in the open, and do something about the shortcomings."[31] Actually, President Dykstra welcomed the political value of the report. He distributed it to the faculty and at a general faculty meeting on October 4, 1943, urged that its findings be studied carefully. Two weeks later he put it on the agenda of the Board of Regents. At this meeting he arranged for a joint committee consisting of UW Librarian Doane, society Superintendent Alexander, Dean Emeritus Sellery, a member of the Historical Society's Board of Curators, and Fred L. Holmes, an active UW alumnus and another society board member, to review the consultants' findings and urge the regents to begin implementing its recommendations. As a modest start the committee advised the board to provide $5,000 annually to develop a combined card catalog of the two collections, one of the lesser but glaringly obvious recommendations of the report. More significantly, the joint committee proposed that the University assume responsibility for collecting general periodicals and works on the history of Great

---

[30]UW Faculty Document 680L, Theodore C. Blegen and Keyes DeWitt Metcalf, "A Survey of the Libraries of the State Historical Society and the University of Wisconsin," summer, 1943; BOR Minutes, October 16, 1943. In 1945 UW Librarian Doane and Louis Kaplan, his reference librarian, compiled some additional data comparing Wisconsin's library expenditures with those of neighboring states. Perhaps the most striking comparison was with Minnesota, a state with an income level and tax base roughly equivalent to Wisconsin's. Like Wisconsin, Minnesota was supporting only one public university. In 1876 the library of the University of Minnesota held 10,000 bound volumes, compared with 8,563 in the UW library, plus 33,347 in the Historical Society collection in the capitol. The two university libraries maintained an even pace until about 1900, when Minnesota began to pull ahead. By 1945 the Minnesota library totalled 1,345,809 volumes, compared with 567,000 in the UW collection, augmented by 334,640 in the Historical Society holdings, for a combined Wisconsin total of 901,640. Doane and Kaplan calculated that the growth of the University of Minnesota library from 1876 to 1945 was 186 percent, while the UW library had grown by only 53 percent and the Historical Society Library by even less—47 percent—in the same period. Gilbert H. Doane, "Some Data Relating to the Library Situation at the University of Wisconsin," memorandum [1945], UHP.

[31]*Capital Times*, October 15 and 18, 1943.

Britain and Latin America "so that the Society may be able to take care adequately on its proper fields of collection, namely Wisconsin and American history." More costly suggestions were for an extension of Bascom Hall to provide additional undergraduate library space and for a joint effort with the Historical Society to secure an appropriation to fill in the court of its building "so as to provide additional library facilities for both the University and the Society."[32] Society member John Thomas Lee, who had raised the alarm about the 1925 University appropriation to build an addition to the society library, again suspected the University of hegemonic designs. "I have observed University politics and policies for many years," he warned Alexander. "You would be well to be on the alert....Cooperation, not union now or ever, should be the watchword."[33]

The regents promptly voted $5,000 to begin work on the combined card catalog and referred the other recommendations to various board committees for further study. At the same meeting, however, the board's Constructional Development Committee recommended a list of post-war building projects. Sixth in priority was a new and separate library building projected to cost $1,618,000, but the committee noted parenthetically the cost might "be reduced should a different plan and structure be adopted."[34] The issue of the nature and location of any expanded library facilities was obviously still unresolved, and the regents evidently gave no consideration to any joint University-society effort to get funding for the long-discussed Park Street transverse addition to the society building. The board discussed the library question at length at its next meeting before voting in January, 1944, to ask the legislature for planning funds for six post-war construction projects totaling $5.6 million, of which a new library was last in priority.[35]

The failure to give more urgency and higher priority to solving the library problems did not escape criticism in the state press. The *Green Bay Press Gazette* and the *Appleton Post Crescent* both chided the University for finding ways to construct a field house, a theater, and a large addition to the Law School during the depression rather than

---

[32]Edward P. Alexander, Gilbert H. Doane, Fred L. Holmes, G.C. Sellery, "Memorandum from a Joint Committee of the University and State Historical Society Summarizing Requests Made of the Regents," October 16, 1943, BOR Papers, 1/1/3, box 59.

[33]Quoted in Lord and Ubbelohde, *Clio's Servant*, p. 373.

[34]"Report of the Regents Committee on Construction and Development," October 14, 1943, BOR Papers, 1/1/3, box 59.

[35]BOR Minutes, November 6, 1943, January 15, 1944.

choosing projects like the library now described as "urgent" needs. President Dykstra was sensitive to such criticism but had trouble explaining why the University could not have imposed an additional student fee as its match for a PWA grant for the general University Library when it did so for the Law Library addition.[36] It was, some observers decided, mostly a matter of questionable University priorities.

The library project got a major boost when an interim legislative committee studying post-war University building requirements decided in the fall of 1944 to recommend $5.8 million for six urgent construction projects. The institution's most critical need, the committee declared, was a new library, which it ranked second after a small safety project to fireproof the stairways and corridors in Bascom Hall. The committee called for an appropriation of $1,791,400 for land acquisition and construction of a new library building. "No one thoroughly familiar with the University," the report declared, "will deny that this is the most important need of the many which exist for new construction."[37] Faculty supporters must have been elated that the solons were more persuaded than either the regents or the campus administration of the seriousness of the library problem. After Governor Goodland showed himself sympathetic to University needs the Board of Regents identified another eleven building projects for a combined total of $12.3 million.

The library, which UW faculty and students had regularly identified throughout the inter-war years as the University's most pressing issue, now seemed on track to be remedied in the immediate post-war period. A University bulletin published in late 1944 confidently promoted the regents' post-war building plans as the way "to keep faith with our State and our Democracy" and serve returning veterans and future generations. "The most desperate and longest felt University need," the document declared, "is a central library."

> Provision for this building was made by the legislature twenty years ago. The appropriation lapsed, however, for reasons which at that time seemed compelling but which need no discussion here. Suffice it to say that whether the appropriation was inadequate or the title to the site was in question, no library was built and students have continued to be crowded into the Historical Library which forty years ago had ample space for both the Historical Society and a University with two thousand students. The Library is an all-

---

[36]See *Green Bay Press Gazette*, December 15, 1943; *Appleton Post Crescent*, January 19, 1944.

[37]BOR Minutes, October 28, 1944; "The Real Need of the University," *WAM*, 46 (December 15, 1944), 2-3; *Capital Times*, December 31, 1944.

University need and it has been recognized as such for many years. From time to time some of our library needs have been met by the establishment of special libraries serving professional students, but the big problem of having space and books for the general students has remained absolutely unsolved.[38]

Anticipation of the post-war construction projects was high during early 1945. In June the legislature appropriated $8 million for University construction, necessitating the trimming back of the regents' list by a third, though the library retained its high priority ranking. The newly created Campus Planning Commission now believed it should be built across from the Historical Society on the east end of the lower campus, and the regents began acquiring land along Lake Street.[39] Later that summer Governor Goodland released planning funds for ten UW construction projects, including $50,000 for the library.[40] In December the regents allotted nearly a quarter of the $8 million appropriation for the construction of the first unit of the new library.[41] The culmination of the long campaign for a new library at last seemed imminent. In keeping with past disappointments, however, these appearances proved deceptive. Getting the new library constructed turned out to be a long and complicated process. That story—of further years of frustrating delays, bureaucratic in-fighting, and another round of legislative lobbying—must remain for a subsequent volume.[42]

"A Sample of Original Wisconsin"

A considerably more successful venture was the creation of the

---

[38]*It's Our Job to Provide Means for Further Education*, Bulletin of the University of Wisconsin, No. 2738, December, 1944, p. 5.

[39]"Report of the Constructional Development Committee," June 27, 1945, BOR Papers, 1/1/3, box 62; *Capital Times*, September 29, 1945.

[40]BOR Minutes, August 11, 1945.

[41]Ibid., December 1, 1945.

[42]A key figure in the post-war efforts to solve the library problem was Louis Kaplan, who joined the UW library staff in 1937 as chief of the reference section. Kaplan's views of the interaction of the University and the Historical Society libraries and his account of his library service over the years are valuable in understanding the special dynamics of the Wisconsin situation. In particular see his account of the long relationship between the University and the Historical Society libraries in Louis Kaplan, "Two Wisconsin Libraries, 1854-1954," *Transactions of the Wisconsin Academy of Science, Arts, and Letters*, 71 (1983), 122-30. See also Kaplan, "The Interaction of Campus Politics and Library Administration," in Gretchen Lagana, *Louis Kaplan and the University Library at the University of Wisconsin-Madison, 1937-1971*, pp. 46-57.

University of Wisconsin Arboretum along the southern shore of Lake Wingra. This project was more the work of a remarkably devoted group of public-spirited Madison citizens, however, than a University-led initiative. As far back as 1855 Increase Lapham had called for an "arboretum" at the University containing "at least one good specimen of each tree and shrub that grows naturally in Wisconsin."[43] With their more pressing problems University leaders absorbed in the daunting task of launching a new academic community on "College Hill" could be pardoned for ignoring Lapham's scheme as more visionary than practical. Whatever landscaping the regents authorized, such as the American elms lining the walkways on either side of the Hill, was intended more for campus beautification than scientific conservation or botanical study. The idea of an outdoor natural history laboratory on or near the campus remained dormant throughout the nineteenth century.

Fortunately, a number of Madison residents were concerned about the growth of the city and the accompanying loss of open green space. In 1892 they formed the Madison Park and Pleasure Drive Association to develop parks and recreational roadways in and around the city. Although some Madisonians saw the association as a self-serving millionaire's club, it purchased and drained rubbish-filled marshes to create a number of privately maintained public areas—Burrows, Tenney, Brittingham, and Henry Vilas Parks—named in honor of some of the prominent contributors. In 1908 the city belatedly adopted a half-mill tax for park purposes, followed two decades later by a city park commission. Since one of the MPPDA purposes was pleasure driving, it planted trees and constructed roadways in and around its parks and elsewhere, such as the Willows Drive along University Bay on Lake Mendota. Henry Vilas Park, situated on the north shore of Lake Wingra with a small but growing zoo, was probably the association's finest achievement. Several members owned other land on Lake Wingra, and the association secured options and planned a roadway along the shore. In conjunction with the University, in 1907 the group commissioned John Nolen, a prominent landscape architect of Cambridge, Massachusetts, to develop a comprehensive plan for Madison's park development. Nolen submitted two reports—one for the city and the other for the University—in 1909 and 1911. In particular, he called for the creation of a large city park to surround Lake Wingra and connect with the

---

[43]Increase A. Lapham, "The Forest Trees of Wisconsin," *Transactions of the Wisconsin State Agricultural Society*, 4 (1855), 195-251.

existing Henry Vilas Park. He also urged the University to develop an arboretum of several thousand acres extending westward from the campus along the shores of Lake Mendota to Eagle Heights. He emphasized the need for haste in obtaining the necessary properties while open land was still relatively cheap, for he foresaw the rapid expansion of the city into its surrounding green space.[44] The Nolen reports, which complemented the 1908 Laird-Cret campus master plan, spurred President Van Hise to acquire the Eagle Heights farm, but he failed in efforts to purchase Picnic Point at this time.

Others shared Nolen's enthusiasm for the beauty of the Lake Wingra area. In 1911 three enterprising Madison businessmen organized the Lake Forest Land Company to develop an exclusive suburb on 840 acres along the south shore of the lake. They platted lots running down to the shore, drew plans for connecting streets and a broad boulevard leading to a central mall, park, and shopping center. Lots ranged in price from $600 to $2,000 depending the size, location, and view, with a series of venetian-style canals providing lake access for interior locations. It was a grandiose scheme, but the lot prices were high for what was regarded as a remote and isolated area. Development costs were also high, as the soft peat subsoil required more fill than anticipated for road construction. By the time the loan company backing the project failed in 1922, only 73 lots had been sold and six houses built, and the Lake Forest Company was never able to extricate itself from the ensuing legal and financial tangles. Empty sidewalks crumbled, roads settled and eroded, and the half-dredged lagoons became weed-choked. The once-promising suburb was soon known as the "Lost City."[45]

Fortuitously, a new civic group, the Madison Parks Foundation, some of whose members had belonged to the earlier Madison Park and Pleasure Drive Association, had just organized for the purpose of acquiring land for public parks. A key figure in the new group was Michael B. Olbrich, a Madison attorney and long-time progressive, who was currently serving as Governor John J. Blaine's executive counsel and adviser. Olbrich was an enthusiastic member of the town-gown Get-Away Club, transplanted wild flowers to his backyard garden, and liked to hike in the Wingra woods with botany Professor E.W. Gilbert

---

[44]John Nolen, *Madison: A Model City* (Boston: American Society of Landscape Architects, 1911).

[45]See Jeffrey Groy, "Men and the Marsh: Lake Forest," *Arboretum News* 30 (Winter, 1981), 1-4, and (Spring, 1981), 1-6.

and other University friends. In 1925 Governor Blaine appointed him to the Board of Regents. Whether Olbrich was the first to conceive the idea of acquiring the Lost City woods and other property around Lake Wingra for a University arboretum is unclear, but he quickly became its most articulate and effective spokesman. He may have picked up on a suggestion by Paul E. Stark, a Madison realtor and member of the Madison Parks Foundation, to build a road around the east and south shore of Lake Wingra and in the process acquire 600 acres for an arboretum. Olbrich thought the group should aim for a larger tract, as much as 2,500 acres. In December, 1927, his eloquence persuaded the regents to approve in principle a rather complicated plan of land swaps with a realty company to gain 30 acres of shore land and to devote the remainder of the Tripp estate, valued at $83,000, to acquire other property adjacent to Lake Wingra and the Nakoma Golf Course through the parks foundation "for a Forest Reserve Arboretum and Wildlife Refuge," with the understanding the Tripp funds would be matched by private donations.[46] Olbrich, who had previously given generously for Madison park development, was confident there would be no problem raising outside funds for land acquisition. The project now had official blessing and the promise of some University help.

This favorable start seemed to evaporate with Olbrich's suicide at the start of the crash in late 1929. Overnight the Arboretum project lost its most eloquent and influential advocate on the Board of Regents and within the Madison community. The onset of the depression, moreover, shifted the demands on private philanthropy to the relief of human suffering rather than land acquisition for what seemed an increasingly improbable and even irrelevant dream; some of those who had pledged funds asked to be released under the new circumstances. For several years Colonel Joseph W. Jackson, who had succeeded Olbrich as the most devoted promoter of the Arboretum scheme, almost despaired of carrying out Olbrich's plan. In October, 1931, Jackson hosted a dinner for the discouraged Arboretum supporters to try to revive the project. He pointed out that federal, state, and local relief funds and labor might be available to develop an arboretum and urged redoubled efforts to create one. His contagious enthusiasm helped to reorganize the parks

---

[46]BOR Minutes, December 7, 1927; "Olbrich Works for Arboretum," *WAM*, 29 (January, 1928), 132. The balance in the Tripp estate, estimated at $83,000 in 1927, was in securities which did not actually yield this much when eventually sold. While useful at the start, the Tripp funds were much less significant than other private contributions in acquiring land for the arboretum. See Arboretum memorandum, December 4, 1943, BOR Papers, 1/1/3, box 60.

foundation as the Madison and Wisconsin Foundation and to launch a fund-raising campaign. In July, 1932, Jackson and other members of his board were able to transfer to the regents the 245-acre Nelson farm on the western shore of Lake Wingra (now the Longenecker Gardens and part of the Curtis Prairie) for which Olbrich had been raising funds when he died.[47] Following up on this start, in the spring of 1933 Jackson persuaded Jessie Bartlett Noe, who was unable to pay the taxes on a partly wooded 190-acre tract next to the Nelson farm, to deed it to the University with a reversion clause.

With nearly 500 acres in hand, the University Arboretum was formally dedicated on June 17, 1934, coincident with a well-deserved University honorary degree for John Nolen, whose 1911 plan had given the idea its original legitimacy. The ceremony honored the many who had worked to realize the dream of creating what Aldo Leopold, an early Arboretum enthusiast who had recently moved from the Forest Products Laboratory to a UW professorship in game management, described as much more than "an outdoor library of horticultural varieties" or "ecological groupings."

> We want to have all these things, but they by no means represent the main idea of what we are trying to express here….Our idea, in a nutshell, is to reconstruct, primarily for the use of the University, a sample of original Wisconsin—a sample of what Dane County looked like when our ancestors arrived here during the 1840s.[48]

Other land acquisitions soon followed. Nakoma resident and prominent Madison baker Louis Gardner made a gift of the 190-acre East Marsh in December, 1935, and later purchased a key parcel of 30 acres along Monroe Street to prevent its development. After a series of complicated maneuvers in March, 1936, Colonel Jackson persuaded C.B. Chapman, one of the partners in the bankrupt Lake Forest Land Company, to deed the 90-acre Island tract on the east end of Lake Wingra. The most complex negotiations involved the Lost City lots, some of whose owners still hoped to profit from their dormant investments. In 1947 Jackson was finally able to get title to the largest remaining parcel of 257 lots, or nearly 53 acres, from the Chapman

---

[47]*Capital Times*, Augurt 28, 1932; *Daily Cardinal*, September 21, 1932.

[48]Aldo Leopold, "What Is the University of Wisconsin Arboretum, Wild Life Refuge, and Forest Experiment Preserve?" in *Our First Fifty Years: The University of Wisconsin Arboretum, 1934-1984* (Madison: University of Wisconsin Arboretum, 1984), pp. 2-3.

estate. Two years later Gertrude Bergstrom, the daughter of Regent Frank Sensenbrenner, himself a generous contributor to other Arboretum land purchases, helped to acquire another 22 lots, but it was 1963 before the Arboretum was able to get the last three Lost City lots. In nearly all of these negotiations Colonel Jackson was the tireless prime mover and promoter.[49]

The last large land purchase was the Grady farm south of Lake Wingra, acquired after much nail-biting by Jackson and other Arboretum supporters in December of 1940. While he was alive Regent Olbrich had often talked with Nettie Grady, who ran a student rooming house near the campus, about the desirability of adding her family farm south of the lake, which had been settled by her father in 1865, to the proposed Arboretum. She was enough captivated by Olbrich's enthusiasm to visit Kew Gardens while on a trip to England to gain information about similar ventures. In 1935 Miss Grady gave the University an option to buy the land for $25,000, but the regents thought the price too high. Even after she reduced it to $18,000, enough to cover a mortgage held by the trustees of the Vilas estate, the board declined to consider it. Jackson frantically sought to raise the funds, and even considered asking the Vilas trustees to buy the Grady tract and hold it until the University could acquire it. Now gravely ill but still eager for the Arboretum to have her land, Miss Grady eventually dropped the price to $13,500 but died before any action could be taken, leaving the land tied up in her estate. Finally persuaded of the value of the tract, the Board of Regents agreed to acquire the parcel provided the Arboretum Committee raised $7,500 of the purchase price. The indefatigable Colonel Jackson persuaded the Grady heirs to extend the option and set out on another round of fund-raising. He was still $3,000 short when, with the option again about to expire, Gertrude Bergstrom sent a check for the balance. After Jackson triumphantly presented the $7,500 to the regents, a more accurate survey revealed the Grady tract was in reality 200 acres instead of the 180 Miss Grady had thought she owned, an unexpected but welcome bonus.[50] By 1942 the Arboretum consisted of 1,100 acres, about half the size of Olbrich's original plan but enough for a multipurpose natural history preserve of the sort he envisioned.

From the first UW authorities had agreed this would be a true

---

[49]For a brief illustrated review of the Lost City, see Vera Jones, "Arboretum History—The Lost City," *News Leaf: Friends of the Arboretum Newsletter*, 7 (February, 1993), 1-2.
[50]BOR Minutes, December 7, 1940.

University Arboretum, administered centrally and available for scientific study by interested faculty and students from any department. Once developed, it would also be open to the public. With the acquisition of the Nelson farm in 1932 President Frank appointed two committees to oversee the long-term development of the facility. The first, an Arboretum Committee made up of technical experts from various disciplines, was chaired by Olbrich's close friend, botanist E.M. Gilbert, with other members drawn from the plant pathology, genetics, forestry, horticulture, geology, and zoology departments, and including Albert F. Gallistel, the superintendent of buildings and grounds, and Maurice E. McCaffrey, the secretary of the Board of Regents. The latter two were to provide invaluable help in the development and expansion of the Arboretum in the years ahead, with Gallistel contributing unmatched knowledge of the campus and its surrounding area and McCaffrey serving as an influential advocate with the regents. The committee recruited Assistant Professor G. William Longenecker of horticulture as executive director of the Arboretum and Professor Aldo Leopold as director of research.[51] A second advisory committee included Colonel Jackson and several other long-standing Madison supporters of the project as well as representatives of state and federal agencies interested in conservation.

Once the Arboretum Committee had developed a multi-part master plan for the long-term development of the facility, the lack of any operating budget seemed an insuperable problem. In the depth of the depression scrounging and improvisation became a way of life. Longenecker persuaded Walter Hanson to become the resident caretaker in 1933, living rent-free in the Nelson farm house with wood-cutting privileges, in return for patrolling the property and guarding against trespassers and fire. Ralph Immell, a member of the Arboretum Advisory Committee and the director of the state Conservation Department, offered 15,000 red and white pine and spruce seedlings from his agency, and William McKay, a Waterloo nurseryman contributed 150 larger evergreens. The biggest problem was labor for tree-planting, land-clearing, and fencing, as student volunteers were inadequate for the large task at hand. During the first year the committee also made use of unskilled workers receiving county relief. This proved not a very reliable source, so it was with some apprehension that the committee agreed to a state offer in the summer of 1934 to establish a transient work camp at the Arboretum housing up to 350 men. The first contin-

---

[51]See ibid., July 17, 1933; *Daily Cardinal*, October 15, 1933.

gent arrived in July, living in tents while they constructed ten wooden barracks, administration and recreation buildings, and a mess hall, the whole complex quickly dubbed Camp Madison.[52] This new manpower, along with the trucks and heavy equipment provided by the Wisconsin Emergency Relief Administration, enabled construction of a road and further clearing, dredging, and planting.

The transients varied considerably in age and skills and not all were satisfactory workers. Few took much interest in the conservation projects on which they were engaged. Gallistel and Jackson thereupon came up with the idea of converting the transient camp into one housing a like number of young men serving in the Civilian Conservation Corps, a recently established federal program under the direction of the Department of the Interior and the Army. The youthful CCC workers lived under Army discipline while working on conservation projects of precisely the sort taking place at the Arboretum. With support from Representative Harry Sauthoff and Governor La Follette, the shift took place in August of 1935. Camp Madison became the only CCC camp located on a University campus, and some of its members enrolled in University or vocational school courses in their spare time.[53] Although federal authorities entered into another four-year agreement with the University in 1940, in November of the following year the government abruptly withdrew all of the CCC personnel and closed Camp Madison. The nation was gearing for war, and the era of free labor at the Arboretum was largely over. While it lasted much was accomplished; estimates valued the six years of CCC work as worth more than a million dollars. Although the Student Board devoted two of its annual student work days, in 1943 and 1944, to tree-planting in the Arboretum, the effort could hardly rival the CCC contribution.[54]

By the end of the Second World War much of the varied layout of the present Arboretum was discernible. A start had been made to create a bird and wild fowl refuge by screening the marshes with trees and bushes along the road. Minnow ponds and lagoons had been dredged to provide for nesting sites and the cultivation of rare bog plants. The Lake Forest woods, now protected, produced an increasing profusion of wildflowers. Thousands of young pines were thrusting upward on some

---

[52]*Daily Cardinal*, July 21, 1934.

[53]BOR Minutes, April 24, 1935, March 9, 1938, May 11, 1940; *Daily Cardinal*, August, 1935, August 5, 1936.

[54]*Daily Cardinal*, April 22, 1943, March 30, 1944, April 18, 1945.

of the once-cleared higher ground. In the center of the Arboretum the Madison Garden Club had planted a spectacular array of lilacs. (After some debate the Arboretum Committee had agreed this imported plant might be included because of its popularity among early Wisconsin settlers, a decision surely welcomed today by the thousands of viewers of the colorful display each spring.) Botanists Norman Fassett, John Thomson, and John Curtis were painstakingly restoring the 60-acre former Nelson pastureland below the Noe woods into a prairie of the sort early settlers had found covering so much of southern Wisconsin. Aldo Leopold, Chauncey Juday, Arthur Hasler, Robert McCabe, and their students were conducting a variety of wild life and limnology experiments. These involved surveys of existing animal species and the effort to create conditions and food supplies needed to sustain others once native to the area, including the seining of carp from Lake Wingra to restore the native fish population. Much, of course, remained to be done on a restoration project that some estimated would take anywhere from a half-century to a millenium to accomplish. Still, it was already abundantly clear the University possessed a unique outdoor living laboratory worthy of Michael Olbrich's vision in 1927.[55]

The Healing Professions

The opening of Wisconsin General Hospital in 1924 revolutionized medical and nursing education at the University and in the state, leading to the most significant new curricular and outreach developments of the inter-war period. Located just west of the Hill on University Avenue, the hospital was the center of a growing medical complex that for the first time provided the facilities and patients needed for a comprehensive program of clinical education in the health-related fields. Like the Arboretum these developments were achieved neither easily nor quickly.

Although the legislation creating the University of Wisconsin in 1848 had authorized a Department of Medicine as one of the four basic units of the new institution, the early presidents and faculty of what was

---

[55]This account of the early history of the Arboretum has drawn heavily on the work of Nancy D. Sachse, whose book, *A Thousand Ages: The University of Wisconsin Arboretum* (Madison: University of Wisconsin Regents, 1965), and article, "Madison: Public Wilderness: The University of Wisconsin Arboretum," *Wisconsin Magazine of History*, 44 (Winter, 1960-61), 117-31, are the best scholarly studies. For a physiographic and programmatic map of the Arboretum in 1943, see "The Arboretum," *Wisconsin Engineer*, 43 (May, 1943), 6.

at first little more than a small preparatory school were in no position to provide medical training. Not until 1886, when a committee of the Wisconsin State Medical Society urged the regents to offer a preliminary course of medical study, did the University launch what the 1887 catalog described laconically as a "special science course, antecedent to the study of medicine." For several years Professor Edward A. Birge, whose zoology courses had treated some of this material, had sole responsibility for the pre-medical course, which included zoology, vertebrate anatomy, histology, physiology, embryology, and bacteriology. Birge was thus a remarkable one-man medical faculty until his responsibilities as the new College of Letters and Science dean necessitated some relief through the appointment of anatomist William Snow Miller and bacteriologist Harry L. Russell in 1892 and 1893, respectively. There was no thought of establishing a medical school as such at this time. The "special science course" was intended to be purely pre-professional, providing interested undergraduates with a grounding in some of the relevant basic science fields before they went elsewhere for professional medical training. That the UW graduates were well-prepared was universally acknowledged by the medical schools receiving them.

This limited objective began to expand as the University matured during the administrations of Presidents Chamberlin, Adams, and especially Van Hise. In 1904 Van Hise recruited Charles R. Bardeen of the Johns Hopkins University Medical School to develop a Department of Anatomy. After graduating from Harvard in 1893, Bardeen had immediately entered the first Johns Hopkins medical class, graduating in 1897 and taking up a teaching position as the school's first professor of anatomy. He sometimes described himself as the first graduate of the Johns Hopkins Medical School, since his name had headed the alphabetical list of the

Dean Bardeen as Seen by Max Otto

initial graduating class, which, he also liked to point out, had included Gertrude Stein.[56] Unstated at the time of Bardeen's arrival in Madison but almost certainly in the minds of both Van Hise and Bardeen, was the expectation that the latter would draw up a plan for a two-year Medical School, which he did in conjunction with L&S Dean Birge, whose college included most of the courses and faculty involved with the pre-medical program. Van Hise persuaded the regents and the legislature to authorize the two-year school in 1907, promptly appointing Bardeen as its dean. The curriculum was a logical expansion of the earlier pre-medical course, providing for two years of basic science and pre-clinical education before students were sent to take their final two years of hospital training at full four-year medical schools in other states. Some Wisconsin physicians were skeptical of the prospects for the UW Medical School on the ground that effective medical education could only be given in large cities with a sufficiently varied patient population. A particularly outspoken critic was Dean William H. Washburn of the recently established Wisconsin College of Physicians and Surgeons in Milwaukee, who had hoped the University might take over his school.

The uneasiness of some members of the state medical profession over the University's growing involvement in health care escalated after a serious typhoid epidemic in 1909 led the Board of Regents to authorize the Medical School to operate a student health clinic. The State Laboratory of Hygiene traced the outbreak to an infected student worker in the kitchen of a popular student boarding house; he subsequently died, along with six other students among the thirty-four reported cases. The typhoid scare was followed almost immediately by an outbreak of diphtheria, leading Bardeen and the Medical School faculty to urge more systematic attention to the health care of the student body. Up to this time the University had largely ignored this problem, apart from the limited role of the two physician directors of men's and women's physical education and a loose arrangement with Madison General Hospital, over whose board Dean Bardeen presided, to admit students needing hospital care. Local Madison physicians objected strongly to what they called "contract medicine" by University doctors serving a student clientele they saw as rightfully theirs. Bardeen met the criticism forthrightly, predicting the day would come when

---

[56]See "Charles R. Bardeen," *Wisconsin Medical Alumni Magazine Quarterly*, 32 (Fall, 1992), 2-22.

health insurance was generally available and the emphasis of physicians could then properly shift to keeping their patients well rather than merely treating their illnesses. He highlighted the self-interest of the critics who objected to the University's efforts to promote the health of its students:

> I think the Regents can see as little reason why they should not hire a physician to look after the students at the students' expense any more than they should not put up dormitories for students because it would interfere with the income of keepers of student rooming houses and boarding houses. They look upon the University as a state and not a city institution, and do not feel that the Madison physicians have a right to object on personal financial grounds to measures taken by the Regents for the welfare of the student body.[57]

The student clinic opened in 1910 in Cornelius House on the lower campus at State and Park Streets. The service was under the direction of Dr. Joseph S. Evans, an experienced specialist in internal medicine, whom Bardeen recruited as student medical advisor and professor of clinical medicine. In its first semester the clinic treated 837 patients out of a student population of 3,500, an indication of its immediate value. Evans' warm personal charm and friendly interest in both his patients and his colleagues in the Madison medical community soon helped to allay some of the criticism of the venture. In 1912 the health service moved to the larger Olin House, just east of the president's residence on Langdon Street, and three years later it acquired the Raymer House next door for a student infirmary.[58]

Although Dean Bardeen's ultimate goal was a comprehensive campus medical center with a complete medical curriculum, at first he concentrated on building the basic medical sciences undergirding the two-year program, strengthening the courses in anatomy, bacteriology,

---

[57]Charles R. Bardeen to John M. Dodson, December 8, 1909, quoted in Paul F. Clark, *The University of Wisconsin Medical School: A Chronicle, 1848-1948* (Madison: Published for the Wisconsin Medical Alumni Association by the University of Wisconsin Press, 1967), p. 19. Dodson had formerly been a prominent Madison physician and was currently serving as dean of the Rush Medical College in Chicago. He had chaired the committee of the Wisconsin State Medical Society that recommended a pre-medical course in 1886.

[58]William A. Mowry, "The University Takes Great Precautions to Guard the Student Health," *WAM*, 31 (February, 1930), 188, 216-7; Charles E. Lyght, "Student Health at the University," ibid., 35 (March, 1934), 155; "University Health Service—A Long and Noble Struggle," *Wisconsin Medical Alumni Quarterly*, 25 (Fall, 1985), 1-4; Clark, *University of Wisconsin Medical School*, pp. 17-21, 221-2.

physiology, and physiological chemistry, and gradually adding faculty specialists in pharmacology and toxicology and pathology. For medical students and the student body as a whole the anatomy lab in the attic of Science Hall, where the dean casually presided over an impressive collection of corpses and skeletons, became the symbol of the developing medical program.[59] Bardeen had a good eye for quality, and two of his early faculty recruits, physiologists Joseph Erlanger and Herbert Gasser, later became Nobel Laureates after leaving Wisconsin. The dean's strategy was summarized in his advice not to recruit big names. "These men are usually over the hump," he explained. "Take men on the make."[60]

In 1914 Bardeen persuaded Dr. William F. Lorenz, the director of the Wisconsin Psychiatric Institute of the new Mendota State Hospital across the lake, to accept an unsalaried joint appointment as associate professor of neuro-psychiatry. A decade later after the completion of Wisconsin General Hospital, Lorenz and his institute physically joined the Medical School, thereby adding an important clinical specialty.[61] Even before relocating to the campus Lorenz began collaborating with the brilliant young pharmacologist Arthur S. Loevenhart in basic research on the arsenical treatment of neuro-syphilis.[62] Loevenhart, physiological chemist Harold C. Bradley, and several other medical faculty members did important research in Washington and Madison for

---

[59]Bardeen's anatomy classes were legendary. He preferred an informal socratic method of teaching and relied on his assistants to make sure the students learned the dry facts of human anatomy. Generations of medical students came to dread his off-the-wall oral examinations. Harold Rusch, who later headed the McCardle Cancer Laboratory, liked to tell the story of Bardeen's inquisition when Rusch and his lab partner, a young woman, had finished dissecting a human arm. Bardeen asked Rusch what muscles would be stimulated when a wedding ring was slipped over the third finger. Rusch responded that they would be the cutaneous branches of the common volar digital nerves. Only partly correct, said the dean, turning to the young woman, who quickly replied, "Every nerve in the human body." That was the answer Bardeen wanted, and he admonished Rusch to "let your mind wander more." Another famous Bardeen question was "What muscle would be first activated upon falling from an airplane?" The answers usually ranged widely, rarely coming up with the expected response—"the anal sphincter." See "Charles R. Bardeen," p. 11.

[60][William S. Middleton?] "Some Personal Insights into the University of Wisconsin Medical Scene (Prior to 1955)," notes evidently for a speech, n.d., UHP.

[61]See Bardeen to Frank, September 8, 1925, Frank Presidential Papers, 4/13/1, box 13.

[62]Loevenhart, the first Jewish member of the medical faculty, was also one of its most distinguished scientists, who built a strong program in pharmacology and toxicology. His early death at the age of fifty was a great loss to the school. See Bardeen, "Arthur S. Loevenhart and the Medical School," *WAM*, 30 (May, 1929), 253, 282.

the Army's Chemical Warfare Service during the First World War, a story whose details remain to be told. By the end of the war Bardeen believed the school was ready to move to a full four-year curriculum if it could get adequate clinical facilities with a sufficiently large patient base. This need was partially met with the construction of the first real campus clinical facilities, a new Student Infirmary in 1919 and the Bradley Memorial Children's Hospital in 1920.[63] Even before their completion both buildings were pressed into service during the great post-war influenza epidemic, which saw even the University Club commandeered as a temporary campus hospital.

Following the war Bardeen stepped up his campaign for a four-year curriculum, arguing that Wisconsin could not for long expect other states to accept its students for the final two years of their training and pointing out that too many Wisconsin medical students were failing to return to the state after completing their education.[64] His warnings were persuasive; on April 25, 1919, Governor Emanuel Philipp approved legislation removing the previous two-year restriction and authorizing the regents to develop a four-year medical school. Only a comprehensive general hospital as a teaching facility was lacking. Bardeen assigned Dr. Evans, the popular director of the student health service, to cultivate the governor. Philipp, a stalwart Republican who had begun his three terms as governor in 1915 deeply suspicious of the University's close ties to the La Follette progressives, had by this time come to appreciate the importance of the institution to the state. In spite of the governor's initial misgivings about the hospital project, Evans and Bardeen persuaded him to call a special session of the legislature in May of 1920 that then approved Philipp's proposal to use the surplus in the 1919 Soldiers' Bonus Fund for the construction of Wisconsin General Hospital as a World War I veterans' memorial. Identifying the hospital as a war memorial made it difficult for the legislators to object, particularly since a new appropriation was not required. Philipp's

---

[63]For the construction of the infirmary the legislature appropriated $43,000, and two wealthy Madison residents, Carl Johnson and Thomas E. Brittingham, each gave $25,000. Most of the funds for the children's hospital were contributed by Professor and Mrs. Harold Bradley and her parents, Mr. and Mrs. Charles R. Crane, in memory of the Bradley's daughter, Mary Cornelia Bradley; the regents provided $18,000.

[64]For examples of Bardeen's detailed arguments in support of clinical training and the development of clinical facilities at Wisconsin, see Bardeen to Birge, November 24, 1919; "Public Needs to Be Met by the Proposed State of Wisconsin General Hospital," Birge Presidential Papers, 4/12/1, box 10, UA; Bardeen, "The Need of a Complete Medical Course at the State University," *Wisconsin Medical Journal*, 18 (April, 1920), 449-52.

political astuteness went further. Anticipating the loss of stalwart control of the state government, he shrewdly urged University authorities to lose no time in starting construction while his administration was still in office. By December, 1920, following the election of progressive John J. Blaine as governor the previous month, the poured concrete foundation of the new hospital was in place.

Then work stopped, for the new governor was as suspicious of the University as Governor Philipp had been six years earlier.[65] Convinced the University had been taken over by the stalwarts, Blaine saw the hospital project as a questionable legacy of the Philipp administration. Arguing that the bonus fund might not be sufficient to cover the projected costs, he held up construction for two years, obliging Bardeen and Evans to mount an eventually successful lobbying effort to get the project underway again. In April of 1922 Bardeen informed President Birge that the medical faculty viewed with "deep concern" the delay in implementing the clear legislative authorization of a four-year medical school with its attendant clinical facilities. "This delay has produced a crisis in the conduct of the medical school which it is our duty to bring to the attention of the Board of Regents," he warned. Further deferral would no doubt result in the departure of key faculty and loss of the existing favorable construction bids. "It is necessary either to go forward or to go backward."[66] Perhaps in response the governor relented, and once construction resumed there were no further problems. Wisconsin General Hospital admitted its first patients on September 29, 1924, and in the fall of 1925 the first clinical class of twenty-five upper division medical students (nineteen men and six women) began their training. After nearly two decades the Van Hise-Bardeen dream of a four-year medical school was a reality.[67]

The new facility served primarily indigent and low income patients. The hospital superintendent, Dr. Robin C. Buerki, reported in 1929 that three-fourths of Wisconsin General patients were referred by family doctors and county judges as public charges whose costs were then shared by the state and their home counties. Another 15 percent were deemed poor enough to be charged a subsidized reduced rate of $5 a

---

[65]See pp. 17-21.

[66]Bardeen to Birge, April 29, 1922, Birge Presidential Papers, 4/12/1, box 28.

[67]See Bardeen, "The Development of Our Medical School," *WAM*, 26 (November, 1924), 6-10. A half-decade later the dean proudly reviewed the school's impressive development in the new facilities. Bardeen, "Medical Progress at Wisconsin," ibid., 32 (October, 1930), 3, 34-6.

day, including all charges. Only 10 percent were private patients paying the full $6-8 daily room rate plus additional fees and charges. Buerki justified the last group on the ground that the hospital should be open on a limited basis to all Wisconsin residents and because UW clinical faculty members, who were not permitted by the Medical School to treat private patients in other Madison hospitals, should be allowed to augment their incomes modestly through this private practice.[68]

The hospital also provided a clinical base for nursing education. In 1924 Bardeen and Evans recruited Helen I. Denne, a young Canadian nurse currently working as a nursing supervisor at Presbyterian Hospital in Chicago, as professor of nursing, with dual responsibilities as superintendent of hospital nursing services and director of a new UW School of Nursing. She got the school under way immediately, enrolling eleven students in the first class in the fall of 1924. Denne resigned upon her marriage in 1937 and was replaced as director by Christina C. Murray, with Denne's assistant, Lila B. Fletcher, taking over the supervision of hospital nursing services.[69] In an unusual arrangement the School of Nursing was budgeted through Bardeen but located administratively in the College of Letters and Science, where its undergraduate students took many of their courses and from which they could receive a bachelor of science degree if they chose to go beyond the basic three-year nursing diploma program. In 1940 the school dropped the diploma option to concentrate on its innovative five-year-plus baccalaureate degree program involving a combination of nursing training and liberal arts education.

Under the five-year nursing curriculum students took regular liberal arts courses in the College of Letters and Science during their first two pre-clinical years, with a rigorous physiology course often serving as a screening device for entry into the clinical part of the program. They then spent twenty-nine months living in the Nurses Dormitory, constructed in 1926 on University Avenue just west of the hospital. Here they took nursing courses in classrooms located in the

---

[68]R.G. Buerki to J.D. Phillips, January 23, 1930, Frank Presidential Papers, 4/13/1, box 78. Buerki also noted that the hospital billed state legislators at the reduced $5 daily rate and waived all other charges. See also Bardeen to Frank, May 18, 1926, on the importance of allowing some private practice income in order to recruit well-qualified clinical physicians. Ibid., box 1.

[69]See William S. Middleton to Dykstra, December 1, 1937, Dykstra Presidential Papers, 4/15/1, box 13, UA.

dorm basement and received clinical training in the nearby hospital. The clinical sequence was closely tied to hospital schedules and the students operated essentially around the clock, providing the hospital with a good deal of unsalaried nursing care while in training. The clinical program required students to live in the Nurses Dormitory and enrollment was accordingly restricted to the number of accommodations there. In recognition of their valuable service to the hospital, the students received room, board, laundry of their uniforms, and eventually a fee-remission scholarship during their clinical training. Following this they normally took additional courses in either the College of Letters and Science or the College of Agriculture in order to meet the requirements for a bachelor of science degree in hygiene, with an appropriate major offered by either of these colleges or after 1939 one in public health nursing offered by the school itself. Shortly after Pearl Harbor the school resumed an accelerated three-year diploma program for the duration of the war and later participated in the U.S. Cadet Nurse Corps program to train nurses for military and essential civilian wartime service.[70]

The UW School of Nursing was the first collegiate nursing program in the state and one of the early ones in the country. Although Director Denne herself possessed only a baccalaureate degree, she was determined to develop a program with academic content and rigor. A small, dignified, self-assured woman, always she commanded respect. In the face of some faculty grumbling that nursing was a vocational rather than an academic subject and was thus unsuited to a university, Denne insisted her school must be an integral part of the institution and its students must meet regular University admission and grading standards and participate in normal student extracurricular activities. She made sure the nursing curriculum included a heavy dose of liberal arts courses and advised students to take the school's five-year degree program rather than the shorter and less academic diploma option. In keeping with University norms, she measured student progress by course credits rather than number of hours, the method commonly used in other nursing schools at this time, and she sought to win academic respectability for the nursing courses and credits. She and some members of her faculty held regular professorial appointments even though they did not have the advanced degrees normally expected for

---

[70]School of Nursing press release, August 28, 1942, Dykstra Presidential Papers, 4/15/1, box 87.

the higher faculty ranks.[71]   As a result of Denne's vision and firm leadership the Wisconsin nursing program was much more academic than was characteristic of most collegiate nursing schools of the day, which often were little different from the multitude of hospital-based schools offering mostly clinical training.[72]

The four-year Medical School naturally required a considerable expansion of its clinical faculty.   Gradually Dean Bardeen recruited additional specialists, often on a part-time basis, in such fields as gastroenterology, orthopedic and plastic surgery, pediatrics, ophthalmology, radiology, anesthesiology, obstetrics and gynecology, and dermatology.   The dean recognized he could not provide University salaries commensurate with what the clinical faculty could earn in private practice.   To attract and hold high quality specialists for the Medical School he developed what came to be called the Bardeen Rule, which permitted the medical faculty to engage in private practice. Under the rule full-time faculty members with clinical specialties could earn as much again through private practice as their official UW salaries.   The Bardeen Rule established limits and controls, but understandably did little to endear itself to Madison physicians who resented the competition from state-salaried specialists.   The critics noisily objected to the medical faculty's use of University offices, equipment, and the Wisconsin General Hospital for private gain.   Even when the faculty members conducted their private practice off campus, they were seen to be shirking their University teaching and research obligations.

The issue was a continuing public relations problem for the Medical School and the University until Bardeen's successor, Dean William S. Middleton, persuaded the full-time medical faculty to give

---

[71]It should be noted, however, that nursing faculty salaries were well below those of other (mostly male) faculty members not only in the Medical School but elsewhere in the University. Upon her appointment as a full professor in 1924, Denne was paid a twelve-month salary of $3,600, plus room, board, and laundry maintenance estimated at $600. In 1930 she received her first and only raise, to $3,850 in salary and $690 in maintenance, but with the salary waivers in 1932 and 1933 these figures were cut to $3,208 and $360, respectively. This remained her annual compensation until her resignation in late 1937. Personnel Cards, UA.

[72]See Clark, *University of Wisconsin Medical School*, pp. 203-8; Signe S. Cooper, "Nursing in Transition: Breaking the Barriers of Tradition: The School of Nursing, 1924-1974," in *A Resourceful University: The University of Wisconsin-Madison in Its 125th Year*, (Madison: University of Wisconsin Press, 1975), pp. 235-44; "50th Anniversary UW-Madison School of Nursing," *Wisconsin Medical Journal*, 73 (September, 1974), 11; National League for Nursing Education, *Proceedings of a Conference on Nursing Schools Connected with Colleges and University*, held at Teachers' College, Columbia University, January 21-25, 1928 (New York: National League for Nursing Education, 1928).

up their private practice and private compensation after 1935. Under the Middleton policy private patients could be treated by the full-time faculty only in consultation with and upon referral of a physician outside the University. Fees for such service were paid into a Medical School clinical practice fund and subsequently distributed among the clinical faculty according to their part in generating the funds, with the continuing restriction that such additional income could not exceed their regular UW salaries. Any excess funds were used for support of research or other school needs. The basic intent of the Bardeen Rule was thus retained by Middleton, but complaints by local doctors about unfair competition diminished considerably. Dean Middleton and President Dykstra also developed what became a general University policy that outside funds could not be used to raise a faculty member's base salary above the amount established by the regents.[73]

The recognition that the Medical School needed to build bridges to the medical practitioners of the state early led Bardeen to create one of the most innovative features of the clinical curriculum, the Wisconsin medical preceptorships. One state physician called the preceptor program the dean's "masterpiece."[74] Convinced that hospital training gave medical students only partial exposure to the problems they would confront in the future, in November of 1926, as the first four-year class was beginning its senior year, the dean met with a group of representative doctors from around the state. He proposed that advanced UW medical students be placed for several months to work with a practicing physician on a master-apprentice basis. While assisting the preceptor, who would gain some prestige by holding a courtesy appointment in the school, the student would learn how to practice medicine in the field and deal with ailments not requiring hospital treatment. Although the preceptor idea was based on ancient practice, Bardeen's plan was none the less a new approach in modern medical education, and it was warmly embraced by the state medical establishment.[75] To make it feasible academically, the senior year was

---

[73]See Middleton to Dykstra, February 3, 1938; Dykstra to Middleton, February 5, 1938, Dykstra Presidential Papers, 4/15/1, box 13; Middleton to Dykstra, April 10, 1940; Middleton to M.E. McCaffrey, April 10, 1940; A.W. Peterson to Dykstra, April 16, 1940; Dykstra to Middleton, April 23, 1940, ibid., box 52.

[74]H.M. Stang to Frank, June 15, 1935, Frank Presidential Papers, 4/13/1, box 171.

[75]Bardeen had conceived the preceptor plan more than a year earlier, even before the first four-year class began its clinical studies, proposing it to the Board of Regents in June, 1925. After studying the plan for a month the regents approved it and authorized the Medical School

lengthened from thirty-two to forty-eight weeks and divided into quarters so each medical student could spend one quarter with an out-state physician. Administered initially by the highly respected Dr. Evans, the program not only added a valuable dimension to UW medical training but also strengthened the Medical School's outreach efforts to work with and serve the Wisconsin medical community.[76]

Like the School of Nursing, the Medical School maintained a dual instructional program for a number of years, regularly admitting more students into the two-year pre-clinical track than it could accommodate for clinical training during the third and fourth years. Competition for admission into the clinical program was keen, since those who were passed over had to try for acceptance by another four-year medical school. The fateful selection process frequently brought disappointment and hard feelings to the losers and their families. During 1935-36 Joseph A. Padway, a prominent La Follette progressive leader in Milwaukee, former state senator, and the general counsel of the Wisconsin Federation of Labor, complained that a Jewish medical student had been discriminated against in not being advanced to the third year. In view of Padway's prominence and political influence, his continuing pursuit of the matter for more than a year resulted in a number of reviews by the admissions committee, the dean, and even President Frank, all of whom professed to be satisfied that the selection process was fair and objective and that the Medical School imposed no quota nor other discrimination against Jewish students. Backed by President Frank, who assured Padway there was "not even a chemical trace of racial or religious consideration in these decisions," the school declined to reverse itself.[77] To avoid such complaints and in recognition

---

to develop a system of clinical professorships to recognize the services of "members of the medical profession who give aid in teaching medical students and who serve without financial compensation." BOR Minutes, June 25, August 5, 1925.

[76]See, for example, Bardeen to Frank, February 13, 1930, Frank Presidential Papers, 4/13/1, box 70.

[77]See W.S. Middleton to Joseph A. Padway, July 9, 1935; Padway to Middleton, May 25, 1936; Middleton to Padway, May 28, 1936; Padway to Frank, June 5, 1936; Middleton to Frank, June 9, 1936; Padway to Frank, June 25, 1936; Frank to Padway, July 10, 1936; Padway to Frank, July 13, 1936; Frank to Padway, July 14, 1936; Padway to Frank, July 31, 1936; R.C. Herrin to Frank, August 14, 1936; Walter J. Meek to Frank, August 14, 1936; Middleton to Frank, August 14, 1936; Middleton to Frank, September 26, 1936; Middleton to Frank, September 28, 1936, Sellery Presidential Papers, 4/14/1, box 13, UA. The quotation is from Frank to Padway, July 10, 1936. Professor Philip P. Cohen, who earned a UW Ph.D. degree in biochemistry in 1937 and a UW M.D. degree in 1938 and then joined and later

of the increasingly difficult task of placing third-year Wisconsin students in other four-year schools, the Medical School decided in 1940 to phase out the separate two-year pre-clinical track effective in 1942.[78]

In the early years of the Medical School Dean Bardeen concentrated on strengthening the basic medical science departments supporting the pre-clinical curriculum. Even as he subsequently developed the clinical disciplines needed for the four-year school, he remained active in and supportive of basic research. In 1934 the school received a large bequest from Miss Jenny Bowman providing $420,000 for fundamental research on the study and cure of cancer.[79] Bardeen headed a committee that visited leading tumor centers and then recommended a program of postdoctoral research fellowships. That way the income from the bequest could support several promising younger scholars studying different aspects of the disease. The first two Bowman fellows, recent M.D. graduates Harold P. Rusch and Frederic E. Mohs, devoted their careers to cancer research and subsequently received regular faculty appointments in the Medical School. The Bowman support for cancer studies was augmented the following year by another windfall, a bequest from Michael McCardle for the promotion of cancer studies. Using a combination of McCardle and federal PWA funds, in 1940 the Medical School constructed the McCardle Memorial Laboratory to house the various interdisciplinary cancer research activities.

Ironically, Dean Bardeen himself died of cancer on June 12, 1935, before the new cancer research program had borne any fruit.[80] His successor, Dr. William S. Middleton, served as dean for the next twenty years except for a break for service with the Army Medical Corps in

---

headed the Medical School's Department of Physiological Chemistry, believed there was indeed an informal Jewish quota applied by the Medical School Admissions Committee. He was convinced that Dean Middleton was unaware of it, however, and declared, "I know for a fact that he would never be a party to anything of that kind." Cohen, oral history interview, 1980, UA.

[78]Middleton to Dykstra, November 20, 1940; C.A. Smith to Dysktra, December 4, 1940, Dykstra Presidential Papers, 4/15/1, box 68; BOR Minutes, December 7, 1940.

[79]See Bardeen, "The Significance of the Bowman Bequest for Cancer Research at Wisconsin," *WAM*, 35 (April, 1934), 184-6.

[80]See "Glenn Frank Statement on Death of C.R. Bardeen," June 13, 1935, Frank Presidential Papers, 4/13/1, box 160; Joseph S. Evans, "In Memorium: Charles Russell Bardeen, 1871-1935," *WAM*, 36 (July, 1935), 295, 327; *Capital Times*, June 12 and 13, 1935; *Wisconsin State Journal*, June 12 and 13, 1935; Fond du Lac *Commonwealth Reporter*, June 13, 1935.

Europe in 1942-45.[81] Middleton had joined the medical faculty as a young physician in 1912 assigned to assist Dr. Evans in the student infirmary. An internist, he was a skilled diagnostician and an awesomely well-organized stickler for detail, even admonishing student nurses when their caps were awry or their stocking seams crooked. A man of selfless personal integrity, he once privately urged President Dykstra to reduce his dean's salary to help meet a University budget cut.[82] Following his appointment as dean, Middleton continued to make hospital rounds every morning, seeing patients and instructing medical and nursing students and interns; then punctually at noon he retreated to his hospital office for a bottle of milk and a short break before going to his dean's office for a long afternoon of administrative work before finally rushing off for a handball match. Middleton once described the Medical School as the product of "Bardeen's brain and Evans' heart." In his history of the early development of the school Paul Clark added Middleton to the founding triumvirate, terming him the consummate "teacher-clinician."

As Clark's designation suggests, Dean Middleton believed the primary mission of the Medical School was the training of new physicians rather than basic medical research. In 1939 he appointed a special committee to study whether it was advisable to provide a more flexible program of study and research for the top 15 percent of medical students. The committee rejected this option but offered a number of other suggestions for curricular change, which on the whole were less significant than the more sweeping changes required for the subsequent

---

[81] See Middleton to Dykstra, April 13 and 14, 1942; Dykstra to Middleton, April 15, 1942, Dykstra Presidential Papers, 4/15/1, box 88.

[82] "One does not care to appear in the light of a martyr," Middleton wrote, "and I would not wish my attitude in this matter discussed." Middleton to Dykstra, May 27, 1938, Dykstra Presidential Papers, 4/15/1, box 13. While appreciative of the offer, Dykstra declined to implement it. Dykstra to Middleton, May 31, 1938, ibid.

accelerated wartime program.[83]   Apart from the cancer initiatives supported by the Bowman-McCardle funds, Middleton was less supportive than Bardeen of the research interests of the medical faculty, though he did institute the practice of monthly reports from his faculty, which he summarized and circulated in the school and shared with Presidents Frank and Dykstra, in order to keep abreast of faculty research and other professional activities.[84]   He promoted biweekly hospital staff meetings for presentations and discussion of the latest developments in various fields of medicine.[85]   He also retained a lively interest in his old Department of Student Health, adding psychiatric counseling and treatment under the direction of Professor Annette Washburne.[86]

Like Bardeen, Middleton had an imperial view of his domain and doggedly fought to reserve expansion space for the Medical School extending to the top of Observatory Hill.   He argued that the 1908 Laird-Cret campus plan had earmarked the territory north of Linden Drive for his school.   He complained in 1938 that expansion of the Extension and Home Economics Building represented "infiltration" by the College of Agriculture eastward into Medical School space.   By 1940 he went so far as to lay claim to the building itself for Medical School needs.   Since such presumption put him on a collision course with the powerful College of Agriculture and its allies among regents and legislators, none of the UW Presidents of the period—neither Frank, Dykstra, nor Fred—accepted Middleton's expansive territorial claims.[87]

---

[83]"Report of the Committee on Special Curriculum," November 25, 1939, Dykstra Presidential Papers, 4/15/1, box 52.   Middleton confessed to Dykstra he was disappointed at the committee's "failure to enunciate certain functional changes in curriculum which I think are fundamental."   Middleton to Dykstra, December 9, 1939, ibid.

[84]See Middleton, "Medical School Activities," October 15, 1935, Frank Presidential Papers, 4/13/1, box 184.

[85]See, for example, "Investigations in Gynecological Endocrinology," including a schedule of staff meetings for the remainder of the semester, October 22, 1935, ibid.

[86]See his initial proposal in Middleton to Frank, December 4, 1935, ibid., box 84.   Though not immediately successful, Middleton persevered until he won modest funding for psychiatric services for students.

[87]Middleton to Dykstra, September 20, 1938; Dykstra to Middleton, September 22, 1938, Dykstra Presidential Papers, 4/15/1, box 34; Middleton to Dykstra, January 25, 1940, ibid., box 52.   Bardeen's defense of Medical School turf was hardly less acute, though he never went so far as Middleton.   In 1930 when construction of the new Children's Orthopedic Hospital required relocation of the home economics practice cottage, Bardeen told President Frank he was willing (over the objections of Abby Marlatt, the director of the home economics program, who favored another location objected to by Agriculture Dean Russell) to move the cottage to

Middleton had more success in persuading the regents to purchase the outstanding medical library of anatomy Professor William Snow Miller following the latter's death in 1939. Appointed initially as an instructor of biology in 1892 to assist Birge in the pre-medical course, Miller had charge of the histology course for most of his career. He also had a lifelong interest in the history of medicine, offering an informal seminar on the subject for interested medical students in his University Club rooms beginning in 1909. By the time of his death he had accumulated an outstanding library of rare historical works on the development of medicine through the ages. Recognizing its value, Dean Middleton badgered President Dykstra and the regents to acquire the collection until the board finally came up with $15,000 for its purchase late in 1940.[88] Buttressed by this library, Dean Middleton subsequently carried on the tradition of William Snow Miller's medical history seminars through the establishment of a professorship in the history of medicine after World War II, one of the first such in the country. Hardly less authoritarian if perhaps less visionary than Bardeen, Middleton too left an indelible mark on the school, expanding and strengthening its clinical program in a number of areas. With Bardeen he certainly deserves to be considered one of the founders of the healing professions at Wisconsin.[89]

The Other Professions

Engineering languished during the early decades of the University, getting at best minimal attention and support required for uneasy compliance with the requirements of the Morrill Land Grant Act of 1862. Engineering lacked the numerous and well-organized farmer

---

the empty lot just north of the Wisconsin High School on Henry Mall. This should be regarded as "a temporary location," however, as the Medical School claimed all the space bounded by University Avenue and Linden Drive between Charter Street and the mall. Bardeen to Frank, March 14, 1930, Frank Presidential Papers, 4/13/1, box 70.

[88]Oscar T. Toebaas to Middleton, April 13, 1940; M.J. Cleary to Dykstra, May 13, 1940; M.E. McCaffrey to Dykstra and Regents Executive Committee, May 17, 1940; Eben J. Carey to Dykstra, June 20, 1940; Carey to Leonard J. Kleczka, June 20, 1940; Middleton to Dykstra, July 10, 1940; James O. Kelley to McCaffrey, September 30, 1940; Middleton to Dykstra, September 30, 1940; A.W. Peterson to Dykstra, October 10, 1940, Dykstra Presidential Papers, 4/15/1, box 68; BOR Minutes, May 11, June 15, October 26, 1940.

[89]The section is based in part on Clark, *University of Wisconsin Medical School*, the most extensive treatment available of the Medical School during the inter-war period, and Curti and Carstensen, *University of Wisconsin*, vol. 2, pp. 480-96.

constituency in the state and in the legislature that provided substantial backing for educational initiatives and research in agriculture.[90] After the Civil War the University at first relied on Army officers directing the required military drill to offer instruction in civil and military engineering. Even when the University began to recruit regular engineering faculty in the late 1870s, the program remained a small and awkward stepchild within the College of Arts. Not until the arrival in 1887 of President Thomas C. Chamberlin, a geologist with applied interests, did engineering receive its first significant administrative support. In winning approval from the regents and the legislature for a fundamental restructuring of the University in 1889, Chamberlin saw to it that one of the four basic academic units was a separate College of Engineering.

Although President Chamberlin soon named deans of three of the four new units (Agriculture, Law, and Letters and Science), inexplicably the College of Engineering remained without a dean for a decade, governed by a board consisting of the senior engineering faculty. Not until 1899 did President Adams recruit John Butler Johnson, a professor of civil engineering at Washington University in St. Louis, as the college's first dean. Energetic and active, Johnson seemed an excellent choice, but he was killed in a tragic accident after only three years in office. His successor, Frederick E. Turneaure, had also taught at Washington University before joining the Wisconsin faculty in 1892. Like Johnson he was a civil engineer and a recognized authority on structural engineering and railway and highway bridge construction. Turneaure served as dean until his retirement in 1937, all the while promoting a traditional view of engineering education that substantially shaped and at the same time limited the college's development. When he retired he was still administering the college informally and remotely from an ancient roll-top desk in his office in the Engineering Building on the Hill, where his secretary, who incidentally herself determined departmental supplies and equipment allocations, also kept an unlocked closet filled with office supplies to which staff members had free access without limit or accounting.[91]

Unlike the College of Agriculture where Dean Harry Russell encouraged his faculty to have advanced degrees and developed a

---

[90]See pp. 767-84.

[91]F. Ellis Johnson, "Report on Administration of the College of Engineering, 1938-1944," January 13, 1945, pp. 5-6, Fred Presidential Papers, 4/16/1, box 32, UA.

synergistic mix of basic and applied scientists working together on agricultural problems, Turneaure thought the primary mission of the College of Engineering was to turn out well-trained engineers, not scientists. As previously noted in Chapter 8, he favored a demanding undergraduate engineering program augmented by on-the-job training over graduate study, even for members of his faculty, a view common among engineering educators prior to World War II. Faculty and student research projects in the College of Engineering were heavily applied, directed at solving problems of specific interest to Wisconsin governmental agencies and industries.

In 1913 Turneaure and Van Hise persuaded the regents to establish the Engineering Experiment Station modeled after the highly successful similar agency for applied research in the College of Agriculture. The engineering station failed to flourish like its agricultural counterpart, however. Turneaure and Van Hise asked the state for a minimum of $10,000 a year to support its research, but by 1918-20 the station's appropriation was only about $3,000, less than half of the research budget provided at its start and far less than that of the agricultural station. There were several reasons why the engineering station did not live up to its early promise. One, certainly, was the absence of federal research funding like that increasingly available to the agricultural station. Another was that on the whole the engineers were less highly trained and research-oriented than their colleagues in the College of Agriculture and also had less adequate laboratory facilities and support. Still another was the failure of Turneaure and the engineering faculty to develop much support from the college's potential constituencies in the state. Even so, Wisconsin progressives were deeply suspicious of the occasional research grants received by the engineering station from industrial sources and were resentful of the outside consulting and patent income enjoyed by Turneaure and some of the engineering faculty. Governor Blaine, for example, feuded with the dean in the mid-twenties over the latter's ex officio membership on the Wisconsin Highway Commission, charging he was too sympathetic to construction interests. Following up Blaine's criticism, a progressive senator in 1927 went so far as to introduce a bill restructuring the commission in order to replace Turneaure, an effort that was repeated in the next biennium.[92] The college's serious identity problems continued throughout the inter-

---

[92]See Edward E. Browne to John J. Blaine, February 4, 1925, John J. Blaine Papers, box 46, SHSW; *Daily Cardinal*, April 14, 1927, May 2, 1929.

war years.[93]

This is not to suggest that the College of Engineering did no research of value. The growing laboratory and testing facilities in the Engineering Building, in the old Chemistry Laboratory north of Science Hall inherited by the chemical engineering department after the chemistry department's move to its new building on University Avenue in 1906, in the engineering shops on the northeast slope of the Hill, and after 1930 in the buildings on the Camp Randall engineering campus enabled the college's faculty and students to undertake a good deal of useful applied research. This ranged widely across the engineering disciplines and included testing the cost and durability of concrete and bituminous surfaces for roadways, the strength of reinforced concrete for structural uses, work on the octane requirements of high compression gasoline engines, slag research for more efficient blast furnace operation, studies of the nature and causes of metal fatigue, improved techniques for welding and electro-plating, devices for air conditioning, and many more. The college's Electrical Standards Laboratory, operated in conjunction with the state Public Service Commission, was used by a number of Wisconsin manufacturers and electric utilities to calibrate their gauges and meters and to test the output of motors and generators. Its Hydraulics Laboratory adjacent to the UW pumping station on the lakeshore included a 220,000 gallon concrete reservoir sixty feet above on the bluff that made possible modeling studies of water flow speed and pressure important in designing dams, locks, and flood and erosion control systems. This facility also included a sanitary laboratory for study of sewage and waste water disposal problems. The college's research and testing facilities expanded steadily during the inter-war period. By 1945 there were more than three dozen specialized laboratories for faculty and student use in the study of various engineering problems.[94] The University's public relations arm, the *Press Bulletin*, regularly applauded the research of the College of Engineering, emphasizing its practical value

---

[93]For background on the development of the College of Engineering in the early twentieth century, see Curti and Carstensen, *University of Wisconsin*, vol. 2, pp. 444-79.

[94]The dramatic growth in the number and sophistication of the engineering research facilities can be seen by comparing the listings in the University catalogs of the period. See, for example, *University of Wisconsin Catalog, 1925-26*, Bulletin of the University of Wisconsin, Serial No. 1354, General Series No. 1130, August, 1926, pp. 221-5, and *General Announcement of Courses, 1944-46 (Catalog)*, Bulletin of the University of Wisconsin, Serial No. 2771, General Series No. 2555, June, 1945, pp. 230-2.

to the state. The engineers may not have equalled their agriculture colleagues in cutting-edge research or in attracting the attention and support of most Wisconsin citizens, but they were well-respected in professional and engineering education circles and were often called on to provide expert advice on engineering problems on campus, in Wisconsin, and elsewhere.

During the Turneaure years the College of Engineering offered a solid but quite traditional and in some respects even a vocational curriculum.[95] In 1925 nearly all of its students were undergraduates taking one of the four-year courses leading to a bachelor of science degree in the five broad areas of engineering: civil, mechanical, electrical, chemical, or mining engineering, with some further specialization possible within each degree track. Another option enabled a student to spread the undergraduate program over five years in order to include with it appropriate work in the College of Letters and Science. At the graduate level the college offered a degree of Master of Science in any of the five branches of engineering, as well as an advanced professional degree (for example, Civil Engineer, Electrical Engineer, and the like) for any of its graduates who spent at least five years in professional work, at least one of them in a position of responsibility, and who presented a satisfactory thesis. While the college also offered the Ph.D. degree, Dean Turneaure did not emphasize its availability, no doubt partly because so few engineering faculty members themselves held doctorates.[96] By 1937, when Turneaure retired as dean, the engineering faculty had added a sixth basic field to the undergraduate curriculum by separating mining and metallurgical engineering.[97] Within the broad field of civil engineering the number of sub-majors expanded to include such options as

---

[95]For example, when Dean Ellis Johnson succeeded Turneaure in 1938 he promptly upset one engineering department chairman by rejecting a requisition to buy a pipe-threading machine for use in laboratory instruction. Johnson told President Dykstra:

> In the first instance, it seemed questionable whether instruction in pipe fitting should be offered for University credit. Second, if such instruction was to be offered that it should be thoroughgoing enough that the student should learn to actually handle a pipe stock rather than merely to place the pipe in an automatic threading machine. Third, the equipment needs of the College of Engineering and the department concerned were so serious in real engineering equipment that such vocational equipment should at least receive secondary consideration.

Johnson, "Report on Administration of the College of Engineering, 1938-44," pp. 13-4.

[96]See *Catalog, 1925-26*, pp. 225-7.

[97]See UW Faculty Minutes, April 7, 1930.

aeronautics, erosion control, highways, railways, city planning, hydraulics, sanitation, and structures. There was also an Engineering and Law option, approved in 1932, which enabled a student to earn an engineering and a law degree over a six-year period.[98] The basic undergraduate engineering degree required 146 credits, in contrast to the normal 120 credits for the letters and science and most other UW baccalaureate degrees.[99]

Turneaure's successor, F. Ellis Johnson, was a 1906 UW electrical engineering graduate who had subsequently taught at Rice, Kansas, and Iowa State, and most recently had served for three years as Dean of the College of Engineering at the University of Missouri. Fifty-three when President Dykstra recruited him to return to his alma mater in 1938, Johnson was in the prime of his professional life with a decade of successful department- and college-level administrative experience at three other universities to draw on. The new dean found much that needed changing in the UW College of Engineering. He quickly concluded that a good part of the faculty was weaker than required for a major engineering college and needed upgrading. In a series of department staff meetings shortly after his arrival he distributed a detailed personnel questionnaire so he could become better acquainted with the qualifications, experience, interests, and long-term objectives of the engineering staff. He announced he would not be disturbed by a large faculty turnover if it were in the best interest of the individual and the institution, pointing out this would allow a department to bring in new blood and free salary funds for differential merit raises for the

---

[98] See ibid., June 6, 1932; UW Faculty Document 410, "Revision of Entrance Requirements to the Law School," June 6, 1932.

[99] *General Announcement of Courses, 1938-1939 (Catalog 1937-1938),* Bulletin of the University of Wisconsin, Serial No. 2347, General Series No. 2131, August, 1938, pp. 240-300.

remaining faculty.

Not surprisingly, a significant part of the engineering faculty found the new order threatening. Fully a quarter of the staff failed to return Johnson's questionnaire, with some complaining it was an invasion of their privacy. The inquiry caused even more unhappiness when the dean penalized those who failed to respond by withholding salary increases, explaining that without the requested information he was unable to evaluate the holdouts. In his first biennial report to President Dykstra and the Board of Regents Dean Johnson observed that "the continued training of faculty men requires that their assigned duties constitute for each a challenge for growth." This should be reflected in "(a) Researches in fundamental and applied science; (b) Applications of research to development of new state industries; (c) Solution by research of the problems of industries or state bureaus; (d) Publications."[100] Under Johnson scholarly activity was to be valued and rewarded as it had not been in the Turneaure era.

Dean Johnson also quickly began restructuring the college, abolishing one department and reorganizing and reducing the total from sixteen to six, mostly by collapsing a number of small departments into a single Department of Civil Engineering. At the same time he pressured several long-time chairmen to step down in favor of younger colleagues. At least two of the deposed chairmen—Otto Kowalke of chemical engineering and Edward Bennett of electrical engineering, each of whom had held their posts for more than two decades—did not take their removal kindly and thereafter gave leadership to the growing opposition to the dean's reforms.[101] In his first year Johnson also

---

[100]Johnson, "Biennial Report, College of Engineering, 1938-40," p. 6, General Presidential Papers, 4/0/2, box 10, UA.

[101]Johnson, "Biennial Report of the College of Engineering, 1940-42," pp. 1-5, General Presidential Papers, 4/0/2, box 11; Johnson, "Report on Administration of the College of Engineering, 1938-44," pp. 4-26. Professor Bennett felt so strongly about what he saw as Dean Johnson's arbitrary conduct that he asked to retire in mid-semester in the fall of 1943, explaining:

> I take the step because it is the last way left to me to protest the demoralizing of this enterprise. This state of demoralization is resulting from a use of administrative powers in the determination of educational policies and in the conduct of faculty affairs that is contrary to the practices, and is, in my estimation, in violation of the laws, under which this College and this University have attained their stature.

Edward Bennett to James W. Watson, October 8, 1943, Fred Presidential Papers, 4/16/1, box 32. For two upbeat post-Kowalke reports on the Department of Chemical Engineering see R.A. Ragatz, "The Department-of-the-Month...Chemical Engineering," *Wisconsin Engineer*, 46

pressured the engineering student body to abandon an ancient college tradition—the colorful St. Patrick's Day parade that had frequently resulted in serious conflict with rival law students, most recently in a destructive State Street riot in 1938—in favor of a college open house to showcase student projects. The first Engineering Exposition attracted forty industry exhibits and displayed seventy interesting student projects. It drew large crowds, enabling the venture to clear a profit of more than a thousand dollars after expenses. About half of the proceeds were divided among the participating student engineering societies and the balance used to furnish a lounge in the main lobby of the Mechanical Engineering Building. Small wonder the dean described the event as "a notable success as a constructive undertaking."[102] Indeed, the Expo was probably the most popular of the various Johnson innovations and promptly became an annual occurrence.

During 1939-40 Johnson moved to reform the college's undergraduate programs to make them less vocational and more professional. As a first step he persuaded the faculty to drop the requirement of shop for all engineering students in the freshman year. Since this shop work was very elementary, abandoning it in favor of more advanced training in subsequent years improved the curriculum while achieving a considerable saving in space and staff salaries.[103] Johnson thought the undergraduate programs in general were too narrowly technical and demanded too much from the average undergraduate student. He favored broadening the engineering baccalaureate degree to include more liberal arts work, though this might, he realized, require increasing the time and credits required. His preference was to shift more of the technical work to the graduate level. In the fall of 1939 Johnson proposed two alternatives to the engineering faculty:

> Either — Reduce the present scientific and technical contents of the four-year engineering curricula to more nearly mere fundamentals and increase economic and social studies sufficiently to provide a broad "humanistic" base. This makes it necessary to leave to graduate years a portion of the technical studies we now consider essential in the undergraduate program. Or — Lengthen the undergraduate program to five years. Spread the present scientific and technical requirements of the four-year curriculum through five

(November, 1941), 5; Bill Jacobson, "Research and Curricula in...Chemical Engineering," ibid., 47 (December, 1942), 8-9.

[102]Johnson, "Biennial Report, College of Engineering, 1938-40," p. 13.
[103]Ibid., p. 8.

years so as to open the opportunity for a parallel band of economic and social studies.

To try to assure that his reform proposals would not be rejected out of hand by parochial-minded departments, he asked that they be considered separately by each of the four professorial ranks across the college. As he later conceded drily, "because it was an innovation this plan was not popular and therefore did not work out well." Nor was he able to orchestrate a consensus through faculty questionnaires and written balloting, even with the assurance that the two tracks might operate together and the five-year option could be phased in gradually. One department supported a five-year, 170 credit degree, but another thought such a change though perhaps desirable was impractical, and still others favored modification of the four-year program. Johnson had managed to stimulate considerable discussion, but the college faculty remained hopelessly deadlocked. After two inconclusive referenda, the dean conceded defeat, suggesting further study of the matter and declaring that "no material change is indicated until such further thought and discussion bring a greater unanimity of opinion."[104] Except for minor changes the engineering curricula were not revised until the war forced the college to make temporary adjustments for the Navy V-12 program.[105]

President Dykstra had recruited Dean Johnson from outside the University, encouraged his efforts to reform the College of Engineering, and stood by him loyally until departing for UCLA in January, 1945. The president must have winced, however, at Johnson's whirlwind campaign for change and his lack of diplomatic finesse in working within UW faculty governance traditions. Dykstra's successor, President E.B. Fred, took little time in deciding he could not ignore the considerable faculty dissatisfaction with Johnson's hard-driving autocratic style. With characteristic off-handed subtlety, shortly after assuming the presidency Fred suggested to Johnson in two conferences during June, 1945, that he thought it might be time for a change in the College of Engineering deanship. When Dean Johnson expressed surprise at this suggestion, the president explained that his view was based on conversations with some of the engineering faculty and

---

[104]Johnson to the Faculty of the College of Engineering, May 11, 1940, in Johnson, "Report on Administration of the College of Engineering, 1938-44," pp. 46-7.

[105]See ibid., pp. 2-29, 40-7.

members of the Board of Regents. Johnson appealed to the regents to investigate the circumstances of his pending ouster, especially what he termed "a campaign of misrepresentation and letters to which members of the Board have been subjected."[106]

The board was not about to overrule its new president, however, and it gave Johnson no satisfaction. At the same time, with the earlier noisy uproar over the firings of Dean Snell and President Frank no doubt in mind, President Fred and the regents preferred to avoid a public spectacle that Johnson's outright dismissal might bring. Instead, during the fall of 1945 Fred worked on Johnson to assure a quiet change. He offered to defer any immediate action until Johnson found another position, or if the dean should decide to remain in Madison to appoint him to a research professorship in electrical engineering at his current salary. By now reconciled to stepping down, in late November Johnson formally requested a leave of absence for the second semester, during which he would continue to hold the title of dean while he sought another position.[107] President Fred then met with the chairmen of the engineering departments and asked their advice on how to administer the college until Johnson's resignation took effect July 1. The group recommended that Professor Morton O. Withey, the chairman of the mechanics department, serve as acting dean. Fred had already consulted privately with Withey about the future of the college and very likely engineered this advice. Later in the year after Johnson's resignation took effect the regents confirmed Withey's appointment as the regular dean.[108]

The removal of Dean Johnson, carried out quietly and with a certain amount of indirection and delicate persuasion, typified what was to be E.B. Fred's seemingly gentle and oblique yet nevertheless sure-footed administrative style during his presidency. The change in leadership immediately reduced the tensions within the College of Engineering that had been mounting since 1938. At the same time Dean Johnson's departure largely postponed dealing with some of the

---

[106]Johnson to President Fred and the Board of Regents, July 21, 1945, Fred Presidential Papers, 4/16/1, box 32.

[107]"Memorandum of Conference with Dean Johnson," November 27, 1945; Johnson to Fred and the Board of Regents, November 26, 1945; Johnson to Fred, December 17, 1945, ibid.

[108]"Memorandum of Conference with Professor M.O. Withey Concerning the Future of the Engineering," December 27, 1945; "Conference on Deanship of College of Engineering," January 2, 1946; "Memorandum of Conference with Dean Johnson," January 8, 1946, ibid.

issues—in particular curricular reform and upgrading the faculty—he had correctly identified as problems. These remained to be addressed in the future.

A more successful and enduring impact on another of the UW professional schools in this period was achieved by Dean Lloyd K. Garrison of the Law School. Garrison succeeded Dean Harry S. Richards, who had died unexpectedly while attending a meeting of the American Law Institute on Agency in Boston in 1929. Richards was a recognized national leader in legal education who left his successor what Harvard Dean Roscoe Pound called "one of the great law schools of the country." It is not too much to say that Dean Richards virtually singlehandedly created the modern UW Law School following his appointment in 1903. As soon as he could he moved the school from the state capitol to the campus and shifted from a mostly part-time instructional staff of practicing lawyers and judges to a professional faculty of full-time legal scholars. Another achievement was to raise the school's admission standards and broaden and strengthen the academic content of its courses. Over some reluctance on the part of the then largely practitioner faculty, he converted the curriculum to the new case method of instruction. In 1905 he raised the entrance requirements to include completion of one year of college-level work; two years later the school increased this to two years of pre-law education. Wisconsin was the first public law school to adopt this entrance prerequisite and only the fifth in the country, following the example of Harvard, Columbia, Pennsylvania, and Chicago. Twenty years later the American Law School Association, of which Wisconsin was a charter member and Richards served as president in 1914-15, made this a standard requirement for institutional membership. Just before his death Richards succeeded in raising the UW entrance qualification to three years of pre-law study.[109] Under Dean Richards' leadership the Law School offered one of the first summer law programs in the country beginning in 1908, established a chapter of the honorary Order of the Coif (then called Theta Kappa Nu) that same year, added a practical component to the curriculum in 1916 by requiring the students to spend

---

[109]H.S. Richards to President Frank and the Board of Regents, October 8, 1926, Frank Presidential Papers, 4/13/1, box 32. The entrance requirements were further strengthened in 1937 by requiring students to have either a baccalaureate degree or a grade point average of 1.3 (on a 3.0 scale) on three years of pre-legal study. BOR Minutes, June 19, 1937; Lloyd K. Garrison, "Memorandum of Entrance Requirements for the Law School," June 3, 1937, Sellery Presidential Papers, 4/14/1, box 8.

a six month apprenticeship in a law office, and launched the *Wisconsin Law Review* in 1920 as a vehicle for student and faculty legal scholarship. Richards was so highly regarded that when word of his death reached the campus Professors Page and Rundell went to Chicago to accompany his body back to Madison, the *Daily Cardinal* highlighted the news with a heavy black border, and President Frank closed the University on the day of his funeral, for which the law faculty and student body marched silently in a body down State Street to Grace Episcopal Church for the service.[110]

Lloyd Garrison brought a different but equally influential management style to the Law School. Recruited by President Glenn Frank in early 1932 after a lengthy search, Garrison at thirty-four was a prominent liberal New York attorney specializing in bankruptcy and labor law but had no previous academic experience.[111] He possessed an innovative and decidedly Frank-like vision of legal education, however. Under his leadership the Law School expanded the case method of instruction to include the broader social and economic context that shaped the law. This new functional approach to the study of law had been tentatively explored by Richards and others in the late twenties but the economic upheaval of the great depression added a big impetus to the trend during the next decade. The changed emphasis was reflected in Garrison's own free-wheeling one-credit course for first-year students, "Introduction to Law," and in the team-taught course he and other law faculty members developed with the political science department on "Law in Society." Under Garrison's leadership the faculty reorganized the first-year program to emphasize the origins and development of American law so the students would, as the dean explained to the Board of Regents in 1933, "see it as a whole and perceive, by its growth in the past, the possibilities and need of its adaptation in the future to changing social and economic conditions."[112] Later the school experimented with a number of topical one-credit courses designed to give students some exposure to areas of the law they needed to understand without becoming experts in the details

---

[110]See H.S. Richards, "The Law School," *WAM*, 27 (August, 1926), 329-30; W. Scott Van Alstyne, Jr., "The University of Wisconsin Law School, 1868-1968: An Outline History," *Wisconsin Law Review* (1968), pp. 326-9.

[111]See "Appoint Law Dean: Lloyd Garrison Named to Post Left Vacant by Death of Dean Harry S. Richards in 1929," *WAM*, 33 (March, 1932), 175.

[112]Garrison, "Report of the Dean of the Law School for the Academic Year 1932-33," p. 4, Frank Presidential Papers, 4/13/1, box 147.

developed through the case study approach.[113] Garrison's growing stature as a legal educator led to his election in 1937 as president of the American Association of Law Schools. He also served as a trustee of Howard University, 1935-50, and as a member of the Harvard University Board of Overseers, 1938-44.

One of Dean Garrison's early moves, in 1933, was to organize the Law School Alumni Association, which he utilized to raise scholarship and loan funds for needy students after discovering that well over half of his student body was wholly or partially self-supporting, with many students having difficulty dividing their time between full-time study and a heavy work schedule. At first he thought the association might also help place students after graduation, but decided to start a regular placement bureau in 1935, staffed initially by a recent graduate, John C. Stedman.[114] The alumni association provided useful support when Garrison had to raise funds to repay a loan from the William F. Vilas Estate Trust for a library annex to the Law Building in 1938. In addition to soliciting the alumni for contributions and pledges, Garrison persuaded the regents to impose a special segregated library building fee on current and future law students.[115]

The Law Library addition, still in use, is the most visible legacy of the Garrison era. Upon its completion in 1940 the dean organized a faculty-student work day to move books by means of a human chain into the new facility. This was followed later by an impressive two-day dedication celebration involving national and state leaders of the bar. One of the most striking features of the new library was a large mural dominating the main reading room painted by the University's artist-in-

---

[113]"Memorandum on One Credit Courses" [1938?], Dykstra Presidential Papers, 4/15/1, box 29.

[114]Garrison to Frank, March 1 and 2, April 15, 1935, Frank Presidential Papers, 4/13/1, box 164. A native of Sturgeon Bay, Stedman was the first UW law student to undertake Ph.D. studies, with a joint program in law and economics and a dissertation on public utilities. After setting up the placement bureau he remained on the law faculty for the duration of his career.

[115]In addition to trying to raise private funding, Garrison considered but abandoned the idea of including a law student dormitory with the library so as to generate a revenue stream to help amortize a loan for the building project. See Garrison to Dykstra, December 20, 1937; Dykstra to Garrison, January 5, 1938; Garrison, "Law Alumni—Possible Donors," memorandum, December 10, 1937, Dykstra Presidential Papers, 4/15/1, box 8; Dykstra to Garrison, September 19, 1938, ibid., box 29. In the end the Wisconsin University Building Corporation borrowed funds from the trustees of the Vilas Estate for part of the library addition costs, and Garrison planned to have the Law School Alumni Association issue its own thirty-year notes to repay the Vilas Estate. Garrison, "Memorandum to the Faculty," January 5, 1940, ibid., box 47.

residence, John Steuart Curry, that commemorated the freeing of the slaves. The mural had originally been commissioned for the new Department of Justice building in Washington but was rejected after its subject matter was deemed too controversial and Curry declined to change his sketch. Garrison, who as a one-time officer of the National Urban League had long had an interest in Negro advancement, immediately persuaded Curry to paint his mural for the new Law Library, where it remains as a major example of Curry's artistry and a testament to Garrison's abolitionist heritage.[116]

Dean Garrison was fully committed to one aspect of the Wisconsin Idea, the La Follette-Van Hise concept of active public service by the UW faculty. He himself set an example for his faculty by frequent national service as a mediator and advisor on labor policy, by serving as the initial chairman of the National Labor Relations Board in 1934 and later as a member of a federal mediation panel to settle the bitter 1937 steel strike.[117] In Garrison's first year as dean he augmented the school's long-standing apprenticeship requirement by creating several postgraduate fellowships to enable top law graduates to spend a fourth year of study and research in public law, with an apprenticeship involving rotational assignments working in various state agencies. "The plan," he told Frank and the regents, "is to produce leaders of the bar with a broad intellectual background and a sense of public obligation."[118] Gradually the Law School recruited faculty members with a strong social science orientation who emphasized the broad context of current societal problems in order to produce more relevant legal solutions. The new thrust in Wisconsin legal education was typified by the appointments of Jacob H. Beuscher in 1935 (after several years of part-time teaching) and J. Willard Hurst in 1937. Beuscher developed a pioneering interest in land and farm law and Hurst became an eminent legal historian of American economic development.

Garrison's outspoken liberal views and frequent public service did not escape criticism. In the fall of 1938 one of the regents, Judge

---

[116]Van Alstyne, "University of Wisconsin Law School," p. 331.

[117]See pp. 272-8, 443.

[118]Garrison, "Report of the Dean, 1932-33," pp. 2-3. "I am convinced," Garrison told a foundation official from whom he sought additional support for the plan, "that the best, and possibly the only hope of bringing about in this country much needed reforms in the administration of justice and in government, lies in the development of a new generation of leaders equipped for the task and aware of the problems." Garrison to Guy Moffett, January 16, 1933, Frank Presidential Papers, 4/13/1, box 131.

August C. Backus of Milwaukee, complained that the Law School was suffering as a result of Garrison's frequent absences. The dean had spent the summer of 1938 as a member of a U.S. commission investigating Swedish and British labor relations and was planning to spend the fall term on a Guggenheim grant to study labor conditions in England. "I feel that lending Garrison has hurt the law school," Judge Backus told President Dykstra and the board. "He went once, and now he's gone again. Maybe he'll go again, and then again after that. We're running our law school without a dean."[119] Dean Garrison subsequently drew the ire of state conservatives, including Governor Heil who had recommended its passage, when in the spring of 1941 he testified against a bill barring the Communist Party from the ballot in Wisconsin and later urged its veto. The governor was further offended shortly afterward by Garrison's Citizenship Day address in Milwaukee, in which the dean advocated accepting German domination of Europe and the Japanese conquests in Asia rather than be drawn into war. Instead Garrison urged a permanent alliance between the United States and Britain to use sea power to contain any further aggression.[120] Considerably more hawkish in his foreign policy views, the governor declined to speak after Garrison's remarks. "I don't want to be called on," Heil snapped. "I don't want to follow that man. I'm mad and I might say something that I might be sorry for tomorrow."[121]

As earlier when he sought to bar students with "obnoxious minds" from the University,[122] the governor requested the regents to investigate "obnoxious elements on the faculty," citing particularly Dean Garrison's recent opposition to the anti-communist legislation. Regent President A.J. Glover went so far as to ask the dean for a written explanation of his position on the issue, but when Garrison promptly complied with a detailed seven-page response that would have done credit as a legal brief, the board took no action other than to assure Heil that individual regents were looking into the matter.[123] President Dykstra had a hand in

[119]*Wisconsin State Journal* and *Capital Times*, October 14, 1938.

[120]Garrison, "Address Delivered at the Citizenship Day Ceremonies in Milwaukee," May 18, 1941, Dykstra Presidential Papers, 4/15/1, box 65.

[121]*Capital Times* and *Daily Cardinal*, May 19, 1941.

[122]*Daily Cardinal*, July 16, 1940.

[123]Statement by Regent F.J. Sensenbrenner to the Board of Regents, May 27, 1941, BOR Papers, 1/1/3, box 56; Garrison to A.J. Glover, May 23, 1941, Dykstra Presidential Papers, 4/15/1, box 65; *Capital Times*, May 24 and 27, 1941; *Daily Cardinal*, May 27 and 28, 1941; *Wisconsin State Journal*, June 5, 1941.

devising this innocuous strategy and took comfort from editorials in the state press denouncing the governor for an assault on free speech. Otherwise Dykstra followed his customary strategy of saying nothing to excite the irascible governor. "I have a strong feeling that if and when such little outbursts occur the quieter the University is," he told federal Judge Wiley Rutledge, a UW alumnus and future Supreme Court justice who had written Heil supporting Garrison, "...the better off we all are. I want no case to become a celebrated case unless it is necessary."[124]

Garrison left his post in 1942 for service with the National War Labor Board, along with a number of other law faculty members and a large part of the student body.[125] Indeed, by 1943 nine of the full-time faculty and the two senior law librarians were on wartime service of various kinds, leaving only four faculty members, including Acting Dean Oliver Rundell, and one librarian to handle the school's greatly reduced wartime enrollment of only 48 students in 1943-44 (in contrast to the pre-war total of 384). During the war Garrison kept in sporadic touch with Law School affairs and made an occasional visit, but his interest seemed to diminish over time. After inconclusive negotiations with President Fred during the spring and summer of 1945,[126] Garrison

---

[124]Dykstra to Wiley Rutledge, June 9, 1941, Dykstra President Papers, 4/15/1, box 65. During the next year Garrison went out of his way to keep the more conservative regents informed about the close ties and services of the Law School to the bar and businesses of the state. See Garrison to Arthur T. Holmes, December 13, 1941, ibid., box 82.

[125]See Garrison to Dykstra, December 31, 1942, ibid., box 103.

[126]During the spring of 1945 President Fred and Garrison corresponded about Garrison's return and discussed the matter in person twice, once in Washington in April and again in Madison in May. There is no record of their discussions, though one suspects Garrison may have raised questions about his UW salary, which had been set at $10,000 in 1932 and because of the depression waivers had remained at $8,400 since. At least Garrison twice expressed concern that he be reimbursed for his travel expenses in connection with his visit to Madison, which suggests that he did not quite view the trip as a return "home." In July President Fred consulted with state Supreme Court Justice John D. Wickhem, a former law faculty member, about Garrison. Fred's summary of the discussion is of interest:

> Judge Wickhem feels that Dean Garrison is a valuable man and should be retained on the University staff if possible. He is well aware of the fact that Lloyd Garrison is difficult to live with, or rather uncomfortable at times. On the other other hand, two important contributions have been made by Dean Garrison to the Law School: (1) The *morale* of the Law School has been greatly improved and two distinguished lawyers have been brought to the campus: Professor Charles Bunn and Professor J.W. Hurst. (2) Wisconsin *rates* above Michigan and Marquette. In fact it rates very much better in the east than it ever has in the past. These two contributions are a result of Dean Garrison's attractive personality and intimate knowledge of law. Judge Wickhem hopes that we will be able to retain Dean Garrison and things [thinks] that we should have the

decided not to come back to Madison but instead returned to private practice in New York City, where for a time he held a part-time law professorship at New York University. The regents promptly confirmed Rundell as the regular Law School dean until his retirement in 1953. Garrison left an activist and social science stamp on the school that was profound and enduring. The Garrison era lasted only a decade, but it was colorful, productive, and gave the Law School its first real national visibility.

As has been noted elsewhere, one of President Frank's more significant and lasting reforms was the separation in 1930 of the School of Education from the College of Letters and Science as a distinct coordinate unit under its own dean, Charles J. Anderson.[127]   The unusual "coordinate" feature, largely the handiwork of L&S Dean George Sellery, set the UW school apart from most other teachers colleges in the country by assuring continuing close ties with the rest of the University, especially the College of Letters and Science. As Dean Anderson described the arrangement in his first University catalog, the School of Education automatically included all faculty who taught the upper level courses used for most secondary school teaching majors and minors: agriculture, botany, chemistry, commerce, economics, English, French, geography, German, history, home economics, Italian, journalism, Latin, library science, mathematics, music, physics, physiology, Spanish, speech, zoology.[128] The list grew longer in later catalogs as other majors were added. These outside faculty members had full rights to participate and vote in Education faculty meetings. Joint faculty appointments with other colleges, notably Letters and Science, continued to be easily arranged and common. Education methods faculty responsible for teacher training and supervision of practice teaching in a particular subject were ordinarily members of the appropriate academic disciplinary department as well, which had a large

---

the subject with various lawyers throughout the State.

The tenor of this discussion indicates that Fred and the regents may have been concerned about how far they should go with respect to meeting Garrison's salary expectations and perhaps other considerations in trying to attract the dean back. Fred, "Memorandum of Conference with Justice John D. Wickhem," July 11, 1945, Fred Presidential Papers, 4/16/1, box 11. See also Garrison to Fred, March 6, 1945; Fred to Garrison, March 23, 1945; Garrison to Fred, May 18, 1945; A.W.P.[eterson] to Fred, May 28, 1945, ibid.

[127]See pp. 103-7.

[128]*General Announcement of Courses, 1931-32 (Catalog 1930-31)*, Bulletin of the University of Wisconsin, Serial No. 1739, General Series No. 1513, July, 1931, p. 347.

voice in the methods faculty member's appointment.

During the period of this volume the relationship between the School of Education and its parent college remained extremely close. The same L&S faculty leaders who faithfully attended and spoke at college faculty meetings also regularly served on School of Education committees and appeared at its faculty meetings, sometimes playing a leading role in debate. From the available records it appears that throughout these years for the most part both groups welcomed and considered their partnership to be natural and fruitful, though there was occasional resentment when L&S representatives blocked or modified a proposal put forward by some of the regular education faculty. An example was English Professor Helen White's outspoken opposition to a children's literature library and a full elementary teacher training program, which as a result did not come into being until after World War II.[129] While the character and extent of the collaboration between the letters and science and the education faculties changed and to a considerable extent eroded in later years, the coordinate feature certainly prevented the sense of academic isolation often felt by education faculty members in other universities.[130]

The chief mission of the School of Education was to train teachers at the junior and senior high school levels. Accordingly, the school consisted of several smaller specialized departments concerned with art education and men's and women's physical education, a much larger Department of Education embracing a variety of pedagogical specialties, including child development, educational psychology, curriculum, and educational administration, and a Department of Educational Methods consisting of those faculty members who offered specialized methods courses and supervised practice teaching in the various major and minor subject fields. Such faculty usually held a joint appointment in the related academic department of either the College of Letters and Science or the College of Agriculture and were associated with Wisconsin High School, a six-year secondary school operated by the University since

---

[129]Lola Pierstorff, oral history interview, 1979, UA. According to Pierstorff, White had ill-concealed disdain for teacher training in general, a view probably shared by other L&S faculty members who, like White, directed their interest to maintaining the rigor of the school's subject area majors.

[130]For generally supportive views of the L&S-School of Education relationship by regular education faculty members, see oral history interviews with Lindley J. Stiles (1979), Glen Eye (1979), Wilson B. Thiede (1979), Warren H. Southworth (1979), John J. Goldgruber (1979), John Anderson (1978), and Milton O. Pella (1979), all at UA.

1911 to provide a place for teacher training and curriculum development. Located in its own building on Henry Mall on the agriculture campus, Wisconsin High by the thirties had become a respected college preparatory school attracting a student body of about three hundred made up largely of children of UW faculty members and the Madison elite. In addition to smaller classes than those of the regular Madison high schools, Wisconsin High offered a more experimental and progressive curriculum with such features as an integrated arts program spanning most of the grades, health instruction in all grades including eventually sex education, and the first high school course in Russian language and culture in Madison.[131] Its chief value to the School of Education, however, was to provide a clinical setting for the supervised practice teaching of its advanced students.

Since the bulk of the school's academic program was at the upper-class level, most of its undergraduate students transferred into it as juniors from one of the four-year colleges, usually Letters and Science. After achieving autonomy in 1930, the school reduced its enrollment somewhat by requiring a 1.25 grade point average (on the 3.0 scale then in use) and a successful interview and speech examination by a faculty selection committee. Thereafter the students were required to maintain at least this level of grade performance. Dean Anderson liked to boast that the overall grade point average of education students was consistently higher than in any other undergraduate unit of the University.[132] Campus skeptics, however, attributed this to the influence of the school's selectivity requirement on its grading practices. During the 1930s the School of Education typically enrolled between six hundred and eight hundred undergraduates, roughly 8 percent of the student body and about two-thirds of the undergraduate enrollment of the College of Engineering. Reflecting the common view that teaching was largely a female occupation, women tended to outnumber men by a 2 to 1 margin in the undergraduate program, as was true of those granted University teaching certificates. Men predominated in the graduate program, especially in the field of educational administration. The school operated a large summer program primarily for teachers taking additional academic work in their teaching fields or working on advanced degrees.

---

[131]Goldgruber, oral history interview.

[132]"Report of the Dean of the School of Education, 1937-38," p. 2, General Presidential Papers, 4/0/2, box 7.

Apart from the continuing influence of letters and science faculty, the School of Education's curriculum offered fairly standard training for prospective secondary school teachers, a mix of education theory and methods courses coupled with supervised practice teaching at Wisconsin High or other nearby schools. One innovative feature beginning in 1926 was a major in dance, the first in the country, in recognition of the strong women's dance program developed by Professor Margaret H'Doubler of the Department of Women's Physical Education.[133] The performances of her student dance group, Orchesis, were a staple part of extracurricular campus entertainment throughout this period. After a major review in 1938-39 the School of Education made several changes in its professional curriculum aimed at making it more child-centered. Three new required laboratory courses were added to the undergraduate program: "The Child: His Nature and His Needs," "The School and Society," and "The Nature and Direction of Learning." Reflecting this desire to offer more work in elementary education, Dean Anderson also launched a campaign for an elementary laboratory school.[134] Another significant curricular change was the addition of a major in applied (or studio) art, which was approved by the University faculty only with the understanding that it might be reassigned to another school or college at some future time.[135]

Beginning with the Frank administration the University made a much more concerted and effective effort to work with the secondary schools of the state to assure that entering students were adequately prepared for college-level work, an endeavor in which the School of Education played a substantial part. The University was essentially an open admissions institution requiring only graduation from an accredited secondary school and a recommendation from the student's high school principal. The faculty had previously tended to assume that its role at the apex of the state's educational system was primarily to uphold

---

[133]L&S Faculty Minutes, October 18, 1926; UW Faculty Document 291, "Dance Major in the Course in Physical Education for Women," October 27, 1926.

[134]"Report of the Dean of the School of Education, 1938-40," General Presidential Papers, 4/0/2, box 10; "Report of the Committee on the Undergraduate Curriculum," January 9, 1939, Dykstra Presidential Papers, 4/15/1, box 24; UW Faculty Minutes, January 8, 1940; UW Faculty Document 589, Graduate School Faculty, "Off-Campus Graduate Seminary Work in Elementary Education," January 8, 1940.

[135]Education Faculty Minutes, May 22, 1939; UW Faculty Minutes, June 5, 1939; UW Faculty Document 573, School of Education Faculty, "Major in Applied Art Leading to Degree B.S. (Applied Art)," June 5, 1939.

rigorous academic standards. Often this policy gave the appearance of being applied with little regard for the human cost in student failures and drops. Generations of students joked with gallows humor about the extra railroad cars needed to carry failed students home after their first semester or year in Madison. In late 1927 the new UW registrar, Frank Holt, noting the high mortality rate at the University, warned a PTA audience that as many as 900 freshmen were in danger of being dropped for poor academic work. He subsequently gave a well-publicized estimate that 1,700 students overall were in jeopardy, a figure amounting to 23 percent of the student body.[136] The actual number of students dropped that semester, as the *Press Bulletin* pointed out with evident relief, turned out to be much lower—"only 433."[137] The figure was nevertheless high enough to demonstrate the validity of President Frank's concern for better articulation with the state's high schools regarding the University's academic expectations.

The primary vehicle for this was the new Bureau of Educational Records and Guidance under the leadership of Registrar Holt and Professor V.A.C. Henmon, a prominent psychologist and former director of the School of Education. The bureau was the University's first sustained effort at centralized institutional research, aptitude testing, and the academic counseling of entering students. Over the next several years Holt and Henmon worked closely with secondary school principals, superintendents, and teachers across the state to develop a statewide aptitude testing program to identify the high school seniors who should be encouraged to go on to college, eventually adopting a test created for this purpose by Henmon himself. In 1931 the bureau, responding to a request by the L&S Fish Curriculum Committee and again in collaboration with the secondary schools, spearheaded the development of a series of subject area achievement tests to evaluate knowledge learned in high school so entering students could be placed at the right level in their University courses.[138] Coupled with more

---

[136] *Capital Times*, December 13, 1927, February 5, 1928; *Daily Cardinal*, December 14, 1927.

[137] *Press Bulletin*, March 21, 1928; *Daily Cardinal*, March 15, 1928.

[138] Chaired by the popular and flamboyant history Professor Carl Russell Fish, the committee's membership included Dean Anderson of the School of Education and represented the first systematic review of the University liberal arts curriculum in more than a decade. The Fish Committee had in mind more systematic institutional research than the University had yet undertaken, perhaps reflecting some skepticism about relying too heavily on aptitude or intelligence testing alone:

systematic academic advising during the University's four-day Freshman Days orientation program at the start of each fall semester—another bureau initiative—the achievement tests helped to assure that freshmen signed up for a set of courses more in keeping with their ability. By 1938 the School of Education was administering these standardized aptitude and achievement tests to more than 75,000 Wisconsin high school students each year.[139] In working with high school teachers during the 1930s to construct and update these tests, UW education and letters and science faculty members were developing a much closer relationship between the University and the lower schools of the state, one that had a beneficial side effect in helping to standardize the content of college preparatory courses.

The School of Education regularly hosted conferences for various state education groups. Dean Anderson also encouraged education faculty to visit schools throughout the state to offer advice and maintain contact with UW alumni. During 1939-40, for example, twenty-five education faculty members visited eight schools in nearly every part Wisconsin from Superior and Sturgeon Bay in the north to Beloit and Cassville in the south. Another outreach activity was the "Teachers Radio Round Table" program offered on Monday afternoons as 4:15 during the school year. The format involved a discussion by three UW faculty members of some educational issue of interest to teachers, who were encouraged to continue the exchange in their own staff meetings.[140] So close were these links by the end of our period that local school districts usually sought the advice of School of Education faculty and administrators in appointing a new superintendent, and the school had

---

The Bureau of Records, with the aid of the School of Education and the Committee on High School Relations, is requested to undertake the experimental work necessary to develop standardized high school achievement and ability tests for the purpose of determining aptitudes and scholastic promise. It is understood that the college and university records of students taking these tests shall be carefully studied and the relation of these records to high school achievement and ability tests be determined.

UW Faculty Document 362, "Report of the L&S Committee on Curriculum Changes," June 2, 1930.

[139]Anderson to George C. Sellery, May 3, 1937, Sellery Presidential Papers, 4/14/1, box 1; Anderson to Dykstra, April 7, 1938, Dykstra Presidential Papers, 4/15/1, box 1; Gustav J. Froehlich, *The Prediction of Academic Success at the University of Wisconsin, 1909-1941*, Bulletin of the University of Wisconsin, General Series No. 2358, Serial No. 2574, October, 1941, pp. 7-36.

[140]"Report of the Dean of the School of Education, 1938-40."

great influence in shaping the certification requirements of the State Department of Public Instruction.[141] Accompanying this increased collaboration was a decision by the School of Education in 1931 to abandon its accreditation of the college preparatory high schools of the state, a function dating back to the late nineteenth century, in favor of the more general DPI supervision.[142]

Agriculture was perhaps not a profession in the same sense as engineering, law, and teaching, but by 1925 the College of Agriculture was surely one of the strongest and most diversified of the specialized academic units of the University. Its towering reputation as probably the best agricultural college in the nation if not the world was based mostly on its path-breaking scientific research and the high quality of its graduate training, as well as on its pioneering statewide extension activities, rather than on its undergraduate programs. Undergraduate enrollment in agriculture declined steadily after the First World War until by the mid-1920s it was only a third of the pre-war level.[143] This was less true of the college's subsidiary unit, the School of Home Economics, whose female staff and student body seemed something of an anomaly in the primarily male college. Because of the association the school offered a much more solid science-based curriculum than was typical of most other home economics programs. Home economics enrollments remained steady during the twenties and surprisingly grew during the depression even as the number and proportion of women in the student body was declining. By 1940 the school accounted for about 7 percent of the undergraduate student body, only slightly less than that of its much larger and better funded parent college.[144] By the time of President Glenn Frank's appointment in 1925 the decline in agriculture enrollments led the Board of Regents to question the traditional University funding priorities favoring the college and to freeze its budget pending a review of its activities. Frank's failure to conduct such a review and to adjust the college's budget to reflect its reduced enrollment was one of the complaints against him by the La Follette

[141]Eye, Anderson, and Pella, oral history interviews.

[142]Anderson to Frank, September 25, 1931, Frank Presidential Papers, 4/13/1, box 109.

[143]In 1914-15, 762 students were enrolled in the college's two undergraduate degree programs, the Long and Middle Courses; by 1924-25 the number had declined to 256. *University of Wisconsin Catalogue, 1914-1915*, Bulletin of the University of Wisconsin, Serial No. 735, General Series No. 539, May, 1915, p. 844, and ibid., *1924-25*, Bulletin of the University of Wisconsin, Serial No. 1315, General Series No. 1092, May, 1925, p. 875.

[144]L. Joseph Lins, "Fact Book for History of Madison Campus," notebook, 1983, UHP.

regents during the early thirties leading up to his firing in 1937.[145]

The heart of the College of Agriculture's undergraduate curriculum was the Long Course, a regular four-year baccalaureate program of 133 credits in required and elective courses of which 24 elective credits were to be taken outside the college. After a major curricular review in 1939 the total number of credits was reduced to 124 with 20 taken outside the college. Previously the college had dropped the requirement, in effect at the beginning of this period, that students in the Long Course must have at least six months of practical experience in farming in order to graduate with a bachelor of science (agriculture) degree. Students without this background experience were placed on farms during several summers. Another undergraduate option was the Middle Course, a two-year program designed to serve those who wanted a more applied and less general scientific education. Students taking this option were required to have at least a year of farming experience and upon completing the program received a diploma with the title Graduate in Agriculture. By 1940 so few students were enrolling in the two-year program that the college faculty decided to drop it.[146] A third option was the non-degree Farm Short Course consisting of two fifteen-week sessions over two winters designed for young working farmers who could spend only a limited amount of time in classes in Madison. The content of the short course was intensely practical and some of the classes were broken up into five-week modules to accommodate the work schedules of the students.

As the Farm Short Course suggests, much of the academic program of the College of Agriculture involved outreach education to serve the farmers and agricultural communities of the state. The college had pioneered in extension education beginning in the late nineteenth century, gradually reaching out to all parts of the state through a network of agricultural extension agents and through such activities as Farmers' Week, Women's Week in Home Economics, and various specialized meetings and non-credit short courses. The appointment of Chris Christensen as agriculture dean in 1931 gave a new direction to some of these outreach activities. Much enamored of the Danish folk school movement, Christensen sought to broaden and enrich the cultural life of Wisconsin's rural communities through an expansion of the

---

[145]See pp. 215-8, 303-12.

[146]UW Faculty Minutes, October 7, 1940; UW Faculty Document 602, College of Agriculture Faculty, "Changes in Requirements," October 7, 1940.

college's traditional extension work. An example was his recruitment of the midwestern regional painter John Steuart Curry in 1936 as the college's artist-in-residence, the first such appointment in the country. He encouraged Curry to focus on rural themes in his own work and to offer instruction to rural residents interested in developing their painting skills and artistic understanding. The result was a lively Wisconsin regional art movement by the 1940s. These agricultural extension activities, by far the most comprehensive and successful of any undertaken by the University in this period, are described more fully in the next chapter.

Academically, the reputation of the College of Agriculture rested on the notable scientific achievements of its faculty and the high quality of its graduate training, which attracted some of the top graduate students in the country and from abroad. Dean Harry Russell had determined this result early in the twentieth century by departing from the conventional view of an agriculture college and developing a number of basic science departments: agricultural bacteriology, agricultural chemistry (later biochemistry), experimental breeding (later genetics), and plant pathology. He built these on an array of more conventional applied departments: agronomy, economic entomology, horticulture, poultry husbandry, soils, veterinary science, animal husbandry, dairy husbandry, agricultural economics, agricultural education, agricultural engineering, and agricultural journalism. During the 1930s Dean Christensen developed several others: dairy industry, rural sociology, and wildlife management. The relationships between the college's basic scientists and the applied and extension faculty were very close, frequently involving joint departmental appointments and collaborative research. Indeed, Russell's oft-used three-legged stool metaphor—emphasizing the inseparable partnership of research with teaching and extension—aptly described the composition of not only the college but also its departments. Deans Russell and Christensen used their position as director of the Agricultural Experiment Station to focus the interdisciplinary resources of the college on a variety of applied problems of concern to Wisconsin farmers. One can understand President Frank's reluctance to pursue the 1925 regents' mandate to cut back the agriculture program, for much of the national stature of the University as well as its popularity throughout the state was derived from its College of Agriculture.

The Liberal Arts

President Frank's passion for the reform of undergraduate education was focussed mostly on the University's large College of Letters and Science, whose numerous departments attracted a majority of UW undergraduates and whose elementary courses in English, mathematics, and the basic sciences served the entire undergraduate student body. The college also housed a number of upper division professional programs: education (until it was spun off as an autonomous school in 1930), commerce (made an autonomous school in 1943), journalism, music, nursing, and pharmacy. After the University took over responsibility for the state's Library School in 1938 it too was assigned to the college. During the inter-war period Letters and Science regularly accounted for between 55 and 65 percent of the total campus enrollment and a slightly higher proportion of the undergraduates.

As L&S enrollment grew, its programs expanded apace. Between 1925 and 1945 the college added new Departments of Art History, Comparative Literature, Comparative Philology (later Linguistics), and Slavic Languages, made separate Departments of Geography/Geology and Philosophy/Psychology, divided the Department of Romance Languages into the Department of French and Italian and the Department of Spanish and Portuguese, and separated Sociology and Social Work from Economics, subsequently adding Anthropology to the new department.[147] In short, the college, whose curriculum embodied that of the original university in 1849, was by this period a good-sized university within itself. Small wonder that President Van Hise, in advocating the development of more applied education against those who like L&S Dean Birge feared undermining the traditional undergraduate liberal arts curriculum, could argue with confidence: "...it is fortunate that in this university the college of letters and science became so firmly established before agriculture and engineering were established. So strong are the liberal arts and pure science, that I have no fear that the college of letters and science will lose its leading position in the University."[148]

---

[147]*University of Wisconsin Catalog, 1925-26*, pp. 58-218; *General Announcement of Courses, 1944-46 (Catalog)*, pp. 35-117. Apart from the loss of the Schools of Education and Commerce, about the only other shrinkage in the expanding L&S empire in this period was the decision, necessitated by the depression, to abolish the small Department of Semitic Languages and Hellenistic Greek.

[148]From remarks at a Town and Gown meeting in 1903, quoted in George C. Sellery, *E.A. Birge: A Memoir* (Madison: University of Wisconsin Press, 1956), p. 39.

Small wonder, too, that Glenn Frank saw Alexander Meiklejohn's Experimental College as only the first step in a larger objective, the reform of the sprawling College of Letters and Science.[149]

Frank was not alone in believing the college needed change. Bart McCormick, formerly head of the Wisconsin Alumni Association and currently the influential director of the state teachers association and secretary of the UW Board of Visitors, led the campaign for an autonomous School of Education in the late 1920s, using his position on the visitors' board to pressure President Frank on the issue. McCormick viewed Dean Sellery's L&S college as the chief obstacle to an independent education school and concluded the college needed major overhauling. The 1928 visitors' report, written by McCormick, was particularly blunt in laying the basis for a separate School of Education:

> In the judgment of this board the numerous departments assembled with varying degrees of coherence and functional unity in the College of Letters and Science, as a whole, are seriously lacking in worth while educational objectives. The departments of this college which have maintained worthwhile educational ideals in spite of the organization, are seriously handicapped by being submerged in a large, unwieldy administrative machine, lacking any definite purpose. This department of the University has long since outgrown its administrative shell, and has lacked the elements necessary to build a new one in keeping with its remarkable numerical and functional expansion. The present conglomerate organization does not stimulate the developing of clear and purposeful educational objectives in its members and thus becomes an effective barrier to progress. The Board of Visitors thus recommends an early and efficient reorganization of the College of Letters and Science into a coordinate college of functional units.[150]

President Frank's incessant praise of the Experimental College, with his implied criticism of the quality of education in Letters and Science, eventually led the L&S dean to defend his college with a public counterattack in the spring of 1929. Sellery's provocative remarks to a freshman convocation praising the quality of L&S teaching and raising questions about the work of the Experimental College angered the president and led him for a time to consider replacing Sellery as dean. Frank also questioned whether the Knaplund Committee, appointed by Sellery to

---

[149]Frank to Meiklejohn, January 16, 1926, Alexander Meiklejohn Papers, box 32, SHSW, and Glenn Frank Papers, Northeast Missouri State University, Kirksville.

[150]"Report of the Board of Visitors," March 7, 1928, BOV Papers, 2/1/1, box 1, UA. McCormick's strong and controversial views may have led President Frank to draw back from giving him a University appointment after gaining regents approval for it the previous June.

review the Meiklejohn experiment during 1928-29, would give it a fair evaluation.[151]

With a critical President Frank on one flank and the Board of Visitors on another, the beleaguered Dean Sellery decided to prove that his faculty colleagues were open to change. Sellery formally raised the question of reviewing the general L&S degree requirements during a college faculty meeting on October 21, 1929. The faculty had already approved modifications of the commerce and journalism programs, and informal conversations seemed to suggest support for additional curricular changes in the college as a whole. Chemistry Chairman J.H. Mathews moved that the dean appoint "a representative committee" to make a study and prepare recommendations.[152] Sellery complied on November 4, naming a twelve-member committee chaired by master lecturer and history Professor Carl Russell Fish and significantly including a representative from the Experimental College, political science Professor John Gaus.[153]

Soon the entire University was debating how to reform liberal education in the L&S college. On December 12, for example, a student committee—with representatives of the Women's Self-Government Association, the Wisconsin Men's Union Board, and the *Daily Cardinal*, an appointee each of the deans of medicine, law, engineering, and the Graduate School, and three named by the L&S administration—met at the University Club to begin planning a report it ultimately would share with the Fish Committee.[154]   Meanwhile, another student committee—informally established and dubbed "Committee B"—also took to the field, co-sponsoring with the Athenae Literary Society several public

Carl Russell Fish

---

[151]See pp. 187-92.

[152]L&S Faculty Minutes, October 21, 1929.

[153]Sellery to members of the Committee on the Curriculum, November 4, 1929, Frank Presidential Papers, 4/13/1, box 85.   Chairman Fish had taught for one semester in the Experimental College, but was dissatisfied with the experience and had declined to continue his involvement.

[154]*Daily Cardinal*, December 13, 1929, February 26, 1930; *Capital Times*, February 26, 1930.

talks and discussions, including one on April 3 with President Frank as the special guest speaker.[155] Frank's address, "The Post-Eliot Era In Liberal Education," was the fourth in a series that advocated the perspective of progressive educationists and backers of the Experimental College.[156] For a time curricular reform was the major topic of campus discussion. Meanwhile, as the Fish Committee hammered out its report, Dean Sellery disappointed the students by announcing that initial faculty consideration of the document would, as always, occur in a closed meeting.[157]

The Fish Committee submitted its report on April 17, 1930, following which a delighted President Frank crafted an exuberant press release stressing its "far-reaching educational significance for students and far-reaching financial significance for taxpayers."[158] After five lively meetings the L&S faculty voted on May 20 to approve a slightly revised set of recommendations. The new rules sought to enhance the undergraduate learning experience by making it more flexible yet more rigorous.[159] Attainment examinations and extended opportunities for advanced independent study encouraged ambitious high school students and underclassmen to apply themselves to their studies. Comprehensive examinations in the major maintained academic pressure on juniors and seniors. A Junior Graduate in Liberal Studies certificate, to be awarded at the end of the sophomore year, provided a measure of recognition for departing students who had demonstrated marginal interest or ability and were denied the opportunity to continue. Another provision, accommodating a legislative mandate passed in 1929, allowed anyone to enroll as a non-degree candidate and thereby take courses without regard to the usual curricular requirements. The influence of the Experimental College was reflected in a provision for a standing faculty Committee on the Curriculum and Methods of Instruction and in a recommendation that three new wide-ranging courses be offered for underclassmen. The

---

[155]*Daily Cardinal*, April 3, 4, and 5, 1930; *Capital Times*, April 5, 1930.

[156]J.K. Hart presented the first talk on the topic, "Current Academic Immoralities"; Dean Max McConn of Lehigh University spoke next on "Democracy and the Curriculum"; and Ohio State educational philosopher Boyd H. Bode discussed "Liberal Education and the Philosophy of Life." *Daily Cardinal*, April 3, 1930.

[157]*Capital Times*, April 23 and 24, 1930; *Daily Cardinal*, April 23, 1930.

[158]Press release, April 19, 1930, Frank Papers, Kirksville.

[159]L&S Faculty Minutes, April 28, May 5, 12, 19, and 20, 1930; L&S Faculty Document 45, "Report of the L&S Committee on Curriculum Changes," April 17, 1930; UW Faculty Document 362; Fish, "How The Faculty Looks at the Curriculum Changes," *WAM*, 31 (June, 1930), pp. 351, 387.

most controversial provision established a new and higher grade require-ment for promotion to the junior class (with the losers being consoled with one of the new liberal studies certificates). Believing it would prove to be politically impossible to drop students with an otherwise passing record, Dean Sellery took the floor to argue unsuccessfully against this change.[160] In the end this requirement never went into effect because almost immediately enrollment began to decline as a consequence of the depression; even proponents of the requirement, including President Frank, recognized it was no time to further reduce University enrollment and income. Implementation of the other reforms varied.[161] Although the Fish Committee's measures were incremental rather than sweeping in their purpose, they nevertheless satisfied Sel-lery's objective of demonstrating his college's openness to curricular change and in fact attracted a good deal of national attention.[162]

A decade later, after prompting by President Dykstra who like Glenn Frank was interested in facilitating more interdisciplinary educa-tion, the College of Letters and Science mounted another curricular review. Dykstra had first suggested to the University Committee in December of 1938 that it undertake an evaluation "of teaching aims and methods, with special reference to the long-time objectives of university instruction." The committee demurred, pointing out the great diversity among the various schools and colleges and suggesting this was a matter best left to their separate faculties.[163] Dykstra next wrote Dean Sellery requesting the L&S college to undertake such a study. The president noted the University Committee's advice for a diversified strategy and said he agreed this was "the right method of approach." In light of the current criticism and interest in educational processes Dykstra thought it a good idea "occasionally to turn to some of the general problems of

---

[160]The new requirement effectively excluded any student with a grade point average of less than 1.1 on the current 3.0 scale and put those with a gpa lower than 1.3 at risk of being dropped for a year at the end of the sophomore year. As Dean Sellery pointed out, this would mean the old "Gentleman's C" no longer sufficed for promotion or graduation, even though such students could transfer to the top Ivy League schools.

[161]George C. Sellery, *Some Ferments at Wisconsin, 1901-1947: Memories and Reflections* (Madison: University of Wisconsin Press, 1960), pp. 40-4.

[162]See correspondence in Carl Russell Fish Papers, box 8, SHSW. Fish was asked to write articles about the Wisconsin reforms for *Science and Society*, the *Journal of Higher Education*, and the American Association of University Professors. See Raymond Walters to Fish, September 25, 1930; W.H. Cowley to Fish, November 17, 1930; Fish to H.W. Tyler, November 12, 1930, ibid.

[163]See pp. 351-4.

education which lie at the heart of university procedures." While a university was quite different from an industrial organization, it would nevertheless be useful to "appraise our practices, reconsider objectives and know much more about ourselves than we do." Sounding rather like his repudiated predecessor, the president observed: "Perhaps the whole field of college instruction has had little exploring because the scholarly interests of our faculties are specialized and departmentalized."

Dykstra concluded by posing a series of ten questions, "which are puzzling me...and that I should like to have some help in finding the answers." The queries in effect proposed a comprehensive and continuing educational survey of the University and were revealing indicators of the president's thinking. Their scope was in fact breathtaking, ranging from uncertainty about "a broad educational objective" for the L&S college and the University, to the appropriateness of current entrance and credit requirements. In between, they questioned the suitability of existing academic programming for the great bulk of the UW student body.[164] Like Frank, Dykstra obviously believed the external world was changing and that the University must respond accordingly. But his difference in tone and tactic was striking. President Frank had offered his critical ideas publicly and assertively, in the process often antagonizing and alienating the very faculty members whose support he needed to bring about meaningful change. Dykstra, on the other hand, raised his points privately, diffidently, and with careful regard to collegial feelings and prerogatives. Within a few years the effectiveness of this tentative approach would be demonstrated in a series of significant collaborative faculty-administration reforms.

Dean Sellery quickly responded by appointing the Committee on Curriculum and Educational Procedure following approval by the L&S faculty on March 20, 1939, of his recommendation for such a study. The nine-member committee was an impressive group, consisting of eight prominent L&S scholars and the secretary of the faculty, and chaired by chemistry Professor Farrington Daniels.[165] Not only was Daniels a respected scientist, he also had a solid record of work on important campus-wide bodies, including the Committee on Courses and

---

[164]Dykstra to Sellery, March 14, 1939, Dykstra Presidential Papers, 4/15/1, box 37.

[165]In addition to Daniels, the committee included Professors E.M. Gilbert, Harold Groves, Grayson Kirk, L.E. Noland, H.A. Pochmann, R.L. Reynolds, I.S. Sokolnikoff, and W.F. Twadell, and C.A. Smith, secretary of the faculty.

the University Committee. His selection suggested that the Daniels Committee would take a broad view of its charge. Like the earlier Fish Committee, the Daniels Committee had more to concern itself with than simply a new president's broad vision of the University of the future. It was instantly involved in a heated debate over the curriculum and instruction in the College of Letters and Science. Soon the committee was swamped with advice and importunities from student groups, individual faculty members, the Faculty Teachers' Union, the president, and others.

Although Daniels and his colleagues tried to take these varied constituencies into account, in the end they were guided by the constraints of a continuing tight University budget. The result was a rather narrow report in the spring of 1940 that "endeavored to recommend only practicable changes which can go into effect next year." Not surprisingly, no one was fully satisfied. A radical student group expressed its deep disappointment in the respectful tones characteristic of students of the day:

> Your efforts to revise the curriculum of the College of Letters and Science must certainly be regarded as a laudable step toward an improved curriculum. We feel, however, despite the claims of an over-exuberant press, the report does not "place the University of Wisconsin among the American universities leading in the task of modernizing its teaching work."[166]

The Teachers' Union complained that the report was fragmented and generally deficient.[167] The Daniels Committee's major recommendation was for three new interdisciplinary courses—a one-credit Freshman Forum, a three-credit Senior Survey later called Contemporary Trends, and a new course on the History and Significance of Science. While this outcome was modest, the courses were feasible in a period of tight budgets and were soon in place, with the president himself helping to plan and teach in the Freshman Forum. The new offerings were designed as electives open to all undergraduates across the campus. As the committee explained in its report, it "sought to broaden the intellectual opportunities of those who come to the University even for a short time and to help them to fill better their future places in the state and the nation, and sought to do this without lowering scholastic standards

---

[166] Open letter to the Daniels Committee from Flora Wovschin, chairman of the ULLA Curriculum Committee, *Daily Cardinal*, February 27, 1940.

[167] *Wisconsin State Journal*, February 9, 1940.

in any way."[168] The most significant and lasting of the Daniels Committee recommendations turned out to be the launching of the study of the history of science at the University. Out of it came one of the earliest and in time one of the most respected academic departments in this field in the country, as well as the development of a major specialized library collection supporting its work.

That President Dykstra had hoped the Daniels Committee might go further in its curricular review and recommendations is suggested by the alacrity with which he embraced a proposal by the University faculty in January, 1940, to create a more ambitious study group. Although the impetus for this University-wide committee was the serious budget cut imposed by Governor Heil in his first term, in the faculty debate Dykstra advocated a standing committee "to study educational problems" more broadly. The resulting compromise was a special, not a standing, Committee on Quality of Instruction and Scholarship, with a mandate that both the University Committee and President Dykstra broadened as the committee set about its work.[169] Dykstra's academic leadership might have appeared hesitant and tentative, but unlike his predecessor he was careful to respect faculty prerogatives and to work through his academic deans. Although the resulting changes were incremental rather than sweeping, they proved more enduring than Glenn Frank's more ambitious reform plans.

Between 1925 and the eve of the Second World War University enrollments grew by 44 percent, in the process more than recovering from the temporary decline experienced in the early years of the great depression. This could not be said of the UW operating budget nor of the classroom and other academic facilities needed to serve a growing student body. Both lagged seriously behind the growth in the student body. Not until 1944 were the regents able to restore the last of the faculty and staff salary waivers imposed as part of the depression budget

---

[168]UW Faculty Document 591, "Report of the Faculty of the College of Letters and Science on Curriculum and Educational Procedure," March 4, 1940; UW Faculty Minutes, March 4, 1940. The L&S faculty had received the Daniels Committee report, L&S Faculty Document 68, on February 12, 1940. Debate began that day and continued through February 19, 26, and 27, 1940. On February 27 the L&S faculty approved the revised report, which became UW Faculty Document 591 and was approved by the Board of Regents on March 9, 1940.

[169]See pp. 353-6.

cuts more than a decade before. Nor was the board able to do much about the large and growing backlog of unmet campus construction needs that had to be deferred during the depression and war years. Still, it was impressive how well the University adapted to adversity, taking advantage of private and federal funds to add or remodel some facilities when state funding was unavailable, generally maintaining and in some instances improving faculty and program quality, and launching a number of new curricular initiatives designed to expand and enrich the educational enterprise. At a time when UW students and faculty alike could easily have lost heart, their collective esprit remained remarkably high, their faith in their University's greatness and promise undimmed.

13.

The Boundaries of the Campus

As an institution of the state, the University of Wisconsin was from the beginning assumed to have a public service mission. At first this primarily involved on-campus instruction. Before long, however, the University became involved with other public educational agencies and its personnel began to move off campus, figuratively and often literally. Also, by the late nineteenth century, UW faculty research, particularly in the natural sciences, was helping significantly to improve the quality of life in Wisconsin. The growing complexity of these varied efforts led to a recognition of the need to assure that University scholarship reached those Wisconsin residents who might benefit from its findings. Gradually around the turn of the century a variety of University agencies were developed for this purpose. Chief among them were the University Summer Session, the College of Agriculture's Cooperative Extension Service, and the University Extension Division. To these was added during the inter-war period the educational radio station WHA, a powerful new means of connecting the University with the public. Together these various outreach agencies expressed what became widely known as the "Wisconsin Idea," embodied in the proud slogan "the boundaries of the campus are the boundaries of the state."

The University and the Schools

By the mid-1920s a close relationship had developed between the University and other components of Wisconsin public education. Indeed, the earliest University outreach activity occurred prior to the Civil War, when President Henry Barnard (1859-60) devoted more attention

757

to his cherished teachers' institute movement than he did to his University duties. President Thomas C. Chamberlin (1887-92) continued this tradition of UW assistance to the common schools, while at the same time encouraging the state's developing public high school movement. The increasingly numerous secondary schools promised for the first time to provide the University with significant numbers of adequately prepared students. First, however, their teachers needed better training, especially in the modern laboratory- and field-based sciences. Chamberlin—a prominent geologist—in 1887 encouraged Professor John W. Stearns to set up a summer school on the UW campus to begin addressing this problem. A professor of pedagogy and psychology as well as head of the Wisconsin Teachers Association and editor of the *Wisconsin Journal of Education*, Stearns was uniquely qualified to bridge the wide academic gulf between most of the UW faculty and the personnel of the lower schools. In 1889 the legislature began making the first of a number of annual appropriations to support Stearns' Summer School for Teachers.[1] Prominent University faculty readily agreed to teach in the Summer Session, leading President Charles Kendall Adams (1892-1901) to observe enthusiastically in 1896, "There is no question but that the School has materially improved the teaching of science and other branches in the high schools of the state."[2]

By the First World War summer schooling had become a solid and respectable feature of the University's instructional program, no longer limited to teacher training, though teachers continued throughout the inter-war years to be the largest component of the summer student body. Indeed, at first the regents resisted the recommendations of Presidents Chamberlin and Adams that the board formally sponsor Stearns' Summer School for Teachers, since most of the students were not candidates for a degree. Unexpectedly, significant numbers of regular UW stu-

---

[1]The legislature declined to fund the program for 1893 due to the competing Columbian Exposition in Chicago, which led to the cancellation of that summer session.

[2]Quoted in Scott H. Goodnight, *The Story of the Origins and Growth of the Summer School and the Summer Session, 1885-1940* (Madison: Office of the Summer Session, 1940), p. 26. Among the University faculty offering courses were Edward A. Birge (physiology and zoology), William W. Daniells (chemistry), Franklin H. King (physics and botany), Lucius Hermitage (Latin), and John W. Stearns (psychology and teaching methods). President Chamberlin worked informally with the students, probably in his field of geology. This discussion of the UW Summer Session relies heavily on Goodnight's history and John W. Jenkins and Barry Teicher, "Origins and History of the UW Summer Session" in *Education In Summer: 100 Years At UW-Madison* (Madison: Division of Summer Sessions and Inter-College Programs, 1985).

dents began enrolling in summer courses either to enrich their programs or to speed their progress toward a degree. Wary of overstepping its bounds, however, the board hesitated, even after the legislature unilaterally increased the University budget and pointedly granted specific enabling legislation in 1897. Two years later, with increasing numbers of students remaining in Madison for summertime study, the regents half-heartedly came up with a rather awkward solution. The Summer School for Teachers, still under the direction of Professor Stearns, would continue as a semi-independent enterprise dedicated primarily to serving teachers. Additionally, and running simultaneously with Stearns' school, a new UW Summer Session, led by Letters and Science Dean Edward A. Birge, would sponsor courses for regular degree-seeking students. In 1904, with the advent of the high-energy Van Hise administration (1903-1918), the board consolidated the two complementary summer programs and appointed history Professor Dana C. Munro director. When Munro left for Princeton in 1906, his administrative duties were taken up by another historian, George C. Sellery, whose developing administrative skills would lead him in time to the L&S deanship. Birge, Munro, and Sellery all aimed to give the summer school academic respectability. By the time Scott H. Goodnight succeeded Sellery in 1912, the UW Summer Session had developed into a permanent, reputable, and effective instructional and service agency of the University.

Director Goodnight also gave special attention to extracurricular needs of summer students. While serving as assistant director in 1911, Goodnight arranged with Dr. Joseph S. Evans of the student infirmary to provide health care in the summer. "Hundreds of teachers enter wearied from the work of the school year and in poor physical condition," explained Goodnight in 1914. "They eagerly avail themselves of the opportunity for free medical advice, and in the great majority of cases they leave the session in better health than upon their arrival." Goodnight's summer sessions office funded this special service until 1924, when the regents placed the infirmary on a full twelve-month operating basis, open to every registered student year-round. In 1913 Goodnight developed the University's innovative summer tent colony. Located on the shore of Lake Mendota west of the campus on the Eagle Heights farm, the colony provided inexpensive but serviceable living facilities for dozens of married summer students and their families. In addition to its attractive rustic setting, the tent colony made University study possible for many teachers who otherwise could not afford to relocate to Madison. Albert F. Gallistel, the University superintendent of buildings and grounds, deserved much of the credit for the success and popularity of the colony. He and his wife lived at the colony each season, cultivating a remarkably supportive and close-knit community. They were so popular with the residents that beginning about 1932 the colony became affectionately and widely known as Camp Gallistela.[3]

Goodnight, whom President Van Hise appointed as the University's first dean of men in 1916, administered the Summer Session as director and then dean (beginning in 1930) through 1942.[4] The program thrived during the 1920s, with enrollments growing from fewer than 2,000 before World War I to more than 5,000. Teachers regularly comprised about half the total. The Summer Session achieved a degree of national prominence during the period, with surveys identifying it as one of the largest programs for teachers, behind only those of Columbia and Chicago.[5] Summer brought a somewhat different set of student disciplinary issues: the appropriateness of shorts as campus clothing, the appearance of men's topless swim suits on University beaches in violation of a city ordinance, and the increased temptation of unchaperoned picnics and dancing parties. In 1923 Graduate School Dean Charles S. Slichter proposed that the graduate summer term be lengthened from six to nine weeks, to encourage the progress of summer-only master's degree students, most of them educators. Goodnight and the University faculty eventually supported the change, which took effect in 1927.[6]

Another notable development occurred at this time. During the summer of 1924 and in cooperation with Director Goodnight, the Madison YWCA provided scholarships for eight young working women selected from a pool of one hundred applicants to enroll in three lower-

---

[3]On health care services see "Summer Session Annual Report for 1914," n.d., p. 25, UW-Madison Summer Sessions and Inter-College Programs Office. On the tent colony see Goodnight, *Story of the Origins and Growth*, pp. 48-50; "University 'City' Will Soon Spring Up on Lake Mendota," *WAM*, 35 (May, 1934), 230.

[4]Prior to 1916 Goodnight, whose academic rank was associate professor of German, had served as the de facto dean of men through his position as chairman of the faculty Student Life and Interests Committee. In 1930 President Glenn Frank changed Goodnight's summer session title from director to dean.

[5]In the fall of 1925 the UW Summer Session enrollment of 5,017 ranked third nationally, behind Columbia University's 12,700 and the University of Chicago's 5,800. *Capital Times*, September 30, 1925.

[6]UW Faculty Minutes, December 6, 1926, UA; UW Faculty Document 294, Graduate School Faculty, "Nine-week Graduate Courses in the Summer Session," December 6, 1926, UA.

division English, economics, and physical education courses. The experimental objective, as reported by Goodnight in his annual report for 1924, was to bring "into comradeship and mutual appreciation and helpfulness, girls in industry and girls in college."[7] Forty-one scholarships were available in 1925, but this time for special, sub-freshman-level classes more suitable to the students' limited academic backgrounds. Goodnight, for his part, suspected that the program might have been "better amalgamated with the session as a whole."[8] In 1926 President Frank appointed an advisory committee that included representation from the University, the YWCA, and organized labor. Frank also arranged the first official UW financial support, under summer session auspices, for what by then was known as the School for Workers in Industry, which promptly ran a deficit of nearly $700—much greater than the shortfall for any other summertime program. In 1927 men were first admitted to the program and an executive secretary and field agent, Alice Shoemaker, was hired to canvass the state for additional financial support. Yet the deficits continued throughout the decade while concerns of organized labor overpowered those of the founders, producing further isolation of the program on campus. By 1930 Director Goodnight had concluded that the University had become an inappropriate provider of exceedingly expensive sub-freshman-level courses that might better be taught at public vocational schools located in the state's industrial centers. The School for Workers in Industry would remain permanently at the University, although its administrative connection with the Summer Session was severed in 1932.[9]

The depression had a drastic effect on summer study. Between 1931 and 1932 summer enrollments declined precipitously to 3,724, a drop of 26 percent. Competition for funding among the University's several schools and colleges resulted in a unanimous recommendation of the academic deans—not including Goodnight—that the 1933 Summer

---

[7]Quoted in Goodnight, *Story of the Origins and Growth*, pp. 65-6.

[8]Ibid., p. 67.

[9]For overviews of the School for Workers and its relations with the UW Summer Sessions, see Ernest E. Schwartztrauber, *The University of Wisconsin School for Workers: Its First Twenty-five Years* (Madison: University of Wisconsin School for Workers, 1949); Howard S. Miller, *Summer Sessions, 1885-1960: A Seventy-Fifth Anniversary Review* (Madison: University of Wisconsin Summer Session, 1960), pp. 28-30; Dagmar Schultz, "The Changing Political Nature of Workers' Education: A Case Study of the Wisconsin School for Workers" (Ph.D. diss., University of Wisconsin-Madison, 1972); Robert W. Ozanne, *The Labor Movement in Wisconsin: A History* (Madison: State Historical Society of Wisconsin, 1984), pp. 153-5.

Session be cancelled in response to a drastic state budget cut. Perhaps more in touch with the wishes of Wisconsin teachers and school administrators, however, the regents anguished over the deans' proposal and finally compromised by putting the Summer Session on a self-supporting basis, promising to dock faculty summer salaries to make up for any revenue shortfall. Dean Goodnight and the teaching staff labored under this fiscal burden until 1938 when an improved economy allowed the board to resume guaranteed salary commitments. Other institutions also faced difficult enrollment and financial problems. A typical response among the University's rivals was to reduce graduate degree credit requirements and shorten the summer term in order to attract more summer students.[10] Goodnight ineffectually cried "unfair competition" even as the UW session's relative enrollment position failed to deteriorate as he predicted. Nevertheless, the dean's complaints helped convince the University faculty in late 1939 to shorten the longer summer term from nine to eight weeks while also leaving the six-week session in place.[11]

Dean Goodnight in 1942

---

[10]UW's principal rivals were Teachers College of Columbia University, Northwestern University, and the Universities of Chicago, Michigan, and Iowa.

[11]L&S Dean George Sellery remained a friend of the Summer Session. In late 1938 he offered a successful resolution to the UW faculty to establish a special committee to consider and report on the length of the session. UW Faculty Minutes, November 7, 1938. The committee roster was distinguished, including J.D. Hicks (chairman), C.J. Anderson, S.M. Corey, F. Daniels, M.H. Ingraham, W.F. Twaddell, and E.E. Witte. UW Faculty Minutes, December 5, 1938. The committee reported in November, 1939, offering two plans: the first for a single eight-week session, and the second for a combination six/eight-week session. The faculty discussed and tabled the report. Ibid., November 6, 1939; UW Faculty Document 585, "Report of Special Committee on Length of the Summer Session," November 6, 1939. The faculty met again two weeks later in special session to receive a revised report. This time the faculty voted to approve a six/eight-week session, with undergraduates encouraged to enroll in the longer term. UW Faculty Document 585A, "Revised Report of the Special Committee on Length of the Summer Session," November 20, 1939; UW Faculty Minutes, November 20, 1939. The Board of Regents approved this faculty action to take effect in the summer of 1940. BOR Minutes, January 19, 1940, UA.

Goodnight used the occasion of the wartime year-round calendar of 1942 to resign his summer session deanship. The regents replaced him with education Professor John Guy Fowlkes, an energetic and progressive advocate for professional educators who had run a highly respected school administrators' program during the summer for over a decade. In appointing Fowlkes the authorities guaranteed that the Summer Session would remain alert to the needs of its base constituency—the school people of Wisconsin.[12]

Wisconsin educators found many professional reasons to visit the University campus besides formal summer study. In 1926 the men's physical education department began running what would become a nationally respected coaching clinic, and the College of Engineering organized a unique program for engineering teachers in 1927. Throughout the inter-war period the College of Agriculture maintained its long-time commitment to providing in-service instruction for agricultural teachers of the state. In 1934 the speech department offered the first of several well-received summer drama and speech institutes. The School of Education, under Professor Fowlkes' initiative, in 1929 began sponsoring annual institutes for educational administrators. The depression brought new challenges. In 1932 the school hosted a meeting of more than five hundred principals and superintendents from five states to explore ways to meet the educational problems of the deepening economic slump. During the 1930s and 1940s the School of Education conducted annual summer teachers' institutes, opened a retraining program for unemployed teachers, assisted teachers in restructuring their courses in light of the depression, and offered suggestions on how to meet the wartime teacher shortage.

These non-credit institutes, conferences, and clinics benefited from the long-standing University tradition of close cooperation among the institution's various parts. While the sponsoring academic departments usually provided most of the staffing, faculty members from other schools and colleges frequently contributed their special expertise. The Memorial Union and the Division of Dormitories and Commons helped with arrangements for meeting rooms, food service, and overnight accommodations. Often Scott Goodnight and his small summer session staff or the University Extension Division offered experienced assistance in planning and publicity. Whatever the nature of involvement, the

---

[12]The regents accepted Goodnight's resignation following the 1942 session and immediately named Fowlkes as his successor. BOR Minutes, September 26, 1942.

events typically ran as their organizers wished with essentially no friction and much institutional collaboration.

Besides helping to manage campus-based programs, the University Extension Division also provided off-campus credit and non-credit services to Wisconsin educators. In 1928, for example, teachers accounted for a fifth of the division's correspondence course registrants. That same year Extension helped organize a special state-wide Parents Teachers Association study course. In 1930 Extension offered a new course for teachers of history to help them gain familiarity with important sources of data and analysis. As the depression deepened, many school boards were forced to cut the pay of their teachers, who then had to curtail their usual summer studies in Madison or elsewhere. At the same time, however, the pressures to upgrade the educational attainments of high school instructors continued largely unabated. Teachers thus had to find more economical ways to continue their professional studies. In response the University Extension Division began offering more evening classes at locations throughout the state. This built on the program launched in 1927 with the Wisconsin Vocational Directors Association and its leader George P. "Hammy" Hambrecht to assist the state's county-based vocational schools with their adult education programs.

Other University staff members also spent time away from the campus working with their fellow Wisconsin educators. There was usually a good UW representation at the annual state teachers convention in Milwaukee. In 1928, for example, President Frank addressed the group and Professors C.J. Anderson and Walter Agard participated in the program. The next year the association arranged for more than a dozen UW professors to work with various of its subgroups. Coincidentally, the University was taking steps to upgrade the status of the School of Education by separating it from the College of Letters and Science, a move much applauded by Wisconsin school groups.[13] President Frank's concern for Wisconsin's public school establishment did not of course go unnoticed, and in 1930 the Wisconsin Superintendents and Principals Association asked him to address its annual convention on recent changes influencing Wisconsin high school-UW relations. Frank and forty-seven of his University colleagues also participated in the teachers association meeting being held concurrently in Milwaukee. The UW president was a leading critic of depression-era

---

[13]See pp. 103-8.

cuts in education spending and used his 1932 address at the annual meeting of superintendents and principals to publicize his objections. President Dykstra took over Frank's keynoter role at professional education meetings in 1937, joining the substantial number of UW faculty members participating in the conventions. A more concrete form of University cooperation with state educators came in 1935, when the School of Education and the Graduate School opened an experimental two-year master's degree program in education at the state teachers colleges in Eau Claire and Stevens Point. Deemed a success by 1937, the program thereafter expanded to serve teachers in ten cities across Wisconsin.[14]

Several other UW departments offered direct services to school-age children of the state. The largest and most comprehensive example was Wisconsin High School, located on the Henry Mall at University Avenue. Taken over from the Madison Academy in 1911 and moved to its own new building in 1914, Wisconsin High functioned under the direction of the School of Education as a laboratory of secondary school-level innovation and as the site for supervised practice teaching for education majors. Over time the school gained a reputation for high quality college preparatory instruction with an enrollment of about 400 young people coming substantially from the families of University employees and Madison-area professionals.[15] The School of Journalism may have been the earliest University department to host groups of high school students from across Wisconsin after 1919 when Professor Willard G. Bleyer organized its first annual conference of high school student editors. The events typically lasted two days and met in the Wisconsin High School building or the Memorial Union.[16] During the summer of 1927 music Professor Edgar B. "Pop" Gordon recruited sixty-five fifth and sixth grade students for an experimental course in the teaching of music. The effort was a resounding success, and it encouraged Gordon's departmental colleagues to join him in setting up the school's summer Music Clinic in 1929. Over the years the program

---

[14]UW Graduate Faculty Minutes, October 18, 1935; UW Graduate Faculty Document 11, Frank Presidential Papers, 4/13/1, box 179, UA; *Press Bulletin*, December 8, 1937.

[15]For a review of the school's history to 1929, including a discussion of its relation to Alexander Meiklejohn's Experimental College, see John Dixon, "Wisconsin High, An Experiment," *WAM*, 30 (January, 1929), 115, 140.

[16]During 1937 the *Daily Cardinal* offered additional opportunities to high school editors by allowing some of them to work as "guest reporters" for the paper. *Daily Cardinal*, November 27, 1937.

regularly attracted hundreds of enthusiastic participants. By 1941 the schedule included a clinic faculty concert, a summer session band concert, an informal sing, an all-state orchestra and chorus festival concert, and an all-state band festival concert.[17] At a different level, during the summer of 1935 the School of Education opened an experimental program for nursery and elementary school children that emphasized "observation, demonstration, and experimentation." By 1937 the continuing program had become known as the campus Laboratory School.[18]

There were also a number of liaison arrangements defining the process of admitting students for regular University study. These took place at various institutional levels according to the particular academic needs. During the nineteenth century the University and the public schools developed a high school visitation and accreditation procedure that guaranteed admission for graduates of approved programs.[19] The University's part of this approval process took place under the direction of the faculty Committee on High School Relations and involved regular inspection and consultation with participating high schools by UW faculty members. Under the influence and energetic assistance of Registrar Frank Holt and Professor V.A.C. Henmon, President Frank sought to expand the program through a state-wide psychological testing program designed to identify high school students who should be encouraged to go on to college studies. To gain the cooperation of other Wisconsin higher education leaders, in 1927 Frank assumed leadership of a special committee on institutional cooperation of the Association of Wisconsin Presidents and Deans. Holt addressed the association in 1929 on the early results of the program, which continued to expand throughout the 1930s, eventually using an aptitude test designed by Henmon. The depression curtailed the University's high

---

[17]The *Daily Cardinal* of July 9, 1938, boasted that the Music Clinic was "a result of Wisconsin pioneering and of the university's desire to be of service to all of the people in the state."

[18]*Press Bulletin*, May 11, 1938. The *Daily Cardinal* for July 9, 1938, contains a good historical overview of the Laboratory School. See also L.E. Luberg, "They Learn From Children," *WAM*, 40 (February, 1939), 116-7. The school was so successful that in 1940 the Board of Regents approved a University Extension Division proposal to sponsor a similar program in Milwaukee in cooperation with the public schools and the state teachers college there. BOR Minutes, January 19-20, 1940; UW Faculty Document 589, Graduate School Faculty, "Off-Campus Graduate Seminary Work in Elementary Education," January 8, 1940.

[19]Merle Curti and Vernon Carstensen, *The University of Wisconsin: A History, 1848-1925* (Madison: University of Wisconsin Press, 1949), vol. 2, pp. 233-66.

school visitation and consultation service, until in the spring of 1932 the faculty adopted new regulations substituting approval by the state Department of Public Instruction for the UW inspection program. With regard to advanced standing and graduate admissions, the University worked through the L&S Committee on Normal School Relations, the UW faculty Committee on Advanced Standing, and the presidents and deans association. Thus throughout the inter-war period the University maintained many, varied, and constructive relationships with the rest of Wisconsin's educational establishment.

Improving Agricultural and Rural Life

With the adoption of the federal Morrill Land Grant College Act in 1862, the University's involvement with Wisconsin agriculture was assured, though there was initial faculty resistance to including applied studies in the curriculum. The Morrill Act authorized each state legislature to designate an institution to receive a substantial federal land grant in return for offering practical instruction in engineering and agricultural science. The University accepted Wisconsin's land grant designation in 1866 after Dane County pledged $40,000 to buy land for an experimental farm on the western edge of the campus. Two years later the regents appointed W.W. Daniells to manage the facility and teach courses in agriculture and chemistry. Unfortunately for Daniells' new "department," however, not many students enrolled in it. Before long the young professor was obliged to teach only the regular chemistry course and manage the farm, which the regents expected to pay its expenses while incidentally supplying the campus with firewood. Few Wisconsin farmers saw any reason to send their sons to the University to study agricultural science, when everyone knew that farming was an art, best learned through practical experience at home. In Wisconsin—as elsewhere in the early decades of the University—the day of scientific agriculture and commercial farming had not yet arrived.[20]

---

[20]This section is based heavily on four works: W.H. Glover, *Farm and College: The College of Agriculture of the University of Wisconsin, A History* (Madison: University of Wisconsin Press, 1952); E.R. McIntyre, *Fifty Years of Cooperative Extension in Wisconsin, 1912-1962* (Madison: Cooperative Extension Service, 1962); Edward H. Beardsley, *Harry L. Russell and Agricultural Science in Wisconsin* (Madison: University of Wisconsin Press, 1969); and John W. Jenkins, *A Centennial History: A History of the College of Agricultural and Life Sciences at the University of Wisconsin-Madison* (Madison: College of Agricultural and Life Sciences, 1991).

This situation began to change during the 1880s. The recently formed Wisconsin Dairymen's Association launched a campaign to persuade farmers to shift from grain production to dairying, inasmuch as it was increasingly clear they could not profitably compete with the great wheat farms of Kansas, Nebraska, and the Dakotas. Hiram Smith, a successful farmer and association leader, early appreciated the importance of science and education in this effort. In 1880 he organized a series of farmers' meetings around the state where thriving producers could share the secrets of their success. After he was appointed to the Board of Regents he used his position to energize the University's inchoate agricultural program.

Smith's greatest contribution as a regent was to hire biologist William Arnon Henry, a recent graduate of Cornell University, to direct the work. Henry appreciated the vital need to persuade Wisconsin farmers to take advantage of science-based agricultural knowledge. In 1881 he convinced the legislature to fund a small research project, whose results he publicized throughout the state. Two years later the legislature funded his proposal for a UW Agricultural Experiment Station, which in 1887 joined the new national system created by the federal Hatch Act of 1886. Still, Smith and Henry chafed under President Bascom's liberal arts orientation and participated in a broadly based effort to persuade the legislature to set up a specialized college of agriculture and shift the land grant and other federal support it. To head off this divisive threat, Smith's regent colleagues responded in 1885 by creating the Farm Short Course, a highly practical twelve-week training program for young men planning to make a career of farming. To Henry's surprise, the short course soon flourished, and for the first time the University could be said to be meeting the agricultural instruction mandate of the Morrill Act. The separation movement collapsed, due partly to legislative funding of a new Farmers' Institute program based on Hiram Smith's earlier farmers' meetings. The institutes provided a regular means to showcase University research findings to thousands of state farmers. By 1889, when a general University restructuring transformed the agriculture department into the College of Agriculture, the land grant vision had taken firm root in Wisconsin.

William Henry presided over the College of Agriculture as dean from 1891 to 1907. He also carried the title, conferred in 1887, of Director of the Experiment Station. Much of the college's effectiveness during this period derived from the almost complete lack of undergraduate interest in agricultural instruction, which freed college faculty to make full use the special state and federal funding for scientific research. The result was a steady stream of practical developments in dairy production, animal nutrition, plant growth and diseases, soil fertility, and agricultural engineering. The Farmers' Institutes operated as a major college outreach mechanism. Typically structured as two-day winter events at locations throughout the state, the varied institute programs—heavily staffed by college experts—enabled participants to share information and to become personally acquainted with each other and with college staff members. Readily available institute bulletins summarized each year's proceedings. The institutes were buttressed by more formal and intensive short courses. The Farm Short Course in Madison remained the mainstay, particularly after 1896 when Dean Henry placed it under the energetic direction of agronomist Ransom A. Moore. A more specialized Dairy Short Course opened in 1890 to train factory operators. Both courses became models for subsequent campus-based programs and over time graduated hundreds of college enthusiasts throughout the commercial farming community. Professor Moore capitalized on this in 1901 by organizing the Wisconsin Agricultural Experiment Association, which involved short course alumni in the college's agronomy field tests and in an effective seed and plant distribution network.

Ironically, the seemingly unbounded success of the institutes and other farmers' meetings, short courses, and the experiment association helped produce conditions that threatened the college's future. By the turn of the century Dean Henry was complaining that these popular programs, combined with increased demand for credit teaching, were monopolizing his staff's time and seriously undermining its scientific productivity upon which the entire program depended. State funds could be counted on to provide instructors for the growing numbers of full-time degree students. Local funds were inadequate, however, to meet the ever-growing demand of practicing farmers for up-to-date scientific and technical information. Henry therefore turned for help to the federal government. The eventual result was the Adams Act of 1906, which significantly limited its appropriations "only to paying the necessary expenses of conducting original researches or experiments."[21]

---

[21]Quoted in Norwood Allen Kerr, *The Legacy: A Centennial History of the State Agricultural Experiment Stations, 1887-1987* (Columbia, Missouri: Missouri Agricultural Experiment Station, University of Missouri-Columbia, 1987), p. 49.

While the Adams Act did not pay for outreach activity, it indirectly addressed Henry's concerns by freeing some funding from the Hatch Act of 1886 and 1890 for extension work.[22] Pleased with the progress of his college, proud of his leading role in gaining passage of the Adams Act, and probably weary of political intrigues against him, Dean Henry resigned his position at the University in 1907. He had played a critical role in building the College of Agriculture.

He was succeeded as dean and director by bacteriology Professor Harry L. Russell. A Wisconsin native and UW graduate who was widely traveled and highly respected for his scientific accomplishments and business acumen, Russell shared his predecessor's commitment to the land grant college vision. At the same time his brusque, hard-hitting, no-nonsense style was in sharp contrast to Henry's easy-going, folksy approach to the college's farming and legislative constituencies. Russell was nevertheless better suited for the University that President Van Hise was building in the early twentieth century, an institution with distinct institutional structures designed to provide a variety of applied services to the people of Wisconsin.

Russell's commitment to the Van Hise vision was reflected in his efforts to formalize and expand the outreach function of his college. The dean expanded on Henry's model by staffing each college department with personnel in all three functional areas—teaching, research, and extension. Russell and the agriculture faculty soon likened this arrangement to the "three-legged stool" used in milking cows. Each leg supported the others and all made vital contributions to the overall departmental and college programs. On another front, Russell lobbied first in Wisconsin and later in Washington for a system of jointly funded and directed county-based agricultural agents, envisioned as college instructional emissaries. The first three Wisconsin agents took to the field in 1911, with their ranks expanded considerably with federal support through the national Cooperative Extension Service in 1914. As elsewhere, Wisconsin's land grant agricultural college administered the statewide program, and Dean Russell gained the additional title of Director of Cooperative Extension. American participation in World War I created extreme pressure to expand agricultural production, and the new agricultural extension agents played

---

[22]In addition to supporting scientific research, the Hatch Acts required that the stations "verify experiments" and engage in "printing and distributing the results." Quoted in ibid., p. 50.

an important role in providing a variety of coordinating services. In fact, by war's end this coordinating role had come to characterize a major part of their duties, and in the process the College of Agriculture expanded its ties to rural Wisconsin.

The inter-war period was particularly difficult for American farmers, in Wisconsin no less than in the nation as a whole. The end of the war in 1918 began an economic and social upheaval that persisted in varying forms over the next three decades. The expanded production of the war years triggered a general collapse of farm commodity prices following the armistice. During the next decade farmers' income steadily declined while their expenses continued to rise. The growing number of farm bankruptcies mushroomed during the great depression of the 1930s, accelerating the earlier trends of farm consolidation and the movement of rural people from the land into the cities. American protectionist tariff policies hurt agricultural exports and New Deal remedies emphasized farm controls and production quotas. Wisconsin farmers were by this time heavily into dairying, which provided them somewhat greater stability and less dependence on exports than other commercial farmers. Still, the depression occasioned milk strikes, dumping, organized resistance to foreclosures, and other occasional violence in the once peaceful Wisconsin countryside. To a considerable extent the various New Deal programs were only palliatives, for it took World War II to end the depression. For farmers the war brought renewed demands for massive food and other farm production, even as the needs of the armed services reduced the available farm manpower. Throughout these turbulent years the College of Agriculture sought to help Wisconsin farmers and homemakers adjust to the changing conditions.

At first Dean Russell and his staff found it difficult to change their production-oriented perspective that had previously served the state and nation so well. The dean believed the most efficient and economical farmers would weather the hard times and be in a position to prosper after it passed. Wisconsin progressives in particular disagreed with the growth approach of Russell's Cooperative Extension Service, which they viewed as favoring the larger, more commercially successful farmers. The dean and his assistant director, K.L. Hatch, responded in their 1924 annual report that successful merchandizing of farm products was based on high quality output.

It is useless to try to develop a market for "mongrel" crops. It is destructive to agriculture to deal in "scrub" stock. Both roads lead to disaster. The future of American agriculture cannot rest secure on such a foundation of sand. The popular cry, "We know enough about production, now give us a better marketing system," must not be interpreted literally. *We know altogether too little about production to meet market demands.* We do not need less production effort, but more effort to produce what will appeal to the demands of the market. In our present effort to "solve the marketing problem" we must not overlook the fact that the road to the farm market begins at the first milepost—"the selection of seeds and sires."[23]

Under such headings as "The Economical Production of Meat" and "Alfalfa Eliminates Drain of Feed Bill on Farm Profits" Russell and Hatch proudly described the technical assistance available through agricultural extension, most of which emphasized improved production techniques.

As the average Wisconsin farmer's situation continued to deteriorate, during the next few years the College of Agriculture began to modify its advice. In 1925, for example, Russell and Hatch for the first time organized their annual report explicitly around the economic question, asking: "Which Way Now? More Dairying or More Sources of Income?" They also announced greater college support for the development of marketing cooperatives, an approach the college had given some attention to since 1913, and extended their interest to the quality of rural life.[24] The 1926 extension report went even further in suggesting new college priorities under the title *Agriculture's Triple Seal: Orderly Marketing, Quality Goods, Economical Production.*[25] Its frontispiece proclaimed the new UW president's rather cryptic social welfare perspective:

> Knowledge of production alone may make a man a slave.

---

[23]H.L. Russell and K.L. Hatch, "Mileposts on the Road to Market," in *Mileposts on the Road to Market,* Annual Report of the Extension Service of the College of Agriculture, University of Wisconsin, Circular 167, January, 1924, p. 3.

[24]*Which Way Now? More Dairying or More Sources of Income?* Annual Report of the Extension Service of the College of Agriculture, University of Wisconsin, Madison, Circular 181, February, 1925, pp. 3-5, 11. Under the heading, "State-Wide Service for the Home," p. 10, the report asserted: "By elimination of its drudgery, by helping to insure freedom from disease, and by increasing happy and wholesome recreation, rural life in Wisconsin can be greatly enriched. When women in rural homes are satisfied, contented, and happy, agriculture thrives and the future of rural Wisconsin is assured."

[25]*Agriculture's Triple Seal: Orderly Marketing, Quality Goods, Economic Production,* Annual Report of the Extension Service of the College of Agriculture, University of Wisconsin, Madison, Circular 193, February, 1926.

Knowledge of distribution alone may make a man a plutocrat.
Knowledge of consumption alone may make a man a parasite.
Knowledge of all three makes a man an effective citizen of democracy.
Glenn Frank,
President, University of Wisconsin

By the end of the decade the college had moved a long way from its earlier emphasis on improved production, and its programming reflected more of President Frank's approach than Dean Russell's. By this time the college was sponsoring 123 annual institutes on cooperative marketing, and the county agents were working hard to organize and help run new ones. There was renewed interest in improving rural life and culture, with the addition of women's sections to farmers' meetings on campus and across the state, efforts to introduce the experience of the Danish folk school movement into the Farm Short Course curriculum and elsewhere, the creation of a Department of Rural Sociology, and application of adult education themes in home economics extension work.[26] Harry Russell's College of Agriculture was now performing services he had not envisioned at the start of his deanship. One of the most significant of these was the important role played by its agricultural economists in helping to settle the long and bitter controversy over state land use policy for northern Wisconsin. Beginning with Dean Henry in the 1890s and continuing under Dean Russell through the mid-1920s, the college had consistently promoted the colonization by farmers of the "cutover" northern third of the state, whose once rich forest lands had provided the basis for the earlier lumbering industry. Russell in fact had located most of his pre-war county agricultural agents there to further the process in conjunction with several branch experiment stations intended to demonstrate the agricultural potential of the region.[27] Both Henry and Russell opposed

---

[26] "Adult education for women means better citizens, it means hope for the next generation, it means power to raise standards of living," declared the last annual extension report under Dean Russell. "The community grows because of human interest aroused in its every enterprise. Adult education gives to farm women knowledge which permits them to increase the family income. Better than all else, adult education gives a woman faith in herself." *Forces Building Farm Life: Good Roads, Spare Time, Beauty, All Year Job*, 1929-30 Annual Report of the Extension Director, College of Agriculture, University of Wisconsin, Circular 242, February, 1931, p. 43.

[27] Dean Henry had established the first branch station in Superior in 1905. Stations in Ashland and Iron River followed in 1906. The College of Agriculture assigned J.E. Delwiche the task of organizing and running these and additional northern branch stations that numbered

reforestation of the cutover lands in favor of expanding farm acreage to meet expected growth of demand for food products. They also stood to profit personally from their investments in some of the many colonization companies seeking to attract immigrants to the region. After the war Russell's agricultural engineering department operated the largest stump removal program in the country. The college obtained, packaged, and distributed surplus military explosives, instructed farmers in their use, and provided direct assistance in the work. Following the economic collapse of 1920, prices and demand for food declined and the northern colonization slowed and then stopped entirely. Indeed, many northern colonists abandoned their disappointingly unproductive farms, where fertility of the thin soils declined significantly after a few years and where the short growing season limited the choice of crops. The northern counties and townships now found themselves in possession of numerous abandoned properties and a rapidly eroding tax base incapable of providing necessary services to their remaining scattered residents.

Thoughtful members of the agriculture faculty recognized it was time for a new land use policy for the north country, encouraged by a new federal program to protect watersheds through the reforestation of cutover lands in the northern United States. The Wisconsin legislature followed with a modest reforestation act in 1927. The following year agricultural economics Professor Benjamin H. Hibbard and colleagues analyzed the Wisconsin cutover question and issued a comprehensive if controversial bulletin report, *Tax Delinquency In Northern Wisconsin.*[28] The report demolished the case for northern farm colonization, argued cogently for land-use controls through rural zoning, and urged new initiatives to encourage reforestation and recreational use of the currently unproductive lands. Without pointing fingers, the bulletin nevertheless demonstrated the bankruptcy of the college's earlier colonization policy. To Dean Russell's credit, he had already changed his mind about northern colonization, and he subsequently lobbied in

---

six by the 1920s. Glover, *Farm and College*, pp. 143, 145, 211, 219.

[28]B.H. Hibbard, John Swenehart, W.A. Hartman, and B.W. Allin, *Tax Delinquency in Northern Wisconsin*, Bulletin 399, Agricultural Experiment Station, University of Wisconsin, Madison, June, 1928. Other bulletins issued by Hibbard and his colleagues at about this time included: *Tax Burdens Compared* (1927), *Who Pays for the Highways?* (1929), and *Use and Taxation of Land in Lincoln County, Wisconsin* (1929). See Stephen C. Smith, "Utilizing and Conserving Natural Resources," in *Achievements in Agricultural Economics, 1909-1984, University of Wisconsin-Madison*, Marsha Cannon, ed. (Madison: Department of Agricultural Economics, UW-Madison, April, 1984), p. 17.

1929 for the Wisconsin bill that became the nation's first state-level enabling legislation for rural zoning.[29] Russell also was the founder and leading advocate of the Wisconsin school forest movement, which helped to promote reforestation. College economists continued to advocate the new approach, along with the northern county agricultural agents who provided a variety of assistance to residents and townships seeking to rebuild their depressed local economies.

The resolution of the northern cutover debate, including Harry Russell's belated support of the reforestation conservationists, helped define the final years of the dean's administration. His long-standing progressive critics, including some vocal foes in the legislature, ignored his shift, however, and continued to attack him and the College of Agriculture for its supposed "farm-it-all" expansionist policies. To some extent, as Russell's biographer has observed, the dean and his college were convenient scapegoats for those whom the deteriorating farm economy was punishing severely and seemingly interminably.[30] After all, Russell and the college had merely been carrying out the original land grant ideal, which assumed ever-increasing agricultural productivity as a positive force in American life. Had not agricultural exports helped generate the capital needed for American industrialization during the nineteenth century? Had not the astonishing output of American farms played a key part in securing victory in the First World War? Indeed, prior to the 1920s the notion of agricultural "overproduction" on any broad and sustained scale would have been incomprehensible to most Americans.

Only slowly did the seriousness of the problem of agricultural surpluses become evident to such traditional advocates of commercial farming as Dean Russell. Even then their solutions emphasized greater efficiency over cooperative marketing, the panacea of the progressives. Consequently, Russell received little recognition for his significant

---

[29]Observed Russell in 1928: "The belief was long held that the plow would follow the woodsman's axe and that much of these timbered areas would be ultimately in golden grain and rich green alfalfa and clover. Now we know there is time to grow one or more crops of pulp or lumber before these undeveloped acres that are suitable for cropping will be needed for farm use....The [experiment] station is being asked to supply the technical information that will permit of the best use of Wisconsin's millions of acres of idle land that today are a load on the financial resources of our government." Quoted in Vernon Carstensen, *Farms or Forests: Evolution of a State Land Policy for Northern Wisconsin, 1850-1932* (Madison: College of Agriculture, University of Wisconsin, Madison, July, 1958), p. 91. Carstensen's volume provides a detailed analysis of the issue.

[30]Beardsley, *Harry L. Russell*, p. 136.

strengthening of the college's agricultural economics department, which produced much of the policy guidance and practical assistance that finally resolved the cutover problem as well as leadership for the widespread establishment of agricultural marketing cooperatives across the state. Nor did the dean receive much credit for the creation of the Department of Rural Sociology, a program favored by Wisconsin progressives that previously had operated as a small unit of agricultural economics. Following a series of vicious personal attacks by progressive state Senator John Schumann during the 1929 budget debates, Russell resigned his deanship effective July 1, 1930, to assume direction of the Wisconsin Alumni Research Foundation. No doubt glad to be in a less politically visible position, he nevertheless had reason to be satisfied with his accomplishments as dean. He had built a strong scientific base for the college; equally important, he had made sure it thoroughly meshed with the college's teaching and outreach missions.

Early in 1931 President Frank chose Chris L. Christensen, the executive secretary of the Federal Farm Board, to succeed Russell as dean and director. The search process had taken several months longer than expected, perhaps because the president wanted to be sure the appointment would not further damage his deteriorating relationship with the newly elected progressive governor, Phillip F. La Follette. Frank needed an agriculture dean who could resonate with his relatively moderate political views without at the same time offending the La Follette progressives and their strong pro-cooperative stance. There were few such candidates in the conventional pool of the land grant institutions, most of them conservative biological scientists in the Henry and Russell mold. Eventually someone—perhaps Wisconsin's U.S. Senator "Young Bob" La Follette[31]—recommended Christensen, the

---

[31]Ira L. Baldwin, oral history interview, 1983, UHP.

highest ranking advocate of marketing cooperatives in the federal government. An agricultural economist and enthusiastic student of Danish agricultural economy and rural folk culture, Christensen impressed Frank as exactly the right man for the job.

President Frank announced his choice of the thirty-six-year-old Christensen on January 6. "He brings to the difficult and urgent problems that center in the economic life of rural Wisconsin, a background, an equipment, and a personal devotion of interest that singularly fit him for this strategically important post in Wisconsin's public service," effusively asserted Frank's press release.[32] "Farmers must organize to market effectively," proclaimed an approving *Capital Times* headline quoting Christensen on January 21, after the regents formally affirmed his appointment. The University budget request was before the legislature at this time, and in early February Frank used an appearance at a progressive-dominated joint finance committee hearing to boast of Christensen's selection, which had "been dictated by the determination...that in the twenty-five years ahead the College of Agriculture shall give to the economic side of the farm problems of Wisconsin as able, as distinguished, and as productive leadership as has been given to the scientific side of agriculture during the last twenty-five years."[33] A few weeks later, in an address to a joint Madison Kiwanis-Rural Federation meeting, Christensen struck exactly the right chord by declaring, "one of the things which agriculture needs today is closer and more efficient cooperation. Organized business has taught us that the answer to organization is more organization."[34]

Cooperation remained Dean Christensen's primary emphasis throughout the 1930s. "The more one analyzes the complexity of modern society," he observed in 1938, "the more likely is he to accept

---

[32]Press release, January 6, 1931, Frank Presidential Papers, 4/13/1, box 92; *Daily Cardinal*, January 7, 1931.

[33]Committee on Joint Finance Minutes, February 6, 1931, p. 57, General Presidential Papers, 4/0/5, box 25, UA.

[34]Chris L. Christensen, "Group Action Needed to Help Meet Farm Situation," address before Kiwanis-Rural Federation meeting, Madison, March 30, 1931, in Christensen, *Addresses, 1931* (bound volumes of mimeographed speech texts and other memorabilia labeled by year), p. 6, Accession 91/29, box 1, UA. Later in his remarks Christensen observed: "There must be development of group thinking which will bring with it coordination of production, distribution and consumption. This relationship has been most forcefully expressed by President Glenn Frank in the following manner." He then repeated Frank's aphorism, quoted earlier in this chapter, on the relationship between production, distribution, consumption, and democracy.

the view that cooperation among individuals and among groups is an inevitable development. Cooperation is the very essence and price of progress."[35]   As an active teaching member of the agricultural economics department, Christensen spoke on cooperation to student classes and to campus visitors, to legislators in Madison and farmers across the state, and to listeners of University radio station WHA. He also recruited a former USDA colleague, Asher Hobson, to head the department in 1932. An expert on international agricultural economics and cooperative advocate, Hobson shared Christensen's and Frank's moderate Republican politics and worked closely with Wisconsin farmers as they formed and operated their own purchasing and marketing cooperatives. Other departmental faculty members joined the effort. Rudolph K. Froker, a future dean of the college, convinced Agricultural Adjustment Administration officials to help fund cooperative work in Wisconsin. Marvin Schaars and Henry Bakken published the first college textbook on cooperatives. Schaars, Bakken, Christensen, and others worked with farm leaders to convince the state legislature to enact laws mandating school and college course work in cooperatives. Meanwhile, the department sponsored annual short courses on the management of cooperatives and issued bulletins with topics such as "An Economic Study of the Milwaukee Milk Market" and "The Road to Better Marketing."[36]

Even with the new emphasis on cooperatives, the College of Agriculture continued to provide its farmer constituents with the kind of scientific and technological support they had learned to expect over the preceding half-century. There were major advances in the organization of the Dairy Herd Improvement Association, orchestrated by faculty in animal husbandry and the growing legion of county agricultural extension agents. From the detailed records produced by the association, college geneticists and other scientists learned by selective culling of the herds to reduce the incidence of Bang's Disease or brucellosis, which caused spontaneous abortion in cattle. Later college biochemists and dairy scientists introduced the egg yolk extender, the first practical means of preserving bull semen for artificial insemination. "In the short space of a year since this method was developed,"

---

[35]Christensen, "Essentials In Successful Cooperation," excerpts from an address before the Third Annual Cooperative Management Conference, East Lansing, Michigan, March 23, 1938, in Christensen, *Addresses, 1938*, p. 34.

[36]Marvin A. Schaars, *The Story of the Department of Agricultural Economics, 1909-1972* (Madison: University of Wisconsin, 1972), p. 48.

reported Christensen in 1940, "it has been adopted by all of Wisconsin's artificial breeding associations, so that it already serves in the breeding of some 15,000 to 20,000 cows."[37] Similarly impressive advances occurred in crop production. In 1932, for example, college agronomists introduced the first Wisconsin corn hybrid, distributed it through R.A. Moore's venerable Wisconsin Agricultural Experiment Association, and provided impetus for the formation of several state-based commercial seed companies.[38] The combined effort of college geneticists, plant pathologists, and horticulturalists produced an improved potato that served as the basis for another new seed stock industry.[39] Lessons learned from the work with corn and potatoes helped lead to the quickly ubiquitous Vicland oats strain in 1941. Pasture and forage work benefitted from advances in alfalfa production and the application of fertilizers.[40]

While neither Dean Christensen nor President Frank generally supported the New Deal, the College of Agriculture nevertheless helped to implement important federal depression-era initiatives.[41] Perhaps

---

[37]Christensen, "Progress Report—1938 to 1940—and an Evaluation of the Present Program and Facilities of the College of Agriculture," submitted to President C.A. Dykstra and the Board of Regents, October 1, 1940, p. 22, College of Agriculture Papers, 9/1/1-8, box 1, UA; *AI in Wisconsin: The Story of Artificial Insemination Research*, vol. 1, no. 2 of *Research for a Growing Wisconsin Pamphlet Series* (Madison: College of Agricultural and Life Sciences, June, 1984).

[38]The names of the Blaney, Spangler, and Tracy seed companies are familiar throughout Wisconsin and beyond.

[39]The leaders of this research were Professors G.H. Rieman, R.A. Brink, and D.C. Cooper.

[40]See Laurence F. Graber, *Mister Alfalfa* (Madison: GRA-MAR, 1976), pp. 438-43; Clinton J. Chapman, oral history interview, 1972, UA. Due to their energetic and effective proselytizing throughout Wisconsin Graber and Chapman became widely known respectively as "Mr. Alfalfa" and "Mr. Fertilizer."

[41]"For the first time in our history," lamented Christensen in 1938, "the resources of government are devoted to reducing the supplies of the necessities of life. This, at a time when the President, himself, proclaims that one-third of the population is under-fed, under-clothed, and under-housed." Christensen, "A Look Ahead for the Cooperative Movement," address presented at the opening session of the 14th Annual Conference of the American Institute of Cooperation, Pullman, Washington, July 11, 1938, in Christensen, *Addresses, 1938*, p. 131. Christensen similarly opposed federal restraint of international trade, or what he called "economic isolation." Christensen, "Some Economic Problems With Which Agriculture is Confronted," address delivered in Janesville, Wisconsin, January 9, 1934, in Christensen, *Addresses, 1934*, p. 2. For a complementary perspective see Glenn Frank, *America's Hour of Decision: Crisis Points in National Policy* (New York: Whittlesey House, McGraw-Hill, 1934), pp. 200-1. Christensen's recruitment of Asher Hobson to head the agricultural economics department in 1932 highlighted his view of the importance of world trade in

most visible in Wisconsin was the Upper Mississippi Soil Erosion Station, popularly known as the Coon Valley experiment. Established in 1931 and located in the rugged "driftless" region south of La Crosse, the unique program sought to test contour plowing and other techniques to restore productivity in a badly eroded and misused landscape. "Instead of blundering expensively into means of control," observed Christensen in 1934, "the federal government is there seeking to cope with natural problems in a most natural manner....Attention is being given to practically every phase that may come into the operation of the farms of that area—farm management, field cropping, soils management, forestry and game production."[42] The creation of the federal Rural Electrification Administration in 1935 accelerated the process of bringing electricity to farms in Wisconsin and elsewhere. In the first two years county extension agents helped organize ten REA cooperatives delivering electric service to nearly 5,500 Wisconsin farms. Already in the late 1920s agricultural engineering extension specialists had begun offering annual short courses in rural electrification. As Dean Christensen pointed out in 1936, the college was "interested in helping to make available, at the lowest rates consistent with good management, electricity for lighting our farm homes and farm buildings and operating such machinery on the farm as may be efficiently and economically operated by 'white' power."[43]

Two unique Wisconsin initiatives bolstered the federal efforts in the conservation and management of natural resources. The first built upon the work of the college's agricultural economists during the late 1920s to replace large-scale farming in the cutover region. "Loggers and tourists no longer used the eggs and vegetables that brought in pocket money," observed extension historian E.R. McIntyre. "The spirit of

---

reducing American crop surpluses.

[42]The program involved 750 farms with 90,000 total acres. Christensen, "The Functions and Program of the College of Agriculture," report submitted to President Dykstra, June 30, 1938, p. 12, College of Agriculture Papers, 9/1/1-8, box 1; Christensen, "Shall We Conserve Our Greatest Natural Resource?" address delivered at meeting of the Wisconsin Council of Agriculture, Omro, October 20, 1934, in Christensen, *Addresses, 1934*, p. 148. Christensen found the working relationship with federal authorities "satisfactory," even though the college experienced "some difficulty from time to time" because U.S. officials hesitated to "delegate sufficient authority" in running the program. Christensen, "Report for the Regional Meeting, Land Grant College Association, Urbana, Illinois, October 11-12, 1937," September 25, 1937, in Christensen, *Addresses, 1937*, p. 186.

[43]Christensen, "Turn On the Light," address at Fourth Annual Rural Electrification Short Course, October 22, 1936, in Christensen, *Addresses, 1936*, p. 209.

the remaining settlers vanished like the last spark of a hemlock holocaust. "[44] In May, 1933, the Oneida County Board, taking advantage of the state enabling legislation of 1929, passed the nation's first rural zoning ordinance, asserting unprecedented public control of land use in the county. In anticipation of this event, college extension personnel helped organize and advise the local residents while Dean Christensen and other college staff assisted in drafting the ordinance. Subsequently, and against initial USDA opposition, Christensen encouraged his agricultural agents in other counties to follow Oneida County's lead. Agricultural economics faculty members aided by publishing helpful circulars on the process and its anticipated benefits. By 1934, eighteen additional county ordinances were in effect (thirty-seven by 1948), removing nearly five million marginal agricultural acres from cultivation.

The second Wisconsin initiative involved the appointment of Aldo Leopold, the assistant director of the Forest Products Laboratory and author of the influential book *Game Management*, to a new chair of game management in Department of Agricultural Economics. "The basic problem," Leopold argued, "is to *induce the private landowner to conserve on his own land*, and no conceivable millions or billions for public land purchase can alter that fact."[45] Leopold conducted important research in his fledgling field, spread his gospel throughout the state and nation, participated wholeheartedly in the Coon Valley experiment, and served as the first research director of the University's new Arboretum, Wildlife Refuge, and Forestry Preserve.[46]

Dean Christensen placed great emphasis on enhancing the quality of country life in Wisconsin. "Our goal," the dean explained in 1936,

is to help farmers create a rural economy and culture that will enable honest, industrious and intelligent people to live upon the land with their full share of joys and satisfactions. We must help develop agriculture so as to afford an opportunity for living standards in the country comparable to those afforded young people who choose other walks of life. To create conditions on the land that will attract to it superior youth who will utilize their talent in the raising of better livestock and the growing of better crops and the building of

[44]McIntyre, *Fifty Years*, p. 233.
[45]Quoted in Curt Meine, *Aldo Leopold: His Life and Work* (Madison: University of Wisconsin Press, 1988), p. 321. Emphasis in original. Meine's is the definitive scholarly biography of Leopold.
[46]See pp. 704-8.

better farms to the end that they may attain and maintain better rural living.[47]

A healthy agricultural society required "home grown" leadership, which meant "that farm youth must be given the same educational opportunity as the boys and girls of our urban centers." Christensen was also a strong advocate of "family-sized farm ownership" as a means "to build self- respect and to stabilize the community and the state. It is essential for a program of soil conservation, and it is the cornerstone in the successful development of community and cooperative enterprise." "Farming," he stressed, "is a way of living as well as a way of making a living."[48]

While Christensen's emphasis was greater, the college had for decades sought to improve the quality of rural life. Shortly after his appointment in 1907 Dean Russell arranged to take over the home economics program initiated by the College of Letters and Science. Reopened in 1909 after a year of transitional planning and reorganization, the department replaced its previous liberal arts emphasis with a science-based nutritional program that attracted the first significant numbers of women undergraduates to the college. By the mid-1920s department extension specialists were regularly organizing statewide homemakers' programs in clothing, food, household management, and child nutrition. The annual Farmers' Week on campus began offering special programs for farm women and children and changed the event's title to the more inclusive Farm Folks' Week. In 1929 the home economics department began reaching Wisconsin homemakers on a regular basis through WHA radio's new "Homemakers' Hour" program. The college's rural sociology work paralleled the home economics effort. Beginning in 1911 and continuing through 1916, Professor C.J. Galpin of the agricultural economics department organized annual two-week summertime Country Life Conferences on campus. In 1922, J.H. Kolb, Galpin's successor,

---

[47]Chris Christensen, "Looking Ahead in Extension Work," address to the Twenty-Fourth Annual Conference of Extension Workers, Madison, October 27, 1936, in Christensen, *Addresses, 1936*, p. 227.

[48]Christensen, "Some Economic Problems With Which Agriculture is Confronted," address at Janesville, January 9, 1934, in Christensen, *Addresses, 1934*, p. 4; Christensen, "How Educate for a New Rural Citizenship?" excerpts from an address before 4-H Club Leaders Recognition Banquet, Beaver Dam, February 20, 1940, in Christensen, *Addresses, 1940*, pp. 20-1; Christensen, "What Place Has Culture In the Life of the Farmer?" excerpts from an address at the Wisconsin Council of Agriculture Get-Together Conference, Madison, November 3, 1939, in Christensen, *Addresses, 1939*, p. 167.

staged the first of many inter-war Rural Church Conferences that sought to educate and train rural community activists. This well-respected and successful short course program helped persuade Dean Russell to upgrade the status of Kolb and his colleagues by moving them into a new free-standing Department of Rural Sociology.

As with the cooperative movement, the Christensen-era contributions to rural life were more evolutionary than revolutionary. Responding to increased demand for service, for example, the college slowly added home economists to the county-based extension staff. In 1933, seeking further to highlight the new broader program content, the college changed the title of Farm Folks' Week to Farm and Home Week. That year Extension also organized several "5-H" Clubs, intended "to provide educational, social, and service opportunities" for 4-H Club graduates.[49] Dean Christensen, with the help of Director V.E. Kivlin, took the lead in reorienting the faltering Farm Short Course around the model of the Danish folk schools, about which the dean was both an enthusiast and an acknowledged expert. Through the introduction of new cultural material and broader social activities, Christensen revitalized the short course curriculum—now commonly referred to as the Farm Folk School—to encourage a better sense of pride and community among its students and staff. Illustrative of Christensen's contagious enthusiasm for the folk school movement, he recruited sociologist John Barton and regional fiction writer August "Augie" Derleth to work intensively with the students. He also played a central role in 1936 in creating the nation's first university artist-in-residence program, funded by the Brittingham Trust. The initial appointee was the regional artist John Steuart Curry, who worked with short course students and more generally throughout Wisconsin as an advocate of "regional art as a force for rural culture."[50] Although Christensen was unsuccessful in his perennial campaigns to raise money for a short course dormitory, he did manage to arrange for a limited number of campus residence hall accommodations for short course students who had difficulty finding short-term private housing at reasonable rentals.

After Pearl Harbor the emphasis of the College of Agriculture abruptly reverted to the earlier all-out, full-production model

---

[49]McIntyre, *Fifty Years*, p. 203.
[50]Copy of Board of Regents resolution, approved by Harold Wilkie, September 13, 1936, in Christensen, *Addresses, 1936*, p. 192a.

championed by Deans Henry and Russell. As long-time Associate Experiment Station Director Noble Clark observed, college scientific and technological research again occupied a central role "because the federal administration has declared the nation's needs for food are second only to ships, war weapons, and munitions." As in the past, Extension provided the crucial link between laboratory and farm, helping to produce a 40 percent increase in Wisconsin agricultural output between 1940 and 1944. "It is generally agreed," Clark pointed out after the war, "that the new crop varieties and the new farm practices developed in the agricultural experiment station, and carried to the farmers by the agricultural extension service, were a major factor in making the increased production possible."[51] Agricultural and home extension agents also helped in other important ways, such as supporting the Victory Garden program, 4-H activity, and war-related conferences and radio broadcasts. Indeed, so important did federal officials consider the Cooperative Extension Service that they placed it under the War Food Administration from 1943 to 1947.

Throughout the inter-war period the College of Agriculture was always the University's most significant and widespread presence in the state. From stump removal to conservation and reforestation, from production to cooperation, electrification, and the revitalization of rural life, the college proved itself highly adaptable in helping rural Wisconsin residents meet the challenges of their rapidly changing circumstances. Whatever the product of college research—scientific, technological, economic, or social and cultural—it flowed dependably from the college to Wisconsin farmers through its several venerable communication conduits—including the farmers' meetings and short courses, as well as bulletins and other publications—and through the newer county agent system and educational radio.

"The Beneficent Influence of the University"

When Glenn Frank assumed the UW presidency in 1925 he inherited a University Extension Division responsible for most outreach programming other than the agricultural activities of Dean Russell's

---

[51] "Research in the Wisconsin Agricultural Experiment Station That Has a Bearing on the War Effort or National Emergency," April 1, 1942, College of Agriculture Papers, 9/1/3/1-8, box 1; "The University of Wisconsin in World War II" (unpublished manuscript [ca. February, 1951]), p. 19, General Presidential Papers, 4/0/3, box 109, UA.

Cooperative Extension Service. The division had operated under the same leadership since its inception early in the Van Hise administration.[52] The central figure was Dean Louis E. Reber, whom President Van Hise had recruited from the engineering school at the Pennsylvania State College in 1907. Reber's charge was to organize and administer a comprehensive outreach program then being advocated by a number of Wisconsin progressives and supportive UW faculty. "I shall never be content until the beneficent influence of the University reaches every family in the state," proclaimed Van Hise in 1905. "This is my ideal of a state university."[53] Charles McCarthy of the Legislative Reference Bureau and the Wisconsin Library Commission urged the president to carry this out by setting up a separate extramural agency to provide a number of services, including vocational education for the many state youths who were dropping out of school and going to work in industry. A faculty committee concurred in October, 1906, and about the same time Van Hise appointed the first three staff members—Henry E. Legler, Frank A. Hutchins, and William H. Lighty— assigned entirely to non-agricultural University outreach work. Shortly after they began work Van Hise appointed Reber to direct the effort and persuaded the legislature to appropriate $20,000 specifically to support the new University Extension Division, whose institutional status was considered equivalent to the University's academic colleges.

The University Extension Division—or General Extension, as it was often called—required a no-nonsense, technically-oriented administrator to assure that the new agency fulfilled its founders' vision of social amelioration. Reber, forty-nine when he came to Wisconsin, was such a man.[54] During his first few years at Wisconsin he structured

---

[52]A general University Extension program flourished for at time in Madison during the Chamberlin and Adams administrations of the 1890s. It tried to provide the "cultural side" of University scholarship to the public primarily through faculty lectures. See Curti and Carstensen, *University of Wisconsin*, vol. 1, pp. 547, 715, 721-31. Our discussion of the University Extension Division relies heavily on ibid., vol 2, pp. 549-94; Frederick M. Rosentreter, *The Boundaries of the Campus: A History of the University of Wisconsin Extension Division, 1885-1945* (Madison: University of Wisconsin Press, 1957); Clay Schoenfeld, *The Outreach University: A Case History in the Public Relationships of Higher Education* (Madison: University of Wisconsin-Madison Office of Inter-College Programs, 1977); and Chester Allen, "University Extension in Wisconsin," 3 vols. (unpublished manuscript, 1955), University Extension Division Papers, 18/1/8, UA.

[53]Van Hise address to the Wisconsin Press Association, February, 1905, quoted in Curti and Carstensen, *University of Wisconsin*, vol. 2, pp. 88-9.

[54]Chester Allen viewed Reber as "an engineer and an executive, not an idealist. He saw

the division into four well-functioning programmatic units or departments, each with its own specialized staff, and set up six district offices outside of Madison to link the division more closely with its public at the grassroots level.[55] The Department of Correspondence and Class Study offered University expertise to a thriving market initially dominated by out-of-state commercial vendors.[56] Lighty had begun developing this department in 1906, and in conjunction with Reber he would preside over it for the next two decades. The department offered courses—mostly non-credit, but a few for academic credit—through the mail and at selected local sites, such as public schools, libraries, and manufacturing plants. Madison-based instructors wrote most of the vocationally oriented and commercially published texts, which soon came into widespread use and helped bring national fame to the division. The courses included professional, technical, vocational, and liberal arts offerings, and by 1912 had enrolled a five-year total of nearly 8,000 participants.[57]

---

his objective, and he lost no time in creating an organization. He spared no effort to accomplish his purpose in the shortest and best way." Allen, "University Extension," vol. 1, p. 20.

[55]Unlike Harry Russell's "three-legged stool" staffing model at the College of Agriculture, the founders of the University Extension Division favored a separate arrangement. Charles McCarthy held strongly to this view, as did the "Report of the Sub-Committee on Credit University Extension Work," submitted to President Van Hise on October 16, 1906. "In the opinion of the committee," stated the report, "much, if not substantially all, of the work must be done by a specially selected staff, under the various departments, and the rules regarding the work should be assimilated to current practice in the ordinary work of the University." Quoted in ibid., vol. 1, Appendix B. Reber affirmed this position on March 3, 1908, in a letter to Van Hise pointing out the problems associated with using resident faculty for extension work:

> In order to get the desired results, it is necessary to secure as rapidly as possible, special teachers in practically all of the various lines of work. While the instructors in the University are cooperating with the extension officers cordially, several difficulties confront us. It is impossible, for example, satisfactorily to explain delays to people scattered throughout the state though they may seem reasonable to those who understand the conditions. The instruction in Extension work being extra, is obliged to wait upon other interests. A few days delay or other irregularities from this cause react seriously as a hindrance to growth.

Quoted in ibid., vol. 1, p. 36.

[56]According to a 1906 survey by McCarthy and engineering Professor J.G.D. Mack, over 35,000 Wisconsin residents were paying about $.8 million annually for commercial correspondence courses. Maurice M. Vance, *Charles Richard Van Hise: Scientist Progressive* (Madison: State Historical Society of Wisconsin, 1960), p. 109.

[57]A bulletin issued by Secretary Lighty in late 1907 described the wide array of correspondence subjects:

> The work of the correspondence study department as at present organized, plans

In an effort to formalize the previously random practice across the University, the Department of Instruction by Lectures became the official UW faculty speaker's bureau. During 1913-14, for example, it arranged 158 short non-credit courses of two or three meetings and 910 single lectures for off-campus audiences. Frank A. Hutchins, previously a colleague of McCarthy at the library commission and an early advocate of the division, organized the Department of Debating and Public Discussion. Hutchins and his staff of ten prepared and circulated loose-leaf notebooks containing up-to-date materials on important issues of the day. This "package library" service provided information for high school debate teams and local public policy deliberations. Perhaps even more than the other units, the Department of General Information and Welfare reflected the progressive ideology of the division's founders as it sought through several sub-departments or bureaus to improve social work services and the cultural life of the state.[58] When the Navy Department decided to set up correspondence and other general educational programs for its sailors beginning in 1913, Secretary of the Navy Josephus Daniels turned to Dean Reber's staff as the acknowledged national experts on the subject.

Reber early focussed much of his attention on Milwaukee, the state's major urban center. In accordance with an agreement reached with President Van Hise before he left Pennsylvania, Reber opened a Milwaukee field office in late 1907 or 1908. District Representative Kenneth G. Smith, a former engineer and teacher educator, thereupon began developing a program that would eventually evolve into the University of Wisconsin-Milwaukee. Between 1909 and 1913 Reber opened additional field offices in Oshkosh, Wausau, Superior, Eau

---

to give one or more courses in the following lines: Agriculture. Business and Industry. Engineering. Electrical, Mechanical, Steam, Stationary, Civil and Sanitary, etc., Mechanical Drawing. Highway Construction. The languages, French, Italian, Spanish, German, Greek, Latin. History, Ancient, Medieval, and Modern. Home Economics. Political Economy. Political Science. Sociology. Philosophy. Education, Mathematics. English and Literature. Physical Science. Bacteriology, Botany, Geology, Chemistry, Astronomy, etc. Law. Pharmacy. Music.
Quoted in Allen, "University Extension," vol. 1, p. 35. For a glowing description of the correspondence department's accomplishments from the progressive point of view see Frederic C. Howe, *Wisconsin: An Experiment in Democracy* (New York: Charles Scribner's Sons, 1912), pp. 144-5.

[58]Reber appointed sociologist John L. Gillin to head the Department of General Information and Welfare. Its sub-units included the Bureaus of Municipal Information, Social Center Development, Visual Instruction, and Community Music.

Claire, and La Crosse, but the Milwaukee outpost remained the crucial one. By 1912 Smith's resident staff included at least nine additional instructors and field organizers. Much of the vocational and technical instruction advocated by McCarthy occurred in Milwaukee. In the process of developing the general information and welfare department, moreover, in 1910 Reber approved the creation of a Milwaukee-based Institute of Municipal and Social Service. It sponsored lectures, conferences, field trips, and other activities, all intended "to establish in Milwaukee a center of study, information, and training in social reform, Social Welfare, and Municipal efficiency." The institute promised to assist local citizens "to learn and apply more perfectly the laws of SCIENTIFIC PHILANTHROPY to the conduct of public and private affairs in the city."[59]

Reber's division and its supporters were committed to helping the University play an increasingly active and comprehensive role in the life of the state and its people, one in keeping with progressive reform ideology. During most of the new agency's first decade progressive Republicans dominated state politics and provided strong support, even giving the division its own dedicated category in the state budget separate from the rest of the University. In 1912 Charles McCarthy published his primer on state government activism, *The Wisconsin Idea*, which outlined the history of progressive legislation in Wisconsin and celebrated the culminating legislative session of 1911. McCarthy stressed the idealism of the University generally, the good works of its College of Agriculture, and especially the value—at the time more anticipated than accomplished—of the University Extension Division. McCarthy further praised the wisdom of recent legislation establishing a system of county vocational schools under a state board of vocational education, with the extension dean as an ex officio member.[60] He looked forward to the results of a study sponsored by the new state Board of Public Affairs that he expected would bring "a thorough readjustment" of all public education in Wisconsin to infuse it with progressive values.[61] Meanwhile, a Saturday Lunch Club, including University and other progressives, was meeting weekly at the University Club or elsewhere near the campus to discuss common objectives and

---

[59]Quoted in Allen, "University Extension," vol. 1, p. 68.

[60]Although he did not mention this in his account, McCarthy had been instrumental in securing passage of the legislation.

[61]Charles McCarthy, *Wisconsin Idea* (New York: Macmillan Company, 1912), p. 152.

strategies. Among its members were Robert M. La Follette, Sr., Charles McCarthy, Frank Hutchins, Charles Van Hise, Louis Reber, and William Lighty.[62] The progressives were riding high.

Of course, not everyone in Wisconsin shared the progressives' values and enthusiasm for remaking society. Indeed, even as McCarthy's *Wisconsin Idea* was gaining wide publicity for the state, Dean Harry Russell angered many of Senator La Follette's followers by blocking extension division sponsorship of a number of rural institute programs—some with obviously partisan agendas—in what he regarded as agricultural extension territory. Van Hise sided with Dean Reber in the conflict, but Russell eventually had his way by appealing over the president's head to his supporters on the Board of Regents. As the election of 1914 approached, critics campaigned energetically against progressive excesses, frequently citing allegedly partisan programs of the University Extension Division. Did Wisconsin have a state university, demanded the conservatives, or was it a university state? The anti-progressive, anti-University rhetoric struck a responsive chord with much of the electorate, which was also influenced by the negative findings emerging from the so-called Allen Survey, named for project director William H. Allen. The public affairs board had appointed him in the spring of 1914 to conduct a detailed review of the University. President Van Hise orchestrated a devastating reply to Allen, but it came too late to influence the vote. In November Milwaukee stalwart Republican Emanuel L. Philipp won the governorship and, in a chilling move for the University, appointed Allen to his staff.

Happily, Governor Philipp proved to be no blind ideologue and he soon began to revise his negative view of the University. He and President Van Hise gradually established amicable relations that would characterize the next six years of stalwart rule. Still, for the University the stalwarts brought mostly a holding period, which was complicated by American entry into the war in 1917. The structure of the Extension Division allowed for impressively flexible programmatic responses to the wartime challenges, though without much of its regular staff, many of whom, including Dean Reber, departed for military and related war

---

[62]The club boasted about two hundred members and met from 1911 to 1929. Topics proposed for 1912 included: The Idea of Trust Regulation, The Government of the Capitol City, The Wisconsin Law Providing for Commission Government, The Express Companies, Water Powers, The Doctrine of State's Rights, Interstate Rate Regulation, The High Cost of Living, and Is There a Lumber Trust? See Roger W. Axford, "William Henry Lighty, Adult Education Pioneer" (Ph.D. diss., University of Chicago, 1961), pp. 7-8, 275-9.

service. Correspondence Director William Lighty, whom Van Hise had passed over for the top post in 1907, took charge as acting dean. In Reber's absence Lighty evidently used his position to undermine the dean's authority by complaining to certain regents about his allegedly arbitrary and harsh administrative style.[63] President Van Hise might have resolved or at least managed these personnel conflicts, but his unanticipated death right after the armistice left the division facing the post-war challenges in some disarray.

The regents quickly designated L&S Dean Edward A. Birge, the University's elder statesman, to succeed Van Hise. At sixty-seven, the one-time acting UW president (1900-03) showed little enthusiasm for his new job, which he viewed strictly as an obligation and interim assignment. If Birge realized the post-war era demanded major adjustments throughout the University, he had no intention of leading the way. That would be up to his successor. His forbearance led William Lighty to consider him generally "indifferent, if not mildly opposed" to the work of the Extension staff.[64] It was in this context that Dean Reber resumed his administration of the division in 1919. The following year John J. Blaine, a strongly partisan progressive Republican, captured the gover-

---

[63]On March 9, 1918, President Van Hise wrote to Reber about the previous day's regents meeting:

> Two regents said that they had been informed that your methods in the extension division were so arbitrary that it was impossible to cooperate satisfactorily with you; also in a number of cases that there had been added to this temper, which had made cooperation more difficult. They had the belief that because of these things there was not proper harmony and cooperation in the extension division, and that the best results could not be secured while the present state of affairs existed. I declined to make an investigation relating to the alleged facts during your absence, and said that the matter must necessarily go over until your return. I am sorry to be obliged to send the above statement to you, but it would scarcely be fair to you to withhold what occurred.

Following further discussion among the regents three months later, Van Hise, on June 7, again cautioned Reber: "So far as yourself are concerned, it was agreed that I should talk with you about certain asperities. This I shall do when you return, and shall not attempt to cover the matter by letter." Both letters in Van Hise Presidential Papers, 4/10/1, box 69, UA.

[64]In mid-1926 Lighty addressed a memorandum to Chester D. Snell, the new acting dean of extension, containing Lighty's observations on the views of various UW personalities, including Birge, toward the division. W.H. Lighty, "Attitude of the Residence Faculty Toward Correspondence-Study Teaching and the Reorganized Extension Work," n.d., William H. Lighty Papers, box 26, SHSW. Lighty failed to credit Birge's extensive outreach experience speaking to off-campus audiences, particularly during the early years of University Extension in the 1890s, his early guidance of the UW Summer Session, or his long work with the state geological and natural history survey. Perhaps Birge's "indifference" related more to Lighty than extension.

norship from stalwart Philipp. Blaine's victory seemed on its face to presage a resurgence of the pre-war progressive movement that had nurtured the division's early development. But the times had changed. The collapse of farm prices following the war brought hard times to Wisconsin farmers, a key element of the progressives' constituency, and limited state revenues for more activist programs. Governor Blaine was suspicious of the University, moreover, because of the faculty "Round Robin" manifesto criticizing Senator La Follette's anti-war views. The prospects for extension consequently seemed considerably less bright than before the war. In 1923 Dean Reber, approaching sixty-five and in declining health, requested that President Birge allow him to retire. Birge demurred, arguing that the next president, whom he expected to be named shortly, should make the appointment.

Notwithstanding these difficulties and Dean Reber's growing disenchantment with his job, the Extension Division flourished during the early 1920s. By mid-1924 the division had accumulated a total of 100,803 enrollments in correspondence and extramural study, with 20,935 new participants added in the 1922-24 biennium. During the same two-year period 987 communities used the package library service, with 369 also sponsoring educational lecture programs and musical performances; 493 cities and villages utilized the municipal reference service; 430 client groups worked with the Bureau of Community Development; and 1,400 organizations borrowed educational motion pictures and lantern slides.[65] Each of these programs had been established before the war, all had proven their value and popularity with the Wisconsin public, and Dean Reber had wisely allowed their staffs to carry on with a minimum of organizational tinkering. Fortuitously, the legislature had earlier granted the division permission to retain its surplus fee income rather than return it to the state general fund as other units of the University were required to do. This encouraged Reber and his colleagues increasingly to cultivate revenue-producing activities. A characteristic result was the replacement of free community health programs with profitable graduate seminars for practicing physicians of the state. Thus in a period of stable University appropriations the division actually enjoyed growing operating funds with which to carry

---

[65]These figures appeared as part of Regent Kronshage's public relations campaign for the University conducted just prior to the appointment of Glenn Frank to the UW presidency. *WAM*, 26 (March, 1925), pp. 182-4. Also see "Report of the Dean of the University Extension Division, Three Year Period Ending June 30, 1925," marked "original report," 1925, University Extension Division Papers, 18/1/1, box 18.

on an expanding array of public service programming.

Two key administrative initiatives involved the Milwaukee extension district. In 1923 the legislature approved a $150,000 appropriation for a permanent downtown facility. This action came after an extensive study by a friendly legislative committee, assisted and encouraged by Reber who stressed the difficulties of working in widely dispersed and poorly furnished rented and borrowed facilities and the greater service and efficiencies that would accompany proper accommodations. Reber also promised that the new building would allow extension to develop a unique social work training program. "It is believed that the needs of the state in this respect should be met by the University in Milwaukee," he pointed out. "The demand for workers with the juvenile courts, for probation officers, for truant officers, for home-service workers, for police women, and many other types of workers for community and welfare is great."[66] With the new building the University would have its own permanent outpost in Milwaukee. The second initiative followed closely upon the building appropriation and was another crucial step in the evolution of the Milwaukee unit. The Milwaukee normal school had established a two-year liberal studies program in 1919 to serve ex-soldiers eligible for educational benefits through the Wisconsin Bonus Law and the U.S. Veteran's Bureau. By 1923 this funding was scheduled to end, though there was continued demand for such a junior college program. The Milwaukee extension unit seemed the logical alternative sponsor since it offered a wide array of liberal arts courses during late afternoon and evening hours. It already offered a daytime curriculum, moreover, which had been established in 1919 for veterans preparing to enter the UW College of Engineering in Madison as juniors. In April, 1923, Lighty addressed a memo to Dean Reber discussing the possibility for "the University Extension Division to administer Junior College work in Milwaukee." Lighty outlined options for a freshman/sophomore curriculum, including geography and geology, psychology, English, foreign languages, mathematics, history, science, and drawing, arguing that with the addition of a single instructor the current staff could handle the teaching load. The matter remained unresolved throughout the spring semester, after which Dean Reber left

---

[66]*Appendix to Bill No. 160, S., Report* in re the *Necessity of Providing a Building for the University Extension Division in the City of Milwaukee, Prepared for the Legislative Committee Appointed to Investigate this Matter* (Prepared by the Dean's Office, University Extension Division, November 25, 1922), p. 10, University Extension Division Papers, 18/1/1, box 60.

Madison to vacation along the Atlantic coast. The impatient Lighty thereupon met to discuss the idea with President Birge and L&S Dean Sellery, both of whom suggested waiting for completion of the new building. Lighty disagreed, arguing that the "psychological moment" for further expansion in Milwaukee had arrived. Early in August he addressed a memorandum to Birge again pressing his case. This time the president agreed to bring the matter to the regents, who on September 5, 1923, voted "That the Extension Division be authorized to hold day classes in freshman and sophomore work for credit in Letters and Science and Engineering, at the Milwaukee Branch."[67]

Considerable private communication underlay the regents' decision. In a memo addressed to the board and dated August 31 President Birge defined the questions involved. Notwithstanding Lighty's rosy April staffing estimate, Birge reckoned a $12,000 added annual expense would have to be covered through increased fee income. More significantly, he cautioned that the proposal "involves a policy of great importance, since the Division proposes to offer regular full-time class work to students of a type which it has never before attempted to reach." He pointed out that because the issue arose during the vacation period, the UW faculty had been unable to consider the matter. Instead, Birge had convened a "conference of some 20 leading" faculty members from the colleges involved. L&S Dean Sellery urged "great circumspection" in a program that should be temporary and only modestly publicized by the division. Summarizing his colleagues' views, Sellery declared "there was no enthusiasm for it." Engineering Dean Turneaure and his faculty were more supportive, "favoring a modest program, partly as an experiment." Birge offered no recommendation, in keeping with the recent report of a committee of the Wisconsin Conference of State Boards, which advocated that public junior colleges be operated only under the auspices of local educational agencies and the state normal schools. Under this plan the University was to be involved only as the recipient of larger numbers of well-prepared upperclass transfer students.[68] State

---

[67]Lighty to Reber, April 9, 1923, Birge Presidential Papers 4/12/1, box 45, UA; Lighty to Reber, July 27, 1923; Lighty to Birge, August 11, 1923, Lighty Papers, box 16; BOR Minutes, September 5, 1923. For Lighty's later observations on this episode see Lighty to F.O. Holt, March 26, 1936; Lighty, "Address to the Milwaukee Extension Faculty," October 23, 1936, Lighty Papers, boxes 44 and 82.

[68]Birge to Each Regent, August 31, 1923, Birge Presidential Papers, 4/12/1, box 45; Committee on Junior Colleges appointed by the Conference of State Boards, December 8, 1921, "Report on Junior Colleges for Wisconsin," December 29, 1922, attached to C.J.

Superintendent of Public Instruction and Regent John Callahan, however, wished to see the proposal "tried out," and Milwaukee Regent Gilbert E. Seaman was "firmly of the opinion that enlargement of the work is desirable and necessary to meet the present demand," which need not end with the veterans. "If these courses are extended," emphasized Seaman, "I trust the University as a whole, including the Campus Faculty, will find it possible to support them whole-heartedly."[69]

Immediately following the regents' affirmative vote, Dean Reber issued a notice for distribution throughout the Milwaukee area. "Beginning with the opening of the fall semester, September 20, 1923," he announced, "the University Extension Division of the University of Wisconsin will organize regular day classes in first and second year college studies for graduates of high schools with the appropriate credentials for University admission." Ignoring the veterans, whose interest he evidently took for granted, Reber directed his attention to local high school graduates who were unable to take up full-time collegiate studies in Madison or elsewhere away from home. Even so, the local press essentially ignored the modest publicity effort.[70] Subsequent Extension Division catalogs continued Reber's moderate tone and emphasized the program's close association with the regular UW undergraduate curriculum. There was no suggestion of a temporary or experimental program as envisioned by at least some of the original supporters: "These courses are carried on with the supervision of the College of Letters and Science and the College of Engineering, and carry full university credit. Students desiring to complete the first two years of a university course while living in Milwaukee may do so in

---

Anderson to Birge, January 3, 1923, ibid., box 31. Members of the committee included C.J. Anderson (representing State Superintendent John Callahan), V.G. Barnes (representing High School Principals' Association), H.W. Kircher (representing City Superintendents' Association), C.G. Pearse (representing state normal school presidents), and G.C. Sellery (representing President Birge).

[69]John Callahan to M.E. McCaffrey, August 30, 1923; Gilbert E. Seaman to McCaffrey, September 3, 1923, BOR Papers, 1/1/3, box 37, UA. Anticipating they would be unable to attend the September 5 regents meeting, Callahan and Seaman submitted their views in writing to Regent Secretary McCaffrey.

[70]Reber, notice on dean's office stationary, September 5, 1923, Birge Presidential Papers, 4/12/1, box 45. Reber's announcement in Milwaukee was reported in the Milwaukee *Sentinel* for September 7, 1923. Neither the *Capital Times* nor the *Wisconsin State Journal* mentioned the regent vote on the program, although they did report other aspects of the meeting in their September 6 editions.

these classes."[71]

The expanded day program was moderately successful from its inception. Full- and part-time enrollments in the letters and science credit classes increased from 30 at the beginning in 1923-24, to 52 a year later, and 79 in September, 1925. Meanwhile, registrations in the full-time engineering course declined from around 100 in 1923-24 to about 60 in 1925-26. Extension officials expected this drop as the veterans completed their studies. Over the same period participation in a non-credit, vocationally oriented commerce sequence established for the war veterans in 1919 dropped from a high of 56 to only 15. As a whole, the day program attracted only a small part of the total extension classroom clientele in Milwaukee, where late afternoon and evening classes (both credit and non-credit) consistently outdrew the former, sometimes by more than tenfold.[72] While the number of students enrolled in the letters and science freshman/sophomore work indicated only a modest local demand during the first few years, the program's ability to endure quietly provided a comfortable means for the Madison faculty to become accustomed to maintaining small departmental outposts in the big city. Although only moderately important at the time, this evolving program would ultimately help to produce the downfall of Reber's successor, Chester D. Snell, and to further the progress of the Milwaukee Center toward full university status.

Meanwhile, as Dean Reber awaited the appointment of a new University president, he sought an appropriate extension building in Milwaukee. Frustration abounded as Milwaukee city officials slowly considered plans for a new civic center, somewhere within which they hoped to place the new extension facility. At first they thought the city might contribute the site, leaving the full appropriation of $150,000 for construction. This plan collapsed, however, and high downtown land prices soon made clear that the original appropriation was inadequate to complete the project as envisioned. Stymied, the dean and his special regent committee sought alternatives and finally identified an old school building that could be purchased and refitted with the available funds. Governor Blaine objected to this strategy, however, because the appropriation had called for the construction of a new rather than the remod-

[71]*General Catalogue of University College Courses and Day and Evening Classes in Milwaukee, 1924-1925, University Extension Division*, Bulletin of the University of Wisconsin, Serial No. 1287, General Series No. 1064 [1924], p. 7.

[72]Miscellaneous enrollment statistics, College of Agriculture Papers, 18/1/1, box 16.

eling of an existing building. To resolve what seemed a minor technical problem, University authorities asked the recently convened 1925 legislature to modify the 1923 appropriation to permit the erection "or purchase" of an acceptable structure.[73]

Unanticipated controversy now suddenly overwhelmed the effort to acquire a Milwaukee extension building. One well-orchestrated campaign was led by Edward A. Fitzpatrick, the recently appointed graduate dean at Milwaukee's Jesuit Marquette University. Fitzpatrick had worked with William H. Allen on his critical survey of the University in 1915 and later had served as secretary of the Wisconsin State Board of Education, an ineffective educational oversight agency created by the Philipp administration until it was disbanded in 1923. Fitzpatrick complained to the Senate Committee on Education and Public Welfare, which was considering the UW request, that extension's full-time day program might injure Marquette and other private schools in Milwaukee:

> If, as is variously rumored, the proposal for the building at Milwaukee is merely the beginning of the development of a college here which will be a branch of the University, then it is our deliberate judgment that such an institution might *possibly* affect injuriously Marquette University and certainly would be wasteful expenditure of public funds to duplicate existing educational facilities furnished by private agencies.[74]

Before proceeding further, the senators requested an attorney general's opinion on the constitutionality of the building plans for the Milwaukee Extension Center.

On May 4 Attorney General Herman L. Ekern, a long-time La Follette progressive, issued an unequivocal opinion in the University's favor. He first decided, in agreement with the Marquette University position, that the state constitution prohibited "the establishment of a department or college as a part of the state university at any other place than at or near the seat of state government" in Madison. The question thus was "whether the proposed university extension activities at Milwaukee come within the constitutional prohibition so interpreted." Ekern's conclusion was that they did not:

---

[73]Reber to Glenn Frank, September 22, 1925, with enclosure, "Memorandum Re A Building for the University Extension Division in Milwaukee," September 21, 1925, Frank Presidential Papers, 4/13/1, box 13.

[74]Edward A. Fitzpatrick to Senator Teasdale, February 18, 1925, ibid., box 14. Emphasis in original.

> The work which may be taken by a student through the university extension is not confined to any one college but may be in any college of the university with proper credit upon completion. It is, therefore, what its name implies, an extension of the work of all the colleges and in no sense constitutes the establishment of any new department or college. It merely furnishes an additional point of contact for the established department or college.[75]

In other words, the Extension Division's functional role was only that of a conduit between the University's academic colleges and departments in Madison and the Wisconsin public.

Concern about the proposed Milwaukee extension building also developed in Madison, where there had always existed latent concern about the possibility of losing state agencies to Milwaukee. Thus even before Dean Fitzpatrick made his objections, Regents Daniel Grady and Harry L. Butler opposed the building project as tending toward the establishment of a University branch in Milwaukee.[76] A similar concern may have been behind Senator Garey's decision to withdraw the enabling legislation from consideration by the full senate, even after the attorney general's opinion affirming its constitutionality. The Madison *Capital Times* asked editorially if there was a plot for "Detaching the Capitol and University From Madison By Piecemeal?" The paper reviewed Milwaukee press coverage of the campaign by Dean Reber and the special regent committee to obtain the proposed extension building and predicted a second effort to establish a "branch capitol" in Milwaukee. Editor Evjue doubted the constitutionality of such schemes, Attorney General Ekern's opinion notwithstanding, and warned that Madison had "a valid right to insist that administrative and legislative officials of the state have no right to make changes that are in plain violation of the state constitution."[77] The controversy over the constitutionality of the University's presence in Milwaukee would continue for

---

[75]Herman L. Ekern to C.B. Casperson, May 4, 1925, Attorney General Papers, General Correspondence, Series 629, box 152, SHSW. For statements of the Marquette and Extension Division positions see Edward A. Fitzpatrick to Ekern, March 14, 1925; Walter D. Corrigan to Ekern, March 17 and 25, 1925; WHL [Lighty], "Preliminary Notes on the Wisconsin Constitutional Mandate to Establish a State University as Related to the University Extension Building, Milwaukee," April 18, 1925, University Extension Division Papers, 18/1/1, box 7.

[76]Fitzpatrick to Ekern, March 14, 1925. Fitzpatrick explained that he had not been the first to question "the authority of the University to establish a branch in Milwaukee or at any other place. This question was not raised by us originally but by Mr. Daniel Grady, a member of the Board of University Regents and in the Board itself, and if I am not mistaken, Mr. Harry Butler of Madison, who was a member of the Board at the time, concurred in the opinion."

[77]*Capital Times*, January 20, 1926.

decades to come.

President Birge's retirement and the appointment of Glenn Frank as his successor in 1925 gave Dean Reber his long-sought opportunity to recommend a successor to head the Extension Division. His choice was Chester D. Snell, the director of extension at the University of North Carolina, and he promptly began trying to arrange a meeting between Frank and Snell in the fall of 1925. Snell informed Reber he was willing to discuss the UW extension post with Frank, although he already had made tentative plans to spend the 1926-27 academic year completing the residency requirement for his doctoral work in educational administration at Columbia University. The reluctant candidate sent Frank an article he had recently published in the UNC *Alumni Review* outlining the outreach program he had shaped at North Carolina. According to Snell his unit operated "as far as possible through the avenue of regular university channels," stressing the involvement of the resident departments whose efforts were "strengthened" by a well-organized and dedicated extension staff. "Those who have visited the University to study its extension program," he asserted, "have found virtually the entire University engaged or interested in serving the State." Snell's views accorded with Frank's needs, and on April 13, 1926, the two enjoyed a productive first visit at the University of Virginia. "I am certain that great things are just ahead for Wisconsin under your leadership," Snell wrote Frank effusively a few days later, "and I hope I shall be able to play a real part in working out with you and putting into operation plans for bringing about the newer relationship between the University and the State which you have vividly outlined." On April 28 the UW Board of Regents officially accepted Reber's resignation and approved Frank's recommendation to appoint the youthful Snell acting dean at an impressive annual salary of $7,500, the same salary then earned by such long-time veteran deans such as Charles Slichter, Harry Russell, and George Sellery.[78]

"Your appointment enthusiastically confirmed by board," Frank wired Snell on April 30. The local press took a similar upbeat view of the selection. The *Wisconsin State Journal* told its readers that "Mr. Snell is said to have achieved one of the most conspicuous successes in

---

[78]Reber to Frank, November 16 and 24, 1925, January 22, 1926, Frank Presidential Papers, 4/13/1, box 14; "The University That Is Not In Chapel Hill," reprint, *Alumni Review* (February, 1926), enclosed with Snell to Frank, April 1, 1926; Snell to Frank, April 16, 1926, ibid., box 15; BOR Minutes, April 28, 1926. Snell began his tenure at Wisconsin at the same salary with which Reber finished.

the country's education history in making extension in his state." The *Daily Cardinal* reported that Snell came "highly recommended" by President Emeritus Birge and Dean Reber.[79] The *Capital Times* quoted Reber's support for the appointment: "I really think, in electing him, the board of regents has secured the best man in the United States for this position." Even Reber's veteran extension rival, William Lighty, whom the dean had explicitly rejected as an appropriate successor, sent enthusiastic word to Snell "to tell you how gratifying to me and to many of us here on the campus is the decision to bring you here." He saw the appointment as a significant feature of Glenn Frank's much-heralded University renaissance:

> We believe ourselves fortunate in the leadership of our brilliant young president, in whom we have confidence, and now we count ourselves fortunate again that he has chosen you with all your wholesome young energy as one of his most important deans. We are eager to get back of a real constructive policy and program for extramural education in Wisconsin. Once again we hope to proceed to build up the aspirations conceived, communicated and sustained by Van Hise.[80]

Such praise must have been heady stuff for the young man from North Carolina.

Already, however, the seeds of Chester Snell's undoing at Wisconsin were being planted. Either by accident or design, the University's announcement of the Snell appointment obscured the new division head's extreme youth and inexperience for such a position by misstating his age as thirty-six (he was only thirty) and the length of his tenure as director at North Carolina as six years (actually less than five).[81] The announcement also neglected to mention that Snell had not resigned his North Carolina position, but instead would be on leave while serving at Wisconsin. Similarly, there was no explanation for Snell's designation as acting dean and the press failed to comment on it. In the beginning

---

[79]According to Reber the University announcement invoked the name of President Birge to indicate that Snell's appointment was based on merit and not political considerations. "Memoranda for Mr. Snell," n.d., p. 12, University Extension Division Papers, 18/1/1, box 60.

[80]*Wisconsin State Journal* and *Capital Times*, April 28, 1926; *Daily Cardinal*, April 29, 1926; Lighty to Snell, April 29, 1926, Lighty Papers, box 24.

[81]The *Wisconsin State Journal* and *Milwaukee Journal* for April 28, 1926, and the Milwaukee *Sentinel*, for April 29, 1926, gave Snell's age as thirty-six. More tellingly, so too did the University's own *Press Bulletin* for May 5, 1926. *Who's Who In America*, e.g., 34 (1966-67), gives Snell's birth date as November 24, 1895.

Snell viewed his appointment at Wisconsin as a personal educational venture, which might or might not become permanent, and he therefore regarded the acting designation as appropriate. His correspondence with President Frank indicates that Snell's assignment eventually would be to head the division on a part-time basis and the rest of the time work directly with the president on educational policy and administration. Frank, in other words, was agreeing to act as Snell's mentor in exactly those fields he had planned to study for his doctorate at Columbia University. Presumably the promise of real-world experience at the heart of a major institution of higher education appealed to Snell as at least equivalent in value to the Ph.D. studies he was foregoing at Columbia.[82] Unfortunately for him and indeed the entire University Extension Division, President Frank's forte was as an impresario and not a mentor, and eventually the extension head would be forced to strike out on his own.

The first year of Snell's administration appeared virtually flawless as the president and acting dean worked to refurbish the University's image of public service through the Extension Division. In October of 1926 the University *Press Bulletin* issued a statement by Snell that sounded much like Van Hise's vision of extension:

> We must see to it that the learning of this University is ever linked closely to the life of the state in terms of practical service...making all the knowledge and all the insight of the university available to men and women throughout Wisconsin for economic betterment, the intellectual stimulation, and the spiritual enrichment of their lives. This is the spiritual charter of University Extension in Wisconsin. Its greatest days are ahead.

Snell saw the challenge "not to rest on laurels won, but to unite again, enter new fields, and preserve for the nation the spirit of the pioneer." President Frank, for his part, promised to "make extension less and less a separate arm of the University and more and more the channel through which the whole University will function in the life of the State."[83] This in fact was the closest Frank ever came to providing

---

[82]Snell remained on leave from North Carolina until 1928. See Louis R. Wilson, *The University of North Carolina, 1900-1930: The Making of a Modern University* (Chapel Hill: University of North Carolina Press, 1957), pp. 417-9. See also Snell to Frank, December 10, 1925; Snell to Frank, April 16, 1926; Frank to Snell, telegram, April 21, 1926, Frank Presidential Papers, 4/13/1, box 15; Snell to Frank, April 18, 1927; Frank to Snell [ca. September, 1927], University Extension Division Papers, 18/1/1, box 14.

[83]*Press Bulletin*, October 6, 1926; Frank, "Future Policies and Programs in University

general policy guidance to his young lieutenant.

Snell meanwhile embarked on a comprehensive program of internal reorganization of his division. Some of his reforms were innocuous and technical in nature, seeking increased efficiency in academic and fiscal record keeping. Others were of greater significance, involving a painful shuffling and replacement of staff members with little regard for quality of work or seniority. The most notable change involved the district field staff, which Snell removed from Professor Lighty's supervision and put in his own office under the close direction of Chester Allen, whom he promoted from the Appleton outpost. In the fall of 1926 Snell informed Lighty that extension staff members were no longer allowed to communicate directly with field personnel, but instead must forward everything through Allen for the dean's approval. "To follow this procedure," explained Snell, "will enable the working out of a correlated long-term program of field work." Perhaps Dean Emeritus Reber had heard reports of this development when he wrote to President Frank from Paris that he trusted Snell would "not go too fast in making changes" and that he had always hoped the division might "come to the point of giving greater independence to individual lines of work."[84]

Snell also set to work on the situation in Milwaukee, where the immediate problem was to complete arrangements for the new building. Prior to his arrival in Madison, the regents had purchased a site for $45,000 and asked Arthur Peabody, the state architect, to plan the facility. Snell promptly joined forces with Peabody and began working with Milwaukee legislators Polakowski and Morris to win passage of a special appropriation of $175,000 to augment the $105,000 remaining from the 1923 appropria-tion. During the spring of 1927 Polakowski and Snell issued a printed circular outlining the need for quick action:

> This bill was introduced separately from the regular University budget just as

---

Extension," text of address delivered to the University Extension Division faculty meeting, May, 1927, Glenn Frank Papers, Northeast Missouri State University, Kirksville. For a similar statement on the "channel" theme see Frank, "The University of Wisconsin—A Look Backward and Forward," *Wisconsin Blue Book, 1927* (Madison: State of Wisconsin, 1927), p. 368.

[84]Snell to Lighty, "Approaches to Field Men," memorandum, October 6, 1926, Lighty Papers, box 26; Reber to Frank, December 25, 1926, Frank Presidential Papers, 4/13/1, box 33. Reber softened his remarks somewhat by adding: "Do not misunderstand me. I have absolute faith in Mr. Snell if he stays with the job long enough. I like his initiative and the confidence he has in himself. He seems to be able to keep the good will of the people of the Division."

was Bill 160S in 1923, for the initiative for the development of the University
Extension work in Milwaukee (and throughout the State) has always come
primarily from the people. While the 1923 bill was supported almost solely
by the people of the State, the present Bill 191S also has the active support of
University officials and the Board of Regents.

Although perhaps accurate, this gratuitous slap at University authorities
did little to allay concerns in Madison about the political dangers inherent in University expansion in Milwaukee. The bill passed, and construction could now proceed.[85]

In approving the 1927-28 University budget, the regents evaluated
Snell's progress, removed the "acting" designation from his title, and
added $1,000 to his original $7,500 salary. "They expressed unanimous gratification over the reorganization work in Extension so far,"
Frank reported to Snell; "they said the 'wrecking' job had been done in
a masterly manner, that the cutting out of dead wood was done effectively." The president had sought to raise Snell's salary to $10,000, but
the board wanted to wait until "at least the beginning of the show of
positive results in increased service of Extension, rather than the negative phase through which it passed under your first year of administration." The disappointed Snell angrily dashed off a handwritten reply to
Frank, but decided against sending it. The draft bemoaned what he
considered his inadequate pay, declared he would have returned to
North Carolina if he had received this news in spring, and laid part of
the blame for the lack of "positive results" on regent and presidential
inaction. He indicated his displeasure with Frank and the planned
mentoring relationship by opting to remain full-time with extension
rather than to undertake studies of the University business office and
other schools and colleges where "waste and dead timber" were apparently rife. The response Snell did send the president was nearly as
hostile. He emphasized the year's positive results, which he complained
had not been reported to the board because of Frank's admonition to
"'tell them as little as possible.'" The extent of his isolation was now
dawning on Snell, and he blamed Frank for failing to provide him with
official marching orders. He intended the future to be different: "I

---

[85]Reber and the special regent committee, consisting of Miss Leola Hirschman and
Theodore Kronshage, had worked with Milwaukee officials to obtain the desired site for
$45,000. "Memoranda for Mr. Snell," pp. 4-6; BOR Minutes, October 17, December 2,
1925, January 20, 1926. Snell enclosed a pamphlet entitled *The University Extension Building
in Milwaukee* with a letter to Frank, on March 24, 1927. Frank Presidential Papers, 4/13/1,
box 34.

should like to have in writing exactly what positive results I am to show and how I should show or exhibit them."[86] Such explicit direction was not Frank's style, and no detailed instructions were forthcoming. The dean was left to shape and portray division policy according to the president's vaguely expressed thoughts, now increasingly focussed on the theme of adult education. Taking a cue from Dean Russell's energetic publicist Andrew Hopkins and his agricultural journalism department, Snell's most effective innovation was to hire an editor from the Forest Products Laboratory, T.J. Mosely. Mosley went to work as the division's first full-time public relations man, soon producing a breezy article for the *Wisconsin Alumni Magazine* under the title, "University Extension Widens Its Scope." "Adult Education," Mosely reported, "is University Extension hitting on all six and being used as a vehicle for social service rather than institutional propaganda. Looked at in this way, it is not such a brand-new experiment after all, in Wisconsin." He described the revitalized field force and new bureaus designed to bring the expertise of UW faculty members in economics, sociology, commerce, engineering, education, and medicine to constituencies throughout the state. Above all Mosely praised the leadership of Dean Chester D. Snell, who "is no faddist in his declared effort to embody the ideals of Adult Education in the program of the University Extension Division....The objective may be expressed as the fulfillment of individual and community living through education."[87]

Notwithstanding Snell's reforms, the Extension Division remained a minor and somewhat isolated sub-agency of the University. The cause was structural, dating back to its inception in the early years of the Van Hise administration when Charles McCarthy and his fellow progressives insisted on a separate, dedicated extension staff to do the specialized work they believed the resident faculty was largely unsuited to perform. For the College of Agriculture, Dean Russell had operated from a very

---

[86]Frank to Snell, typed at home [ca. Sunday, August 28, 1927]; Snell to Frank, handwritten letter, not sent, September, 1927, University Extension Division Papers, 18/1/1, box 14. Snell to Frank, October 7, 1927, Frank Presidential Papers, 4/13/1, box 52. On Snell's earlier views about returning to North Carolina, his expectation for a larger UW salary, and the central importance of President Frank in Snell's decision to come to Madison, see Snell to Frank, April 18, 1927, University Extension Division Papers, 18/1/1, box 14.

[87]T.J. Mosley, "University Extension Widens Its Scope," *WAM*, 29 (February, 1928), 159, 184. According to Clay Schoenfeld, by 1929 Snell's main contribution was to "sell" extension division programming, new or not. *Outreach University*, pp. 115-6.

different assumption, shaping his outreach agency by fully integrating the extension staff into each of its academic departments. It was clear to many by the 1920s that the agriculture model was the more effective of the two, and President Frank was among those who recognized its superiority. It was Snell's article proclaiming North Carolina extension's ability to work through "regular university channels" that had made him an attractive candidate for the UW extension job. Frank expected Snell to work the same magic in Wisconsin. Dean Snell, confronting the basic fact of his division's structural isolation, soon encountered the same difficulties that had plagued Reber: how to recruit regular UW faculty members to cooperate with his bureaus in their public service work? Unlike agricultural extension, whose staff was closely integrated with the regular agriculture faculty, Snell's division tended to be viewed as a poor and distant relation obliged to compete with the campus teaching and research priorities of the schools and colleges. Lacking the federal funding that supported agricultural extension, moreover, Snell's chief weapon was rhetorical but largely unsatisfactory—to appeal for University cooperation.

The new six-story Milwaukee Extension Building, located at 619 State Street, was completed and put into service in September, 1928. At a festive dedication ceremony presided over by Dean Snell, who called the event "an Adult Education rally," Governor Fred Zimmerman formally presented the facility to President Frank, who was joined on the platform by representatives of some fifty Milwaukee educational and social agencies as well as by Milwaukee Mayor Hoan, Regent President Grady, and University Business Manager Phillips. Frank criticized conventional schooling for producing too many young citizens who were "inflexibly committed to American civilization as it is, stamped with the qualities of unquestioning defenders of the present status instead of the qualities of questioning pioneers." The Milwaukee Center, he promised, would work with adults to reverse this dismal trend. "We must develop an adult education which will give us better adults, who will give us better schools, which will give us a better education, which will give us a better social order. For the school and the social system must be saved together or they will sink together." Central to this agenda was a new, cutting-edge liberal studies program to begin with the fall term. These new non-credit courses, Snell declared, would "provide the means whereby the intelligent adult may keep step with modern thought and knowledge in the fields he wants to explore without having to tie himself to scholastic apron strings."[88]

The Milwaukee liberal studies program drew much of its inspiration from Alexander Meiklejohn's Experimental College, which had opened the previous year. The Milwaukee project had its origins in a small "Adult Education Conference" in Snell's Madison office on December 10, 1927. Participants included President Frank, Meiklejohn, Acting Professor of Education Joseph K. Hart, William Lighty, T.J. Mosley, UW rural sociologist J.H. Kolb, and Charles Purin and M.R. Schnaitter of the Milwaukee Center. According to the conference minutes, Snell opened the meeting by announcing that he hoped to undertake an adult education experiment in Milwaukee whose lessons later would be extended to evening instruction classes and correspondence work. "One big objective," he said, "would be to get away from both the subject-by-subject machinery of instruction and the passive-listener attitude on the student's part." The ensuing discussion was wide-ranging and enthusiastic if also sometimes rambling and even incoherent. Professor Hart, a professional visionary, proposed "a transformation of teaching technique" so the instructor might "be released from a sense of the subject-matter" and "be able to sense the viewpoint of the group." Professor Lighty wondered "what is an adult?" Professor Schnaitter objected to rigid distinctions between "vocational" and "humanistic" subjects. The conference—more an adult education love fest than a planning session—adjourned with a request from Snell that the participants confer among themselves and send suggestions to him. During the next few months Professors Hart and Meiklejohn offered advice, Lighty objected to certain features of the evolving plan, and Purin and Schnaitter worked out the curriculum. Characteristically, President Frank had no suggestions for the detailed plan.[89]

Shortly before opening the new Milwaukee Extension Building the

---

[88]Snell's characterization of the ceremony appeared in Snell to Governor Fred R. Zimmerman, July 12, 1928, Frank Presidential Papers, 4/13/1, box 52. For quotations from the ceremony see *Milwaukee Journal*, September 19, 1928. The facility contained twenty-five classrooms, four science laboratories, seventeen staff offices, and could accommodate 3,000 evening and 500 daytime students. Yet by 1929 overcrowding had developed, requiring several classes to meet at the public library. Within a few years the building developed a two-foot tilt toward State Street. See Elisabeth Holmes, compiler and editor, *The Urban Mission Anticipated: A Biography of the UW Extension Center in Milwaukee* (Milwaukee: University of Wisconsin-Milwaukee Foundation, 1976), p. 8.

[89]"Minutes of Adult Education Conference," December 10, 1927; Snell to Frank, January 19, March 2, 1928, Frank Presidential Papers, 4/13/1, box 52.

division issued its formal announcement of the "Foundation Courses in Liberal Education Leading to the Liberal Education Certificate." The program would offer, "without paralleling the usual college subjects in content or method, a series of courses aiming to give the foundations of a liberal education." The aim was to concentrate on process- as well as content-learning:

> To give an opportunity for adults to acquire an education which involves more than the obtaining of information and skill—an education which will lead to emancipation from a "drifting with the group" opinion; an education which will engender capacity for self criticism; and above all, an education which will create a feeling for those things that make life richer and more significant.

Courses would be organized around the traditional lecture format or take the form of "co-operative group activities in which the instructor functions as guide and advisor." Subject groups included philosophy, social science, history, language-literature, art, and biological and physical sciences. Each non-credit course would meet for seventeen weeks, and completion of ten courses would qualify the student for a Certificate in Liberal Education. Anyone could participate. Instructors for the first semester represented a wide range of backgrounds, from UW's well-known philosophy Professor Max Otto to nutritionist Dorothy Wiepking and Rabbi Samuel Hirshberg of Milwaukee to fifteen scientists from the University of Chicago.[90]

Dean Snell was concerned with much more than a new adult education venture in Milwaukee. In 1927 he abolished the old superintendent position as superfluous—the dean planned to spend considerable time in the city overseeing the center's work and progress on the new building—and the next year he recruited Charles Purin to direct the freshman-sophomore program, which he considered of great importance to the center.[91] By early 1929 he had thoroughly revamped Milwau-

---

[90]*Foundation Courses in Liberal Education Leading to the Liberal Education Certificate, University Extension Division*, Bulletin of the University of Wisconsin, Serial No. 1530, General Series No. 1304, August, 1928.

[91]In his effort to recruit Purin, Snell sent a bulletin describing the legislature's support for the development of the Milwaukee Center and added: "While little is said in the enclosed pamphlet concerning the Junior College, for the reason that the adult work appeals more to the members of the legislature, yet the freshman and sophomore work will receive our greatest attention and development during the next several years." Snell to Charles M. Purin, Hunter College, New York City, May 19, 1927, Frank Presidential Papers, 4/13/1, box 34.

kee's extension leadership. He first hired M.R. Schnaitter to take charge of the late afternoon and evening program emphasizing adult liberal and vocational non-credit work and a smattering of college-level courses. In 1927 the dean tried to remove Assistant Professor Chauncey Batchelor, the current Milwaukee English department chairman, who allegedly favored scholarship over teaching and whose outspoken criticism of the center administration and faculty was well-known and unappreciated. Batchelor fought his demotion and dismissal through 1929 when the regents finally affirmed Snell's decision.[92] He then recruited Malcolm Shaw MacLean, whose formal academic credentials were superior to Batchelor's, to take over the English chairmanship. About the same time Snell brought in Malcolm Little, a former colleague at the University of North Carolina, to oversee the center's administrative affairs as assistant director, and promoted Purin to the new director's position, with responsibility limited to academic affairs. As Snell reported to President Frank, these last appointments completed his reorganization of the Milwaukee program.[93]

These changes took place in the face of a continuing and confusing institutional ambivalence about the relationship between the Milwaukee extension program and the University in Madison. As the attorney general's opinion of 1925 had pointed out, the academic departments in Madison were the official sponsors of the freshman and sophomore credit courses. At the same time the University Extension Division was responsible for the overall center administration as well as for all non-credit work, which involved full- and part-time division staff and occasionally regular University faculty. Assistant Director Little functioned almost exclusively as Dean Snell's representative in Milwaukee, concerning himself with budgets, personnel, and other administrative matters. Professor Purin reported to Snell but also consulted frequently with the various Madison academic departments about their involvement with the center. At times the arrangement worked well and progress was obvious, as when the division succeeded in obtaining eleven scholarships for day students in 1927 and setting up an academic counseling

---

[92]Batchelor's dismissal at Milwaukee was an early reflection of developing tensions there. For the flavor of the controversy see *Capital Times*, June 18, 19, and 22, November 16, December 2, 1929; *Daily Cardinal*, July 4, November 17 and 19, December 3, 1929; *WAM*, 31 (January, 1930), 160; Snell to C.C. Batchelor, May 17, 1927, Frank Presidential Papers, 4/13/1, box 34; Purin to the Board of Regents, December 2, 1929, BOR Papers, 1/1/3, box 42; BOR Minutes, June 22, October 9, 1929; Holmes, *Urban Mission Anticipated*, p. 16.

[93]Snell to Frank, January 10, 1929, Frank Presidential Papers, 4/13/1, box 67.

service the following year. Yet, as the Batchelor case revealed, friction was unavoidable when scholarly and administrative goals came into conflict, sometimes arousing concern among Madison faculty members. Extension engineering Professor H.P. Wood resigned in 1927, for example, complaining to the regents that the division had suppressed his work at the center. The next year Snell and Madison chemistry department Chairman Mathews debated at length but failed to agree on appropriate research expectations for center faculty members, with the dean arguing for a heavy emphasis on teaching in the "junior college" program.[94] These disagreements were but symptoms of possible future trouble, however, for on the whole the 1920s were good years for Snell, the division, and especially the progress of the Milwaukee Center.

The great depression brought problems but also opportunities for the Extension Division. Shortly after the stock market crash in late 1929 Dean Snell predicted the "business drop" meant favorable conditions for extension because more people would welcome inexpensive educational opportunities close to home.[95] Events soon began to confirm this view. Even as enrollment in credit work at the Milwaukee Center declined, the number of students registering for classes in other Wisconsin localities increased dramatically. By late 1932, with the depression in full force, Snell was advocating free college-level classes for unemployed Wisconsin workers. The legislature agreed to provide $30,000 for this program in 1933, which, along with federal Civil Works Administration adult education funding, increased enrollment at the Milwaukee Center and enabled the division to respond to strong demand throughout the state. During 1932 Snell was part of a state-wide committee to develop plans for vocational and extension-based educational opportunities for recent high school graduates unable either to find jobs or attend college full time.[96] The division also stepped up

---

[94]The debate began when Snell wrote to G.G. Town, a chemistry instructor at the Milwaukee Center. After discussing his policy governing extension research funding, Snell observed: "As I understand it, there is already enough knowledge and data produced in the field of chemistry to keep a man busy the rest of his life trying to master it." Snell to Town, December 19, 1928, ibid. The subsequent exchange between Mathews and Snell defined a major conceptual gulf between the two men and, more significantly, between Snell and the general University faculty. J.H. Mathews to Snell, December 21, 1928; Snell to Mathews, December 27, 1928, ibid.

[95]*Daily Cardinal*, November 26, 1929.

[96]"Tentative Draft," memorandum based on March 11, 1932, meeting of John Callahan, George Hambrecht, Frank Holt, E.G. Doudna, and Snell; *Educational Plans for High School Graduates*, Bulletin Prepared By a State Committee of Callahan, Hambrecht, Doudna, and

its efforts to enroll school teachers for post-graduate study and even to offer special secondary-level courses within the public schools to supplement the standard curriculum.[97]

These creative responses could not overshadow the tensions and problems exacerbated by the depression, however. As Chester Allen, Dean Snell's field staff director and close associate, later recalled, "It was a period in which the confusion increased and the basic horrid human traits of suspicion, selfishness, pessimism, and fear gripped a surprisingly large number of people."[98] Part of the trouble derived from the division's isolated and financially precarious position within the University. Graduate Dean Charles S. Slichter, for example, proposed unsuccessfully in 1930 that Snell's deanship be abolished in favor of a less expensive extension governing committee consisting of the University academic deans. Concerned about the likely cost to his budget, Snell angered Wisconsin progressives by declining to provide extension support for a state-level committee studying minimum wages and safety regulations for working women and children. In response to growing complaints, the dean countered with a four-part series of articles in the *Capital Times* that tried to answer the critics while presenting a positive image of the division.[99] Meanwhile, relations between Snell and President Frank continued to deteriorate. In early 1930, for example, the dean defensively requested (but did not receive) a written statement of objectives for the coming biennium. Two years later Snell felt betrayed when Frank considered absorbing the division budget into that of the rest of the University. In early 1934 Frank disappointed Snell in remarks about extension at a University faculty meeting and later angrily rebuked the dean after learning from a newspaper article that Snell had unilaterally—and improperly—entered into agreements with three county normal schools to provide what amounted to junior college programs at their institutions.

As in the past the situation in Milwaukee was the most vexing.

Snell, n.d., Frank Presidential Papers, 4/13/1, box 122.

[97]See John L. Bergstresser, "Classes Go to the Student," *WAM*, 39 (April, 1938), 213-6.

[98]Allen, "University Extension," vol. 2, p. 38.

[99]The *Capital Times* announced these essay topics while the actual headlines varied considerably: "Adult Education as a State and University Function" (January 27, 1931), "The University Extension Division in Terms of Social Results" (January 28), "Is the University Extension Division Attempting to Build a Branch University in Milwaukee?" (January 29), and "Extension Dept. Planning To Aid In the Solution of State Economic, School Problems" (January 30).

The most troublesome problem was how to support a resident faculty adequate to staff the freshman/sophomore program when the latter depended largely on unpredictable fee income. At first Snell's strategy was to cut the related support costs as much as possible. As the depression deepened, he turned to the idea of reducing, or at least being able quickly to reduce, the teaching staff as required. Thus in mid-1933 Snell wrote suggestively to Frank about the drastic staff cuts then being applied at Rutgers University.[100] The following January he asked the president for authority to issue one-year contracts to all assistant professors up for appointment, rather than the usual three-year commitments. Then hastily, apparently before receiving any official response from Frank, he and Professor Purin began informing the targeted staff members of the new contract policy. Soon near-panic gripped the center, deepened by widespread distrust of the dean whom several junior staff members suspected had ulterior motives in their cases. Chauncey Batchelor's ordeal in the late 1920s came to mind, as well as a more recent and continuing conflict between Snell and Albert Croft, an outspoken sociology instructor due for promotion to assistant professor. The perception grew that Snell was arbitrary and autocratic in dealing with the center. In May President Frank informed Snell he was prepared to guarantee the usual three-year contracts for assistant professors, but Snell nevertheless offered terminal one-year appointments to five apparently troublesome but academically competent staff members and refused to renew the expiring three-year appointment of Assistant Professor of Zoology Donald C. Boughton, who was then completing two years of research leave.

Boughton responded by circulating an open letter to his Milwaukee colleagues severely criticizing the dean's administration. It set off a chain of events that eventually resulted in the widely publicized firing of Chester Snell. Even to this day, after the publication of at least three accounts of the affair, many of the details remain obscure.[101] Indeed, the bitter litany of charges, denials, counter-charges, and innuendo that characterized the remainder of Snell's administration in 1934 and much

---

[100]Snell to Frank, June 30, 1933, Frank Presidential Papers, 4/13/1, box 138. The headline of the enclosed clipping from an unidentified newspaper read: "RUTGERS DROPS 47 FROM ITS FACULTY." Future events at Wisconsin would show that Snell favored this tactic for the Extension Division.

[101]See Rosentreter, *Boundaries of the Campus*, pp. 142-4; Schoenfeld, *Outreach University*, pp. 119-21; Holmes, *Urban Mission Anticipated*, pp. 15-26. Allen's unpublished "University Extension," vol 2, pp. 90-125, bitterly offers a pro-Snell interpretation.

of 1935 provided ample proof that regardless of the merit of the charges he had lost control of his unit. For that reason alone the regents concluded they needed to make a change in the division's leadership. This they did in April, 1935, after conducting a series of closed hearings in Madison and Milwaukee beginning the previous November. Much of the testimony from the Madison-based extension staff was negative in content and tone. This was particularly true of Professor Lighty, whose displeasure with Snell was widely known and shared by many campus faculty members and administrators who had grown to resent the dean's tendency to bypass normal lines of authority and appeal directly to the regents and legislature for special consideration of his division. The situation in Milwaukee was less clear-cut, reflecting a major rift in the forty-member full-time staff. Perhaps eight or ten young faculty turks (who used the American Federation of Teachers local union as their main vehicle of protest) constituted Snell's main critics. They were opposed by most of their more senior colleagues, some of whom served at the dean's pleasure in relatively well-paying administrative posts. In his defense Snell offered some irrelevant but highly inflammatory innuendo, suggesting sexual improprieties by the unnamed but easily identified married daughter of a UW regent, an AFT union official, and several Milwaukee Center employees. Although the lurid charges drew the attention for a time of a legislative committee investigating the University, if anything they confirmed the regents in their resolve to remove the dean.[102]

As Chapter 4 argues, the Snell episode reflected badly on the University and Glenn Frank and in turn helped lead to the president's own downfall in early 1937. Largely overlooked in the Snell affair was the involvement of the regular University faculty through its University Committee. At the time Snell proposed dropping the customary three-year contracts for assistant professors, the committee was working with the campus administration and regents to find ways of reducing the University budget while protecting faculty appointments. One of its key members was Mark Ingraham, who was also chairman of the mathematics department. Ingraham learned of Snell's new personnel policy

---

[102]The 1,021-page transcript of the regent hearings makes fascinating reading while at the same time providing little clarification of the facts of the matter. See "Investigation by Special Committee of the Board of Regents of the University of Wisconsin as to Conditions in the University of Wisconsin Extension Division Center at Milwaukee, Wisconsin: Testimony November 7, 1934, November 21, 1934, January 11, 1935, March 4, 1935, March 9, 1935" (bound transcript, n.d.), BOR Papers, 1/6/3, box 1.

through discussions with William E. Roth, an assistant professor of mathematics in Milwaukee whose job apparently was in jeopardy. Ingraham naturally reacted to the news in terms of faculty tenure, and alerted his University Committee colleagues to what he considered a dangerous precedent. During the summer of 1934 he spoke and corresponded with Snell, expressing his opposition to the dean's approach, and he almost certainly worked with President Frank earlier that spring in identifying funds to guarantee three-year appointments for the Milwaukee assistant professors.[103] Precisely what else Ingraham and his colleagues did about the issue is unknown, but the transcript of the regent investigation reveals an unusually single-minded concern on the part of Regent Harold Wilkie to determine whether Snell had respected University faculty prerogatives at the center. The significance of this is two-fold. First, Dean Snell lost whatever campus support he might have had by appearing to violate faculty prerogatives and undermine the Madison faculty's efforts to protect faculty contracts and tenure. Second, his actions forced the University tacitly to recognize the Milwaukee Center staff as full-fledged UW faculty members with customary Madison faculty rights and privileges. The "great circumspection" urged by Dean Sellery in 1923 no longer applied.

To replace Snell the regents named Frank O. Holt as extension dean in April, 1935. A decade earlier Holt, then the superintendent of schools in Janesville, had sought the extension job from which Reber was then retiring. President Frank had selected Snell instead, but, impressed with Holt's quality, had appointed him University registrar and general supervisor of an expanding student services program. Holt's judgment about institutional policy and skill at public relations were masterful, and over the years he had developed into one of the president's closest advisors. As dean he soon demonstrated his keen sense of the division's role within the University and its capacity to serve the wider public. For the first year he retained his registrar's position and worked almost entirely out of that office. Division staff members thus found themselves largely on their own for day-to-day activities, but after a period of moderate confusion they responded productively and with increasingly improved morale. Following the firing of President Frank in early 1937 and the appointment of Curtis Merriman as the new registrar, Holt moved into the dean's office in the

---

[103]Snell to Mark H. Ingraham, chairman, University Committee, July 14, 1934, and Ingraham to Snell, July 17, 1934, University Faculty Papers, 5/96/2, box 2, UA.

Extension Building near Agricultural Hall and began involving himself more directly in extension affairs. Like Agriculture Dean Christensen next door, he quietly emphasized cooperation and collegiality, rejecting Snell's authoritarian style in favor of one more in keeping with Wisconsin tradition.

Dean Holt took a more affirmative approach in Milwaukee, proclaiming his intention to transform the center into an integral branch of the University. He made it clear to the Milwaukee teaching staff that he recognized and supported their status as full-fledged University faculty, sometimes even boasting that their scholarly credentials were every bit as impressive as those of their mentors in Madison. He rescinded all of Snell's planned firings, began holding regularly scheduled faculty meetings, and encouraged the formation of a new faculty Committee of Seven that eventually came to play an important role in institutional governance. Although the divisive Snell affair had left a legacy of hard feelings, under Holt's wise leadership it soon began to appear as an aberration and a more enduring spirit of collegiality quietly emerged. Holt also cultivated the center's instructional ties with Madison by publicizing the successful experience of Milwaukee students who transferred to the Madison for their junior and senior years. He even arranged for the *Daily Cardinal* to report regularly on Milwaukee campus events as part of day-to-day University life. Meanwhile, technical and liberal studies programs continued to serve an adult constituency with a broad array of non-credit offerings. The most substantial indication of Holt's success in integrating the Milwaukee Center with the Madison campus came early in 1941 when the University faculty approved the establishment of a limited program of graduate studies in Milwaukee.[104]

Dean Holt capitalized on the University faculty's growing acceptance of the freshman/sophomore program at Milwaukee to encourage further development of freshman class centers throughout the state. In this he continued more than redirected Snell's initiatives, but his superior public relations skills and wide contacts with the education establishment of the state produced better results. He also received encouragement from President Dykstra. Following the success of experimental programs in Antigo and Rhinelander, a group of educational officials met in June, 1935, to discuss the prospects for the further development of junior colleges throughout the state. Holt was an active participant,

---

[104]UW Faculty Document 612, Graduate School Faculty, "Report on Graduate Work in Milwaukee," February 3, 1941; UW Faculty Minutes, February 3, 1941.

encouraging local public and county normal and vocational schools to sponsor college freshman programs in conjunction with the Extension Division. During the next two academic years sixteen units in thirteen towns and cities other than Milwaukee enrolled more than 430 students. Participation dropped to less than 300 in 1937-38, a reflection of the improved economy and the projected end of state aids for collegiate studies at vocational schools. The policy of the Extension Division next shifted to reducing the number of extramural instructional sites for junior college work and emphasizing to local school officials the virtues of University-provided instruction over that available from high school teachers. The operation of off-campus University freshman study centers was beginning to take firm institutional root when American entry into the Second World War suddenly, if temporarily, brought about the suspension of the program for the duration. The rapid expansion of the University centers following the war would quickly validate the division's ground-breaking efforts during the 1930s, when its depression-spawned program had enabled several thousand Wisconsin young people to begin their University undergraduate studies while living at home, far from the Madison campus. At the same time, the expanded presence of University instructors around the state produced a number of unanticipated controversies. In 1933, for example, Instructor Albert Croft of the Milwaukee Center aroused the objections of Roman Catholic officials though his sociological critique of Church doctrines and activities. Three years later an extension history instructor in Wausau, T. Harry Williams, upset local residents by remarking that Lincoln's Gettysburg address was an excellent example of political propaganda. Wausau officials demanded Williams' removal from the local center staff, but after reviewing the case Holt refused to yield and threatened to close the center if Williams were forced out. The critics reluctantly backed down. In 1937, with anti-Japan sentiment in the state rising, the division was at first unable to place extension English Instructor S.I. Hayakawa, a Canadian of Japanese ancestry. Finally the Rhinelander Center agreed to take him. A Kenosha Center English instructor set off a storm of controversy in 1940 by assigning Thomas Wolfe's controversial novel, *Look Homeward Angel*. In this instance Dean Holt ordered the book removed from the class reading list.[105]

After Dean Holt took charge of the new University Public Service

---

[105]Rosentreter, *Boundaries of the Campus*, pp. 164-70, provides a good analysis of these controversies. For another reference to Hayakawa, see p. 565.

Department in 1943, the following year the regents selected Lorentz H. Adolphson, a division political scientist, to head the Extension Division. As in the transition between Reber and Snell, the University was about to enter a new phase of development. Adolphson's task was thus to plan extension's post-war contributions. He took over a unit considerably stronger and better integrated with the rest of the University than had been the case in 1925. The Milwaukee Center had developed into an established and well-accepted outpost offering lower-division credit-instruction through a resident faculty in the state's largest city. Its post-war prospects seemed bright. While currently inactive, the division's pre-war freshman centers scattered around the state had helped to condition the Madison faculty and the public to the value of lower division UW credit instruction at the grassroots. Indeed, the occasional controversy over staffing and academic freedom reflected the seriousness with which the public viewed this emerging educational opportunity. There was also growing public awareness of how general extension staff members were working effectively with Engineering, Commerce, Medicine, and other campus units to expand the long tradition of bringing University expertise to the people of Wisconsin.

Educational Radio

During the inter-war years radio broadcasting emerged as a revolutionary new means of mass communication. Marconi's successful wireless telegraphic transmission across the Atlantic ushered in the radio age in 1901, soon followed by important developments in vacuum tube engineering that made possible wireless telephonic communication of speech and music. There followed after World War I a period of program innovation and near-chaos, as hundreds of aspiring commercial and educational broadcasters vied for the use of the limited number of frequencies and as the federal government haltingly groped for a workable form of regulation. From 30 stations and 60,000 sets in 1922, American radio broadcasting burgeoned to 733 stations and 7.3 million sets just five years later. The first broadcasting networks emerged (the National Broadcasting Company in 1926 and the Columbia Broadcasting System in 1927), nurturing a highly lucrative and influential advertising industry. Federal regulation through the new Federal Communications Commission in 1934 brought a more peaceful era of vastly improved signal and program quality, with the result that the 1930s and 1940s marked the heyday of radio as an entertainment medium. Two more networks took shape (the Mutual Broadcasting System in 1934 and the NBC Blue Network—later the American Broadcasting Company—in 1942). National audiences as large as fifteen million listened regularly to Jack Benny, Bob Hope, and other entertainers; advertising receipts exceeded $215 million in 1940; and the number of receiving sets in the U.S. reached nearly 77 million by 1948.[106]

Educational radio at the University of Wisconsin developed within and to a minor extent helped to shape the larger context. In 1914 Edward Bennett, a professor of electrical engineering, performed wireless telegraphic experiments on campus, constructed a transmitter, and obtained experimental license designation 9XM from the federal authorities.[107] The next year he arranged for transfer of the license to Earle M. Terry, an assistant professor of physics, who also had built his own apparatus and was ready to begin experimental transmissions. Terry and his students soon were in frequent wireless telegraphic contact with university research laboratories in other states. Unexpectedly, "ham" operators across the countryside listened in and reported on the quality of reception. In December, following the example of A. Hoyt Taylor at the University of North Dakota, Terry, in association with the U.S. Weather Bureau office on campus, began broadcasting scheduled weather reports for his surprisingly enthusiastic ham audience, now numbering in the hundreds.[108] The forecasts were so well received that Terry decided to try another kind of broadcast, reporting in code on the February, 1917, UW-Ohio State basketball game played at the Armory on the lower campus. Terry constantly refined his transmitter, located

---

[106]See W. Rupert MacLaurin, *Invention and Innovation in the Radio Industry* (New York: Macmillan Company, 1949); "Radio," in *Concise Dictionary of American History*, Thomas C. Cochran, advisory editor, and Wayne Andrews, editor (New York: Charles Scribner's Sons, 1962); Gleason L. Archer, *History of Radio to 1926* (New York: American Historical Society, Inc., 1938); Gleason L. Archer, *Big Business and Radio* (New York: American Historical Company, Inc., 1939); John S. Penn, "The Origin and Development of Radio Broadcasting at the University of Wisconsin to 1940" (Ph.D. diss., University of Wisconsin, 1958), pp. 5-12. This section is based largely on information presented by Penn, although our analysis runs counter to Penn's negative portrayals of UW Presidents Birge and Frank and his largely uncritical treatment of such individuals as Earle M. Terry, William H. Lighty, H.L. Ewbank, and Edward Bennett. Ewbank served as Penn's major professor for the Ph.D.

[107]The U.S. Department of Commerce issued experimental licenses as authorized by the Radio Act of 1912. By 1916 the department had issued fifteen licenses, including Bennett's.

[108]Between 1914 and 1916 four universities began wireless telegraphic broadcasting. These included North Dakota, Nebraska Wesleyan, the University of Nebraska, and UW.

in the basement of Science Hall at Park and Langdon streets, and focussed the remainder of his experimental energies on the improvement of vacuum tubes, which increasingly seemed capable of producing telephonic or voice transmissions. Bennett and Terry were mostly interested in the science and engineering of radio transmission, however, with only a marginal concern for programming. By the time of American entry into World War I, Terry was well along in the process of constructing a continuous wave transmitter for use in the physics department's new facility, Sterling Hall, located next to the Chemistry Building on the southwest slope of University Hill.

The war proved a boon both for the UW station and for Terry personally. The War Department in April of 1917 abruptly ordered the shut-down of all domestic radio stations to protect national security, but Terry arranged for 9XM to remain operational for experimental purposes, the country's single exception to the ban. Hoyt Taylor (who had worked with Terry at Wisconsin early in the century) had helped make this arrangement in his capacity as director of communications at the Naval District Headquarters at Great Lakes, Illinois. The objective was to perfect submarine radio reception and the experiment involved frequent broadcasting tests between Madison and Great Lakes. Later in 1917 Terry also arranged with the Army Signal Corps to train operators (expanded in 1918 to include technicians) and to perform other tests. With this backing, Terry and student C.M. Jansky, Jr., constructed a new apparatus and transmitted for the first time a clear 9XM voice message. His war work enhanced Terry's stature within the University. In 1917 he was promoted to associate professor and between 1916 to 1919 his salary was increased from $2,000 to $3,325. This institutional recognition was particularly gratifying in light of Terry's previously undistinguished application-oriented career in the highly theoretical UW physics department, involving eight years as an instructor and seven additional years as an assistant professor.[109]

Prior to the war Terry and a few of his academic colleagues elsewhere had stumbled upon the notion of radio *broadcasting* through their experiments involving ham operators and weather forecasts. This voice use of radio contrasted with that of the commercial sector dominated by American Marconi, General Electric, and Westinghouse, which antici-

---

[109]In 1920 Terry received another major salary increase to $4,000. As with most faculty salaries of the era, Terry's remained static through 1925-26, when he received a raise of $250. Personnel Cards, UA.

pated the primary use of the new medium for individual-to-individual communication. With the end of wartime restrictions, 9XM and other experimental stations at educational institutions began to expand their scheduled broadcasts significantly. At Wisconsin Terry and student assistant Malcolm Hanson in 1919 began making occasional evening hour-long broadcasts of recorded music. Early in 1921 9XM added live programming to its now-staple voice weather and phonograph offerings. Extension division music Professor E.B. Gordon took charge of the latter, quickly expanding his programs to include a modest element of instruction. Later that year, on March 11, 1921, 9XM made its first "remote" broadcast of a Men's Glee Club concert in Music Hall. About the same time agricultural journalism Professor Andrew Hopkins began providing scripted news materials on the work of his agriculture colleagues. The next fall, through a cooperative arrangement with the Wisconsin Department of Agriculture and Markets, 9XM began daily price reports on livestock, poultry, butter, eggs, cheese, potatoes, and hay. Basketball season brought the first of many remote broadcasts from the Armory, made possible by a line strung through the maze of underground campus heating tunnels between Sterling Hall and the lower campus gym. As the Wisconsin experience demonstrated, the pioneering phase of radio was passing, and the U.S. Department of Commerce responded by abolishing all experimental designations. On January 13, 1922, 9XM entered the open radio market as station WHA.

The period from early 1922 through mid-1926, when WHA encountered staggering difficulties with federal regulation, encompassed important programming and policy developments. As early as 1921 the growing demands associated with programming had begun to distract Professor Terry and his assistants from their scientific work. The following year Terry sought partial relief by inviting Andy Hopkins to provide more material about the College of Agriculture. Recognizing a golden public relations opportunity, Hopkins enthusiastically convened a college Radio Committee that organized a daily noontime program focussing on farm and home topics. The hour-long show was an immediate hit among rural listeners and would remain so through many years and numerous mutations. Terry likewise turned to School of Music Director Charles H. Mills, whose unit was always seeking audiences for its performing groups. The result was a continuing series of well-received concerts by the Men's Glee Club, the UW Band, the UW Orchestra, the Choral Union, numerous smaller ensembles, and solo performers. To mobilize other campus resources, Terry turned to the

Extension Division's most energetic proponent of University outreach, William H. Lighty. By March, 1922, Lighty had convinced President Birge to appoint a special University Radio Committee representing all parts of the campus. Soon an impressive array of late afternoon and evening lectures, concerts, and campus news reports began to entertain and edify a listening audience within a range of a hundred to a thousand miles, depending on the time of day and atmospheric conditions. Even in this early stage, however, campus scholars soon recognized that the talent demands of the new medium were insatiable and increasingly time-consuming. A quiet undercurrent of discontent and resistance began to develop, fed in part by Lighty's often aggressive manner and his identification with the Extension Division. By mid-decade, popular and willing campus radio lecturers were becoming scarce.

University policy concerning WHA reflected the nascent and generally ambiguous status of radio broadcasting during the early 1920s. The regents, for example, had never explicitly considered whether the institution ought to operate a radio broadcasting station. While they had taken official possession of the 9XM and WHA licenses, those credentials were viewed merely as necessary legal authority for physics laboratory experiments. As with Harry Steenbock's concern to patent his vitamin D research, the board was reluctant to undertake unusual organizational ventures whose relevance and outcome were unclear. Throughout the Birge administration WHA received no direct budgetary support. Terry himself had to recruit Hopkins, Mills, and Lighty to provide enough programming to fill the broadcast time required for retaining the WHA license. Not until Birge agreed to appoint the special faculty Radio Committee was the University administration involved in the operation at all. Like most Americans of the day, the president initially viewed radio broadcasting as an entertaining "toy," and only slowly realized its serious cultural and educational potential.[110] Birge established two additional radio policies, both of them essentially defensive.

---

[110] On November 27, 1922, Birge wrote to R.B. Howell about his evolving opinion of WHA: "As these developments have taken place the possibilities and values of social, civic, economic advancement have grown, and the place of the radio broadcast as a constructive factor through the wider possession and use of authentic useful knowledge in the advancement of civilization has become more and more manifest." Quoted in Penn, "Origin and Development," p. 163. Birge may in fact have been more advanced than most university administrators of the day. In 1923 Lighty surveyed the National University Extension Association and found a predominating view that radio was merely an amusement of no particular value to the academic world. Ibid., p. 25.

The first required every University speaker to submit a manuscript of his or her talk to the president well in advance of the scheduled broadcast. The purpose was to assure that the speaker did not make inappropriate or otherwise embarrassing remarks. The second forbade any shared broadcast between WHA and other stations involving commercial announcements. Throughout the Birge administration the status of WHA at the University was tentative and experimental.

In Glenn Frank the University gained a president who appreciated the great educational and public relations value of the new medium. As Frank settled into his new responsibilities, however, WHA began to encounter an increasingly inhospitable external environment driven by the new broadcasting networks. Their associated radio advertising requirements forced commercial stations relentlessly to extend and standardize their hours of broadcasting and geographical coverage. WHA was managing to provide some excellent programming but only intermittent service resulting from Terry's frequent need to shut down his equipment for repairs, technical improvements, and school recesses. With the number of stations proliferating nationally, Secretary of Commerce Herbert Hoover began assigning more than one station to each of the ninety available frequencies and encouraging them to cooperate in their scheduling. This arrangement worked adequately for WHA until May of 1925 when commercial station KYW of Chicago expanded its broadcast hours to conflict with those of WHA, which now included broadcasts three evenings each week as well as substantial weekday afternoon programming. Simultaneous broadcasting by the two stations would not work, KYW would not compromise, and WHA was forced to curtail its offerings before shutting down completely for summer vacation. Scheduling conflicts continued throughout the 1925-26 academic year, with KYW forcing WHA to cancel its coverage of UW football games in favor of KYW's broadcasts of University of Chicago contests. Conditions deteriorated further after a 1926 federal court ruling in *U.S. v Zenith* invalidated Secretary Hoover's modest regulatory powers. Suddenly a mad scramble of licensed and unlicensed stations disrupted the airwaves. Public outrage led to passage of the Radio Act of 1927 that directed a new Federal Radio Commission to bring the atmospheric babel under control. Working in unexplored territory and without adequate legislative guidance the commission consistently favored the more powerful commercial stations and networks. The results were disastrous for the poorly funded educational stations, many of which soon passed out of existence. The number of educational stations declined from 94 in 1927 to 49 by March of 1931. At Wisconsin Professor Terry and his helpers persevered until the commission in March of 1929 assigned WHA to the 940 kilocycle frequency, which promised for the first time in years to accommodate a decent programming schedule, though one restricted to daytime hours.[111] This was unfortunately Terry's last victory, for he died unexpectedly shortly thereafter.

Meanwhile, President Frank was haltingly developing a more positive and inclusive radio policy. In the fall of 1925, during Frank's first semester on the job, the president received separate visits about WHA by physics Chairman Charles Mendenhall and William Lighty. Mendenhall pointed out the heavy burden on Professor Terry and urged that the University either provide adequate funds for a properly staffed and accommodated radio operation or close it down. Lighty recommended the appointment of yet another special radio programming committee. Disinclined by nature to act with dispatch and busy with more pressing matters, Frank at first did nothing. With regard to Mendenhall's concerns, the president's short-term options were limited, but he eventually arranged for minor yet explicit University budget support to begin in 1926-27. Frank may have been skeptical of Lighty's advice because of Reber's recent rejection of his long-time lieutenant for the extension deanship.[112] Still, the following March Frank pleased Lighty by essentially reappointing the special committee previously designated by President Birge. In the fall he named a more inclusive programming group with an Executive Committee chaired by Professor Terry. In addition to Lighty, the Executive Committee also included Lighty's new chief, Acting Dean Chester Snell, and representatives from Journalism, Speech, Agriculture, and Music. The committee's makeup suggested an expanded vision for WHA rejecting its early balkanized programming, which too often had reflected the continuing competition between the Extension Division and the College of Agriculture. Under the new arrangement Lighty's rather partisan influence

---

[111]Prior to this assignment, the Federal Radio Commission forced WHA to share a succession of frequencies with various stations. None of the arrangements was entirely workable, as broadcasting range was occasionally limited to an unsatisfactory twenty-five miles.

[112]Lighty interpreted Frank's perspective differently. In 1947 he recalled: "President Frank did not seem to visualize the potentialities of the radio station. He seemed reluctant to give it any support from the President's office. At times it was felt that he was perfectly willing for the broadcast activities to come to an end." Quoted in Penn, "Origin and Development," pp. 281-2.

quickly faded. The leadership transition was completed soon after Terry's death, with operational control placed under electrical engineering Professor Edward Bennett and programming under the joint leadership of speech Professor Henry L. Ewbank, who now chaired the Program Committee, and Agriculture's Andy Hopkins.[113]

A broader conception of educational radio in Wisconsin soon emerged. During the fall of 1929 Bennett, Ewbank, and Hopkins began discussing the possibility of consolidating WHA with Stevens Point station WLBL, operated by the State Department of Agriculture and Markets. The two stations had previously shared a frequency for a short time with good results. The proposed new station, WIS, would satisfy Federal Radio Commission programming requirements, ease the financial burden on the University and the agriculture and marketing department, and, most importantly, provide statewide coverage. Its several educational and public service purposes would involve adult education programming on such topics as agricultural and home economics, health, and conservation, and would facilitate wider discussion of public issues. It would also provide supplementary educational services for rural schools and foster educational experimentation. In January, 1930, the University submitted a request for the merger to the federal commission, which considered the matter for eighteen months before deciding against it.[114] As a result WHA was for a time in a sort of conceptual limbo, unsure whether it was an entity of the University or more broadly of the state. This ambiguity was expressed in the station's funding after University officials and Governor Phillip La Follette agreed early in 1931 that WHA should be removed from UW's biennial budget request. When the legislature failed to provide separate funding, however, La Follette had to arrange financing through the State

---

[113]Penn offers a more negative evaluation of President Frank's relations with WHA, referring to Andrew Hopkins' stated view that he was "lukewarm" and Lighty's estimate that he was indifferent. Penn himself observes that Frank's apparently unenthusiastic attitude was "typical of the university administrators across the country." None of these conclusions takes into account the difficult financial and institutional problems faced by Frank (and his fellow presidents) that placed great constraints upon the setting up of expensive new initiatives with arguably dubious educational benefits. See Penn, "Origin and Development," pp. 305-8.

[114]The politics of this effort were complicated and messy and involved officials from the University and the state government as well as members of the Wisconsin congressional delegation. Not only did certain commercial stations oppose the consolidation, but so too did residents of Stevens Point, who feared the service they currently were receiving would be curtailed. The episode concluded after the University Radio Committee, recognizing that the prospects were hopeless, requested that the application be withdrawn.

Emergency Board. This ad hoc arrangement worked satisfactorily and continued for several years. With the failure of the consolidation effort, the advocates of educational radio at the University and in state government sought another method of uniting WHA and WLBL. This time they resorted to a direct land line, which finally linked the stations in January of 1933. "Wisconsin now controls and operates what is probably the first state-owned radio chain in the country," observed the *Daily Cardinal.* "The improvement is looked upon as a powerful force in strengthening the feeling of unity among residents of the different parts of the state."[115] Virtual state-wide coverage was finally a reality, although occasional and sometimes extended interruptions in the connection would plague the mini-network for years to come.

Although its funding remained precarious throughout the depression, WHA programming expanded as the station sought new and varied ways to serve the Wisconsin public. WHA programmers saw the station both as a voice of the University and a conduit between the various agencies of state government and the people of Wisconsin. As early as 1929 programs and series were provided by the Wisconsin Conservation Commission, the Department of Public Instruction, and the State Board of Health. By 1932 the state industrial, tax, and insurance commissions, the Bureau of Personnel, the State Historical Society, the State Geological Survey, and the U.S. Forest Products Laboratory also were contributing. WHA also began to feature political issues, as in a "freedom of speech forum" inaugurated by President Frank in April of 1931. "Here," explained Professor Ewbank to Governor La Follette, "we believe the audience is entitled to a full presentation of each viewpoint by a believer in that theory. Until the listener has heard each theory presented by its friends he is not well qualified to render judgment."[116] During the 1932 election campaign WHA provided air time to each candidate on the statewide ballot. All active parties participated and Ewbank reported a "large and favorable" listener response.[117] In 1931 WHA installed a remote studio at the State Capitol for public service programming. "Wisconsin, as usual, takes the lead," declared Henry

---

[115]*Daily Cardinal*, January 7, 1933.

[116]WHA almost immediately received praise from the American Civil Liberties Union for the new series. Ibid., April 24, 1931. In Ewbank to Phil La Follette, July 29, 1932, quoted in Penn, "Origin and Development," pp. 362-3, Ewbank refers to the series, which he mistakenly dates from March, 1931, as the "Radio Forum." It eventually became more widely known as the "Political Education Forum."

[117]Quoted in Penn, "Origin and Development," p. 364.

Goddard Leach, the editor of *Forum* magazine. "These programs should be of inestimable good in eliminating stupid prejudice and raising the political morale of the electorate."[118]

Campus-based programming also flourished. Musical, agricultural, and homemaking shows continued to attract an expanding base of listeners. In 1929 UW students began offering programs, first with a series of entertaining variety shows and later with dramatic productions via the "Cardinal Hour" and the "Wisconsin Players." During the spring of 1930 extension division faculty members Edgar Gordon and Mary D. Webb conducted an experiment to determine the effectiveness of radio instruction. Gordon taught music and Webb taught current events to 6th, 7th, and 8th grade classes in Dane County. Professor Ewbank, who chaired the special University Radio Research Committee set up to supervise the project, concluded that such offerings were valuable when qualified subject-matter teachers were unavailable and particularly when used as a supplement to standard classroom work. This experiment, and the advent of WHA's first full-time program director, Harold B. McCarty, led to the inauguration of the "Wisconsin School of the Air" in October of 1931, with an initial offering of ten courses each week. By 1933 more than 22,000 children were listening from their classrooms throughout the state, and the number expanded to 325,000 by 1940.[119] In the spring of 1931 WHA offered its first formal non-credit course, on elementary Spanish, for adult listeners. The course was repeated in the fall and was succeeded by others on play writing, aeronautics, child study, and typewriting. This was followed by WHA's broadcasting sessions of actual University courses. The first, on Tuesday mornings, included noisy "sky-rocket" greetings from the 280 students enrolled in music Professor Charles H. Mills' music appreciation class. Faculty members in other departments followed Mills' lead, and in October, 1933, WHA inaugurated the "Wisconsin College of the Air." "In this time of depression, the state-owned radio stations have shown their ability to provide educational opportunities to compensate for retrenchments in school, home, farm and personal budgets," observed the University Radio Committee in summarizing its recent programming accomplishments for the Federal Radio Commis-

---

[118]*Daily Cardinal*, September 22, 1934, and quoted in Penn, "Origin and Development," pp. 365-6.

[119]For a good overview see Ralph W. Johnson, "The Wisconsin School of the Air," *Wisconsin Academy Review* (June, 1989), pp. 33-9.

sion. "The WHA and WLBL stations are the only ones in Wisconsin which have planned comprehensive programs of education for people who, because of financial or geographical barriers, are unable to continue their education."[120]

The remaining years before the war brought further if sometimes stressful development. WHA relocated from the physics department to the old campus heating plant behind Science Hall formerly occupied by the Department of Mining and Metallurgy of the College of Engineering. To pay for the remodeling, the regents arranged for federal depression relief grants successively from the Civil Works Administration and Federal Emergency Relief Administration. Work started in early 1934 and continued haltingly into the next year. By December of 1934 construction had progressed far enough to allow the station to begin broadcasting from the facility, now called Radio Hall. The new quarters included three studios, five offices, and a comfortable reception and observation area—truly palatial compared with the previous make-shift accommodations in Sterling Hall.[121] In 1935 WHA's operations budget improved markedly, rising from $16,000 to $20,000, when the legislature placed the station administratively with WLBL under the State Department of Agriculture and Markets. In 1938 Governor Phil La Follette accomplished a wholesale governmental reorganization, which in September included the transfer of WHA and WLBL to the University and the formation of a policy-making State Radio Council. Two months later, however, conservative Republican Julius Heil defeated La Follette in the gubernatorial election, and early in 1939 a compliant legislature rescinded the reorganization. The two stations then returned to agriculture and marketing until 1941 when the legislature once again assigned them back to the regents and provided a healthy budget increase to $47,640. Actually, these shifts in administration had little day-to-day effect on WHA programming, because the station's operation always remained firmly in the hands of campus officials.

Even more than Glenn Frank, President Clarence Dykstra recognized the potential of educational radio and considered WHA an integral and valuable part of the University. He rejected *Capital Times* editor William Evjue's attacks on a foundation-funded radio research project

---

[120]Quoted in Penn, "Origin and Development," p. 375.
[121]Total cost of the remodeling project was $18,232, of which the University paid $4,200. WHA made further improvements from 1936 through 1938 with funding from a Works Progress Administration grant.

and otherwise defended the station vigorously. To monitor and guide WHA's progress on a continuing basis, he established a standing faculty University Radio Committee. Dykstra often associated the station with the University's public service mission. "What better medium do we have for attaining that fine ideal than radio?" he asked a conference of educational broadcasters in Chicago in December, 1937. "What more effective means of reaching all people and achieving the goal of truly democratic education?"[122] Dykstra subsequently worked effectively with Governor La Follette on the short-lived 1938 reorganization effort and later helped persuade Governor Heil to return WHA and WLBL to the University. By the beginning of the war an experienced and confident WHA radio network was in place to help the University and the state meet the challenges of wartime mobilization.

The Expanding Public Service Tradition

Already well-established by the end of the nineteenth century, the University's commitment to public service broadened considerably in response to the Wisconsin progressive movement. With their belief in an activist state, the progressives saw education as a key long-term instrument for the effort to reshape society. While the University Extension Division was the major new organizational development resulting from the progressive impulse, it was by no means the only University effort to reach out to a wider public in these years. Increasingly the campus-based State Laboratory of Hygiene provided indispensable service for testing water samples and other public health services. The University similarly provided space and support for the state Toxicology Laboratory, the federal

---

[122]C.A. Dykstra, "What Shall We Do With Radio?" address before the National Conference on Educational Broadcasting, Chicago, Illinois, December 1, 1937, Dykstra Presidential Papers, 4/15/1, box 143, UA, and quoted in Penn, "Origin and Development," pp. 420-1.

Forest Products Laboratory, the Madison area office of the U.S. Weather Service, the Wisconsin Geological and Natural History Survey, and the Wisconsin Academy of Science, Arts, and Letters. After opening in 1924, the Wisconsin General Hospital enabled the Medical School to develop clinical programs that brought state-of-the-art medical care to low-income Wisconsin residents from all parts of the state. The Medical School's preceptor program developed useful ties to physicians around the state and smoothed the way for its continuing education program and lending library of the latest medical research findings. Other UW colleges and schools—notably Engineering, Law, Education, and Commerce—also worked with their special constituencies, sometimes directly and often with the help of Extension Division, WHA radio, and Summer Session officials. During the 1930s the Science Inquiry organized interdisciplinary campus research on a variety of problems of current interest to the state and nation. Individual faculty members spoke frequently to service clubs and other off-campus groups about their scholarly specialties. A good example was Professor Joseph H. "Matty" Mathews, the long-time chairman of the chemistry department, who was in great demand to discuss his leadership of the emerging field of scientific crime detection.

The University served the public in less formal ways as well. Following its opening in 1928, the Memorial Union provided social, recreational, and cultural activities for UW alumni and on occasion Madison area residents. With the addition of the Union Theater wing in 1939, the University offered the finest facility for musical and dramatic presentations in the city of Madison, most of which were open to and patronized by the general public. The University Arboretum was likewise open to the public for educational and recreational use. The acquisition of Picnic Point in 1941 extended the area of University-owned shore line offering public access to Lake Mendota, including several bathing beaches and boat rentals at the University Boathouse behind the Armory. Indeed, without the University's presence the residents of Madison would have had little public access to their largest lake. Throughout the inter-war years the University expanded its athletic facilities and attracted ever larger crowds of spectators for its intercollegiate athletic contests, especially in football, basketball, and boxing. Increasingly, Badger teams came to symbolize the state as well as the University. For some Wisconsin residents with little or no other contact with the campus, they *were* the University.

Two expressions in common usage described this wide-ranging

public service function of the University. The first was the "Wisconsin Idea," popularized by Charles McCarthy in 1912 to summarize the various ameliorative activities of the Wisconsin progressive movement, including those of the University. After the stalwarts returned to power with the election of Governor Emanuel L. Philipp in 1914, the term increasingly referred more narrowly to University public service. Related to the key University role in the Wisconsin Idea was the phrase "the boundaries of the campus are the boundaries of the state." It is not clear exactly who coined these words or when they were first used, though President Van Hise had vaguely referred to such a comprehensive public service objective in his 1904 inaugural address. As the University Extension Division evolved, leaders such as Dean Reber frequently invoked the image if not the exact phrase. In early 1938 as the Dykstra administration was getting under way, the University published a bulletin describing its outreach activities, *A Story of Public Service: The Boundaries of the Campus Are the Boundaries of the State.*[123] "It is the story of a great vision," Dykstra declared in the forward, "carried on through the years until it has become part and parcel of the history of the State and its University."

The president had it right.

---

[123]Edited by Robert Foss, Bulletin of the University of Wisconsin, Serial No. 2281, General Series No. 2065, January, 1938.

14.

Two Difficult Decades

For scarcely four years during the two decades covered by this volume—only between 1925 and 1929—was the University able to operate under more or less normal conditions. During the remainder of the period campus life was severely disrupted by the ravages of the great depression and by mobilization for the Second World War. Not until the 1950s did more ordinary circumstances return, and by then the swollen post-war enrollments had doubled the size and forever changed the nature of the institution. The story of the University in the interwar years is thus largely one of adapting to rapidly changing and mostly unfavorable external conditions. How the University handled adversity and adapted to new circumstances, how its leaders endeavored to uphold the morale of the faculty and students in difficult times, and how its members sought to preserve and even enhance its quality in an unpromising environment are the significant themes running throughout this volume. In this the University of Wisconsin was hardly unique, of course, for colleges and universities across the country faced similar difficult challenges and choices in these years. A number of the University's problems were unique, however, as were some of its responses, and the latter occasionally offered creative leadership to American higher education in general.

Weathering the Politics of Ideology

The University had prospered greatly during the first two decades of the twentieth century, when Wisconsin progressives came to see it as a potentially significant engine of political reform and social change in the state. For them a key issue was therefore who should lead the institution and assure that it lived up to their vision of its promise and utility. The University stood at the apex of the state's educational system and its reach extended to every corner of Wisconsin. In the right hands its ability to help in the progressives' hoped-for transformation of society was enormous. After the turn of the century two members of the UW Class of 1879 were in a position to bring this about: Governor Robert M. La Follette, the leader of the progressive faction of the dominant Wisconsin Republican Party, and his choice to lead their alma mater, UW President Charles R. Van Hise. The two men favored a broadened reform and public service mission for the University. During La Follette's governorship (1901-07) they developed a close alliance to implement it.

Even after La Follette left Madison for the U.S. Senate he continued his close interest in the University and his support of Van Hise, until the latter's public criticism of the senator's anti-war stand in the First World War brought an irretrievable break in their friendship. La Follette and his followers were convinced Van Hise had sold out to the conservative (or stalwart) Republicans who had taken control of the state government in 1915. They were also dissatisfied with the man the regents chose to succeed Van Hise after his unexpected death in 1918, Letters and Science Dean Edward A. Birge, whom they considered too old and conservative to give the University the dynamic reformist leadership they desired. Although La Follette used all of his considerable political influence to try to determine Birge's successor in 1925, the regents passed over the senator's candidate and appointed instead a youthful New York editor and prominent liberal Republican publicist, Glenn Frank. Lacking the La Follette family imprimatur, from the beginning President Frank was suspect in the eyes of some Wisconsin progressives. Although Frank was undeniably progressive in his political views, was committed to the reform of undergraduate education along the lines favored by progressives across the country, and was fully supportive of the expanded public service mission demanded by the progressives for the University, he remained an outsider, distrusted by Wisconsin progressive leaders and only tolerated by much of the UW faculty. Chief among his political opponents were Senator La Follette's two sons, who inherited leadership of the progressive movement in the state following the senator's death in mid-1925: Young Bob, who took over his father's seat in the United States Senate, and Phil, who directed the La Follette organization in Wisconsin and in the process served three terms as governor during the 1930s.

Very likely the La Follette brothers considered Glenn Frank a potential rival and early concluded that his ill-disguised political ambitions required that he be discredited or eliminated. Old Bob had never for long tolerated any strong rival for leadership of the state progressive movement and his sons were no more forbearing. Whatever their motivation, the La Follettes did little to conceal that they did not like Glenn Frank. As governor, Phil La Follette went out of his way to humiliate the UW president and undermine his administration. When this did not suffice to drive Frank from his post, the governor engineered Frank's dismissal early in 1937 by a compliant progressive majority on the Board of Regents. Frank's firing after a widely publicized open hearing was a shocking and for Wisconsin an unprecedented intrusion of partisan politics into the management of the University. It generated national condemnation and revealed a dark side of La Follette progressivism. It also blighted the governor's further political aspirations in the state and the country.

While the La Follette-picked successor to Frank, Cincinnati city manager Clarence A. Dykstra, had only marginally stronger academic credentials and experience than his predecessor, he turned out to be a better administrator and, no doubt to the La Follette brothers' relief, showed no interest in a Wisconsin or national political career. Dykstra's honeymoon was short, however, for in 1938 Governor La Follette lost his bid for a fourth term to a conservative Milwaukee industrialist, Julius Heil. Heil was suspicious of Dykstra as a creature of the La Follette progressive regents who had appointed him. During his first year in office the governor approved a bill to reorganize the Board of Regents to make it more independent and thereby give the University more protection from future gubernatorial meddling. In the process Heil retained only one member of the old board, one of the minority supporters of Glenn Frank; his other appointees, mostly stalwarts, proved over time to be devoted to the University's welfare.

An impulsive maverick, the unpredictable Heil was new to Wisconsin politics and took only limited direction from other stalwart Republican leaders. Unfortunately for Dykstra, the governor was largely self-educated and had no ties to the University nor any particular interest in education. During the governor's first term the UW president had to contend with a budget cut nearly as severe as those imposed by Phil La Follette on Glenn Frank in the depths of the depression. Dykstra's patient, low-key work in educating Heil about the many valuable services performed by the University, especially those helping the state and nation prepare for World War II, eventually paid off with more sympathetic budgetary treatment during the second Heil administration, which coincided with the entry of the United States into the war. Before then both Dykstra and the University were increasingly involved in national defense activities. After Pearl Harbor the war emergency took precedence over all else for the remainder of Dykstra's career at Wisconsin until his departure for the top administrative post at UCLA in early 1945.

It seems ironic that the University suffered through more political interference and niggardly support in the inter-war years from its professed friends, the Wisconsin progressives, than from their opponents, the supposedly tight-fisted, business-oriented stalwarts. More often than not the progressives dominated state government in this period. Between 1920 and 1944, for example, they won eight of the twelve gubernatorial elections; the stalwarts only three. Most of the time the progressives controlled one or both houses of the legislature and its key committees. Progressive appoin-tees predominated on the Board of Regents, which ought to have provided reassurance that the University was in good hands. Yet the University's treatment by progressive politicians was usually anything but friendly and generous. Governor Blaine shocked other progressives, including the La Follettes, with his miserly treatment and almost paranoid obsession to purge the University of alleged stalwart influences. While Phil La Follette's options as governor during the depression were more sharply constrained, that alone did not account for his repeated meddling in University affairs and his draconian University budgets. The two stalwart governors of the period—Walter Kohler and Julius Heil—were considerably more supportive of the University, though it took the initially-suspicious Heil some time to gain an appreciation of its importance to the state.

Very likely this seeming paradox was because the progressives had greater and less realistic expectations of the University. Their ideology led them to regard it as one of the most important institutions in the populist state they were creating, but they had only mixed success in shaping it to their liking. The stalwarts, having no such lofty ambitions, took the University as they found it and generally thought it worthy of their support. Perhaps as populists the progressives had trouble accepting the reality of the University. Though it was a low-tuition, essentially open-admissions school in these years—a true people's university—and though it directly benefitted countless thousands of Wisconsin residents each year through its low cost or free extension services, it was also undeniably an elite institution, highly regarded as such nationally. The most distinguished members of its faculty were able to command relatively high salaries even in the depression. Put crudely in terms that were unspoken but widely assumed, one measure of the University's success was how many of its graduates would subsequently be members of the state's elites of the next generation. The stalwarts, with less aversion to elites whether of institutions or individuals, had no problem with this reality and in fact expected their University to be so ranked and dedicated. This difference in expectations was part of the larger progressive-stalwart ideological contest in the inter-war years. Unfortunately, the partisan wrangling usually victimized the University, resulting in reduced budgetary support and making the institution and its leadership much more of a political football than was healthy for either the school or the state it served.

Creative Boot-Strapping

Considering their serious budget problems, University leaders were able to accomplish a remarkable amount of new construction and remodeling of campus facilities in the inter-war period. They made good use of the regents' 1925 creation, the Wisconsin University Building Corporation, for a number of projects, of which the most important were the construction of several residence halls along the shore of Lake Mendota. These included the first men's dormitories on campus since the 1880s: Tripp and Adams Halls and the related Van Hise refectory, and subsequently the nearby eight-unit Kronshage complex. Equally impressive and needed was the large five-unit women's dormitory, Elizabeth Waters Hall, very likely the finest and most elegant in the country when it opened in 1940. By enabling the University to skirt the state constitutional prohibition against bonded indebtedness, the WUBC also made possible the construction of the Field House and the Memorial Union and its later theater addition. The WUBC device was less useful for general building purposes because its projects required a predictable revenue stream against which the regents' captive corporation could first borrow construction funds and then repay the mortgage indebtedness while also covering the operating expenses. Dormitories, athletic facilities, and a student union could generate reliable program revenue for this purpose. Classrooms, laboratories, and other academic facilities could not, so addressing these needs was a much more difficult and mostly insoluble problem except in the late 1920s when for a brief time more generous state appropriations enabled some badly needed remodeling (such as the theater and undergraduate library in Bascom Hall) and new construction (the Mechanical Engineering Building on the west campus).

The federal Public Works Administration created by Franklin Roosevelt's New Deal as an anti-depression weapon offered another way to accomplish some campus construction in the 1930s. Since the state government was unwilling to supply the required matching funds, University leaders had to develop some complicated and creative funding packages to take advantage of these federal funds. PWA grants were thus mostly limited to helping with WUBC projects such as the Kronshage men's dormitory complex, Elizabeth Waters Hall, and the Union Theater, where the University's match could be assured from dormitory rentals, food service, ticket receipts, and other program revenue. The only purely academic facility to be built with PWA funds was the library addition to the Law School Building, for which matching funds were generated through a loan from the Vilas Trust and a special library fee charged law students.

President Dykstra was sensitive to complaints he had not done more to use PWA funding for critically needed academic facilities, particularly a new University library. Such criticism overlooked the constraints under which he and the regents had to operate, however. Neither budget-strapped governors nor their legislatures during the depression were willing to provide matching funds for new UW buildings at a time when enrollments had fallen sharply and other state needs seemed more urgent. Wisconsin citizens and their representatives traditionally prided themselves on the open access and low tuition of their state university, moreover. It is inconceivable that the regents, governors, or legislatures of the period would have approved a new general undergraduate fee earmarked to help finance UW academic facilities or for any other purpose.

The wonder is not that Dykstra ignored important University building needs, but that he was able to accomplish as much construction and remodeling as he did in such difficult times. He and President Frank before him must more than once have blessed Regent President Kronshage and his colleagues for devising the Wisconsin University Building Corporation and gaining its approval by state political leaders so the University could in effect bond itself for certain revenue-generating building projects. Theirs was an innovative creation of broad applicability, which later pointed the way to the present State Building Commission. It was also a useful model for other public universities constrained by similar state constitutional restrictions.

An even more daring and far-reaching innovation was the Wisconsin Alumni Research Foundation, also approved in 1925 by the same Board of Regents that devised the WUBC, though it is less clear the regents fully understood WARF's implications and potential. WARF was based on a simple yet new and truly revolutionary idea: that a university might (indirectly) patent and market the products of faculty research in order to generate revenue to support more faculty research. In the past universities had defined their mission to preserve, generate, and transmit knowledge, not to restrict access to it nor profit from their role in developing new findings. With the notable exception of William T. Evjue's *Capital Times* (whose criticism came only later), many Wisconsin progressives who were otherwise suspicious of educational foundations created by wealthy industrialists like Andrew Carnegie and John D. Rockefeller had few concerns about WARF. It was a Wisconsin invention, one controlled by prominent Wisconsin alumni for the benefit of their alma mater. It might indeed provide the means by which their University could flourish while remaining under public control, free of the golden chains of the tainted money of the "malefactors of great wealth."

Although WARF was created in response to a specific problem—how to handle Professor Harry Steenbock's vitamin D irradiation process so as to generate income while protecting the state's dairy industry—its value to the University was soon apparent. Within five years the WARF trustees were able to begin making a steady and growing number of grants to support University research activities. By easing the impact of depression budget cuts, WARF funds helped to preserve and strengthen the UW faculty research base, especially in the biological and physical sciences, at a time when other universities were obliged to cut back both their younger faculty and their support of research. Steenbock's request that WARF funds should not be restricted to his discipline of biochemistry but rather be used to support scientific research more generally throughout the University extended WARF's impact. Two decades after the foundation's creation WARF was generating a substantial annual revenue stream that dwarfed its creators' expectations and was the envy of other major universities lacking such a means to capitalize on faculty research. WARF's great growth and impact would occur in the post-war years, but by 1945 it was evident that the fortuitous creation of two decades before was to be a key factor in maintaining the University as one of the country's major research institutions. WARF was positioning the University to compete successfully for the growing volume of post-war federal research funding.

Even as state appropriations were eroding, the University showed it could mobilize support from alumni, students, and other benefactors. Throughout the inter-war years UW leaders increasingly turned to private sources for help with special projects, though not on a systematic basis. The most spectacular illustration of this determination to develop new sources of support was the drive to collect funds for construction of the Memorial Union in the 1920s. This was the University's first capital campaign—to use the terminology of later fund raisers—and it took the better part of a decade. Although the alumni gave major leadership and support, the effort was sparked by the undergraduate Men's Union Board, and students—both men and women—played a significant part in its success by purchasing life memberships and otherwise raising money for a building most of them knew could not be constructed during their years in Madison. Such devotion to their campus community is one of the striking characteristics of the UW student body in these years. It was rewarded by an unprecedented advance in responsible student government when, despite the uneasiness of some alumni leaders, University authorities approved a plan that gave students majority control of the Memorial Union Council, the new facility's immediate governing body. At a time when colleges and universities, including Wisconsin, were expanding their supervision of extracurricular student life and reasserting their *in loco parentis* responsibilities, such confidence was a refreshing break with prevailing skepticism about how far students could be trusted to manage a complex and costly enterprise. Subsequent experience proved it was not misplaced.

Another lengthy boot-strap effort, this one by public-spirited Madison residents including several regents and alumni, led to the acquisition and development of the University Arboretum in the 1930s and 1940s. The Arboretum enabled University researchers, headed by Professors Aldo Leopold and John Curtis, to recreate a 60-acre prairie of the sort that had earlier covered much of southern Wisconsin and to experiment with restoring the natural habitat of some of the wildlife species once native to the area. In both ventures the University gave pioneering leadership to the study of environmental issues that were to become much more fashionable in the post-war decades. The 1260-acre

Arboretum quickly became a valuable living laboratory for UW scientists and their students as well as a sylvan oasis for Madison residents increasingly distanced from open space by their ever-expanding urban environment.

Several substantial bequests, mostly from alumni concerned to help in the further development of their alma mater, also enabled the University to undertake some significant new ventures in the inter-war period. The sizable estate of J. Stephens Tripp, a wealthy Chicago attorney, provided some of the funds needed for the construction of the Tripp and Adams men's dormitory complex and the Memorial Union in the 1920s. A decade later the Bowman and McArdle bequests helped launch the Medical School on the study of the causes and treatment of cancer, now one of its premier specialties.

What turned out to be a more troublesome bequest, but one of continuing importance to the University, was the Brittingham Family Trust, created in 1924 by the will of Thomas E. Brittingham, a prosperous lumberman and former UW regent. The trust was unusual in that all of its proceeds were to be used to support University activities but were to remain under the control of and be dispensed by the Brittingham family. The first Brittingham grant, at the request of President Frank in 1926, was to pay the large salary of Alexander Meiklejohn after he was recruited by Frank to launch the Experimental College. Following an unfortunate controversy in 1930 over the extent of the Brittingham family's control of the trust for which Frank and several headstrong regents were largely at fault, University authorities stopped their requests and the family ceased making grants for several years. The dispute was mostly over principle rather than substance, because the Brittinghams had not sought to direct the use of their grants other than to ask that they be for short-term projects not otherwise fundable in the regular University budget. The break was especially untimely because such private support was more than ever needed by the University in the depression.

After six years and a change of heart, memory, and membership among the regents, the rift was mended and Brittingham funds began to flow once again, this time mostly in support of the arts on campus. The first of the renewed Brittingham grants was spectacular and drew national attention: the appointment of the prominent regional painter John Steuart Curry to the faculty of the College of Agriculture as the University's first artist-in-residence, with the assignment to document the state's agricultural heritage and to develop a rural arts program. Another Brittingham grant in 1939 brought the talented young Danish pianist Gunnar Johansen to the School of Music as its first artist-in-residence, beginning an association that lasted throughout the remainder of his career and life. The following year Brittingham funds made possible the appointment of the Belgian Pro Arte Quartet as artists-in-residence when its members were unexpectedly stranded in Madison following the German attack on their country. The arrangement was intended initially to provide only temporary hospitality, but as the war dragged on it became permanent. The successor Pro Arte Quartet remains today a proud campus adornment.

Just as the Wisconsin Alumni Research Foundation and the Bowman and McArdle bequests demonstrated the benefit of flexible private funding to support faculty research, so the Brittingham trust illustrated as nothing else in this period the value of such money to enrich the cultural life of the campus. The Brittingham artist-in-residencies also showed the creativity of UW leaders in conceiving what were at the time rather uncommon, even daring, uses of discretionary funds. What other public American university would have come up with the idea, let alone have the audacity, to appoint a nationally prominent artist to its agriculture faculty, or have the vision to sponsor a world-famous touring string quartet as part of its music school? WARF and the Brittingham Trust showed the advantages of being able to draw on private but University-dedicated funds for worthy purposes for which state appropriations could not be obtained. Their example undoubtedly underlay the decision by President Fred and the regents not long after the war to create the University of Wisconsin Foundation to undertake more aggressive and systematic private fund-raising.

Greater Faculty Responsibility and Authority

Regardless of the pleasant and close-knit character of the UW community with its active faculty social life centered in the University Club and an interlocking network of dining clubs, the inter-war period was not an entirely happy one for faculty members. They and their University were often under attack by suspicious politicians, critical editors, and worried parents. They had to endure the first general salary reductions since the 1860s—the depression salary waivers—which in some cases persisted for more than a decade. The depression and even more the war disrupted academic programs, increased staff turnover especially among the younger faculty, raised teaching loads, and for nearly two decades kept the campus in a state of seemingly permanent uncertainty and flux. The two UW presidents of the period, Glenn Frank and Clarence Dykstra, were regarded by most of the faculty as outsiders with only marginal academic qualifications to lead a great university. They were as a result more tolerated than admired, though Dykstra's tactful leadership gradually won faculty support for several significant changes in faculty governance and undergraduate education. In contrast, there was warm faculty enthusiasm for the widely admired inside leader, Agriculture Dean E.B. Fred, when the regents named him to the presidency in early 1945. Not since the retirement of President Birge two decades earlier had the campus been led by a president who commanded such high faculty respect.[1]

In one major area the faculty gained significantly from the serious campus difficulties and sometimes defensive presidential leadership of these years. Lacking a solid base of faculty support, Presidents Frank and Dysktra were inclined to listen to faculty views and respect the faculty's governance structure. Frank had to learn the importance of this the hard way, notably after the early demise of his cherished Experimental College, which foundered in part because its over-exuberant and heavy-handed implementation alienated much of the faculty. Still, the growth of faculty power owed as much to the times as to the needs of the presidents to win faculty support. The difficult problems confronting the presidents and regents in this period were ideally suited to building up the authority of the faculty. The chief instrument for this was the University Committee, whose official status as the elected representative of the entire faculty gave it a justification to study and offer recommendations on any issue of faculty concern, of which there were many in these years. Recognizing that its power was essentially moral rather than legal, the committee used its rather tenuous authority wisely, aware that the respect of the Board of Regents and University administrators had to be earned through collegial rather than confrontational faculty leadership.

For the second round of salary waivers in 1933 President Frank and the regents were more than willing to accept the University Committee's thoughtful plan for an equitable graduated system of cuts based

---

[1]At 93, Birge was at this time still active in his limnology laboratory in the Biology Building—not yet named in his honor. That would come after his death in 1950 at the age of 98.

on salary level. By not taking a stand in the regents' controversial firing of President Frank in 1937, the committee and the faculty gained the privilege of being consulted on the selection of the next president, a practice President Dykstra and the regents then extended to the appointment of academic deans and institutionalized in the selection of President Fred in 1945. Dykstra carried this democratic ethos further by reminding the faculty of its right, which had fallen increasingly into disuse, of reporting each year the departmental preference for the appointment of its chairman. By 1942 when the faculty with Dykstra's encouragement created the present four interdisciplinary faculty divisions, each with an elected executive committee to advise the deans on new or changed courses and the awarding of tenure, the UW faculty possessed more real authority in campus governance than existed at any other major American university. By working responsibly to help deal with the depression and war crises and by firmly defending faculty rights, as in the Athletic Board's 1935 stand-off with the Board of Regents over control of intercollegiate athletics, the faculty gained increased respect and much greater influence in what had traditionally been considered management responsibilities reserved for the president, deans, and the regents. The present term "shared governance" to describe the interaction of the campus community had not yet been invented, but the concept certainly moved a giant step forward in these years.

The Continuing Pursuit of Quality

Surprisingly, the serious problems and mostly bleak external environment accompanying the depression and war years did not weaken the University as much as might be expected. Indeed, the challenges seemed to draw the campus closer together, creating a sense of loyalty and esprit among the faculty and student body that their later more cynical successors might consider curious but nevertheless admirable.

In spite of the recurring cutbacks and dislocations, the faculty continued to take pride in the University and endeavored to maintain its quality. One faculty initiative was particularly important in this regard. The University Committee won not only regent but faculty approval of an extraordinarily wise budget-balancing policy in the depression: to cut back the number of the temporary teaching staff and reduce all faculty salaries enough so as to uphold tenure, honor fixed-term appointments, and generate sufficient budgetary flexibility to allow some promotions and essential new appointments at all levels during the crisis. If the size of the faculty declined somewhat during the depression, it would be hard to make the case that its quality deteriorated as well. On the contrary, the general lack of academic jobs enabled the University to retain a more experienced faculty than normally, especially at the junior level. The deans' ability to continue making some appointments at all levels, moreover, permitted them to strengthen several important curricular areas and even launch a few new activities. Of growing significance was the Graduate School's creation of the University of Wisconsin Press in 1937, begun by Dean Fred with a grant of WARF funds to publish scholarly books by UW faculty members. A considerable number of academic departments improved themselves through judicious replacements, often adding new specialties and sub-disciplines in the process. In good times and bad UW faculty members continued to win major academic honors and awards, literary prizes, and scholarly fellowships. In a few cases the products of their research, notably Harry Steenbock's vitamin D irradiation process and Karl Paul Link's blood-thinner dicumarol, helped build WARF's endowment and its ever-expanding support of UW research.

The best known example of curricular innovation at Wisconsin in these years was the Experimental College, begun in 1927 before the depression made such ambitious and costly pedagogical ventures difficult to sustain. The college closed in 1932, partly a victim of the depression but even more of the hubris of its architects, Alexander Meiklejohn and Glenn Frank, who in their zeal to promote it nationally as the solution to the problems of undergraduate liberal education neglected to convince Wisconsin parents and their own UW colleagues of its worth. Still, the example of the Experimental College helped to encourage other curricular changes at Wisconsin in these years. It was surely no accident that Dean Bardeen announced his innovative preceptor program for fourth-year medical students at the very time Meiklejohn was publicly fleshing out his plan for the Experimental College. Bardeen remained a warm supporter of the Meiklejohn experiment to the end. If only in reaction, the influence of the Experimental College can be seen in some of the 1930 Fish Committee's recommendations, even more in the broad interdisciplinary and contemporary thrust of the Daniels Committee report in 1940, and especially in the Integrated Liberal Studies Program launched in 1948. These curricular reforms and more aimed to improve the quality of the educational experience at

Wisconsin, for despite Meiklejohn's and Frank's doubts about the commitment of their campus colleagues to more effective teaching, this remained a continuing concern for the faculty throughout the inter-war years.

Accompanying the curricular changes was a significant expansion of the University's off-campus instructional activities. To be sure, the College of Agriculture had been taking its services into every corner of the state since the late nineteenth century. Its agricultural extension program continued to develop throughout this period through a growing network of experiment stations and county agents. Under Dean Christensen the college broadened its focus in the 1930s beyond its traditional emphasis on efficient agricultural production to include cooperative marketing and the quality of rural life, the latter exemplified in John Steuart Curry's regional art program.

With considerable misgiving President Van Hise had allowed the University Extension Division to undertake non-credit instruction in Milwaukee, not wanting to be seen as drawing students from Marquette University and the Milwaukee Teachers College. Birge was likewise unenthusiastic but acquiesced in the expansion of extension courses in Milwaukee during his presidency. Both presidents were concerned lest any University presence in Milwaukee generate political pressures to develop a UW branch in the state's largest city, one that might eventually threaten the support and status of the home campus in Madison as the state's major university. The need for expanded educational opportunities for Milwaukee-area veterans returning from the First World War, however, led the Milwaukee-based extension staff to begin offering classroom instruction in several collegiate subjects, first in engineering and commerce. By 1923 this special post-war activity had expanded to cover the first two years of liberal arts degree work. That year the legislature also provided funds to construct a downtown Milwaukee extension building to provide classroom space for the now-considerable array of credit and non-credit instruction being offered by the resident Milwaukee extension faculty. What Van Hise and Birge had feared was slowly but surely taking place.

President Frank's head of the Extension Division, Dean Chester Snell, saw the University's budgetary and enrollment reductions during the early years of the depression as fortuitously offering both a need and an unusual opportunity to expand his empire. His division operated primarily on low-overhead fee income generated from the students enrolled in its courses, which were expected to be largely self-supporting. The depression increased the number of regular degree students unable to afford full-time residence in Madison, but who welcomed the opportunity to continue their academic work on a part-time basis locally. Snell had no trouble finding local school officials delighted to gain some prestige through association with the University by allowing their classrooms to be used in the evening by extension instructors—occasionally their own moonlighting high school teachers—offering college-level courses for UW academic credit. Although Snell and subsequently President Frank were dismissed by the Board of Regents for reasons mostly unrelated to this expansion of the University Extension Division's activities, extension credit instruction around the state continued to expand until the program was suspended during World War II. It resumed thereafter on a permanent and more ambitious basis, gradually growing into the present cluster of two-year campuses operated by the University Center System.

The development of a University-operated radio broadcasting network constituted another major expansion of University educational and information services. Although related experimentation had been taking place on campus since the early 1900s, physics Professor Earle M. Terry deserves most of the credit for setting up and developing University station WHA, which was initially licensed with the experimental designation 9XM in 1914 and began transmitting on a more or less regular basis in 1917. Federal authorities authorized a regular license and the station's present designation in 1922. Terry and his colleagues spent the rest of the decade tinkering with and improving equipment, developing a programming format, struggling to gain an institutional foothold within the University, and trying to compete with increasingly powerful and overbearing commercial stations. Chaos reigned in the airways for a time until early 1929, when WHA's situation improved markedly with a new and better frequency assignment, even though it allowed daytime broadcasting only.

Although WHA's funding and formal institutional status remained precarious for the rest of the 1930s, major advances occurred. The naming of Harold B. McCarty in 1931 as the first full-time program director bore fruit almost immediately with the inauguration of the "Wisconsin School of the Air," soon followed by the "Wisconsin College of the Air" and improved musical, farm, and home programming. Meanwhile, after considerable difficulty WHA and state station WLBL in the Stevens Point area, which broadcast crop reports for the Wisconsin Department of Agriculture and Marketing, were linked in

1933 to form perhaps the nation's earliest public radio network, thereby enabling campus programmers consistently to reach most of the state. Never before had the University possessed an educational tool of such reach and potential power. While only a harbinger of the much larger and more comprehensive state radio network to come, these developments were surely among the most significant of the inter-war period.

The dislocations brought by the Second World War were if anything more severe and required more adjustments even than those resulting from the great depression. Regular male enrollments fell precipitously during the war years and were only partly replaced by the several thousand service men and women assigned to the campus for differing periods of time in a variety of wartime training programs. For the first time in the University's history women students outnumbered the men in the regular student body, taking control of the *Daily Cardinal*, the *Badger*, the Student Board, and other student organizations. Like many of the male students, a substantial part of the faculty also left the campus for war service, either in uniform or for work in various war agencies. Those remaining had to adapt to numerous changes in their normal routine—working under a compressed year-round trimester calendar, developing new war-related courses, and administering and teaching in the diverse service programs, some of which, like the Navy Radio School, offered little more than elementary vocational training. For a time the Army and Navy took over most of the campus student housing—all of the UW residence halls except Elizabeth Waters and the Nursing Dormitory, the University Club, and a number of the Langdon Street fraternity houses leased by the University for service use. Workers attracted to Madison for work in area war plants competed for the private housing traditionally available to students. Housing the regular student body during the war years was thus a considerable challenge both for the students and for residence halls Director Donald Halverson and the deans of men and women. The latter resorted among other expediencies to leasing temporarily-empty fraternity houses for use by women students and the military programs.

The need to replace faculty members departing on short notice and to staff some of the specialized service programs required frequent staffing adjustments and much temporary hiring. For this the deans and departments often had to compromise their usual hiring standards, sometimes drafting faculty wives to teach elementary foreign language or mathematics courses. It would be hard to argue that the University's academic standards and quality did not decline somewhat during the war years, but not from a lack of will nor a determination to play a useful role in the national war effort.

An Uncommon Community

What strikes a later observer as one of the most remarkable characteristics of the University of Wisconsin before World War II is the degree to which it functioned as a close-knit, mutually-supportive academic community. In spite of its growing size and complexity and regardless of differing views about how to deal with its problems, its members regularly showed a high degree of respect and concern for each other and for the institution of which they were a part. Although the campus was comprised of a number of diverse groups, often with competing interests, most of the time they showed remarkable zeal in defending and promoting their University. One thinks, for example, of the daring public relations and lobbying campaign undertaken by the Board of Regents to defeat Governor Blaine's harsh University budget in 1925, one of the most decisive examples of the regents' rejection of a governor in the state's history. One is reminded, too, of the regents' general tolerance and defense of campus dissent, whether by left-leaning faculty members, critical *Daily Cardinal* editors, radical student groups, or even an over-zealous Governor Heil seeking to cleanse the campus of un-American elements. The two presidents of the period, Glenn Frank and Clarence Dykstra, though outsiders with no Wisconsin background, were likewise staunch in their defense of academic freedom and free speech at the University. The assumption by UW authorities of greater *in loco parentis* responsibilities in these years did not include to any appreciable degree censorship of student expression.

The faculty, too, time and again showed remarkable devotion to their academic community. Harry Steenbock's decision to assign the patent for his vitamin D irradiation process to WARF for the broad support of UW faculty research was but one example of this community spirit. Another was the plan developed by the members of the University Committee—all of them high-salaried senior faculty—for the salary waivers imposing larger graduated reductions on those with the highest salaries. Indeed, in spite of a relatively modest salary scale intensified by the depression waivers, most UW faculty members did not view the University as a temporary way station but rather as a supportive place to make a life-long academic career. Although the depression greatly reduced faculty mobility throughout the country, the general pattern of relative stability in UW faculty ranks long antedated the 1930s. Younger faculty members wanted to stay in Madison if they could; their elders likewise were rarely attracted elsewhere. To a great extent for both, the University *was* their profession. In contrast to more recent faculty attitudes, UW faculty members in these years considered their involvement in external professional activities to be complementary but clearly subsidiary to their University appointments and loyalty.

One reason for this institutional devotion, certainly, was faculty pride in the University's academic stature. This was at bottom self-respect, but it fostered a determination to maintain the University's national standing through active scholarly work and high standards for appointment and promotion. Equally important was the faculty's growing involvement and authority in institutional governance. By the Second World War the University was known for its remarkably collegial and highly democratic system of faculty government. Wisconsin faculty members typically thought of the institution as *their* University. In fact, they had more influence over general policy and more control over matters of greatest faculty concern than was true of most other major American universities. Underlying the expansion of faculty authority in these years was the thoughtful way the faculty addressed problems and carried out its responsibilities. The approach was nearly always collegial rather than confrontational. Guided by its University Committee, which normally included some of the wisest campus leaders, the faculty did not so much seek greater power for its own sake as to demonstrate a devotion to the welfare of the University that earned the respect and trust of regents, presidents, deans, and the rest of the UW academic community. From that trust flowed an increasing delegation of authority and sharing of governance responsibilities, based largely on moral rather than legal authority.

No less than the regents and the faculty, throughout the period the students also sought to improve their campus community. This student proprietary spirit manifested itself in a number of ways: in the successful drive to raise funds to build the Memorial Union, in the Hoofers' construction of the lakeshore ski jump and Observatory Hill toboggan runs, in the spirited defense of the University when it was under attack by John Chapple in 1931 and in the resulting Student Public Relations Committee to continue to promote the University around the state, in the collective efforts to alleviate depression hardship, in the campaign for better and non-discriminatory housing, in such ritual activities as the

Varsity Welcome, Freshman Week, Venetian Nights, Senior Swingout, the Pipe of Peace ceremony, and even the St. Pat parades, and, most impressive of all, in the all-University student work days to improve the campus. UW students were proud of their University and wanted to excel in their undertakings, whether in athletic or forensic contests or dramatic productions, in the ambitious reach and quality of the student-organized Union Concert Series, or even in the big-name dance bands hired for major student proms. A substantial part of the student body read the *Daily Cardinal* with interest and respect, and was not surprised but indeed expected the national awards it won with monotonous regularity. Finally, and not least, students reacted with pride to the achievements of their teachers, for they understood instinctively that the stature of their University rested first of all on the quality of its faculty.

In short, the University of Wisconsin in 1945 was a remarkably resilient and confident institution. It had met the hardships of depression and the trials of war with pride and resourcefulness—as an uncommon *community*. Whatever challenges the post-war years might bring, the campus could face them with the advantage of an enviable tradition of spirit and commitment.

Appendix 1.

The Evolving Face of the Campus

Major Land Acquisitions, Construction, and Remodeling
1925-45[1]

Land Acquisitions[2]
College of Agriculture
Gregg Farm (1925), 99.25 acres valued at $28,000, to expand the Hill Farm in Madison
Torger Thompson Estate (1929), 1,158 acres, Dane County
Wetmore Farm (1930), 68.2 acres, $2,605, for Coddington Branch Station, Waushara County
Stroeh Farm (1931), 160.6 acres, $9,000, LaCrosse County
Thomas Farm (1931), 243 acres, $7,500, to expand Spooner Branch Station, Washburn County
Prange Farm (1934), 60 acres, $300, to expand Hancock Branch Station, Waushara County
McGown Farm (1936), 40 acres, $400, Portage County
Hanawa Company (1941), 310 acres, Blackhawk Island, Juneau County
C.D. Parsons (1941), 40 acres, $10,200, to expand Hill Farm, Madison
Wisconsin University Building Corporation (1945), 120 acres, $20,000, Rieder Farms expansion of the Hill Farm, Madison[3]

---

[1]This information is derived from a number of manuscript sources, especially "Land Sales and Purchases," General University Papers, 0/0/5, folio 1, UA; Alden Aust, "A Tabular History of the University of Wisconsin: Including the Date of Construction, the Architect, the Size in Cubic Feet, and the Approximate Cost of Construction," June 4, 1937, Buildings: Dates and Costs, Subject File, UA; undated and unattributed manuscript giving a physical history of the University from 1848 to 1959, Campus Planning and Development Subject File, UA.

[2]This section does not include the acquisition of a number of lots in the immediate campus area, notably on Park Street, on and south of University Avenue, and along Langdon and Lake Streets, the latter for the proposed University Library.

[3]This represented the legal transfer of the Rieder Farms to the University from its WUBC corporate captive. Actually, the College of Agriculture had been leasing and making improvements to the property since 1931, and the Board of Regents had approved the $20,000 purchase in 1938.

Miles Farm (1945), 60 acres, Fayville Prairie, Jefferson County
Backus Farm (1945), 40 acres, $12,000, to expand Eagle Heights
Farm, Madison
Arboretum
Madison Parks Foundation (1932), 140 acres, $60,000
Lake Forest Company, Madison Parks Foundation, etc. (1932),
238.6 acres, $109,000
Madison Parks Foundation & Madison Realty Company (1932),
33.4 acres
Jessie B. Noe (1933), 190 acres, $47,500
Frank W. and Mary C. Hoyt (1934), 71.8 acres, $28,000
Lake Forest Company (1936), 280 acres, $20,000 for The Island
and Gardner Tracts
Wingra Land Company (1937), 12.2 acres
Madison Parks Foundation (1937), 13.4 acres
Mortgage Securities Company (1941), 53.6 acres
Grady Farm (1941), 197 acres
Gay Investment Company (1943), 10.5 acres, $4,509
Milwaukee Extension Center
City of Milwaukee (1926), 3 lots, $45,000
Marshall & Ilsey Bank (1938), 1 lot, $45,000
City of Milwaukee (1938), 6 lots
Picnic Point
Alice M. Young (1941), 128.9 acres, $205,000
President's Home, 130 North Prospect Avenue
John M. Olin Estate (1926), 8 lots in University Heights, Madison
University Club, 803 State Street
University Club House Association (1933), .35 acre, transfer

New Construction[4]
Adams Hall (1925-26), 1520 Tripp Circle
Tripp Hall (1925-26), 1510 Tripp Circle
Refectory (1926), 1515 Tripp Circle
Nurses Dormitory (1926), 1402 University Avenue
Bascom Hall west wing and theater (1926), 500 Lincoln Drive
Chemistry Building (later Chamberlin Hall) east wing (1926-27), 425
North Charter Street

---

[4]This section omits many small construction projects, mostly involving barns, sheds, and
other buildings on the various University farms in Madison and outlying the branch stations.

Agriculture Hall Library addition (1929), 1450 Linden Drive
Service Memorial Institutes (1926-28), 470 North Charter Street
Field House (1929-30), 1450 Monroe Street
Orthopedic Hospital (1930-31) (later Children's Hospital), 1415 Linden Drive
Mechanical Engineering Building (1931), 1525 University Avenue
Student Infirmary addition (1931), 1300 University Avenue
Tent Colony Cottage (1932), Eagle Heights Farm
Carillon Tower (1934), 1150 Observatory Drive
Music Hall Annex (1934), 925 Bascom Mall
Artist-in-Residence Studio (1936), 432 Lorch Street
Agronomy Seed Building (1936), 1930 Linden Drive
University Hospital, 7th floor addition (1936), 1300 University Avenue
Kronshage Men's Residence Halls, 1650 Kronshage Drive
    Three units (1938)
    Five units and refectory (1939)
Memorial Union Theater addition (1938-39), 800 Langdon Street
Law Library addition (1938-39), 957 Bascom Mall
McArdle Memorial Laboratory (1938-40), 420 North Charter Street
Elizabeth Waters Hall (1938-40), 1200 Observatory Drive
Home Management House (1940-41), 1430 Linden Drive

Major Remodeling
President's Home (1925-26), 130 North Prospect Avenue
Stadium improvements and east enclosure (1927), 1440 Monroe Street
    Restrooms under Stadium (1936)
Biology Building Vivarium, second floor and pent house (1927), 430 Lincoln Drive
    Addition (1931)
Memorial Union basement excavation and expansion (1933), 800 Langdon Street
Kleinhenz Hall (Short Course Dining Hall) addition (1934), 1815 Linden Drive
Chemistry Building ultracentrifuge (1936), 425 North Charter Street
    Addition (1939)
Library School relocation and remodeling (1938), 811 State Street[5]

_____

[5]The former Phi Kappa Psi fraternity house, located next door to the University Club and

Appendix 1.

Administration Building addition (1939), 831 State Street
Biochemistry Building addition (1939), 420 Henry Mall
Heating Plant addition (1939), 1225 University Avenue
Wisconsin High School (1940), 425 Henry Mall
Naval Armory (1942), 1610 University Avenue

built in the early 1920s on the site of the former home of John W. Sterling, the first professor
and for a time head of the University.

Appendix 2.

The Evolution of UW Academic Programs 1925-45[1]

College of Agriculture
Agricultural Bacteriology
Agricultural Chemistry
    Name changed to Biochemistry in 1938
Agricultural Economics
Agricultural Education
Agricultural Engineering
Agricultural Journalism
Agronomy
Animal Husbandry
Dairy Husbandry
    Divided into two departments—Dairy Husbandry and Dairy Industry—in 1940
Economic Entomology
Genetics
Forestry
    Program assigned to Forest Products Laboratory in 1934
Home Economics
Horticulture
Plant Pathology
Poultry Husbandry
Rural Sociology
    Separated from Agricultural Economics and given department status in 1931
Soils
Veterinary Science

---

[1]This list is derived from University catalogs and faculty and regent documents and is intended to reflect the structural changes in the University's academic programs during the period. Because of space limitations it does not attempt to show changes in the course offerings of individual departments, although these would give a fuller picture of the evolution and growth of the academic enterprise. Interested readers will find this information readily available in the catalogs.

College of Engineering
Chemical Engineering
Civil Engineering
    Absorbed many small instructional "departments" in 1940
Drawing (a service unit primarily for underclass students)
Electrical Engineering
Mechanical Engineering
Mechanics
    Given department status in 1940
Mining, Metallurgy, and Geology
    Name changed to Mining and Metallurgy in 1940

College of Letters and Science
Art Education
    Assigned solely to School of Education in 1940
Art History and Criticism (established in 1925)
Astronomy
Botany
Chemistry
Classics
    Greek
    Latin
    Semitic Languages (dropped in 1932)
Comparative Literature (established in 1926)
Comparative Philology (established in 1932; forerunner of Linguistics)
Economics
    Commerce
        Separated from Economics and given school status within L&S in 1927; made independent in 1944
    Industrial Relations
    Sociology, Anthropology, and Social Work
        Separated from Economics and given department status in 1930
Education, School of
    Given coordinate independent status in 1930
English
Experimental College (1927-32)

Geology and Geography
    Divided into separate departments in 1929
German
History
History of Science (established in 1942)
Irish (established in 1938 after legislative directive)
Journalism
    Given school status within L&S and master's degree authorized in 1927
Library School
    Originally sponsored by the state Free Library Commission in association with the University
    Absorbed administratively into L&S in 1937
    Raised to a graduate program in 1938
Mathematics
Meteorology
    Limited program offered by U.S. Weather Bureau staff
Music, School of
    Master of Music degree authorized in 1936
Nursing, School of
    Budgeted in Medical School; academic programs administered by L&S
Pharmacy
    Three-year curriculum expanded to four-year program in 1932
    Given school status within L&S in 1939
Philosophy and Psychology
    Divided into two departments in 1927
Physics
Polish
    Established in 1937 after legislative directive
    Renamed Slavic Languages in 1944 upon offering Russian
Political Science
Romance Languages
    French
    Italian
    Spanish
    Portuguese (after 1926)
    Divided into two departments—French and Italian, and Spanish and Portuguese—in 1930
Scandinavian Languages

Speech
Zoology

School of Education *(Initially a professional school within the College of Letters and Science; granted "coordinate" independent status in 1930)*
Educational Organization and Administration
Educational Measurements and Scientific Techniques
Educational Psychology
Educational Supervision and Methods
Elementary Education
History of Education
Secondary Education
Men's Physical Education and Athletic Coaching
    Master's degree authorized in 1927
Women's Physical Education
    Undergraduate major in dance after 1926
    Master's degree authorized in 1927
Professional Training of Teachers (established in 1926)
Rural Education (established in 1926)
Curriculum Construction (established in 1926)
Vocational Guidance and Vocational Education (established in 1926)
After 1931 reorganization
Art Education (with L&S until 1940)
    Applied art baccalaureate major offered in 1939
Education
    Elementary Education
    Educational Organizations and Administration
    Educational Supervision
    Educational Curricula and Objectives
    Instructional Procedures
    Measurements, Statistics, and Scientific Techniques
    Guidance and Welfare
    Educational Psychology
    History of Education
    Philosophy of Education
    Educational Sociology
    Special Fields, including Home Economics Teaching

Educational Methods
Industrial Education
Physical Education—Men
Physical Education—Women

Law School

Admission requirements raised in 1926 from two to three years of pre-law study Innovative four-year Doctor of Juridical Science (SJD) degree introduced in 1933 involving thesis and practicum Admission requirements raised in 1937 to either a baccalaureate degree or 1.3 gpa (on a 3-point scale) in three years of pre-law study

Medical School *(Full four-year M.D. program begun in 1925; parallel two-year program dropped in 1940)*
Anatomy
Hygiene
Medical Bacteriology (separated from Pathology in 1935)
Medicine (Renamed Medical Division in 1929)
    General Medicine
    Clinical Pathology
    Therapeutics
    Pediatrics
    Dermatology
    Medical Jurisprudence
        Medical Ethics added in 1926
    Neuro-Psychiatry
        Neuropsychiatry given department status in 1930
    Physical Medicine (after 1944)
Pathology and Bacteriology
    Pathology assigned to Medical Division in 1935
Pharmacology and Toxicology
    Assigned to Medical Division in 1935
Physiological Chemistry
    Assigned to Medical Division in 1935
Physiology
    Assigned to Medical Division in 1935
Surgery (Renamed Surgical Division in 1929)
    General Surgery

Orthopedic and Plastic Surgery
    Divided in 1935, with Oral and Plastic Surgery given
    separate department status
Urology
Opthamology, Rhinology, and Otolaryngology
    Divided in 1935, with Otolaryngology and Rhinology
    given separate department status
Physical Therapy
    Combined with Radiology in 1929 and given department
    status
    Masters degree program in Physical Therapy after 1940
Radiology
Obstetrics and Gynecology
    Given department status in 1929; reassigned to Surgical
    Division in 1936
Anesthesia
    Given department status in 1934
Two-year combined pre-medical baccalaureate program offered
with L&S; increased to three years in 1935
Baccalaureate degree program in Medical Technology offered with
    L&S after 1940
One-year certificate program in Physical Therapy offered with
Schools of Nursing and Education after 1940
Baccalaureate degree program in Occupational Therapy offered
with School of Education after 1943

School of Nursing *(Budgeted in Medical School; academic program*
    administered by L&S; three-year professional diploma and five-year
    baccalaureate degree)
Dietetics
Medicine and Surgery
Nursing
Therapeutics
Public Health Nursing (after 1939)

University Extension Division
Department of Debating and Public Discussion
Department of Group and Community Service (renamed Depart
ment of Public Service in 1927)

Bureau of Instruction by Lectures (renamed Lectures and
Short Courses in 1927)
Bureau of Municipal Information
Bureau of Visual Instruction
Bureau of Community Development
Postgraduate Medical Instruction
Bureau of Economics and Sociology (after 1927)
Bureau of Dramatic Activities (after 1927)
Bureau of Business Information (after 1927)
> Renamed Department of Business Administration after
> 1938
Field Organization (after 1927)
Office of the Editor (after 1932)
Milwaukee Center (after 1927)
Day School
Evening School
Speech Clinic (after 1935)
Department of Extension Teaching (after 1928)
Correspondence Study

Division of Physical Education *(A separate instructional unit responsible for the required freshman-sophomore physical educa tion courses)*

Men's Physical Education and Intramural Athletics
Intercollegiate Athletics (Men)
Women's Physical Education and Sports
Degree work in men's and women's physical education offered
through the School of Education
Participation in supervised team sports and marching band gained
exemption from physical education requirement in 1928
Two-year physical education requirement reduced to freshman year
in 1933
Wartime physical education requirement increased to two years for
women and continuously during each semester for men begin-
ning in 1942

Summer Session

Gradual expansion of course offerings throughout the period
Six- and nine-week terms offered beginning in 1927

On self-sustaining basis in 1933-37 (no guaranteed instructional salaries)
Nine-week term reduced to eight weeks in 1940
Wartime calendar offered summer trimester in 1942-45

Military Science *(Responsible for the Army Reserve Officers Train ing Program)*
ROTC enrollment included exemption from physical education requirement

Division of Social Education *(Established in 1935 to recognize the extracurricular instruction offered by the Memorial Union and the Division of Residence Halls)*

Appendix 3.

After the Experimental College

Alexander Meiklejohn's and Glenn Frank's Experimental College did not die after it closed in 1932. In a real sense it lives still, especially in the hearts of those of its fast-dwindling remaining guinea pigs and advisers and in their recorded recollections of the Camelot they created along the shores of Lake Mendota for a brief time between 1927 and 1932.

The closing of the college soon brought a scattering of its staff. Gaus was on leave and did not teach in the college in its final year, nor did "Doc" Agard. Agard remained at Wisconsin for the rest of his career, eventually chairing the Department of Classics and continuing to be known as a master teacher and gentle advocate of liberal causes and curricular reform. Gaus stayed another decade before moving to Harvard, as a visiting professor in 1942 and permanently in 1947. The end of the experiment gave Carl Bögholt time to finish his doctoral dissertation, after which he received a regular faculty appointment in the Department of Philosophy where he too developed a reputation as one of the University's great teachers. Laurence Saunders and Paul Raushenbush left the University, but Raushenbush remained in Madison, advising the La Follette progressives on social and economic issues and helping to develop and administer Wisconsin's pioneering unemployment compensation law after 1931. Malcolm Sharp moved to the University of Chicago in 1933, while Bob Havighurst went to Ohio State. After the college closed its doors in 1932, Chairman Meiklejohn requested a leave of absence and moved to Berkeley, California, where he started a new adult education venture, the San Francisco School of Social Studies, which operated precariously from 1934 to 1942. Probably for personal financial reasons, twice in the mid-thirties Meiklejohn returned to Madison to teach philosophy for a semester before retiring from the University in 1938 at the age of sixty-six on a Wisconsin pension of $67.52 per month.[1]

---

[1]Theda A. Carter to Meiklejohn, August 29, 1938, Alexander Meiklejohn Papers, box 31, SHSW. See also Mark H. Ingraham to Meiklejohn, July 28, August 11, 1938, ibid.; M.E. McCaffrey to Meiklejohn, June 6, 1938, box 32, ibid.; Meiklejohn to Max Otto, June 2 [1933], Max Otto Papers, box 2, SHSW. Although he did not draw a salary from the Univer-

As the college wound down during 1931-32, Chairman Meiklejohn sought to preserve the jobs of those advisers—chiefly the graduate assistants—who did not have a claim to on-going appointments in the regular academic departments. He persuaded President Frank to endorse a directive that declared with respect to reappointments, promotions, and salaries "the members of the Experimental College staff are to be regarded as regular members of the departments to which they have been assigned and are to be dealt with as if they have been teaching in the regular courses."[2] Frank may have thought he was simply confirming the rights of the regular faculty members, but Meiklejohn used the statement on behalf of the graduate assistants, sometimes describing it to departmental chairmen as a presidential "ruling."[3] There was no question about the right of the regular faculty members serving in the Experimental College to resume full-time positions in

---

sity after the Experimental College closed except for the two semesters he taught in 1935 and 1936, Meiklejohn objected strenuously and repeatedly to taking any salary cut during the depression. See Meiklejohn to Frank, June 27, August 21, October 24, November 25, 1932; Meiklejohn to BOR, October 24, 1932; McCaffrey to Meiklejohn, June 30, November 4, 1932, January 24, 1933; Frank to Meiklejohn, December 5, 1932, Meiklejohn Papers, box 32. Because of the uncertain funding of his San Francisco School, Meiklejohn proposed tentatively to return to teach in the second semester of 1934-35, but President Frank told him the philosophy department could not plan its staffing on the basis of a "'floating population'" of faculty, and that by this time there was "no provision in department plans or in the budget for this." Meiklejohn to Frank, August 1, November 13, 1934; Frank to Meiklejohn November 8, 1934, ibid. It was probably Meiklejohn's dissatisfaction over the University's decision to reduce his salary in keeping with the general faculty salary cuts during the depression that precipitated his decision to retire for reasons of ill health in 1938. See Sellery to Meiklejohn, May 13 and 21, June 6, 1938; Meiklejohn to Sellery, May 17 and 25, and May [undated draft], 1938; McCaffrey to Meiklejohn, June 6, 1938, ibid. Meiklejohn's concern for his personal finances was understandable. While he was employed at Brown and Amherst he had qualified for a retirement pension from the Carnegie Foundation for the Advancement of Teaching. Because he had not resumed academic employment at a Carnegie-associated college within a year after he left Amherst in 1924, however, he lost all claim to a Carnegie pension for his 27 years of Brown-Amherst service. Meiklejohn tried repeatedly in the 1920s, 1930s, and 1940s to get the Carnegie Foundation to make an exception and overlook the brief gap between his Amherst and his Wisconsin employment, but the foundation trustees refused, fearing legal complications with other claimants in similar circumstances. See, for example, Meiklejohn to President Carmichael, September 20, November 10, 1948; Howard J. Savage to Meiklejohn, November 12, December 2, 1948, ibid., box 8.

[2]Experimental College memorandum, May 6, 1931, Meiklejohn Papers, box 32. Frank's endorsement to Meiklejohn's document typed on Experimental College stationery stated: "This is an accurate statement of the meaning of the legislation creating the Experimental College. Glenn Frank".

[3]See, for example, Meiklejohn to McGilvary, March 30, 1932, ibid.; Meiklejohn to Otto, March 30, April 2, 1932; Otto to Meiklejohn, April 1, 1932, Otto Papers, box 2.

their home departments. For the younger staff—the graduate assistants—the problem was difficult, and largely insoluble regardless of presidential intentions and departmental good will. Here Meiklejohn found himself trapped by the close relationship he had worked out with President Frank rather than with Dean Sellery in making appointments to his staff. The dean, he complained to Frank, recognized no responsibility for the Experimental College staff. "This is, I presume," he admitted, "connected with the fact that, in accordance with my arrangement with you, our decisions upon personnel have not been taken by me to him but have gone directly to you."[4]

Meiklejohn, moreover, had usually managed to persuade the president to agree to higher salaries for the advisers than were paid for comparable teaching appointments in the departments. He now found departmental chairmen, whose budgets were severely constrained by the depression, unwilling to take on higher-cost men, however deserving, especially if this meant depriving their own departmental assistants of an appointment. To Meiklejohn it seemed a matter of simple justice for the University to take care of his staff after the Experimental College closed, and without a reduction of their salaries. To the departments, justice at a time their enrollments and budgets were declining was not such a simple matter; it also involved equity for their own staff.[5]

After the college closed its doors in June of 1932, Meiklejohn's urgent pleas to President Frank sufficed to generate funding in 1932-33 for the former advisers who did not hold regular departmental appointments. As the depression deepened, however, the president's sup-

---

[4]Meiklejohn to Frank, March 8, 1932, Meiklejohn Papers, box 32. On another occasion Meiklejohn complained to his patron: "You and I have agreed on the general principle that they [the Experimental College advisers] should have the same security as other men in the departments, but meanwhile Dean Sellery and the department heads do not accept the agreement....Can we do anything at once so that these men know where they stand and what to count on at the end of the year? It isn't a good time for being uncertain about your job." Meiklejohn to Frank, October 7, 1931, ibid. Frank showed this letter to Dean Sellery, who promptly wrote a handwritten letter to Meiklejohn stating his conviction that the Experimental College staff had "the same (but no greater) claim as other L&S teachers." Sellery to "A.M.," November 4, 1931, ibid.

[5]See the extended discussion of the problem of higher Experimental College salaries involving Meiklejohn and Professor R.E. Neil Dodge, the chairman of the English department, in 1931 and 1932: Meiklejohn to Dodge, March 25, April 3 and 21, May 25 and 28, 1931; Dodge to Meiklejohn, March 25, April 7 and 16, May 27, 1931; Walter R. Agard to Meiklejohn, May 22, 1931; Meiklejohn to Dodge, March 28, May 11, 1932; Dodge to Meiklejohn, March 29, 1932; Dodge to H.H. Giles, March 24 and 28, June 4, 1932; Giles to Meiklejohn, May 8, 1932, ibid., box 31.

port—and funds—evaporated, and Meiklejohn and the tenured advisers grew increasingly frantic about the fate of their younger colleagues. One of the advisers angrily wrote President Frank:

> Issues are of course generally obscured; and this one is doubtless obscured by troublesome problems of scholastic policy, departmental administration, and depression finance. When all qualifications have been made, however, these young men seem to be victims of a deplorable clash of personalities among their elders.
>
> ...Some of us have at times shown our confidence in the University administration; but this matter seems fit only for protest. It is an inexcusable breach of faith on the part of Dean Sellery and yourself.[6]

Everyone, it seemed, was on edge over the unhappy situation. When Meiklejohn, now on leave in California where he was launching his new adult education center, accused the English Department of failing to act "as men of honor" in disregarding President Frank's pledge of equal treatment for the former Experimental College staff, Professor Dodge exploded:

> To which I can only answer that if my honor depends on my being able to reason so subtly, God help my honor. Because Giles is to be treated as a member of the department, he is apparently to be kept for another year, though to keep him means to turn out some other member of the department. For of course instructors serve on one-year appointments; and since enrollment in our English courses fell off 20% in 1931-32 and an additional 20% in 1932-33, the departmental staff must be cut down to meet the shrinkage; and the only way of cutting down ordinarily practiced, I suppose, is by not renewing some of the one-year appointments.
>
> May I suggest again that our difference is a matter of interpretation? You and I interpret the President's language differently....We do not believe that honor is involved. Nor do we care to have it suggested that we are not capable of watching over our honor ourselves.
>
> You may wish to know that, to the best of my memory, I have at no time had communication with or from President Frank on the status of either Giles or Beecher.[7]

Before he left for a new job at the University of Chicago Law School, Malcolm Sharp worked out a plan whereby several of the older and more financially secure advisers—those "who are in both psychological and economic condition to help," he told Meiklejohn—would contribute money to enable John and Harriet Powell, the most destitute of the

---

[6]Malcolm Sharp to Frank, March 11, 1933, ibid., box 27. Sharp sent a copy of his letter to Meiklejohn with the comment: "At the present juncture, it seems that this can do no harm, and has a chance of doing some good." Sharp to Meiklejohn, March 11, 1933, ibid.

[7]Dodge to Meiklejohn, March 27, 1933, ibid., box 31. Meiklejohn graciously responded, "I can see that my remarks to you about 'honor' and 'obligation' were unnecessary and irrelevant." Meiklejohn to Dodge, April 2 [1933], ibid.

former Experimental College staff, to spend the 1933-34 year organizing the defunct college's records.[8] It was a sad and inglorious way to end an adventure begun with such high hopes only a scant few years earlier. The end of the experiment did not mean the end of the distinctive esprit and warm camaraderie developed among the college's members. Quite the contrary. Some 250 people attended the closing banquet in Tripp Commons in June, 1932, at which Meiklejohn complained that the University had "crucified" his experiment.[9] For many members of the college its aura grew ever brighter with the passing years. A former student reported in a survey conducted by the Powells in 1933 that he was "in constant contact" with his fellow guinea pigs. "I should add," he commented, "that I think the Exp. College students are maintaining acquaintanceships more than any group in the *process of disbanding* that I have ever known or heard of."[10] A group of midwestern Ex-Collegers organized a reunion at the University of Chicago in 1942 to mark the tenth anniversary of the college's closing and managed to get questionnaire responses from more than half of the 327 students who had been enrolled in the college during its brief life. "I don't think there has ever been a fellowship quite like that one," one of the younger advisers who could not attend told Meiklejohn.[11] "I classify the years I spent in the Experiment College as the brightest I have ever spent," echoed a former student. Recalled another alumnus, now a CIO labor organizer:

> The first year with the Greeks got me far enough away from myself and my day-to-day world for a bird's-eye view of a great civilization, but again and again I found myself forced to search my own judgments and prejudices and to examine the values of our contemporary institutions....Never before or since have I experienced such pleasurable and painful intellectual tossing around.[12]

At the close of the reunion Chairman Meiklejohn reminded the group they were still a fellowship, "studying the same lessons, grappling with

---

[8]Sharp to Meiklejohn, April 3, 1933, ibid. See also Sharp to Meiklejohn, April 18, May 8 and 25, 1933, ibid.; "Doc" [Walter R. Agard] to Meiklejohn, May 7, 1933, ibid., box 1; John W. Powell to Meiklejohn, Wednesday [1933], ibid., box 24. The following year Meiklejohn brought Powell to San Francisco to work in his new adult education school.

[9]*Daily Cardinal* and *Capital Times*, June 5 and 6, 1932.

[10]Kenneth Decker, questionnaire, p. 9, Meiklejohn Papers, box 55. Emphasis in original.

[11]Giles to Meiklejohn, May 7, 1942, ibid., box 31.

[12]Walker H. Hill, ed., *Learning and Living: Proceedings of an Anniversary Celebration in Honor of Alexander Meiklejohn, Chicago, May 8-10, 1942* (Chicago: The Editor, 1942), pp. 107-8.

the same problems, attempting to interpret the same principles, pushing forward the same undertakings, which challenged us all ten years ago. And that means the Experimental College did not die. It lives in you."[13]

In May, 1957, twenty-five years after the closing of the college, its members held a second reunion at Annapolis, Maryland, on the campus of St. John's College, whose great books approach to education made it a congenial host. For those who could not attend, the gathering was widely covered in the press and recorded in published *Proceedings* and on an LP recording of Alexander Meiklejohn's address to the group and his traditional reading of his favorite poets. A highlight was the announcement that 115 Ex-Collegers and friends of Meiklejohn had created a fund totaling $3,180 to support a new Alexander Meiklejohn Award for Academic Freedom by the American Association of University Professors.[14]

The third Experimental College reunion was, appropriately, held in Madison in June of 1962, partly to mark the thirtieth anniversary of the closing of the college but also to celebrate the ninetieth birthday of its founder. The organizers made a special effort to get as many letters of greeting as possible from the alumni, most of whom were now passing the half-century mark themselves. Jenkin Lloyd Jones, the editor of the *Tulsa Tribune*, regretted he could not attend, because he was "bursting with curiosity to see what happened to all those scapegraces who claimed they were philosophizing when they were simply loafing."[15] Another absentee, Victor Wolfson, who as a member of the first class had organized the Experimental College Players and later became a prominent Broadway playwright, sent an affectionate telegram to Meiklejohn:

> Will I ever forget that peaceful morning when you rose and said: "Well now we are born." Yes, we were born and I've never gotten over that birth trauma, or the years that followed in our marvellous booby hatch. I am still in shock and intend to remain in this delicious condition the rest of my life, dear Alec and I thank you for it.[16]

Most of the reminiscences struck a more serious note, but all paid warm tribute to Meiklejohn, the master teacher. Carroll Blair, another veteran of the first class, who had achieved notoriety as a Communist activist in

---

[13]Ibid., pp. 113-4.
[14]Delos Otis to "Ex-Colleger," July, 1958, Meiklejohn Papers, box 32.
[15]Jenkin Lloyd Jones to Meiklejohn, May 2, 1962, ibid.
[16]Victor Wolfson to Meiklejohn, telegram, June 6, 1962, ibid.

the 1930s, thanked Meiklejohn for "teaching us that valuable ability to indulge in doubt....also for teaching us the complexity of life and thought; the often contradictory nature of phenomena—in short the dialectical approach to the world and ourselves."

You have blazed a trail and have never abandoned the goals you moved toward all these years. Strange that many of us who brashly thought in our youth that we knew better than you, still find ourselves following the marks you placed on the trees years before![17]

The high point of this reunion was the announcement of the formation of the Alexander Meiklejohn Experimental College Foundation, whose first project was a gift of $7,000 to the University to create the Alexander Meiklejohn Lectureship on the Meaning and Methods of Education for Freedom.[18]

Nor did the University community forget Alexander Meiklejohn and his Experimental College. In 1939 and 1940 the student chairman of the Memorial Union Forum Committee, Leon Epstein, engaged in protracted negotiations to bring Meiklejohn back to Madison for a series of lectures. In announcing Meiklejohn's Great Hall lecture in the summer of 1939, Epstein declared that the Union was "at last bringing 'home' one of the university's greatest teachers."[19] In 1947 Clay Schoenfeld, the editor of *The Wisconsin Alumnus* magazine, solicited a retrospective article—"The Experimental College Ten Years After"—to commemorate the College's birth, which Schoenfeld mistakenly placed a decade later than the actual beginning in 1927![20] The following year the College of Letters and Science began a new Integrated Liberal Studies Program offering an integrated curriculum to a select number of

---

[17]Carroll W. Blair to Meiklejohn, March 23, 1962, ibid.

[18]Agard to Alec and Helen Meiklejohn, January 1, 1963, ibid., box 1; Fred Harvey Harrington to Ernest P. Strub, February 19, 1963; Strub to Harrington, February 21, 1963; Dave Connolly to "Ex. Coll. Alumni," August 15, 1963, ibid., box 32.

[19]*Daily Cardinal*, July 4 and 18, 1939. "We 'liberals' here-abouts have managed successfully, I think, to criticize our Marxist enemies without bringing on an abrogation of free speech," Epstein wrote in a letter about a follow-up lecture by Meiklejohn. "But our problem in this respect is by no means settled, and perhaps it would provide basis for an address this spring. Of course you may have something more interesting in mind." Leon Epstein to Meiklejohn, February 28, 1940, Meiklejohn Papers, box 32. See also Epstein to Meiklejohn, June 12, August 18, December 13, 1939, January 5, 1940, ibid. After graduation from Wisconsin and military service in World War II, Epstein earned a Ph.D. degree from the University of Chicago and returned to Madison in 1948 to teach political science, eventually serving as department chairman and then dean of the College of Letters and Science between 1965 and 1969.

[20]Clay Schoenfeld to Meiklejohn, February 12, 1947, Meiklejohn Papers, box 31.

freshmen and sophomores, a development that former Ex-College adviser Doc Agard helped design and implement. While the ILS Program was neither a carbon copy nor a direct descendant of the Experimental College, its lineage was clear. Meiklejohn returned to Madison to be feted and give an address sponsored by the philosophy department in the spring of 1949, again for a speech in the Memorial Union Theater in 1951, and yet again in the fall of 1963 for the first Alexander Meiklejohn Lecture given by his friend Stringfellow Barr.[21] The next June Meiklejohn returned to Madison, this time to receive the honorary degree of Doctor of Letters, proudly escorted on the occasion by Professor Robert Pooley, the first director of the ILS Program. Meiklejohn was especially touched by President Fred Harvey Harrington's praise for the Experimental College during the exercises. "I hope the words are recorded," he wrote to the Gauses afterward in his still-firm hand. "They give ground for satisfaction for all of us who took part in the daring venture of 37 years ago."[22] Six months later Alexander Meikle-

---

[21]For correspondence about this event, see Agard to Alec and Helen Meiklejohn, January 1 and 18, March 18, June 15, July 9 and 19, September 20, 1963; Meiklejohn to Agard, January 10, 1963, ibid., box 1; Elizabeth Tarkow to Dr. and Mrs. Meiklejohn, October 4, 1963, ibid., box 32. When Barr changed his mind about staying three days as Meiklejohn and the planning committee had intended so he would have more contact with UW faculty and students, Agard wrote his friend: "This changes our plans (deplorably) doesn't it? Please change the 'worksheet' to get all we can out of Winkie! Or should we try someone else who will be more cooperative?" Winkie [Stringfellow Barr] to Agard, July 12, 1963, with undated Agard note to Meiklejohn, ibid., box 1.

[22]Meiklejohn to John and Jane Gaus, July 2, 1964, ibid., box 14. See also Harrington to Meiklejohn, February 26, 1964, ibid., box 32; Robert C. Pooley to Meiklejohn, May 5, 1964, ibid., box 31. Meiklejohn himself may have raised the question of an honorary degree, for he at least was aware of the effort to arrange one as early as 1957. On January 27 of that year Agard wrote him: "Now to two points I have for some time been meaning to discuss with you Alec. (1) The degree. I promptly presented the idea to the phil. dep't, who must make the recommendation to A.[ndrew] Weaver's Hon. Deg. Com. Carl B-[ögolt] tells me that the dep't just puts off doing anything. The fact is only two in the dept (Carl and [Albert] Ramsperger) were here when you were, & the rest are (at best) a heterogeneous lot. It is too late for action this year, but I shall keep at it. What a pity that the U. in so many ways is torpid and unimaginative! A few degrees have been given to former teachers here, but very few, & as far as I know they have all been scientists who discovered something in bacteriology, etc. Apparently discoveries in the humanistic field are less appreciated. But I shall keep on trying...." Agard to Alec and Helen Meiklejohn, January 27, 1957, ibid., box 1. A few months before receiving the honorary degree Meiklejohn had been awarded the first Presidential Medal of Freedom by President Lyndon Johnson in ceremonies at the White House for his devotion to civil liberties, a selection originally made by the late President Kennedy. One is tempted to speculate, however, that the recognition from the institution many of whose faculty had once scorned him probably meant as much to Meiklejohn as this high honor from his

john was dead at the age of ninety-two.

College reunions are commonplace, and rarely are they noteworthy for anything but sentimental recollections of lost youth. Like the college itself, the reunions of the Ex-Collegers were different—notable not just for the enthusiasm of the participants but also for the intellectual quality of their program of speakers and their serious discussion of important issues. When they got together the Ex-Collegers seemed always to be trying to recreate the old free-wheeling give-and-take dialogue they had experienced in the dens of Adams Hall and the sessions in the New Soils Building many years before. They also reflected an abiding loyalty to alma mater and a continuing zest and quest for learning that any university would be proud to have instilled in its graduates.[23]

At the same time, it must be recognized that not all of the members of the Experimental College were similarly affected by the Meiklejohn spell. Some of the faculty participated only briefly and, like Carl Russell Fish, left disillusioned.[24] Many of the students also dropped out, transferring to programs on the Hill or leaving the University entirely. The steadily declining enrollment throughout the five years of the experiment cannot be whistled away by enthusiastic Ex-College partisans. In 1986 when Professor Ralph W. Johnson of University Extension's radio station WHA was seeking to track down Experimental College alumni for a program of recollections about the college, one of the his contacts cautioned him not to rely just on the Alexander Meiklejohn Foundation staff for leads. "Many grads appear to be completely alienated by the Foundation," he reported. "Those turned off by the school you've got to reach."[25]

---

country.

[23]Those attending the 65th Experimental College reunion in Madison on April 28-29, 1993—a corporal's guard of less than two dozen and most of them in their eighties—agreed this would be their last formal gathering. None of them liked the idea of one day returning as the lonely last survivor to figuratively lock the door of memories of their great adventure with Alexander Meiklejohn.

[24]On the basis of his year as an Experimental College adviser, Fish denied that Ex-College students were mostly "cranks"; the great majority, he told one skeptic, "are remarkably like the normal type of student I am dealing with all the time." Although he had learned from the experiment, he nevertheless had serious reservations: "I do not think it is ideal. I would make drastic changes at once." Fish to A. C. Kingsford, June 10, 1929, Carl Russell Fish Papers, box 8, SHSW.

[25]L. Edmands to Ralph W. Johnson, October 24, 1986, xerox copy courtesy of Professor Johnson.

Even some of the alumni who participated Experimental College reunions harbored doubts about the value of the experiment for which they had been proud guinea pigs. Two illustrations, collected from participants at the fiftieth reunion of the College in Madison in 1982, will suffice:

From Frederick Gutheim, First Class

> I value the many friendships with faculty and students that I formed at the Experimental College 1927-29, but in my view history has overtaken this educational venture. The University of Wisconsin repudiated it. Other educational experiments seem of equal importance as well as greater continuity. Its great accomplishment in creating the sophomore program to study American civilization has been institutionalized as "American studies." Much as I revere Alexander Meiklejohn, I believe we must turn his picture to the wall and venture forward on our own—as he would, I am sure, wish us to do. I see no alternative. Organized alumni efforts to replicate the Experimental College or memorialize its experience are inescapably retrogressive. I believe you cannot go back, relive earlier experiences, give them to others and anyone who tries is bound to find himself lying about it.[26]

From Phillips L. Garman, Third Class

> It is difficult for me to draw many current applications or keys from our studies of Athenian and early twentieth century civilization. Contrary to Doc's hopes, Aristotle seems more relevant than Plato, although one can derive more pleasure from reading the latter....our recent leaders seem more like Alcibiades than Pericles, although the world is far more complex and horrifying....
>
> To say it swiftly and pass on among the damned: lovely a man as Alec and the others were, enjoyable as the experience was, I came to think of the educational theory as benighted.
>
> The older I get the more radical I become. Although my radicalism goes in the direction of anarchy and individualism, I have not got over a feeling that education ought to be strict. That men—boys—at least, *I* was a boy—are better served by more directed and stringently appraised study. Bright boys (and we were many bright boys) especially need management because there is otherwise no inducement to read with discipline or insight, or to read difficult material, in so permissive an environment. Only single-minded, verified, incontrovertible geniuses should be free to run on their own reins.
>
> But I see that you all have a contrary enthusiasm, so I shall merely wave in passing at the convocations and the publishing projects.

---

[26]"Reflections—a Half Century Later," *AMECF Quarterly*, 1 (December, 1982), 7.

But with affection.[27]

Perhaps the most thoughtful evaluation of the experiment came from one of the members of the last class, John Reddin of Manitowoc, who later became a journalist and an editor of the *Milwaukee Journal*. Reddin's comments were written in the form of an unpublished letter-to-the-editor in response to a December, 1940, article by UW alumnus Maurice Zolotow in the *American Mercury* recalling "Bohemia on the Campus" in the early thirties. Zolotow had lived in Adams Hall as a freshman in 1931-32 with, but not a part of, the last Experimental College class, a year he nostalgically described as the last year of Bohemia in Madison. Reddin objected strenuously to Zolotow's lumping the Ex-College guinea pigs with other UW exotics of that era and calling them "instinctive bohemians" who "infected all who came near them with the virus of their bonhomie and defiance of rules."[28] Reddin's recollections are worth quoting at length as a fitting epitaph to the now nearly forgotten Camelot by the Lake:

> Actually, the Experimental College was nothing more than "a group of people reading the same books." That was Meiklejohn's definition of a college, and we fit it beautifully. The books were not unusual—The Education of Henry Adams, the Autobiography of Lincoln Steffens, Plato and assorted Greeks, Middletown, the Rise of American Civilization, and others that people beyond eighth grade intelligence were reading. We were trying to get an education—trying to develop intelligence, to build individual sets of references that would enable us to meet "human situations."
>
> If we were queer, it was only because our approach was different. Instead of going to classes, we worked individually, guided by advisors with whom we met in individual and group conferences. The general college meeting every Monday morning at which Meiklejohn usually presided was the nearest thing to a class we had—and it was a combination chapel and bull session. If we studied physics, they told us where the laboratory was and let us go to it, with help if we wanted it, alone if we didn't. Men like Stuart Chase, Lewis Mumford and Clarence Darrow would drop around for a day or a week and live and talk with us. We were there to learn and were allowed to make use of every means imaginable.
>
> Our informality was our greatest radicalism. We dressed as we pleased, and pretty much did as we pleased. Our regulations were little more than the obligations any half-way intelligent person recognizes in the society in which he lives. It is easy to convince a man who has gone through formal college courses that a little knot of unkempt youngsters in bathing suits,

---

[27]Ibid., p. 16. Emphasis in original.
[28]Maurice Zolotow, "Bohemia on the Campus: Sex, Poetry, and the Higher Emancipation in Wisconsin," *American Mercury*, 68 (December, 1939), 472.

shorts, or dirty slacks, lying around on the grass or dangling their feet from a pier, are not showing the diligence one might expect from students. It took more than a cursory glance to realize that they were probably worrying about the price system, or arguing about the Phaedo, or trying to define "justice", or telling their advisor that the period paper just assigned was ridiculously silly, ill-conceived and generally inadequate. It bothered more conventional observers to see guinea pigs tossing a football around or walking about with men they called Doc or John or "D" or Bob, knowing those men were teachers and deserving of more respect. It was hard for somebody who had to sit for hours on end listening to dry lectures given by desiccated scholars to understand what an evening playing "Murder" and munching "brownies" at Meiklejohn's home had to do with education.

Talk was our forte. We talked from breakfast to lunch, from lunch through dinner and sometimes on to breakfast again. From Solon to sex, from Japan's invasion of China to Ruth Etting, from the football team to Kant—everything was grist, and we kept the mill running twenty-four hours a day. The den, the community room in every dorm house, was the class-room in which we secured as much of our education as anywhere else. Students from "the hill" who lived in the same dorms couldn't but gather that we were wasting time when we held bull sessions while they struggled with math or the next day's French lessons. The fact that they had to work for grades while nobody said a word to us if we stayed in bed all day or spent a week swimming or playing bridge instead of studying bothered them. The fact that we didn't stay in bed all day or waste too much time wasn't under-standable either—unless one appreciated the sense of obligation most of us had, the love we learned to feel for the satisfaction of holding up our end in discussions, of discovering some thought in something that had escaped us previously, of the feeling of power an idea can give.

It is easy to see why we were thought queer. And we did rather revel in that reputation. It wouldn't have been human for us not to exaggerate our queerness. Our hair probably did grow longer than necessary at times, we probably did leave our trousers unpressed as added atmosphere, we did undoubtedly dramatize a studied casualness, a false indifference, a feigned superiority, an air of indolence. But underneath we took ourselves with sophomoric seriousness. We felt the weight of the world's problems on our shoulders, and that we would solve them all by the end of two years we seldom if ever doubted. Our queerness was all stage setting. We were intensely jealous of the set, too, and the real "queeries", however much Zolotow believes it now, were never part of us.

What the College did to us is hard to assess. It was an exciting experi-ence. It was a hundred things at once. Above all, it was satisfying. It gave us tolerance, eagerness, faith—or, at worst an appreciation of them, a desire for them, a commitment to them. It may not have given us the tools with which to overpower all the troubles of America, but it gave us the abiding belief that the troubles were worth curing, that the tools were worth trying to make or find. And we would try....

One picture stays with me:

It is the Memorial Union—a dining hall, and not the Music Room. The

College was closing, and we final guinea pigs had come to hear the death knell. Glenn Frank, stiff and cold and nervous, poured out a spouting of dictionary words that floated heavily after him as he made a hurried and embarrassed exit when the honors had been done.

Then a slight, intense, almost mystic little man began to talk. I don't know to this day what he said. It doesn't matter much. His appeal always affected my emotions [more] than my intellect, unless I could read him or think over what he said away from his presence. The picture I remember is of the room when he had finished talking. Everyone was on his feet. For a moment there was tremendous clapping. Then silence, and for several moments nobody moved. Everyone watched that little man. It was almost a spell. A spell that broke slowly, and when it finally broke found us all staring embarrassedly, red-faced at one another. Embarrassed and red-faced because every person in that room knew that the gulping in his throat and the mist in his eyes were in the eyes and throats of everyone else. We shuffled about a few minutes, muttered gruffly to one another and stampeded for the door. With that moment the Experimental College became a report to the University—a report that lies dust covered on some forgotten shelf. But for us, that moment crowned the most exciting years we shall probably ever know.

That man was, of course, Alexander Meiklejohn; he was the Experimental College. He was its soul—the idealism, the moving spirit, the intelligence that made it tick. Like Socrates, he was called a dangerous man by legislators and perennial world-savers. And maybe he was dangerous. He wanted us to become educated. To him that meant "being able to see, in any set of circumstances, the best response which a human being can make to those circumstances." That is dangerous to placid, unquestioning conventionalism....And so, perhaps, he was a dangerous man. Perhaps that made him queer, and so, made us queer. But to us it made him great and living with him for two years wa[s] a privilege that was worth anything—even being included among the bohemians in mis[s]hapen memories.[29]

[29]John Newcomb Reddin, "Guinea Pigs vs. Bohemia" (unpublished manuscript, ca. 1940), Meiklejohn Papers, box 56. So far as can be determined, Reddin's thoughtful rejoinder was never published.

Bibliographical Note

Source materials for the period covered by this volume are abundant and easily available in Madison to the researcher. Indeed, thanks initially to the efforts of Merle Curti and Vernon Carstensen, the authors of the first two volumes in this series, *The University of Wisconsin: A History, 1848-1925* (Madison: University of Wisconsin Press, 1949), a University Archives was established that now possesses a rich and well-organized documentary collection. It enabled us to avoid many of the difficulties encountered by our two predecessors. In addition to a wealth of documentary materials, the archives has an impressive iconographic collection, which made possible the recent publication of Arthur Hove's (with the editorial assistance of Anne Biebel) *The University of Wisconsin: A Pictorial History* (Madison: University of Wisconsin Press, 1991). Anyone interested in pursuing the University's history during the inter-war years is strongly advised to begin at the University Archives.

As our footnote citations indicate, we relied heavily on a few key University Archives collections. Most helpful were the presidential papers of E.A. Birge, Glenn Frank, George C. Sellery (acting), and Clarence A. Dykstra, as well as several series of presidential papers arranged by subject. Not only is the general correspondence voluminous, but so too are the numerous official and unofficial reports, documents, speech texts and the like that were instrumental in defining this period of University history. The papers of the Board of Regents also were crucial, including the official minutes of the board, its executive committee, and other associated bodies, as well as files of documents and correspondence. Less frequently of help but nevertheless indispensable were the University Faculty papers, consisting primarily of minutes of faculty meetings and official faculty documents, as well a disappointingly small number of records of important faculty committees. Finally, we should call attention to the papers of the University business manager. As one would expect, this collection contains considerable technical data on nearly any University project costing money, but it also contains an impressive body of policy and other supporting information not found elsewhere.

The University Archives also maintains collections—varying greatly in quality—from the several sub-units of the University. The papers of the College of Letters and Science were especially helpful, including

874

both correspondence and subject files of the dean and his staff as well as smaller departmental and individual faculty member collections. The College of Agriculture collection is perhaps even more comprehensive, but also more complex and difficult to use. Other notable collections include those of the Graduate School, the University Extension Division, the Medical School, the Summer Session, and the Deans of Men and Women (and other student affairs materials).

In addition, the University Archives also maintains numerous miscellaneous resources. Complete sets of publications and other serial documents that were especially useful to us include the annual University budgets, University catalogues and bulletins, the *Daily Cardinal*, the *Octopus*, the *University of Wisconsin Press Bulletin*, the *Wisconsin Alumni Magazine* (*Wisconsin Alumnus*), and the *Badger*. Other resources of occasional value include personnel employment card files for the period, departmental file drawers, and biographical and subject file collections. The University Oral History Project, an agency of the archives, has a collection of approximately four hundred taped interviews, many of them relevant for the inter-war period. The archives' iconographic collection was the source of most of the photographs contained in this volume.

Several non-University archives provided valuable assistance. The manuscript collections of the State Historical Society of Wisconsin made available papers of government officials and other individuals outside the University who had occasion to associate with it as well as papers of a number of faculty members. Most important in this study were the collections of John J. Blaine, Herman Ekern, Zona Gale, Julius P. Heil, Theodore Kronshage, Philip F. La Follette, Michael Olbrich, Alexander Meiklejohn, and Max C. Otto. The Library of Congress holds the great bulk of La Follette family papers, particularly those of Robert M. La Follette, Sr. Aside from the University of Wisconsin Archives, the best collection of Glenn Frank's papers is at the archives of Northeast Missouri State University at Kirksville. The documentary evidence regarding University of California President Sproul's recruitment of UW President Dykstra to UCLA is to be found at the archives of the University of California at Berkeley. The UCLA archives has good supplementary data on Dykstra's years in Madison.

During the course of our research the authors have developed a rather substantial archives for the University History Project, which we assume will eventually be absorbed into the University Archives.

During the mid-1980s, for example, we acquired the University Club's modest yet important archives. The project also obtained more than 130 taped oral histories, written reminiscences, and other kinds of information from University alumni and staff members who had been associated with the institution during the inter-war period or otherwise were knowledgeable about it.[1] Finally, the project canvassed all academic depart

---

[1]Some, but not all, of the contributors listed below are cited in the chapter footnotes. Those who were omitted also were of significant value in the study, however, as they provided important background information. The authors wish to thank one and all. The parenthetical notations indicate the type of contribution: W=written, OH=taped oral history, I=interview, and M=miscellaneous. All contributions are on file with the University History Project: Margaret P. Addison (W), Kenneth E. Anderson (OH), Aaron Arnold (W), William C. Atten (W), Ira L. Baldwin (OH), Hollis W. Barber (W), Richard Bellman (W), Eleanor Granger Benda (OH), Beatrice C. Bice (W), James E. Bie (OH), George L. Bird (W), Willard W. Blaesser (OH), Julia Bogholt (OH), Gustav Bohstedt (OH), Gladys L. Borchers (OH), Fredrich A. Buerki (OH), S. Lee Burns (OH), Guy T. Buswell (OH), Porter Butts (OH), Mrs. Porter Butts (M), Lois E.A. Byrns (W), Marguerite Christensen (OH), Franklin W. Clark (OH), Wilbur J. Cohen (W), Hubert A. Conner (OH), Signe S. Cooper (W/OH), Merle Curti (I), Scott Cutlip (I), Elmer G. Dahlgren (OH), Jean Davis (W), Bob De Haven (OH), Allan D. Dickson (W), Robert M. Dillett (OH), Franz Dykstra (M), Janet Smith Ela (OH), Benjamin G. Elliott (OH), William O. Farber (W), David Fellman (OH), Delbert L. Gibson (OH), Alice (Christensen) Gjerde (OH), Ruth B. Glassow (OH), Mr. & Mrs. Thomas R. Green (W/OH), Lee S. Greene (W), Florence Whitaker Gross (OH), Lawrence E. Halle (OH), Donald L. Halverson (OH), Fred Harvey Harrington (OH), Maurice L. Hartung (OH), William Hay (I), Harriet Hazinski (OH), Gunther W. Heller (W/M), Paul S. Henshaw (OH), Thomas J. Higgins (I), E.M. Hildebrand (W), Asher Hobson (OH), Virginia V. Hoebel (OH), Fred Holt (OH), Olaf A. Hougen (OH), Mark H. Ingraham (OH), Leslie G. Janett (W), Elmer S. Junker (W/OH), Louis Kaplan (M), Dorothy Keenan (W/OH), Ellen D. Kistler (W), Paul Klein (W/OH), Dorothy Knaplund (W/OH/I), Cecelia Shestock Konkel (OH), Harold Kubly (OH), Robert Lampman (M), Eileen Martinson Lavine (OH), John W. Lehman (W/OH), Mr. & Mrs. Arno T. Lenz (OH), Angeline G. Lins (OH), Jean G. Linton (W/OH), Katherine D.K. Lower (W/OH), Eldor A. Marten (OH), Albert E. May (OH), John Mayor (W/OH), L.S. McClung (W/OH), Donald W. Miller (W), J. Duain Moore (OH), Harland W. Mossman (OH), Leslie F. Orear (M), Otto E. Mueller (OH), William Q. Murphy (OH), John P. O'Brien (OH), Frederic S. Orcutt (OH), Ronald Ostrander (OH), David G. Parsons (OH), Ray L. Pavlak (W), Charles A. Pearce (W), Glenn S. Pound (OH), Carver Puestow (I), Elizabeth H. Rasmussen (OH), Willard L. Roberts (W), Barbara Hammond Robinson (OH), George W. Robinson (OH), A.H. Rogers (OH), Erna C. (Brambora) Rollefson (OH), Ragnar Rollefson (OH), Allan F. Saunders (W), Herbert A. Schmidt (OH), Clay Schoenfeld (OH), Max O. Schultze (W), Joseph E. & Emily Shafer (W/OH), Elizabeth H. Shands (M), Jasper B. Shannon (OH), Gordon & Agnes Shipman (W), Alton John Simpson (OH), John T. Skinner (W), Henry Ladd Smith (OH), Mary Bunting Smith (W), Newell J. Smith (OH), Elizabeth B. Stahmer (W), Fredrick J. Stare (W), John F. Stauffer (OH), Hugh R. Stiles (W), Fannie Taylor (OH), Robert Taylor (I), Carl Thompson (OH), John W. Thomson (OH), Wilbert R. Todd (OH), Stanislaw M. Ulam (OH), Irving & Carlyn Ungra (OH), Mary M. (Taylor) Vinje (OH), Virginia Walker (OH), John B. Washbush (I), Grace G. Wegner (OH), Kenneth W. Wegner (OH), Bernard A. Weisberger (M), Victor Weiss (OH), Frederick L. Wellman (W), W. Norris Wentworth (OH),

ments of the University for histories they might have prepared. This collection is small but growing.

There is a growing secondary literature on the University's history. Probably the most insightful on the inter-war period as a whole is Mark H. Ingraham's essay, "The University of Wisconsin, 1925-1950," in Allan G. Bogue and Robert Taylor, eds., *The University of Wisconsin: One Hundred and Twenty-Five Years* (Madison: University of Wisconsin Press, 1975). Ingraham's biography of the influential faculty leader and graduate dean of the period, *Charles Sumner Slichter: The Golden Vector* (Madison: University of Wisconsin Press, 1972), also offers important insights into the life of the University generally. George C. Sellery's *E.A. Birge: A Memoir* (Madison: University of Wisconsin Press, 1956) and his memoir *Some Ferments at Wisconsin, 1901-1947: Memories and Reflections* (Madison: University of Wisconsin Press, 1960) provide heartfelt though less detached analyses. Lawrence H. Larsen's *The President Wore Spats: A Biography of Glenn Frank* (Madison: State Historical Society of Wisconsin, 1965) is the only full-scale treatment of Frank. There is none of President Dykstra. Other particularly notable works on the University's history include: W.H. Glover, *Farm and College: The College of Agriculture of the University of Wisconsin, A History* (Madison: University of Wisconsin Press, 1952), Edward H. Beardsley, *Harry L. Russell and Agricultural Science in Wisconsin* (Madison: University of Wisconsin Press, 1969), Aaron J. Ihde, *Chemistry, as Viewed from Bascom's Hall: A History of the Chemistry Department at the University of Wisconsin in Madison* (Madison: Department of Chemistry, UW-Madison, 1990), and Robert J. Lampman, ed., *Economists at Wisconsin, 1892-1992* (Madison: Department of Economics, UW-Madison, 1993). Copies of these and other books may be found at the University Archives as well as in the general UW-Madison library collection.

Clarance & Dorothy Westring (OH), Edwin & Gladys Wiig (OH), Lester Wilkin (W), Logan T. Wilson (OH), Dorothy Wirtz (OH), Melvin H. Wunsch (W), Charles C. Wurth (OH), Telle C. Yelle (OH), Theodore W. Zillman (OH), Maurice E. Zolotow (OH)

Photographic References

For the convenience of readers wishing to know the source and negative numbers of the photographs used in the two sections of illustrations, this information is provided below. Three of the photographs (on pp. 322, 332, and 620) are from the Iconographic Collections of the State Historical Society of Wisconsin, identified by the prefix WiH. All of the remaining photographs are from the University Archives.

First Section: p. 321, top, X25 2745; p. 321, bottom, M-5 263; page 322, top, WiH(X3)48655; p. 322, bottom, M190; p. 323, top, M194; p. 323, bottom, M221; p. 324, top, X25 1415; p. 324, bottom, X25 2233; p. 325, top, X25 2739; p. 325, bottom, M207; p. 326, top, X25 1288; p. 326, bottom, X25 2751; p. 327, top, X25 2257; p. 327, bottom, X25 2742; p. 328, top, X25 887; p. 328, bottom, X25 2743; p. 329, top, M92; p. 329, bottom, PM 1669-B; p. 330, top left, X25 2736; p. 330, top right, X25 1071; p. 330, bottom left, X25 1445; p. 330, bottom right, M214; p. 331, top left, X25 88; p. 331, top right, 25 2746; p. 331, bottom, M96; p. 332, top, X25 2238; p. 332, bottom, WiH(X3)48980; p. 333, top, M205; p. 333, bottom, X25 822; p. 334, top, X25 2735; p. 334, bottom, M86; p. 335, top, X25 2633; p. 335, bottom, X25 2734; p. 336, top, X25 2748; p. 336, bottom, X25 2732.

Second section: p. 607, top, X25 2745; p. 607, bottom, M209; p. 608, top, M218; p. 608, bottom, M192; p. 609, top, X25 1912; p. 609, bottom, X25 2752; p. 610, top, M204; p. 610, center, X25 1354; p. 610, bottom, M213; p. 611, top, X25 1358; p. 611, bottom, X25 2737; p. 612, top, M109; p. 612, bottom, M206; p. 613, top, X25 1347; p. 613, bottom, X25 1344; p. 614, top, M99; p. 614, bottom, X25 1350; p. 615, top, X25 1495; p. 615, center, X25 1495; p. 615, bottom, M211; p. 616, top, X25 1280; p. 616, bottom, X25 2741; p. 617m top, M71; p. 617, bottom, M107; p. 618, top left, M125; p. 618, top right, M102; p. 618, bottom, M191; p. 619, top left, M201; p. 619, top left center, M202; p. 619, top right center, M203; p. 619, top right, M220; p. 619, bottom left, M200; p. 619, bottom right; p. 620, top, M215; p. 620, bottom, WiH(D487)8218; p. 621, top, M87; p. 621, bottom, X25 2738; p. 622, top, X25 2693; p. 622, bottom, X25 1455.

Index

Aamodt, Olaf S., 497
Abbott, Edith, 181-2
Academic programs: evolution of, 853-60
Academic freedom, 9, 128-30, 131, 284-91,
    320, 384-400, 845; affirmed, 469-70
Academy, The, 523
Action, 624
Adams Act (1906), 769
Adams, Charles Kendall, 8-9, 642, 644,
    685-7, 758
Adams Hall, 67, 119-20, 123, 168, 169,
    174, 176, 177, 195-6, 197, 198, 204,
    210, 415, 869, 871, 568, 571, 572, 577,
    662, 670, 833; photo of, 609
Adams, Harry, 311
Adams, Henry, 170, 170n
Adkins, Homer, 203
Administration reform, 113-5, 133-9
Admission requirements, 556-7
Adolphson, Lorentz H., 815
Adult education, 107-13, 764, 773, 773n,
    803-6, 808, 809n, 822. *See also*
    Extension Division, University
African-Americans. *See* Negroes
Agard, Walter R., 468, 764; and civil
    liberties, 389, 543, 547n; and the
    Experimental College, 164n, 165-6,
    166n, 172, 174, 483, 861, 868n; and
    University Club, 533, 543, 547n
Agricultural Chemistry, Department of. *See*
    Biochemistry, Department of
Agricultural Experiment Station, 513, 747,
    768
Agricultural Extension Service. *See*
    Cooperative Extension Service
Agricultural Hall, 291, 693, 813
Agriculture, College of, 8, 108, 110, 114,
    270, 497-8, 745-7, 767-84, 853
Alexander, Edward P., 695, 697
Alexander, Walter, 260
All-University Religious Convocation, 116-
    7, 279, 285
All-University Research Council, 133, 157-
    60
All-University Study Commission, 91-2,

151, 151n, 160, 165
Allen, Chester, 112, 801, 809
Allen, Robert S., 274
Allen, William H., 789
Alumni Loyalty Fund, 42
Alumni Records Bureau, 591
Alumni, University of Wisconsin: and
    financial support, 41-2. *See also*
    Wisconsin Alumni Association
"America and the War" series, 426
American Association of University
    Professors (AAUP), 233, 468, 470
American Association of University
    Women, 518
American Civil Liberties Union, 179
American Federation of Teachers, 252-3,
    468, 811
American Institute of Cooperation, 269
American Legion, 390
American Mercury, 293-6
American Student Union, 385-90, 394
America's Hour of Decision (Frank), 276-7
Amherst College, 25, 31, 32, 46, 89, 90,
    93, 144-7, 150, 155, 165, 166, 207,
    592, 862n
Andersen House for women, 580, 581
Ann Emery Hall for women, 568, 577
Anderson, Charles J., 309-10, 764; as
    candidate for president, 456n; and
    creation of School of Commerce, 451;
    and creation of independent School of
    Education, 104-5, 107; as dean of
    School of Education, 739, 741, 744
Anderson, Marian, 629
Anderson, Rasmus B., 517n
Anti-Semitism, 389, 427n, 478, 478n,
    498n; and *Daily Cardinal*, 635-40; in
    fraternities and sororities, 673-4; in
    housing, 119, 545, 676-7; in Medical
    School, 545, 719; in sports, 676
Anti-war movement, 393-5
Antigone (Sophocles), 174
Apex Club, 119
Arboretum. *See* University Arboretum
Arden Club, 580, 624

879

Arden House, 580
Armory (Gym), 78, 117, 261, 516, 589, 590, 602, 643, 653, 658, 664, 665, 817, 818, 828
Army Air Corps: mechanics training program, 416; meteorology training program, 420-2; campus recruiting, 417
Army Specialized Training Reserve Program (ASTRP), 433, 437, 439,
Army Specialized Training Program (ASTP), 420-2, 431, 437-8
Artist-in-Residence. *See* Curry, John Steuart
Associated Press, 87
Association of Wisconsin Presidents and Deans, 138
Athletics: basketball, 653-5; and Big Ten Conference, 267, 644; board, 258, 260-9, 467; bowling, 517, 658; boxing, 621, 655-6; crew, 656-7; discrimination in 676; football, 645-52; intercollegiate, 642-57; intramural and recreational, 657-61; and military trainees during WW II, 435; reform of, 253-69; women's, 660-1. *See also* Stadium; Cheerleaders; Field House; Hoofers Club
Aurner, Robert, 522
Aust, Franz, 678
Avery, Robert, 678
Aydelotte, Frank, 31
Ayres, Edmund D., 534

Babcock, Stephen M., 582
Bacchanals of Euripides, The, 175
Bachhuber, Ruth, 634, 635-6, 640
Backus, August C., 301, 379-80, 737
Badger (Yearbook), 86-7, 435, 623, 625, 642
Badger Club, 582
Bag rush, 663; photos of, 617
Bakken, Henry, 778
Baldwin, Ira L., 233-4, 498, 508, 512, 522; death of daughter, 669; and University Club, 528, 539
Band, 376, 648-9
Bard College, 89
Bardeen, Charles R., 21n, 125, 219, 246; anatomy classes, 712n; supports Experimental College, 115, 841; and hiring faculty, 475, 498-9; as dean of

School of Medicine, 709-23; and preceptor plan, 115, 841
Barnard Hall, 119, 374, 417, 431, 434, 563, 572, 575, 576
Barnard, Henry, 5, 757-8
Barton, John, 783
Baruch, Bernard, 147
Bascom, Lelia, 533, 544, 544n
Bascom Hall (Main), 4, 21, 38, 71, 74, 78, 283, 309, 319, 402, 602, 648, 693, 695, 698, 699, 834, 850
Bascom Hill. *See* "Hill," the
Bascom, John, 3-4, 6-8, 23, 33
Basketball, 653-5
Batchelor, Chauncey, 807
Bayliss, Zoe, 417n
Bean, Ernest F., 543
Beautification days on campus, 551
Beck, Carl, 310
Becker, Gerhard, 625
Becker, Howard, 497
Beer, 670-2
Behr, Sam, 176
Bennett, Edward, 266, 502, 729, 816, 822
Bennington College, 89
Bergendahl, Florence, 468
Berger, Meta, 248
Bergstresser, John, 194, 204, 206
Bergstrom, Gertrude, 705
Bernard, Carl, 658
Beuscher, Jacob H., 498, 736
Biemiller, Andrew J., 379
Bietila, Paul and Walter, 660
Big Ten Conference, 267, 644
Biochemistry, Department of, 487-9
Biology Building (Birge Hall), 693
Birge, Edward A., 709; and athletics, 645; and budget cuts, 39-43; on collegiality of faculty, 512-3; as dean of L&S, 8-10, 12; on dining clubs, 519; on faculty governance, 464-5; and Glenn Frank, 54, 59, 71; on Grady resolution, 125-6; and hiring faculty, 475; and Milwaukee Junior College, 792-3; on patent rights, 68; photo of, 321; appointed president, 790, 830; public relations of, 81n; retires, 62-3, 346; salary of, 56; search for successor of, 3-4, 14-22, 29, 30, 35; and Summer Session, 759; on undergraduate liberal arts curriculum,

748; and WHA radio, 819-20; and Wisconsin Idea, 11-2

Birkenmajer, Jozef A., 490n

Blacks. *See* Negroes

Blaesser, Willard, 178n, 410, 410n, 411n, 567n

Blaine, John J., 17-8, 714, 790, 791; and academic freedom, 128-9; activism of, 19-20; and Board of Regents, 19-20, 44-5; and Frank appointment, 61-2, 75; photo of, 322; and Roscoe Pound, 21-38; and University budget, 39

Blair, Carroll, 176, 178, 866-7

Blegen, Theodore G., 695-7

Bleyer, Willard G., 203, 203n, 207-8, 765

Blood drives, 425

Bloodgood, F.J., 248

Board of Public Affairs, 38

Board of Regents: and John Bascom, 4, 8; and John J. Blaine, 19-20, 44-5; and budget during WW II, 448-9; and Paul A. Chadbourne, 6; and decision-making during WW II, 416, 446-9; enlarged, 19; and Glenn Frank, 51-8, 64-5, 224, 297-302, 303-15; and Julius P. Heil, 378-81; and Emanuel Philipp, 18-9; photos of, 321, 324; and preparations for war, 403-4; search for successor to Birge, 3-4, 63

Board of Visitors: and educational reform, 95-100, 103; on Experimental College, 151; members of, 182

Boat House, 658

Bögholt, Carl M., 166n, 483, 547n, 861, 868n

Bohstedt, Gustav, 429, 497, 512

Bouda, Francis, 679

Boughton, Donald C., 252, 810

Bowling, 517, 658

Bowman, Jennie, 491, 720

Boxing, 655-6; photo of match in Field House, 621

Bracher, Frederick, 493

Bradley Committee, 597

Bradley, Harold C., 157, 255, 712, 713n; supports Glenn Frank, 296; and Memorial Union, 121, 592, 597, 598, 603; photo of, 610; and student discipline, 195-6, 196-8, 204; and University Club, 533

Bradley Memorial Children's Hospital, 713

Brandeis, Elizabeth, 478n, 543, 547n

Brandeis, Louis D., 86

Brayton, Aaron M., 280

Breit, Gregory, 496, 505

Brittingham, Mary, 155, 236

Brittingham, Thomas E., 155, 236, 713n

Brittingham, Thomas E., Jr., 236-43, 307

Brittingham Trust, 236-43, 837

Browder, Earl, 386

Brown, Bill, 436

Brown, Dorothy, 641

Brown, Edward J., 309

Brown, Ray, 255, 259-60

Brunette, E.F., 253

Buck, Philo M., 490; writes "America and the War" series, 426

Budgets, University, 5, 17, 38-41; and Clarence Dykstra, 352-3, 359, 368-9, 370-8, 378-84; and Glenn Frank, 134-7, 215-7, 219-26; wartime, 403-4

Buerki, Robin C., 714-5

Buildings: construction of, 141, 684, 834, 836, 850-1; fund, 449; proposals for, 452-3, 458; remodeling of, 851-52. *See also* Camp Randall Stadium; Dormitories; Field House; Housing; Memorial Union; University Library

Bullis, Harry A., 302-3, 307, 310, 457-8

Bunn, Charles W., 498, 738n

Bureau of Business Information, 373

Bureau of Educational Records and Guidance, 97-8, 100-2, 123, 204, 207, 556-7, 743

Burke, Arthur E., 441, 542-9

Burke, Robert, 679-80

Burkhardt, Frederick H., 497

Burris, Robert H., 489

Burrus, Jefferson D., 254

"Bush," The, 668-9

Butler, Harry L., 28, 30, 46, 797

Butts, Porter F., 121, 583n; and Memorial Union, 592, 600, 603, 604-5; photo of, 610

Byrne, Eugene H., 484

Cabell, James Branch, 86n

Caldwell, Otis W., 31

Callahan, John, 298, 794; as regent supports Frank for president, 54-8;

supports Frank as president, 301, 304; and replacement for Frank, 340-2; as regent supports Roscoe Pound for president, 26-8, 30, 36, 38

Callan, James, 359-60

Calvary Lutheran Church, 559, 560

Camp Randall, 643n

Camp Randall Stadium. *See* Stadium

Campbell, Richard V., 498

Campbell, Ruth, 577

Campbell, William J., 459

Campus Liberal Association, 390

Campus Plan of 1908, 67, 350, 513n, 702, 722

Campus Planning Commission, 458n

Cancer research, 491. *See also* McArdle Memorial Laboratory

Capital Times. See Evjue, William T.

Card, William M., 492

Carillon Tower, 851

Carlson, Andrew J., 308

Carnegie, Andrew, 126

Carnegie Foundation for the Advancement of Teaching, 147

Carns, Marie L., 499

Carstensen, Vernon, xi-xii

Cashman, John E., 34, 125, 128, 132, 359; favors new library building, 689, 692

Casida, Lester E., 498

Casperson, C.H., 126

Cassidy, Frederic G., 492

Cattell, J. McKeen, 86n

Censorship, 129, 285-7, 289, 294, 314, 446-8, 627-8, 632

Century Magazine: Frank as editor of, 24,47, 49-51, 64-5, 76, 82; Meiklejohn's article in, 143, 146, 147-8, 168

Chadbourne Hall, 407, 417, 431, 434, 563, 572, 575, 576

Chadbourne, Paul A., 6

Chairmen of departments: appointments of, 464-5n, 470

Challenge, The, 300

Chamberlin, Thomas C., 8-9, 724, 758

Chapman, C. B., 704

Chapman, Clinton J., 497

Chapple, John, 177, 282-8, 630, 677

Charter House for women, 580

Cheerleaders, 643

Chemistry Building, 817

Chi Phi fraternity, 114

Child, William Washburn, 31

Christensen, Chris L., 269-70, 294, 302, 344, 444, 746-7, 776-83, 842; as candidate for president, 456n; photos of, 326

Citizenship Day, 391-2

Civil Affairs Training School, 437

Civil liberties, 387-400; and Japanese during WW II, 427-9

Civilian Conservation Corps (CCC), 707; photo of, 334

Civilian Pilot Training program, 413, 430

Clancey, Joseph, 360

Clark, Franklin W., 437

Clark, Harry Hayden, 492

Clark, Noble, 783

Clark, Paul F.: on Dean Charles Bardeen, 475; and Experimental College, 186; opposes racial discrimination at University Club, 543, 547, 547n, 548

Clark, Warren W., 302

Classics, 170, 174-5

Claus, Robert, 679-80

Clausen, Fred, 261, 633n

Cleary, Michael J., 380, 449, 458

Clouds, The (Aristophanes), 174

Coakley, Maurice, 361

Coeducation, 5-7, 181-2, 248-50

Coffman, Lotus D., 58, 307

Cohen, Philip P., 499

Coleman, Joe, 315

College Hill. *See*, "Hill," the

College Women's Club, 518

Columbia University, 24, 25, 31, 89, 173, 389, 476, 480, 486, 487, 557, 640, 686, 733, 760, 798, 800

Combs, Jessie, 299

Commerce Magazine, 624

Commerce, School of, 110, 114, 373, 450

Committee for Constitutional Rights, 290

Committee on Cooperation, 100

Committee on Curriculum and Educational Procedure, 423, 753-5

Committee on Emergency Educational Policy, 409

Committee on High School Relations, 766

Committee on Physical Education, 258

Committee on Student Personnel, 441

Committee on Student Defense Problems, 411

Committee on Student Life and Interests, 244-50, 256, 446, 564-7; and housing, 568-9, 573

Committee on Student Discipline, 245, 247, 587

Committee on the Curriculum and Methods of Instruction, 751. *See also* Fish Curriculum Committee

Committee on the Quality of Instruction and Scholarship, 351-8, 502-4

Commons, John R., 68, 157, 162, 242, 492n; and failure to hire Milton Friedman, 477-82; hosts "Friday Nights," 512n; salary of, 156n; and search for University president, 29, 36, 58

Communism, 181, 278-9, 290-2, 300, 385-400

Communist Party of the United States, 178-9, 284-5, 386. *See also* Youth Communist League

Community of Scholars: the University as, 510-50

Comparative Literature, Department of, 490

Conant, James B., 307-9

Congo's eating co-op, 561-2

Constitutional Education League, 386

Construction of buildings, 141, 684, 834, 836, 850-1; remodeling, 851-52

Consultative Committee on Retrenchment Policies, 226, 232

Cooperative Extension Service, 108, 513, 745-7, 757, 770-2, 778, 780-4, 842

Coranto House for women, 580

Cornell University, 31, 144, 175n, 420n, 486, 512, 658, 686, 768

Correspondence and Class Study, Department of, 786

Correspondence courses during WW II, 414, 430

Council Against Intolerance, 427n

Counselors, faculty and WW II, 408

Country Life Conferences, 782

Course in Humanities, 164n

Crane, Mr. and Mrs. Charles R., 713n

Creative Arts, School of, 114

Credit Union, UW, 278

Cret, Paul. *See* Campus Plan of 1908

Crew, 656-7

Crisis Confronting the University of Wisconsin, The, (Birge), 42

Croft, Albert, 810, 814

Croly, Herbert, 147, 148-9

Cubberley, Ellwood P., 24n

Curriculum: committees on, 423, 743, 750-2, 753-5; during WW II, 423

Curry, John Steuart: as artist-in-residence, 270, 491, 494, 736, 747, 783, 837, 842; photo of, 332

Curti, Merle, xi-xii, 506; and Arthur E. Burke affair, 543-4, 546-8; hired, 486; writes "America and the War" series, 426

Curtis, John, 708, 836

Dahlke, Gerald O., 583-4n

Daily Cardinal, 623; and academic freedom, 285-7, 289-91, 627; "America and the War" series, 426; history of, 83-4, 83n; opposes racial discrimination at University Club, 545; opposes ROTC, 288-92, 673; on regents' attempt to limit UW Press, 447; and story on illegal student drinking, 627-8; and WW II, 410, 425

Daily Worker, 179-80

Dairy industry, 69, 270

Dairy Short Course, 769

Dammen, Arnold, 670-1

Dance program, 742

Dances and proms, 668; during WW II, 437, 440. *See also* Parties

Daniells, W.W., 767

Daniels Curriculum Committee, 423, 753-5

Daniels, Farrington, 296, 351-2, 544, 753-5; photo of, 331

Daniels, Josephus, 787

Darbo, Rolf, 567n

Dating program during WW II, 425

Daughters of the American Revolution, 629

Davenport, Herbert J., 31

Davis, Parke H., 643

Davis, Richard, 635; photo of, 619

Davis, Susan, 408n

Dawson, Percy M., 166n

Debating and Public Discussion, Department of, 787

Denne, Helen I., 533, 715-7

Department system, 349-50; and appointment of chairmen, 464-5n, 470; size of, 510-1. *See also* Divisions, faculty

Depression. *See* Great depression

Dewey, John, 88, 131, 290

Dickie, Helen A., 499

Dickson, Campbell, 194

Dies Committee, 385, 386-7, 388, 390, 395

Dies, Martin, 385, 395-6

Dillon, Myles, 490

Dining clubs, 518-27. *See also* University Club

Disabled veterans: post-war plans for, 439-40

Discipline, student: enforcement of, 118-9, 564-9; at Experimental College, 195-8; and doctrine of *in loco parentis*, 7, 562-7; and Student Court, 118, 587

Discrimination, 674: and anti-Semitism, 119, 389, 427n, 478, 478n, 498n, 545, 635-40, 673-7, 719; by fraternities, 675; in honorary fraternities, 676; in housing, 119, 427-8, 545, 674, 676-7, 681-2; and Japanese during WW II, 427-9; racial, 441, 542-9, 629, 673, 676; in sports, 676. *See also* Civil liberties

Divisions, faculty, 133-4, 356-7, 470-1, 840. *See also* Department system

Doane, Gilbert H., 695, 697

Dodge, R.E. Neil, 864

Dollard, John, 121, 592

Doran, Madeleine, 492, 495

Dormitories, 119-20, 123, 562-3, 568, 576-9. *See also* Adams Hall; Barnard Hall; Chadbourne Hall; Elizabeth Waters Hall; Housing; Kronshage Dormitory Complex, Tripp Hall

Dormitories and Commons, Department of: and WW II training, 416

Dormitories Committee, 196-8, 204

Doroszewski, Witold, 490n

Dos Passos, John, 179

Downer, George F., 264, 655

Doyle, James E., 311, 570, 588n, 634, 639, 640

Draft: deferments, 408; registration, 409. *See also* Selective Service

Drake, L. E., 547

Drama, 174-5, 182-3

Draper, Lyman C., 687

Dress code, 566

Drew, Wallace T., 314

Duffield, Eugene S., 205-6

Duggar, Benjamin M., 497, 505, 521

Dupee, Gordon, 382

Durand, Loyal, 104

Durgin, Jean, 665

Dvorak, Raymond, 496, 649

Dykstra, Clarence A., xii, 12, 320, 508, 831-2, 839; advocates more academic training during WW II, 418-20, 434; and anti-Semitism and control over the *Daily Cardinal*, 637, 638; and appointment of department chairmen and divisional committees, 470-1; background of, 342-3; and civil liberties, 384-400; commencement address and WW II, 415; and creation of School of Commerce, 451-2; construction of buildings under, 834; and College of Engineering, 731-3; faculty reaction to, 345-6; family of, 346-8; and friction with military during WW II, 417-9; and failure to hire Milton Friedman, 478-82; and Julius Heil, 366-9, 370-8, 378-84, 398-400; and conflict between Gov. Heil and Dean Garrison, 737-8; leadership of during WW II, 441-5; and L&S modifications, 752-5; hires Sinclair Lewis, 494; and library inadequacies, 694-5; and new library, 697; mangement style of as president, 466-7; opposes housing discrimination, 428n; photos of, 324, 335; and postwar influx of veterans, 440, 441; and preparations for war, 400-6; and Pro Arte Quartet, 491; resignation of, 453-5; and salaries of professors in Medical School, 718; and University budget, 352-3, 359, 368-9, 370-8, 378-84; war-related research, 429-30; and WHA radio, 825-6; writes "America and the War" series, 426; and WW II, 407-8, 411

Dykstra, Franz, 346-7, 454n

Dykstra, Lillian, 348

Eagle Heights farm, 702

Earley, James S., 478n

Eastman, Max, 179

Easum, Chester V., 484, 507; writes "America and the War" series, 426
Ebling, Walter H., 498
Eccles, Mark, 492
Edgerton, Alanson H., 101
Edman, Irwin, 173
Edson, Charles F., 486
Education, School of, 95-8, 103, 104-7, 110, 739-45, 749, 856-7
Education and Engineering Building (Engineering Building), 684, 693, 724
Education of Henry Adams, The, 170, 170n, 204
Educational radio, 815-26. *See also* WHA radio
Educational reform: and adult education, 107-13; and College of Education, 104-7; and elective system, 143-4; and Extension Division, 107-13; and faculty initiatives, 94-6; of Glenn Frank, 64-6, 66n, 87-113, 115, 143-50, 748-52; and freshman orientation, 101-2, 664; and Grady resolution, 123-4; and Alexander Meiklejohn, 89, 111, 123, 170-2, 181; and Memorial Union, 120-3; and progressivism, 123-4, 126, 132; and ROTC, 130-1; and radicalism of UW, 131-2; and research funding, 123-4; and student life, 116-20; and undergraduate advising, 96-8; and University reorganization, 133-4; in University's schools and colleges, 113-5. *See also* Experimental College
Ekern, Herman L., 24n, 28, 33, 38, 45, 46, 380, 446-7, 796-7
Elective system, 143-4
Electra (Euripides), 174
Elizabeth Waters Hall, 463, 575-6, 660, 662, 833, 834, 844; photo of, 609
Ellingson, Lloyd, 659
Elsom, James C., 643
Eltzman, E.T., 279-80
Elvehjem, Conrad A., 507
Elwell, Fayette H., 450-2; and failure to hire Milton Friedman, 481
Ely, Richard T., 9
Ely, Stephen L., 446-8
Emergency Board, 222, 224, 226, 301, 362, 374-5, 377, 381-2
Emergency Inventions Development

Council, 429-30
Emergency Relief Administration: and Arboretum, 707
Emery, Annie Crosby, 564, 586
Engineering, College of, 8, 109-10, 115, 405, 723-33, 854; hiring of faculty by, 499-502; and WW II training, 416, 431-2
Engineering Exposition, 667, 730
Engineering Foundation, 126
Englund, Gene, 655
Enrollment, 16-7, 223, 230, 277-8, 552-5; in Experimental College, 168-9, 192-5; effect of great depression on, 552-4; during WW II, 419, 422, 436, 463, 554-5; during inter-war years, 474
Epstein, Leon D., 387-90, 678, 867
Erickson, Theodore C., 499
Erlanger, Joseph, 712
Euthenics Club, 426
Evans, Evan, 42-3
Evans, Joseph S., 24n, 564, 711, 713, 759
Everett, Walter G., 167n
Evjue, William T.: on European affairs, 394; opposes foundation and private support of University, 126-7, 236-43, 825-6, 835; and firing of Glenn Frank, 294, 316; supports new library, 697; questions constitutionality of Milwaukee Extension Center, 797; supports free speech for *Cardinal*, 289-92; on cuts in faculty salaries, 228-9; on job of University president, 75-6; criticizes University secrecy, 81n, 697
Ewbank, Henry L., 822, 823, 824
Experimental College, 841; activism of, 483; aftermath of, 861-73; budget for, 183-4; and coeducation, 181-2; and committee to investigate, 749-50; criticisms of, 183-4; discipline at, 195-8; downfall of, 200-9, 211; enrollment in, 168-9, 192-5; evaluation of, 171, 209-11; facilities for, 119-20, 195-9, 199n; faculty of, 123, 165-7, 167-8n, 482-3; faculty reaction to, 106, 115, 155, 183-9, 201-3; final report on, 202-8; Frank lays foundation for, 87-90, 93-4, 138, 683, 749; influence of, 751; Jews at, 193-4; Meiklejohn's appointment, 90-3, 138, 139-40, 151-5, 482; Meiklejohn's

background for, 144-50; Meiklejohn's salary, 155-6; opening of, 164-7; organization of, 143-4, 156-64; photo of class of, 612; planning of, 154-6; Players, 174-5; radicalism of, 176-80; recruitment of students for, 193-5, 199; relations with University, 172, 175-6, 190-1; Sellery's criticism of, 183-9, 201-3; student evaluation at, 171; and undergraduate education, 100, 114

Extension and Home Economics Building, 722, 813

Extension Center Building, Milwaukee, 112, 251, 792, 795-7, 804, 806, 842

Extension Division. *See* University Extension Division

Extracurricular activities of students, 661-80

Faast, Ben, 261

Faculty: and athletics, 261-3, 266-9; bowling league, 517; collaboration among, 512-5; committee on public functions, 78; cuts in, 224; deadwood on, 216, 223-4, 319-20; denounces La Follette, 14-5, 15n, 17-8, 18n, 312; description of, 474; Divisions, 356-7, 470-1, 840; on Frank's dismissal, 314-5; and governance, 338-41, 348-58, 445-6, 464-509; hiring of, 474-6, 476n; meetings of, 471-2, 473; parking for, 223; reaction to Experimental College, 159-64; reaction to Frank's appointment, 58-63; and dispersal of research funds, 472; retention of during great depression, 474; retooling of during WW II, 422; and rights, 131; salaries, 16-7, 20, 137, 141, 150, 155-6, 218, 223-6, 226-36, 503-4; as a community of scholars, 510-50; and selection of E. B. Fred as president, 455-8; size of departments, 510-1; teaching loads of, 370-1; tenure of, 468-70, 492; and University Committee, 30. *See also* Great depression

Faculty-Student Committee on Student Defense Problems, 411

Fallon, William, 267

Fallows House for women, 581

Farm Folk School, 783

Farm Folks' Week, 782, 783

Farm Short Course, 110, 269-70, 746, 768, 769, 783

Farmers' Institutes, 110, 769

Farmers' Week, 746, 782

Fascism, 363, 385

Fassett, Norman, 708

Federal Farm Board, 269

Feinsinger, Nathan P., 498

Female College, 6

Field House, UW, 46, 254-5, 284, 407, 461, 606, 643n, 653-4, 698, 833

Filene, Edward A., 31, 48, 52, 54, 111, 274-5

Finnegan, James E., 301

First Congregational Church, 559, 561-2

Fish, Carl Russell, 128, 663n, 750; death of, 484-5; criticizes Experimental College, 160-1, 869; photo of, 331; salary of, 156n. *See also* Fish Curriculum Committee

Fish Curriculum Committee, 115, 743, 750-2

Fitzpatrick, Edward A., 796

Fleming, Ed, 600n

Fleming, G. James, 676; photo of, 619

Fletcher, Lila B., 715

Flexner, Abraham, 147

"Flying Badgers," 413

Fontanne, Lynn, 603-4

Food Research Institute (Stanford), 133

Football, 645-52

Forest Products Laboratory, U.S., 405, 684

Foster, Finley K.M., 627

Foster, Harold E. "Bud," 264, 655

Foster, William Z., 176-7

Fourth Tuesday Club, 520-1

Fowlkes, John Guy, 533, 763

Fox, Philip G., 477, 540n

Frank, Glenn, Jr., 49, 73-4, 346

Frank, Glenn, Sr., xii, 12, 31, 839; on academic freedom, 128-30, 131, 284-6; accepts presidency, 57-8; administration of, 134-40, 350; adult education reform, 107-13; and College of Agriculture, 745-6; and Arboretum, 706; arrives in Madison, 73-80; assessment of, 317-20; and athletics, 253-69; background of, 47-53; and Brittingham Trust (University of Wisconsin Trust), 236-43; as candidate for presidency, 51-8, 64-5;

and Chris L. Christensen, 269-70, 294; and continuing education for teachers, 764; criticism of, 213-4, 293-7; death of, 304, 317; and School of Education, 97-9, 103-5; on educational reform, 64-6, 66n, 87-113, 115, 143-50, 748-52; and Experimental College, 100, 106, 143-63, 200-9, 294, 841, 862-4, 873; and Extension Division, 99, 107-13, 250-3, 798-813; calls on faculty to solve societal problems, 514; and faculty governance, 467; firing of, 299-315, 378-9; and freshman orientation, 101-2; and Grady resolution, 123-34; and high school visitation and consulting service, 766; and hiring faculty, 475; and Philip F. La Follette, 60-2, 297-9, 302; relation with legislature, 134-8; and library inadequacies, 694-5; management style of, 465-6; and Alexander Meikeljohn, 149-56, 294, 475; and Memorial Union, 120-3, 592, 599, 604; and Michael Olbrich, 63-4, 140; photos of, 323, 608; political aspirations of, 315-7; politics of, 49-51, 313-4, 830-1; as president, 70-3; reactions to appointment, 58-63; and religion on campus, 116-8, 278-80, 558-9; and reorganization of University, 133-9; and ROTC on campus, 130, 287-9; salary of, 150, 235-6, 302; and Albert Schmedeman, 230; and George Clarke Sellery, 61, 139-40, 163-4, 183-8; and student discipline, 118-20; and student facilities, 119-21; and student speakers program against discrimination, 677, 678; and Summer Session, 761; and University budget, 134-7, 215-7, 219-26; and WHA radio, 820-1, 822n

Frank, Mary Smith, 48-9, 57n, 73-5, 213, 213n, 249-50, 271, 348, 445

Frank, Milton, 522

Frankenburger, David B., 519

Fraternities: buyers cooperative, 567, 585; organization of, 583-6; and pledges, 566, 586, 663

Frautschi, Lowell E., 523, 590n, 598; photo of, 610

Fred, Edwin B., 270, 341-2, 402, 502, 505, 533, 839; as dean of Agriculture, 444; appointed president, 439, 455-8; and College of Engineering, 731-3; and government service during WW II, 443; and hiring faculty, 500; on Law School, 738n; photo of, 331; and Science Inquiry, 514; style of, 461

Free speech, 288-92, 388-9, 845. *See also* Academic freedom

Freedom and the College (Meiklejohn), 146-7

Freehoff, William A., 382, 452

Freshman Days orientation, 101-2, 123

Freshman Glee Club, 176

Freshman Orientation Week, 102, 664

Freshman Welcome, 142

"Friday Nights," 512n

Friday Noon Luncheon Club, 517, 526

Friedman, Milton, 476-82

Froker, Rudolph K., 498, 778

Fulcher, Paul, 626

Fuller Opera House, 590, 668

"Functional Organization of Faculty Forces, A." *See* Divisions, faculty

Gaelic and Irish Studies, 490

Gale, Joseph W., 499

Gale, Zona: educational reform of, 131; feminism of, 248; and Glenn Frank, 50-6, 59, 63, 68, 73, 214, 294-5; on Frank's dismissal, 304-7, 310; on Grady resolution, 126; photo of, 321; on University funding, 42, 71; and search for successor to Birge, 24-30, 34, 36-7; writing of, 179, 180

Gallistel, Albert F., 573, 679, 706, 707, 760

Galpin, C.J., 782

Game Management (Leopold), 781

Gamma Alpha, 511

Gardner, Edward H. "Ned," 592

Gardner, Louis, 704

Garey, Senator, 797

Garman, Phillips L., 870-1

Garnett, Arthur C., 547n; writes "America and the War" series, 426

Garrison, Ellen Jay, 271

Garrison Lloyd K., 271-7, 290, 294, 296, 340n, 405, 443, 498, 733, 734-9

Garton, John, 360

Gasser, Herbert, 712

Gates, Clough, 31, 340, 573; as an anti-Frank regent, 299, 302, 304, 309-11
Gaumnitz, Erwin, 477
Gaus, John M., 508, 547n, 750; and Experimental College, 165-7, 166n, 170, 483, 861; as presidential candidate, 340n
Gausewitz, Alfred L., 498
Gelfan, David, 407
General Education Board, 68, 125-6
General Information and Welfare, Department of, 787
German House for women, 579-80
Gerth, Hans, 497
Get-Away Club, 517, 702
Gettleman, Ben, 223
GI Bill, 460
Giessel, Helen, 416n
Gilbert, E.M., 706
Gilbert, G.L., 223
Gillin, John L., 787n
Givens, Willard, 308
Glicksman, Harry, 424n, 428, 543, 547n
Glover, Arthur J., 379, 381, 396, 737
Glowacki, Stan, 641
God Damned Independents ("GDIs"), 634, 639, 640
Golemgeske, John, 265
Goodland, Walter S., 42, 448-9, 458, 459; and new library, 699-700
Goodnight, Scott H., 21n, 582; and anti-Semitism and control over the *Cardinal*, 637-8; opposes anti-Semitism, 675; on Athletic Board, 260; bans open-house parties during WW II, 423n; and Committee on Student Life and Interests, 244-50, 256, 446, 564-7, 568-9; anti-Communist position of, 388-9, 392; and discipline of students, 72, 118-9, 244-50, 681; and Fraternity Buyers Cooperative, 567, 585; opposes hazing of students, 586; and *Octopus*, 627; photos of, 329, 608; retirement of, 460; and student drinking alcoholic beverages, 670; and student government, 588; and Summer Session, 759-63; supports building student union, 591, 597; and University Personnel Council, 410-1
Gordon, David, 179-81
Gordon, Edgar B. "Pop," 114, 765, 818,
824
Governance and faculty, 338-41, 348-58, 445-6, 464-509; and awarding of research funds, 472
Graber, Laurence F., 497
Grade point average, 566, 752
Graduate School, 11, 227, 229-30, 270
Grady, Daniel, 23, 28, 30, 797; and athletics, 258-60, 267; and Clarence Dykstra, 362; and selection of Glenn Frank as president, 54, 73, 298, 301, 304, 309-10, 344; on private funding for University, 67-8, 125
Grady, Nettie, 705
Grady resolution, 67-8, 71, 76, 76n, 123-34, 155, 236, 239, 259
Grant County Herald, 43
Graves, Frank P., 31, 35
Great depression, 141-2, 215, 845-6; effect on UW, 502-5; and Extension Division, 808; and faculty governance, 467-8; faculty salaries, 226-36, 503-4; and high school visitation and consultation service, 766; and hiring, 483; and library budget, 694-700; and retention of faculty, 474; effect on student life, 278-92; and Summer Session, 761-2; and University budget, 215-26
Greeley, Louise Troxell, 570, 573, 575, 576-9, 581; photo of, 329
Green, Commander, 428n
Gregory, Charles W., 519
Griebsch, Max, 496
Groves, Harold, 131, 221, 476-82, 483, 547n
Groves House for women, 581
Gunderson, Adolph, 44, 344
Gutheim, Frederick, 176, 870
Guyer, Michael F., 156n, 157, 491

H.P.C. Bulletin, 624
Hagen, Oskar F., 489, 507, 508
Haight, George I., 41-3, 46, 84, 122, 126; and Memorial Union, 591n, 594, 595, 599
Halburn House for men, 582-3n
Hall, Howard L., 498
Hall, Norris F., 307-8, 496, 547n
Halverson, Donald L., 562, 572, 600, 670-1, 844; and discipline in Experimental

College dorms, 197, 198; and housing during WW II, 421; and woman's dorms, 576-9; and WW II school for Navy cooks and bakers, 416
Hambrecht, George P. "Hammy," 764
Hanley, Miles L., 492
Hanna, Hilton, 676
Hanson, Malcolm, 818
Hanson, Walter, 706
Harder, Pat, 417, 652
Hardin, Clifford M., 498
Hare, Michael, 603
Haresfoot Club review, 516, 591, 668; photos of, 334, 613
Harlow, Harry F., 497
Harrington, Fred Harvey, 486, 548-9, 868
Harris, Abram, 48, 53-4
Harris, John W., 499
Harshaw, Myron, 310
Hart, Edwin B., 487, 488; photo of, 326
Hart, Joseph K., 111, 111n, 112-3, 805
Harvard University, 24n, 25, 29, 31, 33, 35-7, 49, 89, 91n, 91-3, 95n, 120, 143, 144, 170n, 200n, 210, 307, 308n, 317, 340n, 346, 386, 401n, 420n, 452, 456, 493, 496, 506n, 508n, 597, 695, 709, 733, 735
Hasler, Arthur D., 496, 708
Hastings, Edwin G., 532-3, 538n
Hatch Act (1886), 768, 769-70
Hatch Act (1890), 769-70
Hatch, K.L., 771-2
Haugen, Einar J., 495
Havighurst, Robert J., 172, 861
Hayakawa, S. Ichiye, 624, 814
Haydon, A. Eustace, 173
Hayes, Carlton, 24
Haynes, Winifred, 624
Haywood, "Big," Bill, 278-9, 582
Haywood House for men, 582
H'Doubler, Margaret, 516, 742
Heil, Julius P., 316, 352-3; and academic freedom, 397-400; and Board of Regents, 378-81; and budget, 368-9, 370-8, 381-4, 403-4; career of, 364-7; and civil liberties, 392-400; and Clarence Dykstra, 466-7, 831-2; and Lloyd Garrison, 737-8 and WW II, 392-3, 394-5, 400-4
Heironimus, John Paul, 544

Heitmeyer, Rev., 281
Hengell, Father Harry C., 117, 279-80, 281, 559
Henmon, V.A.C.: and Bureau of Educational Records and Guidance, 98, 100-1, 743; and Experimental College, 203n; and Milwaukee Extension Center, 112; opposes physical education requirement, 287; develops scholastic aptitude test, 557, 766
Henry, William Arnon, 7, 768-70, 773-4
Herb, Raymond G., 496, 505
Hesseltine, William B., 485
Hetzel, Ralph D., 341, 456
Heun, Howard T., 267
Hibbard, Benjamin H., 774
Hicks, John D., 485-6, 533
Higby, Chester P., 484
"Hill," the, 74, 78, 132, 167, 171, 172, 176, 183, 200, 207, 208, 210, 431, 466, 684, 693, 708, 724, 726; as Bascom Hill, 183, 320, 425, 559, 662, 663, 664, 665, 666, 680, 684; as College Hill, 701; as University Hill, 4, 5, 6, 7, 817
Hill, A. Ross, 31
Hillel Foundation of B'nai B'rith, 560
Hilsenhoff, Ray L., 566
Hirsch, Elroy "Crazylegs," 417, 652
Hirschfelder, Joseph O., 496
Hirshberg, Rabbi Samuel, 806
History, Department of, 483-7
History of Art, Department of, 489-90
Hoan, Daniel W., 502n
Hobson, Asher, 260, 497, 522, 541-2
Hodgkins, Walter J., 380, 398, 446, 454-5, 459
Hohlfeld, Alexander, 156n, 162-3, 496
Holloway, William O., 281
Holmes, Arthur T., 380, 398
Holmes, Fred L., 40, 307, 310, 697
Holt, Frank O., 97, 100-1, 138, 211, 253, 269, 284, 391, 417, 743, 766; as candidate for president, 456n; and citizenship program, 391; and Committee on Cooperation, 100-1; on Glenn Frank's effectiveness, 212-3n; and Freshman Week, 101-2; and Milwaukee Extension Center, 813-4; and public relations, 138, 284; as registrar and director of Bureau of Educational

Records and Guidance, 97-8, 743; and state-wide testing of high school students, 766; and student speakers program, 284, 677, 678; appointed dean of University Extension, 253, 269, 812; and University Personnel Council, 410; as University Vice President for External Relations, 443; welcomes WAVES, 417

Holt, M. Leslie, 496, 547

Home Economics, School of, 745, 746

Home Week, 783

Homecoming, 648; photo of, 616

"Homemakers' Hour" (WHA radio), 782

Hones, Kenneth S., 299

Hoofers Club: photo of ski jump, 621; photo of toboggan slide, 620; and sailboats, 658; and ski jump at Muir Knoll, 658-60; and WW II ski patrol, 413n

Hoover, Herbert, 176, 316

Hopkins, Andrew W., 83, 818, 822

Horn, Charles L., 395

Hotchkiss, William O., 21n, 513

Hougen, Olaf A., 500, 501

Housing, 568-86; discrimination in, 427-8, 674, 676-7, 681; of military trainees, 431-2; off-campus, 563-4; and Summer Session tent colony, 759-60. *See also* Dormitories

Hrdlička, Aleš, 173

Huber, Henry, 132

Hughes, Merritt Y., 492, 495

Hull, C. L., 160, 168-9

Hunt, Elizabeth, 581

Hurst, J. Willard, 498, 736, 738n

Hutchins, C. P., 646

Hutchins, Frank A., 785, 787, 788

Hutchins, Robert, 418

Hyde, Grant M., 40, 83, 530-1

"*I*" *Gotist*, 624

Immell, Ralph M., 413, 706

In loco parentis, 7, 244-50

Indiana University, 418, 644, 658, 696,

Industrial Workers of the World (IWW), 278-9

Inefficiency Club, 521-2

Ingraham, Mark, 233-4, 811-2; as candidate for president, 456n; as club member, 527; on collegiality of UW

administration, 467n, 549-50; and creation of School of Commerce, 451; and Committee on Quality of Instruction and Scholarship, 353-8, 502-4; as dean of L&S, 444; national posts held by, 468, 508; photo of, 327; and selection of E.B. Fred as president, 455n; and tenure at the Milwaukee Extension Center, 811-2; and training soldier-students, 420

Institute for Research in Social Sciences (North Carolina), 133

Institute for the Study of Law (Johns Hopkins), 133

Institute of Human Relations (Yale), 133

Institute of Municipal and Social Service, 788

Institute system, 133-4

Instruction by Lectures, Department of, 787

Integrated Liberal Studies Program, 320

Inter-Church Council. *See* University Religious Council

Intercollegiate Athletics, 642-57

International Education Board, 71

International Harvester, 178, 364

Interracial housing for women (Groves House), 581

Interstate Commerce Commission, 32

Intramural and recreational athletics, 657-61

Iron Cross (men's honorary society), 589

Irwin, Malcolm R., 498

Issue, The, 88, 88n

Jackson, Joseph W., 703-7

Jacobs, Herbert, 291

Janda, Harold F., 501

Jansky, C.M., Jr., 817

Japanese people: discrimination against, 427-9

Jastrow, Joseph, 72, 74

Jensen, Merrill, 486

Jerome, Harry, 203, 477

Jessup, Walter A., 31

Jewish students, 119, 193-4, 193n, 557-8. *See also* Anti-Semitism

Johansen, Gunnar, 491, 494, 838

Johnson, Alvin, 147

Johnson, Carl, 135, 713n

Johnson, F. Ellis, 501-2, 667, 728-33

Johnson, James, 511

Johnson, John Butler, 724
Johnson, Marvin J., 489
Johnson, Ralph W., 869
Joint Committee on Finance (Wis.), 134-5, 231, 372-3, 375
Joint Committee on Social Control, 245
Jones, Burr W., 519
Jones, Chester Lloyd, 450, 495, 514
Jones, Jenkin Lloyd, 866
Jones, John D., 458, 459
Jones, L. R., 505
Jones, Tom, 264, 649, 658
Jorgenson, Allen, 635
Journalism, School of, 110
Juday, Chauncey, 708
"Junior Woman," 280-1

Kadushin, Rabbi Max, 560
Kahlenberg, Louis, 162, 172n, 208-9, 465
Kansas City Post, 59
Karney, Rex, 636
Kasten, Lloyd A., 496
Keitt, George W., 352-5
Keyes, Elisha, 8
Kiekhofer, William H. "Wild Bill": as candidate for president, 456n; as director of School of Commerce, 450; and appointment of Glenn Frank, 23; photo of, 330; popularity of, 94; on collapse of stock market, 141; on student attrition, 94; and Student Initiative Plan, 113-4; and University Club, 533, 535-7; and "W" Day, 664
Kircher, H.W., 104
Kirk, Grayson L., 389, 496
Kivlin, V.E., 408n, 783
Kleczka, Leonard J., 380
Kleene, Stephen C., 496
Kluckhohn, Clyde K., 597
Knaplund, Paul, 213n, 508; and Experimental College, 160-2, 187, 189-92, 749-50; as chairman of history department, 485-6; and racial discrimination at University Club, 547; resident at University Club, 528
Knox, Frank, 405
Kohler, Walter, J., Sr.: elected governor, 131-2, 135n, 215, 691; defeated as governor, 230; as regent supports construction of Memorial Union, 591;

and University budget, 136-8, 141, 832; appoints regents, 379; as outgoing regent, 23
Kolb, J.H., 782, 783, 805
Korecz, Emerick, 675
Kotz, John, 655
Kowalke, Otto, 500, 501, 502, 729
Kresky, Michael, 361
Kronshage men's dormitory complex, 407, 421, 431, 432, 433, 438, 574-7, 662, 833, 834
Kronshage, Theodore, Jr., 574; on Experimental College, 187; and Grady resolution, 125-6; and Memorial Union, 595; photo of, 321; public relations efforts of, 81; searches for successor to Birge, 23-8, 30, 33-7; and selection of Frank, 54-6, 59; and University budget, 39-41, 45, 135, 137, 216-8, 223; urges University reform, 13-21; and WUBC, 67
Ku Klux Klan, 50
Kurylowicz, Jerzy, 490

La Follette, Belle, 21, 21n, 25, 38, 61, 283
La Follette, Fola, 313
La Follette, Mary, 25
La Follette, Philip F., 672; and Arboretum, 707; and Birge's successor, 18, 21, 25, 33-4; and budget of University, 135, 137, 138-9, 215-7, 219-24; downfall of, 358-64; and Glenn Frank, 60-2, 201, 213n, 297-9, 830-1; and dismissal of Glenn Frank, 302-15, 317-9; elected governor, 131, 179, 215; and great depression, 226-30, 277; and Julius Heil, 264-5; and Memorial Union, 595; photo of, 322; radicalism of, 282-3; and WHA radio, 822-3
La Follette, Robert M., Jr., 18n; helps oust Frank, 318; and search for University president, 23, 26, 33-4; as U.S. Senator and governor, 830-1; defeated as U.S. Senator, 317; and University budget, 218
La Follette, Robert M., Sr., 788; agenda for University, 17; and Edward A. Birge, 21-3; denounced by faculty ("round robin" resolution), 14-5, 15n, 17-8, 18n; and Grady resolution, 123-4;

and Michael Olbrich, 45; and Roscoe Pound, 21-38; reelection of, 18; on search for University president, 32; and University budget, 40-1; association with Van Hise, 14-6, 17, 830; and Wisconsin Idea, 10-1, 31-2

La Follette's Magazine, 40, 68, 124

La Guardia, Fiorello, 405

La Maison Française, 580

Labor unions, 595

Laing, Gordon, 31

Laird, Warren P. *See* Campus Plan of 1908

Lampman, Robert, 386, 387n, 388-90

Land acquisitions, 849-50; Eagle Heights farm, 702; Picnic Point, 680, 702

Landman, Rabbi Sol, 560, 676

Langdon Hall for women, 568, 577

Langdon Street, 7, 290, 291, 428n, 431, 463, 560n, 571n, 577, 581, 584, 590, 592, 603, 626, 648, 666, 674, 679, 711, 817, 844

Langer, Rudolph E., 496

Language programs, 374, 490

Lardy, Henry A., 488-9

Larkin, Beulah, 427

Larson, G. L., 260

Lash, Joseph P., 386

Lathrop Hall, 589, 597, 601

Lathrop, Henry B., 183

Lathrop, John H., 4-5

Law Building, 666, 735, 834

Law, James R., 307

Law, School of, 8, 115, 215, 271-7, 498, 733-9, 857; Alumni Association of, 735; and cane-tossing tradition, 667; Library of, 735-6

Le Grand, Roger W., 636; photo of, 619

Leach, Henry Goddard, 823-4

League for Defense of American Principles, 282

League for Independent Political Action, 131

League for Industrial Democracy, 176

League of Nations, 49, 50, 55, 128, 426

League to Enforce Peace, 49

Leake, Chauncey, 173

Lee, John Thomas, 688, 698

Legislature, Wisconsin: activism of, 7-8; and Board of Regents, 4; and University budgets, 5, 17, 38-41, 45-6, 215-8, 220-4

Legler, Henry E., 785

Leith, Charles K., 505, 506, 514

Lenroot, Irvine L., 45

Leonard, William Ellery, 118-9, 180, 245, 389, 493; photo of, 330

Leopold, Aldo, 490, 522, 781; and Arboretum, 704, 706, 708, 836; photo of, 330

Lescohier, Don, 477

Letters and Sciences, College of (L&S), 854-6; cuts in, 224; Dykstra on, 347; independence of, 95-5; organization of, 8; reform of, 113-5, 748-55; relations to Experimental College, 159-64. *See also* Ingraham, Mark; Sellery, George Clarke

Letters, College of, 6-7

Lewis, Robert H., 427n, 431-2

Lewis, Sinclair, 493-5; photo of, 615

Library. *See* Law, School of, Library; Medical Library Service; State Historical Society of Wisconsin; University Library

Library Science, School of, 110, 540, 748

Lighty, William H., 785, 788, 799, 801; and academic freedom, 447; and adult education, 110-2; and correspondence courses, 110-2, 786; and Milwaukee Extension Center, 792-3, 805, 811; as acting dean of University Extension, 789, 790; and WHA radio, 85, 819, 821

Lindbergh, Charles A., 180

Link, Karl Paul, 237-8, 241-3, 488, 841

Linton, Ralph, 497

Lippmann, Walter, 146

Literary Guild, 52

Little, George, 255-8; and athletics, 651, 654, 657

Little International, 662

Little, Malcolm, 807

Little New Deal, 362

Lobeck, A.K., 173

Loevenhart, Arthur S., 125, 712

Logos Club, 526

Longenecker, G. William, 706

Loomis, Orland S., 448

Loraine Hotel, 74

Lorenz, William F., 268, 712; and University Club, 537-8, 540n

Lovett, Robert Morss, 23, 26-31, 34, 38, 47, 181-2, 290

Lowell, A. Lawrence, 89
Lumpkin, Rev. H.H., 283
Lunt, Alfred, 603-4
Luther Memorial Church, 560
Lysistrata (Aristophanes), 182-3

Maas, W.C., 384
MacBain, Harold L., 24
MacDuffie, Cyrus C., 496
MacGregor, Fred H., 128-9, 320
Mack, J.G.D., 786n
Mack, Julian E., 496
MacLean, Malcolm Shaw, 807
Madison Garden Club, 708
Madison Literary Club, 517, 520
Madison Park and Pleasure Drive
  Association, 701
Main Hall. *See* Bascom Hall
Mann, Horace, 5
Manning, Hazel, 533-4
Maple Bluff, 315
Maple Bluff Country Club, 131, 213
Marching Band, 648-9
Marlatt, Abby, 722n
Marquette University, 251, 796, 842
Martinson, Eileen, 641
Mascots, 649
Mason, Max, 23-4, 24n, 592, 593
Masten, Mabel G., 499
Mathews, J. Howard "Matty," 465n, 750,
  808, 826, 827; photo of, 330; and WW
  II Committee on Emergency Educational
  Policy, 409
Mathews, Lois Kimball, 565
Maurer, Irving, 280
Mayland, Ed, 629
McArdle Memorial Laboratory, 491, 720
McArdle, Michael, 491, 720
McCabe, Robert, 708
McCaffrey, Maurice E., 55-6, 307, 311,
  706
McCarthy, Charles, 785, 786n, 788, 828
McCarthy, Joseph R., 317
McCarty, Harold B., 824, 843
McClure Newspaper Syndicate, 57
McCormick, Bart, 99, 104, 749
McCoy, Elizabeth, 498
McGilvary, E.B., 152-3, 156, 173
McGovern, Francis, 310
McKay, William, 706

McNutt, Paul V., 420n
McVey, Frank L., 31
Mead, Daniel W., 507
Mead, George W., 298-9, 301, 571n
Mead, Margaret, 429
Mead, Warren J., 521
Meanwell, Walter E., 263-7, 528, 653-5,
  656
Mechanical Engineering Building, 110, 141,
  413, 452, 666, 684, 693, 730, 834
Mechanics and Engineering, College of, 8
Medical Library Service, 112
Medicine, School of, 17, 115, 270-1, 405,
  498-9, 708-15, 717-22, 857-8; salaries
  of professors in, 718; and WW II
  training, 416, 432-3. *See also* Nursing,
  School of; Wisconsin General Hospital
Meek, Walter J., 443, 508
Meiklejohn, Alexander, 112, 117, 749,
  841; and adult education conference,
  805; and aftermath of Experimental
  College, 861-8; appointment of, 90-3,
  138, 139-40, 149-56, 475, 482-3;
  background of, 93, 144-50, 290; and
  Brittingham Trust, 236-40, 243; on
  coeducation, 181-2; educational reform
  of, 89, 111, 123, 170-2, 181; final
  report on Experimental College, 202-9;
  Frank's support of, 139-40, 294; founds
  League for Independent Political Action,
  131; presented Medal of Freedom, 868n;
  opening of Experimental College, 164-7;
  photo of, 612; as possible president, 25,
  32, 46; salary of, 108, 155-6, 156n; on
  student discipline, 196-200, 199n. *See
  also* Educational reform; Experimental
  College
Meiklejohn, Donald, 167n
Meiklejohn, Gordon, 193
Meiklejohn, Helen, 175
Mekeel, H. Scudder, 429
Meloche, Villiers W., 496, 534
Memorial Union, 120-3, 346, 348, 836; and
  beer sales, 670-2; and bowling, 658;
  military services during WW II, 425,
  435; and outbreak of WW II, 407, 409,
  410, 412; need for, 589-605; photos of,
  610, 611; theater, 591n, 595, 602-5,
  668, 698-9, 833, 834
Memorial Union Building Committee, 138,

591, 595
Mencken, H. L., 86, 86n, 293
Mendenhall, Charles E., 156, 505, 821
Mendota, Lake, 120, 158, 169, 196, 209, 278, 284, 290-2, 570, 576, 589, 658, 662, 664, 666, 701-2, 759, 828, 833, 861
Merriam, Charles E., 307
Merriman, Curtis, 460, 812
Metcalfe, John C., 390
Metcalfe, Keyes DeWitt, 695-7
Meves, Donald, 424
Meyer, Balthasar H., 31-2
Meyer, Ernest, 293-7
Meyer, Ovid O., 499
Meyer, Roland K., 496
Middleton, George, 61-2
Middleton, William S., 270-1, 443, 499, 717-23; photo of, 328
Military Relations Board, 436
Military Science, Department of, 860; during WW II, 412. *See also* Reserve Officer Training Corps
Millar, James D., 360
Miller, J. L., 415n
Miller, William Snow, 709
Milliken, Robert A., 31
Mills, Charles H., 521, 818, 824
Milwaukee Association of Commerce, 43
Milwaukee County Federation of Teachers, 252
Milwaukee Extension Center, 251-4, 791-2, 804-9, 813-5, 842
Milwaukee Journal: supports UW building plans, 458
Milwaukee Junior College, 792-7
Michigan State College (University), 658, 696
Moe, John, 624
Mohr, Charles, 655
Mohs, Frederic C., 491, 720
Moore, Ransom A., 769
Morgan, J.P., 180
Morgan, Thomas "Dad," 668
Morphy, "Major" E.W., 496, 648-9
Morrill Land Grant Act, 5-6, 767
Morrow, Anne, 180
Morse, Caryl, 311
Mortar Board House, 580
Mortensen, Otto A., 499

Morton, Walter, 478n, 480n, 482-3, 526
Mosby, Wade H., 635
Mosely, T.J., 803, 805
Mossman, Harland W., 499
Mucks, Arlie, Sr., 261
Mumford, Lewis, 173
Munro, Dana C., 759
Murphy, Francis T., 360
Murphy, Robert B.L., 307, 523; photo of, 619
Murray, Christina C., 715
Music. *See* Band; Marching Band; Dvorak, Raymond, 496, 649; Mills, Charles H.; Morphy, "Major" E.W.
Music Clinic, 765-6
Music Hall, 78, 534, 664, 685, 818

Nafziger, Ralph, 83
Nardin, F. Louise, 21n, 183, 244-50, 565, 597
Nation, 24
National Academy of Sciences, 127-8
National Association of Professional Men's Clubs, 77
National Defense Mediation Board, 402
National Defense Research Committee, 394
National Industrial Recovery Act, 271-2
National Labor Relations Board, 271-6
National Progressives of America, 363
National Recovery Administration, 264-5
National University Extension Association (NUEA), 111
National Youth Administration, 278
Navy Radio School, 414-5, 416, 417, 431; photo of students in, 336
Navy ROTC: proposal for, 438, 439
Neal, Norman P., 498
Neale-Silva, Eduardo, 496
Negroes, 386; and Arthur E. Burke affair, 542-9; and housing discrimination, 427n; opposition to discrimination against, 428-9. *See also* Discrimination
Negus, Fred, 652
Neilson, William Allen, 24, 25, 31
Nelson, Philip E., 378
Nestigen, Edward, 393
Nettels, Curtis P., 484
Neufeld, Maurice, 174-5
Neutrality, international, 392-3
New Deal, 270-7, 365

New Republic, 146, 148
New School for Social Research, 147
New Student, 624
Newman, Edwin, 389
Newman, Morton, 634-5, 639
Niebuhr, Reinhold, 117
Night life of students, 669-70
Noe, Jessie Bartlett, 704
Noer, Frederick J., 289, 633n
Nolen, John, 701-2, 704
North Hall, 4, 7, 67, 563, 662
Northwestern University, 35, 47, 48, 53, 58, 60, 265, 485, 644, 650, 651
"Number 9" research fund, 472, 473n
Nursing, School of, 426-7, 684, 715-7, 858

Observatory Hill, 120, 158, 570, 575, 658, 660, 722, 846
Octopus ("Octy"), 305, 376, 624, 626
O'Dea, Andrew, 643, 656
O'Dea, Pat, 650
Ogg, Frederic A., 508
Ohio State University, 267, 342, 496, 644, 652, 696, 816, 861
Olbrich, Michael B.: and selection of Frank, 43-5, 54-6, 63-4, 71, 74; and student housing, 120; suicide of, 140-1; and University Arboretum, 702-3; on University's budget, 135, 138; and launching of WARF, 69
Olin House, 74, 348
Olin, John M., 56
Olson, Julius E., 78, 296, 495, 507
O'Neill, James M., 161-2
O'Shea, Michael V., 180
Otis, Delos S., 166n
Otto, Max C., 23, 60, 117, 173, 189, 228-9, 447, 448, 547n, 806; and anti-Semitism and control of the *Cardinal*, 637; radicalism of, 279-80, 283, 286, 290, 320
Owen, Sally, 661; photo of, 619

Pacifism, 407, 672-3
Padway, Joseph A., 719
Page, William H. "Herbie," 157, 667
Pan Hellenic and Inter-Fraternity councils, 424-5
Parents Teachers Association study course, 764

Parkway Theater, 602, 668
Parsons, Kenneth H., 498
Parties: ban on open-house during WW II, 423n. *See also* Proms and dances
Patent rights, 68-9
Paxson, Frederic L., 484, 506, 689
Peabody, Arthur, 801-2
Peace Federation, 393
Pearson, Drew, 274
Pease, Arthur Stanley, 190
Penicillin, 487
Perkins, Frances, 272-3, 276
Perlman, Selig, 426, 478n, 547n; writes "America and the War" series, 426
Peters, Margedant, 624
Peterson, A.W., 522: as director of Business and Finance, 460-1; as UW comptroller, 381, 383, 402, 434, 440, 443, 454n, 577, 591n
Peterson, William H., 487
Pfankuchen, Llewellyn, 496
Phi Beta Kappa, 51, 676
Philipp, Emanuel L., 11, 17, 18-9, 33, 713, 789, 828
Phillips, J.D., 73, 138, 138n, 222-4, 260, 263-4, 572, 597
Phillips, Paul H., 488-9
Phillips, William B., 166n
Physical Education, Division of, 859
Phytogeography of Nebraska (Pound), 36
Picnic Point, 120, 571n, 662, 662n, 680, 702, 828
Pipe of Peace Ceremony, 665; photo of, 615
Pochmann, Henry A., 492
Pohle, Ernst A., 499
Polish language instruction, 490
Politics of Industry, The (Frank), 49
Pollard, Leslie K., 418, 438
Pooley, Robert C., 547n
Post, Gaines, 486; writes "America and the War" series, 426
Potter, Pitman, 128
Potter, Van R., 491
Pound, Roscoe, 21, 25-38, 47, 52, 53, 55
Powell, John Walker, 166n, 193n, 864-5
Presbyterian Student Center (Pres House), 559
Princeton University, 66, 89, 686, 759
Pro Arte String Quartet, 491, 838

Progressive Club, 672
Progressive Education Association, 88
Progressive Party, 277, 297, 305, 360, 672, 829-30
Progressivism, 7-8, 123-4, 126
Proms and dances, 668; during WW II, 437, 440
Public relations, UW, 39-44, 81-7
Public Works Administration (PWA), 672, 834; and Camp Randall Stadium, 647n; and McArdle Memorial Laboratory, 720; and new men's dorms, 573-4, 834; and Memorial Union, 602-3
Publications, student, 623-42
Purdue University, 263, 644, 652, 655, 658
Purin, Charles, 805, 806-8, 810
Purnell, William H., 668
Pyre, James F.A. "Sunny," 257, 646

Q Club, 520
Quintana, Ricardo B., 492

Racket Club, 675
Radicalism, 19, 177-81, 279-92, 384-400
Radio: commercial broadcast of football games, 650. *See also* WHA radio
Radio Hall, 825
Ragatz, Roland A., 501
Ramsperger, Albert, 868n
Ranney, Donald, 567-70
Rathskeller (Memorial Union), 601-2; photo of, 611
Raushenbush, Paul, 166, 861
Rawleigh, W.T., 241-2
Reber, Louis E., 99, 108, 250-1, 784-99, 801, 828
Recruitment, student, 199-200
Reddin, John, 871
Reforestation, 774-5
Reis, Alvin C., 302-3
Religion on campus, 116-7, 279-80, 285-6, 557-62. *See also* Jewish students
Remodeling projects, 851-2
Republican Program Committee, 316
Research: funding, 123-34, 468, 472; "Number 9" fund, 472, 473n; war related, 429-30. *See also* Grady resolution; Wisconsin Alumni Research Foundation
Research Committee, 472-3

Reserve Officer Training Corps (ROTC), 130-1, 287-9, 290-1, 385, 402, 404, 433n, 633, 673; proposal for Navy ROTC, 438, 439
Retirement age, mandatory, 471
Reynolds, John W., 690
Reynolds, Robert L., 412, 484, 547n
Rice, William Gorham, 128, 272
Richards, Harry S., 139, 166, 271, 733-4
Richards, Raymond, 298, 301
Richardson, Victor P., 44
Riker, Joyce, 491
Rinelli, Alfred. 675
Riordan, J.P., 260
Rockefeller Foundation, 125
Rockefeller, John D., 126
"Rocking Chair" incident, 118-9, 245
Rocking Horse, 624
Rockwell, Ethel T., 112
Rodeo. *See* Little International
Roe, Frederick W., 23, 160, 162
Roeseler, Robert O., 496
Roethe, Edward J., 360-1, 378, 380
Rogers, Alfred T., 27, 44
Rogers, Samuel G.A., 166, 494, 507
Rogers, Will, 177
Roland, Merwyn, 359
Rollefson, Ragner, 496
Roosevelt, Franklin D., 27, 270-7, 313-4, 359, 834
Rosenberry, Marvin B., 71
Ross, Edward A., 35, 51, 59, 156n, 162, 556, 675n
Rostovtzeff, Michael I., 484
Rotary Club of Madison, 77, 451, 517, 518n
Roth, William E., 812
"Round robin" resolution, 14-5, 15n, 17, 312
Rowing, 656-7
Royal Bengal Bicycle Riders Club, 523
Ruedisili, Chester H., 424, 547n
Rundell, Oliver S., 276, 443, 533, 539, 547, 738
Runge, Clara T., 318
Rural Church Conferences, 782
Rural Electrification Administration (REA), 780
Rural Progress, 315-6
Rural zoning, 774-5, 781

Rusch, Harold P., 491, 712n, 720
Russell, Bertrand, 51
Russell, Dora, 119, 294
Russell, Harry L., 23-4, 69, 71, 125-6, 131, 137, 139, 237, 269, 472, 513, 709, 770-6; and hiring faculty, 475, 497-8; photos of, 325, 326
Rutgers University, 810, 810n
Ruthven, Alexander G., 396-8

Sachse, William L., 486; writes "America and the War" series, 426
Salaries: of Birge, 56; faculty, 16-7, 20, 137, 141, 150, 155-6, 218, 223-36, 503-4; of Glenn Frank, 150, 235-6, 302; in School of Medicine, 718; Meiklejohn's, 108, 155-6, 156n; of presidents, 150, 235; of Sellery, 108; of Snell, 798; of Slichter, 108, 156n, 798; and waivers, 226-36
Salter, John T., 496
Salter, Leonard A., Jr., 547n
Sarah Lawrence College, 89
Sarles, William B., 498
Saturday Lunch Club, 14, 788
Saunders, Laurance J., 166n, 861
Sauthoff, Harry, 131, 707
Schaars, Marvin, 778
Schafer, Joseph, 688
Schindler, John, 88
Schmedeman, Albert G., 230-1, 596
Schmidtmann, John C., 32, 120, 188, 571n
Schnaitter, M. R., 805, 807
Schoenfeld, Clarence (Clay), 394, 673-4, 867
Schofield, John M., 282, 283
School and Society (Showerman), 190n
School for Workers in Industry, 760-1
Schreiner, Dave, 652
Schumann, John C., 137, 776
Science Hall, 7, 67, 562, 693, 712, 726, 817, 825
Science Inquiry, 514
Scott, Walter Dill, 48, 53, 58
Seaman, Gilbert E., 794
Seevers, Maurice H., 499
Selective Service, 400-1, 404, 408-9
Sellery, George Clarke: and anti-Semitism and control of the *Cardinal*, 636-8; and athletics, 268-9; on ceremony, 79; opposes independent School of Education, 749; and Experimental College, 93, 106-7, 157, 172, 183-9, 201-3, 208, 211, 863-4; and Frank's dismissal, 311-2; and failure to hire Milton Friedman, 477-82; and hiring faculty, 475, 500; and hiring history faculty, 484-5; and modifications in L&S program, 750-5; and new library, 697; criticism of Meiklejohn, 156, 160-4; and Milwaukee Junior College, 793; photos of, 323, 327; as president, 337-9, 346; reforms of, 352, 355; and ROTC, 288, 290-1, 402; and salary cuts, 234-5; salary of, 108; as skeptic of Frank, 61, 134, 138-40, 214; opposes student frivolousness during WW II, 423-4; and Summer Session, 759, 762n; retirement of, 443-4; and requirements for tenure, 492; and undergraduate advising, 96-7; on University budget, 219; and UW Press, 447; on admitting women to Rathskeller, 601-2; during WW II, 412
Senior Swingout, 665-6; photo of, 615
Senior thesis, 692
Senn, Alfred, 490
Sensenbrenner, Frank J., 380, 398, 459
Service Memorial Institutes building, 684
Sevringhaus, Elmer L., 543, 547n
Shands, Hazel L., 498
Sharp, Frank C., 166n, 255
Sharp, Lauriston, 121-2, 598, 599
Sharp, Malcolm P., 166, 166n, 175, 178, 179, 861, 864
Sharp, Walter R., 496
Shaw, George Bernard, 175
Shearer, Conrad, 359
Sheasby, Fred, 137
Sherman, Stuart P., 25, 157
Shoemaker, Alice, 761
Sholts, Arthur, 247
Showerman, Grant M., 156n, 189-90, 190n, 507
Shrimsky, Israel, 594
Shuster, W. Morgan, 49
"Sifting and winnowing," 9, 124, 392, 399, 469. *See also* Academic freedom
Sigma Delta Chi, 300
Silk, Leonard S., 628n
Simonsen, Lee, 603

Sinykin, Gordon, 306
Six O'clock Club, 526
Ski jump (Muir Knoll), 658-60; photo of, 621
Ski patrol, 412-3, 413n; photo of, 336
Sky rocket, 78, 291, 310, 407, 648, 664; described, 664n
Slavic Languages, Department of, 490
Slichter, Charles S.: on administration of University Extension, 809; and intercollegiate athletics, 645; and Experimental College, 162, 173, 196-7; defends Glenn Frank, 296; and dispute between Frank and Gov. La Follette, 219-20; and Karl Paul Link, 237, 241; attempts to raise private funds for research, 132; and University Research Committee, 237, 472; retirement of, 270, 296; salary of, 108, 156n, 798; favors longer Summer Session, 760; and WARF, 69
Slichter, Sumner H., 456
Smith, Alfred E., 176
Smith, Charles A., 82
Smith Club, 518
Smith, Ed, 676
Smith, Hiram, 7, 768
Smith, Howard L., 72
Smith, Kenneth G., 787
Smith, Walter M., 688, 689-90
Snell, Chester D.: supports adult education, 111-2, 842-3; appointed dean of University Extension, 107-8, 138-9, 798; firing of, 809, 810-2; and Milwaukee Extension Center, 795, 801, 804-9; photo of, 328; and public relations, 803; and reforms of University Extension, 801; salary of, 107-8, 798, 802; and WHA radio, 821. *See also* University Extension Division
Social Education, Division of, 860
Society for Promotion of Research and Conversation (SPRC), 526
Soils Building, 169, 869
Solalinde, Antonio G., 496
Sororities: organization of, 583-6; and pledges, 566, 586, 663
Sorum, C. Harvey, 496
South Hall, 4, 6, 184, 662
Soviet Union, 385-7. *See also* Communism

Spanish House for women, 580
Spears, Clarence W., 260-9, 310, 651-2, 654-5
Sproul, Robert G., 453
St. Francis House, 560
St. Patrick's Day celebration, 666-7, 730; photo of, 618
St. Paul's Roman Catholic Chapel, 559
Stadium (Camp Randall), 255, 392, 415, 431, 463, 643, 746-7, 647n, 653
Stakes of War, The (Frank), 49
Stark, Paul E., 703
State Board of Affairs, 134
State Capitol, 668
State Federation of Labor, 125
State Historical Society of Wisconsin, 685-700
State Street, 13, 14, 21, 74, 223, 314, 431, 527, 539, 545, 559, 560, 650, 663, 666, 668, 690, 730, 734
Staudenmayer, George, 42
Stauffer, John, 512
Stayton, William G., 86n
Stearns, John W., 758
Stebbins, Joel, 173, 505, 506, 547
Stechow, F.E.G., 489-90
Stedman, John C., 498, 735
Steenbock, Harry, 514; gives patent to WARF, 68-9, 487, 515, 835, 845; photo of, 332
Steffens, Lincoln, 48
Stegner, Wallace E., 493, 507
Steinman, Samuel, 281, 630-1; photo of, 619
Stemm, Blanche, 568-9n
Stephenson, Carl, 484
Sterling, John, 5
Sterling Hall, 693, 817, 818, 825
Steve, William F., 422
Stewart, Walter W., 31
Stiehmm, Reuben H., 499
Stock market crash, 141
Stock Pavilion, 130, 174, 363, 516, 590, 602, 638, 662
Stoddard, Lothrop, 49
Stoke, Harold W., 443, 496
Stouffer, Samuel A., 497
Stoute, Argyle, 445n
Stovall, William D., 491
Stradley, Bland A., 267

Strawn, Silas H., 222
Student Athletic Board, 258
Student Board, 393, 681-2
Student Clinic, 711
Student Court, 118, 587
Student Employment Office, 555
Student government, 586-9
Student Infirmary, 713, 759
Student Initiative Plan, 113-4
Student League for Industrial Democracy, 290-1
Student League for Intellectual Freedom, 284, 677
Student Public Relations Committee, 677-8
Student Senate, 118
Student Speakers Bureau (truth squads), 284, 677-8
Student War Council, 411-2, 416, 425, 426
Students: academic freedom of, 384-400; admissions requirements for, 556-7; advising of, 96-7; anti-war movement among, 393-5; and Committee on Student Life and Interests, 244-50, 260, 568-9, 573; cutting classes during WW II, 424; description of, 555-8; discipline of, 7, 118-9, 195-8, 244-50, 564-9, 587; dormitories for, 119-20, 123, 562-3, 568; dress code for, 566; enrollment of, 16-7, 94-5, 168-9, 192-4, 419, 422, 436, 463, 474, 552-5; extracurricular activities of, 661-80; and frivolousness during WW II, 423-4; government by, 118-20, 169; grade point average (minimum), 566, 752; and housing 568-86; and idea of *in loco parentis*, 7, 244-50; and malaise of at end of WW II, 440; and Memorial Union, 120-3; publications by, 623-42; radicalism of, 19, 177-81, 279-92, 384-400; recruitment, 199-200; religious activities of, 116-7, 557-8; and resentment toward military during WW II, 435-7; and tuition, 137, 375-7; women, 280-2
Stuhldreher, Harry, 268, 652
Sturtevant, John L., 42
Summer Session, 859-60
Summer School for Teachers, 758-63
Sunday, Billy, 47, 65, 66
Suzzallo, Henry, 31
Swan, Rev. Alfred W., 447, 559

Swarthmore College, 89

Tabard Inn for women, 580, 581
Taft, William Howard, 31-2, 49
Tate, John T., 342
Tatum, Arthur L., 499
Taylor, Harold A., 497
Taylor, Hoyt, 817
"Teachers Radio Round Table," 744
Teachers' Union, 374
Tent colony, 759-60
Tenure, 468-70, 492
Terry, Earle M., 816-22, 843
Thayer, Donald, 385, 394
Theaters: in Madison, 590, 602, 668. *Also see* Memorial Union, theater
Thistlethwaite, Glenn, 257-8, 651
Thomas, Edward A., 540, 541
Thomas, John, 708
Thomas, Norman, 176
Thompson, Jack, 625
Thornton, Madeline J., 499
Three Squares Club, 561
Thwaites, Reuben Gold, 685-7
Titus, William A., 182
Topchevsky, Morris, 173
Torrie, James H., 498
Town and Gown dining club, 131, 213, 215, 517, 519-20
Trewartha, Glenn T., 421
Trilling, Blanche M., 538, 660
Tripp Hall, 67, 119-20, 123, 158, 195-6, 197, 415, 568, 571, 572, 577, 662, 670, 833; photo of, 609
Tripp, J. Stephens, 196
Troxell, Louise, 250, 269, 565. *See also* Greeley, Louise Troxell
Truax, Donald, 311
Tuition, 137, 375-7
Turneaure, Frederick E., 131, 724-8; and hiring faculty, 475, 499-500; and Milwaukee Junior College, 793; photo of, 325; and University Club, 537; and University West End Club, 517n
Turner, Frederick Jackson, 24n, 506, 645
Twenhofel, William H., 245
Twombly, John, 6

Uhl, Willis L., 103
Uncensored News, 283-4

Union. *See* Memorial Union
Union Council, 121, 176
Unions, labor, 595
United States Armed Forces Institute (USAFI), 430
United States Army Institute (USAI): correspondence program, 414, 430
United States Geological Survey, 429
University Arboretum, 679, 700-8, 836-7
University Archives, xii
University Boat House, 658
University City, 120-1, 572
University Club, 11, 14, 348, 527, 527-42, 838; discriminates against blacks in housing (Burke affair), 441, 542-9; and housing for military trainees during WW II, 431; photos of, 333; as temporary hospital, 713
University Committee, 30, 150-1, 231-3, 236, 245, 268, 341-2, 351-7, 839, 840; development of, 470; and tenure system, 468-70, 811-2
University Control (Cattell), 72, 72n
University Elective Service, 411-2
University Extension Division, 11, 99, 107-13, 138, 764, 784-813, 842, 858-9; and Army Institute correspondence program, 414, 430; and WW II training, 413
University Heights Poetry Club, 517
University Hill. *See* "Hill," the
University Hospital. *See* Wisconsin General Hospital
University Jubilee of 1904, 10-1
University League, 271, 278, 518
University League for Liberal Action, 385-90, 393-4, 402, 634
University Library, 685-700; inadequate acquisitions budgets, 694-700; need for new building, 452, 458; satellites, 692-4. *See also* State Historical Society of Wisconsin
University Methodist Church, 560
University of California (president's office and Berkeley campus), 420n, 484, 485n, 486n, 506n, 686, 696
University of California at Los Angeles (UCLA), 342, 453-4, 453n
University of Chicago, 8, 23, 27, 31, 35, 97, 173, 265, 267, 290, 307, 308, 354, 418, 440, 476, 481, 497, 544, 593, 594,

644, 646, 651, 733, 760, 806, 820, 861, 864, 865
University of Illinois, 24, 96, 522, 644, 655, 696
University of Iowa, 31, 44, 101, 103, 644, 652, 696
University of Michigan, 9, 96, 263, 265, 396-8, 485, 644, 646, 651-2, 658, 686, 696
University of Minnesota, 58, 96, 260, 265, 307, 308, 342, 395, 418, 452, 644, 646, 650, 651, 658, 695, 696
University of Missouri, 417, 676
University of North Carolina, 107, 798-9
University of Wisconsin Press Bulletin, 83
University of Wisconsin Foundation: creation of, 461
University of Wisconsin Press, 59, 446-8, 841
University Personnel Council, 410, 567
University Planning Commission, 458n
University Press Bureau, 40, 83
University Religious Council, 558-9
University Research Committee, 237
University War Council, 411
University West End Club, 517
Upper Mississippi Soil Erosion Station (Coon Valley experiment), 780

V-12 Naval Training Program, 420-2, 432-3, 437-8
Vail, Harry "Dad," 656
Vallier, Betty, 435
Van Doren, Carl, 24-8
Van Hise, Charles R.: and athletics, 646-7; collegiality of, 464; criticized for supporting applied research, 72-3; death of, 3; description of presidency of, 10-2; and faculty governance, 349-50; and hiring faculty, 474-5; inaugural address, 10, 589; denounces La Follette's anti-war stance, 14-5; and men's dorms, 67; opposes Milwaukee Extension Center, 251; outreach philosophy of, 784-5; and ties with progressives, 10-2, 830; and public relations, 81n; and student government, 586-7; succesor of, 24n
Van Hise Refectory, 67
Van Slyk, Napoleon, 8
Van Vleck, Edward B., 156n, 505

Van Vleck, John H., 496
Varsity Welcome, 78-9, 664
Vasiliev, Alexander A., 484, 508, 528
Venetian Night celebrations, 666
Vergeront, Barbara M., 380
Veterans: plans for post WW II, 439-40, 441, 460
Veterans' Council, 460
Victory Garden program, 784
Vilas, family and Trust: estate, 705; family home used by College Women's Club, 518; La Follette offends Regent Vilas, 10; loan for Law School library annex, 735, 735n, 834; park and zoo, 649, 701-2
Villa Maria, 568
Villard, Oswald Garrison, 24
Vivas, Eliseo, 190
"Voice for Victory" pledge, 425

"W" Club, 176, 265, 267, 290, 649, 664
"W" Day, 664
W.S.G.A. Bulletin, 624
Wagner, George, 521
Wahlin, Hugo B., 429-30
"Wake Up, America," 405
Wallerstein, Ruth C., 495, 547n
Walrus Club, 524-6
Walsh, John J., 655-6
War Manpower Commission, 420
Washburn, William H., 710
Washburne, Annette C., 499, 722
Waters, Elizabeth, 26, 182
Waters, John E., 386
Waters, Ralph M., 499
Watrous, James S., 242, 489-90, 628; photo of, 619
Watson, Kenneth M., 501
Watts, O.P., 500
Wausau Daily Record-Herald, 42
Wayland Baptist Student Center, 560
Weaver, Andrew T., 260-3, 267, 522, 604, 868n
Weaver, Warren, 188, 255-8, 456
Webb, Mary D., 824
Weekly Cardinal, 84
Wehrwein, George S., 497
Weil, Richard, 175
Weiss, Victor F., 366-9
Wendt, Kurt F., 501

Werner, A. Matthias, 380, 456, 457n
Wesley Methodist Foundation, 560, 561
WHA radio, 63, 84-5, 405, 407, 782, 815-26, 843
Wheeler, Crawford, 591
White, Helen C., 495, 507, 740; and University Club, 534, 536, 538, 539, 543, 547n, 548
Whitehead's God affair, 446-8
Wickhem, John, 307, 435, 738n
Wicks, Virginia, 581
Wiepking, Dorothy, 806
Wiggam, Albert E., 56, 66n
Wilcox, Walter W., 497
Wild, Robert, 135
Wilkie, Harold M., 132, 223, 227-8, 235, 241, 260-1, 268, 289, 298-301, 304-7, 309-11, 316, 318, 340, 361, 537, 812
Wilkie, Horace, 588n
Wilkinson, Julia M., 183-4, 444-5
Willard, Daniel, 86n
Willard, John E., 496
Williams, Frankwood, 173
Williams, T. Harry, 814
Willkie, Wendell, 316
Wilson, Gertrude, 502n
Wilson, Hampden, 385
Wilson, Perry W., 498
Wilson, Woodrow, 86, 89
Wirka, Herman W., 499
Wisconsin Achievement Testing Program, 101
Wisconsin Agricultural Experiment Association, 769, 779
Wisconsin Alumni Association, 41-2, 83, 126, 258, 302, 591
Wisconsin Alumni Magazine, 41-2, 84
Wisconsin Alumni Research Foundation (WARF), 501, 509, 776, 835-6; and dicumarol, 488; founding of, 69-70, 473n; during great depression, 229-30, 269-70, 278; importance of, 489; and postdoctoral research grants, 468; receives patent from Steenbock, 68-9, 487, 515, 835, 845; and Warfarin, 488
Wisconsin Alumnus, 867
Wisconsin Athletic Review, 624, 649
Wisconsin City Superintendents' Association, 95-6
"Wisconsin College of the Air," 824

Wisconsin Country Magazine, 624
Wisconsin Education Association, 97-8
Wisconsin Engineer, 624, 642
Wisconsin General Hospital, 39, 684, 708
Wisconsin High School, 346, 740-1, 765
Wisconsin Idea, 11, 13, 31-2, 86, 108, 271, 757, 828
Wisconsin Idea, The (Charles McCarthy), 788, 789, 828
Wisconsin Institute for National Defense, 405
Wisconsin Institute on the Affairs of the Commonwealth, 110
Wisconsin Law Review, 624
Wisconsin League of Municipalities, 128
Wisconsin Literary Magazine, 176, 624
Wisconsin Men's Union, 589-92, 599-600, 836
Wisconsin Octopus. See Octopus
Wisconsin Players, 428
Wisconsin Preceptor Plan, 115, 718-9
Wisconsin Press Association, 86
Wisconsin Railroad Commission, 31-2
"Wisconsin School of the Air," 824
Wisconsin State Defense Council, 442
Wisconsin State Journal: receives Brittingham's letter on Link gift, 243; supports Callan bill, 360; on rumors about deans of men and women, 245; prints Dykstra's photo soon after Frank's firing, 339; on Frank's arrival in Madison, 70, 75-6; on Heil's Communist purge idea, 398; on La Follette's early part in Frank ouster, 299; features mother's plea to clean up University morals, 281-2; on Otto as a liability, 280; on separation of regents and politics, 379; and selection of Birge's successor, 30, 35; on Snell's appointment, 799; on student enrollments, 94
Wisconsin Student Association, 410, 434
Wisconsin Student Independent, 624
Wisconsin Teachers Association, 43
Wisconsin Union Committee, 435
Wisconsin Union Concert Series, 590
Wisconsin Union Directorate, 425
Wisconsin Union film committee, 428
Wisconsin Union Service Committee, 435
Wisconsin Union. *See* Memorial Union

Wisconsin University Building Corporation (WUBC), 66-7, 120, 138n, 196, 376-7, 540, 572-5, 581, 595, 653, 833, 834
Wisconsinite, 624
"Wiskits," 411
Wisnicky, Walter, 497
Withey, Morton O., 508, 732
Witte, John M., 635
Witte, Edwin E., 495-6; and failure to hire Milton Friedman, 479
Witzmann, Edgar J., 499
Wolfson, Victor, 866
Women: Andersen House, 580, 581; athletics, 660-1; and civil defense and community activity during WW II, 408; Charter House, 580; closing hours for dormitories for, 566, 586; College Women's Club, 518; and *Cardinal* leadership, 641; discipline of, 248-50, 280-1; dormitories for, 563, 568, 576-9; and Department of English, 495; Fallows House, 581; German House for, 579-80; effect of great depression on enrollment of, 553-4; Groves House, 581; *La Maison Française*, 580; admitted to Memorial Union's Rathskeller, 601-2; Mortar Board House, 580; expanded opportunities for during WW II, 426-7; Marine trainees arrive on campus, 431; Meiklejohn on, 181-2; organizations exclusively for, 518, 524-6; and Senior Swingout, 665-6; Spanish House, 580; as students, 5-7, 374; Tabard Inn, 580, 581; and University Club, 535-7, 543; effect of WW II on enrollment of non-residents, 554
Women Accepted for Voluntary Service (WAVES), 417, 431
Women's Army Corps (WAC), 433
Women's Athletic Association, 660-1
Women's Building Corporation, 581
Women's Christian Temperance Union, 628, 671
Women's Elective Service, 408, 411
Women's Emergency National Training Service (WENTS), 426
Women's Self-Government Association (WSGA), 410, 426, 566, 577, 586, 588-9, 601

Women's Week in Home Economics, 746
Wood, H.P., 808
Woodburn, James G., 501
Work day projects, 678-80; photos of, 622
Workers in Industry School, 181, 761
Works, George A., 267
World War I, 11-2, 14
World War II, 407-63; boom and bust, 431-41; coming of, 384-5, 392-3; governance and administration during, 441-55; mobilizing for, 408-30; preparing for peace, 455-63. *See also* Veterans
World Court, 128
Wright, Frank Lloyd, 297

X Club, 520

Yale University, 98-9, 133, 210, 308, 484, 650

Ye Olde Warre Clubbe, 522-3
Ygdrasil Literary Society, 517
Young, Edwin, 457n
Young, Karl, 28-9
Young, Kimball, 203n, 246-7, 497
Young Men's Christian Association (YMCA), 116, 290, 393, 412, 413, 543, 558, 589-90, 629
Young Women's Christian Association (YWCA), 116, 558, 580-1, 760, 761
Youth Communist League, 300, 360, 386, 398
Youth Committee Against War, 393-4

Zawacki, Edmund I., 490n
Zdanowicz, Casimir D., 508-9
Zimmerman, Fred R., 135, 135n, 298, 653, 690
Zolotow, Maurice, 291, 871-3

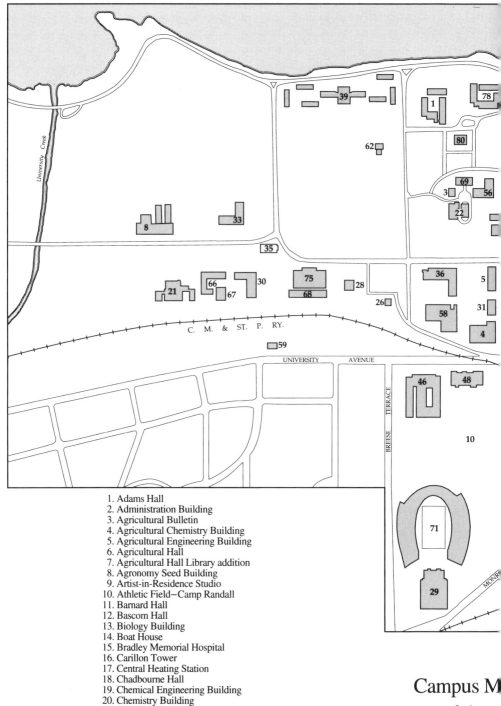

1. Adams Hall
2. Administration Building
3. Agricultural Bulletin
4. Agricultural Chemistry Building
5. Agricultural Engineering Building
6. Agricultural Hall
7. Agricultural Hall Library addition
8. Agronomy Seed Building
9. Artist-in-Residence Studio
10. Athletic Field−Camp Randall
11. Barnard Hall
12. Bascom Hall
13. Biology Building
14. Boat House
15. Bradley Memorial Hospital
16. Carillon Tower
17. Central Heating Station
18. Chadbourne Hall
19. Chemical Engineering Building
20. Chemistry Building
21. Dairy Barn
22. Dairy Building−Hiram Smith Hall
23. Education and Engineering Building
24. Electrical Laboratory/
      Industrial Arts Laboratory/Machine Shops
25. Elizabeth Waters Hall
26. Entomology Building
27. Extension Division/Home Economics Building

Campus M
of the
University of W
1945